Wadsworth
Thomson Learning.

Australia • Canada • Denmark • Japan • Mexico
New Zealand • Philippines • Puerto Rico
Singapore • South Africa Spain • United
Kingdom • United States

James S. Nairne
Purdue University

Psychology
THE ADAPTIVE MIND

Second Edition

Psychology Editor: Stacey Purviance
Development Editor: Penelope Sky
Editorial Assistants: Erin Conlon, Amy Wood
Marketing Manager: Joanne Terhaar
Marketing Assistant: Jenna Burrill
Project Editor: Tanya Nigh
Print Buyer: Karen Hunt
Permissions Editor: Bob Kauser
Production Service: Thompson Steele, Inc.
Text and Cover Designer: Cuttriss and Hambleton
Art Editor, Photo Researcher, Copy Editor, Illustrator, Compositor: Thompson Steele, Inc.
Cover Printer: Phoenix Color
Printer/Binder: Von Hoffman Press

For more information contact

Wadsworth/Thomson Learning
10 Davis Drive
Belmont, CA 94002-3098
USA
www.wadsworth.com

International Headquarters
Thomson Learning
290 Harbor Drive, 2nd Floor
Stamford, CT 06902-7477
USA

UK/Europe/Middle East
Thomson Learning
Berkshire House
168–173 High Holborn
London WC1V 7AA
United Kingdom

Asia
Thomson Learning
60 Albert Street #15-01
Albert Complex
Singapore 189969

Canada
Nelson/Thomson Learning
1120 Birchmount Road
Scarborough, Ontario M1K 5G4
Canada

Library of Congress Cataloging-in-Publication Data

Nairne, James S.
   Psychology : the adaptive mind / James S. Nairne. —2nd ed.
      p.   cm.
   Includes bibliographical references and indexes.
   ISBN 0-534-35766-0 (alk. paper)
   1. Psychology. I. Title.
   BF121.N27 1999
   150—dc21   99-16382
                           CIP

TO VIRGINIA AND STEPHANIE

About the Author

James S. Nairne is Professor of Psychological Sciences at Purdue University in West Lafayette, Indiana. He received his undergraduate training at the University of California, Berkeley and his Ph.D. in psychology from Yale University. As a graduate student, he was recruited to provide demonstrations for all sections of introductory psychology at Yale, and he has been an enthusiastic teacher of introductory psychology ever since. He is an active researcher in cognitive psychology, specializing in human memory, and he's published dozens of articles in professional journals. He is currently an associate editor for the *Journal of Memory and Language*, a consulting action editor for *Memory*, and he is a member of the editorial board of the *Journal of Experimental Psychology: Learning, Memory, and Cognition.*

Brief Contents

Contents   ix

Preface   xxv

The Tactics of Psychological Research 2

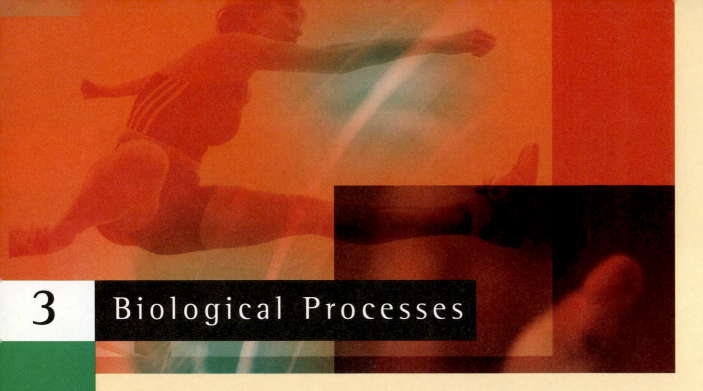

3 Biological Processes

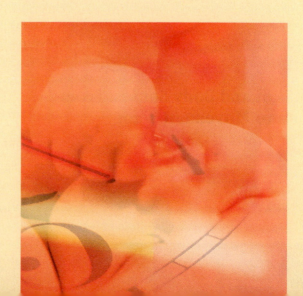

5 Sensation and Perception

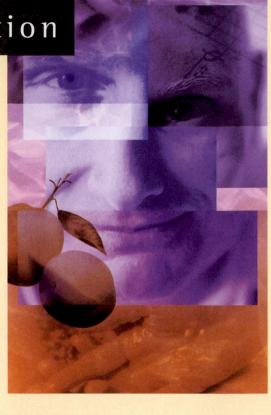

Consciousness 6

7 Learning from Experience

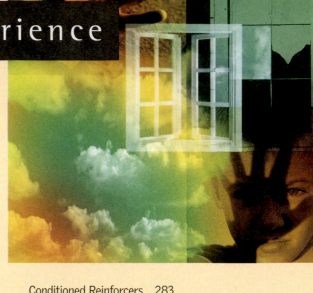

Remembering and Forgetting 8

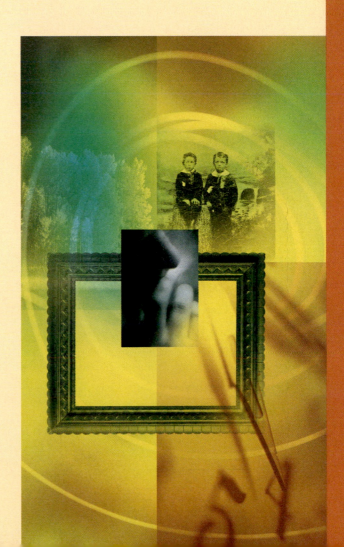

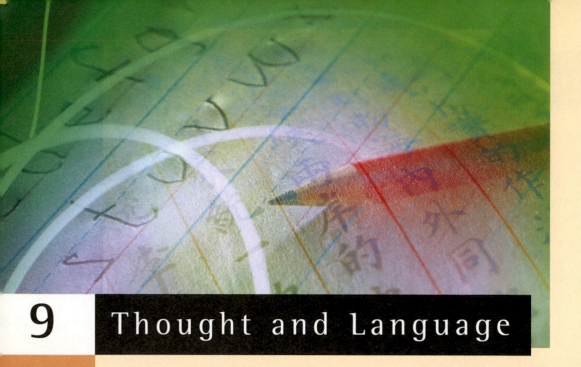

9 Thought and Language

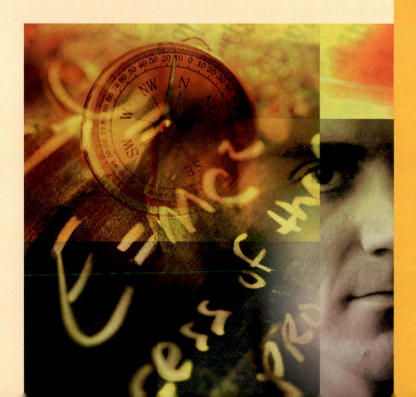

11 Motivation and Emotion

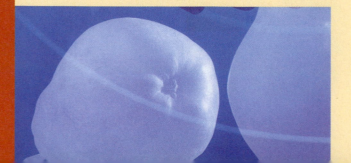

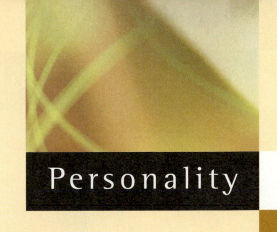

Personality 12

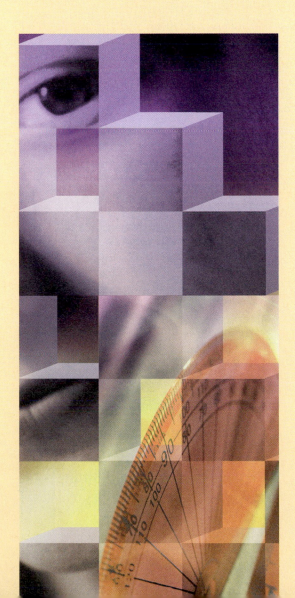

13 Social Psychology

15 Therapy

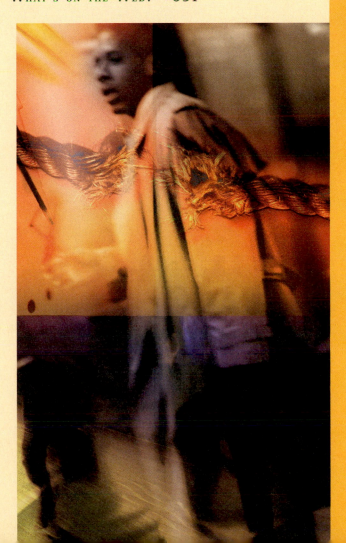

Preface

To the Instructor

One of the first hurdles we face as instructors of introductory psychology is convincing students that psychology is more than just the study of abnormal behavior. Introduce yourself as a psychologist and you're likely to get a response such as "Don't analyze me!" or "I'd better watch what I say around you!" It takes time for students to realize that psychology is a vast interdisciplinary field that includes all aspects of both normal and abnormal behavior. Even after exposure to its breadth, the topics of psychology can remain mysterious and forbidding. Take a look at a typical chapter on learning, for example, and its contents seem to bear little resemblance to our everyday understanding of what it means to "learn." There are extended discussions of drooling dogs and key-pecking pigeons, but little about the connection between conditioning procedures and the learning problems we face on a daily basis.

In *Psychology: The Adaptive Mind*, I focus extensively on the function and purpose of psychological processes. Instead of leading with the facts and methods specific to a topic, I introduce each topic as a kind of "solution" to an adaptive or conceptual/practical "problem." For example, if you want to understand how we learn about the signaling properties of events (problem), we can look to classical conditioning (solution). Notice the shift in emphasis: Instead of topic followed by function, it's function followed by topic. This is what I call the adaptive problem-solving approach, and it offers a number of advantages:

1. The student has a reason to follow the discussion.
2. Because the discussion is about an adaptive or conceptual problem, it naturally promotes critical thinking. The student sees the connection between the problem and the solution.
3. The adaptive problem-solving theme extends across chapters.
4. The organization provides an effective learning framework.

Each chapter is organized around a set of adaptive or conceptual and practical problems that (a) focus the discussion on the functional relevance of the material and (b) demonstrate that we think and act for adaptive reasons. For example, classical conditioning is introduced as a solution to an adaptive problem: How do we learn about the signaling properties of events? Similarly, electrochemical transmission in the nervous system is introduced as the solution to the adaptive problem of communicating internally; the experimental method is introduced as a solution to the conceptual problem of determining the causes of behavior, and so on.

When behavior is viewed as the product of adaptive systems, psychology begins to make more sense. Students learn that behaviors (including the methods of psychologists!) are reactions to particular problems. When we emphasize adaptiveness we relax our egocentric view of the world and increase our sensitivity to why behavior is so diverse, both within and across species. Our appreciation of individuality and diversity is enhanced by the understanding that differences are natural consequences of adaptations to the environment.

CONTENT CHANGES SINCE THE FIRST EDITION

Please note that in addition to expanding the discussions of numerous topics and introducing new ones, I've improved the clarity of the narrative, rewritten parts that seemed a bit too technical in the first edition, and provided hundreds of new references, many from 1997 and 1998. I have also incorporated directly into the text the material that appeared at the end of the chapters as separate "Adaptive Mind" sections.

Chapter 1: An Introduction to Psychology
- New section on the early contributions of women
- New section on culture

Chapter 2: The Tactics of Psychological Research
- Expanded coverage of zero correlations and scatter plots
- Expanded discussion of correlations and causality, including the third variable problem

Chapter 3: Biological Processes
- Expanded coverage of neurotransmitters
- Expanded section on communication within the brain, including neural networks
- New discussion of family studies and their role in the nature-nurture controversy

Chapter 4: Human Development
- New section on egocentrism
- New sections on temperament and childhood friendships
- Expanded discussion of adult development, including a new section on the family life cycle
- New sections on growing old in our society, ageism, and end-of-life decisions

Chapter 5: Sensation and Perception
- Expanded discussion of receptive fields
- Expanded discussion of higher-level detection
- New section on motion perception
- Expanded discussion of audition

Chapter 6: Consciousness
- Expanded discussion of attention deficit disorder
- New discussion of jet lag
- New discussion of sleep deprivation
- Expanded coverage of sleep disorders

Chapter 7: Learning from Experience
- Expanded coverage of partial reinforcement and shaping
- Expanded coverage of punishment
- Expanded coverage of social learning

Chapter 8: Remembering and Forgetting
- Expanded coverage of auditory memory
- Expanded coverage of repetition and distributed practice
- New discussion of false memories
- New section on repressed memories
- Expanded coverage of the neurobiology of memory

Chapter 9: Thought and Language
- Expanded coverage of language comprehension
- Expanded coverage of language in chimpanzees

- Expanded coverage of the value of heuristics

Chapter 10: Intelligence

- Expanded coverage of fluid and crystallized intelligences
- Expanded coverage of mental retardation
- New section on creativity
- New section on emotional intelligence

Chapter 11: Motivation and Emotion

- Expanded coverage of achievement motivation
- Expanded coverage of pheromones
- Expanded coverage of anger and happiness

Chapter 12: Personality

- Expanded discussion of personality tests, including new coverage of the MMPI and TAT tests
- Streamlined discussion of Freud's psychodynamic theory
- Expanded discussion of self-monitoring and the person-situation debate

Chapter 13: Social Psychology

- Expanded discussion of person perception, including new coverage of stereotypes and physical appearance
- New section on prejudice
- Expanded coverage of attributional biases
- Expanded coverage of persuasion and self-perception theory
- New section on deindividuation
- Expanded coverage of group decision making
- New section on the determinants of facial attractiveness

Chapter 14: Psychological Disorders

- Expanded discussion of panic attacks
- New section on suicide
- New discussion of the bio-psycho-social perspective
- New section on cultural influences

Chapter 15: Therapy

- New section on group therapy
- New section on family therapy

Chapter 16: Stress and Health

- Updated coverage of external and internal stressors
- Updated coverage of the immune response
- New Inside the Problem on adaptation and the immune response

NEW AND REVISED FEATURES

- An appealing new design adds interest but not clutter.
- Figures and photos have been updated.
- Glossary terms and definitions now appear in the margins.
- The outlines at the beginning of every chapter have been expanded.
- Learning Goals at the beginning of every section and a Test Yourself review at the end of every section give students regular opportunities to check their understanding.
- Concept Summaries throughout each chapter help students review important themes, approaches, or subject areas.
- Comprehensive chapter summaries let students review important points without having to take extensive notes or wade through lots of text again.
- Annotated Recommended Readings for every chapter include brief

descriptions of relevant books and articles to steer students toward further investigation.

- Text connections to the CD-ROM PsychNow! are highlighted throughout.

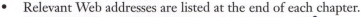

- Relevant Web addresses are listed at the end of each chapter.
- InfoTrac College Edition URLs and suggested search terms appear at the end of each chapter.
- **http://psychology.wadsworth.com** At the end of each chapter, students are encouraged to visit our text-specific Web site, which offers practice quizzes, hypercontents, updates, critical thinking questions, and discussion forums.

TEACHING AND LEARNING SUPPLEMENTS

Psychology: The Adaptive Mind is supported by a state-of-the-art teaching and learning package.

Study Guide (0-534-36774-7)

Prepared by Janet Proctor of Purdue University with a Language Enhancement Guide by Mary Beth Foster of Purdue University. This is a revision of the last edition. All test items have answers with rejoinders.

Thomson Learning Web Tutor™ (0-534-76578-5)

This on-line ancillary helps students succeed by taking the course beyond classroom boundaries to a virtual environment rich with study and mastery tools, communication tools, and course content. Professors can use WebTutor to provide virtual office hours, post their syllabi, set up threaded discussions, track student progress with the quizzing material, and so on. For students, WebTutor offers real-time access to a full array of study tools, including flashcards (with audio), practice quizzes and tests, on-line tutorials, exercises, discussion questions, Web links, and a full glossary. Professors can customize the content in any way they choose, from uploading images and other resources, to adding Web links, to creating their own practice materials.

Instructor's Resource Guide (0-534-36778-X)

By Charles Grah of Austin Peay State University and Gregory Robinson-Reigler of the University of St. Thomas at St. Paul. This update of the last edition contains the following for each chapter in the text:

- Detailed chapter outlines
- Learning objectives
- Lecture elaborations
- Making connections
- Incorporating diversity
- Focus on research
- Demonstrations and activities
- Student critical thinking journal
- Answers to critical thinking questions
- Suggested readings
- InfoTrac College Edition key words
- Film and video suggestions
- Supplements correlation grid
- Guide for the first day of instruction

Instructor's Resource Guide ASCII Version (0-534-36781-X MAC and 0-534-36782-8 WIN)

This is the electronic version (ASCII) of the Instructor's Resource Guide.

Test Bank (0-534-36775-5)

By Shirley-Anne Hensch of the University of Wisconsin, Center. In this update of the last edition you will find approximately 4035 test items:

- Approximately 195 multiple-choice items, 40 sentence-completion questions and 20 essay questions for each text chapter.
- Ten new items are designed for use as an on-line quiz and ten items are taken from the second edition Study Guide.
- Each test item (about 20 per chapter) will have the following information in the margin: section and page references, type of question, correct answer, and Study Guide and on-line quiz alerts.
- Each chapter opener includes a section grid that maps the test items for each sub-topic in the text chapter.

Thomson Learning Testing Tools™ (0-534-36779-8 MAC and 0-534-36780-1 WIN)
This is the electronic version of the Test Bank.

Transparency Acetates (0-534-36776-3)
Approximately 100 text figures are available in this acetate package.

Electronic Transparencies (0-534-36777-1)
The complete set of transparencies is available on a cross-platform CD-ROM in Adobe Acrobat. The disk has a one-time download of Acrobat Reader for easy viewing of the electronic slides

Web Site
http://psychology.wadsworth.com
Wadsworth's PsychStudy Center contains the ten test items per chapter for the on-line quiz, as well as all the basic PsychStudy Center amenities: practice quizzes, hypercontents, updates, critical thinking questions, and discussion forums, teaching tips, and InfoTrac College Edition links.

CNN Today Videos: Introductory Psychology
Volume 1 (0-534-36634-1); Volume 2 (0-534-50420-5)
Exclusive to Wadsworth. The CNN Today Video is course-specific to help you launch lectures and to encourage discussion. Organized by topics covered in a typical course, these 60-minute videos contain many exciting clips. Qualified adopters will each receive one free video.

Integrator Online™ CD-ROM for Introductory Psychology (0-534-35746-6)
Designed for use in any teaching and learning situation from standard lecture to full Internet delivery, this CD-ROM is directly linked to the content of each chapter. The faculty version of Integrator Online includes CourseWeaver Online™, which allows you to deliver course materials via local lecture, individual computers, or Internet links, interactive activities, study sessions, and simulations. Alternatively, students can use the CD-ROM on their own to explore activities, complete homework, or practice for quizzes.

Powerpoint for Introductory Psychology by Linda Lockwood, Metropolitan State College (0-534-26624-XMAC and 0-534-26623-1WIN)
Covering the 16 most commonly taught topics in Introductory Psychology, this PowerPoint presentation features many figures pulled directly from Wadsworth psychology texts. Fully functional and ready to use, you may also personalize the presentation by editing the material, importing your own images and text, or exporting into your own pre-existing PowerPoint presentation.

ACKNOWLEDGMENTS
Writing this textbook has been a unique experience for me. College professors live relatively solitary professional lives; we interact a lot with students and colleagues, but we're not usually part of a team, especially one of the size required to produce a textbook such as *Psychology: The Adaptive Mind*. My publisher deserves enormous

credit for organizing the team and for helping me carry out my original plan for the book. Particular thanks are due to Bill Roberts and Craig Barth, for demanding that the book have a "soul," as well as a distinctive author voice. I am also very grateful to Ken King and Jay Honeck for convincing me to write the book in the first place.

I've had the opportunity to work with a number of talented individuals during the writing and production of this book. My editor on the first edition, Jim Brace-Thompson, was very influential in shaping the book and deserves enormous thanks (and credit). My current editor, Stacey Purviance, took over from JBT with vigor and an astonishing amount of intelligence and savvy. She understood the book from the beginning and is probably its most effective spokesperson. I've also been fortunate to work with two gifted developmental editors, Joanne Tinsley and Penelope Sky. Both are true professionals and influenced the book in many ways. Penelope did a great job in particular with the art and photo scheme for the second edition. Thanks. The second edition also received an enormous boost from Greg Robinson-Riegler who helped craft the fine concept summary tables (among other things).

On the production side, the captain of the second edition team was Tanya Nigh, who held together the tight production schedule and coordinated the efforts at Wadsworth. Special thanks go to Nicole Barone at Thompson Steele, Inc.; she was an absolute pleasure to work with—competent, friendly, and always there when I called.

Of course, I could never have written this book without the help and guidance I received from the reviewers listed below. I hope they can see their mark on the book because it's substantial.

REVIEWERS OF THE FIRST EDITION

Karin Ahlm	DePauw University
Mary Ann Baenninger	Trenton State College
Daniel R. Bellack	Trident Technical College
Ira Bernstein	University of Texas at Arlington
Kenneth Bordens	Indiana University–Purdue University at Fort Wayne
Nancy S. Breland	Trenton State College
James Calhoun	University of Georgia
D. Bruce Carter	Syracuse University
John L. Caruso	University of Massachusetts–Dartmouth
Regina Conti	Colgate University
Eric Cooley	Western Oregon State College
Randall Engle	University of South Carolina, Columbia
Roy Fontaine	Pennsylvania College of Technology
Nelson L. Freedman	Queen's University, Ontario, Canada
Richard Froman	John Brown University
Grace Galliano	Kennesaw State College
Eugene R. Gilden	Linfield College
Perilou Goddard	Northern Kentucky University
Tim Goldsmith	University of New Mexico
Joel Grace	Mansfield University
Charles R. Grah	Austin Peay State University
Terry R. Greene	Franklin & Marshall College
George Hampton	University of Houston–Downtown
Linda Heath	Loyola University of Chicago
Phyllis Heath	Central Michigan University
Shirley-Anne Hensch	University of Wisconsin Center–Marshfield/ Wood County
Michael Hillard	University of New Mexico
Vivian Jenkins	University of Southern Indiana
James J. Johnson	Illinois State University
Timothy Johnston	University of North Carolina at Greensboro
John Jung	California State University–Long Beach
Salvador Macias III	University of South Carolina at Sumter
Carolyn Mangelsdorf	University of Washington
Edmund Martin	Georgia Tech

Michael McCall	Ithaca College
Laurence Miller	Western Washington University
Carol Pandey	Pierce College
Blaine F. Peden	University of Wisconsin–Eau Claire
William J. Pizzi	Northeastern Illinois University
Anne D. Simons	University of Oregon
Stephen M. Smith	Texas A & M University
John E. Sparrow	University of New Hampshire–Manchester
Irene Staik	University of Montevallo
Robert Thompson	Shoreline Community College
Diane Tucker	University of Alabama–Birmingham
John Uhlarik	Kansas State University
Lori Van Wallendael	University of North Carolina at Charlotte
Fred Whitford	Montana State University
Carsh Wilturner	Green River Community College
Deborah Winters	New Mexico State University

We offer special thanks to the following professors and their students for conducting student reviews of the manuscript.

F. Samuel Bauer	Christopher Newport University
Gabriel P. Frommer	Indiana University
R. Martin Lobdell	Pierce College
Robert M. Stern	The Pennsylvania State University
The students of	Dominican College

REVIEWERS OF THE SECOND EDITION

Glen M. Adams	Harding University
Jeffrey Adams	St. Michael's College
Marlene Adelman	Norwalk Community College
Robert Arkin	Ohio State University
Cheryl Arnold	Marietta College
Nolan Ashman	Dixie College
Elaine Baker	Marshall University
Charles Blaich	Wabash College
Dawn Blasko	Pennsylvania State University–Erie
Susan Bovair	College of Charleston
Stephen E. Buggie	University of New Mexico
Brian Burke	University of Arizona
James Butler	James Madison University
James F. Calhoun	University of Georgia
Kenneth Carter	Emory University
Jill Cermele	Drew University
Catherine Cowan	Southwest State University
Patricia Crowe	North Iowa Community College
Timothy Curran	Case Western Reserve University
Robert M. Davis	Indiana University–Purdue University, Indianapolis
Crystal Dehle	Idaho State University
Gina Dow	Denison University
Susann Doyle	Gainesville College
Patrick Drumm	Ohio University
Maryann Dubree	Madison Area Tech College
Peter Dufall	Smith College
Joseph Ferrari	DePaul University
Paul Foos	University of North Carolina–Charlotte
Kathleen Flannery	Saint Anselm College
Susan Frantz	New Mexico State
William R. Fry	Youngstown, State University
Grace Galliano	Kennesaw State University
Stella Garcia	University of Texas–San Antonio
Robert Gehring	University of Southern Indiana
Judy Gentry	Columbus State Community College
Sandra Goss	University of Illinois at Urbana-Champaign
Lynn Haller	Morehead State University
Suzy Horton	Mesa Community College
Wendy James-Aldridge	University of Texas–Pan American
Cynthia Jenkins	Creighton University

Scott Johnson	John Wood Community College
Robert Kaleta	University of Wisconsin–Milwaukee
Deric Kenne	Mississippi State University
Stephen Kiefer	Kansas State University
Kris Klassen	North Idaho College
Stan Klein	University of California–Santa Barbara
Richard Leavy	Ohio Wesleyan University
Judith Levine	State University of New York–Farmingdale
Arlene Lundquist	Mount Union College
Molly Lynch	University of Texas-San Antonio
Salvador Macias III	University of South Carolina–Sumter
Douglas W. Matheson	University of the Pacific
Yancy McDougal	University of South Carolina–Spartanburg
Susan H. McFadden	University of Wisconsin
Glenn E. Meyer	Trinity University
David B. Mitchell	Loyola University Chicago
William Nast	Bishop State Community College
Donald Polzella	University of Dayton
Pamela Regan	California State University–Los Angeles
Linda Reinhardt	University of Wisconsin–Rock County
Catherine Sanderson	Amherst College
Stephen Saunders	Marquette University
Susan Shapiro	Indiana University-East
John E. Sparrow	University of New Hampshire–Manchester
Jon Springer	Kean University
Tracie Stewart	Bard College
Bethany Stillion	Clayton College and State University
Thomas Swan	Siena College
Dennis Sweeney	California University–Pennsylvania
Thomas Timmerman	Austin Peay University
Peter Urcuioli	Purdue University
Lori R. Van Wallendael	University of North Carolina-Charlotte
David Wasieleski	Valdosta State University
Diane Wentworth	Fairleigh Dickinson University
Lisa Weyandt	Central Washington University
Fred Whitford	Montana State University
Steve Withrow	Guilford Tech Community College

Many colleagues and students at Purdue also played a very important role in creating the final product, often suffering through questions about one research area or another, especially Peter Urcuioli. One of my graduate students, Fabian Novello, helped me a great deal on the first edition as did Alicia Knoedler, Georgia Panayiotou, and Esther Strahan. Undergraduates Jennifer Bataille, Lauren Baker, and Kate Gapinski—now all graduated—read portions of the manuscript and also provided valuable feedback. Julie Smith, as always, helped me in innumerable ways, especially with the references and glossary.

Finally, and perhaps most importantly, I want to thank my family. Everyone, including my parents, experienced the writing of this book in one way or another. My wife and daughter, Virginia and Stephanie, lived the book as I did, and I dedicate it to them with love.

James S. Nairne

To the Student

Psychology is the scientific study of behavior and mind. It can be a tough subject, but I think you'll find it's rewarding and fascinating. Throughout this book there are dozens of specific studies and hundreds of isolated facts, but my main goal is for you to understand psychology in a way that will be useful throughout your life. Toward that end, I try hard to show you how particular behaviors, cognitive processes, and emotions help you solve important adaptive problems every day.

WHAT DO WE MEAN BY "THE ADAPTIVE MIND"?

I take the view that everything we do is influenced, in part, by our need to solve—or adapt to—problems in our environment. By "problem" I simply mean the challenges we need to meet, or the demands we need to resolve, as we move through everyday life. For example, before you can act or respond to something, your brain needs to communicate with the environment and with the rest of your body. To solve this adaptive problem—communicating internally—your body uses the nervous system, the endocrine system, and the genetic code. Our survival also depends frequently on our ability to communicate with each other. Again, how to communicate with others is a problem that we need to solve. In this case, the solution—or adaptation—was the development of verbal and nonverbal language.

I hope it's easy to see that our behaviors and thoughts can be seen as solutions (adaptations) to problems or demands. Each chapter begins with three or four adaptive or conceptual problems like the ones described above, and throughout the chapter I show you how these particular problems are solved by the body and mind.

I invite you to browse back through the rest of the preface for a preview of how this book is organized. And I hope you will soon begin applying what you learn to situations in your daily life. The study of psychology may be challenging, but above all else it is relevant to everything we do. Have fun!

James S. Nairne

An Introduction to Psychology

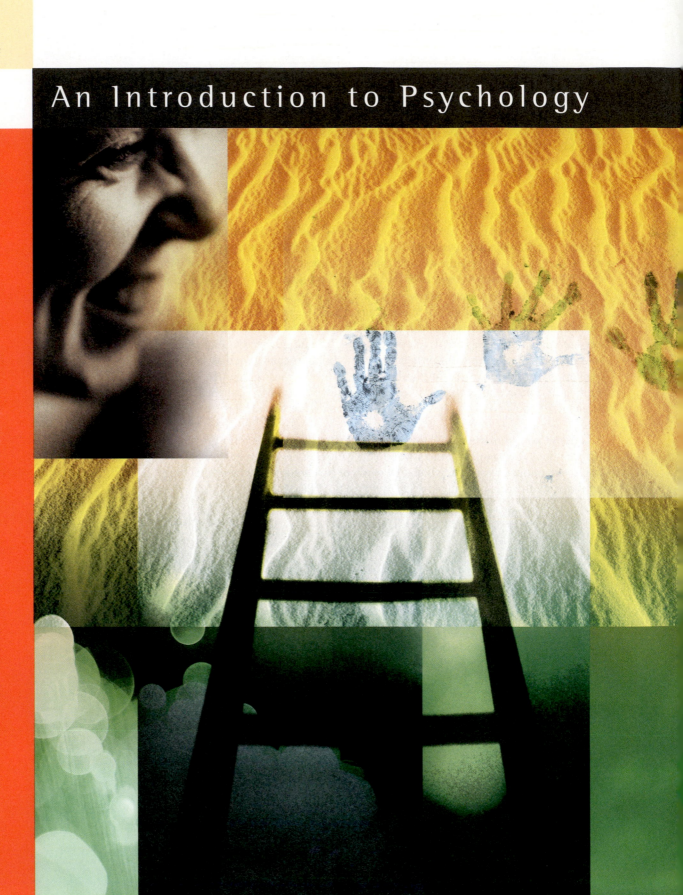

Welcome to the study of **psychology**—the scientific study of behavior and mind. If this is your first psychology course, expect to be surprised by what you find covered in this book. People often assume that psychology is concerned exclusively with the study of mental illness—that is, "crazy" people, mental "breakdowns," or activities designed to put you in touch with your "inner child." It's true that many psychologists treat psychological problems, but the image of psychology that is depicted on afternoon talk shows, or in the self-help books that line the shelves of your local bookstore, is very often misleading. Overall, psychologists tend to focus just as much on the study of *normal* behavior as they do on abnormal behavior.

Why is the focus on everyday, normal behavior? Well, when you suffer from a psychological problem, such as depression, it usually means that there's been a breakdown in normal psychological functioning. The problem may be due to some kind of "broken brain," or a set of faulty internal beliefs, or maybe you've just learned to act in a way that is causing adjustment problems. To understand the abnormal, it's essential that we understand normal functioning first, in the same way a medical doctor must understand the characteristics of healthy bodies before he or she can understand sickness and disease.

Even more important, as you'll discover, one of the main goals of psychology is to map out the essentials of behavior and mind—how people act, think, and feel. Psychologists are actively building a knowledge base about how people and animals behave, and they're using this knowledge to build a systematic science of behavior and mind. By studying what's been learned in psychology, you can expect to receive a number of tangible benefits.

1. You will see how psychologists have acquired the ability to predict behavior in a variety of situations. By observing the world, psychologists have discovered the causes and expressions of many different kinds of behavior, both normal and abnormal. What you learn should enable you to better understand your own actions, as well as those of the people around you.

2. You will learn about techniques that can help you control and improve your behavior. Modern psychology has something to say about everything from the treatment of irrational fears (such as the fear of spiders) to the development of effective study skills—even to the design of the kitchen stove.

3. You will be exposed to a method of inquiry that will teach you how to think critically about yourself and about others. You will learn how researchers ask questions about behavior, how they draw conclusions about cause and effect, and how they develop theories that allow them to predict the circumstances in which particular behaviors will occur.

4. You will discover why people differ in their actions, thoughts, and feelings. Most psychologists believe that human actions are governed by general principles, but any given instance of behavior—such as how you will act at dinner tomorrow night—is almost always determined by multiple causes. Your actions are shaped by your current environment, the culture in which you were raised, and the genetic material passed along to you by your biological parents. Much of psychology is concerned with the study of individual differences among people.

From time to time, you will learn things about yourself that may be difficult to match up with the familiar image of everyday experience. You will discover, for example, that your personal memories are not always accurate; instead, what you remember may simply be an elaborate reconstruction of the past created by adaptive memory mechanisms in your brain. You will learn that some of the beliefs you

psychology
The scientific study of behavior and mind.

Most psychologists believe that human thoughts and emotions arise ultimately from complex activities in the brain.

hold about yourself—how you act and treat others—are not rock solid and unchanging, as you might think; instead, they can be easily changed in the face of a demanding environment. You may even start to question the amount of control you actually have over your own behavior. We'll consider the possibility (although with a critical eye) that your actions are controlled by unconscious forces, biological drives, and external stimuli that are not under direct willful control.

So be forewarned: The content of this textbook may make you feel uncomfortable at times. What you'll learn will likely change the way you view yourself, the world, and others around you. That may seem like a rather tall order at the moment, but it's one I hope you find intriguing as you begin your journey into the adaptive mind.

Previewing the Conceptual Problems

To help tackle the subject matter of psychology, each of the chapters in this textbook is organized around groups of *problems,* usually adaptive problems, that relate to everyday life. The purpose of this organizational scheme is to show you how people use psychological processes to help them adapt to their environment.

For example, one of the most important things that you learn about in your environment is that certain events are reliable predictors, or signals, of other events. If you're walking along a mountain path and hear a sudden rattling sound, it's useful to know that a dangerous snake might be lurking nearby. In Chapter 7, "Learning from Experience," you'll learn about a procedure that psychologists use to study how people learn about signals in their environment. This procedure, called *classical conditioning,* is a kind of solution to an important problem: how we learn about signals. Similarly, in Chapter 3, "Biological Processes," you'll learn how each of us communicates information internally through the vast communication network of the nervous system. Internal communication is a crucial problem for your body to solve: If a bicyclist weaves suddenly into the path of your car, the message needs to be communicated quickly and efficiently to the muscles controlling the foot-to-brake connection. The body uses its internal neural networks to solve problems connected with internal communication.

When you encounter each new topic in a chapter, you should ask yourself the following question: How does the psychological process under discussion help me solve an adaptive problem in my life? Each of us is constantly adjusting our actions, often in a flexible and strategic way, to meet the needs of new conditions as they arise. We each carry around with us a kind of psychological tool kit, acquired either from learning or naturally as a by-product of evolution, that helps us initiate, direct, and control our behavior. For most of the topics in the coming chapters, you'll see how these adaptive tools can be used to solve the various obstacles and survival problems we face. (For a slight look ahead, you can find some of these tools listed in Table 1.1.)

TABLE 1.1
Examples of Adaptive, Conceptual, and Practical Problems

	Chapter	Problem to Be Solved	Example	Solution Tools
Adaptive problems	3	Communicating internally	A bicyclist weaves suddenly into the path of your car.	Electrochemical transmission in the nervous system.
	7	Learning what events signal	You hear a rattling tail on a mountain path.	Interevent associations acquired through classical conditioning
	8	Remembering over the short term	You try to remember a telephone number as you cross the room.	Rehearsal in short-term memory
	13	Interpreting the behavior of others	A shadowy figure emerges suddenly from an alleyway.	Knowledge-based social schemas used to predict outcomes
Conceptual and practical problems	2	Determining the causes of behavior	Sally watches a violent TV program and becomes aggressive.	Experimental research
	10	Conceptualizing intelligence	Andy is excellent at fixing mechanical devices but is terrible at reading and math.	Psychometric tests designed to measure the mind
	14	Defining abnormality	Lucinda hears voices and thinks she's immortal.	*Diagnostic and Statistical Manual of Mental Disorders*
	15	Treating the mind	Ralph is mired in the depths of depression.	Psychoactive drug therapy or "insight" therapy

Note: The solution tools shown in the far-right column will be discussed in detail in the relevant chapters.

In some instances, our focus will veer slightly away from adaptive problems toward more practical problems that psychologists seek to solve, either to advance basic knowledge or to help troubled individuals in need. For instance, what are the best strategies to use to understand the cause of a behavior (Chapter 2)? What are the best ways to conceptualize and then measure something abstract such as intelligence (Chapter 10)? Intelligence is not something that can be measured directly, like height or weight; it can only be inferred by measuring various aspects of behavior. How can abnormal behavior be classified, and, once identified, how can it be treated (Chapter 14)? These are practical problems that psychologists attempt to solve, and learning about the solutions and how they're reached is key to understanding how modern psychology works.

In this first chapter, you'll be exposed to three broad topics, which you can think of as conceptual problems that psychologists have attempted to solve. Each is designed to help acquaint you with the scientific study of behavior and mind: (1) What is the proper way to define and describe psychology? (2) How did current psychological perspectives evolve? (3) What is the proper focus for modern psychology?

LEARNING GOALS

1. Give the modern definition of psychology.
2. Discuss the different ways to study the mind scientifically.
3. Describe what psychologists do, distinguishing among clinical, applied, and research psychologists.

Defining and Describing Psychology

As defined earlier, psychology is the scientific study of behavior and mind. The word comes from the Greek *psyche*, which translates as "soul" or "breath," and *logos*, which means the study or investigation of something (as in bio*logy* or physio*logy*). The word *psychology* was not in common use before the nineteenth century, and it did not actually become an independent subject matter of science until around the middle of the nineteenth century (Boring, 1950). Up to that point, "the study of the mind," as psychology was widely known, was conducted mainly by philosophers and physiologists. Neither Sigmund Freud nor Ivan Pavlov, for example, were trained in psychology, despite their reputations as famous psychologists.

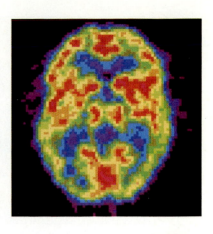

Notice that today's definition of psychology is quite precise—it is not simply the study of the mind, but rather it is the *scientific* study of *behavior* and mind. The emphasis on science, and particularly the scientific method, helps to distinguish psychology from the closely related field of philosophy. The essential characteristic of the scientific method, as you'll see in Chapter 2, is *observation:* Scientific knowledge is always based on some kind of direct or indirect observation. Psychologists collect observations, look for regularities, and then generate predictions based on what they've observed.

By mind, psychologists usually mean the contents and processes of subjective experience: sensations, thoughts, and emotions. Behavior and mind are kept separate in the definition because only behavior can be directly measured by the scientific observer. Psychologists interpret the term behavior in a quite general way. Besides referring to obvious actions such as moving, talking, gesturing, and so on, many psychologists consider the activities of cells within the brain (as measured through physiological recording devices) and the expressions of thoughts and feelings (as revealed through oral and written responses) to be types of "behavior."

The term *behavior* can mean many things to a psychologist—overt actions, thoughts and feelings as revealed through written reports, and even recordings of electrical activity in the brain.

? CRITICAL THINKING

Do you think it's possible to study behavior independently of the mind? Or, does all behavior result from the actions of a willful mind? Cockroaches, snails, and starfish all behave, but do they have minds?

THE INVISIBLE MIND: HOW CAN IT BE STUDIED?

It's worthwhile to pause for a moment and think about how difficult it is to study the mind. Imagine that you accidentally unearth a small black box that is capable of responding to questions by displaying answers on a small screen. You give the box a quick once over and find that it appears to act intelligently. You ask it questions; it responds appropriately. What kind of strategy might you use to discover how this box works? In an important sense, your task is similar to the one facing the psychologist: There is an intelligent object—in the case of a psychologist, it's a human being—and the object responds to questions and appears to think intelligently. Yet it's not immediately obvious how or why that object works the way that it does. The internal mechanisms and processes are hidden, locked away within an external shell.

First, because the box is intelligent, you might begin by asking it to *tell* you how it works (see Figure 1.1). Instruct the box to look inward, to reflect on the internal mechanisms responsible for its intelligence. This approach is likely to yield lots of useful and interesting data, but it creates a potentially serious problem: How can you tell whether the box's insights, once delivered, are accurate? The box could be lying, or simply misunderstand its own operating mechanisms. What the box thinks is going on may not, in fact, be an accurate representation of reality. As you'll see later in this chapter, psychologists have faced similar problems in their efforts to understand the mind. People are often capable of providing detailed accounts of why they act the way they do. But the psychologist faces the difficult task of separating fantasy and fabrication from reality. It's difficult to rely entirely on self-reports, although they can be useful sources of data, unless an alternative

mind
The contents and processes of subjective experience: sensations, thoughts, and emotions.

behavior
Observable actions such as moving, talking, gesturing, and so on; behaviors can also refer to the activities of cells, as measured through physiological recording devices, and to thoughts and feelings, as measured through oral and written expression.

(a)   (b)   (c)

FIGURE 1.1

Studying the Mind

It is difficult to study the mind because mental events are not directly observable. Using the analogy of a black box, these three panels depict some of the ways that one might attempt to study the mind: (a) Ask the box itself for insight; (b) pry the box open to see what's inside; or (c) measure the box's behavior and look for regularities.

way exists to verify the accuracy of the claims (Crutcher, 1994; Ericsson & Simon, 1993; Payne, 1994).

Second, you might simply pry the box open to see what you find inside. This is obviously something a psychologist can't do, although examining the internal structure of the human brain is an active area of research in psychology (you'll find out how this is possible in Chapter 3). Yet here, too, potential problems loom. Suppose you find billions of little objects with long threadlike tails that appear to be interconnected in a vast network. What do they mean? These bizarre internal objects themselves require explaining, and even if you succeed in determining their function, you face further obstacles. For one thing, you run the risk of breaking the machine by prying it open and examining its working parts. Moreover, understanding any one of these objects doesn't necessarily tell you how the machine as a whole operates. The intelligent behavior of the box could be the result of many components working together, in ways that can't be understood by studying the individual parts in isolation.

Third, leaving the box intact, you might try to understand how it works by looking for regular patterns in its behavior. You could measure things such as the time it takes the box to answer questions, the number of errors it makes, how long it takes the box to forget previous responses, and so on. By measuring and describing the box's behavior—its limits and range of abilities—you could start to make intelligent guesses about how the box operates. This last approach is probably closest to the way most modern psychologists approach their subject matter. They observe behavior in a systematic way, looking for regular patterns, in order to develop ideas that can then be tested through more observations of behavior.

In general, to understand the mysteries of the mind—such as the origins of sensations, thoughts, and emotions—psychologists must first and foremost study how the body behaves. Psychologists believe that this is the only reasonable scientific approach, because the mind itself cannot be observed directly. Psychologists observe behavior, along with the environmental conditions that cause changes in behavior, and use these observations to draw inferences about the structure and content of mental processes. In Chapter 2, we'll discuss some of the methods that psychologists use to accomplish these ends.

WHAT PSYCHOLOGISTS DO

You now know that a psychologist is someone who is engaged in the scientific study of behavior and mind. But, what do psychologists actually do on a daily basis? How do they earn a living? Where do they work? As shown in the "Concept Summary" table on the next page, we can divide the job description into three main categories: *clinical psychologist, applied psychologist,* and *research psychologist.* These are not meant to be exclusive "either-or" categories—for example, clinical psychologists often

CONCEPT SUMMARY
Types of Psychologists

Type of psychologist	Guiding Focus	Primary Workplace	Examples of What They Do
Clinical psychologists	The diagnosis and treatment of psychological problems	Clinics Private practice Academic settings	Counsel clients suffering from adjustment problems or more severe psychological problems; evaluate diagnostic techniques and therapy effectiveness.
Applied psychologists	Extending psychological principles to practical problems in the world	Private industry Schools Academic settings	Help performance of students in school; improve employee morale and performance at work; design computers so that humans can use them efficiently.
Research psychologists	Conduct research to discover the basic principles of behavior and mind	Academic settings Private industry	Conduct experiments on the best study method for improving memory; assess the impact of daycare on child's attachment to his/her parents; observe the effects of others on a person's helping behavior.

work in applied settings and conduct research—they're designed simply to represent a useful way of generally subdividing the profession.

Clinical Psychologists

To most people, a psychologist is someone who diagnoses and treats psychological problems—such as depression, anxiety, phobias, or schizophrenia—or gives advice on such things as how to raise children or get along with your boss. Professionals who deal with these kinds of problems are called **clinical psychologists,** and they typically work in clinics or in private practice delivering human services such as psychotherapy or counseling. Distinctions are often made between clinical and counseling psychologists, although the dividing line between the two is not clear and firm. *Counseling psychologists* are more likely to deal with adjustment problems (marriage and family problems), whereas clinical psychologists tend to work with more severe psychological disorders. Together, clinical and counseling psychologists make up the majority of psychologists. In fact, over half of all the professionals working in psychology are actively involved in the treatment of mental health (American Psychological Association, 1993).

Applied Psychologists

Not all psychologists are concerned with understanding and treating abnormal behavior or with helping people adjust. Another category of professional psychologists tends to focus on average, "normal" people (we'll consider what it means to be normal or abnormal in Chapter 14). The goal of applied psychologists is to extend the principles of scientific psychology to practical, everyday problems in the real world. **Applied psychologists** work in various settings. For example, a *school psychologist* might work with students in primary and secondary schools to help them perform well academically and socially; an *industrial/organizational psychologist* might be employed in industry to help improve employee morale, train new recruits, or help managers establish effective lines of communication with their employees. *Human factors psychologists* play a key role in the design and engineering of new products: Why do you think telephone numbers are seven digits long, grouped in three then four (e.g., 555-9378)? How about traffic lights—why red and green? Does it make a difference whether the word *delete, remove,* or *erase* is used in a word processing program? These are examples of practical problems that have occupied the attention of human factors psychologists (Proctor & Van Zandt, 1994).

Research Psychologists

At the university or college level, you are likely to find **research psychologists** who collect data on both basic and applied issues in psychology. Research psychologists conduct experiments or collect observations in an attempt to discover the basic principles of behavior and mind; they, too, are usually associated with a

clinical psychologists
Professional psychologists who specialize in the diagnosis and treatment of psychological problems.

applied psychologists
Psychologists who try to extend the principles of scientific psychology to practical, everyday problems in the world.

research psychologists
Psychologists who conduct experiments or collect observations designed to discover the basic principles of behavior and mind.

specialty. *Biopsychologists,* for instance, seek to understand how biological or genetic factors influence and determine behavior. *Personality psychologists* are concerned with the internal factors that lead people to act consistently across situations, and also with the determinants of individual differences in behavior. *Cognitive psychologists* focus on higher mental processes such as memory, learning, and reasoning. *Developmental psychologists* study how behavior and internal mental processes change over the course of a lifetime. *Social psychologists* are interested in how people think about, influence, and relate to each other. These are just a few of the specialties that research psychologists adopt. As you work your way through the chapters of this text, you will be exposed to a wide range of research interests.

Psychologists and Psychiatrists

Finally, you might be wondering about the differences between psychologists and **psychiatrists.** Psychiatrists are medical doctors who specialize in psychological problems. To become a psychiatrist you must graduate from medical school and then complete further specialized training in the subject matter of psychology. Like clinical psychologists, psychiatrists are involved in the treatment of mental disorders, but unlike psychologists, they are licensed to prescribe drugs.

As you'll see in Chapter 15, drug therapy is often useful for treating the physical problems that sometimes create or accompany problems of the mind. Helpful changes can occur as a result of drug therapy, and there is an ongoing debate among mental health professionals about whether psychologists should be allowed to prescribe drugs (e.g., DeNelsky, 1996; Hayes & Heiby, 1996). At present, it is not unusual for psychologists and psychiatrists to work together. A clinical psychologist, for example, might refer a client to a psychiatrist if he or she suspects that a physical problem might be involved.

TEST YOURSELF 1.1

Test your knowledge about how best to define and describe psychology by deciding whether each the following statements is true or false. (You will find the answers in the Appendix.)

1. Psychologists use the term *behavior* to refer only to observable responses, such as moving, talking, and gesturing. Internal events, such as thoughts and feelings, therefore fall outside of the domain of scientific psychology. *True or False?*

2. Psychology did not exist as a separate subject matter of science 150 years ago. To explore questions about behavior and mind, it was necessary to spend the majority of your time studying philosophy and/or physiology. *True or False?*

3. Clinical psychologists are generally interested in diagnosing and treating psychological problems such as depression or schizophrenia. *True or False?*

4. Psychiatrists differ from psychologists primarily in their focus of interest. Psychiatrists tend to work on severe and chronic problems, such as schizophrenia, whereas psychologists treat milder problems, such as phobias and anxiety disorders. *True or False?*

Tracing the Evolution of Psychological Thought

The field of psychology may have a relatively short past, but it has a long and distinguished intellectual history. Thousands of years ago, the Greek philosopher Aristotle (384–322 B.C.) wrote extensively on such topics as memory, sleep, and sensation. These are topics, of course, that today form an important part of the subject matter of psychology. It was Aristotle who first argued that the mind could

psychiatrists
Medical doctors who specialize in the diagnosis and treatment of psychological problems. Unlike psychologists, psychiatrists are licensed to prescribe drugs.

be seen as a kind of *tabula rasa*—a blank tablet—upon which experiences are written to form the basis of knowledge. The idea that knowledge arises directly from experience, a philosophical position known as **empiricism**, continues to be an important theme in modern psychological thought.

MIND AND BODY: ARE THEY THE SAME?

As mentioned earlier, the intellectual roots of modern psychology lie in the disciplines of both *philosophy* and *physiology*. In a sense, psychology has always occupied a kind of middle ground between these two areas (Bolles, 1993; Hunt, 1993). Philosophers such as Aristotle, Plato, and others helped to frame many of the fundamental questions that occupy the attention of psychologists today: Where does knowledge come from? What are the laws, if any, that govern sensation? What are the necessary conditions for learning and remembering?

Physiologists, on the other hand, attempt to understand the workings of the human body. Years of research on the mechanics of physical movement and the anatomy of sensory systems produced volumes of data that were later used to develop a *scientific* understanding of behavior and mind. In 1833 the German physiologist Johannes Müller published an enormously influential *Handbook of Human Physiology* that proposed links between the nervous system and a variety of psychological effects. By the 1860s, clear connections had been established between certain types of brain damage and the loss of mental function, such as the ability to produce or comprehend spoken language. Advances in our knowledge of the physical operation of the brain continue to shape the kinds of theories that psychologists propose. I'll discuss some of these advances in Chapter 3, and also later in this chapter.

Descartes' Solution

To question the relationship between the physical *body*, as studied by the physiologists, and the *mind*, as studied by philosophers, is fundamental to psychology. Are the mind and body separate and distinct, or are they one and the same? Do they interact in ways we can understand? Can we learn anything about one by studying the other? In the seventeenth century, the French philosopher *René Descartes* (1596–1650) argued that the mind and body must be kept separate: The physical body, he claimed, cannot "think," nor is it possible to explain "thinking" by appealing to physical matter. He did allow for the possibility, however, that one could importantly influence the other. The *mind*, he argued, can initiate and control the actions of a mechanical *body* through the pineal gland, a small structure at the base of the brain (see Figure 1.2).

Descartes helped to frame the mind–body problem clearly, and his attempt at describing the human body in machinelike terms had an important influence on generations of physiologists. His specific ideas about the body turned out to be largely incorrect—the pineal gland, for example, plays a role in producing hormones, not muscle movements—but some of his ideas remain influential today. It was Descartes, for instance, who first introduced the concept of a *reflex*. Reflexes are automatic, involuntary reactions of the body to events in the environment. As you'll see in Chapter 3, reflexes play a very important role in our survival. But his solution to the mind–body problem did little to advance the scientific study of mind. Talking about the mind as something separate from the physical world places the subject matter of psychology outside the boundaries of science. The scientific method is based on observation, and it's impossible to study something scientifically that cannot be observed in some way.

Mind Equals Brain Activity

Modern psychologists approach the mind–body problem quite differently than Descartes did. They reject the separation of mind and body and assume the two are one and the same. What we call the "mind" today is considered to be nothing

? **CRITICAL THINKING**

Psychology is the scientific study of behavior and mind. Is it really surprising then that its intellectual roots lie in physiology and philosophy?

FIGURE 1.2

Descartes and the Reflex

René Descartes introduced the concept of the reflex, which he described as an automatic, involuntary reaction of a mechanical body to an event in the world. He identified the mediating structure as the pineal gland, shown here as a tear-shaped object in the back of the head.

empiricism
The idea that knowledge comes directly from experience.

more than brain activity; put simply, the mind is what the brain does. As you'll see throughout this text, there is an extremely close link between the operation of the brain and behavior. Many psychological problems appear to come directly from problems in the operation of the brain, and many of the symptoms can be treated effectively through biological means (usually the administration of drugs).

NATURE OR NURTURE: WHERE DOES KNOWLEDGE COME FROM?

Philosophers and psychologists have also been keenly interested in determining the origins of knowledge. Where does knowledge come from? As noted earlier, Aristotle adopted an empiricist position: He believed that knowledge comes entirely from our day-to-day experiences. Empiricism can be contrasted with a philosophical position called **nativism**, which holds that certain kinds of knowledge and ideas are inborn, or innate.

Nativists believe that babies arrive into the world knowing certain things, and this knowledge cannot be accounted for simply by experience. For example, the German philosopher Immanuel Kant (1724–1804) believed that humans are born with a certain mental "structure" that determines how they perceive the world. People are born with a natural tendency, he argued, to see things in terms of cause and effect and to interpret the world in terms of space and time (Bolles, 1993; Wertheimer, 1987). Nativists do not necessarily believe that *all* knowledge is present at birth, but they reject the idea that all knowledge comes directly from experience. For a better understanding of the nativist position, you can take a look at the accompanying feature, "Inside the Problem."

Darwin's Theory of Evolution

By the last half of the nineteenth century, the writings of Charles Darwin (1809–1882) were becoming quite influential in the debate about the origins of knowledge. Darwin proposed that all living things are essentially the end products of an extended period of evolution, guided by the principles of natural selection. Cats have fur, seals have thick skin, and babies cry because these physical and behavioral traits have been passed along, and selected for, during the evolutionary history of the species. By *natural selection*, Darwin meant that some individuals are better than others at overcoming obstacles and solving the problems present in their environment. Because animals compete for survival and for opportunities to reproduce, those inherited characteristics that enhance survival and reproduction will be the traits most likely to persist from generation to generation. If an inborn tendency to cry, for example, helps to communicate feelings about hunger effectively, then crying increases the likelihood that one will live long enough to pass this natural tendency on to offspring. Such tendencies are selected for naturally because they are *adaptive*—they improve the chances for meeting the needs demanded by the environment (Darwin, 1859, 1871).

Notice the emphasis is on *inherited* tendencies. Darwin believed that the principles of natural selection apply to characteristics that pass from parents to their offspring—not only physical traits, but behavioral and psychological ones as well. It was later learned that the principal vehicle for the transmission and expression of these inherited traits is the genetic material that resides inside the cells of the body. During development, the activity of the genes, together with other internal and external influences, gives rise to the physical structure of the brain and the rest of the body.

By emphasizing the adaptive value of inherited characteristics, including psychological characteristics, Darwin was destined to have an enormous influence on the thinking of psychologists (Dennett, 1995). If natural selection plays a role in the evolution of mental abilities, for instance, then it becomes easier to accept the idea that people might inherit certain ways of thinking or of viewing the world (the *nativist* position). Researchers now commonly argue, for example, that

Charles Darwin believed that both physical and psychological characteristics were selected for their adaptive value.

nativism
The idea that certain kinds of knowledge and ideas are innate, or present at birth; innate ideas do not need to be learned.

Inside the Problem   Are We Born Knowing?

In each chapter you will encounter special sections, such as this one, designed to bring you a bit more deeply "inside the problem" under discussion. The point of these sections is to expand the discussion in the text, perhaps by providing a demonstration or particularly relevant study, or simply to discuss things from a slightly different angle or perspective.

As you can probably guess, the question of whether humans are born knowing fundamental things about their world is extremely difficult to answer. For one thing, no one is really sure at what point experience begins. We could draw a line at birth and say that any knowledge or abilities that exist at that very moment are innate, but, as you'll see in Chapter 4, the environment can exert tremendous influences on embryos as they develop in the womb. We can never eliminate the influence of experience completely—in fact, the very act of assessing knowledge is itself a kind of experience. So we're always faced

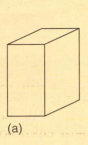
(a)

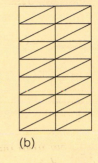
(b)

FIGURE 1.3
From Bolles, 1993

with the tricky problem of disentangling which portions of the knowledge we observe are inborn and which are produced through experience.

One attack on the problem, proposed by a school known as *Gestalt psychology*, was to demonstrate that people use certain organizing principles of perception that cannot be altered by experience. Take a look at Figure 1.3. If I showed you (a) and then (b), do you think you could easily rec-

ognize that (a) is in fact embedded in (b)? It's not easy to see, is it? More important, it doesn't really matter how many times I show you (a). Even if I force you to look at (a) 100 times, it's always going to be difficult to find when you look at (b). The reason, according to the Gestalt psychologists, is that humans are born with a certain fixed way of viewing the world. The visual system, in this case, naturally organizes the sensory input in (b) in such a way that (a) is masked. These organizing principles are innate, and experience cannot change them (Ellis, 1938).

I'll have more to say about organizing principles when we take up the topics of sensation and perception in Chapter 5. At that time, we'll return to this issue of experience and its effects on perception, and you'll see that experience is not always irrelevant to perception. In fact, there are many cases in which the knowledge we gain from experience fundamentally affects the way we perceive the world.

---

humans have an inherited predisposition to acquire language, much as birds have an inherited predisposition to fly (Pinker, 1994).

Nature and Nurture

Today, it is widely recognized that most psychological phenomena—intelligence, emotion, personality—are influenced, at least in part, by innate genetic factors. At the same time, most psychologists agree that personal experience also plays a critically important role in thought, emotions, and behavior. How a genetic message is expressed depends on an interaction between the message coded in the genes and environmental effects that occur during development. With respect to the origins of knowledge, recognition of this interaction has led virtually all psychologists to the following important compromise: The study of mind and behavior requires that one appeal to the effects of *nature* (innate factors) as well as *nurture* (experience). So, the solution to the nature versus nurture debate isn't nature *or* nurture—it's nature *plus* nurture.

You'll be reading more about the relative contributions of nature and nurture to the understanding of psychological effects in the coming chapters. From an adaptive perspective, it makes sense that both factors are commonly involved. The newborn infant, for example, arrives into the world with a tool kit of basic reflexes that helps the child to survive. At the same time, it would make no sense to "hardwire" the brain with fixed responses to all environmental events. We live in a constantly changing world, and it is to our advantage that we can shape our responses to best meet the needs of individual situations. One of the challenges continually

Certain physical characteristics, such as camouflage, are selected for in nature because they are adaptive—they improve the chances of an organism surviving.

Separated at birth, the Mallifert twins meet accidentally.

Copyright Charles Adams/*The New Yorker Magazine.*

faced by psychologists is how to discover the respective roles that innate and learned factors play in any given instance of behavior.

THE FIRST SCHOOLS: PSYCHOLOGY AS SCIENCE

The first psychological laboratory was established in 1879 at the University of Leipzig by a German professor named Wilhelm Wundt (1832–1920). Wundt was a medical doctor by training, and early in his career he worked with some of the great physiologists of the nineteenth century. Fittingly, his laboratory was established during the time he spent as a professor of *philosophy*. (Remember, the intellectual roots of psychology lie at the union of philosophy and physiology.) Wundt is traditionally recognized as the founder, or father, of modern psychology, and 1879 is seen as the year that psychology finally emerged as a unique field separate from philosophy and physiology. Prior to Wundt, there were no official psychology departments nor official psychologists (Bolles, 1993).

It is noteworthy that the birth of psychology is identified with the establishment of an experimental laboratory. Wundt's background in physiological research convinced him that the proper approach to the study of mental events was to conduct experiments. He believed that controlled observations should be collected about the phenomena of mind in the same way that one might observe twitching frog legs in an effort to understand the principles of nerve conduction. Wundt wasn't quite sure that all mental processes could be studied in this way, but he committed himself wholeheartedly to the use of scientific techniques.

To get a brief glimpse of what life was like in Wundt's laboratory, imagine spending hour after hour, day after day, listening to the steady ticking of a metronome or listening for the first sound of an iron ball dropping onto a platform. Your task? Press a button at the very first moment you hear each sound. If you prove talented at this task, Professor Wundt might give you the additional task of pressing a button at the exact moment you become aware of your perception of the sound. What's the difference between hearing a sound and your perception of the sound? About one-tenth of a second in your reaction time. This may sound silly to you, and far removed from the proper subject matter of psychology, but Wundt believed that small differences in reaction times were important clues in his ongoing investigation of the mind.

Structuralism

Wundt (1896) was convinced that the proper focus for psychology should be the study of immediate conscious experience, by which he meant the things that people sense and perceive when they reflect inward on their own minds. Immediate experience to Wundt was best described in terms of *elements*—primarily sensations and feelings—and it was the job of the psychologist to (1) identify these elements, and then (2) discover how they combine to produce meaningful wholes. This general approach was later named **structuralism** by one of Wundt's students, Edward Titchener (1867–1927). Structuralists believe that psychologists should seek to understand the *structure* of the mind by breaking it down into elementary parts, much like a chemist might try to understand a chemical compound (Titchener,

structuralism
An early school of psychology; structuralists attempted to understand the mind by breaking it down into its basic constituent parts, much like a chemist might try to understand a chemical compound.

1899). (There are actually some important differences between structuralism as practiced by Titchener and the more general approach advocated by Wundt, but these differences are beyond the scope of this textbook.)

One problem with structuralism, however, is that while you can directly observe and measure a chemical compound, it's not possible to directly observe the internal workings of the human mind. Mental events are subjective and personal, and they can't be recorded in the same way that a wavelength of light or the frequency of a sound can be recorded. The structuralists' solution to this problem was to develop a technique called **systematic introspection,** which required people to provide *rigorous* descriptions, or self-reports, of their own internal experiences. In principle, anyone can turn attention inward and observe his or her active mental life. If you're trained properly, the structuralists argued, your observations become systematic enough to build a science of psychology.

Trained introspectionists spent hours trying to isolate and describe the fundamental elements found in simple sensations. Wundt believed that the resulting self-reports were of immense value to psychology, especially in conjunction with more objective measures like reaction time. Structuralists like Wundt and Titchener tended to pick rather simple events to study, such as the perception of a sound or color, because these events were assumed to be easier to break apart. One result of the effort was the amassing of volumes of data about elementary sensory experiences. Titchener's laboratory, for example, was one of the first to document that complex tastes could be broken down into combinations of four elementary tastes: salty, bitter, sour, and sweet (Webb, 1981).

Functionalism

Once psychology was legitimized by Wundt as an independent subject matter of science, psychology departments began to spring up rapidly throughout the world. This was particularly true in North America, where literally dozens of laboratories were established in the last two decades of the nineteenth century (Hilgard, 1987). Titchener, for example, immigrated to the United States and established his own psychological laboratory at Cornell University. By 1890 psychologists already had available to them a number of professional journals reporting the results of research, as well as a number of highly influential textbooks of psychology (e.g., James, 1890). In 1892 the American Psychological Association was founded, and an American who had trained under Wundt in Germany, G. Stanley Hall (1846–1924), was installed as its first president. By 1905 the Association had elected its first woman president, Mary Whiton Calkins.

North American psychologists, however, quickly began to veer away from the strict structuralist approach advocated by many European psychologists. Whereas the structuralists tended to focus exclusively on the *content* of immediate experience, dissecting the mind into parts, North American psychologists worried more about the *function* of immediate experience. What is the *purpose* of the mental operations that underlie immediate experience? How are the components of mind *used* to achieve this end? Because the emphasis was on function rather than content, this school of thought became generally known as **functionalism.** Functionalists believe that it's not the analysis of structure but the analysis of function and purpose that should occupy the attention of psychologists (Angell, 1903; Dewey, 1896; James, 1890).

Functionalists such as William James (1842–1910) and James Rowland Angell (1869–1949) were convinced that it's not possible to understand a whole like the mind by simply looking at its parts—that's like trying to understand a house by analyzing the underlying bricks and mortar (James, 1884). It's necessary to first understand the goal—what specifically is being attempted by the mental operation—then you can try to decipher how the individual parts work together to achieve that goal. For example, to understand how memory works you must first

Wilhelm Wundt, circa 1912, established the first psychological laboratory at the University of Leipzig in 1879.

systematic introspection
An early investigative technique used to study the mind; systematic introspection required subjects to look inward and provide rigorous descriptions of their own internal experiences.

functionalism
An early school of psychology; functionalists believe that the proper way to understand mind and behavior is to analyze their function and purpose. You can only truly understand a mental process, functionalists argue, by first knowing the purpose of the mental process.

William James, shown here in 1868, was convinced that to understand a mental process, it's important to consider its function—how does it help the individual solve problems in the environment?

John Watson, who rejected the study of the mind in favor of the study of observable behavior, is shown here at age 30.

behaviorism
A school of psychology proposing that the proper subject matter of psychology is directly observable behavior and the situations that lead to changes in behavior, rather than immediate conscious experience.

consider the purpose of memory—what specific kinds of problems do our memory systems help us solve as we work our way through the day?

Darwin's ideas about evolution through natural selection were extremely influential in the development of this way of thinking. If you want to analyze the color markings on a butterfly's wings, a Darwinian theorist would argue, you must ask how those markings help the butterfly survive. Similarly, when analyzing the operations and processes of mind, a functionalist would argue, we need to focus first on the adaptive value of those operations—how they help people solve the problems they face.

Functionalism had a liberalizing effect on the development of psychology in North America. It greatly expanded the range of topics that were acceptable for scientific psychology to cover. For example, it became important to study how an organism interacts with its environment, which led to an early emphasis on learning (Thorndike, 1898) and to the study of individual differences (how people differ). Later, some functionalists turned their attention to applied issues, such as how people solve practical problems in industry and in educational settings (e.g., Taylor, 1911). To a functionalist, just about any aspect of behavior or mind was considered fair game for study, and psychology in North America boomed.

Behaviorism

The distinctive shape of psychology was destined to undergo an even more radical transformation in the first two decades of the twentieth century. Although functionalism and structuralism differed in their emphasis, both schools of thought still considered the fundamental problem in psychology to be understanding immediate conscious experience. The great functionalist William James, in particular, is well known for his superb analysis of the content and purpose of *consciousness*, which he compared to a flowing and ever-changing stream (see Chapter 6). Around 1900, the technique of introspection—looking inward to observe one's own mind—remained the dominant method of analysis in the tool kit of the experimental psychologist.

Yet not all psychologists were convinced that self-observation, even when systematic, could lead to consistent and valid scientific data. By definition, observations are personal, so there is no way to be certain that the recorded observations accurately reflect the internal workings of the mind, or are representative of all people (remember our earlier problem with the black box?). It was also recognized that introspection might change the mental operations being observed. If you're concentrating intently on documenting the elements of a banana, it seems likely that you are experiencing "banana" in an atypical way—not as something to eat, but rather as a complex collection of sensations. Introspection also limited the range of populations and topics that could be covered—it's difficult to ask someone with a severe mental disorder, for example, to introspect systematically on his or her condition (Marx & Cronan-Hillix, 1987).

For these and other reasons, psychologists started to question the usefulness of studying immediate conscious experience. Increasingly, a shift began toward the study of *behavior*. The intellectual leader of this new movement was a young professor at Johns Hopkins University named John B. Watson (1878–1958). Watson believed that psychology should discard all references to consciousness or mental events. Such events cannot be publicly observed, he argued, and therefore fall outside of the proper domain of science. Observable behavior should be the proper subject matter of psychology; consequently, the task for the scientific researcher is to discover how changes in the environment can lead to changes in measurable behavior. Because of its emphasis entirely on behavior, Watson called this new way of thinking **behaviorism** (Watson, 1913, 1919).

Behaviorism had an enormous impact on the development of psychology, particularly in North America. Remember, the psychology of Wundt and James was the psychology of mind and immediate experience. Yet by the second and third decades of the twentieth century, references to consciousness or immediate experience had largely vanished from the psychological vocabulary, as had the technique of systematic introspection. Researchers now concerned themselves with measuring behavior, especially in animals, and noting how carefully controlled laboratory experiences could change behavior (Skinner, 1938; Hull, 1943). Influential psychologists such as B. F. Skinner (1904–1990) were able to provide repeated demonstrations of the practical value of the behaviorist approach. Skinner discovered principles of behavior modification—how actions change with the application of reinforcement and nonreinforcement—that are now widely used in such settings as mental hospitals, schools, and the workplace (Skinner, 1969). We'll discuss these principles in some detail in Chapter 7.

The behaviorist approach dominated psychology for decades. However, as you'll see later in this chapter, its influence was not to last forever. To help you put things in perspective, the "Concept Summary" table on page 19 summarizes the three main schools of psychology's early days.

PIONEERS: THE INFLUENCE OF WOMEN

As noted earlier, Mary Whiton Calkins was elected president of the American Psychological Association in 1905. It's worth drawing special attention to this accomplishment because women have often been overlooked in historical treatments of psychology (Scarborough & Furumoto, 1987). The success of Mary Calkins is especially noteworthy considering the significant discrimination against women in the early days of psychology. Calkins, for example, was denied admittance to Harvard University (as were all women), and she was only allowed to take classes with William James as a "guest" graduate student. She passed the final examinations for the Ph.D. but was never officially awarded the degree.

Calkins made a number of contributions to the science of psychology, including the development of the paired-associate learning technique (a method for studying memory that is still in use today), and she was a major contributor to philosophy as well. The first woman to receive a Ph.D. in psychology was Margaret Floy Washburn (in 1894) who went on to become the second woman president of the American Psychological Association in 1921. Washburn's early contributions were in the structuralist tradition—she published her dissertation in one of Wundt's journals—and later she became very well known for her book *The Animal Mind* (1908) and for her behavioral views on consciousness.

Calkins and Washburn are notable examples of women pioneers in psychology, but they were hardly alone. A number of others overcame significant hardships to become active contributors to the developing science. For example, Christine Ladd-Franklin was famous for her early work on color vision, and Lillien Martin, who also made significant contributions in perception, rose to head the department at Stanford University in 1915. In the coming chapters, you'll read more about the contributions of women to psychology, and you'll find that women continue to be among the most important contributors to psychological thought.

FREUD AND THE HUMANISTS: THE INFLUENCE OF THE CLINIC

At roughly the same time psychology in America was undergoing its identity crisis, a medical doctor practicing in Vienna was mounting his own kind of psychological revolution. Although Sigmund Freud (1856–1939) had been trained as a neurologist (someone who studies the nervous system), his insights were to come not from the laboratory but from his experiences as a practitioner, or clinician. Freud regularly encountered patients whose physical problems turned out to be psychological in origin. His efforts to develop effective methods of treatment for these disorders led him to an all-encompassing theory of mind that was to influence legions of future psychologists and psychiatrists (Freud, 1900, 1910, 1940).

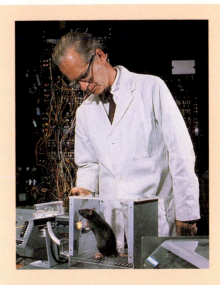

B. F. Skinner, shown here with one of his famous "Skinner boxes," championed the behaviorist approach and was one of the most influential psychologists of the twentieth century.

Mary Whiton Calkins, the first woman president of the American Psychological Association.

Margaret Floy Washburn, the first woman to receive a Ph.D in psychology.

Sigmund Freud, developer of psychoanalysis, is shown here in the early 1920s.

psychoanalysis
A term used by Freud to describe his theory of mind and system of therapy.

Psychoanalysis

Freud called his theory of mind and system of therapy **psychoanalysis.** The term is appropriate because Freud believed that the mind and its contents—the *psyche*—must be *analyzed* extensively before effective treatments can begin. In his view, psychological problems need to be solved through *insight*: The patient, or client, needs to understand exactly how his or her memories and other mental processes lead to problem behaviors. For this reason, psychoanalysis is often referred to as a form of "insight" therapy.

One of Freud's unique contributions was the emphasis he placed on *unconscious* determinants of behavior. Freud believed each person houses a kind of hidden reservoir in the mind, filled with memories, urges, and conflicts that guide and control actions. By unconscious, he meant that these conflicts and memories cannot be accessed directly through conscious introspection—you might try, but your mind blocks you from consciously experiencing certain feelings and memories on your own. If you accept Freud's reasoning, it follows that psychology should not be based solely on the study of immediate experience because conscious awareness can often be misleading. People's thoughts as well as their behaviors, Freud argued, are the by-products of unconscious forces that are well beyond current awareness.

Though Freud was basically working outside of mainstream developments in scientific psychology, he too would have rejected systematic introspection as a viable technique for the analysis of mind—but for reasons different from the behaviorists'. Freud believed that recording immediate experience was of interest, but only as a way of discovering hidden conflicts and desires. Freud relied instead on the analysis of dreams—which he believed were largely symbolic—and the occasional slip of the tongue as his primary investigative data. He spent long hours listening to his patients relate their latest dreams or fantasies in the hope of discovering some symbolic key that would unlock the contents of his patients' unconscious minds. His complex analyses of the mind and its symbols led him to develop a theory of how the unconscious mind defends itself from those seeking to unlock its secrets. We'll consider this theory, as well as its applications for the treatment of psychological disorders, in more detail in Chapters 12 and 15.

In addition to stressing unconscious influences on behavior, Freud believed that childhood experiences play an important role in shaping adult behavior. He suggested that children go through stages of psychological development and that progression through the stages depends on a complex interplay between innate sexual urges and experience. He proposed, for example, that boys become erotically attached to their mothers during childhood and consequently experience anxiety about potential castration by their father. These urges and anxieties are unconscious, of course, so the adult male is unlikely to consciously remember any of these conflicts. Freud's theory was considered shocking when it was first introduced (Freud lived during the highly moralistic Victorian era), and it continues to be criticized today. For example, Freud has been criticized for being biased against women (Lerman, 1986; Masson, 1984). However, there is no denying the impact of psychoanalytic thought. Psychodynamic theories of human personality—those that stress unconscious forces in determining behavior—continue to be influential in modern psychology.

The Humanistic Response

As noted, Freud's influence was substantial, especially among clinicians seeking to provide effective therapy for psychologically disturbed patients. The familiar image of the client lying on a couch talking about his or her childhood, while the therapist silently jots down notes, is a fairly accurate description of the way early

CONCEPT SUMMARY
Approaches to the Study of Psychology

General Focus	Specific Approach	Important Figure(s)	Focuses of Approach
Research	Structuralism	Wundt, Titchener	Determining the structure of immediate conscious experience through the use of *systematic introspection,* in which one attempts to describe the fundamental elements associated with simple thoughts and sensations.
	Functionalism	James, Angell	Determining the *functions* of conscious experience through the use of introspection, naturalistic observation, and the measurement of individual differences. Influenced by Darwin, it greatly expanded the range of topics studied in psychology.
	Behaviorism	Watson, Skinner	Establishing laws of observable *behavior*. The approach rejects the study of immediate conscious experience and mental events, unless they are defined in terms of observable behavior. It was the dominant approach to scientific psychology until the "cognitive revolution" of the 1950s.
Clinical	Psychoanalytic	Freud	Analyzing personality and treating psychological disorders by focusing on *unconscious* determinants of behavior. Also contends that childhood experiences play an important role in shaping adult behavior.
	Humanistic	Rogers, Maslow	Each person's unique self, and capacity for growth. A reaction against Freud, it emphasized that humans are basically good, and have a unique capacity for self-awareness, choice, responsibility, and growth.

psychoanalysis was performed. However, not all psychologists were comfortable with this approach. Freudian psychology paints a dark and pessimistic view of human nature. It presents human actions as the product of unconscious animalistic urges related to sex and aggression. Moreover, it dismisses any awareness that people might have about why they act the way they do as symbolic and misleading; instead, people's actions are really motivated by deeply hidden conflicts of which they are unaware.

In the 1950s negative reactions to Freud's view of therapy and mind led to the development of a new movement known as **humanistic psychology.** Humanistic psychologists such as Carl Rogers (1905–1987) and Abraham Maslow (1908–1970) rejected the pessimistic views of Freud and focused instead on what they considered to be the human's unique capacity for self-awareness, choice, responsibility, and growth. People are not helpless unknowing animals, the humanists argued, controlled by unconscious forces—they are ultimately in control of their own destinies and can rise above whatever innate sexual or animalistic urges they possess. Humans are built for personal growth, to seek their fullest potential, to become all they are capable of being (Maslow, 1954; Rogers, 1951).

The optimistic message of the humanists was to play a significant role in theories of personality development, as well as in the treatment of psychological disorders. Carl Rogers, for example, promoted the idea of *client-centered therapy,* in which the therapist is seen not as an analyst or judge, but rather as a supporter and friend. Humanistic psychologists believe that all individuals have a considerable amount of untapped potential that must be nurtured by an empathetic therapist. This idea remains influential among modern psychological approaches to therapy (see Chapters 12 and 15).

? CRITICAL THINKING

Although Freud was not technically a psychologist—he was a medical doctor—would you classify him as a clinical, an applied, or a research psychologist?

humanistic psychology
A movement in psychology that emerged largely as a reaction against the pessimism of Freud. Humanistic psychologists focus on people's unique capacity for choice, responsibility, and growth.

Carl Rogers helped develop the humanistic perspective, which focuses on our unique capacity for self awareness, responsibility, and growth.

TEST YOURSELF 1.2

Test your knowledge about how thinking in psychology developed by answering the following questions. (You will find the answers in the Appendix.)

1. Most modern psychologists believe that the mind and the body are:
   a. controlled by different sections of the pineal gland.
   b. best considered as one and the same.
   c. separate, but both can be studied with the scientific method.
   d. best studied by philosophers and physiologists, respectively.

2. Fill in the blanks in the following paragraph. Choose your answers from the following set of terms: behavior, behaviorism, emotions, empiricists, functionalists, introspection, structuralists, thoughts.

   Functionalists and structuralists used the technique of ___introspection___ to understand immediate conscious experience. The ___structuralists___ believed that it was best to break the mind down into basic parts, much like a chemist would seek to understand a chemical compound. The ___empiricists functionalists___ were influenced by Darwin's views on natural selection, and focused primarily on the purpose and adaptive value of mental events. ___Behaviorism___, founded by John Watson, steered psychology away from the study of immediate conscious experience toward an emphasis on ___behaviorism___.

3. Freud's psychoanalysis differs from Rogers' humanistic approach in which of the following ways?
   a. Psychoanalysis is "client-centered" rather than "therapist centered."
   b. Psychoanalysis is designed to promote self-awareness and personal growth.
   c. Psychoanalysis minimizes the influence of early childhood experiences.
   d. Psychoanalysis is designed to reveal hidden urges and memories related to sex and aggression.

Understanding the Focus of Modern Psychology

LEARNING GOALS

1. Describe what it means to adopt an eclectic approach.
2. Discuss the origins and meaning of the cognitive revolution.
3. Describe recent develops in biology and how they have influenced modern psychology.
4. Discuss why psychologists think cultural factors are important determinants of behavior and mind.

eclectic approach
The position adopted by many psychologists that it's useful to select or adopt information from several sources—one need not rely entirely on any single perspective or school of thought.

The subject matter of psychology has undergone substantial changes since Wundt established the first psychological laboratory in 1879. Vigorous arguments have taken place—often lasting for decades—about the proper focus for psychology (mind or behavior?) and about how to conceive of human nature (e.g., is there free will?). You shouldn't be too surprised by the presence of controversy, however. Remember, the discipline is only a little over a century old. Psychology is still getting its theoretical feet wet.

As we greet the twenty-first century, the majority of psychologists have turned away from a strict allegiance to one school of thought, such as behaviorism or psychoanalysis, and have adopted a more **eclectic approach.** The word *eclectic* in this context means that one selects or adopts information from many different sources rather than relying entirely on one perspective or school of thought. Eclecticism is common among both clinicians working in the field and research psychologists working primarily in the laboratory.

In the case of the clinical psychologist, the best technique often depends on the preferences of the client and on the particular problem at hand. For instance, some kinds of phobias—irrational fears of things like heights or spiders—can be treated effectively by focusing on the fearful behavior itself and ignoring its ultimate origin. (We don't need to know why you're afraid of snakes; we can just try to deal with the fear itself.) Other kinds of problems may require the therapist to determine how factors in childhood contribute to and prolong maladaptive adult behavior. Modern clinical psychologists tend to pick and choose among perspectives in an effort to find the approach that works best for their clients.

Research psychologists also tend to take an eclectic approach. For example, depending on the circumstance, a researcher might try to determine the genetic or biological origins of a behavior or seek simply to describe the conditions under which the behavior occurs. If it is possible to catalog when and under what environmental conditions a behavior occurs, the behavior can be modified in a number of positive ways. Researchers recognize that it's possible to understand behavior and mind from many different perspectives, at many different levels of specificity.

Three additional trends or perspectives have become quite influential in recent years. Modern psychologists remain eclectic, but increasingly you'll find them appealing to *cognitive*, *biological*, and *cultural* factors to explain behavior. Because of the special emphasis these factors currently receive, I highlight them briefly in the following sections.

THE COGNITIVE REVOLUTION

By the 1950s, many psychologists had grown uncomfortable with the strict idea, promoted by behaviorism, that behavior is the only proper subject matter for psychology. Researchers began to show renewed interest in the fundamental problems of consciousness and internal mental processes (Miller et al., 1960; Neisser, 1967). A shift away from behaviorism began, and this movement, which is still going strong, is known generally as the **cognitive revolution.** The word *cognitive* refers to the process of knowing or perceiving; as you may remember from our earlier discussion, cognitive psychologists are research psychologists who study things like memory, learning, and reasoning.

There are a number of reasons why psychologists have returned to the study of internal mental phenomena. One factor is the refinement of research techniques that enable investigators to infer the characteristics of mind directly from observable behavior. Recording such regularities in behavior as reaction times or forgetting rates can provide detailed information about internal mental processes, provided the experiments are conducted properly. You'll learn about some of the specific tactics of psychological research in Chapter 2, and in subsequent chapters you'll see how those techniques have been applied to the study of the mind as well as behavior.

Another important factor that helped fuel the cognitive revolution was the development of the computer, which became a model of sorts for the human mind. Computers function through an interplay between *hardware*—the fixed structural features of the machine such as the internal chips and the disk drives—and *software*, the programs that tell the hardware what to do. Although the human mind cannot be compared directly to a computer, it's useful to conceive of behavior as reflecting the interplay between biological (or genetic) factors—that is, the hardwired structures of the brain and nervous system—and the tactics and strategies (the software) we learn from the environment. Cognitive psychologists tend to develop explanations of behavior based on appeals to *information processing systems*—internal structures in the brain that have developed to process or manipulate information from the environment in ways that help to solve problems (see Chapters 8 and 9).

As you'll discover throughout this book, behavior is often influenced by people's beliefs and by the manner in which they think. Everything from perceptions and memories, to decisions about what foods to eat, to our choice of friends is critically influenced by prior knowledge and beliefs. Many psychologists are convinced as well that the key to understanding certain psychological disorders, such as depression, lies in the analysis of an individual's thought patterns.

cognitive revolution
The shift away from strict behaviorism, begun in the 1950s, characterized by renewed interest in fundamental problems of consciousness and internal mental processes.

Inside the Problem   The Psychology of Stoves and Doors

At the very beginning of the chapter, I mentioned that psychologists have something to say about a variety of topics—even the design of the kitchen stove. You may not have thought too much about the role of psychology in stove design, but remember: Between every object and its successful use is a user, a human being. It's this human factor that often determines whether the product will be a success or a disaster. Let's see how a modern psychologist might analyze proper and improper stove design.

Does your stove look like the one depicted in the left panel of Figure 1.4? Mine does. There are four burners, arranged in a rectangle, and four control knobs that line up horizontally along the front (or sometimes the back). Your job as a user is to learn the relationship, or what

psychologists call the *mapping*, between the control knobs and the activation of each burner. In this case you need to learn that the far left knob controls the back burner on the left. Or is it the front burner on the left? If you have a stove like this, which is psychologically incorrect, the odds are that you have trouble remembering which knob controls which burner. Many a time, I've placed a pot of water on one of the burners and turned a control knob, only to find moments later that I've turned on the wrong burner. The reason is simple: The stove has been designed with an unnatural mapping between its controls and the burners. (By the way, the stove came with the house.)

"Mapping" is easier to understand when you look at a psychologically correct design, as depicted in the middle panel of

Figure 1.4. Notice in this case that the arrangement of the burners naturally aligns with the controls. The left-to-right display of the control knobs matches the left-to-right arrangement of the burners. There is no need to learn the mapping in this case—it's obvious at first sight which knob you need to turn to activate the appropriate burner. Alternatively, if you want to keep the rectangular arrangement of the stove top, then simply arrange the control knobs in a rectangular manner that matches the burners, as shown in the far right panel. The point is that there are natural and unnatural ways to express the relationship between product control and product function. Taking advantage of the natural mapping requires that you consider the human factor—in this case, the fact that humans tend to rely on spatial

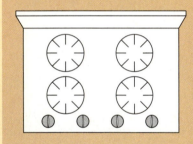 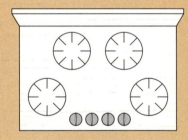 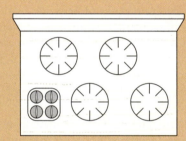

FIGURE 1.4
The Human Factors of Stove Design
The stove on the left does not provide a natural "mapping" between the control knobs and the burners and is therefore difficult to use. The stoves in the middle and on the right provide psychologically correct designs that reduce user errors.

Depressed individuals tend to think in rigid and inflexible ways, and some forms of therapy are directed specifically at challenging these entrenched thoughts and beliefs. You'll see many references to thoughts and cognitions as we investigate a range of psychological phenomena. For a closer look at how cognitive factors can even influence the design of the kitchen stove, see the accompanying feature, "Inside the Problem."

DEVELOPMENTS IN BIOLOGY

An equally important contributor to the focus of modern psychology has been the substantial developments in the understanding of the *biological* underpinnings of behavior. Over the years researchers have uncovered fascinating links between structures in the brain and the phenomena of behavior and mind (see Figure 1.5). It is now possible to record the activity of brain cells directly, and it's been discovered that individual brain cells often respond to particular kinds of events in the environment. For example, there are cells in the "visual" part of the brain that

Examples of psychologically incorrect and correct door designs.

similarity (left knob to left burner; right knob to right burner).

Doors provide additional excellent examples of psychologically correct and incorrect design. Take a look at the first door shown in the series of photos. I'm sure you've seen a door like this, with a single bar that needs to be pushed or pulled. But how many times have you slammed yourself into the wrong side of the bar, leaving yourself with an unopened door and a rapidly growing bruise? People do this all the time, even when the door in question is one they use (or misuse) on a regular basis. The middle door shows another example of bad design. In this instance, there is a large flat plate bearing the word PULL. This design is faulty because large flat plates naturally lead us to push, not pull. The fact that the door requires the PULL sign in large letters is one indication of a rather significant design flaw. Do you want to see a psychologically correct door design? The door in the far right panel is unambiguous and easy to use: The flat plates naturally induce us to push, and the top plate on the left tells which side to push. Simple enough—that is, if you take the human factor into account.

As we've stressed in this chapter, all humans interact with the world with a kind of adaptive tool kit—people use certain strategies and have certain natural tendencies that help them to adapt to the ever-changing experiences of the world. People are naturally inclined to push on large flat things because this tendency is usually adaptive: If the object has a large flat side, you can use the entire weight of your body, through pushing, to produce movement. But if a product, like a door, works against this natural tendency, it can be extremely difficult to use. It's critical therefore that people's natural behavioral tendencies be taken into account at some point during the design process.

respond actively only when particular colors, or patterns of light and dark, are shown to the eye. Cells in other parts of the body and brain respond to inadequate supplies of nutrients by "motivating" one to seek food.

Moreover, technology is now allowing psychologists to take "snapshots" of mental life in action. As you'll see in Chapter 3, it is now possible to create images of how activities in the brain change as the mind processes different things in its environment. These pictures of the brain in action can help researchers understand normal as well as abnormal brain activity. For example, it's possible to record brain activity during depression, extreme anxiety, or even during auditory and visual hallucinations. This information is useful in helping researchers pinpoint where problems in the brain potentially lie and in acting as a kind of road map for treatment.

Great strides have been made as well in the understanding of brain chemistry—that is, of how natural drugs inside the brain control the range of behaviors people are capable of expressing. It turns out that certain psychological problems,

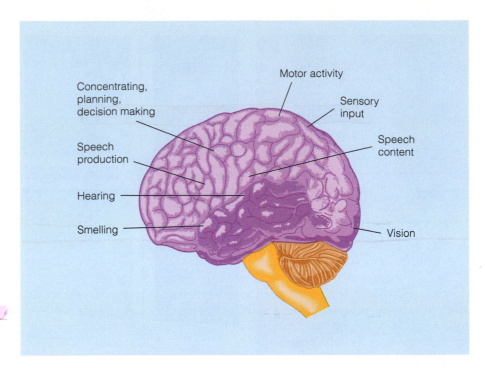

FIGURE 1.4
Specificity in the Brain
Researchers have discovered that certain functions in the body appear to be controlled by specific areas of the brain. Developments in the biological sciences continue to have an enormous impact on the thinking of psychologists.

such as depression and schizophrenia, may be related to imbalances among the chemical messengers in the brain. These developments, which we'll discuss in detail in Chapters 3, 14, and 15, are shaping the way psychological theories are constructed and how psychological problems are treated.

RECOGNIZING CULTURE

It's not possible to characterize modern psychological thinking without also discussing the concept of culture and the role it plays in behavior and mind. By **culture,** psychologists generally mean the shared values, customs, and beliefs that are characteristic of a group or community. Cultural groups can be based on obvious things, such as ethnicity, race, or socioeconomic class, but also on political, religious, or other factors (e.g., those who share the same sexual orientation might be considered as a cultural group). Culture is a broad construct, and its influences can be found in virtually all aspects of behavior and mind.

Recognizing that culture exerts a strong influence on our thoughts and actions may seem obvious to you, but it was largely ignored in mainstream psychology for many years. In the introductory textbook that I used as a college student, group influences were not discussed except for a mere three paragraphs covering why individuals might differ in intelligence. Psychologists have always recognized that behavior is influenced by the environment, which can mean one's culture, but it was the behavior of individuals in isolation rather than the behavior of individuals in groups that received the most attention. Researchers spent their time looking for universal principles of behavior, those that cut across all people in all groups, rather than exploring how the shared values of a community might affect how people think and act. The search for universal principles is still actively pursued today, but cross-cultural factors are now considered to be an integral part of the story of psychology (Cooper & Denner, 1998).

There were a few notable psychologists who paid attention to culture early on, especially in attempting to explain cognitive and social development. Over half a century ago, the Russian psychologist Lev Vygotsky proposed that children's thoughts and actions originate from their social interactions, particularly with parents. Vygotsky believed that it's not possible to understand the mind of a child without carefully considering the child's social and cultural world. In an important

culture
The shared values, customs, and beliefs that are characteristic of a group or community.

Cultural groups can be based on obvious things, such as ethnicity, race, or socioeconomic class, but also on political, religious, and other factors.

sense, the properties of a child's mind are actually created by his or her social and cultural interactions. At first, these ideas were not very influential in psychology, partly because Vygotsky died young in the 1930s, but they've recently been rediscovered by psychologists and are now being actively pursued. (You'll read a bit more about Vygotsky in Chapter 4.)

Why have cultural factors finally become so important to psychologists? There are number of reasons, but perhaps most importantly, studies continue to show that culture matters, even when studying basic psychological principles such as memory (DiMaggio, 1997; Mullen, 1994), perception (Davies & Corbett, 1997), and reasoning (Li et al., 1996). Most psychologists now realize that a full understanding of behavior and mind cannot be achieved without considering the individual in his or her social and cultural context. Cultural factors play a role in how we think, interact with each other, and even in how we see the world.

SOLVING PROBLEMS WITH THE ADAPTIVE MIND

Psychologists are in the business of explaining behavior—discovering general principles—but the thoughts and actions of most people appear to be everchanging. Pick any two people (or animals for that matter), put them in the same situation, and you may well see two different reactions. Take your closest friend—can you predict how he or she will react to a new experience with any kind of certainty? Or think about the number of times you've been surprised or even shocked by the reaction or moodiness of someone you thought you knew.

It's difficult to predict behavior because everyone's view of the world is highly personal and subjective. No two people have exactly the same experiences; no two people are born with exactly the same physical or genetic attributes (even identical twins have *some* differences). Behavior is virtually always determined by multiple causes, so it's hard to gather the information needed to generate a reasonable prediction. At the same time, psychologists are convinced that people and animals do not act in haphazard ways; there are reasons why people act the way they do, and it is the job of the psychologist to discover exactly what those reasons might be. The cause of a particular behavior may lie completely in the environment: It might be that you've been rewarded or punished for acting a certain way in the past, and those experiences are continuing to control your behavior. Alternatively, your actions might arise from the operation of some internal biological system that may not even be under your direct willful control.

As I mentioned at the beginning of the chapter, each of the chapters in this textbook is organized around a set of adaptive or practical *problems*. The problem-solving approach is designed to promote the idea that we think and act for adaptive reasons; we use our psychological tool kit to help us solve problems every day. But this theme is also designed to provide you with a direct link between the topic discussions and

CRITICAL THINKING

Behavior can be difficult to predict but still be governed by understandable principles. Think about how hard it is to predict the weather or even the movement of a ball rolling down an inclined plane. Would you claim that these activities are not controlled by principled "laws of nature"?

the real world. For instance, in Chapter 13, you'll learn about a topic in social psychology called attribution theory. Why? Because attribution theory deals with a very important everyday problem: How do we assign a cause to someone's behavior? You constantly need to interpret the behavior of others, whether it's the sudden anger of a friend or the disapproving look of a professor. At first glance, attribution theory may seem like an abstract topic, but it's actually quite relevant to your life.

The problem-solving approach is also intended to encourage you to think critically about the material. Rather than just memorizing the facts about a topic, you should try to make the connection between the topic under discussion and solving the adaptive or practical problem. For example, how exactly does a procedure like classical conditioning, which we'll discuss in Chapter 7, help psychologists understand how people learn about the signaling properties of events? Exactly how does a diagnostic procedure like the DSM-IV help psychologists understand and diagnose psychological problems?, and so on.

Finally, and perhaps most important, the problem-solving approach is designed to help promote a common theme of understanding across the chapters. Psychology gains cohesion when behavior is viewed as the product of an adaptive mind. You are encouraged to understand that behaviors, as well as the methods of psychologists, are reactions to problems faced. Emphasizing adaptiveness will increase your sensitivity to the diversity of behavior, both within and across species. Individuals respond and react to unique situations, use strategies that are culturally bound, and are influenced by their individual biological states.

TEST YOURSELF 1.3

Test your knowledge about the focus of modern psychology by answering the following questions. (You will find the answers in the Appendix.)

1. According to the eclectic approach, in choosing the best technique to use in therapy, you should consider:

   a. the specific unconscious urges that are driving behavior.
   b. the training and biases of the therapist/researcher.
   c. the preferences of the client and the particular problem under investigation.
   d. the availability of relevant monitoring equipment.

2. Fill in the blanks in the following paragraph. Choose your answers from the following set of terms: biology, cognitive, computer, cultural, philosophy.

   Over the past several decades psychologists have returned to the study of internal mental phenomena such as consciousness. This shift away from strict behaviorism has been labeled the ___COGNITIVE___ revolution. An important factor that helped fuel this revolution was the development of the ___COMPUTER___ which became a model of sorts for the human mind. Developments in ___BIOLOGY___ are also playing an important role in shaping modern psychology and in creating effective treatments for psychological problems.

3. Increasingly, psychologists are appealing to cultural factors to help explain human behavior. Which of the following statements about culture and psychology is false?

   a. Cultural influences were largely ignored by psychologists for many years
   b. Culture influences social processes but not basic psychological processes such as memory or reasoning.
   c. A few notable psychologists, such as Lev Vygotsky, studied cultural influences many decades ago.
   d. By culture, psychologists mean the shared values, customs, and beliefs that are characteristic of a group or community.

Solving the Problems

At the end of every chapter, you'll find a section that summarizes the main points of the chapter from the perspective of our "problems to be solved." This is a good point to stop and think about the facts and theories you've read about and to try to see how they relate to the particular problems we've discussed. In this chapter, my primary goal was to introduce you to the science of psychology. I framed our discussion around three main problems.

◉ **Defining and Describing Psychology.** Psychology is the scientific study of behavior and mind. Notice that this definition makes no specific reference to psychological problems or to any kind of abnormal behavior. Although many psychologists (especially clinical psychologists) do indeed work to promote mental health, applied psychologists and research psychologists tend to work primarily on normal populations of individuals. The goal of the scientific study of behavior and mind is to discover general principles that can be applied widely to help people adapt more successfully—in the workplace, in school, or at home.

◉ **Tracing the Evolution of Psychological Thought.** Even though psychology has existed as a separate subject matter of science for little more than a century, people have pondered the mysteries of behavior and mind for thousands of years. Psychology has its primary roots in the areas of philosophy and physiology. Thinkers in these fields addressed several fundamental psychological issues, such as the relation between the mind and the body, and the origins of knowledge. Most psychologists solve the mind–body problem by assuming that the two are essentially one and the same—thoughts, ideas, and emotions are considered to arise out of the biological processes of the brain. It is also common for psychologists to assume that many basic kinds of behaviors originate from natural ingrained tendencies (nature) as well as from lifetime experiences (nurture).

Once the discipline of psychology was established by Wundt in 1879, vigorous arguments ensued over the proper way to characterize and study the mind. Structuralists, such as Wundt and Titchener, believed the world of immediate experience could be broken down into elements, much like how a chemist seeks to understand a chemical compound. The functionalists argued instead that the proper focus should be on the function and purpose of behavior. The behaviorists, on the other hand, rejected the world of immediate experience in favor of the exclusive study of behavior. Added to the mix were the insights of Sigmund Freud, with his emphasis on the unconscious mind, and the arguments of the humanists, who strongly advocate free will and the power of personal choice.

◉ **Understanding the Focus of Modern Psychology.** Each of the psychological perspectives that were influential in psychology's first century remain influential to a certain extent today. But most modern psychologists adopt an eclectic approach—they pick and choose from the perspectives based on the problem at hand. The study of behavior remains of primary importance, but the world of inner experience is also considered fair game for study, as evidenced by the cognitive revolution and by recent developments in the biological sciences. Psychologists also increasingly point to cultural factors in their attempts to explain behavior and mind.

The problem-solving approach in this book is based on the concept of the adaptive mind: People, as well as other animals, use their mental machinery—rooted in the biological processes of the brain—to achieve certain fundamental ends. Individuals adjust their actions in a continuing effort to solve the problems that arise from ever-changing environmental conditions.

An Introduction to Psychology Chapter Summary

Psychology is the scientific study of behavior and mind, and of how people differ as a result of biological and environmental influences and cultural context. Psychological understanding lets us predict, control, and improve behavior.

Defining and Describing Psychology

STUDYING THE MIND

Self-reports: People describe their thoughts and feelings.

Biological analysis: Scientists study the brain directly.

Behavioral observation: Psychologists infer how the mind works from how the body behaves.

WHAT PSYCHOLOGISTS DO

Clinical: Diagnose and treat problems; give advice.

Applied: Help normal people in practical settings improve performance.

Research: Collect data on basic and applied issues through research and observation.

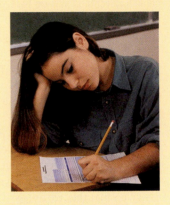

Tracing the Evolution of Psychological Thought

The intellectual roots of psychology are in philosophy and physiology.

MIND AND BODY

Descartes: The mind is separate from the body, which it controls through the pineal gland.

Modern psychologists: The mind and the body are the same because the mind is what the brain does.

WOMEN

Mary Calkins: First female president of APA. Developed paired-associate learning technique. Completed work for a Ph.D. in psychology but was denied the degree by Harvard on the basis of her gender.

Margaret Washburn: First woman to receive a doctorate in psychology; second female president of APA.

Christine Ladd-Franklin: Did significant early work on color vision.

Lillien Martin: Made significant contributions in perception.

KNOWLEDGE

Empiricism: We learn everything through experience (Aristotle).

Nativism: Some knowledge is inborn (innate), including cause and effect, space and time.

Darwin: Natural selection guides *evolution;* tendencies (genes) are inherited.

PSYCHOANALYSIS

Freud: Neurologist and clinician analyzed the mind and the unconscious determinants of behavior through dreams and free association.

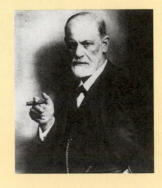

THE FIRST SCHOOLS

Structuralism: Wundt established an experimental lab to study the components of immediate experience, how they sum to a meaningful whole.

Functionalism: North American psychologists studied the adaptive purpose (*function*) of immediate experience.

Behaviorism: Immediate conscious experience cannot be observed, so behavior is the proper subject of psychology. *Watson* led this movement.

HUMANISM

Rogers and *Maslow* rejected Freud's pessimism and focused on positive traits. People control their destinies and can attain their full potential.

Understanding the Focus of Modern Psychology

The *eclectic* approach draws from diverse sources and uses various methods.

COGNITION

The process of knowing (learning, memory, reasoning) is as important as behavior.

BIOLOGY

Brain structure and activity, and genetic inheritance and makeup, are linked to thought and behavior.

CULTURE

Shared values, customs, and beliefs; race and class; and political and religious factors all influence the thoughts and actions of group members.

Terms to Remember

psychology, 4

DEFINING AND DESCRIBING PSYCHOLOGY

mind, 7
behavior, 7
clinical psychologists, 9
applied psychologists, 9
research psychologists, 9
psychiatrists, 10

TRACING THE EVOLUTION OF PSYCHOLOGICAL THOUGHT

empiricism, 11
nativism, 12
structuralism, 14
systematic introspection, 15
functionalism, 15
behaviorism, 16
psychoanalysis, 18
humanistic psychology, 19

UNDERSTANDING THE FOCUS OF MODERN PSYCHOLOGY

eclectic approach, 20
cognitive revolution, 21
culture, 24

Recommended Readings

Hunt, M. (1993). *The story of psychology.* New York: Anchor Books. A highly entertaining look at the history of psychology from the musings of the ancient Greek philosophers to modern theoretical approaches.

James, W. (1890). *The principles of psychology.* New York: Holt. (Reprinted Harvard University Press, 1983.) It's worth taking a look at James' classic work. The writing is poetic, the insights are many, and remember—this was once used as an introductory textbook in psychology!

Hilgard, E. R. (1987). *Psychology in America: An historical survey.* New York: Harcourt Brace Jovanovich. A fascinating first-hand account of the history of American psychology. The book contains many personal anecdotes collected by the author.

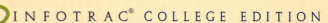

INFOTRAC® COLLEGE EDITION

For additional readings, explore Infotrac College Edition, your online library. Go to:
http://www.infotrac-college.com/wadsworth

Hint: enter the search terms: History of psychology, Behaviorism, Psychoanalysis, Humanism, Cognitive Psychology.

What's on the Web?

Bad Human Factors Designs

(www.baddesigns.com/examples.html)

Ever get frustrated with the stupid way that someone designed the things you work with everyday? Have trouble telling the difference between the buttons on your stereo? Can't figure out which side of the door to push to get out? This site is full of stupid human factors designs, complete with pictures. Surf around, and see if you can do some intelligent redesigning!

History of Psychology Timelines

(wysiwig://245/http:/www.geocities.com/Athens/Delphi /6061/en_linha.htm)

(www.cwu.edu/~warren/today.html)

A couple of impressive sites—the first gives you an extensive chronology of events that helped to shape psychology. The second provides you with a "clickable calendar"—every date of the year is linked to a list of events in the history of psychology that happened on that date! Find out what happened in the history of psychology on October 8!

History of Psychology Web Site

(http://elvers.stjoe.udayton.edu/history/welcome.htm)

This is a fantastic site, with a list of over 100 "clickable" names that will give you a description of how that person contributed to the advancement of psychology. The list ranges from Aristotle to St. Thomas Aquinas to Christine Ladd-Franklin to B.F. Skinner. You can even sort the list of historical figures according to their birthdate—see if any famous figures share your birthday!

The Wadsworth Psychology Study Center Web Site

See http://psychology.wadsworth.com/ for practice quiz questions, hypercontents, updates, critical thinking exercises, discussion forums and more! The Wadsworth Psychology Study Center provides a wealth of information fully organized and integrated by chapter.

The Tactics of Psychological Research

Todd leaned backed on his bed, headphones firmly in place, and cranked up the volume. He couldn't hear the message playing backward on the tape, the one announcing the arrival of the Antichrist. He noticed nothing at all in particular, in fact, but he didn't feel much like going to church on Sunday either.

Is it possible to influence people through the use of hidden messages—that is, messages presented at levels too low to be seen or heard? Some believe that such messages are everywhere, hidden from the naked eye by evil advertisers and dark-natured rock stars. What do you think? Are there secretive messages lurking about in advertisements, or flowing backwards on the sound track of your favorite CDs? People who believe in such *subliminal stimuli* (*subliminal* means "below threshold") assume these messages are responsible for much of society's ills, such as our sudden buying urges or especially abnormal thoughts (Key, 1973).

Fortunately, research psychologists have looked at the topic of subliminal influence and have discovered very little need for concern (e.g., Merikle & Skanes, 1992; Greenwald et al., 1991). There's almost no evidence that messages such as these are actually used by advertisers, and even if they are, their influence is probably minimal at best. The topic is of interest to us, however, because the subject of this chapter is the strategies and tactics of psychological research. How do psychologists determine whether events in the environment, such as subliminal messages, really affect mind and behavior?

As you remember from Chapter 1, psychology is a scientific enterprise. Its methods rely on *observation*, on information gathered in through the senses. Because observation is the ultimate authority in psychology, psychologists use the **scientific method** as their main tool for investigating behavior and mind. This means that if you want to understand the effect of subliminal messages on the mind, your first step is to employ the scientific method. Reduced to its barest essentials, the scientific method contains four important steps (see Figure 2.1).

1. *Observe.* The scientific method always begins, appropriately, with *observation*. In psychology, we choose the behavior of interest and begin recording its characteristics as well as the conditions under which the behavior occurs.

2. *Detect regularities.* Next, the researcher looks for *regularities* in the observations that have been collected—are there certain consistent features that the behaviors show, or conditions under which the behaviors commonly appear?

---

scientific method

An investigative method that generates empirical knowledge—that is, knowledge derived from systematic observations of the world. It involves forming a hypothesis on the basis of initial observations, and then testing the hypothesis with further observations.

FIGURE 2.1

Steps in the Scientific Method

The four major steps in the scientific method. The first step, shown in the first panel, is observation; here, the rat is observed jumping toward a checkerboard panel on the left. In step two, the researcher looks for regularities in behavior and notes that the rat, over repeated trials, consistently jumps to the checkerboard on the left. In step three, the researcher generates a hypothesis (If I move the checkerboard to the right, the rat will jump to the right), and in step four, the researcher tests the hypothesis. Here the hypothesis has turned out to be wrong. The rat is jumping left rather than following the checkerboard.

OBSERVE

Rat receives food for jumping through checkerboard panel on left

DETECT REGULARITIES

Over trials, rat consistently chooses to jump toward the checkerboard panel on left

GENERATE HYPOTHESIS

Rat has learned to associate checkerboard with food, so if checkerboard is moved to the right, then the rat will jump to the right

OBSERVE

Rat jumps to the left, suggesting rat has learned that jumping left produces food

3. *Generate hypothesis.* In step three, the researcher forms a *hypothesis*, which is essentially a prediction about the characteristics of the behavior under study. Hypotheses are normally expressed in the form of testable if-then statements: If some set of conditions is present and observed, then a certain kind of behavior will occur.

4. *Observe.* Finally, the predictions of the hypothesis are checked for accuracy—once again through *observation*. If new data are consistent with the prediction of the hypothesis, the hypothesis is supported.

Notice that the scientific method is anchored on both ends by observation. The kinds of observations that are collected in the first and last steps aren't always the same, as you'll discover in this chapter, but some kind of observation always begins and ends the scientific process. This means that psychological terms need to be defined in a way that allows you to observe. To make certain that terms and concepts meet this criterion, psychologists typically use what are called **operational definitions,** which define concepts specifically in terms of how those concepts can be measured (Levine & Parkinson, 1994; Stevens, 1939). For example, "intelligence" might be defined operationally as performance on a psychological test, and "memory" might be defined as the number of words correctly recalled on a retention test. If your goal is to investigate the topic of subliminal influence, you first need to develop an operational definition for "subliminal influence." Can you think of one? I'll return to the topic of subliminal messages later in the chapter.

operational definition
Defining concepts in terms of how those concepts are measured.

Previewing the Practical Problems

The primary goal of most psychologists is understanding. Psychologists want to know what causes behavior; they want to understand how internal processes, or external events in the environment, conspire to produce the remarkable diversity of human thought and action. However, understanding is not always easy to achieve, nor is it the only acceptable goal of psychology. Sometimes it is enough merely to describe and predict. Consider television sets, refrigerators, or computers. Most of us have no idea how these things work, nor could we fix them if they broke, but we know how to use them to enrich our lives. The same might be said of psychology; we may not always understand why people act the way they do, but if we can catalog *when* people will act in a particular way, we gain more effective control over our environment.

In this chapter you'll be introduced to the general tactics and strategies that underlie psychological research. The discussion focuses on four practical problems that researchers

Psychologists want to understand what causes people to act in common and distinctive ways.

investigating behavior and mind often attempt to solve. In each case, I'll discuss the technical solutions to these problems, and we'll pay particular attention to the pitfalls that can hinder the research process.

First, what are the proper techniques for observing and describing behavior? One of the most important steps in any psychological research project is to choose a behavior of interest and begin recording its characteristics. However, observation in research is more than just casual looking or listening—the methods of observation must be systematic.

Second, how can one predict behavior? Once a set of behavioral data has been collected and described, the researcher typically begins to think about the possibility of prediction. Descriptive research yields facts about behavior. But we need a different set of techniques to decide when and how the behavior will occur again in the future. Prediction is of value because it allows for more effective control of future environments.

Third, what are the ways to determine the underlying causes of behavior? To determine causality it is necessary to conduct *experimental research*. The researcher must systematically manipulate the environment in order to determine the effect of that manipulation on behavior. If conducted properly, experiments allow the researcher to understand *why* behavior occurs or changes in a particular situation.

Fourth, what procedures ensure that research participants are treated ethically? Is it proper for the psychologist to lurk in the shadows, carefully recording your every move in some grand attempt to advance scientific knowledge? Is it proper to experiment on animals—depriving them of food or water or destroying portions of their brain—simply to learn about the mechanisms underlying behavior? These are not easy questions to answer for any branch of science.

Observing and Describing Behavior: Descriptive Research

Because observation is so important to psychological research, it is appropriate that we begin with a discussion of descriptive research. **Descriptive research consists of the tactics and methods that underlie the direct observation and description of behavior.** At face value, the act of observation seems simple enough—after all, most people can watch and record the behavior of themselves or others. However, it's actually easy to be misled, even when the goal is simply to record behavior passively (Rosenthal & Rosnow, 1969; Rosnow & Rosenthal, 1996).

Let's suppose that you want to observe the behavior of preschoolers in the local day-care center. You arrive with cameras and recording devices in hand and begin systematic observations of the children at play. After a few moments, you notice that the children distract easily—many seem uneasy and hesitant to engage in the activities suggested by the teacher. Several children show outward signs of fear and eventually withdraw, crying, to a corner of the room. Later, in describing your results, you conclude that children in day-care centers adjust badly, and some even show early signs of poor psychological health.

It shouldn't take much thought to recognize that your research strategy may suffer from a basic problem. Whenever you observe the actions of someone else, the very act of observing can affect the behavior you're recording. In the case of the day-care center, it's likely that your unexpected presence in the center (with cameras and the like) made the children feel uncomfortable and led them to act in ways that were not representative of their normal behavior. Psychologists refer to this condition as a problem of reactivity. **Reactivity** occurs whenever an individual's behavior is changed in some way by the process of being observed. It's called "reactivity" because the subject's behavior is essentially a *reaction* to the observation process (Orne, 1969; Webb et al., 1981). The children are probably

LEARNING GOALS

1. Describe the goals and pitfalls of descriptive research.

2. Explain how psychologists conduct naturalistic research.

3. Discuss the gains and costs of case studies and surveys.

4. Explain how statistics can summarize and help interpret data.

descriptive research
The tactics and methods that underlie the direct observation and description of behavior.

reactivity
The extent to which an individual's behavior is changed as a result of being observed; the behavior becomes essentially a reaction to the process of being observed.

not naturally hesitant and distracted—they were simply startled by you and your recording devices.

One of the negative consequences of reactivity is that your observations are likely to lack external validity. **External validity** refers to how well the results of an observation generalize to other situations or are representative of real life (Campbell & Stanley, 1966; Cook & Campbell, 1979). If a child's behavior is largely a reaction to your presence as an observer, it is clearly not representative of real life. More generally, even if these children are naturally fearful, your one set of observations cannot guarantee that your conclusions are representative of how children at other day-care centers will act. To improve external validity, you must record the behavior of children at another day-care center, or preferably many day-care centers, to see whether similar patterns of behavior emerge.

NATURALISTIC OBSERVATION: FOCUSING ON REAL LIFE

One way that researchers try to reduce the problem of reactivity and improve external validity is to observe behavior in natural settings using noninterfering measures (Martin & Bateson, 1993; Timberlake & Silva, 1994). In **naturalistic observation,** the researcher records only naturally occurring behavior, as opposed to behavior produced in the laboratory, and makes a serious effort not to interfere with the behavior in any way. Because the recorded behavior is natural and has not been manufactured by the researcher, the recorded data are generally considered to be representative of real life (of course, it is also necessary to repeat the observations in different settings to be sure the results generalize). Also, if the subjects are unaware of being observed, their behavior cannot simply be a reaction to the observation process. Naturalistic observation has been used with great success by psychologists as well as by *ethologists*, biologists who study the behavior of animals in the wild (Goodall, 1990; Lorenz, 1958).

But how is it possible to observe behavior in a way that is truly noninterfering? To observe natural behavior directly, researchers sometimes use a technique called *participant observation*, in which the observer attempts to become a part of the activities being studied. For example, in the 1950s a group of psychologists infiltrated a doomsday cult group by passing themselves off as true believers. This particular cult preached the impending end of the United States, on a particular date, from a natural disaster. Once they were on the inside, the psychologists were able to record and study the reactions of the cultists when the inevitable day of

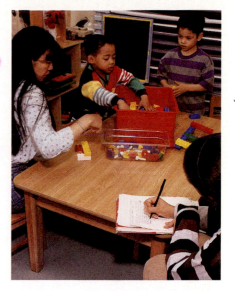

Psychologists need to worry about the problem of reactivity: Are the behaviors being observed simply a reaction to the observation process? If the behavior of these children is changed as a result of the observer's presence, then the observations may not generalize well to other situations.

external validity
The extent to which the results of an observation generalize to other situations or are representative of real life.

naturalistic observation
A research technique that involves recording only naturally occurring behavior as opposed to behavior produced in the laboratory.

In naturalistic observation, the researcher records only naturally occurring behavior, as opposed to behavior produced in the laboratory, and a concerted effort is made not to interfere with the behavior in any way.

? **CRITICAL THINKING**

Do you see any ethical problems with the technique of participant observation? After all, isn't the researcher misleading people by assuming a false identity?

doom failed to materialize (Festinger, et al., 1956). In another classic project that you'll read more about in Chapter 14, a group of researchers had themselves committed to local mental hospitals—they complained of hearing voices—in an effort to obtain an honest record of patient life inside an institution (Rosenhan, 1973). Participant observation could easily be used in our day-care center example: You could simply introduce yourself as a new teacher, rather than as a researcher, and hide your cameras or other recording equipment.

Another useful technique is to measure behavior indirectly, by looking at the *results* of a behavior rather than the behavior itself. For example, you might be able to learn something about the eating or shopping habits of teenagers at the local mall by measuring the content and quality of the litter they leave behind. Administrators at museums have been able to determine the popularity of various exhibits by noting how quickly floor tiles in front of each wear out and need to be replaced (Webb et al., 1981) (see Figure 2.2). Neither of these examples requires direct observations of behavior; it is the aftereffects—the products—of the behavior that provide the insightful clues.

Naturalistic observation is an effective technique for gaining a record of natural behavior, but it can also be used to verify the results of laboratory experiments (Miller, 1977; Timberlake & Silva, 1994). To gain control over a behavior, and to understand what causes an action to be performed, researchers usually manipulate the behavior directly through an experiment. Because it is difficult to conduct experimental research in natural settings, laboratory studies usually generate concerns about external validity. For instance, most studies of human memory have been conducted in the laboratory by having subjects learn lists of words (Bruce, 1985; Neisser, 1978). But to what extent are the psychological principles gleaned from such studies relevant to learning and remembering in natural settings? To answer this question psychologists also record natural instances of remembering and forgetting, such as eyewitness accounts of naturally occurring events, to determine whether the patterns resemble those collected in the lab (e.g., Conway et al., 1994). For reasons that will become clear later in this chapter, naturalistic observation, by itself, is a poor vehicle for determining causality. However, it can be used effectively to gather basic information about a phenomenon and, in conjunction with laboratory research, to establish the generality of psychological principles.

FIGURE 2.2

Naturalistic Observation of Behavioral Results

In a study conducted at the Chicago Museum of Science and Industry, researchers gauged the popularity of exhibits by noting how quickly the vinyl tiles in front of each display needed to be replaced. The live chick-hatching exhibit proved to be extremely popular.

CASE STUDIES: FOCUSING ON THE INDIVIDUAL

Another widely used descriptive research technique is the case study. In a **case study,** the researcher focuses on a single case, usually an individual, in order to accumulate a great deal of information about a psychological topic (Bromley, 1986; Elmes et al., 1995; Heiman, 1995). Because a great deal of information is collected about the background and behavior of one person, case studies give the researcher a very important historical perspective that aids in forming hypotheses about the possible causes of a behavior or psychological problem.

There are many famous examples of case studies. If you visit your local bookstore, you're certain to find books written about interesting cases; often the subjects suffer from psychological disorders. For example, you may have heard of Chris Sizemore, popularized in the movie *The Three Faces of Eve*, who coped with emotional distress by shifting among three distinct and quite different personalities (Thigpen & Cleckley, 1957). *Sybil*, depicted in a television miniseries of the same name, was the subject of another famous case study of multiple personality disorder (now known as dissociative identity disorder). One of the most influential psychological theories of the twentieth century, the psychoanalytic theory of Sigmund Freud, was based primarily on descriptive data derived from case studies.

However, like naturalistic observation, the case study methodology suffers from some limitations (Yin, 1998). By focusing on just a single case, researchers essentially place all of their theoretical eggs in one basket. This means that questions are often raised about external validity: Are the experiences of the research subject truly representative of others (Liebert & Liebert, 1995)? Sybil's frightening descent into dissociative identity disorder may or may not be representative of how psychological disorders normally develop. Another problem with case studies is that the claims of the individual under study are often difficult to verify. If the observations of the single subject are somehow tainted with inaccuracies—if the subject is lying, for example—the entire study must be viewed with suspicion. Once again, as with naturalistic observation, case studies are excellent vehicles for generating hypotheses but are generally ineffective for determining cause-and-effect relationships.

SURVEYS: FOCUSING ON THE GROUP

Whereas a case study focuses on a single individual, psychologists use a **survey** to sample reported behavior broadly, usually by gathering responses from many people. Most surveys are administered in the form of a questionnaire—individuals, or groups of individuals, are asked to answer questions about some personal behavior or psychological characteristic. You are of course familiar with the opinion surveys conducted by political campaigns or by the news media to capture the current attitudes of voters. Surveys can also be used purely for research purposes, to gain valuable descriptive information about behavior and mind. For example, researchers can use a survey to determine the widespread psychological aftereffects of a significant environmental disaster (Dooley et al., 1992), or to determine whether problems such as depression are more likely in elderly people who suffer financial hardships (Krause & Liang, 1993).

Figure 2.3 shows results of a survey conducted to assess some current beliefs of practicing psychotherapists. Michael Yapko (1994) asked 869 psychotherapists with differing degrees of academic training to respond to questions about the use of hypnosis as a technique for recovering forgotten or "repressed" memories of prior events. As you may know, hypnosis is sometimes used by therapists as a memory aid to help troubled clients recover forgotten instances of trauma. Ninety-seven percent of Yapko's (1994) survey respondents agreed that hypnosis is a worthwhile tool in psychotherapy, and nearly 54% were convinced that hypnosis can be used to recover memories of actual events as far back as birth. More

case study
A descriptive research technique in which the research effort is focused on a single case, usually an individual.

survey
A descriptive research technique designed to gather limited amounts of information from many people, usually by administering some kind of questionnaire.

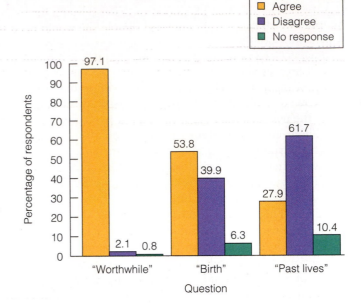

FIGURE 2.3

Opinions about Hypnosis
Selected results from the Yapko (1994) survey of psychotherapists show the percentage of respondents who agreed, disagreed, or gave no response to the following statements: "Hypnosis is a worthwhile psychotherapy tool," "Hypnosis can be used to recover memories of actual events as far back as birth," and "Hypnosis can be used to recover accurate memories of past lives."

than one in four of the respondents actually believed that hypnosis can be used to recover accurate memories of past lives.

Surveys can be significant, if conducted properly, because they provide researchers with valuable insight into what people believe. In this case, Yapko's data are alarming because they reveal how widespread misinformed views can be, even among professional psychotherapists. As you'll find in Chapters 6, 8, and 12, there is little, if any, scientific evidence to support the belief that memories recovered through hypnosis are especially accurate, nor is there any scientific evidence to support the existence of past lives (remembered or otherwise)! These survey findings point to the need for improved education and training, at least for this group of respondents. However, as you'll see shortly, before survey results like these can be accepted as truly representative of a target group, such as practicing psychotherapists, the researchers must ensure that the participants in the survey have been sampled randomly.

Sampling from a Population

The point of a survey is to gather lots of observations to help determine the characteristics of a larger group or population. If the population of interest is extremely large, such as everyone between ages 18 and 25 in the United States, researchers must decide how to select a representative subset of individuals to measure. A subset of individuals from a target population is referred to as a *sample*.

A researcher needs to consider a number of technical details when sampling from a population. For example, it is easy to end up with an unrepresentative, or *biased*, sample unless the proper precautions are taken (Weisberg et al., 1989). Let's imagine that a researcher named Rosa wants to know how often college-aged adults practice safe sex. She puts an ad containing a toll-free telephone number in selected college newspapers. Her hope is that students will call the number and answer questions about their sexual practices. However, not every college-aged student in the country will choose to participate, so Rosa will certainly end up with only a subset, or sample, of the population of interest. Do you think the data collected from her subset will be truly representative of college students?

In this case, the answer is clearly "no," because the method of sampling depends on people *choosing* to participate. Volunteers tend to produce biased samples, because people who volunteer usually have strong feelings or opinions about the study (Rosenthal & Rosnow, 1975). Think about it—would you call in and tell a researcher that you regularly fail to practice safe sex? Representative samples are produced through **random sampling,** which means that everyone in the target population has an equal likelihood of being selected for the survey. In principle, for Rosa to achieve a truly unbiased sample she would need to sample randomly from the entire population of college students—everyone in the group must have an equal chance of being selected. Because this is difficult to achieve in practice, Rosa will probably need to limit herself to sampling randomly from the population of students going to her particular college.

Now let's return to the Yapko's (1994) survey in which 869 practicing psychotherapists gave their views on the use of hypnosis as an effective memory aid. The results showed that some psychotherapists erroneously believe that memories recovered through hypnosis are accurate. Unfortunately, however, Yapko did not use a random sample of psychotherapists in his study—he simply asked therapists who attended certain conventions and workshops for their opinions. His data may therefore suffer from a volunteer problem that limits their generalizability. Only psychotherapists with strong opinions about hypnosis may have chosen to participate. To claim his results are truly representative of psychotherapists as a whole, he would need to use random sampling.

Even if a proper sample of the population has been selected, surveys can suffer from additional problems (Taylor, 1997; Weisberg et al., 1989). Because large numbers of people need to be tested, it is not usually possible to gain in-depth information about the behavior or opinion of interest. For example, researchers who use surveys are typically unable to obtain detailed historical information of the sort that can be collected in a case study. The basic data in a survey also consist of self-reports, and people cannot always be counted on to provide accurate observations. Some people lie or engage in wishful thinking, while others answer questions in ways they think might please the researcher. The results of a survey can also depend on the particular wordings of the questions, or even on the order in which the questions are asked. Surveys can be written in ways that minimize these risks—for example, particular questions can be asked several times with slightly different wording to check on the consistency of the participant's responses—but inaccuracies in responding are always a concern and difficult to eliminate.

If conducted properly, surveys can be great vehicles for obtaining general information from a target population. If the sample is truly random, concerns about external validity are reduced. But as with the other descriptive research methods that we've discussed, surveys rarely provide definitive information about behavior and mental processes. They are best used in conjunction with other techniques, such as case studies or naturalistic observation, in a broadly based research effort.

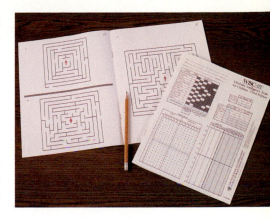

Psychologists use psychological tests to predict and select as well as to help decipher the fundamental components of mind.

PSYCHOLOGICAL TESTS: ASSESSING INDIVIDUAL DIFFERENCES

A major area of descriptive research in psychology is psychological testing. Psychological tests, which come in a variety of forms, are designed primarily to measure individual differences among people. For example, *achievement tests* measure a person's current level of knowledge or competence in a particular subject (such as mathematics or psychology) compared to others'; *aptitude tests* are designed to measure a person's potential for success in a given profession or area of study. Researchers also use various kinds of intelligence and personality tests to classify ability, or to characterize a person's tendencies to act in consistent ways.

Psychological tests have enormous practical value, as well as value in helping to advance basic research (Anastasi, 1985). Intelligence tests can be used to identify children who might need extra help in school or who are gifted and can benefit from an enriched curriculum; for adults, intelligence test scores are sometimes used to predict future performance on the job (Ree & Earles, 1992; Wagner, 1997).

random sampling
A procedure for selecting a representative subset of a target population; the procedure guarantees that everyone in the population has an equal likelihood of being selected for the sample.

CONCEPT SUMMARY
Observational Research Methods

Specific Method	Description	Advantages and Disadvantages
Naturalistic observation	Record naturally occurring behavior	A: Behavior is natural; results are generalizable D: Research lacks control, can't determine cause
Case studies	Gather a great deal of information on a single case	A: Gives historical perspective D: Difficulties in generalization based on one case
Surveys	Gather responses from many participants	A: Can easily gather large amounts of information D: Sampling bias; subjects misrepresenting selves
Psychological tests	Measure individual differences between people	A: Potential practical uses; assess basics of mind D: Difficulties in test construction and validation

Psychologists also analyze test performance to answer fundamental questions about the mind. For example, data collected from psychological tests have been used to tackle questions such as: Do people have a fixed amount of intelligence, present at birth, or do they have multiple kinds of intelligence that rise and fall with experience? Do people have consistent personality traits, such as honesty or pleasantness, or do their behaviors change haphazardly across situations? You'll hear more about these specific questions when we treat psychological tests in more detail in Chapters 10 and 12.

STATISTICS: SUMMARIZING AND INTERPRETING THE DATA

At the end of most research projects, regardless of the method used, the researcher is faced with lots of observations to analyze (i.e., from the final step in the scientific method). These observations, or data, need to be organized and summarized into a form that allows for interpretation. The ultimate goal is to find regularities in the observations so that effective hypotheses can be formulated and tested. When observing children in a day-care center, for instance, an investigator normally collects information from many children, along with repeated observations of the same child, in an effort to make certain that the results can be generalized. It would be inappropriate simply to pick and choose from the results, based on what looks interesting, because selective analyses of data can introduce systematic biases into the interpretation (Barber, 1976; Rosenthal, 1994).

Central Tendencies

If the collected observations can be expressed in the form of some kind of number, it is possible to calculate *statistics*, or values derived from mathematical manipulations of the data, to summarize and interpret the results. For any set of numerical observations, such as how often day-care providers wash their hands during a fixed period of diaper changing, it is useful to begin with a measure of *central tendency*, or the value around which scores tend to cluster. You are probably familiar with the **mean**, which is the arithmetic average of a set of scores. To calculate a mean, you simply add up the numbers representing each observation and divide the total by the number of observations. So, if Jack washed his hands 4 times, Sally 9 times, Kim 4 times, Jessica 5 times, and Rowena 8 times, the mean of these scores would be 6 (4 + 9 + 4 + 5 + 8 = 30; 30 ÷ 5 = 6). The mean summarizes the observations into a single representative number: On average, day-care providers in your study washed their hands 6 times while changing diapers. Notice that in this case none of the workers actually washed his or her hands exactly 6 times. The mean provides only an estimate of central tendency; it does not indicate anything about particular scores.

mean
The arithmetic average of a set of scores.

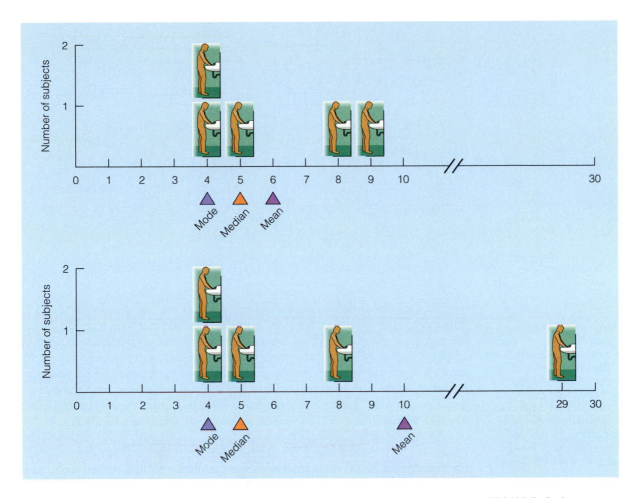

FIGURE 2.4

Comparing the Mean, the Median, and the Mode

The top row shows the differences between the *mean* (arithmetic average), the *median* (middle point in a set of scores), and the *mode* (most frequently occurring score) for handwashing behavior at a day-care center. The bottom row shows how the mean can be affected by an extreme score, someone who washes his hands 29 times. Notice that the extreme score has no effect on the median or mode.

Other measures of central tendency include the **mode,** which is the most frequently occurring score (in the handwashing example the mode is 4), and the **median,** which is the middle point in the set of scores. The mode has the advantage that it always represents a real score—someone actually washed his or her hands 4 times—and it is easy to calculate. Calculating the median takes a bit more work. First, order the scores from smallest to largest (4, 4, 5, 8, 9), then look for the middle score. With the handwashers, half the scores fall below 5, and half fall above, so 5 is the median. If the number of scores is even, with no single middle score (e.g., 4, 4, 5, 6, 8, 9), the median is often calculated by taking the midpoint of the two middle scores (the midpoint between 5 and 6 is 5.5).

Researchers usually like to compute several measures of central tendency for a set of scores. The mean is an excellent summary of the average score, but it can sometimes be misleading. Suppose, for example, that Sally is replaced at the day-care center by Anthony, who suffers from an abnormal compulsion to wash his hands. Anthony washes his hands 29 times during the recording period. If we replace Sally with Anthony, we now have the following set of scores: 4, 4, 5, 8, 29. The arithmetic average, or mean, will shift rather dramatically—from 6 to 10—because of Anthony's extreme score, but neither the mode nor the median will change at all (see Figure 2.4). Because of the way they are calculated, means are very sensitive to extreme scores—the value shifts in the direction of the extreme score. On the other hand, the mode and the median are unaffected. In our example, the median or the mode is probably a better summary of the behavior than the mean.

Variability

In addition to calculating measures of central tendency, researchers are also quite interested in summarizing **variability,** or how much the scores in a set differ from one another. The mean indicates the average, but it provides no information about

---

mode
The most frequently occurring score in a set of scores.

median
The middle point in an ordered set of scores; half of the scores fall at or below the median score, and half fall at or above the median score.

variability
A measure of how much the scores in a distribution of scores differ from one another.

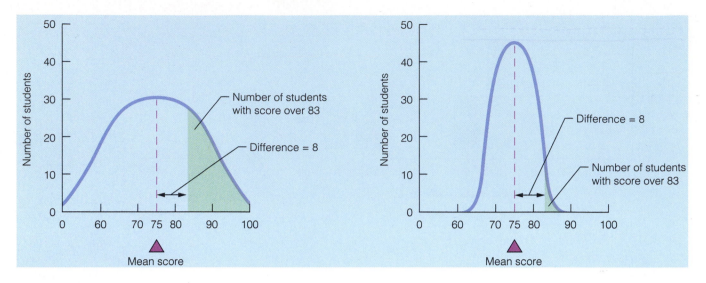

FIGURE 2.5
Variability
Researchers are often interested in variability, or the extent to which scores in a set differ from one another. Each of these two distributions has the same average, or mean, but the distribution on the left has more variability. Notice that the difference between the mean and a particular score, such as 83, is the same in the two cases. But scoring 8 points above the mean is highly unusual in the distribution on the right, and more common in the distribution on the left. If you received a score of 83, which class would you rather be in?

 CRITICAL THINKING

Grade point average is typically calculated using the mean. Suppose the mean was replaced with a grade point mode or a grade point median. What would be the advantages and disadvantages of calculating grade point in this way?

range
The difference between the largest and smallest scores in a distribution.

standard deviation
An indication of how much individual scores differ or vary from the mean in a set of scores.

descriptive statistics
Mathematical techniques that help researchers describe their data.

inferential statistics
Mathematical techniques that help researchers decide whether recorded behaviors are representative of a population or whether differences among observations can be attributed to chance.

how far apart the individual scores are from each other. To see why variability is important, think about your last exam score. Let's assume that you received a 79 and the average score was 75. What can you conclude about your performance? Your best guess is that you did about average because your score was relatively close to the mean. But perhaps not. If the scores were all bunched toward the middle, your performance might have been spectacular—in fact, a 79 could have been the highest grade in the class. Thus, researchers need to know more than the average of a set of scores—they also need to know something about variability (see Figure 2.5).

Several measures of variability are available to researchers. A simple one is the **range,** which measures the difference between the largest and smallest scores in the distribution. If the highest score in the class was a 90 and the lowest score a 50, the range would be 90 − 50 = 40. A more widely used index is the **standard deviation,** which provides an indication of how much individual scores vary from the mean score. It's calculated by (1) finding the difference (or deviation) of each score from the mean, (2) squaring those deviations, (3) finding the average, or mean, of the squared deviations, and (4) calculating the square root of this average. We'll return to the concept of standard deviation later in the text, particularly in Chapter 10, because psychologists often define psychological characteristics, such as intelligence, in terms of how far away a measured score "sits" from the mean in a distribution of scores.

Inferential Statistics
Statistics such as the mean and the standard deviation help researchers *describe* their data; as such, they form a part of what is generally called **descriptive statistics.** But it is also possible to use statistics to draw inferences from data—to help *interpret* the results. Researchers use **inferential statistics** to decide (1) whether the behaviors recorded in a sample are representative of some larger population, or (2) whether the differences among observations can be attributed to chance or to some characteristic of the subjects or the environment.

Inferential statistics are based on the laws of probability. Researchers always assume that the results of an observation, or group of observations, might be attributable to unknown chance factors. For example, suppose that you find that male day-care providers wash their hands 5.8 times a day on average, whereas female providers wash 6.2 times a day (a difference of 0.40). Is there really a gender difference in handwashing behavior? It could be that your recorded gender difference is accidental and unrepresentative of a true difference. Maybe if you had recorded handwashing behavior on a different day you would have found that male day-care providers wash their hands more often. It is in your interest, then, to determine how representative your handwashing data are of true handwashing behavior.

Inside the Problem   Intuitive Statistics

Most people are intuitive statisticians, whether they recognize it or not. For example, when you meet someone new, you no doubt try to determine which of his or her actions represent the real person and which are only momentary quirks. You spend time trying to determine the collective beliefs of your friends, and you worry about how your beliefs might differ from theirs. It's natural and reasonable to act in this way, because everyday statistical intuitions help you describe and summarize your environment.

Unfortunately, there's some evidence to suggest that we're often not very good everyday statisticians. Let's consider an example taken from a study by Fong, Krantz, and Nisbett (1986) involving a statistical principle called the *law of large numbers*. Imagine that you've just visited a new restaurant and had a spectacular meal. You confidently recommend the place to all your friends and decide to visit there as a group. But this time, the meal is a disaster—the food is overcooked and the service is bad. What conclusion would you draw? If you're like most people, you will give a *deterministic* answer, which means that you will come up with some reason or excuse to explain the new experience. You might assume, for example, that the chef has changed, or that the group's expectations were simply too high.

Let's consider another example that demonstrates the same point. You're a rabid baseball fan who has been following the career of the home team's new shortstop. The kid had a spectacular first year and won Rookie of the Year honors. In the off-season, he was awarded a new contract worth millions, and expectations are high when the new season rolls around. But his second year turns out to be disappointing; his average drops 30 points and his home run production is down. What would you conclude? Is he slacking off? Is he living off his press clippings?

In both cases, your conclusions are flawed from a statistical perspective. The

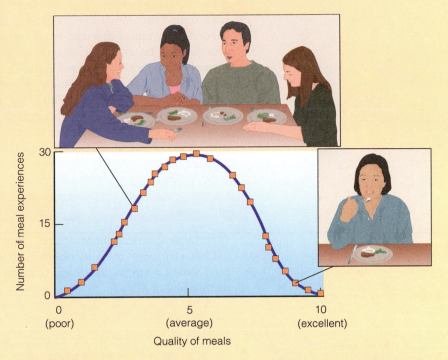

FIGURE 2.6
The Law of Large Numbers
The larger the sample size, the more likely it is that the sample will accurately represent the true average of the population. Any single small sample may or may not reflect the average. If you have a great meal one time at a restaurant, that doesn't mean it represents the average meal at the restaurant. Further sampling may yield results closer to the average.

error lies in your assumption that the original small sample of behavior provided a reliable indication of true characteristics. You have failed to recognize that variability is virtually always a significant part of data collection, whether you're talking about the behavior of a restaurant or the behavior of a person. Statistically, small samples of behavior—such as one meal in a restaurant or one year in the big leagues—cannot be expected to provide reliable indications of true quality or average ability. To achieve an accurate representation, you need to collect lots of observations. This is essentially the *law of large numbers:* The larger the sample size, the more likely the conclusions will accu-

rately represent the population of interest (see Figure 2.6).

Is there any way to avoid these kinds of errors? One answer is education: If you ask doctoral-level scientists with training in statistics to comment on the restaurant or rookie examples, they will tend to give statistical rather than deterministic answers. They will point to the concept of variability and say things like "There are probably more instances of restaurants that serve an occasional excellent meal than ones that serve only excellent meals," or "You hit it lucky at an inconsistent restaurant" (Fong & Nisbett, 1991). So there's hope for us all—as long as we listen to the statistics teacher!

Through the use of inferential statistics, researchers attempt to determine the likelihood, or probability, that the collected pattern of data might have occurred by chance. More specifically, you need to ask: If there is really no true gender difference in handwashing behavior, how often would you expect to find, if handwashing behavior was sampled on any particular day, that females would wash their hands 0.40 times more than males? The details of the procedures are beyond the scope of this text, but if you find that the probability of the recorded observations being due to chance is extremely low, then your findings can be treated as *statistically significant*. In most psychological studies, the probability that an outcome is due to chance must be lower than .05 (5%) for the outcome to be accepted as statistically significant. This means you can treat a female handwashing advantage of 0.40 as significant only if that difference occurs less than five times out of a hundred by chance factors alone. To find out more about our "intuitive" sense of statistical reasoning, turn back to the "Inside the Problem" feature on page 43.

TEST YOURSELF 2.1

To test your knowledge of descriptive research methods, fill in the blanks with one of the following words or terms: reactivity, external validity, case study, random sampling, survey, mean, median, mode, standard deviation. (You will find the answers in the Appendix.)

1. The middle point in an ordered set of scores is the _____.

2. The _____ technique, which focuses on the study of a single instance of a behavior or condition, is open to criticism because its results may lack _____; that is, the results may not generalize or be representative of the population as a whole.

3. When behavior changes as a result of the observation process, the recorded data are said to suffer from a problem of _____.

4. The descriptive research technique used to gather limited amounts of information from many people is called a _____

Predicting Behavior: Correlational Research

Facts are the important outcomes of descriptive research—researchers collect observations systematically and then describe them in ways that yield useful summaries of natural or laboratory behavior. However, psychologists are rarely satisfied with simply describing behavior; they like to use what they've learned to make predictions about behavior in the future. For example, after observing and describing the academic performance of someone in high school, a psychologist might want to predict how well that individual will perform in college. As we discussed earlier, prediction allows you to determine which individuals are likely to perform in a certain way in the future. Thus, the manager of a company can select the best potential employee based on present performance; the school administrator can manage a student's curriculum to maximize future performance.

CORRELATIONAL RESEARCH

One way to predict future performance is to determine whether a *relationship* exists between two measures of behavior: the one recorded in the present and the one expected in the future. Psychologists often use a statistical measure called a **correlation** to help make this determination. A correlation tells you whether two

correlation
A statistic that indicates whether two variables are related or vary together in a systematic way; correlation coefficients vary from +1.00 to −1.00.

The building skills of the young girl on the left may or may not be predictive of a professional career in architecture.

variables, or measures that can take on more than one value (such as a test score), vary together systematically. Correlations are computed by gathering observations on both measures of interest from a single set of individuals and then computing a mathematical index called a *correlation coefficient.* A correlation coefficient gives the researcher a feel for how well the value of one variable, such as job success, can be predicted if the value of a second variable, such as an achievement test score, is known.

When there is a correlation between two measures of behavior, those behaviors tend to vary together in some way. In the day-care example, there is probably a strong correlation between the number of diapers changed during the day and the number of times the caretakers wash their hands. The two measures vary together—the more diapers changed, the more frequently hands are washed. In this particular case, we have a *positive correlation,* which means that the two measures move in the same direction—the more of one, the more of the other. A *negative correlation* exists when the two measures still vary together but in opposite directions. For example, there is a negative, or inverse, relationship between the number of hours that Beverly practices on the piano and the number of errors she makes during her recital performance. The more she practices, the fewer errors she is likely to make. A relationship still exists—we can predict one when we know the other—but the correlation is negative.

Calculating a correlation coefficient requires that you collect observations from a relatively large number of individuals. Moreover, you need to collect data initially on *both* behavioral measures. The details of the calculation are beyond the scope of this text, but *variability* among the collected observations is an important ingredient of the calculation. If calculated properly, correlation coefficients always range between +1.00 and −1.00. The absolute value of the coefficient (the range between 0 and 1 without the sign) indicates the *strength* of the correlation. The closer the value is to 1.00 (either positive or negative), the greater the relationship between the two measures and the more likely you are to predict correctly. The sign of the coefficient indicates whether the correlation is positive or negative. Positive correlations fall within the range from 0 to +1.00; negative correlations fall within the range from 0 to −1.00.

Figure 2.7 shows how positive and negative correlations can be represented graphically, in the form of a *scatter plot.* Each point in a scatter plot represents a

FIGURE 2.7

Positive and Negative Correlation
Two examples of scatter plots. Each point shows an individual's scores on each of the two variables. (a) In a strong positive correlation, the values for both variables move in the *same* direction; that is, as more diapers are changed, more hands are washed. (b) In a negative correlation, the values for the two variables move in *opposite* directions; that is, as more time is spent practicing, fewer errors are made during the recital.

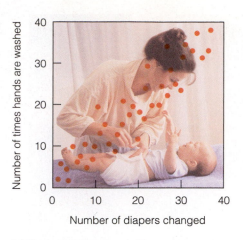

(a) Strong positive correlation

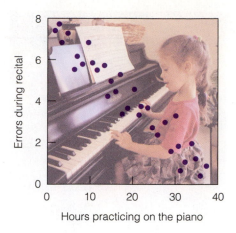

(b) Strong negative correlation

person's scores on the two measures. In figure (b) you can find, for a particular person, how many hours he or she spent practicing and the number of errors made during the recital. Once the correlation has been computed, it can then be applied to new individuals who have a score on only one of the measures. So, if a correlation is present, you can predict how many errors Natasha will make during her recital by simply knowing how many hours she practiced. The closer the correlation is to 1.00 (positive or negative), the more accurate your prediction is likely to be. This is the logic used by most college admissions committees—they know there is a correlation between SAT and college performance, so they try to predict how well people will do in college by looking at their SAT scores.

Zero Correlations

When a correlation coefficient is not statistically different from zero, the two behavioral measures are said to be *uncorrelated*. Technically, this means that knowing the value of one measure does not allow you to predict the value of the second measure with an accuracy greater than chance. Imagine, for example, trying to predict college grade point average and by measuring how many times people wash their hands during the day. In this case, the correlation is almost certainly zero—you can't use hand-washing behavior to predict GPA. It's important not to confuse the concept of a zero correlation with negative correlation. If the correlation between two variables is zero, no statistical relationship is present—a value on one behavioral measure reveals nothing about the other behavioral measure. In a negative correlation a clear relationship exists, it's just that the values move in opposite directions. For a look at how people sometimes misinterpret zero correlations, see the accompanying feature, "Inside the Problem."

Behavioral measures rarely correlate perfectly—most correlations are only moderate. This means that when researchers make predictions about behavior based on correlations, the accuracy of their predictions will usually be limited. For example, the correlation between scores on the SAT and the grade point average of college freshmen is only +0.40, not 1.0 (Donlon, 1984). Researchers can use SAT scores to predict college performance at greater than chance levels, but the test's predictive abilities are far from perfect (Stricker et al., 1996). Similarly, the correlation between height and weight is only about +0.60; on average, taller people do tend to weigh more, but there are obviously exceptions to this general rule. Correlation coefficients give researchers some important predictive ability, but they do not completely capture the variability present in the world.

CORRELATIONS AND CAUSALITY

Determining that a relationship exists between two measures of behavior is important because it helps people make educated guesses about their environment. It is

Inside the Problem   Predicting the Future

Do you believe in *precognition,* commonly defined as the ability to predict the future? Do you believe that some individuals have knowledge about the future that they've obtained through extrasensory means? There is certainly plenty of anecdotal evidence. Jennifer, who dreams vividly about the death of her grandmother, awakens to a phone call announcing that her grandma has died. Bradley, who senses a terrible plane crash on the drive home from work, is surprised to learn about an actual crash on the evening news.

But let's think about such occurrences from the perspective of what we've learned about correlations. In a sense, when psychologists conduct correlational research they are attempting to predict the future (although not through extrasensory means). They want to know whether the value on one variable, such as SAT scores, predicts how people will perform in the future on a second variable, such as college GPA. For the sake of argument, let's suppose that we track the performance of a psychic named Eleanor who claims her dreams predict the future. We measure her performance over the course of many years on two variables. One variable corresponds to the number of times she dreams about a plane crashing in a given year; the other measures the number of planes that actually crash in that year. If you believe in precognition, you would expect to find a positive correlation between these two variables. That is, as the number of Eleanor's dream predictions about plane crashes goes up, so should the number of actual crashes.

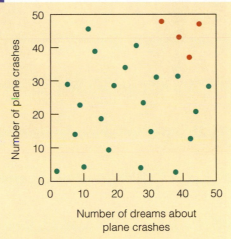

FIGURE 2.8

Zero Correlation
This scatter plot shows a zero correlation between variables measuring dreaming about plane crashes and planes actually crashing. Notice that overall it is not possible to predict the value on one of the variables by knowing a value on the other, although sometimes high values on each variable occur together (marked in orange).

But what if there is really no relationship between these two variables? What if the likelihood of Eleanor dreaming about a plane crash is uncorrelated with the probability of an actual crash? Under these conditions, the relationship between the two variables might look like the scatter plot depicted in Figure 2.8. Remember, when a correlation is near 0, there is no way consistently to predict the value of one variable when given the other. Sometimes a high value on one of the variables will be associated with a high value on the other variable; other times it will be associated

with a low value. If no relationship exists between the two variables, then we shouldn't be able to estimate the number of plane crashes based solely on our knowledge of Eleanor's dreams.

But let's think more carefully about what a zero correlation means in this context: It means that in some years, when Eleanor has lots of dreams about planes crashing, there will also be lots of planes that crash. Notice that the scatter plot shows several instances where a high value on the dreaming variable is associated with a high value on the plane crashing variable (marked in orange). Does this mean that in these selected years Eleanor possessed an uncanny ability to predict the future? Not necessarily, because these points could have occurred by chance. To get a true feeling for Eleanor's predictive ability, you need to look at the entire plot. As you can see, there are also years in which Eleanor predicted that lots of planes would crash and not very many did so, and other years where many planes crashed but few dreams were reported.

The point to remember is that when two variables are unrelated, we cannot predict what will happen—sometimes dreams will be associated with plane crashes and sometimes they won't. The mistake many people make is to look *only* at the cases where the two variables appear to be related. Remember, if there is no such thing as precognition—if the correlation is truly zero—then by chance we should expect to find situations where dreaming about plane crashes really is connected with unfortunate airline disasters!

---

useful to know if someone who acts in a certain way at time 1 is likely to act in a predictable way at time 2. Suppose, for example, that psychologists could demonstrate a meaningful correlation between the amount of violence that a child watches on television and how aggressively that child will act later in life. Knowing about such a relationship would probably influence the behavior of parents and might even lead to a social outcry for the monitoring of televised violence.

Correlations are useful devices for helping psychologists describe *how* behaviors co-occur in our world, but they are of only limited value when it comes to understanding *why* behaviors occur and co-occur. The presence of a correlation between two behaviors may help psychologists predict, but correlations do not allow them to determine causality. A correlation between watching violence on television and later aggression does not mean that television violence causes aggression, even if the correlation is perfect.

Do children model what they see on television? Many psychologists believe they do.

<blockquote>
? CRITICAL THINKING

Pat doesn't make any decisions in her life without consulting a psychic. She's convinced that most of what the psychic tells her about her future comes true. Given what you know about correlations and causality, how might you convince her otherwise?
</blockquote>

Third Variables

The main reason why it's not possible to determine causality from a correlation has to do with the presence of other potentially uncontrolled factors in the situation. Two variables can appear to be connected—that is, they might rise or fall together in a regular way—but the connection could be due to a common link with some third variable. Let's consider an example close to home. It's commonly argued, correctly, that annual income will be higher if a person graduates from college. Put in terms of a correlation, annual income is positively correlated with years of schooling. Does that mean that a good education *causes* better jobs and higher income? Perhaps, but not necessarily. There could be a third factor lurking around that explains the relationship.

Think for a moment about the kinds of people who go to college. Do they represent a random sample of the population as a whole? Of course not. College students tend to be brighter, they tend to come from better secondary schools, they tend to be people who have worked hard and succeeded in high

CONCEPT SUMMARY
Correlational Patterns

Question to Be Addressed	Pattern of Correlation	Interpretation
How does the number of diaper changes *relate to* the number of hand washings?	Positive	The more diaper changes, the more hand washings; the fewer diaper changes, the fewer hand washings. (more/more; fewer/fewer)
How does performance on the SAT *relate to* college GPA?	Positive	The greater the score on the SAT, the higher the GPA; the lower the score on the SAT, the lower the GPA.
How does the amount of piano practice *relate to* the number of errors during a recital?	Negative	The more practice, the fewer errors are made; the less practice, the more errors are made.
How does the amount of time spent partying *relate to* college GPA?	Negative	The more time spent partying, the lower the GPA; the less time spent partying, the higher the GPA.
How does a person's shoe size *relate to* his or her score on an intelligence test?	No correlation	Knowing one's shoe size tells you nothing about his or her IQ test score and vice-versa.

school, and they also tend to come from families that are in the higher income brackets (college is expensive). None of these other factors is controlled for in the calculation of a correlation. You can predict with a correlation, but you can't isolate the particular factor that is responsible for the relationship. College students might end up with higher incomes because they're smarter, work harder, are richer, or because they're better educated. Any or all of these factors could be contributing to the relationship that the correlation describes (Cook & Campbell, 1979).

Now let's return to the example we considered earlier—the relationship between TV violence and aggression. Can you think of any third variable that might explain the correlation? One possibility is that aggressive children simply like to watch violent programs on television. It is not the violence on TV that is causing the aggression, it is the child's aggressive tendencies that are leading to the choice of programs. Still other factors could be involved— perhaps children who are allowed to watch violence on television tend to be raised in households where aggression or lashing out is the normal way of dealing with life's problems. Once again, correlations describe relationships, but they typically provide no insight into cause and effect. To determine causality, as you'll see shortly, researchers cannot simply describe and predict behavior; they must manipulate it.

> **experimental research**
> A technique in which the investigator actively manipulates or alters some aspect of the environment (defined broadly) in order to observe the effect of the manipulation on behavior.

TEST YOURSELF 2.2

Test your understanding of correlations by identifying whether the following statements represent positive, negative, or zero correlations. (You will find the answers in the Appendix.)

1. The more Larry studies his psychology, the fewer errors he makes on the chapter test:
   NEGATIVE

2. As Sadaf reduces her rate of exercising, her heart rate begins to slow:
   POSITIVE

3. The longer that Yolanda waits for her date to arrive, the higher her blood pressure rises:
   POSITIVE

4. Eddie finds no relationship between the frequency of plane-crash dreams and the number of planes that actually crash: _0 CORRELATION_

Determining Why Behavior Occurs: Experimental Research

If the ultimate goal of most psychologists is to establish the causes of behavior, what research strategy will allow them to do so? Suppose you wanted to determine whether, in fact, watching violent programs really does cause later aggression. What specific steps should you take? You must be certain that if there is an increase in aggressive behavior after a violent television program has been watched, then it is indeed the television violence that is responsible for the change. Alternative possibilities need to be eliminated, or at least accounted for, before you can confidently conclude that things are causally related. As you've just seen, the mere description of a relationship is not sufficient— correlation does not imply causation. Establishing causality requires *control*, one of the most important functions of an experiment.

In **experimental research,** the investigator actively manipulates or alters some aspect of the environment in order to observe the effect of that manipulation on behavior. By the term *environment*, psychologists can mean just about

> **LEARNING GOALS**
>
> 1. Define experimental research and explain why experiments are conducted.
>
> 2. Discuss the differences between independent and dependent variables.
>
> 3. Explain what is meant by experimental control and how it allows for the determination of causality.
>
> 4. Describe the problems created by expectancies and biases and how these problems are solved.

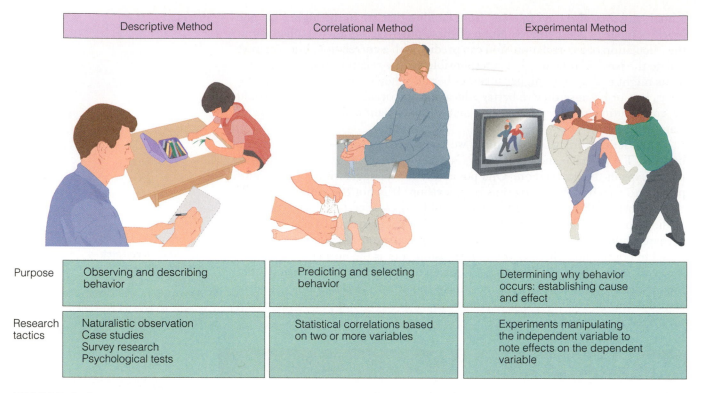

Descriptive Method	Correlational Method	Experimental Method

	Descriptive Method	Correlational Method	Experimental Method
Purpose	Observing and describing behavior	Predicting and selecting behavior	Determining why behavior occurs: establishing cause and effect
Research tactics	Naturalistic observation Case studies Survey research Psychological tests	Statistical correlations based on two or more variables	Experiments manipulating the independent variable to note effects on the dependent variable

FIGURE 2.9

Summary of Major Research Methods
The chart summarizes the purpose and research tactics for the three major research methods: descriptive research, correlational research, and experimental research.

anything. For instance, they might manipulate the external setting (room temperature, lighting, time of day), a person's internal state (hunger, mood, motivation to perform), or social factors (presence or absence of an authority figure or popular peer group). The particular manipulation is determined by the researcher's hypothesis. As mentioned earlier, hypotheses in psychology are usually expressed in the form of if-then statements about behavior: If some set of conditions is present and observed, then a certain kind of behavior will occur. The purpose of the experiment is to set up the proposed conditions and see what happens.

To examine the role of television violence on aggressive behavior, an experimenter would directly manipulate the amount of violence the person watches. Perhaps one group of children would be picked by the experimenter to watch a violent superhero cartoon while a second group watches the playful antics of a lovable purple dinosaur. The experimenter would then carefully measure the effect of the manipulation on the behavior of interest: aggression. This strategy of directly *manipulating* the viewing habits, rather than simply observing them, is the essential feature of the experimental approach. Notice the difference from correlational research, in which the investigator would simply record the viewing habits of lots of children and then measure later aggressive acts. It is only through a direct manipulation by the experimenter, as you'll see shortly, that control over the environment can be exercised and causality determined. Figure 2.9 compares experimental research to the other two approaches we've discussed, observational and correlational.

INDEPENDENT AND DEPENDENT VARIABLES

The aspect of the environment that is manipulated in an experiment is called the **independent variable.** Because it is a *variable* (that is, something that can take on more than one value), any experimental manipulation must consist of at least two different conditions. In our example, the independent variable is the amount of television violence observed by the children, and the two conditions are (1) watching a violent program, and (2) watching a nonviolent pro-

independent variable
The aspect of the environment that is manipulated in an experiment. It must consist of at least two conditions.

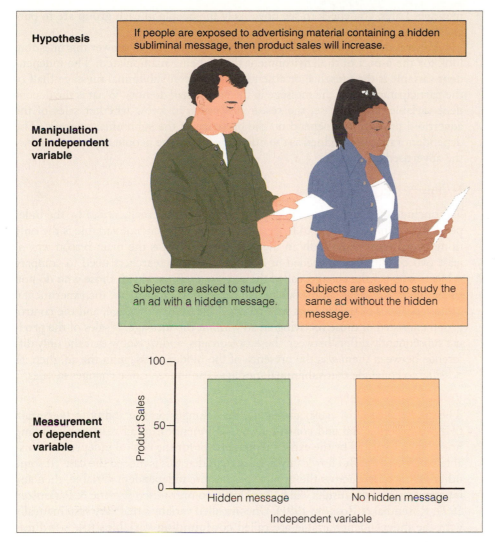

Hypothesis

If people are exposed to advertising material containing a hidden subliminal message, then product sales will increase.

Manipulation of independent variable

Subjects are asked to study an ad with a hidden message.

Subjects are asked to study the same ad without the hidden message.

Measurement of dependent variable

Product Sales

100

50

0

Hidden message   No hidden message

Independent variable

FIGURE 2.10

The Major Components of an Experiment

The hypothesis is tested by manipulating the independent variable and then assessing its effects on the dependent variable. If the only thing changing systematically in the experiment is the independent variable, the experimenter can assume that changes in the independent variable are *causing* the changes measured by the dependent variable.

gram. The aspect that is manipulated is called an *independent* variable because the experimenter produces the change, independently of the subject's wishes, desires, or behavior.

The behavior that is measured or observed in an experiment is called the **dependent variable.** In our example, the dependent variable is the amount of aggressive behavior that is seen following the exposure to the violent or nonviolent program. The experimenter manipulates the independent variable, the level of TV violence, in order to observe whether the behavior measured by the dependent variable, aggression, changes. Notice that the experimenter is interested in whether the dependent variable *depends* on the experimental manipulation (hence the name *dependent* variable).

Now let's return to the topic that opened this chapter: subliminal perception. Can evil advertisers improve product sales by hiding messages such as "BUY NOW" in their advertising material? Remember, a subliminal message is presented below a person's normal threshold for perception. You won't be able to consciously see or notice the message, but it will presumably exert an effect nonetheless. Let's begin by forming the hypothesis: If people are exposed to advertising material containing a hidden subliminal message, then product sales will increase (see Figure 2.10). To test this prediction, you might give two groups of people an advertisement to study. One group receives an ad containing a hidden message and the other group receives the same advertisement without the

dependent variable
The behavior that is measured or observed in an experiment.

message. Later, you check to see how likely the people in each group are to purchase the product described in the ad.

What is the independent variable in this experiment? To answer this question, look for the aspect of the environment that is being manipulated: The independent variable is the presence or absence of the secret subliminal message (half of the participants receive the message in the ad and half do not). What is the dependent variable? In this case, the researcher wants to know whether sales of the advertised product will depend on the presence of the subliminal message. The dependent variable is defined as the number of times the people in each group buy the advertised product.

EXPERIMENTAL CONTROL

To conclude that changes in the dependent variable are really *caused* by the independent variable, you need to be certain that the independent variable is the only thing changing systematically in the experiment. This is the main reason why at least two conditions are needed in an experiment. Researchers need to compare subjects who get the change, called the *experimental group,* with those who do not, called the *control group.* In the subliminal perception experiment, the experimental group consisted of the subjects who received the hidden message, and the control group consisted of those receiving an ad without the message. If sales of the product subsequently differs between these two groups, and we know that the only difference between them was the presence of the hidden message in the ad, then it's possible to conclude that subliminal messages can indeed cause changes in sales.

Confounding Variables

The determination of cause and effect, then, hinges on the ability to be certain that the experimental and control groups are identical in all respects, including how they are treated by the experimenter, except for the critical independent variable manipulation. But how can you be certain that this is indeed the case? If some other factor differs across the groups, besides the independent variable, then any interpretation of the results will be hopelessly compromised (Levine & Parkinson, 1994; Rosenthal & Rosnow, 1991). Uncontrolled variables that vary systematically with the independent variable are called **confounding variables** (the word *confound* means to throw into confusion or dismay). Suppose, for example, that researchers decide to use one kind of advertisement in the experimental condition and a different advertisement in the control condition. This would introduce a confounding variable because any differences in sales could then be attributed to the effectiveness of the individual ad, or the product advertised, rather than to the presence or absence of the subliminal message. Changes in the dependent variable could not then be attributed uniquely to the manipulation of the hidden message.

One solution to the problem of confounding variables is to try to equate the groups by holding constant all of the factors that might vary along with the experimental manipulation. You could give everyone exactly the same advertisement, for instance, and conduct the experimental session at the same time of day for both groups. In addition, you would want to make certain that subjects in both groups are given the same amount of time to study the ad and the same length of time to buy, or indicate that they'll buy, the advertised product. Any factor that might affect the likelihood of purchase, other than the independent variable manipulation, should be controlled—that is, held constant—across the different groups. When potential confounding variables are effectively controlled, allowing for the determination of cause and effect, the experiment is said to have **internal validity.**

Knowing what factors to worry about comes, in part, from experience. The more you know about the phenomenon under study, the more likely you are to identify and control variables that can lead to confounding. Consumer researchers recognize, for example, that it's essential to give everyone the same advertisement

confounding variable
An uncontrolled variable that changes along with the independent variable.

internal validity
The extent to which an experiment has effectively controlled for confounding variables; internally valid experiments allow for the determination of causality.

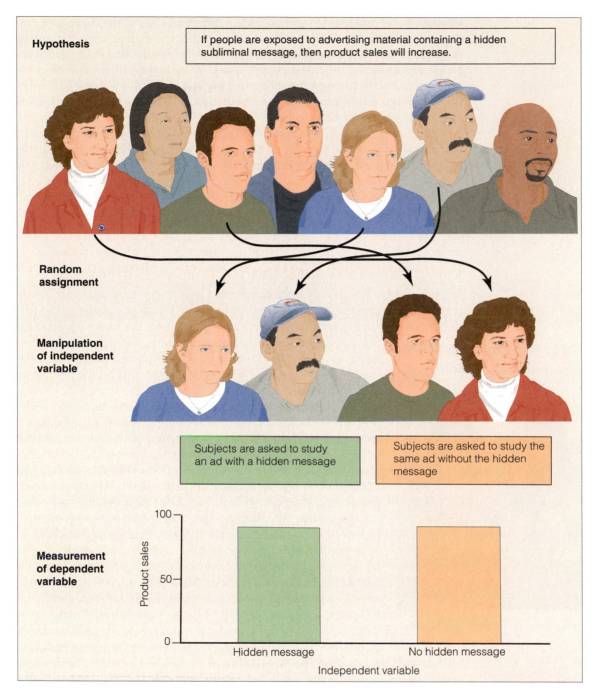

Hypothesis

If people are exposed to advertising material containing a hidden subliminal message, then product sales will increase.

Random assignment

Manipulation of independent variable

Subjects are asked to study an ad with a hidden message

Subjects are asked to study the same ad without the hidden message

Measurement of dependent variable

Product sales

100

50

0

Hidden message   No hidden message

Independent variable

FIGURE 2.11

Random Assignment

In random assignment, the experimenter ensures that each participant has an equal likelihood of being assigned to any of the groups or conditions in the experiment. Here, people are randomly assigned to the two levels of the independent variable. Random assignment increases the chances that unique subject characteristics will be represented equally in each condition.

and product in the experimental and control conditions; obviously, some ads or products will be liked better than others regardless of whether they contain hidden messages. But other variables, such as the length of the participants' hair or their eye color, probably have no effect on buying behavior and need not be controlled for.

Random Assignment

Still, the problem of subject differences remains—how can experimenters ever be certain that their two groups of subjects are equivalent? People differ in many ways: intelligence, affection for certain products, motivation to perform, and so on. Researchers cannot hold all of these factors constant. Just think about the task of finding two or more groups of subjects with exactly the same amount of intelligence, likes and dislikes, and motivation to perform. It would be impossible. The solution to the problem of intrinsic subject differences lies in the concept of random assignment, which is similar to the random sampling used for survey research. In **random assignment,** the experimenter ensures that each participant has an equal chance of being assigned to any of the groups or conditions in the experiment. At the outset, each subject is assigned randomly to a group. Neither the subject nor the experimenter voluntarily chooses which group is assigned; the assignment is governed by chance.

Random assignment does not eliminate differences among people—some subjects will still be more intelligent than others, and some will be more naturally inclined to buy an advertised product than others. Random assignment simply increases the likelihood that these differences will be equally represented in each of the groups (see Figure 2.11 on page 55). As a result, the researcher knows that group differences on the dependent variable cannot easily be attributed to some special characteristic of the individual subjects.

EXPECTANCIES AND BIASES IN EXPERIMENTAL RESEARCH

Individuals who arrive ready to participate in a psychology experiment are almost certain to have expectations about what will happen. People are rarely passive participants in research; they almost always attempt to guess the true purpose of the

Subjects who participate in research studies usually have expectations about the research. They expect certain things to happen, and these expectations can potentially influence the results.

project. These expectations can sometimes affect a subject's behavior in ways that cloud interpretation of the results (Barber, 1976; Rosenthal & Rosnow, 1969). Let's suppose that on the first day of class your teacher randomly selects half of the students, including you, to participate in a special enrichment program. You receive instruction in a special room, with carefully controlled lighting and temperature, to see whether your learning will improve. The rest of the students, forming the control group, are left in the original classroom. The end of the semester arrives and, sure enough, the enrichment group has consistently performed better than the control group. What can you conclude from these results?

Technically, this seems to be a well-designed experiment. It includes both an experimental and a control group, the subjects were randomly assigned to groups, and we can assume that all other known potentially confounding variables were carefully controlled. But there is still a problem. The subjects in the enrichment group *expected* to perform better, based on their knowledge about the experiment. After all, they were selected to be in an enrichment group. Consequently, these students may have simply tried harder, or studied more, in an effort to live up to the expectations of the researcher (or at least to what they *perceived* the expectations of the researcher to be). At the same time, subjects in the control group were aware that they were failing to get special instruction; this knowledge might have lowered their motivation to perform, leading to poorer performance. The fact that the groups differed in what they learned does not necessarily mean that the enrichment program itself is responsible.

There are two main ways that researchers can control for these kinds of *expectancy effects*. First, the investigator can be somewhat misleading in initially describing the study. Subjects can be deceived, or misled, in a way that disguises the true purpose of the experiment. This approach raises obvious ethical questions, although it is possible, under some conditions, to omit telling the subjects some critical feature of the study without severely violating ethical standards. (I'll return to the issue of ethics in research later in the chapter.)

Second, the investigator can try to equate expectations for both the experimental and control groups. For example, the researchers can lead the control group to believe that they, too, are receiving an experimental treatment. This

random assignment
A technique ensuring that each participant in an experiment has an equal chance of being assigned to any of the conditions in the experiment.

technique is often used in drug studies. Participants in both the experimental and control groups receive a pill or an injection, but the drug is actually present only in the medication given to the experimental group. The control subjects are given a **placebo**—an inactive, or inert, substance (a "sugar pill") that looks just like the true drug (Shapiro, 1960; White et al., 1985).

Blind Controls

The kind of experimental procedure described above is often used in a **single-blind study.** That is, the subjects are kept "blind" about the particular group in which they have been placed (experimental or control). Single-blind studies effectively control for subject expectancies because the subjects don't know which group they are in. This means that any expectations that might be present are likely to be equally represented in both groups. It is even possible to inform the subjects that some of them will be given a placebo—the inactive pill or injection—as long as no one knows who is in which group. Notice that the single-blind technique does not eliminate subject expectancies; it simply reduces the chances that expectancies will contribute more to the experimental group than to the control group (or vice versa).

The subjects participating in the experiment aren't the only ones who expect certain things to happen—the experimenter does too (Rosenthal, 1966). Remember, it is the experimenter who formulated the hypothesis. Experimenters are often convinced that behavior will change in a certain way, and these expectations can influence the results. Imagine, for example, that a researcher has developed a drug designed to cure all forms of influenza. The researcher has worked hard on its development but still needs convincing scientific evidence to show that it is effective. So the researcher designs a single-blind experiment composed of two groups of flu-suffering subjects. One group receives the drug and the other a placebo. Later, after analyzing the results, the researcher is satisfied to report that indeed people in the experimental group recovered more quickly than those in the control group.

There are two ways that the experimenter's expectations might influence these results. First, there is always the possibility that the overzealous investigator has deliberately manufactured results consistent with the hypothesis. Such intentional errors on the part of researchers are probably rare, but they have been documented on occasion in most branches of scientific research (for a discussion, see Barber, 1976; Broad & Wade, 1982). A second and more likely possibility is that the experimenter has unknowingly influenced the results in subtle ways. Perhaps, for example, he or she gave slightly more attention to the flu-stricken people in the experimental group; the researcher expected these people to get well and so was more responsive to changes in their medical condition. Alternatively, the researcher might simply have been more encouraging to the people who actually received the drug, leading them to adopt a more positive outlook on their chances for a quick recovery. Such biases are not necessarily deliberate on the part of the researcher. Nevertheless, these unintentional effects can cloud a meaningful interpretation of the results.

The solution to experimenter expectancy effects is similar to that for controlling subject expectancies—simply keep the researcher blind about the assignment of subjects to groups. If those administering the study do not know which subjects are receiving the experimental treatment, they are unlikely to treat members of each group differently. Obviously, someone needs to know the group assignments, but the information can be coded in such a way that the person doing the direct observations remains blind about the condition. To control for both experimenter and subject expectancies in the same context, a **double-blind study** is conducted, in which neither the subject nor the observer is aware of who is in the experimental and control conditions. Double-blind studies, often used in drug research, are considered to be an effective way for reducing bias effects.

placebo
An inactive, or inert, substance that resembles an experimental substance.

single-blind study
An experimental design in which the participants do not know which of the conditions to which they have been assigned (e.g., experimental versus control); it's used to control for subject expectancies.

double-blind study
An experimental design in which neither the participants nor the research observers are aware of who has been assigned to the experimental and control groups; it's used to control for both subject and experimenter expectancies.

Inside the Problem   Extending Memory Principles Under Water

Researchers typically choose to investigate basic psychological principles in the laboratory, where they can control the phenomenon of interest. Establishing cause and effect requires that the environment be manipulated systematically—potential confounding variables need to be controlled for. But herein lies a dilemma: By investigating behavior in the laboratory and exercising rigorous control, are researchers discovering things about behavior and mind that are specific to the laboratory and unrepresentative of real life?

Fortunately, it is possible to conduct well-controlled experiments in real-world settings. Such experiments, where feasible, provide useful information about behavior in natural settings and allow researchers to help establish the generalizability of laboratory findings. Let's take a look at a study in which researchers attempted to extend laboratory principles about memory to a practical setting: the ability of scuba divers to remember safety information while under water (Martin & Aggleton, 1993).

As you'll learn in Chapter 8, laboratory research has established that people often remember things better if they're tested in conditions that resemble those present during original learning. Dozens of studies have been conducted examining so-called "context effects," in which the conditions present during learning and later remembering are either matched or mismatched. But the vast majority of these studies have been conducted in laboratory settings using artificial word lists (Davies & Thomson, 1988). Martin and Aggleton wanted to see whether similar principles applied in the real-life environment of the scuba diver.

One of the hazards that any scuba diver must face is *decompression;* as the diver moves from deep water to shallow water, the changes in water pressure can have potentially damaging effects on the body. It is essential that divers understand and remember basic information about pressure and depth, such as the data published in standardized decompression tables.

Martin and Aggleton (1993) asked 40 scuba divers to memorize and then remember data from standard decompression tables. But they manipulated the conditions of initial learning and testing by randomly assigning each of the divers to one of four groups: (1) those who learned the decompression data on dry land and then had their memory tested in the same context, on dry land; (2) those who learned the data under water while diving and were tested later on dry land; (3) those who learned the data on dry land but were tested under water; and (4) those who both learned and remembered the data while diving under water.

What was the *independent variable* in this experiment? It was the manipulation of the match between the initial learning conditions and the testing environment (dry land or under water). Groups 1 and 4 studied the materials and were then tested in the same environments, whereas groups 2 and 3 had mismatched learning and testing environments. The *dependent variable* in this experiment—the divers' memory for the decompression data—was measured by recording how often they answered

GENERALIZING EXPERIMENTAL CONCLUSIONS

Properly designed experiments enable an investigator to determine the causes of behavior. The determination of causality is possible whenever the experimenter has sufficient control over the situation to eliminate factors other than the experimental manipulation as contributors to a change in behavior. But experimental control is not always gained without a cost. Sometimes in the search for appropriate controls, the researcher creates an environment that is sterile or artificial and not very representative of situations in which the subject normally behaves. The results of the experimental research then cannot easily be generalized to real-world situations. As you learned previously, researchers use the term *external validity* to refer to how well results generalize across subjects and situations.

Consider again the issue of television violence and aggression: Does one really cause the other? A number of experimental studies have been conducted to explore this question (Friedrich-Cofer & Huston, 1986), but most have been conducted in the laboratory under controlled conditions. Subjects are randomly assigned to groups who watch violent programs or neutral programs, and their behavior is then observed for aggressive tendencies, again under controlled conditions. In one recent study, preschool children were exposed to neutral or aggressive cartoons and then were given the opportunity to play with aggressive toys (such as guns); more aggressive acts were recorded for the children who watched the violent cartoon (Sanson & di-Muccio, 1993). These results clearly demonstrate that witnessed violence can increase the likelihood of aggressiveness. But this does not necessarily mean that these children would act similarly in their homes, or that the effects of

? CRITICAL THINKING

Experiments are sometimes criticized because they are considered artificial. Many psychology experiments use college students in introductory psychology courses as participants. Do you feel there is a problem in generalizing the findings from these studies to the whole population?

questions about the data correctly. (All of the participants, whether wet or dry, wrote their answers on waterproof plastic sheets). The results of the experiment are shown in Figure 2.12, which presents the mean number of correct responses for each of the four groups.

According to standard laboratory findings, when conditions are matched between original learning and testing, people should remember things better. This is exactly what happened in the Martin and Aggleton study. The divers remembered the critical decompression data better when they learned and were tested in the same kind of environment (dry or wet). As you can see, the divers in groups 1 and 4 answered more questions correctly than the divers in groups 2 and 3. Thus, the experiment was successful in extending laboratory findings to a natural environment. But even more important, something of great practical value was learned: If divers want to remember vital safety information while under water, it's best for them to learn that information while they're diving, not while on dry land.

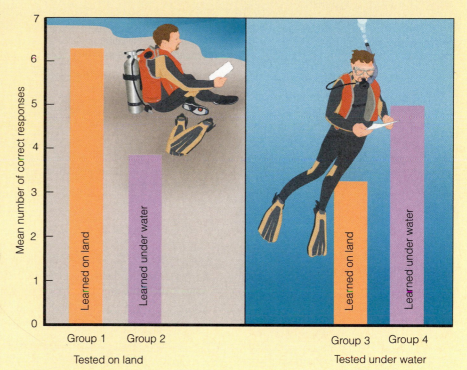

FIGURE 2.12

Context Effects in Remembering

This graph summarizes the results of the Martin and Aggleton (1993) underwater memory study. When testing occurred on land, decompression tables learned on land were remembered better than those learned under water; when testing was done under water, it was better to have learned the tables under water.

the brief exposure to violence will be long lasting. In short, the experiment may lack external validity. Concerns about generalizability should not, however, be taken as a devastating critique of the experimental method—results demonstrated in the laboratory often do generalize to real-world environments. But it's legitimate to raise questions about how widely the results apply. As you might expect, we'll return to the problem of external validity in later chapters.

TEST YOURSELF 2.3

Try answering the following questions to test your knowledge about experimental research. (You will find the answers in the Appendix.)

1. Fill in the blanks with the terms *independent* or *dependent*.

   In experimental research, the researcher actively manipulates the environment in order to observe its effect on behavior. The aspect of the environment that is manipulated is called the ___INDEPENDENT___ variable; the behavior of interest is measured by the ___DEPENDENT___ variable. To draw conclusions about cause and effect, the experimenter must make certain that the ___INDEPENDENT___ variable is the only thing changing systematically in the environment.

2. Javier wants to determine once and for all whether the presence of Leonardo DiCaprio in a movie increases the box office take. He randomly forms two groups of subjects. One group sees *Titanic*, starring DiCaprio, and the other group sees *Barney's Big Adventure*,

CONCEPT SUMMARY
The Experimental Method

Research Question (variables in bold)	Independent Variable (experimenter *manipulates*)	Dependent Variable (experimenter *measures*)
Does **watching television violence** affect **aggression**?	Experimenter *manipulates* the amount of exposure to TV violence.	Experimenter *measures* the amount of aggression displayed.
Does **exposure to subliminal messages** have an effect on **product sales**?	Experimenter *manipulates* whether or not subjects receive a hidden message.	Experimenter *measures* product sales.
Does **forming images of words** to be remembered enhance **memory for those words**?	Experimenter *manipulates* whether or not subjects form images of words as they're being presented.	Experimenter *measures* memory for the words.

without DiCaprio. Sure enough, the DiCaprio movie is later rated as more enjoyable than the movie starring the purple dinosaur. Javier concludes that DiCaprio movies are sure winners. What's wrong with this experiment?

a. The dependent variable—DiCaprio versus Barney—is confounded with the content of the movie.
b. The independent variable—DiCaprio versus Barney—is not the only factor changing across the groups.
c. Nothing has been manipulated—it's really a correlational study.
d. Experiments of this type require independent variables with at least three levels.

3. Random assignment is an important research tool because it helps the researcher control for potential confounding variables. Which of the following statements about random assignment is true? Random assignment:

a. eliminates individual differences among people.
b. ensures that some participants will get the experimental treatment and others will not.
c. increases the likelihood that subject differences will be equally represented in each group.
d. controls for bias by ensuring that biased subjects will be placed in the control group.

Treating Research Participants Ethically: Human and Animal Guidelines

As you've seen, knowledge in psychology comes from observation, but observing others requires that psychologists invade, to a certain extent, the personal environment of the research participants. Earlier you were introduced to the problem of *reactivity:* The use of observational techniques can importantly change the way people behave. Although psychologists have developed techniques for reducing reactivity—designing noninterfering measures, keeping subjects blind about their actual role in the study, fooling subjects into thinking the observer is really a part of the environment—each method raises some significant ethical questions. Is it appropriate to deceive subjects into thinking they are not really being recorded? Is it appropriate to withhold treatment from some participants, through the use of placebos, in the interest of achieving proper experimental control? To deal with such issues, formal organizations such as the American Psychological Association (APA) develop and publish ethical guidelines and codes of conduct that members are expected to follow (American Psychological Association, 1992; Fisher & Younggren, 1997).

LEARNING GOALS

1. Explain the principle of informed consent.
2. Discuss the roles of debriefing and confidentiality in research.
3. Discuss the ethical issues involved in animal research.

All psychologists have a professional responsibility to respect the rights and dignity of other people. This responsibility is recognized around the world (Leach & Harbin, 1997), and it goes beyond simple research activities; the code of conduct applies to all psychologists' activities, from administering therapy to working in the field to giving testimony in the courtroom. First and foremost, respecting the rights of others means showing concern for their health, safety, and welfare; no diabolical mind-altering treatments that may permanently affect the participants are allowed, even "in the name and pursuit of science." Psychologists are expected to act responsibly in how they advertise their services, how they represent themselves in the media, and how they charge and collect their fees.

INFORMED CONSENT

The cornerstone of the code of ethical conduct is the principle of **informed consent.** Participants in any form of research or therapy must be informed, in easy-to-understand language, of any significant factors that could affect their willingness to participate (Mann, 1994; Meisel & Roth, 1983). Physical and emotional risks should be explained as should the general nature of the research project or of the therapeutic procedures that will be used. Once informed, participants must then willingly give their written consent to participate in the research. They should understand as well that if they choose not to participate, for whatever reason, they will suffer no negative consequences for withdrawal.

To study the behavior of people in natural settings, such as the willingness of bystanders to help others in need, sometimes requires that the researcher mislead or withhold information from the people being observed.

But informed consent can raise a significant problem for the researcher. Individuals cannot give truly informed consent unless they understand the details of the project, yet full disclosure could critically affect their behavior in the study. You've seen that it is often necessary to keep subjects blind about group assignments so that their expectations won't affect the outcome of the study. Imagine that you were interested in studying how readily the bystanders at an accident will come to the aid of a victim. To gain experimental control, you might stage a mock accident in the laboratory, in front of waiting research subjects, to see how they react. Conducting the study in the laboratory would enable you to investigate the likelihood of intervention under a variety of conditions (such as whether the subject is alone or with others in the room when the accident occurs). But subjects in this situation would need to be misled—you certainly could not fully inform them about the procedure by telling them that the accident is not real.

The psychological research community recognizes that it is sometimes necessary to use deception as part of a research procedure. Not all psychologists agree with this conclusion (Baumrind, 1985; Ortmann & Hertwig, 1997), but it represents the majority opinion. According to the APA code of ethics, deception in research is justified only if the prospective scientific, educational, or applied value of the study is clear, and there is no way to answer the research questions adequately without deceiving the subjects in some way. It is agreed also that whatever deception might be involved, it should not be of a type that could cause subjects physical or emotional harm or affect their willingness to participate in the study. Experimenters have a responsibility, once again, to respect the rights and dignity of research participants at all times. Most universities and colleges make certain that subjects' rights are protected by requiring investigators to submit detailed descriptions of their studies to oversight review committees before any human or animal subjects can be tested. If a study fails to protect the subjects adequately, permission to conduct the study is denied.

informed consent
The principle that before consenting to participate in research, people should be fully informed about any significant factors that could affect their willingness to participate.

DEBRIEFING AND CONFIDENTIALITY

Two other key ingredients of the psychologist's code of ethical conduct are the process of *debriefing* and the maintenance of *confidentiality*. Psychologists are expected to debrief subjects fully at the end of the experimental session, meaning that everyone involved is to be informed about the general purpose of the study. **Debriefing** is intended to clear up any misunderstandings that the subject might have about the research and to explain in detail why certain procedures were used (Gurman, 1994; Holmes, 1976). Certainly if deception was a part of the study, the full nature of the deception should be disclosed during the debriefing process. Debriefing gives the researcher an opportunity to counteract any anxieties that the subject might have developed as a result of the research. If the subject failed to help the victim of a staged accident, for example, the experimenter could explain that bystander passivity is a characteristic of most people (Darley & Latané, 1968).

Finally, once the participation is completed, the subject's right to privacy continues. Psychologists are obligated to respect the privacy of the individual by maintaining **confidentiality**—the researcher or therapist is not to discuss or report confidential information obtained in research or in therapy without the permission of the individual. Confidentiality makes sense for more than just ethical reasons. Research subjects, as well as people seeking help for psychological problems, are likely to feel more comfortable with the process, and to act more naturally, if they are convinced that their right to privacy will be respected.

THE ETHICS OF ANIMAL RESEARCH

In laboratories all over the world, animals actively participate in basic research. They're pressing metal bars for food, receiving small doses of electrical stimulation in the brain, and being raised in enriched environments designed to improve their ability to learn. Although animals are probably used in less than 10% of all current psychological research studies, the famous "laboratory rat" has been an incredibly important source of basic data in the discipline for decades (Coile & Miller, 1984). As you'll see in later chapters, many of the most significant psychological principles were originally discovered through the study of animal behavior (Domjan & Purdy, 1995).

Why use animal subjects? The most often cited reason is for experimental control. It is possible to raise and house nonhuman subjects in relatively ideal environments. Researchers can control diet, experience, and genetic background and thereby eliminate many of the potentially confounding variables that plague research with human subjects. Researchers can also study phenomena such as life-span development in ways that cannot be accomplished with human subjects. Studies that would take 70 or 80 years with humans take only a few years with rats. Nonhuman subjects are sometimes used because they are thought to contain simple, rather than complex, internal structures and systems. The basic biological machinery that underlies learning, for example, has been studied extensively with sea slugs; the number of neural connections in a sea slug is tiny compared with the billions of connections residing in a human brain. Research with nonhuman subjects often serves as a vehicle for developing hypotheses that can later be tested, when feasible, with humans.

But is research with animal subjects ethical? There can be no informed consent in animal research, as animal rights activists point out. Does sufficient justification exist for the invasive procedures sometimes used in animal research—for example, is it okay to permanently destroy a part of a cat's brain in order to learn about how localized brain structures control behavior? Obviously, the use of animals in research is a highly controversial subject. Many millions of dollars are spent every year by animal rights groups; many of these groups oppose any sort of animal research (see Hubbel, 1990). Other critics question the intrinsic value of animal studies, arguing that an understanding of animals reveals little about human functioning and may even mislead researchers into drawing inappropriate

debriefing
At the conclusion of an experimental session, informing the participants about the general purpose of the experiment, including any deception that was involved.

confidentiality
The principle that all personal information obtained from a participant in research or therapy should not be revealed without the individual's permission.

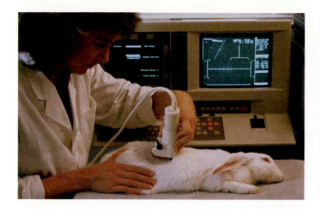

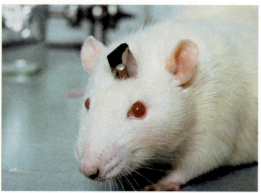

They've Saved More People Than 911.

Perhaps you didn't know that rats and mice have been part of just about every important medical discovery of this century. Well, now you know. To learn more about the benefits of animal research, call 202-457-0654 or write 818 Connecticut Ave. NW Washington DC 20006. FOUNDATION for BIOMEDICAL RESEARCH

Many important insights in psychology have come from the study of animals, but using animals as laboratory subjects raises serious ethical questions.

conclusions (see Ulrich, 1991). In one survey of animal rights activists, 85% advocated the complete elimination of all animal research (Plous, 1991).

Despite the claims of these critics, the majority of psychologists believe that animal research has enormous value. They base their belief on the fact that animal studies have repeatedly led to significant breakthroughs in both the understanding of behavior and psychological disorders and in medical and biological research (see Miller, 1985, 1991). To cite one instance, animal research in psychology over the past two decades has led to breakthroughs in our understanding of depression, as well as to the development of drugs that lessen the symptoms of this disorder (see Chapters 14 and 15). Similarly, through the study of monkeys' natural fear of snakes in the wild, psychologists have learned about how phobias (such as the fear of heights or the fear of being locked in small places) might be learned by imitating the behavior of one's parents rather than through a traumatic life experience (see Chapter 7). In virtually every chapter in this textbook, you will be exposed to psychological principles that have been gained from research with nonhuman subjects.

Moreover, it is important to understand that the American Psychological Association enforces strict guidelines with regard to the ethical treatment of nonhuman subjects. Psychologists who conduct research using animals are expected to treat their subjects humanely. They are responsible for ensuring the animal's proper care, and any treatments that cause discomfort, pain, or illness must be

CRITICAL THINKING

Can you think of any circumstances in which it might be ethical to conduct research with animals even though the results won't generalize to humans?

avoided unless absolutely necessary. When surgical procedures are performed, the animals must be given the appropriate anesthesia, and proper medical procedures must be followed to eliminate infections and minimize pain. Failure to stick to these standards can result in censure or termination of membership by the governing body of the association.

The issue of animal research is controversial, in part, because of misinformation. Experiments that inflict pain and suffering on animals are extremely rare and do not fairly characterize the majority of animal studies (see Coile & Miller, 1984). It's also the case that psychologists haven't done a very good job of promoting the true value of animal research (Johnson & Morris, 1987). At the same time, all researchers must recognize that the nature of the research subject can importantly determine one's results. Findings established from research with nonhuman subjects may, in fact, not always apply to humans—because animals have evolved to solve different problems than humans. Despite these legitimate concerns, animal research continues to be a valuable tool in the search for an understanding of behavior and mind (see Miller, 1991).

TEST YOURSELF 2.4

You can test what you've learned about ethics and research by answering the following questions. (You will find the answers in the Appendix.)

1. Fill in the banks.

   All psychologists have a responsibility to respect the rights and dignity of other people. To ensure that research participants are treated ethically, psychologists use (a) informed _____CONSENT_____, which means that everyone is fully informed about the potential risks of the project, (b) _____CONFIDENTIALITY_____, which assures that the subject's right to privacy will be maintained, and (c) _____DEBRIEFING_____, which is designed to provide more information about the purpose and procedures of the research.

2. Sometimes it is necessary to deceive research participants in some way, such as keeping them blind about group assignments, so that expectations won't determine the outcome. Most psychologists believe that deception:

   a. is always justified as long as it furthers scientific knowledge.
   b. is never justified unless the research involves clinical treatment.
   c. is justified, but only under some circumstances.
   d. is not necessary if you design the project correctly.

3. The majority of psychologists believe that animal research has enormous value. But some question the ethics of using animals primarily because:

   a. no real scientific advancements have come from animal research.
   b. animals are often treated cruelly.
   c. animals can give no informed consent.
   d. animal research is too expensive.

Solving the Problems

Psychologists rely on a set of established research tools. The facts and theories that make up the discipline of psychology have arisen from the systematic application of these tools. Understanding research methodology is important because the conclusions reached in research studies are inevitably influenced by the methods that have been used. Whether the recorded behavior of children in a day-care center will accurately represent real life, for example, depends on what the methods of observation have been. In addition, the extent to which an experiment has the capacity to determine whether television violence causes aggression depends on the experimenter's use of the proper controls and selection of subjects that are representative of the population of interest. In this chapter I divided our discussion of the methods of psychological research into four main problem areas.

Observing and Describing Behavior. Descriptive research consists of the methodologies that underlie the observation and description of behavior. In *naturalistic observation,* the researcher observes behavior in natural settings rather than in a laboratory environment. Naturalistic observation is a useful technique for generating research ideas and for verifying whether conclusions reached in the lab generalize to more realistic settings. In *case studies,* the focus is on a single instance of a behavior or psychological phenomenon. This technique allows the researcher to obtain lots of background information on the individual being studied, but the results may not always generalize to wider populations. In *survey research,* behavior is sampled broadly, usually by gathering responses from many people in the form of a questionnaire. Surveys typically provide information that is representative of the group being examined, but the amount of information that can be gathered is usually limited. Finally, through *psychological tests,* differences among individuals can be quantified.

Once the observational data have been collected, they are summarized through the application of *statistics.* Such statistics include measures of central tendency—the mean, median, and mode—and measures of variability, or how far apart individual scores are from each other in a set of scores. Researchers also use *inferential statistics,* based on the laws of probability, to test hypotheses. Inferential statistics can help the researcher decide whether a difference between an experimental and a control group, for example, is likely to have occurred by chance.

Predicting Behavior. In *correlational research,* the researcher tries to determine whether a relationship exists between two measures of behavior. For instance, does high school grade point average predict college performance? Correlation coefficients, which provide an index of how well one measure predicts another, are statistics that vary between +1.00 and −1.00. Correlations are useful primarily because they enable the researcher to predict and select. If employers know, for example, that there is a correlation between achievement test scores and job performance, they can use someone's score on an achievement test to predict that person's success on the job. Correlations are useful tools for predicting and selecting, but they do not allow the researcher to draw conclusions about causality.

Determining Why Behavior Occurs. If researchers want to know whether an activity, such as watching violence on television, *causes* a change in behavior, they must conduct an *experiment.* In doing so, the researcher manipulates the environment in a systematic way and then observes the effect of that manipulation on behavior. The aspect of the environment that is manipulated is called the *independent variable;* the measured behavior of interest is called the *dependent variable.* To determine that the independent variable is really responsible for the changes in behavior, the researcher must exert experimental control—the only thing that must be changing systematically is the experimenter's manipulation of the independent variable. Researchers conducting experiments encounter a variety of potential pitfalls, including subject and experimenter expectancies, that need to be controlled. Control strategies include the use of random assignment and blind research designs.

Treating Research Participants Ethically. Scientific psychology is based on observation, and observing others requires that researchers invade, to a certain extent, the personal environment of their subjects. As a result, it is important that all researchers maintain a strict code of ethical conduct. An important safeguard is informed consent, which is designed to guarantee that participants will be informed of any significant factors that could influence their willingness to participate. Other ethical standards govern proper debriefing and the maintenance of confidentiality. All researchers, regardless of the nature of the research, have a professional responsibility to respect the rights and dignity of their research subjects. This applies not only to human participants but also to animals whenever they are used as part of the research process.

Psychological Research Chapter Summary

Psychology is the scientific study of behavior and mind, and of how people differ as a result of biological and environmental influences and cultural context. Psychological understanding lets us predict, control, and improve behavior.

Observing and Describing Behavior: Descriptive Research

Scientists study the mind by using the scientific method, in which they (1) observe, (2) detect regularities, (3) generate a hypothesis, and (4) observe again.

NATURALISTIC OBSERVATION

Behavior is observed in natural settings with noninterfering measures.

TESTS

Various psychological tests measure individual differences.

CASE STUDIES

Intense focus on a single case yields historical information that can be used to generate hypotheses.

STATISTICS

Data analyses reveal regularities in psychological observations that are needed to test effective hypotheses.

SURVEYS

Responses gathered from many people help establish generality.

Predicting Behavior: Correlational Research

In addition to describing current behavior, psychologists use what they've learned to make predictions about future behavior.

CORRELATIONAL RESEARCH

A *correlation* helps determine whether there is a relationship between two variables, or measures of behavior.

CORRELATIONS AND CAUSALITY

A correlation between two measures of behavior helps prediction, but does not allow for the determination of causality.

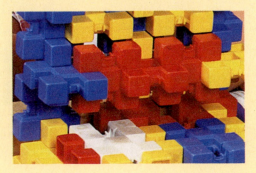

Determining Why Behavior Occurs: Experimental Research

Determining causality requires *control*, an important feature of a psychological experiment.

VARIABLES

Independent variable: The aspect of the environment that is manipulated in an experiment.

Dependent variable: The behavior that is measured or observed in an experiment.

EXPECTANCIES AND BIASES

Researchers must account for the fact that expectations and biases can affect the subject's behavior in ways that distort experiment results.

EXPERIMENTAL CONTROL

At least two conditions must be included as part of an independent variable manipulation. Members of the **control group** are usually not exposed to the treatment; those in the **experimental group** are.

GENERALIZING CONCLUSIONS

Necessary experimental controls can limit the relevance of results to other subjects and situations.

Treating Research Participants Ethically: Human and Animal Guidelines

Psychologists must respect the rights of their subjects, showing concern for their health, safety, and welfare.

INFORMED CONSENT

Research participants must understand any factors that could affect their willingness to participate.

DEBRIEFING/CONFIDENTIALITY

To *debrief* means to inform research participants about the purpose of the completed study. *Confidentiality* protects the participant's privacy.

ANIMAL RESEARCH

Although APA guidelines require that animals be treated humanely, controversy remains over their use in psychological research.

Terms to Remember

scientific method, 34
operational definition, 35

OBSERVING AND DESCRIBING BEHAVIOR

descriptive research, 36
reactivity, 36
external validity, 37
naturalistic observation, 37
case study, 39
survey, 39
random sampling, 41
mean, 42
mode, 43
median, 43
variability, 43
range, 44
standard deviation, 44
descriptive statistics, 44
inferential statistics, 44

PREDICTING AND SELECTING BEHAVIOR

correlation, 46

DETERMINING WHY BEHAVIOR OCCURS

experimental research, 51
independent variable, 52
dependent variable, 53
confounding variable, 54
internal validity, 54
random assignment, 56
placebo, 57
single-blind study, 57
double-blind study, 57

TREATING RESEARCH PARTICIPANTS ETHICALLY

informed consent, 61
debriefing, 62
confidentiality, 62

Recommended Readings

Stanovich, K. E. (1998). *How to think straight about psychology* (5th ed.). Reading, MA: Addison-Wesley. Provides an in-depth discussion of how to evaluate empirical evidence in psychology and avoid faulty conclusions.

Snodgrass, J. G., Levy-Berger, G., & Haydon, M. (1985). *Human experimental psychology*. New York: Oxford University Press. An excellent resource for designing experiments, setting up apparatus, testing subjects, analyzing and interpreting data, and writing up the results of research.

Pelham, B. W. (1999). *Conducting experiments in psychology: Measuring the weight of smoke*. Pacific Grove, CA: Brooks/Cole. A new book that describes the essentials of research methods using many real-life examples and hands-on activities.

INFOTRAC® COLLEGE EDITION

For additional readings, explore Infotrac College Edition, your online library. Go to:
http://www.infotrac-college.com/wadsworth

Hint: enter the search terms: Participant observation, Survey research, Psychological tests, Experimental design, Psychological research methods.

🌐 What's on the Web?

The Junk Science Homepage

(www.junkscience.org)

This page presents "all the junk that's fit to debunk." It's a very interesting site, chock full of phony claims and questionable science—a veritable feast for the skeptical types! Although many of the articles do not relate specifically to psychology, it's still a great site to visit to get a feel for the dogged skepticism of a scientist.

Psychology Research on the Net

(psych.hanover.edu/APS/exponnet.html)

This page is part of the American Psychological Society Web site, and offers links to a dizzying array of research projects that will give you an idea of the range of phenomena that psychologists investigate. The projects linked to this site run the gamut of every area in psychology, from Clinical to Social to Cognitive. Participate in projects on decision making, giving directions, anger, and irrational food beliefs, and dozens of others.

Psychexps

(www.olemiss.edu/projects/PsychExps/Exps/experiments.html)

This site allows you to test yourself as a subject in some strictly experimental studies, the majority of which would be conducted by research psychologists in the area of cognition. Find out how accurate and how quick you are at tasks like mental rotation, word recognition, and face recognition.

The Wadsworth Psychology Study Center Web Site

See http://psychology.wadsworth.com/ for practice quiz questions, hypercontents, updates, critical thinking exercises, discussion forums and more! The Wadsworth Psychology Study Center provides a wealth of information fully organized and integrated by chapter.

Biological Processes

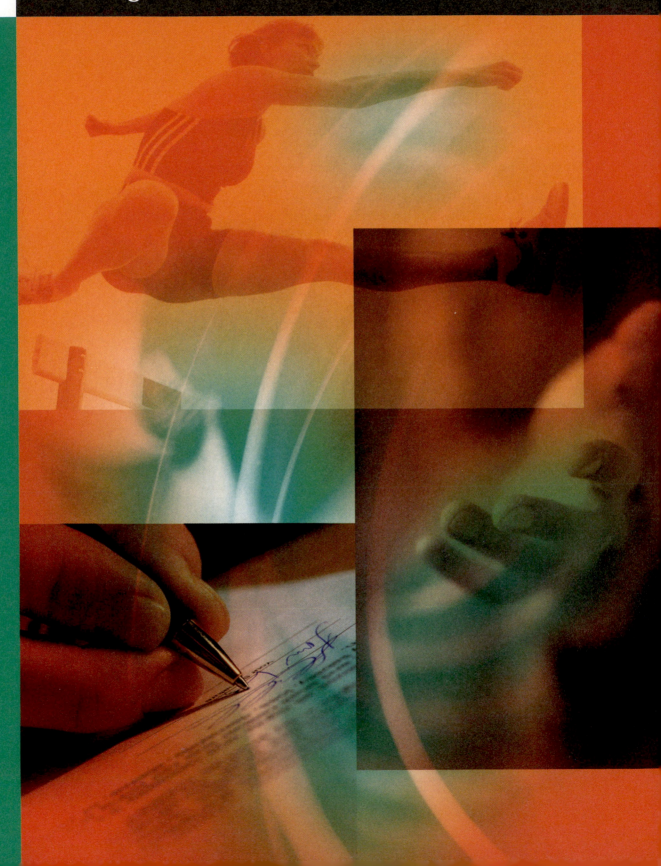

After days and nights of incredible labour and fatigue, I succeeded in discovering the cause of generation and life; nay, more, I became myself capable of bestowing animation upon lifeless matter. . . . I see by your eagerness, and the wonder and hope which your eyes express, my friend, that you expect to be informed of the secret with which I am acquainted.

MARY WOLLSTONECRAFT SHELLEY,
FRANKENSTEIN

neuroscience
An interdisciplinary field of study directed at understanding the brain and its relation to behavior.

Nearly two decades ago, a group of young adults, searching for a heroin high, injected themselves with a homemade version of a "designer" drug. It was supposed to simulate the effects of heroin, but sloppy lab work produced a substance that permanently redesigned the users' brains. One of the chemical components essentially destroyed a tiny region of their midbrains. The users became frozen in their bodies—their minds remained active, but each lost the ability to communicate or move about freely. It was only a small mix-up in the recipe, and the drug affected only a tiny portion of the brain, but the consequences were truly devastating for the users.

You probably already know and accept that there is a close connection between the brain and the movements of the body. So it should be no surprise to you that damage to the brain can dramatically influence the body's ability to move. But remember, most scientists believe that *all* behavior arises from the activities of the brain—not just things like walking, breathing, or maintaining a beating heart, but your intimate thoughts and feelings as well. Virtually every time you think, act, or feel, biological activity in your brain is playing a critical, if not primary, role. To the psychologist this means that psychological disorders, such as schizophrenia or clinical depression, are products of the brain as well—but they are by-products, perhaps, of what might be considered a "broken" brain.

This chapter introduces you to the field of **neuroscience,** which studies the connection among the brain, the mind, and behavior. Although I'll focus primarily on the brain, your behavior is actually controlled by a broader system that

FIGURE 3.1

The Central Nervous System
The central nervous system consists of the brain and the spinal cord.

Brain

Spinal cord

includes the spinal cord as well as the connections that the brain makes to muscles, sensory organs, and other internal structures in the body. More specifically, the brain and spinal cord comprise what is called the **central nervous system** (see Figure 3.1). An additional network of nerves, the **peripheral nervous system,** acts as the communication link between the central nervous system and the rest of the body. It's the job of the peripheral nervous system to relay messages from the central nervous system to the muscles that produce actual responses. Later in this chapter, I'll expand on these basic divisions of the nervous system and outline their various functions in greater detail. I'll also return to the frozen users mentioned above, and you'll see exactly where their problem lies.

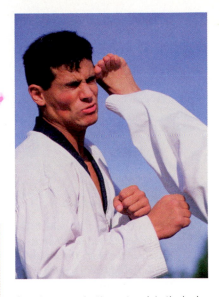

A vast communication network in the body helps us monitor the environment and produce quick adaptive responses when they're needed.

Previewing the Adaptive Problems

Our discussion of biological processes is divided into four central problems of adaptation. Each problem can be viewed as a challenge to be resolved by the systems in your body to help you survive and adapt successfully to the environment. As you'll soon see, these biological solutions provide important insight into the workings of the adaptive mind.

First, how does your body, particularly the nervous system, communicate internally? One reason behavior is often adaptive is that people are able to monitor their environment continuously and produce quick responses that best fit the needs of the situations they face. If a child trying to catch a bouncing ball runs suddenly into the path of your car, you step quickly on the brake and the child is saved. These nearly instantaneous world-to-behavior links are possible because of a complex communication network linking the outside world to the brain.

Second, how does your brain initiate and coordinate behavior? The nervous system may handle the complicated task of receiving and communicating information, but information by itself does not translate into hand movements, quick reactions, or artistic creativity. Somehow the body must assign meaning to the information it receives and coordinate the appropriate responses.

Third, how does the body regulate growth and other internal functions? Besides relying on the rapid transmission of information from one point to the next, the systems in your body also have widespread and long-term internal communication needs. To resolve these needs, structures in the body control the release of chemicals into the bloodstream that serve important regulatory functions, influencing growth and development, sexual behavior, the desire to eat or drink, and even emotional expression.

Fourth, how does the body store and transmit the genetic code? The genetic blueprint that you inherited from your parents determines much of who you are and what you have the potential to become. Molecules that carry the genetic code influence more than simply eye color, height, or hair color. Intelligence, personality, and even susceptibility to mental disorders have at least some genetic basis. You'll learn how the body transmits genetic material to its offspring, thereby helping to ensure survival of the species.

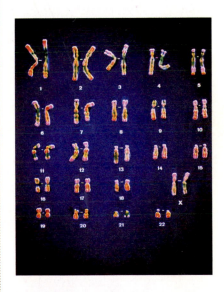

The genetic blueprint is inherited from the mother and father, and importantly shapes our physical and psychological characteristics.

Communicating Internally: Connecting World and Brain

Strike a match and hold it an inch or so away from the tip of your index finger. Now move it a bit closer. Closer. Closer still. Let the flame approach and momentarily touch the flesh of your finger. On second thought, skip this experiment. Experience has already given you a pretty good idea of the consequences of finger–flame combinations. Flame approaches flesh, and you withdraw your finger quickly, automatically, and efficiently. Let's consider the nervous system mechanisms that underlie this kind of reaction, because it represents one of the simplest and purest kinds of world-to-brain communications.

central nervous system
The brain and the spinal cord.

peripheral nervous system
The network of nerves that links the central nervous system with the rest of the body.

CRITICAL THINKING

A reflex is a type of adaptive behavior that does not arise directly from activity of the brain. If you were building a body from scratch, what types of reflexes would you build in and why?

neurons
The cells in the nervous system that receive and transmit information by generating an electrochemical signal; neurons are the basic building blocks of the nervous system.

sensory neurons
Neurons that make initial contact with the environment and carry the message inward toward the spinal cord and brain.

interneurons
Neurons that make no direct contact with the world but rather convey information from one neuron or processing site to another.

motor neurons
Neurons that carry information away from the central nervous system to the muscles and glands that directly produce behavioral responses.

glial cells
Cells in the nervous system that do not transmit or receive information but that perform a variety of functions, such as removing waste, filling in empty space, or helping neurons to communicate efficiently.

myelin sheath
An insulating material that protects the axons of some neurons and helps to speed up neural transmission.

reflexes
Largely automatic body reactions—such as the knee jerk—that are controlled primarily by spinal cord pathways.

dendrites
The branchlike fibers that extend outward from a neuron and receive information from other neurons.

The main components of the nervous system are individual cells, called **neurons,** that receive, transmit, and integrate information. The language that neurons use to communicate is electrochemical; that is, it's part electrical and part chemical. Neurons come in three major types—*sensory neurons, interneurons,* and *motor neurons*—that differ physically from one another, and serve quite different functions.

1. **Sensory neurons** make the initial contact with the environment and are responsible for carrying the message inward toward the spinal cord and brain. The heat of the flame excites receptor regions in the sensory neurons in your fingertip, which then pass the message along to the spinal cord.

2. **Interneurons,** the most plentiful type of neurons, make no direct contact with the world but rather convey information from one internal processing site to another. Interneurons in the spinal cord receive the message from the sensory neurons, then pass it on to the motor neurons.

3. **Motor neurons** carry the messages and commands away from the central nervous system to the muscles and glands that directly produce the behavioral response. In the match example, which is depicted in Figure 3.2, the motor neurons contact the muscles of the finger, which leads to a quick and efficient finger withdrawal.

The nervous system also contains **glial cells,** which greatly outnumber neurons (by a factor of about ten to one) but do not directly communicate messages on their own. The details are beyond the scope of our discussion, but glial cells perform a variety of functions in the nervous system, such as removing waste, filling in empty space, and helping neurons to communicate efficiently (see Kimelberg & Norenberg, 1989). Some types of glial cells wrap around portions of neurons, acting as a kind of insulation. This insulation, called the **myelin sheath,** protects the neuron and helps speed up neural transmission. Unfortunately, glial cells also play an important role in some kinds of brain dysfunction, including brain cancer and Alzheimer's disease (Saitoh et al., 1997).

You may have noticed that so far the brain hasn't figured into our discussion of fingers and flames. Actually, the message is passed upward to the brain, through the activity of more interneurons, and it is in the brain that you consciously experience the heat of the flame. But in situations requiring a quick response, as in the case of a flame touching your finger, the nervous system is capable of producing a collection of largely automatic reactions. These reactions, called **reflexes,** are controlled primarily by spinal cord pathways. A reflex requires no input from the brain. If your spinal cord were to be cut, blocking communication between most of the body and brain, you wouldn't feel the pain or react with a facial grimace, but your finger would still twitch. Reflex pathways allow the body to respond quickly to environmental events in a relatively simple and direct way. People don't think or feel with their spinal cords, but reflex pathways are an important part of our ability to adapt successfully to the world.

THE ANATOMY OF NEURONS

Before it's possible to understand how information passes from one neuron to another—how the message actually moves between world and brain—it's important to consider the basic anatomical hardware of these cells. As shown in Figure 3.3 on page 76, neurons typically have four major structural components: *dendrites,* a *soma,* an *axon,* and *terminal buttons.* For any communication system to work properly, it must have a way to receive information, a way to process any received messages, and a means for sending any appropriate response on its way. The four structural components of the neuron play these distinct roles in the communication chain.

The **dendrites,** which look like tree branches extending outward from the main body of the cell, are the primary information receivers. A sensory neuron

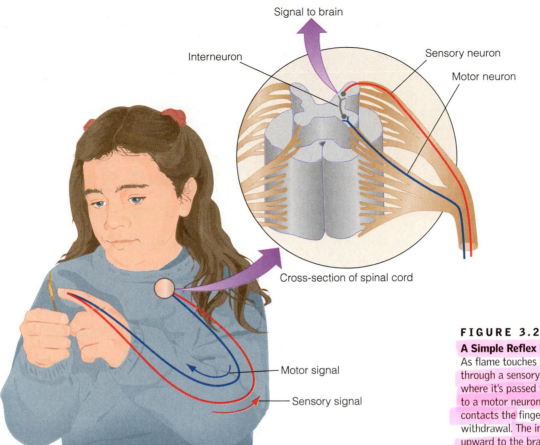

Signal to brain

Interneuron

Sensory neuron

Motor neuron

Cross-section of spinal cord

Motor signal

Sensory signal

FIGURE 3.2

A Simple Reflex Pathway
As flame touches flesh, the information travels through a sensory neuron to the spinal cord, where it's passed to an interneuron and then on to a motor neuron. The motor neuron then contacts the finger muscles, causing a quick *reaction* withdrawal. The information is also passed upward to the brain, where the experience of pain occurs.

passes information about a burning flame along to an interneuron by interacting with the interneuron's dendrites. A particular neuron may have thousands of these dendritic branches, allowing the cell to receive input from many different sources. Once received, the message is processed in the **soma,** the main body of the cell. The soma is also the cell's metabolic center, and it's the place where genetic material is stored.

The **axon** is the cell's transmitter device. When a neuron transmits a message, it sends an electrical signal called the *action potential* down its axon toward other neurons. Axons are essentially biological transmission cables, although the action potential in a neuron is considerably slower and quite different from the electrical currents in your house's wiring. Axons can vary dramatically in size and shape; in some cases, they can be several feet in length. Near its end, the axon branches out in preparation to make contact with other cells. At the tip of each branch are tiny swellings called **terminal buttons.** Chemicals released by these buttons play an important part in passing the message on to the next neuron.

Neurons don't actually touch. The **synapse** is a small gap between cells, typically between the terminal buttons of one neuron and the dendrite or cell body of another. It is into this gap that the chemicals released by the terminal buttons flow. The synapse and the chemicals released into it are critical factors in the body's communication network, as you'll see next.

NEURAL TRANSMISSION: THE ELECTROCHEMICAL MESSAGE

Neurons may differ in size and shape, but the manner and direction of information flow is predictable and consistent.

Dendrites → Soma → Axon → Terminal buttons

soma
The cell body of a neuron.

axon
The long tail-like part of a neuron that serves as the cell's transmitter device.

terminal buttons
The tiny swellings at the end of a neuron's axon that contain chemicals important to neural transmission.

synapse
The junction, or small gap, between neurons, typically between the terminal buttons of one neuron and the dendrite or cell body of another neuron.

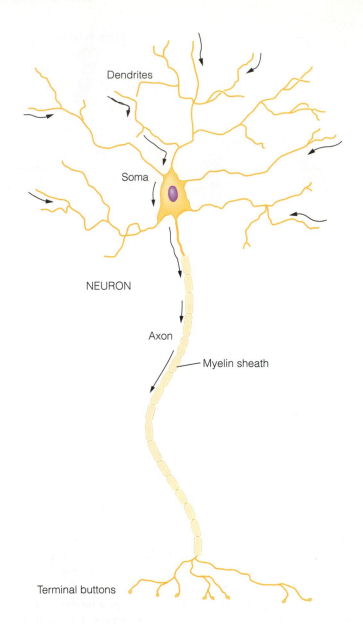

Dendrites

Soma

NEURON

Axon

Myelin sheath

Terminal buttons

FIGURE 3.3

The Components of a Neuron
The *dendrites* are the primary information receivers, the *soma* is the cell body, and the *axon* is the cell's transmitter device. The myelin sheath that surrounds the axon helps speed up neural transmission. At the end of the axon are the *terminal buttons*, which contain the chemical messengers.

Information usually arrives at the dendrites from multiple sources—many thousands of contacts might be made—and is passed along to the soma. Here all the messages that have been received sum together; if sufficient energy is present, an action potential will be generated (see below). The action potential travels down the axon toward the terminal buttons, where it causes the release of chemicals into the synapse. These chemicals move the message from the end of the axon to the dendrites of the next neuron, starting the process all over again. That's the general sequence of information flow: Messages travel electrically from one point to another within a neuron, but the message is transmitted chemically between neurons. Now let's consider each of these processes in more detail.

The Resting Potential
Neurons possess electrical properties even when they are neither receiving nor transmitting messages. Specifically, a tiny electrical charge, called the **resting potential**, exists between the inside and outside of the cell. This resting potential is created by the presence of electrically charged atoms and molecules, called *ions*, that are distributed unevenly between the inside and outside of the cell. The main ions in neural transmission are positively charged *sodium* and *potassium* ions and negatively charged *chloride* ions.

resting potential
The tiny electrical charge in place between the inside and outside of the resting neuron.

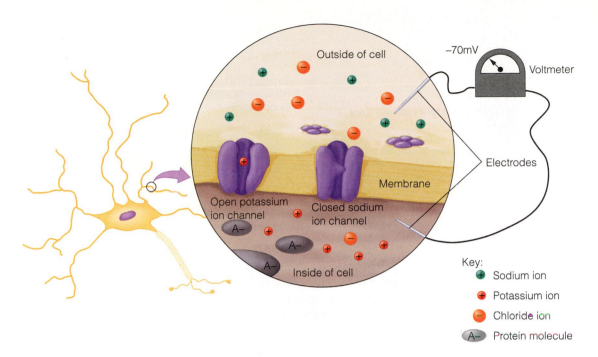

Key:
- Sodium ion
- Potassium ion
- Chloride ion
- A– Protein molecule

Normally, ions will distribute themselves evenly in an environment, through a process called *diffusion*. However, they are unable to do so around a resting neuron because free movement is blocked by the neuron's cell wall, or *membrane*. The membrane of a neuron is selectively permeable, which means that it only allows certain ions to pass in and out through special ion "channels." As shown in Figure 3.4, when the neuron is resting, the sodium and chloride ions are concentrated outside of the cell and the potassium ions are largely contained inside. These unequal concentrations are maintained, in part, by a sodium-potassium pump that actively moves ions into and out of the cell. If you measured the electrical potential of the neuron with an electrode, you would find that the fluid inside the cell is *negative* with respect to the outside (between −60 and −70 millivolts). This negative charge defines the resting potential for the cell. Most of the negative charge comes from large protein molecules inside the cell, which are too big to pass through ion channels.

Why is it adaptive for neurons to have a resting potential? It's likely that the resting potential helps the cell respond quickly when it is contacted by other neurons. When one neuron communicates with another, it releases chemicals that change the nature of the contacted neuron's membrane. Ions that are normally outside the cell can rush in quickly through newly opened channels. This changes the electrical potential inside the cell, which, as you'll see shortly, can lead to the production of an action potential.

Generating an Action Potential

For a neuron to stop resting and generate an **action potential,** the electrical potential inside the cell must become less negative. Changes in internal potential occur as a result of contact from other neurons. Two types of messages can be passed from one neuron to the next: excitatory messages and inhibitory messages. If the message is *excitatory*, the membrane of the contacted neuron changes and sodium ions begin to flow into the cell. This process, called **depolarization,** moves the electrical potential of the cell from negative toward zero and increases the chances that an action potential will be generated. When the message is *inhibitory*, the opposite happens: The cell membrane either pushes more positive ions out of the cell or allows negative ions to move in. The result is **hyperpolarization:** the electrical potential of the cell becomes more negative, and the chances of an action potential decrease.

FIGURE 3.4
The Resting Potential
Neurons possess electrical properties even when they are neither receiving nor transmitting messages. The resting potential is a tiny negative electrical charge across the inside and outside of the resting cell, created by an uneven distribution of ions across the cell membrane. Ion movement occurs through special channels in the membrane.

action potential
The all-or-none electrical signal that travels down a neuron's axon.

depolarization
The change in a neuron's electrical potential from negative toward zero; depolarization usually occurs when positive ions flow into the cell as a result of neural communication.

hyperpolarization
An increase in the negative electrical potential of a neuron, reducing the chances of the cell generating an action potential.

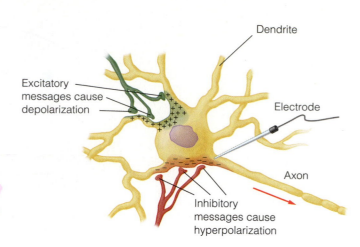

It's important to remember that any given neuron in the nervous system is in contact with many other neurons. As a result, small changes in potential regularly occur in many input regions of the neuron as messages are received (see Figure 3.5). Near the point where the axon leaves the cell body, in a special trigger zone called the *axon hillock*, all of the excitatory and inhibitory potentials combine. If enough excitatory messages have been received—that is, if the electrical potential inside the cell has become sufficiently less negative—an action potential will be initiated. If not, the resting potential of the axon will be maintained.

Action potentials are generated in an *all-or-none* fashion; that is, they will not begin until sufficient excitatory input has been received, but once the firing threshold is reached, they always travel completely down the length of the axon to its end. The process is somewhat analogous to the firing of a gun. Once sufficient pressure is delivered to the trigger, a bullet will fire and move down the barrel in a characteristic way. Action potentials, like bullets, also travel forward in a way that is independent of the intensity of the messages that caused the firing. Bullets don't travel farther or faster if you pull the trigger harder.

Action potentials also travel down the axon in a fixed and characteristic way. It really doesn't matter whether the neuron is carrying a message about pain or pleasure; the characteristics of the signal won't vary from one neuron to the next, or from one point on the axon to the next. The overall speed of transmission, however, depends on the size and shape of the axon; in general, the thicker the axon, the faster the message will travel. Impulse speed varies among neuron types in a range from about 2 to 200 miles per hour (which is still significantly slower than the speed of electricity through a wire or printed circuit).

One feature that increases the speed of transmission in many neurons is the myelin sheath, which, as mentioned earlier, is built from a type of glial cell. Myelin provides an insulating wrap for the axon, like the plastic around copper wiring in your house. At regular points, there are gaps in the insulation, called *nodes of Ranvier*, that permit the action potential to jump down the axon rather than traveling from point to point. This method of transmission from node to node is called *saltatory conduction*; it comes from the Latin word *saltare* which means "to jump." The myelin sheath speeds transmission and it also protects the message from interference from other neural signals.

Neurotransmitters: The Chemical Messengers

When the action potential reaches the end of the axon, it triggers the release of chemical messengers from small sacs, or vesicles, in the terminal buttons (see Figure 3.6). These chemical molecules, called **neurotransmitters,** spill out into the synapse and interact chemically with the cell membrane of the next neuron (called the *postsynaptic membrane*). Depending on the particular characteristics of this membrane, the neurotransmitter will transfer either an excitatory or an inhibitory message.

neurotransmitters
Chemical messengers that relay information from one neuron to the next. They are released from the terminal buttons into the synapse, where they interact chemically with the cell membrane of the next neuron; the result is either an excitatory or an inhibitory message.

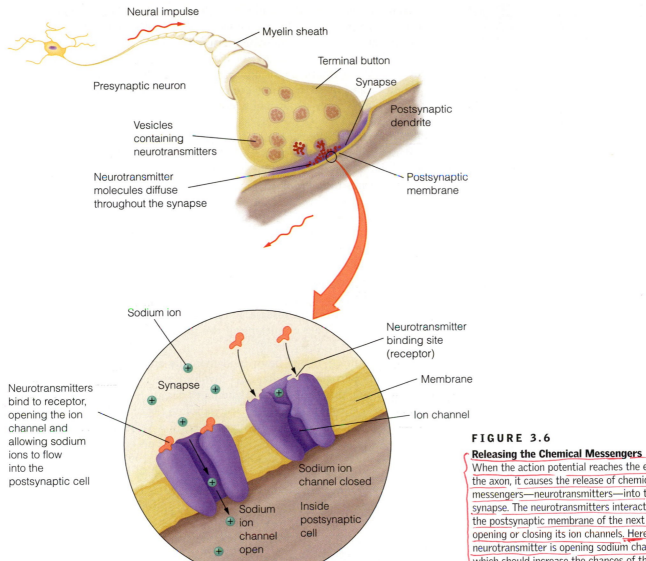

Neural impulse

Myelin sheath

Terminal button

Presynaptic neuron

Synapse

Postsynaptic dendrite

Vesicles containing neurotransmitters

Neurotransmitter molecules diffuse throughout the synapse

Postsynaptic membrane

Sodium ion

Neurotransmitter binding site (receptor)

Neurotransmitters bind to receptor, opening the ion channel and allowing sodium ions to flow into the postsynaptic cell

Synapse

Membrane

Ion channel

Sodium ion channel closed

Inside postsynaptic cell

Sodium ion channel open

FIGURE 3.6

Releasing the Chemical Messengers

When the action potential reaches the end of the axon, it causes the release of chemical messengers—neurotransmitters—into the synapse. The neurotransmitters interact with the postsynaptic membrane of the next neuron, opening or closing its ion channels. Here, the neurotransmitter is opening sodium channels, which should increase the chances of the receiving cell initiating its own action potential.

The released neurotransmitter molecule acts as a kind of key in search of the appropriate lock. The substance moves quickly across the synapse—it takes only about 1/10,000 of a second—and activates receptor molecules contained in the postsynaptic membrane. Depending on the particular type of receptor molecule that is present, the neurotransmitter will then either increase or decrease the electrical potential of the receiving cell. When the message is excitatory, the neurotransmitter causes channels in the postsynaptic membrane to open, allowing positive sodium ions to flow into the receiving cell. When the message is inhibitory, negative chloride ions are allowed to enter the cell and positive potassium ions are allowed to leave. It's worth emphasizing that neurotransmitters, by themselves, are neither excitatory nor inhibitory. It is really the nature of the receptor molecule that determines whether a particular neurotransmitter will produce an excitatory or inhibitory effect; the same neurotransmitter can produce quite different effects at different sites in the nervous system.

Dozens of neurotransmitters have been identified in the brain, along with their various functions. The neurotransmitter **acetylcholine** is a major messenger in both the central and peripheral nervous systems; it acts, for example, as the primary transmitter between motor neurons and muscles in the body. When released into the synapse between motor neurons and muscle cells, acetylcholine tends to

? CRITICAL THINKING

The speed of neural transmission is quite slow, at least relative to the speed of processing in a computer chip. How do you think it's possible for people to make quick, seemingly instant, decisions? Hint: Could large groups of neurons acting together be involved?

acetylcholine

A neurotransmitter that plays several roles in the central and peripheral nervous systems, including the excitation of muscle contractions.

For much of recorded history, psychological disorders were attributed to possession by evil spirits. Today, psychologists recognize that some disorders are the result of brain malfunctioning.

dopamine
A neurotransmitter that often leads to inhibitory effects; decreased levels have been linked to Parkinson's disease and increased levels have been linked to schizophrenia.

serotonin
A neurotransmitter that has been linked to sleep, dreaming, and general arousal and may also be involved in some psychological disorders such as depression and schizophrenia.

GABA (gamma-amino-butyric acid)
A neurotransmitter that may to play a role in the regulation of anxiety; it generally produces inhibitory effects.

create excitatory messages that lead to muscle contraction. The neurotransmitter **dopamine** often produces inhibitory effects that help dampen and stabilize communications in the brain and elsewhere. Inhibitory effects help to keep the brain on an even keel and allow us to do things like produce smooth voluntary muscle movements, sleep without physically acting out our dreams, and maintain posture. If neurotransmitters had only excitatory effects, there would be an endless chain of communication, producing a blooming, buzzing ball of confusion in the brain.

Dopamine is of particular interest to psychologists because it's thought to play a role in schizophrenia, a serious psychological disorder that disrupts thought processes and produces delusions and hallucinations. When schizophrenic patients take drugs that inhibit the action of dopamine, their hallucinations and delusions are sometimes reduced or even eliminated. It has been speculated that perhaps an excess supply of dopamine is partly responsible for the disorder (O'Donnell & Grace, 1998; Sigmundson, 1994; Snyder, 1976). Further support linking dopamine and schizophrenia has come from the study of Parkinson's disease. This movement disorder apparently results from the underproduction of dopamine. Parkinson's patients are often given the drug L-dopa, which increases the levels of dopamine in the brain, to reduce the tremors and other movement problems that result from the disease. For some patients, however, one of the side effects of L-dopa can be a mimicking of the thought disorders characteristic of schizophrenia (Braff & Huey, 1988).

Neurotransmitters in the brain fundamentally affect people's thoughts and actions, but the particular mechanisms involved are not well understood. We know, for example, that people with Alzheimer's disease have suffered destruction of cells that play a role in producing acetylcholine (Mash et al., 1985; Quirion, 1993). Since memory loss is a common problem for Alzheimer patients, a close connection may exist between acetylcholine and certain kinds of memory functioning (Hasselmo et al., 1996; McDonald & Crawley, 1997). We also know that **serotonin,** another neurotransmitter that often acts in an inhibitory fashion, affects sleep, dreaming, and general arousal, and may also be involved in such psychological disorders as depression, schizophrenia, and obsessive-compulsive disorder (Potter & Manji, 1993; McAllister-Williams et al., 1998; Thomsen, 1994, 1998). As you'll learn in Chapter 15, some medications used to treat depression, such as Prozac, act by modulating the effectiveness of serotonin. Similarly, researchers have suspected for some time that a neurotransmitter called gamma-amino-butyric acid (**GABA**) probably plays an important role in the regulation of anxiety. Many oft-prescribed medications for anxiety (e.g., tranquilizers such as Valium) act to regulate GABA in the brain.

In each of these cases, however, researchers still face the difficult task of determining the specific neural pathways and mechanisms involved. At this point, much of the link is correlational rather than causal. We know that as the levels of particular neurotransmitters vary in the body, so too do the symptoms of various disorders. This is useful information for treatment, but it doesn't establish a definitive cause-and-effect link between neurotransmitters and psychological characteristics.

Drugs and the Brain

Because the transmission of messages *between* neurons is chemical, chemicals that are ingested into the body can significantly affect the communication networks in the brain. Some drugs, called *agonists,* mimic the action of neurotransmitters. For example, the nicotine in cigarette smoke can act like the neurotransmitter acetylcholine. Nicotine has a general stimulatory effect in the body, such as increasing the heart rate, because it produces excitatory messages in much the same way as acetylcholine.

CONCEPT SUMMARY Neurotransmitters and Their Effects		
Neurotransmitter	**Nature of Effect**	**Involved In . . .**
Dopamine	Generally inhibitory*	Dampening and stabilizing communication in the brain and elsewhere; helps ensure smooth motor function. Plays a role in both schizophrenia and Parkinson's disease
Acetylcholine	Generally excitatory*	Communication between motor neurons and muscles in the body, leading to muscle contraction. May also play a role in Alzheimer's disease.
Serotonin	Generally inhibitory*	Regulating sleep, dreaming, and general arousal. Also may play a role in some psychological disorders, including depression.
GABA	Generally inhibitory*	The regulation of anxiety; tranquilizing drugs act on GABA to decrease anxiety.

*Note: No neurotransmitter, on its own, is excitatory or inhibitory; the specific nature of a neuron's action depends on specific characteristics of the receiving cell's membrane.

Other drugs act as *antagonists,* which means that they oppose or block the action of neurotransmitters. The lethal drug curare, which South Americans sometimes use on the tips of hunting arrows and blowdarts, is antagonistic to acetylcholine. Curare blocks the receptor systems involved in muscle movements, including those muscles that move the diaphragm during breathing. The result is paralysis and likely death from suffocation.

In the early 1970s membrane receptor systems were discovered in the brain that react directly to *morphine*, a pain-killing and highly addictive drug derived from the opium plant (Pert & Snyder, 1973). It turns out that we have receptor systems that are sensitive to morphine because the brain produces its own morphinelike substances called **endorphins.** Endorphins serve as natural painkillers in the body. They are thought to act as *neuromodulators,* or chemicals that modulate (increase or decrease) the effectiveness of neurotransmitters. Apparently, the brain

endorphins
Morphine-like chemicals that act as the brain's natural painkillers.

Many natural substances—such as coffee, curare, and the common groundcover St. John's Wort—contain ingredients that affect the action of neurotransmitters in the body and brain.

Inside the Problem   "Animal Electricity" and the Neural Impulse

Mary Wollstonecraft Shelley, in her classic novel *Frankenstein,* used an electrical storm to infuse life into her monstrous creation. Even in her time, the early nineteenth century, people recognized that the neural impulse had a powerful electric component. In fact, the formal linking of electricity to the initiation of behavior in the nervous system dates back to the work of an Italian named Luigi Galvani in the last two decades of the eighteenth century. Galvani noticed that when the severed legs of frogs were hung from brass hooks connected to iron rods, they would sometimes twitch in the presence of electric storms or when static electricity was discharged nearby.

This rather odd discovery led Galvani to begin experimenting with the relationship between electrical activity and muscle movement. He eventually learned that he could control and initiate the twitching movements by touching one end of a frog leg with a metal rod, touching the other end with a rod of a different metal, and then touching the free ends of the two rods together. We now know Galvani had formed a rudimentary kind of wet battery with this procedure and was electrically stimulating the movement, but he didn't recognize this fact at the time. Galvani assumed that the leg was naturally generating "animal electricity," which he tried to capture by piling up frog legs in various ways. (You don't need frog legs to generate electricity, as Alessandro Volta showed several years later with the development of the first inorganic battery in 1800.)

Galvani's discovery eventually led to the development of practical batteries, but it also helped convince people that the behavior of living things might be governed by understandable forces of nature. Remember, two centuries ago the relationship between the physical body and behavior was by no means clearly established. It was still popular to attribute the initiation of behavior to spiritual forces. Galvani's work suggested that behavior might be studied and controlled in the laboratory, in the same way that forces of nature could be studied and controlled. For example, if

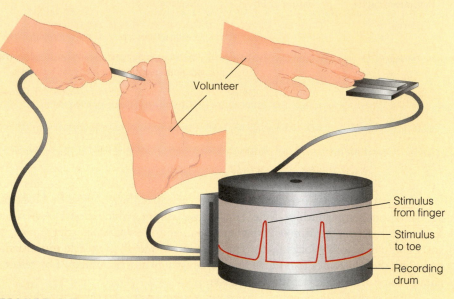

Volunteer

Stimulus from finger

Stimulus to toe

Recording drum

FIGURE 3.7

Measuring the Speed of Neural Transmission
Helmholtz trained volunteers to press a response button whenever they felt a touch. By comparing reaction times for touches on various parts of the body, Helmholtz was able to obtain a reasonably accurate measure of the speed of neural transmission.

the initiation of motor movements is governed by a physical force such as electricity, perhaps there might be a way to measure something like the speed of internal messages in the body. A preliminary solution to this problem was worked out in 1849 by Hermann von Helmholtz.

By this time, mental processes had become associated with brain activity. But the idea that the brain decides on an action and then carries it out by delivering a message to the muscles was still undeveloped. Then, as today, the initiation of movement seemed to be instantaneous with the willful decision. Think about it: There is certainly no personal sense of a delay between deciding to lift your hand and then lifting it. But Helmholtz showed, through a clever experiment, that the initiation of a movement does indeed occur in real time—the farther a message has to travel in the body, the longer it takes to initiate the movement.

Helmholtz's experiment was straightforward. He trained a volunteer to press a key whenever he felt a touch to his body (see Figure 3.7). The subject's reaction time to press the key was the measure of interest and formed the dependent variable in

the experiment. The experimental manipulation, or independent variable, was where on the body the touch occurred. Helmholtz began the experiment by touching the subject on the toe and measuring the reaction time to press the key; next, he moved the point of contact higher up, near the thigh, and again measured the subject's speed in pressing the key. He found that it took the subject less time to press the key when touched on the thigh than when touched on the toe. To calculate the speed of the neural message, Helmholtz simply divided the distance between the two points of stimulation by the difference in reaction times, and he arrived at a remarkably accurate measure of the speed of neural transmission. More important, his estimate of neural speed, which he deduced was between 100 and 200 miles per hour, proved that the initiation of movement is not instantaneous in the body but rather is relatively slow. The fact that messages travel at a rate well below the speed of electricity confounded researchers of the time but provided a further indication that willful actions are importantly limited by the characteristics of the physical body.

has evolved systems for releasing endorphins under conditions of stress or exertion to reduce pain and possibly to provide pleasurable reinforcement (Hoffmann, 1997; Schedlowski et al., 1995). We'll return to the study of drugs, particularly their effects on conscious awareness, in Chapter 6.

THE COMMUNICATION NETWORK

Up to this point, we've tapped briefly into the electrochemical language of the nervous system. You've seen how information is transmitted electrically within a neuron, through the flow of charged ions, and how one neuron signals another through the release of chemical messengers. But understanding the dynamics of neuron-to-neuron communication is only part of the story.

Most brain researchers agree that if we are ever to unravel the complex relationship between the brain and mind, we must understand how neurons work together. A vast communication network permeates the brain, involving the operation of thousands of neurons, and the manner in which these cells interact is of critical importance. Behaviors, thoughts, feelings, ideas—they don't arise from the activation of single neurons; instead, it is the *pattern of activation* produced by groups of neurons operating at the same time that underlies both conscious experiences and complex behaviors. It is therefore necessary to pay attention to the specific ways in which neurons are connected and the means through which those connections can be modified by experience (Kandel, 1991).

Information is also communicated in the nervous system through the rate at which neurons generate action potentials. The *firing rate* of a neuron is defined by the number of action potentials it generates per unit of time. The firing rate is subject to some natural limitations. For instance, a **refractory period** follows the generation of an action potential, during which more action potentials cannot be generated. But neurons are still able to fire off a relatively steady stream of messages in response to environmental stimulation. Many neurons even appear to have spontaneous firing rates, which means that they generate a steady stream of action potentials even with little or no apparent input from the environment.

A continuously active cell is adaptive for the nervous system because information can be communicated by either increasing or decreasing the spontaneous firing rates of its neurons. The color red, for example, might be experienced when particular cells in the brain increase their pattern and frequency of firing, whereas green may be linked to a decrease in the generation of action potentials (see Figure 3.8 on page 84). In this way, more information is effectively coded into the system. (You'll learn more about how color is processed in the visual system in Chapter 5.) Changes in firing rate, along with the global patterns of activation among large groups of cells, are ultimately responsible for most complex psychological phenomena.

Neural Networks

Because the brain contains roughly 100 billion neurons, it's quite impractical to try to map out individual neural connections. So how can we ever hope to discover how everything works together to produce behavior? One solution is to study neural patterns in lower organisms, whose circuits of neurons are less complex and more easily mapped. Another option is to try to simulate activities of the mind—such as simple learning and memory processes—by creating *artificial* networks of neurons on computers.

Computerized **neural networks** have been created in a variety of shapes and sizes (Caudill & Butler, 1990), but all share some fundamental properties. For example, all neural networks are built from individual processing *units*, roughly representing model neurons, that become active when information is received. Rules exist for determining how unit activations originate and change with time; an excellent summary of these rules can be found in the writings of David

refractory period
The period of time following an action potential during which more action potentials cannot be generated.

neural networks
A term used to describe computer simulation models of neural communication networks in the brain.

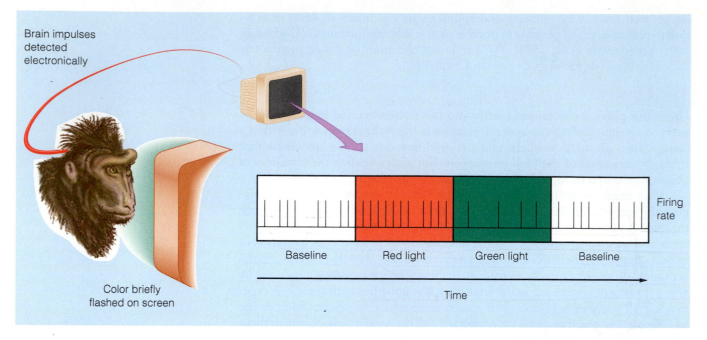

FIGURE 3.8

Changes in Firing Rates
Information is partly communicated through changes in the firing rates of neurons. Here, neurons in the monkey's brain increase their firing rate, relative to baseline, when a red stimulus appears, and decrease their firing rate, relative to baseline, when a green stimulus appears.

Rumelhart and Jay McClelland (1986), two leaders in the development of artificial networks. You can think about the activation of a unit in a neural network as comparable to the firing rate of an action potential in a real neuron.

As in the human nervous system, the individual processing units in artificial neural networks do not act alone. Meaningful concepts are usually represented by the activity in groups of units rather than by the activity of a single unit. A mental representation, such as the image of a friend named Paul, is *distributed* as a pattern of activity across several processing units in a group. For example, the blue circles on the right in Figure 3.9a might represent the letters P, A, U, and L, which collectively form the name PAUL; the red circles on the left might stand for some of the components of Paul's image—such as his wire glasses, his red hair, his mustache, and his round nose. Notice that each unit plays a specific role within a general pattern that represents your friend and his name. Your concept of Paul is represented by the activity pattern across the units as a whole, not by the activity of any single unit.

Units in a neural network are *connected*, such that the activation of one unit will affect the activation of other units. The particular pattern of connections among units is important because it determines how the network as a whole will operate. In the real nervous system, the network of neuron-to-neuron connections is also critical because it determines which brain regions are activated by information received from the environment. In Figure 3.9a, each of the input units (red) on the left is connected to each of the output units (blue) on the right. This means that activation of the first unit on the left will affect the activation of *all* of the units on the right.

At this point, no one has come close to achieving anything resembling an artificial brain, but simple computerized networks have been developed that show brainlike properties. For example, neural networks can recognize objects when given incomplete information and can perform reasonably well if artificially damaged. If a subset of input units is turned off, perhaps mimicking damage to the brain, activation of the remaining units should still be sufficient to reproduce the correct output response. This is an adaptive characteristic of both neural circuits in the brain and neural networks. Each is able to sustain damage, or lesion, and still produce the correct responses.

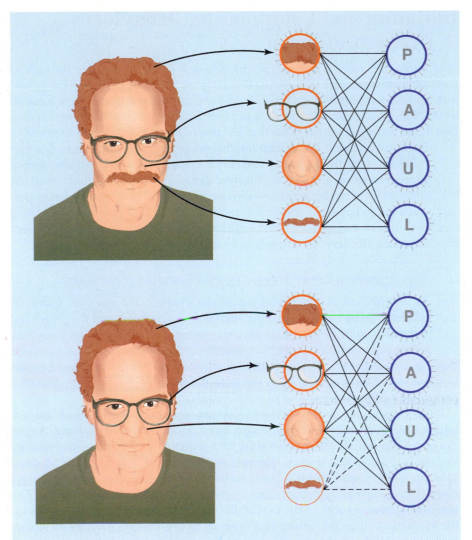

FIGURE 3.9
A Simple Neural Network
Neural networks are built by connecting simple processing units. In our example, the various features of Paul's face are connected with processing units corresponding to the letters of his name. Notice that each of the facial units is connected with all of the letters in his name. This means that if Paul shaves off his mustache (b), you will still be able to recall his name through activation of the remaining features.

TEST YOURSELF 3.1

Test your knowledge about neurons and how they communicate. Select your answers from the following list of terms: dendrites, soma, axon, terminal buttons, action potential, neurotransmitters, refractory period. (You will find the answers in the Appendix.)

1. The main body of the cell, where excitatory and inhibitory messages combine:

   _____

2. The long tail-like part of a neuron that serves as the cell's main transmitter device:

   _____

3. The all-or-none electrical signal that travels to the end of the axon, causing the release of chemical messengers: _____

4. The branchlike fibers that extend outward from a neuron and receive information from other neurons: _____

5. Acetylcholine, serotonin, GABA, and dopamine are all examples of

   _____

Initiating and Coordinating Behavior: A Division of Labor

As a whole, the nervous system has a lot of tough problems to solve through its communication network of neurons. Besides generating the right physical behaviors, and mental processes such as thinking and feeling, the brain keeps constant track of more mundane things, such as maintaining a beating heart, controlling breathing, and signaling the body that it's time to eat. If your body is deprived of food or water, or if its constant internal temperature is compromised, something must motivate you to seek food, water, or the appropriate shelter. Moreover, although you may not have thought about it too much, even the simplest of everyday activities—producing spoken language, walking, perceiving a complex visual scene—require a great deal of coordination among the muscles and sensory organs of the body. To accomplish such different functions, the nervous system divides its labor.

THE CENTRAL AND PERIPHERAL NERVOUS SYSTEMS

As I explained at the beginning of the chapter, the nervous system is divided into two major parts: the central nervous system and the peripheral nervous system. The central nervous system, consisting of the brain and spinal cord, acts as the central executive of the body. Decisions are made here, and messages are then communicated to the rest of the body via bundles of axons called **nerves**. The nerves outside the brain and spinal cord form the peripheral nervous system.

It is through the peripheral nervous system that muscles are actually moved, internal organs are regulated, and sensory input is moved toward the brain. As you can see in Figure 3.10, the peripheral nervous system is further subdivided into the somatic and autonomic systems. Information travels toward the brain and spinal cord through *afferent* (sensory) nerve pathways; *efferent* (motor) nerve pathways carry central nervous system messages outward to the muscles and glands. The **somatic system** consists of the nerves that transmit sensory information toward the brain, as well as the nerves that connect to the skeletal muscles to initiate movement. Without the somatic system, information about the environment could not reach the brain, nor could we begin a movement of any kind. The **autonomic system** controls the more automatic needs of the body, such as heart rate, digestion, blood pressure, and the activities of internal glands. These two systems work together to ensure that information about the world is communicated to the brain for interpretation, that movements are carried out, and that the life-sustaining activities of the body are continued.

One critical function of the autonomic system, besides performing the automatic "housekeeping" activities that keep the body alive, is to affect the body's ability to handle and recover from emergency situations. The *sympathetic division* of the autonomic system prepares the body for emergencies by triggering the release of chemicals that put it in a state of readiness (such as by increasing heart rate, blood pressure, and breathing rate). After the emergency has passed, the *parasympathetic division* calms the body down by slowing heart rate and lowering blood pressure. Parasympathetic activity also helps increase the body's supply of stored energy that may have been reduced as a result of dealing with an emergency situation.

RESEARCH TECHNIQUES FOR DETERMINING BRAIN FUNCTION

Before we embark on a detailed examination of the structure and function of the brain, it's useful to consider some techniques that researchers use to decide exactly what functions the different parts of the brain serve. The anatomical features of the nervous system as a whole—the various nerve tracts and so on—can be stud-

---

LEARNING GOALS

1. Describe the basic organization of the nervous system.
2. Explain the techniques that researchers use to study the brain.
3. Describe the major structures of the brain and the functions associated with each structure.
4. Describe how the two hemispheres divide and coordinate brain functions.

---

nerves
Bundles of axons that make up neural "transmission cables."

somatic system
The collection of nerves that transmits information toward the brain and connects to the skeletal muscles in order to initiate movement; part of the peripheral nervous system.

autonomic system
The collection of nerves that controls the more automatic needs of the body, such as heart rate, digestion, blood pressure, and so on; part of the peripheral nervous system.

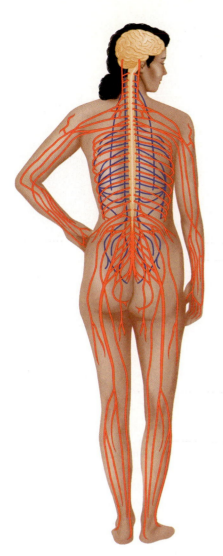

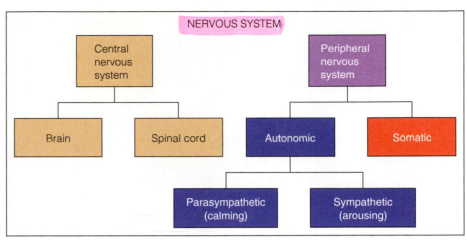

FIGURE 3.10
The Nervous System
The human nervous system includes the central nervous system, which contains the brain and the spinal cord, and the peripheral nervous system, which contains various subsystems. (Based on Kalat, 1996).

ied through dissection of the body. But the dissection of brain tissue, which contains billions of neurons, tells only a limited story. To determine the architecture of the brain, researchers need to rely on a broader set of tools. We'll briefly consider three general techniques: (1) the study of brain damage from injury or disease, (2) methods that allow the researcher to activate (or "talk" to) the brain directly, and (3) methods that allow researchers to "listen" to the brain in action.

Brain Damage and Lesion
The study of brain damage is one of the oldest available methods for determining brain function. A patient arrives with some specific, localized region of damage—such as a blow to the right side of the head—and complains of a particular problem, such as trouble moving the left side of his or her body. In this way, a basic link can be established between a brain area and a behavior or function. As early as the middle of the nineteenth century it was known that damage to isolated areas on the left side of the brain creates distinct patterns of speech difficulties. Destruction of *Wernicke's area* (named after its discoverer) results in a patient who cannot easily understand spoken language (Wernicke, 1874); damage to *Broca's area* results in a patient who can understand but not produce spoken language (Broca, 1861). Cases like these support the idea that different psychological and behavioral functions are controlled by specific areas of the brain.

Unfortunately, relying on case studies of brain injury has its limitations. For one thing, researchers must wait for the specific injury of interest to present itself

This patient, who may be suffering from a form of brain damage, is having his memory assessed at a memory disorders clinic.

for their inspection. To make matters worse, the patient usually must die before the full nature of the injury can be established, usually through an autopsy. In addition, most instances of brain damage, either from an accident or from a tumor or a stroke, produce very general and widespread damage. So it is difficult to know exactly which portion of the damaged brain is responsible for the behavioral or psychological problem. As we saw in Chapter 2, case studies can be rich sources of information, but the researcher typically lacks important controls.

To establish a true structure–function relationship, it is necessary to observe in a controlled way the effects of systematic and localized removal of tissue. Researchers have taken advantage of the fact that brain tissue contains no pain receptors to explore brain function in lower animals, particularly rats. It's possible to destroy, or *lesion*, particular regions of an animal's brain by administering an electric current, injecting chemicals, or cutting tissue. Even here it is difficult to pinpoint the damage exactly (because everything in the brain is interconnected), but lesioning techniques have become increasingly more accurate in recent years. There are chemicals, for example, that can selectively damage neurons in the brain without damaging neighboring nerve pathways (Bergvall et al., 1996; Jarrad, 1993). The lesioning procedure is then followed by controlled examination of the animal's behavior to see how it is affected. Animal research of this form has led to significant advances in our understanding of the brain although, as you learned in Chapter 2, some have questioned the ethics of such research.

Talking to the Brain

It is also possible to talk to the brain directly by capitalizing on the electrochemical nature of the communication network. Essentially, messages can be created where none would have normally occurred. Researchers can inject chemicals that serve to excite, rather than destroy, the neurons in a particular area of the brain. Alternatively, researchers can insert small wire electrodes into brain tissue, allowing an area's cells to be stimulated electrically. The researcher initiates a message externally, then observes any changes in behavior.

Electrical stimulation techniques have been used primarily with animals. It's possible to implant an electrode in such a way as to allow an animal to still move freely about in its environment (see Figure 3.11). A small pulse of current can then be delivered to various brain regions whenever the researcher desires. Studies have shown that electrical brain stimulation can cause animals to suddenly start eating,

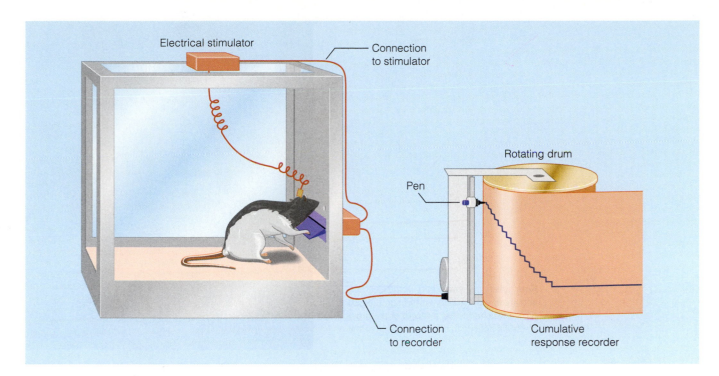

FIGURE 3.11
Electrical Stimulation
A rat presses a bar and a small pulse of electric current is delivered to the brain. Stimulation of certain brain areas appears quite rewarding to the rat, leading it to press the bar at a very rapid rate.

drinking, engaging in sexual behavior, or preparing for an attack. Using electrical stimulation, researchers have found that certain areas in the brain act as pleasure centers in rats, leading them to engage repeatedly in whatever behavior led to the stimulation (Olds, 1958; Leon & Gallistel, 1998). For example, if rats are taught that pressing a metal bar leads to electrical stimulation of a reward area, they will press the bar thousands of times an hour. (The natural inference, of course, is that the stimulation is pleasurable, although we really have no way to tell what a concept like "pleasure" means to a rat.)

The electrical stimulation technique is often used by researchers to link behavior to patterns of activity in specific areas in the brain. For example, a behavior that is produced by stimulation of brain region X but not by stimulation of brain region Y suggests that region X plays at least some role in the overall behavior. Still, the precise mapping of behaviors to brain locations remains a difficult task. It is always possible to argue, for example, that a stimulated area is required to produce a particular behavior but that it does not act alone—it might serve only as a communication link, or relay connection, to some other brain region that actually starts the behavior.

Under some circumstances, it has been possible to stimulate cells in the human brain and note the behavioral effects. During certain kinds of brain surgery (such as surgery to reduce the seizures produced by epilepsy), the patient is kept awake and the brain is stimulated from time to time with an electrode. Because there are no pain receptors in the brain, the patient typically receives only a local anesthetic prior to the surgery (along with some drugs for relaxation). Keeping the patient awake is necessary because the surgeon can stimulate an abnormal area, prior to removal, to make sure that vital capabilities such as speech or movement will not be affected. Electrical stimulation under these conditions has caused patients to produce involuntary movement, hear buzzing noises, and in some rare instances even experience what they report to be memories (Penfield & Perot, 1963).

Listening to the Brain

Brain lesioning and electrical stimulation are popular and effective research tools, but they are *invasive* in the sense that they require making contact with (or even

? CRITICAL THINKING

Does it bother you that researchers often try to generalize the results of studies of rats to humans? If so, does it also bother you that some of the basic principles of genetics were derived from the study of pea plants?

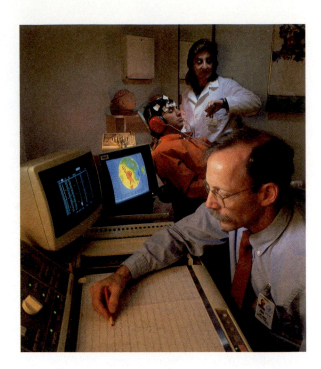

Researchers can eavesdrop on the electrical activity of a person's brain through the EEG device which provides a record of the gross electrical activity in different regions of the brain.

destroying) actual brain tissue. Fortunately, there are other techniques, which can be applied more readily to the study of humans, that essentially eavesdrop on the brain without any penetration of the skull. The **electroencephalograph (EEG)** is a device that simply monitors the gross electrical activity of the brain. Recording electrodes attached to the scalp measure global changes in the electrical potentials of thousands of brain cells in the form of line tracings, or brain waves. The EEG is useful not only as a research tool but also for diagnostic purposes (Barcelo & Gale, 1997). Brain disorders, including psychological disorders, can sometimes be detected through abnormalities in brain waves (John et al., 1988; Lee, E-K., 1998; Sponheim et al., 1994).

An actual picture of the brain's anatomical structures, including abnormalities in brain tissue, can be obtained through a **computerized tomography scan** (or **CT scan**). CT scanners use computers to detect how highly focused beams of X rays change as they pass through the body at various angles and orientations. CT scanners are most often used by physicians to detect tumors or injuries to the brain, but they can also be used to determine whether there is a physical basis for some chronic behavioral or psychological disorder.

Other imaging devices are designed to obtain a snapshot of the *active* brain at work. These techniques help the researcher determine how various tasks, such as reading a book, affect individual parts of the brain. In **positron emission tomography (PET),** the patient ingests a harmless radioactive substance, which is then absorbed into the cells of brain regions that are metabolically active. When the person is performing a specific kind of task, such as speaking or reading, the active areas of the brain absorb more of the ingested radioactive material. The PET scanner then develops a pictorial blueprint that reveals how the radioactive substance has distributed itself over time. It is assumed that those parts of the brain with the most concentrated traces of radioactive material probably play a significant role in the task that the subject is performing.

In recent applications of this technique, a kind of radioactive water is injected into the body that allows the PET scanning device to measure blood flow in the brain. Images of how blood flow changes when regions of the brain are active and inactive are considered to be reliable indicators of how activity in the brain changes from moment to moment (Raichle, 1994).

electroencephalograph (EEG)
A device used to monitor the gross electrical activity of the brain.

computerized tomography scan (CT scan)
The use of highly focused beams of X rays to construct detailed anatomical maps of the living brain.

positron emission tomography (PET)
A method for measuring how radioactive substances are absorbed in the brain; it can be used to detect how different tasks activate different areas of the living brain.

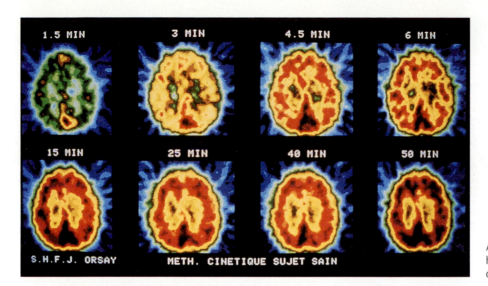

A series of eight PET scans demonstrate how a harmless radioactive substance is absorbed over time into the cells of active brain regions.

Another technique that can be used to isolate both structure and function in the brain is **magnetic resonance imaging (MRI).** MRI has two main advantages over PET scanning: It doesn't require the participant to ingest any chemicals, and it's capable of producing extremely detailed, three-dimensional images of the brain. MRI technology capitalizes on the fact that atoms behave in systematic ways in the presence of magnetic fields and radio-wave pulses. Although expensive to build and use, MRIs have proven to be excellent diagnostic tools for spotting brain damage, tumor growth, and other abnormalities.

More recent applications of what is called "functional MRI" use the MRI technology to map changes in blood oxygen use as a function of task activity. Functional MRI, like PET scanning, is currently being used to help isolate structure–function relationships in the brain (Binder et al., 1994; Engel et al., 1994). So far, this new technique has helped to isolate the brain regions associated with visual processing, language, attention, and even memory (Gabrieli, 1998; Schacter et al., 1998). There is some evidence to suggest that functional MRIs may help psychologists distinguish between true and false memories: When we remember something that did not in fact occur, the blood flow patterns in the brain are unique compared to the remembering of an actual event. Exactly what these

magnetic resonance imaging (MRI)
A device that uses magnetic fields and radio-wave pulses to construct detailed, three-dimensional images of the brain; "functional" MRIs can be used to map changes in blood oxygen use as a function of task activity.

(a) The magnetic resonance imaging device (MRI) is capable of isolating both structure and some function in the brain.
(b) MRIs produce extremely detailed images of the brain and are thereby excellent diagnostic tools for spotting damage, tumor growth, and other physical abnormalities.

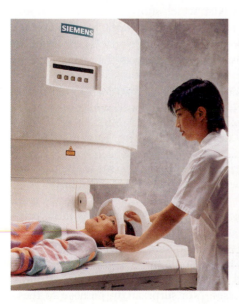

(a)

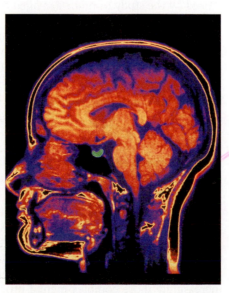

(b)

CONCEPT SUMMARY
Brain Investigation Techniques

Technique	Overview	What Can It Show?
Brain damage and lesion	Associate areas of brain damage with changes in behavioral function.	The areas of the brain that may be responsible for different functions.
Electrical brain stimulation	Use electrical or chemical stimulation to excite brain areas.	How activation of certain brain regions affects behavior.
EEG (Electro-encephalograph)	Use electrodes to record gross electrical activity of the brain.	How overall activity in the brain changes during certain activities, such as sleeping, and may allow for detection of disorders.
Computerized tomography (CT) scan	X rays are passed through the body at various angles and orientations.	Tumors or injuries to the brain, as well as the structural bases for chronic behavioral or psychological disorders.
Positron emission tomography (PET)	A radioactive substance is ingested; active brain areas absorb the substance; PET scanner reveals distribution of the substance.	How various tasks (like reading a book) affect different parts of the brain.
Magnetic resonance imaging (MRI)	Monitors systematic activity of atoms in the presence of magnetic fields and radio-wave impulses.	A three-dimensional view of the brain, serving as a diagnostic tool for brain abnormalities, such as tumors. Functional MRI allows for observation of brain function.

results mean is still a matter of heated debate, but everyone agrees that functional MRI is potentially a very useful tool.

BRAIN STRUCTURES AND THEIR FUNCTIONS

Having discussed some of the research tools that scientists use to map out brain structure and function, let's now turn our attention to the brain itself. Remember, it is within the brain that mental processes are presumed to be represented, through the simultaneous activities of billions of individual neurons. Particular regions in the brain are thought to contribute unique features to an experience, helping to create a psychological whole. Thus, your perception of a cat is not controlled by a single cell, or even by a single group of cells, but rather by different brain areas that detect the color of the fur, recognize a characteristic meow, or even generate the expectation that the cat will saunter into the room because you just put down the food dish. The contributions of specific brain regions are underscored by the study of brain-damaged patients, which shows that people can lose specific kinds of mental abilities. For instance, someone might lose knowledge about living things but not about inanimate things (Kandel, 1991), or a person might lose the ability to see moving objects but not objects that are stationary (Zeki, 1992).

I'll divide our discussion of the brain into sections that correspond to the brain's three major anatomical regions: the *hindbrain*, the *midbrain*, and the *forebrain*.

The Hindbrain: Basic Life Support

The **hindbrain**, which is the most primitive part of the brain, sits at the juncture point where the spinal cord and brain merge (see Figure 3.12). "Primitive" is an appropriate term for two reasons. First, structures in the hindbrain act as the basic life-support system for the body—no creative thoughts or complex emotions originate here. Second, from the standpoint of evolution, the hindbrain is the oldest part of the brain. Similar structures, with similar functions, can be found throughout the animal kingdom. You can think of the hindbrain as a kind of base camp, with higher structures that are situated farther up into the brain controlling increasingly more complex mental processes. Not surprisingly, damage to these lower regions of the brain seriously affects the ability of the organism to survive.

hindbrain
A primitive part of the brain that sits at the juncture point where the brain and spinal cord merge. Structures in the hindbrain, including the medulla, pons, and reticular formation, act as the basic life-support system for the body.

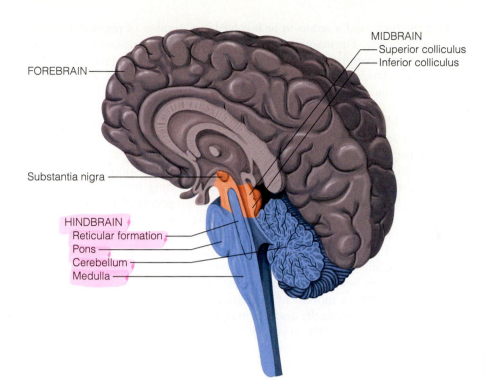

FOREBRAIN

MIDBRAIN
Superior colliculus
Inferior colliculus

Substantia nigra

HINDBRAIN
Reticular formation
Pons
Cerebellum
Medulla

FIGURE 3.12
The Hindbrain
Shown here are the various structures of the human hindbrain. The hindbrain acts as the basic life-support system for the body, controlling such things as heart rate, blood pressure, and respiration.

As you can see in Figure 3.12, the hindbrain contains several important anatomical substructures. The *medulla* and the *pons* are associated with the control of heart rate, breathing, blood pressure, and reflexes such as vomiting, sneezing, and coughing. Both areas serve as pathways for neural impulses traveling to and from the spinal cord (the word *pons* means "bridge"). These areas are particularly sensitive to the lethal effects of drugs such as alcohol, barbiturates, and cocaine.

The hindbrain also contains the *reticular formation*, a network of nerves linked to the control of general arousal, sleep, and possibly specific movements of the head (Robbins, 1997; Siegel, 1983). Damage to the reticular formation can lead to the loss of consciousness. Finally, at the base of the brain sits a structure that in general appearance resembles a smaller version of the brain. This is the **cerebellum** (which means "little brain"), a structure involved in the preparation, selection, and coordination of complex motor movements such as hitting a golf ball, playing the piano, or writing (Yamaguchi et al., 1998). No one is certain about the exact role the cerebellum plays in movement—it may help guide movement through the integration of sensory information—but it clearly serves a vital function. The cerebellum may be involved in other functions as well; for instance, brain imagining studies have shown that the cerebellum becomes active during language, memory, and reasoning tasks (Schmahmann & Sherman, 1998).

The Midbrain: Neural Relay Stations

The **midbrain**, which lies deep within the brain atop the hindbrain, is enveloped by other structures that make up the forebrain. Perhaps because of its central position, the midbrain and its accompanying structures receive input from multiple sources, including the sense organs. The *tectum* and its component structures, the *superior colliculus* and *inferior colliculus*, serve as important relay stations for visual and auditory information and help coordinate reactions to sensory events in the environment (such as moving the head in response to a sudden sound).

The midbrain also contains a group of neurons, collectively called the *substantia nigra*, which release the neurotransmitter dopamine from their terminal buttons. As you saw earlier in the chapter, dopamine tends to produce inhibitory

cerebellum
A hindbrain structure at the base of the brain that is involved in the coordination of complex motor skills.

midbrain
The middle portion of the brain, containing such structures as the tectum, superior colliculus, and inferior colliculus; midbrain structures serve as neural relay stations and may help coordinate reactions to sensory events.

effects in the body, and it seems to be involved in a number of physical and psychological disorders. For example, the rigidity of movement or continuous muscle twitches and tremors that characterize Parkinson's disease apparently result from decreased levels of dopamine in the brain. Indeed, the death of neurons in the substantia nigra is believed to be the cause of the disorder (Jenner, 1990; Keller & Rueda, 1998). Exactly why this portion of the midbrain degenerates is not known, although environmental toxins may be contributors (Kuhn et al., 1998; Snyder & D'Amato, 1986).

A number of important developments in the understanding and treatment of Parkinson-like disorders have resulted from investigating the substantia nigra. Do you remember the frozen users described in the opening to the chapter? The faulty part of the drug recipe produced a chemical component, called MPTP, that destroyed the substantia nigra. The loss of these dopamine-producing cells is assumed to be responsible for the users' loss of movement. Ironically, this tragic accident proved to be of great value to researchers of Parkinson's disease. By studying these individuals, along with the component MPTP, researchers were able to confirm the link between the production of dopamine in the substantia nigra and the rigidity of movement that characterizes Parkinson's disease. It has even been possible to mimic the disorder in animals through the administration of MPTP (Schneider et al., 1994; Snyder & D'Amato, 1986).

More recently, some of the frozen users have participated in a controversial transplant procedure involving brain tissue from aborted fetuses. There is some evidence that injecting portions of the substantia nigra from such fetuses into damaged adult brains can reverse Parkinson-like symptoms, although the results are by no means clearcut (see Lindvall et al., 1989). This research does, of course, raise some serious ethical questions. Many people object to fetal tissue research of any kind. Proponents of transplant studies counter that this research is quite likely to lead to breakthroughs in the restoration of damaged or lost brain function in suffering human beings.

The Forebrain: Higher Mental Functioning

Moving up past the midbrain we encounter the **forebrain** (see Figure 3.13). The most recognizable feature of the forebrain is the **cerebral cortex,** the grayish matter full of fissures, folds, and crevices that covers the outside of the brain (*cortex* is the Latin word for "bark"). The cortex is quite large in humans; it accounts for approximately 80% of the total volume of the human brain (Kolb & Whishaw, 1990). We'll look at the cerebral cortex in depth after a review of the other structures of the forebrain.

Beneath the cerebral cortex are subcortical structures, including the thalamus, the hypothalamus, and the limbic system. The **thalamus** is positioned close to the midbrain and it's an important gathering point for input from the various senses. Indeed, the thalamus is thought to be the main processing center for sensory input before that information is sent out to areas in the upper regions of the cortex. Besides acting as an efficient relay center, information from the various senses is probably combined in some way here.

The **hypothalamus,** which lies just below the thalamus, is important in the regulation of eating, drinking, body temperature, and sexual behavior. In experiments on lower animals, administering electric current to different regions of the hypothalamus initiates a variety of behaviors. For example, male and female rats will show characteristic sexual responses when one portion of the hypothalamus is stimulated (Marson & McKenna, 1994; Pfaff & Sakuma, 1979), whereas damage to another region of the hypothalamus can seriously affect regular eating behavior (Sclafani, 1994). (I will have more to say about the neural basis of hunger in Chapter 11.) The hypothalamus also plays a key role in the release of hormones by the pituitary gland; you'll read about the actions of hormones when we discuss the endocrine system.

forebrain
The outer portion of the brain, including the cerebral cortex and the structures of the limbic system.

cerebral cortex
The outer layer of the brain, considered to be the seat of higher mental processes.

thalamus
A relay station in the forebrain thought to be an important gathering point for input from the senses.

hypothalamus
A forebrain structure thought to play a role in the regulation of various motivational activities, including eating, drinking, and sexual behavior.

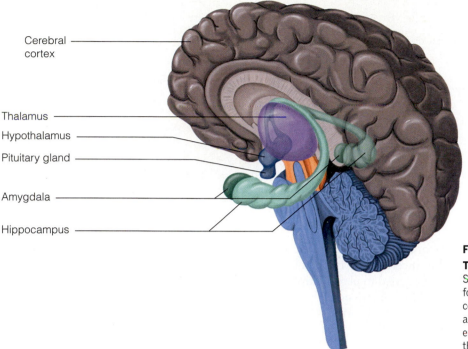

Cerebral cortex

Thalamus

Hypothalamus

Pituitary gland

Amygdala

Hippocampus

FIGURE 3.13
The Forebrain
Shown here are the various structures of the forebrain, including the limbic system and the cerebral cortex. Structures in the limbic system are thought to be involved in motivation, emotions, and memory. The cerebral cortex is the seat of higher mental processes.

The **limbic system** is composed of several interrelated brain structures, including the amygdala and the hippocampus. The *amygdala* is a small, almond-shaped piece of brain (*amygdala* means "almond") that has been linked to a variety of motivational and emotional behaviors, including fear, aggression, and defensive behaviors (Davis & Lee, 1998; Aggleton, 1993). Destruction of portions of the amygdala in lower animals, through brain lesioning, can produce an extremely passive animal—one that will do nothing in response to provocation. The *hippocampus* (Greek for "seahorse," which it resembles anatomically) is thought to be important to the formation of memories (Eichenbaum et al., 1994). People with severe damage to the hippocampus sometimes live in a kind of perpetual present—they are aware of the world around them, and they recognize people and things known to them prior to the damage, but they remember almost nothing new. These patients act as if they are continually awakening from a dream; experiences slip away, and they recall nothing from only moments before. (I'll return to disturbances of this type, and memory loss in general, in Chapter 8.)

The Cerebral Cortex

On reaching the cerebral cortex, we finally encounter what is considered to be the seat of the higher mental processes. Thoughts, the sense of self, the ability to reason and solve problems—each arises as a result of neurons firing in patterns somewhere in specialized regions of the cerebral cortex. The cortex is divided into two *hemispheres*, left and right. The left hemisphere controls the sensory and motor functions for the right side of the body, and the right hemisphere controls these functions for the left side of the body. A structure called the *corpus callosum*, which I'll discuss later, serves as a communication bridge between the two hemispheres.

Each hemisphere can be further divided into four parts, or *lobes:* the *frontal, temporal, parietal,* and *occipital* (see Figure 3.14). These lobes (or at least parts of them) appear to control particular body functions, such as visual processing by the occipital lobe and language processing by the frontal and temporal lobes. A slight warning is in order here, however: Although researchers have discovered that

? CRITICAL THINKING

Do you think it's possible that personality is completely localized in one portion of the brain? If so, how could you explain the fact that someone's personality can seem to change depending on the situation?

limbic system
A system of structures thought to be involved in motivational and emotional behaviors (the amygdala) and memory (the hippocampus).

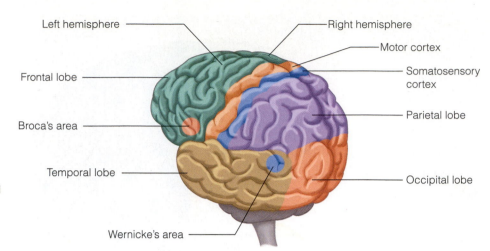

FIGURE 3.14

The Cerebral Cortex
The cerebral cortex is divided into two hemispheres—left and right—and each hemisphere can be divided further into four parts, or lobes. The lobes appear specialized to control particular functions, such as visual processing in the occipital lobe and language processing by the frontal and temporal lobes.

particular areas in the brain seem to control highly specialized functions, there is almost certainly considerable overlap of function in the brain. Most brain regions are designed to play multiple roles in helping us think or act.

How can we possibly assign something like a "sense of self" to a specific area of the cerebral cortex? Once again, the evidence is primarily correlational—some portion of the cortex is damaged, or stimulated electrically, and behavioral changes are observed. We know, for example, that damage to the frontal lobe of the cortex can produce dramatic changes in an individual's personality. In 1850 a railroad foreman named Phineas Gage was packing black powder into a blasting hole when, accidentally, the powder discharged, driving a thick iron rod through the left side of his head (entering just below his left eye and exiting the left-top portion of his skull). The result was a three-inch hole in his skull and a complete shredding of a large portion of the left frontal lobe of his brain. Remarkably, Gage recovered, and with the exception of the loss of vision in his left eye and some slight facial paralysis, he was able to move about freely and perform a variety of tasks. But he was "no longer Gage" in the minds of his friends and acquaintances—his personality had completely changed. Whereas prior to his injury he was known to all as someone with "a well-balanced mind" and as "a shrewd businessman," after the meeting of brain and iron rod he became "fitful, irreverent, indulging at times in the grossest profanity (which was not previously his custom)" (Bigelow, 1850).

CONCEPT SUMMARY
Brain Areas, Structures, and Functions

Brain Area	General Function	Structures and Specific Function
Hindbrain	Basic life support	**medulla** and **pons**: associated with the control of heart rate, breathing, and certain reflexes **reticular formation**: control of general arousal, sleep, and some movement of the head **cerebellum**: involved in preparation, selection, and coordination of complex motor movement
Midbrain	Houses neural relay stations	**tectum** (components are **superior colliculus** and **inferior colliculus**): relay stations for visual and auditory information **substantia nigra**: group of neurons that release the neurotransmitter dopamine
Forebrain	Higher mental functions	**thalamus**: initial gathering point for sensory input; information combined and relayed here **hypothalamus**: helps regulate eating, drinking, body temperature, and sexual behavior **amygdala** (part of **limbic system**): linked to fear, aggression, and defensive behaviors **hippocampus** (part of **limbic system**): important to the formation of memories **cerebral cortex**: the seat of higher mental processes, including sense of self, and the ability to reason and solve problems.

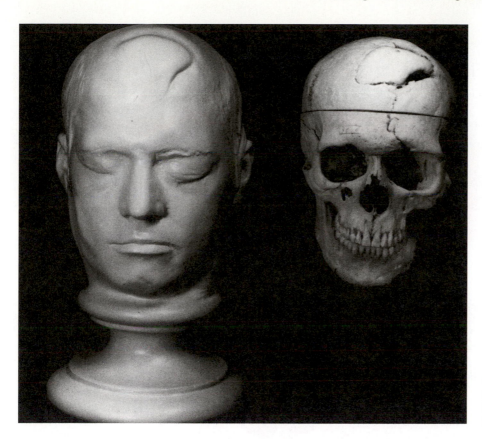

After a blasting accident substantially damaged the frontal lobe of Phineas Gage's brain, he was "no longer Gage" in the opinion of his friends and acquaintances.

The **frontal lobes** are the largest lobes in the cortex and are thought to be involved in a variety of functions including planning and decision making, certain kinds of memory (particularly developing strategies for remembering), and personality (as our discussion of Phineas Gage indicated). The frontal lobes were once the site of a famous surgical operation, the prefrontal lobotomy, which was performed on people suffering from severe and untreatable psychological disorders. The operation was performed to calm the patient and reduce symptoms, which it sometimes did, but the side effects were often severe. Patients lost their ability to take initiative, or make plans, and they often appeared to lose their social inhibitions (like Gage). For these reasons, the operation fell out of favor as an acceptable treatment for psychological disorders.

The frontal lobes also contain the *motor cortex*, which controls the initiation of voluntary muscle movements, as well as areas involved in language production and, possibly, higher-level thought processes (Baldo & Shimamura, 1998; Butler et al., 1993). Broca's area, which is involved in speech production, is located in a portion of the left frontal lobe in most people. The motor cortex sits at the rear of the frontal lobe in both hemispheres; axons from the motor cortex project down to motor neurons in the spinal cord and elsewhere. If neurons in this area of the brain are stimulated electrically, muscle contractions—the twitch of a finger or the jerking of a foot—can occur. Even more interesting, researchers have discovered an intriguing relation between body parts and regions of the motor cortex. It turns out that there is a mapping, or *topographic* organization, in which adjacent areas of the body, such as the hand and the wrist, are activated by neurons that sit next to each other in the motor cortex.

This kind of organization is actually found in many regions of the cerebral cortex. For example, the **parietal lobe** contains the topographically organized *somatosensory cortex*, through which people experience the sensations of touch, temperature, and pain. Thus, the brush of a lover's kiss on the cheek excites

frontal lobe
One of four anatomical regions of each hemisphere of the cerebral cortex, located on the top front of the brain; it contains the motor cortex and may be involved in higher-level thought processes.

parietal lobe
One of four anatomical regions of each hemisphere of the cerebral cortex, located roughly on the top middle portion of the brain; it contains the somatosensory cortex, which controls the sense of touch.

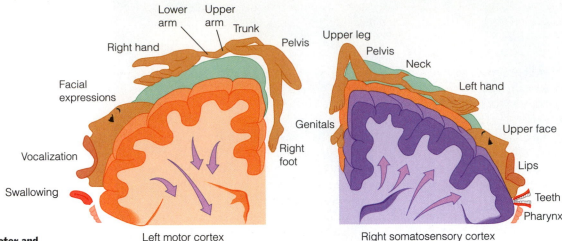

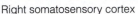

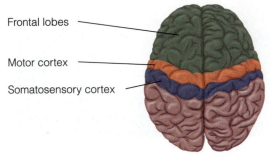

FIGURE 3.15

Specialization in the Motor and Somatosensory Cortex

The motor cortex is located at the rear of the frontal lobes in each cerebral hemisphere. In a systematic body-to-brain relationship, adjacent parts of the body are activated by neurons in adjacent areas of the cortex. The somatosensory cortex, which controls the sense of touch, is located in the parietal lobes of each hemisphere; again, there is a systematic mapping arrangement. Notice that for each type of cortex, the size or amount of the representation relates to degree of sensitivity.

neurons that lie close to neurons that would be excited by the same kiss to the lips. In addition, as Figure 3.15 demonstrates, there is a relationship between sensitivity to touch (or the ability to control a movement) and size of the representation in the cortex. Those areas of the body that show particular sensitivity to touch or are associated with fine motor control (such as the face, lips, and fingers) have relatively large areas of neural representation in the cortex.

The **temporal lobes,** which lie on either side of the cortex, are involved in processing auditory information received from the left and right ears. As you'll see in Chapter 5, there is a close relationship between the activities of particular neurons in the temporal lobe and the perception of certain frequencies of sound. As noted earlier, one region of the temporal lobe, Wernicke's area, appears to control language comprehension (the ability to understand what someone is saying). A person with damage to Wernicke's area might be able to repeat a spoken sentence aloud with perfect diction and control yet not understand a word of it; brain imaging studies also reveal that Wernicke's area becomes active when people are asked to perform tasks that require meaningful verbal processing (Abdullaev & Posner, 1997). For most people, the speech area is localized in the temporal lobe of the *left* cerebral hemisphere.

Finally, at the far back of the brain sit the **occipital lobes,** where most visual processing occurs. I'll consider the organization of this part of the brain in more detail in Chapter 5; for now, recognize that it is here, in the far back of the brain, that the information received from receptor cells in the eyes is analyzed and turned into visual images. The brain paints an image of the external world through a remarkable division of labor—there appear to be separate processing stations in the occipital lobe designed to process color, motion, and form independently (Shapley, 1990). Not surprisingly, damage to the occipital lobe tends to produce

temporal lobe
One of four anatomical regions of each hemisphere of the cerebral cortex, located roughly on the sides of the brain; it's involved in certain aspects of speech and language perception.

occipital lobe
One of four anatomical regions of each hemisphere of the cerebral cortex, located at the back of the brain; visual processing is controlled here.

highly specific visual deficits—the person might lose the ability to recognize a face, a contour moving in a particular direction, or a color (Zeki, 1992).

THE DIVIDED BRAIN

Nowhere is the division of labor in the brain more evident than in the study of the two separate halves, or hemispheres, that make up the cerebral cortex. Although the brain is designed to operate as a functional whole, the hemispheres are *lateralized*, which means that each side is responsible for performing some unique and independent functions (Hellige, 1990). As you've seen, the right hemisphere of the brain controls the movements of the left side of the body, whereas the left hemisphere handles the body's right side. This means that stimulating a region of the motor cortex in the left cerebral hemisphere would cause a muscle on the right side of the body to twitch. Similarly, if cells in the occipital lobe of the right cerebral hemisphere are damaged or destroyed, a blind spot develops in the left portion of the visual world. Lateralization undoubtedly serves some adaptive functions. For example, it may allow the brain to divide its labor in ways that produce more efficient processing.

Figure 3.16 shows how information received through the eyes travels to one side of the brain or the other. If you are looking straight ahead, an image originating from the left side of your body (the left visual field) falls on the inside half of the left eye and the outside half of the right eye; receptor cells in these locations transmit their images to the back of the *right* cerebral hemisphere. Both eyes project information directly to each hemisphere, as the figure shows, but information from the left visual field goes to the right hemisphere and vice versa. By capitalizing on the nature of these neural pathways, as you'll see in a moment, researchers can present information initially to one side of the brain or the other.

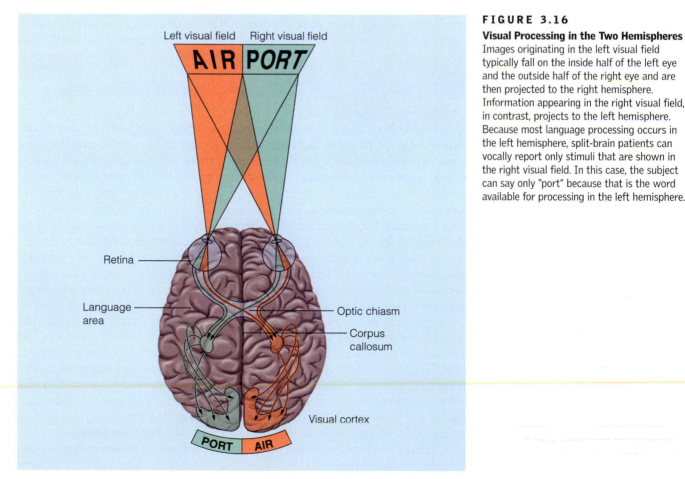

FIGURE 3.16

Visual Processing in the Two Hemispheres
Images originating in the left visual field typically fall on the inside half of the left eye and the outside half of the right eye and are then projected to the right hemisphere. Information appearing in the right visual field, in contrast, projects to the left hemisphere. Because most language processing occurs in the left hemisphere, split-brain patients can vocally report only stimuli that are shown in the right visual field. In this case, the subject can say only "port" because that is the word available for processing in the left hemisphere.

It's adaptive for both sides of the brain to process information from the environment; otherwise, this person would probably have difficulty developing a coordinated response to this rapidly arriving ball.

Under normal circumstances, if an object, such as a car, approaches you from your left side, the information eventually arrives on both sides of your brain. There are two reasons why this is the case. First, if you turn your head or eyes to look at the object—from left to right—its image is likely to fall on both the inside and the outside halves of each eye over time. It might start off represented only on the inside half of the left eye, but as your eyes turn, the outside half will soon receive the message. Second, as we noted earlier, a major communication bridge— the **corpus callosum**—connects the two brain halves. Information arriving at the right hemisphere, for example, is transported to the left hemisphere via the corpus callosum in just a few thousandths of a second (Saron & Davidson, 1989). This transfer process occurs automatically and requires no head or eye turning.

Splitting the Brain

If you think about it, you'll realize that it's important for both sides of the brain to receive information about objects in the environment. To see why, imagine what visual perception would be like for someone without a corpus callosum—someone with a "split brain." Suppose an object appears suddenly, with great velocity, in the person's left visual field. There's no time to move the head or eyes, only time for a kind of reflexive response. Our patient would be incapable of a coordinated response since the image would be registered only in the right hemisphere. Because the right side of the brain contains the machinery to control only the left side of the body, a fully coordinated body response could not be initiated. Moreover, the split-brain patient would be unable to name the menacing object, because the language comprehension and production centers are located, typically, on the left side of the brain.

Let's consider another experiment for our hypothetical patient. Suppose that we flash the word AIRPORT on a screen, very quickly, but arrange it so that the first part of the word, AIR, appears in the left visual field and the second part, PORT, appears in the right visual field. What do you think the patient will report seeing? The answer is the word PORT, because that's the image received by the left hemisphere—the place where the language centers are located. The language part of the brain wouldn't even know that AIR had been presented, because the image would remain locked in the visual centers of the right hemisphere.

Actually, our hypothetical patient, as well as a version of the study that was just described, is *real* (Gazzaniga, 1970). There are a number of individuals who have

corpus callosum
The collection of nerve fibers that connects the two cerebral hemispheres and allows information to pass from one side to the other.

split brains. Some were born without a corpus callosum (Sanders, 1989); others had their communication gateway severed on purpose by surgeons seeking to reduce the spread of epileptic seizures (Springer & Deutsch, 1989). Epilepsy is a kind of electrical fire storm in the brain that spreads across the cortex, producing convulsions and loss of consciousness. Cutting the communication gateway from one hemisphere to another creates a kind of fire break that limits epileptic seizures to one half of the brain. Cutting the corpus callosum is a rarely used procedure because modern antiepileptic drugs are able to control seizures for most patients. However, it has proven effective in some instances for patients who fail to respond to medication.

The two hemispheres of split-brain patients are not broken or damaged by the operation; information simply cannot easily pass from one side of the brain to the other. In fact, the behavior of split-brain patients appears to be remarkably normal. It's extremely unlikely that you would be able to identify one of them in a crowd. Their behavior appears normal because most input from the environment still reaches both sides of their brain. These patients can turn their heads and eyes freely as they interact with the environment, allowing information to fall on receptor regions that transmit to both hemispheres. The abnormal nature of their brain becomes apparent only under manufactured conditions like those encountered by our hypothetical patient and through the personal anecdotes that these patients sometimes report.

Much of the work on split-brain individuals was conducted by the late Nobel Prize-winning neuroscientist Roger Sperry and his colleagues. In one classic study by Gazzaniga, Bogen, and Sperry (1965), a variety of images (pictures, words, or symbols) were presented visually to either the left or right visual fields of split-brain subjects. As with our hypothetical patient, when an image was shown to the right visual field, it was easily named because it could be processed by the language centers of the left hemisphere. For left visual field presentations, the patients remained perplexed and silent. It was later learned, however, that their silence did not mean that the brain failed to process the image. If split-brain patients were asked to *point* to a picture of the object just shown, they could do so, but only with the *left* hand (e.g., Gazzaniga & LeDoux, 1978). The brain had received the input but could not respond verbally.

Although split-brain patients behave relatively normally after surgery, they do report that sometimes their right and left hands act as if they have minds of their own. These reports are anecdotal, of course, and need to be viewed with some caution. Patients have claimed that it is difficult to read something, such as a newspaper or a book, unless it is held by the right hand; the left hand, which maps to the nonverbal right hemisphere, apparently has no interest in reading as a leisure activity (Preilowski, 1975). It has been claimed that the two hemispheres occasionally compete, sometimes over bizarre things like what clothes to wear. One patient reported buttoning a blouse with one hand while, at the same time, unbuttoning the blouse with the other. Again, it's difficult to know what to make of these claims, or to know how accurately they have been reported, but it does seem likely that independent processing activities can go on simultaneously in the two hemispheres of the brain. Some researchers have even suggested that each side may have its own kind of separate consciousness (Kandel, 1991; Victor, 1996).

Hemispheric Specialization

The available evidence strongly indicates that the two hemispheres of the cerebral cortex are specialized to perform certain kinds of tasks. The right hemisphere, for example, appears to play a more important role in spatial tasks, such as fitting together the pieces of a puzzle or orienting oneself spatially in an environment. Patients with damage to the right hemisphere characteristically have trouble with spatial tasks, as do split-brain patients who must assemble a puzzle with their right hand (Kalat, 1992). The right hemisphere may also be involved in some important aspects of emotional processing (Spence et al., 1996). The left

? CRITICAL THINKING

Besides as a treatment for epilepsy, can you think of any situations in which having a split brain might actually be beneficial compared to having a unified brain?

Inside the Problem   Studying Lateralization in Intact Brains

The study of split-brain patients has produced a number of compelling findings supporting lateralization in the brain. But we don't need a split-brain patient to study hemispheric specialization. Techniques are available that work well with normal individuals and that don't require multimillion-dollar imaging equipment. All we need is a willing subject and some carefully calibrated equipment to record the time it takes to perform certain kinds of tasks. Let's work through the experimental logic that underlies one such procedure: the *concurrent activities paradigm.*

In the concurrent activities paradigm, volunteers are asked to perform two tasks at the same time; and their performance on each task is timed. As you know from personal experience, it's often difficult to do two things at once—it usually takes longer to perform each task and your accuracy decreases. Performance is slow and less accurate under these conditions because the brain has limited resources. When two tasks need to be performed, processing in the brain is divided, or shared, across two activities. The concurrent activities paradigm also assumes that if two tasks draw on resources from the *same* side of the brain, performance will be slower than if the tasks are controlled by different sides of the brain (or the tasks are controlled equally by both sides of the brain). Thus, by varying the types of tasks and measuring

how much one task slows down performance on the other, researchers can infer how activities are specialized in a particular hemisphere.

To see how this process works in practice, imagine that we ask a subject to tap a telegraph key, as quickly as possible, with either the right or left index finger. Because of the way the brain is wired, we know that tapping the right index finger should be controlled primarily by the left side of the brain, whereas left-hand tapping should be controlled by the right side. We now ask the subject to perform a second task, such as reading words aloud from a screen, at the same time as the rapid-fire finger tapping. If the new task slows down the tapping more for the right hand than for the left hand, we can assume that the new task is controlled primarily by the left hemisphere. The idea once again is that if one hemisphere controls both tasks at the same time, the tapping will slow down more (see Figure 3.17).

In fact, the concurrent activities procedure has produced results that are consistent with the findings gathered from the study of brain-damaged patients and from the results of imaging techniques like the PET scan. Corina, Vaid, and Bellugi (1992) found that repeating English words aloud slowed the rate of finger tapping more for the right hand than for the left hand, but copying symbolic gestures (such as the "thumbs up" signal) showed no differential

effect. This is exactly the result we would predict if speech and language processing are located primarily in the left hemisphere. Tapping with the right hand and repeating English words aloud both draw on resources from the same (left) hemisphere, so performance on both tasks is slowed. However, copying symbolic gestures does not require the use of specialized language centers and may not be lateralized, so performance is not differentially affected.

But be warned: We should not accept results like these uncritically. To draw conclusions about hemispheric specialization from such results requires blind acceptance of a number of assumptions that have not been tested directly. For example, in the Corina and colleagues (1992) study no measure of brain activation was reported, so we have no way of telling whether the resources of the brain were actually being taxed by these two tasks or whether, in fact, the two tasks were really competing for the limited resources. What makes findings like these compelling is that they fit well into an overall pattern of results. When the results of the Corina study are interpreted in light of what we know from the study of split-brain patients and from imaging studies like the PET procedure, a strong case can be made for lateralized language centers. In short, making a convincing case in psychological research often requires a multipronged attack.

hemisphere—perhaps in part because of the lateralized language centers—clearly contributes more to verbal tasks such as reading and writing.

Still, you should understand that a great deal of cooperation and collaboration goes on between the hemispheres. They interact continuously, and most mental processes, even language to a certain extent, depend on activity that arises in both sides of the brain. You think and behave with a whole brain, not a fragmented one. Moreover, if one side of the brain is damaged, regions in the other hemisphere can sometimes take over the lost functions (Gazzaniga et al., 1996). Specialization in the brain exists because it is sometimes adaptive for the two hemispheres to work independently—much in the same way that it is beneficial for members of a group to divide components of a difficult task, rather than trying to cooperate on every small activity (Hellige, 1993).

Over the last two decades or so, there has been an explosion of interest—often by people operating at the fringe of scientific psychology—in assigning a variety of psychological phenomena to the different sides of the brain. It has been sug-

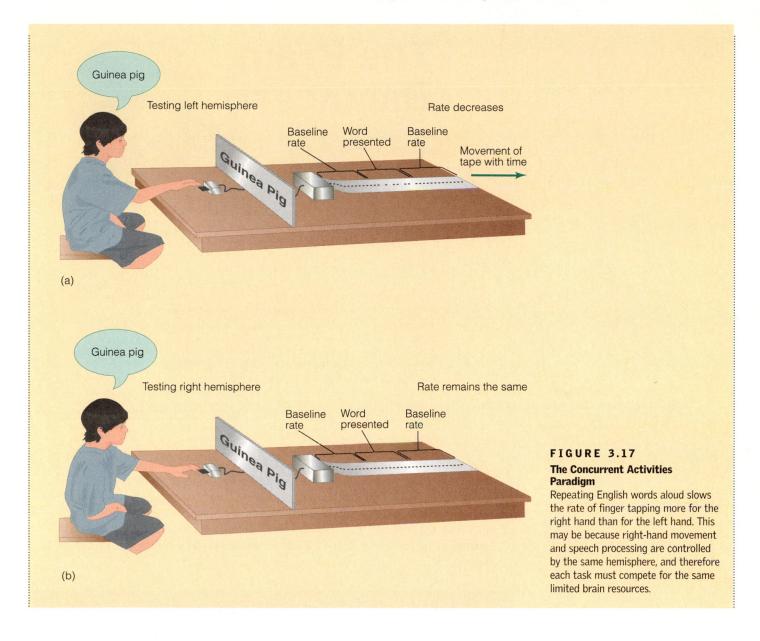

FIGURE 3.17

The Concurrent Activities Paradigm
Repeating English words aloud slows the rate of finger tapping more for the right hand than for the left hand. This may be because right-hand movement and speech processing are controlled by the same hemisphere, and therefore each task must compete for the same limited brain resources.

gested, for example, that the right side of the brain is holistic rather than analytic and accounts for such varied activities as fantasy, dance, and music appreciation. The left side of the brain is argued to be the rational mind, controlling not only language but also mathematical and scientific abilities. I once encountered a man who, after offering his left hand in greeting, claimed: "I'm trying to develop my right hemisphere"—he apparently felt that shaking with his right hand promoted too much left brain thinking. Companies have even started marketing packages designed to teach people to become more right brained or left brained in their approach to the world, or to develop ways to synchronize the two sides of the brain (see Druckman & Swets, 1988).

At present, there is little if any scientific evidence to support such claims. It's extremely unlikely that people can learn to develop a particular side of the brain, or that individuals will ever be properly classified as "right brained" or "left brained." There is also no scientific rationale for proposing that a particular thinking style can be attributed to one hemisphere and not to the other (Hellige, 1990). Adding to the confusion is the fact that proper experimental studies are rarely, if

The Brain Balancer!

Studies have shown that each side of the brain has different strengths. For instance—creativity lies in the right side of the brain. Further studies have shown that people are dominant in one side of their brain. It is also a known fact that only 10% of the brain is generally used. Think of all that brain power going to waste!

This needn't be you! With this kit, you will discover which side of your brain is dominant. Next, you will find out how to strengthen your less dominant half. Once your brain is equally balanced, there is no stopping!

Inner equilibrium brings outer equilibrium! With your brain's halves working together, you will increase your self-confidence, creativity, and ability to solve problems. **This will positively affect your life!**

With less of life's little annoyances to worry about, you can then concentrate on developing the 90% of the brain that is unused. It is believed that this is where motivation, intuition, and other such powers lie. The possibilities for personal, intellectual, and occupational growth are endless!

So, call and order your **BRAIN BALANCER** kit today! With a 30-day money-back guarantee, you have nothing to lose and everything to gain! The kit includes the **BRAIN BALANCER** booklet, workbook, and tape.

There is little, if any, scientific evidence to support claims of the type made in this advertisement. (From Kalat, 1996)

ever, conducted. Far too often the striking and newsworthy claims are based on anecdotal reports or poorly designed studies. For example, students who listened to tapes designed to stimulate synchronization of the hemispheres were found to perform better on a variety of tasks than students who weren't exposed to the tapes. But the students who participated were fully informed about the potential benefits of the tapes, so their task improvements could easily be attributed to a placebo effect (for further discussion, see Druckman & Swets, 1988).

TEST YOURSELF 3.2

Test what you've learned about research into brain structures and their functions. Fill in each blank with one of the following terms: EEG, PET scan, hindbrain, midbrain, forebrain, cerebellum, hypothalamus, cortex, frontal lobes, limbic system, corpus callosum. (You will find the answers in the Appendix.)

1. A "primitive" part of the brain that controls basic life support functions such as heart rate and respiration: _____

2. A structure thought to be involved in a variety of motivational activities, including eating, drinking, and sexual behavior: _____

3. The portion of the cortex believed to be involved in higher-order thought processes (such as planning) as well as the initiation of voluntary motor movements: _____

4. A structure near the base of the brain that is involved in coordination of complex activities such as walking and playing the piano: _____

5. A device that is used to monitor the gross electrical activity of the brain: _____

Regulating Growth and Internal Functions: Extended Communication

The human body actually has two communication systems. The first, the connective network of the nervous system, starts and controls most behaviors—thoughts, voluntary movements, and sensations and perceptions of the external world. Electrical activity, forming the neural impulse, moves rapidly down axons, like sparks traversing the fuses of firecrackers tied in series, forcing the release of neurotransmitters that complete the communication chain. But the body also has long-term communication needs. For example, the body must initiate and control growth and provide long-term regulation of numerous internal biological systems. Consequently, a second communication system has developed: a network of glands called the **endocrine system,** which uses the bloodstream, rather than neurons, as its main information courier. Chemicals called **hormones** are released into the blood by the various endocrine glands and serve to control a variety of internal functions.

The word *hormone* comes aptly from the Greek *hormon*, which means "to set into motion." Hormones play a role in many basic, life-sustaining activities in the body. Hunger, thirst, sexual behavior, and the "fight-or-flight" response are all regulated in part by an interplay between the nervous system and hormones released by the endocrine glands. Again, the fact that the body has two communication systems rather than one makes sense from an adaptive standpoint. One system, communication among neurons, governs transmissions that are quick and detailed; the other, the endocrine system, initiates the slower but more widespread and longer-lasting effects. In the following section, I'll consider the endocrine system in more detail and then consider how hormones influence some fundamental differences between men and women.

THE ENDOCRINE SYSTEM

The chemical communication system of the endocrine glands differs in some important ways from the rapid-fire electrochemical activities of the nervous system. On the one hand, communication in the nervous system tends to be *localized*, which means that a given neurotransmitter usually affects only cells in a small area. On the other hand, hormones have widespread effects. Because they are carried by the blood, they travel throughout the body and interact with numerous target sites. Also in contrast to neurotransmitters, hormones have long-lasting effects. Whereas neural communication operates in time scales bordering on the blink of an eye, the endocrine system can produce effects lasting minutes, hours, or even days. In some animals, for example, it is circulating hormones that prepare the organism for seasonal migration or for hibernation. Thus, the endocrine system provides the body with a mechanism for both widespread and long-term communication that cannot be produced by interactions among neurons.

Although the endocrine and nervous systems communicate in different ways, their activities are closely coordinated. Structures in the brain (especially the hypothalamus) stimulate or inhibit the release of hormones by the glands; once released, these chemicals then feed back and affect the firing rates of neural impulses. The feedback loop balances and controls the regulatory activities of the body. The hypothalamus is of particular importance because it controls the pituitary gland. The **pituitary gland** is a kind of master gland that controls the secretion of hormones in response to signals from the hypothalamus; these hormones, in turn, regulate the activity of many of the other vital glands in the endocrine system. It is the pituitary gland, for example, that signals the testes in males to produce *testosterone* and the ovaries in females to produce *estrogen*—both of critical importance in sexual behavior and reproduction.

endocrine system
A network of glands that uses the bloodstream, rather than neurons, to send chemical messages that regulate growth and other internal functions.

hormones
Chemicals released into the blood by the various endocrine glands to help control a variety of internal regulatory functions.

pituitary gland
A kind of master gland in the body that controls the release of hormones in response to signals from the hypothalamus.

Hypothalamus
Stimulate pituitary gland

Pituitary Gland
Secretes hormones that stimulate the adrenal glands

Adrenal Glands
Secrete norepinephrine and epinephrine into bloodstream

Norepinephrine and Epinephrine
Cause surge of energy; heart rate increases; blood is shunted to areas that require it, away from the stomach and intestine; glucose is made available to the muscles

FIGURE 3.18

The Fight-or-Flight Response
In potentially dangerous situations the endocrine system generates a fight-or-flight response. Hormones are released that produce energizing effects on the body, increasing our chances of survival.

? CRITICAL THINKING

Initiation of the fight-or-flight response clearly has adaptive value. But can you think of any circumstances in which this response might actually lower *the chances of an adaptive response?*

Let's consider one example of the endocrine system at work. You leave a party late, convinced that you can walk the 2-plus miles home without incident. The streets, quiet without the noise of midday traffic, exert a calming influence as you pass the flashing traffic lights and the parked cars. But suddenly, across the street, two shadowy figures emerge from an alleyway and move in your direction. You draw in your breath, your stomach tightens, and your rapidly beating heart seems ready to explode from your chest. These whole-body reactions, critical in preparing you to fight or flee, are created by signals from the brain that lead to increased activity of the endocrine glands. The hypothalamus, acting via the pituitary gland, signals the *adrenal glands* (located above the kidneys) to begin secreting such hormones as *norepinephrine* and *epinephrine* into the blood. These hormones produce energizing effects on the body, increasing heart rate, constricting the blood supply to the stomach and intestines, and increasing the amount of glucose (sugar) in the blood. The body is now prepared for action, enhancing the likelihood of survival (see Figure 3.18).

GENDER EFFECTS

Prior to birth, hormones released by the pituitary gland establish sexual identity, determining whether a child ends up with male or female sex organs. At puberty, an increase in sex hormones (testosterone and estrogen) leads males to develop facial hair and deep speaking voices and females to develop breasts and to begin menstruation. It is now suspected that hormones released during development may even affect the basic wiring patterns of men's and women's brains. Evidence suggests that men and women may think differently as the result of gender-specific activities of the endocrine system.

Psychologists Doreen Kimura and Elizabeth Hampson (1994) report, for example, that the performance of women and men on certain tasks changes significantly as the levels of sex hormones increase or decrease in the body. Women traditionally perform better than men on some tests of verbal ability, and their performance on these tasks improves with high levels of estrogen in their body. Similarly, men show slightly better performance on some kinds of spatial tasks (such as imagining that three-dimensional objects are rotating), and their performance seems to be related somewhat to their testosterone levels. The evidence is correlational, which means that we cannot be sure that it is the hormones that are causing the performance changes, but the data are suggestive of endocrine-based gender differences in thought (Collins & Kimura, 1997).

It's also the case that girls who have been exposed to an excess of male hormones during the initial stages of prenatal development, either because of a genetic disorder or from chemicals ingested by the mother during pregnancy, tend to be particularly tomboyish during development (Resnick et al., 1986), preferring to engage in play activities that are more traditionally associated with boys. In one study reported by Kimura (1992), researchers at UCLA compared the choice of toys by girls who either had or had not been exposed to excess male hormones during early development. The girls who had been exposed to the male hormones tended to prefer the typical masculine activities—smashing trucks and cars together, for example—more than the control girls did.

It's been known for some time that male and female brains may differ anatomically, although such differences have often been exaggerated historically (Shields, 1975). Animal studies have confirmed that male and female *rat* brains differ anatomically; moreover, these differences in rat brains are clearly attributable, in part, to the early influence of hormones (see Hines, 1982, for a review). For humans, the data are less clear and far more controversial. It's been reported that the right cortex of males tends to be slightly thicker than the right cortex of females (see Kimura, 1992), but whether this anatomical difference accounts, even in part, for the superiority that males show in performing certain spatial tasks is unclear. Other studies have reported that sections of the corpus callosum are more elaborate in women, suggesting that the two hemispheres communicate more effectively in females (de Lacoste-Utamsing & Holloway, 1982). However, subsequent researchers have had a difficult time replicating this particular result (see Witelson, 1992).

The evidence supporting gender-based differences in brain anatomy and mental functioning is provocative and should be investigated further. Hormones released by the endocrine system are known to produce permanent changes early in human development, and it's certainly possible that actions later in life are somehow influenced by these changes. But at this point no direct causal link has been established between anatomical differences and the variations in intellectual functioning that are sometimes found between men and women. In fact, some researchers have argued that sex-based differences in brain organization may

There may indeed be gender differences in brain anatomy and functioning, but the decision of girls and boys to engage in stereotypical activities is strongly influenced by the environment as well.

actually cause men and women to act more *similarly* than they would otherwise (De Vries & Boyle, 1998).

In addition, the performance differences that women and men show on certain laboratory tasks aren't very large and don't reflect general ability. Many of the studies report that gender-based differences are extremely small (see Hyde & Linn, 1988). To repeat a theme discussed in Chapter 1, it is extremely difficult to separate the effects of biology (*nature*) from the ongoing influences of the environment (*nurture*). Men and women are faced with different environmental demands and cultural expectations during their lifetimes. Without question, these demands help determine the actions they take, thereby helping promote behavioral differences between the sexes. We will return to gender issues often in later chapters of this text.

TEST YOURSELF 3.3

Test your knowledge about the differences between the endocrine system and the nervous system. For each statement, decide whether the *endocrine* or *nervous* system is the most appropriate term to apply. (You will find the answers in the Appendix.)

1. Communication effects tend to be localized, affecting only a small area:
   _____

2. Responsible for whole-body reactions, such as the fight-or-flight response:
   _____

3. The major determinant of sexual identity: _____

4. Communicates through the release of epinephrine and norepinephrine:
   _____

5. Operates quickly, with time scales bordering on the blink of an eye:
   _____

Storing and Transmitting the Genetic Code: Genetic Influences on Behavior

As you've seen in this chapter, the biological processes that influence how we think and act seem on the whole to be understandable and predictable. PET scans of people engaging in a visual task reveal reliable activity in the occipital lobe of the cortex. Sudden paralysis to the right side of the body allows the physician to predict, usually successfully, that the stroke occurred in the left cerebral hemisphere. But behavior is the main interest of psychology, and it remains remarkably difficult to predict. People typically react differently to the same environmental situation—even if they are siblings raised in the same household. How do we explain the remarkable diversity of behavior, given that everyone carries around a similar 3- to 4-pound mass of brain tissue?

One answer is that no two brains are exactly alike. The patterns of neural activity that are responsible for our behaviors (and thoughts) are uniquely determined by our individual experiences and by the genetic material that we've inherited from our parents. Most of us have no trouble accepting that experience is a critical determinant of individual differences in behavior; but what about genetics? Sure, hair color, eye color, and blood type may be expressions of fixed genetic influences, but how could genetics govern intelligence, personality, or emotionality?

Recognizing that heredity has a role in such characteristics is a given to the psychologist. As you'll see, we'll appeal to genetic principles repeatedly throughout our discussions of the adaptive mind. But it's also important to remember that the genetic code serves two adaptive functions for the human species. First, genes

LEARNING GOALS

1. Describe the basic principles of genetic transmission.

2. Explain how psychologists study genetic influences on behavior.

provide individuals with a kind of flexible blueprint for their physical and psychological development. Second, genes provide a means through which people are able to pass on physical and psychological characteristics to their offspring, thereby helping to ensure continuation of the species.

GENETIC PRINCIPLES

Let's briefly review some of the important principles of genetics. How is the genetic code stored, and what are the factors that produce genetic variability? The genetic message resides within *chromosomes,* which are thin, threadlike strips of DNA. Human cells, with the exception of sperm cells and the unfertilized egg cell, contain a total of 46 chromosomes, arranged in 23 pairs. Half of each chromosome pair is contributed originally by the mother through the egg, and the other half arrives in the father's sperm. **Genes** are segments of chromosome that contain instructions for influencing and creating particular hereditary characteristics. For example, each person has a piece of chromosome, or gene, that helps determine height or hair color and another piece that may determine susceptibility to disorders such as muscular dystrophy or even Alzheimer's disease.

Because humans have 23 *pairs* of chromosomes, they have two genes for most developmental characteristics, or traits. People have two genes, for example, for hair color, blood type, and the possible development of facial dimples. If both genes are designed to produce the same trait (such as nearsightedness), there's little question about the characteristic that will develop (you'll definitely need glasses). But what if the two genes differ—for example, the father passes along the gene for nearsightedness, but the mother's gene is for normal distance vision? Under these conditions, the trait that will be expressed is determined by the *dominant gene;* in the case of vision, the "normal" gene will dominate the *recessive gene* for nearsightedness.

The fact that a dominant gene will mask the effects of a recessive gene means that everybody has genetic material that is not actually expressed in physical and/or psychological characteristics. A person may see perfectly but still carry around the recessive gene for faulty distance vision. This is the reason why parents with normal vision can produce a nearsighted child, or two brown-haired parents can produce a child with blond hair—it depends on the particular combinations of gene types that have been inherited by the child. It's also worth noting that very few traits are governed by just one gene; most traits, even eye and hair color, are influenced by more than one gene.

Another important distinction is between the **genotype,** which is the actual genetic message, and the **phenotype,** which is a person's observable characteristics. The phenotype, such as clear distance vision or brown hair, is controlled mainly by the genotype, but it can also be influenced by the environment. A person's height and weight, for example, are shaped largely by the genotype, but environmental factors such as diet and physical health will contribute significantly to the final phenotype. This is an important point to remember: Genetic blueprints provide the materials from which characteristics develop, but the environment often shapes the final product. Exactly how a genotype is expressed into a phenotype defines the nature–nurture issue in its purest form.

Across individuals, variations in the genetic message arise because there are trillions of different ways that the genetic information from each parent can be combined at fertilization. Each egg or sperm cell contains a random half of each parent's 23 chromosome pairs. According to the laws of probability, this means that there are some 8 million (2^{23}) different combinations that can reside in either an egg cell or a sperm cell. The particular meeting of egg and sperm is also a matter of chance, which means that there are some 64 trillion ways that the genetic material from both parents can be combined at fertilization—and this is from a single set of parents!

GENES AND BEHAVIOR

But we still haven't established the link between genetics and psychology—what is the connection between genotypes, phenotypes, and behavior? Any behavior,

genes
Segments of chromosomes that contain instructions for influencing and creating particular hereditary characteristics.

genotype
The actual genetic information inherited from one's parents.

phenotype
A person's observable characteristics, such as red hair. The phenotype is controlled mainly by the genotype, but it can also be influenced by the environment.

CRITICAL THINKING

In what ways are the environmental experiences of identical twins more similar than those for fraternal twins? Would this still be true if both sets of twins are raised apart from birth?

Genetic background plays an important role in determining physical appearance, but many researchers believe that it also helps to shape certain psychological characteristics.

family studies

The similarities and differences among biological (blood) relatives are studied to help discover the role heredity plays in physical or psychological traits. Family studies rarely provide conclusive evidence because genes and the environment are usually confounded.

twin studies

Identical twins, who share genetic material, are compared to fraternal twins in an effort to disentangle the roles heredity and environment play in psychological traits.

if it is indeed influenced by genetic factors, is likely to be the product of lots of genetic information interacting in complex ways. However, as you'll see throughout this book, there are instances where it is possible to predict, at least on average, things about the psychology of an individual by knowing something about his or her genetic record. Susceptibility to the psychological disorder *schizophrenia* is a case in point. Natural children of parents who have schizophrenia (where either one or both have the disorder) have a greater chance of developing the disorder themselves, when compared to the children of normal parents. This is the case even if the children have been adopted at birth and never raised in an abnormal environment (Gottesman, 1991; Moldin & Gottesman, 1997). Thus, genetic similarity probably plays some role in the increased tendency to develop schizophrenia. (I'll return to this issue in more detail in Chapter 14.)

One way that psychologists study the link between genes and behavior is to investigate family histories in detail. In **family studies,** researchers look for similarities and differences among biological (blood) relatives as a way determining whether heredity has an influence. As you've just seen, the chances of schizophrenia increase with a family history, and there are many other traits that seem to run in families as well (e.g., intelligence and personality). The trouble with family studies, however, is that members of a family share more than just common genes. They are also exposed to similar environmental experiences, so it's difficult to separate the relative roles of nature and nurture in behavior. Family studies can be useful sources of information—it helps to know, for instance, if someone is at a greater than average risk of developing schizophrenia—but they can't be used to establish cause-and-effect links between genes and behavior.

In **twin studies,** a somewhat better technique, researchers compare behavioral traits between *identical* twins, who share the same genetic material, and *fraternal* twins, who were born at the same time but whose genetic overlap is only roughly 50% (fraternal twins can even be of different sexes). In studies of intelligence, for example, identical twins tend to have much more similar intelligence scores than fraternal twins, even when environmental factors are taken into account (Bouchard et al., 1990; Bouchard, 1997). Identical twins make ideal research subjects because researchers can control, at least in principle, for genetic factors. Because these twins have the same genetic makeup, any physical or psychological differences that emerge during development must be attributable to environmental factors. Similarly, if identical twins are raised in different environments but still show similar traits, it's a strong indication that genetic factors are involved in expression of the trait.

I've provided only a brief sample of the study of genes and behavior in this section because we'll be returning to the interplay between heredity and environment throughout many of the later chapters. For now, recognize that the adaptive mind is indeed influenced by the code that is stored in the body's chromosomes. Through the random processes that underlie genetic combinations at fertilization, nature secures diversity within the species—everyone receives a unique genetic blueprint that, in combination with environmental factors, helps determine brain structure as well as human psychology. From an evolutionary standpoint, diversity is of great importance because it increases the likelihood that at least some members of a species will have the necessary tools to deal successfully with the problems of survival.

TEST YOURSELF 3.4

To check on your understanding of genetics, choose the best answer to each of the following statements. (You will find the answers in the Appendix.)

1. The actual genetic information inherited from one's parents: genotype or phenotype?

2. If the two inherited genes for a specific trait differ, which plays a stronger role: dominant or recessive? _____

3. Psychologists can study genetic effects on a variety of characteristics, such as intelligence or susceptibility to schizophrenia, by studying which kind of twins raised in different environments: identical or fraternal? _____

Solving the Problems

To account for the complexities of behavior, modern psychologists accept that our thoughts, feelings, and actions are by-products of active biological systems. The human brain, along with the rest of the nervous system, is a biological solution to problems produced by constantly changing and sometimes hostile outside environments. Fortunately, out of these biological solutions arise those attributes that make up the human mind, including intellect, emotion, and artistic creativity. In this chapter we've considered four central problems of adaptation that we face and effectively solve through our biological systems.

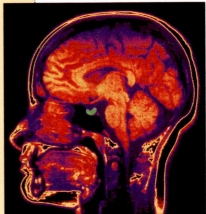

Communicating Internally. Networks of individual cells, called neurons, establish a marketplace of information called the nervous system. To communicate internally, the nervous system has developed an electrochemical language. Messages travel electrically within a neuron, usually from dendrite to soma to axon to terminal button, and then chemically from one neuron to the next. Combining electrical and chemical components creates a quick, efficient, and extremely versatile communication system. Neurotransmitters regulate the rate at which neurons fire, by producing excitatory or inhibitory messages, and the resulting global patterns of activation underlie the behaviors and thought processes that humans are capable of producing.

Initiating and Coordinating Behavior. To accomplish the remarkable variety of functions it controls, the nervous system divides its labor. Through the use of sophisticated techniques, including brain-imaging devices, researchers have begun to map out the localized regions of brain tissue that support particular psychological and life-sustaining functions. At the base of the brain, in the hindbrain region, structures control such basic processes as respiration, heart rate, and the coordination of muscle movements. Higher up are regions that control motivational processes such as eating, drinking, and sexual behavior. Finally, in the cerebral cortex more complex mental processes—such as thought, sensations, and language—are represented. Some functions in the brain appear to be lateralized, which means that they are controlled primarily by one cerebral hemisphere or the other. Through the development of specialized regions of cells, the human brain has become capable of increasingly more adaptive reactions to its changing environment.

Regulating Growth and Internal Functions. To solve its widespread and long-term communication needs, the body uses the endocrine system to release chemicals called hormones into the bloodstream. These chemical messengers serve a variety of regulatory functions, influencing growth and development, hunger, thirst, and sexual behavior, in addition to helping the body prepare for action. Hormones released early in development and on into adulthood may underlie some of the behavioral differences that are found between men and women.

Storing and Transmitting the Genetic Code. Physical and behavioral characteristics are influenced by portions of chromosomes called genes. The particular combinations of genes that are inherited from the parents, along with influences from the environment, dictate the characteristics that an individual will actually display. Psychologists often try to disentangle the relative contributions of genes and the environment by conducting twin studies, comparing the behaviors and abilities of identical and fraternal twins who have been raised in similar or dissimilar environments. When twins show similar behavioral characteristics, even though they have been raised in quite different environments, psychologists assume that the underlying genetic code may be playing an influential role.

Biological Processes Chapter Summary

Most scientists believe that all behavior arises from the activities of the brain. Virtually every time you think, act, or feel, biological activity in your brain is playing a critical role. *Neuroscience* is the study of how the brain, mind, and behavior are interconnected.

Communicating Internally: Connecting World and Brain

Information is received, transmitted, and integrated by neurons, cells that communicate electrochemically.

NEURONS

Structure: Dendrites/soma/axon/terminal button.

Sensory neurons: Carry information to the spinal cord and brain.

Interneurons: Convey information between internal processing sites.

Motor neurons: Carry messages from the central nervous system to the muscles and glands that produce the behavioral response.

NEURAL TRANSMISSION

Messages travel electrically from one point to another within a neuron and chemically, through *neurotransmitters,* from one neuron to another.

COMMUNICATION NETWORK

The pattern of activation produced by groups of neurons operating at the same time underlies both conscious experiences and complex behaviors.

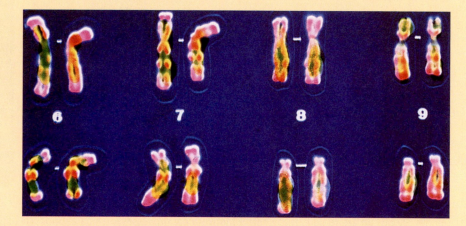

Initiating and Coordinating Behavior: A Division of Labor

A division of labor makes it possible to think, feel, and function physically all at the same time.

NERVOUS SYSTEMS

Central nervous system: The brain and spinal cord, which communicate decisions to the rest of the body through bundles of axons (*nerves*).

Peripheral nervous system: Moves muscles, regulates organs, sends sensory information to the brain. Includes *somatic* and *autonomic* systems.

BRAIN STRUCTURES

Hindbrain: Basic life support through the *medulla, pons, reticular formation,* and *cerebellum.*

Midbrain: Relays visual and auditory messages.

Forebrain: Higher mental functioning through the *cerebral cortex, thalamus, hypothalamus,* and *limbic system.*

BRAIN RESEARCH

Brain damage and lesion: Studying damage can reveal brain function

Talking to the brain through chemical injection or electrodes.

Listening to the brain through noninvasive techniques such as electrical monitoring (EEG), X rays (CT scan), live snapshots (PET), and magnetic imaging (MRI).

BRAIN DIVISIONS

The two *hemispheres* (halves) of the cerebral cortex are *lateralized:* each side is responsible for independent functions.

The *corpus callosum* connects the two cerebral hemispheres.

Regulating Growth and Internal Functions: Extended Communication

Long-term communication requirements are provided by a second system, which uses the bloodstream instead of the nervous system.

ENDOCRINE SYSTEM

Endocrine glands release *hormones* into the blood that interact with the nervous system to regulate basic activities such as the fight-or-flight response.

GENDER EFFECTS

Hormones released by the pituitary gland determine sexual identity before birth and direct sexual maturing at puberty. Endocrine activities may account for basic differences in the way males and females think and behave.

Storing and Transmitting the Genetic Code: Genetic Influences on Behavior

The genetic code provides a flexible blueprint for physical and psychological development. Genes are also a means of transmitting characteristics from one generation to the next, thus continuing the species.

GENETIC PRINCIPLES

Inside the *cell* are 23 pairs of *chromosomes,* threadlike strips of *DNA; genes* are segments of chromosomes that contain instructions for creating or influencing a particular hereditary characteristic. Genes can be *dominant* or *recessive.*

Genotype: The actual genetic message.

Phenotype: A person's observable characteristics.

GENES AND BEHAVIOR

Psychologists study the influence of genetics on behavior through specific kinds of research.

Family studies: Similarities and differences sometimes reveal the influence of heredity.

Twin studies: Researchers compare behavioral traits between identical twins (who share the same genetic material) and fraternal twins (whose genes are only about 50% the same). Traits not accounted for by genetics are attributed to environmental influences.

Terms to Remember

Recommended Readings

Kalat, J. W. (1998). *Biological psychology* (6th ed.). Belmont, CA: Wadsworth. A leading undergraduate textbook on biological psychology. The material discussed in Chapter 3 is covered here in much more detail.

Sacks, O. (1985). *The man who mistook his wife for a hat*. New York: Summit Books. A witty example of the case study approach applied to the neurosciences. Sacks presents examples and anecdotes from patients suffering from various forms of brain damage. All of Oliver Sacks' books are interesting, but this one is a classic.

Gazzaniga, M. S. (1992). *Nature's mind: The biological roots of thinking, emotions, sexuality, and intelligence*. New York: Basic Books. This book is written by a leading neuroscientist, Michael Gazzaniga, who is one of the pioneers in the study of split-brain patients. He provides a fascinating and readable account of the role that biological processes play in mind and behavior.

INFOTRAC® COLLEGE EDITION

For additional readings, explore Infotrac College Edition, your online library. Go to:
http://www.infotrac-college.com/wadsworth

Hint: enter the search terms: Neural transmission, Sympathetic nervous system, Cerebral cortex, Brain imaging, Behavioral genetics.

What's on the Web?

Neurosciences on the Internet

(www.neuroguide.com)

If you want to find information related to the brain or neurosciences, this is the place to do it! A very impressive site that serves as a sort of "clearinghouse" for information on the brain and nervous system. It provides information on neurosurgery and brain disorders, as well as psychiatry and psychology.

Neuroscience for Kids

(weber.u.washington.edu/~chudler/neurok.html)

Yes, the title says "for kids," but this site isn't just for kids. It provides information on the brain and nervous system presented in a straightforward, engaging, and interesting fashion. Think of it as "Sesame Street meets Chapter 3." Included are exercises to let you explore the nervous system, experiments and activities, and links to other neuroscience resources. The site is part of a larger neuroscience site based at the University of Washington.

The Whole Brain Atlas

(www.med.harvard.edu/AANLIB/home.html)

This site has everything you wanted to know about the brain (and every picture you wanted to see!) but were afraid to ask. It provides an extensive and graphic introduction to the brain, offering views of the stroke–damaged brain, a brain with Alzheimer's, and many others. It also provides information on neuro-imaging of the brain.

The Wadsworth Psychology Study Center Web Site

See http://psychology.wadsworth.com/ for practice quiz questions, hypercontents, updates, critical thinking exercises, discussion forums and more! The Wadsworth Psychology Study Center provides a wealth of information fully organized and integrated by chapter.

Human Development

Do you ever wish you could hop into a time machine and start over? Maybe you could return to that point in the third grade where you tripped in front of the whole school, or to middle school—Mrs. Gatherton's English class—where the answer you blurted out became the focus of jokes for months. In fact, while you're at it, why not return to early childhood? If only your parents had been sympathetic, rather than angry, when your efforts at toilet training ended in a messy failure. Things would be very different now, right?

Few psychologists would question the claim that you are, in many ways, a product of your environment. However, as you saw in Chapter 1, philosophers and scientists have debated for centuries about the true origins of knowledge and behavior. If you could rerun your life, controlling your environment, would you really end up as a different person? You might, but it's also quite possible that your personality—your likes and dislikes—is a reflection of the genetic material you inherited from your parents. By now, you probably recognize that there is no simple answer to the classic *nature versus nurture* debate. The origins of behavior and knowledge don't lie exclusively in either nature (genes) or nurture (the environment), but most often in *both*.

The topic of this chapter is human **development,** the age-related physical, intellectual, and social changes that occur throughout an individual's lifetime. If you listen to the discussions of modern *developmental psychologists*—those who study the developmental process—you will repeatedly hear references to the concept of *interaction*. They believe that to understand the origins of any developmental change, it's necessary to view the developing human from the perspective of combined social, cultural, and biological forces (Sigelman & Shaffer, 1995; Zigler & Stevenson, 1993). As you saw in Chapter 3, unique genetic messages compel the body to change over time, but the environment helps determine how those messages are realized. This means that it isn't possible to understand development by attending to any single factor in isolation, be it biological or environmental. Instead, development is better seen as a series of adjustments that the mind and body make to multiple factors. Moreover, these adjustments occur throughout the life span: From conception to death, the developmental process continues (Baltes, 1987; Baltes et al., 1980).

development
The age-related physical, intellectual, social, and personal changes that occur throughout an individual's lifetime.

Previewing the Adaptive Problems

Why do humans need to develop? There's one very straightforward reason: There is no room for a full-sized adult in the mother's womb, so nature is forced to start small. More importantly, however, extending the process of development over time enables humans to fine-tune their physical, intellectual, and social capabilities to better meet the needs of the environments they face (Bjorklund, 1997). Nature has built a certain amount of flexibility, or *plasticity,* into the developmental process that allows the environment to modify the course of development. This flexibility has given us, as individuals and as a species, an exceptional degree of adaptability to environmental influences (Corballis, 1991; Greenough et al., 1987). Keep the adaptive significance of development in mind as you consider the three main developmental problems that are the focus of this chapter (see Figure 4.1).

First, how do we move from fertilized eggs to fully functioning adults, capable of producing our own offspring? The environment helps shape the physical process of growth, and can determine its ultimate outcome, but most physical changes are surprisingly consistent and predictable. In general, the timing of development is a product of evolutionary

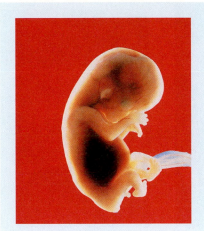
Developing physically

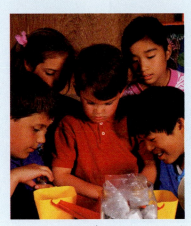
Developing intellectually

Developing socially and personally

FIGURE 4.1
Adaptive Problems of Development
Humans face three main developmental problems: developing physically, intellectually, and socially /personally.

history and reflects the problems of survival that the human species has been required to solve.

Second, how do we develop the intellectual tools needed to solve survival problems? The developmental changes that occur in how people think—what is called cognitive development—are of major importance to psychologists. Intellectually, the newborn is hardly a miniature adult. You'll discover that there are good reasons to believe that infants see and think about the world somewhat differently from adults.

Third, how do we form the social relationships and sense of personal identity needed for personal protection, nourishment, and continuation of the species? Humans are social animals. They are continually interacting with each other, and these relationships help people adapt successfully to their environments. In this section, we'll consider the milestones of social development, beginning with the formation of attachments to parents and caregivers and ending with a discussion of how relationships change in middle and late adulthood.

Developing Physically

To a child, it seems to take forever to grow up. In fact, humans do take a relatively long time to reach full physical maturity, compared to other species. At birth, for example, the brain of a chimpanzee is at about 60% of its final weight, whereas the brain of a human newborn is only at about 25% of its ultimate weight (Corballis, 1991; Lenneberg, 1967). Humans do a lot of developing outside of the womb. Still, the main components of the body—the nervous system, the networks of glands, and so on—develop at an astonishingly rapid rate from the point of conception.

Guided by the genetic code and influenced by the release of hormones by the endocrine system, individuals in the early years change physically at rates that will never again be matched in their lifetimes. To place the growth rate in some perspective, it's been estimated that if children continued to develop at the rate they show in the first two years of life, adults would end up over 12 feet tall and weighing several tons! Fortunately, things slow down considerably after the first few years of life; but they never completely stop—we continue to change physically until the very moment of death.

LEARNING GOALS

1. Describe the physical changes that occur during prenatal development.

2. Discuss growth during infancy and childhood.

3. Describe the physical changes that occur during adolescence.

4. Describe the essential characteristics of the aging body and brain.

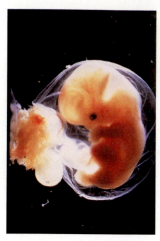

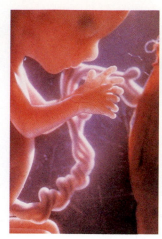

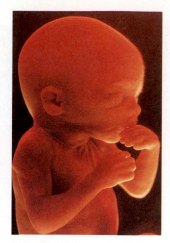

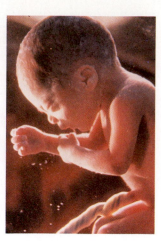

5–6 weeks postconception   4 months   6 months   8 months

The Developing Human

THE STAGES OF PRENATAL DEVELOPMENT

The human developmental process begins with the union of egg and sperm at conception. Within the fertilized egg, or **zygote,** the 23 chromosomes from the father and the 23 chromosomes from the mother pair up to form the master genetic blueprint. Over the next 266 days or so (approximately 9 months), the organism undergoes a steady and quite remarkable transformation. It begins as a single cell and ends as an approximately 7-pound newborn composed of literally billions of cells. The period of development that occurs *prior* to birth is called prenatal development and is divided into three main stages: *germinal, embryonic,* and *fetal.*

The Germinal Period

It takes about two weeks after conception for the zygote, which rapidly begins to divide into more cells, to migrate down from the mother's fallopian tubes (where the sperm and egg meet) and implant itself in the wall of the uterus (often called the womb). The period from conception to implantation, called the **germinal period,** is characteristically fraught with difficulties. In fact, most fertilized eggs fail to complete the process; well over half fail to achieve successful implantation, either because of abnormalities or because the implantation site is inadequate to supply the nutrition needed for proper growth (Roberts & Lowe, 1975; Sigelman & Shafer, 1995).

The Embryonic Period

If successful implantation occurs, the **embryonic period** begins. During the next six weeks, the human develops from an unrecognizable mass of cells to a somewhat familiar creature with arms, legs, fingers, toes, and a distinctly beating heart. Near the end of the embryonic period—in the seventh and eighth weeks after fertilization—sexual differentiation begins. Depending on whether the father has contributed an X or a Y chromosome (the mother always contributes an X), the embryo starts to develop the sexual characteristics of either a male or a female (see Figure 4.2). If the developing embryo has inherited a Y chromosome, it begins to secrete the sex hormone *testosterone*, which leads to the establishment of a male sexual reproductive system. In the absence of testosterone, the natural course of development in humans is to become female.

The Fetal Period

At the ninth week of prenatal development, the **fetal period** begins and continues until birth. Early in the period, the bones and muscles of what is now called the *fetus* start to develop. By the end of the third month, the skeletal and muscular sys-

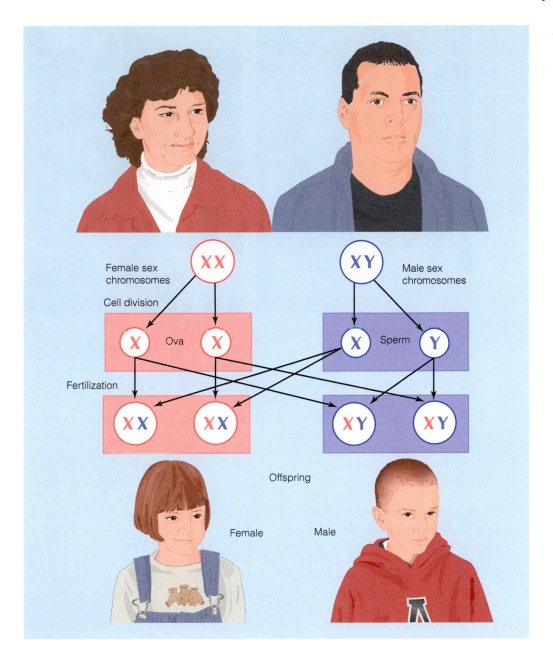

FIGURE 4.2
Genetic Determinants of Gender
Depending on whether the father has contributed an X or a Y chromosome, the child will develop the sexual characteristics of a female or a male.

tems allow for extensive movement—even somersaults—although the fetus at this point is still only about 3 inches long (Apgar & Beck, 1974). By the end of the sixth month, the fetus has grown to over a foot long, weighs in at about 2 pounds, and may even be capable of survival if delivered prematurely. The last three months of prenatal development are marked by extremely rapid growth, both in body size and in the size and complexity of brain tissue. The fetus also develops a layer of fat under the skin during this period, which acts as protective insulation, and the lungs mature in preparation for the baby's first gasping breath of air.

Environmental Hazards
Although the developing child is snugly tucked away within the confines of its mother's womb, it is by no means completely isolated from the effects of the

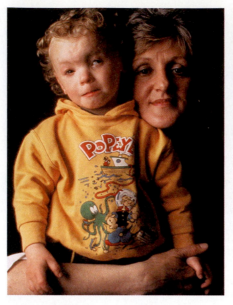

The child on the left is one of thousands born each year with fetal alcohol syndrome. The age of the mother is also a risk factor in pregnancy, but most women over the age of 35, such as the woman on the right, deliver normal, healthy babies.

environment. The mother's physical health and diet, as well as any possible exposure she might have to toxins in the environment, can potentially affect the developing child. Mother and child are linked physically, so if the mother gets sick, smokes, drinks, or takes drugs, the effects can transfer to the developing fetus or embryo. Some psychologists believe that the mother's psychological state, such as her level of anxiety during pregnancy, can exert an effect as well and may even influence the personality of the developing child (e.g., Oldani, 1997).

Environmental agents that can potentially damage the developing child are called **teratogens.** As a rule, the structures and systems of the developing fetus or embryo are most susceptible to teratogens during their initial formation. For example, if the mother contracts German measles (rubella) during the first six weeks of pregnancy, the child is at risk for developing heart defects because it is during this period that the structures of the heart are formed. Figure 4.3 shows the periods of greatest susceptibility—called *critical periods*—for various structures in the body. In general, the embryonic period is the point of greatest susceptibility, although the critical structures of the central nervous system can be affected throughout prenatal development.

The powerful influence of the environment on the developing fetus or embryo should not be underestimated. A pregnant woman who drinks heavily— five or more drinks a day—is at least 30% more likely than a nondrinker to give birth to a child suffering from *fetal alcohol syndrome*, a condition marked by physical deformities, a reduction in the size of certain brain structures, and an increased risk of mental retardation (Kaufman, 1997; Riley et al., 1995; Streissguth et al., 1991). Negative long-term effects can also result from drug consumption—even of over-the-counter and prescription drugs—as well as from improper nutrition, smoking, and possibly excessive caffeine (Day & Richardson, 1994; Sussman & Levitt, 1989).

It's hard to predict with any certainty what effect an environmental agent will have on development because susceptibility is largely a matter of timing and the specifics of the master genetic plan. Some mothers can abuse themselves terribly and still give birth to normal children; others who drink only moderately, perhaps as few as seven drinks a week, may produce a child with significant disabilities (Abel, 1981; Jacobson & Jacobson, 1994). Because the effects of maternal activities are impossible to predict in any particular case, most doctors recommend against playing Russian roulette with the developing fetus or embryo; it's best to stay sober, well fed, and under a doctor's care throughout pregnancy.

teratogens
Environmental agents—such as disease organisms or drugs—that can potentially damage the developing embryo or fetus.

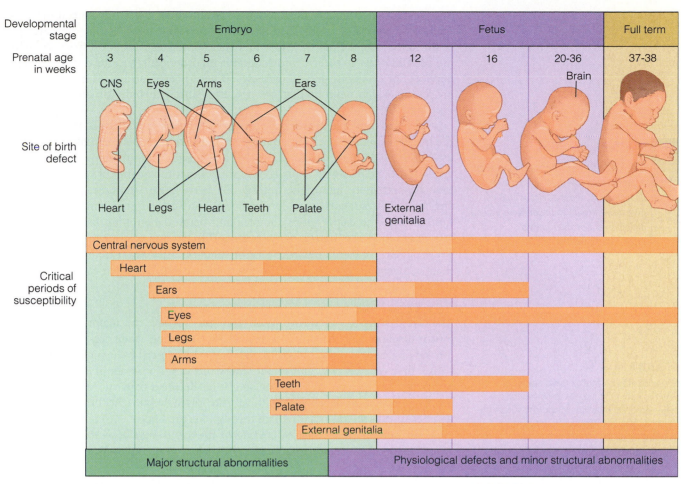

Developmental stage	Embryo						Fetus			Full term
Prenatal age in weeks	3	4	5	6	7	8	12	16	20-36	37-38

Site of birth defect: CNS, Eyes, Arms, Ears, Brain; Heart, Legs, Heart, Teeth, Palate, External genitalia

Critical periods of susceptibility:
Central nervous system
Heart
Ears
Eyes
Legs
Arms
Teeth
Palate
External genitalia

Major structural abnormalities	Physiological defects and minor structural abnormalities

GROWTH DURING INFANCY

Although thus far I've stressed the negative impact of the environment—how maternal illness and environmental agents consumed by the mother can limit or prevent expression of the normal genetic plan—in the vast majority of cases, the environment has a nurturing effect on the developing organism. The internal conditions of the mother's uterus are perfectly tuned for physical development. The temperature is right, the fetus floats cushioned in a protective fluid, and regular nourishment is provided through the umbilical cord and placenta. More often than not, the result is a healthy baby, with normal physical systems, who is ready to take on the world.

The average newborn weighs in at about 7 pounds and is roughly 20 inches in length. Over the next two years, as the child grows from baby to toddler, this weight will quadruple and the child will reach about half of his or her final adult height. Along with the rest of the body, the brain continues its dramatic growth spurt during this period. As mentioned earlier, a newborn enters the world with a brain that is only 25% of its final weight; but by the second birthday, the percentage has increased to 75%. Remarkably, this increase in brain size is not due to the formation of new neurons, as most of the cells that make up the cerebral cortex are in place well before birth (Nowakowski, 1987; Rakic, 1991). Instead, the cells grow in size and complexity, and a number of supporting glial cells are added. Each of us has essentially all the neurons we're going to possess at the moment we're born.

Experience Matters

The fact that substantial numbers of neurons are intact at birth does not mean that the brain of the newborn infant is *mature*—far from it. The brain still needs to build and fine-tune its vast internal communication network, and it needs

FIGURE 4.3

Critical Periods of Susceptibility During Prenatal Development
Specific organs and body parts are at greatest risk from teratogens during certain critical periods of prenatal development. The light part of each bar signifies the period of greatest susceptibility. (Adapted from Sigelman & Shaffer, 1995.)

experience to accomplish this task. During the final stages of prenatal development, and especially during the first year or two after birth, tremendous changes occur in the neural circuitry. More branches (dendrites) sprout off from the existing cells, in order to receive information from other cells, and the number of connections, or synapses, greatly increases. There is even a kind of neural pruning process in which neurons that are not used simply atrophy or die (Dawson & Fischer, 1994).

The key principle at work is *plasticity*. The genetic code does not rigidly fix the internal circuitry of the brain; instead, a kind of rough wiring pattern is established during prenatal development that is filled in during the important first few years of life. Studies with animals have shown that the quality of early experience may be extremely important during this period. For example, rats raised in enriched environments (with lots of social contact and environmental stimulation) show significantly more complex and better functioning brain tissue than rats raised in sterile, barren environments (Greenough et al., 1987; Rosenzweig, 1984). There is also better recovery of function after brain injury if rats spend their recovery time in an enriched environment (van Rijzingen et al., 1997).

FROM CRAWLING TO WALKING

Associated with the maturing brain and muscles are the major milestones in motor development that thrill every wide-eyed parent: when the baby rolls over for the first time, crawls, and walks. Ask parents to describe the highlights of their baby's first year or two, and you'll almost certainly hear about when the baby began to sit up, crawl, stand alone, and walk. Before a baby can do these things, however, adequate development must take place within the brain and in the neuron-to-muscle links that radiate throughout the body.

For example, the insulated coating of the axons (*myelin sheath*), which helps speed up neural transmission, needs to develop. Generally, the nervous system

---

? CRITICAL THINKING

Given that the environment plays such an important role in shaping brain development, what advice would you give new parents to maximize enriched development of their baby's intellectual capabilities?

FIGURE 4.4

Major States of Motor Development
Approximate time periods are given for the major points in motor development. Although psychologists are reluctant to tie developmental milestones to age, most children learn to crawl, stand alone, and walk at about the same age.

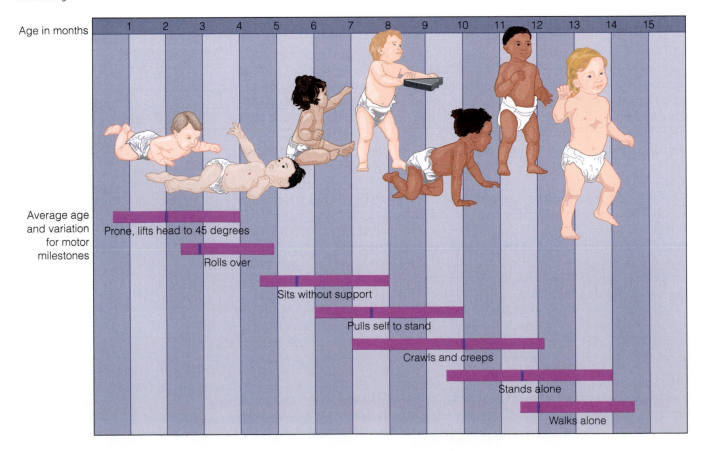

Age in months   1 2 3 4 5 6 7 8 9 10 11 12 13 14 15

Average age and variation for motor milestones

Prone, lifts head to 45 degrees

Rolls over

Sits without support

Pulls self to stand

Crawls and creeps

Stands alone

Walks alone

There are many cultural differences in child-rearing practices. The Indian baby shown on the left, unlike the Caucasian baby on the right, calmly accepts being swaddled to a cradleboard. However, even with the cultural differences, both of these babies should begin crawling and walking at roughly the same time.

matures in an essentially "down and out" fashion—that is, from the head down and from the center out toward the extremities (Shirley, 1933). Infants can lift their heads before they can roll over because the neuron-to-muscle connections in the upper part of the body mature before those in the lower part of the body. Babies crawl before they walk because they are able to control their arms efficiently before they are able to control their legs.

Although psychologists don't like to tie developmental milestones directly to age—because not all children develop at the same rate—most children learn to crawl, then stand alone, and walk at about the same time. Figure 4.4 shows the major stages of an infant's motor development. The sequence of development, from lifting the head to walking alone, is stable, orderly, and predictable. As noted earlier, the baby sits before it stands and crawls before it walks partly because of the way that the nervous system develops. In addition, you can see that associated with each stage is a range of ages, although the range is not large. Roughly 90% of all babies can roll over at 5 months of age, sit without support at 8 months, and then walk alone by 15 months. But, whereas one baby might stand alone consistently at 9 months, another might not accomplish the same feat until nearly 14 months of age.

Individual Differences

What accounts for individual differences? The answer is impossible to pinpoint for most cases, but both nature and nurture contribute. Each individual has a genetic blueprint that uniquely determines when he or she will develop physically, but environmental experiences can speed up or slow down the process to a certain extent (Schmuckler, 1996). Some cultures place higher value on early motor development than others and therefore nurture such development in their children. If a baby is routinely exercised and handled during the early months of life, there is some evidence that he or she will progress through the landmark stages of motor development more quickly (Hopkins, 1991; Zelazo et al., 1972).

But differences such as these are usually small, and they play little, if any, role in determining final motor development. Hopi babies are traditionally swaddled and bound to cradleboards for much of the first year of life, yet these babies begin walking at roughly the same time as babies who are not bound in this manner (Dennis & Dennis, 1940). To learn to walk at a reasonable age, the infant simply needs to be given the opportunity to move around at some point—to "test the waters" and explore things on his or her own (Bertenthal et al., 1994). Hopi babies are bound to cradleboards for only their first nine or ten months; afterward, they are given several months to explore their motor capabilities before they begin to walk (Shaffer, 1993).

Grace and coordination in motor movements take time to develop. This 2-year-old will probably have little trouble bouncing a basketball successfully by the time he enters elementary school.

FROM TODDLERHOOD TO ADOLESCENCE

From the onset of toddlerhood through puberty, the growth rate continues, but at a less rapid pace. The average child grows several inches and puts on roughly 6 to 7 pounds annually. Even though these changes are significant, it's often hard for parents to detect them because they represent only a small fraction of the child's current size (2 inches added to a 20-inch baby are far easier to spot than 2 inches added to someone who is 40 inches tall). More noticeable are the changes that occur in hand-to-eye coordination as the child matures. Three-year-olds lack the grace and coordination in movements that are so obvious in a 6-year-old. The brain also continues to mature, although again at a pace far slower than during prenatal development or during the first two years of life. There is also good evidence to suggest that general processing speed—how quickly people think and react to sudden changes in their environment—increases consistently throughout childhood (Kail, 1991; Kail & Salthouse, 1994).

Between the end of childhood and the beginning of young adulthood lies an important physical and psychological transition period called *adolescence*. Physically, the two most dramatic changes that occur during this time are the adolescent *growth spurt* and the onset of **puberty,** or sexual maturity (the word *puberty* is from the Latin for "to grow hairy"). As with crawling and walking, it's not possible to pinpoint the timing of these changes exactly, particularly for a specific individual, but changes usually start occurring for girls at around age 11 and for boys at about 13. Hormones released by the endocrine system rock them out of childhood by triggering a rapid increase in height and weight accompanied by the enlargement and maturation of internal and external sexual organs.

Maturing Sexually

Puberty is the developmental period during which individuals mature sexually and acquire the ability to reproduce. For the adolescent female, high levels of *estrogen* in the body lead to external changes, such as breast development and broadening hips, and eventually to the beginning of *menarche* (the first menstrual flow) at around age 12 or 13. For boys, hormones called *androgens* are released, leading to the appearance of facial hair, a lower voice, and the ability to ejaculate (release semen) at around age 13 or 14. Neither the initial appearance of menarche nor the first ejaculation necessarily means that the adolescent is ready to reproduce—ovulation and sperm production may not occur until months later—but psychologically these "firsts" tend to be highly memorable and emotional events (Golub, 1992).

puberty
The period during which a person reaches sexual maturity and is potentially capable of producing offspring.

Not all children reach the adolescent growth spurt at the same age. Boys typically lag behind girls by as much as two years.

The onset of puberty is another classic instance of how the master genetic plan interacts with the nurturing effects of the environment. Did you know that the average onset age for menarche has dropped from about 16 in the 1880s to the current 12 to 13? Physically, people are maturing earlier than in past generations, and it's almost certainly not due to genetics. Instead, better nutrition, better living conditions, and improved medical care are responsible for the trend (Tanner, 1990). Even today, in parts of the world where living conditions are difficult, the average age of menarche is later than in industrialized countries such as the United States (Chumlea, 1982). Although the environment does not cause sexual maturation—that's controlled by the genetic code—the environment modulates the expression of the code, either accelerating or delaying the point when changes start to occur (Graber et al., 1995).

REACHING ADULTHOOD

The adolescent years are marked by dramatic changes in appearance and strength. Motor skills, including hand-to-eye coordination, improve to adult levels during the teenage years. As you're undoubtedly aware, there are world-class swimmers and tennis players who are barely into their teens. The brain reaches adult weight by about age 16, although the myelination of the neurons—so critical in early motor development—continues throughout the adolescent years (Benes, 1989; Benes et al., 1994). The continued maturation of the brain can also be seen in the gradual quickening of reaction times that occurs throughout adolescence (Kail, 1991).

When do individuals actually cross the threshold to adulthood? That's a difficult question to answer because becoming an adult is, in some sense, a state of mind. There are differences in how the transition from adolescent to adult is defined across the world. Some cultures have specific rites of passage and others do not. And, as you know, not all adolescents are willing to accept the socially defined responsibilities of adulthood at the appropriate time. But by the time people reach their twenties, they are physically mature and at the height of their physical prowess.

The Aging Body

It's barely noticeable at the time, but most people begin slowly and steadily to decline physically, at least with respect to their peak levels of strength and agility, at some point during their twenties. Unfortunately, the loss tends to be across the board, which means that it applies to virtually all physical functions, from strength to respiration rate to the heart's pumping capacity (Whitbourne, 1985). Individual differences occur in the rate of decline, of course, depending on such factors as exercise, illness, and heredity (I'm sure you can think of a 40-year-old who is in better physical shape than a 25-year-old). But wrinkles, age spots, sagging flesh, and loss of muscle tone are all reliable and expected parts of the aging process.

By about age 50, the average woman begins **menopause,** the period during which the menstrual cycle slows down and finally stops. Ovulation also stops, so women at this point lose the ability to bear children. These events are caused by hormonal changes, in particular by a decline in the level of female hormones in the body. Despite what you might have heard, menopause is not disruptive for all women, either physically or psychologically (McKinlay et al., 1992). The main physical symptoms, such as hot flashes, can be controlled by hormone replacement therapy, and the idea that the majority of women undergo a sustained period of depression or crankiness is simply a myth (Matthews, 1992). Men do not experience "male menopause" because they never menstruate, although some men do lose the ability to father children in their later years because of a decline in the production or activity of their sperm. The loss in reproductive capacity, expressed by the term *climacteric* (meaning "critical time"), does not occur in all men.

Strenuous daily exercise programs, such as those practiced by Olympic athletes, can delay the onset of puberty.

CRITICAL THINKING

How might you test the idea that mental activity or exercise helps to counteract the decline in mental skills that occurs with age? Can you make predictions based on choice of profession? Should people who choose intellectually challenging professions show less mental decline with age?

menopause
The period during which a woman's menstrual cycle slows down and finally stops.

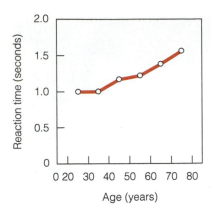

Age and Reaction Time
This figure shows how average reaction time changes between age 20 and age 80 for a cognitive task requiring subjects to match numbers with symbols on a computer screen. Although there is a gradual quickening of reaction time from childhood through adolescence, after age 20 reaction time gradually slows. (Based on Salthouse, 1994.)

dementia
Physically based losses in mental functioning.

The Aging Brain

With age, the brain undergoes significant physical changes. Some individuals suffer brain degeneration—the loss of brain cells—which can lead to senility and, in some cases, to a disabling condition called Alzheimer's disease. But the good news is that the majority of older people never experience these problems; fewer than 1% of people at age 65 are afflicted with **dementia,** the technical name for physically based loss in mental functioning. Although that percentage may rise to as much as 20% for individuals over age 80 (Cavanaugh, 1993), significant losses in mental functioning or mental health are still the exception rather than the rule. The bad news is that everyone loses brain cells with age—the extent of the loss depends on the particular site in the brain (Kemper, 1994; Selkoe, 1992)—and associated declines occur in certain kinds of memory, sensory abilities, and reaction time, as shown in Figure 4.5 (Cavanaugh, 1993; Salthouse, 1994). (Later in this chapter, we'll take a closer look at how memory changes with age.)

The physical changes that occur in the aging brain may not be all bad, however. Neurons are lost, and the loss is apparently permanent, but the remaining neurons may in some instances increase in complexity. In a famous autopsy study by Buell and Coleman (1979), it was found that dendrites were significantly longer and more complex in samples of normal brain tissue taken from elderly adults when compared to those of middle-aged adults (see Figure 4.6). It appears that the brain may compensate for the losses it experiences by making better use of the structures that remain intact. Some researchers have even argued that sustained mental activity in later years may help promote neural growth, thereby counteracting some of the normal decline in mental skills (Black et al., 1991; Coleman & Flood, 1987; Mirmiran et al., 1996). This conclusion is still somewhat speculative, but there does seem to be general agreement that adaptive changes in the brain can occur even in the later stages of the aging process.

FIGURE 4.6

Aging Neurons
Samples of hippocampal neurons taken from people in their fifties, seventies, and nineties, and from adults afflicted with Alzheimer's disease. Notice that the dendrites of the samples actually increase in length and complexity from the fifties to seventies, declining only in late old age or in Alzheimer's disease.

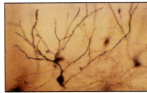

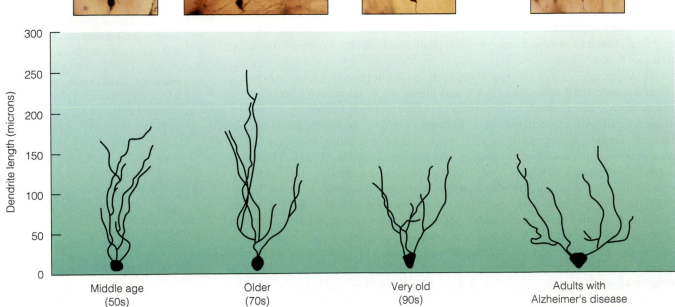

Developing Intellectually

Throughout a person's lifetime, the connections among neurons in the brain are continually changing. New pathways are formed and others are abandoned in response to environmental experiences. The brain's *plasticity*—the ability to change and adjust its connections—is extremely adaptive, especially during the early years of development. Because there is no way for the master genetic plan to predict the environments that a person will encounter after birth, it builds in an intrinsic capacity for change.

    As the brain changes physically in response to the environment, so too do the characteristics of the mind that are of main interest to psychologists. Infants are not born seeing and thinking about the world as adults do. Cognitive processes—how individuals think and perceive—develop over time. As with learning to walk, intellectual development depends on adequate physical maturation within the brain as well as on exposure to the right kinds of experiences. In this section, we'll consider three aspects of intellectual development: How do children learn to perceive and remember the world? How do thought processes change with age? How do individuals develop a sense of right and wrong?

THE TOOLS OF INVESTIGATION

What does the world look like to a newborn child? Is it a complex three-dimensional world, full of depth, color, and texture? Or is it a "blooming, buzzing confusion," as claimed by the early psychologist William James? Let's stop for a moment and think about how a psychologist might answer these questions. Deciphering the perceptual capabilities of an infant is not a simple matter. Babies can't tell us what they see, nor can they move around in ways that allow us to figure out what they see (that is, by avoiding some things and knocking into others).

    Because infants don't communicate as adults do, the analysis of perceptual development requires a researcher to show considerable creativity in his or her methods. It's necessary to devise a way to infer perceptual capabilities from what are essentially immobile, largely uncommunicative infants. Fortunately, babies possess several characteristics that make the job a little easier: (1) they show *preferences*, which means they prefer some stimuli over others; (2) they notice *novelty*, which means they notice new or different things in their environment; and (3) they can *learn* to repeat activities that produce some kind of reward. As you'll see

FIGURE 4.7
The Preference Technique
Babies prefer some visual stimuli over others. In this case, a preverbal infant is demonstrating a preference for a female face by tracking its location across trials. The preference can be determined by simply recording how long the baby looks at each face.

In research by Carolyn Rovee-Collier, infants learn that leg kicking can produce movement of a mobile hanging overhead.

 CRITICAL THINKING

If you were to design a blueprint for a living thing, why do you think it would be important to build in natural preferences?

habituation
The decline in responsiveness to repeated stimulation; habituation has been used as an effective tool to map out the perceptual capabilities of infants.

shortly, researchers have developed techniques that capitalize on each of these tendencies.

The Preference Technique

In the "preference technique" developed by Robert Fantz (1961), an infant is presented with two visual displays simultaneously and the investigator simply records how long the infant looks at each (see Figure 4.7). Suppose that one of the displays shows a male face, the other a female face, and the baby looks at the female face for a significantly longer period of time. By "choosing" to look longer at the female face, the infant has shown a preference. By itself, this preference indicates very little. To infer things about what the baby can really see, it's necessary to present the same two displays a number of times, switching their relative positions from trial to trial. If the baby continues to look longer at the female face even though it appears on the left on some trials and on the right on others, we can infer that the baby has the visual capability to tell the difference between the two displays. The infant "tells" us that he or she can detect differences by exclusively tracking the female face. Notice that we didn't need to ask the baby anything—we simply inferred things about his or her visual system by measuring overt behavior.

Habituation Techniques

One of the preferences babies consistently show is for novelty—they like to look at new things. But, they tend to ignore events that occur repeatedly in their environment without consequence. For instance, if you show newborns a blue-colored card and track how their eyes move (or how their heart rate changes), you'll find that they spend a lot of time looking at the card when it first appears—it's something new. But if you present the same card over and over again, their interest wanes, and they'll begin to look at something else. This decline in responsiveness to repeated stimulation, called **habituation**, provides an effective tool for researchers seeking to map out the infant's perceptual world (Bornstein, 1992; Colombo et al., 1997; Flavel et al., 1993). By acting bored, which is defined operationally by how long they look at the card, babies reveal that they remember the stimulus from its previous presentation and recognize that it hasn't changed. It's as if the baby is saying, "Oh, it's that blue card again."

Habituation can be used to discover specific information about how babies perceive and remember their worlds (DeSaint et al., 1997; Granrud, 1993). For example, suppose we wanted to discover whether newborns have the capacity to perceive color. We could show the blue card for a while, then suddenly switch to a green card that matches on all other visual dimensions (such as size and brightness). If the infant shows renewed interest in the card—treating the stimulus as if it was novel—we can infer that the baby can discriminate, or tell the difference, between blue and green. If, on the other hand, the baby continues to ignore the new green card, it suggests that perhaps the baby lacks color vision at this stage in development. We can also study memory by varying the time that elapses between presentations of the card. If the baby continues to act bored by the blue card even though we insert long pauses between successive presentations, we know that he or she is remembering the card over those particular time intervals.

Using Rewards

A researcher can also gain insight into what a baby sees, knows, and remembers by *rewarding* a simple motor movement, such as kicking a leg or sucking on an artificial nipple, in the presence of particular kinds of events (Siqueland & DeLucia, 1969). For example, in research by Carolyn Rovee-Collier (1993), 2- and 3-month-old infants were taught that kicking their legs could produce movement of a crib mobile hanging overhead. A moving mobile is quite rewarding to babies at this age, and they'll double or triple their rate of leg kicking in a matter of minutes if it leads to movement. We can then study cognitive abilities—such as memory—by taking the mobile away, waiting for some period of time, and then replacing the mobile. If the baby begins leg kicking again at rates comparable to those produced at the end of training, we can infer that the baby has remembered what he or she has learned. We can also change the characteristics of the mobile after training and learn things about a baby's perceptual abilities. For example, if we train an infant with a blue mobile and then switch to a green one, any differences in leg kicking should help to tell us whether the baby can discriminate between green and blue.

THE GROWING PERCEPTUAL WORLD

Based on the use of techniques such as those discussed above, researchers have discovered that babies greet the world with sensory systems that function reasonably well. Although none of these systems is operating at peak efficiency, because their biological equipment is still maturing, babies still see a world of color and shape (Banks & Shannon, 1993). They even arrive with built-in preferences for some colors and shapes. One-day-old babies, for example, respond more to patterned stimuli than to unpatterned ones; as shown in Figure 4.8, they even prefer to look

FIGURE 4.8

Infant Preferences

In the experiment by Johnson and colleagues (1991), babies were shown either a blank stimulus, a stimulus with scrambled facial features, or a face. Each stimulus was positioned over the baby's head and then moved from side to side. The dependent variable measured the extent to which the baby tracked each stimulus by turning his or her head and eyes. As the results show, the babies tracked the face stimulus more than the others. (Graph adapted from Johnson et al., 1991.)

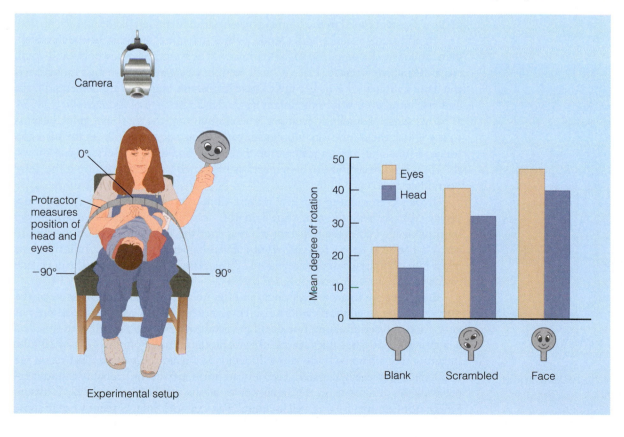

Distinctive reactions to a variety of tastes—such as the ones shown here to lemon, sugar, and salt—have been found in infants immediately after birth.

at correctly drawn faces rather than scrambled faces with features placed in incorrect positions (Johnson et al., 1991; see also Walton & Bower, 1993). Learning, or experience, may play a role in some of these preferences, but it's clear that reasonably sophisticated perceptual processing can occur rapidly after birth.

Newborns also hear reasonably well, and they seem to recognize their mothers' voice within a day or two after birth (DeCasper & Fifer, 1980). Remarkably, there is evidence to suggest that newborns can even hear and remember things that happen *prior* to birth. By the twenty-eighth week, fetuses will close their eyes in response to loud noises presented near the mother's abdomen (Parmelee & Sigman, 1983). Infants will also choose to suck on an artificial nipple that produces a recording of a story that was read aloud to them repeatedly before birth (DeCasper & Spence, 1986). If you think about it, you'll realize that this is an adaptive quality for the newborn to possess. Remember, the newborn needs nourishment and is dependent on others for survival. Consequently, babies who are born into the world with a visual system that can detect shapes and forms and an auditory system tuned to the human voice have an increased likelihood of survival.

In addition to sights and sounds, babies are quite sensitive to touch, smell, pain, and taste. Place a drop of lemon juice in the mouth of a newborn, and you'll see a distinctive grimace. Place a small amount of sugar in the baby's mouth, and the baby will smack his or her lips. These distinctive reactions are present at birth and are found even before the infant has had a single taste of food (Steiner, 1977). A baby's sense of smell is developed well enough that the newborn quickly learns to recognize the odor of its mother's breast (Porter et al., 1992). As for pain and touch, babies will reject a milk bottle that is too hot, and, as every parent knows, the right kind of pat on the baby's back is pleasurable enough to soothe the newborn into sleep.

Babies even seem to perceive a three-dimensional world. When placed on a visual cliff, such as the one shown in the accompanying photo, at roughly 6 months of age babies are reluctant to cross over the apparent drop-off, or cliff, to reach a parent (Gibson & Walk, 1960). Even babies as young as 2 months show heart rate changes when they're placed on the glass portion covering the deep side of the visual cliff (Campos et al., 1970).

But these are infant perceptions, and the infant's world is not the same as the one viewed by an adult. Newborn babies cannot see as well as adults. They're not very good at discriminating fine detail in visual patterns: Compared with the ideal acuity level of 20/20, babies see a blurry world that is more on the order of 20/600, meaning that what newborns see at 20 feet is like what adults with ideal vision see at 600 feet (Banks & Salapatek, 1983). In addition, newborns probably cannot perceive shapes and forms in the same way as adults do (Bornstein, 1992; Johnson, 1997), nor can they hear as well as adults. For example, infants seem to have some

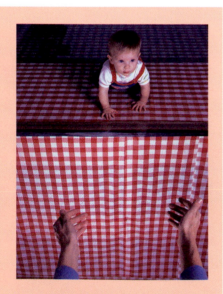

In the visual cliff apparatus, a plate of glass covers the drop-off or "cliff." Beginning at roughly 6 months of age, babies are reluctant to cross over to reach a beckoning parent.

trouble listening selectively for certain kinds of sounds, and infants need sounds to be louder than adults do before they can be detected (Bargones & Werner, 1994).

Infants' perceptual systems improve markedly during the first few months, partly because of continued physical development but also because experience plays a role in the fine-tuning of sensory abilities. Research with nonhuman subjects, such as cats or chimpanzees, has shown that if animals are deprived of visual stimulation during the early weeks or months of life, permanent visual impairments can result (Gandelman, 1992). Thus, perceptual development relies on experience as well as on physically mature sensory equipment.

By the time we leave infancy, our perceptual systems are reasonably intact. Most of the changes that occur during childhood and adolescence deal with the ability to *use* the equipment we have. For example, as children grow older their attention span improves and they are better able to attend selectively to pertinent information. Memory improves throughout childhood, partly because kids learn strategies for organizing and maintaining information in memory. Moreover, as you'll see in Chapters 5 and 8, the way individuals perceive and remember the world depends on what they know about the way the world works. We use our general knowledge about people and events to help us interpret ambiguous stimuli and to remember things that happen in our lives. Perception and memory are influenced by the knowledge gained from experience, which is one of the reasons why perceptual development is really a lifelong process.

DO WE LOSE MEMORY WITH AGE?

What happens to memory as we age? Is there an inevitable decline in the ability to remember? It's quite common for the elderly to report memory problems, such as increased forgetfulness, but there is no simple or straightforward relationship between aging and memory. Some kinds of memory falter badly with age, but other kinds do not. For example, psychologists are now reasonably convinced that the ability to *recall* recent events, such as items from a grocery list, declines with age. However, in certain tests of *recognition*, in which information is re-presented and the task is to tell whether one has seen it before, little or no differences in memory ability are found between the young and the elderly (see Kausler, 1994; Parkin, 1993).

Researchers who study the developmental process typically conduct research using what are called *longitudinal* or *cross-sectional* research designs. In a **longitudinal design,** the same individuals are tested repeatedly over time, at various points in childhood or even on through adulthood. In a **cross-sectional design,** which is conducted over a limited span of time, researchers directly compare performance on some task among *different* people of different ages. For example, Craik and McDowd (1987) used a cross-sectional design to compare recall and recognition performance for two age groups: a "young" group of college students, with an average age of 20.7 years, and an "old" group, volunteers from a senior citizen center, with an average age of 72.8 years. All of the participants were asked to learn memory lists that consisted of short phrases ("a body of water") presented together with associated target words ("pond"). The lists were followed by either (1) an immediate recall test in which the short phrase was given and the subject needed to recall the target word, or (2) a delayed recognition test that required the subjects to decide whether a word had or had not been presented in one of the earlier lists.

In such experiments, attempts are made to match the participants on as many variables as possible—such as educational level and verbal ability—so that the only difference between the groups is *age*. Any performance differences can then be attributed uniquely to the independent variable (age) and not to some other confounding factor (see Chapter 2). The results of the Craik and McDowd (1987) study are shown in Figure 4.9. As you can see, the young subjects outperformed

longitudinal design
A research design in which the same people are studied or tested repeatedly over time.

cross-sectional design
A research design in which people of different ages are compared at the same time.

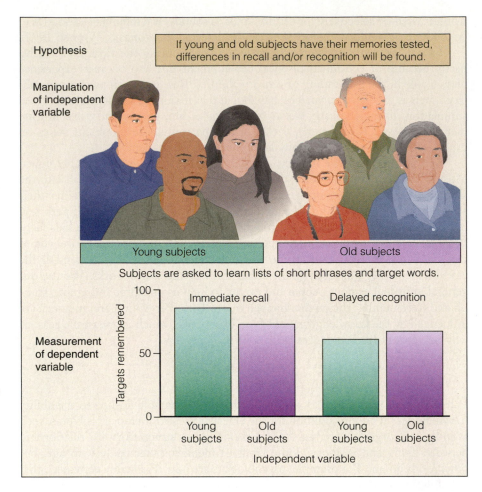

FIGURE 4.9
Memory and Aging
In the study by Craik and McDowd (1987), two groups, one with an average age of 20.7 years and one with an average of 72.8 years, were asked to learn and then recall or recognize target words. Although the "young" subjects recalled more targets than the "old" group, the advantage disappeared for recognition.

the old subjects on the test of recall, but the advantage vanished on the recognition test. Measuring memory loss in the elderly therefore depends on how memory is actually tested. Other studies have shown that performance depends also on the types of materials tested. When older subjects are asked to remember materials that fit naturally into their rich knowledge base, they may even perform better than their younger counterparts (Zacks & Hasher, 1994).

Although most people past age 60 or 70 are able to perform well on certain kinds of memory tests, it is still the case that older people perform quite poorly on some kinds of memory tasks, especially those that require recall. Researchers are actively trying to determine why these memory deficits occur. One possibility is that older adults lose the ability to suppress irrelevant thoughts or ignore irrelevant stimuli (Hasher et al., 1991). Because they are unable to focus selectively on the task at hand, they fail to process the to-be-remembered information in ways

CONCEPT SUMMARY
Research Designs for Studying Development

Type of Design	Overview	Advantages and Disadvantages
Cross-sectional	Researchers compare performance of *different* people of different ages.	A: Faster, more practical than longitudinal. D: Other variables may be *confounded* with age.
Longitudinal	Researchers test the *same* individuals repeatedly over time.	A: Can examine changes in *individuals*. D: Cost-intensive; subject loss over time.

that are conducive to later recall (Craik, 1994). As you'll see in Chapter 8, memory depends greatly on the kinds of mental processing that occur during initial study.

PIAGET AND THE DEVELOPMENT OF THOUGHT

The close connection between what we see and what we know explains why it's difficult for researchers to get a good grasp on how infants *truly* perceive the world. It might be possible for a researcher to demonstrate that a newborn can tell the difference between a purring kitten and a block of wood, but does this mean that the infant really sees what we know of as a *cat*? Babies might coo and smile to the rhythmic sound of music on the radio, but is their internal experience anything close to that of an adult? In some sense, these are philosophical questions rather than scientific ones, but it's important to recognize that it's not easy to talk about a baby's ability to perceive or remember without knowing something about how a baby thinks.

Much of what we know about how thought processes develop during childhood comes from the collective works of a Swiss scholar named Jean Piaget (1929, 1952, 1970). It was Piaget who first convinced psychologists that children think quite differently than adults. Children are not little adults, he argued, who simply lack knowledge and experience; instead, they view the world in a very unique and idiosyncratic way. Piaget believed that everyone is born with a natural tendency to organize the world meaningfully. People construct mental models of the world—called **schemata**—and use these schemata to guide and interpret their experiences. But these schemata are not very adultlike early in development—in fact, they tend not to reflect the true world accurately—so much of early intellectual development is spent changing and fine-tuning our worldviews. One of Piaget's primary contributions was to demonstrate that children's reasoning errors can provide a window into how the schema construction process is proceeding.

Jean Piaget interacts with a group of children in a classroom.

For example, consider the two tilted cups shown at right. If young children are asked to draw a line indicating how the water level in a tilted cup might look, they tend to draw a line that is parallel to the top and bottom of the cup, as shown in the cup on the left, rather than parallel to the ground, as shown in the cup on the right. This kind of error is important, Piaget argued, because children can't have learned such a thing directly from experience (water never tilts that way in real life). Instead, the error reflects a fundamental misconception of how the world is structured. Young children simply have an internal view, or model, of the world that is inaccurate.

Assimilation and Accommodation

As their brains and bodies mature, children are able to use experience to build more sophisticated and correct mental models of the world. Piaget suggested that this process of cognitive development is guided by two adaptive psychological processes: **assimilation** and **accommodation.** Assimilation is the process through which people fit—or assimilate—new experiences into their existing schemata. For example, suppose a small child who has been raised in a household full of cats mistakenly concludes that the neighbor's new rabbit is simply a kind of kitty. The new experience—the rabbit—has been assimilated into the child's existing view of the world: Small furry things are *cats*. The second function, accommodation, is the process through which one changes or modifies existing schemata to accommodate new experiences when they occur. When the child learns that the new "kitty" hops rather than walks and seems reluctant to purr, he or she will need to modify and revise the existing concept of small furry things; the child is forced to change the existing scheme to accommodate the new

schemata
Mental models of the world that people use to guide and interpret their experiences.

assimilation
The process through which people fit—or assimilate—new experiences into existing schemata.

accommodation
The process through which people change or modify existing schemata to accommodate new experiences when they occur.

CONCEPT SUMMARY
Piaget's Stages of Cognitive Development

Stage	Basic Characteristics	Accomplishments	Limitations
Sensorimotor period (birth–2 years)	Schemata about the world revolve primarily around sensory and motor abilities.	Child develops **object permanence**; learns how to control body; learns how to vocalize, and learns first words.	Schemata are limited primarily to simple sensory and motor function; problems in thinking about absent objects (early).
Preoperational period (2–7 years)	Schemata grow in sophistication. Children can think about absent objects, and can use one object to stand for another.	Children readily symbolize objects, and imaginary play is common; great strides in language development.	Children are pre-logical; they fail to understand **conservation**, due to **centration** and a failure to understand **reversibility**; children show **egocentricity** in thinking.
Concrete operational period (7–11 years)	Children gain the capacity for *true* mental operation, i.e., verbalizing, visualizing, mental manipulation.	Understand reversibility and other simple logical operations like categorizing and ordering.	Mental operations remain *concrete,* tied to actual objects in the real world. Difficulty with problems that do not flow from everyday experience.
Formal operational period (11 years–adulthood)	Mastery is gained over *abstract* thinking.	Adolescents can think and answer questions in general and abstract ways.	No limitations; development of reasoning is complete. However, not all reach this stage.

information. Notice that the child plays an active role in constructing schemata by interacting directly with the world (Piaget, 1929).

Piaget believed that children develop an adult worldview by proceeding systematically through a series of four stages or developmental periods: *sensorimotor, preoperational, concrete operational,* and *formal operational.* Each of these periods is tied roughly to a particular age range—for example, the preoperational period usually lasts from age 2 to about age 7—but individual differences may occur in how quickly children progress from one period to the next. Although the timing may vary from child to child, Piaget believed that the *order* in which individuals progress through the stages is invariant—it remains the same for everyone. Let's consider these cognitive developmental periods in more detail.

Some people might have trouble assimilating these objects into their existing schemata for objects in a room.

THE SENSORIMOTOR PERIOD: BIRTH TO TWO YEARS

From birth to about age 2, schemata about the world revolve primarily around the infant's sensory and motor abilities (hence the name **sensorimotor period**). Babies initially interact with the world through a collection of survival reflexes. For example, they'll start sucking when an object is placed in their mouth (called the *sucking reflex*), and they'll automatically turn their head in the direction of a touch or brush on the cheek (called the *rooting reflex*). In an important sense, this means that when an object comes into a newborn's view, that object is interpreted in terms of how it can be sucked. Of course, this behavior is far different from an adult's, but it's *adaptive* for a newborn. These reflexes increase the likelihood that adequate nourishment will follow, and attaining adequate nourishment is a significant problem the newborn needs to solve.

Object Permanence

sensorimotor period
Piaget's first stage of cognitive development, lasting from birth to about 2 years of age; schemata revolve around sensory and motor abilities.

As infants develop intellectually over the first year, they begin to use their maturing motor skills to help them understand how they can voluntarily interact with the world. Babies start to vocalize to gain attention; they learn that they can kick their legs to make sounds; they acquire the ability to reach with their arms to touch or grasp objects. The initial stirrings of symbolic thought also begin during

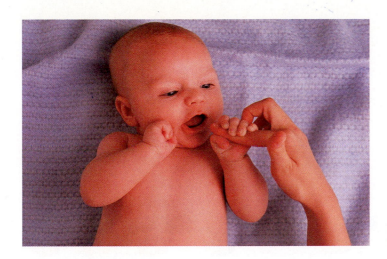

The rooting reflex is adaptive because it helps the newborn receive needed sustenance.

the sensorimotor period. The infant gradually develops the ability to represent things internally as mental images or symbols. Early in the first year, for example, babies lack **object permanence,** which means that they fail to recognize that objects exist when they're no longer in sight. The adjacent photos illustrate how psychologists have measured object permanence. Notice that the baby loses interest when the toy is covered, suggesting that the baby is only capable of thinking about objects that are directly in view. Babies at this point are unable to represent objects symbolically—out of sight equals out of mind. But by the end of the first year, Piaget argued, the child has a different reaction to the disappearance of a favored toy; as object permanence develops, the child will begin to search actively for the lost toy.

According to Piaget, until object permanence develops, babies fail to understand that objects still exist when they're no longer in view. Notice how this boy loses interest when he can no longer see his favorite toy.

THE PREOPERATIONAL PERIOD: TWO TO SEVEN YEARS

From about ages 2 through 7, the child's schemata continue to grow in sophistication. Children in the **preoperational period** no longer have difficulty thinking about absent objects, and they can use one sort of object to stand for another. A 4-year-old, for example, can effortlessly use a stick to represent a soaring airplane or a cardboard box for a stove. The child realizes that these are not the real objects, but he or she can imagine them to be real for the purposes of play. However, as Piaget demonstrated in a number of clever ways, the child still thinks about the world quite differently from an adult. As you'll see momentarily, the child lacks the ability to perform certain basic mental *operations*—hence Piaget's use of the term *preoperational* to describe a child's mental abilities during this period.

Conservation

Something that children at the preoperational stage often fail to understand is the principle of conservation. To understand **conservation,** one needs to be able to recognize that the physical properties of an object can remain the same despite superficial changes in its appearance (see Figure 4.10). If 4- or 5-year-old children are shown two playdough balls of exactly the same size and we ask them which object contains more playdough, most of the children will say that the two balls contain the same amount. But if one of the balls is then rolled into a long sausage-like shape, the children are likely to think that the two quantities of playdough are no longer the same, saying that either the sausage or the ball has more playdough. Children at this age simply do not understand that a basic property of an object, in this case its mass, doesn't change as the object changes shape.

Typically, preoperational children will fail to conserve a basic quantity even if they directly *observe* the change in appearance taking place. Suppose that we ask 5-year-old Sam to pour a cup of water into each of two identical glasses. Sam performs the task and accepts that the two glasses now contain the same amount

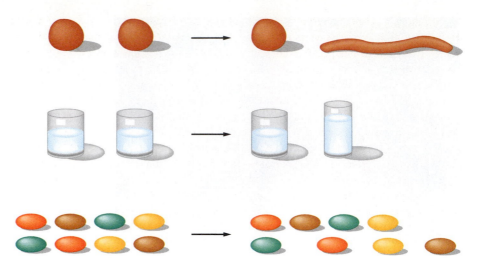

FIGURE 4.10

Examples of Conservation Problems
Understanding conservation means recognizing that the physical properties of objects remain the same even though the objects may superficially change in appearance. Preoperational children often fail conservation problems—they fail to detect, for example, that the objects to the right of the arrows still retain the same volume or number.

of water. We then instruct him to pour the water from one of the glasses into another glass that is tall and thin. Do the glasses now contain the same amount of water? "No," Sam explains, "now the tall one has more water." Sam is not showing any evidence of conservation; he does not yet recognize that how the water looks in the glass has no effect on its volume.

The reason children in the preoperational period make these kinds of errors, Piaget argued, is that they still lack the capacity to think in truly adultlike ways. For example, preoperational children suffer from *centration*—they tend to focus their attention on one particular aspect of a situation and to ignore other aspects. Sam is convinced that the tall glass has more water because he cannot simultaneously consider both the height and width of the glass; he focuses only on the height and therefore is convinced that the taller glass must contain more water. In addition, children at this age have a tough time understanding *reversibility*—they don't understand that one kind of operation can produce change and that another kind of operation can undo that change. For example, Sam is unlikely to consider what will happen if the water from the tall glass is poured back into the original glass. The capacity to understand that operations are reversible doesn't develop until the next stage.

Egocentrism

Piaget also discovered that children in the preoperational period tend to see the world, and the objects in it, from primarily one perspective: their own. Children at this stage have a tough time imagining themselves in another person's position. If you ask a child in the preoperational period to describe what another person will see or think, you're likely to find the child simply describing what he or she personally sees or thinks. Piaget called this characteristic **egocentrism**—the tendency to view the world from your own unique perspective only.

THE CONCRETE OPERATIONAL PERIOD: SEVEN TO ELEVEN YEARS

Between the ages of 7 and about 11, children enter the **concrete operational period** and gain the capacity for true mental *operations*. By mental operations, Piaget meant the ability to perform mental actions on objects—to verbalize, visualize, and mentally manipulate objects. A child of 8 can consider the consequences of rolling a long strip of playdough into a ball before the action is actually performed. The result is that children in the concrete operational period have fewer difficulties with conservation problems because they are capable of reversing operations on objects—they can mentally consider the effects of both doing and undoing an action.

egocentrism
The tendency to see the world from your own unique perspective only, a characteristic of thinking in the preoperational period of development.

concrete operational period
Piaget's third stage of cognitive development, lasting from ages 7 to 11. Children acquire the capacity to perform a number of mental operations but still lack the ability for abstract reasoning.

Children at the concrete operational stage also show the initial stirrings of logical thought, which means they can now mentally order and compare objects and perform more sophisticated classifications. These children can do simple math problems and solve problems that require elementary reasoning. Consider a problem such as the following: Martin is faster than Jose; Jose is faster than Conrad. Is Martin faster or slower than Conrad? Children of 9 or 10 have little trouble with this problem because they can keep track of ordered relations in their heads. Younger preoperational children will probably insist on actually seeing Martin and Conrad race—they cannot easily solve the problem in their heads.

Although concrete operational children possess a growing array of mental operations, Piaget believed that they are still limited intellectually in an important way. The mental operations they can perform remain *concrete*, or tied directly to actual objects in the real world. Children at this age have great difficulty with problems that do not flow directly from everyday experience. Ask an 8-year-old to solve a problem involving four-armed people and barking cats and you're likely to see a blank look on his or her face. Basically, if something can't be seen, heard, touched, tasted, or smelled, it's not going to be something that concrete operational children can easily consider in their heads (although these children can imagine non-real world objects they have encountered, for example, in cartoons or fairy tales). The ability to think truly abstractly doesn't develop until the final stage of cognitive development.

The Formal Operational Period: Eleven to Adulthood

Piaget repeatedly stressed the idea that children tend to think differently from adults. Children's schemata, or mental models of the world, are limited because they lack the proper amounts of biological maturation and experience. These limitations in turn lead to errors in reasoning or judgment, although the child's view of the world can be adaptive for solving the particular problems that children face (as when a baby's viewing of an object as something to be sucked increases the likelihood of obtaining nourishment). But by the time children reach their teenage years, most will be in the formal operational period, during which their thought processes become increasingly more like those of an adult. Neither teenagers nor adults have problems thinking about imaginary or artificial concepts; they can consider hypothetical outcomes, or make logical deductions about places they've never visited or that might not even exist. Teenagers as well as adults can develop systematic strategies for solving problems—such as using trial and error—that are beyond the capability of most preteens.

The formal operational period, which most people reach by their teenage years, is when mastery over abstract thinking is gained.

CRITICAL THINKING

Do you think Piaget's insights about cognitive development have any implications for education? For example, should teachers be giving first- and second-grade children abstract math problems to solve?

The **formal operational period** is the stage in which individuals start to gain mastery over *abstract* thinking. Ask a concrete operational child about the meaning of education, and you'll be likely to hear about teachers and grades. The formal operational adolescent is able to answer the question in a general and abstract way, perhaps describing education as a system organized by parents and the government to foster the acquisition of useful knowledge. Piaget believed that the transition from concrete operational thinking to formal operational thinking probably occurs gradually, over several years, and may not be achieved by everyone (Piaget, 1970). Once it is reached, the adolescent is no longer tied to concrete real-world constructs and can invent and experiment with the possible rather than with the here and now alone.

CHALLENGES TO PIAGET'S THEORY

Most psychologists agree that Piaget's contributions to the understanding of cognitive development have been substantial. He successfully convinced the psychological community that children have unique internal schemata, and he provided convincing demonstrations that those schemata, once formed, tend to change systematically over time. However, not all of Piaget's ideas have withstood the rigors of experimental scrutiny. It's now common for researchers to challenge the specifics of his theory, primarily his assumptions about what children really know and when they know it.

It now seems clear that Piaget was simply wrong in some of his conclusions about the young child's mental capabilities. Children and young infants are considerably more sophisticated in their models of the world than Piaget believed (Flavel et al., 1993; Kuhn, 1992; Spelke, 1991). For example, Piaget was convinced that object permanence doesn't develop until late in the child's first year. Although it's true that children will not search for a hidden toy in the first few months of life, more sensitive tests have revealed that even 1- to 4-month-old infants are capable of recognizing that vanished objects still exist.

In research by child psychologist T. G. R. Bower (1982), very young infants watched as a screen was moved in front of a toy, blocking it from view (see Figure 4.11). Moments later, when the screen was removed, the infants acted surprised if the toy was absent (it could be secretly removed by the experimenter). If objects no longer exist when removed from view, then infants shouldn't be surprised by a sudden absence (see also Baillargeon, 1994; Hofstadter & Reznick, 1996). Other researchers have demonstrated that small infants can show symbolic thought—they understand, for instance, that objects move along continuous paths and do not jump around—and they gain this understanding at points in development far earlier than Piaget imagined (see Mandler, 1992; Spelke et al., 1992).

Problems with the Stage View

Piaget has also been criticized for sticking to the notion of distinct *stages*, or periods of development (Flavel et al., 1993). Piaget recognized that not all children develop cognitively at the same rate, but he remained convinced that a child's thought processes undergo sharp transitions from one qualitative stage to the next. Most modern developmental psychologists believe that cognitive development is better viewed as a process of continual change and adaptation (Siegler, 1996). If we adopted a stage view, as Piaget did, we should expect that once the child undergoes a stage transition—say, from the preoperational stage to the concrete operational stage—the child should relatively quickly show the capacity to perform a variety of new tasks. But this is not usually the case.

Children's thought processes do not seem to undergo rapid transitions; in fact, they often change slowly over long periods of time (Flavel, 1971). For example, it is not uncommon to find a 5-year-old who understands conservation of number but has no idea about conservation of mass or volume. So, a given child might show mental schemata that are characteristic of more than one stage.

formal operational period
Piaget's last stage of cognitive development; thought processes become adultlike, and people gain mastery over abstract thinking.

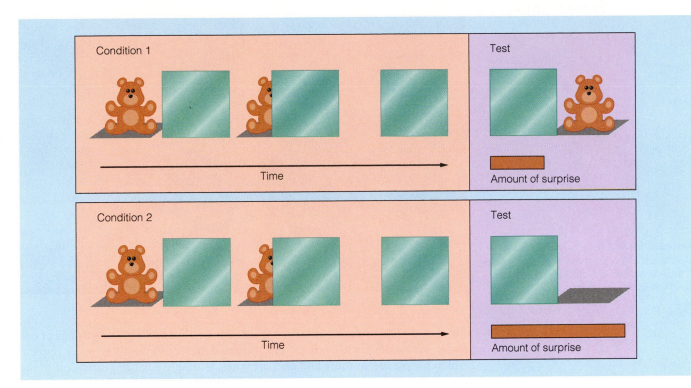

Children in nomadic societies move frequently from place to place and may be able to orient themselves in an environment faster and more efficiently than children raised in fixed locales.

Children are learning to adapt to their world, and to tasks and problems that might occur only in particular situations. So it's not surprising that they act in ways that are difficult to fit into any specific cognitive stage, or that the transitions from one developmental point to the next are not rapid and well-defined (Munakata et al., 1997).

The Role of Culture

Piaget was also rather fuzzy about the mechanisms that produce cognitive change. His demonstrations that infants, toddlers, and school-age children think in fundamentally different ways were brilliant, but he never clearly accounted for the psychological processes that produce those changes (Siegler, 1994; 1996). He also tended to ignore the importance of social context in explaining individual differences in cognitive ability. Cross-cultural research has shown that children across the world develop cognitively in similar ways, but significant cultural differences occur in the rate of development (Matsumoto, 1994). For example, children raised in nomadic societies, which move frequently from place to place, seem to acquire spatial skills (the ability to orient themselves in their environment) earlier and better than children raised in single, fixed locales. Schooling may also be a factor: Ample cross-cultural evidence indicates that people who never attend school may have a difficult time reaching the formal operational stage of thinking, at least as measured through the use of traditional Piagetian tasks (Cole, 1992; Segall et al., 1990).

The idea that we cannot fully understand the development of mental processes without considering social and cultural influences was actually promoted by a Russian psychologist, Lev Vygotsky, around the same time that Piaget was developing and fine-tuning his theoretical ideas. Vygotsky died in 1934, after only a decade of work in psychology, but his ideas continue to exert a powerful influence on modern developmental psychologists (Wertsch &

FIGURE 4.11
Reevaluating Object Permanence
In this experiment by T. G. R. Bower, young infants watched as a screen was moved in front of a toy, blocking it from view. Moments later, the screen was removed and the baby's level of "surprise," defined as a change in heart rate, was measured. In one condition, the toy appeared behind the screen; in a second condition, the toy had vanished. Despite their young age, the babies showed more surprise when the toy was absent, suggesting that object permanence may develop earlier than Piaget suspected.

According to Vygotsky, cognitive abilities arise directly out of the social and verbal interactions that children have with other people, including their friends and relatives.

Tulviste, 1992). Vygotsky argued that cognitive abilities emerge *directly* out of our social interactions with others. He proposed, for example, that inner speech, which people use to think and plan activities, is simply a natural extension of the outer speech that people use to communicate with others. Vygotsky was convinced that intellectual development is tied to social interaction—it grows out of each person's attempts to master social situations. This means that we cannot understand development by considering the individual alone—we must always consider the individual in his or her social context (Vygotsky, 1978).

Beyond Formal Operational Thought

Another active area of controversy surrounding Piaget's theory concerns the issue of adult cognitive development. Does intellectual development really end with the acquisition of formal operational thinking at some point during adolescence, as claimed by Piaget? A number of researchers believe that mastery over abstract thought, which is the hallmark of the formal operational period, is only one part of a much more extensive process of adult cognitive development (Cavanaugh, 1993; Commons et al., 1989; Riegel, 1976). There are probably fundamental differences between adolescent and adult thought processes that cannot be explained without the introduction of new, *postformal* stages of cognitive development.

Currently, there is no general consensus about exactly what these postformal thoughts represent. One popular idea is that postformal cognitive development is characterized by *relativistic thinking*. Adults tend to think about "truth" in a much more relative way than teenagers do; adults recognize, for instance, that the correct answer to a moral dilemma might vary from one situation to the next. Adults are also more tolerant of ambiguity in their thinking than teenagers are (although too much ambiguity in thought is obviously a problem). Adolescent thinking is typically rigid and absolute in the sense that teenagers tend to rely on fixed rules of right and wrong and show little intellectual flexibility (Labouvie-Vief et al., 1987; Perry, 1970).

Other researchers have argued that adolescents are also less capable of thinking about *systems* of ideas. Teenagers who have reached the formal operational stage might be able to deal with abstract ideas, but they will have trouble dealing with higher-order systems of ideas of the type found in a scientific theory (Richards & Commons, 1990). Systematic comparisons among ideas, as in the analysis of the similarities and differences among theories, require postformal thought processes. Ironically, many modern developmental psychologists argue that Piaget himself must have been operating at a level of cognitive development beyond the formal operational stage when he developed his own theory.

MORAL DEVELOPMENT: LEARNING RIGHT FROM WRONG

Developing intellectually means more than just learning to think logically and form correct internal models of the world. As children mature intellectually, they also need to develop *character*. They need to acquire a sense of **morality,** which provides them with a way to distinguish among appropriate and inappropriate thoughts and actions. Piaget had strong opinions on this topic, arguing that the sense of morality is closely tied to one's stage of cognitive development and to one's social experiences with peers. For example, from Piaget's perspective children in the concrete operational stage would not be expected to show sophisticated moral reasoning skills, because morality is basically an abstract concept—something that cannot be handled until the formal operational stage of development. Partly for this reason, the tendency has been to conduct most of the research on moral development on adolescents and adults.

Children need to develop a sense of morality, which helps them tell the difference between appropriate and inappropriate actions.

Kohlberg's Stage Theory

The most influential theory of moral development is the stage theory proposed by Lawrence Kohlberg. Strongly influenced by the writings of Piaget, Kohlberg framed his theory around the idea that individuals progress through an orderly series of stages of moral development (Kohlberg, 1963, 1986). His investigative technique was to give people of various ages a hypothetical moral dilemma and use their solutions to identify their current state of moral development. Let's consider an example, based on Kohlberg (1969).

A woman is stricken with a rare and deadly form of cancer. There is a drug that can save her, a form of radium recently discovered by a druggist in town. But the druggist is charging $2000 for the medicine, ten times what the drug cost him to make. The sick woman's husband, Heinz, tries desperately to raise the money but can raise only half of the needed amount. He pleads with the druggist to sell him the drug at a reduced cost, or at least to allow him to pay for the drug over time, but the druggist refuses. "No," the druggist says, "I discovered the drug and I'm going to make money from it." Frantic to save his wife, Heinz considers breaking into the druggist's office to steal the drug.

What do you think? Should the husband steal the drug? Why or why not? You probably have an answer to this dilemma. But your "Yes, he should steal the drug" or "No, that would be wrong" answer is not of main interest to psychologists. Instead, it is the *reasoning* behind your answer, the kind of intellectual justification that you give, that is important to the psychologist. Kohlberg believed that people can be classified into stages of moral development based on the quality of their reasoning about such moral problems. Although Kohlberg's theory actually proposes as many as six stages of moral development, I'll focus on his three main levels only: the *preconventional*, the *conventional*, and the *postconventional* (see the "Concept Summary" table on page 144).

At the lowest level of moral development—the **preconventional level**—decisions about right and wrong are based primarily on external consequences. Young children will typically interpret the morality of a behavior in terms of its immediate individual consequences—that is, whether the act will lead directly to a reward or to a punishment: "Heinz shouldn't steal the drug because he might get caught and punished" or "Heinz should steal the drug because people will get mad

morality
The ability to distinguish between appropriate and inappropriate actions; a child's sense of morality may be tied to his or her level of cognitive development.

preconventional level
In Kohlberg's theory, the lowest level of moral development, in which decisions about right and wrong are made primarily in terms of external consequences.

CONCEPT SUMMARY
Kohlberg's Stage Theory of Moral Development

Stage	Basis for Moral Judgment	Possible Response to "Was Heinz Right?"
Preconventional	External consequences	Yes: "He can't be happy without his wife." No: "If he gets caught, he'll be put in jail."
Conventional	Social order	Yes: "Spouses are responsible for protecting one another." No: "Stealing is against the law."
Postconventional	Abstract ethical principles	Yes: "Individual lives are more important than society's law against stealing." No: "Laws are necessary in a civilized society; they need to be followed by all to prevent chaos."

? CRITICAL THINKING

Based on what you've learned about moral development, what advice would you give parents who are trying to teach their children about right and wrong?

conventional level
In Kohlberg's theory of moral development, the stage in which actions are judged to be right or wrong based on whether they maintain or disrupt the social order.

postconventional level
Kohlberg's highest level of moral development, in which moral actions are judged on the basis of personal codes of ethics that are general and abstract and that may not agree with societal norms.

at him if his wife dies." Notice the rationale is based on the immediate external consequences of the action rather than on some abstract moral principle.

At the **conventional level** of moral reasoning, people start to justify their actions on the basis of internalized rules. Now an action is right or wrong because it maintains or disrupts the *social order*. Someone at this level might argue that Heinz shouldn't steal the drug because stealing is against the law, or that Heinz should steal the drug because husbands have an obligation to protect their wives. Notice here that the moral reasoning has moved away from immediate individual consequences to societal consequences. Moral behavior is that which conforms to the rules and conventions of society. In general, individuals at the conventional level of moral reasoning tend to consider the appropriateness of their actions from the perspective of the resident authority figures in the culture.

At the final level of moral development, the **postconventional level**, morality is based on abstract principles that may even conflict with accepted standards. The individual adopts a moral standard not to seek approval from others or an authority figure but to follow some universal ethical principle. "An individual human life is more important than society's dictum against stealing," someone at this level might argue. In this case, moral actions are driven by general and abstract personal codes of ethics that may not agree with societal norms.

Evaluating Kohlberg's Theory

The idea that we progress through periods of moral development, from an early focus on immediate individual consequences toward a final principled code of ethics, remains popular among many developmental psychologists (see Damon & Hart, 1992). A number of observational studies have confirmed aspects of Kohlberg's views. For example, people do seem to move through the various types of moral reasoning in the sequence suggested by Kohlberg (Walker, 1989). Furthermore, the link that both Piaget and Kohlberg made between moral reasoning and level of cognitive development has clear merit. But Kohlberg's critics argue that his views lack generality because he ties the concept of morality too closely to an abstract code of *justice*—that is, to the idea that moral acts are those that ensure fairness to the individual (Damon & Hart, 1992).

For example, suppose that your sense of morality is not based on fairness but rather on concern for the welfare of others. You might believe that the appropriate action is always one that doesn't hurt anyone and takes into account the happiness of the affected individual. Under these conditions, as analyzed by Kohlberg, your moral code is likely to lack abstract generality. Your behavior will appear to be driven more by an individual situation than by a consistent code of justice. Psychologist Carol Gilligan (1982) has argued that women in our culture often adopt such a view (a moral code based on caring), whereas men tend to make moral decisions on the basis of an abstract sense of justice. According to Kohlberg's theory, however, this means that women will tend to be classified at a lower level of moral development than men. Gilligan sees this as an unfair and unjustified gender bias.

The Role of Culture

It now appears that Gilligan may have overstated the case for sex differences in moral reasoning. Men and women often think in much the same way about the types of moral dilemmas studied by Kohlberg (Walker, 1989). At the same time, other evidence indicates that important cross-cultural differences occur in moral thinking that are not captured well by Kohlberg's classification system. For example, studies of moral decision making in India reveal striking differences from those typically found in Western cultures. Richard Shweder and his colleagues (1990) found that both Hindu children and adults are likely to find it morally acceptable for a husband to beat a disobedient wife—in fact, keeping disobedient family members in line is considered to be the moral obligation of the head of the family. In the United States, such actions would be widely condemned.

Western cultures also tend to place more value on individualism and stress individual goals more than other cultures, where the emphasis may be on collective goals. These kinds of cultural values and teachings need to be factored into any complete theory of moral development (Miller, 1994). Moreover, education, and the value a culture places on teaching moral values, plays a role as well and can affect the speed with which moral development proceeds (e.g., Snarey, 1995). The bottom line: There is evidence supporting consistency in moral development across the world—that is, people tend to interpret morality first in terms of external consequences and only later in terms of abstract principles—but, not surprisingly, culture exerts its influence in powerful ways (Saltzstein, 1997).

TEST YOURSELF 4.2

Check your knowledge of intellectual development by answering these questions. (You will find the answers in the Appendix.)

1. Pick the appropriate research technique from among the following terms: cross-sectional, habituation, longitudinal, preference, and reward.

    a. Baby learns to kick her leg when a blue, but not a red, card appears. _____

    b. Baby grows bored and stops looking at repeated presentations of the same event. _____

    c. Comparisons are made among three groups of children; each group contains children of a different age. _____

    d. The development of memory is studied by testing the same individual repeatedly throughout his or her lifetime. _____

2. According to Piaget, children develop mental models of the world, called schemata, that change as the child grows. During the preoperational period of development, children often fail to recognize that the physical properties of an object can stay the same despite superficial changes in its appearance (e.g., rolling a ball of dough into a sausage shape doesn't change its mass). Piaget referred to this ability as:

    a. conservation
    b. object permanence
    c. accommodation
    d. relativistic thinking

3. Pick the appropriate level of moral development, as described by Kohlberg. Possible answers include conventional, preconventional, and postconventional.

    a. Actions are justified on the basis of whether or not they disrupt social order. _____

    b. Actions are justified on the basis of abstract moral principles. _____

    c. Actions are justified on the basis of their immediate consequences. _____

Developing Socially and Personally

Human beings do not develop in isolation. We are social animals, and our social and emotional relationships critically affect how we act and view ourselves. For infants, relationships with caregivers—usually their parents—guarantee them adequate nourishment and a safe and secure environment. For children, the social task is to become part of a social group and thereby learn what it means to get along with peers and follow the rules and norms of society. For adults, whose social bonds become increasingly intimate, the task is to learn to accept responsibility for the care and support of others. As with most aspects of development that you've learned about, social and personal development is a continuous process that is shaped by innate biological forces as well as by learned experiences.

FORMING BONDS WITH OTHERS

Think again about the problems faced by the newborn infant: limited motor skills, somewhat fuzzy vision, yet a powerful sustained need for food, water, and warmth. As I've noted, to gain the nourishment needed to live, as well as to gain protection from danger, the newborn relies on interactions with others—usually the mother—to stay alive. The newborn forms what psychologists call **attachments,** the strong emotional ties to one or more intimate companions. The need for early attachments is so critical that many researchers believe that innate, biologically driven behavioral systems may be involved in their formation (Bowlby, 1969, 1988).

According to child psychiatrist John Bowlby, both caregiver and infant are preprogrammed from birth to respond to certain environmental signals with attachment behavior. The newborn typically cries, coos, and smiles, and these behaviors lead naturally to attention and support from the caregiver. It's no accident that adults like to hear babies coo or watch them smile—these preferences may be built directly into the genetic code (Bowlby, 1969; Sigelman & Shaffer, 1995). At the same time, the baby arrives into the world with a bias to respond to care and particularly to comfort from the caregiver. Newborns imitate the facial expressions of their parents (Maratus, 1998), for example, which presumably enhances their social interactions with mom and dad (Bjorklund, 1997; Heimann, 1989).

Notice that both the infant and the caregiver are active participants in a reciprocal relationship—the attachment is formed because both parties are prepared to respond with bonding to the right kind of environmental events. The bond usually is formed initially between baby and mother because it is the mother who provides most of the early care (Lamb et al., 1992).

When a mother nurses her newborn child, she is providing more than just the food needed for survival. Her "contact comfort" helps to ensure that the attachment bond she forms with her child will be a secure one.

THE ORIGINS OF ATTACHMENT

The idea that humans are predisposed genetically to form strong emotional attachments makes sense from an adaptive standpoint—it helps to ensure survival. But what determines the strength or quality of the attachment? Differences clearly exist in the quality of the bond that forms between infant and caregiver—some infants are securely attached to their caregivers, others are not. Research with animal subjects suggests that one very important factor is the amount of actual *contact comfort*—the degree of warm physical contact—provided by the caregiver.

Contact Comfort

In some classic research on early attachment, psychologist Harry Harlow noticed that newborn rhesus monkeys, when separated from their mothers at birth, tended to become attached to soft cuddly things left in their cages, such as baby blankets. If one of these blankets was removed for cleaning, Harlow noticed, the monkeys would became extremely upset and cling to it frantically when returned. Intrigued,

attachments
Strong emotional ties formed to one or more intimate companions.

If forced to choose between two surrogate mothers, baby monkeys prefer a soft and cuddly cloth "mother" to a wire one, even when the wire mother provides the food.

Harlow began a series of experiments in which he isolated newborn monkeys and raised them in cages with a variety of surrogate, or artificial, "mothers" (Harlow & Zimmerman, 1959). In one experimental condition, baby monkeys were raised with a mother consisting simply of wire mesh fitted with an artificial nipple that delivered food; in another condition, the babies were exposed to a nippleless cloth mother made of the same wire mesh but wrapped in a soft terrycloth and a padding of foam rubber.

The idea behind the experiment was to see which of the two surrogate mothers the monkeys preferred. If early attachments are formed primarily to caregivers who provide nourishment—that is, infants love the one who feeds them—we would expect the monkeys to prefer and cling to the wire mother, since it provides the food. But in the vast majority of cases, the monkeys actually preferred the cloth mother. If startled in some way, perhaps by the introduction of a foreign object into the cage, the monkeys ran immediately to the cloth mother, hung on tight, and showed no interest in the wire mother that provided the food. Harlow and his colleagues concluded that *contact comfort*—the warmth and softness provided by the terrycloth—was the primary motivator of attachment (Harlow et al., 1971).

Children housed in a Romanian hospital dubbed "the children's Auschwitz."

For obvious reasons, similar experiments have never been conducted with human babies. However, we have every reason to believe that human infants are like rhesus infants in their desire and need for contact comfort. Many studies have looked at how children fare in institutional settings that provide relatively low levels of contact comfort (Hodges & Tizard, 1989; Provence & Lipton, 1962; Spitz, 1945). Children reared in orphanages with poor infant-to-caregiver ratios (e.g., one caregiver for every 10–20 infants), on average, show many more developmental problems than children reared in less deprived environments (Shaffer, 1993). Over the past decade, you may have seen news reports of orphaned children in Romania who, for some time, were literally "warehoused with minimal food, clothing, heat, or caregivers" (Kaler & Freeman, 1994). When the social and intellectual functioning of these orphans is compared to children reared at home, the orphans show significant and sometimes severe deficits (Kaler & Freeman, 1994).

Temperament

Clearly, the emotional and physical responsiveness of parents to their infants is an important predictor of the quality of the parent-child bond (Ainsworth et al., 1978; Cox et al., 1992). The quality of the attachment, in turn, can either enhance or hinder the normal developmental process. Physical contact is a necessary part of a quality attachment, but what determines whether the infant will receive the contact he or she needs? One contributing factor is the baby's **temperament,** the general level of his or her emotional reactivity. Difficult or fussy babies tend to elicit fewer comforting and responsive reactions, and the quality of the attachment between parent and child suffers as a result (Thomas & Chess, 1977).

Psychologists who study temperament have found that infants can be categorized into types. As you might guess, some babies are *easy;* they're basically happy, readily establish daily routines, and tend not to get upset very easily. Other babies are *difficult;* they have difficulty accepting new experiences, establishing routines, and maintaining a pleasant mood. Fortunately, only about 10% of babies fall into this difficult group, and about 40% of sampled babies are readily classified as easy (Thomas & Chess, 1977). The remaining 50% are more difficult to categorize. Some babies are "slow-to-warm-up," which means they roughly fall between easy and difficult and show a mixture of different temperaments.

Many psychologists now believe that these differences in moodiness, or temperament, can't be explained by simply appealing to the environment. Babies are probably born easy or difficult, although experience certainly plays some kind of role (Rothbart & Ahadi, 1994; Soudino et al., 1996). One possibility is that biological factors, tied to specific structures in the brain, control a baby's degree of emotional reactivity. Jerome Kagan has discovered that infants tend to be either *inhibited*—they're generally shy and fearful of unfamiliar people or new events— or *uninhibited*—they show little negative reaction to the unfamiliar or novel. Kagan believes that natural differences in the activity levels of certain brain structures contribute to these inhibited and uninhibited temperaments (Kagan, 1997; Kagan & Snidman, 1991).

If temperament is based in biology, then you might expect it to remain the same, or be stable, across the life span. In other words, if you're a moody baby, then you should be a moody adolescent and a moody adult. In general, research has supported this conclusion (Caspi & Silva, 1995; Schwartz et al., 1996). Infants who seem very shy or inhibited tend to be classified in a similar way as they age. There is also evidence that identical twins, who share the same genetic material, show more similarities in temperament than do fraternal twins or regular siblings raised in the same home (Braungart et al., 1992). As you'll see when you read Chapter 12, which covers personality, genetic factors probably influence many aspects of personality, not just temperament.

TYPES OF ATTACHMENT

Once attachments are formed, there are systematic differences in the types of bonds that are formed. To investigate these differences, psychologists have used a technique called the **strange situation test.** This test can be used to classify 10- to 24-month-old children into three main attachment groups (e.g., Ainsworth & Wittig, 1969; Ainsworth et al., 1978). The idea behind the test is to subject the child gradually to a stressful situation and note how his or her behavior toward the parent changes. After arrival in the lab, the parent and child are ushered into a waiting room filled with toys; the child is encouraged to play with the toys. Various levels of infant stress are then introduced. A stranger might enter the room, or the parent might be asked to step out for a few moments leaving the child alone. Of main interest to the psychologist are several dependent measures

temperament
A child's general level of emotional reactivity.

strange situation test
Gradually subjecting a child to a stressful situation and observing his or her behavior toward the parent or caregiver. This test is used to classify children according to type of attachment—secure, resistant, or avoidant.

of stress or discomfort: Initially, how willing is the child to move away from the parent and play with the toys? How much crying or distress does the child show when the parent leaves the room? How does the child react to the parent when the parent comes back into the room—does the child greet and cling to the parent, or does he or she move away?

Most infants—approximately 70%—react to the strange situation test with what psychologist Mary Ainsworth calls *secure attachment*. With the parent present, even if the situation is new and strange, these children play happily and are likely to explore the room looking for interesting toys or magazines to shred. But as the level of stress increases, they become increasingly uneasy and clingy. If the mother leaves the room, the child will probably start to cry but will calm down rapidly if the mother returns.

About 10% of children show a pattern called *resistant attachment;* these children react to stress in an ambiguous way, which may indicate a lack of trust for the parent. Resistant children will act wary in a strange situation, refusing to leave their mother's side and explore the room, and they do not deal well with the sudden appearance of strangers. If the mother leaves the room, they cry, yet they are unlikely to greet the mother with affection on her return. Instead, these children act ambivalent, scorning their mother by temporarily resisting her affection.

The final group of children—about 20%—show a pattern of *avoidant attachment*. These children demonstrate no strong attachment to the mother in any aspect of the strange situation test. They are not particularly bothered by the appearance of strangers in the room, nor do they show much concern when the mother leaves the room or much interest when she returns. Ainsworth discovered that the parents of these children tend, on average, to be unresponsive and impatient when it comes to the child's needs and may even actively reject the child on a regular basis (Ainsworth, 1979). Why? It's difficult to tell because the parent-child relationship depends on several factors: the particular personality characteristics of the parent, the temperament of the child, and the child-rearing practices of the culture (see the "Inside the Problem" feature on page 150 for more information on cultural differences in child-rearing practices).

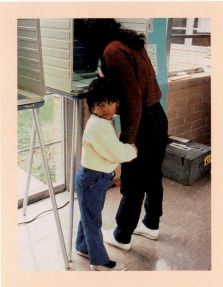

How children react when they are in a strange situation provides insight into the type of attachment they've formed with their parent or caregiver.

? CRITICAL THINKING

Do you think the findings of the strange situation test would change if the test was conducted in the child's home? Why or why not?

DO EARLY ATTACHMENTS MATTER LATER IN LIFE?

Given that infants can be easily divided into these attachment groups by around age 1, it's reasonable to wonder about the long-term consequences. For instance, are the avoidant children doomed to a life of insecurity and failed relationships? There is evidence to suggest that children with an early *secure* attachment do indeed have some social and intellectual advantages, at least throughout middle and later childhood. For example, teachers rate these children as more curious and self-directed in school (Waters et al., 1979). By age 10 or 11, securely attached children also tend to have more close and mature relationships with their peers than children who were classified as insecurely attached (Elicker et al., 1992).

However, early patterns of attachment are not perfect predictors of later behavior. One problem is stability: Sometimes a child who appears to be insecurely attached at 12 months can act quite differently in the strange situation test a few months later (Lamb et al., 1992). In addition, a child who has a particular kind of attachment to one parent may show quite a different attachment pattern to the other. It's also important to remember that when psychologists talk about predicting later behavior based on early attachment patterns, they are referring mainly to correlational studies. As you learned in Chapter 2, it's not possible to draw firm conclusions about causality from simple correlational analyses. The fact that later behavior can be predicted from early attachment patterns does not mean that early bonding necessarily causes the later behavior patterns—other factors might be responsible. For instance, children who form secure attachments in

Inside the Problem   Culture and Child Rearing

Did you know that, on average, it's more difficult to get a child raised in a Western industrialized country, such as the United States, to go to bed at night than it is for a child raised in Guatemala? A child from the United States is also more likely to demand and cling to a favored toy, such as a blanket or a teddy bear. Why? The answer lies partly in the fact that parents in the United States typically require their children to sleep alone, or at least in a separate room. In the United States, sleeping in the same room or bed with parents is thought to foster dependency, which is seen as an undesirable personality trait in children. But in most other countries of the world, including Guatemala, isolating children at bedtime is considered inappropriate and even shocking (Morelli et al., 1992). In Guatemala, Mayan mothers sleep in the same bed with their children at least until the infants reach toddlerhood. Perhaps not surprisingly, Mayan infants go to bed easily and do not require complex bedtime rituals of the type seen in most U.S. homes.

It's also been found that mothers in the United States tend to hold and touch their babies less often, on average, than mothers in some other cultures do. In one study, the parenting styles of middle-class mothers in Boston were directly compared with those of Gusii mothers in the African country of Kenya. For both cultures, the type of contact that the mothers displayed toward their babies was observed and carefully recorded (Richman et al., 1992). It turned out that the Boston mothers were far more likely to leave their children to their own devices (in playpens and infant seats) than the Gusii mothers, who instead chose to hold and cuddle their babies much of the time. On the other hand, the researchers also discovered that the Gusii mothers rarely made direct eye contact with their children and talked to them far less than the American mothers did.

What accounts for these differences? Why do American mothers touch their babies less but talk to them more? The answer lies partly in the particular beliefs that parents have about their children and partly in the customs of the cultures. For example, it's widely believed among Gusii mothers that their babies are incapable of understanding speech until age 2. As a result, idle conversations with the infant are thought to be wasteful and of little value. It's also considered inappropriate—a kind of cultural taboo—in Gusii society to look directly into someone's eyes during a conversation. This probably explains why Gusii mothers rarely make direct eye contact with their infants. Mothers in the United States have a quite different set of cultural beliefs; they are confident that their babies respond to language very early in development, and they believe that sustained eye contact is an excellent and appropriate way to communicate. The U.S. culture also places high value on independence and self-reliance. Depositing the baby or toddler in a playpen is not considered a heartless act by most U.S. mothers—it's a way to break dependence and encourage independence.

Many researchers believe that an emphasis on instilling independence early in life, which is a common practice in the United States and other Western industrialized countries, affects the kinds of attachment bonds that are formed during childhood. Earlier in the chapter we discussed a technique called the strange situation test, in which the behavior of infants in a new situation is recorded under various levels of stress (ranging from the entrance of a stranger to the parent leaving the child alone). This test has been administered to children in many different cultures of the world, and some interesting cross-cultural differences in childhood behavior have been recorded. For example, it's been found that children from both the United States and Germany are far more likely to show avoidant attachment than children raised in Japan (Cole, 1992; van

infancy typically have caregivers who remain warm and responsive throughout childhood, adolescence, and adulthood. So it could be that securely attached infants tend to have successful and meaningful relationships later in life because they live most of their lives in supportive environments.

Friendships

There's no question that early attachments are important. But the relationships formed *after* infancy, especially during later childhood and adolescence, also significantly affect our social behavior. Under the right circumstances, there are good reasons to believe that individuals can counteract negative experiences that occur during infancy or childhood (Lamb et al., 1992). The significance of friendship is a case in point. Psychologists now recognize that a child's social network—the number and quality of his or her friends—has a tremendous impact on social development and well-being (Berndt, 1988; Hartup & Stevens, 1997).

Children with friends interact more confidently in social situations, they are more cooperative, and they report higher levels of self-esteem (Newcombe & Bagwell, 1995). Children with friends, compared to those without friends, are also less likely to seek help for psychological problems, and they're more likely to be

Some cultures encourage children to sleep in the same room or bed as their parents; other cultures do not.

Ijzendoorn & Kroonenberg, 1988). Remember, avoidant children show little or no strong attachments; they are not bothered by the appearance of strangers in the room, nor do they seem distressed when their mother leaves the room. Some researchers believe that these cultural differences in attachment result from the fact that parents in the United States and Germany spend less time with their children, choosing instead to foster independence and autonomy. Children in Japan, on the other hand, spend very little time away from their mother during the first year or so of life.

It's important to understand that this decision of whether or not to stress independence can be more than simply a matter of cultural choice. Many of the child-rearing strategies that occur throughout the world are driven by the special problems faced by the society. For instance, middle-class mothers in the United States, Germany, and Japan do not face immediate survival problems. The child left momentarily unattended in the playpen is not likely to be attacked by a predator. But in some societies of the world, particularly nomadic societies, the infant's survival is a constant and pressing concern.

Child-rearing practices are also affected by how the society has historically framed its economy. In agricultural societies, children are encouraged early in life to work in teams and to think of themselves as dependent on the actions of the group. In hunting societies or in nomadic societies that are constantly on the move, self-reliance and permissiveness are more likely to be stressed because parents often need to travel great distances alone in search of food. The unique problems faced by the culture determine the way parents rear their children and, consequently, have a significant affect on how the children learn to behave.

seen as well-adjusted by teachers and adult caretakers. Such trends are true for young children and adolescents, and continue on into adulthood (Berndt & Keefe, 1995). When you read Chapter 16, which deals with stress and health, you'll find that social support—particularly our network of friends—predicts how well we're able to cope and deal with stressful situations and how well we're able to recover from injury or disease. This is just as true for children as it is for adults (Hartup & Stevens, 1997).

Obviously, general conclusions like these need to be qualified a bit. For example, the quality (or closeness) of the friendship matters, as does the identity of the friends. If you have very close friends who recommend drug use or a life of crime, then the developmental consequences will be less than ideal. It's also unclear at this point what aspects of friendship matter most. For instance, people often share similarities with their friends (such as common attitudes and values). Does this mean that friends merely play the role of reinforcing our values and making us more secure in our attitudes? In-depth research on friendships is ongoing, in part, because psychologists recognize the value of friendship across the life span. When asked to rank what is most important in their lives, children, adolescents, and adults often pick "friends" as the answer (Klinger, 1977).

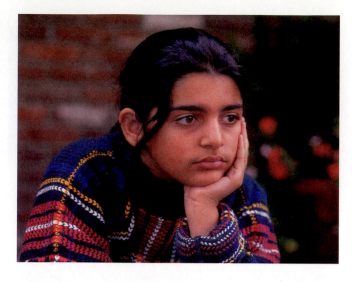

The quality of a child's social network—the number and quality of friends—can have a tremendous influence on his or her social development and well-being.

CHILD CARE: A CAUSE FOR CONCERN?

What about child care and its long-term impact on development? Most parents of preschool children face a dilemma: Do I stay at home and provide full-time care for my child, or do I work outside the home and place my child in child care? In contemporary American society, *day care* often turns out to be the answer, although it is not always a choice made voluntarily by the parent. For many, day care has simply become an economic necessity. The last several decades have seen a steady rise in the number of mothers employed outside of the home. In 1960, for example, 16.5% of mothers with children under 3 years of age worked outside of the home; by the middle 1980s, the figure had risen to over 50%; by 1995, it was over 60% (Lamb & Sternberg, 1990; Hofferth, 1996).

What are the long-term consequences of day care? Does leaving children in the hands of nonparental caretakers, often for many hours a day, have dire consequences on their social and mental development? Fortunately, the answer turns out to be "no" for most children, and day care may even have positive effects on social and cognitive development. It's been reported that preschoolers who spend time in quality day-care centers adjust better in school—they are more sociable and popular among their classmates—than children who have received full-time care at home (Andersson, 1992). The day-care experience may also help speed up intellectual development, at least for some children. Recently, Caughy and colleagues (1994) found that day-care participation during the first three years of life was positively associated with improved reading and math skills, although the results applied only to children who lived in home environments classified as low in emotional support and intellectual stimulation.

Placing a child in day care has simply become an economic necessity for many parents.

In the mid-1980s it was widely reported that children in day care were more likely to form insecure attachments (avoidant or resistant) than children who receive full-time home care (e.g., Belsky, 1988). More recent studies have failed to replicate these findings or have found the differences to be quite small (Clarke-Stewart, 1989; Lamb, 1998; Roggman et al., 1994). But still, psychologists acknowledge that day care can have detrimental effects under some circumstances. It's important to recognize that "day care" is a multifaceted concept—the term can mean anything from occasional babysitting by a neighbor for a few hours a week, to care by nonparental relatives, to extended care by licensed professionals in for-profit day-care centers. Consequently, it's difficult to draw general conclusions about day care that will be of much use.

Wide variations also exist in the *quality* of the service provided during day-care hours and in the quality of care that the child receives at home. Factors such as how early in life the child enters a program and whether the child attends regularly or intermittently may be important (Lamb & Sternberg, 1990). As with most environmental effects, the role that day care plays in the life of a child will depend on many factors interacting together, including the individual characteristics of the child, the parents, the home environment, and the quality and quantity of the service provided. But the consensus among researchers is fairly positive at this point: For the vast majority of children, regular day care will have no negative long-term consequences on development, and it may even have substantial benefits (Scarr, 1998).

FORMING A PERSONAL IDENTITY: ERIKSON'S CRISES OF DEVELOPMENT

One of the most important parts of social development is the formation of **personal identity**—a sense of self, of who you are as an individual and how well you measure up against peers. We recognize ourselves—that is, that we represent a unique person different from others—quite early in our development. Children as young as 6 months of age will reach out and touch an image of themselves in a mirror; by a year and a half, if they look into a mirror and notice a smudge mark on their nose, they'll reach up and touch their own face (Butterworth, 1992; Lewis & Brooks-Gunn, 1979).

As noted earlier in the chapter, many psychologists are convinced that people use social interactions—primarily the ones with parents during childhood and with peers later in life—to help them come to grips with who they are as individuals. One of the most influential theories of how this process of identity formation proceeds is the stage theory of Erik Erikson. Erikson (1963, 1968, 1982) believed that personal identity is shaped by a series of psychosocial *crises* that each person must confront at a characteristic stage in development (see "Concept Summary," next page).

Part of the process of developing socially and personally is the development of personal identity. Ellen demonstrates self-awareness as she discovers her nose in the mirror's reflection.

Infancy and Childhood

As you know, for the first few years of life babies are largely at the mercy of others for their survival. According to Erikson, this overwhelming dependency leads infants to their first true psychosocial crisis, usually in the first year of life: *trust versus mistrust*. Psychologically and practically, babies face an important problem: Are there people out there in the world who will meet my survival needs? Resolution of this crisis leads to the formation of an initial sense of either trust or mistrust, and the infant begins to develop some basic knowledge about how people differ. Some people can be trusted and some cannot. It is through social interactions, learning who to trust and who not to trust, that the newborn ultimately resolves the crisis and learns how to deal more effectively with his or her environment.

As the child progresses through toddlerhood and on into childhood, other fundamental conflicts appear and need to be resolved. During the "terrible twos," the child struggles with breaking his or her dependence on parents. The crisis at this point, according to Erikson, is *autonomy versus shame or doubt*: Am I capable of independent self-control of my actions, or am I generally inadequate? Between the ages of 3 and 6, the crisis becomes one of *initiative versus guilt*: Can I plan things on my own, with my own initiative, or should I feel guilty for trying to carry out my own bold plans for action? In late childhood, beginning around age 6 and ending at around age 12, the struggle is for a basic sense of *industry versus*

personal identity
A sense of who one is as an individual and how well one stacks up against peers. Erik Erikson's theory postulates that personal identity is shaped by a series of personal crises that each person confronts at characteristic stages of development.

CONCEPT SUMMARY
Erikson's Stages of Personal Identity Development

Life Period	Stage	Conflicts Revolve Around . . .
Infancy and childhood	Trust vs. mistrust (first year of life)	Developing a sense of trust in others; are there others present who will fulfill my needs?
	Autonomy vs. shame or doubt ("terrible twos")	Developing a sense of self control; can I control my own actions?
	Initiative vs. guilt (ages 3–6)	Developing a sense of one's own drive and initiative; can I carry out plans? should I feel guilty for trying to carry out my own plans?
	Industry vs. inferiority (ages 6–12)	Developing a sense of personal ability and competence; can I learn and develop new skills?
Adolescence and young adulthood	Identity vs. role confusion (adolescence)	Developing a single, unified concept of self, a sense of personal identity; who am I?
	Intimacy vs. isolation (young adulthood)	Questioning the meaning of our relationships with others; can I form a committed relationship with another person, or will my personal insecurities lead to isolation?
Adulthood and older adulthood	Generativity vs. stagnation	Concern over whether one has contributed to the success of children and future generations; older adulthood have I contributed to the community at large?
	Integrity vs. despair	Acceptance of one's life—successes and failures; am I content, looking back on my life?

inferiority: Can I learn and master new skills, can I be industrious and complete required tasks, or do I lack fundamental competence?

Again, what's important in determining how these crises will be resolved is the quality of the child's interactions with parents, peers, and other significant role models. If 5-year-old Roberta's parents repeatedly scold her for taking the initiative to get her own drink of milk, she may develop strong feelings of guilt for trying to become independent. According to Erikson, children with highly critical parents or teachers can acquire a self-defeating attitude toward themselves that carries over later in life. Children who resolve these crises positively learn to trust themselves and their abilities and acquire a strong positive sense of personal identity.

Adolescence and Young Adulthood

By the time we reach adolescence, our intellectual development has proceeded to the point where we naturally begin to consider personal qualities that are pretty general and abstract. In particular, Erikson argued, adolescents have to deal with the fundamental crisis of *identity versus role confusion.* They become concerned with testing roles and with finding their true identity: Who am I? What kind of person do I really represent? In a very real sense, the teenager acts as a kind of personality theorist, attempting to integrate various self-perceptions about abilities and limitations into a single unified concept of self. Erikson (1968) coined the term *identity crisis* to describe this transition period, which he believed is often filled with turmoil.

Observational studies of how adolescents actually come to grips with the identity crisis reveal many individual differences (Offer & Schonert-Reichl, 1992; Peterson, 1988). Not all teenagers become paralyzed with identity "angst" and anxiety—most, in fact, show no more anxiety during this transition period than at other points in their lives. Individual differences also occur in how young people commit to a particular view of themselves (Marcia, 1966). Some adolescents choose an identity by modeling others: "I'm honest, open, and cooperative because that's the way I was brought up by my parents." Others develop a personal identity through a soul-searching evaluation of their feelings and abilities. Some

Erik Erikson

adolescents even reject the crisis altogether, choosing instead not to commit to any particular view of themselves. The specific course or path an individual takes depends on many factors, including his or her level of cognitive development, the quality of the parent-child relationship, and outside experiences (Compas et al., 1995).

Entrance into young adulthood is marked by the crisis of *intimacy versus isolation.* Resolution of the identity crisis causes us to question the meaning of our relationships with others: Am I willing or able to form an intimate, committed relationship with another person? Or will my insecurities and fears about losing independence lead to a lifetime of isolation and loneliness? People who lack an integrated conception of themselves, Erikson argued, cannot commit themselves to a shared identity with someone else. Some have argued that this particular conclusion may be more applicable to men than women (Gilligan, 1982). Historically, women have been forced by societal pressures to deal with intimate commitments—raising a family and running a home—either at the same time as, or before, the process of searching for a stable personal identity. This trend may well be changing, however, because more women are establishing professional careers prior to marriage.

Erik Erikson would probably argue that this young man is concerned with testing roles and finding his true identity.

Adulthood, Middle Age, and Beyond

With the establishment of career and family arrives the crisis of *generativity versus stagnation.* The focus at this point shifts from resolving intimacy to concern about children and future generations: Am I contributing successfully to the community at large? Am I doing enough to assure the survival and productivity of future generations? Failure to resolve this crisis can lead to a sense of meaninglessness in middle life and beyond—a condition Erikson calls *stagnation.*

For some people, especially men in their 40s, this point in psychosocial development is marked by soul-searching questions about personal identity reminiscent of those faced in adolescence (Gould, 1978; Levinson et al., 1978). According to psychologists such as Gould and Levinson, the so-called "midlife crisis" arises as people begin to confront their own mortality—the inevitability of death—and as they come to grips with the fact that they may never achieve their lifelong dreams and goals. There is no doubt that this can be an emotionally turbulent period, but recent evidence suggests that the midlife crisis is a relatively rare phenomenon. It gets a lot of attention in the media, and it's certainly consuming for those affected, but probably fewer than 5% of people in middle age undergo anything resembling a turbulent midlife crisis (McCrae & Costa, 1990).

The final stage in the process of psychosocial development, which occurs from late adulthood to the point of death, is the crisis of *integrity versus despair.* It is at this stage in people's lives, Erikson argued, that they strive to accept themselves and their pasts—both failures and successes. Older people undergo a kind of life review in an effort to resolve conflicts in the past and to find ultimate meaning in what they've accomplished. If successful in this objective search for meaning, they acquire wisdom; if unsuccessful, they wallow in despair and bitterness. An important part of the process is the preparation for death and dying, which I'll discuss in more detail near the end of the chapter.

Is this man going through a turbulent midlife crisis as he begins to confront his own mortality?

Evaluating Erikson's Theory

Erikson's stage theory of psychosocial crises has been enormously influential in shaping how psychologists view personal identity development. Among its most important contributions is the recognition that personal development is a lifelong process. Individuals don't simply establish a rigid personal identity around the time they reach Piaget's formal operational stage; the way that people view themselves and their relationships changes continually throughout their lives. Erikson's theory is also noteworthy for its emphasis on the role of social and cultural interactions in shaping human psychology. Human beings do not grow up in a kind of psychological vacuum; the way people think and act is critically influenced by their interactions with others, as Erikson's theory fully acknowledges (Douvan, 1997; Eagle, 1997).

Nevertheless, Erikson's theory suffers from the same kinds of problems as any stage theory. Although there may be an orderly sequence of psychosocial crises that people confront, overlap occurs across the stages (Whitbourne et al., 1992). As noted earlier, the search for identity is not confined to one turbulent period in adolescence—it is likely to continue throughout a lifetime. Furthermore, like Piaget, Erikson never clearly articulated *how* a person actually moves from one crisis stage to the next: What are the psychological mechanisms that allow for conflict resolution, and what determines when and how they will operate (Achenbach, 1992)? Finally, Erikson's theory of identity development, although useful as a general organizing framework, lacks sufficient scientific rigor. His concepts are vague enough to make scientific testing difficult.

GENDER-ROLE DEVELOPMENT

In our discussion of Erikson's theory, I touched briefly on the role of *gender* in establishing personal identity. It's been argued that women are sometimes required to struggle with questions about intimacy and relationships before addressing the identity crisis, as the burden of establishing a home and rearing children typically falls on their shoulders. But gender is itself a kind of identity; children gain a sense of themselves as male or female quite early in life, and this *gender identity* has a long-lasting effect on how individuals behave and on how others behave toward them.

The available evidence suggests that the rudimentary foundations of gender identity are already in place by the age of 2 or 3. Children at this age recognize that they are either a boy or a girl (Thompson, 1975), and they sometimes even give stereotyped responses about gender when asked. For example, when shown a picture of an infant labeled as either a boy or a girl, 3-year-olds are more likely to identify the infant "boy" as the one who is strong, big, or hard and the infant "girl" as the one who is weak, small, and soft (Cowan & Hoffman, 1986). But children at this age have not developed sufficiently to recognize gender as a general and abstract characteristic of individuals. They might believe, for instance, that a boy can become a girl by changing hairstyle or clothing (Marcus & Overton, 1978). To understand that gender is a stable and unchanging condition requires some

? CRITICAL THINKING

How well do Erikson's ideas describe your own personal identity development? Are you going through any fundamental crisis at the moment, or are you aware of having solved one in the past?

Children are often rewarded for acting in ways that are gender-role appropriate.

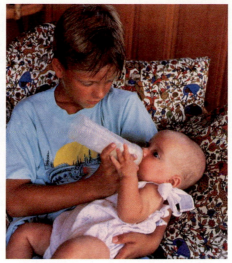

Children often act in accordance with well-specified gender roles, but not always.

ability to conserve—to recognize that the qualities of objects remain the same despite superficial changes in appearance.

By the time children are firmly entrenched in elementary school, gender is seen as a permanent condition—"I'm a boy (or a girl) and I always will be." At this point, children tend to act in accordance with reasonably well-established **gender roles**—specific patterns of behavior consistent with how society dictates males and females should act. Children at this age have strong opinions about how boys and girls should behave, what occupations they should have when they grow up, and how they should look. Can you imagine the reaction that a 7-year-old boy might receive if he walked into his second-grade class wearing a dress, or with his fingernails polished a bright shade of pink?

Nature or Nurture?

How do these firm ideas about gender roles develop? Are they the inevitable by-product of biological differences between male and female brains, or do they grow out of experience? We encountered this issue in Chapter 3, where we considered the evidence supporting gender-based differences in brain anatomy and functioning. Although data suggest that hormones released by the endocrine system early in development may account for some gender differences in behavior and thought (Kimura, 1992), psychologists are just as likely to appeal to the environment to explain gender-role development.

According to *social learning* accounts of gender-role development, children learn to act in a masculine or feminine manner because they grow up in environments that reward them for doing so. Parents across the world quickly set up what Sigelman and Shaffer (1995) call "gender-role curriculums" to reinforce particular types of behavior from their male and female children. The socialization process begins the moment the new parents learn the answer to their question, "Is it a boy or a girl?" Parents become preoccupied with dressing Adorable Ginnie in pink bows and Active Glenn in blue. Television and movies continue the process: Children are exposed to hour after hour of stereotypical children acting in gender-appropriate ways (Hansen, 1989; Lovdal, 1989). Studies have indicated, for example, that children who watch a lot of television are more likely to prefer toys that are "gender appropriate" than children who watch little television (McGhee & Frueh, 1980).

One of the by-products of growing up under the gender-role curriculum is the establishment of **gender schemas** (Bem, 1981). A gender schema is an organized set of beliefs and perceptions held about men and women. Once established, these schemas guide and direct how individuals view others, as well as their own behavior. For example, as a male, my gender schema might direct me to judge my behavior as well as the behavior of other men with respect to such general concepts as "strength," "aggression," and "masculinity." We encountered the concept

CRITICAL THINKING

Do you think that we as a society should work hard to eliminate specific gender roles? Do you believe that men and women can ever be taught to think and act similarly?

gender roles
Specific patterns of behavior that are consistent with how society dictates males and females should act.

gender schemas
The organized sets of beliefs and perceptions held about men and women.

of schemas (or schemata) earlier in the chapter when we talked about Piaget, and I'll have more to say in later chapters about schemas and the role they play in directing behavior. For the moment, you can think of schemas as little knowledge packages that people carry around inside their heads. Gender schemas are acquired through learning, they set guidelines for people's behavior, and they underlie the expectations that people hold about the appropriateness of actions. As you can probably guess, gender schemas are generally adaptive—they help us interpret the behavior of others—but they can lead to inaccurate perceptions of specific individuals and even to discrimination.

THE FAMILY LIFE CYCLE

Among the more significant environmental influences on adult personal and social development are the transitions connected with family life. Should I get married? Should I have children? If so, how many children and when? As you're certainly aware, how you answer these questions will depend on many factors, including your personality, the culture in which you were raised, and perhaps even your

There are increasing numbers of nontraditional families, including gay and lesbian couples who are raising children.

genetic or biological background as well. You hear a lot about the traditional nuclear family—husband, wife, 2.5 kids—but it's largely a myth, at least when defined literally as a marriage in which neither partner has been divorced, where there are no stepchildren, and where mom is the homemaker and dad is the principal breadwinner.

There is considerable diversity in the structure of the modern family (Dremen, 1997). Divorce is an unfortunate fact of life for many families as is the need for two or more paychecks. There are also increasing numbers of nontraditional families: single parents who have never been married, families where dad stays at home and mom works, and gay and lesbian couples who are raising children. The good news is that you can expect children to develop normally in each of these cases, regardless of the family structure, although certainly divorce and economic hardships exert a psychological toll on children and parents alike (e.g., Kalter, 1998). The concept of "family" is also importantly culture-bound. In many cultures, for instance, there is an extended family structure in which parents, children, grandparents, and other relatives live together in the same household.

From the perspective of understanding development, though, it's clearly important to pay attention to what's going on in the family. Whatever form it takes, the family structure will exert a strong influence on a person's thoughts and actions. Psychologists refer to the transitions, or the sequence of stages, that families move through over time as the **family life cycle** (Duvall, 1977). Each stage in the cycle defines a unique set of issues or problems that need to be confronted and solved. Often, psychologists tie the different stages in the family life cycle to the ages of the children. For example, it's easy to see that families with preschool children are faced with problems (e.g., child care) that are different from the problems faced by families with young teenagers or families with children who are ready to leave the nest.

Viewing adult development in terms of environmental events in the family, such as having a newborn in the house, reinforces the idea that development should not be viewed solely in terms of physical age; instead, human development is better seen as a complex interaction between physical aging and the problems defined by the environment. Presumably, parents with infant children are confronted with many of the same problems, regardless of whether they chose to start their family in their early 20s or late 30s. Decisions about whether to have children, for instance, are often determined by economic concerns (Surra, 1998) and decisions about parenting style must be made by all parents, whatever their ages. The changes that occur throughout development are virtually always shaped by

family life cycle
The transitions, or sequences of stages, that families move through. In many models of the family life cycle, the stages are tied to the age of the children.

powerful forces in the environment, and the influence of the family is a perfect case in point.

Once again, the exact nature of the family life cycle will depend on the particular family structure. Most of the research on family life cycles has been conducted with traditional family structures—that is, heterosexual couples with children rather than extended families, childless families, or even single-parent families. More work needs to be done on nontraditional family structures because the unique problems and needs that arise in these environments will tell us much about the behaviors of those involved (Rowland, 1991).

GROWING OLD IN SOCIETY

With the passage of time, and the inevitable physical declines that accompany the aging process, come constant new challenges for the developing individual. That is not to say that all of the changes that greet us in our older years are negative—far from it. In fact, some kinds of intelligence seem to increase with age (see Chapter 10): marital satisfaction often grows (Carstensen, 1995), and many elderly people remain actively involved in the community and report high levels of contentment (Lawton et al., 1992). One recent survey found that people in their seventies, on average, report more confidence in their ability to perform tasks than do people in their fifties (Wallhagen et al., 1997)!

At the same time, there are definite hurdles in the pathways of the elderly, many related to health care. The elderly need more physical care, require more doctor visits, and can be at an economic disadvantage due to retirement. Although most elderly adults do not live in nursing homes, many are in need of continuing care. Whatever form this care takes, it is likely to be expensive. Nursing homes, on average, cost $37,000 per year in 1993, and the costs have continued to rise (Belsky, 1999). To make matters worse, the bulk of the costs often must be borne by family members because Medicare (health care for the elderly funded by the federal government) doesn't cover custodial, or chronic, care. The scope of the problem should not be underestimated, especially as the "graying of America" continues. Over the next 50 years, there is expected to be a large increase (perhaps as much as sixfold) in the number of people over age 85.

Ageism

From a psychological perspective there are other obstacles that adults face as they grow old in society. One such problem is **ageism,** or prejudice against an individual based on his or her age. We'll discuss the basis for prejudice, and particularly the formation of stereotypes, in detail in Chapter 13. For the moment, it is sufficient for you to understand that we all have beliefs about the personal traits and behaviors of individuals belonging to groups. The elderly comprise such a group, and one's attitudes and beliefs toward the elderly can affect their ability to cope with the problems of everyday life.

Stereotypes about the elderly are complex and depend on cultural factors and the age of the individual holding the stereotype, but surveys often reveal beliefs that are inaccurate. Palmore (1990) has listed some of the more common myths, including the belief that most elderly people are sick, in mental decline, disabled and therefore unable to work, isolated and lonely, and depressed. In each of these cases, the negative stereotype is misleading or simply not true. Most elderly people are not sick or disabled and, as mentioned earlier, research indicates that the elderly may, on average, be more contented and less prone to depression than younger people (Lawton et al., 1992; Palmore, 1990). Not surprisingly, negative stereotypes tend to lead to negative consequences, including the fact that older people are generally evaluated less positively (Kite & Johnson, 1988) and may be subject to job discrimination (Kite, 1996).

As you'll learn in Chapter 13, stereotypes are not all bad. In fact, they can be quite adaptive. Like schemas, stereotypes help us organize and make predictions

ageism
Discrimination or prejudice against an individual based on physical age.

Many negative stereotypes about the elderly are untrue. The majority of elderly people are not sick or disabled; they live active lives.

about the world, and the beliefs that accompany stereotypes are not necessarily negative. For example, people tend to believe that the elderly are kinder, wiser, more dependable, and have more personal freedom than younger people (Palmore, 1990). Many of these assumptions are counter to the facts. Beliefs such as these, although not necessarily accurate, can lead to a kind of favorable discrimination that helps to counteract the negative stereotypes mentioned above. One of the lessons of social psychology is that how we view others is often tied to our expectations; age can be a powerful determinant of what those expectations will be.

DEATH AND DYING

As we close our discussion of the developmental process, it's fitting that we turn our attention to the final stage of life: death and dying. It's common to hear people say that death is a part of living, but it's a part of living most people would choose to avoid. It's the process of death that troubles people most—the unpredictability, the uncertainty, the inability to understand what the end will be like. There are many psychological aspects to death, and to the dying process, including how people come to grips with their own mortality and how they grieve and accept the loss of others. One of the most influential approaches to the dying process is the stage theory of Elisabeth Kübler-Ross (1969, 1974).

Kübler-Ross proposed that people progress through five distinct psychological stages as they face death. She based her theory on a set of extensive interviews conducted with hundreds of terminally ill patients. Her fundamental insight was that people appear to react to their own impending death in a characteristic sequence: (1) *denial*—"There must be some terrible mistake"; (2) *anger*—"Why is this happening to me?"; (3) *bargaining*—"What can I do to stop this terrible thing?"; (4) *depression*—"Blot out the sun because all is lost"; and (5) *acceptance*—"I am ready to die." As a stage theorist, Kübler-Ross essentially implied that people move through each of these five stages, from denial to acceptance, as a normal part of their emotional acceptance of death.

Kübler-Ross' views on the dying process have been highly influential, both in psychological and medical circles, primarily because she was one of the first people to treat the topic of dying thoroughly and systematically. She sensitized legions of physicians to the idea that denial, anger, and depression are normal reactions to dying and that they should be treated with respect rather than dismissed out of hand. However, most psychologists today are not convinced that people progress through a fixed set of orderly stages in the way Kübler-Ross described. There are simply too many individual differences to support the theory. Not all dying people move through distinct emotional stages, and, even if they do, the stages do not seem to follow any particular set order. Stages might be skipped, might be experienced out of order, or might alternate, with the person being angry one day and accepting the next. In sum, there is no firm evidence to support a stage approach to the process of dying.

Many psychologists find it more appropriate to talk about *dying trajectories*. A dying trajectory is simply the psychological path people travel as they face their impending death. Different people show different trajectories, and the shape and form of the path depends on the particular illness as well as on the personality of the patient (Bortz, 1990; Glaser & Strauss, 1968). Trajectories are preferred to stages because stages imply that all people react to impending death in fixed and characteristic ways. But there is no right or wrong way to deal with dying—some people may react with anger and denial, others with calm acceptance. The best that witnesses to the dying process can do is offer support and allow the individual to follow his or her own unique path.

End-of-Life Decisions

One current topic of particular interest to psychologists is the decision-making processes that surround the end of life. Should people have the right to control

The shape and form of the final dying trajectory depends on the particular illness, the conditions of care, and the personality of the individual.

how and when they die, especially if they're faced with a poor quality of life (e.g., constant pain, immobility, or dependency)? Is suicide, assisted suicide, or "pulling the plug" justified under any circumstance? In some sense, these are legal and ethical questions rather than psychological ones, but questions about controlling the end of life occupy the attention of many people, especially the elderly.

There has been very little research conducted on the psychological factors that influence end-of-life decisions. It seems likely that religious convictions, value systems, life satisfaction, and even fear of death play a role in how people feel about the various end-of-life options. A recent study by Cicirelli (1997) confirms these expectations. Older adults, ranging in age from 60 to 100, were asked their views of various end-of-life options. Each person was given sample decision situations such as the following:

> Mrs. Lee is an elderly widow who has terminal bone cancer. She has had chemotherapy to try to cure the cancer but it has not helped her, and the side-effects from the chemotherapy itself have been difficult to deal with. She is slowly getting worse, and the pain is unbearable. Drugs for pain help some, but leave her in a stupor.

The participants were then asked to make judgments about various end-of-life options, such as strive to maintain life, refuse medical treatment or request that it be removed, commit suicide, or allow someone else to the make the decision about terminating life. Cicirelli (1997) found that people were often willing to endorse more than one option, but the majority opinion was to strive to continue life (51% of the participants endorsed this view). Psychosocial factors, such as religious convictions and fear of death, played a significant role in the decision-making process. For example, there was a significant minority who favored the ending of life under these circumstances, but these individuals tended, on average, to be less religious, to value the quality of life more, and to have a greater fear of death.

TEST YOURSELF 4.3

Test your knowledge about social and personal development by answering the following questions. (You will find the answers in the Appendix.)

1. The strange situation test is often used to study attachment. Identify the type of attachment that best characterizes the following reactions: avoidant, resistant, or secure.

   a. When Mom leaves the room, the child begins to cry, but calms down rapidly when she returns. _____

b. When Mom leaves the room, the child couldn't care less. There is little reaction or interest when she returns. _____

c. When Mom leaves the room, the child cries but shows little or no affection on her return. _____

d. When Mom is in the room, the child refuses to leave her side and does not react well to the sudden appearance of strangers. _____

2. According to Erik Erikson, adolescents face a psychosocial crisis called *identity versus role confusion*. Current research suggests that:

a. This is a time of rebellion for all adolescents.
b. Erikson made a mistake—no such crisis occurs.
c. The identity crisis has mostly a genetic basis.
d. Not all teenagers suffer anxiety during this period.

3. Gender identity doesn't develop until a child enters elementary school—it's only at that point that gender-role curricula begin to exert an effect. *True or False*?

4. Which of the following statements about the elderly and growing old in society are true and which are false?

a. Most elderly people are sick and disabled.
b. Stereotypes about the elderly are always harmful.
c. Most elderly people have little, if any, confidence in their abilities.
d. The elderly, on average, would rather die than suffer the consequences of a painful and terminal disease.

Solving the Problems

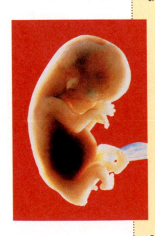

As people grow from infancy through childhood and on to adulthood, they experience fundamental changes in physical, intellectual, and social functioning. For the most part, these developmental changes can be viewed as *adaptive* reactions to environmental change as individuals grow and learn from experience. It's adaptive that humans are born with a genetic blueprint flexible enough to allow them to change how they think and behave in the most appropriate way. Humans are not born as biological machines, predestined to develop according to a fixed and inflexible plan. Instead, they are better viewed as individuals born with genetic potential that is realized, or not, based on experiences with the environment.

In many ways, this chapter on human development acts as a *précis*—or concise summary—of the topics you'll encounter throughout the book. Understanding human development requires that we take into account all aspects of the psychology of the individual: how people change physically; learn to perceive, think, and remember; and develop as social animals. Thus, you can think about the adaptive problems in this chapter as opening acts for the remaining chapters in the book.

Developing Physically. Individuals begin life as a fertilized egg, or zygote, which contains genetic material packed into chromosomes received from the mother and father. Prenatal development—which is divided into the germinal, embryonic, and fetal stages—takes place between conception and birth. The body develops rapidly during this time and is especially susceptible to both positive and negative influences from the environment. Infancy and childhood are marked by rapid growth in height and weight and by a further maturing of the nervous system. One of the by-products of nerve cell maturation is motor development. The major milestones in motor development—crawling, standing alone, walking—occur at similar times for most individuals, in part because of the systematic manner in which the nervous system develops.

As people move through adolescence and into early adulthood, their physical systems continue to change. Puberty is the developmental period in which individuals mature sexually, and it's marked by dramatic changes in physical appearance driven primarily by the release of gender-specific hormones. Once people reach their twenties, their bodies become physically mature, and most begin a gradual across-the-board decline in physical ability. Some declines occur in mental ability over time, especially in old age, although significant losses in mental functioning or mental health are still the exception rather than the rule. There is evidence to suggest that losses in the number of brain neurons may be counteracted by increases in the complexity of the remaining nerve cells. In general, there are individual differences in how the aging process proceeds; both the positive and negative consequences of aging are affected by one's genetic blueprint as well as by lifestyle choices (for instance, how much one exercises).

Developing Intellectually. Psychologists use the term *cognitive development* to refer to the changes in intellectual functioning that accompany physical maturation. Several innovative techniques have been used to map out the internal perceptual world of infants. Newborns have remarkably well-developed tools for investigating the world around them: they can see, hear, smell, feel, and taste, although not at the same level as they will later in childhood. Individuals leave infancy with well-developed perceptual systems and use the experiences of childhood to help fine-tune and use their sensory equipment.

Much of what we know about how thought processes develop during infancy and childhood comes from the work of Jean Piaget. Piaget's theory of cognitive development proposes that children use mental models of the world—called schemata—to guide and interpret ongoing experience. Central to the theory is the idea that as children grow physically, and acquire new experiences, their mental models of the world change systematically. Piaget argued that children pass through a series of cognitive stages (sensorimotor, preoperational, concrete operational, and formal operational) characterized by unique ways of thinking. Piaget's theory has been criticized for a number of reasons, but the idea that children do not function as "little adults" continues to be widely accepted among developmental psychologists. Piaget's theory is complemented by Lawrence Kohlberg's theory of moral development. Like Piaget, Kohlberg proposed a stage theory, suggesting that individuals pass through qualitatively different levels of moral development, which differ in the extent to which moral actions are seen as driven by immediate external consequences or by general abstract principles.

Developing Socially and Personally. Humans use relationships with others to help them solve the problems that arise throughout development. Infants, burdened with limited motor skills and immature perceptual systems, form attachments with others to gain the sustenance they need for survival. Both the infant and the caregiver are active participants in the attachment process and are prepared to respond, given the right kinds of environmental events, with mutual bonding. Ainsworth identified three main categories of attachment—secure, resistant, and avoidant—that may have long-term consequences. In general, the responsiveness of the parent early in life is a significant but not inevitable influence on the relationships formed later in life.

Another aspect of social development is the formation of personal identity—a sense of who one is as an individual. Erik Erikson argued that personal identity is shaped by a series of "psychosocial" crises that individuals confront over the life span. During infancy and childhood, individuals address questions about their basic abilities and independence and learn to trust or mistrust others. During adolescence and adulthood, individuals deal with the identity crisis and come to grips with their roles as participants in intimate relationships. In the later years, individuals struggle with questions of accomplishment, concern for future generations, and meaning. Other important aspects of social development include the learning of gender roles—how each person learns to think and act as a member of a gender group—and the critical influences of the family structure. The chapter ended with a discussion of the social and psychological factors that confront the elderly and some of the important stages and decisions that accompany death and dying.

Human Development Chapter Summary

Developing Physically

The environment helps shape the physical process of growth, and can determine its ultimate outcome, but most physical changes are surprisingly consistent and predictable.

THE STAGES OF PRENATAL DEVELOPMENT

The fertilized egg is referred to as the zygote. Prenatal development is divided into three main stages. The *germinal period* is the period from conception to implantation. The *embryonic period* occurs over the next six weeks. The *fetal period* goes from the ninth week to birth, and includes the development of skeletal and muscular systems.

GROWTH DURING INFANCY

The average newborn weighs about 7 pounds and is approximately 20 inches in length. Over the next two years, there is tremendous physical development and increasing complexity of brain networks. The newborn's brain shows *plasticity*; changes are constantly occurring in neural circuitry.

FROM CRAWLING TO WALKING

Generally, the nervous system develops from the head down and from the center out. The sequence of development, from lifting the head to walking alone, is stable and predictable. Both nature and nurture contribute to individual differences.

FROM TODDLERHOOD TO ADOLESCENCE

General processing speed and coordination show great improvement. *Adolescence* is an important physical and psychological transition period that features the *growth spurt* and the onset of *puberty*.

REACHING ADULTHOOD

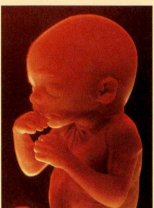

By the twenties, people are physically mature and at the height of their physical prowess. A small decline begins to occur in the twenties. Some individuals suffer brain degeneration with age, but fewer than 1 percent of people at age 65 are afflicted with *dementia*, or physically based loss in mental functioning.

Developing Intellectually

The developmental changes that occur in how people think (cognitive development) are of major importance to psychologists. There are good reasons to believe that infants see and think about the world differently than adults.

THE TOOLS OF INVESTIGATION

In the *preference technique*, an infant is presented with two visual displays simultaneously, and the researcher notes how long the infant looks at each. Researchers also use *habituation*, the decline in responsiveness to repeated stimulation, by *rewarding* simple motor movements investigate infants' preferences and abilities. TA researchers can also gain insight into infants' abilities.

THE GROWING PERCEPTUAL WORLD

Babies greet the world with sensory systems that function reasonably well. They show preferences for some colors and shapes; they recognize their mothers' voice within a day or two after birth; they are sensitive to smell, taste, and touch, and they seem to perceive a three-dimensional world.

PIAGET AND THE DEVELOPMENT OF THOUGHT

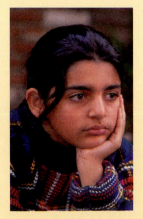

Piaget believed that everyone is born with a natural tendency to organize the world meaningfully, and do so through the use of *schemata*. Cognitive development is guided by assimilation (one fits new experiences into existing schemata) and accommodation (one modifies existing schemata to accommodate new experiences).

THE SENSORIMOTOR PERIOD: BIRTH TO TWO YEARS

From birth to age two, schemata revolve primarily around the infant's sensory and motor abilities. The infant gradually develops the ability to represent things internally, as shown in their development of *object permanence*.

THE PRE-OPERATIONAL PERIOD: TWO TO SEVEN YEARS

Although schemata are growing in sophistication, the children still lack the ability to perform basic mental operations. They fail to understand *conservation*. They show *centration* and don't understand *reversibility*. They also show *egocentrism*, viewing the world from their own perspective.

THE CONCRETE OPERATIONAL PERIOD: SEVEN TO ELEVEN YEARS

Children gain the capacity to verbalize, visualize, and mentally manipulate objects. They show the initial stirrings of logical thought. However, mental operations remain concrete, tied to actual objects in the world.

THE FORMAL OPERATIONAL PERIOD: ELEVEN TO ADULTHOOD

By the time children reach their teenage years, most will be in the formal operational period, when their thought processes become increasingly more like those of an adult. They can use systematic strategies for solving problems; mastery is gained over abstract thinking.

MORAL DEVELOPMENT: LEARNING RIGHT FROM WRONG

Kohlberg proposed three major levels of development. At the *preconventional level*, decisions about right and wrong are based primarily on external consequences. At the *conventional level*, people start to justify their actions on the basis of internalized rules, and whether an action maintains or disrupts the social order. *Postconventional*, morality is based on abstract principles that may even conflict with accepted standards. Kohlberg's critics argue that his views lack generality.

Developing Socially and Personally

Social relationships help people adapt successfully to their environments.

FORMING BONDS WITH OTHERS

Newborns form attachments, strong emotional ties to one or more intimate companions. Some believe both caregiver and infant are preprogrammed from the baby's birth to respond to environmental signals with attachment behavior.

THE ORIGINS OF ATTACHMENT

Harlow demonstrated that early attachments are formed primarily on the basis of *contact comfort*, rather than nourishment. Another important factor is *temperament*, the general level of emotional reactivity.

TYPES OF ATTACHMENTS

The *strange situation test* has been used to investigate differences in attachment bonds. The child is subjected gradually to a stressful situation and behavior is observed. Most children show *secure attachment*, while some show *resistant* or *avoidant* attachments.

FORMING A PERSONAL IDENTITY: ERIKSON'S CRISES OF DEVELOPMENT

Erikson believed that *personal identity* is shaped by a series of psycho-social crises. During infancy and childhood, the crises experienced include *trust vs. mistrust, autonomy vs. shame or doubt, initiative vs. guilt,* and *industry vs. inferiority*. During adolescence and young adulthood, we experience *identity vs. role confusion*. Entrance into young adulthood features the crisis of *intimacy vs. isolation*. As career and family are established, the conflict is *generativity vs. stagnation*, and in later adulthood we face the conflict of *integrity vs. despair*.

GENDER ROLE DEVELOPMENT

The foundations of gender identity are in place by age 2 or 3, and by the time children are in grade school, they tend to act in accordance with *gender roles*. *Gender schema* guide and direct our perceptions and behaviors.

THE FAMILY LIFE CYCLE

There is diversity in the structure of the modern family. Psychologists refer to the transitions that families move through as the family life cycle. Development is a complex interaction between physical aging and the problems defined by the environment (e.g., one's family).

GROWING OLD IN SOCIETY

The elderly face challenges presented by physical decline and society. *Ageism* is prejudice against an individual based on his or her age. Some of the more common myths claim that the elderly are sick, in mental decline, or depressed.

DEATH AND DYING

Kübler-Ross proposed that people progress through five stages as they face death: denial, anger, bargaining, depression, and acceptance. Many psychologists find it more appropriate to speak in terms of *dying trajectories*, the paths people travel as they face their impending death.

Terms to Remember

development, 118

DEVELOPING PHYSICALLY

zygote, 120
germinal period, 120
embryonic period, 120
fetal period, 120
teratogens, 122
puberty, 126
menopause, 127
dementia, 128

DEVELOPING INTELLECTUALLY

habituation, 130
longitudinal design, 133
cross-sectional design, 133
schemata, 135
assimilation, 135
accommodation, 135
sensorimotor period, 136
object permanence, 137
preoperational period, 137
conservation , 137
egocentrism, 138
concrete operational period, 138
formal operational period, 140
morality, 143
preconventional level, 143
conventional level, 144
postconventional level, 144

DEVELOPING SOCIALLY AND PERSONALLY

attachments, 146
temperament, 148
strange situation test, 148
personal identity, 153
gender roles, 157
gender schemas, 157
family life cycle, 158
ageism, 159

Recommended Readings

Tanner, J. M. (1990). *Fetus into man: Physical growth from conception to maturity* (Rev. ed.). Cambridge, MA: Harvard University Press. A classic book on development providing all the details on physical growth and development.

Hayflick, L. (1994). *How and why we age*. New York: Ballantine. Another excellent summary of the biological factors involved in the aging process; it's very informative and easy to read.

Flavell, J. H., Miller, P. H., & Miller, S. A. (1993). *Cognitive development* (3rd ed.). Englewood Cliffs, NJ: Prentice-Hall. An interesting undergraduate textbook, written by leading developmental researchers, covering all aspects of cognitive development. It includes detailed discussions of Piaget, Vygotsky, and other leading theorists.

Bornstein, M. H., & Lamb, M. E. (1992). *Developmental Psychology: An advanced textbook* (3rd ed.). Hillsdale, NJ: Erlbaum. A superb account of cutting edge research in developmental psychology. This book covers all aspects of human development, from perceptual to social.

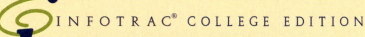

INFOTRAC® COLLEGE EDITION

For additional readings, explore Infotrac College Edition, your online library. Go to:
http://www.infotrac-college.com/wadsworth

Hint: enter the search terms: Motor development, Cognitive development, Moral development, Psychosocial development, Death and dying.

🌐 What's on the Web?

Child Development Web Site

(idealist.com/children/)

This site is ". . . .a meeting place for parents, students of development and early childhood education, and professionals who work with children." It provides a wealth of information related to child development, as well as tutorials on various theories of development such as Erikson's and Freud's.

Adolescence: Change and Continuity

(www.personal.psu.edu/faculty/n/x/nxd10/adolesce.htm)

This site can help you gain some insight into the turbulent years of adolescence. You can choose to explore basic domains, such as social transitions that occur in adolescence; you can explore the important contexts of adolescence, such as schools, family, and peer groups; and you can explore how certain issues such as achievement, sexuality, and delinquency interact with this developmental stage.

AARP Webplace

(www.aarp.org/)

This is the official Web site of the American Association for Retired Persons, and provides some very useful information about the process of aging. What new medical breakthroughs will affect the aging population? What is the typical "profile" of the older American? Find out with a trip to this site.

The Wadsworth Psychology Study Center Web Site

See http://psychology.wadsworth.com/ for practice quiz questions, hypercontents, updates, critical thinking exercises, discussion forums, and more! The Wadsworth Psychology Study Center provides a wealth of information fully organized and integrated by chapter.

Sensation and Perception

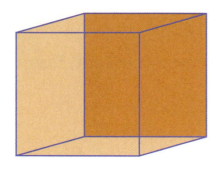

FIGURE 5.1
The Necker Cube

sensations
The elementary components, or building blocks, of an experience, such as a pattern of light and dark, a bitter taste, or a change in temperature.

perception
The collection of processes used to arrive at a meaningful interpretation of sensations; through perception, the simple components of an experience are organized into a recognizable form.

You bolt upright, breathing heavily, startled awake by an uncertain sound. The rumbling of distant thunder rolls overhead; the rain, gentle now, creates a soft and steady patter on the roof. Awake, you listen. A variety of sounds beckon your interpretation: the hum of the fish tank filter, the irregular ticking of what must be the gas heater cooling, the creak of a settling floorboard. There is even the distant sound of your cat making a late-night visit to the litter box. Normal sounds, you tell yourself, nothing to spark concern. Sinking back into the warmth of your bed, you shut your eyes and try to clear your mind. It's nothing—you're okay—but the silence continues to tell its story . . .

Each of us is constantly bombarded by messages from the environment. Some come in the form of light energy, bouncing in all directions off objects in the real world; others, like strange "bumps in the night," arrive as regular changes in air pressure. Many of these messages will ultimately get translated into an electro-chemical language for delivery deep within the brain. The products of this translation process, and their subsequent interpretation, serve as our focus in this chapter. We turn now to the important psychological processes of sensation and perception. It is through sensation and perception that we primarily build and define the world of immediate experience.

To help understand the difference between the psychological terms *sensation* and *perception*, consider the image shown in Figure 5.1. It's a geometric figure, a cube, but it exists at another level of description as well. It consists of lines, angles, patterns of light and dark, colors, and so on. These elementary features—the building blocks of the meaningful image—are processed by the visual system, through reasonably well understood physiological systems, and the products are visual **sensations**. Psychologists have historically thought of sensations—such as a pattern of light and dark, a bitter taste, a change in temperature—as the fundamental, elementary components of an experience. **Perception** is the collection of processes used to arrive at a meaningful interpretation of sensations. The simple components are usually organized by higher-order activities (which are less well understood) into a recognizable form—in this case you perceive a *cube*.

Now, let's think more closely about what "interpretation" means in this context. Look closely at the cube once again. Stare at it for a while. The lines, the angles, and the colors remain fixed, but the cube itself appears to shift its shape from moment to moment. For a time, the shaded surface of the image is the front of the cube; then, in the next instance, it forms the back of the cube. First you see it from one perspective, and then from another. How is this possible? Certainly the image on the page remains fixed; the reflected light is not changing systematically with time. The answer lies in the *interpretation* of the sensory image. In this case, the message delivered to the brain is ambiguous. Because more than one interpretation of the physical image is possible, the brain engages in a perceptual dance, shifting from one interpretation to the other (Gaetz et al., 1998). As you'll see later when we discuss each of the sensory systems in detail, sometimes the brain gets it wrong altogether—in those cases, perceptual illusions may be produced.

Previewing the Adaptive Problems

To appreciate how the brain actually builds its internal representation of the outside world, we'll discuss each of the sensory systems from the perspective of three important adaptive problems. Each is a fundamental problem that our sensory systems need to

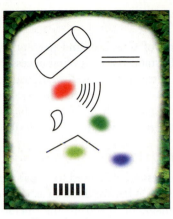

Translating the message   Extracting the message   Producing stable interpretations
                                 components

Figure 5.2
Adaptive Problems of Sensation and Perception
To build its internal representation of the outside world, the brain needs to solve three fundamental
adaptive problems for each of its sensory systems : (1) translating the message from the environment
into the language of the nervous system; (2) extracting the elementary components of the message,
such as colors, sounds, simple forms, and patterns of light and dark; and (3) building a stable
interpretation of those components once they've been extracted.

solve, regardless of whether it's light, sound, or some other kind of information that we're
trying to interpret (see Figure 5.2).

First, how does the external message from the environment get translated into the
language of the nervous system? As you learned in Chapter 3, communication in the nervous system is fundamentally an electrochemical process. When the outside world begins
to "talk" to the brain, the message arrives in a variety of forms that are not electrochemical. For example, you see by means of reflected light, which arrives in the form of
electromagnetic energy; you hear by interpreting sound vibrations, or repetitive changes
in air pressure. In a sense, it's like trying to listen to someone who speaks a language you
don't understand. The brain needs an interpreter—a process through which the incoming message can be changed into an understandable form. The translation process is
called **transduction** and it's accomplished in a different way for each of the sensory
systems.

Second, how do the elementary components—the sensations—get extracted from
the message? Once the environmental message has been successfully translated—
appearing now in the form of neural impulses—the important message components need
to be extracted or pulled out of the complex sensory pattern. To accomplish this feat, the
newly formed sensory code is delivered from the translation sites to processing stations
deep within the brain. Along each pathway, which differs for each of the sensory systems, are localized regions specialized to perform unique sensory functions.

Third, how does the brain build a stable and long-lasting interpretation of these components once they've been extracted? Although the sensory pathways may successfully
break down the environmental message into a series of much simpler components, a significant problem remains: How do these extracted features, represented as the activities of
many thousands of neurons, combine to produce perceptual experiences? You see objects,
not patterns of colored light and dark; you hear melodies, not sequences of irregularly
timed sounds. The biological bases of perception—the processes that produce the interpretation—are still poorly understood, but you'll discover that the brain uses certain principles of organization that may well cut across all of the senses.

transduction
The process by which external messages
are translated into the internal language of
the brain.

Vision: Building a World of Color and Form

Our discussion of sensation and perception begins with vision: the sense of sight. To understand vision, it's first necessary to discuss how the physical message—light—is translated into the language of the brain. Next, we'll trace some of the pathways in the brain that are used to extract the basic components of the visual message. Finally, we'll tackle the topic of visual perception: How does the brain create its stable interpretation of the light information it receives?

TRANSLATING THE MESSAGE: VISUAL TRANSDUCTION

The physical message delivered to visual receptors, **light,** is a form of electromagnetic energy. What we think of as visible light is actually only a small part of an electromagnetic spectrum that includes other energy forms, such as X rays, ultraviolet rays, and even radio and television waves (see Figure 5.3).

Light is typically classified by two main physical properties. The first is *wavelength*, which corresponds to the physical distance from one energy cycle to the next. Changes in the wavelength of light are generally experienced, psychologically, as changes in color, or **hue.** If you look at Figure 5.3, you'll discover that we see wavelengths ranging from only about 400 to 700 nanometers (billionths of a meter). Psychologically, these wavelengths are experienced as colors ranging roughly from violet to red. The second physical property is *intensity*, which corresponds to the amount of light falling on an object. Changes in intensity are generally experienced as increases or decreases in **brightness.**

Light originates from a source, such as the sun or a light bulb, and usually enters the eye after bouncing off objects in its path. Most of the time light is a mix-

light
The small part of the electromagnetic spectrum that is processed by the visual system. Light is typically classified in terms of *wavelength* (the physical distance from one energy cycle to the next) and *intensity* (the amount of light falling on an object).

hue
The dimension of light that produces color; hue is typically determined by the wavelength of light reflecting from an object.

brightness
The aspect of the visual experience that changes with light intensity; in general, as the intensity of light increases, so does its perceived brightness.

FIGURE 5.3

Light and the Electromagnetic Spectrum
Visible light is actually only a small part of the electromagnetic spectrum, which includes such other energy forms as X rays and radio and TV waves. Changes in the wavelength of light from about 400 nanometers to 700 nanometers are experienced as changes in color; short wavelengths are seen as violets and blues; medium wavelengths as yellows and greens; and long wavelengths as reds.

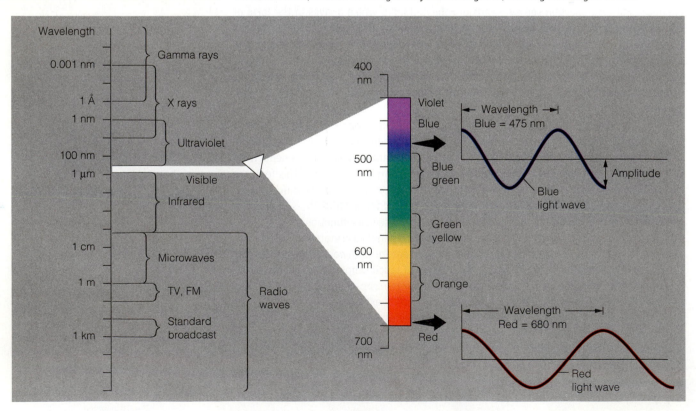

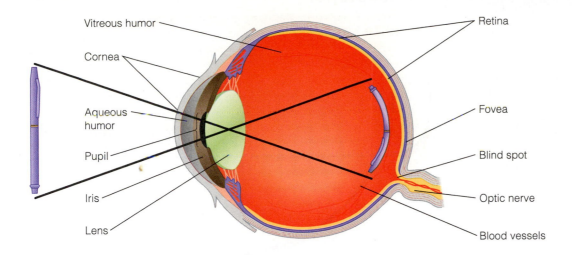

Vitreous humor

Cornea

Aqueous humor

Pupil

Iris

Lens

Retina

Fovea

Blind spot

Optic nerve

Blood vessels

FIGURE 5.4

The Human Eye
Light enters the eye through the cornea, pupil, and lens. As the lens changes shape in relation to the distance of the object, the reflected light is focused at the back of the eye where, in the retina, the visual message is translated.

ture of many different wavelengths; after hitting an object, some of these wavelengths are absorbed—which ones depends on the physical properties of the object—and the remaining wavelengths reflect outward, where they eventually enter the eyes. It is here, in the eyes, that the important translation process occurs.

Entering the Eye

The first step in the translation process is to bring the incoming light energy to the light-sensitive receptor cells that sit at the back of each eye. When light bounces off an object, the reflected wavelengths are scattered about. They then need to be brought back together—or focused—for a clear image to be processed. In the human eye, the focusing process is accomplished by the **cornea,** the protective outer layer of the eye, and by the **lens,** a clear, flexible piece of tissue that sits behind the pupil.

As shown in Figure 5.4, light first passes through the cornea and the pupil before traveling through the lens. The **pupil,** which looks like a black spot, is actually a hole in a ring of colored tissue called the **iris.** The iris gives the eye its distinctive color (a person with green eyes has green irises), but the color of the iris plays no real role in vision. Relaxing or tightening the muscles around the iris changes the size of the pupil, thereby regulating the amount of light that enters the eye. In dim light, the pupil gets larger, which allows more light to get in; in bright light, the pupil gets smaller, allowing less light to enter. As light passes through the pupil, it is also restricted to the central portions of the lens, where there are fewer optical distortions (Thibos et al., 1990).

The lens focuses the light on the sensory receptors, which are at the back of the eye, much like the lens in a camera focuses light on film. But whereas in a camera focusing typically involves changing the distance between the lens and the film, in the human eye focusing is accomplished by changing the shape of the lens itself. This process, known as **accommodation,** is influenced by the distance between the lens and the object being viewed. When an object is far away, the lens is relatively long and thin; as the object moves closer, muscles attached to the lens contract and the lens becomes thicker and rounder. As you age, the lens loses some of this flexibility, making the accommodation process far less efficient (Fukuda et al., 1990). This is one of the reasons people typically require reading glasses or bifocals when they reach middle age. The corrective lenses in the glasses support the accommodation process, which the eyes can no longer successfully perform on their own.

cornea
The transparent and protective outer covering of the eye.

lens
The flexible piece of tissue that helps focus light toward the back of the eye.

pupil
The hole in the center of the eye that allows light to enter; the size of the pupil changes with light intensity.

iris
The ring of colored tissue surrounding the pupil.

accommodation
In vision, the process through which the lens changes its shape temporarily in order to help focus light on the retina.

Inside the Problem   Dark Adaptation

You arrive at the movie theater early, as usual, and settle into your seat. You've picked your spot with care—midway up, clean floor, nobody in the row directly in front of you. The lights dim, the movie begins, and you start to relax. A short time later, the door swings open and an awkward-looking fellow wanders in late, looking for a seat. He appears to bounce from side to side down the aisle, occasionally stopping to peer into a row with a confused look on his face. You can see him fine; he, on the other hand, appears to be nearly blind. The reason, of course, is that your eyes have adjusted to the dark, whereas his have not.

When you move from a brightly lit environment to a dark one, it takes about 20-25 minutes for your eyes to adjust, a process known as **dark adaptation.** Why does the adjustment process take so long? To discover the answer, we need to turn our attention once more to the rods and cones. As mentioned earlier, visual transduction occurs when light reacts chemically with photopigments in the receptor cells. In bright light, many of these photopigments break down, or become "bleached," and are no longer useful for generating a neural impulse. When you enter a dark movie theater from a bright environment, your receptor cells simply don't have enough of the depleted photopigments to detect the low levels of illumination. The photopigments need to be regenerated by the cells, a process that takes time. As long as there is enough light around, you won't have much of a problem because your eyes never completely run out of photopigment; difficulties arise only in dark environments, where your receptor cells need to operate at peak efficiency.

The timing of the adaptation process is shown in Figure 5.5. This dark adaptation curve is produced by measuring the smallest amount of light that people can reliably see, plotted as a function of time spent in the dark. Over 20–25 minutes, smaller and smaller amounts of light are needed to achieve accurate detection. Sensitivity increases, once again, because the visual receptor cells are recovering from their

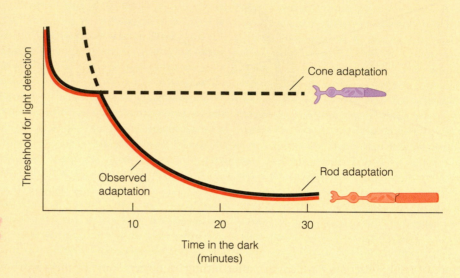

FIGURE 5.5

The Dark Adaptation Curve
Your eyes gradually adjust to the dark and become more sensitive; that is, you are able to detect light at increasingly low levels of intensity. The rods and cones adapt at different rates and reach different final levels of sensitivity. The dark adaptation curve represents the combined adaptation of the two receptor types. Notice that at about the 8-minute mark there is a point of discontinuity; this is where further increases in sensitivity are due to the functioning of the rods.

earlier interactions with bright light, which broke down the visual pigments, requiring those pigments to be regenerated.

Notice that a break, or point of discontinuity, occurs at about the 8-minute mark in the dark adaptation curve. To help understand its cause, think about the following two empirical facts: (1) If the light source used to measure sensitivity is of a particular color (such as green), then after the break point in the curve the color will seem to become gray. (2) If the light source used to measure sensitivity is presented only to the fovea, the dark adaptation curve will level off at about the 8-minute mark, and no further increases in sensitivity will be found. Based on what you already know about the visual system, can you deduce why the curve "breaks" in this fashion?

The explanation is that the rods and the cones adapt to the dark at different rates. Early in the dark adaptation function,

the cones show the most sensitivity, but they achieve their maximum responsiveness rather quickly. After about 7 or 8 minutes in the dark, the rods, which can detect quite low levels of illumination, begin to take over. Since cones are needed to detect color, a green light source presented at a low level of illumination will appear colorless. In addition, if the light source is presented only to the fovea, where there are no rods, the dark adaptation curve will cease to improve beyond the point of maximum cone sensitivity.

To psychologists, the dark adaptation curve provides more than just a measurement of how the eyes adjust to the dark. It provides strong support for the contention that the human visual system relies on two types of receptor systems, each with quite different properties and each operating most efficiently under different conditions of illumination.

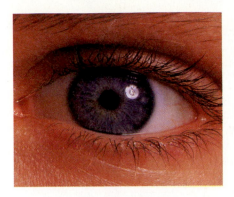 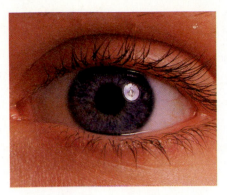 

One of the functions of the pupil is to regulate the amount of light entering the eye. In bright light, the pupil gets smaller, allowing less light to enter; in dim light, the pupil gets larger allowing more light to enter.

Light completes its journey when it reaches a thin layer of tissue, called the **retina,** that covers the back of the eye. It is here that the electromagnetic energy actually gets translated into the inner language of the brain. Embedded in the retina of each eye are about 126 million light-sensitive receptor cells that *transduce*, or change, the light energy into the electrochemical impulses that characterize neural processing. The translation process is chemically based. Each of the receptor cells contains a substance, known as a *photopigment*, that reacts to light. The light causes a chemical reaction that ultimately leads to a neural impulse, completing the initial translation process. Thus, what begins as a pattern of electromagnetic information ends as a pattern of electrochemical signals: the language of the brain.

You may have noticed in Figure 5.4 that the focused image on the retina is actually inverted, or upside down. This may seem strange, given that we don't see an upside-down world. The inverted image is created by the optical properties of the lens, although its existence did confuse early investigators of vision. It's important to remember that we don't actually see with our eyes. Our perceptual world is built in our brains. The main function of the eyes is simply to solve the problem of transduction and pass the information forward to the brain. The brain later corrects the inversion problem and we see a stable, orderly, and right-side-up world.

Rods and Cones

There are two types of receptor cells contained in the retina: **rods** and **cones.** Of the roughly 126 million receptor cells within each eye, about 120 million are rods and 6 million are cones. Each receptor type is named for its visual appearance—rods are generally long and thin, whereas cones are short, thick, and tapered to a point. Rods are the more sensitive visual receptors; they can generate visual signals when very small amounts of light strike their surface. This makes rods useful at night and in any situation in which the overall level of illumination is low. Rods also tend to be concentrated along the periphery, or sides, of the retina. This is one reason that dim images can sometimes be seen better out of the corners of your eyes.

Cones tend to be concentrated in the very center of the retina, bunched in a small central pit called the **fovea** (which means "central pit"). Unlike rods, cones need relatively high levels of light to operate efficiently, as the accompanying "Inside the Problem" feature discusses. Cones perform a number of critical visual functions. For example, cones are used for processing fine detail, an ability called **visual acuity.** Cones also play an extremely important role in the early processing of color, as we'll discuss later.

Early Processing in the Retina

Once the electrochemical signal is generated by a rod or a cone, it's passed along to other cells in the retina, particularly *bipolar cells* and *ganglion cells*, where further processing occurs (see Figure 5.6). Even at this early stage in visual processing,

dark adaptation
The process through which the eyes adjust to dim light.

retina
The thin layer of tissue that covers the back of the eye and contains the light-sensitive receptor cells for vision.

rods
Receptor cells in the retina, located mainly around the sides of the retina, that transduce light energy into neural messages; these visual receptors are highly sensitive and are active in dim light.

cones
Receptor cells in the central portion of the retina that transduce light energy into neural messages; they operate best when light levels are high, and they are primarily responsible for the ability to sense color.

fovea
The "central pit" area in the retina where the cone receptors are located.

visual acuity
The ability to process fine detail in vision.

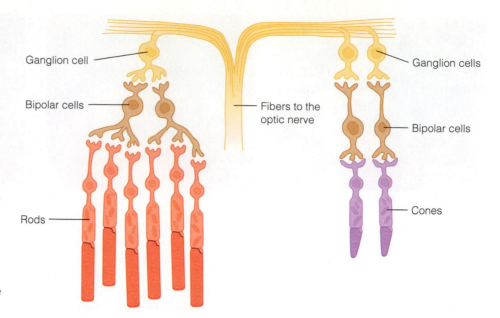

FIGURE 5.6

Rods, Cones, and Receptive Fields
Rods and cones send signals to other cells in the retina. Each ganglion cell has a receptive field. Ganglion cells in the fovea which receive input from cones, tend to have smaller receptive fields than ganglion cells in the periphery, which receive input from rods. The fovea provides better detail, and the sides of the eyes are more sensitive to low levels of light.

cells in the retina are beginning to interpret the incoming visual message. For example, the ganglion cells have what are called **receptive fields,** which means they receive input from a group of receptor cells and respond only when particular patterns of light shine across the retina (Shapley, 1990; Shapley & Kaplan, 1989).

This concept of a receptive field is a very important one. The fact that a cell, such as a ganglion cell, receives input from a number of receptor cells means that it can pass on higher-order information to the brain. For example, many cells in the retina have what are called *center–surround* receptive fields. These cells will respond one way—perhaps increasing their firing rate—when light falls on one region of the retina, and the opposite way—decreasing their firing rate—when light falls in a nearby region (see Figure 5.7). This means that information about how light is actually spread out across the retina can be sent to the brain. One by-product is that we can easily detect *edges:* the brain can tell where light stops and starts. As you'll discover shortly, cells have increasingly more complex receptive fields the farther up you travel in the brain.

The visual signals generated by the ganglion cells eventually leave the retina, en route to the deeper processing stations of the brain, through a collection of nerve fibers called the *optic nerve.* The optic nerve consists of roughly 1 million axons that wrap together to form a sort of visual transmission cable. Because of its size, at the point where the optic nerve leaves each retina there is no room for visual receptor cells. This creates a biological **blind spot** because there are no

receptive field
In vision, the portion of the retina that, when stimulated, causes the activity of the neuron to change.

blind spot
The point where the optic nerve leaves the back of the eye.

CONCEPT SUMMARY
Comparing Rods and Cones

Characteristic	Rods	Cones
Number	Approximately 126 million per retina	Approximately 6 million per retina
Shape	Generally long and thin	Short, thick, tapered to a point
Location	Concentrated in the periphery of the retina	Concentrated in the center of the retina, the *fovea*
Sensitivity		
—Light	Sensitive at low levels of illumination	Not very sensitive at low levels of illumination
—Detail	Not sensitive to visual detail	High level of sensitivity to detail; high *visual acuity*
—Color	Indistinguishable among different wavelengths	Three types, each maximally sensitive to a different wavelength

receptor cells in this location to transduce the visual message. Interestingly, people normally experience no holes in their visual field; as part of its interpretation process, the visual system fills in the gaps to create a continuous visual scene (Durgin et al., 1995; Ramachandran, 1992). You can locate your blind spot by following the exercise described in Figure 5.8 on page 178.

EXTRACTING THE MESSAGE COMPONENTS: VISUAL PATHWAYS

After leaving the retina, the patterns of neural activation flow along each optic nerve until they reach the *optic chiasm* (from the Greek word meaning "cross"), where the information splits into different tracts leading to the separate hemispheres of the brain (see Figure 5.9). Information that has been detected on the right half of each retina (from the left visual field) is sent to the right hemisphere, and information falling on the left half of each retina (from the right visual field) projects to the left hemisphere. The majority of the visual signals move directly toward a major relay station in the thalamus called the *lateral geniculate nucleus*; other signals, perhaps 10% of the total, detour into a midbrain structure called the *superior colliculus*.

Significant processing and interpretation of the visual message occurs along these pathways. Neuroscientists currently believe that there are two primary visual pathways from the retina through the lateral geniculate nucleus. One pathway, often called the P-channel, is specialized to process color, texture, and possibly depth; the other, called the M-channel, seems to process movement (Livingstone & Hubel, 1988; Schiller et al., 1990; Shapley, 1990). At the same time, processing in the superior colliculus, a somewhat more primitive structure, controls our ability to localize objects in space by moving the head and eyes (Sparks, 1988). One of the hallmarks of the visual system is that many of these activities are carried out simultaneously, through what is called **parallel processing**. Many different brain regions work together, in parallel, to pull the essential features out of a visual message.

Feature Detectors

From the lateral geniculate nucleus, the visual message moves toward the back of the brain, primarily to portions of the occipital lobe. Here, in the primary visual cortex, further elements of the visual message are picked out and identified. For

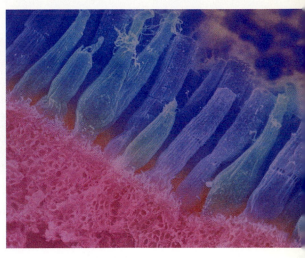

Each human retina contains two types of photoreceptor cells: rods and cones. As shown in this color-enhanced photo, the rods are rod-shaped in appearance and the cones are cone-shaped.

parallel processing
Processing that occurs in many different brain regions at the same time, in parallel.

FIGURE 5.7

Center-Surround Receptive Fields
Receptive fields in the retina often have a center-surround arrangement. Light falling in the center of the field has an opposite effect from light falling in the surround. In panel (a) light in the center of the field produces an excitatory response (shown by the color green); in panel (b) light falling in the surround produces an inhibitory response (shown by the color purple). When light falls equally in both regions, shown in panel (c), there will be no net increase in the cell's activity.

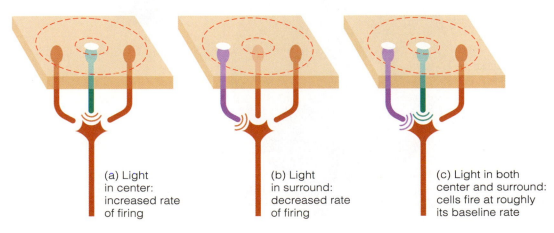

(a) Light in center: increased rate of firing

(b) Light in surround: decreased rate of firing

(c) Light in both center and surround: cells fire at roughly its baseline rate

FIGURE 5.8
The Blind Spot
To experience your blind spot, simply close your left eye and focus with your right eye on the boy's face. Then, hold this book only a few inches from your face and slowly move it away till the pie mysteriously disappears. Notice that your brain fills in the spot—complete with the checkerboard pattern.

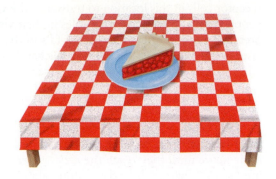

example, David Hubel and Torsten Wiesel (1962, 1979) discovered **feature detectors** in the visual cortex of cats and monkeys. Feature detectors are cells that respond best to very specific visual events, such as patterns of light and dark. One type of feature detector, which Hubel and Wiesel called a *simple cell*, was found to respond actively only when a small bar of light was shone into a particular region of the retina. Cells of this type also turned out to be orientation specific, which means that the visual bar needed to be presented at a particular angle in order for the cell to respond.

The properties of these cells were discovered by measuring neural impulses in individual cells, using implanted recording electrodes. An example of this type of experiment, and the equipment used, is shown in Figure 5.10. Remember, there are no pain receptors in the brain, which makes it possible for researchers to explore the reactions of brain cells without causing an animal severe discomfort. The recorded cells were found to increase, decrease, or show no changes in their

feature detectors
Cells in the visual cortex that respond to very specific visual events, such as bars of light at particular orientations.

FIGURE 5.9
The Visual Pathways
Input from the left visual field falls on the inside half of the left eye and the outside half of the right eye and projects to the right hemisphere of the brain; input from the right visual field projects to the left hemisphere. Visual processing occurs at several places along the pathway, ending in the visual cortex, where highly specialized processing takes place.

Center

Left visual field

Right visual field

Optic nerve

Thalamus

Superior colliculus

Visual cortex

Retina

Optic nerve

Optic chiasm

Lateral geniculate nucleus of the thalamus

Superior colliculus

Left visual cortex   Right visual cortex

(occipital lobes)

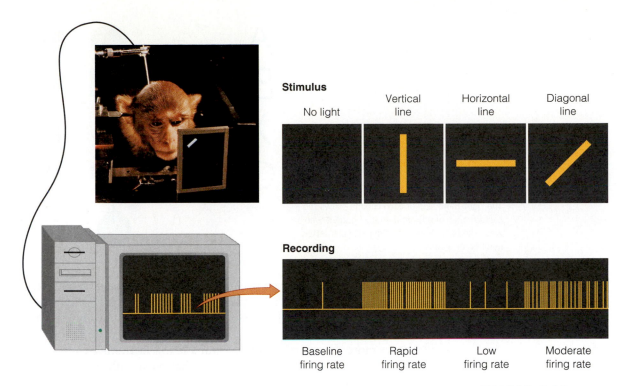

FIGURE 5.10

Feature Detectors in the Visual Cortex
Hubel and Wiesel discovered feature detectors in the brains of cats and monkeys that increase their firing rates to specific bars of light presented at particular orientations.

firing rates in response to specific visual stimuli shown to the eye. In Figure 5.10, experimenters are recording the reaction to the presentation of a small bar of light presented at a particular angle. Again, Hubel and Wiesel found that certain feature detectors in the monkey's brain would react to this stimulus, and not to others, and only when the bar was shown at this particular angle.

Hubel and Wiesel also discovered that feature detectors are not randomly organized in the visual cortex. Rather, there is a kind of master plan to the organization in the brain. Cells that respond to stimuli shown at a particular orientation, say 20 degrees, tend to sit together in the same "columns" of brain tissue. If a recording electrode is moved across neighboring columns, cells show regular shifts in their orientation specificity. So, if cells in a particular column A respond to bars at an angle of 20 degrees, then cells in a physically adjacent column B might respond actively only to bars presented at a 30-degree angle. This is generally thought to mean that cells in the visual cortex break down the visual message in a systematic and highly organized way.

Higher-Level Detection

Obviously, the brain is sensitive to more than just bars, or orientation-specific patterns of light and dark. Hubel and Wiesel also found cells that responded selectively to more complex patterns—for example, corners, edges, bars that moved through the visual field, and bars that displayed a certain characteristic length. Other researchers have found cells—once again in monkey brains—that respond most actively to *faces*. Moreover, to get the most active response from these cells, the face needed to look realistically like a monkey—if the face was distorted or cartoonish, the cells did not respond as actively (Perrett & Mistlin, 1987). There's even evidence suggesting that some cells are "tuned" to respond selectively to certain kinds of facial expressions (Hasselmo et al., 1989).

In humans, researchers have collected evidence of how the brain parses the visual message by studying brain-damaged patients. When certain parts of the human brain are damaged because of stroke or injury, the result is often very selective, even bizarre, visual problems. For example, one kind of damage in the brain can produce a condition called *prosopagnosia*, in which a person loses the ability to

? CRITICAL THINKING

Can you think of any reason why it might be adaptive for the brain to first break the visual pattern down into basic features—such as a bar or a pattern of light and dark—before recombining those features together into a unified whole?

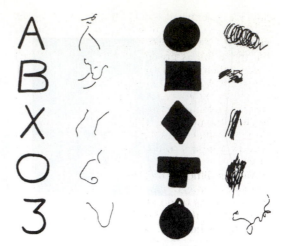

The right-hand side of each column shows the performance of a brain-damaged patient who was asked simply to copy the particular letter, number, or shape.

recognize faces. An affected person can fail to recognize acquaintances, family members, or even his or her own reflection in a mirror (Farah, 1994)! In another condition, called *akinetopsia*, patients possess normal vision only for objects at rest; if an object is placed in motion, it seems to vanish, only to reappear if it becomes stationary once more. Conversely, patients with a lesion in another cortical location might show the most sensitivity to objects that move rather than stay stationary (Zeki, 1992).

Additional evidence for specialization in the human brain has come from studies using PET scanning procedures. In this procedure, the subject ingests a harmless radioactive substance that is then absorbed into the cells of brain regions that are metabolically active. A visual event of some kind is presented, and the researcher can then observe which areas of the brain are activated. Using this technique, researchers have discovered that certain areas of the brain respond selectively to patterns of dots that *move* across the visual field (Dupont et al., 1994). Other areas respond selectively to object tasks, such as matching faces, but not to spatial tasks, such as finding dots in an array (McIntosh et al., 1994). Still other areas of the brain may be selectively involved in the processing of mental *images*, such as mentally visualizing a letter in upper- or lowercase (Kosslyn et al., 1993).

Results like these indicate that the human brain, like the monkey brain, divides its labor. Certain regions of the cortex are specifically designed to process particular parts of the visual message. In other words, there is specificity in the organization and function of the brain. The exact role that each of these parts plays in vision remains to be worked out, and it's quite possible that particular cells

Many areas in the human brain appear to respond selectively to visual motion. The highlighted regions, derived from PET scanning, show areas of the human brain that react more to a moving visual stimulus than to a stationary one.

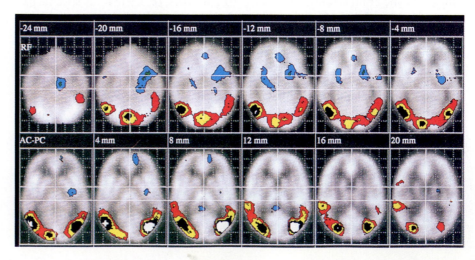

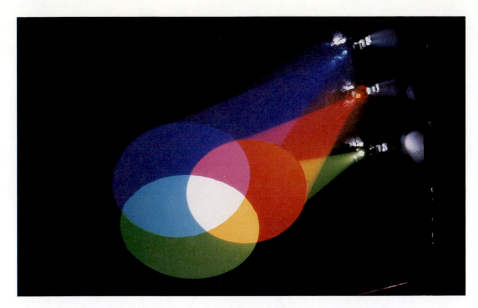

Additive mixing of lights with different wavelengths can create a variety of perceived colors—even white.

or regions of the brain perform more than one function (Schiller, 1996), but the mysteries of how the brain solves the basic problems of vision are beginning to unravel.

Color Vision: Trichromatic Theory

One of the most significant things the brain pulls out of the visual message is color. It turns out that color information is processed along the entire visual pathway: Retina → lateral geniculate nucleus → visual cortex. In the retina, as you'll see shortly, early color information is extracted by comparing the relative activations of different types of cone receptors; higher up in the brain, messages encounter cells that are "tuned" to respond only to particular colors.

Earlier you learned that color is determined primarily by the wavelength of light reflected back into the eye. In general, short wavelengths (around 450 nanometers) produce blues, medium wavelengths (around 530 nanometers) produce greens, and long wavelengths (around 670 nanometers) produce reds. White light, which most people would classify as colorless, is actually a combination of all of the wavelengths of the visible spectrum. The reason your neighbor's shirt looks red is because chemical pigments in the fabric of the shirt absorb all but the long wavelengths of light; the long wavelengths are reflected back into the eyes, and you see the shirt as red. But in a sense, the object itself, the shirt, is truly colorless; you perceive the object as red only because the shirt has "rejected," by reflecting outward, those forms of electromagnetic energy that your visual system will shortly classify as red.

When reflected wavelengths reach the retina, they cause cones in the fovea to become active. Physiological analysis of the human eye has revealed three types of cone receptors: One type generates neural impulses primarily to *short* wavelengths (420 nanometers); another type responds most energetically to *medium* wavelengths (530 nanometers); and a final type responds most to *long* wavelengths (560 nanometers) of light. The sensitivity of a particular cone type actually spreads across a relatively broad range of individual wavelengths and is determined by the photopigment that the receptor contains (Bowmaker & Dartnall, 1980; Schnapf & Baylor, 1987). Figure 5.11 shows the sensitivities for each of the cones, as well as for the rods.

The **trichromatic theory** of color vision proposes that color information is extracted through the activations of these three types of cones (trichromatic means "three-color"). An early version of the trichromatic theory was proposed in the nineteenth century by Thomas Young and Hermann von Helmholtz—long before modern techniques had verified the existence of the different cone types.

trichromatic theory
A theory of color vision proposing that color information is extracted by comparing the relative activations of three different types of cone receptors.

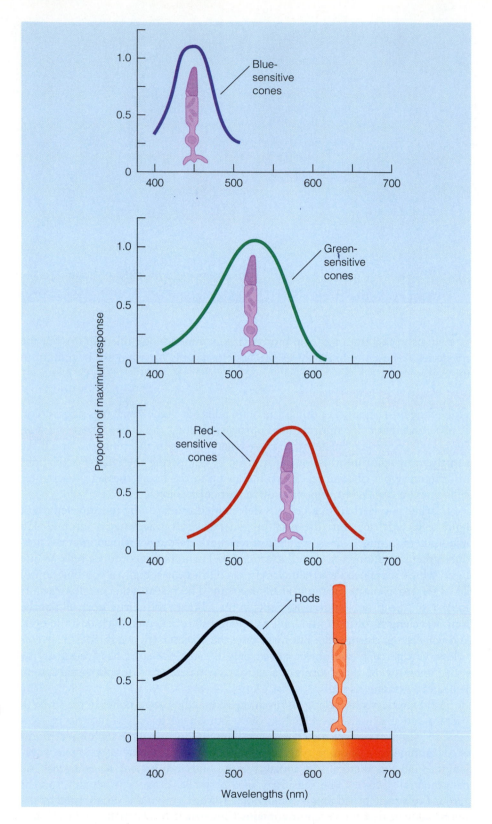

FIGURE 5.11

Receptor Sensitivity Curves
Blue-sensitive cones are most likely to respond to short wavelengths of light; green-sensitive cones respond best to medium wavelengths; red-sensitive cones respond best to long wavelengths. On the sensitivity curve for rods, notice that rods are not sensitive to long wavelengths of light. (Based on Jones & Childers, 1993.)

As the basis for their theory, Young and Helmholtz used the fact that most colors can be matched by mixing three basic, or *primary*, colors. They suggested that the brain must determine the color of an object by comparing the relative activation levels of three primary receptors. When just one receptor type is strongly activated, you see one of the primary colors. For example, when a short wavelength

cone is strongly activated, you might see something in the violet to blue region of the spectrum; when a medium cone is active, you would see something resembling green. For long wavelengths, which activate the third type of cone, you sense the color red. All other colors, such as a pumpkin orange, are sensed when more than one of the receptor types is activated. Most colors correspond to a mixture of wavelengths and are sensed by comparing the activations of the three receptors.

The trichromatic theory explains a number of interesting aspects of color vision. For example, it explains certain kinds of color blindness. At times, nature makes a mistake and fills someone's red cones with green photopigment or the green cones with red photopigment (Boynton, 1979). Under these rare conditions, which affect more males than females, individuals are left with two rather than three operational cone receptors. The trichromatic theory predicts that *dichromats*—people with two rather than three cone types—should lose their ability to discriminate successfully among certain colors. Indeed, people who lack either the red or green cone type have a great deal of trouble distinguishing red from green. Other types of cone loss can produce trouble with blue–green discriminations. The particular type of color deficiency depends on the particular type of lost receptor.

Color Vision: Opponent Processes

The physiological evidence, combined with the color mixing and color blindness patterns, provides strong support for the trichromatic theory. But the theory fails as a complete account of color vision. For one thing, the trichromatic theory has a problem with *yellow*. Human observers seem convinced that yellow is every bit as "pure" a color as red, green, and blue; even 4-month old infants prefer dividing the color spectrum into four color categories rather than three (Bornstein et al., 1976). In addition, most people also have no problem reporting a yellowish red or a bluish green but almost never report seeing anything resembling a yellowish blue or, for that matter, a greenish red. Why?

It turns out that certain colors are specially linked, such as blue and yellow, and red and green. You can discover this for yourself by taking a look at Figure 5.12. You'll find that if you stare at a vivid color like red for awhile and then switch over to a blank white space, you will see an *afterimage* of its *complementary* color. Exposure to red produces an afterimage of green; exposure to blue results in an afterimage of yellow. Also, when you mix complementary colored lights, you get white, or at least various shades of gray (Hurvich & Jameson, 1951). The special status of yellow, in conjunction with the linking of complementary colors, is quite difficult for the trichromatic theory to explain.

The difficulties with the trichromatic view were recognized in the nineteenth century by the German physiologist Ewald Hering. Hering proposed an alternative view of color vision: **opponent-process theory**. He suggested that there

opponent-process theory
A theory of color vision proposing that cells in the visual pathway increase their activation levels to one color and decrease their activation levels to another color—for example, increasing to red and decreasing to green.

must be mechanisms in the visual system (i.e., cells) that respond positively to one color type (such as red) and negatively to another (such as green). Instead of three primary colors, Hering proposed six: *blue*, which is linked to *yellow* (therefore solving the problem with yellow); *green*, which is linked to *red*; and finally, *white*, which is linked to *black*. According to the opponent-process theory, people have difficulty perceiving a yellowish blue because activation of, say, the blue mechanism is accompanied by inhibition, or decreased activation, of the yellow mechanism. A yellowish red does not present a problem in this scheme because yellow and red are not linked in an opponent fashion.

Like Young and Helmholtz, Hering was operating in a kind of physiological vacuum—there was no solid physiological evidence for either a three-receptor system or for specially linked opponent-process cells. We know now that such evidence does exist. For example, in addition to the discovery of the different cone photopigments, researchers have found cells at various points in the visual pathway that do indeed code color information in an opponent-process fashion (see DeValois & DeValois, 1980). The rate at which neural impulses are generated by these cells increases to one type of color (for example, red) and decreases to another (green).

So what underlies our ability to detect such a vast array of colors in the world? The visual system pulls color information out of the visual message by relying on multiple processing stations. Color information is extracted first at the retinal level through the activations of different cone types; further up in the brain, opponent-process cells fine-tune and further process the message. Although the specific pathways and combination rules have yet to be fully worked out, this means that some sort of merging of the trichromatic and opponent-process views best characterizes our current knowledge about color extraction.

PRODUCING STABLE INTERPRETATIONS: VISUAL PERCEPTION

Let's return, for a moment, to the cube in Figure 5.1. You've seen how the electromagnetic energy bouncing off the page gets translated into an electrochemical signal, and how specialized regions of the visual pathway break the message down—the brain extracts lines, edges, colors, even angles of orientation from the visual scene. But your fundamental perception is still of a cube—an object with form, not some complex combination of elementary particles.

To understand how the human brain can perceive "wholes" with visual machinery that seems designed to analyze parts, it helps to remember that perception is only partly determined by what comes in through the eyes. People also rely a great deal on their knowledge and their expectations to construct what they see. Let's consider a simple example: Take a look at the two images depicted in

? CRITICAL THINKING

Based on what you've learned about color vision, why do you think traffic lights change between red and green?

CONCEPT SUMMARY
Comparing Trichromatic and Opponent-Process Theory

Theory	Stage of Processing	Processing Mechanism	Basic Description
Trichromatic	Early in the retina	Three different cone types, maximally sensitive to short, medium, or long wavelengths of light	Brain compares the relative activity levels among the three cone types to determine the color of a stimulus; helps to explain certain types of color blindness (e.g., *dichromats*)
Opponent-process	Later in the visual pathway	Three types of mechanisms (e.g., cells) that respond positively and negatively to certain color pairs (red-green; blue-yellow; black-white)	Mechanism responds positively to one member of a particular color pair (e.g., blue) and negatively to the other (e.g., yellow); helps to explain complementary-color afterimages and prominence of yellow as a primary color

(a)

(b)

FIGURE 5.13

Prior Knowledge and Perception
Whether you detect meaningful images in (a)
and (b) depends on how much prior knowledge
you bring to perceptual interpretation. (From
Coren, Ward, & Enns, 1994.)

Figure 5.13. If you were raised in North America, you probably have no trouble
seeing the image in panel (a): It's the word SKY, written in white, against a solid
black background. Panel (b), on the other hand, appears to be a meaningless collection of black shapes. Actually, panel (b) also shows the word SKY, but it's written in Chinese calligraphy. People who can read English, but not Chinese, see
panel (a) as a meaningful image; if Chinese is your native language, and you can't
read English, panel (b) presents the meaningful image (Coren et al., 1987). Thus,
prior knowledge plays a critical role in helping people interpret and organize what
they see.

We also typically use one part of a visual display to help us interpret other
parts. Exactly the same visual event is shown in positions 2 and 4 of the following
two lines:

A 13 C D E F G

10 11 12 13 14 15 16

but you "see" the letter B or the number 13 depending on the surrounding events.
The surrounding letters and digits act as *context* and generate expectations about
what appropriate whole is likely to be present in positions 2 and 4. In some cases,
how the elements are arranged in a visual display can even cause people to see
things that aren't really there. Is there a white triangle embedded in the middle of
Figure 5.14? It sure looks like there is, but the perception is really an illusion—
there is no physical stimulus, no reflected pattern of electromagnetic energy on
the retina, that corresponds to the triangular form. Yet, you interpret the pattern
as a triangle.

FIGURE 5.14
Illusory Contours
Can you see the white triangle embedded in
this figure? No physical stimulus corresponds to
the triangular form. Nonetheless, people
interpret the pattern as a triangle.

Psychologists have recognized for some time that there is more to perception
than what meets the eye. Our perceptual world is constructed through a combination of two important kinds of mental activities: First, as we've been discussing
throughout the chapter, the visual system performs an analysis of the actual sensory message, the pattern of electromagnetic information on the retina.
Psychologists refer to this as **bottom-up processing**—the processing that starts
with the actual physical message. Second, we also use our knowledge, beliefs, and
expectations about the world to interpret and organize what we see, something
psychologists call **top-down processing**. Perception always reflects a combination of these two processes. What you see is determined by what's out there in the
world, but also by what you expect to be out there.

Principles of Organization

You may remember that in Chapter 1 we briefly discussed the possibility that
people are born with certain organizing principles of perception that cannot be
altered by experience. This point of view was championed by a group of
researchers known as *Gestalt psychologists* (the word *Gestalt* translates from the
German as "configuration" or "pattern"). According to the Gestalt psychologists,

bottom-up processing
Processing that is driven by the actual
physical message delivered to the senses.

top-down processing
Processing that is driven by one's beliefs
and expectations about how the world is
organized.

(a)

(b)

FIGURE 5.15

Separating Figure from Ground
We have a natural tendency to divide any visual scene into a discernible "figure" and "ground." This task can be difficult, as with the painting (b); or it can be easy but ambiguous (a): Which do you see a vase, or a pair of profiles?

people see objects as well-structured and organized wholes because they are born with tendencies to *group t*he incoming visual message in sensible ways. For example, people have a natural, automatic tendency to divide any visual scene into a *figure* and a *ground*—we see the wine glass as separate from the table, the printed word as separate from the page. The rules governing the separation of figure and ground are complex, but as you can see from Figure 5.15, the task is easy or hard depending on whether strong or weak cues are available to guide the interpretation.

The Gestalt psychologists outlined a number of compelling and systematic rules, known generally as the **Gestalt principles of organization,** that govern how people organize what they see:

1. *The law of proximity.* If the elements of a display are close to each other—that is, they lie in close spatial proximity—they tend to be grouped together as part of the same object. Here, for example, you see three groups of dots, rather than a single collection.

Proximity

2. *The law of similarity.* Items that share physical properties—that physically resemble each other—are placed into the same set. Thus, here you see rows of X's and rows of O's rather than mixed-object columns.

Similarity

3. *The law of closure.* Even if a figure has a gap, or a small amount of its border is missing, people tend to perceive the object as complete.

Closure

Gestalt principles of organization
The organizing principles of perception proposed by the Gestalt psychologists. These principles include the laws of proximity, similarity, closure, continuation, and common fate.

4. *The law of good continuation.* If lines cross or are interrupted, people tend to see continuous lines that flow in a continuous direction. In the figure at the top of the next page, you have no trouble perceiving the snake as a whole object, even though part of it is blocked from view.

Continuation

5. *The law of common fate.* If things appear to be moving in the same direction, people tend to group them together. Here, the moving dots are classified together as a group, with some fate in common.

Common
fate

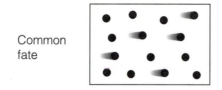

Object Recognition

By imposing organization on the visual scene, these natural grouping rules simplify the problem of recognizing objects. Psychologist Irving Biederman (1987, 1990) suggests that the Gestalt principles of organization may help the visual system break down complex visual messages into components called *geons* (short for "geometric icons"). Geons are simple geometrical forms, such as blocks, cylinders, wedges, and cones. From a collection of no more than 36 geons, Biederman argues, more than 150 million possible complex and meaningful objects can be created—far more than people would ever need to capture the richness of their perceptual world. This means that once the brain is familiar with the basic geons, it acquires the capability to recognize the basic components of any perceptual experience. Just as the 26 letters of the alphabet form the basis for an incredible variety of words, geons form the alphabet for building any object that a person might see.

One of the attractive features of Biederman's theory, which he calls **recognition by components,** is its ability to explain how people can successfully identify degraded or incomplete objects. Nature rarely provides all the identifying characteristics of a physical object: cars are usually partially hidden behind other cars; a hurried glimpse of a child's face in a crowd might be all the information that reaches the eye. Yet the viewer has no trouble recognizing the car or the child. According to Biederman (1987), only two or three geons can be sufficient for the rapid identification of most objects.

To illustrate, Biederman asked subjects to identify objects such as the ones shown in the left column of Figure 5.16. In some cases, the items were presented intact; in other conditions, the images were made more difficult to see by removing bits of information that either maintained (the middle column) or disrupted (the right column) the component geons. Not surprisingly, people had no problem recognizing the objects in the middle column but had considerably more trouble when the geons were obscured. In fact, Biederman found that identification of the right-column objects was almost impossible—most subjects in this condition failed to identify any of the objects correctly.

As currently developed, Biederman's theory of object recognition is quite successful in explaining the results of experiments like the one just described. But it remains to be seen whether it will provide a complete account of object recognition. For example, not all researchers are convinced that a relatively small set of

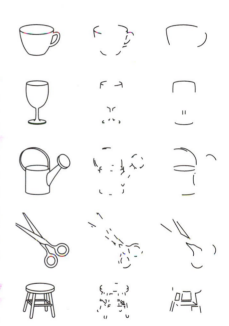

FIGURE 5.16

Recognition by Components
Biederman proposed that we recognize visual forms in part by extracting simple geometric forms—geons—from the visual message. Degraded versions of the objects on the left are in the other columns. We have no trouble recognizing the objects in the middle column but most of us cannot identify those in the right column. This is because the geons are degraded in the right column but not in the middle column. (From Biederman, 1990.)

recognition by components
The idea proposed by Biederman that people recognize objects perceptually via smaller components called *geons*.

basic shapes is sufficient to allow us to discriminate among all objects (Liu, 1996). Many objects share basic parts, yet we are able to quickly and efficiently tell them apart. Moreover, there may be certain kinds of objects in the world, such as faces, that are perceived and remembered immediately as wholes, without any breaking down or building up from parts (Farah et al., 1998). As you learned earlier, there appear to be cells in the brain that respond selectively to faces; there are also certain kinds of brain damage that make recognizing faces, but not other kinds of objects, difficult or impossible. We are capable of recognizing an enormous range of objects in our world, without hesitation, and it may well be that our brains solve the problems of object recognition in a number of different ways.

The Perception of Depth

The ability to recognize objects and forms, perhaps as a product of inborn principles of organization, is only part of the story of perception. In addition to recognizing figures as separate from backgrounds, people also see those figures in depth. In fact, the ability to perceive depth is one of the most amazing capabilities of the visual system. Think about it: The visual message that arrives for processing at the retina is essentially two-dimensional. Yet, somehow, people are able to extract a rich three-dimensional world from the "flat" image plastered on the retina. How is this possible? Moreover, as we discussed in Chapter 4, the ability to perceive depth develops relatively early in life. Infants as young as a few months can clearly tell the differences between the shallow and deep sides of a visual cliff (Campos et al., 1970; Gibson & Walk, 1960).

The ability to extract depth from the visual message results from a combination of bottom-up and top-down processing. People use their knowledge about objects, in combination with bottom-up processing of the actual visual message, to create a three-dimensional world. For example, the brain knows and adjusts for the fact that distant objects produce smaller reflections on the retina. Thus, if you see two people that you *know* to be of comparable height, but the retinal images they produce are of different sizes, your brain figures out that one person must be standing closer than the other. Experience also makes it clear that closer objects tend to block the images of objects that are farther away: If your view of a TV screen is blocked by a human form, you can be reasonably certain that your friend is standing in *front* of the television.

Another cue for distance, one that artists often use to depict depth in paintings, is *linear perspective*. As shown in the accompanying photos, parallel lines that recede into the distance tend to converge toward a single point. Generally, the farther away two lines are, the closer together those lines will appear to be. The relative *shading* of objects in a scene can provide important clues as well: If one object casts a shadow on another, you can often tell which of the two is farther away. Objects that are far away also tend to look blurry and slightly bluish. If you look at a realistic painting of a mountain scene, you'll see that the distant hills lack fine detail and are painted with a tinge of blue.

The depth cues that we've been considering are called **monocular depth cues,** which means they require input from only one eye. A person can close one eye and still see a world full of depth, based on the use of monocular cues such as the ones we discussed above. But the brain also uses **binocular depth cues;** these are cues produced by two eyes, each with a slightly different view of the world. Hold your index finger up about an inch or so in front of your eyes. Now quickly close and open each eye in alternation. You should see your finger jumping back and forth as you switch from one open eye to the other. The finger appears to move because each eye has a slightly different angle of view on the world, producing different images in each retina.

The differences between the locations of the images in the two eyes is called **retinal disparity.** It's a useful cue for depth because the amount of disparity changes with distance from a point of fixation. If you're looking at a bicycle that

monocular depth cues
Cues for depth that require input from only one eye.

binocular depth cues
Cues for depth that depend on comparisons between the two eyes.

retinal disparity
A binocular cue for depth that is based on location differences between the images in each eye.

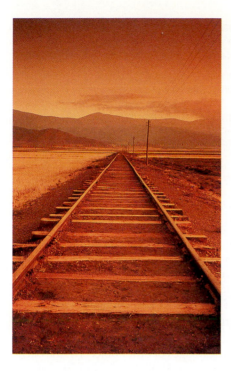

Can you identify the types of cues present in these "flat" pictures that allow us to perceive depth?

is ten feet away, then the image of a child who is five feet away (or fifteen feet away) will produce more retinal disparity. The farther away the object is from the fixation point, the greater will be the differences in the two retinal images. The brain derives depth information, in part, by calculating the amount of disparity between the image in the left eye and the image in the right eye. The brain can also use the degree that the two eyes turn inward, called **convergence,** to derive information about depth. The closer an object is to the face, the more the two eyes need to turn inward, or converge, in order to see the object properly.

Motion Perception

Not only do we see a three-dimensional world, but we also experience a world full of movement. Cars speed by us as we walk, birds soar and dive through the sky, and leaves rustle in the wind. Our ability to perceive motion effortlessly is extremely adaptive. Movement helps us determine the positions of objects over time, and it helps us to identify objects as well. For example, movement gives us information about shape, because we are able to see the object from more than one viewpoint, and it also helps us solve figure–ground problems—once an object begins to move, we can easily separate its image from a background that remains stationary.

How do we perceive movement? You might think that the brain could solve this problem by simply tracking the movement of images across the retina. Although this is true to a certain extent, motion perception turns out to be more complex. Images are constantly moving across our retinas, as we turn our eyes or walk about, but we don't necessarily see objects as moving. In addition, sometimes we perceive motion when there is, in fact, no actual movement in the environment. Think about those flashing arrows you see in front of stores or motels—they beckon us in, but they're actually made up of still lights that are blinking on and off at regular intervals. We experience an illusion of motion, called the **phi phenomenon,** even though nothing in the environment is actually moving. We experience a similar illusion of motion every time we watch a movie. Movies are really nothing more than still pictures presented rapidly in succession, but we certainly experience smooth and flowing movement of the characters.

convergence
A binocular cue for depth that is based on the extent to which the two eyes move inward, or converge, when looking at an object.

phi phenomenon
An illusion of movement that occurs when stationary lights are flashed in succession.

CONCEPT SUMMARY
Depth Cues

Type of Cue	Cue	Description
Monocular	Relative size	Comparably-sized stimuli that produce different-sized retinal images are perceived as varying in distance from the observer.
	Overlap	Closer objects tend to block the images of objects further away.
	Linear perspective	Parallel lines that recede into the distance appear to converge on a single point.
	Shading	Shadows cast by objects on other objects assist in depth perception.
	Haze	Distant objects tend to look blurry and slightly bluish.
Binocular	Retinal disparity	The differences between the locations of the images in the two eyes; the amount of disparity changes with distance from a point of fixation.
	Convergence	The closer the stimulus, the more the eyes turn inward toward one another.

As we discussed earlier, there appears to be a specific pathway in the brain that is designed to help us process movement, and there are a variety of cells in the cortex that respond to movement when it occurs (Newsome et al., 1995). Changes in the retinal image, changes in the motion of the eyes, as well as changes in the relative positions of objects in the environment all contribute to our general perception of movement. For example, our brain infers movement when the retinal image of one object changes over time, but the images of other objects in the background do not. As with depth, there are many cues in the environment that can help in the interpretation process.

Perceptual Constancies

Yet another rather remarkable feature of the human visual system is its capacity to recognize that an object remains the same even though the image in the retina might be constantly changing. As a case in point, consider how the size of an object's retinal image decreases with distance. As you walk away from a parked car, the size of its retinal image becomes smaller and smaller—so small, in fact, that it eventually resembles the image that might be reflected from a toy car held at arm's distance. Do you ever wonder why your car has mysteriously been transformed into a toy? You don't, of course, because your visual system maintains a stable interpretation of the image, as a car, despite the changes in retinal size.

When you perceive an object, or its properties, to remain the same even though the physical message delivered to the eyes is changing, you are showing what is called a **perceptual constancy**. In the case of the car, it is *size constancy*—the perceived size of the car remains constant even though the actual size of the reflected image is changing with distance. Figure 5.17 provides an example of *shape constancy*. Consider how many changes occur in the reflected image of a door as it slowly moves from closed to open. Yet you still recognize it as a door, not as some bizarre shape that evolves unpredictably over time. Size and shape constancies turn out to be related, both result, at least in part, from the visual system's use of cues to determine distance. Both are also extremely adaptive characteristics. In most instances, the object does, in fact, remain constant—only its reflected image changes.

To see what kind of cues might be used to produce constancy, take a look at Figure 5.18. Take particular note of the rectangular shapes on the ground marked as A, B, and C. You see these planters as the same size and shape, in part, because of the texture patterns covering the ground. Each of the open boxes covers three texture tiles in length and an additional three in width. The actual retinal image, however, differs markedly for each of the shapes (take a ruler and measure the physical size of each shape). You interpret and see them as the same because your experiences in the world have taught you that size and distance are related in systematic ways.

We show perceptual constancies for a variety of object dimensions. In addition to size and shape constancy, the brightness and color of an object can appear

perceptual constancy
Perceiving the properties of an object to remain the same even though the physical properties of the sensory message are changing.

FIGURE 5.17

Shape Constancy

Think about all the changes in the image of a door as it moves from closed to open. Yet we perceive it as a constant rectangular shape.

to remain constant, even though the intensity and wavelength of the light changes. Once again, these characteristics help us maintain a stable and orderly interpretation of a constantly changing world. Think about how chaotic the world would appear if you saw a new and different object every time the physical properties of its reflected image changed. For example, instead of seeing the same dancer gliding across the floor, you might be forced to see a string of dancers each engaged in a unique and unusual pose.

Perceptual Illusions

Of course, the perception of constancy is not gained without a cost. In its effort to maintain stability in image interpretation, the visual system can be tricked—**perceptual illusions,** or inappropriate interpretations of physical reality, can be created. Take a look at the two people sitting in the room depicted in Figure 5.19 on page 192. The girl sitting on the right appears much taller than the girl sitting on the left. In reality, these two are approximately the same size. You're tricked because your brain uses cues in the environment—combined with the belief that rooms are vertically and horizontally rectangular—to interpret the size of the inhabitants. Actually, as the rest of the figure shows, it is the room, not the difference in size of the girls, that is unusual.

Based partly on your expectations about the shape of rooms, and partly on the unique construction of the room, as you look through the peephole you think

perceptual illusions
Inappropriate interpretations of physical reality. Perceptual illusions often occur as a result of the brain's using otherwise adaptive organizing principles.

FIGURE 5.18

Constancy Cues

We see these three planters, marked A, B, and C, as matching in size and shape partly because of depth cues in the environment: Each covers three tiles in length and three in width.

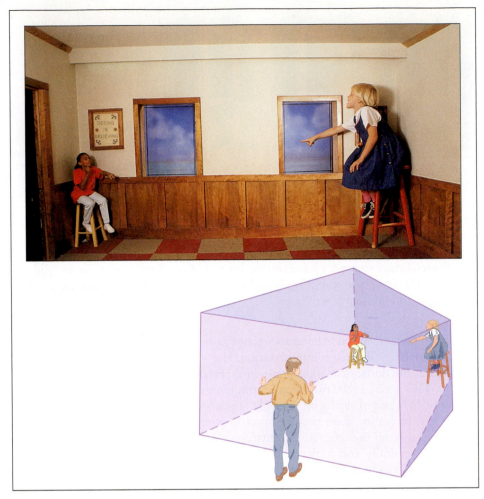

FIGURE 5.19

The Ames Room
The girl on the right appears much taller than the girl on the left. But this is an illusion induced by the belief that the room is rectangular. In fact, the sloping ceiling and floors provide misleading depth cues. To the viewer looking through the peephole the room appears perfectly normal. This famous illusion was designed by Adelbert Ames.

you're looking at two people who are the same distance away from your eyes. But the person on the left is actually farther away, so a smaller image is projected onto the retina. Because the brain assumes the two are the same distance away, it compensates for the differences in retinal size by making the person on the right appear larger (Dorward & Day, 1997).

The Ponzo illusion, shown in Figure 5.20(a), operates in a similar way. You see two lines that are exactly the same size as quite different because the linear perspective cue—the converging parallel lines—tricks the brain into thinking that the horizontal line near the top of the display is farther away. Because it has the same size retinal image as the bottom line (remember, the two are physically the same size) the brain compensates for the distance by making the top line appear larger. Figure 5.20(b) shows a similar illusion: The monsters are really the same, but the one on the top certainly appears larger!

Similar principles underlie perception of the Müller-Lyer illusion, which is shown in Figure 5.21. The vertical line with the wings turned out (a) appears longer than the line with the wings turned in (b), even though each line is identical in length. As (c) shows, this particular illusion may have a real-life model—the interior and exterior corners of a room or building. Notice that for the outside corner of this building, the wings are really perspective cues signaling that the front edge is thrusting forward and the walls are sloping away. For the inside corner, the perspective cues signal the opposite—-the inside edge is farther away. In the Müller-Lyer illusion the two lines produce the same retinal image, but your visual system assumes that (a), which is just like the interior corner, is likely to be farther away, and consequently must be larger in size.

(a)

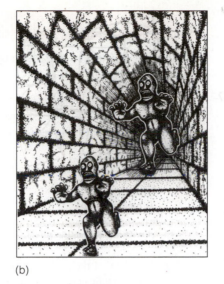

(b)

FIGURE 5.20
Illusion of Depth
These two figures based on the Ponzo illusion show that depth cues can lead to perceptual errors. In (a) the horizontal lines are actually the same size, as are the monsters in (b). (From Shepard, 1990.)

Interestingly, if the Müller-Lyer illusion is based on our experiences with rooms and buildings, we can speculate about what it would be like to be raised in an environment with few rectangular corners. We can predict that a person who has limited experience with rectangular corners might actually be less susceptible to the illusion because he or she will be unlikely to interpret the wings as cues for depth. Indeed, when a group of Navajos who had been raised in traditional circular homes (called *hogans*) were tested for the illusion, they were more likely to consider the lines as equal in length, although there was still evidence of the illusion among those who were tested (Leibowitz, 1971; Pedersen & Wheeler, 1983). It's unlikely that experience alone can account for the perceptual illusions that we've discussed, even the Müller-Lyer illusion, but it's reasonable to assume that experience can exert an influence, possibly on the magnitude or intensity of the illusion that is produced.

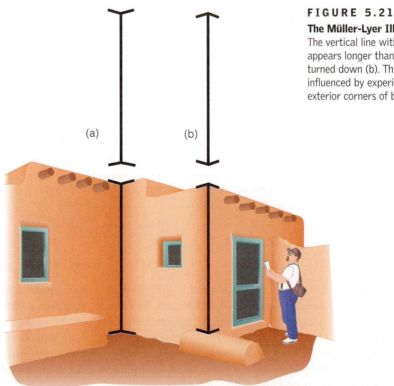

(a)   (b)

(c)

FIGURE 5.21
The Müller-Lyer Illusion
The vertical line with the wings turned up (a) appears longer than the line with the wings turned down (b). This particular illusion may be influenced by experiences with the interior and exterior corners of buildings (c).

TEST YOURSELF 5.1

Check your knowledge about vision by answering the following questions. (You will find the answers in the Appendix.)

1. To test your understanding of how the visual message is translated into the language of the brain, choose the best answers from among the following terms: accommodation, cones, cornea, fovea, lens, opponent-process, pupil, receptive field, retina, rods, trichromatic.

    a. The "central pit" area where the cone receptors tend to be located: _____

    b. Receptors that are responsible for visual acuity, or our ability to see fine detail: _____

    c. The process through which the lens changes its shape temporarily in order to help focus light: _____

    d. The "film" at the back of the eye that contains the light-sensitive receptor cells.

    e. The protective outer layer of the eye.

2. Decide whether each of the following statements about how your brain extracts message components is true or false.

    a. Visual messages tend to be analyzed primarily by structures in the superior colliculus, although structures in the lateral geniculate are important too. *True or False?*

    b. It's currently believed that information about color and movement are probably processed in separate pathways in the brain. *True or False?*

    c. The opponent-process theory of color vision makes it easier to understand why most people think there are four, rather than three, primary colors (red, green, blue, yellow). *True or False?*

    d. Some feature detectors in the brain are "tuned" to respond only when certain patterns of light are shown into the eye at specific angles of orientation. *True or False?*

3. Test your knowledge about visual perception by filling in the blanks. Choose your answers from the following terms: binocular depth cues, bottom-up processing, convergence, monocular depth cues, perceptual constancy, perceptual illusion, phi phenomenon, retinal disparity, recognition by components, top-down processing.

    a. The part of perception that is controlled by our beliefs and expectations about how the world is organized: _____

    b. Perceiving an object, or its properties, to remain the same even though the physical message delivered to the eyes is changing: _____

    c. An illusion of motion: _____

    d. The depth cue that is based on calculating the degree to which the two eyes have turned inward: _____

    e. The view that object perception is based on the analysis of simple building blocks, called geons: _____

Hearing: Identifying and Localizing Sounds

Imagine the world without sound. You wouldn't hear music, or speech, or laughter. Hearing enriches our life and, like vision, it serves a variety of very adaptive functions. For example, sounds help us identify and locate objects in our path. It is through sound that we are able to produce and comprehend the spoken word. Even our most private sense of self—the world inside our heads—often appears in the form of an inner voice, or an ongoing speech-based monologue (see Chapter 8).

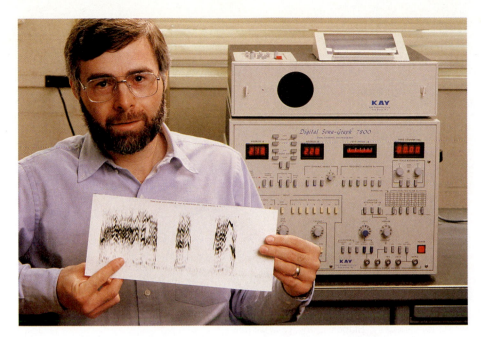

This researcher is holding a spectrogram, which records how the intensity and frequencies of sounds change over time.

TRANSLATING THE MESSAGE: AUDITORY TRANSDUCTION

The physical message delivered to the auditory system, **sound,** is a form of energy, like light, that travels as a wave. However, sound—unlike light—is mechanical energy and requires a *medium* (such as air or water) in order to move. Sound begins with a vibrating stimulus, such as the movement of vocal cords, the plucking of a tight string, or the pounding diaphragm of a stereo speaker. The vibration pushes air molecules out into space, where they collide with other air molecules, and a kind of traveling chain reaction begins.

The rate of the vibrating stimulus determines the *frequency* of the sound, defined as the number of times the pressure wave moves from peak to peak per second [measured in units called *hertz*, where 1 Hz = 1 cycle (repetition)/second]. Psychologically, when the frequency of a sound varies, people hear changes in **pitch,** which corresponds roughly to how high or low a tone sounds. For example, middle C on a piano has a frequency of 262 Hz, whereas the highest note on a piano corresponds to about 4000 Hz. Humans are potentially sensitive to frequencies from roughly 20 to 20,000 Hz, but we are most sensitive to frequencies in the 1000 to 5000 Hz range (Gulick et al., 1989; Sivian & White, 1933). Many important sounds fall into this range of maximum sensitivity, including most of the sounds that make up speech.

The other major dimension of sound is *amplitude*, the measured height a sound wave reaches. Psychologically, changes in amplitude are experienced as changes in *loudness*. As the wave increases in amplitude, it generally seems louder to the ear. The amplitude of a wave is typically measured in units called *decibels* (dB). To give you some perspective, a normal conversation measures around 60 dB, whereas an incredibly loud rock band can produce sounds over 100 dB. (Just for your information, prolonged exposure to sounds at around 90 decibels can produce permanent hearing loss.)

Entering the Ear

Let's follow a sound as it enters the auditory pathway (see Figure 5.22). We saw that in the visual system, an optical pathway focuses the light energy onto the visual receptors. In the auditory system, sounds travel toward the auditory receptor cells through the ears. The external flap of tissue usually referred to as the "ear" is known technically as the **pinna;** it helps capture the sound, which then funnels down the auditory canal toward the *eardrum,* or **tympanic membrane.**

sound
The physical message delivered to the auditory system, a mechanical energy that requires a medium such as air or water in order to move.

pitch
The psychological experience that results from the auditory processing of a particular frequency of sound.

pinna
The external flap of tissue normally referred to as the "ear"; it helps capture sounds.

tympanic membrane
The eardrum, which responds to incoming sound waves by vibrating.

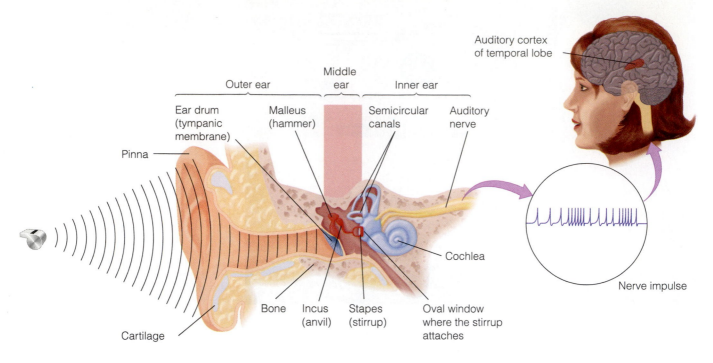

Auditory cortex
of temporal lobe

Middle
ear

Outer ear   Inner ear

Ear drum   Malleus   Semicircular   Auditory
(tympanic   (hammer)   canals   nerve
membrane)

Pinna

Cochlea

Bone   Incus   Stapes   Oval window
        (anvil) (stirrup)   where the stirrup
                             attaches

Cartilage

Nerve impulse

FIGURE 5.22

The Structures of the Human Ear
Sound enters the auditory canal and causes the
tympanic membrane to vibrate in a pattern
that is then transmitted through three small
bones in the middle ear to the oval window.
The oval window vibrates, causing fluid inside
the cochlea to be displaced, which moves the
basilar membrane. The semicircular canals are
part of our sense of balance.

middle ear
The portion between the eardrum and the
cochlea containing three small bones (the
malleus, incus, and stapes) that help to
intensify and prepare the sound vibrations
for passage into the inner ear.

cochlea
The bony, snail-shaped sound processor in
the inner ear, where sounds get translated
into nerve impulses.

basilar membrane
A flexible membrane running through the
cochlea that, through its movement,
displaces the auditory receptor cells, or hair
cells.

The tympanic membrane responds to the incoming sound wave by vibrating.
The particular vibration pattern, which differs for different sound frequencies, is
then transmitted through three small bones in the **middle ear:** the *malleus* (or
hammer), the *incus* (or anvil), and the *stapes* (or stirrup). These bones help intensify the vibration pattern and prepare it for passage into the fluid-filled inner ear.
Within the inner ear lies a bony, snail-shaped sound processor called the **cochlea;**
here, the sound energy gets its initial translation into the internal language of the
nervous system.

Transduction in the Cochlea
The third bone in the middle ear, the stapes, is connected to an opening in the
cochlea called the *oval window*. As the stapes vibrates, it causes fluid inside the
cochlea to displace a flexible membrane, called the **basilar membrane,** that runs
throughout the cochlear shell. Transduction takes place through the activation of
tiny auditory receptor cells, called *hair cells*, that lie along the basilar membrane.
As the membrane starts to ripple—like a cat moving under a bedsheet—tiny hairs,
called *cilia*, that extend outward from the hair cells are displaced. The bending of
these hairs causes the auditory receptor cells to fire, creating a neural impulse that
travels up the auditory pathways to the brain (see Figure 5.23).

Different sound frequencies trigger different movement patterns along the
basilar membrane. Higher frequencies of sound cause the membrane to be displaced the most near the oval window; low frequencies produce a traveling wave
that reaches its peak deep inside the spiraling cochlea. As you'll learn shortly, the
receptor cells that are activated the most by any particular sound pattern help the
brain detect information about pitch. If hair cells near the oval window are
responding the most, the incoming sound is perceived as high in pitch. If many
cells along the membrane are active, and the most active ones are far away from
the oval window, the incoming sound is perceived as low in pitch.

EXTRACTING THE MESSAGE COMPONENTS: AUDITORY PATHWAYS

Less is known about the auditory pathways than about the visual route toward the
cortex, but there are some general similarities worth noting. The neural impulses
generated from the hair cells leave the cochlea in each ear along the *auditory nerve*.

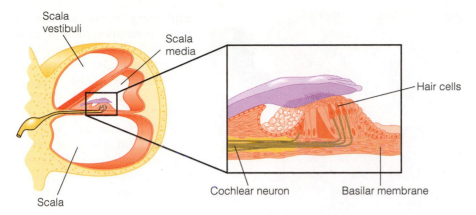

Scala vestibuli

Scala media

Hair cells

Cochlear neuron

Basilar membrane

Scala

FIGURE 5.23

The Basilar Membrane
This figure shows an open slice of the cochlea. Sound vibrations cause fluid inside the cochlea to displace the basilar membrane that runs throughout the cochlear shell. Different frequencies trigger different patterns along the membrane. Transduction takes place through bending hair cells. The hair cells nearest the point of maximum displacement will be stimulated the most, which helps the brain code information about pitch.

Messages that have been received in the right ear travel mainly along pathways leading to the left hemisphere of the brain; left-ear messages go primarily to the right hemisphere. Like in the visual system, auditory nerve fibers also appear to be "tuned" to transmit a specific kind of message. In the visual system, the ganglion cells transmit information about regions of light and dark on the retina. In the auditory system, fibers in the auditory nerve pass on rough *frequency* information. Electrophysiological measurements of individual auditory nerve fibers show tuning curves—for example, a fiber might respond best to an input stimulus of around 2000 Hz and less well to others (Ribaupierre, 1997).

Extracting Pitch

Complex sounds, such as speech patterns, are built from combinations of simple sound frequencies. The auditory system pulls out information about the simple frequencies, which correspond to different pitches, in several ways. Pitch is determined, in part, by the particular place on the basilar membrane that is active. For example, as we discussed earlier, activation of hair cells near the oval window leads to the perception of a high-pitched sound. This is called the **place theory** of pitch perception (Békésy, 1960): We hear a particular pitch because certain hair cells are responding actively. "Place" in this instance refers to the location of the activated hair cell along the basilar membrane.

Place theory helps to explain certain kinds of hearing loss. For example, as people grow older they typically have trouble hearing the higher frequencies of sound (such as those in whispered speech). Why might this be so? Most sounds that enter the auditory system activate, to at least some extent, those hair cells nearest the oval window. Cells in the interior portions of the cochlea respond actively only when low-frequency sounds are present. Thus, if receptor cells wear out from years of prolonged activity, those nearest the oval window should be among the first to do so. Place theory thus explains, in part, why older people have difficulty hearing high-pitched sounds.

Despite its successes, place theory does not offer a complete account of pitch perception. One problem with place theory is that hair cells do not act independently—often, many are activated in unison. As a result, it's thought that the brain must also rely on the *rate* at which cells fire their neural impulses. According to **frequency theory**, pitch is determined partly by the frequency of neural impulses traveling up the auditory pathway: The higher the rate of firing, the higher the perceived pitch. Like place theory, frequency theory does a reasonable job of

place theory
The idea that the location of auditory receptor cells activated by movement of the basilar membrane underlies the perception of pitch.

frequency theory
The idea that pitch perception is determined partly by the frequency of neural impulses traveling up the auditory pathway.

Prolonged exposure to intense noise can create hearing loss.

explaining many aspects of pitch perception, but it runs into difficulties with high-frequency sounds. Because of their *refractory periods*, individual neurons cannot fire fast enough to deliver high-frequency information. To solve this problem, the brain tracks the patterns of firing among large groups of neurons. When groups of cells generate neural impulses rapidly in succession, they create *volleys* of impulses that provide additional clues about the pitch of the incoming message (Wever, 1949).

In summary, the brain uses several kinds of information to extract pitch. Remember that for vision, specifically color vision, the brain uses information from multiple cone receptors as well as from opponent-process cells located in the upper regions of the brain. To detect pitch, the brain uses information about where on the basilar membrane activation is occurring (*place theory*) as well as the rate at which signals are generated (*frequency theory*). Neither place nor frequency information, by itself, is sufficient to explain our perception of pitch—both kinds of information are needed and used.

The Auditory Cortex

The auditory message eventually reaches the auditory cortex, which is located mainly in the temporal lobes of the brain. Cells in the auditory cortex are frequency-sensitive, which means that they respond best to particular frequencies of sound. There is also a well-developed organizational scheme, just as in the visual system. Cells that sit in nearby areas of the auditory cortex tend to be tuned to similar frequencies of sound. For example, cells that respond to low-frequency sounds are clustered together in one area of the auditory cortex, whereas cells responsive to high-frequency sounds sit in another area (Scheich & Zuschratter, 1995).

There also appear to be cells in the auditory cortex that respond best to complex combinations of sounds. For example, a cell might respond only to a sequence of tones that moves from one frequency to another, or to a burst of noise (Pickles, 1988). In animals, cortical cells have also been discovered that respond only to sounds that exist in the animal's natural vocabulary, such as a particular "shriek," "cackle," or "trill" (Wollberg & Newman, 1972). In people, PET scans have shown that specific areas of the brain "light-up" when complex auditory sequences are played, such as eight-note melodies (Zatorre et al., 1994). Much remains to be learned, though, about how complex sounds—such as patterns of speech—are represented in the cortex.

PRODUCING STABLE INTERPRETATIONS: AUDITORY PERCEPTION

Say the phrase "kiss the sky," then repeat it aloud in rapid succession. Now do the same thing with the word "stress" or "life." You'll notice that your perception of

Think about how easily you can listen to an orchestra with many different instrument sounds and pick out the sound of the trumpet, violin, or piano.

what you're saying undergoes some interesting changes. "Kiss the sky" begins to sound like "kiss this guy"; "stress" will probably turn into "dress" and "life" into "fly." This is a kind of auditory analogue to the Necker cube that we discussed at the beginning of the chapter.

Organizing the Auditory Message

As with the ever-changing cube, there is not always a straightforward mapping between the physical and the psychological interpretation of a sound event. The brain is often faced with auditory ambiguity—it seeks meaning where it can, usually by relying on established organizational rules (Bregman, 1990; Hirsh & Watson, 1996). As with vision, the brain separates the incoming auditory stream into figure and ground; it tends to group auditory events that are similar and that occur close together in time. Sound frequency, for example, can be used as a grouping cue to distinguish among voices. Females generally speak at higher frequencies than males. As a result, it is easier to tell the difference between a male and a female talking than it is to tell the difference between two speakers of the same gender.

The fact that the brain organizes and imposes structure on incoming sound messages should not come as much of a surprise. Think about how easily you can listen to a band or orchestra, filled with many different instruments, and pick out the trumpet, violin, or piano. Think about how easily you can focus on the intriguing voice of your date, to the exclusion of other voices, while in the midst of a noisy party. Moreover, the ability to identify and organize sounds increases with experience. People use their knowledge and expectations, through top-down processing, to interpret the incoming auditory sequence. Car mechanics, after years of experience, can identify an engine problem simply by listening to the particular "knocking" that the engine makes; cardiologists, as a result of experience, can use the intricacies of the heartbeat to diagnose the health of a cardiovascular system.

Prior knowledge not only influences how we perceive sounds, it also influences how we produce sequences of sounds. Try saying the following aloud, and listen closely to the sounds:

Marzi doats n doze edoats n lidul lamzey divey.

? CRITICAL THINKING

Can you think of any songs that you like now but didn't like when you first heard them? One possibility is that you've learned to organize the music in a way that makes it more appealing.

Recognize anything familiar? Well, actually this is a well-phrased lesson in the dietary habits of familiar barnyard animals; it's taken from a popular 1940s song (Sekular & Blake, 1990). (Here's a hint: Mares eat oats and . . .) With a little knowledge, and some expectations about the content of the message, you should eventually arrive at an agreeable interpretation of the lyric. Notice how once you've arrived at that interpretation, the same groupings of letters produce quite a different reading aloud.

Sound Localization

Another adaptive characteristic of the auditory sense is the ability to use incoming sounds to figure out location. For example, if you're driving down the street fiddling with your car radio and hear a sudden screech of brakes, you're able to determine the source of the sound rapidly and efficiently. How do you accomplish this feat? Just as comparisons between the retinal locations of images in the two eyes provide information about visual depth, message comparisons between the ears help people *localize* objects in space.

Let's assume that the braking car is approaching yours from the left side. Because your left ear is closer to the source of the sound, it will receive the relevant sound vibrations slightly sooner than your right ear. If an object is directly in front of you, the message will arrive at both ears simultaneously. By comparing the arrival times between the left and right ears, the brain is able to localize the sound fairly accurately. What's amazing is that these arrival time differences are extremely small. For example, the maximum arrival time difference, which occurs when an object is directly opposite one ear, is only about 600 *micro*seconds (a microsecond is 1/10,000 of a second).

Another important cue for sound localization is *intensity*—more precisely, intensity differences between the ears. The sound that arrives first—to either the left or right ear—will be somewhat louder, or more intense, than the sound arriving second. Again, these intensity differences are not large, and they depend partly on the frequency of the arriving sound, but they are useful cues for sound localization. Thus, your brain can calculate the differences in arrival times between the two ears, plus any differences in intensity (or loudness), and use this information to localize the source (Giguere & Abel, 1993).

TEST YOURSELF 5.2

Check your knowledge about the auditory system by determining whether each of the following questions is true or false. (You will find the answers in the Appendix.)

1. Sound is a form of mechanical energy that requires a medium, such as air or water, in order to move. *True or False?*

2. According to the frequency theory of pitch perception, the location of activity on the basilar membrane is the primary cue for determining pitch. *True or False?*

3. Sound pressure causes tiny hair cells, located in the pinna, to bend, thereby generating a neural impulse. *True or False?*

4. The separation of a sensory message into figure and ground occurs for vision but not for hearing. *True or False?*

5. We use multiple cues to help us localize a sound, including comparisons of arrival times and intensity differences between the two ears. *True or False?*

The Skin and Body Senses: From Touch to Movement

Our perceptual experiences might appear to be driven primarily by what comes in through our eyes and ears. We communicate through the spoken word; we usually identify objects through vision. But imagine a world without physical contact. It's through a lingering kiss, or the brush of a hand against a cheek, that our experiences often gain meaning. Skin contact builds its own perceptual world: You can detect the location of a light switch in the dark, feel the warmth of a fire, or experience the pain of an accidental cut.

It's relatively easy to appreciate the adaptive significance of the skin and body senses. You need to be able to detect the presence of a spider crawling up your leg; if a blowing ember from the fireplace happens to land on your forearm, it is certainly adaptive for you to respond quickly. It's also important for us to be able to detect and control the movement and position of own bodies. We need to know, for example, if we're hanging upside down or the current positions of our arms and legs. Human sensory systems have developed not only to detect the presence of objects in the environment but also to provide accurate information about the body itself.

In this section of the chapter you'll learn about three skin senses—touch, temperature, and pain—as well as the body senses related to the perception of movement and balance. In each case, as in our earlier discussions, the environmental message needs to be translated, transmitted to the brain, and interpreted in a meaningful fashion.

LEARNING GOALS

1. Explain how sensory messages delivered to the skin—touch and temperature—are translated and interpreted within the brain.

2. Describe how we perceive and interpret pain.

3. Discuss the operation and function of the body senses: movement and balance.

TOUCH

In the case of touch or pressure, the physical message delivered to the skin is mechanical. An object makes contact with the body—perhaps your fingers actively reach out and initiate the contact—and receptor cells embedded in the skin are disturbed. The mechanical pressure on the cell (it is literally deformed) produces a neural impulse, and the message is then transmitted to the spinal cord and up into the brain.

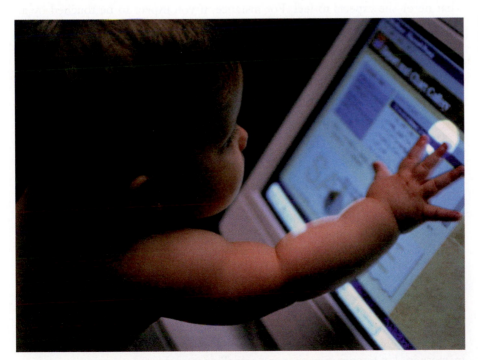

Humans use the sense of touch to acquire information about shape, firmness, texture, and weight.

The fact that these people can take a "snow bath" in the middle of winter demonstrates how the perception of temperature can be influenced by psychological factors.

cold fibers
Neurons that respond to a cooling of the skin by increasing the production of neural impulses.

warm fibers
Neurons that respond vigorously when the temperature of the skin increases.

Currently, it's believed that there are several different types of pressure-sensitive receptor cells in the skin. Some respond to constant pressure; others respond best to intermittent pressure, such as a tapping on the skin or a stimulus that vibrates at a particular frequency (Bolanowski et al., 1994). As with vision and hearing, touch information is transmitted up the neural pathway through distinct channels to processing stations in the brain, where the inputs received from various points on the body are combined (Bolanowski, 1989). One kind of nerve fiber might carry information about touch location; other fibers might transmit information about whether the touch has been brief or sustained.

At the level of the *somatosensory cortex*, located in the parietal lobe of the brain, a close connection is found among regions of the skin and representation in the cortex (Prud'homme et al., 1994). As you learned in Chapter 3, the cortex contains multiple "body maps," where adjacent cortical cells have areas of sensitivity that correspond to adjacent areas on the skin. Moreover, as in the visual cortex, some areas are represented more elaborately than others. For example, a relatively large amount of cortical tissue is devoted to the hands and lips, whereas the middle portion of the back, despite its size, receives little representation in the cortex. Maybe that's the reason why we kiss to display intense affection rather than simply pat someone on the back. There's a lot more cortex devoted to the lips than to the back.

Virtually everyone has the ability to recognize complex objects exclusively through touch. When blindfolded, people show near-perfect identification of common objects (such as toothbrushes and paperclips) after examining them by active touch (Klatzky et al., 1985). Active skin contact with an object produces not only shape information but information about firmness, texture, and weight. Moreover, as with seeing and hearing, a person's final interpretation of an object depends on a mixture of what the person feels and what he or she expects to feel. For instance, if you expect to be touched by an object on a particular finger, you are more likely to identify the object correctly (Craig, 1985). There are also measurable changes in blood flow in the somatosensory cortex when a person simply expects to be touched (Drevets et al., 1995).

TEMPERATURE

At present, researchers have only a limited idea of how the body records and processes the temperature of an object. Electrophysiological research has detected the presence of **cold fibers** that respond to a cooling of the skin by increasing the production of neural impulses, as well as **warm fibers** that respond vigorously when the temperature of the skin increases. But the behavior of these temperature-sensitive receptor systems is not particularly well understood (Zotterman, 1959).

We do know, however, that the perception of warm and cold is only indirectly related to the actual temperature of the real-world object. To demonstrate, try plunging one hand into a bowl of cold water and the other hand into a bowl of hot water. Now place both hands into a third bowl containing water sitting at room temperature. The hand that was in the cold water will sense the water as warm; the other hand will experience it as cold. Same water, same temperature, but two different perceptual experiences. The secret behind this perceptual enigma lies in understanding that it is the temperature *change* that determines your perception. When your cold hand touches warmer water, your skin begins to warm; it is the increase in skin temperature that you actually perceive.

At times, these perceptual processes can lead to temperature "illusions." For instance, metal seems cooler than wood even when both are at the same physical temperature. Why? Because metal is a better conductor of heat than wood, so it absorbs more warmth from the skin. Consequently, the brain perceives the loss of heat as a cooler physical temperature.

EXPERIENCING PAIN

Pain is a very unique kind of sensory experience. It is not a characteristic of the external world that the brain seeks to interpret, such as an object or an energy source. Rather, **pain** is an adaptive reaction that the body generates in response to any stimulus that is intense enough to cause tissue damage. The stimulus can be just about anything. It can come from outside or inside the body; it doesn't even need to be particularly intense (consider the effect of salt on an open wound).

Little is known about pain receptors in the skin, although cells have been discovered in some animals that react to painful stimuli (such as intense heat) by sending signals to the cortex (Dong et al., 1994). Pain is a complex psychological experience, however, and it often relies on much more than just a physical stimulus. There are well-documented examples of soldiers who report little or no pain after receiving serious injuries in battle; the same is true of many individuals entering an emergency room. In addition, certain non-Western cultures use rituals that should, from a Western perspective, inflict great pain but apparently do not (Melzak, 1973).

Gate-Control Theory

The interplay between the physical and the psychological in pain perception forms the basis for the **gate-control theory** of pain (Melzak & Wall, 1965, 1982). The basic idea is that the neural impulses generated by pain receptors can be blocked, or gated, in the spinal cord by signals produced in the brain. If you've just sliced your finger cutting carrots on the kitchen counter, you would normally feel pain. But if a pan on the stove suddenly starts to smoke, the pain seems to evaporate while you try to prevent your house from burning down. According to the gate-control theory, the brain can block the critical pain signals from reaching higher neural centers when it is appropriate to do so.

How is the gating action actually carried out? Once again, the details of the mechanisms are unclear, but there appear to be two types of nerve fibers that are responsible for opening and closing the gate. So-called "large" fibers, when stimulated, produce nervous system activity that closes the gate; other, "small" fibers, when stimulated, inhibit those neural processes and effectively open the gate. External activities—such as rubbing or placing ice on a wound—also apparently stimulate the large fibers, which close the gate preventing further passage of the pain message toward the brain. Again, the details of the neural circuitry remain to be worked-out, and it's probably worth noting that the neural connections proposed in the original gate-control theory proved to be incorrect, but the idea of a pain gate that opens and closes remains popular among researchers.

In addition to gating the pain signals, as we discussed in Chapter 3, the brain can also control the experience of pain through the release of chemicals called *endorphins*, which produce pain-killing effects like those obtained through morphine. The release of endorphins is thought to account, in part, for those instances in which pain should be experienced, but is not. For example, sometimes swallowing a sugar pill can dramatically reduce pain even though there is no physical reason why sugar should be effective (a "placebo" effect). The locus of such effects, and other analgesic procedures such as acupuncture, might lie in the brain's internal production of its own antipain medication.

pain
An adaptive response by the body to any stimulus that is intense enough to cause tissue damage.

gate-control theory
The idea that neural impulses generated by pain receptors can be blocked, or gated, in the spinal cord by signals produced in the brain.

The vestibular sense helps people maintain balance by monitoring the position of the body in space.

THE KINESTHETIC SENSE

The word **kinesthesia** literally means "movement"; when used in connection with sensation, the term refers to the ability to sense the position and movement of one's body parts. For example, as you reach toward a blossoming flower, feedback from your skin, tendons, muscles, and especially joints helps you maintain the correct line toward the target. The kinesthetic sense shares many properties with the sense of touch—a variety of receptor types in the muscles that surround the joints react to the physical forces produced by moving the limbs (Gandevia et al., 1992; Verschueven et al., 1998).

The nerve impulses generated by the kinesthetic receptors travel, as in touch, to the somatosensory cortex. It is presumed that at the level of the cortex, there are increasingly complex cells that respond only when body parts, such as the arms, are placed in certain positions (Gardner & Costanzo, 1981). But, the psychological experience of movement is most likely influenced by multiple factors, as with other kinds of perception (Jones, 1988). The visual system, for example, provides additional feedback about current position, as does the sense of touch.

THE VESTIBULAR SENSE

We have another complex receptor system, attached to the cochlea of the inner ear, that responds not only to movement but also to acceleration and to changes in upright posture. Each ear contains three small fluid-filled **semicircular canals** that are lined with hair cells similar to those found in the cochlea. If you quickly turn your head toward some object, these hair cells are displaced and nerve impulses signaling acceleration are transmitted throughout the brain. Some of the nerve fibers project to the cortex; others direct messages toward the eye muscles, so you can accurately adjust your eyes as your head is turning.

The vestibular system is also responsible for the sense of balance. If you tilt your head, or encounter a 360-degree loop on a roller coaster, receptor cells located in other inner ear organs, called **vestibular sacs,** quickly transmit the appropriate orientation information to the brain. Continual disturbance of the semicircular canals or the vestibular sacs can produce dizziness, nausea, and motion sickness (Lackner & DiZio, 1991).

kinesthesia
In perception, the ability to sense the position and movement of one's body parts.

semicircular canals
A receptor system attached to the inner ear that responds to movement and acceleration and to changes in upright posture.

vestibular sacs
Contain receptors thought to be primarily responsible for the sense of balance.

TEST YOURSELF 5.3

Check your knowledge about the skin and body senses by answering the following multiple choice questions. (You will find the answers in the Appendix.)

1. Alicia holds her left hand in a bowl of cold water and her right hand in a bowl of hot water. She then transfers both hands to a bowl containing water at room temperature. She finds that left hand now feels warm and her right hand cool. Why?

   a. Cold and hot fibers rebound after continued activity.
   b. It's temperature *change* that determines perception.
   c. She expects a change, therefore a change is experienced.
   d. Opponent-process cells in the cortex are reacting.

2. According to the gate-control theory, psychological factors can influence the perception of pain by:

   a. channeling pain signals to the occipital lobe.
   b. reducing the supply of endorphins in the body.
   c. blocking pain signals from reaching higher neural centers.
   d. blocking pain receptors from relaying messages to the spinal cord.

3. The vestibular sacs contain receptor cells that help us maintain our sense of balance. Where are they located?

   a. in the lateral geniculate nucleus
   b. in the superior colliculus
   c. in the joints and limbs of the body
   d. in the inner ear

The Chemical Senses: Smell and Taste

We end our review of the individual sensory systems with the chemical senses, *smell* and *taste*. We receive a vast array of messages from the environment, but few carry as much emotional impact as chemically based input. You can appreciate the touch from a loving caress, or the visual beauty of a sunset, but consider your reaction to the smell of decaying meat, or to the distinctive taste of milk left a bit too long in the sun! Smells and tastes are enormously adaptive because they possess powerful signaling properties; like other animals, humans learn to avoid the off-odor or the bitter taste.

The perception of both smell and taste begins with the activity of receptor cells, called **chemoreceptors,** that react to invisible molecules scattered about in the air or dissolved in liquids. These receptors solve the translation problem and project the newly formed neural impulses toward the brain. Psychologically, the two senses are related: Anyone who has ever had a cold knows that things "just don't taste right" with a plugged nose. You can demonstrate this for yourself by holding your nose and trying to taste the difference between an apple and a piece of raw potato. In fact, people can identify a taste far more efficiently if they are also allowed a brief sniff (Mozell et al., 1969). Let's consider each of these chemical senses in a bit more detail.

SMELL

The technical name for the sense of smell is **olfaction,** which comes from the Latin word *olfacere* meaning "to smell." Airborne molecules enter through the nose or the back of the throat and interact with receptor cells embedded in the upper region of the nasal cavity (Lancet et al., 1993). Like the receptor systems

chemoreceptors
Receptor cells that react to invisible molecules scattered about in the air or dissolved in liquids, leading to the senses of smell and taste.

olfaction
The sense of smell.

A taster's ability to identify the smell, or "bouquet," of a fine wine depends on the constellation of airborne chemicals produced by the wine, as well as on the experiences of the taster.

that are used to hear and detect motion, the olfactory receptor cells contain tiny hairs, or *cilia*. The airborne molecules are thought to bind with the cilia, causing the generation of a neural impulse. Receptor fibers then move the message forward to the *olfactory bulb*, located at the bottom front region of the brain. From here, the information is sent to several areas in the brain.

Studies have shown that people probably have up to a thousand or more different kinds of olfactory receptor cells (Buck & Axel, 1991). It's not yet known whether each receptor type plays a special role in the perception of a particular odor, but there's almost certainly no simple one-to-one connection. For one thing, olfactory receptor cells are often activated by more than one kind of chemical stimulus. In addition, most odors are complex psychological experiences (Carrasco & Ridout, 1993; Kauer, 1987). People have no problem recognizing the smell of frying bacon, or the aroma of fresh coffee, but a chemical analysis of these events fails to reveal the presence of any single defining molecule. Clearly, the ability to apply the label "frying bacon" to a set of airborne chemicals arises from complex perceptual processes. It's even possible to produce smell *illusions*—if you are led to expect that a particular odor is present, even though it is not, you are likely to report detecting its presence (O'Mahony, 1978).

The neural pathway for smell is somewhat unusual, compared with the other sensory systems that we've discussed, because connections are made with forebrain structures such as the amygdala, hippocampus, and the hypothalamus (Buck, 1996). As you learned in Chapter 3, these areas have been linked with the regulation of feeding, drinking, sexual behavior, and even memory. It's speculation, but part of the emotional power of olfactory cues might be related to the involvement of this motivational pathway. Certainly in lower animals, whose behavior is often dominated by odor cues, brain structures such as the hypothalamus and the amygdala seem likely to play a major role in the animal's reaction to odors in its environment.

Many animals release chemicals, called *pheromones*, that cause highly specific reactions when detected by other members of the species. Often pheromones induce sexual behavior or characteristic patterns of aggression, but a variety of reactions can be produced. Ants, for example, react to the smell of a dead member of the colony by carrying the decaying corpse outside the nest (Wilson, 1963).

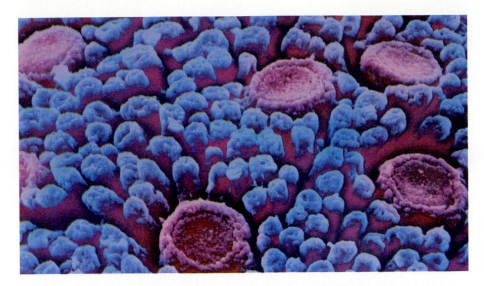

Taste buds, which contain the receptor cells for taste, are embedded within the folds of the papillae (shown here as the large, circular objects).

So far, much to the disappointment of the perfume industry, no solid support has been found for human pheromones; at least, no scents have been discovered that reliably induce sexual interest (although scents can certainly become associated to people that are arousing).

TASTE

Smell's companion sense, taste, is known by the technical term **gustation,** which comes from the Latin *gustare* meaning "to taste." Unlike odors, which are difficult to classify, there appear to be four basic tastes: sweet, bitter, salty, and sour. When psychologists use the term *taste*, they are referring to the sensations produced by contact with the taste receptors; they are not referring to the overall richness of the psychological experience that accompanies eating. Typically, the term **flavor** is used to describe the meal experience. Flavor is influenced by taste, smell, and the visual appearance of the food, as well as by expectations about the quality of the meal.

Taste receptors are distributed throughout the mouth, but mainly occur across the tongue. If you coat your tongue with a mouthful of milk and glance in a mirror, you'll see that your tongue is covered with tiny bumps called *papillae*. The **taste buds,** which contain the actual receptor cells, are embedded within the folds of the papillae. Currently, lots of questions remain about how the transduction process for taste actually occurs. One possibility is that taste stimuli directly penetrate the membrane of the receptor cell, causing the cell to fire; another idea is that taste stimuli simply alter the chemical structure of the cell membrane (Shirley & Persaud, 1990; Teeter & Brand, 1987). In any case, the neural impulse is generated and passed up toward the brain.

The neural pathway for taste takes a more traditional route than the one for smell: Information is passed toward the thalamus and then up to the somatosensory area of the cortex (Rolls, 1995). Little work has been done on how cortical taste cells react, although taste-sensitive cells have been discovered (Scott et al., 1994; Yamamoto et al., 1981). Stronger evidence for taste "tuning" has been found in analysis of the receptor fibers, but, as with many of the other senses, a given receptor cell seems to react to a broad range of gustatory stimuli. The neural code for taste is probably determined, to some extent, by the particular fiber that happens to react and by the relative patterns of activity across large groups of fibers.

The brain can produce stable interpretations of taste stimuli, but the identification process is complex. For one thing, prior exposure to one kind of taste often changes the perception of another. Anyone who has ever tried to drink orange juice after brushing his or her teeth understands how tastes interact. To some

? CRITICAL THINKING

Some smells and tastes are truly disgusting and lead to characteristic facial expressions and reactions. Can you think of any adaptive reasons why we might have such reactions? How might reactions of disgust help us or others to survive?

gustation
The sense of taste.

flavor
A psychological term used to describe the gustatory experience. Flavor is influenced by taste, smell, the visual appearance of food, as well as by expectations about the food's quality.

taste buds
The receptor cells on the tongue involved in taste.

extent, the interaction process depends on the similarity of successive tastes. For example, a taste of a sour pickle, but not a salty cracker, will reduce the "sourness" of lemon juice. There are even natural substances that can completely change the normal perception of taste. One substance extracted from berries, called "miracle fruit," turns extremely sour tastes (such as from raw lemons) sweet. Another substance, taken from the leaves of a plant found in India and Africa, temporarily eliminates the sweet taste of sugar.

TEST YOURSELF 5.4

Check your knowledge about smell and taste by filling-in the blanks. Choose the best answer from among the following terms: chemoreceptors, flavor, gustation, hypothalamus, olfaction, olfactory bulb, pheromones, taste, taste buds. (You will find the answers in the Appendix.)

1. The general term for receptor cells that are activated by invisible molecules scattered about in the air or dissolved in liquids: _____

2. One of the main brain destinations for odor messages: _____

3. A psychological term used to describe the entire gustatory experience: _____

4. The technical name for the sense of smell: _____

5. The technical name for the sense of taste: _____

From the Physical to the Psychological

Throughout this chapter, you've learned that there is a kind of transition from the physical to the psychological. Messages originate in the physical world, but our conscious experiences of those messages can be driven by expectations and beliefs about how the world is organized. We *interpret* the physical message, and this means that our conscious experience of the sensory message can be different from the one that is actually delivered by the environment.

In the field of **psychophysics,** researchers search for ways to describe the transition from the physical to the psychological in the form of mathematical laws. By quantifying the relationship between the physical properties of a stimulus and its subjective experience, psychophysicists hope to develop *general* laws that apply across all kinds of sensory input. Let's consider some examples of how such laws are established.

STIMULUS DETECTION

Psychophysics is actually one of the oldest research areas in psychology; it dates back to the work of Wilhelm Wundt, Gustav Fechner, and others in the nineteenth century. One of the first questions these early researchers asked was: What is the minimum amount of stimulus energy needed to produce a sensation? Suppose I present you with a very faint pure tone—one that you cannot hear—and gradually make it louder. At some point you will hear the tone and respond accordingly. This point is known as the **absolute threshold** for the stimulus; it represents the level of intensity that lifts the stimulus over the threshold of conscious awareness. One of the early insights of psychophysicists such as Fechner was the realization that absolute thresholds, on average, are really not absolute— that is, there is no single point in an intensity curve at which detection reliably begins. For a given intensity level, sometimes people will hear the tone, other times not (the same situation applies to detection in all the sensory modalities, not

LEARNING GOALS

1. Explain the psychology of stimulus detection including the technique of signal detection.

2. Define difference thresholds, and explain Weber's Law.

3. Discuss stimulus adaptation and its adaptive value.

psychophysics
A field of psychology in which researchers search for ways to describe the transition from the physical stimulus to the psychological experience of that stimulus.

absolute threshold
The level of intensity that lifts a stimulus over the threshold of conscious awareness; it's usually defined as the intensity level at which people can detect the presence of the stimulus 50% of the time.

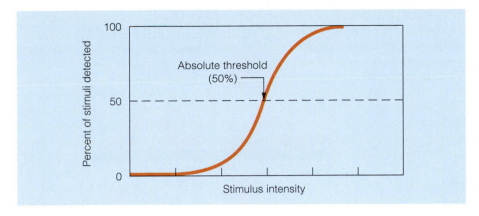

FIGURE 5.24
Absolute Threshold
The more intense the stimulus, the greater the likelihood that it will be detected. The absolute threshold for detection is defined as the intensity level at which we can detect the presence of the stimulus 50% of the time.

just auditory). For this reason, absolute thresholds were redefined as the intensity level at which people can detect the presence of a stimulus 50% of the time (see Figure 5.24).

It might seem strange that a person's detection abilities change from moment to moment. Part of the reason is that trial-to-trial observations turn out to be "noisy." It is virtually impossible for a researcher to control all the things that can potentially affect someone's performance. For example, a subject might have a momentary lapse in attention that causes him or her to miss a presented stimulus on a given trial. Some random activity in the nervous system might even create brief changes in the sensitivity of the receptor systems. Experimenters try to take these factors into account by presenting the subject with many detection opportunities and averaging performance over trials to determine the threshold point.

Psychologists have also tried to develop reasonably sophisticated statistical techniques to pull the truth out of noisy data. Human observers often have built-in biases that influence how they respond in a detection environment. For example, people will sometimes report the presence of a stimulus even though none has actually been presented. Why? Sometimes the observer is simply worried about missing a presented stimulus, so he or she says "Yes" on every trial. To control for these tendencies, researchers use a technique called **signal detection** that mathematically compares *hits*—in which a stimulus is correctly detected—to *false alarms*—in which the observer claims a stimulus was presented when it actually was not.

Four types of outcomes can occur in a detection situation. Besides hits and false alarms, the subject can also fail to detect a stimulus when it was actually presented—called a *miss*—or correctly recognize that a stimulus was, in fact, not presented on that trial—called a *correct rejection*. These four outcomes are shown in Figure 5.25 on page 210. Researchers compare these outcomes over trials in an attempt to infer a subject's true detection ability.

To see why it's important to compare different outcomes, imagine that Lois is participating in a simple detection experiment and that her strategy is to say "Yes, a stimulus occurred" on every trial (even when no stimulus was actually presented). If the researcher pays attention only to hits, it will appear as if Lois has perfect detection ability—she always correctly identifies a stimulus when it occurs. But saying "Yes" on every trial will also lead to false alarms—she will say "Yes" on trials when no stimulus was actually presented. By comparing hits and false alarms, the researcher is able to determine whether her high number of "hits" is really due to detection ability or whether it's due to some other strategic bias on her part. If Lois can truly detect the stimulus when it occurs, she should show lots of hits and very few false alarms.

CRITICAL THINKING

Can you think of any occupations requiring detection—such as air traffic controller—in which it might be advantageous to be biased toward saying "Yes" that a stimulus has occurred?

signal detection
A technique that can be used to determine the ability of someone to detect the presence of a stimulus.

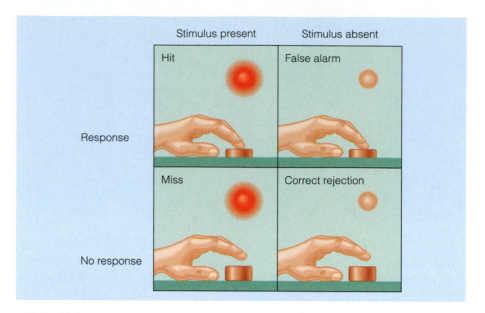

FIGURE 5.25
Signal Detection Outcomes
There are four possible outcomes in a signal detection experiment. If the stimulus is present and correctly detected, it's called a *hit;* if the stimulus is absent but the observer claims it's present, it's a *false alarm*. A *miss* is when the stimulus is present but not detected, and a *correct rejection* is when the observer correctly recognizes that the stimulus was not presented.

DIFFERENCE THRESHOLDS

Researchers in psychophysics have also been concerned with the measurement of **difference thresholds:** the smallest difference in the magnitude of two stimuli that an observer can detect. Suppose I present you with two tones, each equally loud. I then gradually increase the intensity of one of the tones until you notice it as being louder than the other (called the *standard*). How much of a change in magnitude do I need to make for you to detect the difference? As with absolute thresholds, the required amount changes a bit from one moment to the next, but an important general principle emerges.

It turns out that detection of a *just noticeable difference* (or *jnd*) in magnitude depends on how intense the standard was in the first place. If you have your stereo cranked up, small changes in the volume will not be noticed; but if the volume starts out low, the same changes are likely to produce a very noticeable difference. If you're at a rock concert and your friend Gillian wants to tell you something, she needs to yell; if you're in a library, a whisper will do. We can state this relationship more formally as follows: The jnd for stimulus magnitude is a constant proportion of the size of the standard stimulus. In other words, the louder the standard stimulus (the stereo), the more volume will need to be added before a difference in loudness will be detected. This general relationship, called **Weber's law,** doesn't work just for loudness—it applies across all the sensory systems. If the lights in your house go off, two candles will make the room a lot brighter than one; if the lights are on, the addition of one or two candles will lead to little, if any, noticeable increase in brightness (see the accompanying photos). Weber's law demonstrates once again that the relationship between the physical and the psychological is not always direct—increases in the magnitude of a physical stimulus will not always lead to increases in the psychological experience.

difference threshold
The smallest difference in the magnitude of two stimuli that an observer can detect.

Weber's law
The principle stating that the ability to notice a difference in the magnitude of two stimuli is a constant proportion of the size of the standard stimulus. Psychologically, the more intense a stimulus is to begin with, the more intense it will need to become for one to notice a change.

The addition of a single candle to a brightly lit room has little effect on perceived brightness (left photo); but when a candle is added to a dimly lit room (right photo), the increase in brightness will be quite noticeable.

SENSORY ADAPTATION

There is one other feature of all sensory systems that was stressed by the early researchers in psychophysics. Sensory systems are more sensitive to a message when it first arrives than to its continued presence. Through **sensory adaptation,** the body quickly adapts, by reducing sensitivity, to a message that remains constant—such as the feel of a shirt sleeve on your forearm, your hand resting on your knee, or the hum of computers in the background. Think about what the world would be like without sensory adaptation. The water in the pool would never warm up; the smell of garlic from last night's dinner would remain a pervasive force; you would constantly be reminded of the texture of your sock pressing against your foot.

Adaptation is a feature of each of the sensory systems that we've described. Images that remain stable on the retina will vanish; this doesn't normally occur because the eyes are constantly moving and refreshing the retinal image. If you are presented with a continuous tone, your perception of its loudness decreases over time (Evans, 1982). If auditory adaptation didn't occur, no one would ever be able to work in a noisy environment. Human sensory systems are designed to detect *changes* in the incoming message; sensitivity is reduced to those aspects of the message that remain the same.

sensory adaptation
The tendency of sensory systems to reduce sensitivity to a stimulus source that remains constant.

TEST YOURSELF 5.5

Check your understanding of psychophysics by deciding whether each of the following statements is true or false. (You will find the answers in the Appendix.)

1. The intensity level that is required to barely perceive a stimulus varies across individuals, but remains constant for any given individual. *True or False?*

2. A "false alarm" occurs in signal detection when an observer claims a signal was present when, in fact, it was not. *True or False?*

3. According to Weber's law, the detection of a just noticeable difference in magnitude is constant across all intensity levels. *True or False?*

4. Sensory adaptation is a characteristic of all sensory systems. *True or False?*

Solving the Problems

To navigate successfully in the world, we rely on multiple sensory systems. As you've seen, the external world itself is not very user-friendly—it bombards the body with energy-based messages, but none arrives in a form appropriate for the language of the brain. Moreover, the messages that sensory systems receive are complex and ever-changing. Thus, the body faces three fundamental problems of adaptation: How can the external message be translated into the internal language of the nervous system? How do the elementary components get extracted from the message? Finally, how does the brain build a stable and long-lasting interpretation of the message components once they've been extracted?

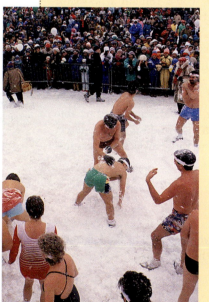

Translating the Message. To solve the translation problem, the body relies on the activation of specialized receptor cells that respond, appropriately enough, by generating neural impulses in the presence of particular energy sources. In the visual system, receptor cells—rods and cones—react to light; in the auditory system, sound energy leads to movement of the basilar membrane, which in turn causes tiny hair cells to generate a neural impulse. The body also has specialized receptors that react to pressure on the skin, free-floating chemicals in the air, and the relative position or movement of muscles. Each of these receptor systems acts as a kind of "translator," changing the messages delivered by the external world into the electrochemical language of the nervous system.

Extracting the Message Components. Once translated, the sensory message receives further processing in the brain to extract the message components. A variety of neural pathways seem specialized to look for particular kinds of sensory information. For example, opponent-process cells in the lateral geniculate region of the brain are specialized to process color; they signal the presence of one kind of color by increasing the rate that they generate neural impulses, and they signal another kind of color by decreasing their firing rate. Similarly, highly specialized cells in the visual cortex respond only to particular patterns of light and dark that appear in the eye. One kind of cell might respond only to a bar of light presented at a particular orientation; another cell might respond only to a pattern of light that moves in a particular direction across the retina.

In the auditory cortex, the brain extracts information about the frequencies of sound in an auditory message. Psychologically, changes in frequency correspond to changes in perceived pitch. The brain detects frequency information by noting the particular place on the basilar membrane where hair cells are stimulated and by noting the rate at which neural impulses are generated over time. It's not unusual for the brain to rely on multiple kinds of processing to extract a particular message component. The perception of color, for instance, relies not only on opponent-process cells but also on the relative activations of three different cone types that reside in the retina.

Producing Stable Interpretations. To establish a coherent, stable interpretation of the sensory message, people use a combination of bottom-up and top-down processing—beliefs and expectations work with the actual sensory input to build perceptions of the external world. The fact that people are able to maintain a constant and stable interpretation of events in the world is really a quite remarkable accomplishment. As we noted at the beginning of the chapter, the pattern of light reflected from a continuously moving object changes continuously with time, yet you have no trouble recognizing a dancer moving effortlessly across the stage. You also have no trouble recognizing the voice of a friend in a crowded room, even though the actual auditory message reaching your ears may be filled with frequency information from many different voices.

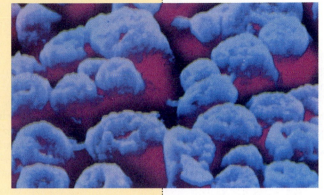

The brain solves the problems of perception, in part, by relying on organizational "rules." For example, we are born with built-in tendencies to group message components in particular ways. Figures are separated from ground, items that share physical properties are perceived together, and so on. But we also rely on prior knowledge for help in the interpretation process. We use what we know about how cues are related in the environment to arrive at sensible interpretations of ambiguous objects. For instance, if two parallel lines converge in the visual field, the brain assumes that the lines are moving away—like railroad tracks moving off in the distance. Such top-down processing is usually extremely adaptive—it helps us maintain a stable interpretation—although in some cases, perceptual illusions can be produced.

Sensation and Perception Chapter Summary

Vision: Building a World of Color and Form

To understand vision, it's necessary to understand how the physical message—light—is translated into the language of the brain. What pathways in the brain are used to extract the basic components of the visual message? How does the brain create a stable interpretation?

TRANSLATING THE MESSAGE: VISUAL TRANSDUCTION

Light is classified by two main physical properties, *wavelength*, and *intensity*. Light reflected from an object passes through the *cornea*, then through the *pupil* (the middle of the *iris*). The *lens* undergoes accommodation, sending the incoming light to a thin layer of tissue, the *retina*. The visual receptors (rods and cones) are located here. The rods are more light sensitive, are located primarily in the periphery of the retina, and are useful at low levels of illumination. The cones tend to be concentrated in the center of the retina (in the *fovea*), need more light to operate, and are responsible for processing fine detail and color. *Bipolar* and *ganglion* cells process the message and send it to the brain via the *optic nerve*.

EXTRACTING THE MESSAGE COMPONENTS: VISUAL PATHWAYS

From the retina, patterns of activation flow to the *optic chiasm* and then to a relay station in the thalamus, the *lateral geniculate nucleus*. Many processing activities are carried out simultaneously, via *parallel processing*. In the visual cortex, *feature detectors* respond to particular aspects of a stimulus, such as orientation and patterns of light and dark. The *trichromatic theory* of color vision proposes that color information is extracted through the activation of three different types of cones. The opponent-*process theory* proposes mechanisms in the visual system that respond positively to one color type and negatively to others. Both theories account for certain aspects of color vision.

PRODUCING STABLE INTERPRETATIONS: VISUAL PERCEPTION

Perception involves both *bottom-up processing* (which starts with the actual physical message) and *top-down processing* (application of knowledge and expectation) People have a natural tendency to group incoming visual messages according to *Gestalt principles of organization*, which include the laws of *proximity*, *similarity*, *closure*, and *good continuation*. Depth is perceived with the aid of *monocular depth cues* and *binocular depth cues*, the latter include *convergence* and *retinal disparity*. Visual perception also demonstrates perceptual constancy; perceived properties (such as size) remain the same even though the physical message to the eye is changing. *Perceptual illusions* are inappropriate interpretations of physical reality.

Hearing: Identifying and Localizing Sounds

Hearing enriches our lives, and like vision, it serves a variety of adaptive functions. Sounds help us identify and locate objects in our path. It allows us to produce and comprehend the spoken word. Even our private self often appears in the form of an inner voice.

TRANSLATING THE MESSAGE: AUDITORY TRANSDUCTION

The auditory system receives *sound*, which varies in *frequency* and *amplitude*. Sound enters through the pinna and travels through the tympanic membrane, to the *middle ear*, and finally, the inner ear and the cochlea. Vibration of fluid in the cochlea displaces the *basilar membrane*, which causes auditory receptors (*hair cells*) to be activated.

EXTRACTING THE MESSAGE COMPONENTS: AUDITORY PATHWAYS

According to the *place theory* of pitch perception, we hear a particular pitch because certain hair cells are responding actively. According to *frequency theory*, pitch is determined in part by the frequency of neural impulses traveling up the auditory pathway. Both theories explain aspects of pitch perception. Final processing of the message occurs in the auditory cortex.

PRODUCING STABLE INTERPRETATIONS: AUDITORY PERCEPTION

Prior knowledge helps the brain organize and impose structure on incoming sound messages. Sound localization involves message comparisons between the ears (arrival time and intensity).

The Skin and Body Senses: From Sense to Movement

Although perceptual experiences seem to be driven primarily by seeing and hearing, physical contact is extremely important, allowing us to detect touch, temperature, and pain.

TOUCH

There are several types of pressure-sensitive receptors in the skin. Touch information is transmitted through distinct channels to processing stations in the brain. There, the *somatosensory cortex* (in the *parietal lobe*) processes the message.

EXPERIENCING PAIN

Pain is an adaptive reaction that the body generates in response to any stimulus intense enough to cause tissue damage. According to the *gate-control theory* of pain, neural impulses generated by pain receptors are gated in the spinal cord by signals produced by the brain; the brain can block critical signals from reaching higher neural centers when appropriate. The brain also controls the experience of pain through the release of chemicals called *endorphins*, which produce morphine-like effects.

TEMPERATURE

Cold fibers respond to a cooling of the skin by increasing the production of neural impulses; *warm fibers* respond vigorously when the temperature of the skin increases. Temperature change is important in determining temperature perception.

THE KINESTHETIC SENSE

Kinesthesia refers to the ability to sense the position and movement of one's body parts. Nerve impulses generated by kinesthetic receptors travel to the somatosensory cortex.

THE VESTIBULAR SENSE

The *vestibular sense* responds to movement, acceleration, and changes in upright posture. Each ear contains *semicircular canals* that help us detect the position of the head. *Vestibular sacs* are responsible for our sense of balance.

The Chemical Senses: Smell and Taste

Smells and tastes are adaptive because they possess powerful signaling properties; like other animals, humans learn to avoid bad odors or bitter tastes. The perception of smell and taste begins with *chemoreceptors*.

SMELL

Olfaction occurs as airborne molecules enter the nose or back of the throat and interact with receptors in the nasal cavity. The message travels to the olfactory bulb in the brain. People probably have up to 1000 different types of olfactory receptor cells. Many animals release *pheromones*, chemicals that cause highly specific (often sexual) reactions when detected by other members of a species.

TASTE

Gustation is smell's companion sense. There appear to be four basic tastes: sweet, salty, bitter, and sour. Taste buds containing the taste receptors are embedded within *papillae* (tiny bumps) on our tongue. Neural messages for taste travel toward the thalamus and then to the somatosensory area of the cortex.

From the Physical to the Psychological

Messages originate in the physical world, but our conscious experience of those messages can be driven by expectations and beliefs about how the world is organized. In the field of *psychophysics*, researchers try to describe the transition from the physical to the psychological in the form of mathematical laws.

STIMULUS DETECTION

The *absolute threshold* for a stimulus is the level of intensity that lifts it over the threshold of conscious awareness. These are not absolute; a more precise definition is the intensity level at which people can detect the presence of a stimulus 50% of the time. To account for response biases, researchers developed a technique known as *signal detection* that mathematically compares *hits* to *false alarms*.

SENSORY ADAPTATION

One important adaptive function of sensory systems is *sensory adaptation*, through which the body quickly adapts to a stimulus by reducing sensitivity to messages that remain constant, such as the feel of a shirt sleeve on your arm.

DIFFERENCE THRESHOLDS

A *difference threshold* is the smallest difference in the magnitude of two stimuli that an observer can detect. Detection of a *just noticeable difference* (jnd) depends on how intense the standard was in the first place. According to *Weber's law*, the jnd for stimulus magnitude is a constant proportion of the size of the standard stimulus.

Terms to Remember

sensations, 170
perception, 170
transduction, 171

VISION

light, 172
hue, 172
brightness, 172
cornea, 173
lens, 173
pupil, 173
iris, 173
accommodation, 173
dark adaptation, 175
retina, 175
rods, 175
cones, 175
fovea, 175
visual acuity, 175
receptive field, 176
blind spot, 176
parallel processing, 177
feature detectors, 178
trichromatic theory, 181
opponent-process theory, 183
bottom-up processing, 185
top-down processing, 185
Gestalt principles of organization, 186
recognition by components, 187
monocular depth cues, 188
binocular depth cues, 188
retinal disparity, 188
convergence, 189
phi phenomenon, 189
perceptual constancy, 190
perceptual illusions, 191

HEARING

sound, 195
pitch, 195
pinna, 195
tympanic membrane, 195
middle ear, 196
cochlea, 196
basilar membrane, 196
place theory, 197
frequency theory, 197

THE SKIN AND BODY SENSES

cold fibers, 202
warm fibers, 202
pain, 203

gate-control theory, 203
kinesthesia, 204
semicircular canals, 204
vestibular sacs, 204

THE CHEMICAL SENSES

chemoreceptors, 205
olfaction, 205
gustation, 207
flavor, 207
taste buds, 207

FROM THE PHYSICAL TO THE PSYCHOLOGICAL

psychophysics, 208
absolute threshold, 208
signal detection, 209
difference threshold, 210
Weber's law, 210
sensory adaptation, 211

Recommended Readings

Goldstein, E. B. (1999). *Sensation and Perception* (Fifth Edition). Pacific Grove, CA: Brooks/Cole. This is an excellent undergraduate textbook filled with interesting demonstrations. It covers most of the material presented in Chapter 5, but in much greater depth.

Shepard, R. N. (1990). *Mind sights.* New York. W. H. Freeman. This provocative book is full of wonderfully original visual tricks and illusions. Accompanying the drawings are concise scientific explanations of the illusions. The two "monsters" shown in Figure 5.20 come from this book.

INFOTRAC® COLLEGE EDITION

For additional readings, explore Infotrac College Edition, your online library. Go to:
http://www.infotrac-college.com/wadsworth

Hint: enter the search terms: Visual perception, Pattern recognition, Motion perception, Optical illusions, Speech perception, Signal detection.

What's on the Web?

Cow's Eye Dissection

(www.exploratorium.edu/learning_studio/cow_eye/index)

Yes, you read that right. This sight, part of the wonderful Exploratorium site, provides you with the opportunity to dissect the eye of a cow on-line—turns out there's a fair amount of similarity between our eyes and a cow's eyes. A fun way to find out more about the eye.

Illusionworks

(www.illusionworks.com)

Nothing's quite as fascinating as a visual illusion. They're fun to look at, and intriguing to learn about. This site presents a variety of visual illusions, and provides interesting and informative explanations of the processes that are responsible.

Seeing, Hearing, and Smelling the World

(www.hhmi.org/senses/)

While many Web sites allow you to learn more about vision (arguably the "#1 sense"), relatively few are devoted to the other major senses. This site allows you to investigate these more "neglected" senses, with articles like "A Secret Sense in the Human Nose?" and "Sniffing Out Social and Social Signals."

The Wadsworth Psychology Study Center Web Site

See http://psychology.wadsworth.com/ for practice quiz questions, hypercontents, updates, critical thinking exercises, discussion forums and more! The Wadsworth Psychology Study Center provides a wealth of information fully organized and integrated by chapter.

Consciousness

consciousness
The subjective awareness of internal and external events.

The development of technologies such as the EEG, shown here, are providing psychologists with a "window" through which the internal activities of the brain can be observed.

Stop for a moment and take a look inside your own head. Try to grab hold of conscious thought and take it for a ride. Forget about its contents—ideas, images, sounds—concentrate only on the movements from thought-to-thought-to-thought-to-thought. Notice the transitions, the ways that ideas and feelings spring forth, only to disappear a moment later. Would you call the movements bumpy? Smooth? The American psychologist William James was convinced that consciousness should be described as a personal, always changing, sensibly continuous *flow*. Consciousness isn't something that can be chopped up in bits, he argued: "words such as 'chain' or 'train' do not describe it fitly . . . a 'river' or 'stream' are the metaphors by which it is most naturally described" (James, 1890, p. 233).

Studying the characteristics of **consciousness,** which can be defined as our subjective awareness of internal and external events, was one of the main jobs of psychologists in the nineteenth century. In fact, if you had taken a psychology course at the turn of the century, the subject matter would likely have been defined as "the science which describes and explains the phenomena of consciousness" (Ladd, 1896, p. 1). With the rise of behaviorism, however, psychologists shifted away from the study of internal experience toward an emphasis on behavior. Techniques like introspection, which required people to look inward and comment on their own internal thoughts, fell strongly out of favor. Most psychologists became convinced that internal observations were difficult, if not impossible, to confirm objectively. So by the early part of the twentieth century, the behaviorists were arguing forcefully that "psychology must discard all reference to consciousness" (Watson, 1913, p. 163).

Even today, it's relatively easy to understand why the behaviorists were dissatisfied with the study of internal experience. Turning inward and asking questions about the contents of consciousness is "like asking a flashlight in a dark room to search around for something that doesn't have any light shining upon it. The flashlight, since there is light in whatever direction it turns, would have to conclude that there is light everywhere" (Jaynes, 1976, p. 23). It's tough to study the properties of an object when your only tool of discovery is the object itself.

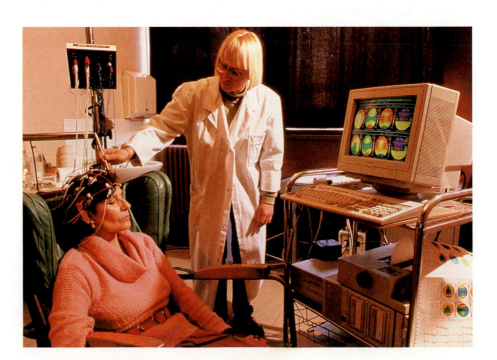

Consciousness by its very nature is a deeply personal experience. It's not something that can be measured easily like a knee jerk or the speed of a rat running through a maze for food.

In recent years, however, the study of consciousness has emerged from its intellectual dark age and has regained a measure of respectability (Milner & Rugg, 1992). One contributing factor has been the development of technologies such as the electroencephalograph (EEG) and positron emission tomography (PET). These devices provide a clear window into the activities of the brain, so there's no longer a need to depend on potentially unreliable techniques like introspection. It's possible now to listen objectively to the brain and to measure how internal activity changes over time. Many neuroscientists are convinced that consciousness can ultimately be linked directly to patterns of neural activity in the brain, although no biological seat of consciousness has yet been discovered (Horgan, 1994). Clearly, as our tools of discovery have broadened, so too has our willingness to explore the workings of the inner world of the mind.

Previewing the Adaptive Problems

Psychologists define *consciousness* as the subjective *awareness* of internal and external events—but what does it really mean to be aware? Intuitively, everyone has a reasonably good idea of what the term means. To be aware is to experience the here and now, to experience the past in the form of memories, to think internally and develop a guiding "view of the world" (Klatzky, 1984). Awareness has the additional property that it can be focused: You can choose to attend to that bug walking up the page of your text, to the beautiful sunset outside your window, or to the voice of your roommate telling you to turn out the light. You can also use conscious thought to develop strategies for behavior; you can think about what you want to say or do and you can imagine the outcomes of those actions without actually performing the behaviors. You can also use conscious thought to imagine the content of other minds—to predict the behavior of other people and to understand their motivation (Weiskrantz, 1992).

It also helps to remember that many actions are controlled by processes that operate *below* levels of awareness. To take an extreme case, you're not aware of the processes controlling your heartbeat or breathing rate, yet these functions carry on like clockwork in the body. Your awareness also takes on different properties when you sleep, when you're hypnotized, or when you take certain types of drugs. We'll focus on some of these properties of consciousness in this chapter, and you'll see how altering awareness helps people solve certain adaptive problems. For a visual summary of the problems that will be addressed in this chapter, take a look at Figure 6.1 on page 222.

First, how do people set priorities for mental functioning? Whatever conscious awareness might be, it's pretty clear that there's often not enough of it to go around. There are limits to the number of things that a person can think about at the same time, or to the number of tasks that they can perform. Have you ever tried to solve a difficult thought problem while someone talks nearby? Obviously, it's critical for people to be selective about what they choose to focus on.

Second, what roles do sleep and dreaming play for the adaptive mind? Sleep clearly serves an adaptive function, as does dreaming. Some researchers believe that we sleep in order to give the brain a chance to rest and restore itself from the day's activities. Others believe that sleep protects us during periods when our sensory equipment is unlikely to function well (such as at night). Dreaming, with its sometimes bizarre imagery, may help us work out hidden conflicts or simply help us exercise the neural circuitry of the brain.

Third, why do certain chemicals, or drugs, produce profound alterations in awareness? You may have heard about the mind-bending alterations of consciousness that are produced by taking psychoactive drugs, such as LSD or mescaline. What you may not know, however, is that the biological processes that produce the changes are natural and

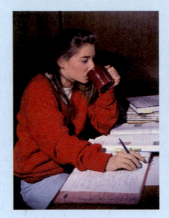

Setting priorities for mental functioning

Sleeping and dreaming

Altering awareness: Psychoactive drugs

Altering awareness: Induced states

FIGURE 6.1

Adaptive Problems of Consciousness
Here are the four adaptive problems that we consider in this chapter.

important ingredients of the adaptive mind. Consuming psychoactive drugs can have harmful and long-lasting consequences, but it's important to understand that artificial drugs operate, in part, by tapping natural adaptive systems.

Fourth, what happens under hypnosis and meditation, two other techniques that seem to alter awareness significantly? Hypnosis is a procedure that induces a heightened state of suggestibility in a willing participant—can it serve an adaptive purpose? Through hypnosis, it's possible to break bad habits (such as smoking), drastically reduce the experience of pain, and eliminate nausea in a patient undergoing chemotherapy. The techniques of meditation have proven effective in the treatment of stress and psychological disorders. You'll discover that both hypnosis and meditation can be used to alter awareness in ways that have adaptive benefits.

Setting Priorities for Mental Functioning: Attention

As you saw in Chapter 5, the world is a smorgasbord of sensory information. Nature delivers an astonishing variety of sights, sounds, and smells. You don't experience every sight and sound, of course; you sample selectively from the table based on your current needs. If you're searching desperately for a child lost in a shopping mall, you focus on the familiar sound of the child's voice or the color of his or her shirt. If you're trying to determine what's for dinner tonight, you sniff the air for the smell of cooking pot roast or simmering spaghetti sauce. You notice those things that are important to the task at hand—you shift through, block out, and focus on those messages that are needed for solving the particular problem that you face.

Psychologists use the term **attention** to refer to the internal processes people use to set priorities for mental functioning. For adaptive reasons, the brain uses attention to focus selectively on certain parts of the environment while ignoring others. Obviously, the concepts of attention and consciousness are closely linked—you are consciously aware of only those things that receive some measure of attention. But why is awareness selective? One reason is that the resources of the brain and nervous system are limited. The brain has only so many neurons, and there are limits to how fast and efficiently these neurons can communicate. These limitations in resources require us to make choices about which parts of the environment to process (Broadbent, 1958; Kahneman, 1973).

LEARNING GOALS

1. Define attention and discuss its adaptive value.

2. Discuss how experiments on dichotic listening can be used to study attention.

3. Describe automaticity and its effects on awareness.

4. Discuss disorders of attention such as visual neglect and attention deficit disorder.

attention
The internal processes people use to set priorities for mental functioning.

In addition, even if the resources were unlimited, it would still be in our interest to make choices about the things relevant to our goals. In a mystery novel, certain events are relevant clues for solving the murder and others are "red herrings"—irrelevant points that lead the reader in the wrong direction and delay solving the crime. The trick is to be selective in deciding which components enter into the equation. A first-rate detective knows not only what to look for, but also what information to avoid. The same is true for even the simplest kind of action, such as walking across the room or reaching for a cup. The visual and motor systems must focus on the objects in the person's *path*, not every single object in the room. If people looked at and thought about everything, they might suffer interference from irrelevant input. Prioritizing mental functioning is an important part of the coordination and control of human actions (Allport, 1989).

EXPERIMENTS ON ATTENTION: DICHOTIC LISTENING

Experimental control over the phenomenon of attention began in the 1950s with the development of the **dichotic listening** technique (Broadbent, 1952; Cherry, 1953). As shown in Figure 6.2, in a typical experiment subjects are asked to listen to spoken messages presented individually to each ear through headphones. To promote selective attention, the subject's task is to *shadow*, or repeat aloud, one of the two messages while essentially ignoring the other. This kind of listening is called *dichotic*, meaning "divided into two," because two messages are involved, delivered separately into each of the two ears.

A dichotic listening experiment requires the subject to listen to two voices at the same time. Have you ever tried to watch television while someone next to you is filling you in on the details of his or her latest escapade? Not an easy task. In fact, in all likelihood you had to either ignore one of the two, or switch back and forth from one message to the other. This is essentially what happens in a dichotic listening experiment. By being forced to repeat one of the messages aloud, subjects appear to process the other message poorly. For example, if at the end of the experiment subjects are given a surprise test for the unattended message, they can usually remember very little, if anything, about its content. They might pick up on the fact that one speaker was male and the other female, but they remember virtually nothing else about the second message (Cherry, 1953; Moray, 1959).

At the same time, people don't just shut off the part of the world that is not bathed in the spotlight of attention. If they did, their actions wouldn't be very adaptive because the world is constantly changing. Some new, possibly critical, situation could suddenly arise. Instead, the brain appears to monitor many things at

CRITICAL THINKING

Can you think of any circumstances where your brain attends to things of which you are not aware?

dichotic listening
A technique in which different auditory messages are presented separately and simultaneously to each ear. Usually the subject's task is to shadow, or repeat aloud, one of the messages while ignoring the other.

Attended channel:
"Four-score and seven years ago our fathers ..."

"Four-score and seven years ago our fathers ..."

Unattended channel:
"When asked the question, 'what is consciousness?' we become conscious of consciousness ..."

FIGURE 6.2

The Dichotic Listening Technique
In dichotic listening, a subject is asked to listen to different spoken messages presented simultaneously to each ear and to shadow—or repeat aloud—one of the messages while ignoring the other. The task taps the ability to *attend* selectively.

The cocktail party effect. By using the processes of attention, it's possible to filter out competing conversations in a noisy environment. But if someone from across the room suddenly speaks your name, you'll probably notice it.

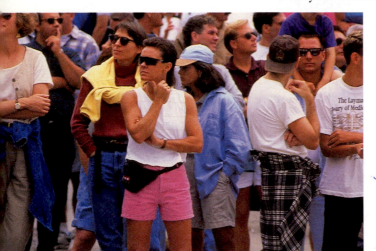

When searching for someone in a crowd, people use the processes of attention to key in on selected features, such as height or the color of a shirt.

cocktail party effect
The ability to focus on one auditory message, such as a friend's conversation at a party, and ignore others; the term also refers to the tendency to notice when one's name suddenly appears in a message that one has been actively ignoring.

the same time, although the monitoring may be minimal and beyond your current awareness.

A case in point is something called the **cocktail party effect.** Imagine you're at a large party, filled with noisy conversation, and you're trying really hard to hear what your date is saying. In all likelihood, you won't be consciously aware of the conversations around you; if I were to interrupt you and ask you to repeat what the couple standing next to you had been discussing, you probably couldn't do it. You successfully filter out these competing messages by using the processes of attention. Now suppose that someone across the room suddenly speaks your name. The odds are that you'll turn your head immediately. People in dichotic listening experiments have shown the same effect: They appear to ignore the contents of the unattended message, but if their name is suddenly spoken in the unattended channel, they notice and remember it later. This is the cocktail party effect and it suggests that our brains are aware of more things than we think.

Another compelling example of how people can monitor many things at the same time comes from an experiment by Treisman (1960), again using the dichotic listening technique. People were presented with compound sentences such as "Against the advice of his broker, the naive investor panicked" in one ear and "Released from his cage, the little lamb bounded into the field" in the other (see Figure 6.3). Subjects were asked to attend to the message in just one of the ears by repeating it aloud, but in the middle of some of the sentences Treisman switched things around—the second half of each sentence moved to the opposite ear. Thus, in the attended ear the subject heard something like "Against the advice of his broker, the little lamb bounded into the field," whereas in the unattended ear the message became "Released from his cage, the naive investor panicked." The interesting finding was that about 30% of the time subjects continued to repeat the meaningful sentence ("Against the advice of his broker, the naive investor panicked") even though the message had switched midway from the attended to the unattended ear. Moreover, many of the subjects reported being unaware that the message had switched.

Attended channel:
"Against the advice of his broker the little lamb bounded into the field."

"Against the advice of his broker, the naive investor panicked."

Unattended channel:
"Released from his cage the naive investor panicked."

FIGURE 6.3

Treisman's "Ear-Switching" Experiment
At one point in a dichotic listening experiment by Treisman, unknown to the participant, the to-be-shadowed message was suddenly switched to the unattended channel. Interestingly, subjects often continued to repeat portions of the meaningful sentence even though it was now presented in the unattended ear.

The cocktail party effect and the findings of the ear-switching experiments suggest that the brain does not simply filter out what goes on in the unattended message. It focuses the spotlight of attention on the task at hand, but it carries on at least some unconscious monitoring of the rest of the environment as well. If something else important happens, the brain shifts the spotlight of attention and allows the new event to enter conscious awareness. In Treisman's experiment, the brain must have been following the meaning of the messages in both ears, even though the people who participated were only aware of monitoring one thing. Exactly how all this works has been the subject of considerable debate over the last several decades (Cowan, 1995; Pashler, 1998), but the process itself is clearly adaptive. Humans wouldn't live for long in a world where they processed only those things in the realm of immediate awareness. But what about subliminal messages hidden in advertisements? Do they work? See the accompanying "Inside the Problem" feature on page 226 for a discussion of the effectiveness of subliminal messages

PROCESSING WITHOUT ATTENTION: AUTOMATICITY

The idea that the brain and body are doing things beyond current awareness may seem strange at first, but not if you think about it. After all, when's the last time you thought about breathing, or keeping your heart beating, or walking, or even forming words from your repertoire of spoken sounds? You can drive a car and carry on a conversation at the same time—you don't need to focus an attentional spotlight on every turn of the wheel or pressing of the brake. These things occur automatically. In the case of driving, people have developed a skill that demands less and less attention with practice.

Psychologists use the term **automaticity** to refer to fast and effortless processing that requires little or no focused attention (Logan, 1991). When you practice a task, such as playing Mozart on the piano, overall speed steadily improves. You may even reach a point where performing the task seems automatic—Mozart rolls off your fingertips with such ease that you're not even consciously aware of finger movement. Automatic processes, once they develop, no longer seem to require conscious control. The mind is free to consider other things, while the task itself is performed without a hitch. Many of the activities that people take for granted—such as reading, talking, and walking—are essentially automatic processes.

If you practice a task for extended periods, such as juggling, your performance may become automatic. Automatic processes, once acquired, no longer require much conscious control.

automaticity
Fast and effortless processing that requires little or no focused attention.

Inside the Problem   Subliminal Messages

Is it possible to influence people by presenting subliminal messages—that is, messages presented at levels so hard to detect that they essentially bypass conscious awareness? We briefly considered this topic in Chapter 2, when experimental methods were discussed, but it's worthwhile to consider the topic again as we discuss attention. You've seen how the brain uses attention to prioritize mental functioning; automatic processes can also develop that lead to fast and effortless behaviors that require little or no conscious thought. So, from an adaptive perspective, it's certainly reasonable to assume that people might be influenced by things that bypass conscious awareness. But do these messages work?

At this point, it's not possible to determine whether advertisers really try to influence people subliminally (the advertisers are not talking) or, in fact, whether the subliminal tapes that people buy to lose weight or gain confidence really do present the promised embedded messages (some evidence suggests that the messages might not even be present). It is possible, however, to conduct controlled experiments where messages are purposely embedded in advertisements or on tapes. Dozens of such studies have been conducted (Druckman & Bjork, 1991; Merikle, 1988; Rosen & Singh, 1992); the general consensus seems to be that the effects of subliminal influence are mild or nonexistent.

For example, it is sometimes claimed that subliminal messages lead to enhanced memory. In a study by Vokey and Read (1985), three or four instances of the word SEX were inserted into vacation slides; the words were placed into the pictures in such a way that they were not directly noticeable but could be detected easily if pointed

out by the experimenters. Immediately after viewing the slides, or after a delay, subjects were given a memory test for the slides. Even though we know in this instance that the message was actually there and could be detected, the subjects showed no improvement in the recognition of the slides relative to the proper control groups.

In a study by Rosen and Singh (1992), the embedded messages were of three types: (1) the word SEX, (2) a picture of a naked woman and several phallic symbols, or (3) the word DEATH combined with pictures of skulls. The "embeds" were placed in black-and-white print ads for liquor or cologne, and subjects were asked to view each ad as part of an experiment on advertising effectiveness. No direct mention was made of the embeds, which were present in some of the ads but not in others. This study is noteworthy because it used a variety of measures of advertising effectiveness to check for effects of the subliminal messages. None of these measures turned out to be affected in any significant way by the hidden information.

With regard to self-help tapes, again the data are clear. Greenwald and his colleagues (1991) recruited subjects to help evaluate the effectiveness of tapes designed to improve either memory or self-esteem. Unknown to the subjects, however, the labels on some of the tapes had been switched, and those who thought they were listening to a self-esteem tape were actually given a memory tape, and vice versa. After regular listening, people seemed to improve on posttests of self-esteem or memory, but it didn't matter which tape the subject had actually been given. A weight-loss study by Merikle and Skanes (1992) produced similar results.

Subjects improved as a result of participating in the study (in this case, they lost weight), but it didn't matter whether the tape actually contained the subliminal message, or even if the subjects had listened to a tape at all!

Why the improvement? Certainly, one would think, people would stop buying these tapes if they were completely ineffective. From a psychological perspective, though, it's important to remember that those who buy such tapes are motivated to improve. Thus, the people who volunteer for a weight loss study may simply be more conscious of their weight during the course of the experiment (Merikle & Skanes, 1992). Alternatively, a tape may act as a kind of placebo, leading to improvement because the listener believes in its magical powers. If subliminal self-help is placebo-related, we would expect the subject to improve regardless of whether the message was, in fact, actually embedded in the background. All that's necessary is that subjects think they are receiving something that will work.

So what can we conclude about subliminal messages? Is it possible to alter behavior without awareness? Perhaps. Most psychologists believe that a person's behavior can be affected under conditions in which no subjective conscious awareness is present (Greenwald et al., 1995). As you'll discover in Chapter 8, people often "remember" without awareness, and everyone regularly performs tasks (such as walking or talking) without thinking about it. But it's a bad idea to waste a lot of time worrying about subliminal conspiracies. There's not much evidence that these messages exist, and even if they do, their influence is minimal at best.

It's possible to measure how automaticity develops through what is called a *divided attention task* (Logan, 1988). In a typical experiment, people are asked to perform two tasks at the same time, such as playing a piece by Mozart on the piano while simultaneously trying to remember a short list of unrelated words. Automaticity is demonstrated when one task, the automatic one, fails to interfere with performance on the other task (Hasher & Zacks, 1979; Shiffrin & Schneider, 1977). Clearly, if you've just learned to play the Mozart piece, your mind will need to focus on every note, and you'll have enough trouble just getting through it without error, let alone recalling a list of words. But if you're an accomplished pianist—if your Mozart performance has become automatic—you can let your fingers do the playing and your mind can concentrate on remembering the word list.

Notice the relationship between automaticity and awareness, because it tells us something important about the function of consciousness. The better you are at performing a task—the more automatic the task has become—the less likely you are to be aware of what you're doing. This is a very important characteristic of mental functioning. If we assume that the resources of the brain and nervous system are limited, then automaticity can help free up needed resources for conscious thought. Environmental conditions can change at any moment, so we often need to use consciousness as a kind of work space to develop new and creative strategies for behavior. So, people use consciousness for handling the new and demanding, while relying on the steady and effortless processes of automaticity to keep moving and acting in a normal way.

DISORDERS OF ATTENTION

We've stressed the link between attention and consciousness because, in many respects, attention is the gateway to consciousness (Ellis & Hunt, 1993): We only become conscious of things that receive some measure of attention. It follows that if the brain systems that control attention were to be damaged in some way, you should expect to find a corresponding loss in conscious awareness. Brain researchers have used clinical cases of brain damage to examine this possibility, and they are in the process of mapping out what appear to be attention-related areas of the brain (Posner & Rothbart, 1992). Let's briefly consider two examples of attentional disorders that may be related to brain dysfunction: *visual neglect* and *attention deficit disorder.*

Visual Neglect

It's been known for some time that damage to the right parietal lobe of the cerebral cortex can produce an odd and complex disorder of attention called **visual neglect** (see Figure 6.4 on page 228). People suffering from visual neglect show a tendency to ignore things that appear toward the left side of the body (remember from earlier chapters that the right side of the brain tends to be involved in processing things on the left side of the body). Visual neglect can cause people to read only from the right side of pages and copy only the right side of pictures. They may even dress, shave, or apply makeup to only the right side of the body (Bisiach & Rusconi, 1990). It's as if an entire side of their visual field has vanished from awareness. Fortunately, the condition sometimes recovers with time, although it's often associated with other kinds of processing deficits in the brain (Kerkhoff et al., 1994; Mesulam, 1987). It can also arise from damage to the left side of the brain, which then creates problems in the right visual field, but it occurs more frequently with right-brain damage (Posner, 1993).

Is the brain really shutting off all visual information that it receives from one side of the body? Probably not. In one study, a patient suffering from visual neglect was shown drawings of two houses. One house was normal in appearance; the other was normal on the right side but had bright red flames and smoke billowing out from a window on its left side. The patient was asked to choose which of the two houses she would prefer to live in. "The houses look the same to me," she reported, presumably because she was attending only to the right side of each picture. Nevertheless, she consistently chose to live in the house without the flames (Marshall & Halligan, 1988). This suggests that even though the brain mechanisms underlying conscious *awareness* had been damaged, her brain was still able to use the available information to help determine the appropriate behavior (Bisiach, 1992).

CRITICAL THINKING

In what ways are the symptoms of visual neglect similar to the symptoms of the split-brain patients that were discussed in Chapter 3?

visual neglect
A complex disorder of attention characterized by a tendency to ignore things that appear on one side of the body, usually the left side.

FIGURE 6.4
Visual Neglect
Patients suffering from visual neglect might consciously detect no differences between these two houses. But they would probably choose to live in the house without the flames.

Attention deficit disorder is sometimes, but not always, associated with problems of hyperactivity.

attention deficit disorder
A psychological condition, occurring most often in children, marked by difficulties in concentrating or in sustaining attention for extended periods.

Attention Deficit Disorder

The right hemisphere of the brain may also be involved in **attention deficit disorder,** a psychological condition characterized by difficulties in concentrating. Individuals with attention deficit disorder have trouble sustaining attention for extended periods—they're easily distracted and often cannot finish tasks that they begin. It's one of the most common psychological problems in school-aged children, although it probably affects only about 3–5% of all children (Cantwell, 1996). In addition to having attention problems, which hurt schoolwork, children with attention deficit disorder are sometimes hyperactive and impulsive—they squirm and fidget continuously and regularly blurt out answers to questions before the questions have even been completely asked (Barkely, 1997). Attention problems are not always associated with hyperactivity, although the diagnosis is often known generally as attention deficit/hyperactivity disorder (Barlow & Durand, 1999).

There is some evidence that attention deficit disorder might be caused by mild damage, or malfunctioning, of the right hemisphere of the brain. In one study researchers measured the amount of time that it took children to turn their eyes to the left to see an unexpected visual stimulus. It was found that children with attention deficit disorder showed a different pattern of eye-movement times than children without the disorder (Rothlind et al., 1991). Because leftward eye movements are controlled by the right hemisphere of the brain, these findings were interpreted to mean that the problem relates to a specific deficit in right-hemisphere brain functioning.

But the brain mechanisms involved in attention deficit disorder are still largely unknown. PET scan studies, for instance, have indicated that various regions of the brain, including the frontal lobes, may be selectively involved (Zemetkin et al., 1990). It's unlikely that any single brain location is responsible, because the disorder is quite complex and can manifest itself in a variety of ways. There are even ongoing debates about the disorder's proper definition (Barkley, 1997; Shaywitz et al., 1994). So, it may take some time before researchers arrive at a complete neurological understanding of the problem.

What about treatment? The news on this front is promising. It turns out that a majority of children who have attention problems can be helped with a combination of medication and directed training. Children with attention problems need to learn coping strategies to help them perform well in school and in social settings. A complete training program typically includes teaching study skills, such as learning to write down important information (rather than relying on memory) and offering rewards for sitting still and not being disruptive in social interactions. Medications, such as Ritalin, seem to help concentration and they often reduce hyperactivity and disruptive behavior. It's interesting to note that Ritalin, as well as many other drugs that are used to treat attention deficit disorder, actually comes from a class of drugs—called stimulants—that generally serve to increase nervous system activity. You'll read more about stimulants later in this chapter, but in low doses, Ritalin appears to increase a person's ability to concentrate and focus attention (Mattay et al., 1996).

Finally, it's worth mentioning that there is some concern among psychologists that attention deficit disorder may be overdiagnosed at the present time. It's important to be cautious about applying the label "attention deficit disorder" to a child simply because he or she may have troubling sitting still in school or in paying attention. All children are restless from time to time, and certainly most ignore their parents in some situations, but that doesn't mean that medication and/or a directed training program is in order. Children with true attention deficit disorder are usually identified quite early in childhood, by around age 3 or 4. They have trouble in social settings and don't make friends easily; their behavior, either because of the hyperactivity or the difficulties in concentration, is simply too much for their peer group to bear.

TEST YOURSELF 6.1

To test your knowledge about how we set priorities for mental functioning, try deciding whether each of the following statements about attention and its disorders is true or false. (You will find the answers in the Appendix.)

1. The "cocktail party effect" suggests that we cannot attend to more than one message at a time; we focus our attention on one thing and the rest of the environment is effectively filtered out. *True or False?*

2. In dichotic listening tasks, people are presented with two auditory messages, one in each ear, and the task is to repeat one of the messages aloud while essentially ignoring the other. *True or False?*

3. If a task—like playing Mozart on the piano—has become automatic, then you can perform a second task—like remembering a list of letters—without interfering with performance on the first task. *True or False?*

4. When visual neglect is caused by damage to the right side of the brain, people seem not to notice things that appear on the right side of the body. *True or False?*

5. Attention deficit disorder is primarily a learned disorder that can easily be treated by special skills training. *True or False?*

Sleeping and Dreaming

To set priorities for mental functioning, we focus our attention selectively in an effort to solve the problems of particular environments and tasks. For example, if you're trying to read a book, you focus on the visual features of the page and try to block out distracting sounds. If you're listening to music, you might close your eyes so that you can fully appreciate the rhythms and harmonies of the sound patterns. However, when you redirect your attention, you're not really changing anything fundamental about the processes of consciousness; instead, you're simply altering the *content* of conscious awareness. In the case of sleep, however, the change is more fundamental—you are no longer consciously aware of the external world, as you are in a waking state, yet your mind is still actively processing something, possibly a dream. For this reason, sleep is sometimes referred to as a different "state" of consciousness.

BIOLOGICAL RHYTHMS

To understand sleep, you first need to understand that we live in a world full of rhythms and cycles, both in the environment (day to night, the seasons, etc.) and

LEARNING GOALS

1. Discuss biological rhythms and how they are controlled.

2. Describe the various stages and characteristics of sleep.

3. Discuss the function and adaptive significance of sleep.

4. Discuss the function and current theories of dreaming.

5. Describe the various disorders of sleep.

within our bodies. The regular daily transition from waking awareness to sleep is an example of one kind of cycle in the body called a *biological rhythm*. Actually, many body functions work in cycles, which is something that we share with all other members of the animal kingdom. Sleep and waking vary daily, along with body temperature, hormone secretions, blood pressure, and other processes (for a review, see Aschoff & Wever, 1981). Activities that rise and fall along a 24-hour cycle are known as **circadian rhythms** (*circa* means "about," and *dies* means "day"). Other biological activities may follow cycles that are either shorter or longer. The female menstrual cycle operates on an approximately 28-day cycle, for example, whereas changes in appetite and the ability to perform certain tasks may change several times throughout the day.

What controls these internal rhythms? Certainly regular changes in blood pressure or internal body temperature are not under our conscious control. You don't consciously alert the endocrine system that it's time to secrete hormones or actively instruct some portion of your brain that your body temperature needs to start rising. These functions are controlled automatically by structures in the brain, called **biological clocks,** that trigger the needed activities at just the right time. These clocks schedule the internal functions of the body and make sure that everything is performing as it should. Animal research has determined that a particular area of the hypothalamus, called the *suprachiasmatic nucleus,* may play a key role in regulating the clock that controls circadian rhythms (Ralph et al., 1990; Schwartz, 1996). But it's thought that the human brain probably has several clocks, each controlling its own function such as body temperature or activity level (Johnson & Hastings, 1986).

Setting Our Internal Clocks

The environment turns out to play a critical role in helping our brains synchronize their internal biological clocks. Light is a particularly important controller, or

circadian rhythms
Biological activities that rise and fall in accordance with a 24-hour cycle.

biological clocks
Brain structures that schedule rhythmic variations in bodily functions by triggering them at the appropriate times.

FIGURE 6.5

Pacing the Internal Clock
Light strongly influences our internal biological clocks. If you were suddenly forced to live without darkness, you would still sleep a normal 8 hours (shown by the length of the bar). But sleep onset times would probably drift. For example, if you usually fall asleep at 11:00 P.M. and wake at 7:00 A.M., after a while you might find yourself becoming sleepy at 2:00 A.M. and rising at 10:00 A.M.

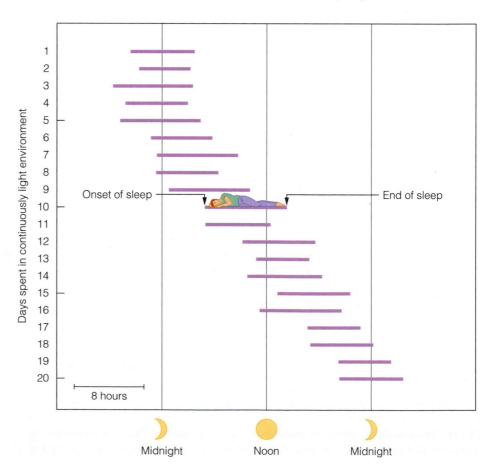

The activity levels of many animals are controlled by internal clocks that are "set," in part, by the environment. Bears are active during the warm summer months and hibernate during the winter.

zeitgeber (meaning "time giver"), of the pacing of internal clocks (Czeisler et al., 1989). If you were suddenly forced to live in a continuously dark or light environment, you would still sleep regularly (although your sleep activities may be disrupted somewhat). But the timing of the sleeping and waking cycles would drift and lose their connection with night and day (see Figure 6.5). Rather than falling asleep at your usual 11:00 P.M. and waking at 7:00 A.M., after a while you might find yourself becoming sleepy at 2:00 A.M. and rising at 10:00 A.M. People use light during the day, as well as the absence of light at night, as a way of setting their internal sleep clock.

The fact that the environment is so important in maintaining internal body rhythms makes considerable adaptive sense. Remember, the environment also operates in synchrony with universal cycles. The sun rises and sets approximately every 12 hours. There are daily changes in air pressure and temperature caused, in part, by the continuous rotation of the earth about its axis. It's perfectly reasonable to assume that animals, including humans, have adapted to remain in harmony with these cycles. As the cold of winter approaches, birds fly south for the warmer temperatures and the more plentiful food supplies; other animals stay put and prepare for hibernation. These changes in behavior are sensible adaptations to fixed changes in the environment that are not under the animal's direct control.

Jet lag is a good example of how the environment can play havoc with our internal clocks. When you travel to a new time zone, especially if you move east (which shortens your day), your usual signals for sleeping and waking become disrupted—it gets light and dark at unusual times for you. The net result is that you have trouble going to sleep, you get up at the "wrong" time, and you generally feel lousy. Your body needs to reset its clocks, in line with your new environment, and this process takes time. This is one reason why diplomats and business travelers often arrive at their destinations a few days before an important event or meeting; it gives them time to adjust their internal clocks and shrug off the jet lag.

CRITICAL THINKING

Can you think of any workplace environments that might lead to symptoms similar to jet lag?

THE CHARACTERISTICS OF SLEEP

As I mentioned earlier, the transition from waking to sleep is sometimes described as a change in one's *state* or level of consciousness. Rather than being "death's counterfeit" (as Shakespeare called it), sleep does involve some awareness, although the focus of that awareness no longer connects directly to events in the world. The sticky problem facing researchers, of course, is that they cannot directly measure the subjective experience (because the subject is unresponsive). What researchers *can* do is eavesdrop on the electrical activity of the brain,

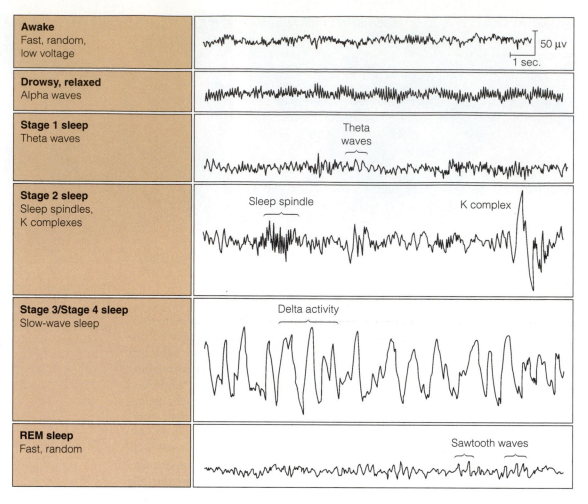

FIGURE 6.6

EEG Patterns Associated with Sleeping and Wakefulness

As we move from a waking state into sleep, characteristic changes occur in the electrical activity of the brain. Generally, as we become drowsy and move through the four stages of sleep, our brain waves become slower and more regular and show more amplitude. But during REM sleep, when we are presumed to be dreaming, the EEG shows a pattern more closely resembling the waking state. (From Hauri, 1982.)

through EEG recordings, and infer things about changes in the sleeper's state of consciousness by looking at how the patterns of brain activity change over time.

As you may recall from Chapter 3, the *electroencephalograph*, or EEG, is a device that monitors the electrical activity of the brain. Electrodes are attached to the scalp, and changes in the electrical potentials of large numbers of brain cells are recorded in the form of line tracings, or brain waves. It's possible to record EEG-based brain waves at any time, including when someone is asleep. The EEG was first applied to the sleeping brain in the 1930s, and by the 1950s researchers had discovered some very intriguing and unexpected things about the sleep process. For example, EEG tracings revealed that sleep is characterized by cyclic changes in brain activity and that at certain points the electrical activity of the sleeping brain bears a striking similarity to the brain activity of a person who is wide awake (Aserinsky & Kleitman, 1955; Dement & Kleitman, 1957).

Figure 6.6 presents typical EEG recordings made during waking and sleep states. The main things to notice are (1) the *height*, or amplitude, of the brain waves; (2) the *frequency*, or number of cycles per second (usually described in Hertz); and (3) the *regularity*, or smoothness, of the pattern. Regular high-amplitude waves of low frequency reflect neural synchrony, meaning that large numbers of neurons are working together. In the first row of tracings, measured when a subject was awake, you'll see no evidence of neural synchrony—the EEG pattern is fast and irregular, and the waves are of low amplitude. Presumably, when people are awake and focusing their attention on some task, the brain is busy dividing its labor; lots of cells are working on specialized individual tasks, so the combined brain activity tends to look irregular. In contrast, when the brain is in a relaxed state, it produces **alpha waves,** which have a higher amplitude and cycle in a slower, more regular manner.

Stages 1–4 of Sleep

As you settle down for the night and prepare for sleep, the fast and irregular wave patterns of the waking state are soon replaced by slower, more synchronized alpha waves. You're not really asleep at this point—just relaxed, and perhaps a little drowsy. The first official sign of sleep—what is called *stage 1* sleep—is marked by a return to waves that are bit lower in amplitude and slightly more irregular. The dominant wave patterns of stage 1 sleep are called **theta waves;** as you can see in Figure 6.6, they're different from the patterns found in the waking state. But even here, people will often report that they're not really asleep; instead, they might claim that their thoughts are simply drifting.

The second stage of sleep, *stage 2* sleep, is defined by another change in the EEG pattern. Specifically, the theta activity that defines stage 1 sleep begins to be interrupted occasionally by short bursts of activity called *sleep spindles.* There are also sudden, sharp waveforms from time to time called *K complexes.* You're definitely asleep at this point, although your brain still shows some sensitivity to events in the external world. Loud noises, for example, tend to be reflected immediately in the EEG pattern by the triggering of a K complex (Bastien & Campbell, 1992). Your brain reacts, as revealed by the K complex, but you're not really consciously aware of the environment. For instance, you won't do a very good job of responding to signals delivered by an experimenter (say, by raising your finger or hand).

The final two stages of sleep, *stage 3* and *stage 4,* are progressively deeper states and show more synchronized slow-wave brain patterns called **delta activity;** for this reason, these stages are sometimes called delta or *slow-wave sleep.* Notice that the wave patterns in Figure 6.6 appear large (high in amplitude) and cycle slowly compared to the patterns of the earlier sleep stages. You're really asleep now, and tough to arouse (Kelly, 1991). If I shake you awake during slow-wave sleep, you won't be very responsive. You'll act confused and disoriented, and it'll take quite some time for you to reach a normal state of conscious awareness.

REM Sleep

It's fair to characterize the transition from stage 1 to stage 4 sleep as moving from a light to a deep sleep. Not surprisingly, other internal measures of arousal, such as breathing rate, heart rate, and blood pressure, decline regularly as you progress through each of the stages. But about 70–90 minutes into the sleep cycle, something very unexpected happens—abrupt changes appear in the entire physiological pattern. Heart rate increases rapidly and becomes more irregular; twitching movements might begin in the hands, feet, and face; in males, the penis becomes erect, and in females vaginal lubrication begins; the eyes begin to move rapidly and irregularly, darting back and forth or up and down behind the eyelids. The EEG pattern loses its synchrony and takes on low-amplitude, irregular patterns that resemble those of the waking state. But you're not awake—you've entered *paradoxical,* or **REM** (rapid eye movement), sleep.

REM sleep is called "paradoxical" for an obvious reason: The electrical activity of the brain during REM sleep resembles the "awake" pattern, yet people are actually deeply asleep. Their muscle tone is extremely relaxed, and they're relatively difficult to arouse. But as the EEG indicates, the brain is extremely active during this period—if the person is jostled awake from REM sleep, he or she will

CRITICAL THINKING

Can you think of any adaptive reasons why sleep occurs in stages? What might be the advantage to starting off in a light sleep and moving to a deeper sleep?

alpha waves
The pattern of brain activity observed in someone who is in a relaxed state.

theta waves
The pattern of brain activity observed in stage 1 sleep.

delta activity
The pattern of brain activity observed in stage 3 and stage 4 sleep; it's characterized by synchronized slow waves. Also called slow-wave sleep.

REM
A stage of sleep characterized by rapid eye movements and low-amplitude, irregular EEG patterns similar to those found in the waking brain. REM is typically associated with dreaming.

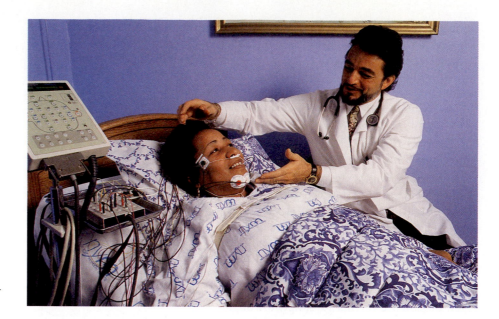

In sleep disorders clinics, the changes in the gross electrical activity of the brain are monitored throughout the night.

seem instantly alert. As noted above, this contrasts sharply with the reaction of people who are awakened from the early stages of sleep, when they're likely to act confused or even deny that they've been asleep. Perhaps most interesting, people who awaken from REM sleep are likely to report an emotional and storylike *dream*. In fact, REM-based dreaming is reported well over 80% of the time, even in people who have previously denied that they dream (Goodenough, 1991; Snyder, 1967).

There is still some debate among sleep researchers about the exact relationship between the REM state and dreaming. It's true that people often report dreaming if they're awakened during REM, but dreaming also seems to occur during the earlier stages of sleep. Haven't you ever experienced a dream moments after going to sleep? Most people have, but it's unlikely that your brain was in an official REM state. Systematic studies of dreaming and the sleep stages have revealed conflicting results. Some studies report low levels of dreaming during non-REM stages (Dement, 1978); other studies have found the percentages to be relatively high (over 50%; see Foulkes, 1985). It remains an open question whether dreaming is an exclusive result of REM, which seems unlikely, or whether dreaming is simply highly correlated with REM activity. I'll have more to say about the REM state momentarily, when we consider the function of dreaming.

The Sleep Cycle

Over the course of an average night, most adults cycle through the various stages of sleep, including REM sleep, about four or five times. Each sleep cycle takes about 90 minutes: You progress from stage 1 through stage 4, then back from stage 4 toward stage 1, ending in REM (see Figure 6.7). This sequence remains intact throughout much of the night, but the amount of time spent in each stage changes as morning approaches. During the first cycle of sleep, the majority of time is spent in stages 3 and 4 (slow-wave sleep), but REM sleep

FIGURE 6.7
Sleep Cycles
During an average night, most adults pass through the various stages of sleep four or five times. A complete cycle usually takes about 90 minutes. As the figure shows, as morning approaches, we tend to spend more time in REM sleep, presumably dreaming. (Based on Kalat, 1996.)

| | 11 P.M. | | 12 A.M. | | | 1 A.M. | | 2 A.M. |

| Sleep stage | A | 1 | 2 | 3 | 4 | 3 | 2 | REM | 1 | 2 | 3 | 4 | 3 | 2 | 3 | 2 | REM | 1 |

Why do people sleep? It could be to restore or repair depleted resources, but research suggests that vigorous activity during the day does not necessarily change one's sleeping patterns.

tends to dominate the later cycles. The total amount of time spent in REM sleep, presumably dreaming, increases and the interval between successive REM states becomes shorter (Ellman et al., 1991). In fact, by the end of the night, stage 4 seems to disappear and you end up spending almost all of your time in REM sleep (Webb, 1992). As you're aware, many dreams seem to occur toward the end of the sleep period, and these are the dreams you're most likely to remember.

THE FUNCTION OF SLEEP

If you sleep 8 hours a night and you live to the ripe old age of 75, you'll have spent a quarter century with your eyes closed, your limbs lying useless at your sides, and your outstretched body seemingly open to attack. Doesn't this seem a bit strange? Think about it. What could be the adaptive value, beyond the exercising of neurons during REM sleep, of redirecting the focus of awareness inward, away from the potential threats of predators lurking about in the environment?

Repairing and Restoring

Researchers aren't exactly sure why people sleep, but a number of plausible hypotheses have been offered. One possibility is that sleep functions to *restore or repair* the body and brain. The daily activities of waking life produce wear and tear on the body, and some mind/brain "down time" may be needed to put things back in order. There are definitely periods during sleep, especially slow-wave sleep, when the metabolic activity of the brain is dramatically lowered (Sakai et al., 1979). Moreover, if people are deprived of sleep for any extended period of time, their ability to perform complex tasks, especially those requiring problem solving, deteriorates (Linde & Bergstrom, 1992).

But is the brain really working overtime during sleep—repairing disorganized circuits or restoring depleted resources? In general, there isn't strong empirical support for this idea (Horne, 1988). Many restorative activities do go on during

3 A.M.			4 A.M.				5 A.M.		6 A.M.				7 A.M.
2	3	2	REM	1	2	3 2 A 1	REM	A 1 A	2		REM		

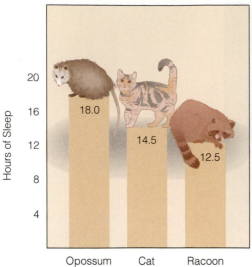

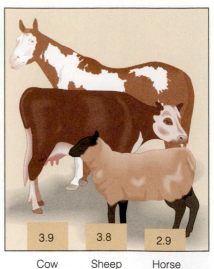

FIGURE 6.8

Sleep Times for Various Species
Large grazing animals, such as cows and horses, eat frequently and are quite vulnerable to surprise attacks from predators. As the figure shows, such animals tend to sleep very little. Small, quick animals, such as cats and rodents, are less vulnerable to attack and sleep a great deal.

sleep, but these activities are not confined just to sleep. They occur regularly throughout the day, so sleep does not appear to be special in this regard. There also doesn't appear to be a strong relationship between the amount of activity in a day and the depth and length of the sleep period that follows. Sleep researchers have tried to tire people during the day by having them engage in vigorous exercise or spend a long day at a shopping center or amusement park, but no great changes in their subsequent sleep patterns have been observed (Horne & Minard, 1985). Rest and restoration may be one of the important consequences of a good night's sleep, but that's clearly not the whole story.

Survival Value

Another possibility is that sleep is simply an adaptive response to changing environmental conditions, a form of behavior that is useful because it increases the likelihood that we will survive. Humans rely a lot on their visual systems; as a result, we aren't very efficient outside at night in low levels of illumination. Our ancestors could have moved about at night looking for food, trying to avoid being eaten or killed by some lurking predator, but it was probably a better idea for them to stay put in a cave somewhere until dawn. Sleep thus became adaptive—particularly sleeping at night—because it stopped people from venturing forth into a hostile environment.

We can find evidence in support of this idea by looking closely at the sleeping patterns of animal species in the wild. If sleep is an adaptive reaction to light–dark cycles and susceptibility to predators, then we might expect animals that rely on senses other than vision to be active primarily at night, when vision-based predators would be at a hunting disadvantage. This is indeed the case for mice, rats, and other rodents. Second, large animals that must eat continuously and can't easily find places to hide should sleep very little. And, indeed, grazing animals such as sheep, goats, horses, and cattle, which are vulnerable to surprise attack by predators, sleep only a few hours a day (see Figure 6.8). In one study, researchers found that body weight and susceptibility to attack could explain the majority of the differences among the sleeping patterns of different species (Allison & Chichetti, 1976).

Sleep Deprivation

Earlier I mentioned that our ability to perform complex tasks is disrupted if we haven't received much sleep. This shouldn't come as too much of a surprise— you've probably performed an all-nighter at some point, only to find yourself irritable and not good for much the next day. But how serious is prolonged sleep deprivation? From time to time people have tried to remain awake for very long periods—approaching two weeks—and the results have been generally negative: some of the symptoms were slurred speech, sharp declines in mental ability, and even the development of paranoia and hallucinations. Although severely sleep-deprived individuals can appear normal for brief periods, extensive loss of sleep generally wreaks havoc on virtually all aspects of normal functioning (Coren, 1996).

Even more dramatic are the consequences in animal studies. When rats and dogs are deprived of sleep for extended periods, the results are often fatal. Sleep deprivation disrupts the ability of the animal to regulate internal functions, such as temperature, and leads to considerable loss of weight (despite an increased intake of food). The immune system also starts to fail, along with various organs in the body. After roughly three weeks of no sleep, the survival rate among these animals is virtually zero—they all die (Coren, 1996; Rechtschaffen & Bergmann, 1995). Fortunately, people don't ever reach these levels of sleep deprivation, because we simply can't stay awake. Indirectly, however, sleep loss contributes to thousands of deaths each year, mostly through traffic accidents and job-related mishaps.

The Function of REM and Dreaming

It's easy to see how sleep itself might have developed as an adaptive response, whether to repair, restore, or protect the organism struggling to survive. But why are there stages of sleep? Why, if people want to protect or rest the body, do they spend a significant amount of time in such an internally active state as REM sleep? Since REM sleep is strongly correlated with the recall of dreams, does dreaming serve some unique biological or psychological function? Unfortunately, at this point we have no definitive answers to these questions.

It's not clear whether REM sleep is even a necessary component of normal functioning. It's possible to deprive people selectively of REM sleep by carefully monitoring the EEG and then waking the person whenever characteristic REM patterns appear in the recordings. Unlike the findings for sleep loss in general, losing significant amounts of REM sleep usually does not lead to dramatic effects. People may show a bit more irritability (compared to controls who are shaken awake during non-REM periods), and their performance on tasks requiring logical reasoning and problem solving is hurt, but the level of impairment is not large (Ellman et al., 1991). Some forms of severe depression even appear to be helped by REM sleep deprivation, and some effective antidepressant drugs suppress REM sleep as a side effect (Vogel et al., 1990).

On the other hand, some intriguing changes do occur in sleep *patterns* after periods of REM deprivation. Sleep researchers have noticed that on the second or third night of REM deprivation it is necessary to awaken the subject with much greater frequency. When people lose sleep, particularly REM sleep, their bodies attempt to make up for the loss during the next sleep period by increasing the total amount of time spent in the REM stage. The more REM sleep lost, the more the body tries to make it up the next night. This tendency, known as **REM rebound,** is one reason why many researchers remain convinced that REM sleep serves some unspecified but extremely important function in the brain. One possibility, explored in the accompanying "Inside the Problem" feature on page 238, is that REM sleep plays a role in strengthening or consolidating certain kinds of memories.

Wish Fulfillment

Why do we dream? Historically, psychologists have tended to view dreaming as an extremely important psychological phenomenon. Sigmund Freud believed that dreams, once interpreted, could serve as a "royal road to the unconscious." Freud believed that dreaming was a psychological mechanism for *wish fulfillment*, a way to satisfy forbidden wishes and desires—especially sexual ones. He believed that dreams often look bizarre because the objects within our dreams tend to be symbolic. We hide our true feelings because our wishes and desires are often too

REM rebound
The tendency to increase the proportion of time spent in REM sleep after a period of REM deprivation.

Inside the Problem   Does REM Sleep Help Us Learn?

For decades sleep researchers have considered the possibility that activities during sleep may help strengthen, or *consolidate,* certain kinds of memories. As we'll discuss in Chapter 8, people who learn a list of words just before going to sleep remember those words better than people who learn the same words just prior to the start of a busy day. But the fact that sleeping after learning leads to better memory does not mean that sleep is responsible for the improvement. It could be that sleeping improves memory only because the activities of a busy day *interfere* with new learning. It's not that sleeping strengthens memory; rather, remaining active leads to the establishment of new memories that interfere with old ones.

However, a group of researchers in Israel has shown that a particular stage of sleep, REM, may at least play a role in promoting certain kinds of learning (Karni et al., 1994). Karni and colleagues asked subjects to solve a perceptual puzzle task that required detecting a small target pattern in a complex visual array. In earlier research it had been found that performance on this task improved with practice and, more important, that most of the improvement seemed to occur 8 to 10 hours after a practice session. This finding encouraged Karni and his colleagues to investigate (1) whether performance would also improve if subjects spent the 8 to 10 hours asleep, and (2) whether certain stages of sleep might be more important than others in promoting the learning consolidation process.

A group of subjects was asked to practice this perceptual task just before going to sleep. Three experimental conditions were then investigated. In one condition, the subjects were allowed a normal night's sleep, without interruption. In a second condition, the subjects were awakened by a ringing bell every time their brain waves, as measured by EEG, revealed that they had entered a REM stage. In a third condition, sleep was again disrupted, but only when the EEG signaled a period of slow-wave sleep (stages 3 and 4). In the morning, everyone was asked to perform the perceptual task again.

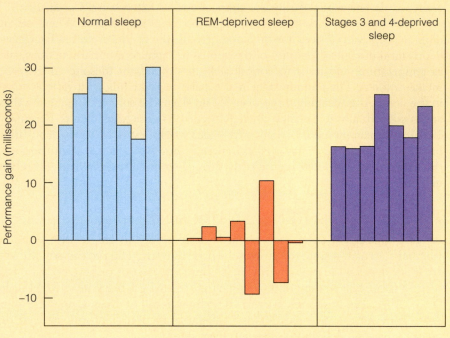

FIGURE 6.9
Performance Gains After Deprived and Nondeprived Sleep
Each bar shows the gain or loss on a morning perceptual task for an individual subject in the experiment. Notice that in the REM-deprived condition, subjects showed little or no performance gain. (Data from Karni et al., 1994.)

The results of this experiment are shown in Figure 6.9. The data show how much performance on the perceptual detection task improved from night to morning across the three conditions. The main finding of interest was that performance on the task did indeed improve after sleeping, but only if the subjects had been allowed normal levels of REM sleep. The subjects who had been REM-deprived showed essentially no improvement in the task; in other words, they failed to learn from the practice session. Moreover, it wasn't just the fact that they were repeatedly awakened that impaired learning; subjects in the slow-wave interruption condition were awakened just as often, on average, yet still showed considerable improvement in performance.

These results suggest that activities during REM sleep are needed to consoli-date some forms of learning overnight. But what are these activities? It's unclear at this point, but Karni and his colleagues speculate that the neurotransmitter *acetylcholine* (ACh) may be involved. Studies with animals have shown that ACh increases in the brain during REM sleep. This important neurotransmitter is thought to play a role in storing memories. As we mentioned in Chapter 3, memory problems are common in patients suffering from Alzheimer's disease, and it's known that neurons in the brain that produce ACh often degenerate during the disease. Thus, ACh may be needed to consolidate the storage of experience, explaining why REM activity is important in the consolidation process.

disturbing to be allowed to come to consciousness directly. To Freud, for example, the appearance of a cigar or a gun in a dream (in fact, any elongated object) might represent a penis, whereas a tunnel (or any entryway) could stand for a vagina. To establish the true meaning of the dream, Freud believed that it was necessary to distinguish between the dream's **manifest content**—the actual symbols of the dream—and its **latent content,** which are those hidden desires that are too disturbing to be expressed directly.

Since the time of Freud, psychologists have been more reluctant to search for hidden meaning in dreams. Although certain kinds of dream events cut across people and cultures (people often dream of flying or falling, for example), and most people have the unsettling experience of recurring dreams, interpretation is often in the eye of the beholder. Whether a cigar represents a penis, or just a cigar, isn't immediately obvious even to the most thoughtful or well-trained psychologist. Moreover, just because you repeatedly dream about being chased by a poodle that looks like your brother Ed doesn't mean that the dream is significant psychologically. A troubling dream, for example, might simply lead you to wake up suddenly and think about what has just occurred. As a result, the dream becomes firmly ingrained in memory and likely to occur again.

Activation-Synthesis

An alternative view, the **activation-synthesis hypothesis** of Hobson and McCarley (1977; Hobson, 1988), proposes that dreaming is a consequence of random activity in the brain. During REM sleep, for reasons that are not particularly clear, cells in the hindbrain tend to spontaneously activate the higher centers of the brain. This activity could arise simply to exercise the brain circuitry (Edelman, 1987), or it could be a consequence of random events in the room (e.g., the cat snoring or a mosquito buzzing around your face). Whatever the reason, the higher brain centers have evolved to interpret lower brain signals in meaningful ways. Thus, the brain creates a story in an effort to make some sense out of the signals that it's receiving. But in the activation-synthesis view, there's little of psychological significance here: Dreams typically represent only a "random synthesis of neurological activity" (Weinstein et al., 1991).

The activation-synthesis hypothesis has received a lot of attention among sleep researchers because it takes into account how biological activity in the brain changes during sleep. It also provides another explanation for why dream content is often bizarre: Since the activated signals that produce dreams are random in nature, the brain has a tough time creating a story line that is meaningful and consistent. Ironically, this view implies that there may be some psychological significance to reported dreams after all, but not for the reasons suggested by Freud. The biological mechanisms that generate the REM state are not psychologically driven, but the brain's *interpretations* of those purely physiological activities may have psychological meaning. The story your brain creates probably tells us something about how you think when you're awake (Antrobus, 1991; Foulkes, 1985).

The activation-synthesis hypothesis is an intriguing alternative to the traditional Freudian view, but much remains to be worked out. The theory is a bit vague and consequently difficult to test. Moreover, as noted earlier, we also dream during non-REM states and the theory, at present, focuses primarily on brain activity that occurs during REM sleep. It is also of interest to note that REM activity is commonplace in numerous organisms other than humans (Durie, 1981). Virtually all mammals experience REM, as do birds and some reptiles, such as turtles. Moreover, human infants spend a remarkable amount of time in REM sleep; even human fetuses show REM patterns in the womb. I suppose it's possible to argue that a fetus dreams, but does it make sense to propose that the fetus is working out some hidden sexual conflict or spinning an internal story in an effort to make sense of random activity?

? CRITICAL THINKING

The activation-synthesis hypothesis proposes that dreams arise from the interpretation of random neural activity. Yet many people dream of flying, falling, or being unprepared for a test. How do you explain the fact that people have similar dreams if dreaming results from random neural activity?

manifest content
According to Freud, the actual symbols and events experienced in a dream.

latent content
According to Freud, the true psychological meaning of dream symbols, which represent hidden wishes and desires that are too disturbing to be expressed directly.

activation-synthesis hypothesis
The idea that dreams represent the brain's attempt to make sense out of the random patterns of neural activity generated during sleep.

CONCEPT SUMMARY
Functions of Sleep and Dreaming

Why Do We Sleep?

Theory	Description	Evaluation
Repair and restoration	Sleep restores and/or repairs the body and brain.	Not strongly supported by data; restorative activities of the body are not limited to sleep. Changes in physical activity do not lead to consistent changes in subsequent sleep patterns.
Survival value	Sleep increases chances of survival.	Receives some support from observation of sleep patterns in different species of animals.

Why Do We Dream?

Theory	Description	Evaluation
Wish fulfillment (Freud)	Dreaming is a psychological mechanism, for fulfillment of wishes, often sexual in nature. Dreams include both a *manifest* and *latent content*.	Difficult to assess; psychologists are reluctant to ascribe hidden meaning to dreams. The meaning of dreams is in the eye of the dreamer.
Activation synthesis	Dreaming is a consequence of random activity that occurs in the brain during REM sleep. The brain creates a story to make sense of these random signals.	Theory is vague and difficult to test. Dreaming is not limited to REM sleep.
Problem solving	Dreaming helps us focus on our current problems in order to find solutions.	Evidence is weak and anecdotal.

We've discussed two prominent views of dreaming—Freud and activation-synthesis—but there are others. For example, some psychologists have suggested that dreams serve a problem-solving function. We may dream to focus our attention on particularly troubling current problems in order to work toward possible solutions (Cartwright, 1991; Fiss, 1991). But the evidence for the problem-solving view is also weak, relying mainly on anecdotes rather than systematic research (Blagrove, 1996; Domhoff, 1996). It's safe to assume that REM sleep and dreaming reflect some important property of the adaptive mind, but at the moment major questions remain unanswered.

DISORDERS OF SLEEP

We end our treatment of sleep and dreaming with a brief discussion of sleep disorders. Psychologists and other mental health professionals divide sleep disorders into two main diagnostic categories: (1) *dyssomnias*, which are problems associated with the amount, timing, and quality of sleep and (2) *parasomnias*, which are abnormal disturbances that occur during sleep. Let's consider some prominent examples of each type.

Dyssomnias

The most common type of dyssomnia is **insomnia,** a condition marked by difficulties in initiating or maintaining sleep. Everyone has trouble getting to sleep from time to time, and everyone has awakened in the middle of the night and been unable to get back to sleep. For the clinical diagnosis of insomnia, however, these difficulties need to be chronic—lasting for at least a month. It's been estimated that perhaps 30% of the population suffers from some degree of insomnia, although the number of truly severe sufferers is thought to be closer to 15% (Bootzin et al., 1993; Gillin, 1993). There are many potential causes for the condition, including stress, emotional problems, alcohol and other drug use, as well as medical conditions. Some kinds of insomnia may even be learned—for example, children who regularly fall asleep in the presence of their parents often have trouble getting back to sleep if they wake up later alone in their room (Adair et al., 1991). Presumably, these children have learned to associate going to sleep with the presence of a parent and consequently cannot return to sleep without the parent present.

insomnia
A chronic condition marked by difficulties in initiating or maintaining sleep, lasting for a period of at least one month.

Whereas insomnia is characterized by an inability to sleep, in **hypersomnia** the problem is *too much* sleep. People who are diagnosed with hypersomnia show excessive sleepiness—they're often caught catnapping during the day, and they complain about being tired all the time. The cause of this condition is unknown, although it has been suggested that genetic factors might be involved (Parkes & Block, 1989). Excessive sleepiness can also be caused by infectious diseases, such as mononucleosis or chronic fatigue syndrome, and by a sleep disorder called *sleep apnea*. Sleep apnea is a relatively rare condition in which the sleeper repeatedly stops breathing throughout the night, usually for short periods lasting up to a minute or so. The episodes typically end with the person waking up gasping for breath. Because these episodes occur frequently throughout the night, the affected person feels tired during the day. Significant sleep apnea problems are found in perhaps 1%–2% of the population, although a higher percentage of individuals may experience occasional episodes (Kales & Kales, 1984).

There is yet another even rarer sleep disorder, called *narcolepsy*, that is characterized by sudden extreme sleepiness. Sleep attacks can occur at any time during the day and can last from a few seconds to several minutes. What makes this disorder unusual is that the person seems to directly enter a kind of REM-sleep state. They lose all muscle tone and can even fall to the ground in a sound sleep! Fortunately, not all instances of narcolepsy are this extreme, although it can be a disabling condition. There is some evidence to suggest that the disorder may have a genetic link (Barlow & Durand, 1999). Again, it is very rare and probably affects only a few people in a thousand.

Parasomnias

The second category of sleep disorders, parasomnias, includes such abnormal sleep disturbances as nightmares, night terrors, and sleepwalking. **Nightmares** are frightening and anxiety-arousing dreams that occur primarily during the REM stage of sleep. They inevitably cause the sleeper to awaken; if they recur frequently, they can lead to the symptoms of insomnia. What causes nightmares? No one is certain at this point, although frequent nightmares may indicate the presence of a psychological disorder.

Night terrors, which occur mainly in children, are terrifying experiences in which the sleeper awakens suddenly in an extreme state of panic—the child may sit in bed screaming and will show little responsiveness to others who are present. Night terrors are not considered to be serious indicators of psychological or medical problems, and they tend to go away with age. Finally, **sleepwalking** occurs when the sleeper rises during sleep and wanders about. Sleepwalking happens mainly in childhood, tends to vanish as the child reaches adolescence, and is not thought to result from a serious psychological or medical problem. It's interesting to note that both night terrors and sleepwalking occur during periods of non-REM sleep, which suggests that neither may be related entirely to dreaming.

hypersomnia
A chronic condition marked by excessive sleepiness.

nightmares
Frightening and anxiety-arousing dreams that occur primarily during the REM stage of sleep.

night terrors
A condition in which the sleeper, usually a child, awakens suddenly in an extreme state of panic; not thought to be associated with dreaming.

sleepwalking
A condition in which the sleeper rises during sleep and wanders about; not thought to be associated with dreaming.

TEST YOURSELF 6.2

To check your understanding of sleep and dreaming, try answering the following questions. (You will find the answers in the Appendix.)

1. Try to choose the EEG pattern that best fits the following descriptions. Choose from the following: alpha waves, delta activity, K complex, sleep spindles, theta waves, REM.

   a. The characteristic pattern found in stage 1 sleep: _____

   b. Often triggered by loud noises during stage 2 sleep: _____

   c. Another name for the slow-wave patterns that are found during stage 3 and stage 4 sleep: _____

   d. The characteristic pattern of paradoxical sleep: _____

2. Which of the following statements is most consistent with the view that we sleep because it keeps us away from hostile environments during times when we can't see well?

   a. Sleep deprivation leads to a breakdown in normal functioning.
   b. Fearful dreams make us wary of venturing outside.
   c. Cats sleep more than cows.
   d. People sleep less as they age.

3. Diagnose the following sleep disorders based on the information provided. Choose from the following: hypersomnia, insomnia, nightmare, night terror, sleep apnea, sleepwalking.

   a. Difficulty initiating and maintaining sleep: _____
   b. Sleeper awakens suddenly, screaming, but the EEG pattern indicates a period of non-REM sleep: _____
   c. Sleeper repeatedly stops breathing during the night, usually for short periods lasting less than one minute: _____
   d. An anxiety-arousing dream that usually occurs during the REM stage of sleep: _____

Altering Awareness: Psychoactive Drugs

The rhythmic cycles of sleep reveal how conscious awareness can shift in dramatic ways as the electrical activity of the brain changes. We haven't talked much about the biological factors that control these brain changes, but it shouldn't surprise you to learn that the brain's chemical messengers, the neurotransmitters, are primarily responsible. The start of REM sleep, for example, appears to be controlled by neurons in the hindbrain, particularly the *pons*, that release acetylcholine (Amzica & Steriade, 1996). In studies with animals, it's been found that levels of acetylcholine in the cortex are highest during REM and waking states and drop to lower levels during the stages of slow-wave sleep (Jasper & Tessier, 1969). Exactly when we fall asleep, and how long we sleep, may be affected by the actions of the neurotransmitter *GABA*; wakefulness and general arousal have been linked to *norepinephrine* and *dopamine*.

The brain is a kind of biochemical factory, altering moods and shifting awareness by enhancing or inhibiting the actions of its various neurotransmitters. As we've discussed previously, the brain sometimes reacts to stress or injury by releasing brain chemicals called *endorphins*, which reduce pain and serve to generally elevate mood. Altering awareness chemically in such a fashion is highly adaptive, because the delay of pain can allow an organism to escape from a life-threatening situation.

If you allow an external agent, such as a drug, to enter your body, it too can radically alter the delicate chemical balance that controls awareness and other mental processes. Obviously, drugs can have tremendously beneficial effects, especially in the treatment of psychological and medical disorders (see Chapter 15). But drugs can have negative effects as well, even though they might seem to change awareness in a highly pleasurable way. As you probably know, drug *abuse*, particularly of alcohol and tobacco, is directly or indirectly responsible for hundreds of thousands of deaths annually in the United States (Coleman, 1993). In this section, we'll consider the actions of drugs labeled **psychoactive**—those that affect behavior and mental processes through alterations of conscious awareness.

DRUG ACTIONS AND EFFECTS

Psychologists are interested in psychoactive drugs for two main reasons. First, they produce powerful effects on behavior and mental processes. Second, they can help us understand more about the neural mechanisms that cause behavior. Psychoactive drugs, like most natural drugs produced by the brain, exert their

LEARNING GOALS

1. Compare neurotransmitters with psychoactive drugs.
2. Discuss the different categories of psychoactive drugs and provide examples from each.
3. Discuss the psychological factors that influence the effects of psychoactive drugs.

psychoactive drugs
Drugs that affect behavior and mental processes through alterations of conscious awareness.

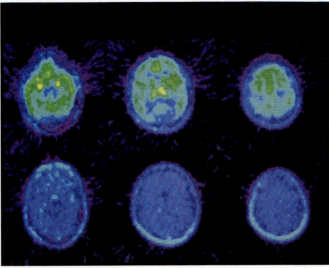

This series of PET scans shows how administration of an opium-like drug affects general activity in the brain. The first PET scan in the top row shows a normal active brain; the last PET scan in the bottom row shows diminished activity after the drug has taken full effect.

effects primarily by changing the normal communication channels of neurons. Neuron-to-neuron communication can be affected in a variety of ways. Some drugs, such as *nicotine*, duplicate the action of neurotransmitters by actually attaching themselves to the receptor sites of membranes; this mimicking action allows the drug to produce the same effect as the brain's natural chemical messenger. Other drugs depress or block the action of neurotransmitters; some sleeping pills, for instance, decrease norepinephrine or dopamine stimulation. The psychoactive drug *fluoxetine* (known commercially as Prozac) has been used successfully to treat depression; it acts by slowing the process through which the neurotransmitter serotonin is broken down and taken back up into the transmitting cell (Kramer, 1993).

Over time, repeated use of a drug can cause changes in the way the body reacts. For example, a drug **tolerance** can develop, which means that increasing amounts of the drug will be needed to produce the same physical and behavioral effects. Tolerance is a kind of adaptation that the body makes to compensate for the effects of the drug. **Drug dependency** is often linked with the development of tolerance—dependency is manifested as either a physical or a psychological *need* for continued use (Woody & Cacciola, 1997). With physical dependency, the person typically experiences **withdrawal** symptoms when he or she stops taking the drug. These are clear, measurable physical reactions such as sweating, vomiting, changes in heart rate, or tremors. Drug dependency is the primary cause of substance abuse, although the mechanisms that lead to dependency are still a matter of some debate. At this point, it's not certain whether dependency develops as a consequence of "urgings" produced by biological withdrawal, or whether people essentially learn to become dependent on the drug with repeated use (Tiffany, 1990).

CATEGORIES OF PSYCHOACTIVE DRUGS

It's useful to classify psychoactive drugs into one of four categories—depressants, stimulants, opiates, and hallucinogens—based on their specific mind-altering characteristics. We'll briefly examine each type and then conclude with a discussion of some psychological factors involved in drug use.

Depressants

In general, drugs classified as **depressants** slow, or depress, the ongoing activity of the central nervous system. *Ethyl alcohol*, which is present in beer, wine, and distilled drinks, is a well-known example of a depressant. Biochemically, alcohol appears to lead to an increase in either the secretion or general effectiveness of the

? CRITICAL THINKING

Do you believe that psychoactive drugs should be legalized for recreational use? If not, how can you justify the availability of alcohol, nicotine, and caffeine?

tolerance
An adaptation that the body makes to compensate for the continued use of a drug such that increasing amounts of the drug are needed to produce the same physical and behavioral effects.

drug dependency
A condition in which an individual experiences a physical or a psychological need for continued use of a drug.

withdrawal
Clear and measurable physical reactions, such as sweating, vomiting, changes in heart rate, or tremors, that occur when a person stops taking certain drugs after continued use.

depressants
A class of drugs that slow or depress the ongoing activity of the central nervous system.

Despite its pleasurable properties, too much alcohol consumption can have severe negative consequences on your health and well-being.

neurotransmitters GABA and dopamine. Both usually act as inhibitory messengers in the brain, so neurons in a number of vital brain centers become inhibited (Suzdak et al., 1986). Drinkers feel "high" after a few drinks in part because the drug produces a calming effect on the body, which leads to a reduction in anxiety (Oscar-Berman et al., 1997). By the way, animals also find the effects of alcohol quite reinforcing—they will perform tasks that yield small amounts of alcohol as a reward (Wise & Bozarth, 1987).

As the consumption of alcohol increases, more complex psychological effects emerge because those brain centers that control judgment become sluggish from inhibition. As you're undoubtedly aware, after a few drinks people often start acting in ways that are contrary to their normal behavioral tendencies (Steele & Josephs, 1990). The normally demure become loud and aggressive; the sexually inhibited become flirtatious and provocative. These behavioral changes are produced, in part, because alcohol reduces self-awareness. Drinkers are less likely to monitor their behaviors and actions closely, and they tend to forget about any problems that are currently bothersome (Hull & Bond, 1986).

These carefree moments are stolen at a cost, of course, because the body eventually reacts to the drug in a more negative way. Fatigue, nausea, and depression are likely consequences of overconsumption. If too much alcohol is consumed, the results can be fatal. Alcohol poisoning, which comes from drinking large quantities of alcohol in a short period of time, often leads to death. The indirect costs are great as well: As activity in the sympathetic nervous system slows, so too does reaction time, which increases the chances of an accident while driving or in the workplace. Countless people die every year as a result of alcohol-related incidents.

Barbiturates and *tranquilizers* are also classified as depressant drugs. Both are widely prescribed for the treatment of anxiety and insomnia, and they produce effects in the brain similar to those induced by alcohol (the neurotransmitter GABA is again involved; Gardner, 1997). Like alcohol, at low doses tranquilizing agents tend to produce pleasurable feelings of relaxation. But at higher doses your ability to concentrate easily is lost, memory is impaired, and speech becomes slurred. Barbiturate use also commonly leads to tolerance and dependency. With continued use, your metabolism changes, so that larger and larger doses of the drug are required to obtain the same effect, and you become physically and psychologically dependent on the drug. Tranquilizers (such as the widely prescribed Valium and Xanax) are less habit forming than barbiturates and for this reason are more likely to be prescribed.

Stimulants

A **stimulant** is a drug that increases central nervous system activity, enhancing neural transmission. Examples of stimulants include *caffeine, nicotine, amphetamines,* and *cocaine*. These agents generally increase alertness and can affect mood by inducing feelings of pleasure. The morning cup of coffee is an excellent example of how a stimulant in low doses—caffeine—can improve your mood significantly and even increase concentration and attention. Other effects of stimulants include dilated pupils, increased heart and respiration rate, and decreased appetite. In large doses, stimulants can produce extreme anxiety and even convulsions and death.

Both amphetamines and cocaine produce their stimulating effects by increasing the effectiveness of the neurotransmitters norepinephrine and dopamine.

stimulants
A class of drugs that increases central nervous system activity, enhancing neural transmission.

Dopamine seems to be primarily responsible for the positive, reinforcing qualities of these drugs (Wise & Rompre, 1989). Research has shown that animals will work hard to administer themselves drugs that increase the activity of dopamine-based synapses. In the case of cocaine, which is derived from the leaves of the coca plant, the drug blocks the reabsorption of both norepinephrine and dopamine. When reabsorption is blocked, these transmitter substances are able to exert their effects for a longer period of time. Cocaine produces intense feelings of euphoria, although the effects of the drug wear off relatively quickly. A half hour or so after the drug enters the body, the user "crashes," in part because the drug has temporarily depleted the user's internal supply of norepinephrine and dopamine. Regular use of cocaine produces a number of harmful side effects, including intense episodes of paranoia and even hallucinations and delusions (Stein & Ellinwood, 1993).

The flowering opium plant.

Opiates

Drugs classified as **opiates** (also sometimes called *narcotics*) depress nervous system activity, thereby reducing anxiety, elevating mood, and lowering sensitivity to pain. Well-known examples of opiates include opium, heroin, and morphine. As you learned previously, morphine—which is derived from the flowering opium plant—acts on existing membrane receptor sites in the nervous system. Its pain-killing effects and pleasurable mood shifts (it's named after Morpheus, the Greek god of dreams) apparently arise from the fact that it mimics the brain's own chemicals, specifically *endorphins*, which are involved in reducing pain. Opiates, however, can produce strong physical and psychological dependence. The body is changed with continued use; once usage is stopped, the body rebels with intense and prolonged withdrawal symptoms.

People who are regular users of opiates such as heroin or morphine suffer in many ways, despite any fleeting pleasures that might immediately follow drug use. Kicking an opiate habit is extremely tough because the withdrawal symptoms—which can include everything from excessive yawning, to nausea, to severe chills—last for days. Users who opt for the normal method of administration—intravenous injection—run additional risks from disease, especially HIV. Longitudinal studies of heroin addicts paint a grim picture, addicts tend to die young (at an average age of about 40) from a variety of causes including suicide, homicide, and overdose (Hser et al., 1993).

Hallucinogens

For the final category of psychoactive drug, **hallucinogens** (sometimes called *psychedelics*), the term "psychoactive" is particularly apt. *Hallucinogens* play havoc with your normal internal construction of reality. Perception itself is fractured, and the world becomes awash in fantastic colors, sounds, and tactile sensations. Two of the best known examples of these drugs, *mescaline* and *psilocybin*, occur naturally in the environment. Mescaline comes from a certain kind of cactus, whereas psilocybin is a type of mushroom. Both of these drugs have been used for centuries, primarily in the context of religious rituals and ceremonies. Since the 1960s, they have served as potentially dangerous recreational drugs for those seeking alternative realities.

Lysergic acid diethylamide (LSD) is a synthetic version of a psychedelic drug. LSD is thought to mimic the action of the neurotransmitter serotonin (Strassman, 1992); the drug acts on specific serotonin-based receptor sites in the brain, producing stimulation. For reasons that are not particularly clear, variations in sensation and perception are produced. A typical LSD experience, which can last for up to 16 hours, consists of profound changes in perception. Some users report a phenomenon called *synesthesia*, which is a blending of sensory experiences—colors may actually feel warm or cold, and rough textures may begin to sing. Also for

opiates
A class of drugs that reduces anxiety, lowers sensitivity to pain, and elevates mood; opiates often act to depress nervous system activity.

hallucinogens
A class of drugs that tend to disrupt normal mental and emotional functioning, including distorting perception and altering reality.

CONCEPT SUMMARY
Psychoactive Drugs

Category	Examples	General Effects
Depressants	Ethyl alcohol Barbiturates Tranquilizers	Believed to enhance the effectiveness of GABA and dopamine, which often act as inhibitory messengers in the brain. Produce pleasurable feelings of relaxation, but at high doses concentration and memory are impaired.
Stimulants	Caffeine Nicotine Amphetamines Cocaine	Amphetamines and cocaine may work primarily by increasing the effectiveness of dopamine and norepinephrine. Stimulants tend to increase alertness, elevate mode, and produce physical changes such as increased heart and respiration rate.
Opiates	Opium Morphine Heroin	Depressing of nervous system activity, resulting in reduced anxiety, mood elevation, and lower sensitivity to pain. Can produce strong physical and psychological dependence.
Hallucinogens	LSD Mescaline Psilocybin Marijuana	Produce variations in sensation and perception. LSD is believed to mimic the action of serotonin. Some users report *synsthesia*, a blending of sensory experiences. Marijuana leads to a general sense of well-being and heightened awareness of normal sensations. Negative side effects can include anxiety, fearfulness, and panic.

Marijuana.

unknown reasons, a user's experience can turn sharply wrong. Panic or depression can develop, increasing the likelihood of accidents and personal harm. Users also sometimes report the occurrence of "flashbacks," in which the sensations of the drug are reexperienced long after the drug has presumably left the body.

Marijuana, which comes from the naturally occurring hemp plant *Cannabis*, can also be classified as a hallucinogenic drug. It is unusual to see profound distortions of perceptual reality with this drug, however, unless large amounts are ingested. Marijuana is usually smoked or swallowed, and its effects last around 4 hours. Users typically report a melting away of anxiety, a general sense of well-being, and more notice is given to normal sensations. Changes in the perception of time and its passage are sometimes reported, along with increased appetite. The pleasant effects of the drug are usually followed by fatigue and sometimes sleep.

As with other hallucinogenic drugs, marijuana does not always produce a pleasant experience. Some users report anxiety, extreme fearfulness, and panic (Fackelmann, 1993). A number of studies have shown that marijuana use impairs concentration, motor coordination, and the ability to track things visually (Moskowitz, 1985); these side effects probably contribute to the likelihood of traffic accidents when driving under the influence. Less is known about the long-term effects of regular use, but there's some evidence that marijuana may impair the formation of memories (Hooker & Jones, 1987; Miller & Branconnier, 1983; Millsaps et al., 1994). On the positive side, marijuana may help reduce some of the negative symptoms of chemotherapy (e.g., nausea), and in some cases it's proved helpful in treating eye disorders such as glaucoma. But the medical evidence in this area remains controversial.

PSYCHOLOGICAL FACTORS

Among the more interesting characteristics of psychoactive drugs, especially to psychologists, are the sharp differences that can be seen in the effects of these drugs. Two people can take the same drug, in exactly the same quantity, but experience completely different mind-altering effects. A small amount of LSD consumed by Teo produces a euphoric "religious experience"; the same amount for Jane produces a frightening descent into a whirlpool of terror and fear. Why? Shouldn't the pharmacological effects on the neurotransmitters in the brain produce similar or at least consistent psychological effects?

The answer is that the psychological effects are influenced by many factors. The environmental setting in which a drug is taken, for example, is known to affect the experience. Smoking marijuana for the first time in a car speeding 75 miles per hour might seriously limit the anxiety-reducing effects of the drug. Many users report that familiarity with the drug's effects is also important—users claim that you need to "learn" to smoke marijuana or take LSD before the innermost "secrets" of the drug are revealed. In fact, experienced users of marijuana have been found to experience a "high" after smoking a cigarette they only *thought* was marijuana; similar effects did not occur for novice users (Jones, 1971). Both familiarity and the environment affect the user's *mental set*—his or her expectations about the drug's harmful and beneficial consequences. Finally, the user's physical state is critical. Some people develop resistance or tolerance to a drug faster than others do. The experience of a drug may even depend on such mundane things as whether the person has eaten or is well rested.

TEST YOURSELF 6.3

Test your knowledge about psychoactive drugs by picking the category of drug that best fits each of the following statements. Choose from among these terms: depressant, hallucinogen, opiate, stimulant. (You will find the answers in the Appendix.)

1. Increases central nervous system activity: _Stimulant_

2. Reduces pain by mimicking the brain's own natural pain-reducing chemicals: _opiate_

3. Tends to produce inhibitory effects by increasing the effectiveness of the neurotransmitter GABA: _barbiturates & tranquilizers = depressants_

4. Distorts perception and may lead to flashbacks: _hallucinogens_

5. The type of active ingredient found in your morning cup of coffee: _caffeine_

Altering Awareness: Induced States

The setting is Paris, late in the year 1783. Dressed in a lilac silk robe, German-born physician Franz Anton Mesmer works to restore the delicate balance of universal fluids within his patients. He attaches large magnets to each patient's sides—the better to affect their animal magnetism—and then rhythmically passes an iron rod, in large wavelike motions, over their outstretched bodies. His patients quickly fall into a trancelike state: They can still talk and move their limbs on command, but each appears to have entered an alternative form of consciousness; each appears to have lost all forms of voluntary control. Upon later awakening, many feel better, apparently cured of their various physical and psychological problems.

Although Mesmer himself eventually fell into disrepute, rejected by the scientific community of his time, the phenomenon of "mesmerizing" did not. Today, of course, we recognize that the artificial state of awareness he induced in his patients had nothing to do with magnets or the balancing of universal fluids. Modern psychologists would explain the bizarre behavior of Mesmer's patients as an example of hypnosis. **Hypnosis** can be defined generally as any form of social interaction that produces a *heightened state of suggestibility* in a willing participant. It is of interest to psychologists, like the related topic of meditation, because it's a technique that is specifically designed to alter conscious awareness. As you'll see shortly, hypnosis has some highly adaptive properties.

LEARNING GOALS

1. Describe the physiological and behavioral effects of hypnosis.

2. Discuss whether hypnosis can be used effectively as a memory aid.

3. Describe the dissociation and role-playing accounts of hypnosis.

4. Describe the physical, behavioral, and psychological effects of meditation.

hypnosis
A form of social interaction that produces a heightened state of suggestibility in a willing participant.

LE MAGNÉTISME ANIMAL
Importante Découverte par M.ʳ Mesmer, Docteur en Médecine, de la Faculté de Vienne en Autriche.

Magnetic "cures." In the latter part of the 18th century, Anton Mesmer helped to promote the belief that physical and psychological problems could be "cured" by passing magnets over the body.

CRITICAL THINKING

Under what circumstances do you think it might be adaptive for someone to enter a heightened state of suggestibility?

The Phenomena of Hypnosis

Despite some two centuries of work on the topic, our understanding of hypnosis remains incomplete. Researchers are not sure at this point whether hypnosis is truly an altered state of awareness or simply a kind of social play acting designed simply to please the hypnotist. But we do know a few things about what hypnosis is not. For one thing, people who are hypnotized never really enter into anything resembling a deep sleep. The word *hypnosis* does come from the Greek *hypnos* meaning "to sleep," but hypnosis bears little physiological relation to sleep. The EEG patterns of a hypnotized subject, along with other physiological indices, more closely resemble those of someone who is relaxed rather than deeply asleep (Graffen et al., 1995). Moreover, certain reflexes that are commonly absent during sleep, such as the knee jerk, are still present under hypnosis (Pratt et al., 1988).

Another myth is that only weak-willed people are susceptible to hypnotic induction. Everyone appears to be susceptible to a degree, in the sense that we all show heightened suggestibility under some circumstances. There are individual differences among people—hypnotic suggestibility scales indicate that only about 20% of the population are highly hypnotizable (Hilgard, 1965)—but it's not clear what factors account for these differences. Personality studies have shown that people who are easy to hypnotize are not weak-willed or conforming, although they may have more active imaginations that people who resist hypnosis (Nadon et al., 1991).

A variety of methods can be used to induce the hypnotic state. The most popular technique is one where the hypnotist, acting as an authority figure, suggests to the client that he or she is growing increasingly more relaxed and sleepy with time: "Your eyes are getting heavier and heavier, you can barely keep your lids open," and so on. Often the client is asked to fixate on something, perhaps a spot on the wall or a swinging pendulum. The logic here is that eye fixation leads to muscle fatigue, which helps convince clients that they are indeed becoming increasingly relaxed. Other approaches to induction rely more on subtle suggestions (Erickson, 1964), but in general no one method is necessarily better than any other. In the words of one researcher, "The art of hypnosis relies on not providing the client with grounds for resisting" (Araoz, 1982, p. 106).

Once they're hypnotized, a person becomes highly suggestible, responding to commands from the hypnotist in ways that seem automatic and involuntary. The

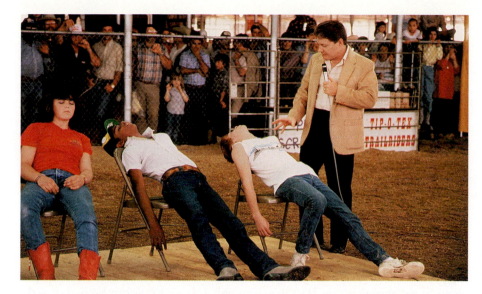

Although hypnosis is often used for entertainment purposes, it can have considerable clinical value.

hypnotist can then use his or her power of suggestion to achieve adaptive ends, such as helping people kick unwanted habits like smoking or overeating. Anesthetic effects are also possible at certain deep stages of hypnosis. Hypnotized patients report less pain during childbirth (Harmon et al., 1990) and typically suffer less during dental work (Houle et al., 1988). It's even been possible to perform major surgeries (such as appendectomies) using hypnosis as the primary anesthesia (Kihlstrom, 1985). Research is ongoing to determine the biological basis for these striking analgesic effects. It was once thought, for example, that the release of endorphins by the brain might be responsible, although this possibility now seems less likely (Moret et al., 1991).

If you ever visit a stage hypnotist, you're likely to witness an astonishing variety of hypnotically induced behaviors. One impressive demonstration is **catalepsy:** One of the hypnotized person's limbs is placed in some unusual position (perhaps raising a leg or an arm in the air), and the subject then retains this position rigidly for long periods of time without any signs of tiring. Perceptual effects are also common. The volunteer, acting as a kind of robot, appears to see or hear things that are not really there; perhaps the subject carries on conversations with imaginary people or ignores loud noises that would normally cause someone to jump. Perceptual changes of this sort have sometimes been reported in the laboratory. In a number of these studies, researchers have looked for hypnotically based changes in vision. Susceptibility to perceptual illusions, for instance, can sometimes be reduced under hypnosis, although the data overall are not especially clear-cut (Kihlstrom, 1985). There has also been work demonstrating that perception of time can be altered under hypnosis, leading to underestimation of the hypnotic period (St.-Jean et al., 1994).

Memory Enhancement

One frequent claim is that hypnosis can dramatically improve *memory*, a phenomenon called **hypnotic hypermnesia.** Perhaps you've heard of criminal cases where hypnotized witnesses suddenly and miraculously recalled minute details of a horrific crime. In one famous kidnapping case from the 1970s, a bus driver was buried 6 feet underground along with 26 children inside a tractor trailer. Later, under hypnosis, he was able to reconstruct details of the kidnapper's license plate—digit by digit. There is a long-standing belief among many psychotherapists that hypnosis is an excellent tool for uncovering hidden memories of abuse or other forms of psychological trauma (Pratt et al., 1988; Yapko, 1994). There have even been a number of well-publicized examples of *age regression* under hypnosis, in which the subject mentally traveled backward to some earlier place (such as his or her second-grade classroom) and was able to recall numerous details.

catalepsy
A hypnotically induced behavior characterized by an ability to hold one or more limbs of the body in a rigid position for long periods without tiring.

hypnotic hypermnesia
The supposed enhancement in memory that occurs under hypnosis; there is little if any evidence to support the existence of this effect.

? **CRITICAL THINKING**

Can you think of any situations in which memories accessed through hypnosis should be admitted in court? Why or why not?

Unfortunately, there is little hard evidence to support these phenomena scientifically. A patient's memory may indeed improve after a hypnotic session, but this fact does not allow us to conclude that the hypnotic state was responsible for the improvement (Spiegel, 1995). One possibility is that hypnotic induction procedures (the relaxation techniques) simply create effective and supportive environments in which to remember (Geiselman et al., 1985). Another problem is that it's often difficult to judge whether memories recovered during hypnosis are, in fact, accurate representations of what actually occurred. You may "remember" a particularly unfortunate experience from the second-grade classroom, but can you be sure that this traumatic episode indeed occurred as you remember it?

As you'll see in a moment, hypnotized people often adopt roles designed to please the hypnotist. What appear to be memories, then, are sometimes *fabrications*—stories that the subject unintentionally makes up to please the hypnotist. For this reason, many states have banned the use of hypnotic testimony in criminal court cases. It's simply too difficult to tell whether the memory recovered after hypnosis is accurate or a product of suggestion by the hypnotist. Controlled experiments in the laboratory have been unable to find good evidence for true memory enhancement—at least, memory enhancement that can be tied directly to the properties of hypnosis (Dinges et al., 1992; Steblay & Bothwell, 1994).

EXPLAINING HYPNOSIS

Even if a hypnotized person is experiencing some kind of altered form of consciousness, there is considerable debate about exactly how this so-called state should be explained. As noted earlier, the EEG patterns of someone in a hypnotic deep sleep resemble the patterns of someone in a relaxed waking state; in fact, there do not appear to be any reliable physiological measures that can be used to define the hypnotized condition. So, how do we explain the heightened suggestibility? Currently, there are two prominent interpretations of hypnosis: (1) hypnosis is a kind of dissociation, or true splitting of conscious awareness, and (2) hypnosis represents a kind of social role playing. Let's consider each of these ideas in more detail.

Hypnotic Dissociations

Some researchers have argued that hypnosis produces what are called **hypnotic dissociations** in the subject. By "dissociations," it is meant that the individual experiences a kind of splitting of consciousness where multiple forms of awareness coexist (Hilgard, 1986, 1992). Hilgard (1986) has argued, for example, that conscious awareness in a hypnotized subject is actually divided into separate components. One stream of consciousness follows the commands of the hypnotist, perhaps feeling no effects of painful stimulation, while another stream, the hidden observer, is painfully aware of the true stimulation.

Some researchers believe that hypnosis leads to a dissociation or "splitting" of conscious awareness.

Hilgard has supported his position with experiments in which subjects are hypnotized and asked to submerge one arm into a bucket of extremely cold ice water (a common procedure to test for the analgesic effects of hypnosis). "You'll be aware of no pain," the subject is told, "but that other part of you, the hidden part that is aware of everything going on, can signal any true pain by pressing this key." A button is made available which the subject is allowed to press, at will, with the nonsubmerged hand. It turns out that people press this key repeatedly—reporting the pain—and the key presses become much more frequent the longer the arm is kept submerged. During hypnosis, as well as afterward, the subjects claim to have no knowledge of what the nonsubmerged hand is doing. There is a hidden part of consciousness, Hilgard argues, that maintains realistic contact with what's going on; it is the other hypnotized stream of awareness that feels no pain.

This idea that conscious awareness is divided or split during hypnosis may seem mystical, strange, and worthy of skepticism. But as I've made clear many

hypnotic dissociation
A hypnotically induced splitting of consciousness during which multiple forms of awareness coexist.

times, the brain often divides its labor to arrive at adaptive solutions. You walk and talk at the same time, and you certainly don't consciously think about picking up each leg and putting it down while making a point in the conversation. The idea that consciousness is regularly dissociated, or divided, is not really an issue to most psychologists; it's accepted as a given, as a normal part of psychological functioning. But whether it is correct to characterize *hypnosis* as a true splitting of consciousness is still a matter of debate.

Social Role Playing

Most of the skepticism about hypnosis comes from the fact that hypnotized subjects often seem eager to please the hypnotist by acting in accordance with a kind of hypnotized role. The behavior of a hypnotized person is easily modified by expectations and by small changes in the suggestions of the hypnotist. For example, if people are told prior to being hypnotized that a rigid right arm is a prominent feature of the hypnotized state, then rigid right arms are likely to be reported after hypnosis even when no such specific suggestion is made during the induction process (Orne, 1959). It often appears as if subjects are trying desperately to "do whatever they can to achieve the suggested effects" (Kihlstrom & McConkey, 1990).

A number of researchers have suggested that hypnotic behavior may, in fact, simply be a kind of social role playing. Everyone has some idea of what hypnotized behavior looks like—to be hypnotized, you must fall into a trance state and act slavishly in compliance with the all-powerful hypnotist. So when people agree to be hypnotized, they implicitly agree to act out this role (Barber et al., 1974; Sarbin & Coe, 1972; Spanos, 1982). People have not actually lost voluntary control over their behavior; rather, they follow the lead of the hypnotist and obey his or her every command because they think, perhaps unconsciously, that involuntary compliance is an important part of what it means to be hypnotized (Lynn et al., 1990). Once again, this may not be a decision that is made consciously; it's better to characterize the process as "creative role engagement, where people generate the sensations, subjective experiences, and mental representations scripted by the hypnotic context" (Lynn et al., 1990, p. 172).

Quite a bit of evidence exists to support this role playing interpretation of the hypnotic state. One compelling finding is that essentially all hypnotic phenomena can be reproduced with *simulated subjects*—people who are never actually hypnotized but who are told to *act* as if they are hypnotized as part of an experiment (Spanos, 1986, 1996). Moreover, many of the classic phenomena—such as posthypnotic suggestions—turn out to be controlled mainly by subject expectations rather than by the whims of the hypnotist. For example, if subjects are told to respond to some cue, such as tugging on their ear every time they hear the word *psychology*, they will often do so after hypnosis. However, posthypnotic suggestions of this kind turn out to be effective only if the subjects believe they are still participating in the experiment; if the hypnotist leaves the room, or if the subjects believe the experiment is over, they stop responding appropriately to the cue (see Lynn et al., 1990, for a review).

MEDITATION

Hypnosis is a procedure that produces an altered state of awareness—heightened suggestibility—after interactions have taken place between a willing subject and someone trained in the appropriate induction techniques. In **meditation,** it is the participant alone who seeks to manipulate awareness. Most meditation techniques require you to perform some time-honored mental exercise, such as concentrating on repeating a particular string of words or sounds called a *mantra.*

The variations in awareness achieved through meditation, as with hypnosis, are often described in mystical or spiritual ways. Meditators report, for example, that they are able to obtain an expanded state of awareness, one that is characterized by a pure form of thought unburdened by self-awareness. There are many

meditation
A technique for self-induced manipulation of awareness, often used for the purpose of relaxation and self-reflection.

Daily meditation sessions can produce significant reductions in anxiety and improve physical and psychological well-being.

forms of meditation and numerous induction procedures; most trace their roots back thousands of years to the practices of a variety of Eastern religions.

Daily sessions of meditation have been prescribed for every sort of physical and psychological problem. As with hypnosis, the induction procedure usually begins with relaxation, but the mind is kept alert through focused concentration on breathing, internal repetition of the mantra, or efforts to clear the mind. The general idea is to step back from the ongoing stream of mental activity and set the mind adrift in the oneness of the universe. Great insights, improved physical health, and release from desire are some of the benefits that are reported.

Scientifically, it's clear that meditation *can* produce significant changes in physiological functions. Arousal is lowered, so heart rate, respiration rate, and blood pressure tend to decline. EEG recordings of brain activity during meditation have revealed what appears to be a relaxed mind—specifically, there is a significant increase in alpha wave activity (Benson, 1975). Such changes are, of course, to be expected during any kind of relaxed state and do not necessarily signify anything special about a state of consciousness. Indeed, there appear to be no significant differences between the physiological patterns of accomplished meditators and those of nonmeditators who are simply relaxing (Holmes, 1987). At this point, researchers have little to say about the subjective aspects of the meditative experience—whether, in fact, the meditator has indeed merged with the oneness of the universe—but most researchers agree that inducing a relaxed state once or twice a day has beneficial effects. Daily meditation sessions have apparently helped people deal effectively with chronic anxiety and other psychological disorders (Eppley et al., 1989).

TEST YOURSELF 6.4

Check on what you've learned about hypnosis and meditation by deciding whether each of the following statements is true or false. (You will find the answers in the Appendix.)

1. The EEG patterns of a hypnotized person resemble those of non-REM sleep. *True or False?*

2. Hypnosis improves memory under some circumstances because it reduces the tendency to fabricate, or make things up, to please the questioner. *True or False?*

3. Hypnotic dissociations represent a kind of splitting of consciousness, where more than one kind of awareness is present at the same time. *True or False?*

4. Hilgard's "hidden observer" experiments provide support for the social role playing explanation of hypnosis. *True or False?*

5. Meditation leads primarily to alpha wave rather than theta wave EEG activity. *True or False?*

Solving the Problems

Studying conscious awareness is not an easy task for a psychologist. Consciousness is by its very nature a subjective, personal experience. It is a difficult concept to define objectively, and appealing to the scribblings of an EEG pattern or to a pretty picture from a PET scanning device may, in the minds of many, fail to capture the complexities of the topic adequately. Is consciousness some classifiable thing that can change its state, like water as it freezes, boils, or evaporates? For the moment, psychologists are working with a set of rather loose ideas about the topic, although conscious awareness is agreed to have many adaptive properties. We considered four adaptive characteristics of consciousness in this chapter; each revealed ways that the adaptive mind adjusts in order to solve problems faced in the environment.

Setting Priorities for Mental Functioning The processes of attention allow the mind to *prioritize* its functioning. Faced with limited resources, the brain needs to be selective about the enormous amount of information it receives. Through attention, people can focus on certain aspects of the environment while ignoring others; through attention, people can adapt their thinking in ways that allow for more selective and deliberate move- ment toward a problem solution. Attentional processes enable the brain to *divide* its processing. People don't always need to be consciously aware of the tasks they perform; automatic processes allow one to perform multiple tasks—such as driving a car and following a conversation—at the same time. Certain disorders of attention, including visual neglect and attention deficit disorder, provide some insights into attention processes. In both of these cases, which may be caused by malfunctioning in the brain, the person's ability to adapt to the environment is compromised.

Sleeping and Dreaming Sleep is one part of a daily (circadian) rhythm that includes wakefulness, but sleep itself turns out to be composed of regu- larly changing cycles of brain activity. Studies using the EEG reveal that people move through several distinct stages during sleep, some of which are characterized by intense mental activity. Sleeping may allow the brain a chance to rest and restore itself from its daily workout, or it may simply be adaptive as a period of time out. Lying relatively motionless in the dark recesses of some shelter may have protected our ancestors at night when their sensory equipment was unlikely to function well. Whether dreaming, which occurs during the REM period of sleep, is an effective solution to some pressing problem faced by the organism remains unclear. Some psychologists believe that dreaming may reveal conflicts that are normally hidden to conscious awareness, or that dreaming may be one way to work out currently troubling prob- lems. A third possibility is that dreaming is simply a manifestation of the brain's attempt to make sense of spontaneous neural activity.

Altering Awareness: Psychoactive Drugs Psychoactive drugs alter behavior and awareness by tapping into natural brain systems that have evolved for adaptive reasons. The brain, as a biochemical factory, is capable of reacting to stress or injury by releasing chemicals (neurotransmitters) that help reduce pain or that shift mood in a positive direction. Many of the drugs that are abused regularly in our society activate these natural systems. As a result, the study of psychoactive drugs has enabled researchers to learn more about communication systems in the brain. There are four main categories of psychoactive drugs. *Depressants,* such as alcohol and barbiturates, lower the ongoing activity of the central nervous system. *Stimulants,* such as caffeine, nico- tine, and cocaine, stimulate central nervous system activity by increasing the likelihood that neural transmissions will occur. *Opiates,* such as opium, morphine, and heroin, depress nervous system activity by mimicking the chemicals involved in the brain's own pain con- trol system. Finally, *hallucinogens,* such as LSD, play havoc with the user's nor- mal internal construction of reality. Although the mechanisms involved are not known, it's believed that LSD mimics the actions of the neurotransmitter sero- tonin.

Altering Awareness: Induced States Two techniques have been designed specifically to alter conscious awareness: hypnosis and meditation. Hypnosis is a form of social interaction that induces a heightened state of sug- gestibility in people. Hypnotic techniques usually promote relaxation, although, once achieved, brain activity under hypnosis more closely resembles the waking rather than the sleeping state. In meditation, it is the participant alone who manipulates awareness, often by mentally repeating a particular word or string of words. The biological mechanisms of both hypnosis and

meditation are poorly understood at present, but each has some positive consequences. Pain and discomfort can be significantly reduced through hypnotic suggestion, whereas the continued use of meditation has been linked to the reduction of stress and anxiety.

Consciousness Chapter Summary

Consciousness is the subjective awareness of internal and external events. It is a deeply personal experience and cannot be measured or analyzed easily. Neuroscientists think consciousness is the reflection of neural activity in the brain.

Setting Priorities for Mental Functioning: Attention

Attention refers to the internal processes we use to set priorities for mental functioning. The brain uses attention to focus selectively on certain parts of the environment and not others.

DICHOTIC LISTENING

Different messages are presented simultaneously to each ear, and the subject tries to repeat one message aloud while ignoring the other.

AUTOMATICITY

Mental processing is fast and easy, requiring little or no focused attention.

ATTENTION DISORDERS

- *Visual neglect:* The tendency, caused by damage to the right (or left) parietal lobe, to ignore everything on the left (or right) side of the body.
- *Attention deficit disorder:* A psychological condition found most often in children, characterized by distractibility, often with impulsivity and/or hyperactivity.

Sleeping and Dreaming

When we sleep we are no longer consciously aware of the external world, but our minds are still actively processing something. Sleep may be an adaptive reaction to light-dark cycles and susceptibility to predators. Researchers use the *electroencephalograph (EEG)* to monitor electrical activity in the brain during sleep.

BIOLOGICAL RHYTHMS

The internal cycles that control sleep and waking and other physical processes are controlled by structures in the brain that trigger rhythmic variations at appropriate times.

FUNCTIONS OF SLEEP

To *repair* and *restore* the body and brain. To respond adaptively to changing conditions for the sake of *survival*.

SLEEP DISORDERS

- *Dyssomnias:* Problems associated with the amount, timing, and quality of sleep (*insomnia, hypersomnia, narcolepsy*).
- *Parasomnias:* Abnormal disturbances of sleep (*nightmares, night terrors, sleepwalking*).

Delta activity

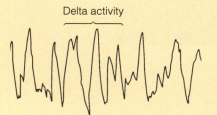

SLEEP CHARACTERISTICS

During sleep we experience repeated cycles of brain activity, each about 90 minutes long.

- *Stage 1:* "Drifting"
- *Stage 2:* Asleep but still dimly sensitive to the external world.
- *Stages 3 & 4:* Progressively deeper sleep
- *REM sleep:* Abrupt physiological changes; brain waves look "awake"; most dream activity occurs here.

REM AND DREAMING

REM sleep may serve an important function in the brain, such as strengthening certain kinds of memories. Dreams may be a form of *wish fulfillment* (Freud); the *activation-synthesis hypothesis* holds that dreaming is a product of random activity in the brain.

Altering Awareness: Psychoactive Drugs

External agents taken into the brain can radically alter the chemical balance that controls awareness. Psychologists are interested in psychoactive drugs because of their effects on mental processes and behavior and because they increase our understanding of neural mechanisms.

ACTIONS AND EFFECTS

The normal communication channels of neurons are altered in a variety of ways. Repeated use of a drug can change the way the body reacts.

- *Tolerance:* Increasing amounts of the drug are required to produce the desired effects.
- *Dependency:* Either a physical or a psychological need for continued use.
- *Withdrawal:* Measurable physical reactions to discontinued use.

CATEGORIES

- *Depressants:* Slow the activity of the central nervous system.
- *Stimulants:* Increase central nervous system activity.
- *Opiates (narcotics):* Depress the nervous system activity and reduce anxiety and sensitivity to pain.
- *Hallucinogens (psychedelics):* Drastically alter normal perception.

PSYCHOLOGICAL FACTORS

- *Environmental setting*
- *Familiarity with effects*
- *Physical state*

Altering Awareness: Induced States

HYPNOSIS

Any form of social interaction that produces a *heightened state of suggestibility* in a willing participant. Associated phenomena include:

- *Catalepsy:* A limb remains rigidly in an unusual position for a long time.
- *Hypnotic hypermnesia:* Dramatically improved memory.

EXPLAINING HYPNOSIS

In the absence of reliable psychological measures, the hypnotized condition is defined by:

- *Hypnotic dissociation:* Multiple awarenesses coexist.
- *Social role playing:* Subjects adopt a role designed to please the hypnotist.

MEDITATION

Self-induced altered awareness achieved through emptying the mind by relaxing and concentrating on breathing or *mantra* (repetition of specific sounds), or through related techniques. Daily meditation can cause significant physiological changes and may reduce anxiety.

Terms to Remember

consciousness, 220

SETTING PRIORITIES FOR MENTAL FUNCTIONING

attention, 222
dichotic listening, 223
cocktail party effect, 224
automaticity, 225
visual neglect, 227
attention deficit disorder, 228

SLEEPING AND DREAMING

circadian rhythms, 230
biological clocks, 230
alpha waves, 233
theta waves, 233
delta activity, 233
REM, 233
REM rebound, 237
manifest content, 239
latent content, 239
activation-synthesis hypothesis, 239
insomnia, 240
hypersomnia, 241
nightmares, 241
night terrors, 241
sleepwalking, 241

ALTERING AWARENESS: PSYCHOACTIVE DRUGS

psychoactive drugs, 242
tolerance, 243
drug dependency, 243
withdrawal, 243
depressants, 243
stimulants, 244
opiates, 245
hallucinogens, 245

ALTERING AWARENESS: INDUCED STATES

hypnosis, 247
catalepsy, 249
hypnotic hypermnesia, 249
hypnotic dissociation, 250
meditation, 250

Recommended Readings

Coren, S. (1996). *Sleep thieves.* New York: The Free Press. Written for the layperson by a top research psychologist, this book presents a convincing case for the importance of a good night's sleep.

Jaynes, J. (1976). *The origin of consciousness in the breakdown of the bicameral mind.* Boston: Houghton Mifflin. This is a fascinating and provocative book, full of speculations about the origins of consciousness. Jaynes argues that conscious awareness developed relatively recently in human history and that ancient peoples from Mesopotamia to Peru were unable to think as we can today.

Dennett, D. C. (1991). *Consciousness explained.* Boston: Little, Brown and Company. Written by a philosopher, this book challenges the traditional commonsense view of consciousness. Generally easy to read—Dennett is a great writer—and it contains much food for thought.

INFOTRAC® COLLEGE EDITION

For additional readings, explore Infotrac College Edition, your online library. Go to:
http://www.infotrac-college.com/wadsworth

Hint: enter the search terms: Visual neglect, Altered states of consciousness, Stages of sleep, REM sleep, Drugs and behavior, Hypnotic effects.

What's on the Web?

CHADD (Children and Adults with Attention Deficit/Hyperactivity Disorder)

(http://www.chadd.org/)

No doubt you've heard something about "ADHD" and related problems, and now you've read a bit about it. This site will provide with some more useful information about the disorder. Find out the basics of ADHD with the provided fact sheets and FAQ.

The Sleep Well Index

(www.stanford.edu/~dement)

One of the best sites on the Web for finding out more about sleep. Find out about snoring, dreams, insomnia, sleep aids, and much more. The site boasts a clickable index of dozens of sleep-related topics. Do you have "restless leg syndrome?"

The Quantitative Study of Dreams

(psych.ucsc.edu/dreams/)

Few topics pique the curiosity of the psychology student more than dreams. Why do we dream? What do dreams mean? The previous chapter provided some suggestions —this site will allow you to explore the question in more depth. The folks at this site provide details on their dream research, as well as information for those who wish to explore their own dreams.

The Wadsworth Psychology Study Center Web Site

See http://psychology.wadsworth.com/ for practice quiz questions, hypercontents, updates, critical thinking exercises, discussion forums and more! The Wadsworth Psychology Study Center provides a wealth of information fully organized and integrated by chapter.

Learning from Experience

Have you ever eaten something unusual, maybe clam pizza, and then felt sick afterward? I bet you were reluctant to try that particular item again. Even the sight of the food is still probably enough to make you check for the availability of the nearest restroom. Now think about something quite different—a rat pressing a bar for a pellet of food. Assume the rat shows remarkable consistency in its behavior, pressing the bar only when a flashing light comes on and never when the light is off. Is there any connection between the two—the behavior of the rat and your reaction to an unfortunate culinary experience? Both involve learning, but do humans and animals learn in the same way? Is there any relationship between learning about what foods to avoid and pressing a bar for food?

Historically, researchers have studied learning in relatively simple kinds of situations, often using animal subjects such as rats, pigeons, or sea snails. In fact, much of what you'll read about in this chapter comes from animal research. Using animals as models to understand human psychology makes sense when you consider that all species—even sea snails—need to learn in order to survive. Many psychologists believe that all organisms, including humans, share a "library" of similar learning mechanisms (Roitblat & von Ferson, 1992). It's generally accepted that there are common principles, or laws of learning, that can be applied widely across situations and species.

Figure 7.1 shows the results of an experiment comparing the learning and memory abilities of pigeons, monkeys, and humans (Wright et al., 1985). All participants were required to learn short sequences of items, from briefly presented lists, and then to remember those items a short time later. (Pigeons identified items by pecking lighted disks; monkeys and human subjects pressed levers.) The details of the experiment and the specifics of the results aren't really important for us here. What is important are the similarities in performance across species. Notice how regular the changes are across the various conditions. For example, all types of subjects remembered items that occurred near the end of a list best when test delays were short, but they remembered items at the beginning of the list best when delays were long. For this task, at least, it doesn't really matter whether you are a pigeon, a monkey, or a human. This suggests that the animal–human gap is probably narrower than you think—there are striking similarities in learning and performance that cut across species (Wright, 1990). This is something you should keep in mind as you read through the research presented in this chapter.

Previewing the Adaptive Problems

What exactly is learning? Most people view learning as simply the process of acquiring knowledge. You go to school, you take classes, you learn something about how the world works. In essence, that's the same way that psychologists think about learning. However, as you learned in Chapter 2, psychologists like to define concepts in terms of how those concepts can be measured. "Knowledge" cannot be measured directly—you could crack someone's head open, but all you're going to find are neurons and glial cells. Instead, **learning** is defined in terms of behavior—more precisely, as a relatively permanent change in behavior, or potential to respond, that results from experience. Notice that the emphasis is on changes in *behavior*. Unlike acquired knowledge, behavior is something we can directly observe. We make inferences about learning and the acquisition of knowledge by observing behavior and noting how behavior changes over time.

learning
A relatively permanent change in behavior, or potential to respond, that results from experience.

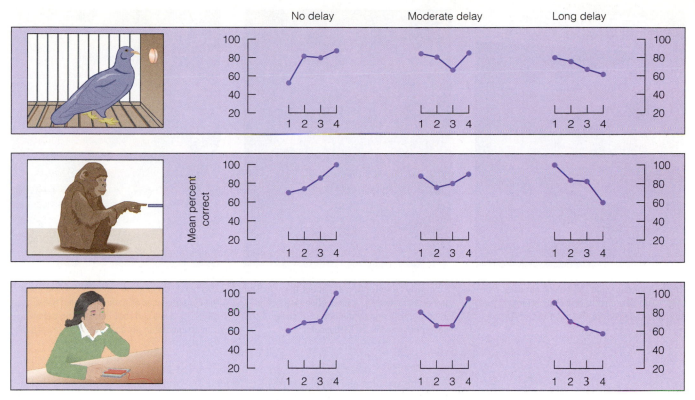

Position of item in list

FIGURE 7.1

Learning in Pigeons, Monkeys, and People

Most animal species, including humans, may share basic learning mechanisms. In this experiment by Anthony Wright and his coworkers, pigeons, monkeys, and people were required to learn lists of four visual items, then remember them after various delays. Notice that it doesn't really matter whether the subject is a monkey, a pigeon, or a human—each remembers items at the end of the list best after no delay, items at the beginning and end of the list equally well at the moderate delay, and items first in the list best at the long delay. (Graphs from Wright et al., 1985.)

Of course behavior can sometimes change as a result of experience in ways that we would not want to classify as learning. For example, your behavior might change because you forgot something, such as a telephone number you've recently dialed. Or suppose you're stuck in bed for two days with a high fever; your behavior is certainly going to change—you sleep a lot more than normal—but these changes will not have anything to do with learning. The concept of learning is reserved for those cases where behavior changes in a way that reflects the experience—people change their behavior, either as a reaction to the experience or as a result of practice, to maximize adaptive behavior in the future.

One final point to note in the definition of learning is the phrase *potential to respond*. Sometimes people acquire knowledge but don't change their behavior in any way that reflects what they've learned. For example, you've now learned the textbook definition of *learning*. But is your behavior going to change? Not likely, unless you need to retrieve the information during an examination. You've probably also learned a great deal about the location of fast-food restaurants in your community. But your behavior isn't going to reflect that knowledge unless you're hungry. It's important to keep in mind the relationship between learning and *performance*—to demonstrate that learning has occurred, it needs to be reflected in actual behavior (Wasserman & Miller, 1997).

The bright colors and screeching sirens of a fire engine are designed to draw our attention, and to signal the need for us to get out of the way.

It's clearly adaptive to learn about the signaling properties of events. A distinctive rattle on a mountain trail signals the potential strike of the western diamondback rattlesnake.

This family dog has no problem learning about the consequences of hanging around the dinner table. She's learned that her begging behavior is instrumental in producing a tasty reward of yogurt.

In this chapter our discussion revolves around four simple adaptive problems that are solved, in part, by our ability to learn. To meet the needs of constantly changing environments, everyone must use experience to modify and improve his or her performance. The particular problems we'll be discussing may appear simple at first, but they lie at the heart of many kinds of adaptive behavior.

First, it's important to recognize significant events when they occur and react to them appropriately. We also need to learn to ignore events that occur repeatedly but have no immediate consequence. The shrill cry of an infant, the screech of automobile brakes—these sounds demand our attention and cause us to react. Humans and animals notice sudden changes in their environment; they notice those things that are new and potentially of interest. However, its important to note that our reactions to these novel events change with repeated experience, and these changes are controlled by some of the most basic and important of all learning processes.

Second, it's useful to learn about the signaling properties of stimuli, or events, in the environment. When does one event predict that a second event is likely to follow? Many things that happen in our world signal the fact that other events will occur. For instance, you know that lightning precedes thunder and that the rattling of a tail can signal the bite of a venomous snake. Often, you can't *do* anything about the co-occurrence of such events, but if you recognize the relationship, you can respond accordingly (you can take cover or move to avoid the snake).

Third, it's essential that we learn about the consequence of our behavior. All species, sea snails as well as people, need to learn that when they act in a certain way, their behavior has consequences. The child who flicks the tail of a cat once too often receives an unwelcome surprise. The family dog learns that if he hangs around the dinner table, an occasional scrap of food might very well come his way. Behaviors are instrumental in producing rewards and punishments, and it's clearly adaptive for us to learn when and how to act.

Fourth, sometimes we need to learn by simply observing others. Often, our most important teachers are not our own actions and their consequences, but the actions of others. People learn by example, as does most of the animal kingdom. Observational learning has considerable adaptive significance: A teenager learns about the consequences of drunk driving, one hopes, not from direct experience but from observing others whose fate has already been sealed. A young monkey in the wild learns to be afraid of snakes not from a deadly personal encounter but from observing her mother's fear.

It's adaptive for all living things to notice sudden changes in the environment. In this case, the unexpected appearance of a red-tailed hawk elicits distinctive orienting reactions from an opossum family.

Learning about Events: Noticing and Ignoring

Let's begin with the first problem: How do we learn to notice and ignore events that occur and repeat in our world? We're constantly surrounded by sights, sounds, and sensations—from the sound of traffic outside the window, to the color of the paint on the wall, to the feel of denim jeans against our legs. As you learned in Chapter 6, it's not possible to attend to all of these stimuli. Instead, you need to prioritize your mental functioning because the human nervous system has limited resources. And this is not just a human problem: Animals, too, have limited resources, and they constantly need to decide whether events in their environment are important or unimportant. Not surprisingly, there are basic psychological processes that help people and animals determine which events should continue to receive a measure of attention and which should not.

LEARNING GOALS

1. Define the orienting response and discuss its adaptive value.

2. Describe and compare habituation and sensitization.

3. Distinguish between short-term and long-term habituation.

HABITUATION AND SENSITIZATION

As you learned in Chapter 4, humans are programmed from birth to notice *novelty*; when something new or different happens, we pay close attention. Suppose you hear a funny ticking noise in your car engine when you press the gas pedal. When you first notice the sound, it occupies your attention. You produce an **orienting response**, which is a kind of automatic shift of attention toward the new event. Perhaps you lean forward and listen; you may even repeatedly press the gas pedal to establish a link between acceleration and ticking. But after driving with the problem for a while, your behavior changes—the ticking becomes less bothersome, and you may even stop reacting to it altogether. Your behavior in the presence of the event changes with repeated experience, which is the hallmark of learning.

When you slow or stop responding to an event that has become familiar through repeated presentation, you are demonstrating **habituation;** you may

orienting response
An inborn tendency to shift one's focus of attention toward a novel or surprising event.

habituation
The decline in the tendency to respond to an event that has become familiar through repeated exposure.

remember that we talked about this process in some detail in Chapter 4. Most birds will startle and become agitated when the shadow of a hawk passes overhead, but their level of alarm will rapidly decline if the object is presented repeatedly and there is no subsequent attack (Tinbergen, 1951). It makes sense for animals to produce a strong initial orienting response to a sudden change in their environment. If a bird fails to attend quickly to the shape of a potential predator, it's not likely to survive. Through the process of habituation, organisms learn to be *selective* about the things they orient toward. They attend initially to the new and unusual but subsequently ignore events that occur repeatedly without significant consequence.

Sensitization occurs when responsiveness to an event *increases* with repeated exposure. Sensitization, like habituation, is a general learning phenomenon found throughout the animal kingdom. Both habituation and sensitization are natural responses to repeated events—they help us respond appropriately to the environment. Whether you will become more or less responsive in any specific situation depends on the relative strengths of the habituation and sensitization processes (Groves & Thompson, 1970). Generally, increases in responsiveness—sensitization—are more likely when the repeated stimulus is intense. For example, if you are exposed to repetitions of a very loud noise, you become "sensitized" to the noise—your reactions become more intense and prolonged with repeated exposure. If the noise is relatively modest in intensity, repeated exposure may lead to decreases in responsiveness. Habituation and sensitization also depend importantly on the timing of presentations—that is, whether the repetitions occur close together or widely separated in time (Haerich, 1997; Staddon, 1998).

SHORT- AND LONG-TERM EFFECTS

Habituation and sensitization are both examples of learning because they produce changes in behavior as a function of experience. However, researchers have spent more time studying habituation than sensitization. The effects of sensitization generally tend to be short-lived (Domjan, 1998), whereas habituation can produce either short-term or long-term effects. Researchers use the term *short-term habituation* to refer to instances in which the loss in responsiveness produced by habituation is only temporary. The sea snail of the genus *Aplysia*, for example, produces a distinctive defensive reaction (gill retraction) when a particular portion of its body, the mantle shelf, is touched. Repeated tapping of the mantle shelf produces habituation of the gill response, but the effect is short-lived. After a short rest period, if the mantle shelf is tapped again, the sea snail's habituated response returns to its original level of reaction (Kandel & Schwartz, 1982).

In *long-term habituation*, the loss in responsiveness lasts for an extended period. For example, when placed in a new environment cats are often skittish when they eat. The slightest sound or movement is likely to send them scurrying under the nearest piece of furniture. With time the animal learns, and the adjustment is typically long-lasting (see Figure 7.2). Drug tolerance, which we discussed in Chapter 6, is often classified as an example of long-term habituation. In humans, an initial dose of 100 to 200 milligrams of morphine produces profound sedation or even death, but morphine-tolerant subjects are capable of receiving over 100 times that amount without negative effects (Baker & Tiffany, 1985). The body's response to the drug changes after repeated use—that is, the body *habituates* to the drug. The exact nature of the learning that occurs as tolerance develops is still a matter of some debate (Siegel, 1983, 1989), but tolerance shows clearly how responsiveness to an event can change as a consequence of repeated exposure.

Because it is a general kind of learning process that occurs throughout the animal world, habituation is often used as a psychological model for understanding how behaviors change with experience. Some learning theorists, for example,

sensitization
An increase in the tendency to respond to an event that has been repeated; sensitization is more likely when a repeated stimulus is intense.

FIGURE 7.2
Long-Term Habituation
Organisms notice sudden changes in the environment, but they learn to ignore them if they occur repeatedly. For an eating cat, a novel sound leads initially to panic and escape, but if the sound is repeated over days, the cat habituates and continues eating without the slightest reaction.

have used short- and long-term habituation as the basis for proposing sweeping theories about the structure of basic learning and memory systems (Staddon, 1998; Wagner, 1981). A number of neuroscientists have used habituation and sensitization as tools for mapping out the fundamental neural mechanisms of learning (Cleary et al., 1998; Groves & Thompson, 1970). Moreover, as we discussed in Chapter 4, psychologists who are interested in development have used habituation as an experimental technique for discovering the content of an infant's mind (Bornstein, 1992).

As adaptive organisms, humans rely on simple learning processes such as habituation to help conserve their limited resources. The world is full of events to be noticed, far more than anyone can ever hope to monitor. Orienting responses guarantee that people will notice the new and unusual, but through habituation we learn to ignore those things that are repeated but are of no significant consequence. People are thereby able to solve a very important problem—how to be selective about the events that occur and recur in the world. However, there is more to learning than just noticing and ignoring events; it is equally important to learn about relationships between events, as you'll see in the next section.

TEST YOURSELF 7.1

Check your knowledge about noticing and ignoring by choosing the best answer for each of the following descriptions. Choose from the following terms: habituation, orienting response, sensitization. (You will find the answers in the Appendix.)

1. When Shawn practices his trumpet he tries repeatedly to hit a high C note. The first time he tries, his roommate says nothing. By the third try, his roommate is banging on the door telling him to be quiet: _____

2. First-time driver Alonda reacts by screaming and slamming on the brakes when a passing car horn sounds: _____

3. Kesha loves clocks and has six different varieties in her apartment. Strangely, she never notices any ticking noises: _____

4. Your cat Comet used to startle and jump three feet in the air whenever you ground your gourmet coffee beans in the morning. Now he never seems to notice:

   _____

5. Drug users often develop tolerance, which means that after repeated use they need larger doses of the drug to achieve the same effects. Tolerance may be considered an example of: _____

Learning What Events Signal: Classical Conditioning

Everyone knows that a flash of lightning cutting across the sky means that a clap of thunder is likely to follow; experience has taught you to *associate* lightning with thunder. You also know that a sour smell coming from the milk means it probably won't taste very good. In each of these cases, you've learned an association between two events—more specifically, you've learned that one event signals the occurrence of the other. This knowledge is clearly adaptive because it allows you to prepare yourself for future events. You know to cover your ears or to avoid drinking the milk. In this section, we'll consider how simple associations like these are learned and reflected in performance.

The scientific study of elementary associations actually began around the turn of the century in the laboratory of a Russian physiologist named Ivan P. Pavlov (1849–1936). Pavlov developed a technique, now known generally as **classical conditioning,** that proved useful for investigating how elementary associations are formed. According to most accounts, Pavlov didn't start off with a burning desire to study learning. His main interest was in digestion, which included the study of how dogs salivate, or drool, in the presence of a variety of foods. People salivate when food is placed in their mouths, as do dogs, because saliva contains certain chemicals that help in the initial stages of digestion. However, to his annoyance, Pavlov found that his dogs often began to drool much too soon—before the food was actually placed in their mouths. Pavlov referred to these premature droolings as "psychic" secretions, and he began to study why they occurred, in part, to avoid future contamination of his digestion experiments.

THE TERMINOLOGY OF CLASSICAL CONDITIONING

Pavlov recognized immediately that "psychic" secretions developed as a result of experience. At the same time, he was keenly aware that drooling in response to food is *not* a learned response. He recognized that the presentation of certain kinds of stimuli, which he called **unconditioned stimuli (USs),** automatically lead to responses, which he called **unconditioned responses (URs).** For example, food is an unconditioned stimulus that automatically produces salivation as an unconditioned response. Neither dogs nor humans need to be taught to drool when food is placed in their mouths; rather, this response is a reflex similar to the jerking of your leg when the doctor taps you just below the knee. The occurrence of an unconditioned response (salivation) after presentation of an unconditioned stimulus (food in the mouth) is *unconditioned*—that is, no learning, or conditioning, is required.

The problem facing Pavlov was that his dogs began to drool merely at the *sight* of the food dish or even at the sound of a food-bearing assistant entering the room. Food dishes and the footsteps of arriving assistants are not unconditioned stimuli that automatically cause a dog to salivate. Drooling in response to such stimuli is learned; it is *conditioned*, or acquired as a result of experience. For this reason, Pavlov began referring to the "psychic" secretions as **conditioned responses (CRs)** and to the stimuli that produced them as **conditioned stimuli (CSs).** (Actually, it is thought that Pavlov meant to use the phrases *conditional stimuli* and *conditional responses*, to stress the role of experience, but the word *conditional* was translated incorrectly from the Russian as "conditioned.")

Let's take footsteps as an example. The sound of an approaching feeder leads to drooling because the dog has learned that the sound *signals* the appearance of the food. Footsteps and food bear a special relation to each other in time: When the footsteps are heard, the food is soon to arrive. To use Pavlov's terminology, the footsteps are acting as a conditioned stimulus that produces salivation, a conditioned response, in anticipation of food. This is not unlike what happens to you

CRITICAL THINKING

Can you think of any reason why it might be adaptive to begin the digestive processes before food actually gets into the mouth?

classical conditioning
A set of procedures, initially developed by Pavlov, used to investigate how organisms learn about the signaling properties of events. Classical conditioning leads to the learning of relations between events—conditioned and unconditioned stimuli—that occur outside of one's control.

unconditioned stimulus (US)
A stimulus that automatically produces—or elicits—an observable response prior to any training.

unconditioned response (UR)
The observable response that is produced automatically, prior to training, on presentation of an unconditioned stimulus.

conditioned response (CR)
The acquired response that is produced to the conditioned stimulus in anticipation of the arrival of the unconditioned stimulus. Often, the conditioned response resembles the unconditioned response, although not always.

conditioned stimulus (CS)
A neutral stimulus (one that does not produce the unconditioned response prior to training) that is paired with the unconditioned stimulus during classical conditioning.

when your mouth begins to water as your waiter arrives with a delicious looking meal. Conditioned stimuli typically lead to conditioned responses after the conditioned stimulus and the unconditioned stimulus have been *paired* together in time—the footsteps (the CS) reliably occur just before presentation of the food (the US). However, as you'll see shortly, simply pairing two events together does not always lead to the formation of this kind of association.

ACQUIRING THE CS–US CONNECTION

What are the necessary conditions for establishing a connection between a conditioned stimulus and an unconditioned stimulus? It helps to remember

In the summer of 1934, the Russian physiologist Ivan Pavlov watched one of his experiments on "psychic" secretions in dogs. Notice the dog's cheek, which is fitted with a device for measuring salivation.

the following general rule: A conditioned stimulus will acquire signaling properties, leading to the production of a conditioned response, whenever it provides *information* about the occurrence of the unconditioned stimulus (Rescorla, 1992). If a bell (CS) is struck just before the delivery of food (US), and the bell–food pairings are continued over time, the dog will begin to salivate (CR) whenever the bell (CS) is struck (see Figure 7.3 on page 268). An association is formed in this case because the bell provides information about the delivery of the food—the dog knows that food will be arriving soon after it hears the bell. This rule helps to explain a wide variety of experimental findings.

1. For an effective association to form, the conditioned stimulus needs to be presented *before* the unconditioned stimulus. If the two are presented at the same time (*simultaneous conditioning*), or if the conditioned stimulus is presented *after* the unconditioned stimulus (*backward conditioning*), little evidence of conditioning will be found. In both of these cases, the conditioned stimulus provides no information about when the unconditioned stimulus will appear, so conditioned responding does not develop. There are some exceptions to this general rule (e.g., Matzel et al., 1988; Rescorla, 1980), but usually the conditioned stimulus needs to be presented first, before the unconditioned stimulus, for effective conditioning.

2. The unconditioned stimulus needs to follow the conditioned stimulus *closely in time*. Pavlov found that if there is a long delay between when the bell (CS) is struck and when the food (US) is delivered, dogs usually don't form a connection between the bell and the food. As the gap between presentation of the conditioned stimulus and presentation of the unconditioned stimulus increases, one becomes a less efficient signal for the arrival of the other—that is, the conditioned stimulus provides less useful information about the appearance of the unconditioned stimulus. Once again, there are exceptions to the rule (DeCola & Fanselow, 1995), but generally if the gap between the conditioned stimulus and the unconditioned stimulus is long, only a weak association forms.

3. The conditioned stimulus needs to *uniquely* predict the unconditioned stimulus. If the unconditioned stimulus also occurs at times when the conditioned stimulus has not been presented, conditioned responding will not usually develop. For example, in one study Rescorla (1968) presented a tone (CS) to rats, followed by a mild electric shock (US). Shock is an unconditioned stimulus that causes animals to jump (UR) prior to any conditioning. In one group, the shock was presented

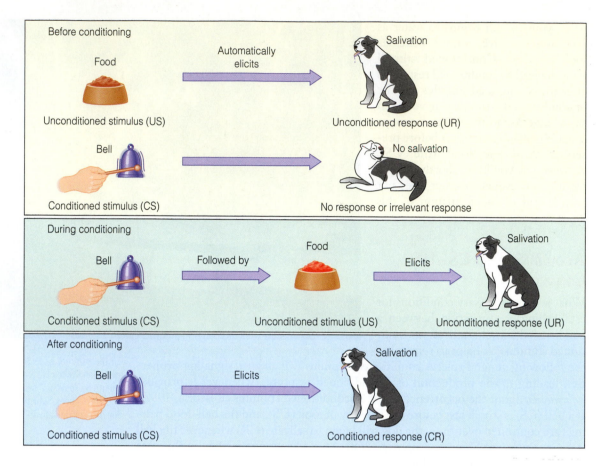

FIGURE 7.3

Classical Conditioning

Through classical conditioning, organisms learn about the signaling properties of events. The presentation of an unconditioned stimulus (US), leads to an automatic unconditioned response (UR) prior to training. A neutral stimulus (one that does not produce a relevant response before conditioning) is paired closely in time with a US. Eventually, the animal learns that this conditioned stimulus (CS) predicts the occurrence of the US and begins to show an appropriate conditioned response (CR) on presentation of the CS. Although here the CR and the UR are the same, they needn't be.

both after the tone and also during periods when the tone was absent. The rats in the first group quickly began displaying a fear response, freezing (the CR), when they heard the tone, but there was little evidence of conditioned responding in the second group (see Figure 7.4). Notice that in this second group, the tone did not clearly indicate when shock would occur in the session, because the shock also occurred when there was no tone. The tone did not provide sufficient information about the occurrence of the shock, so it failed to become a strong signal for the shock.

4. The conditioned stimulus needs to provide *new* information about the occurrence of the unconditioned stimulus. If there are already stimuli in the environment that signal the unconditioned stimulus, then presenting yet another stimulus before the unconditioned stimulus leads to little or no learning. Suppose you teach some rats that a tone is as a reliable signal for the shock. Now, after the rats have learned to freeze to the tone, you start turning on a light at the same time as you sound the tone. Both the light and the tone are then followed by the shock.

CONCEPT SUMMARY	
Factors Affecting Classical Conditioning	
Factor	**Relation to Conditioning Effectiveness**
Timing relationship between CS and US	CS should usually be presented *before* the US. The US should usually follow the conditioned stimulus *closely in time.*
Informativeness of CS	The CS should *uniquely* predict the US. The CS should provide *new* information about the occurrence of the US (blocking).

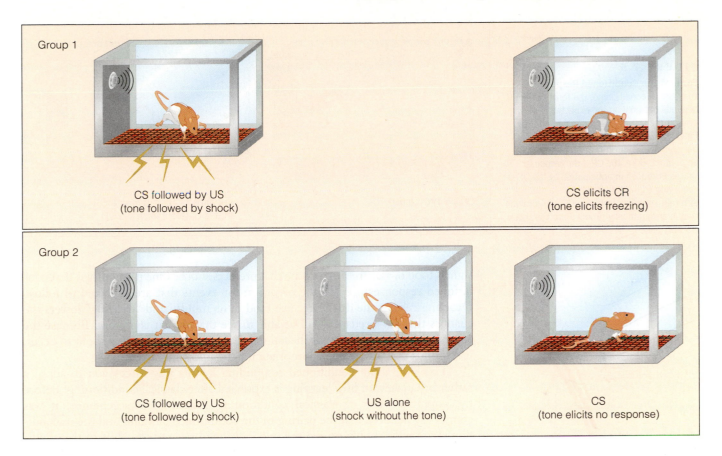

FIGURE 7.4

Informational Rules in Classical Conditioning

For a CR to develop to a CS, the CS needs to provide information about the occurrence of the US. In an experiment by Rescorla (1968), every time an auditory CS sounded for rats in Group 1, a shock US followed closely (left panel). The animals quickly learned to freeze in anticipation of the shock (right panel). For rats in Group 2, the shock was presented after the sound (left panel), but also during times when the sound was not turned on (middle panel). These animals showed no evidence of freezing to the sound (right panel), presumably because it did not provide sufficient information about the US occurrence.

Under these conditions, rats don't typically learn that the light, too, is a reliable signal for the shock (e.g., Kamin, 1968). This result is called *blocking* because the tone appears to block learning to the light. The light is always presented just before the shock, but no conditioning occurs. Why? Because the light provides no *new* information about the occurrence of the shock—the tone already tells the rat that the shock is about to occur, so the rat learns nothing about the light.

These four examples illustrate why learning researchers have adopted what is sometimes called a *cognitive* view of classical conditioning. Through classical conditioning, we learn that one event signals another event when the first event uniquely predicts, or provides information about, the second event. Rats and people don't acquire associations between conditioned stimuli and unconditioned stimuli in a *passive* way, through the simple pairing of the events in time. Rather, they actively process their environment—they seek to establish when events predict, or even cause, the occurrence of other events.

? CRITICAL THINKING

Why do you think it's adaptive to learn associations only when the conditioned stimulus provides new *information about the unconditioned stimulus? Can you think of any situations in which it might be useful to learn that many stimuli predict the appearance of the unconditioned stimulus?*

CONDITIONED RESPONDING: WHY DOES IT DEVELOP?

The learning of an association between the conditioned stimulus and the unconditioned stimulus—that is, that one signals the appearance of the other—does not really explain conditioned responding. Why should dogs drool to a bell that

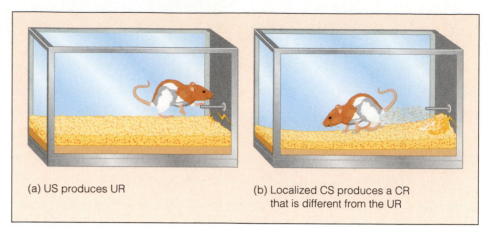

FIGURE 7.5

Form of the Conditioned Response
In classical conditioning, the form of the CR depends not only on the expected US but also on the CS itself. In an experiment by Pinel and Treit (1979), rats attempted to bury an electric prod that produced shock on contact. Here, the CR—the response that is produced in anticipation of the US— is burying (right panel), which is a quite different response from the UR, withdrawal, that is automatically produced to the shock US (left panel).

(a) US produces UR

(b) Localized CS produces a CR that is different from the UR

signals food or rats freeze to a tone that predicts shock? One possibility is that conditioned responses prepare the organism for events that are expected to follow. Drooling readies the dog to receive food in its mouth, and "freezing" lowers the chances that any predators will be able to see that the rat is present. Because the conditioned stimulus informs the animal that a significant event is about to occur, it responds in a way that is appropriate for the upcoming event.

Thinking about conditioned responding in this way forces you to adopt a rather broad view of how learning is expressed after classical conditioning. Before the cognitive view of classical conditioning gained wide acceptance, it was commonly believed that the pairing of the conditioned stimulus and the unconditioned stimulus simply caused the unconditioned response to shift to the conditioned stimulus. Pavlov was convinced, for example, that the conditioned stimulus acts as a kind of substitute for the unconditioned stimulus—organisms respond to the conditioned stimulus as if it were essentially identical to the unconditioned stimulus.

However, this view makes the unique prediction that organisms should always produce a conditioned response that is identical, or at least highly similar, to the unconditioned response. Dogs should always *drool* to a stimulus that predicts the arrival of food; rats should always *jump* to a stimulus that predicts shock. But as you've seen, rats will freeze rather than jump to a signal predicting shock. Over the last several decades a number of experimental findings have shown that the traditional stimulus-substitution view of classical conditioning is incorrect.

1. The response to the conditioned stimulus depends not only on the unconditioned stimulus, but also on the properties of the conditioned stimulus itself (Holland, 1977; Rescorla, 1988). As noted earlier, a tone that signals shock causes rats to freeze, but rats will try to bury or cover up a more localized stimulus that predicts shock. For example, as shown in Figure 7.5, if rats learn that touching a bar in the cage means they will get shocked, they will try to cover the bar with material from the bottom of the cage (Pinel & Treit, 1979). Pigeons will peck a lighted disk that signals food but will show little or no change in behavior to a tone that predicts food (Nairne & Rescorla, 1981). In both of these cases, the conditioned response that is present after training doesn't look very much like the unconditioned response.

2. In some cases, a conditioned response will appear that is actually *opposite* in direction to the unconditioned response. For example, when injection of the drug *epinephrine* is used as an unconditioned stimulus, it produces a decrease in the secretion of stomach acids as an unconditioned response. A stimulus that signals the impending injection of this drug, however, leads to an *increase* in secretions as a conditioned response. When a conditioned response acts in the opposite direction from an unconditioned response, it is called a *compensatory response*. Some

Inside the Problem   Developing Taste Aversions

On St. Thomas in the Virgin Islands, researchers Lowell Nicolaus and David Nellis encouraged captured mongooses to eat eggs laced with carbachol, a drug that produces temporary illness. After 5 days of eating eggs and getting sick, the still-hungry mongooses reduced their consumption of eggs to around 37% of their normal consumption level (Nicolaus & Nellis, 1987). In a very different context, in a research program designed to combat the negative effects of chemotherapy, young cancer patients were allowed a taste of some unusually flavored ice cream just before the onset of their normal chemotherapy—a treatment that typically produces nausea and vomiting. Several weeks later, when offered the ice cream, only 21% of the children were willing to taste it again (Bernstein, 1978).

Both of these situations represent naturalistic applications of classical conditioning. Can you identify the critical features of each? How do these two examples involve the learning of a relation between two events, a conditioned stimulus and an unconditioned stimulus, that largely occurs outside the organism's control? First, let's look for the unconditioned stimulus—the stimulus that unconditionally produces a response prior to training. In both of these cases, the unconditioned stimulus is the illness-producing event, either the drug carbachol or the cancer-fighting chemotherapy. The response that is automatically produced, unfortunately for the participants, is stomach distress. Children don't need to learn to vomit from chemotherapy; a mongoose doesn't need to be taught to be sick after receiving carbachol. These are inevitable consequences that require no prior conditioning.

Now, what is the conditioned stimulus—the event that provides information about the occurrence of the unconditioned stimulus? In these examples, it is the taste of the food, either the eggs or the ice cream, that signals the later onset of nausea. It's worth noting that the children were aware that their nausea was produced by the chemotherapy, not the ice cream, yet an association was still formed

between the taste of the ice cream and a procedure that led to sickness. A conditioned response, feelings of queasiness to the food, was produced whenever the opportunity to eat was presented. Taste aversions are easy to acquire. They often occur after a single pairing of a novel food and illness.

It is extremely adaptive for people and mongooses to acquire taste aversions to potentially dangerous foods—it is in their interest to avoid those events that signal something potentially harmful. In the two studies we've just considered, the researchers investigated the aversions for a particular reason. Mongooses often eat the eggs of endangered species (such as marine turtles). By baiting the nests of mongoose prey with tainted eggs and establishing a taste aversion, scientists have been able to reduce the overall rate of egg predation. Similar techniques have also been used to prevent sheep from eating dangerous plants in the pasture (Zahorik et al., 1990).

In the case of chemotherapy, Illene Bernstein was interested in developing

methods for *avoiding* the establishment of taste aversions: Cancer patients who are undergoing chemotherapy also need to eat, so it's critical to understand the conditions under which aversions are formed. Taste aversions often develop as a side effect of chemotherapy. Patients tend to avoid foods that they've consumed just before treatment, potentially leading to weight loss that impedes recovery. Researchers have found that associations are particularly likely to form between *unusual* tastes and nausea. Broberg and Bernstein (1987) found that giving children an unusual flavor of candy just before treatment reduced the likelihood of their forming aversions to their normal diet. These children formed a taste aversion to the candy rather than to their normal diet. Another helpful technique in preventing taste aversions from developing is to ask the patient to eat the same, preferably bland, foods before every treatment. Foods that do not have distinctive tastes and that people eat regularly (such as bread) are less likely to elicit taste aversions.

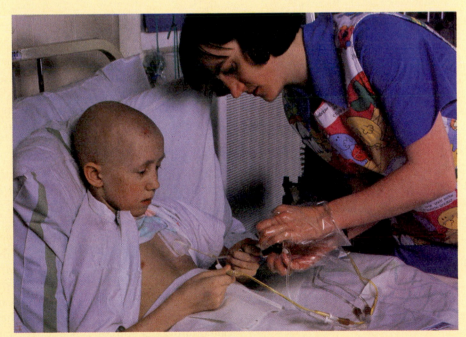

For children undergoing the rigors of chemotherapy, like this young boy suffering from leukemia, it's important to prevent taste aversions from developing as a negative side effect of the treatment. Broberg and Bernstein (1987) found that giving children an unusual flavor of candy just prior to treatment reduced the chances of a taste aversion forming to their normal diet.

researchers have argued that compensatory responses help offset a drug's effects, perhaps playing a role in the development of drug tolerance (Siegel, 1983). (As we discussed earlier, drug tolerance can also be viewed as an example of habituation; it is not yet clear whether tolerance develops from the learning processes involved in classical conditioning, from habituation, or from both.)

3. The occurrence of a conditioned response after learning also depends on how the subject feels about the unconditioned stimulus. If you've learned that a bell signals the delivery of food, your response to the bell will depend on how you feel about the food. Experiments of this type have been conducted by Rescorla and his colleagues, using rats and pigeons as subjects. Hungry rats were taught that a light signaled the delivery of food. After conditioning, the animals were given unlimited access to the food or were spun around on a phonograph turntable after eating to produce temporary discomfort. In both cases, the animals stopped responding to the conditioned stimulus even though its signaling properties remained intact (Holland & Rescorla, 1975). The rats stopped responding, presumably, because they either felt sick or were no longer interested in the food. (Don't worry, the effects of the spinning were temporary, and the rats' appetites quickly returned to normal.)

The take-home message is that the form of the conditioned response depends on many things. As a rule, the idea that classical conditioning turns the conditioned stimulus into a literal substitute for the unconditioned stimulus—or that organisms simply learn to respond to the conditioned stimulus in the same way that they automatically respond to the unconditioned stimulus—cannot account for the complexities in responding just described. Robert Rescorla (1988) put it this way: "Pavlovian conditioning is not the shifting of a response from one stimulus to another. Instead, conditioning involves the learning of relations among events that are complexly represented, a learning that can be exhibited in various ways" (p. 158). Learning such relations among events can be quite adaptive, as the "Inside the Problem" feature on page 271 discusses.

SECOND-ORDER CONDITIONING

Pavlov also discovered that conditioned stimuli possess a variety of properties after conditioning. For example, he found that a conditioned stimulus can be used to condition a second signal. In **second-order conditioning,** an established conditioned stimulus, such as a tone that predicts food, is presented immediately following a new event, such as a light; the unconditioned stimulus itself is never actually presented. In such a case, the pairing of the tone with the light can be sufficient to produce conditioned responding to the light.

An example from Pavlov's laboratory helps to illustrate the procedure. One of Pavlov's associates, Dr. Frolov, first taught a dog that the sound of a ticking metronome signaled the application of meat powder in the mouth. The dog quickly started to drool in the presence of the ticking. A black square was then presented, followed closely by the ticking. After a number of these black square–metronome pairings, even though the ticking was never followed by food powder on these trials, the dog began to drool in the presence of the black square. The dog drooled in response to the square because it signaled the ticking, which the dog had previously learned signaled the food (see Figure 7.6).

The fact that conditioned stimuli can be used to condition other events is important because it greatly expands the number of situations in which classical conditioning applies. It is not necessary for an unconditioned stimulus to be present in a situation in order for you to learn something about its occurrence. For example, most children quickly learn that the word *no* can signal a very unpleasant consequence (e.g., being forced to stand alone in a corner); but, luckily for parents, the word *no* can then be paired with many other events without the need to actually deliver the unpleasant consequence. So, the parent

second-order conditioning
A procedure in which an established conditioned stimulus is used to condition a second neutral stimulus.

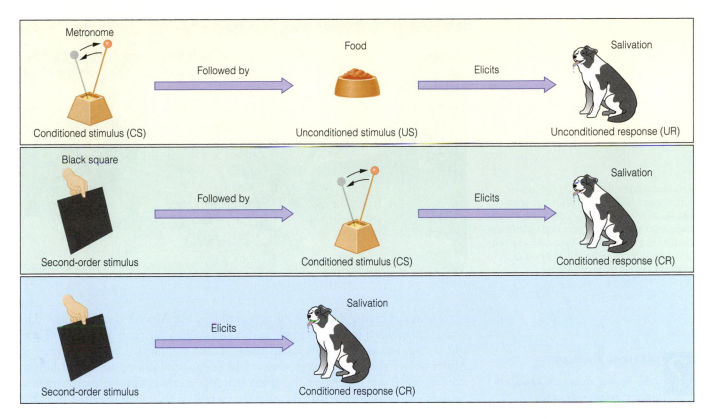

FIGURE 7.6
Second-Order Conditioning
In second-order conditioning, an established CS is used in place of a US to condition a second signal. In Dr. Frolov's experiment, a ticking metronome was first paired with food; after repeated pairings, the ticking elicited salivation as a CR. Next, a black square—which did not produce salivation initially—was paired with the ticking (no US was presented). After repeated pairings, the presentation of the black square began to produce salivation.

can simply point to a container of ant poison and say "No," and the child will get the picture.

Advertisers often rely on second-order conditioning to help sell products. For example, consider the logic behind using celebrities to endorse products. Advertisers are trying to get you to form a link, or association, between the product and feelings of pleasure or enjoyment. Most people like Michael Jordan because he is linked to something they enjoy—great skill on the basketball court. The product, such as a long-distance telephone service, is then paired with Jordan in an effort to get you to associate it with pleasurable consequences. The product becomes a signal for something that leads to enjoyment—this is a kind of second-order conditioning, and it's been used for decades in the marketplace.

STIMULUS GENERALIZATION

Pavlov also noticed that a response produced to the conditioned stimulus tended to generalize to other, related events. If a tone of a particular pitch was conditioned as a signal for food, other tones that sounded similar also produced salivation—even though they had never actually been presented. When a new stimulus produces a response similar to the one produced by the conditioned stimulus, **stimulus generalization** has occurred.

A famous example of stimulus generalization was reported in a study of classical conditioning conducted around 1920 by John Watson and Rosalie Rayner. They presented Albert, an 11-month-old infant, with a white rat (the conditioned stimulus), which he liked, followed by a very loud noise (the unconditioned stimulus), which he did not like. Not surprisingly, this unconditioned stimulus produced a strong, automatic fear reaction: Albert cried (the unconditioned response). After several pairings of the rat with the loud noise, little Albert began to pucker his face, whimper, and try to withdraw his body (all conditioned responses) immediately at the sight of the rat. (By the way, many psychologists question the ethics of this experiment.)

stimulus generalization
Responding to a new stimulus in a way similar to the response produced by an established conditioned stimulus.

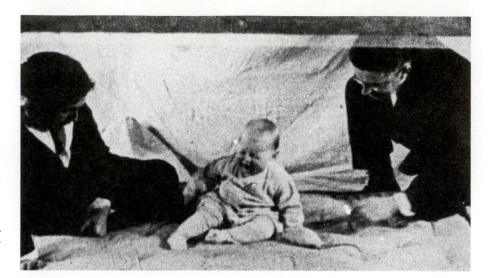

This photo, taken from a 1920 film, shows Little Albert reacting with dismay to a white rat. As described in the text, this rat had previously been paired with a very unpleasant noise. On the right is the famous behavioral psychologist John Watson: to the left of Albert is Watson's colleague, Rosalie Rayner.

However, crying when the rat appeared was not Albert's only response. His crying generalized to other stimuli, such as a rabbit, a fur coat, a package of cotton, a dog, and even a Santa Claus mask. These stimuli had been presented to Albert before the conditioning session had begun, and none had caused him to start crying. It was concluded, therefore, that Albert cried at the sight of them now because of his experience with the rat; he generalized his crying response from the white rat to the other stimuli.

As a rule, stimulus generalization occurs when a new stimulus is *similar* to the conditioned stimulus (see Figure 7.7). If you get sick after eating clams, there's a good chance you'll avoid eating oysters; if you've had a bad experience in the dentist's chair, the sound of the neighbor's high-speed drill may make you uncomfortable. Generalization makes adaptive sense: Things that look, sound, or feel the same often share significant properties. It really doesn't matter whether it's a tiger, a lion, or a panther leaping at you—you should run all the same.

STIMULUS DISCRIMINATION

Watson and Rayner did find that Albert showed *no* tendency to cry when he was presented with a block of wood. He perceived a difference between white furry or fluffy things and things that were not white and fluffy. This is called **stimulus discrimination;** it occurs when you respond to a new stimulus in a way that is different from your response to the original conditioned stimulus. Through stimulus discrimination, you reveal that you can distinguish among stimuli, even when those stimuli share properties.

When stimuli *do* share properties—for example, two tones of a similar pitch—people often need experience to teach them to discriminate. The natural tendency is to generalize—that is, to treat similar things in the same way. Albert certainly could tell the difference among rats, rabbits, and Santa Claus masks; what he needed to learn was which of those white, furry things signaled the unfortunate noise. In many cases, the development of stimulus discrimination requires that one directly experience whether or not the unconditioned stimulus will follow a particular event. If event A is followed by the unconditioned stimulus but event B is not, then you learn to discriminate between these two events and respond accordingly.

EXTINCTION: WHEN CSs NO LONGER SIGNAL THE US

Remember our general rule: A conditioned stimulus becomes a good signal when it provides *information* about the occurrence of the unconditioned stimulus. So what happens when the conditioned stimulus stops predicting the appearance of

stimulus discrimination
Responding differently to a new stimulus than one responds to an established conditioned stimulus.

FIGURE 7.7
Stimulus Generalization
After conditioned responding to a CS is established, similar events will often produce conditioned responding, too, through stimulus generalization. For example, if a red light is trained as a CS, then similar colors that were not explicitly trained will also produce responding if tested. Notice that the less similar the test stimulus is to the training CS, the less generalization occurs.

an unconditioned stimulus? In the procedure of **extinction,** the conditioned stimulus is presented repeatedly, after conditioning, but is no longer followed by presentation of the unconditioned stimulus. Under these conditions, the conditioned stimulus loses its signaling properties because it stops predicting the appearance of the unconditioned stimulus. Not surprisingly, conditioned responding gradually diminishes as a result. For example, if we continued to place the white rat in little Albert's crib but no longer followed the rat's appearance by the noise, we would be carrying out the procedure of extinction. After a while, it's likely that Albert would no longer cry when he saw the rat.

Notice the similarity between the procedure of extinction and the concept of habituation. Both involve the repeated presentation of an event accompanied by a gradual loss in responding. The difference between them is that extinction involves a loss in responding that has been acquired as a result of conditioning—you change your behavior because the conditioned stimulus no longer signals the presence of another significant event. In habituation, no prior learning or conditioning is required to produce the changes that result from repeated exposure. You naturally orient toward sudden changes in your environment—no learning is required—but you'll learn to ignore those events that repeatedly occur without significant consequence.

extinction
Presenting a conditioned stimulus repeatedly, after conditioning, without the unconditioned stimulus, resulting in a loss in responding.

CONCEPT SUMMARY
Major Phenomena of Classical Conditioning

Phenomenon	Description	Example: Pavlov's dogs
Second-order conditioning	An established CS is presented immediately following a new event; after several pairings, this new event may come to elicit responding.	After a dog has been conditioned to salivate in response to a CS (tone), the CS is presented immediately following a new signal (e.g., a light). After several pairings, the light then may come to elicit responding.
Stimulus generalization	A new stimulus produces a response similar to the one produced by the conditioned stimulus.	After a dog has been conditioned to salivate in response to a CS (e.g., a red light), the same response may be produced by a similar stimulus (e.g., an orange or purple light).
Stimulus discrimination	The response to a new stimulus is different from the response to the original CS.	After a dog has been conditioned to salivate in response to a CS (light), the response does not occur to a different stimulus, such as a ringing bell.
Acquisition	Conditioned responding becomes stronger with repeated CS–US pairings.	The more times a dog hears the stimulus (tone) paired with the US (food), the stronger the conditioned response becomes.
Extinction	Conditioned responding diminishes when the CS (after conditioning) is presented without being followed by the US.	After a dog has been conditioned to salivate in response to a CS (tone), the tone is presented repeatedly without the US (food). Responding to the CS lessens.
Spontaneous recovery	Conditioned responding that has disappeared in extinction recovers spontaneously with the passage of time.	After extinction, a dog no longer responds to the CS (tone). After a rest period, the dog once again will respond when presented with the CS (tone).

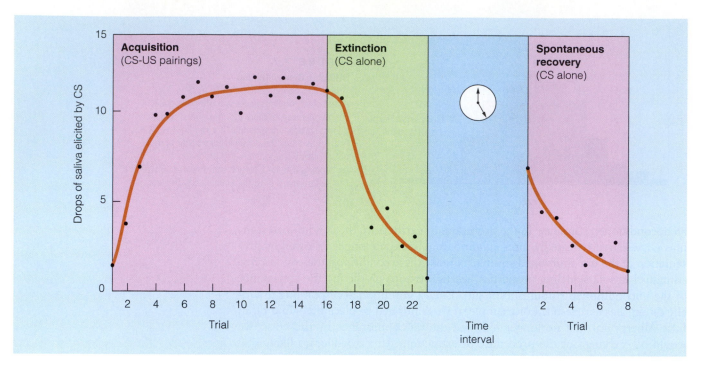

FIGURE 7.8

Training, Extinction, and Spontaneous Recovery

During training, Pavlov found that the amount of salivation produced to the CS initially increased and then leveled off as a function of the number of CS–US pairings. During extinction, the CS is repeatedly presented without the US, and conditioned responding gradually diminishes. If no testing of the CS occurs for a rest interval following extinction, spontaneous recovery of the CR will often occur if the CS is presented again.

Spontaneous Recovery

Sometimes conditioned responding that has disappeared as a result of extinction will recover spontaneously with the passage of time. **Spontaneous recovery** is the recovery of an extinguished response after a period of nonexposure to the conditioned stimulus (see the far right panel in Figure 7.8). In Pavlov's case, his dogs stopped drooling if a bell signaling food was repeatedly presented alone, but when the bell was rung again the day after extinction the conditioned response reappeared (although often not as strongly). Spontaneous recovery is another example of why it is important to distinguish between learning and performance. At the end of extinction, the conditioned stimulus can seem to have lost its signaling properties, but when it is tested after a delay, we see that at least some of the learning remained (see also Bouton, 1991).

CONDITIONED INHIBITION: SIGNALING THE ABSENCE OF THE US

During extinction, you learn that a conditioned stimulus no longer signals the appearance of the unconditioned stimulus. As a result, you stop responding to a stimulus that once elicited a response, because you no longer anticipate that the unconditioned stimulus will follow. You've not forgotten about the unconditioned stimulus; instead, you've learned something new: A conditioned stimulus that used to signal the unconditioned stimulus no longer does.

In **conditioned inhibition,** you learn that an event signals the *absence* of the unconditioned stimulus, but the signal is not typically a previously conditioned stimulus. To create an inhibitory conditioned stimulus, we take a neutral stimulus, one that has no signaling properties, and arrange for it to be a reliable signal for the absence of the unconditioned stimulus. There are a variety of ways to do so, but common to all is the presentation of the new event under conditions in which

spontaneous recovery
The recovery of an extinguished conditioned response after a period of nonexposure to the conditioned stimulus.

conditioned inhibition
Learning that an event signals the absence of the unconditioned stimulus.

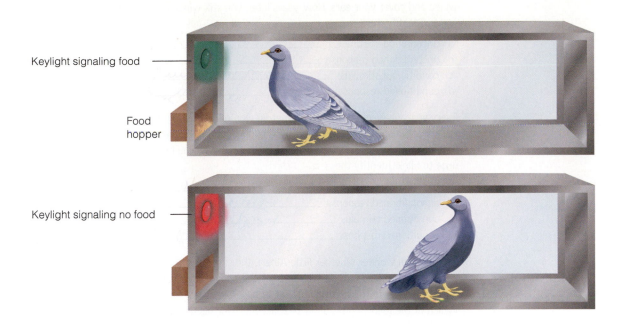

Keylight signaling food

Food hopper

Keylight signaling no food

FIGURE 7.9
Conditioned Inhibition
In conditioned inhibition, the CS provides information about the absence of the US. Pigeons will approach and peck at a keylight CS that signals the appearance of food (upper panel), but they will withdraw from a keylight CS signaling no food (lower panel). Notice that the withdrawal response is an indication that the red light has become a conditioned inhibitor—a CS that predicts the absence of food.

the unconditioned stimulus is normally expected but is not delivered (Williams et al., 1992). For example, if dogs are currently drooling to a bell that predicts food, then putting the bell together with a light and then following this compound (bell + light) with no food will establish the light as a conditioned inhibitor for food. The animal learns that when the light is turned on, food does not follow the bell.

What change in behavior is produced by a conditioned stimulus that predicts the absence of something? Inhibitory learning can be expressed in various ways, but as a rule, the inhibitory conditioned stimulus will produce a reaction that is in some way the *opposite* of that produced by a signal that predicts the appearance of the unconditioned stimulus. For example, if a conditioned stimulus signaling food produces an increase in responding, then an inhibitory conditioned stimulus will lead to a decrease in the normal amount of responding. Several experiments have shown that pigeons and dogs will approach a signal predicting food but will withdraw from a conditioned stimulus signaling the absence of food (see Figure 7.9) (Hearst & Franklin, 1977; Jenkins et al., 1978).

The conditions required for establishing the presence of conditioned inhibition are complex and need not concern us here, but it is important to appreciate the intrinsic value of an inhibitory signal. It's just as adaptive to know that a significant event will *not* occur as it is to know that the event will occur. For example, you understand that when your traffic light is green, it is unlikely that a car will travel directly into your path. Therefore, the green light signals to you that it's safe to go forward. Inhibitory stimuli often act as "safety signals," telling people when potentially dangerous events are likely to be absent or when dangerous conditions are no longer present.

TEST YOURSELF 7.2

Check your knowledge about classical conditioning by answering the following questions. (You will find the answers in the Appendix.)

1. Growing up, your little sister Leah had the annoying habit of screaming, at the top of her lungs, every time she stepped into her bathwater. Her screaming always made you

wince and cover your ears. Now, years later, you still wince every time you hear running water. Identify the

   a. unconditioned stimulus: _____ *Leah crying*

   b. unconditioned response: _____ *[handwritten]*

   c. conditioned stimulus: _____ *water running*

   d. conditioned response: _____ *[handwritten]*

2. Every year when you visit the optometrist, you get a puff of air blown into your eye to test for glaucoma. It always makes you blink. Just before the puff is delivered, the doctor typically asks you if you're "ready." Now, whenever you hear that word, you feel an urge to blink. Identify the

   a. unconditioned stimulus: _____ *Puff of air*

   b. unconditioned response: _____ *[handwritten]*

   c. conditioned stimulus: _____ *ready?*

   d. conditioned response: _____ *blink*

3. People often wonder whether little Albert, the subject in the Watson and Rayner experiment, grew up filled with fear and anxiety. Suppose I told you that he suffered no long-term effects from the experiment and, in fact, later grew his own fluffy white beard. Which of the following probably best accounts for his normal development?

   a. Conditioned inhibition

   b. Stimulus generalization

   c. Spontaneous recovery

   (d.) Extinction

5b
PsychNow!

Learning about the Consequences of Behavior: Instrumental Conditioning

LEARNING GOALS

1. Define instrumental conditioning and discuss the law of effect.

2. Explain what is meant by the discriminative stimulus.

3. Define reinforcement and distinguish between positive and negative reinforcement.

4. Discuss different schedules of reinforcement and compare their effects on behavior.

5. Explain how complex behaviors can be acquired through shaping.

6. Define punishment and distinguish between positive and negative punishment.

instrumental conditioning
A procedure for studying how organisms learn about the consequences of their own voluntary actions; they learn that their behaviors are instrumental in producing rewards and punishments. Also called **operant conditioning**.

Classical conditioning answers an important survival question: How do we learn that certain events signal the presence or the absence of other events? Through the processes tapped by classical conditioning, we learn to expect that certain events will or will not occur, at certain times, and we react accordingly. But our actions under these conditions typically don't have any effect on the pairing of the signal and the unconditioned stimulus. Usually, occurrences of the conditioned stimulus and the unconditioned stimulus are outside our control. For example, you can't change the fact that thunder will follow lightning; all you can do is prepare for an event (thunder) when a prior event (lightning) tells you it's coming.

In another type of learning, studied through a procedure called **instrumental conditioning** (or **operant conditioning**), we learn that our own *actions*, rather than conditioned stimuli, lead to outcomes. If a child is allowed to watch an hour of television as a reward for cleaning her room, she learns that her behavior is *instrumental* in producing rewards; by *operating* on her environment, she produces a pleasing consequence. Some technical differences exist between instrumental and operant learning situations, but for our purposes it is sufficient simply to remember that both involve learning about the consequences of behavior. Notice, though, how classical conditioning differs from instrumental conditioning: In the former, you learn that events signal outcomes; in the latter, you learn that your own actions or behaviors produce outcomes (see Figure 7.10).

THE LAW OF EFFECT

The study of instrumental conditioning actually predates Pavlov's historic work by several years. In 1895, Harvard graduate student Edward Lee Thorndike (1874–1949), working in the cellar of his mentor William James, began a series of

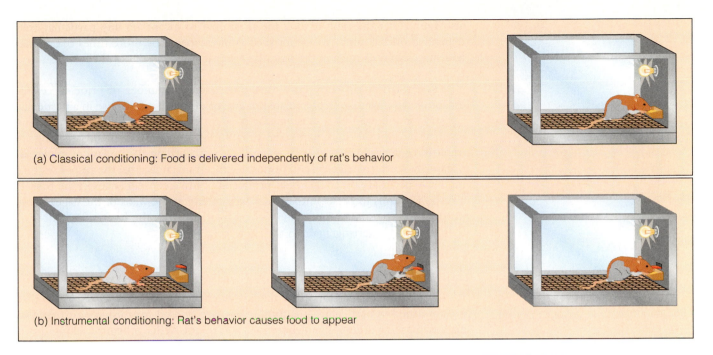

(a) Classical conditioning: Food is delivered independently of rat's behavior

(b) Instrumental conditioning: Rat's behavior causes food to appear

FIGURE 7.10

Classical versus Instrumental Conditioning

In classical conditioning (top row), food is delivered independently of the rat's behavior. The light CS signals the automatic arrival of the food US. In instrumental conditioning (bottom row), the rat must press the bar in the presence of the light in order to get the food. The light serves as a discriminative stimulus telling the rat that pressing the bar will now produce the food.

experiments on "animal intelligence" using cats from around the neighborhood. He built a puzzle box, which resembled a kind of tiny prison, and carefully recorded the time it took for the cats to escape. The boxes were designed so that escape was possible only through an unusual response, such as tilting a pole, pulling a string, or pressing a lever (see Figure 7.11). On release, the cats received a small amount of food as a reward.

Thorndike specifically selected escape responses that were unlikely to occur when the animals were first placed in the box. In this way, he could observe how the cats learned to escape over time. Through trial and error, the cats eventually learned to make the appropriate response, but the learning process was gradual. Thorndike

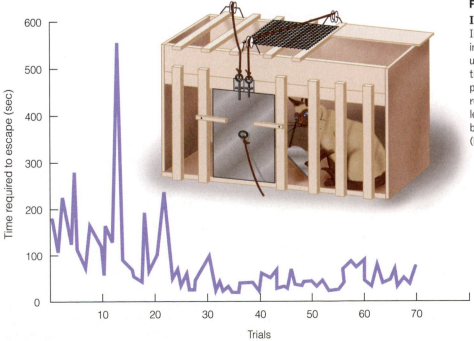

FIGURE 7.11

Instrumental Conditioning

In Thorndike's famous experiments on animal intelligence, cats learned that some kind of unusual response—such as pressing a lever or tilting a pole—allowed them to escape from a puzzle box. The graph shows that the time required to escape gradually diminished over learning trials. Here the cat is learning that its behavior is instrumental in producing escape. (Based on Weiten, 1995.)

also found that the time it took for an animal to escape on any particular trial depended on the number of prior successful escapes. The more times the animal had successfully escaped in the past, the faster it could get out of the box on a new trial.

The relationship between escape time and the number of prior successful escapes led Thorndike to formulate the **law of effect:** If a response in a particular situation is followed by a satisfying or pleasant consequence, it will be strengthened; if a response in a particular situation is followed by an unsatisfying or unpleasant consequence, it will be weakened. According to the law of effect, all organisms learn to make certain responses in certain situations; the responses that regularly occur are those that have produced positive consequences in the past. If a response tends to occur initially (e.g., scratching at the walls of the cage) but is not followed by something good (such as freedom from the box), the chances of that response occurring again in the situation diminish.

THE DISCRIMINATIVE STIMULUS: KNOWING WHEN TO RESPOND

It's important to understand that the law of effect applies only to responses that are rewarded in particular situations. If you are praised for raising your hand in class and asking an intelligent question, you're not likely to begin walking down the street repeatedly raising your hand. You understand that raising your hand is rewarded only in a particular situation, namely, the classroom lecture. What you really learn is something like the following: If some stimulus situation is present (the classroom), and you act in a certain way (raising your hand), then some consequence will follow (praise).

B. F. Skinner (1938) referred to the stimulus situation as the **discriminative stimulus.** He suggested that a discriminative stimulus "sets the occasion" for a response to be rewarded. Being in class—the discriminative stimulus—sets the occasion for question-asking to be rewarded. In some ways, the discriminative stimulus shares properties with the conditioned stimulus established in classical conditioning. For example, you often find *stimulus generalization* of a discriminative stimulus: If a pigeon is trained to peck a key in the presence of a red light, the bird will later peck the key whenever a light of a similar color is turned on. If you're rewarded for asking questions in psychology, you might naturally generalize your response to another course, such as economics, and raise your hand there. Conversely, *stimulus discrimination* also occurs, usually after experiencing reward in one situation but not in another. You may learn, for instance, that raising your hand in psychology class leads to positive consequences, but a similar behavior in your economics class is frowned on by the professor. In such a case, one setting (psychology) acts as an effective discriminative stimulus for a certain instrumental response, but another setting (economics) does not.

Over the years, learning researchers have argued about exactly what is learned about the discriminative stimulus in instrumental conditioning, especially in studies with animal subjects. For example, if a rat is taught to press a lever to receive food, does the rat learn simply to press the lever whenever it is there? Does the reward merely "stamp in" an association between a discriminative stimulus (the lever) and a response (pressing)? For many years, this was the traditional view in psychology: Instrumental conditioning leads to the formation of associations between stimuli and responses (Hull, 1943).

However, most psychologists now believe that more is learned in instrumental conditioning than connections between discriminative stimuli and responses. For example, it seems likely that the animal also learns something about the reward itself. Just as in classical conditioning, responding in the presence of the discriminative stimulus depends on how the animal feels about the reward—if a rat is taught to press a lever for a reward, and then the value of the reward is somehow changed, the rat will change its behavior accordingly (Colwill & Rescorla, 1986). This suggests that the animal learns not only about the discriminative stim-

law of effect
The idea that if a response in a particular situation is followed by a satisfying or pleasant consequence, it will be strengthened; if a response in a particular situation is followed by an unsatisfying or unpleasant consequence, it will be weakened.

discriminative stimulus
The stimulus situation that sets the occasion for a response to be followed by reinforcement or punishment.

ulus and the response but also about the specific reward that follows the response (Colwill, 1994; Colwill & Delameter, 1995).

THE NATURE OF REINFORCEMENT

The law of effect states that responses will be strengthened if they are followed by a pleasant or satisfying consequence. By "strengthened," Thorndike meant that a response was more likely to occur in the future in that particular situation. But, what defines a pleasant or satisfying consequence? This is a tricky problem because the concept of a "pleasant" or "satisfying" event is highly personal—what's pleasant for me might not be pleasant for you. Moreover, something that's pleasing at one time might not be pleasing at another. Food, for example, is "positive at the beginning of Thanksgiving dinner, indifferent halfway through, and negative at the end of it" (Kimble, 1993).

For these reasons, psychologists use a technical term—**reinforcement**—to describe consequences that *increase* the likelihood of responding. As you'll see, it's popular to distinguish between two major types of reinforcement: *positive* and *negative*.

Positive Reinforcement

When the *presentation* of an event after a response increases the likelihood of the response occurring again, **positive reinforcement** has occurred. Usually, the presented event is an *appetitive stimulus*—something the organism likes, needs, or has an "appetite" for. According to Thorndike (1911), an appetitive stimulus is "one which the animal does nothing to avoid, often doing such things as to attain or preserve it" (p. 245). Food and water are obvious examples, but responses can be reinforcing, too (such as sexual activity or painting a picture). Remember, though, it's not the subjective qualities of the consequence that matter—what matters in defining positive reinforcement is an *increase* in a tendency to respond. As long as you're more likely to act in a certain way again, after a consequence has been delivered, then the consequence qualifies as positive reinforcement.

Psychologists have discovered that it's sometimes possible to predict when the presentation of an event will be reinforcing by appealing to the concept of a behavioral *bliss point*. By bliss points, psychologists mean baseline tendencies to respond to events. Everyone has a certain desire to eat, drink, listen to music, play volleyball, study for school, and so on. These baseline levels of satisfaction, which presumably differ from one person to the next, are called bliss points. According to the *response deprivation theory* of reinforcement, an event will be reinforcing as long as presenting it allows someone to move toward his or her natural bliss point for that event (Allison, 1989; Timberlake, 1980). If you have been deprived of eating for a while, you have fallen below your natural bliss point for eating and therefore will find the presentation of food to be positively reinforcing. Once you've eaten, food loses its reinforcing value because you've already reached your natural bliss point for eating. This is the reason why food is no longer reinforcing shortly after you finish a large meal.

Importantly, the response deprivation theory predicts that the presentation of *any* event or response, in principle, can serve as positive reinforcement (see also Premack, 1962). If you have been deprived of responding to an event for long enough (that is, you have fallen below your bliss point), the presentation of that event should be reinforcing. Most children, for example, would rather color than do math problems (presumably because the bliss point for coloring is naturally high). However, if children are deprived of doing math problems for long enough, so that they fall below their natural bliss point for math, the opportunity to do math can actually serve as positive reinforcement (see Konarski, 1985; Timberlake, 1980).

Negative Reinforcement

With **negative reinforcement,** the *removal* of an event after a response increases the likelihood of that response occurring again. In most cases, negative

? CRITICAL THINKING

Can you think of a case where presenting an unpleasant event actually increases the likelihood of the response that produces it?

reinforcement
Response consequences that increase the likelihood of responding in a similar way again.

positive reinforcement
An event that, when *presented* after a response, increases the likelihood of that response occurring again.

negative reinforcement
An event that, when *removed* after a response, increases the likelihood of that response occurring again.

CRITICAL THINKING

When you study for an examination, or try to do well in school, are you seeking positive reinforcement or negative reinforcement?

escape conditioning
A situation in which a response can reduce or eliminate an unpleasant stimulus, such as when a rat escapes an ongoing shock by jumping over a barrier.

avoidance conditioning
A situation in which a response can prevent the delivery of an aversive stimulus, such as when a rat learns to jump over a barrier to avoid a shock.

reinforcement occurs when a response allows you to eliminate, avoid, or escape from an *unpleasant* situation. For instance, you hang up the phone on someone who is criticizing you unfairly, shut off the blaring alarm clock in the morning, or walk out of a movie that is boring you to tears. These responses are more likely to occur again in the future, given the appropriate circumstance, because they lead to the removal of something negative—criticism, noise, or boredom. But, as you may have guessed, the event that is removed doesn't have to be unpleasant—it simply has to increase the likelihood of the "contingent" response (the response that led to the removal).

Researchers who study negative reinforcement in animals have historically used two kinds of learning procedures: escape conditioning and avoidance conditioning. In **escape conditioning,** the animal learns that a response will end some kind of unpleasant stimulus. For example, a rat might learn that jumping over a short barrier separating one part of the cage from another will terminate a mild electric shock. The jumping response is reinforced because it allows the animal to escape from a negative situation (see the top row in Figure 7.12). In **avoidance conditioning,** the response the animal learns *prevents* the negative situation from occurring. For example, if the mild electric shock is signaled by the appearance of a light, the rat might learn to jump over the barrier as soon as the light appears, thus *avoiding* exposure to the shock. Once again, the avoidance response is reinforced by the elimination of something negative (see the bottom row in Figure 7.12).

Students are often confused by the term *negative reinforcement* because they think negative reinforcement is a bad thing. Actually, whenever psychologists use the term *reinforcement*, both positive and negative, they are referring to outcomes

FIGURE 7.12
Escape versus Avoidance Conditioning
In escape conditioning (top row), a response is negatively reinforced because it ends an aversive event. The rat learns that jumping over a short barrier will terminate a mild electric shock. In avoidance conditioning (bottom row), the rat learns to make a response that prevents the aversive stimulus from occurring; here, the rat learns to avoid the shock by jumping when the light comes on. Often, the animal will learn first to escape from, and then to avoid, an aversive event.

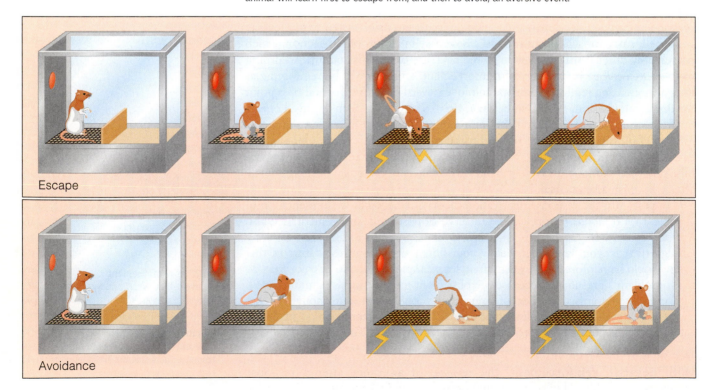

Escape

Avoidance

CONCEPT SUMMARY
Positive and Negative Reinforcement

Consequence	Description	Example
Positive reinforcement	The *presentation* of an event after a response increases the likelihood of the response occurring again.	Juan's parents reward him for cleaning his room by giving him $5. The presentation of $5 increases the likelihood that Juan will clean his room again.
Negative reinforcement	The *removal* of an event after a response increases the likelihood of the response occurring again.	Hannah's parents nag her continually about cleaning up her room. When she finally cleans her room, her parents stop nagging her. The removal of the nagging increases the probability that Hannah will clean her room again.

that increase the probability of responding. The terms *positive* and *negative* simply refer to whether the response ends with the presentation of something or the removal of something. In both cases, the result is a rewarding aftereffect, and we can expect the response that produced the reinforcement to occur again in that situation.

Conditioned Reinforcers

Sometimes a stimulus can act like a reinforcer even though it seems to have no intrinsic value. For example, money will serve as a satisfying consequence even though it's only a well-made piece of paper marked with interesting engravings. However, having money predicts something of intrinsic value—you can buy things—and this is what gives it its reinforcing value. In the same way, if a stimulus or event predicts the absence or removal of something negative, then its presentation is also likely to be reinforcing. Stimuli of this type are called **conditioned reinforcers** because their reinforcing properties are acquired through learning (they are also sometimes called "secondary" reinforcers to distinguish them from more "primary" reinforcers such as food or water). These stimuli are reinforcing because they signal the presence or absence of other events.

SCHEDULES OF REINFORCEMENT

The law of effect implies that behaviors are more likely to be repeated if they are *followed* by positive or negative reinforcement. As in classical conditioning, however, the development of an instrumental response depends greatly on how often, and when, the reinforcements are actually delivered. It is necessary to teach someone that his or her behavior uniquely predicts the reward—if you deliver the reward in a haphazard way, or when the behavior in question has not occurred, learning can be slow or nonexistent (Dickinson & Charnock, 1985).

Most of the research done on the acquisition of instrumental responding has been concerned with the scheduling of reinforcements. A **schedule of reinforcement** is simply a rule used by the experimenter to determine when particular responses will be reinforced (Ferster & Skinner, 1957). If a response is followed rapidly by reinforcement every time it occurs, the reinforcement is said to be on a *continuous* schedule. If reinforcement is delivered only some of the time after the response has occurred, this is called a **partial reinforcement schedule.** There are four major types of partial reinforcement schedules: fixed-ratio, variable-ratio, fixed-interval, and variable-interval. Each produces a distinctive pattern of responding (see Figure 7.13 on page 284).

Fixed-Ratio Schedules

Ratio schedules of reinforcement require you to produce a certain *number* of responses before receiving reinforcement. In a **fixed-ratio schedule,** the number of required responses is fixed and doesn't change from one trial to the next. Suppose you are paid a dollar for every 100 envelopes you stuff for a local marketing firm. This schedule of reinforcement is referred to as an "FR 100"

conditioned reinforcer
A stimulus that has acquired reinforcing properties through prior learning.

schedule of reinforcement
A rule that an experimenter uses to determine when particular responses will be reinforced. Schedules may be fixed or variable, ratio or interval.

partial reinforcement schedule
A schedule in which reinforcement is delivered only some of the time after the response has occurred.

fixed-ratio schedule
A schedule in which the number of responses required for reinforcement is fixed and does not change from trial to trial.

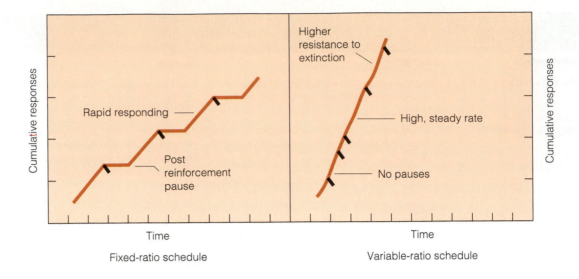

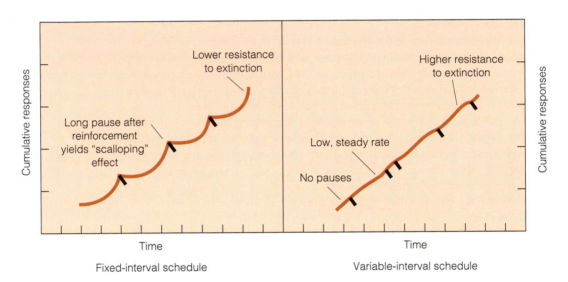

FIGURE 7.13

Schedules of Reinforcement
Schedules of reinforcement are rules that the experimenter uses to determine when responses will be reinforced. Ratio schedules tend to produce rapid rates of responding because reinforcement depends on the number of responses. Interval schedules tend to produce lower rates of responding because reinforcement is delivered only for the first response after a specified time interval. In the cumulative response functions plotted here, the total number of responses is plotted over time.

(fixed-ratio 100) because it requires 100 responses (envelopes stuffed) before the reinforcement is delivered (a dollar). You can stuff the envelopes as quickly as you like, but you must produce 100 responses before you get the reward.

Fixed-ratio schedules typically produce steady, consistent rates of responding because the relationship between the instrumental response and the reinforcement is clear and predictable. For this reason, assembly-line work in factories is often reinforced on a fixed-ratio schedule. The only behavioral quirk occurs when the number of required responses is relatively large. For example, if you have to pick 10 bushels of grapes for each monetary reward, you are likely to pause a bit in your responding immediately after the tenth bushel. This delay in responding after reinforcement is called the *postreinforcement pause*. Pausing after reinforcement is easy to understand in this situation—after all, you have to do a lot of work before you receive the next reward. But it can be an important factor to consider when choosing the most appropriate schedule for a given work environment.

If you stop delivering the reinforcement after the fixed number of responses has occurred, you can expect the individual to change his or her behavior accordingly. Eventually, the individual will simply stop responding. Similar to what happens in classical conditioning, the introduction of nonreinforcement following a period of training is called *extinction*. How quickly subjects stop responding, or extinguish their behavior, when reinforcements are no longer delivered is determined partly by the reinforcement schedule in effect. Fixed-ratio schedules typically produce rapid rates of extinction because it quickly becomes clear that something about the schedule has changed—the reinforcement no longer occurs after the required number of responses has been produced.

Variable-Ratio Schedules

A **variable-ratio schedule** also requires that a certain *number* of responses be made before a reward is given. (This is the defining feature of a ratio schedule.) However, with a variable-ratio schedule, a different number of responses may be required on each trial. Reinforcement may be delivered after the first response on trial 1, after the seventh response on trial 2, after the third response on trial 3, and so on. It's called a variable-ratio (VR) schedule because the responder never knows how many responses are needed to obtain the reward (that is, the number of responses *varies*, often in a random fashion).

Variable-ratio schedules differ from fixed-ratio schedules in that you can never predict which response will get you the reward. As a result, these schedules typically produce high rates of responding, and the postreinforcement pause, seen in fixed-ratio schedules, is usually absent (after all, the next response might get you the reward again). Gambling is an example of a variable-ratio schedule; because of chance factors, a gambler wins some bets and loses others, but the gambler never knows what to expect on a given bet.

The unpredictability of reward during a variable-ratio schedule makes it difficult to eliminate a response trained on this schedule when the response is no longer reinforced. Consider the typical compulsive slot machine player: Dollar after dollar goes into the machine; sometimes there's a payoff, more often not. Even if the machine breaks and further payments are never delivered (thus placing the responder on extinction), many gamblers would probably continue playing long into the night. On a variable-ratio schedule, it's hard to see that extinction is in effect because you've never been able to predict when reinforcement will occur.

Fixed-Interval Schedules

In an *interval* schedule of reinforcement, the reward is delivered for the first response that occurs following a certain interval of time; if a **fixed-interval schedule** (FI) is in effect, the time period remains constant from one trial to the next. Suppose we reward a pigeon with food when it pecks a lighted response key after 2 minutes have elapsed. In this case, we would be using an "FI 2 min." schedule. Note that the pigeon must still produce the response to receive the reward. (Otherwise the learning procedure would not be instrumental conditioning.) Pecking just doesn't do any good until at least 2 minutes have elapsed.

You shouldn't be surprised to learn that fixed-interval schedules typically produce low rates of responding. Because no direct association exists between how much you respond and the delivery of reinforcement—you're rewarded only when you respond after the interval has passed—it doesn't make sense to respond all the time. Another characteristic of fixed-interval schedules is that responding slows down after reinforcement and gradually increases as the end of the interval approaches. If the total number of responses is plotted over time in a cumulative response record, the net effect is a *scalloping* pattern of the type shown in Figure 7.13.

To appreciate scalloping, consider how people generally study in school. Because "reinforcement" occurs only on fixed test days, students often wait until the week (or night) before the test to start studying the material. Studying behavior increases gradually throughout the test-to-test interval and peaks on the night before the exam. (Actually, studying is not reinforced on a true fixed-interval schedule because you must take the test on a specific day; in a true fixed-interval schedule, you can respond anytime after the fixed interval has elapsed and still get reinforcement.)

variable-ratio schedule
A schedule in which a certain number of responses is required for reinforcement, but the number of required responses typically changes from trial to trial.

fixed-interval schedule
A schedule in which the reinforcement is delivered for the first response that occurs following a fixed interval of time.

CONCEPT SUMMARY
Schedules of Reinforcement

Type of Schedule	Description	Example	Effect on Behavior
Continuous	Response is followed rapidly by reinforcement every time it occurs.	Every time Duane cleans his room, his parents give him $1.	Leads to fast acquisition of response, but response is easily extinguished.
Partial	Response is followed by reinforcement only some of the time.	Sometimes, Duane gets $1 after he cleans his room.	Acquisition is slower, but learned response is more resistant to extinction.
—fixed ratio	The number of responses required for reinforcement is fixed.	Duane gets $1 every 3 times he cleans his room.	Duane cleans his room consistently with a pause in cleaning after each $1; he stops quickly if reward stops.
—variable ratio	The number of responses required for reinforcement varies.	Duane gets $1 after cleaning his room a certain number of times, but the exact number varies.	Duane cleans his room consistently with few pauses; he continues to clean his room even if the reward isn't delivered for a while.
—fixed interval	Reinforcement is delivered for the first response after a fixed interval of time.	Every Tuesday, Duane's parents give him $1 if his room is clean.	Duane doesn't do much cleaning until Tuesday is approaching; he stops quickly if reward stops.
—variable interval	Reinforcement is delivered for the first response after a variable interval of time.	On some random weekday, Duane gets $1 if his room is clean.	Duane cleans his room consistently and doesn't stop even if the reward isn't delivered for a while.

Variable-Interval Schedules

When a **variable-interval schedule (VI)** is in effect, the allotted time before a response will yield reinforcement changes from trial to trial. For example, we may deliver reinforcement for a response occurring after 2 minutes on trial 1, after 10 minutes on trial 2, after 30 seconds on trial 3, and so on. Variable-interval schedules are common in everyday life. Suppose you are trying to reach someone on the telephone, but every time you dial you hear a busy signal. To be rewarded, you know that you have to dial the number and that a certain amount of time has to elapse, but you're not sure exactly how long you need to wait.

Like variable-ratio schedules, variable-interval schedules help eliminate the pause in responding that usually occurs after reinforcement. The rate of extinction also tends to be slower in a variable-interval schedule because of the uncertainty created about when the next reinforcement will be delivered. From the responder's point of view, the next response could very well produce the desired

variable-interval schedule
A schedule in which the allotted time before a response will yield reinforcement changes from trial to trial.

Through shaping—in which reinforcements are delivered for successive approximations of a desired behavior—it is possible to produce some unusual behaviors in animals. These rabbits are shown in the early stages of training for an advertisement that featured them popping out of top hats (circa 1952).

reward, so it makes sense to continue steady responding. For responding to cease, you need to recognize that the relationship between responding and reinforcement has changed.

There are many different types of reinforcement schedules. The four partial schedules we have considered here are representative and demonstrate the remarkable consistency in behavior that scheduled reinforcements can produce. Moreover, as Skinner (1956) has argued, these principled behaviors are universal—the postreinforcement pause, for example, occurs regardless of the specific response, the nature of the reinforcement, or the species receiving the training. Reward, and the pattern with which it is delivered, exerts a powerful influence on everyday actions.

? CRITICAL THINKING

Do you think fishing is reinforced on a variable-interval schedule of reinforcement or a variable-ratio schedule? How might the answer depend on the skill of the person doing the fishing?

ACQUISITION: SHAPING THE DESIRED BEHAVIOR

In principle, you should be able to gain control over any behavior, such as getting your dog to sit or shake hands, by reinforcing the appropriate response according to a specified schedule. For example, if you use a variable-ratio schedule to train your dog to sit, and you use food as a reward, then your dog should continue to sit on command even when food is not available as a reward. In this case, the dog knows that sitting is reinforced only some of the time, so failure to receive a reward doesn't necessarily weaken the response.

In practice, however, it can be difficult to train a behavior if the behavior is not likely to occur initially. How do you reward your dog for sitting if the dog never sits on command in the first place? Most people train a dog by yelling "Sit," pushing the dog's bottom down, and stuffing a food reward in its mouth. Under these conditions, however, they are not really establishing the proper instrumental relationship between the dog's own behavior and the delivery of a reward. They have actually set up a kind of classical conditioning procedure—the dog is taught that having his bottom pushed downward is a *signal* for an inviting (food) unconditioned stimulus. This might work, but it does not teach the animal that its own behavior is instrumental in producing the outcome. What you want your dog to learn is that the word *sit* is a discriminative stimulus that signals that a behavior (sitting) is instrumental in producing some kind of reward.

To solve this problem, Skinner (1938) developed a procedure called **shaping**, in which reinforcement is delivered for successive *approximations* to the desired response. Instead of waiting for the complete response—here, sitting to the command "Sit"—to occur, you reinforce some part of the response that is likely to occur initially. For instance, you might reward your dog for simply approaching you when you say, "Sit." As each part of the response is acquired, you become more strict in your criteria for what constitutes a successful response sequence. Skinner and others have shown that incredibly complex sequences of behavior can be acquired using the successive-approximation technique of shaping.

Practical Applications

Not surprisingly, shaping also works quite well as a technique for modifying behavior in people. (In Chapter 15, you'll see how shaping can be applied in therapy to modify maladaptive thoughts, lessen fears, and help individuals handle stressful situations.) Disturbed children who can't communicate have been taught to speak by reinforcing verbal sequences with candy or cereal. Whereas the child might be reinforced initially for any kind of verbal utterance, gradually the reward is withheld until the child produces a more natural flow of sounds.

The same kind of training can be used with adult patients who are suffering from severe psychological disorders. Patients with serious mental problems sometimes lack normal living skills—for example, they might lose the ability to clean or bathe themselves properly or communicate effectively with others. Social skills can be trained, through shaping, leading to a significant improvement in the quality of the patient's life (e.g., Benton & Schroeder, 1990; Wong et al., 1993).

shaping
A procedure in which reinforcement is delivered for successive approximations of the desired response.

Inside the Problem   Superstitious Behavior

Have you ever noticed the odd behavior of a professional baseball player as he approaches the batter's box? He kicks the dirt (a fixed number of times), adjusts his helmet, hitches up his trousers, grimaces, swings toward the pitcher a few times, and adopts a characteristic crouch. Basketball players, as they prepare to make a free throw, endlessly caress the ball with their hands, bounce it a certain number of times, crouch, pause, and release. Such regular patterns are a player's signature—you can identify who's in the batter's box or up at the line by watching these ritualistic preparation patterns.

Let's analyze these behaviors from the perspective of instrumental conditioning. According to the law of effect, these odd patterns of behavior must have been reinforced—they occurred, perhaps by chance, and were followed by a reward (a hit or a successful free throw). But because the pairing of the behavior with its consequence was really accidental, psychologists refer to this kind of reinforcement as *accidental* or *adventitious reinforcement*. In the player's mind, however, a cause-and-effect link has been formed, and he acts in a similar fashion again. Once the player starts to perform the behavior on a regular basis, it's likely that the behavior will continue to be accidentally reinforced, although on a partial schedule of reinforcement. (Can you identify the particular schedule?) The result is called a superstitious act, and because of the partial sched-

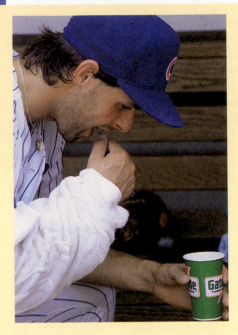

Many athletes perform odd rituals on a regular basis. This professional baseball player feels the need to brush his teeth vigorously before every time up at the plate. A learning theorist might argue that the player's bizarre behavior was somehow accidentally reinforced in the past, forming a superstitious cause-and-effect link between teeth brushing and successful performance.

ule (a variable-ratio one), it is difficult to eliminate.

In 1948, B. F. Skinner developed an experimental procedure to mimic and gain control over the development of superstitious acts. He placed hungry pigeons in a chamber and delivered bits of food every 15 seconds, irrespective of what the bird happened to be doing at the time. In his own words: "In six out of eight cases the resulting responses were so clearly defined that two observers could agree perfectly in counting instances. One bird was conditioned to turn counterclockwise about the cage, making two or three turns between reinforcements. Another repeatedly thrust its head into one of the upper corners of the cage. A third developed a "tossing" response, as if placing its head beneath an invisible bar and lifting it repeatedly" (Skinner, 1948, p. 168).

Remember, from the experimenter's point of view, no cause-and-effect relationship existed between these quirky behaviors and the delivery of food. Researchers since Skinner have replicated his results, but with some added caveats (Staddon & Simmelhag, 1971). For example, many of the behaviors that Skinner noted are characteristic responses that birds make in preparation for food; therefore, some of the strange behaviors Skinner observed might have been natural pigeon reactions to the expectation of being fed rather than learned responses. Nevertheless, the point Skinner made is important to remember: From the responder's point of view, illusory connections can form between behaviors and outcomes. Once these connections have been made, if the behaviors recur, they might continue to be accidentally reinforced and thus serve as the basis for the familiar forms of superstitious acts.

Shaping also has enormous applications for teaching, both inside and outside of the classroom. B. F. Skinner and others long advocated for the use of shaping as a technique for learning. Mastery of subject matter can be broken down into small steps accompanied by lots of positive reinforcement. Many computer programs used in schools and at home follow the shaping format—start small and gradually increase the requirements for reward. Shaping is also a great technique for sports activities. To teach someone an effective golf swing, it's best to begin by rewarding simple contact between the club and the ball. Later, the teacher can fine-tune the person's swing by offering praise only when the mechanics of the swing are more technically correct. See the accompanying "Inside the Problem" feature.

BIOLOGICAL CONSTRAINTS ON LEARNING

Is it really possible to teach any response, in any situation, provided that you have enough time and an effective reinforcer? Probably not. Many psychologists believe that there are biological constraints, perhaps based on the genetic code, that limit the responses that can be taught. Thorndike, in his early studies of cats in puzzle boxes, noted that it was basically impossible to increase the probability of yawning or of certain reflexive scratching responses in cats through the application of reinforcement.

Similar observations were reported later by animal trainers Keller and Marion Breland (1961). The Brelands, who were former students of B. F. Skinner, encountered some interesting difficulties while attempting to train a variety of species to make certain responses. In one case, they tried to train a pig to drop large wooden coins into a piggy bank (for a bank commercial). They followed the shaping procedure, where successive approximations of the desired sequence are reinforced, but they could not get the pig to complete the response. The animal would pick up the coin and begin to lumber toward the bank but would stop midway and begin "rooting" the coins along the ground. Despite their using punishment and nonreinforcement of the rooting response, the Brelands could never completely eliminate the response. They encountered similar problems trying to teach a raccoon to put coins in a bank.

> We started out by reinforcing him for picking up a single coin. Then the metal container was introduced, with the requirement that he drop the coin into the container. Here we ran into the first bit of difficulty: he seemed to have a great deal of trouble letting go of the coin. He would rub it against the inside of the container, pull it back out, and clutch it firmly for several seconds. However, he would finally turn it loose and receive his food reinforcement. Then the final contingency: we [required] that he pick up [two] coins and put them in the container.
>
> Now the raccoon really had problems (and so did we). Not only could he not let go of the coins, but he spent seconds, even minutes, rubbing them together (in a most miserly fashion) and dipping them into the container. He carried on this behavior to such an extent that the practical application that we had in mind—a display featuring a raccoon putting money into a piggy bank—simply was not feasible. The rubbing behavior became worse and worse as time went on, in spite of nonreinforcement. (Breland & Breland, 1961, p. 682)

In the cases of the pig and the raccoon, biological tendencies connected with feeding and food reinforcement interfered with the learning of certain response sequences. Pigs root in connection with feeding, and raccoons rub and dunk objects related to food (Domjan, 1998). These natural tendencies are adaptive responses for the animals—at least with respect to feeding—but they limit what the animals can be taught. Learning psychologists must always remember that behavior is a joint product of biology (nature) and experience (nurture), and both must be taken in account in a full description or account of learning.

PUNISHMENT: LOWERING THE LIKELIHOOD OF A RESPONSE

Up to now, we have considered how the chances of a response increase, in the presence of a discriminative stimulus, when the response leads to reinforcement. If your behavior is instrumental in producing an appetitive event (positive reinforcement) or in removing something unpleasant (negative reinforcement), you're likely to behave in a similar fashion in the future. But the law of effect has another side: Thorndike claimed that if a response is followed by an unsatisfying or unpleasant consequence, it will be weakened. The term **punishment** is used to refer to consequences that decrease the likelihood of responding. Like reinforcement, punishment comes in two forms: *positive* and *negative*.

Positive Punishment

When a response leads to the *presentation* of an event that lowers the likelihood of that response occurring again, this is **positive punishment**. Notice, as with reinforcement, the concept is defined in terms of its effect on behavior—lowering the likelihood of responding—rather than on its subjective qualities. Usually,

punishment
Consequences that decrease the likelihood of responding in a similar way again.

positive punishment
An event that, when *presented* after a response, lowers the likelihood of that response occurring again.

CONCEPT SUMMARY
Comparing Punishment and Reinforcement

Punishment—Consequences that *Decrease* the Likelihood of Responding

Outcome	Description	Example
Positive punishment	Response leads to the presentation of an event that decreases the likelihood of that response occurring again.	Little 5-year-old Skip nearly runs into the street; his mother pulls him back from the curb and gives him a brief tongue-lashing. This decreases the likelihood that Skip will run into the street.
Negative punishment	Response leads to the removal of an event that decreases the likelihood of that response occurring again.	Little 5-year-old Skip keeps teasing his 3-year-old sister at the dinner table. His mom sends him to bed without his favorite dessert. Withholding the dessert decreases the likelihood that Skip will tease his sister at the dinner table.

Reinforcement—Consequences that *Increase* the Likelihood of Responding

Outcome	Description	Example
Positive reinforcement	Response leads to the presentation of an event that increases the likelihood of that response occurring again.	Little 5-year-old Skip helps his mom do the dishes. Mom takes him to the store and lets him pick out any candy bar he wants. Letting Skip pick out a candy bar increases the likelihood that he'll help with the dishes.
Negative reinforcement	Response leads to the removal of an event that increases the likelihood of that response occurring again.	Little 5-year-old Skip has been such a good helper all week that his mom tells him that next week, he doesn't have to do any of his scheduled chores. Relieving Skip of his scheduled chores increases the likelihood that he'll be a good helper.

however, positive punishment occurs when a response leads directly to the presentation of an *aversive* outcome. As a parent, if your child hassles the cat with her new toy, you could scold the child loudly whenever she engages in the behavior—this qualifies as positive punishment. Provided the aversive event—the scolding—is intense enough, the instrumental response that produced the punishment—hassling the cat—will tend to disappear rapidly or become *suppressed*.

Negative Punishment

When the *removal* of an event after responding lowers the likelihood of that response occurring again, **negative punishment** has occurred. For example, if a response leads to the removal of a positive outcome, you are unlikely to respond in that way again. Instead of scolding your child for hassling the cat, you could simply take her toy away. You are removing something she likes when she engages in an inappropriate behavior—this qualifies as negative punishment. Similarly, if you withhold your child's weekly allowance because his or her room is messy, you are punishing the child by removing something good—money. As with positive punishment, negative punishment is recognized as an effective training procedure for rapidly suppressing an undesirable response.

What accounts for the rapid suppression of the response that is punished? It seems likely that people simply learn the associative relationship between their behavior and the particular outcome. You learn about the consequences of your actions—that a particular kind of behavior will lead to a relatively unpleasant consequence. In this sense, we don't really need two different explanations to account for the behavior changes produced by reinforcement and punishment; the only major difference is that behavior increases in one situation and declines in the other. In both cases, people simply use their knowledge about a behavior and its consequences to maximize gain and minimize loss in a particular situation.

Practical Considerations

In principle, punishment is a quite effective technique for suppressing an undesirable behavior. However, difficulties often arise in everyday practice. For example, it can be hard to gauge the appropriate strength of the punishing event. When the

negative punishment
An event that, when *removed* after a response, lowers the likelihood of that response occurring again.

punishment is aggressive or violent, such as the forceful spanking of a child, you run the risk of hurting the child either physically or emotionally. At the same time, if a child feels ignored, yelling at him or her can actually be reinforcing because of the attention it provides. Children who spend a lot of time in the principal's office may be causing trouble partly because of the attention that the punishment produces. In cases such as this, punishment leads to the exact opposite of the intended result.

You also need to recognize that punishment only *suppresses* a behavior; it does not teach someone how to act appropriately. For instance, spanking your child for lying might reduce the lying behavior, but it will not teach the child how to deal more effectively with the social situation that led to the initial lie. To teach the child about more appropriate forms of behavior, you would need to reinforce some kind of alternative response. You must teach the child a positive strategy for dealing with situations that can lead to lying. That's the main advantage of reinforcement over punishment: Reinforcement teaches you what you should be doing—how you should act—whereas punishment only teaches you what you shouldn't be doing.

Punishment can also produce undesirable side effects, most notably anger, resentment, and aggression. Studies with animals in the laboratory have shown that aggressive behavior is often a consequence of punishment procedures. Animals that are shocked together in the same experimental context will often attack one another throughout the shock duration (Domjan, 1998). Parents who punish their children regularly, without alternative reinforcement, invite future resentment and a loss in the quality of the relationship with their child. Few psychologists deny that punishment can be an effective means for stopping a behavior, and it may even be a desirable consequence in some circumstances (e.g., running into the street or sticking a fork into an electrical outlet). But punishment, by itself, is rarely a sufficient technique—it needs to be supplemented with alternative strategies for behaving which provide the opportunity for a little tender loving care (positive reinforcement).

TEST YOURSELF 7.3

Check your knowledge about instrumental conditioning by answering the following questions. (You will find the answers in the Appendix.)

1. For each of the following statements, decide which term best applies: negative punishment, positive punishment, negative reinforcement, positive reinforcement.

   a. Stephanie is grounded for arriving home well past her curfew:
   _____

   b. Greg receives a bonus of $500 for exceeding his sales goal for the year:
   _____

   c. Nikki gets a ticket, at double the normal rate, for exceeding the posted speed limit in a school zone: _____

   d. Little Mowrer cries all the time when her Mom is home because Mom always comforts her with a kiss and a story: _____

   e. With Dad, Mowrer is a perfect angel because crying can be followed by a stern lecture that lasts for an hour or more: _____

2. Identify the schedule of reinforcement that is at work in each of the following situations. Choose from the following: fixed-interval, fixed-ratio, variable-interval, variable-ratio.

   a. Rowena feels intense satisfaction after she calls the psychic hotline, but only when a psychic named Darlene reads her future: _____

   b. Prana likes to visit the Monster Truck rally because they always have good corn dogs: _____

c. Sinead constantly watches music television because her favorite show "Puck Live" comes on from time-to-time at odd hours: _____

d. Mohamed has just joined a coffee club—he gets a free pound of gourmet coffee after the tenth pound that he buys: _____

e. Charlie hangs around street corners for hours at a time. Occasionally, a pretty woman walks by and gives him a smile: _____

Learning from Others: Observational Learning

The world would be a very unpleasant place if you could only learn about the consequences of your behavior through simple trial and error. You could learn to avoid certain foods through positive punishment, but only after eating them and experiencing an unpleasant consequence. Through escape and avoidance conditioning, children might learn not to play in the street, provided they leap away from the oncoming traffic in time. You could learn to avoid illegal drugs, but only if you have a bad experience, such as an arrest or a risky overdose. Clearly, it's sometimes best not to undergo the experiences that lead to learning.

In the wild, rhesus monkeys show an adaptive fear response in the presence of snakes. Because snakes are natural predators of monkeys, it makes sense for monkeys to avoid them whenever possible. But how do you suppose that fear is originally acquired? According to a strict interpretation of the law of effect, the animal must learn its fear through some kind of direct reinforcement or punishment—that is, through trial and error. This means that a monkey would probably need to approach a snake and be bitten (or nearly bitten) before it could learn to fear the snake; unfortunately, this single learning experience is likely be fatal much of the time. This suggests that trial- and-error learning is not always adaptive, especially when you're learning about something dangerous or potentially harmful.

Fortunately, it turns out that it's possible to learn a great deal without trial and error—by simply observing the experiences of *others*. People and animals can learn by example, and this kind of learning, called **observational learning** or **social learning,** has considerable adaptive value. In the wild, newly weaned rats acquire food habits by eating what the older rats eat (Galef, 1985); red-winged blackbirds will refuse to eat a certain food if they have observed another bird getting sick after it has eaten the food (Mason & Reidinger, 1982); chimpanzees in the wild learn how to use stone tools to crack open nuts by observing older chimpanzees eating (Inoue-Nokamura & Matsuzawa, 1997). Rhesus monkeys, it turns out, acquire their fear of snakes partly through social learning rather than through direct experience (Mineka, 1987). They watch other monkeys in their environment showing fear in the presence of a snake and thereby acquire the tendency to show fear themselves. It's also possible to learn by observing the mistakes of others—if one bird watches another bird consistently choosing an incorrect response for food, the bird doing the observing is more likely not to make the same mistake (Templeton, 1998).

MODELING: LEARNING THROUGH EXAMPLE

What conditions produce effective observational learning? One important factor is the presence of a significant role model. People naturally tend to imitate, or **model,** the behavior of significant others, as do most members of the animal kingdom. You probably learned a lot of things by watching your parents or your teachers—even though you may never have been aware of actually doing so. Research has shown that observational learning is particularly effective if the model has positive characteristics, such as attractiveness, honesty, perceived competence, and some kind of social standing (Bandura, 1986; Brewer & Wann, 1998). It's also more likely if you observe the model being rewarded for a particular action, or if the model's behavior is particularly successful.

In one classic study, Bandura and his colleagues showed nursery-school children a film that portrayed an adult striking, punching, and kicking a large, inflatable, upright "Bobo" doll. Afterward, when placed in a room with Bobo, many of these children imitated the adult and violently attacked the doll (Bandura et al., 1963). In addition, the chances of the children kicking the doll increased if the adult was directly praised in the film for attacking Bobo ("You're the champion"). Bandura (1986) has claimed that the responses acquired through observational learning are especially strengthened through *vicarious reinforcement*, which occurs when the model is reinforced for an action, or weakened through *vicarious punishment*, in which the model is punished for an action. A clear parallel therefore exists between the law of effect and observational learning; the difference, of course, is that the behavior of others is being reinforced or punished rather than one's own.

Albert Bandura did much of the early pioneering work on observational learning (you'll find more discussion of his work in Chapter 12). Bandura believes that much of what we learn from an experience depends on our existing beliefs and expectations. You are unlikely to learn much from a model, for example, if you believe that you are incapable of ever performing the model's behavior. You can watch a great pianist, or singer, or athlete, but you're not likely to imitate his or her behavior if you feel that you're incapable of performing the task. Our beliefs about our own abilities—which Bandura refers to as "self-efficacy"—significantly shape and constrain what we gain from observational learning.

We naturally tend to imitate, or model, the behavior of significant others. Modeling is adaptive because it allows us to learn things without always directly experiencing consequences.

PRACTICAL CONSIDERATIONS

It's easy to see how the techniques of observational learning might be used to improve or change unwanted behaviors. Many studies have shown that observation of a model performing some desirable behavior can lower unwanted or maladaptive behavior. Children have been able to reduce their fear of dental visits (Craig, 1978) or impending surgery (Melamed & Siegel, 1975) by observing films of other children effectively handling their dental or surgical anxieties. Clinical psychologists now use observational learning as a technique to deal with specific fears and as a method for promoting cooperative behavior among preschoolers (Granvold, 1994).

At the same time, it's just as important to recognize that observational or social learning can lead to undesirable effects. For example, it's been estimated that children now witness thousands of reinforced acts of violence just by watching Saturday morning cartoons. Although the causal connection between TV violence and personal aggression has not been firmly established (Freedman, 1988), the consensus among psychologists clearly supports a link (Hearold, 1986). In addition, it can be difficult for a society to overcome unproductive stereotypes if they are repeatedly portrayed through the behavior of others. Many gender-related stereotypes, such as submissive or helpless behavior in females, continue to be

Observational learning has powerful consequences that are not always what we intend. Children model the behavior of significant role models, even when the model acts in a way that lacks adaptive value.

? CRITICAL THINKING

Given what you've learned about modeling, do you now favor the passage of laws that will control the amount of violence shown on television? Why or why not?

represented in TV programs and movies. By the age of 6 or 7, children have already begun to shy away from activities that are identified with members of the opposite sex. Although it's unlikely that television is entirely responsible for this trend, it's widely believed that television plays an important role (Ruble et al., 1981).

Even if people don't directly imitate or model a particular violent act, it's still likely that the observation itself influences the way they think. For instance, witnessing repeated examples of fictional violence distorts people's estimates of realistic violence—they are likely to believe, for example, that more people die a violent death than is actually the case. This can lead individuals to show irrational fear and to avoid situations that are in all likelihood safe. People who watch a lot of television tend to view the world in a fashion that mirrors what they see on the screen. They tend to think, for example, that a large proportion of the population are professionals (such as doctors or lawyers) and that few people in society are actually old (Gerbner & Gross, 1976). It's not just the imitation of particular acts we need to worry about: Television and other vehicles of observational learning can literally change or determine our everyday view of the world (Bandura, 1986).

TEST YOURSELF 7.4

Check your knowledge about observational learning by deciding whether each of the following statements is true or false. (You will find the answers in the Appendix.)

1. Observational learning, like classical conditioning, typically involves learning about events that occur outside of your control. *True or False*?

2. People are more likely to imitate the behavior of a role model if the model is observed being rewarded for his or her behavior. Bandura refers to this reward process as vicarious reinforcement. *True or False*?

3. Observational learning is usually a passive process. Our beliefs and expectations about how well we can perform the model's behavior play little or no role. *True or False*?

4. Most psychologists believe that television is a powerful vehicle for observational learning. *True or False*?

5. Clinical psychologists now use observational learning to treat specific fears, such as phobias. *True or False*?

Solving the Problems

As organisms struggle to survive in their environments, their capacity to learn—that is, to change their behavior as a result of experience—represents one of their greatest strengths. Psychologists have long recognized the need for understanding how behavior changes with experience; historically, research on learning predates research on virtually all other topics, with the possible exception of basic sensory and perceptual processes.

Even today, the study of learning in one form or another is the cornerstone for much of psychology. In attempting to understand and treat mental disorders, clinical psychologists often seek their answers in an individual's prior experiences. To understand the dynamics of group behavior, social psychologists appeal increasingly to the effects of prior experience. Cognitive psychologists, as you'll see in the next two chapters, consider experience to be perhaps the most important determinant of the content and structure of thought and other mental processes. Indeed, it is difficult to find an area of psychology that does not consider learning to be fundamental to its enterprise.

In this chapter, we've concentrated on relatively basic learning processes. To meet the needs of changing environments, all organisms must solve certain types of learning problems, and the principles of behavior that you've learned about apply generally across animal species.

Learning about Events. Everyone—people and animals—needs to *recognize* new events when they occur. Novel, or unusual, events lead to an orienting response, which helps ensure that we'll react quickly to sudden changes in our environment. The sound of screeching automobile brakes leads to an immediate reaction; you don't have to stop and think about it. At the same time, no one can attend to all the stimuli that surround us, so you must learn to ignore events that are of little adaptive significance. Through the process of habituation, characterized by the decline in the tendency to respond to an event that has become familiar, you become selective about responding to events that occur repeatedly in your environment.

Learning What Events Signal. We also need to learn about what events *signal*—it's helpful to know, for example, that green traffic lights mean you can move your car forward freely and that red lights mean you should stop. Signals, or conditioned stimuli, are established through classical conditioning. Events that provide information about the occurrence or nonoccurrence of other significant events become conditioned stimuli. A conditioned stimulus elicits a conditioned response, which is a response appropriate for anticipating the event that will follow.

Learning about the Consequences of Behavior. It's also important to learn about the *consequences* of our actions. People need to learn that when they act a certain way, their behaviors produce outcomes that are sometimes pleasing and sometimes not. In instrumental conditioning, the presentation and removal of events after responding can either increase or decrease the likelihood of responding in a similar way again. When a response is followed by reinforcement, either positive or negative, the tendency to respond in that way again is strengthened. When a response is followed by punishment, either positive or negative, you are less likely to behave that way again. It's also important to consider the schedule of reinforcement. Schedules affect not only how rapidly you will learn and respond, but also the pattern of responding and how likely you are to change your behavior if the reinforcement stops.

Learning from Others. Through observational or social learning, we imitate and model the actions of others, thereby learning from example rather than from direct experience. We study how other people behave and how their behavior is reinforced or punished, and we change our own behavior accordingly. Observational learning can have a number of effects, both positive and negative, on the individual and on society.

Learning from Experience Chapter Summary

Learning is a relatively permanent *change in behavior*, or in *potential to respond*, that results from experience. Common principles of learning can be applied widely across situations and species; much of what we know comes from animal research.

Learning about Events: Noticing and Ignoring

Because the nervous system has limited resources we cannot attend to every stimulus in the environment. Basic psychological processes help us prioritize our mental functioning.

HABITUATION AND SENSITIZATION

Habituation occurs when one slows or stops responding to an event that has become familiar through repeated responding. *Sensitization* occurs when responsivness to an event *increases* with repeated exposure. These are both general learning phenomena found throughout the animal kingdom.

SHORT- AND LONG-TERM EFFECTS

Researchers have focused on habituation, rather than sensitization, and have established that habituation can have either short-term or long-term effects. *Short-term habituation* refers to instances when the loss in responsiveness is short-lived. In *long-term habituation,* the loss in responsiveness lasts for an extended period.

Learning What Events Signal: Classical Conditioning

It's important to learn about the signaling properties of stimuli, or events in the environment. We need to learn that one event predicts that a second event is likely to follow. It may not be possible to do anything about the co-occurrence of the events, but we can respond accordingly.

THE TERMINOLOGY OF CLASSICAL CONDITIONING

Unconditioned stimuli are stimuli that lead to automatic responses termed *unconditioned responses.* After repeated pairing with an unconditioned stimulus, a *conditioned stimulus* can come to elicit a *conditioned response.* An association between the CS and US has been acquired.

CONDITIONED RESPONDING: WHY DOES IT DEVELOP?

The conditioned stimulus does not simply serve as a "substitute" for the unconditioned stimulus. Sometimes the CS and US lead to different responses. The CR depends on the US and also on the properties of the CS. In some cases, a CR may appear that is opposite to the unconditioned response. The CR will generally be a response that is appropriate for the arrival of the US.

STIMULUS GENERALIZATION

Stimulus generalization occurs when a new stimulus produces a response similar to the one produced by the conditioned stimulus.

EXTINCTION

If the conditioned stimulus is presented repeatedly, and is no longer followed by the unconditioned stimulus, the conditioned stimulus loses its signaling properties and conditioned responding diminishes.

ACQUIRING THE CS–US CONNECTION

For an effective association to be formed, the CS must be presented *before* the US, the US must follow the CS *closely* in time, the CS needs to *uniquely predict* the US, and needs to provide *new* information about the US.

SECOND-ORDER CONDITIONING

An established conditioned stimulus (e.g., a tone that predicts food) is presented immediately following a new event, such as a light; the unconditioned stimulus itself is never presented. In this case, the pairing of the tone and the light can produce conditioned responding to the light.

STIMULUS DISCRIMINATION

Stimulus discrimination occurs when one responds to a new stimulus in a way that is different from the response to the original stimulus.

CONDITIONED INHIBITION: SIGNALING THE ABSENCE OF THE US

Conditioned inhibition occurs when one learns that an event signals the *absence* of the unconditioned stimulus. This new event is presented under conditions where the unconditioned stimulus is normally expected, but not delivered.

Learning about the Consequences of Behavior: Instrumental Conditioning

All species need to learn that when they behave in a certain way, the behavior has consequences. Behaviors play an important role in producing rewards and punishments, so it's clearly adaptive for us to learn when and how to act.

THE LAW OF EFFECT

In his experiments, Thorndike found that if a response is followed by a satisfying consequence, it will be strengthened; if a response is followed by an unsatisfying consequence, it will be weakened. This is the *law of effect*.

THE NATURE OF REINFORCEMENT

When the presentation of an event after a response increases the likelihood of the response occurring again, *positive reinforcement* has occurred. When the removal of an event after a response increases the likelihood of the response occurring again, *negative reinforcement* has occurred. *Escape conditioning* and *avoidance conditioning* are two of the learning procedures used to study negative reinforcement. *Conditioned reinforcers* are stimuli that acquire reinforcing properties through learning (e.g., money).

ACQUISITION: SHAPING THE DESIRED BEHAVIOR

Training a behavior can be accomplished through *shaping*, which refers to reinforcing *successive approximations* to the desired behavior.

PUNISHMENT: LOWERING THE LIKELIHOOD OF A RESPONSE

Punishment refers to consequences that decrease the likelihood of responding. *Positive punishment* occurs when the presentation of an event decreases responding. *Negative punishment* occurs when the removal of an event decreases responding.

THE DISCRIMINATIVE STIMULUS: KNOWING WHEN TO RESPOND

The law of effect applies only to responses that are rewarded *in particular situations*. The situation is termed the *discriminative stimulus*.

SCHEDULES OF REINFORCEMENT

A *schedule of reinforcement* is a rule used to determine when responses will be reinforced. In a *continuous schedule*, every response is followed by reinforcement; in a *partial schedule*, reinforcement is delivered only after some responses. Partial schedules include *fixed ratio*, *variable ratio*, *fixed interval*, and *variable interval*.

BIOLOGICAL CONSTRAINTS ON LEARNING

Many psychologists believe that there are biological constraints, perhaps in the genetic code, that limit the responses that can be taught.

Learning from Others

Often, our most important teachers are the actions of others; people, as well as most of the animal kingdom, learn by example. Learning through observation of others has considerable adaptive significance.

MODELING: LEARNING THROUGH EXAMPLE

People naturally tend to model the behavior of significant others. Observational learning is especially likely if the model has positive characteristics, or is observed being rewarded.

PRACTICAL CONSIDERATIONS

Observational learning (like punishment), can lead to undesirable effects, as in the case of children modeling the violence they see on TV.

Terms to Remember

learning, 260

LEARNING ABOUT EVENTS

orienting response, 263
habituation, 263
sensitization, 264

LEARNING WHAT EVENTS SIGNAL

classical conditioning, 266
unconditioned stimulus (US), 266
unconditioned response (UR), 266
conditioned response (CR), 266
conditioned stimulus (CS), 266
second-order conditioning, 272
stimulus generalization, 273
stimulus discrimination, 274
extinction, 275
spontaneous recovery, 276
conditioned inhibition, 276

LEARNING ABOUT THE CONSEQUENCES OF BEHAVIOR

instrumental conditioning, 278
operant conditioning, 278
law of effect, 280
discriminative stimulus, 280
reinforcement, 281
positive reinforcement, 281
negative reinforcement, 281
escape conditioning, 282
avoidance conditioning, 282
conditioned reinforcer, 283
schedule of reinforcement, 283
partial reinforcement schedule, 283
fixed-ratio schedule, 283
variable-ratio schedule, 285
fixed-interval schedule, 285
variable-interval schedule, 286
shaping, 287
punishment, 289
positive punishment, 289
negative punishment, 290

LEARNING FROM OTHERS

observational learning, 292
social learning, 292
modeling, 292

Recommended Readings

Domjan, M. (1998). *The principles of learning and behavior* (4th ed.). Pacific Grove, CA: Brooks/Cole. A leading undergraduate textbook on learning. The material discussed in Chapter 7 is covered here in much more detail.

Mackintosh, N. J. (1974). *The psychology of animal learning.* London: Academic Press. A classic. This is the bible for anyone interested in the history and theoretical development of basic learning research. It's a professional-level text, but very interesting and easy to read. Believe me, it's worth a look if you're interested in learning in animals.

Skinner, B. F. (1948). *Walden Two.* New York: Macmillan. This is behaviorist B. F. Skinner's famous work of fiction describing how the principles of behavior modification might be used to create a utopian society. Interesting and controversial.

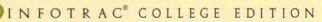

INFOTRAC® COLLEGE EDITION

For additional readings, explore Infotrac College Edition, your online library. Go to:
http://www.infotrac-college.com/wadsworth

Hint: enter the search terms: Habituation, Classical conditioning, Schedule of reinforcement, Consequences of punishment, Observational learning.

🌐 What's on the Web?

Animal Training at Sea World

(www.seaworld.org/animal_training/atcontents.html)

After reading this chapter, you no doubt are aware that the basic principles of learning are instrumental (pun intended) in training animals to do the fantastic tricks they do at parks like Sea World. This Web site provides you with an overview of basic learning principles, presented within the context of the training they do at Sea World. It's a very interesting explanation of basic learning principles in an applied context.

B. F. Skinner Foundation

(www.lafayette.edu/allanr/skinner.html)

This Web site is devoted to the legendary learning researcher. It provides a wealth of information about B.F. Skinner and his legacy, as well as a biography—penned by Skinner himself.

Dr. P's Dog Training

(www.uwsp.edu/acad/psych/dog/dog/htm)

Like the Sea World site described above, this site allows you to see the principles of learning applied to animal training. Learn how teach an old dog new tricks with a visit to this site. It provides a wealth of information about dog training, including selections on assistance dogs, martial arts for dogs, and dog-sledding.

The Wadsworth Psychology Study Center Web Site

See http://psychology.wadsworth.com/ for practice quiz questions, hypercontents, updates, critical thinking exercises, discussion forums and more! The Wadsworth Psychology Study Center provides a wealth of information fully organized and integrated by chapter.

8 Remembering and Forgetting

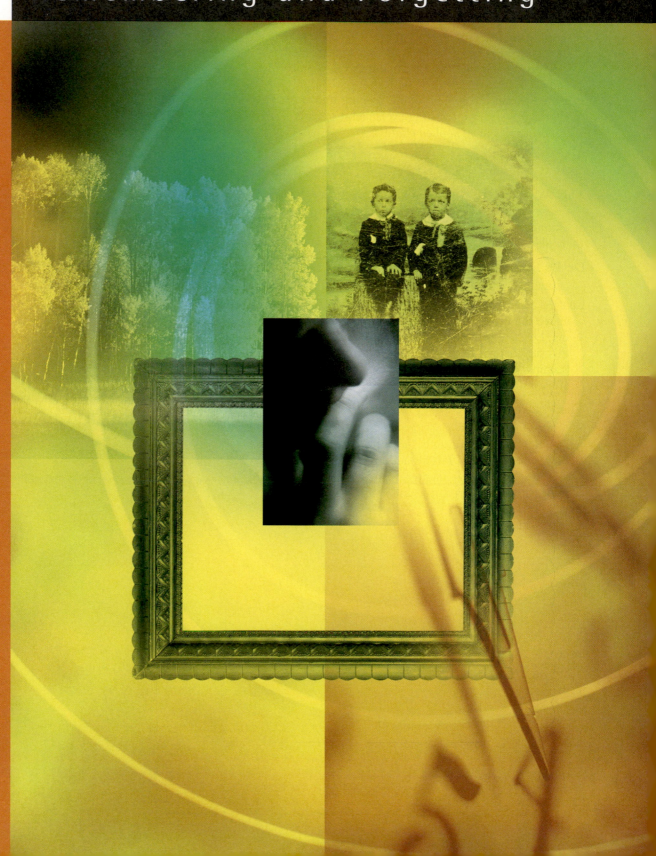

W hat if the flow of time suddenly fractured and you were forced to relive the same 10 minutes, over and over again, in an endless cycle? You might be driving your car, or reading a book; it wouldn't matter—at the end of the interval you'd begin again, back at the same fork in the road, or the same location on the page. Think about how this might affect you. You wouldn't age, but would you be able to endure?

The answer, I suspect, depends on your capacity to remember and forget. If you've seen the movie *Groundhog Day*, you'll remember that Bill Murray's character was caught in a kind of time warp—he was forced to relive the same day over and over. To make matters worse, he was fully aware of his condition. Like Murray, if your memories remained intact from one cycle to the next, if you were aware of the endless repetition, life would quickly become unbearable. But, if your memories were erased before each new 10-minute interval, you'd lack awareness of your hopeless plight; your life, albeit in an abbreviated form, would continue as usual. It is through **memory**—broadly defined as the capacity to preserve and recover information—that concepts like the past and the present gain meaning in our lives.

Researchers have discovered that certain brain injuries, or neurological disorders, actually mimic some of the conditions just described. Individuals suffering from *anterograde amnesia* appear normal at first sight—their social skills and language abilities are intact—but they are forever locked in the past. They recognize no one new, not even the professionals who have been treating them for extended periods. They can't remember what they ate for breakfast or the year in which they are living. Each morning begins like the previous one, devoid of any sense of recent personal history. They read the same magazines; they experience the same grief over the death of a loved one (Ogden & Corkin, 1991).

However, even these amnesics preserve some components of memory functioning. They retain the ability to communicate, which requires remembering the meaning of words and the rules for how to string words together. They still have a basic understanding of the world and the objects in it. They even remember personal experiences, as long as those experiences happened before the point of serious brain dysfunction. A world truly without memory would be devoid of thought and reason. You would never learn; you would never be able to produce spoken language or understand the words of others; your sense of personal history would be lost, and thereby much or all of your personal identity.

memory
The capacity to preserve and recover information.

encoding
The processes that determine and control the acquisition of memories.

storage
The processes that determine and control how memories are stored and maintained over time.

retrieval
The processes that determine and control how memories are recovered and translated into performance.

Previewing the Adaptive Problems

L ike learning, memory is not something that can be directly observed. It is an *inferred* capacity, one that psychologists assume must be operating in situations where people act on the basis of information that is no longer physically present. To understand how memory works, we need to consider how memories are formed (**encoding**), how memories are maintained once they are encoded (**storage**), and how the stored information is recovered and translated into performance (**retrieval**). Each of these psychological processes is depicted visually in Figure 8.1; we'll examine them in more detail as we work through some adaptive problems that memory systems help solve.

First, we need some kind of internal machinery for remembering information over the short term. Consider the interpretation of spoken language. Because speech unfolds one word at a time, it is necessary to remember the early part of a sentence, after it has

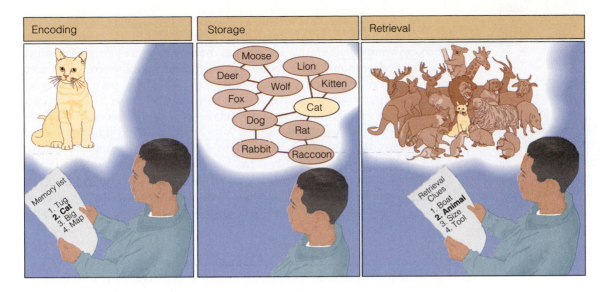

FIGURE 8.1

Basic Memory Processes

Human memory consists of three principal processes: *encoding,* which determines and controls how memories are initially acquired; *storage,* which determines how memories are represented and maintained over time; and *retrieval,* which controls how memories are recovered and translated into performance. In panel 1, how the subject thinks about the word CAT will affect how that word is encoded into memory. Panel 2 shows how CAT might be stored in long-term memory through the activation of existing knowledge structures. In panel 3, the subject uses the cue ANIMAL to help retrieve the memory of CAT.

receded into the past, in order to comprehend the meaning of the sentence as a whole. Likewise, in the performance of most mental tasks, such as solving math problems, certain bits of information need to be retained during the ongoing solution process. Try adding 28 + 35 in your head without remembering to carry the 1 (or subtract 2 if you round the 28 up to 30). By establishing short-term memories, we are able to prolong the incoming message, giving us more time to interpret it properly.

Second, once information leaves the immediate present, it needs to be stored internally so that we can recover it quickly at the appropriate place and time. To establish effective long-term memories, you can process, or think about, information in ways that will aid encoding and promote long-term storage. For example, forming a visual image of a to-be-remembered item increases its durability in memory. It also helps to think about the meaning of the item or to relate the item to other material that has already been stored. We'll consider these techniques in some detail, and provide some tips that can help you improve your own ability to remember.

Third, as we interact with the world, we're constantly required to recover images of the immediate and distant past. But what initiates an act of remembering? What causes you to remember your appointment with the doctor this afternoon, or what you had for breakfast this morning, or a fleeting encounter with a stranger yesterday? Most researchers believe that the retrieval of stored memories is triggered by other events, or cues, encountered in the environment.

Fourth, it's upsetting to forget, but forgetting turns out to have considerable adaptive properties—it keeps us current and prevents us from acting in ways that are more appropriate for yesterday than for today. It's the study assignment that you need to complete *today* that is critical, not the one from yesterday or the week before. It is your *current* phone number that you need to remember, not the one from a previous apartment or from the home you lived in as a child.

Remembering over the Short Term

When environmental information reaches the senses, we rely on two memory systems to help prolong the incoming message over the short term. The first, called **sensory memory**, keeps the message in a relatively pure, unanalyzed form. Sensory memories are like fleeting snapshots of the world. The external message is represented in accurate detail—as a kind of picture or echo—but the sensory representation usually lasts less than a second. The second system, **short-term memory**, is a limited-capacity "working memory" that we use to hold information, after it has been analyzed, for periods lasting on the order of a minute or two. Short-term memories are also rapidly forgotten, but they can be maintained for extended periods through internal repetition. We'll take a look at each of these systems and consider some of their important properties.

VISUAL SENSORY MEMORY: THE ICON

When you watch a movie or a television program, you experience a continuous flow of movement across the screen. As you probably know, the film does not actually contain moving images; it is composed of still pictures, separated by periods of darkness, that are presented rapidly in sequence. People perceive a continuous world, some researchers believe, because the nervous system activity left by one picture lingers for a brief period prior to presentation of the next (Massaro & Loftus, 1996). This extended nervous system activity creates a sensory "memory" that helps to fill the gap, thereby providing a sense of continuous movement.

In vision, the lingering sensory memory trace is called an *icon* and the sensory memory system that produces and stores icons is known as **iconic memory** (Neisser, 1967). It's relatively easy to demonstrate an icon: Simply twirl a flashlight about in a darkened room and you will see a trailing edge. You can obtain a similar effect on a dark night by writing your name in the air with a sparkler or a match. These trails of light are not really present in the night air; they arise from the rapidly fading images of iconic memory, which act as still photographs of the perceptual scene. These images allow the visual sensations to be extended in time so that the brain can more efficiently process the physical message it receives.

sensory memory
The capacity to preserve and recover sensory information in a relatively pure, unanalyzed form; sensory memories are usually accurate representations of externally presented information and last for only a second or less.

short-term memory
A limited-capacity "working memory" system that people use to hold information, after it has been analyzed, for periods usually lasting less than a minute or two. Short-term memory is the system we use to temporarily store, think about, and reason with information.

iconic memory
The system that produces and stores visual sensory memories.

The trails of light created by a whirling sparkler are caused by visual sensory memories, which act as "still photographs" of the perceptual scene.

The Sperling Task

How can icons actually be measured in the laboratory? Over 30 years ago a graduate student in psychology named George Sperling (1960; also see Averbach & Coriell, 1961) developed a clever set of procedures for studying the properties of iconic memory. Using an apparatus called a *tachistoscope*, which presents visual displays for carefully controlled durations, Sperling showed people arrays of 12 letters arranged in rows. For example:

X L W F

J B O V

K C Z R

The subject's task was a simple one: Look at the display and then report the letters. Sounds easy, but the presentation time was extremely brief—the display was shown for only about 50 milliseconds (1/20 of a second). Across several experiments, Sperling found that people could report only about 4 or 5 letters correctly in this task (out of 12). But more important, they claimed to see an image—an icon—of the *entire* display for a brief period after it was removed from view.

Sperling considered these results puzzling: If all 12 letters get registered in this short-lived memory system, as the subjects claimed, why can they only report 4 or 5 letters correctly? He reasoned that there were two possibilities. First, despite what the subjects believe, recall might be limited because only 4 or 5 letters can actually be read from the display in such a short presentation time. Second, the entire display might be read and stored accurately, but its memory fades before subjects have time to report everything they've seen. Again, it was the second alternative that matched what the subjects reported: People were convinced that they saw an image of the entire display but claimed that it faded before everything could be recovered for recall.

Sampling from the Icon

To test between these alternatives, Sperling devised a way to sample selectively from the icon. Rather than asking subjects to recall everything from the display, he asked them to report only the letters shown in a particular row. After the display was turned off, he presented a tone. If the pitch of the tone was high, medium, or low, the task was to report the top, middle, or bottom row of the display, respectively (see Figure 8.2). Sperling called this new condition *partial report* because only a portion of the display needed to be recalled. Performance on these

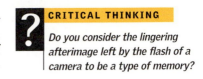

FIGURE 8.2

The Partial Report Technique
A tone sounds after presentation of the display, indicating which row of letters is to be recalled. As the subject attempts to recall them, the visual iconic memory fades and becomes increasingly less accurate. When recall of only part of the display is required, most of the relevant information can be reported before the image has been completely lost.

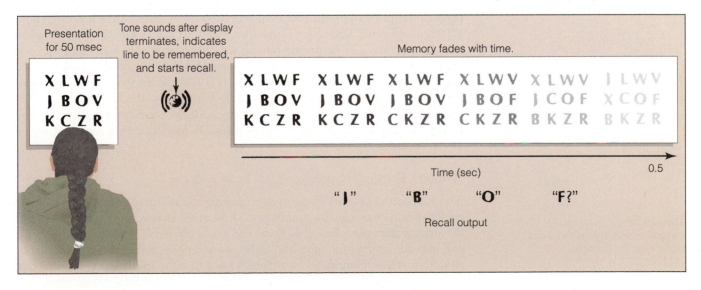

partial report trials was then compared to the original *whole report* condition, which required the recall of all 12 letters. As Sperling anticipated, performance improved dramatically in the new condition—subjects reliably reported almost all of the row letters correctly.

To appreciate Sperling's experiment, it's important to remember that subjects always heard the tone *after* the display had been turned off. There was no way to predict which of the three rows would be cued on a particular trial, so the entire display *must* have been available in memory after the letters were removed. Otherwise, people would have been correct on only one-third of the trials—those trials where the cue signaled the row that they happened to be reading. Requiring recall of only a portion of the display, rather than the entire display, improved performance because it was possible for subjects to report the relevant information before the iconic image had completely faded. In further experiments, by delaying presentation of the tone, Sperling was able to measure how quickly the sensory memory was actually lost. He discovered that the fleeting image—the iconic memory—was indeed short-lived; it disappeared in about a half-second.

In the years since Sperling first developed his partial report technique, psychologists have discovered that performance in this task is more complex than Sperling first thought. For example, Sperling assumed that iconic memory simply decayed away with the passage of time. However, current evidence indicates that people may perform poorly after a delay because they become confused about *where* items were presented in the display (Yeomans & Irwin, 1985). Thus, information is not lost from iconic memory in the way that a television picture is lost after the set is turned off; instead, the image becomes more inexact—subjects may simply forget the item's spatial location (its row) rather than the item itself (Greene, 1992).

CRITICAL THINKING

Can you think of a reason why it might be adaptive for icons to be lost so quickly?

AUDITORY SENSORY MEMORY: THE ECHO

Psychologists assume that we have separate sensory memory systems for each of the sensory modalities. In the auditory system, for example, there is a lingering *echo*, or **echoic memory.** Pure sounds can be held for brief intervals to help auditory perception. In Chapter 5, you learned about how the brain calculates arrival time differences between the ears to help localize sounds. However, in order to compare arrival times, the first sound needs to be retained until the second one arrives; echoic memory may help fill the gap. As noted earlier, echoic memory is also widely believed to play a key role in language processing, perhaps to help retain exact replicas of sounds during sentence and word processing (Crowder, 1976; Nairne, 1990).

How can echoic memory be measured? In a technique used by Efron (1970), people were presented with a series of very brief tones, each lasting less than about 1/10th of a second. The task was to adjust a light so that it appeared exactly when each tone ended. The surprising finding was that people always thought the tone ended later than it actually did. People reported hearing the tone for a brief period after it physically had been turned off. Efron (1970) argued that the perception of this "phantom tone" was actually caused by a memory—the lingering "echo" of echoic memory. As in visual sensory memory, auditory sensory memory is believed to last for only a brief period of time—probably for less than a second (Cowan, 1995; Cowan et al., 1990).

SHORT-TERM MEMORY: THE INNER VOICE

The function of sensory memory is to maintain a relatively exact replica of the environmental message, for a short period, as an aid to perceptual processing. But sensory memory plays little role in the conscious *experience* of the immediate present; instead, internal thoughts and feelings are represented as short-term memories. Short-term memory is the system we use to temporarily store, think about,

echoic memory
The system that produces and stores auditory sensory memories.

Short-term memories help us maintain information, such as telephone numbers, over relatively brief time intervals.

and reason with information. The term "working memory" is sometimes used because this temporary storage system often acts as a kind of mental scratchpad, allowing us to store the components of a problem as we work toward a solution (Baddeley, 1992; Nairne, 1996).

Memory researchers believe that there are three important questions that need to be answered about short-term memory. *First*, what kind of code is used to maintain information over the short term? *Second*, how and why is information forgotten from short-term memory? *Third*, what is the capacity of short-term memory—that is, how much information can we actually maintain over the short term? We'll consider each of these questions in the following sections.

The Short-Term Code

Unlike sensory memories, short-term memories are not brief copies of the environmental message. They consist instead of the by-products, or end results, of perceptual analyses. Consider the letters M O N E Y. In this case, the environmental message is visual. Electromagnetic energy bounces off the page, enters through the eyes, and is processed visually. But your internal thoughts are not about curves, straight lines, or letters. Your thoughts are likely to be about what the message stands for—in this case, a word that has meaning. If you do a little introspection, you'll also notice that you think in a kind of inner *voice*. Notice that you can repeat the word MONEY silently to yourself, either quickly or slowly, and if you like, you can even insert internal pauses after each repetition. There is nothing visual about this repetition process; you have *recoded*, or translated, the visual message into another form—a kind of inner voice.

The notion that people often use an inner voice to store information over the short term is supported by the types of errors that are made during short-term recall. When recalling from short-term memory, people invariably make errors that are acoustically based. Mistakes tend to *sound* like correct items even when the stimulus materials have never actually been presented aloud (Conrad, 1964; Hanson, 1990). For example, suppose you're given five letters to remember—B X R C L—but you make a mistake and misremember the fourth letter. Your error will probably be a letter that sounds like the correct one—you will probably incorrectly remember something like T or P. Notice that C and T and P all sound alike, but they *look* nothing alike. It is believed that errors tend to be acoustic because

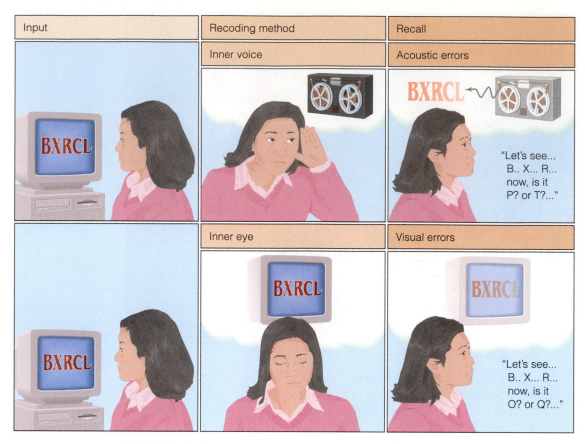

FIGURE 8.3
Recoding and Memory Errors
Short-term memories consist of the by-products, or results, of perceptual analyses. People recode, or translate, the environmental message into other forms. The top row presents the normal case, in which the subject recodes the visually presented message into an inner voice. Notice that recall errors are likely to sound like the letters that were actually presented. Alternatively, if to-be-remembered information is recoded into an inner eye, shown in the bottom row, we would expect recall errors to be similar visually to the original message.

people recode the original visual input into an inner voice rather than an inner "eye" (see Figure 8.3).

Short-term memories are typically stored acoustically, but you are capable of coding information internally in a variety of ways. For example, information is sometimes stored over the short term in the form of visual images (Baddeley, 1992). To illustrate, stop for a moment, close your eyes, and count the number of windows in your house or apartment. People usually perform this task by visualizing the rooms, one by one, and counting the number of windows they "see." Nevertheless, we probably rely more on an inner voice, rather than an inner eye, when remembering things over the short term because we're often called on to interpret and produce spoken language. It makes sense to think in a way that is compatible with the way we communicate. Psychologists also believe that it may be easier to store information about the temporal order of occurrence—which is also essential in language processing—when information is stored acoustically rather than visually (Glenberg & Fernandez, 1989; Hanson, 1990; Penney, 1989).

Short-Term Forgetting

What about forgetting? Everyone knows that it can be tough to remember telephone numbers or directions long enough to write them down. It is possible to prolong short-term memories indefinitely by engaging in **rehearsal,** which is the process of internal repetition, assuming that you have the time and resources to

rehearsal
A strategic process that helps to maintain short-term memories indefinitely through the use of internal repetition.

continue the rehearsal process. (Think about the word *rehearsal* as re-*hear*-sal, as if listening to the inner voice.) Without rehearsal, as you'll see shortly, short-term memories are quickly lost (Atkinson & Shiffrin, 1968).

In an early investigation of short-term forgetting, Lloyd and Margaret Peterson (1959) asked students to recall short lists of three letters (such as CLX) after delays that ranged from 3 to 18 seconds. The task sounds easy—remembering three letters for less than half a minute—but the experiment had an unusual feature: No one was allowed to rehearse, or think about, the letters during the delay interval. To prevent rehearsal, the students were asked to count backward by threes aloud until a recall signal appeared. You can try this experiment for yourself: Just ask someone to read you three letters, then try immediately counting backward by threes from the number 832, and finally have your friend signal you to recall after about 10 to 20 seconds. Under these conditions, you'll probably find that you forget the letters relatively quickly. In the Petersons' experiment, the students were reduced to guessing after about 10 to 15 seconds of counting backward (see Figure 8.4).

Actually, a task like the Petersons' underestimates how quickly information is forgotten from short-term memory when you're not rehearsing. When people are trying to remember material, as in the Petersons' experiment, they're sometimes able to "cheat" by rehearsing and counting backward at the same time (although it's difficult to do). If the task is redesigned so that everyone believes that the contents of short-term memory will *not* be tested but then a surprise test is given, material is forgotten after only a second or two (Muter, 1980; Marsh et al., 1997; Sebrechts et al., 1989). Thus, short-term memory is an excellent system for maintaining information over the short term, but only if you're paying attention. In the absence of rehearsal, short-term memories are quickly lost.

Why is information forgotten so rapidly in the absence of rehearsal? Some researchers believe that short-term memories are lost spontaneously with the passage of time, through a process called *decay*, unless those memories are kept active through rehearsal (Baddeley, 1992; Cowan et al., 1997). You may remember that we mentioned decay earlier as a possible mechanism for explaining the rapid forgetting of sensory memories. Other researchers believe that short-term forgetting is caused by *interference* from new information or because people confuse current memories with past memories (Crowder & Neath, 1991; Keppel & Underwood, 1962; Nairne, 1990, 1996). A third possibility is that both decay and interference operate together to produce information loss. We'll return to the general question of what causes forgetting at a later point in the chapter.

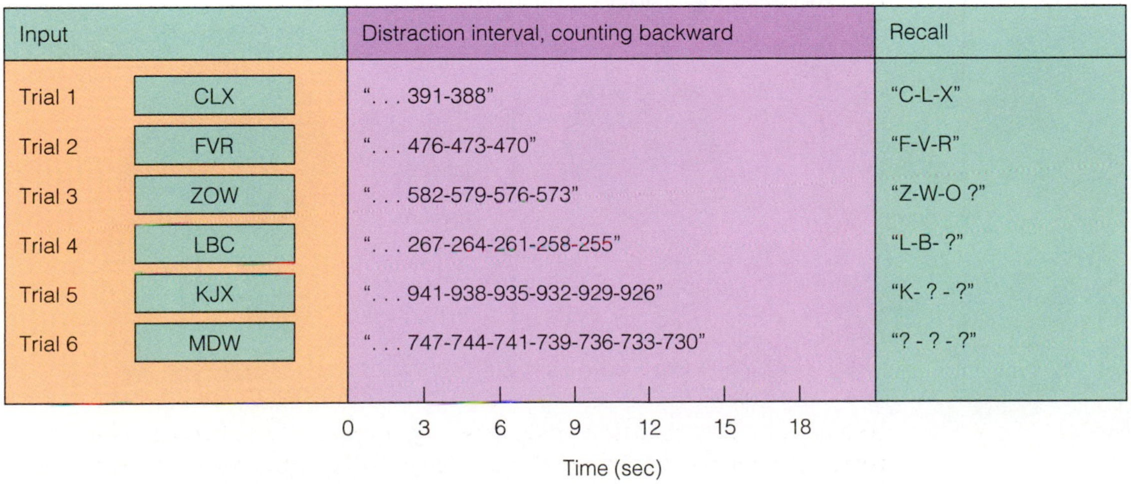

FIGURE 8.4

The Petersons' Distractor Task
On each trial, subjects were asked to recall three letters in correct order, after counting backward aloud for from 3 to 18 seconds. The longer the subjects counted, the less likely they were to recall the letters correctly.

Input		Distraction interval, counting backward	Recall
Trial 1	CLX	"...391-388"	"C-L-X"
Trial 2	FVR	"...476-473-470"	"F-V-R"
Trial 3	ZOW	"...582-579-576-573"	"Z-W-O ?"
Trial 4	LBC	"...267-264-261-258-255"	"L-B- ?"
Trial 5	KJX	"...941-938-935-932-929-926"	"K- ? - ?"
Trial 6	MDW	"...747-744-741-739-736-733-730"	"? - ? - ?"

0   3   6   9   12   15   18

Time (sec)

Short-Term Memory Capacity

How much information can actually be stored over the short term—that is, what's the capacity of short-term memory? Research has shown that short-term **memory span**—which is defined as the number of items a person can recall in the exact order of presentation on half of the tested memory trials—is typically about seven, plus or minus two items. In other words, short-term memory span ranges between five and nine incoming items (Miller, 1956). It's easy to remember a list of four items, but quite difficult to remember a list of eight or nine items (which is one of the reasons why telephone numbers are seven digits long).

Some psychologists believe that the capacity of short-term memory is limited because it takes time to execute the process of rehearsal. To illustrate, imagine you're asked to remember a relatively long list of letters arranged this way:

$$\textbf{CA\quad TFL\quad YBU\quad G}$$

First, try reading this list aloud, from C to G. You'll find that several seconds elapse from start to finish. Now, imagine cycling through the list with your inner voice, as you prepare for short-term recall. It turns out that the C to G cycling takes a similar amount of time inside your head (Landauer, 1962).

Remember, however, items stored in short-term memory are forgotten in a second or two, so the first part of the list will tend to be forgotten during execution of the last. By the time you're finished with the last letter and return to the beginning of the list, the early items have already been lost from memory. You can think about this relationship between forgetting and rehearsal as roughly like juggling (see Figure 8.5). To juggle successfully, you need to win a constant battle against gravity. You throw the dinner plates up, and gravity pushes them down. To prevent one of the plates from crashing, it's necessary to catch and toss it back up in the air before gravity runs it into the ground. Similarly, you need to return to

memory span
The number of items that can be recalled from short-term memory in their proper presentation order on half of the tested memory trials.

FIGURE 8.5

The Capacity of Short-Term Memory
The amount of information that can be stored in short-term memory depends on the process of rehearsal, which you can think of as roughly analogous to juggling. You need to return to each rapidly fading short-term memory trace, and reactivate it through rehearsal, before it is permanently lost or forgotten. Forming "chunks" from the to-be-remembered material makes it easier to rehearse and therefore increases the amount of information that can be retained.

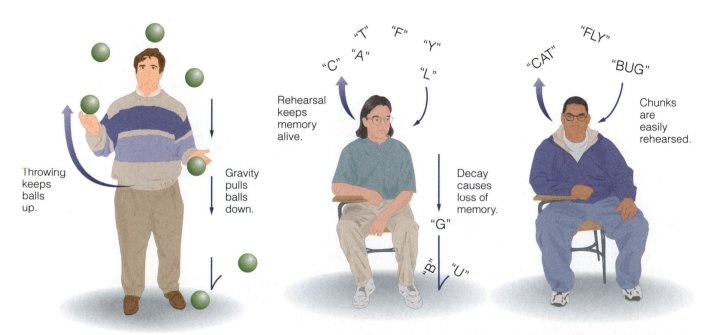

Throwing keeps balls up.

Gravity pulls balls down.

Rehearsal keeps memory alive.

Decay causes loss of memory.

Chunks are easily rehearsed.

the rapidly fading short-term memory trace and reactivate it through rehearsal before the "forces" of forgetting render the memory unobtainable. It's a race between two opposing forces—rehearsal and forgetting.

This means that there should be a close link between the rate of rehearsal (or internal speech) and the size of the memory span. The sooner the rehearsal cycle is completed and begun again, the fewer opportunities there will be for information loss. This relationship is supported by a number of experimental findings. For example, over the short term, it's more difficult to remember lists of long words (such as *conversation, rhinoceros*) than it is to remember lists of short words (such as *top, bat, sit*). It takes longer to cycle through a list of long words using the inner voice, so more of these items are likely to be forgotten (Baddeley et al., 1975; Schweickert et al., 1990). It also takes longer to count to ten in Arabic than it does in English. Consequently, people who speak English can remember longer lists of digits over the short term than those who speak Arabic (Naveh-Benjamin & Ayres, 1986). Finally, children's ability to remember information over the short term improves with language development; as they learn to speak more fluently, their rate of rehearsal improves, which leads to an improved ability to recall information from short-term memory (Hitch & Halliday, 1983).

Chunking

As a general rule, memory span is roughly equal to the amount of material that can be internally rehearsed in about two seconds (which usually turns out to be about seven plus or minus two items). To improve your ability to remember over the short term, then, it's best to figure out a way to rehearse a lot of information in a short amount of time. One effective technique is **chunking**, which involves rearranging the incoming information into meaningful or familiar patterns called *chunks*. Remember that long list of letters presented earlier (CA TFL YBU G)? Perhaps you saw that the same list could be slightly rearranged:

CAT   FLY   BUG

Forming the letters into words drastically reduces the time it takes to repeat the list internally (try saying CAT FLY BUG over and over internally). In addition, once you remember a chunk, it's easy to recall the letters—in most cases, words are great storage devices for remembering sequences of letters. Of course, the trick lies in finding meaningful chunks in what can appear to be a meaningless jumble of information.

The ability to create meaningful chunks, thereby improving memory span, often depends on how much you know about the material that needs to be

Expert chess players recognize familiar configurations in a chess game and can recreate them easily from memory (left); however, when chess pieces are arranged randomly on a board (right), which precludes the chunking of familiar patterns, experts show memory similar to novices.

? CRITICAL THINKING

Do you think it's an accident that local telephone numbers are seven digits long? Why do you suppose the telephone company encourages you to group the numbers into chunks—for example, 449-5854?

chunking
A short-term memory strategy that involves rearranging incoming information into meaningful or familiar patterns.

remembered. Expert chess players can re-create most of the positions on a chess-board after only a brief glance—as long as a meaningful game is in session (Chase & Simon, 1973). They recognize familiar attack or defense patterns in the game, which allows them to create easy-to-rehearse chunks of position information. Similar results are found when electronics experts are asked to remember complex circuit board diagrams (Egan & Schwartz, 1979). In both cases, if the materials are arranged in a more or less random fashion (for example, the chess pieces are simply scattered about the board), the skilled retention vanishes, and memory reverts to normal levels.

TEST YOURSELF 8.1

Check your knowledge about remembering over the short term by deciding whether each of the following statements best describes sensory memory or short-term memory. (You will find the answers in the Appendix.)

1. Information is forgotten in less than a second: _____

2. Information is stored as a virtually exact copy of the external message: _____

3. Information can be stored indefinitely through the process of rehearsal: _____

4. System measured through Sperling's partial report procedure: _____

5. Recall errors tend to sound like the correct item even when the item is presented visually: _____

6. May help us calculate message arrival time differences between the two ears: _____

7. Span is roughly equal to the amount of material that you can say to yourself in two seconds: _____

8. Capacity is improved through chunking: _____

long-term memory
The system used to maintain information for extended periods of time.

Storing Information for the Long Term

Many of the processes used to store information over the short term also play a key role in the storage of information for the long term. Once material drops from short-term memory—the seat of conscious awareness—it becomes part of **long-term memory,** the system used to maintain information for extended periods. Most psychologists believe that the capacity of long-term memory is effectively unlimited, which means that there are really no limits on the amount of material that can be stored. However, exactly what enters long-term memory, as well as the durability of the information that is stored, depends on the processing activities used to encode the information for storage. To promote effective long-term storage, it's important to encode information in certain ways during initial presentation. In this section, we'll consider the kinds of encoding activities that lead to effective long-term storage, but first we'll broadly look at the general kinds of information that are stored.

WHAT IS STORED IN LONG-TERM MEMORY?

Stop for a moment and think about your first kiss. The recollection (assuming you can remember your first kiss) is probably tinged with a measure of warmth, intimacy, and perhaps embarrassment. Do you remember the person's name, the situation, the year? Memories of this type, in which people recall some personal moment from their past, are called **episodic memories**—they are composed of particular events, or episodes, that happened to you personally. Most experimental research on remembering involves episodic memory because people typically are asked to remember information from an earlier point in the experiment. The task is to remember an *event*, such as a word list, that forms a part of the personal history of the participant.

Now, think of a city in Europe that is famous for its fashion and fine wine. The correct response is *Paris*, but did you "remember" or "know" the answer? What about the square root of nine, or the capital city of the United States? These are certainly memories, in the sense that you have preserved and recovered information from the past, but "remembering" these answers feels

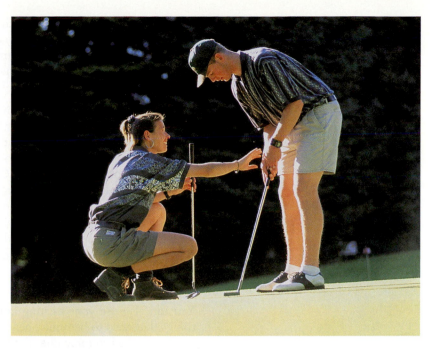

It's difficult to teach skills associated with procedural memory, like golf, because procedural memories tend to be inaccessible to conscious awareness.

vastly different from remembering your first kiss. When you show someone what you know about the world but make no reference whatsoever to a particular episode from your past, you are using **semantic memory** (*semantic* refers to "meaning"). It is through semantic memory that people record facts and remember the rules they need to adapt effectively in the world.

Finally, try to remember how to tie your shoes, drive a car, or ride a bike. The knowledge about how to *do* things, to perform certain tasks, is called **procedural memory.** Most skills, including athletic prowess, rely on the establishment of procedural memories. Procedural memories differ from episodic and semantic memories in a fundamental way: They rarely produce any conscious experience of "remembering." Most people have a difficult time consciously reporting how to tie their shoes or ride a bike. They can do these things, but people find it extremely difficult to put the knowledge they have into words. Procedural memories are among the simplest of all memories to recover, but, ironically, they are among the most difficult for psychologists to study—they seem inaccessible to conscious awareness (Tulving, 1983). For a summary of these memory types—episodic, semantic, and procedural—see the concept summary table below.

ELABORATION: CONNECTING MATERIAL WITH EXISTING KNOWLEDGE

As a general rule, if you want to remember something over the long term, you should relate the material to your existing knowledge. We all house an incredibly rich collection of information in long-term memory, stored as episodic, semantic,

episodic memory
A memory for a particular event, or episode, that happened to you personally, such as remembering what you ate for breakfast this morning or where you went on vacation last year.

semantic memory
Knowledge about the world, stored as facts that make little or no reference to one's personal experiences.

procedural memory
Knowledge about how to do things, such as riding a bike or swinging a golf club.

CONCEPT SUMMARY
Varieties of Long-Term Memory

Type of Memory	Description	Example
Episodic	Memories in which we recall a personal moment from our past.	Wanda, the mail carrier, remembers that yesterday 10 inches of snow fell, making the daily mail delivery very difficult.
Semantic	Knowledge about the world, with no specific reference to a particular past episode.	Wanda knows that mailing a letter first-class costs 33 cents; she also knows that it costs more to send something via express mail.
Procedural	Knowledge about *how* to do something.	Wanda drives along the streets of her mail route effortlessly, without really thinking about it.

? CRITICAL THINKING

When you take a test in one of your college courses, is the test primarily tapping episodic, semantic, or procedural memory?

and procedural memories. This existing knowledge can be used to enrich, or elaborate, the material you're trying to remember. Through **elaboration,** the process of relating input to other things, meaningful connections can be established that ease later recovery of the stored material.

Think about Meaning

In its simplest form, elaboration involves just thinking about the *meaning* of information that you want to remember. In an experiment by Craik and Tulving (1975), people were asked questions about single words such as MOUSE. In one condition, the task required everyone to make judgments about the sound of the word (Does the word rhyme with HOUSE?); in another condition, people were required to think about the meaning of the word (Is a MOUSE a type of animal?). Substantially better memory was obtained in this second condition. Presumably, thinking about meaning, rather than sound, causes people to form more connections between presented events and other things in memory. The deeper and more elaborative the processing, the more likely that memory will improve (Craik & Lockhart, 1972).

Notice Relationships

You can also use your existing knowledge to look for relationships among the things that need to be remembered, to organize what you need to learn. Suppose you were asked to remember the following list of words:

NOTES PENCIL BOOK NEWSPAPER MUSIC COFFEE

If you think about what the words mean and look for properties that the words have in common—perhaps things that you would take to a study session or a lecture—you are engaging in what psychologists call *relational processing*. Relational processing is a kind of elaboration, and it turns out to be an extremely effective strategy for promoting long-term retention (Hunt & Einstein, 1981).

Once again, relational processing works because you are embellishing, or adding to, the stimulus input. If you're trying to remember the word PENCIL and you relate the word to an involved sequence of events depicting a morning lecture, you have created a richer and more elaborate memory record (see Figure 8.6). Later, when you try to remember this particular word, there are likely to be lots of cues that will help remind you of the correct response. Thinking about music, newspapers, drinking coffee—any of these can lead to the correct recall of PENCIL. You will also be better able to discriminate the correct memory record, when you think of it, from other things in memory that can interfere with the retrieval process.

Notice Differences

Connections help memory, but it's also important to specify how the material you want to remember is different from other information in long-term memory. If you simply encode the fact that PENCIL is a writing implement, you might incorrectly recall things like PEN, CHALK, or even CRAYON when later tested. Instead, you need to specify the event's occurrence in some detail—we are talking about a yellow, Number 2 pencil, not some crayon—so that the memory record becomes *unique*. Unique memory records are remembered better because they are easier to distinguish from other related, but not appropriate, material in memory (Waddill & McDaniel, 1998).

Psychologists use the term **distinctiveness** to refer to how unique or different a memory record is from other things in memory (Neath, 1998; Schmidt, 1991). One of the common by-products of elaboration is a distinctive, and therefore easy-to-remember, memory record. By comparing the item that you're trying to remember with other things in memory, you'll notice how the item both shares properties with other information (elaboration) and is unique or different (Craik & Jacoby, 1979; Hunt & McDaniel, 1993). Generally, if you want to

elaboration
An encoding process that involves the formation of connections between to-be-remembered input and other information in memory.

distinctiveness
A term used to refer to how unique or different a memory record is from other things in memory. Distinctive memory records tend to be recalled well.

Nonrelational processing	Relational processing

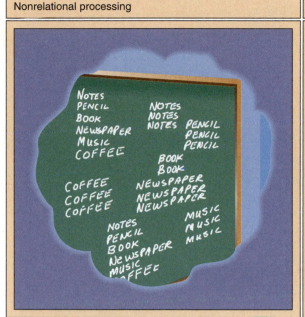 

remember something particularly well you should concentrate on encoding both item similarities as well as differences. (Some kinds of events seem to lead automatically to distinctive memory records, as the accompanying "Inside the Problem" feature on page 316 shows.)

IMAGERY: REMEMBERING THROUGH VISUALIZATION

Another way to produce an elaborative and distinctive memory record is to form a visual image of the material when it's first presented. If you're trying to remember COFFEE, try forming a mental picture of a steaming hot, freshly brewed full mug. **Visual imagery** is the process used to construct an internal image, perhaps using the same brain mechanisms used to perceive events in the physical world (Farah, 1988). Forming mental pictures is an effective memory strategy because it naturally leads to elaborate, rich encodings. Mental pictures require you to think about the details of the material, and these details create a distinctive memory record.

Let's consider some encoding techniques, called *mnemonic devices*, that specifically make use of visual imagery and elaboration to aid long-term remembering. **Mnemonic devices** (*mnemonic* means "pertaining to memory") are special mental tricks that help people think about material in ways that lead to effective everyday remembering. These devices were originally developed by the Greeks (Yates, 1966), so they've been around for a long time. As we describe each strategy in detail, look for ways to apply what you learn to your own practical memory problems.

The Method of Loci

One of the oldest mnemonic devices is the *method of loci* (*loci* is Latin for "places"). According to legend, the technique traces back to an ancient Greek named Simonides, who used it to identify the participants in a large banquet that had ended abruptly in tragedy. Simonides had apparently delivered a lecture at the banquet but was called away just before a portion of the building collapsed, killing many of the diners. To identify the bodies, Simonides formed a visual image of the room and used the seating assignments to reconstruct the guest list.

The **method of loci,** like most mnemonic devices, relies on visual imagery as its major encoding vehicle. The technique begins with the choice of some real-world pathway that is easy to remember, such as moving through the rooms in your house or along some familiar route to work or school. The to-be-remembered

FIGURE 8.6
Relational Versus Nonrelational Processing
We often remember things better if we engage in relational processing, which means we relate to-be-remembered items together in some way. On the right, the items on the memory list are transposed into an imaginary scene. Relational processing can be contrasted with nonrelational processing, in which memory items are simply repeated or rehearsed individually (as on the left). Nonrelational processing usually leads to poor long-term memory.

visual imagery
The processes used to construct an internal visual image, perhaps using the same brain mechanisms used to perceive events in the physical world.

mnemonic devices
Special mental tricks that help people think about material in ways that improve later memory. Most mnemonic devices require the use of visual imagery.

method of loci
A mnemonic device in which you choose some pathway, such as moving through the rooms in your house, and then form visual images of the to-be-remembered items sitting in various locations along the pathway.

Inside the Problem   Flashbulb Memories

Do you remember what you were doing when you first heard about the tragic bombing of the Federal Building in Oklahoma City?

Although we've concentrated on how to use elaboration strategically, distinctive memory records are sometimes created automatically, even when no conscious attempt has been made to remember. **Flashbulb memories** are rich records of the circumstances surrounding emotionally significant and surprising events (Brown & Kulick, 1977). Flashbulb memories have been reported for such events as the assassination of John F. Kennedy, the attempted assassination of Ronald Reagan, the Space Shuttle *Challenger* disaster, and the start of the Gulf War. People who experience flashbulb memories are convinced they can remember exactly what they were doing when they first heard the shocking or surprising news. Playing in school, watching television, talking on the phone—whatever the circumstance, people report vivid details about the events surrounding their first exposure to the news. Do you remember what you were doing when you first heard the verdict in the O. J. Simpson trial? How about the tragic bombing of the Federal Building in Oklahoma City?

Some psychologists speculate that the high arousal levels produced by events of this type lead people to encode the surrounding events in a highly distinctive and elaborative manner. It's as if a giant flash goes off, burning the details surrounding the episode into your brain. From an adaptive standpoint, it makes sense to propose that the brain is designed to remember significant events that might affect your future ability to survive. Not all events are created equal from a survival perspective, and it is certainly in your interest to remember the details that surround events that are of great personal significance.

Surprisingly, however, a number of reports have questioned the accuracy of this kind of memory. Neisser and Harsch (1992) asked college students one day after the Space Shuttle *Challenger* exploded to describe exactly how they first heard the news. The details were recorded, then three years later the same students were asked to recollect their experiences. Everyone tended to be highly confident about their recollections, yet there was not much agreement between the original and the delayed memories. The students thought they were remembering things accurately, but the data proved otherwise. The fact that the memories were poor suggests that the psychological experience of flashbulb memories—that is, the strong conviction that one's memories are accurate—may be related more to the emotionality of the original experience than to the presence of a rich and elaborative memory record.

One factor that apparently needs to be considered is the *importance* of the event to the person doing the remembering. A study by Martin Conway and his colleagues (1994) looked at how well people could remember hearing about the resignation of the British Prime Minister Margaret Thatcher, which occurred in October of 1991. Within 14 days of the resignation, hundreds of participants around the world were asked by Conway and his research team to record the details of how and when they first heard the news. Only people who claimed to remember these details were allowed to participate. Two years later, everyone was tested again, and the researchers discovered dramatic forgetting—but the forgetting occurred primarily for people who lived outside Great Britain. The British subjects remembered personal details about the event far more accurately than did subjects who lived in other countries. The resignation of the prime minister was clearly a more emotionally significant event to the British people; this factor may help to explain why the accuracy of their flashbulb memories was greater.

In many ways, the inaccuracies that have been found in recalling flashbulb memories are as interesting to memory researchers as the accuracies. As you'll see later in this chapter, people often misremember prior events yet think they're remembering things well. The reason is that an important part of remembering is based on *reconstruction* of prior events rather than literal reproduction. People tend not to store literal records of events in their brain; instead, they use their general knowledge to help them decide what must have occurred in a particular situation. This strategy is adaptive because it saves people from having to store minor details, but it can lead to inaccuracies in what they remember.

FIGURE 8.7
The Method of Loci
To-be-remembered items are mentally placed in various locations along a familiar path. These items should be easy to remember because the use of visual imagery promotes an elaborate memory trace and because the stored locations are easy to access.

material—suppose that you wanted to remember a list of errands—is then systematically placed, in your mind, at various locations along the path. It's important to form a visual image of each memory item and to link the image to a specific location along the chosen route. So, if you wanted to remember to pay the gas bill, you might form a mental picture of a large check made out to the gas company and place it in the first location on your path (such as the entry hall in your house).

Depending on the size of your pathway, you can store a relatively large amount of material using this method. At the end of encoding you might have 15 different errands stored. Overdue library books might be linked to the living room sofa, clean shirts encased in plastic might be draped across the kitchen counter, or big bags of dog chow might be associated with a dog on the television screen (see Figure 8.7). To recover the material later, all you need to do is walk along the pathway in your mind, "looking" in the different locations for the objects you've stored (Higbee, 1988). The method of loci is an effective memory aid because it forces you to use imagery—creating an elaborative and distinctive record—and the stored records are easy to recover because the storage locations are easy to access.

The Peg-Word Technique

The **peg-word method** is similar to the method of loci in that it requires you to link the to-be-remembered material to specific memory *cues*, but the cues are usually based on rhymes rather than specific mental pathways. Figure 8.8 shows one popular set of rhyme cues, or *pegs*, that can be used with this technique. The strategy, once again, is to link an image of the to-be-remembered material with an image of the peg. You might picture your overdue library books inside a hamburger bun, a bag of dog chow sitting inside a shoe, or some clean shirts hanging from a tree. To recover the memory records, you simply start counting, and the peg word should lead you to the image of the to-be-remembered errand. One is a bun—return books; two is a shoe—buy dog chow; three is a tree—pick up shirts.

An alternative version of the peg-word method, called the *linkword system*, has been used successfully to assist in learning foreign language vocabulary (Gruneberg et al., 1994). Suppose you wanted to remember the French word for rabbit (*lapin*). While studying, think of an English word that sounds like the French word; perhaps the word *lap* would do for *lapin*. Next, think about the meaning of the French word, and try to form a visual image of the result linked to

? CRITICAL THINKING

If people think primarily in terms of an inner voice, then why is visual imagery such an effective technique for improving memory?

flashbulb memories
Rich memory records of the circumstances surrounding emotionally significant and surprising events.

peg-word method
A mnemonic device in which you form visual images connecting to-be-remembered items with retrieval cues, or pegs.

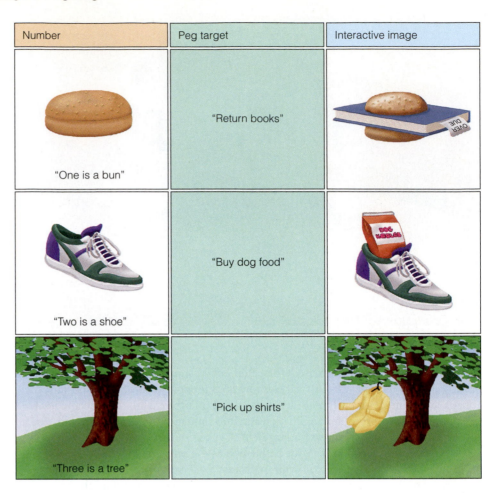

Number	Peg target	Interactive image
"One is a bun"	"Return books"	
"Two is a shoe"	"Buy dog food"	
"Three is a tree"	"Pick up shirts"	

FIGURE 8.8

The Peg-Word Technique

Images of to-be-remembered material are linked visually to the images of specific rhyme cues, or pegs. The interactive visual image produces an elaborative memory trace, and the peg cues are easy to access.

the English rhyme. For example, you could imagine a white furry rabbit sitting in someone's lap. When the word *lapin* then appears later on a test, the English rhyme should serve as an effective cue for bringing forth a remembered image of the rabbit (*lap* acts as a kind of peg word for rabbit). This method has been shown to produce nearly a doubling of the rate of learning for vocabulary words (Raugh & Atkinson, 1975).

The Visual Code

Visual imagery helps memory, but let's pause for a moment and think about the nature of the visual code. Are the images we form inside our head when we try to remember anything like the images produced through actual perception (e.g., where the brain actually processes a message from the environment)? Over the past several decades, lots of research has been conducted exploring the psychological and neurological characteristics of mental images (Kosslyn & Koenig, 1992; Rouw et al., 1997). For the most part, researchers have focused on the following questions: (1) Do remembered images follow the same laws as images produced directly through perception? (2) Do remembered and perceived images activate the same neural mechanisms and pathways in the brain? As you'll see, examination of these questions has produced some intriguing results.

Without looking, try forming a visual image of a penny or a quarter. You use coins every day, so this should be a fairly easy task. If you're like most people, you're probably convinced that you can form an accurate representation from memory of such an object. Now, try to reproduce the image on paper—simply draw the president depicted on the coin, which direction he is facing, and so on. Despite the apparent vividness of the image, it's likely that your performance will turn out to be mediocre at best. People are simply unable to reproduce the main

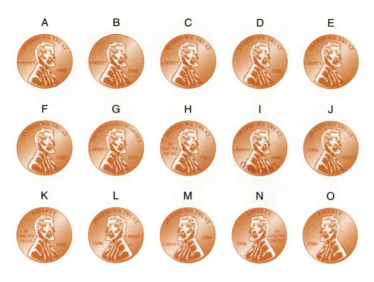

FIGURE 8.9

Can You Recognize a Penny?
Most of us think we can form an accurate mental image of a penny, but we often have difficulty picking a true penny from a group of alternatives. Can you find the real penny in this display taken from the Nickerson and Adams (1979) experiment?

features of the coin very accurately, despite the belief that they can see an accurate representation in their head. Even more surprisingly, it is difficult for people even to recognize the correct coin when it is presented along with incorrect versions of the coin. For a display like the one shown in Figure 8.9, fewer than half of the subjects are likely to pick out the right penny (Nickerson & Adams, 1979; for a British version of the experiment, see Jones & Martin, 1992). Certainly if you were looking at a coin, you would be able to trace the features accurately, so people's images—if they are, in fact, visual—are only fuzzy, relatively inaccurate representations of physical reality.

At the same time, there is a sense in which mental pictures do indeed act visual. For example, try forming a visual image of a rabbit standing next to a rat. Now ask yourself, does the rabbit in your image have whiskers? If I measure your reaction time, it turns out that you will answer a question like this more quickly if you imagine the rabbit standing next to a rat instead of an elephant (Kosslyn, 1983). This is exactly the kind of result we'd expect if you were looking at an actual picture—the larger the object is represented in the picture, the easier it is to "see." In another experiment by Stephen Kosslyn and his colleagues, people were asked to form a visual image of a map like the one depicted in Figure 8.10 on page 320. Notice that there are certain landmarks in this map, including a lighthouse and a collection of huts. Once the image was formed, subjects were asked to focus on one of the landmarks (such as the lighthouse) and then to mentally "scan" to a second landmark (such as the huts) as quickly as possible. Kosslyn and his colleagues found that the time it took people to complete the scan depended on the physical distance between the landmarks on the map. The greater the distance between the locations, the longer it took subjects to complete the scan (Kosslyn et al., 1978). This suggests that people represented the spatial relations among the landmarks in their image in the same way that the spatial relations were presented on the map.

Additional experiments have shown that both mental imagery and normal visual perception may rely on the same neurological mechanisms in the brain (Farah, 1988). For example, techniques that map the activity of brain regions have shown that imagery and perception activate the same regions of the occipital lobe (Kosslyn & Koenig, 1992). Other studies have indicated that people have trouble storing a visual image in their head while they are also performing a visually based tracking task, such as finding locations on a map (Baddeley & Lieberman, 1980). There are even brain-damaged patients who appear to have corresponding impairments in both imagery and visual perception (Levine et al., 1985). For example, some patients whose brain damage has caused them to lose their color vision also have difficulty forming a colorful visual image. Results like these

FIGURE 8.10

Scanning a Mental Image
Kosslyn and his colleagues asked subjects to imagine a map and then scan it from one landmark to another. The time it took depended on the physical distances between landmarks on the actual map. The results suggest that people represent mental images visually.

? CRITICAL THINKING

Given what you've learned about repetition and memory, do you think it's a good idea to have children learn arithmetic tables by rote repetition?

primacy effect
The better memory seen for items near the beginning of a memorized list.

recency effect
The better memory seen for items near the end of a memorized list.

distributed practice
Spacing the repetitions of to-be-remembered information over time.

indicate that there may indeed be an important link between the brain systems involved in perception and those involved in mental imagery (Ishai & Sagi, 1997).

HOW SHOULD MATERIAL BE PRESENTED?

Long-term memory also depends on how material is actually presented during study. For example, if I give you a long list of items to remember, such as ten errands to complete, you will tend to remember the items from the beginning and the end of the list best, regardless of whether you've used any of the mnemonic strategies we've been discussing. This pattern is shown in Figure 8.11, which plots how well items are recalled as a function of their temporal, or serial, position in a list (this graph is often called a *serial position curve*). The improved memory for items at the start of the list is called the **primacy effect;** the end-of-the-list advantage is called the **recency effect.** Memory researchers believe that primacy and recency effects arise because items that occur at the beginnings and ends of a sequence are more naturally distinctive in memory and are therefore easier to recall (Murdock, 1960; Neath, 1993).

The Effect of Repetition

Another aspect of presentation that critically affects long-term memory is *repetition:* If information is presented more than one time it will tend to be remembered better. The fact that repetition improves memory is not very surprising, but it might surprise you to learn that repetition, by itself, is not what leads to better memory. It is possible to present an item multiple times without improving memory—what's necessary is that you use each repetition as an opportunity to encode the material in an elaborative and distinctive manner. If you simply process, or think about, the material in exactly the same way every time it's presented, your memory will not improve very much (Greene, 1992; Herrmann et al., 1993).

How repetitions are spaced out over time is another important factor. Your memory will be better if you distribute the repetitions over time—a technique called **distributed practice.** Practically, this means that all-night cram sessions in which you read the same chapter over and over again are not very effective study procedures. It's better to study a little psychology, do something else, and then return to your psychology. To the extent that you can engage in distributed practice, where you put other activities between the repetitions of the material, your ability to remember the material over the long term will improve (Neath, 1998).

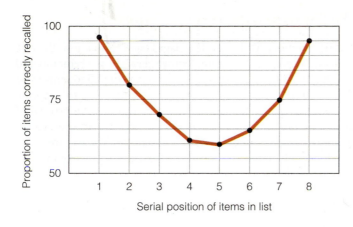

FIGURE 8.11
The Serial Position Curve
When we are asked to recall a list of items, our performance often depends on the temporal, or serial, position of the items in the list. Items at the beginning of the list are remembered relatively well—the *primacy effect*—and so are items at the end of the list—the *recency effect.*

Why does distributed practice lead to the best memory? Again, the answer lies in how you process the material when it is presented. If you engage in massed practice—where you simply reread the same material over and over again without a break—you're likely to think about the material in exactly the same way every time it is presented. If you insert a break between presentations, when you see the material again there is a better chance that you will notice something new or different. Distributed practice leads to memory records that are more elaborate and distinctive.

TEST YOURSELF 8.2

Check your knowledge of how information is stored over the long term by answering the following questions. (You will find the answers in the Appendix.)

1. For each of the following, try to decide whether the relevant memory is episodic, semantic, or procedural.

   a. The capital city of Texas is Austin: _____
   b. Breakfast yesterday was ham and eggs: _____
   c. My mother's maiden name is Hudlow: _____
   d. Executing a perfect golf swing: _____
   e. Tying your shoe laces: _____

2. Your little brother Eddie needs to learn a long list of vocabulary words for school tomorrow. Which of the following represents the best advice for improving his memory?

   a. Say the words aloud as many times as possible.
   b. Write down the words as many times as possible.
   c. Form a visual image of each word.
   d. Spend more time studying words at the beginning and end of the list.

3. For each of the following, decide which term best applies. Choose from: distinctiveness, distributed practice, elaboration, method of loci, peg-word technique.

   a. Visualize each of the items sitting in a location along a pathway:

   _____

   b. Notice how each of the items is different from other things in memory:

   _____

   c. Form connections among each of the items that needs to be remembered:

   _____

   d. Form images linking items to specific cues: _____
   e. Engage in relational processing of the to-be-remembered material:

   _____

Recovering Information from Cues

Can you still remember the memory list from a few pages back? You know, the one based on things that you might take to a morning lecture class? If you remembered the items, such as PENCIL, NOTES, and COFFEE, it's probably because you were able to use the common theme—things at a lecture—as a *cue* to promote remembering. Most psychologists believe that *retrieval*, which is the process of recovering previously stored memories, is guided by the presence of cues, called *retrieval cues*, which are either generated internally (thinking of the lecture scene helps you remember PENCIL) or are physically present in the environment (a string tied around your finger).

THE IMPORTANCE OF RETRIEVAL CUES

A classic study conducted by Tulving and Pearlstone (1966) illustrates the critical role that retrieval cues play in remembering. People were given lists to remember that contained words from a variety of meaningful categories (types of animals, birds, vegetables, and so on). Later, the participants were asked to remember the words either with or without the aid of retrieval cues. Half of the subjects were asked to recall the words without cues (a condition known as **free recall**); the other half were given the category names to help them remember (a condition known as **cued recall**). Subjects in the cued-recall condition recalled nearly twice as many words, presumably because the category names helped them gain access to the previously stored material.

Although these results may not seem surprising, they have important implications for how we need to think about remembering. Consider performance in the free-recall condition. Because people performed poorly, it's tempting to conclude that they either never learned the material or simply forgot many of the items from the list. But the performance of the people who were cued shows that the poor memory resulted from a failure to *access* the relevant stored material. With the right retrieval cues, material that seems to have been lost, or never learned, can be remembered with striking clarity. For this reason, many memory researchers believe that most, if not all, instances of forgetting are really **cue-dependent forgetting.** The information, once it's encoded, is available somewhere in the brain; you simply need the right kind of retrieval cues to gain access.

free recall
A testing condition in which a person is asked to remember information without explicit retrieval cues.

cued recall
A testing condition in which subjects are given an explicit retrieval cue to help them remember.

cue-dependent forgetting
The idea that forgetting is caused by a failure to access the appropriate retrieval cue.

Can you name all of your classmates from the fifth grade? Probably not, but your memory is sure to improve if you're given a retrieval cue in the form of a class photo.

Study	Retrieval match	Retrieval mismatch
Encoding input	Retrieval cue: "Bank"	Retrieval cue: "Bank"

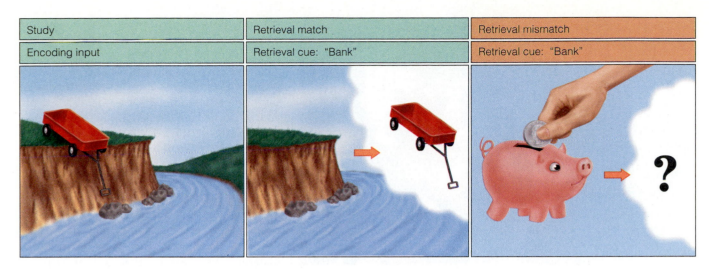

FIGURE 8.12
The Encoding-Retrieval Match
Memory often depends on how well retrieval cues match the way information was originally studied or encoded. Suppose you're asked to remember the word pair BANK—WAGON; during study, you form a visual image of a wagon teetering on the edge of a river bank. When presented later with the retrieval cue BANK, you're more likely to remember WAGON if you interpret the cue as something bordering a river than as a place to keep money.

The Encoding-Retrieval Match

What conditions make retrieval cues effective? Psychologists believe that the effectiveness of a retrieval cue depends in large part on how well the cue *matches* the memory that was encoded. If you think about the sound of a word during its original presentation, rather than its appearance, then a cue that leads you to think about the stored sound will be more effective than a visual cue (some kind of rhyme might work). Similarly, if you think about the meaning of a word during study, then an effective cue will induce you to attend to an appropriate meaning during retrieval.

Let's consider an example. Suppose you were asked to remember the two words BANK and WAGON. You know about the effectiveness of elaborate encodings, so you form a visual image of a WAGON perched on the BANK of a river (see Figure 8.12). Later, BANK is provided as a retrieval cue. Will it help you remember WAGON? Probably, but only if you interpret the retrieval cue BANK to mean a slope immediately bordering a river. If for some reason you think about the BANK as an attractive place to keep money, you probably will not recover WAGON successfully. A retrieval cue will be effective only if it you interpret it in the proper way. By "proper," psychologists mean that the cue needs to be interpreted in a way that matches the original encoding.

The idea that it's important to match encoding and retrieval has a number of interesting implications for remembering. For example, it helps to explain context- or state-dependent remembering. In Chapter 2 we discussed an experiment showing that divers can remember important safety information better if they learn the information while diving rather than on land (Martin & Aggelton, 1993). Presumably, there is a better match between encoding and retrieval when information is learned and tested in the same environment. Another example is childhood, or infantile, amnesia: Most of us have a difficult time remembering things that happened to us when we were very small (before age 4 or 5). However, it's likely that we interpreted the world very differently when we were small. Childhood amnesia may result, then, from a poor match between the present and the distant past. We see and interpret events differently now than we did as children, so we have few effective retrieval cues available for remembering childhood events.

But it takes more than just a proper interpretation of the retrieval cue for it to be effective. According to the **encoding specificity principle,** a specific connection must also be formed between the cue and the to-be-remembered material at the time the material is studied (Tulving, 1983). For example, let's assume that you're asked to memorize the word NURSE. Later, you are given the word DOCTOR as a retrieval cue. DOCTOR and NURSE are naturally related, so

encoding specificity principle
The idea that specific encoding processes determine which retrieval cues will be effective in aiding later memory.

Later, this couple may find it easier to remember their blissful reunion if they're happy rather than sad. How does this conclusion follow from consideration of the encoding retrieval match?

you might think that presenting one would automatically help you remember the other. But presenting DOCTOR as a retrieval cue will be effective for remembering NURSE only if the two words were encoded together during the original learning. If, for whatever reason, you fail to make a connection between DOCTOR and NURSE while you are studying NURSE, DOCTOR will turn out to be a poor memory cue (Tulving & Thomson, 1973).

Transfer-Appropriate Processing

The encoding specificity principle says that for retrieval cues to be effective, they need to be encoded along with the to-be-remembered material. This means that if you want to remember something at a certain place and time, you should pay close attention to the conditions that are likely to be present when you need to remember. You must engage in what psychologists call **transfer-appropriate processing;** that is, you should study the material using the same kind of mental processes that will be required during retrieval. Because of the importance of retrieval cues, performance on a memory test will always depend on the match between the mental processes used during studying and the mental processes required by the test (Ellis & Hunt, 1993).

To illustrate, you've learned at various points in this chapter that elaboration—relating to-be-remembered material to other things—is a generally effective strategy for remembering. But the effectiveness of *any* encoding manipulation will depend on what kind of information is required by the memory test. Let's assume that you're asked to remember the word TUG (see Figure 8.13). If you form a visual image of a tugboat and you are then specifically asked about a tugboat on the memory test, you will probably perform well. But suppose you are asked instead to remember whether the word TUG was printed in upper- or lowercase letters in the study materials. All of the elaboration in the world isn't going to help you unless you have specifically encoded the way the letters were shaped ("TUG," not "tug"). The lesson of transfer-appropriate processing is that you need to consider the nature of the testing environment before you can decide how to study most effectively.

On a practical level, then, this means that you should think about the characteristics of an exam *before* you sit down to study. An essay exam, for example, is a kind of *cued-recall* test—you are given a cue in the form of a test question, and you are required to recall the most appropriate answer. To study for such a test, it is best to practice cued recall: Make up questions that are relevant to the material, and practice recalling the appropriate answer with only the test question as a cue. For a multiple-choice test, which is a kind of *recognition test*, it is necessary to discriminate a correct answer from a group of incorrect answers (called *distractors*). The best way to study for a multiple-choice test is to practice with multiple-choice questions; either make up your own, or use the questions that are often available in study guides.

Do you ever say things to yourself like, "I'll just read the chapter one more time before I go to bed, and I'll ace the exam tomorrow"? Think about this reasoning from the perspective of transfer-appropriate processing—what exactly does the typical exam ask you to do? Exams don't measure the speed or fluency with which the chapter can be *read*. Most exams require you to recall or reproduce material in the presence of cues. Learn the material by reading the chapter, but prepare for the exam by doing the kind of thing that is required by the test. Practice reproducing the material by answering questions from memory, or prac-

transfer-appropriate processing
The idea that the likelihood of correct retrieval is increased if a person uses the same kind of mental processes during testing that he or she used during encoding.

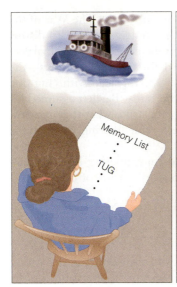

tice discriminating correct from incorrect answers by responding to a variety of multiple-choice questions (Herrmann et al., 1993).

RECONSTRUCTIVE REMEMBERING

Retrieval cues guide remembering in much the same way an incoming physical message guides the processes of perception. As you may recall from Chapter 5, what people "see" really depends on both the incoming environmental message and the expectations they hold about what's "out there." In a similar way, remembering depends on more than just a retrieval cue—beliefs and expectations can color an act of remembering just as they can color what people see and hear. Stop for a moment and try to remember what you had for breakfast two weeks ago. Maybe you skipped breakfast, or gulped down a quick bowl of cereal. It turns out that what you will "remember" in a case like this often corresponds more to habit than to actual fact. If you regularly eat a bowl of cereal in the morning, then eating cereal is what you are likely to recall, even if you broke the routine on that particular day and had a bagel.

Memory Schemas

To understand why memory acts in this way, you need to remember that we store more than just facts in long-term memory—we also store relationships among facts. You know, for example, that houses contain rooms with walls, require insurance protection, and are susceptible to burning down if you're not careful. You know that 2-year-old children drool a lot, fall down, and put things into their mouths. These large clusters of related facts are organized into knowledge structures called **schemas.** Schemas can be about people, places, or activities—we even have them for routines such as going to a restaurant, visiting the local urgent care center, or following daily eating habits. When you remember, you use these organized knowledge packages to help reconstruct the past. So when someone asks you what you ate for breakfast two weeks ago, you can confidently answer "cereal" because you know that cereal is what you usually eat for breakfast. You don't have to remember the specific episode; you can rely on your general knowledge.

The trouble with schema-based remembering is that it can sometimes lead to false memories. You can remember something that is completely wrong—it didn't really happen—yet still be convinced your memory is accurate (remember our earlier discussion of flashbulb memories?). In a well-known experiment conducted over 60 years ago, Sir Frederick Bartlett asked English undergraduates to read an unfamiliar North American Indian folk tale about tribe members who traveled up

FIGURE 8.13

Transfer-Appropriate Processing
It's useful to study material using the same type of mental processes that you'll be required to use when tested. Suppose you form a visual image of a to-be-remembered word during study (panel 1). If the test requires you to recognize an image of the word, you should do well (panel 2). But if the test asks how the word sounds (panel 3) or whether the word was presented originally in upper- or lowercase letters (panel 4), you're likely to perform poorly. You need to study in a way that is appropriate for the test.

schema
An organized knowledge structure in long-term memory.

a river to battle with some warrior "ghosts" (the story's title was "The War of the Ghosts"). In recalling the story some time later, the students tended to distort facts, omit details, and fill in information that was not included in the original version. For example, familiar things were substituted for unfamiliar things—the word *boat* was substituted for *canoe;* "hunting seals" was replaced with "hunting beavers." Because these things were not actually in the story, Bartlett assumed his subjects must have used their prior knowledge to reconstruct what they remembered—even though they were convinced they were remembering the material accurately (Bartlett, 1932).

You can demonstrate how easily schema-based remembering leads to false memories by reading the following list of words aloud to a group of friends:

BED REST AWAKE TIRED DREAM WAKE SNOOZE

BLANKET DOZE SLUMBER SNORE NAP YAWN DROWSY

After you've finished reading the list, ask your friends to write down all the words. The chances are good that someone will remember an item that was not on the list, particularly the word SLEEP. In experiments using lists of related items like these, people have been found to recall nonpresented items, like sleep, nearly 50% of the time (Deese, 1959; Roediger & McDermott, 1995); the chances of false memory increase further when recognition memory is tested—that is, when you're given the word SLEEP and are asked if it was presented on the list (McDermott & Roediger, 1998). What's behind this effect? Obviously, the word SLEEP is highly related to the words on the list. It seems likely that people recognize the relationships among the words and use this knowledge to help them remember. This is a very effective strategy for remembering, but it can lead to false recollections.

Eyewitness Testimony

The fact that memory tends to be reconstructive, leading sometimes to false memories, has important implications for eyewitness testimony. Loftus and Palmer (1974) conducted an experiment in which undergraduates were shown a short film depicting an automobile accident. Later, when questioned about the film, the students were asked to estimate the speed of the cars just prior to the accident. Some students were asked to estimate how fast the cars were going when they *smashed* into each other; others were asked how fast the cars were going when they *contacted* each other. Notice the difference between the words *smashed* and *contacted*—the schema for *smashed* implies that the cars were traveling at a high rate of speed, whereas *contacted* suggests that the cars were moving slowly. As shown in Figure 8.14, subjects who heard the word *smashed* in the question estimated that the cars were traveling about 42 miles per hour; subjects in the *contacted* group gave an estimate of about 10 miles per hour slower.

Once again, these results show that memory is importantly influenced by general knowledge, as well as by expectations. Everyone in the Loftus and Palmer experiment saw the same film, but what people remembered depended on how the questions were worded—that is, on whether people were led to believe that the cars were going fast or slow. In addition to giving estimates of speed, some were asked whether any broken glass was present in the accident scene. When *smashed* was used in the speed question, subjects were much more likely to incorrectly remember seeing broken glass, even though there wasn't any in the original film. By asking the right kinds of questions during testing, it is possible to make people think they experienced things that did not occur. As Loftus (1979, 1991) has emphasized, these findings suggest that caution must be exercised in interpreting the testimony of any eyewitness—reconstructive factors can always be involved.

Overall, though, there is clearly adaptive value to schema-based reconstructive remembering. By relying on preexisting knowledge to "fill in the gaps," or to

? CRITICAL THINKING

Do you think all remembering is reconstructive? What about sensory memory—isn't that a pure kind of remembering?

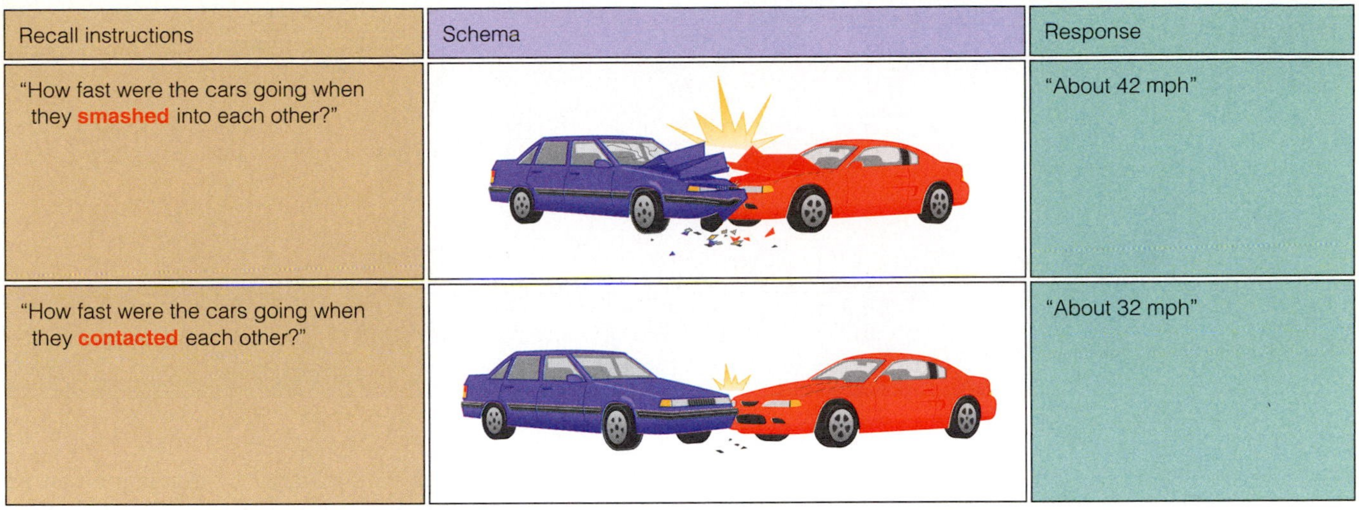

Recall instructions	Schema	Response
"How fast were the cars going when they **smashed** into each other?"		"About 42 mph"
"How fast were the cars going when they **contacted** each other?"		"About 32 mph"

FIGURE 8.14

Schema-Based Remembering
Loftus and Palmer (1974) found that students would remember cars traveling at a faster rate of speed when retrieval instructions used the word *smashed* instead of *contacted*. All subjects saw the same film, but their different schemas for the words *smashed* and *contacted* presumably caused them to reconstruct their memories differently.

help interpret fuzzy recollections, people increase the chances that their responses in new environments will be appropriate—after all, the past is usually the best predictor of the future. People can also use their schematic knowledge to "correct" for any minor details they may have missed during the original exposure. If you already have a pretty good idea of what goes on during a visit to a fast-food restaurant, your mind doesn't need to expend a great deal of effort attending to details the next time you enter a McDonald's. You can rely on your prior knowledge to capture the gist of the experience, even though, on the down side, you may recollect a few things that didn't actually happen.

REMEMBERING WITHOUT AWARENESS: IMPLICIT MEMORY

Up to this point in the chapter we've concentrated on conscious, willful acts of remembering; that is, we've only considered situations where someone is trying to remember something—such as what they ate for breakfast or the words from a memory list. But we often remember things without conscious intent or awareness. You speak, walk to work, recognize someone you know—all these things require memory, but you're usually not explicitly trying to remember anything.

Psychologists use the term **implicit memory** to refer to this kind of remembering (Graf & Schacter, 1985; Roediger & McDermott, 1993). It turns out that implicit memory—remembering without awareness—acts quite similarly to **explicit memory,** the name researchers use to describe conscious, willful remembering. For example, both implicit and explicit memory are strongly influenced by retrieval cues in the environment. If you look at Figure 8.15 on page 328, you'll see some examples of word and picture fragments. Your ability to complete fragments like these improves if you've seen the solution word recently during reading (for example, the word fragment E_E_ _AN_ is easier to solve if the word ELEPHANT has been encountered in the prior 24 hours). But importantly, you don't need to remember seeing the word. Your performance improves even if you don't consciously remember the word, which makes the remembering implicit rather than explicit. However, performance does depend on whether the earlier encounter matches the fragment. If you need to solve a picture fragment, then you're helped more if the earlier encounter was in the form of a picture—such as seeing a picture of an elephant—rather than a word (McDermott & Roediger, 1994; Weldon & Roediger, 1987). Once again, the conditions during testing needed to match the conditions present during the original exposure.

There are situations where implicit memory appears to act somewhat differently from explicit memory. For example, processing strategies that typically improve conscious, willful remembering often have little or no effect on implicit

implicit memory
Remembering that occurs in the absence of conscious awareness or willful intent.

explicit memory
Conscious, willful remembering.

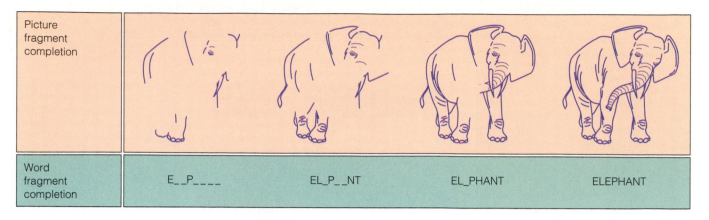

Picture fragment completion				
Word fragment completion	E _ _ P _ _ _ _	EL_ P _ _ NT	EL _ PHANT	ELEPHANT

FIGURE 8.15

Implicit Memory Tests
Here are two examples of implicit memory tests. The subject's task in each case is to complete the picture or word fragment so as to identify the object shown on the far right. In the fragments on the far left, the completion process would be difficult.

? CRITICAL THINKING

Can you think of any ways that advertising agencies might be able to use memory illusions to improve the image of a product?

A prior experience can influence a person's behavior, producing a feeling of déjà vu, even though the memory of that prior experience is beyond awareness.

memory (Roediger et al., 1992). If you elaborate material by thinking about its meaning, your ability to recall that information will improve on most explicit tests of memory, such as recall or recognition. But no similar improvements are usually found when memory is tested using an implicit test, such as solving word fragment problems (Graf et al., 1982). All that seems to matter is that the material be presented in a physically similar way during study and testing.

Memory Illusions

Implicit remembering, like reconstructive remembering, can lead to certain kinds of "memory illusions." *Déjà vu*, in which you feel a sense of familiarity about a location you've never before visited, is an example of such an illusion. You probably encountered a similar location once before, producing a kind of automatic sense of familiarity, but you're unable to pinpoint the particular time and place consciously (see Jacoby & Witherspoon, 1982). A prior experience is influencing your behavior—producing a feeling of déjà vu—but the memory itself is beyond awareness.

In another kind of illusion based on implicit remembering, Larry Jacoby and his colleagues (1989) were able to get people to think certain names were those of famous people when, in fact, the names were not. In step 1 of the experiment, subjects were shown a list of nonfamous names (such as Adrian Marr), which they were asked to remember. In step 2 of the experiment, a longer list was presented that contained three types of items: (a) slightly famous names (such as Minnie Pearl), (b) nonfamous names that were presented on the initial memory list, and (c) nonfamous names that were new to the experiment. For this second list, the task was simply to make a judgment about whether each name was famous. The researchers found that subjects were more likely to think a nonfamous name, such as Adrian Marr, was famous if the name had been part of the earlier memory list. But this "false fame effect" occurred only if the participants failed to recognize the name as having been presented in step 1. The first exposure "tricked" the subjects into thinking the name was famous—probably because the name now seemed familiar—but the trick worked only if the subjects could not explicitly remember having seen the name before in the experiment.

The false fame effect shows how prior experience can affect us in ways that escape awareness. Prior experience can make something seem familiar, but if you can't remember the specific time or place that you encountered the person or object, you can draw erroneous conclusions. Such a process might well account for instances of *cryptomnesia*, or unintentional plagiarism (Brown & Murphy, 1989; Taylor, 1965). Have you ever discovered that one of your "great ideas" was actually suggested to you some time previously by one of your friends? Or perhaps that you had read the idea in a magazine or a book? These are instances in which you have been affected by a prior experience in ways that you cannot consciously remember. The stored memory is affecting your behavior, but the remembering is occurring without conscious awareness.

TEST YOURSELF 8.3

Check your knowledge about how we use cues to help us remember by answering the following questions. Fill in the blanks with one of the following terms: cued-recall, encoding specificity principle, explicit memory, free recall, implicit memory, schema, transfer-appropriate processing. (You will find the answers in the Appendix.)

1. An organized knowledge package that's stored in long-term memory:
   _____

2. Remembering without awareness: _____

3. Studying for a multiple-choice test by writing your own multiple-choice questions:
   _____

4. Retrieval cues must match the information stored in the original memory record:
   _____

5. Remembering material without the aid of any external retrieval cues:
   _____

Updating Memory

Like other storage devices, the mind is susceptible to clutter. Effective remembering often hinges on whether you can successfully discriminate one occurrence from another—you need to remember where you parked your car *today*, not yesterday. You need to remember a current phone number, not some previous one. What if you felt the urge to buy two dozen paper cups every time you entered the grocery store because one time last year you needed paper cups for a party? **Forgetting,** the loss in accessibility of previously stored material, is one of the most important and adaptive properties of your memory system (Bjork, 1989; Kraemer & Golding, 1997).

If you need further convincing that forgetting is adaptive, consider the strange case of a Russian journalist, known as S., who possessed an extraordinary ability to remember. It seems that S., through a fluke of nature, reacted automatically to stimuli in a way that formed unusual and distinctive encodings. When presented with a tone pitched at 500 hertz, S. reported seeing "a dense orange color which made him feel as though a needle had been thrust into his spine" (Luria, 1968, p. 24). For a 3000 Hz tone, S. claimed that it "looks something like a firework tinged with a pink-red hue. The strip of color feels rough and unpleasant, and it has an ugly taste—rather like that of a briny pickle" (p. 24).

S. had a remarkable memory—he could remember grids of numbers perfectly after 15 years—but he suffered a near fatal flaw: He simply could not forget. He had trouble reading books because words or phrases so flooded his mind with previous associations that he had great difficulty concentrating. He would note, for example, small errors in the text: If a character entered the story wearing a cap and in later pages was described without a cap, S. would become greatly disturbed and disappointed in the author. He had trouble holding a job, or even a sustained conversation. For S., the failure to forget produced a truly cluttered mind.

HOW QUICKLY DO WE FORGET?

For most people, once an item has left the immediate present, it is forgotten in a regular and systematic way. How quickly an item is forgotten depends on several

LEARNING GOALS

1. Discuss forgetting, including the contributions of Ebbinghaus, and explain why forgetting is often adaptive.

2. Describe the mechanisms that cause forgetting, including decay and retroactive and proactive interference.

3. Discuss motivated forgetting and the case for and against repression.

4. Describe retrograde and anterograde amnesia and where in the brain memories might be stored.

forgetting
The loss in accessibility of previously stored material.

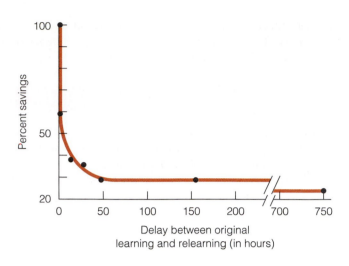

FIGURE 8.16

The Ebbinghaus Forgetting Curve
The German philosopher Hermann Ebbinghaus learned lists of nonsense syllables and then measured how long it would take to relearn the same material after various delays. Shown here are the percent savings found after the delays. (50% savings means it took half as long to relearn the list as it did to learn the list originally; 0% savings means that it took as long to relearn the list as it did to learn the list originally.)

Hermann Ebbinghaus (1859–1909).

factors: how the item was initially encoded, whether it was encountered again at some later time, and the kinds of retrieval cues that are present at the point of remembering. But in general, the course of forgetting looks like the curve shown in Figure 8.16. Most of the forgetting occurs early, but you will continue to forget gradually for a long period following the initial exposure (Wixted & Ebbesen, 1991).

The forgetting curve shown in Figure 8.16 is taken from some classic work by the German philosopher Hermann Ebbinghaus, who was one of the first researchers to investigate memory and forgetting scientifically (Ebbinghaus, 1885/1964). Isolated in his study, he forced himself to learn lists of nonsense syllables (such as ZOK) and then measured how long it took to relearn the same material after various delays (his technique is called the *savings method*). As the graph shows, the longer the delay after original learning, the greater effort Ebbinghaus had to spend relearning the list. The regular form of the Ebbinghaus forgetting function—a rapid loss followed by a more gradual decline—is typical of forgetting in general. Similar forgetting functions are found for a variety of materials, and even for complex skills such as flying an airplane (Fleishman & Parker, 1962) or performing cardiopulmonary resuscitation (McKenna & Glendon, 1985).

Even memories for everyday things, such as the names of high school classmates or material learned in school, are forgotten in regular and systematic ways. In one study, Bahrick (1984) looked at memory for a foreign language (Spanish) over intervals that ranged from about 1 to 50 years. In another study, Bahrick and Hall (1991) examined the retention of high school mathematics over 50 years. In both cases, there was evidence for the rapid loss of recently learned material, followed by more gradual loss, but a considerable amount of knowledge was retained indefinitely. What's surprising about these studies is that a fair amount of the knowledge remained, even though the participants claimed to have not rehearsed or thought about the material in over half a century.

WHY DO WE FORGET?

We can agree that it is adaptive to forget, and we can measure the rate at which information becomes unavailable over time, but what causes forgetting? As we discussed earlier, most memory researchers believe that forgetting is cue dependent—you fail to remember a prior event because you don't have the right retrieval cues. But for many years, psychologists were convinced that memories simply fade with the passage of time, in accordance with a "law of use" (Thorndike, 1914). If you fail to practice a learned habit, such as playing the piano, the habit fades, or *decays*, spontaneously with time.

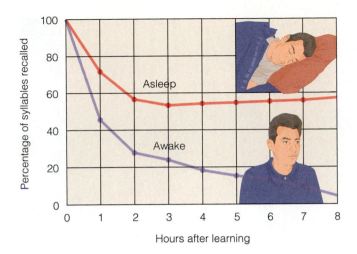

FIGURE 8.17
Interference and Memory
The activities that occur after learning affect how well information is remembered. In this study by Jenkins and Dallenbach (1924), the students showed better memory if they slept during the retention interval than if they remained awake. Presumably, the waking activities interfered with the learning.

However, **decay**—the idea that memories fade just because time passes—alone cannot explain most instances of forgetting. For one thing, as you've seen, memories that appear to have been forgotten can be remembered later under the right retrieval conditions. In addition, people often remember trivial things (such as a joke) for years but forget important things that once received a great deal of practice (such as elementary geometry). Even more significant, just because memories are lost with time doesn't mean that *time* alone is causing the forgetting. A nail left outside becomes rusty with time, but it is not the passage of time that creates the rust—processes other than time (oxidation, in the case of the rusty nail) actually produce the changes.

Retroactive Interference

In forgetting, the "other processes"—which are correlated with the passage of time but are not created by time—often depend on the establishment of other memories. We learn new things all the time, and these new memories compete, or *interfere*, with the recovery of old memories. When you get a new apartment, you work hard to associate your telephone with a new phone number. But after you succeed, it becomes more difficult to retrieve your old number, even if you actively try to remember. The retrieval cue "telephone number" has now become associated to something new; as a result, it loses its capacity to produce the old number. Psychologists use the term **retroactive interference** to refer to cases where the formation of new memories hurts the retention of old memories.

In a classic study of retroactive interference, Jenkins and Dallenbach (1924) asked two students from Cornell University to live in a laboratory for several weeks and learn lists of nonsense syllables either just before bed or early in the morning. The students were tested 1, 2, 4, or 8 hours after learning. The results, which are shown in Figure 8.17, were clear: When the students slept during the delay interval, they remembered more than when they remained awake. Note that a constant amount of time passed in both conditions, so a decay theory would predict no differences between the conditions. The findings suggest that it was the activities that occurred during the students' waking hours that produced the information loss. When awake, the students formed new memories, which interfered with recovery of the old material.

Proactive Interference

But it is not just the learning of new information that produces forgetting. Previously learned information can also produce interference. **Proactive interference** occurs when old memories interfere with the establishment and recovery of new memories. If I try to teach you to remember the word DEATH every time you see the word HAPPY, you can see how prior associations might interfere with the learning process. Seeing the word HAPPY causes you to think of many things

decay
The proposal that memories are forgotten or lost spontaneously with the passage of time.

retroactive interference
A process in which the formation of new memories hurts the recovery of old memories.

proactive interference
A process in which old memories interfere with the establishment and recovery of new memories.

People recall more pleasant than unpleasant experiences, perhaps because they're reluctant to think about and rehearse unpleasant experiences.

? **CRITICAL THINKING**

Can you think of any ways to lessen the influence of proactive interference? Is there any way that you could study information to prevent interference?

that are inconsistent with DEATH. To consider another example, suppose as part of an experiment you're asked to think of PENCIL as a potential weapon to be used in combat. You might be able to think about the word in this way for the experiment, but as time passes you will almost certainly revert back to thinking about PENCIL in the usual way. You might find it difficult to remember PENCIL as a weapon because the word has been used in a different way so many times before. Prior knowledge interferes with the learning and retention of the new material.

Most memory researchers believe that forgetting is usually caused by interference, although it's conceivable that decay might operate in certain situations. One possibility is that decay operates when people remember over the very short term—that is, in sensory memory and short-term memory (Cowan, 1995; Cowan et al., 1997). It's also possible that when people learn new material, older memories are "overwritten" and permanently lost (Loftus & Loftus, 1980). But generally, people don't *lose* material with time; the material simply becomes harder to remember because other things compete and interfere with the retrieval process. As new memories are encoded, old retrieval cues become less effective because those cues are now associated with new things. New experiences can also affect how people interpret retrieval cues that are available, rendering those cues less effective. Successful retention depends on retrieval cues that help discriminate one kind of memory from another. If a particular cue is associated with many things, that cue will not guide the rememberer uniquely to the relevant stored material. Once again, you can see why elaboration is an effective strategy for remembering. If the original event is encoded in an elaborative and distinctive way, the memory record is less likely to be subject to competition from other remembered events.

MOTIVATED FORGETTING

In our earlier discussion of flashbulb memories, it was suggested that highly unusual or emotional events might sometimes lead to distinctive, and therefore easy to remember, memory records. The adaptive value of a system that "stamps in" significant events is easy to understand—remembering these kinds of events could increase our ability to survive. But what about those cases in which it is adaptive to *forget* something, such as a traumatic instance of child abuse or the witnessing of a violent crime?

The idea that the mind might actively repress, or inhibit, certain memory records is an important ingredient of Sigmund Freud's psychoanalytic theory, as you'll see when we discuss personality theories in Chapter 12. Freud introduced **repression** as a "defense mechanism" that people use, unknowingly, to push threatening thoughts, memories, and feelings out of conscious awareness. According to Freud, these repressed memories retain the capacity to affect behavior at an unconscious level but cannot be remembered in the conventional sense. The result is a reduction in the experience of anxiety.

The Evidence for Repression

Modern researchers acknowledge the occurrence of retrieval failure, but they remain undecided about the scientific validity of repression. It's clear that people typically recall more pleasant than unpleasant events (Linton, 1975; Wagenaar, 1986), and painful experiences, such as the pain associated with childbirth, also seem to be recollected less well with the passage of time (Robinson et al., 1980). There are also countless instances, reported mainly in clinical settings, of what appears to be the repression of traumatic experiences.

For example, in one study 475 adults who were undergoing psychotherapy were asked about memories of childhood sexual abuse. Each had reported an incident of abuse during childhood, and each was asked the following specific question: "During the period of time when the first forced sexual encounter happened and your 18th birthday, was there ever a time when you could not remember the forced sexual experience?" (Briere & Conte, 1993). Fifty-nine percent of the people who answered the question responded "yes," suggesting that the memories had been pushed out of consciousness for at least some period of time. In another study supporting the same conclusion, Williams (1992) asked 100 women who had been medically treated for sexual abuse as children—the abuse was documented by hospital and other records—whether they remembered the incident 17 years later. Thirty-eight percent of those responding reported no memory for the abuse, again providing support for the concept of repression.

But do these data really mean that the forgetting was caused by repression? It's possible that people tend to remember positive events because these are the types of events that people rehearse and relate to others. The fact that painful experiences are forgotten with the passage of time can be explained in lots of ways—many things are forgotten with the passage of time, especially those things that are unlikely to be rehearsed. Moreover, there is considerable evidence suggesting that people like to cast themselves in a positive light—people often remember donating more to charity than they actually did, or that they raised more-intelligent children (Cannell & Kahn, 1968; Myers & Ridl, 1979). Many instances of apparent retrieval failure, then, could be due to the reconstructive "recasting" of prior experiences rather than to the active repression of intact memories (see Loftus, 1993).

It's also worth noting that many repressed memories are recovered during the course of therapy. This means that therapists might be indirectly influencing what their clients remember. If you believe that repressed memories of childhood abuse contribute to psychological disorders, then it's reasonable for you as a therapist to explore the early childhood history of your client, perhaps with the expectation of finding abuse. However, as you know, decades of memory research have shown that what people remember is often colored by expectations—people reconstruct what they think must have happened to them previously, and these reconstructions can be inaccurate. No one believes that therapists purposely implant false memories in their clients, but it might happen as an unintentional result of the therapeutic process.

The failure to find solid scientific evidence for the concept of repression does not mean that traumatic events are never forgotten. As Freud noted, a process of

repression
A defense mechanism that individuals use, unknowingly, to push threatening thoughts, memories, and feelings out of conscious awareness.

CONCEPT SUMMARY
Mechanisms of Forgetting

Mechanism	Description	Example
Cue dependence	Failure to remember an event due to a lack of appropriate cues.	Although Susan would recognize a definition of semantic memory on a multiple-choice test, she can't think of it for a fill-in-the-blank test.
Decay	Memories fade with the passage of time.	After only a month of lessons, and then six years of not playing the piano, Shao forgets how to play.
Proactive interference	Old memories interfere with the formation and recovery of new memories.	Bruce is so impressed with the first person he met at the party, he can't remember the names of those he met later.
Retroactive interference	New memories interfere with the recovery of old memories.	Filling out a job application, Seth can only remember his most recent address, not the one before it.
Motivated forgetting	Traumatic experiences are forgotten to reduce anxiety.	Jackie can't remember too much about the day her parents were seriously injured in an accident.

repression might be adaptive in the sense that it can prevent or reduce anxiety. It may also be the case that "forgotten" events continue to exert indirect influences on behavior in ways that bypass awareness. But the data do suggest that memories, whether "recovered" in therapy or simply in the normal course of everyday activities, should not be taken at face value. It is adaptive for people to use prior knowledge, as well as current expectations, to help them remember—but perhaps at the cost that we may sometimes remember things that didn't actually happen.

THE NEUROSCIENCE OF FORGETTING

To explain the instances of forgetting that we've encountered up to this point, we've appealed largely to the actions of normal, adaptive psychological processes. But forgetting can also be caused by physical problems in the brain, such as those induced by injury or illness. Psychologists use the term **amnesia** to refer to forgetting that is caused by some kind of physical problem. (There is another type of amnesia that is psychological in origin—it arises from something called a dissociative disorder—but we'll delay our discussion of this kind of forgetting until Chapter 14.)

Types of Amnesia

There are two major kinds of physically based amnesia: retrograde and anterograde. **Retrograde amnesia** is memory loss for events that happened *prior* to the point of injury (you can think of *retro* as meaning backward in time). People who are in automobile accidents, or who receive a sharp blow to the head, often have trouble remembering the events leading directly up to the accident. The memory loss can apply to events that happened only moments before the accident, or the loss can be quite severe; in some cases, patients lose their ability to recall personal experiences that occurred years before the accident. In most cases, fortunately, these memory losses are not permanent and recover slowly over time (Cermak, 1982).

Anterograde amnesia is memory loss for events that happen *after* the point of physical damage. People who suffer from anterograde amnesia, as we noted at the beginning of this chapter, seem to be forever locked in the past—they are incapable of forming memories for new experiences. The disorder develops as a result of brain damage, which can occur from the persistent use of alcohol (a condition called *Korsakoff's syndrome*), from brain infections (such as viral encephalitis), or, in some cases, as a by-product of brain surgery. One of the most thoroughly studied amnesic patients, known to researchers as H.M., developed the disorder after surgery was performed to remove large portions of his temporal lobes. The pur-

amnesia
Forgetting that is caused by physical problems in the brain, such as those induced by injury or disease.

retrograde amnesia
Memory loss for events that happened prior to the point of brain injury.

anterograde amnesia
Memory loss for events that happen after the point of physical injury.

pose of the operation was to reduce the severity of H.M.'s epileptic seizures; the surgery was successful—his seizures *were* dramatically reduced—but anterograde amnesia developed as an unexpected side effect.

What's Forgotten in Amnesia?

Over the past 25 years, considerable research has been conducted on the problem of anterograde amnesia. Patients such as H.M. have been studied in great detail to determine exactly what kinds of memory processing are lost (Milner, 1966). It was originally believed that patients like H.M. fail to acquire new memories because some basic encoding (or acquisition) mechanisms have been destroyed. It is now clear, however, that these patients can learn a great deal but must be tested in particular ways. If a patient like H.M. is tested indirectly, on a task that does not require *conscious* remembering, performance can approach or even match normal levels.

In one study, Jacoby and Witherspoon (1982) asked Korsakoff's patients with anterograde amnesia to learn homophones for a later memory test. Homophones are words that sound alike but have different meanings and spellings, such as READ and REED. To "bias" a particular interpretation for a given homophone, it was presented as part of a word pair, such as BOOK—READ or, in another condition, SAXOPHONE—REED. (Because the words were presented aloud, the only way to distinguish between the homophones READ and REED was through the accompanying context word BOOK or SAXOPHONE.) Later, the amnesics were asked to recognize the words, but they were unable to do so—they seemed to have acquired none of the presented information. In a second test, however, the homophones were simply read aloud by the experimenter and the subjects' task was to provide the spelling. Surprisingly, if the amnesics had earlier received the pair BOOK—READ, they spelled the test homophone READ, but if the homophone had been paired with SAXOPHONE, they spelled it REED.

These results suggest that the presented homophones were learned by the amnesic patients. The way the subjects spelled the homophone during the test depended on the prior experience. Other experiments have revealed similar findings. For example, amnesics are more likely to complete a word fragment (such as E_E_ _AN_) correctly if they have seen the word before, but if asked to recall the word, their performance falls apart (Graf & Schacter, 1985). Patients who suffer from anterograde amnesia fail to retrieve past experiences whenever they must *consciously* recollect the experience; when the past is assessed indirectly, through a task that does not require conscious remembering, these amnesics often perform at normal levels.

Where Are Memories Stored?

The study of brain-damaged individuals, such as Korsakoff's patients, has also encouraged researchers to draw tentative conclusions about how and where memories might be stored in the brain. We touched on this issue in Chapter 3, when we considered biological processes. At that point special attention was paid to a structure called the *hippocampus*, which most brain researchers believe is critically involved in the formation and storage of memories (Squire, 1992). Damage to the hippocampus, as well as to surrounding structures in the brain, leads to memory problems in a wide variety of species, including humans, monkeys, and rats. Areas surrounding the hippocampus also "light up" in a PET scan when subjects are asked to recall specific material (Raichle, 1994; Squire et al., 1992).

However, no single brain structure, or group of structures, is responsible for all instances of

CRITICAL THINKING

What advice would you give to the family of someone suffering from anterograde amnesia?

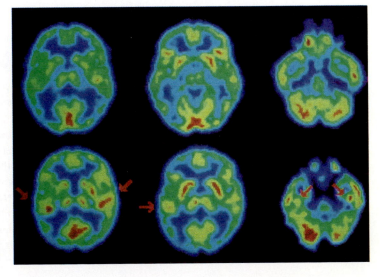

This PET scan shows regions of brain activity during auditory stimulation. The arrows are pointing to areas inside the temporal lobes that become active after words are heard; these same areas are thought to be associated with some kinds of memory.

remembering and forgetting. Things are vastly interconnected in the brain, and activities in one part of the brain often depend on activities in other parts. The regions of the brain that are involved in the storage of memories also depend on the type of processing involved. For example, episodic memory appears to be controlled by different brain regions from those involved in learning and remembering skills (Gabrieli, 1998). There's evidence that emotionally-charged memories may involve a structure in the brain called the amygdala (Phelps & Anderson, 1997), and different brain regions may control the remembering of true and false memories (Schacter et al., 1998).

Certain kinds of memory loss, such as those found in Alzheimer's disease, have been linked to inadequate supplies of neurotransmitters in the brain (Albert & Moss, 1992). But once again, damage to a part of the brain tied to the production of a neurotransmitter (such as acetylcholine) probably has consequences for all regions of the brain that depend on that neurotransmitter. This makes it very difficult to pinpoint where a memory is stored, or even where the processing relevant to the storage of memories takes place. Modern technological advances are supplying researchers with tons of useful information about activity in the brain, but we still have a long way to go before it will be possible to draw anything but tentative conclusions about the physical basis of learning and remembering.

TEST YOURSELF 8.4

Check your knowledge about forgetting and the updating of memory by deciding whether each of the following statements is true or false. (You will find the answers in the Appendix.)

1. Forgetting is usually slow at first and becomes more rapid as time passes. *True or False?*

2. Most psychologists agree that interference rather than decay is primarily responsible for long-term forgetting. *True or False?*

3. Proactive interference occurs when what you learn at Time 2 interferes with what you learned previously at Time 1. *True or False?*

4. Anterograde amnesia blocks the learning of new information. *True or False?*

5. People tend to recall more pleasant than unpleasant events over time. *True or False?*

6. Psychologists believe that the hippocampus is involved in some, but not all, instances of remembering. *True or False?*

Solving the Problems

Time flows continuously, so experiences quickly leave the present and recede backward into the past. To understand the human capacity to preserve and recover this past, we considered some of the fundamental problems that memory systems help us solve.

Remembering over the Short Term. First, to improve perception and aid ongoing comprehension, psychologists assume that people have internal processes that help them maintain information over the short term. In the case of sensory memory, we retain a relatively pure snapshot of the world, or replica of the environmental message. Sensory memories accurately represent the world as recorded by the sensory equipment, but they tend to be short-lived, lasting on the order of a second or less. Short-term memory, in contrast, is the system used to store, think about, and reason with the message once it has undergone perceptual analysis. Items are typically maintained in short-term memory in the form of an "inner voice," and they are forgotten rapidly in the absence of rehearsal. The capacity, or size, of the short-term memory system is determined by a trade-off between the factors that lead to forgetting over the short term (either decay or interference) and the time-limited process of rehearsal.

Storing Information for the Long Term. To store information over the long term, you need to produce elaborate and distinctive memory records. Focusing on the meaning of the input, relating to-be-remembered information to other things in memory, and forming visual images of the input all lead to distinctive memory records that are easily discriminated from other things. Forming a visual image is particularly effective, and many memory aids, or mnemonic devices, are based on the use of imagery. In the peg-word method, for example, the idea is to form a visual image linking the to-be-remembered material to a set of specific memory cues; in the method of loci, the information is linked visually to a particular location or pathway. Long-term memory also depends on how information is actually presented: Items presented near the beginning and end of a sequence

are remembered well, as are items that have been repeated. Spaced or distributed practice turns out to be more effective than massed practice.

Recovering Information from Cues. Most memory researchers believe that successful remembering depends on having the right kinds of retrieval cues. Most forms of forgetting are cue dependent, which means that stored information is not really "lost," it simply is inaccessible because the appropriate retrieval cues are not present. Effective retrieval cues are those that *match* the conditions that were present during original learning. According to the encoding specificity principle, effective retrieval cues also need to be specifically encoded along with the to-be-remembered material. But when people recover information from cues, they also rely on their general knowledge. The past is often reconstructed, and the reconstruction process leads to adaptive, but sometimes inaccurate, recollections of the past.

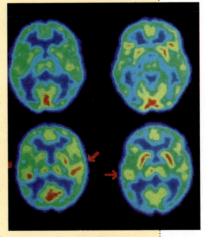

Updating Memory. Forgetting is an adaptive process. If we did not constantly change and update our knowledge about the world, our minds would be cluttered with useless facts, such as where the car was parked last Wednesday. Although the psychological mechanisms of forgetting are still being investigated, it seems unlikely that long-term memories fade as a simple by-product of time. Rather, as we learn new things, previously learned material becomes harder to access. New memories compete and interfere with recovery of the old. With the right kinds of cues, however—cues that discriminate one kind of occurrence from another—previously forgotten material becomes refreshed and available for use once again.

Remembering and Forgetting Chapter Summary

Remembering over the Short Term

It's necessary to have some sort of internal machinery for remembering information over the short term. The performance of most mental tasks requires that certain bits of information be retained throughout the solution process. Short-term memories allow us to prolong incoming messages.

VISUAL SENSORY MEMORY: THE ICON

The *icon* is a lingering visual sensory memory trace. These images allow visual sensations to be extended in time so the brain can more efficiently process the incoming physical message. In a classic series of studies, Sperling compared *whole report* and *partial report,* and found that the icon lasts around ½ second.

SHORT-TERM MEMORY: THE INNER VOICE

Short-term memory is the system we use to temporarily store, think about, and reason with information. Information in short-term memory is typically recoded in the form of an "inner voice." Information in short-term memory is quickly forgotten if not rehearsed, due to decay and interference. Short-term memory capacity is limited, as demonstrated by *memory span,* which is equal to the amount of information that can be rehearsed in about 2 seconds. It can be increased through *chunking.*

AUDITORY SENSORY MEMORY: THE ECHO

Pure sounds can be held for brief intervals to aid in auditory perception. The roles of auditory sensory memory include localization of sounds, and language processing. It's also thought to be extremely brief in duration, probably less than a second. Both visual and auditory sensory memory maintain relatively exact replicas of the incoming stimulus.

Storing Information for the Long Term

Once information is no longer present, it needs to be stored internally so that it can be recovered at the appropriate place and time. In order to establish effective long-term memories, certain types of thinking processes can be employed.

WHAT IS STORED IN LONG-TERM MEMORY?

Episodic memories are those in which we recall some personal moment from our past. *Semantic memories* are things we know about the world, but are not tied to particular episodes from our past. *Procedural memory* refers to our knowledge of how to do things.

IMAGERY: REMEMBERING THROUGH VISUALIZATION

Forming a visual image of presented material is another way to produce an elaborative memory trace. *Mnemonic devices* are special mental tricks that help people think about material in ways that lead to effective remembering. These techniques include the *method of loci* and the *peg-word technique.* Research on visual imagery suggests that "mental pictures" act visual in some ways, not in others. Mental imagery and visual perception may rely on the same neurological (brain) mechanisms.

ELABORATION: CONNECTING MATERIAL WITH EXISTING KNOWLEDGE

Elaboration (relating input to other things) allows us to establish meaningful connections that ease later recovery of the stored material. This can be accomplished by thinking about meaning, noticing relationships, and noticing differences.

HOW SHOULD MATERIAL BE PRESENTED?

Improved memory for items at the start of a list is termed the *primacy effect;* improved memory for items at the end of a list is termed the *recency effect. Repetition* also improves memory, particularly if the repetitions are *distributed* over time.

Recovering Information from Cues

Our interactions with the world require us to recover images of both the immediate and the distant past. The recovery of this information is triggered by other events, or cues, encountered in the environment.

THE IMPORTANCE OF RETRIEVAL CUES

Many researchers believe that most forgetting involves *cue-dependent forgetting*. The information is available, given the right type of cues. According to the *encoding specificity principle*, an effective retrieval cue is one that was associated with the material when it was first encoded. According to the transfer-appropriate-processing principle, material should be studied using the same kind of mental processes that will be used during retrieval.

REMEMBERING WITHOUT AWARENESS: IMPLICIT MEMORY

Implicit memory refers to remembering without awareness. *Explicit memory* refers to conscious, willful remembering. Implicit and explicit memory are similarly affected by retrieval cues, but sometimes behave differently; implicit memory is relatively unaffected by some strategies that help explicit remembering. Implicit memory leads to certain types of "memory illusions."

RECONSTRUCTIVE REMEMBERING

Remembering depends on beliefs and expectations, just as perception does. Remembering is aided by *schemas,* which are large clusters of related facts about people, places, and activities. Schema-based remembering can lead to false memories, as shown in research on eyewitness testimony. However, schema-based reconstructive remembering has considerable adaptive value.

Updating Memory

Forgetting refers to the loss in accessibility of previously stored material, and has considerable adaptive value. It keeps us current, and prevents us from acting in ways that are inappropriate for the present.

HOW QUICKLY DO WE FORGET?

Most forgetting occurs soon after initial exposure. Gradual forgetting continues for a long period. This general pattern of forgetting holds for a wide variety of materials.

MOTIVATED FORGETTING

An important part of Freud's psychoanalytic theory is the assumption that the mind may actively inhibit or *repress* certain memories. While most researchers acknowledge the occurrence of retrieval failure, they remain undecided about the scientific validity of the concept of *repression.*

WHY DO WE FORGET?

The simple passage of time (decay) is not sufficient to explain most instances of forgetting. Rather, both *retroactive interference* (new material interfering with old) and *proactive interference* (old material interfering with new) cause forgetting.

THE NEUROSCIENCE OF FORGETTING

Amnesia refers to forgetting that is caused by some type of physical problem. Retrograde amnesia is memory loss for events that happened prior to the injury. *Anterograde amnesia* is memory loss for events that happen after the point of physical damage. Although the hippocampus is important in the formation of new memories, no single brain structure is responsible for remembering.

Terms to Remember

memory, 302
encoding, 302
storage, 302
retrieval, 302

REMEMBERING OVER THE SHORT TERM

sensory memory, 304
short-term memory, 304
iconic memory, 304
echoic memory, 306
rehearsal, 308
memory span, 310
chunking, 311

STORING INFORMATION FOR THE LONG TERM

long-term memory, 312
episodic memory, 313
semantic memory, 313
procedural memory, 313
elaboration, 314
distinctiveness, 314
visual imagery, 315
mnemonic devices, 315
method of loci, 315
flashbulb memories, 317
peg-word method, 317
primacy effect, 320
recency effect, 320
distributed practice, 320

RECOVERING INFORMATION FROM CUES

free recall, 322
cued recall, 322
cue-dependent forgetting, 322
encoding specificity principle, 323
transfer-appropriate processing, 324
schema, 325
implicit memory, 327
explicit memory, 327

UPDATING MEMORY

forgetting, 329
decay, 331
retroactive interference, 331
proactive interference, 331
repression, 333
amnesia, 334
retrograde amnesia, 334
anterograde amnesia, 334

Recommended Readings

Neath, I. (1998). *Human memory: An introduction to research, data, and theory.* Pacific Grove, CA: Brooks/Cole. A leading undergraduate textbook on memory. The material discussed in Chapter 8 is covered here in much more detail.

Schacter, D. L. (1996). *Searching for memory.* New York: Basic Books. Written by a top memory researcher for a general audience, this book paints a fascinating portrait of how the brain remembers and reconstructs the past. Covers not only the psychology of memory, but it also deals extensively with the biological processes thought to underlie remembering.

Tulving, E. (1983). *Elements of episodic memory.* New York: Oxford University Press. This is a semiautobiographical account of one researcher's profound influence on modern memory theory. Although written as a professional book, it contains many personal observations and anecdotes that bring memory theory alive.

INFOTRAC® COLLEGE EDITION

For additional readings, explore Infotrac College Edition, your online library. Go to:
http://www.infotrac-college.com/wadsworth

Hint: enter the search terms: Short term memory, Long term memory, Autobiographical memory, Visual imagery, Implicit and explicit memory, Amnesia.

What's on the Web?

False Memory Syndrome Foundation

(advicom.net/~fitz/fmsf/)

Few topics in psychology have fueled as much debate as the controversy over so-called "recovered memories" of abuse. As your text discussion points out, the concept of repression is hotly debated in light of the fact that memory can easily be shown to be reconstructive. Learn some more about the debate with a visit to this sight.

Memory (at the Exploratorium)

(www.exploratorium.edu/memory/)

This renowned science museum has an on-line memory exhibition, with some very fun and informative memory demonstrations, facts, and figures. Read about a memory artist, memories for emotional events, and play games with your memory—try to pick the correct penny (it's harder than you think!), and explore some "tricks" for improving your memory.

NASA Applied Cognition Lab

(olias.arc.nasa.gov/cognition/tutorials/index.html)

This particular set of pages at the NASA Web sites provides some fun demonstrations that allow you to explore how your own memory works. Demonstrations provided help you learn the effects of mnemonic devices, interference, and word/picture encoding.

The Wadsworth Psychology Study Center Web Site

See http://psychology.wadsworth.com/ for practice quiz questions, hypercontents, updates, critical thinking exercises, discussion forums and more! The Wadsworth Psychology Study Center provides a wealth of information fully organized and integrated by chapter.

Thought and Language

Wayne Inges, a devious soul, chuckles silently to himself as he completes the deal. "That's right," he says, "center court, floor level—$100 for the pair." Having paid only $50 for the ticket pair himself, Wayne pockets a tidy little profit. But there are more fools in the world, so he decides to buy the tickets back for $150. With game time approaching, and desperation setting in, this time the pair sells for $200. Can you figure out Wayne's total profit for the evening?

To find the answer, your mind begins an internal, goal-directed activity called **thinking.** In its simplest form, thinking, or *cognition*, can be defined as the set of processes used to manipulate knowledge and ideas. Through thought we act on our knowledge in a directed and purposeful way to solve problems, to reason and make decisions, and to understand and communicate with others. Like most other internally based psychological phenomena, it's not possible to measure thinking directly, but much can be learned by observing a thinker and listening to his or her rationales for actions or conclusions.

Let's see, Wayne made $50 on the first transaction but spent $150 to buy the tickets back, so he lost the original $50. He finally sold the pair for $200, so his total profit for the evening must be $50, right? Easy enough. We've used our knowledge about the world, and about mathematics in particular, to work systematically toward a goal. It's easy to see the adaptive value of the process. Thinking increases your ability to survive because you can act on your knowledge in precise, systematic, and purposeful ways.

But, as you may have guessed, our reasoning in this case is completely wrong. We arrived at the wrong answer, as do many others who try this task. Using a slight variation of the same problem, Maier and Burke (1967) found that people come up with the correct answer less than 40% of the time. The correct answer is $100—Wayne paid out a total of $200 ($50 for the first transaction and $150 for the second) and received $300 back from the buyers. Simple subtraction yields the correct answer of $100.

What lies behind the error? The difficulty comes from thinking about Wayne's sales as one continuous event rather than as two separate transactions. This becomes clearer if you frame the problem slightly differently: Wayne bought tickets for Friday night's game for $50 and sold them for $100, then he bought tickets for Saturday's game for $150 and sold them for $200. Under these conditions, people rarely, if ever, make an error. One of the challenges of the modern study of thinking, and problem solving in particular, is to understand why human thought processes are so commonly led astray. How can thought processes that seem so illogical fit snugly into the mold of an adaptive mind?

thinking
The processes that underlie the mental manipulation of knowledge, usually in an attempt to reach a goal or solve a problem.

Previewing the Adaptive Problems

The topics of thought and language actually touch on a wide variety of psychological activities. To think, you need to be aware and possess the capacity to learn. To manipulate the knowledge in your head, you need first to remember. When you solve problems or make decisions, you first need to come up with criteria for what represents an acceptable solution. To express things symbolically in the form of language, you need rules for classifying objects and guidelines for transforming meaning into strings of sounds or symbols.

For centuries, philosophers have struggled to understand the "higher mental processes" of thought and language. More recently, questions about thought and language have formed the focus for *cognitive science*, a diverse field that draws on the work of professionals from a wide variety of disciplines, including psychology, linguistics, philosophy, biology, and even

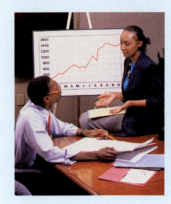

Communicating with others   Classifying and categorizing   Solving problems   Making decisions

FIGURE 9.1

The Adaptive Problems

Thought and language serve a variety of adaptive functions. Summarized here are the four adaptive problems that we'll be considering in this chapter.

engineering and computer science. Once again, we'll discuss the insights of psychologists and cognitive scientists by considering a set of adaptive problems (see Figure 9.1).

First, how do we communicate with others? The ability to communicate, especially through written and spoken language, may well be humanity's greatest success story. No other species on the planet can claim our knack for transmitting knowledge through speech and writing. In fact, the use of language may be the "most pervasive and uniquely human characteristic of the species" (Wasow, 1989). Through language production we transmit thoughts, feelings, and needs to others; through language comprehension we learn and understand.

Second, how do we classify and categorize objects in our world? To make sense of our environment, especially the objects in it, we carve the world into meaningful chunks called *categories.* Can you imagine a world where every encounter was new and unique—a world where no two things shared features in common, where each encounter with a cat, or a bird, or a snake was a new and mysterious experience? The ability to see similarities among things, to classify objects and events into meaningful categories, allows us to simplify our environment and make predictions about how to act.

Third, how do we solve problems like the one posed at the beginning of the chapter? When psychologists talk about problem solving, they're referring to situations in which someone wants to reach a goal, such as solving a math problem or hooking up the new VCR, but how to get from here to there is not immediately obvious. Think about the dozens of practical problems you face and solve each and every day. Did you have trouble finding your keys this morning? Have a difficult time choosing what to wear or what to watch on TV? The adaptive value of problem solving should be relatively obvious—if humans couldn't solve the problem of where to find food and water, or how to woo and win the appropriate mate, *homo sapiens* would quickly follow the path taken by the dinosaurs and the dodo bird.

Fourth, how do we make decisions when confronted with a set of alternatives? Whereas problem solving requires you to move forward toward an unknown solution (which may not even exist), *decision making* requires you to make a choice from among a set of alternatives. Should I buy the tickets for $100, use the money to help pay this month's rent, or gamble the money on the outcome of tonight's game? Note that an important ingredient of decision making is *risk*—choices have consequences, and an incorrect decision can lead to an unpleasant or even fatal outcome.

Communicating with Others

We begin our discussion of thinking, curiously enough, with an extended discussion of language. It might seem funny to lump language and thought together, but the two are closely linked: Language importantly influences the way we think about and view our world. Remember from Chapter 8 how the word *smashed* rather than *contacted* led people to infer and recall things about the meeting of two cars that they would not have otherwise done? Think about the words *doctor* and *secretary*—are you likely to picture a man and a woman, respectively? Do you think twice about a sentence like "The secretary hates his boss"? Words carry significant gender connotations for many. If used inappropriately they become weapons, leading people to expect and draw conclusions about things that are misleading or wrong (Henley, 1989; Mackay, 1983).

DOES LANGUAGE DETERMINE THOUGHT?

How strong is the connection between language and thought? The **linguistic relativity hypothesis** proposes that language *determines* thought (Whorf, 1956). Without a word or a phrase to describe an experience, the experience can only reside, quite literally, out of mind. To test this hypothesis, researchers have turned to nature's laboratory to see how the idiosyncrasies of language affect the way people think across different cultures. In the Philippines, for example, the Hanunoo people have some 92 different names to describe varieties of rice (Anderson, 1990). Deep in the mountainous terrain of the Andes lives a tribe of people called the Quechua who have no word in their language for "flat." Directions are given in terms of body images—such as the *foot*, *belly*, or *head* of a mountain—rather than in terms like *north* or *south* (Hunt & Agnoli, 1991).

According to the linguistic relativity hypothesis, your language determines how you think and perceive the world. Consequently, you might expect the Hanunoo people to see curious things in rice that other cultures, with a more limited "rice" vocabulary, do not. Suppose you took the Quechua out of their familiar environment and put them in a flat terrain, such as a Midwestern cornfield; how might they react? According to the linguistic relativity hypothesis, people who speak only of sharp-angled inclines and precipitous drops might have a difficult time orienting themselves in a flat environment, or even standing up without toppling backwards. This may seem silly, but the idea that thought is a slave to language is very important; it has implications for many things, including education (Lee, 1997).

The Cultural Evidence

In some important cross-cultural research, Eleanor Rosch (published under her former name, Heider) traveled to New Guinea to investigate the perceptual abilities of a tribe called the Dani. For reasons unique to their environment, the Dani's language contains only two basic color terms: *mola* for bright, warm hues, and *mili* for the darker, colder hues. If words completely shape thought, Rosch reasoned, the Dani should have trouble perceiving and remembering colors that lack Dani color names. After showing a wide range of colors, Rosch discovered that volunteers from the tribe had no trouble remembering novel colors that had been presented to them only moments before; moreover, the Dani seemed especially able to learn and remember things about focal colors—red, green, and blue—a result that is also commonly found for English speakers.

Rosch interpreted her results to mean that English speakers and speakers of the Dani language probably perceive the world, at least with respect to color, in very similar ways. Color perception appears to be universal, depending more on the physiology of the visual system than on the particular vocabulary adopted by the perceiver (Heider, 1972). In research conducted after Rosch's pioneering

LEARNING GOALS

1. Evaluate the linguistic relativity hypothesis.
2. Discuss the structure of language and identify its basic units.
3. Discuss some of the factors that contribute to language comprehension.
4. Trace the major milestones of language development.
5. Discuss efforts to produce language in nonhuman species.

linguistic relativity hypothesis
The proposal that language determines the characteristics and content of thought.

study, the same general conclusion has been reached: People seem to see essentially the same world regardless of language particulars (Davies, 1998; Davies & Corbett, 1997).

The cross-cultural evidence has caused the majority of psychologists to conclude that the linguistic relativity hypothesis, taken literally, simply cannot be true. Members of the Hanunoo might be better than their Western counterparts at describing rice, but it's unlikely that rice looks any different to these people. Instead of tottering in the Midwestern cornfield, the Quechua will be able to orient themselves just fine, although they might have difficulty describing their flat environment. All humans share certain fundamental cognitive abilities, and these abilities remain intact even when they're not regularly tapped by the speaker's language and environment.

At the same time, there is little question that language *influences* thought. Both perception and memory depend on prior knowledge, and people often use words as tools to generate expectations that influence cognitive processing. As you learned in Chapter 8, memory for an event depends significantly on how you describe the event to yourself when it originally occurs. The richer the description, or encoding, the more likely you are to remember the event later. If a person has poor language skills, and he or she is unable to encode an event in an elaborate manner, then memory will suffer. Language may not be the sole determinant of thought, but it clearly shapes thought in some significant ways (Lucy, 1997).

THE STRUCTURE OF LANGUAGE

We now turn our attention to language itself. What is language, and how should it be properly defined? If you think about it, birds communicate effectively through the production of acoustic sequences (songs). Some believe that bees can convey information about the exact location of honey through a tail-wagging dance (von Frisch, 1967, but see also Wenner, 1998). Even your dog barks incessantly at outdoor noises in what appears to be an effort to communicate. But to

The Quecha, who live in mountainous regions, have no word in their language for "flat." According to the linguistic relativity hypothesis, one might expect them to have a difficult time orienting themselves spatially in a flat environment.

? CRITICAL THINKING

Do you think the study of color perception is a fair way to test the linguistic relativity hypothesis?

Bees do a characteristic "waggle dance" that may communicate information about the location of honey. But would you say bees have really developed language?

qualify as a true language, the communication system must have rules, known collectively as **grammar,** that allow the communicator to combine arbitrary symbols to convey meaning.

A grammar provides rules about which combinations of sounds and words are permissible and which are not. Grammar has three aspects: (1) **phonology,** the rules for combining sounds to make words; (2) **syntax,** the rules for combining words to make sentences; and (3) **semantics,** the rules used to communicate meaning. In English we would never say something like "The cautious the barked nasty at man poodle." This particular combination of words violates a number of rules of syntax, such as the rule that articles (*the*) and adjectives (*nasty*) come before nouns (*man*). We would also never generate a sentence like "Colorless green ideas sleep furiously." Although this is a well-structured sentence, it suffers from a violation of semantics—it has no meaning. We use our knowledge about semantics to pick the appropriate words (perhaps "people" can sleep furiously, but "ideas" cannot) and to infer connections between words and other things in memory (cautious poodles bark at rather than bite nasty people).

Phonemes and Morphemes

All human languages possess a basic hierarchical structure, which ranges from the fundamental sounds of speech to the more complex levels of spoken conversation. At the bottom of the spoken language hierarchy are **phonemes,** defined as the smallest significant sound units in speech. These speech sounds are produced through a complex coordination of the vocal cords, lungs, lips, tongue, and even the teeth. Table 9.1 lists some examples of phonemes in the English language. Notice that there isn't a simple one-to-one mapping between a given letter of the alphabet and a phoneme. The letter *e*, for example, maps onto one kind of speech sound in the word *head* and a different kind in the word *heat*.

Babies greet the world with the ability to produce a large number of fundamental speech sounds, but they quickly restrict the number to a much smaller set. English speakers use only about 40 to 45 phonemes; other languages may use considerably more or fewer. Japanese speakers, for example, do not differentiate between the phonemes *r* and *l* in their native tongue (which makes it difficult for a native Japanese speaker to hear the difference between *race* and *lace*). English speakers do not meaningfully distinguish the *p* sound in *pause* from the *p* sound in *camp*. In Thai or Hindi, these same sound units carry unique and different mean-

grammar
The rules of language that allow the communicator to combine arbitrary symbols to convey meaning; grammar includes the rules of phonology, syntax, and semantics.

phonology
Rules governing how sounds should be combined to make words in a language.

syntax
Rules governing how words should be combined to form sentences.

semantics
The rules used in language to communicate meaning.

phonemes
The smallest significant sound units in speech.

TABLE 9.1			
Some Examples of English Phonemes			
Symbol	**Examples**	**Symbol**	**Examples**
b	burger, rubble	ng	sting, ringer
ē	easy, zombie	oy	coil, employ
ĕ	enter, metric	r	rat, crust
f	fungus, phone	s	stodgy, best
ĭ	icky, wig	t	tramp, missed
ī	ice, shy	th	that, other
k	kitty, ache	ŭ	ugly, butter
n	newt, annoy		

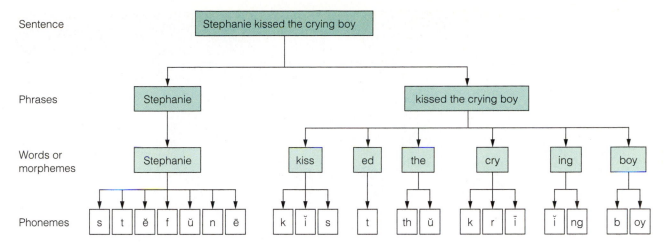

Sentence

Phrases

Words or
morphemes

Phonemes

FIGURE 9.2
The Units of Language
Languages have a basic hierarchical structure,
which includes the fundamental sounds of
speech and the more complex levels of spoken
conversation. Complex rules determine how
words are combined into phrases and sentences
and how fundamental speech sounds
(phonemes) combine to create the smallest
units of meaning (morphemes) and words.

ings. Part of the trick to acquiring a foreign language is mastering the basic phonemes of that language.

At the next level in the hierarchy are **morphemes**—the smallest units of language that carry meaning. Morphemes usually consist of single words, such as *cool* or *hip*, but they can also be prefixes and suffixes. For instance, the word *cool* contains a single morpheme, whereas *uncool* contains two—the root word *cool* and the prefix *un*. The grammar of a language dictates the acceptable order of morphemes within a word—*uncool* has definite meaning in our language, *coolun* does not. The morpheme *s* when placed at the end of a word (*oars*) designates plural. But the phoneme *s* when placed at the beginning of that same word (*soar*) means something entirely different. All told, the average speaker of English knows and uses somewhere between 50,000 and 80,000 morphemes.

Words to Sentences

At the higher levels of the language hierarchy are *words*, *phrases*, and *sentences*. Words combine to form phrases; phrases, in conjunction with other phrases, form sentences. To illustrate, the sentence "Stephanie kissed the crying boy" contains a noun (*Stephanie*) and a verb phrase (*kissed the crying boy*). The verb phrase contains a verb (*kissed*) and a noun phrase (*the crying boy*). Perhaps you can remember diagramming sentences in this way in your high school English class (see Figure 9.2). Breaking sentences into phrases turns out to have psychological meaning—people clearly use phrases when they generate spoken sentences. If I were to accurately time you speaking, for example, I would find that you pause for a moment at the boundaries between major phrases (Boomer, 1965). There are also measurable changes in brain activity that correspond to phrase changes in a sentence (Rösler et al., 1998).

Language researchers have spent decades trying to decipher the rules of syntax that people use to combine words into phrases and phrases into sentences. It was once thought that a single set of rules might be discovered that would effectively capture all of the nuances of sentence generation. Just apply the rules appropriately to words and you've got language. However as the linguist Noam Chomsky pointed out, it's unlikely that such a set of rules exists. To bolster his argument, Chomsky came up with sentences like "Visiting relatives can be a nuisance." It's easy to break this sentence down into its appropriate phrase structure, Chomsky argued, but the phrase structure tells us nothing about what the sentence actually means: Are we annoyed that the relatives are visiting, or is it a nuisance to visit relatives? Both meanings apply to the same phrase structure: Visiting relatives—pause—can be a nuisance. Thus, we cannot capture why or how sentences are generated during a meaningful conversation by appealing simply to the phrase structure.

morphemes
The smallest units in a language that carry meaning.

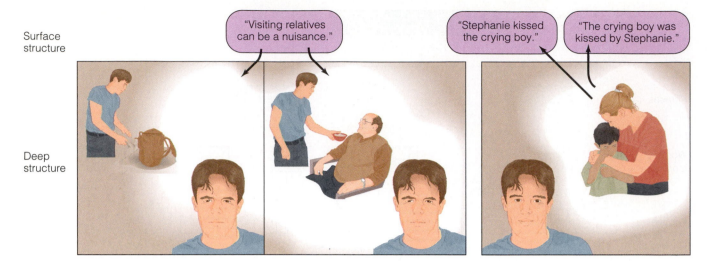

Surface
structure

Deep
structure

FIGURE 9.3

Surface Structure and Deep Structure
The surface structure of a sentence is its "surface" appearance, the literal orderings of words. Deep structure is the underlying meaning of the sentence. This figure shows how the same surface structure—"Visiting relatives can be a nuisance"—can reflect two different deep structures. Similarly, a single deep structure can be transformed into two or more acceptable surface structures.

? CRITICAL THINKING

Based on what you've learned about Chomsky's work, why might it be difficult to program a computer to understand speech?

surface structure
The literal ordering of words in a sentence.

deep structure
The underlying representation of meaning in a sentence.

Surface and Deep Structure

According to Chomsky (1957), to understand how language really works you first need to accept that there is a difference between the "surface" structure of a sentence and its accompanying, more abstract, "deep" structure. The **surface structure** of a sentence corresponds to its superficial appearance (the literal ordering of words), whereas **deep structure** refers to the underlying representation of meaning. Thus, two sentences can have the same surface structure but two different deep structures (the "visiting relatives" example). Or, two different surface structures can arise from the same deep structure ("Stephanie kissed the crying boy"—"The crying boy was kissed by Stephanie").

According to Chomsky, language production requires the transformation of deep structure into an acceptable surface structure (see Figure 9.3). Most language researchers agree with Chomsky on this point, although there are disagreements about how the transformation process actually works (see Wasow, 1989, for a review). Language is clearly more than sets of words or symbols organized in a fixed and rigid way. In the words of psychologist Steven Pinker, there are "hundreds of millions of trillions of thinkable thoughts" (Pinker, 1997) and each can, in principle, be expressed through language in an understandable way. The challenge for language researchers is to discover how this flexibility ultimately arises.

LANGUAGE COMPREHENSION

The flip side of language production—that is, understanding the structure and rules of grammar—is language *comprehension*. How do people use their practical knowledge about the world, and the general context of the conversation, to help them decide what information another person is trying to communicate? This is not a trivial problem because language comprehension presents many difficulties: We don't always hear sounds correctly; words can have many different meanings; the pitch or rhythm in which a phrase is spoken can help or mislead us; and language is full of metaphors that complicate the interpretation process (Lakoff, 1987; Pinker, 1994).

Effective communication seems to rely a great deal on *common knowledge* among speakers (Clark, 1992; Keysar et al., 1998). When you're having a conversation with someone about a mutual friend, you can say "That's typical for him" and there's likely to be no comprehension problem. You both know that the statement refers to your friend, and you both have no trouble listing examples of your friend's "typical" behavior. Similarly, when you hear a statement, you do not simply process the physical energy arriving at your ears into words, phrase structures, and sentences. You make a guess about what the speaker is trying to communicate, perhaps even before he or she makes a sound, and then you use this expectation to interpret the sounds you hear. Thus, in an important sense, language comprehension shares properties with perception: Both rely on a combination of *top-down* and *bottom-up* processing (McClelland & Elman, 1986).

Pragmatic Rules

Language researchers use the term **pragmatics** to describe how practical knowledge can be used both to comprehend the intentions of speakers and to produce an effective response. Consider your response to an *indirect* request like "Could you close the window?" If you process the request directly—that is, if you take its literal interpretation—you might respond, "Yes, I'm capable of putting enough steady pressure on the window to produce closure." You have answered the question, but clearly you have violated some important pragmatic rules. The speaker was making a request, not asking you about your ability to perform the task. In fact, if you had answered the question in this way, the speaker would have probably inferred that you were using *irony* or *sarcasm* in your reply (Gibbs et al., 1995; Lee & Katz, 1998).

The pragmatics of language make comprehension processes a challenge to study. How you interpret someone's words—be they babblings or profound commentary on the hypocrisy of our times—will depend on the shared context of the conversation, as well as on the expectations and beliefs that you bring to the exchange. To facilitate effective communication, there are certain pragmatic guidelines, or maxims, that all good speakers follow (Grice, 1975).

1. Be informative.
2. Tell the truth.
3. Be relevant.
4. Be clear.

If you choose to answer an indirect request literally ("Yes, I can close the window"), then you're not being relevant—you're violating an accepted guideline for communication. If you don't tell the truth, or are purposely vague in answering a request, then you'll soon have trouble finding people who want to talk. By following the simple rules listed above, and by assuming the same for your conversational partner, you can enhance the ease and flow of the conversational process.

LANGUAGE DEVELOPMENT

How does language develop? Are humans born with a genetic blueprint that directs and shapes their communication skills? Or do we acquire language exclusively as a product of experience? Not all people of the world speak the same language, so experience must certainly play an important role. But the majority of language researchers are convinced that babies arrive into the world prepared to learn language, much like they arrive into the world prepared to walk. There is a regularity to language development, as there is to the development of motor skills, that is difficult to explain by appealing simply to the environment (Chomsky, 1986; Pinker, 1994).

The universality of language is apparent even at birth. Most babies cry in similar ways, and they move quickly through vocalization milestones that precede formal language development. By 3 to 5 weeks of age, *cooing*—repeating vowel sounds like "ooooh" and "aaaaah"—has been added to the baby's vocalization patterns. *Babbling*—repeating consonant/vowel combinations such as "kaka" or "baba"—begins in virtually all babies between the ages of 4 and 6 months. Once again, it doesn't matter where you look in the world, this same sequence—crying then cooing then babbling—is found.

Between the ages of 6 and 18 months, experience begins to play a role, shaping and fine-tuning the baby's babblings into language-specific sounds. Babies begin to restrict their vocalizations to the phonemes in the language they hear every day from their parents or guardians; they even acquire a kind of language-

pragmatics
The practical knowledge used to comprehend the intentions of a speaker and to produce an effective response.

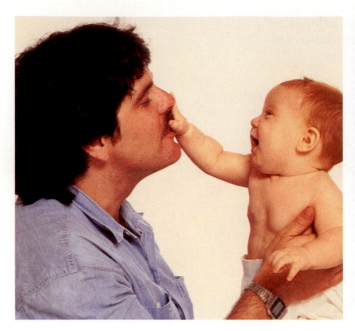

Infants and small children develop rather sophisticated ways to communicate meaningfully (cooing, kicking, pointing, and so on) even though their overt language skills may be limited.

specific "accent" by around 8 months of age (de Boysson-Bardies et al., 1984; Locke, 1994). Simple words—*mama, dada,* and so on—appear by the end of the first year, and by 24 months most babies have developed a vocabulary of nearly 200 words (Nelson, 1973). Language comprehension also develops rapidly during this period—in fact, infants develop the ability to understand the words and commands of language *faster* than they actually learn to produce language.

Child Speak

As every parent knows, infants and young children develop rather sophisticated ways to communicate meaningfully, even though their language production skills may still be limited. An 18-month-old child can point to the bear-shaped jar on the counter and say "ookie" and Mom or Dad immediately knows what the hungry child has in mind. An enormous amount of information can be packed into a single word, even if that word is spoken incorrectly, if its utterance is combined with a gesture, or if the utterance occurs in the right context.

As the child approaches the end of his or her second year of life, a phase of *telegraphic speech* begins. Telegraphic speech involves combining two words into simple sentences, such as "Daddy bad" or "Give cookie." It's called telegraphic speech because, like in a telegram, the child characteristically omits articles (*the*) and prepositions (*at, in*) from communications. But a 2-year-old's first sentences reflect a rudimentary knowledge of syntax: Words are almost always spoken in the proper *order*. For example, a child will reliably say "Want cookie" instead of "Cookie want." During the rest of the child's preschool years, up to around age 5 or 6, sentences become increasingly more complex, to the point where the average child of kindergarten age can produce and comprehend sentences that reveal most of the important features of adult syntax.

It's of enormous interest to psychologists that children develop such sophisticated language skills during their preschool years. After all, few parents sit down with their children and teach them the rules of grammar (such as the differences between present and past tense). Moreover, as we discussed in Chapter 4, children at this age lack the ability to understand most abstract concepts, so they couldn't consciously understand grammatical rules even if parents took the time to try. Children pick up their language skills implicitly; they automatically learn rules for language production.

The rules children learn during their preschool years are revealed partly by the errors that they make. For example, at some point preschoolers acquire the

? CRITICAL THINKING

In normal conversation, how much meaning do you think is typically communicated nonverbally—such as through frowning or folding your arms?

CONCEPT SUMMARY		
Highlights in Language Development		
Age	**Linguistic Highlight(s)**	**Interpretation**
3–5 weeks	*Cooing,* or the repetition of vowel sounds like "oooh" and "aaah"	Both cooing and babbling are vocalization milestones that occur before formal language development, and their occurrence is similar across cultures, highlighting the universality of language.
4–6 months	*Babbling,* or the repetition of vowel-consonant combinations, like "kaka" or "baba"	
6–18 months	Vocalizations become specific to the native language; the first word is spoken by the end of the first year.	Experience plays a role in vocalization as baby's babblings are shaped into language-specific sounds. Language comprehension is rapidly developing.
24 months	Vocabulary of nearly 200 words; child shows *telegraphic speech,* grammatical two-word combinations	Speech reflects knowledge of syntax, as words are almost always combined in the proper order.
Preschool years	Ability to produce and comprehend sentences	Child is now showing most of the important features of adult syntax.

rule "Add *ed* to the ends of verbs to make them past tense." Interestingly, children tend to *overgeneralize* this rule—they say things like "goed" or "falled," which are incorrect in English but represent a correct application of the rule. Notice that *goed* is not something that the child could have learned to use directly from experience. No parent rewards a child for saying *goed,* nor does a child hear the word being used by his or her parents. Rather, the child appears to be naturally "tuned" to pick up communication rules and apply them generally—even if a rule sometimes leads to an incorrect utterance. This natural tendency to learn and apply rules is then shaped by experience as an adult or peer teaches the child that *goed* is incorrect.

Language development continues throughout the school years, as children fine-tune their articulation skills and knowledge about grammar. Vocabulary expands, as does the child's ability to communicate abstract concepts. Ultimately, the sophistication of any child's language ability will depend, at least in part, on his or her level of cognitive development. Children think differently as they age, and their increasingly sophisticated cognitive abilities are reflected in the conversations they generate. You should keep this fact in mind as we turn our attention to language abilities in nonhuman species.

LANGUAGE IN NONHUMAN SPECIES

Psychologists have recognized for decades that nonhuman animals communicate. Anyone who has ever seen a cat indicate that it would rather be inside the house than outside knows this to be true. The question is whether such forms of communication can be called *language.* We know that animals sometimes express things symbolically, and there's little doubt that an animal's actions can convey meaning. But to qualify as a true language the animals would need to possess at least a rudimentary form of grammar—that is, a set of rules for deciding how arbitrary symbols can be combined to convey meaning.

Early attempts to foster language development in chimpanzees, in a form resembling human speech, were not very successful. Chimps were raised in homes, like surrogate children, in an effort to provide the ideal environment for language development. In one case, a chimp named Gua was raised along with the researchers' son, Donald (Kellogg & Kellogg, 1933). Donald and Gua were exposed to the same experiences, and careful attention was paid to rewarding the appropriate vocalizations. But in the end, the Kelloggs had merely produced a fine-speaking son and an effectively mute chimp (legend has it that Donald also developed into an excellent tree-climber). Later efforts to teach chimps to speak yielded the same discouraging results (Hayes & Hayes, 1951).

Chimpanzees lack the vocal equipment needed to produce the sounds of human speech. But chimps can be taught to communicate in relatively sophisticated ways using American Sign Language (left) or by learning to press keys on a board that represent objects such as food or toys (right).

Signs and Symbol Communication

These early attempts were misguided, in a way, because chimps lack the necessary vocal equipment to produce the sounds required for human speech (Hayes, 1952). It's kind of like a bird trying to teach a human to fly by raising a boy in a nest. Without wings, the boy just isn't going to fly. For these reasons, subsequent researchers turned to visual communication mediums. Allen and Beatrice Gardner tried to teach a simplified form of American Sign Language to a chimp named Washoe (Gardner & Gardner, 1969; Gardner et al., 1989). By the age of 4, Washoe was capable of producing about 160 appropriate signs, and apparently she understood a great deal more. Even more impressive was her ability to produce various word combinations, such as "more fruit" or "gimme tickle."

In California, David Premack taught a chimp named Sarah to manipulate plastic shapes that symbolized words (e.g., a plastic triangle stood for the word *banana*). Sarah eventually was able to respond to simple symbol-based sentences that were arranged on a magnetic board (such as "Sarah insert banana into pail"; Premack, 1976). In Georgia, pigmy chimpanzees have been taught to communicate by pressing keys that represent objects such as foods or toys (Rumbaugh, 1977; Savage-Rumbaugh et al., 1986). Again, not only have these chimps learned to associate particular symbols with words or actions, but they've shown the capacity to generate combinations of words by pressing the symbols in sequence (Savage-Rumbaugh et al., 1986).

Work in the Georgia laboratory has also shown that pygmy chimpanzees can understand some spoken English. A chimp named Kanzi can press the appropriate symbol key when a word is spoken (e.g., banana). He can also respond appropriately to a variety of spoken commands. When asked the following: "Can you pour the ice water in the potty?" Kanzi picks up the bowl of ice water, heads to the potty, and carefully pours it in (Savage-Rumbaugh et al., 1993). When asked to "Hide the toy gorilla," Kanzi picks up the toy gorilla and attempts to push it under a fence. Kanzi can even perform these tasks when the command is presented over headphones; this is important because it suggests that Kanzi is not simply responding to subtle cues from his handlers.

Is It Really Language?

These are very impressive demonstrations and are quite convincing when you see them in person or on film. But have chimps like Kanzi really acquired *language?* The jury is still out on this issue. Some psychologists believe that the chimps' behavior simply reflects reinforced learning—like a pigeon who has been taught to peck a key for food—rather than true language ability (Terrace, 1986). At the same time, chimps such as Washoe and Kanzi can apparently generate new combinations of words, and respond to requests that have never been given before. Washoe, for example, learned to respond to environmental events by producing novel signs. On seeing a duck for the first time, she reportedly signed "water bird." Moreover, it's been shown that chimps can acquire these language skills through observing other chimps, without being trained directly (Savage-Rumbaugh et al., 1986).

This debate is nowhere near a firm resolution. Much of the critical evidence (such as Washoe's "water bird") has come primarily from trainer anecdotes, so there is room for multiple interpretations. It's also possible that some of the novel combinations generated by the chimps are simply imitations of their trainers. We just don't know at this point. Most of the psychologists who work with chimps are firmly convinced that the language abilities are real. Kanzi, for example, doesn't seem to follow rigid scripts—he can follow a request that is worded in various ways, which is far beyond what you would expect from a pigeon trained to peck a key.

As you think about this topic for yourself, it's important to keep in mind that chimpanzees have not evolved to understand or produce human language. Chimps have evolved to solve their own problems—problems that arise from their own unique environments. You should avoid, where possible, adopting too egocentric a view of the world. The human mind has evolved to solve human problems, and those problems may or may not overlap with those of other members of the animal kingdom.

TEST YOURSELF 9.1

Check your knowledge about language by answering the following questions. (You will find the answers in the Appendix.)

1. Choose the term that best fits the following descriptions. Choose your answers from the following: deep structure, linguistic relativity, morphemes, pragmatics, phonemes, phonology, semantics, surface structure, syntax.

   a. The smallest significant sound units in speech: _____

   b. The practical knowledge used to understand the intentions of a speaker and to produce an effective response: _____

   c. The idea that language determines the characteristics and contents of thought: _____

   d. The rules governing how words should be combined to form sentences: _____

   e. The smallest units in language that carry meaning: _____

2. Decide whether each of the following statements about language is true or false.

   a. Across the world babies cry, coo, and babble in similar ways. *True or False?*

   b. Children learn the rules of language primarily by copying the words and phrases of their parents. *True or False?*

   c. Telegraphic speech begins toward the end of the child's second year of life. *True or False?*

   d. Chimpanzees lack the vocal equipment needed to produce human speech. *True or False?*

   e. Chimpanzee Kanzi learned to associate symbols with a variety of words, but cannot follow spoken instructions from his trainers. *True or False?*

Classifying and Categorizing

We now turn our attention to another highly adaptive quality of the mind—the ability to classify and categorize objects. By carving the environment into meaningful chunks, people create a world that is manageable, predictable, and sensible. If I tell you I ran into a "redneck" today, you will probably get from my communication a rich supply of unspoken knowledge about my experience—knowledge that goes far beyond the simple words I speak. You will bring to my mention of "redneck" all that you know about the term. You will probably visualize a male; you may well predict what kind of clothes he wears and his general manner of speech; you could presumably imagine his reaction to an act like the burning of the American flag. You might even form some sort of impression about me, depending on whether you view being a redneck as a positive or negative characteristic. What you are doing is enhancing my communication by applying your knowledge about the category "redneck" to it.

A **category** is a class of objects (people, places, or things) that most people agree belong together (Smith, 1989). "Vegetables" is a category that contains such things as peas, carrots, and Brussels sprouts; "psychologists" is a category that includes researchers, clinicians, and applied persons working in the field. Categories allow people to *infer* invisible properties about objects. For example, a kite and a doll share important properties as children's toys, even though the two objects bear little physical similarity to each other. Once you have successfully categorized something, you can make *predictions* about the future. You know, for example, that if you bring your child an object from the category "toy," she is likely to be happy and reward you with a hug.

We'll divide our discussion of classifying and categorizing into three main topics. First, what properties of an object make it a member of a particular category? Second, in making decisions about category membership, do we form and store abstract representations called prototypes? Finally, we'll end the section by briefly considering the structure of categories—when you categorize an object, do you do so in a general or a highly specific manner?

DEFINING CATEGORY MEMBERSHIP

Researchers have spent a lot of time trying to discover the criteria people use to define category membership. What is it about a sparrow that allows us to classify it so effortlessly as a bird? How do we know that a trout is a member of the category "fish" and not something to be used in the garden?

One possibility is that you can easily classify a sparrow as a "bird" because it has certain features that all members of that category share. For example, to be a member of the category "bird," a creature might need to have feathers and be able to do things like sing, fly, and build nests—these are called the necessary or **defining features** of the category "bird." If the object in question has all the defining features, it must be an acceptable member of the category; if the object lacks one or more of these qualities, it must be something else (Medin, 1989). From this standpoint, knowing the right category label for an object is simply a matter of learning the right set of defining features (see Figure 9.4).

But there are problems with this view. It works fine for mathematical categories such as "square" or "triangle," but it breaks down for natural objects. Take the category "vehicle," for example. What are the defining features of a vehicle—something that moves along the ground, has wheels, and can transport people? That applies well to cars and trucks, but what about a surfboard, or a monorail train? Surfboards move through water; monorail trains don't have wheels. What about an elevator, which doesn't have wheels and doesn't move along the ground? Research on natural categories such as birds, vehicles, furniture, and so on demonstrates that people have a tough time identifying and agreeing on just what con-

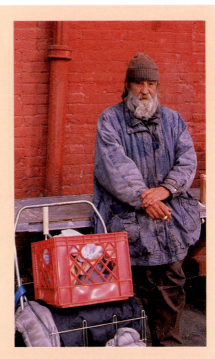

People automatically classify objects, even other people, into well-defined categories. How would you categorize this individual, and what "invisible" properties would you infer about him? Can you predict how he might act in a social situation?

category
A class of objects (people, places, or things) that most people agree belong together.

defining features
The set of features that are necessary to make objects acceptable members of a category (for example, to be a "bird" the object must have wings and feathers, must fly, and so on).

Properties	Generic bird	Robin	Sandpiper	Vulture	Chicken	Penguin
Flies regularly	+	+	+	+	–	–
Sings	+	+	+	–	–	–
Lays eggs	+	+	+	+	+	+
Is small	+	+	+	–	–	–
Nests in trees	+	+	–	+	–	–

FIGURE 9.4

Defining Features of a Category

One way to assign category membership is by defining features. For example, members of the generic category "bird" might be expected to fly regularly, sing, lay eggs, be small, and nest in trees. Unfortunately, people have a tough time identifying and agreeing on the defining features for most natural categories. All of the objects shown here are birds, but they don't necessarily share the same properties. (Based on Smith, 1989.)

stitutes the acceptable defining features of a category (Malt & Smith, 1984; Rosch & Mervis, 1975).

Most natural categories turn out to have *fuzzy boundaries*. For example, in Figure 9.5 on page 358 you can see a series of objects that collectively tap the fuzzy boundary of the category "cup." In an experiment by Labov (1973), people were presented with a selected set of these objects, such as those shown in series 1 through 4, and were required to name each object as it was presented. Labov discovered that as the ratio of cup width to cup depth increased (as the object appeared wider), subjects were increasingly likely to dismiss the "cup" label and characterize the object as a "bowl." But the crossover point was gradual rather than fixed. Even for the object labeled 4, a significant number of people remained convinced that the object was indeed a cup. Results like these suggest that category members have *typical* features that are *characteristic* of the category rather than fixed defining features.

 CRITICAL THINKING

Although categories are usually adaptive, can you think of any instance in which categorizing an object or a person might not be adaptive? How about when you stereotype someone?

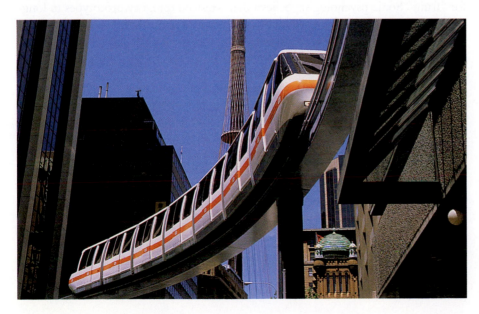

Does this monorail train fit snugly into your category for "vehicle"? If so, what "defining features" does it share with other members of the category?

FIGURE 9.5

Fuzzy Category Boundaries
Are all of these objects members of the category "cup"? Labov (1973) discovered that as the width of the object increased, people were more likely to label it as a "bowl." But the cup category boundary was fuzzy rather than firm; a significant number of people remained convinced that the fourth object was indeed a cup. (From Goldstein, 1994.)

? CRITICAL THINKING

If you wanted to decide whether your friend Bob fits the category "furniture," do you think you would compare him to a prototype (such as a couch or a chair), or would you think about all the things that you've used as a "seat" in your lifetime?

family resemblance
The core features that category members share; a given member of the category may have some but not necessarily all of these features.

prototype
The best or most representative member of a category (such as robin for the category "bird").

category exemplars
Specific examples of category members that are stored in long-term memory.

Family Resemblance

Another way to think about the idea of typical features is in terms of what Rosch and Mervis (1975) have called **family resemblance.** Members of the same category will share certain core features, but it isn't necessary for each member to have them all. Within an extended family, for instance, there may be a characteristic drooping nose, close-set beady eyes, receding hairlines, and a prominent, clefted chin. Cousin Theodore may lack the cleft or the beady eyes, but he could still possess a family resemblance that enables outsiders to easily fit him into the appropriate family. For the category "vehicle," people know that a monorail train doesn't have wheels, and it's not shaped anything like a car, but it moves people along the ground and in this sense fits the category label for most people.

Family resemblance is determined by the collection of core features that an object possesses. Again, members of the same category will share many family features, but it's unlikely that any single member will have them all. If a given object has most of the family features, it will be seen as a good member of the category; if an object has only a few, it will be seen as a poor member of the category. A car, for example, has most of the basic features that people assign to the category "vehicle"; an elevator does not. A robin has most of the features of "bird"; an ostrich or a flamingo has few. Through the notion of family resemblance we can begin to see how natural categories achieve their fuzzy status. There is no absolute set of criteria for what constitutes a vehicle or a bird, there are only good and poor examples of a class of objects that share features (Rosch et al., 1976).

DO PEOPLE STORE CATEGORY PROTOTYPES?

Family resemblance, combined with the idea that there are good and poor members of a category, leads us naturally to the concept of a *prototype*. A **prototype** is the best or most representative member of a category: A robin, for example, is close to the prototype for the category "bird;" an apple resembles the prototype for "fruit." Some psychologists believe that we store category prototypes in long-term memory and use them to help decide category membership. If an object, say a small fuzzy creature with a beak, is similar to the prototype for a certain category, "birds," then we assume that the object must be a member of the prototype's category (Homa, 1984).

However, it isn't necessary to store prototypes to solve categorization problems. Instead, we could simply store all of the category examples (or **category exemplars**) that we encounter. To decide whether a new object is a member of a specific category, we would then compare the object to all of these stored examples rather than to a single prototype. If the object is similar to many examples in a particular category, then we would categorize the object as a member of that category (see Figure 9.6). You should note the main difference between prototype and exemplar views of categorization: In prototype theory, you compare the object to one thing—the prototype; in the exemplar view, the object is compared to many things—the category exemplars.

Whether prototypes or exemplars are used in categorization is currently unknown, although many cognitive psychologists favor the exemplar view (Hintzman, 1986; Medin & Shaffer, 1978; Nosofsky, 1992). The reason is that people seem to know a lot about the individual members of a category. For

Members of the same family often share physical features, creating a family resemblance, but it's unlikely that any single member of the family will share them all.

example, people seem to know about what features go together—such as the fact that small birds are more likely to sing than large birds—and this kind of result is better handled by theories proposing that we store exemplars. Given the flexibility of the human mind, it seems likely that people can solve categorization problems in many different ways. Sometimes we may form prototypes; other times we may rely on rules for deciding category membership; and in many situations we may appeal only to category exemplars (e.g., Erickson & Kruschke, 1998; Smith et al., 1998).

THE HIERARCHICAL STRUCTURE OF CATEGORIES

It turns out that most objects fit nicely into more than one natural category. The reason, in part, is that virtually all categories have a built-in hierarchical structure—there are categories within categories within categories. Consider the class of "living things." Under the umbrella of "living things," we find the category

FIGURE 9.6

Prototypes versus Examplars

How do we decide whether an object is a member of a particular category? According to prototype theory, we compare the object to the abstract "best" example of the category (a generic bird). If the new object is similar to the prototype, it is assigned to the prototype's category. Exemplar theories of categorization propose instead that we compare the new object to all the individual examples of the category that have been stored in memory. Category membership is based on the summed similarity between the new object and the exemplars.

Prototype theory	New object	Compare	Prototype

Exemplar theory	New object	Compare	Individual examples

CONCEPT SUMMARY
Defining Category Membership

View of Categorization	Basis for Categorization	Example
Defining features	Presence of certain features that define membership in the category.	Inez knows that a robin is a bird, because a robin has all of the features that define a bird, such as feathers, wings, and a beak.
Family resemblance	The degree to which category members share certain core features. A *prototype* is the most representative member of a category.	James knows that a robin is a bird, because it shares common features with other members of the bird family. In fact, "robin" would be considered the *prototype* for the category "bird."
Exemplars	All category examples (*category exemplars*) that we encounter are used for categorization.	Semhar knows that a robin is a bird, because it matches so many of the examples of birds stored in her memory.

"animals"; under "animals" there are "cats"; under "cats" there are "Siamese cats"; and so on. Most of the time an object, once it's categorized, can easily be put into another, more general level of abstraction. A cat is an animal, a living thing, an object found on the planet Earth, and so on. These levels differ from one another in terms of their degree of inclusion. The more general the level, the more inclusive it becomes—there are more examples of living things than animals and more cats than Siamese cats (Murphy & Lassaline, 1997).

Some levels in the category hierarchy also appear to have special properties—they are in a sense psychologically privileged. When people refer to an object during a normal conversation, they tend to use what is called its *basic-level* category descriptor. **Basic-level categories** generate the most useful and predictive information (Markman & Wisniewski, 1997). When a furry feline saunters by, you call it a cat, not a living thing or an object found on the planet Earth. The category "cat" provides just the right amount of relevant information. People know you're talking about a four-legged object with fur (rather than the nondescriptive "animal"), but you haven't burdened the conversation with a needless amount of detail ("There's an 18-year-old seal-point Siamese that prefers salmon for dinner").

Basic-level categories tend to be at the intermediate levels of the category hierarchy (see Figure 9.7). The top-level categories, or *superordinates*, are simply

basic-level categories
The level in a category hierarchy that provides the most useful and predictive information; the basic level usually resides at an intermediate level in a category hierarchy.

FIGURE 9.7

Category Hierarchies
Virtually all categories have a built-in hierarchical structure—there are categories within categories within categories. Most things, like this cat, fit nicely into several natural category levels. But when people refer to something during normal conversation, they tend to use its intermediate, or *basic-level*, category label. They call this a "cat" rather than a "living thing," an "animal," or an "18-year-old Siamese cat who likes salmon."

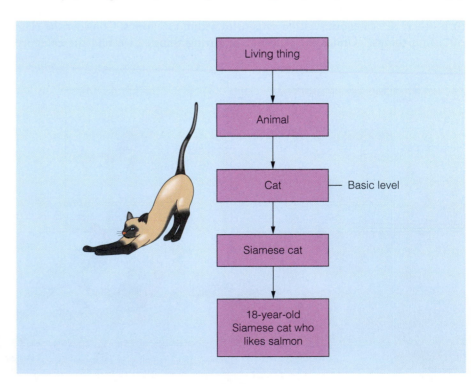

Inside the Problem   Similarity and Categorization

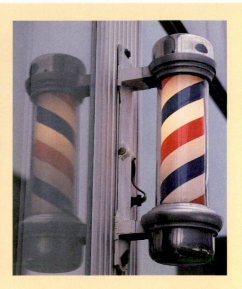

Once upon a time there was an animal, with typical birdlike properties, who wandered into the wrong place at the wrong time. There was a peculiar experiment going on, you see, and the animal was transformed, by accident, into the shape of an insect. Instead of feathers, its body became encrusted in a hardened shell; instead of two legs with pointed feet, it had six legs that looked like sticks. Surprisingly, it went on to live a normal life, and even produced a flock of offspring that looked like birds. If forced to choose, would you call this animal a bird or an insect? Most people still think it's a bird, even though it looks like a bug (after Rips, 1989).

In a study by Gelman and Markman (1986), 4-year-old children were shown two pictures, one of a tropical fish, the other of a dolphin. The children were told that the tropical fish stays underwater to breathe, whereas the dolphin pops above water to breathe. They were then shown a picture of a shark, which was perceptually similar to the dolphin, and were asked: "See this fish? Does it breathe underwater or does it pop above water to breathe?"

Nearly 70% of the 4-year-olds were convinced that the shark breathes underwater even though it looked nothing like a tropical fish (Gelman & Markman, 1986).

Results like these are significant because they violate one of the main tenets of many theories of categorization—classification by similarity. The creature is more similar to an insect in the first case, and a shark certainly looks more like a dolphin than a tropical fish, but people's answers don't reflect the similarity; they choose the category with the least amount of shared features. If natural objects are assigned to categories based on their similarity to a prototype, or to other exemplars, then how can we explain the answers in these two examples?

Researchers are now shifting away from using similarity as the supreme court of appeal for determining category membership. Two things can look very different, or share very few features, yet still be accepted as members of a category. Indeed, the whole concept of "similarity" turns out to be a little fuzzy. For example, is a zebra more similar to a horse or to a

barber pole? The answer, of course, depends on the context. If we're trying to classify the world into "things with stripes" then zebras and barber poles are more similar. It's more useful to think of similarity as a kind of guideline for establishing category membership. Things that are physically similar will usually belong in the same category, but appeals to similarity alone will not be sufficient to explain the richness of people's ability to categorize (Medin et al., 1993; Smith et al., 1998).

In many ways, the ability to place objects effortlessly into categories simply mirrors people's knowledge about the world. People know that objects can change their appearance yet remain fundamentally the same. Children know that two living things from the same category are likely to breathe in the same way, even if those particular examples look nothing alike. Rather than passively comparing features, people seem to classify based on an inference process—does the object in question have properties that fit with one's world view of how things in a particular category should act?

not very descriptive. When people were asked to list the distinguishing features of top-level categories (such as "living things"), Rosch and her colleagues found that only a few features were actually generated (try it yourself: list the properties that characterize "living things"). At the basic level, more properties were generated, and the generated properties tended to be ones that most members of the category share (Rosch et al., 1976). It is of interest to note that basic-level categories are also the category levels that children first learn to use. It is through basic-level categorization that the adaptive mind cuts the world into its most useful and informative slices.

TEST YOURSELF 9.2

Check your knowledge about how people form categories by answering the following questions. (You will find the answers in the Appendix.)

1. For each of the following statements decide on the category term that seems most appropriate. Choose from the following: category exemplars, defining features, family resemblance, prototype.

   a. It must be a bird because all birds have wings, feathers, and a beak.
   _____

   b. It must be a bird because it looks like all the other birds that I've seen.
   _____

   c. It must be a bird because it seems to have some features that are typical of birds.
   _____

   d. It must be a bird because it looks a lot like a robin. _____

2. When people refer to an object, such as your cat, during normal conversation, they tend to use what kind of category descriptor?

   a. Superordinate ("look, it's an object on the planet Earth")
   b. Basic level ("look, it's a cat")
   c. Subordinate ("look, it's a seal-point Siamese")
   d. Functionate ("look, it's something to cuddle")

Solving Problems

In this section of the chapter we'll consider some of the thought processes people use when they consciously seek to solve problems. Obviously, problem solving is an extremely adaptive skill. When you're faced with a problem, such as how to get your car started in the morning, there is a goal, a running motor, and a certain

Certain kinds of problems are well defined, such as trying to find the correct route on a map. Other problems are ill defined and may not even have a solution. Can you decipher the true meaning of the painting on the left?

amount of uncertainty about how to reach that goal. To study the solution process, psychologists typically use problems like the following:

> It's early morning, still dark, and you're trying to get dressed. Your 2-month-old baby, snuggled in her crib at the foot of the bed, sleeps peacefully after a night of sustained wailing. You can't turn on the light—she'll wake up for sure—but the black socks and the blue socks are mixed up in the drawer. Let's see, you recall, I have 5 pairs of black socks and 4 pairs of blue socks. How many socks do I need to take out of the drawer in order to guarantee myself a pair of matching colors?

Notice there is a goal (selecting a pair of matching socks), and it's not immediately obvious how to get from the problem to the solution. Psychologists call this a **well-defined problem** (even though you may have no idea how to solve it) because there is a well-stated goal, a clear starting point, and a relatively easy way to tell when a solution has been reached. Other kinds of problems do not have well-stated goals, clear starting points, or effective mechanisms for evaluating progress—these are called **ill-defined problems.** Ever wonder about the secret of happiness? Maybe you can agree on the starting point (I'm not happy enough), but the goal (happiness) is pretty tough to define, and it's not at all clear how to reach that goal or measure progress.

Most of the research done on the thought processes involved in problem solving has been conducted using well-defined problems, such as our sock problem or those involving math or logic. We'll mainly consider these types of problems in this section, but ill-defined problems can be tackled with some of the same strategies. It's believed that ill-defined problems may sometimes require unique cognitive processes (Jausovec, 1997), but generally the same psychological processes are assumed to operate in the vast majority of problem-solving settings.

THE IDEAL PROBLEM SOLVER

Let's start by considering a set of guidelines that highlight the psychological processes relevant to problem solving. These particular guidelines were developed by psychologists John Bransford and Barry Stein and are recommended in their book *The Ideal Problem Solver* (1993). Bransford and Stein use the letters of the acronym IDEAL to stand for the five major steps that underlie effective problem solving. These steps are briefly described here and are summarized in the concept summary table on page 364.

1. *Identify* the problem. Obviously, before you can solve a problem, you need to recognize that there is, in fact, a problem that needs solving. Strange knocking sounds, little spots of oil, and uneven acceleration are signs of car problems, but they need to be recognized as symptoms before the necessary diagnosis and repairs can begin.

2. *Define*, or represent, the problem information in the most efficient way. Not only is it important to define the goal—What exactly are you trying to solve?—it's also important to correctly interpret the problem components you have to work with. As we discussed previously, the ticket scalping problem that opened the chapter is difficult because most people fail to see that Wayne actually made two *separate* ticket transactions. They tend to think about just *one* pair of tickets, so the cost of the second transaction is applied incorrectly to the first.

3. *Explore* a variety of problem strategies. Once you have identified the problem, defined the goal, and developed some understanding of the information you have to work with, it's time to try to move forward toward a possible solution. To do this, you must decide on a strategy. Most solution strategies amount to "rules of thumb." They don't guarantee a solution, but they can speed up the problem-solving process or at least move you closer to your goal.

4. *Act* on the problem strategy that you chose in step 3. Work through the solution strategy, and as part of the process try to anticipate any dead ends or obstacles that might prevent you from reaching the goal.

well-defined problem
A problem with a well-stated goal, a clear starting point, and a relatively easy way to tell when a solution has been obtained.

ill-defined problem
A problem, such as the search for "happiness," that has no well-stated goal, no clear starting point, or no mechanism for evaluating progress.

CONCEPT SUMMARY The IDEAL Problem Solver		
State of Problem Solving	Description	Example
Identify	Recognize that a problem exists.	In the basement, Greg notices a small amount of water underneath the washing machine.
Define	Represent the problem information in the most efficient way.	Greg notices that there is water dripping down from a pipe above him, just under where the bathroom is.
Explore	Consider possible solutions.	Greg considers trying to fix it himself, asking his handy friend to help, or calling a plumber.
Act	Employ the chosen strategy.	Greg decides to give his friend a call, and watches as he diagnoses and fixes the problem.
Look	Evaluate the effectiveness of the chosen strategy.	Greg notices that the pool of water is gone, and that the pipe has stopped leaking.

5. *Look* back and evaluate the effectiveness of your selected strategy. Have you in fact solved the problem? It's important to identify and correct any errors that have occurred before moving on and trying something new.

If you follow these five problem-solving guidelines, you have approximated the IDEAL problem solver (Bransford & Stein, 1993). Now let's consider some of the processes involved in greater detail.

IDENTIFYING AND DEFINING: PROBLEM REPRESENTATION

To identify and define a problem correctly it's essential to represent the problem information in the correct way. By *problem representation*, psychologists mean that you need to understand exactly what information is given and how that information can potentially be used. Solving a problem is like building a house. If you can't find the right tools, or if you don't know how to use the tools once you've found them, you're unlikely to ever complete the house.

Take the sock problem, for example. The correct answer is three. There are only two colors, so with three samples, you will get two that match. If you're like most people, you let the math get in your way. Did you start worrying about the four to five ratio of blue to black? Did you briefly consider calculating some sort of probability? To solve this problem, you must pay attention to the right problem components—you need to see the problem in the right way. Most people simply fail to detect which information is relevant and which is not. They get hung up with ratios and probabilities and the like. Let's consider another example.

> Dr. Adams is interrupted from his daily rounds by the arrival of a new patient, a child, who has been injured in a fall. "My god!" Adams cries, "It's my son!" Moments later, Dr. Henderson arrives with the same sense of panic and grief. "My son, my dear son," Henderson moans in despair. Is it a tragic mix-up?

You probably solved this one almost immediately, but it demonstrates the point. The two doctors are the mother and the father, which makes it easy to see why both are panicked about their injured son. But the word *doctor*, with its powerful gender connotations, can create an obstacle to correct problem representation. If you initially identify and define the doctors as men, the solution becomes more involved. Seeing the problem in the right way is even more difficult because the doctors have different last names.

Functional Fixedness

The two-doctor problem illustrates a common obstacle to correct problem representation. People allow their preconceptions, even their prejudices, to lock them into an incorrect view of the problem information (Bassok et al., 1995; Dixon & Moore, 1997). Consider another example, illustrated in Figure 9.8, called the Maier two-string problem (after Maier, 1931). Imagine you are standing in a room with two lightweight strings hanging from the ceiling. The strings are hung such

CRITICAL THINKING

Think back to the linguistic relativity hypothesis we discussed earlier. Do you think the "doctor" problem supports the hypothesis?

FIGURE 9.8
The Maier Two-String Problem
Can you figure out a way to tie these two strings together? Notice there's a pair of pliers on the table.

a distance apart that, when holding one of the strings, you cannot reach the other. Using only a pair of pliers, which happens to be sitting on a table in the room, can you tie the strings together?

This is a reasonably difficult problem because most people have a certain set, or fixed, way of viewing the function of pliers. The solution is to tie the pliers to one of the strings and swing it, like a pendulum, while you hold onto the other string. The correct solution, however, requires you to *restructure* the way that you normally think about pliers. Pliers are good for grabbing and holding, but in this case they can serve as pendulum weights, too.

Psychologists use the term **functional fixedness** to refer to this tendency to see objects, and their functions, in certain fixed and typical ways. Doctors are men, pliers are for grabbing, and so on. Functional fixedness is an obstacle to problem solving because it prevents you from recognizing the problem-solving tools that are present in the situation. Now turn to page 366 and try solving the problem illustrated in Figure 9.9. You enter a room in which a candle, a box of tacks, some matches, and a hammer lie on a table. You are told to mount the candle on the wall so that it will still burn properly, using only the objects on the table. Work on the problem for a while; we'll return to its solution shortly.

First, let's stop for a moment and think about the adaptive significance of a concept like functional fixedness. How can such a tendency possibly be adaptive? Wouldn't it be better to consider all possible object uses? Actually, the answer is "no." Most of the time, if you view objects in fixed ways or use fixed strategies that have worked well in the past, you're likely to be successful. After all, pliers usually do solve problems having to do with holding and grabbing, don't they? The problems we've been considering are actually quite artificial—they're set up by psychologists to lead the mind astray in order to provide insight into normal problem-solving methods. Generally, the fact that people tend to rely on well-established habits of perception and thought (sometimes called **mental sets**) is probably an effective overall problem-solving strategy.

Were you able to solve the candle-mounting problem? The correct solution is to dump the tacks out of the box, mount the box on the wall with one of the tacks, and then put the candle in the box (Duncker, 1945). The problem is difficult because most people see the box only as a device for holding the tacks, not as a potential problem-solving tool. They become *fixed* in their views about the

functional fixedness
The tendency to see objects, and their functions, in certain fixed and typical ways.

mental sets
The tendency to rely on well-established habits of perception and thought when attempting to solve problems.

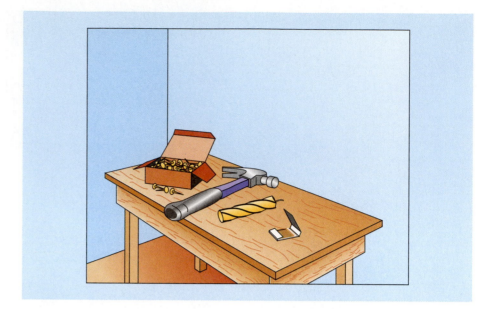

FIGURE 9.9

The Duncker Candle Problem
Using only the materials shown, figure out a way to mount the candle on the wall.

functions of objects, and thereby fail to identify and define all of the available problem tools correctly.

EXPLORING AND ACTING: PROBLEM STRATEGIES

It's important to represent a problem correctly, but problem representation alone cannot guarantee a solution. You also need an arsenal of problem *strategies*—techniques that allow you to move systematically toward a problem solution. Two classes of problem strategies can be used to solve problems: *algorithms* and *heuristics*.

Algorithms and Heuristics

For some well-defined problems you can use **algorithms,** which are step-by-step rules or procedures that guarantee a solution. You can use algorithms to solve simple math problems, for example, because there are fixed rules for addition, subtraction, and so on. As long as you use the rules properly, you will always arrive at the correct solution. Solving anagrams, such as MBLOPRE, is another case in point. There are seven letters in the word, which means there are 5040 possible combinations of the letters. If you systematically work out each of the possible sequences, one will eventually provide a solution to the PROBLEM. But it could take a long time.

Computers are often programmed to use algorithms because computers are capable of examining lots of information very quickly. But algorithms are not always practical strategies for problem solution, even for computers. Consider chess, for example. In principle, it would be possible to use algorithms to play chess—the computer would simply need to consider all of the possible consequences of a particular move. But practically, computers cannot examine all the possible outcomes in a chess game; they can examine only some of them. Consider that there are some 10^{40} possible game sequences, so even if a computer could calculate a game in under one-millionth of one-thousandth of a second, it would still require 10^{21} centuries to examine all the game possibilities (Best, 1989). It could do so; it would just take a very long time. Another problem with algorithms is that they work for only certain kinds of well-defined problems—there is no algorithm, for example, for deciding how to be happy, or for deciding on an appropriate career.

In cases in which it's not feasible to use an algorithm, or in cases in which one is not readily available, it's possible to use **heuristics,** which are essentially problem-solving "rules of thumb." To solve an anagram, especially one with seven

algorithms
Step-by-step rules or procedures that, if applied correctly, guarantee a problem solution.

heuristics
The rules of thumb we use to solve problems; heuristics can usually be applied quickly, but they do not guarantee that a solution will be found.

People use heuristics—"general rules"—when they play chess because the human mind simply cannot examine all the possible moves and their consequences during a game.

letters, it's hardly expedient to use an algorithmic approach, examining all 5040 possible letter sequences. Instead, you turn to heuristics. You know that English words don't usually begin with MB, or end with BL, so you can avoid checking out those possibilities. You can use your knowledge about English words to make guesses about the most likely solution possibilities. Heuristics are extremely adaptive problem-solving tools because they often open the door to a quick and accurate solution. In natural environments, quick solutions can mean the difference between life and death. An organism cannot spend its time wrapped in thought, systematically working through a long list of solution possibilities. Instead, it's adaptive for the organism to guess, as long as the guess is based on some kind of logic.

Means–Ends Analysis

One common heuristic that people use to solve problems is **means–ends analysis,** which attacks problems by devising *means*, or actions, that are designed to reduce the gap between the current starting point and the desired goal, or *ends* (Newell & Simon, 1972). Usually, this strategy requires breaking down the problem into a series of simpler subgoals, in which the appropriate means to an end are more immediately visible. Let's assume that Peter, a normally non-achieving undergraduate, wants to start a relationship with Jill, the brightest student in his psychology class. Obviously, asking Jill out immediately is unlikely to succeed, so Peter breaks the problem down into more manageable components.

First, he reasons, he'll impress her in class by making an insightful comment during the lecture. He now has a new goal, acting intelligent in class, for which there is relatively straightforward means—he needs to study hard so he can master the material. Assuming he is successful (everyone now thinks he is an amazingly insightful young man), he devises a new subgoal: making some kind of sustained contact with Jill. Forming a small study group would be a good means to that end, he surmises, so he approaches the recently impressed Jill with the idea. Notice the key ingredients of the problem-solving strategy: Establish where you are, figure out where you want to be, and then devise a means for effectively getting you from here to there. Often, as in Peter's case, means–ends analysis is made more effective by working systematically through subgoals.

CRITICAL THINKING

Consider a surgical problem. If your life was on the line would you want a doctor who goes by the book, or one who experiments with new techniques that might or might not produce a medical solution?

means–ends analysis
A problem-solving heuristic that involves devising actions, or means, that reduce the distance between the current starting point and the desired end (the goal state).

Inside the Problem

Transferring Strategies across Problems

Solving problems through analogy is one of the most valuable heuristics you can use. But it requires that you see the connection between the problems that you've solved before and the current task at hand. Unfortunately, making the connection turns out to be quite difficult, even if the previous and current problems share many problem features. Consider the following problem, taken from Gick and McGarry (1992):

One Saturday night, at a local country dance, 40 people, 20 men and 20 women, showed up to dance. The dance was a "contra dance," in which men and women face each other in lines. From 8 to 10 P.M., there were 20 heterosexual couples (consisting of one man and one woman each; i.e., two men or women cannot dance together) dancing on the floor. At 10 P.M., however, two women left, leaving 38 people to dance. Could the dance caller make arrangements so that the remaining people could all dance together at the same time in 19 heterosexual couples (p. 638)?

This problem is quite easy for most people to solve. They recognize that 20 men and 18 women cannot be divided into 19 mixed-sex couples, so the answer is "no" (this is sometimes called a "parity" problem). Now take a look at the checkerboard pattern shown in Figure 9.10:

You are given a checkerboard and 32 dominoes. Each domino covers exactly two adjacent squares on the board.

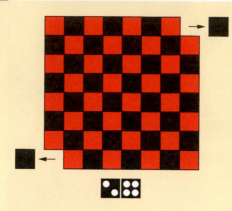

FIGURE 9.10
The Mutilated Checkerboard
The diagonally opposite corners of this checkerboard have been removed. How would you place 31 dominoes on the board so that all of the 62 remaining squares are covered?

Thus, the 32 dominoes can cover all 64 squares of the checkerboard. Now suppose two squares are cut off at diagonally opposite corners of the board. If possible, show how you would place 31 dominoes on the board so that all of the 62 remaining squares are covered. If you think it is impossible, give a proof of why (Gick and McGarry, 1992, p. 625).

This problem turns out to be much more difficult to solve, even though it's actually very similar to the dance problem (it's also a "parity" problem). Just substitute the word "man" for black and the word "woman" for red, and think of the domino as the pairing of a mixed-sex couple. The first problem should serve as an effective analogy for solving the second. But most

people fail to see the connection. In the study by Gick and McGarry (1992), people were first shown how to solve the dance-partner problem and were then asked to solve the checkerboard problem. Very few solved the second problem correctly even though they understood the solution to the first.

What kinds of factors promote successful transfer from one problem-solving situation to another? For one thing, people who have a great deal of experience in a particular area seem better able to draw connections across situations relevant to their expertise than do nonexperts. Experts are able to see what amounts to the deep structure of a problem (its true meaning representation), and they can therefore map one kind of problem to another by noting how the problems are similar (Novick, 1988). Cognitive scientists familiar with parity problems, for example, will have little trouble recognizing the common link between the dance and checkerboard problems.

It also helps if problem-solving hints are provided. In our checkerboard problem, if subjects are told to try using the dance-partner solution as a way of solving the checkerboard problem, performance improves significantly. Finally, it may even help transfer somewhat if your initial attempts at solving the first problem fail. If you get stuck while you're solving one kind of problem and then find yourself stuck in a similar way during a later problem, you tend to use your earlier failure as a way of reminding yourself how you solved the first (Gick & McGarry, 1992).

Working Backward

Another effective heuristic is **working backward**—starting at the goal state and trying to move back toward the starting point. Suppose someone asked you to generate a set of anagrams. How would you proceed? Would you try to generate sets of randomly arranged letters and then see whether a particular sequence forms a word? Of course not. You would start with the solution, the word, and work backward by mixing up the known sequence.

Let's consider another example. You're working on a biology project tracking the growth of bacteria in a petri dish. You know that this particular strain of bacteria doubles every 2 hours. After starting the experiment, you discover that the petri dish is exactly full after 12 hours. After how many hours was the petri dish exactly half full? To solve this one, it's better to work backward. If the dish is full

working backward
A problem-solving heuristic that involves starting at the goal state and moving backward toward the starting point in order to see how the goal state can be reached.

after 12 hours, and it takes 2 hours for the bacteria to double, what did the dish look like after 10 hours? This turns out to be the answer, which is arrived at rather simply if the problem is attacked in reverse.

Searching for Analogies

Finally, another useful heuristic for problem solving is **searching for analogies.** If you can see a resemblance between the current problem and some task that you solved in the past, you can quickly obtain an acceptable solution. Imagine that a man buys a horse for $60 and sells it for $70. Later, he buys the same horse back for $80 and sells it again for $90. How much money did the man make in the horse-trading business? The attentive reader will not miss this one. It's a different version of the ticket scalping problem that opened this chapter. If you see the relationship between the two problems, you're unlikely to suffer the same problem-solving pitfalls you encountered before.

LOOKING AND LEARNING

The ideal problem solver identifies and defines the problem, seeks the best problem representation, and explores and acts on problem strategies. But the whole process is incomplete unless you also *look and learn* from your experience (Bransford & Stein, 1993). Think about a student who tries to use the principles of psychology to improve a test score. The goal is clear—an improved test score—and the student could develop a variety of possible study strategies to enhance performance. However, the ideal problem solver doesn't stop at the final score; the ideal problem solver "debugs" performance in an effort to maximize the information gained.

By analyzing your performance in detail, noting where you made mistakes as well as correct answers, you can determine whether your strategy helped solve one kind of problem, but not another. Through an after-the-fact analysis, you can gain insight into *why* a particular heuristic failed or succeeded. Look and learn from your experience so that the next time, you can do better still.

> **searching for analogies**
> A problem-solving heuristic that involves trying to find a connection between the current problem and some previous problem you have solved successfully.

TEST YOURSELF 9.3

Check your knowledge about problem solving by answering the following questions. (You will find the answers in the Appendix.)

1. Decide whether each of the following problems is *well defined* or *ill defined*. Justify your answer.

   a. Finding your way to a new restaurant in town: _____

   b. Receiving an "A" in your psychology course: _____

   c. Making your lab partner in chemistry fall madly in love with you:

   _____

   d. Baking a cherry cheesecake that won't taste like plumber's caulk:

   _____

2. Try to identify the problem-solving strategy at work in each of the following examples. Choose from the following terms: algorithm, means–ends analysis, working backward, searching for analogies.

   a. On the final exam Myka looks for connections between the physics problem on the test and the ones he worked on while studying. _____

   b. Rachel needs a three-letter word that begins with R to complete the crossword puzzle. She mindlessly considers all possible two-letter combinations, placing them after R until she arrives at an acceptable word. _____

c. Hector really needs an A in his philosophy class, but he has no idea what it takes. He decides to concentrate on writing a really top-notch first paper.

_____

d. Courtney needs to generate a set of anagrams for a school project. To generate each anagram, she starts with a word and then scrambles the letters.

_____

Making Decisions

We turn our attention now to the topic of **decision making,** which deals with the thought processes involved in evaluating and choosing from among a set of alternatives. Obviously, decision making and problem solving are closely related. When you make a decision, you're confronted with a set of alternatives and you must make a choice. The choice is almost always accompanied by *risk*, so it's in your interest to evaluate and select among the alternatives with care. Think about the military strategist on the brink of conflict who must determine whether to attack with vigor or pull back in retreat. Or consider the physician who must choose between a risky treatment that may kill or save a patient with some unsettling probabilities.

Like problem solving, decision making is influenced by how you represent the alternatives in your mind, and by your choice of decision-making strategies. Let's examine how each of these processes affects the choices we make.

THE FRAMING OF DECISION ALTERNATIVES

? CRITICAL THINKING

Do you think problem solving is a part of decision making, or is decision making a part of problem solving?

It turns out that the way the alternatives are structured, called **framing,** has a dramatic influence on the decision-making process. In a study by McNeil and colleagues (1982), practicing hospital physicians were asked to choose between two forms of treatment for a patient with lung cancer: either a surgical operation on the lungs, or a six-week treatment with radiation. Half of the physicians received the following information prior to making the choice:

> Of 100 people having surgery, 10 will die during treatment, 32 will have died by one year, and 66 will have died by five years. Of 100 people having radiation therapy, none will die during treatment, 23 will have died by one year, and 78 will have died by five years.

Put yourself in the doctor's shoes—which would you choose? The other half of the physicians were given the following:

> Of 100 people having surgery, 90 will be alive immediately after the treatment, 68 will be alive after one year, and 34 will be alive after five years. Of 100 people having radiation therapy, all will be alive immediately after treatment, 77 will be alive after one year, and 22 will be alive after five years.

Do you want to change your mind? Actually, exactly the same information is given in each of the choice scenarios. The only difference is that in the first description the treatment outcomes are described, or framed, in terms of who will die, whereas the second description emphasizes who is likely to survive. The treatment consequences are exactly the same in each case. Believe it or not, practicing physicians are more than twice as likely to choose radiation when the choices are death based than when the choices are framed around who will live. Why? The reason probably has to do with the fact that death is abhorrent to physicians. The surgery alternative in the first example clearly states that people will die during the treatment, so it is to be avoided. Interestingly, doctors are even more susceptible to these framing effects than patients who are given the same choices!

This example reinforces the point that human decision making is not always a rational process (at least from an objective perspective). People are prone to inconsistency in their judgments, in part, because our minds weigh information differently in different situations (Kahneman et al., 1982). Let's consider another example. Suppose you were given the choice of winning $40 with a probability of 0.40 or winning $30 with a probability of 0.50. Which would you choose? From a statistical perspective, there is a rational choice based on the *expected value* of each alternative. An expected value is simply the value that you would expect to gain, on average, by choosing one particular alternative many times. Winning $40 with a probability of 0.40 leads to an expected average gain of $16 ($40 × 0.40); winning $30 with a probability of 0.50 leads to an expected value of $15 ($30 × .50). The rational choice, then, is to pick the first alternative, which is what most people do.

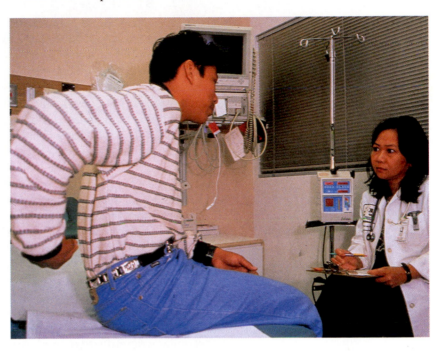

But suppose you were given a choice of winning $40 with a probability of 0.80 or winning $30 with a probability of 1.00. Again, the rational choice is to pick the first alternative (expected values of $32 versus $30), but people tend to act differently in this context. They go for a sure thing. How people weigh decision-making alternatives depends on the particular situation. In general, when people are confronted with situations in which they think they can gain something (such as winning money), they tend to avoid taking risks—they choose certainty. But if the outcomes potentially lead to a loss of some kind (such as someone dying), people are much more likely to take a risk that will limit or avoid the loss.

How doctors interpret treatment options, as well as how the information relevant to those treatments is framed, can critically influence the decision-making process.

Another factor to be considered is the decision maker's interpretation of the problem. In the medical example, the doctors seemed to be acting irrationally, switching choices depending on how the same information was framed. But the treatment problem might have been interpreted quite differently by the doctors in the two situations. For example, when the alternatives were death based, perhaps the doctors readily connected the deaths to the treatment (surgery will kill 10 people and radiation none). In contrast, when the alternatives were framed around who was living, they might have focused on long-term survival and not thought too much about the hazards of treatment (34 people who receive surgery will be alive after five years, but only 22 radiation patients will survive this long). Thus, you cannot assume that the problem information was identical in the two framings—you need to take into account how the problem was actually represented in the mind of the decision maker (Berkeley & Humphreys, 1982; Einhorn & Hogarth, 1981; Jou et al., 1996).

DECISION-MAKING HEURISTICS

When people are forced to choose from among a set of alternatives, most rely on heuristics, or rules of thumb, just as they do when solving problems. These strategies simplify the decision-making process and often lead to correct judgments, but they can sometimes lead you to the wrong decision.

Representativeness

Suppose you're asked to judge the likelihood of some event falling into class A or B. In such a case people often rely on a rule of thumb called the **representativeness heuristic.** They arrive at their decision by comparing the similarity of the object or event in question to the average, or prototypical, member of each class.

representativeness heuristic
The tendency to make decisions based on an alternative's similarity, or representativeness, in relation to an ideal. For example, people decide whether a sequence is random based on how irregular the sequence looks.

It's easiest to demonstrate with an example. Let's assume that your friends, the Renfields, have six children. If B denotes boy and G denotes girl, which of the following two birth order sequences do you think is more likely?

1. B   B   B   G   G   G

2. B   G   G   B   G   B

If you said the second alternative, you're like most people. Actually, according to the rules of probability, the two outcomes are equally likely. Whether your next child will be a boy or a girl doesn't depend on the sex of your previous children—each event is independent of the other. Still, people favor the second alternative because the first sequence clashes with their worldview of randomness. The first sequence just doesn't look like the outcome of a random process—it's not *representative* of randomness.

What if you flipped a coin six times and you got six heads? You'd probably think it was a crooked coin. Again, a sequence of six heads isn't similar to, or representative of, what you think of as a random sequence. You have taken the outcome and compared it to some standard and made your decision accordingly. People use the representativeness heuristic all the time to make decisions in real-world settings. For example, clerks in stores use the type of products that a shopper buys as a way of judging age. If someone loads his or her shopping cart with products normally thought to be representative of an older consumer, the clerk's estimate of the shopper's age increases (McCall, 1994).

Using a heuristic such as representativeness is adaptive and beneficial most of the time, but it can lead to irrational decisions. Imagine that you're leafing through a stack of questionnaires that have been filled out by some adult men. One of the respondents lists his height as 6 feet 5 inches, but his answers are so sloppily written that you can't make out his circled profession—it's either bank president or basketball player (NBA). You need to make a choice: Which is he? Most people choose NBA player because the applicant is tall and apparently not interested in careful writing (Beyth-Marom & Lichtenstein, 1984). But this is actually an illogical choice, because the odds of someone in the sample being a professional basketball player is extremely low—bank presidents outnumber NBA players by a wide margin (probably at least 50 to 1). In choosing basketball player, people have ignored the *base rate*, or the proportion of times that an object or event is likely to occur in the population being sampled.

The representativeness heuristic also dupes people into committing what is called the *conjunction error*. Consider the following: Linda is 31 years old, single, outspoken, and very bright. She majored in philosophy. As a student she was deeply concerned with issues of discrimination and social justice and participated in antinuclear demonstrations. Which of the following alternatives is more likely?

1. Linda is a bank teller.

2. Linda is a bank teller and active in the feminist movement.

In a study conducted by Tversky and Kahneman (1983), 85% of the participants judged alternative 2 to be the more likely. Why? Because Linda's description is more representative of someone active in the feminist movement than it is of a bank teller. But think about it—how can the odds of two things happening together be higher than the likelihood of any one of those events happening alone? Notice that the second alternative is actually a subset of the first alternative and therefore cannot be more likely. Those who choose alternative 2 have acted illogically, at least from the standpoint of the rational decision maker.

Availability

At other times, when asked to estimate the odds of some event occurring, we rely on our memories to help us make our decisions. You are using an **availability heuristic** when you base your estimates on the ease with which examples of the

availability heuristic
The tendency to base estimates on the ease with which examples come to mind. For example, if you've just heard about a plane crash, your estimates of the likelihood of plane crashes increase because "plane crashes" easily come to mind.

People are much more likely to worry when they fly if a recently publicized airline disaster is fresh and "available" in their minds.

event come to mind. Imagine you're asked to estimate the likelihood that you will forget to turn off your alarm clock on Friday night. If you can easily remember lots of instances in which your Saturday morning sleep was interrupted by a blasting alarm, your estimate of forgetting is likely to be high. You have relied on your previous experiences—particularly those experiences that easily come to mind—as a basis for judging probability.

Once again, the availability heuristic is likely to be an adaptive strategy much of the time. But, as with the representativeness heuristic, researchers can arrange situations which make this decision-making practice ineffective. Which do you think is more likely, an English word that begins with the letter K or an English word with K in the third position? By now you're probably skeptical about your first choice, but most people think that English words that begin with K are more likely (Tversky & Kahneman, 1973). In fact, English words that have K in the third position are much more common (the ratio is about 3 to 1). Which do you think is more likely, someone dying from any kind of accident or someone dying from a stroke? Accidents, right? It's not even close. Over twice as many people are likely to die from stroke than from any kind of accident (Slovic et al., 1982). People make the error because examples of the incorrect alternative are more likely to come to mind. It's easier to think of an English word with K in the first position, and accidental deaths get much more publicity than deaths due to stroke.

Anchoring and Adjustment

Judgments are also influenced by starting points—that is, by any initial estimates that you might be given. For example, Tversky and Kahneman (1974) asked people to estimate the number of African countries belonging to the United Nations. Prior to answering, subjects were given a number (between 0 and 100) and were asked to pick the number of countries by moving up or down from this starting point. So, you might be given the number 10 and asked to estimate the number of countries using 10 as a base. For groups that received 10 and 65 as the initial starting points, the estimated number of African countries was 25 and 45, respectively. The judgments were apparently adjusted based on initial estimates, or *anchors*, in a direction that stayed close to the starting point. The smaller the base, the fewer the countries that were estimated.

? CRITICAL THINKING

Try to come up with some examples in your own life in which applying the availability heuristic caused you to change your behavior in some way.

CONCEPT SUMMARY Decision-Making Heuristics		
Heuristic	**Description**	**Example**
Representativeness	We arrive at a decision by comparing the similarity of the object or event to the average member of each class.	Juan meets his new college roommate, Bryce, who is 6'10" and very athletic-looking. Juan assumes that Bryce is a basketball player, probably on scholarship.
Availability	We estimate the odds of some event occurring based on the ease with which examples come to mind.	Stella reads so much in the newspaper about car accidents that she believes her chances of dying in a car accident are greater than her chances of dying from a stroke.
Anchoring and adjustment	Judgments are influenced by initial estimates.	Stacey holds a garage sale and sells two big items early for a total of $150. Throughout the day, she overestimates how much she is making, and is disappointed to learn her actual profit.

In another experiment described by Tversky and Kahneman (1974), one group of people was asked to estimate the product of the following numbers:

$$1 \times 2 \times 3 \times 4 \times 5 \times 6 \times 7 \times 8$$

whereas a second group was asked to estimate the product of the same numbers presented in reverse order:

$$8 \times 7 \times 6 \times 5 \times 4 \times 3 \times 2 \times 1$$

The correct answer in both cases is 40,320. But the first group gave an average estimate of 512, whereas the second group's estimate averaged 2250—quite a difference, given that it's the same problem in both cases. In this example, the early numbers in the sequence serve as the anchors leading to either low or more moderate estimates.

THE VALUE OF HEURISTICS

What are we to make of such an imperfect decision maker? As psychologist Reid Hastie (1991) noted, the heuristic tool user described by Kahneman and Tversky is "an image of a decision maker of 'small brain' attempting to make do with a limited set of useful, imperfect, and not-too-demanding cognitive subroutines" (p. 136).

However, imperfect as heuristics may be there are several points worth making in their favor. First, the use of heuristics may lead to systematic errors under some circumstances, but, as Tversky and Kahneman (1974) have argued, they are usually surprisingly effective. Second, heuristics are economical. Optimal, or rational, decision making can be a complex, time-consuming activity. Strategies that lead to quick decisions with little cost are adaptive even if they sometimes lead to error. Third, to act optimally, in the sense of rational probability theory, you must possess all the information needed to calculate a choice; unfortunately, you often don't have all this information. In these cases, heuristics become useful tools for pointing you in the right direction.

Moreover, as we discussed in the section on framing effects, the fact that people make errors in artificial laboratory situations is somewhat misleading. We can define what the rational decision might be, based on objective information, but people do not always interpret the decision alternatives in the way the researcher intends. We all bring background knowledge to a situation which affects how we think and behave. In the "Linda is a bank teller" example, for instance, people know that there are more bank tellers in the world than feminist bank tellers. People understand a great deal about the frequencies of events in the world—the mistake is made because they're thinking about a single case, Linda, rather than about probabilities in general (Fielder, 1988; Gigerenzer, 1996).

It's important to recognize that just because you make decision errors doesn't mean you're using maladaptive processes. Think back to Chapter 5 and our discussion of perceptual illusions. It's easy to arrange situations in which you might see or hear things that aren't really there, but there is still wide agreement that your visual system is highly adaptive. Just because your visual system can be tricked by an illusion doesn't mean it's a bad system. Similarly, when you make decisions you're relying on adaptive systems that serve you very well in the majority of situations (Gigerenzer, 1997).

TEST YOURSELF 9.4

Check your knowledge about decision making by picking the term that best fits the following statements. Choose your answer from the following: availability heuristic, anchoring and adjustment heuristic, framing, representativeness heuristic. (You will find the answers in the Appendix.)

1. Matt used to fly to visit his parents during the Thanksgiving break, but after seeing nonstop coverage of a gory plane accident, he now chooses to drive.

   _____

2. Larry, a broker, used to tell people that his mutual fund lost money only three times in the last 10 years. Now he tells them that the fund has made money 7 of the last 10 years. He's noticed a very marked improvement in overall sales of the fund.

   _____

3. Kelley sleeps until noon, she parties at night, and she carries around a big backpack the rest of the time. Her neighbor Eileen assumes that Kelley must be a college student.

   _____

4. Graham, who made lots of sales early in the morning, estimates that he and Leslie made $700 from their yard sale; Leslie, who had a big afternoon, puts the estimate at $300.

   _____

Solving the Problems

In this chapter, we've discussed how people use their higher mental processes to communicate, categorize, find solutions to problems, and decide among alternatives. Each of these adaptive problems effectively illustrates how the mind samples from its adaptive tool kit to coexist successfully with its environment.

Communicating with Others. To communicate effectively, humans have developed rules (grammar) for combining arbitrary symbols in meaningful ways to express thoughts, feelings, and needs to others. A proper grammar consists of rules for combining sounds (phonology), rules for constructing sentences from words (syntax), and rules for meaning (semantics). In order to understand how language works, language researchers believe it is important to distinguish between the surface structure of a sentence—the literal ordering of words—and its deep structure, which taps the underlying representation of meaning. To

comprehend the communications of others, we rely on mutual knowledge, or pragmatics, to interpret statements or requests that may be riddled with ambiguity.

Are we born with a natural blueprint for language, or does language develop exclusively as a product of experience? The sequence of language development turns out to be quite universal—it doesn't matter where you look in the world, babies show similar milestones in language development. This finding has led many researchers to the conclusion that people are born ready to learn language in the same way they are born ready to walk. The ability to produce written and spoken language allows people to gather and transmit knowledge in ways that seem to be one of the truly unique characteristics of the human species.

Classifying and Categorizing. When people categorize, or put objects into meaningful groups, they create a world that is more sensible and predictable. Categorization skills enable us to infer invisible properties about objects—if X is a member of category Y, then X will have at least some of the properties of category Y members. As a result, we can make accurate predictions about the things we encounter. How is category membership defined? The evidence suggests that people often rely on family resemblance to make the categorization judgment. Members of the same category tend to share certain basic or core features. At the same time, categories are remarkably flexible; their boundaries are fuzzy, which enables us to classify things adaptively even when those objects may not share all the typical features of the category members. Categories also have structures that are hierarchical—there are categories within categories within categories. An object that fits the category "Siamese cat" also fits the category "animal" or "living thing." Research indicates that we most commonly assign objects to basic-level categories, which tend to be at intermediate levels of the hierarchy.

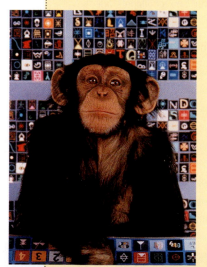

Solving Problems. When people are faced with a problem in their environment, there is a goal, which may or may not be well defined, and it's not immediately obvious how to get from the problem to the solution. What are the thought processes involved in finding an appropriate solution? Using the model of the IDEAL problem solver, good problem solving involves five main steps: (1) identify the problem; (2) define, or represent, the problem; (3) explore strategies for solution; (4) act on those problem strategies; and (5) look and learn from the experience. To identify and define a problem correctly, it's important that you see the problem in the right way. One of the common pitfalls with problem solving is that people allow their preconceptions to influence how they represent problem information. For example, most people fall prey to functional fixedness, or the tendency to see objects and their functions in certain fixed ways.

Each of us uses a variety of problem-solving strategies. Algorithms are procedures that guarantee a solution, but they're often time-consuming and cannot always be applied. Heuristics are problem-solving rules of thumb that can be applied quickly but do not always lead to the correct solution. Examples of problem-solving heuristics include means-ends analysis, working backward, and solving through analogies.

Making Decisions. Decision making involves the thought processes used in evaluating and choosing from among a set of alternatives. When people make decisions, they are confronted with a set of alternatives and are required to make a choice. Choice in decision making is almost always accompanied by risk, so it's adaptive to evaluate and select among the alternatives with care. As with problem solving, decision making is influenced by how the alternatives are viewed or represented. For example, the framing or structuring of the alternatives can affect the decision that is made. We commonly use a variety of decision heuristics, including representativeness, availability, and anchoring and adjustment. Again, these strategies may not always cause us to make the right decision, but they allow us to move quickly and to use past experience.

Thought and Language Chapter Summary

Communicating with Others

The ability to communicate with others through the use of written and spoken language is one of humanity's greatest success stories. Through language production, we transmit thoughts, feelings, and needs to others; through language comprehension, we learn and understand.

DOES LANGUAGE DETERMINE THOUGHT?

The *linguistic relativity hypothesis* proposes that language determines thought; that is without a word or phrase to describe an experience, the experience is literally "out of mind." Cross-cultural evidence suggests that a literal interpretation of this hypothesis cannot be true. But there is little doubt that language influences thought.

LANGUAGE COMPREHENSION

Effective communication relies heavily on *common knowledge* among speakers, and relies on a combination of *bottom-up* and *top-down* processing. The term *pragmatics* is used to describe how practical knowledge is used to comprehend the intentions of speakers and to produce an effective response.

LANGUAGE IN NONHUMAN SPECIES

Early attempts to teach chimps to vocalize were unsuccessful; they lack the necessary vocal equipment for speech. Subsequent researchers have taught chimps to communicate with visual mediums, such as American Sign Language. Chimps have shown the ability to associate particular symbols with words and actions, and understand some spoken English, but not all researchers are convinced that the chimps' achievements constitute true language.

THE STRUCTURE OF LANGUAGE

To qualify as true language, a communication system must have rules, collectively termed *grammar*. Grammar has three aspects: *phonology*, the rules for combining sounds to make words; *syntax*, the rule for combining words to make sentences; and *semantics*, the rules used to communicate meaning. All languages possess a hierarchical structure, ranging from *phonemes* (the smallest significant sound unit in speech) and *morphemes* (the smallest units of language that carry meaning) to words and sentences. According to Chomsky, sentences have a *surface structure* (superficial appearance), and a *deep structure* (underlying representation of meaning). Language production involves the transformation of deep structure into an acceptable surface structure.

LANGUAGE DEVELOPMENT

Researchers believe that all infants enter the world ready to learn language; the universality of language is apparent at birth. Crying, cooing, and babbling are important vocalization milestones. Between 6 and 18 months, experience begins to play more of a role. Simple words appear by the end of the first year. As a child approaches age 2, *telegraphic speech* is shown; the child omits articles and prepositions from communication. Telegraphic speech does reflect a rudimentary knowledge of syntax. Children often *overgeneralize* grammatical rules.

Classifying and Categorizing

To make sense of our environment and the objects in it, we carve the world into meaningful chunks called categories. A *category* is a class of objects (people, places, or things) that most people agree belong together. The ability to see similarities among things, to classify objects and events into meaningful categories, allows us to simplify our environment, and make predictions about how to act.

DEFINING CATEGORY MEMBERSHIP

What criteria do people use to determine category membership? According to a *defining features* approach, things are classified as members of a category if they have certain features that all members of that category share. The view works fine for mathematical categories (e.g., triangle), but breaks down for natural categories (e.g., weapon), which tend to have *fuzzy boundaries*. The *family resemblance* view is that members of a category will share certain core features but it isn't necessary that each member has them all.

THE HIERARCHICAL STRUCTURE OF CATEGORIES

Virtually all categories have a built-in hierarchical structure, with some levels of the hierarchy possessing special properties. *Basic-level categories* are the ones that generate the most useful and predictive information. They tend to be at the intermediate levels of a category hierarchy. Top-level categories or *superordinates* are not very descriptive.

DO PEOPLE STORE CATEGORY PROTOTYPES?

Family resemblance and the fact that there are good and poor members of a category lead to the concept of a *prototype*: the best or most representative member of a category. Prototypes are used to help determine category membership. Alternatively, we may store all category examples (category exemplars) that we encounter, and use these examples to determine category membership.

Solving Problems

Problem solving refers to situations in which someone wants to reach a goal, but the way to do it is not immediately obvious. The ability to solve problems is important for everyday survival. *Well-defined problems* have a well-stated goal, a clear starting point, and a relatively easy way to tell when a solution has been reached. *Ill-defined problems* do not have well-stated goals, clear starting points, or effective mechanisms for evaluating progress.

THE IDEAL PROBLEM SOLVER

The five major steps in problem solving are identifying the problem, defining it (representing it) in the most efficient way, exploring problem strategies, acting on the problem strategy chosen, and looking back to evaluate the effectiveness of the selected strategy.

EXPLORING AND ACTING: PROBLEM STRATEGIES

For some well-defined problems, you can use *algorithms*, step-by-step procedures that guarantee a solution. They are not always practical strategies for problem solving, and they only work for certain types of well-defined problems. When algorithms are not feasible, we may use *heuristics*, or problem solving "rules of thumb." Three common heuristics are *means–ends analysis*, *working backward*, and *searching for analogies*.

IDENTIFYING AND DEFINING: PROBLEM REPRESENTATION

To identify and define a problem, you must understand exactly what information is given and how that information can potentially be used. One obstacle in representation is *functional fixedness*, the tendency to see objects and their functions in certain fixed and typical ways. Generally, the fact that people rely on well-established patterns of perception and thought (*mental sets*) is probably an effective overall strategy.

LOOKING AND LEARNING

The problem-solving process is incomplete unless one looks and learns from their experience. By analyzing one's performance in detail, one can gain insight into why a particular heuristic failed or succeeded.

Making Decisions

Decision making requires a person to make a choice from among a set of alternatives. An important component of decision making is risk. Choices have consequences, so an incorrect decision can lead to unpleasant outcomes.

THE "FRAMING" OF DECISION ALTERNATIVES

The way alternatives are structured (*framing*) has a dramatic influence on the decision-making process. In general, when people are confronted with situations in which they think they can gain something, they tend to avoid taking risks. If the outcomes potentially lead to a loss of some kind, people are more likely to take a risk that will limit or avoid the loss.

THE VALUE OF HEURISTICS

Although heuristics are imperfect, they are usually surprisingly effective. Also, heuristics are economical, because they lead to quick decisions with little cost. Heuristics also are helpful pointing one in the right direction, when not all important information is available.

DECISION-MAKING HEURISTICS

When people are asked to judge the likelihood of some event falling into class A or B, they rely on a rule of thumb termed *representativeness*, which involves comparing the similarity of the event in question to the average member of each class. When asked to estimate the odds of some event occurring, we often rely on an *availability heuristic*, basing estimates on the ease with which examples

of the event come to mind. Both heuristics are beneficial most of the time, but can lead to irrational decisions. Judgments are also influenced by starting points, as reflected in *anchoring and adjustment*.

Terms to Remember

thinking, 344

COMMUNICATING WITH OTHERS

linguistic relativity hypothesis, 346
grammar, 348
phonology, 348
syntax, 348
semantics, 348
phonemes, 348
morphemes, 349
surface structure, 350
deep structure, 350
pragmatics, 351

CLASSIFYING AND CATEGORIZING

category, 356
defining features, 356
family resemblance, 358
prototypes, 358
category exemplars, 358
basic-level categories, 360

SOLVING PROBLEMS

well-defined problem, 363
ill-defined problem, 363
functional fixedness, 365
mental sets, 365
algorithms, 366
heuristics, 366
means–ends analysis, 367
working backward, 368
searching for analogies, 369

MAKING DECISIONS

decision making, 370
framing, 370
representativeness heuristic, 371
availability heuristic, 372

Recommended Readings

Bransford, J. D., & Stein, B. S. (1993). *The ideal problem solver* (2nd ed.). New York: Freeman. A fun book, written by a pair of cognitive psychologists, that is full of great advice on how to solve problems effectively.

Pinker, S. (1997). *How the mind works.* New York: Norton. A witty and fascinating book, written for the layperson, covering all aspects of "mind." Psychologist Pinker successfully brings together work from a variety of disciplines, including evolutionary biology, engineering, neuroscience, and even economics.

Pinker, S. (1994). *The language instinct.* New York: Morrow. In this book, psychologist Pinker specifically addresses language, how it evolved, and whether it truly represents a unique human ability.

INFOTRAC® COLLEGE EDITION

For additional readings, explore Infotrac College Edition, your online library. Go to:
http://www.infotrac-college.com/wadsworth

Hint: enter the search terms: Linguistic relativity, Language development, Animal communication, Problem solving, Decision-making heuristics.

What's on the Web?

Creativity Web

www.ozemail.com.au/~caveman/Creative/

Billed as "resources for creativity and innovation," this Web site includes all manner of techniques for improving one's creative thinking and problem solving. Read about techniques such as "mind mapping" and "lateral thinking," and try to fit them in with the steps of the IDEAL problem solver. Take a stroll around the "creative genius gallery," or take a "mental workout."

Chimpanzee and Great Ape Language Resources on the Internet

www.brown.edu/Departments/Anthropology/apelang.html

This page includes a wealth of links to information on primates and research on their language abilities. Follow the links to the primate homepage or the gorilla homepage. Go into the picture gallery and see if you can tell a Drill Baboon from a Diana Monkey. This is a great resource for more information on apes and their communication skills.

Mind/Brain Resources

http://mind.phil.vt.edu/www/mind.html

You've read all about the field of cognitive psychology. Now find out about the exciting interdisciplinary field of *cognitive science* (mentioned in the chapter introduction), a group of disciplines all working together to fully explain the mysteries of the mind. These fields include such diverse areas as philosophy, computer science, psychology, linguistics, and neuroscience. Explore the common threads that these disciplines share.

The Wadsworth Psychology Study Center Web Site

See http://psychology.wadsworth.com/ for practice quiz questions, hypercontents, updates, critical thinking exercises, discussion forums and more! The Wadsworth Psychology Study Center provides a wealth of information fully organized and integrated by chapter.

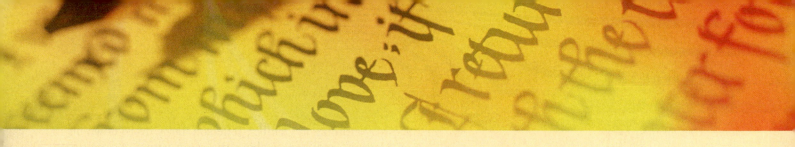

intelligence
An internal capacity or ability that psychologists assume accounts for individual differences in mental test performance. The term is also used to describe the mental processes that underlie the ability to adapt to ever-changing environments.

O n a Saturday morning in October, Jefferson Tarpy drops down his yellow #2 pencil and glances about the room with a cocky grin. Around him, working feverishly, sit dozens of others, similar in age and general appearance, but with pencils raised and sweat collecting on furrowed brows. Jefferson has finished early, as is his custom, and he's just aced the most important standardized test of his life. Next stop: medical school, a top residency, a lifetime of security.

Meanwhile, outside in a park across the street, Larry Steinway has also dropped his yellow pencil. But he doesn't notice. He will need to rely on his attendant to recover it. Although he is physically 22, Larry Steinway's mind drifts in a world occupied by a 4-year-old's thoughts and a 4-year-old's impulses. He uses language only haltingly; his hopes for an elementary school education are limited. Still, he responds quickly when his attendant asks him to calculate the number of seconds elapsing in 65 years, 14 days, and 15 hours. His correct answer includes the requisite number of leap years and arrives in slightly under a minute and a half.

Overhead, oblivious to the exploits of Larry Steinway, flies a single nutcracker in search of a place to deposit his recently harvested supply of pine seeds. On this particular trip, one of many over the past few months, the bird will store its 25,000th seed. Across miles of terrain lie thousands of secret caches, all attributable to this one bird, scattered among the equally numerous storage locations of other nutcrackers. Over the coming winter months, this single bird will successfully revisit its own hiding places, ignoring others, and recover some 80% of the hidden seeds.

These three short sketches each demonstrates behavior that *might* be characterized as intelligent. What do you think? Certainly we can agree that Jefferson Tarpy fits the description of intelligence—ace performer on standardized tests, self-assured; he probably gets all A's and is good at tennis. But what about Larry Steinway—someone who is poor at language, who operates at a mental level far below his physical age? Definitely not intelligent, you say; but then how do you explain his extraordinary calculating skills? Isn't "lightning calculation" an odd but nevertheless intelligent form of behavior? Finally, consider the nutcracker. It can't do geometry or calculus, but could you remember where you put 25,000 seeds scattered across miles of confusing terrain? Don't you think this remarkable ability to adapt to the harshness of winter should be considered a prime example of intelligent behavior?

Most people would have no trouble accepting that Balamurati Krishna Ambati is "intelligent"—after all, at age 12 he was a third-year pre-med student at New York University.

Ten-year-old "savant" Eddie Bonafe was born with severe physical and mental handicaps. But he could reproduce every hymn he heard sung in church on the piano before he had learned to walk. Would you call Eddie "intelligent"?

This little bird, Clark's Nutcracker, can remember the locations of thousands of seeds scattered across miles of confusing terrain. Wouldn't you call that "intelligent" behavior?

Previewing the Conceptual and Practical Problems

It probably won't surprise you to learn that psychologists have had a tough time agreeing on a definition of intelligence. As you've seen, the term can have a variety of meanings. Practically, when psychologists use the term **intelligence,** it's usually in reference to individual differences—specifically, the differences people show in their ability to perform tasks. People clearly differ in ability, and the measurement of these differences is used to infer the capacity called "intelligence." If you think about it, you'll realize that if everyone had the same ability to solve math problems or devise novel and creative ideas, the label "intelligent" would lose its meaning. Psychologists who study intelligence attempt to measure individual differences and then determine how and why those differences occur. One of the important goals is to use the measurement of individual differences to predict such things as job performance and success in school.

The focus of this chapter is the set of conceptual and practical problems that psychologists face in their efforts to understand intelligence. In each of the chapter sections, you'll find that the concept of intelligence has evolved somewhat over time. There are similarities in the ways that psychologists define and measure intelligence, but there are significant differences as well.

First, how should intelligence be conceptualized? It's normal for people to talk of intelligence as if it's some "thing" that is possessed by a person, such as blue eyes, long fingers, or a slightly crooked gait. Yet we cannot see intelligence, nor measure it directly with a stick. Intelligence may not even be best viewed as a single capacity. It may be better seen as a collection of separate abilities. There may be multiple intelligences ranging from the more traditional verbal and math skills to musical ability, mechanical ability, or even athletic ability.

Second, how can we measure the individual differences in performance? Regardless of how we may choose to conceptualize intelligence, there is still the practical problem of measuring how individuals differ. For any particular task, such as performing well in school, there will be a distribution of abilities. Some people will perform extremely well; others will struggle. If these abilities can be measured accurately, through the use of psychological tests, then it should be possible to tailor your activities to fit your skills. You can be advised not to enter cartography school if your spatial abilities are weak, or you can be steered toward a career as a writer or journalist if your verbal abilities are strong.

Third, what are the sources of intelligence? Does intelligent behavior come primarily from your genetic background or from life experiences? In an important sense, the study of intelligence is also an investigation into the plasticity of the mind. Granted that people differ in ability, it is not immediately obvious whether these differences are due to permanent genetic factors or simply to the peculiarities in one's environmental history. Is poor map reading a permanent affliction, resulting from a lack of the right kind of genetic blueprint, or can a superior ability to read maps be taught? Because of the wiring in my brain, am I doomed to forever have trouble fixing that leaky faucet in my kitchen, or can I be taught mechanical skill?

5f
PsychNow!

Conceptualizing Intelligence

From the perspective of the adaptive mind, it makes sense to talk about the adaptive characteristics of intelligence. For example, you might be considered intelligent if you can solve the particular problems that are unique to your environment. It turns out that this is actually a fairly common way for psychologists to think about intelligence (Mathews, 1997; Sternberg, 1997). Adaptive accounts of intelligence present many advantages. For one thing, focusing on adaptation helps to prevent us from thinking that human thoughts and actions are the only proper measuring sticks for intelligent behavior. The fact that

LEARNING GOALS

1. Discuss the psychometric approach to conceptualizing intelligence, including Spearman's two-factor theory.

2. Explain cognitive approaches to conceptualizing intelligence.

3. Discuss Gardner's theory of multiple intelligences.

4. Explain Sternberg's triarchic theory of intelligence.

CRITICAL THINKING

Based on this discussion, how reasonable do you think it is to compare the intelligence of people from one culture to another?

nutcrackers can efficiently hide and relocate thousands of seeds is certainly intelligent from the standpoint of adapting to the harshness of winter (Kamil & Balda, 1990). Understanding that different species (and people) have different survival problems to solve virtually guarantees that we will need to establish a wide range of criteria for what characterizes intelligence.

However, conceptualizing intelligence simply in terms of adaptability does not tell us much about what produces individual differences. People (and nutcrackers) differ in their ability to fit successfully into their environments, even when they're faced with similar problems. We need to understand the factors that account for individual differences. In this section of the chapter, we'll consider four general ways to accomplish this end: (1) the *psychometric* approach, (2) the *cognitive* approach, (3) the theory of *multiple intelligences*, and (4) the *triarchic* theory. Each is designed to provide a general framework for conceptualizing intelligence, with the expressed goal of explaining how people differ in mental ability.

PSYCHOMETRICS: MEASURING THE MIND

We begin with the psychometric approach, which proposes that intelligence is a mental capacity that can be understood by analyzing performance on mental tests. The word **psychometric** literally means "to measure the mind." A person's intelligence is determined by administering a variety of tests that measure his or her specific mental skills, such as verbal comprehension, memory, or spatial ability. The results are then analyzed statistically and conclusions are drawn about underlying mental abilities.

One of the first systematic attempts to treat intelligence in this way was performed in the nineteenth century by Englishman Sir Francis Galton (1822–1911). Galton was a half-cousin of Charles Darwin, and like his famous relative was deeply committed to the idea of "survival of the fittest." He believed that individual differences in ability had their basis in heredity and could be measured through a series of tests of sensory discrimination and reaction time. For a small fee, visitors to Galton's laboratory were given a variety of psychological and physical tests, measuring such things as visual acuity, grip strength, and reaction time to sounds. At the end of the test session they were handed a card with a detailed record of their scores (Hilgard, 1987; Johnson et al., 1985).

Deion Sanders was able to perform at the highest levels in both professional football and professional baseball. Could Deion's skills be used to support the existence of a factor tapping "general athletic ability"?

Galton believed that he was measuring intelligence through performance on his battery of tests. He based his belief partly on the fact that there sometimes appeared to be relationships among the various scores received by a particular individual. If a person tended to score highly on a certain test, such as sensory acuity, he or she tended to score highly on other measures as well. This pattern suggested to Galton that each of the separate tests might be tapping into some general ability—a general intelligence that contributed in some way to each of the different measured skills.

As it turned out, Galton's laboratory investigations into the measurement of intelligence were unsuccessful. His measurements were crude, and his tests were later shown to be poor predictors of actual intellectual performance, such as academic success (Wissler, 1901). For these and other reasons his contributions are of interest primarily for historical rather than scientific reasons. But his general approach captured the attention of other researchers, who went on to develop the psychometric approach in a more rigorous way. Among the more influential of those who carried on the Galton tradition was a mathematically inclined psychologist named Charles Spearman.

Spearman and Factor g

Charles Spearman's principal contribution was the development of a mathematical technique called **factor analysis,** which is a procedure for analyzing the relationships, or correlations, among test scores. The purpose of factor analysis is to isolate the various factors that can account for test performance. For example, as

psychometrics
The use of psychological tests to measure the mind and mental processes.

factor analysis
A statistical procedure developed by Charles Spearman that groups together related items on tests by analyzing the correlations among test scores. It's often used by psychologists to determine underlying common "factors," or abilities.

Sir Francis Galton (1822–1911) and his "anthropometric" laboratory, which he used to measure
intellectual ability.

Galton suggested, it's possible that each of us has a single underlying ability—
intelligence—that helps to explain our performance on mental tests. Alternatively,
there could be multiple factors involved—we might be intelligent in one way, such
as in an ability to remember, and not very intelligent in another, such as in spatial
reasoning. Spearman's technique enabled researchers to check on these possibilities in a systematic way.

To get an idea of how factor analysis works, think about star athletes who
excel in a number of sports. It's natural to assume that good athletes have general
athletic ability that reveals itself in a number of ways. If you were to correlate performance across a variety of skills, you should be able to predict how well they will
perform on one measure of skill, given that you know how well they perform on
others. Good athletes, for instance, should run fast, jump high, and have quick
reflexes. Correlations exist because presumably there is an underlying ability—
athletic skill—that is tapped by each of the individual performance measures.
Similar logic applies to intelligence: Someone who is high (or low) in intelligence
should perform well (or poorly) on many different kinds of ability tests. If there is
general intelligence, you should be able to predict performance on one type of test
(such as math) if you know how well the person performs on other tests (such as
verbal comprehension or spatial ability).

When Spearman (1904) applied factor analysis to the testing of mental ability, he discovered evidence for general intellectual ability. There was a single factor in the analysis, which he called **g** for *general intelligence*, that helped to explain
performance on a wide variety of mental tests. But he also found that it wasn't possible to explain individual test scores entirely by referring to *g*. The correlations
among the test scores were high, but not perfect. He found, for example, that
someone who performed extremely well on a test of verbal comprehension did not
necessarily excel to the same degree on a test of spatial ability. He argued, therefore, that it is necessary to take specific abilities into account, reflected in **s**, that
are *specific* to each individual test (see Figure 10.1 on page 388). So, to predict performance on a test of verbal comprehension, you need a measure of ability that is
specific to verbal comprehension, in addition to *g*.

Hierarchical Models of Intelligence

As you might expect, Spearman's two-factor analysis of intelligence was quite
influential in its time, and it remains influential today. But over the years
researchers have challenged his conclusions, especially the overarching concept of
g. Psychologist L. L. Thurstone, for example, applied a somewhat different version of factor analysis, as well as a more extensive battery of tests, and discovered
evidence for seven "primary mental abilities": verbal comprehension, verbal

? CRITICAL THINKING

*How well does the notion of general
intelligence describe you? If you're
good at one subject, does that predict
how well you do in others?*

g (general intelligence)
According to Spearman, a general factor,
derived from factor analysis, that underlies
or contributes to performance on a variety
of mental tests.

s (specific intelligence)
According to Spearman, a specific factor,
derived from factor analysis, that is unique
to a particular kind of test.

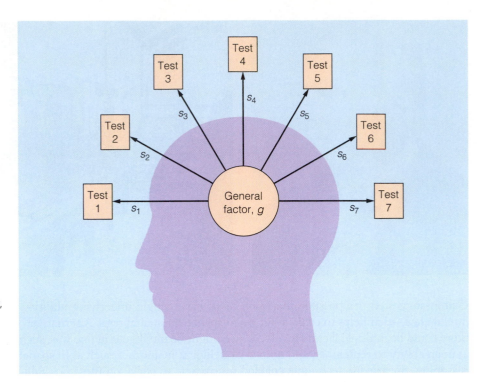

FIGURE 10.1

Spearman's General and Specific Factors
Spearman discovered that to explain performance on a variety of mental tests, it was necessary to consider (1) a common factor, called g for general intelligence, that contributes to performance on all of the tests, and (2) specific factors—labeled here as s_1 through s_7—that are specific to the particular tests.

fluency, numerical ability, spatial ability, memory, perceptual speed, and reasoning (Thurstone, 1938). Thurstone rejected Spearman's notion of a single general intelligence, g, because his analysis indicated that these seven primary abilities are largely independent—just because someone is good at verbal reasoning, for example, doesn't mean that he or she will be good at memory or perceptual speed. If performance on one type of test tells us little or nothing about performance on a second test, it's unlikely that the two tests are tapping the same general underlying ability.

Psychologists have argued for decades about (a) the proper way to apply factor analysis, (b) the particular kinds of ability tests that should be used, and (c) whether single or multiple factors are needed to explain the data (Jensen & Weng, 1994). But the evidence for a central g is hard to dismiss completely, at least when intelligence is defined by performance on tests of mental ability. For this reason, most modern psychometric theories of intelligence retain the concept of general intelligence, but propose more of a hierarchical structure, such as that shown in Figure 10.2. General intelligence, g, occupies a position at the top of the hierarchy, and various subfactors that may or may not operate independently from one another sit at the lower levels. This represents a compromise of sorts between Thurstone's view—that there is more than one primary mental ability—and Spearman's concept of g—general intelligence—but it is a compromise that is supported by the data.

Fluid and Crystallized Intelligence

Other psychologists believe strongly in the notion of general intelligence, but contend that it should be broken down into two separate dimensions: *fluid* intelligence and *crystallized* intelligence (Cattell, 1963, 1998; Horn & Cattell, 1966). **Fluid intelligence** is a measure of your ability to solve problems, reason, and remember in ways that are relatively uninfluenced by experience. It's the type of intelligence that is probably determined primarily by biological or genetic factors. **Crystallized intelligence,** on the other hand, measures acquired knowledge and ability. You learn things about the world, such as how to solve arithmetic problems, and develop abilities that depend on level of schooling and other cultural influences.

fluid intelligence
The natural ability to solve problems, reason, and remember; fluid intelligence is thought to be relatively uninfluenced by experience.

crystallized intelligence
The knowledge and abilities acquired as a result of experience (as from schooling and cultural influences).

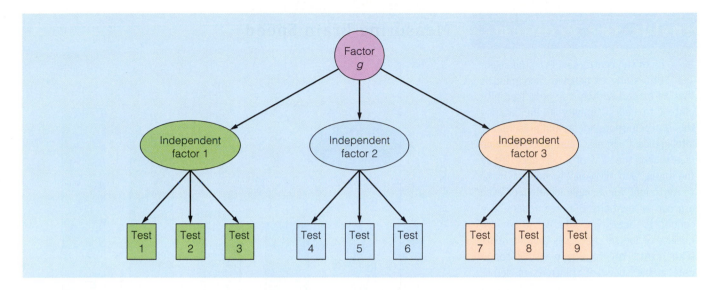

The distinction between fluid and crystallized intelligence is important because it helps to explain how mental abilities change with age and across different cultures (Horn & Noll, 1997). As you'll see later in the chapter, there are reasons to expect fluid and crystallized intelligence to change in different ways as we age. It's also common to find striking differences in people's ability to perform on psychometric tests of mental ability across different cultures and socioeconomic classes. Such differences are difficult to explain from the perspective of general intelligence, unless we assume that an important part of general intelligence is acquired from experience. Distinguishing between fluid and crystallized intelligence can help explain how people who are born with the same amount of natural (fluid) intelligence can end up performing quite differently on tests of mental ability.

FIGURE 10.2
Hierarchical Models
Many psychologists now propose hierarchical models of intelligence, which include elements found in the theories of both Spearman and Thurstone. Like Thurstone, hierarchical models propose separate factors that contribute independently to certain types of tests (for example, factor 1 contributes to tests 1–3, but not to tests 4–9). But, like Spearman, these models also assume that each of the separate factors is influenced by an overall g.

THE COGNITIVE APPROACH

Psychologists who approach intelligence from a psychometric perspective believe that test performance, and test performance alone, is the proper vehicle for defining and measuring intelligence. Psychologists who adopt a cognitive perspective argue instead that intelligence, or at least individual test performance, needs to be understood by analyzing internal mental processes. This kind of analysis typically comes in two forms: (1) measurement of the speed of mental processing, and (2) an analysis of the specific mental operations that produce intelligence thought (Sternberg, 1985).

Mental Speed

Some cognitive psychologists have suggested that intelligence reflects, in part, the speed of transmission among the neural pathways of the brain (see Hunt, 1985; Jensen, 1993; Vernon, 1983). The faster the brain communicates internally, the higher an individual's intelligence. The reason that communication speed might be important is that the brain has limited resources and must quickly allocate, or divide, its processing in order to perform efficiently (see Chapter 6). In support of this position, Jensen and his colleagues typically find a significant correlation between measures of neural communication speed and performance on mental tests of intelligence (Reed & Jensen, 1992; Vernon & Mori, 1992); other researchers have detected a similar relationship and have suggested that genetic factors may play a role (Rijsdijk et al., 1998). For more a detailed discussion of the relation between the speed of neural processing and intelligence, see the accompanying feature, "Inside the Problem" on page 390.

 CRITICAL THINKING

Which do you think contributes the most to performance on an essay exam: fluid or crystallized intelligence?

Inside the Problem   Measuring Brain Speed

One of the central tenets of the scientific study of behavior and mind is that all mental activity can be traced ultimately to neural activity in the brain—thoughts, emotions, ideas, and presumably, intelligence. Currently, researchers have no idea where the seat of intelligence lies in the brain, and it probably doesn't make sense to look for a single location, or even a group of locations. But researchers have sought to determine whether there are general biological processes that correlate with mental ability. One plausible candidate is the speed of transmission across neural pathways. The faster the brain communicates internally, the better its ability to quickly allocate, or divide, its processing in order to perform efficiently. But how is it possible to measure something like the speed of neural processing?

As we discussed in Chapter 3, recording the gross electrical activity of the brain is relatively easy. The procedure is noninvasive, requiring only that several electrodes be attached temporarily to locations on the scalp. Depending on the placement of the electrodes, electrical activity from different parts of the brain can then be recorded. To obtain a measure of the speed of neural processing, Reed and Jensen (1992) attached electrodes to scalp locations that are sensitive to the appearance of visual events. Subjects were seated in a dark room and were presented with a black-and-white checkerboard pattern on a video monitor. Approximately 100 milliseconds after presentation of the stimulus, the brain generates an electrical signal, known as P100, that can be measured in scalp areas over the primary visual cortex.

Reed and Jensen (1992) were not simply interested in the appearance of the P100 signal but rather in the *latency*, or time of appearance, of the signal. People differ in the amount of time it takes for this signal to appear; this latency was assumed by Reed and Jensen to provide an indirect measure of the speed of information processing in the brain. They assumed that short latencies reflected fast processing in the brain and long latencies relatively slower processing. The main question of interest was

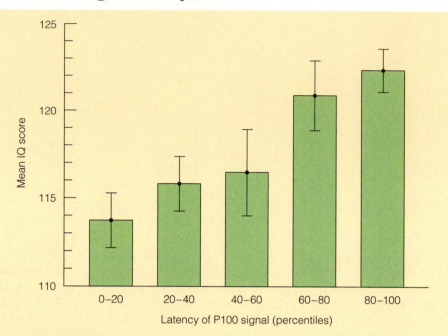

FIGURE 10.3
Signal Latency and IQ
This figure shows how latency, or time of appearance, of the P100 signal relates to the average IQ score. The first bar on the left shows the average IQ score for the 20% of students with the longest latencies; the last bar on the right shows the 20% of students with the shortest latencies. Notice that the higher IQ scores are associated with the students who showed the fastest P100 onset times. (Adapted from Reed & Jensen, 1992.)

whether P100 latency could then be used to predict performance on an intelligence test.

P100 signal times were measured for 147 college students, and each individual's average latency was then compared with his or her score on an independent test of mental ability. Figure 10.3 shows how the intelligence scores varied with P100 latencies. The P100 values are divided into student quintiles, which means that the first bar on the left shows the intelligence scores for the 20% of students with the longest latency values, and the last bar on the right shows the 20% of students with the shortest average P100 latencies. As the data indicate, a relationship appears to exist between latency and performance on the intelligence test. The shorter the latency—that is, the faster the processing in the brain—the higher the intelligence score.

Does this mean that smarter brains are faster brains, as the data might imply? Not necessarily. It's important to remember that conclusions about cause and

effect cannot be drawn from correlational studies like the one conducted by Reed and Jensen. We may be able to predict intelligence scores to some extent by measuring neural processing speed, but that doesn't mean that processing speed is the underlying cause of intelligence. Moreover, the predictive ability of the P100 latencies was far from perfect; they explained only a small proportion of the subject differences that were found in intelligence scores.

Finally, knowledge about the electrical activity of various brain regions is still relatively meager. Researchers are not sure at this point just what the latency of the P100 signal is actually measuring in the brain. It's not a direct measure of the speed of neural impulses—at best, it is an indirect measure that may eventually indicate something about the conduction properties of neurons. Thus, although the Reed and Jensen data are provocative, they cannot tell us with any certainty what neurological processes actually underlie the capacity of intelligence.

Componential Analysis

In addition to measuring the speed of mental processing, cognitive theorists also attempt to identify the specific mental processes that contribute to superior test performance. Robert Sternberg (1977) developed a procedure called *componential analysis* that uses people's reaction times, as well as their error rates, to isolate the mental operations that are tapped by traditional intelligence tests. For example, to isolate the ability to detect relationships among concepts, people might be asked to solve analogies of the following form as quickly as possible: LAWYER is to CLIENT as DOCTOR is to _____? Sternberg argues that intelligent performers are able to infer the relation between the first two components of the analogy quickly (Sternberg & Gardner, 1983). They note, for example, that a LAWYER is typically hired by and works for the CLIENT, and they're able to then map and apply this perceived relation to generate the correct answer (PATIENT). Sternberg believes that intelligent people can generate effective overall plans for attacking problems—they represent problems well and then generate and monitor global strategies for problem solution (see Chapter 9).

Like the psychometric theorists, cognitive theorists hope that once they identify the fundamental components of intelligence, those components can be used to predict and explain individual differences in task performance. If we can get a measure of your ability to analyze analogies, for instance, we might be able to predict how well you will perform on a wide variety of tests of mental ability. Some cognitive theorists have been interested in developing computer software programs that mimic human intelligence, or at least expert thinking in more narrow domains. It may be possible, for instance, to develop a program that can successfully diagnose medical conditions, or solve physics or engineering problems (Simon, 1969, 1992). By conceptualizing intelligence in terms of underlying mental processes and then modeling those processes via computer programs, cognitive theorists hope to go beyond just measuring intelligent behavior to understanding and explaining its causes.

GARDNER'S THEORY OF MULTIPLE INTELLIGENCES

Before we turn to another way of conceptualizing intelligence—the multiple-intelligences approach—let's pause momentarily and return to Larry Steinway, that fictional lightning calculator we met in the opening to the chapter. After reading the previous sections, what do you think psychologists with a psychometric or cognitive bent would have to say about Larry's intelligence? How does someone with a highly specialized skill—lightning calculation—but with otherwise impaired mental abilities fit into these conceptualizations of intelligence? In some respects Larry has a fast brain, but it's highly doubtful that he could solve an analogy problem efficiently, or generate and monitor sophisticated global problem-solving strategies. We can also be sure that Larry will not perform well on a standardized battery of tests, which means that his assigned value of *g* will be far lower than average.

Consider also the gifted athlete, who soars high above the basketball rim but has trouble reading his daughter's nursery rhymes. Or the respected mathematical wizard, full professor at a major university, who has trouble matching her shoes, let alone her socks, in the morning. The point to be made about Larry Steinway, or the athlete or the professor, is that people sometimes show specialized skills or abilities that stand alone, that are not representative of a general ability that cuts across all kinds of behavior. Spectacular skill can be shown in one area accompanied by profound deficits in another. Perhaps more important, these selective skills are often in areas that are *not* traditionally covered by the verbal and analytical battery of commonly used intelligence tests.

Howard Gardner (1983, 1993) argues that traditional conceptions of intelligence need to be broadened to include special abilities or talents of the type we've been discussing. He rejects the idea that intelligence can be adequately conceptualized through the analysis of test performance or artificial laboratory tasks (as used by the psychometric and cognitive approaches). Rather than searching for intelligence, we should understand that human behavior is rich in selective talents and abilities—we need a theory of **multiple intelligences,** not a method for discovering a single underlying *g*. An *intelligence* (rather than "the" intelligence) is defined as "an ability or set of abilities that permits an individual to solve problems or fashion products that are of consequence in a particular cultural setting" (Walters & Gardner, 1986). (Note that Gardner's treatment of intelligence has an adaptive flavor and fits snugly into our general conception of the adaptive mind.) Although Gardner believes that each of these separate intelligences may be rooted in the biology of the brain, each can manifest itself in a variety of ways, depending on one's culture.

Case Studies

Rather than studying intelligent behavior in the laboratory, Gardner uses a case study approach. He studies reports of particular individuals with special abilities or talents, such as superior musicians, poets, scientists, and *savants* like Larry Steinway. He has also looked extensively at the effects of damage to the brain. He has noted, for example, instances in which brain damage can affect one kind of ability, such as reasoning and problem solving, yet leave other abilities, such as musical skill, intact. Based on his research, Gardner has identified what he believes to be seven kinds of intelligence.

1. *Musical intelligence:* the type of ability displayed by gifted musicians or child prodigies
2. *Bodily-kinesthetic intelligence:* the type of ability shown by gifted athletes, dancers, or surgeons who have great control over body movements
3. *Logical-mathematical intelligence:* the type of ability displayed by superior scientists and logical problem solvers
4. *Linguistic intelligence:* the type of ability shown by great writers or poets who can express themselves verbally
5. *Spatial intelligence:* the type of ability shown by those with superior navigation skills or an ability to visualize spatial scenes

multiple intelligences
The notion proposed by Howard Gardner that people possess a set of separate and independent "intelligences" ranging from musical to linguistic to interpersonal ability.

People possess unique abilities that can be considered as types of intelligence. For example, the acrobats on the left certainly possess high levels of bodily-kinesthetic intelligence; Nelson Mandela, shown on the right, rates highly in interpersonal and linguistic intelligence.

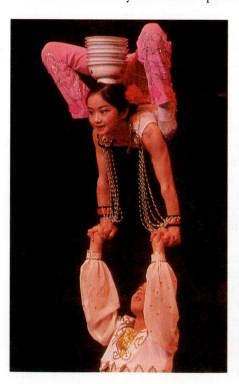

6. *Interpersonal intelligence:* the type of ability shown by those who can easily infer other people's moods, temperaments, or intentions and motivations
7. *Intrapersonal intelligence:* the ability shown by someone who has great insight into his or her own feelings and emotions

Notice that some forms of intelligence, as described by Gardner, are covered well by conventional tests of mental ability. The psychometric and cognitive approaches focus extensively on logical-mathematical intelligence and to some extent on linguistic and spatial intelligence. Some researchers who use the psychometric approach, including L. L. Thurstone, also argue for the need to distinguish among distinct and independent types of intelligence. But researchers who conceptualize intelligence with the psychometric and cognitive approaches rarely, if ever, concentrate on intelligences such as musical ability or great athletic skill. As a result, the multiple-intelligences approach considerably broadens the conceptualization of intelligence.

STERNBERG'S TRIARCHIC THEORY

Most intelligence researchers agree about the need for a multi-pronged attack on intelligence. Not everyone agrees with Howard Gardner's treatment of intelligence, although the framework has been applied successfully in many educational settings (Krechevsky & Seidel, 1998). Some say that Gardner is really talking about multiple talents rather than intelligences, and his theory remains primarily descriptive without much hard scientific evidence. But the majority of psychologists agree with Gardner that intelligence should be broadly conceived—it's not simply performance on a battery of primarily verbal-linguistic or sensory tests.

Robert Sternberg's **triarchic theory** of intelligence is a good example of a recent eclectic approach (meaning it's made up of different elements). Sternberg was trained as a cognitive psychologist, and his theory contains important elements of the cognitive approach. He's convinced that it's important to understand the mental operations that are involved in the planning and execution of specialized tasks. But he also believes that any complete account of intelligence must address behavior outside of the laboratory. For example, what is the form of intelligence that enables people to apply their mental processes creatively to problems that arise in the external environment? Furthermore, how does intelligence relate to the practical experience of the individual? Consequently, he accepts the idea that there may be multiple kinds of intelligence. The term *triarchic* means roughly "ruled by threes" so, not surprisingly, Sternberg's conceptualization of intelligence is divided into three major parts (Sternberg, 1985, 1988).

Analytic Intelligence

Sternberg believes that any complete theory of intelligence must refer in some way to basic analytic skills. Some people are simply better than others at processing information—they're good at representing (or seeing) problems in the right way and can generate effective strategies for solutions. People with high degrees of *analytical intelligence* tend to perform well on conventional tests that tap reasoning and logical-mathematical ability (such as the Scholastic Assessment Test). Because most psychometric tests of intelligence require these kinds of abilities, people who are high in analytic intelligence tend to be assigned a high *g*, for general intelligence. If you know someone who performs well in school, or who claims to be highly intelligent based on a standardized test, he or she is likely to score highly on analytic intelligence.

Creative Intelligence

Sternberg proposes a second kind of intelligence, *creative intelligence*, that expresses how well people are able to cope with new or novel tasks. Being analytic, and processing information well, does not guarantee that you will be creative or be able to apply the skills you've mastered in a new context. The world is full of

triarchic theory
Robert Sternberg's theory of intelligence; it proposes three types of intelligence: analytic, creative, and practical.

CONCEPT SUMMARY
Views of Intelligence

Approach	Example(s)	Intelligence Is ...
Psychometric	Spearman's factor *g* Hierarchical models	A mental capacity that can be understood by analyzing performance on mental tests.
Cognitive	Mental speed Componential analysis	Reflected in the speed of mental processing and the analysis of specific mental operations.
Multiple intelligence	Gardner's multiple intelligences	Seven proposed abilities that permit an individual to solve problems or fashion products that are of consequence in a particular cultural setting.
Triarchic theory	Analytic intelligence Creative intelligence Practical intelligence	The ability to process information analytically; the ability to cope with novel tasks; the ability to solve problems uniquely posed by cultural surroundings.

people who are good in school, or who perform well on assigned tasks, but can't seem to think their way out of a paper bag. They lack creativity and seem to have trouble applying what they've learned. A child who quickly and effortlessly learns to read after acquiring the rudiments of language, for example, is a child who is presumably high in creative intelligence (Sternberg, 1985).

Practical Intelligence

Finally, people differ in *practical intelligence*, which taps how well they fit into their environments. People with lots of practical intelligence solve the problems that are uniquely posed by their cultural surroundings. They mold themselves well into existing settings, and they can select new environments, if required, that provide a better fit or niche for their talents. In a nutshell, these individuals have "street smarts"—they size up situations well and act accordingly. You probably know someone who seems to lack analytic skills—who fails school or drops out—but still manages to succeed quite well in life. They work well with the tools of the environment and manage to do what it takes to succeed.

Sternberg's triarchic theory fits the current trend toward a broadening of the concept of intelligence. Like Howard Gardner's approach, his theory deals with behaviors and skills that are not normally covered by the psychometric and purely cognitive approaches. Triarchic theory, like Gardner's theory, can also be applied successfully in classroom settings where particular types of intelligence can be nurtured and developed (Sternberg, 1998; Sternberg et al., 1998). At the same time, breadth is not gained without some cost—concepts such as practical and creative intelligence are not defined with ringing precision and, consequently, can be somewhat difficult to measure and test. Moreover, even if it is desirable to broaden our conceptualization of intelligence, that doesn't mean that the cognitive or psychometric approaches to intelligence have no value. As you'll see in the next section, psychometric tests are often quite useful in predicting future performance, even though they may be measuring only narrow dimensions of intelligence.

TEST YOURSELF 10.1

For each of the following statements, try to pick the term that best describes the approach to conceptualizing intelligence. Choose your answers from the following: **psychometric, cognitive, multiple intelligences, triarchic theory. (You will find the answers in the Appendix.)**

1. Mitsuko has street smarts—she can mold herself successfully into any situation.

_____

2. Celia wants to measure her intelligence so she volunteers to participate in a reaction time experiment in the psychology department. _____

3. Jeremy flunks most of his classes, but he's a brilliant pianist so he considers himself to be highly intelligent. _____

4. Lucy has just finished an exhaustive battery of mental tests; she's waiting to find out if she has a high *g*. _____

5. Natalie wants to understand the concept of intelligence so she has signed up for a class on factor analysis. _____

6. Verne shows great insight into the feelings of others which makes him score highly on tests of interpersonal intelligence. _____

7. Shelia scored a perfect 4.0 GPA in high school, but has trouble applying what she's learned to new situations. She's beginning to feel like she might not be so intelligent after all. _____

Measuring Individual Differences

We've now discussed some of the ways to conceptualize intelligence theoretically. However, we have yet to discuss in detail how individual differences are actually measured. People differ. Pick just about any attribute—height, weight, friendliness, intelligence—and you're going to find a scattering, or distribution, of individual values. Some people are tall, some are short; some people are friendly, some are not. As we discussed in the previous section, the study of individual differences is important because many psychological concepts, such as intelligence and personality, are defined and measured by individual differences.

If we can get a measure of how you compare to others on some psychological dimension, such as intelligence, it becomes possible to assess your current and future capabilities. **Achievement tests,** for example, measure someone's current level of knowledge or competence in a particular subject (such as math or reading). Researchers or teachers can use the results of an achievement test to assess the effectiveness of a learning procedure or a curriculum in a school. It is also possible to use individual differences to make predictions about the future—how well you can be expected to do in your chosen profession or whether you are likely to succeed in college. **Aptitude tests** measure the ability to learn in a particular area, to acquire the knowledge needed for success in a given domain. Aptitude test results can be used to help choose a career path or even to decide whether to take up something as a hobby, such as car mechanics or the violin.

THE COMPONENTS OF A GOOD TEST

We'll begin by discussing the qualities or characteristics of a "good" test—that is, a test that can be expected to provide a good measure of individual differences. Given that we recognize the need to measure these differences, it's crucial that the measurement device yield information that is scientifically useful. Researchers generally agree on three characteristics that are needed for a good test: *reliability*, *validity*, and *standardization*. Please note that these are characteristics of the *test*, not the person taking the test.

Reliability

The first test characteristic, **reliability,** is a measure of the *consistency* of the test results. Reliable tests produce similar scores from one administration to the next. Suppose we want to measure creativity and we design a test that produces a score from 0 to 100 on a creativity scale. We measure Al and he gets a score of 13; we

achievement tests
Psychological tests that measure your current level of knowledge or competence in a particular subject.

aptitude tests
Psychological tests that measure your ability to learn or acquire knowledge in a particular subject.

reliability
A measure of the consistency of test results; reliable tests produce similar scores or indices from one administration to the next.

Throughout the school years, children regularly take standardized tests that are designed to measure aptitude or achievement.

measure Cynthia and she tops out at 96. Clearly, we conclude, Cynthia is more creative than Al. But is she really? To be sure about the results, we administer the test again and find that the scores reverse. Sadly, our creativity test lacks reliability—it does not produce consistent scores from one administration to the next.

It's important for a test to be reliable because otherwise we cannot draw firm conclusions from the data. Cynthia might be more creative than Al, but the difference in scores could also be just an artifact or failing of the test. On this particular administration Cynthia scored higher, but that's no guarantee that tomorrow's results will yield the same conclusion. One way to measure a test's reliability is to give it to the same group of individuals on two separate occasions. *Test-retest reliability* is then calculated by comparing the scores across the repeated administrations. Often, a correlation coefficient is computed that indicates how well performance on the second test can be predicted from performance on the first. The closer the test-retest correlation comes to a perfect +1.00, the higher the reliability of the test.

Validity

The second test characteristic, **validity,** tells us how well a test measures what it is supposed to measure. A test can yield reliable data—consistent results across repeated administrations—yet not truly measure the psychological characteristic of interest. If a test of creativity actually measures shoe size, then the data are likely to be quite reliable but not very valid. Shoe size isn't going to change much from one measurement to the next, but it has little to do with creativity.

Actually, there are several different forms of validity: *Content validity* measures the degree to which the content of a test samples broadly across the domain of interest. If you're trying to get a general measure of creativity, your test should not be limited to one kind of creativity, such as artistic creativity. For the test to have a high degree of content validity, it should probably measure artistic, verbal, mechanical, mathematical, and other kinds of creativity.

Sometimes psychologists are interested in designing a test that predicts some future outcome, such as job performance or success in school. For a test to have *predictive validity*, it needs to predict this outcome adequately. The Scholastic Assessment Test (SAT) is a well-known case in point. The SAT is designed to predict success in college. So to assess its predictive validity, we need to ask whether the SAT predicts college performance as expressed through a measure such as college grade point average. Various studies have shown that the correlation between

validity
An assessment of how well a test measures what it is supposed to measure. *Content validity* assesses the degree to which the test samples broadly across the domain of interest; *predictive validity* assesses how well the test predicts some future criterion; *construct validity* assesses how well the test taps into a particular theoretical construct.

CONCEPT SUMMARY
Components of a Good Test

Component	Description	Example
Reliability	Consistency of test results	Taking a test twice should yield similar scores each time.
Validity	Does the test measure what it's supposed to?	
—Content	—The degree to which a test samples broadly across the domain of interest	The items on a test of creativity should cover different types of creativity, such as artistic, mathematical, and verbal.
—Predictive	—The degree to which a test predicts some future outcome	Performance on the American College Test (ACT) should correlate with later performance in college classes.
—Construct	—The degree to which a test taps into a particular theoretical construct	Performance on a test of creativity should correlate with other characteristics or indices thought to be associated with creativity.
Standardization	Testing, scoring, and interpretation procedures are kept similar across all administrations of the test.	Everyone who takes the SAT receives the same instructions, uses a #2 pencil and standard answer sheet, and has to complete the test within the same specified period of time.

the SAT scores and grade point averages of college freshmen is somewhere between +0.40 and +0.50 (Donlon, 1984; Willingham et al., 1990). Statistically, this means that we can predict college performance with the SAT at greater than chance levels, although our predictive abilities are not perfect.

There is still another kind of validity, *construct validity*, that measures how well a test taps into a particular theoretical scheme or construct. Suppose we have a theory of creativity that is developed well enough to generate a wide variety of predictions—how creative people act, the kinds of books that creative people are interested in, the susceptibility of creative people to mental disorders, and so on. To have high construct validity, our test must predict performance on each of these separate indices of creativity, rather than on just one. If a test has high construct validity, its scores tend to vary in ways that are predicted by the theory. So if the theory predicts that creative people are more likely to suffer from depression, then people who score highly on the creativity test should have a greater likelihood of being depressed.

Standardization

The third characteristic of a good test of individual differences is **standardization.** When you take a test such as the SAT, or any national aptitude or achievement test, you quickly learn that the testing procedures are extremely rigid. You can break the test seal only at a certain time, the instructions are parroted in monotone by a serious administrator, and your yellow #2 pencil must be put down at an exact tick of the clock. These tests are *standardized*, which means that the testing, scoring, and interpretation procedures are kept similar across all administrations of the test. Rigid adherence to standardization is important because it assures that all test takers will be treated the same.

In fact, the proper interpretation of a test score absolutely demands standardization. Remember, we're concerned with individual differences—it doesn't make much sense to compare two or more scores if different instructions or scoring procedures have been used across the test sessions. A person's score on a test of individual differences can be understood only with respect to a reference group, often called a *norm group*, and everyone within the group must receive the same test and administration procedures. We'll return to this notion of a norm reference group momentarily, as we consider the concept of the IQ.

IQ: THE INTELLIGENCE QUOTIENT

The most famous index of intelligence is the **IQ,** or **intelligence quotient.** The IQ is a single number, derived from performance on a test, and it may well be the most widely applied psychological measure in the world. But how can a single

CRITICAL THINKING

Pick one of your classes in school. Do you think the tests that you've taken so far have been valid? What specific kind of validity are you using as a basis for your answer?

standardization
Keeping the testing, scoring, and interpretation procedures similar across all administrations of a test.

intelligence quotient (IQ)
Originally, mental age divided by chronological age and then multiplied by 100. More recently, defined in terms of deviation from the average score on an IQ test. *See* deviation IQ.

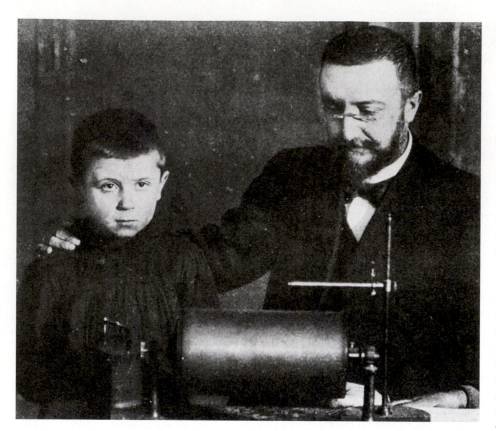

Alfred Binet, shown here with an unidentified child, was commissioned by the French government to develop a test that would help teachers identify students who might have a difficult time grasping concepts in school.

number be used to measure intelligence? This might strike you as odd given our earlier discussion about multiple intelligences and the need to establish a wide variety of criteria for what it means to be intelligent. The key to appreciating the IQ, and to understanding why it is so widely applied, lies in the concept of *validity:* What is the IQ designed to measure, and how successfully does it achieve its goal? As you'll see momentarily, it turns out that IQ does a reasonably good job of predicting what it was designed to predict.

The historical roots of the intelligence quotient trace back about a hundred years, to the work of the French psychologist Alfred Binet and his associate Théopile Simon. Binet and Simon were commissioned by the French government in 1904 to develop a test that would identify children who were considered "dull"—specifically, children who would have a difficult time grasping concepts in school. It was the French government's intention to help these children, once they were identified, through some kind of remedial schooling. Thus, the mission of the test was primarily practical, not theoretical; the charge was to develop a test that would accurately assess individual differences in future academic performance.

Mental Age

Not surprisingly, Binet and Simon designed their test to measure the kinds of skills that are needed in school—such as memory, reasoning, and verbal comprehension. The goal was to determine the **mental age**—or what Binet and Simon called the *mental level*—of the child, which was defined as the chronological age that best fit the child's current level of intellectual performance. Mental age is typically calculated by comparing a child's test score with the average scores for different age groups. For example, let's suppose that an average 8-year-old is able to compare two objects from memory, recognize parts of a picture that are missing, count backward from 20 to 0, and give the correct day and time. An average 12-year-old might be able to define abstract words, name 60 words in 3 minutes, and discover the meaning of a scrambled sentence. If Jenny, who is 8, is able to solve the problems of the typical 12-year-old, she would be assigned a mental age of 12.

Notice that mental age and chronological age do not have to be the same, although they will be on the average (an average 8-year-old should solve problems at the average 8-year-old level). Because intelligence tests are given to lots of children, it's possible to determine average performance for a given age group and then to determine the appropriate mental age for a particular child. By using mental age, Binet and Simon (1916) were able to pinpoint the slow and quick learners and recommend appropriate curriculum adjustments.

In the first two decades of the twentieth century, Binet and Simon's intelligence test was revised several times and was ultimately translated into English for use in North America. The most popular American version was developed by psychologist Lewis Terman at Stanford University; this test later became known as

mental age
The chronological age that best fits a child's level of performance on a test of mental ability. Mental age is typically calculated by comparing a child's test score with the average scores for different age groups.

the *Stanford-Binet* test of intelligence. It was also Terman who popularized the actual intelligence quotient (based on an idea originally proposed by German psychologist William Stern), which is defined as follows:

$$\text{Intelligence quotient (IQ)} = \frac{\text{Mental age}}{\text{Chronological age}} \times 100$$

The IQ is a useful measure because it establishes an easy-to-understand baseline for "average" intelligence—people of average intelligence will have an IQ of 100 because their mental age will always be equal to their chronological age. People with IQs greater than 100 will be above average in intelligence; those below 100 will be below average in intelligence.

Deviation IQ

Defining IQ simply in terms of the *ratio* of mental age to chronological age has some problems. For one thing, it's hard to compare the meaning of the ratio across different ages. If a 5-year-old performed at a level comparable to a 7-year-old, she would be given an IQ of 140 ($7/5 \times 100 = 140$). But if a 10-year-old scored at the level of a 12-year-old, his IQ would be only 120 ($12/10 \times 100 = 120$). Both are performing at levels two years above their chronological age, but they receive very different IQs. Moreover, how much sense does it make to argue that a 30-year-old who performs comparably to a 60-year-old should be given a vastly higher IQ ($60/30 \times 100 = 200$)?

To overcome this problem, most modern intelligence tests retain the term IQ but define it in terms of a *deviation*, or difference, rather than as a ratio. A **deviation IQ** still uses 100 as a baseline average, but a 100 IQ is redefined as the average score in the distribution of scores for people of a certain age. A particular person's IQ is then calculated by determining where his or her test score "sits," relative to the average score, in the overall distribution of scores. (Note that *age* is the "norm group" used for defining the concept of intelligence.) Figure 10.4 shows a frequency distribution of scores that might result from administering a test such as the Stanford-Binet to large groups of people. The average of the distribution is 100, and approximately half of the test takers will produce scores above 100 and the other half, below.

One of the characteristics of modern intelligence tests is that they tend to produce very regular and smooth distributions of scores. With most intelligence tests, for example, not only will the most common score be 100 (by definition), but roughly 68% of the people who take the test will receive an IQ score between 85 and 115. With a distribution such as the one shown in Figure 10.4, we can easily

deviation IQ
An intelligence score that is derived from determining where your performance sits in an age-based distribution of test scores.

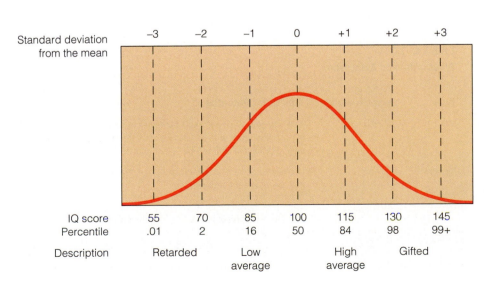

FIGURE 10.4

The Distribution of IQ Scores
IQ scores for a given age group will typically be distributed in a bell-shaped, or normal, curve. The average and most frequently occurring IQ score is defined as 100. Roughly 68% of the test takers in this age group receive IQ scores between 115 and 85, which includes everyone scoring between one *standard deviation* above and below the mean. People labeled as "gifted" (an IQ of 130 and above) or "retarded" (an IQ of 70 or below) occur infrequently in the population.

calculate the percentage of the population apt to receive a particular IQ score. You will find, for example, that approximately 98% of the people who take the test will receive a score at or below 130. Notice once again that IQ in this case is defined in terms of the relative location of a person's score in a frequency distribution of scores gathered from people in the same chronological age group.

EXTREMES OF INTELLIGENCE

Tests such as the Stanford-Binet or the related Wechsler Adult Intelligence Scale have been given to thousands and thousands of people. Consequently, we know a great deal about how IQ scores tend to be distributed in the population. Most people fall within a normal or average range, which covers scores from about 70 to about 130. Individuals who fall above or below this range represent *extremes* in intelligence.

Mental Retardation

A score of 70 or below on a standard IQ test is likely to lead to a diagnosis of **mental retardation,** although other factors (such as daily living skills) contribute to the diagnosis (Fredericks & Williams, 1998). No single test score, by itself, is sufficient to arrive at a diagnosis of mental retardation. A four-level classification scheme has been developed by the American Association on Mental Deficiency. Table 10.1 shows how each category level for retardation is defined—in terms of IQ—and lists some of the adaptation skills that can be expected, on average, for individuals who meet the diagnostic criteria.

What causes mental retardation? There are many possible causes, some genetic and some environmental. Down's Syndrome, for example, is typically associated with low IQ scores and is caused by a genetic abnormality—usually an extra chromosome. Environmental factors during development, such as inadequate nutrition or illness, have also been connected to mental retardation. There are probably hundreds of potential causes for extremely low IQ scores and, once again, a low IQ score does not guarantee the diagnosis.

Giftedness

At the other end of the IQ scale are people considered **gifted,** with IQs at or above approximately 130. Many studies have tracked the intellectual and social accomplishments of gifted children, partly as a means of checking on the validity of the IQ measure. One of the most famous studies was started in the 1920s by Lewis Terman (1925; Terman & Ogden, 1947). Terman was interested in whether children who were identified early in life as gifted would be likely to achieve success throughout their lives. Generally, this turned out to be the case—Terman's gifted subjects earned more college degrees than average, made more money, wrote more books, generated more successful patents, and so on.

CRITICAL THINKING

Do you see any similarities between the way that deviation IQ is interpreted and the way that you normally interpret your test scores in a class?

mental retardation
A label that is generally assigned to someone who scores below 70 on a standard IQ test although other factors, such as one's ability to adapt to the environment, are also important.

gifted
A label that is generally assigned to someone who scores above 130 on a standard IQ test.

TABLE 10.1
Types of Mental Retardation

Type	IQ Range (approximate)	Adaptation Potential
Mild	50–70	May develop academic skills comparable to a sixth-grade educational level; with assistance, may develop significant social and vocational skills, and be self-supporting
Moderate	35–50	Unlikely to achieve academic skills over the second-grade level; may become semi-independent
Severe	20–35	Speech skills will be limited, but communication is possible; may learn to perform simple tasks in highly structured environments
Profound	Below 20	Little or no speech is possible; requires constant care and supervision

Interestingly, these kids also turned out to be both stable emotionally and generally socially adept, which is surprising given the bookworm stereotype that people have of highly intelligent people. Many had successful marriages, and the divorce rate was lower for them than for the general population (Terman, 1954). A more recent study examining gifted children who skipped high school and moved directly to college also found evidence for excellent social adjustment (Nobel et al., 1993). One problem with these data, however, is that the connection between IQ and success is correlational, and there are many potentially confounding factors. High-IQ children, for example, tend to come from economically privileged households, which might help account for later success and emotional stability (Tomlinson-Keasey & Little, 1990).

THE VALIDITY OF INTELLIGENCE TESTING

Do tests that measure intelligence provide a valid measure of intellectual ability? Does IQ, for example, truly tap some hidden but powerful feature of the mind that accounts for individual differences? Do intelligence tests adequately measure the ability to adapt and solve the problems of survival? Remember, the term *validity* has a technical meaning to the psychologist: How well does the test measure the thing that it is supposed to measure? To assess the validity of the IQ, then, we need to ask: How well do the tests that produce IQ scores predict their criterion of interest?

The most widely applied intelligence tests today are the Stanford-Binet, the Wechsler Adult Intelligence Scale (WAIS), and the Wechsler Intelligence Scale for Children (WISC, 3rd edition). These are not the only tests, of course; in fact, if we combine intelligence tests with measures of scholastic aptitude, at least 120 different tests are currently in use (Jensen, 1992). Usually these tests are given for the same reasons that originally motivated Binet and Simon—to predict some kind of academic performance, usually grades in high school or college. From this perspective, IQ passes the validity test with flying colors: IQ, as measured by Stanford-Binet or the Wechsler tests, typically correlates about +0.50 or higher with school grades (Ceci, 1991; Kline, 1991). Notice that the correlation is not perfect, but it is reasonably high when you consider all of the uncontrolled factors that can affect grades in school (motivation, home environment, participation in extracurricular activities, teacher bias, and so on). IQ is also a reasonable predictor of real-world job performance, although its success in this domain is more modest (Ree & Earles, 1992; Sternberg & Wagner, 1993). (For another predictor of real-world job performance, tacit knowledge, see the accompanying feature, "Inside the Problem.")

Critics of IQ often argue that it fails to provide a broad index of intelligence. As we discussed before, it's proper to define intelligence broadly—there are many ways that people can fit successfully into their environments—and it's certain that not all forms of multiple intelligence are tapped by traditional paper-and-pencil IQ tests. This criticism has been recognized for years by the community of intelligence test researchers, and efforts have been made to develop tests that tap a variety of abilities. The influential tests of David Wechsler, for example, were developed in part to measure nonverbal aspects of intellectual ability. The Wechsler tests include not only verbal-mathematical questions of the type traditionally found on the Stanford-Binet test but also nonverbal questions requiring things like the completion or rearrangement of pictures (see Figure 10.5 on page 403). Performance is then broken down into a verbal IQ, a nonverbal (or "performance") IQ, and an overall IQ based on combining the verbal and nonverbal measures.

Labeling Effects

Another potentially serious criticism of IQ concerns the effects of labeling. You take a test as a child, your IQ is derived by comparing your performance with that of other kids your age, and the score becomes part of your continuing academic

CRITICAL THINKING

Do you think it makes sense for elementary schools to use "tracking" systems—that is, to divide children early on into different classes based on performance on standardized tests?

Inside the Problem   Tacit Knowledge and Intelligence

Most psychologists recognize and champion the value of standardized tests of intelligence. Intelligence tests have proven to be excellent predictors of performance in many domains, from school to a wide variety of occupations (Estes, 1992). The general ability index *g* is known to be a reasonable predictor of future performance; in fact, it may be the best predictor that we have for overall job performance (see Jensen, 1993; Ree & Earles, 1992). But as you now know, psychologists are keenly aware of the fact that standard objective tests, such as the ones that measure *g*, are not complete remedies or cures for the problem of predicting future performance. General measures of intelligence still cannot account for all (or even most) of the differences typically found in job performance (Sternberg & Wagner, 1993). A person who scores well on a job-related test may indeed become a good employee, but so might a person who does not score well.

As we've discussed in this chapter, one problem with conventional tests is that they measure intelligence in a rather narrow way. General ability is defined in an academic sense; standardized intelligence tests are full of questions that are quite specific and well defined. One must have certain knowledge in order to perform well; there are right and wrong answers for each question. There's also usually only one path or method for solving the problem. But success on a job typically requires knowledge that is not so cut and dried—there are unspoken rules and strategies that are rarely if ever taught formally. This kind of unspoken practical "know-how" is called *tacit* knowledge, and some psychologists believe that it will turn out to be an even better predictor of job performance than *g* (Wagner & Sternberg, 1985).

Tacit knowledge is rarely if ever assessed on standardized tests of intelligence. It's a kind of knowledge that isn't written in books and it's not usually taught. Instead, it comes primarily from experience—from watching and analyzing the behavior of others. Moreover, people clearly differ in their grasp of job-relevant tacit knowledge. Some managers understand the rules for maximizing the performance of their subordinates better than others do. When tacit knowledge is actually measured, by asking people on the job to make ratings about imaginary job scenarios, it seems to do a reasonably good job of predicting job performance. Sternberg and Wagner (1993) found that tacit knowledge correlates significantly with such things as salary, performance ratings, and the prestige of the business or institution where the person is employed. Moreover, tacit knowledge improves with work experience, which is what you would expect. However, tacit knowledge seems to bear little if any relation to general ability, as measured by *g*. There is almost never a significant correlation with IQ.

The idea that it's useful to develop and use multiple strategies to perform successfully is almost certain to be true. The adaptive mind soaks up knowledge where it can, and as we've seen in earlier chapters, modeling others is an important vehicle for guiding behavior. As it stands now, however, the concept of tacit knowledge, while intuitively plausible, remains slippery scientifically. Critics of Wagner and Sternberg's research have questioned whether tacit knowledge is really anything different from job knowledge (Schmidt & Hunter, 1993). It may not be some human ability, like *g*, that can be tapped by the appropriate test; instead, measurements of tacit knowledge may simply be indices of what has been learned on the job. Other critics have questioned the finding that tacit knowledge fails to correlate significantly with IQ (Jensen, 1993), and they wonder whether adding tacit knowledge really helps predict job performance over and above *g*. Few psychologists question the belief that intelligence is more than a single general ability, but whether tacit knowledge will ultimately be determined to be a separate component of intelligence remains uncertain.

Successful managers understand the unspoken rules and strategies—so-called "tacit knowledge"—that are rarely, if ever, taught directly.

Wechsler Adult Intelligence Scale (WAIS)		
Test	**Description**	**Example**
Verbal scale		
Information	Taps general range of information	On what continent is France?
Comprehension	Tests understanding of social conventions and ability to evaluate past experience	Why are children required to go to school?
Arithmetic	Tests arithmetic reasoning through verbal problems	How many hours will it take to drive 150 miles at 50 miles per hour?
Performance scale		
Block design	Tests ability to perceive and analyze patterns by presenting designs that must be copied with blocks	Assemble blocks to match this design:
Picture arrangement	Tests understanding of social situations through a series of comic-strip-type pictures that must be arranged in the right sequence to tell a story	Put the pictures in the right order:
Object assembly	Tests ability to deal with part/whole relationships by presenting puzzle pieces that must be assembled to form a complete object	Assemble the pieces into a complete object:

FIGURE 10.5

Examples from the WAIS

The Wechsler Adult Intelligence Scale was designed to measure both verbal and nonverbal aspects of intellectual ability. Included here are samples of the various question types. (From Weiten, 1995.)

record. Once the IQ label is applied—you're smart, you're below average, and so on—expectations are generated in those who have access to your score. A number of studies have shown that intelligence labels influence how teachers interact with their students in the classroom. There is a kind of "rich get richer" and "poor get poorer" effect—the kids with the "smart" label are exposed to more educational opportunities and are treated with more respect. Things are held back from the "slow" kids, so they're less likely to be exposed to factors that might nurture academic growth (Oakes, 1985; Rosenthal & Jacobson, 1968).

Labeling effects were particularly serious in the early decades of the twentieth century, when intelligence tests were in their formative stages of development. Tests were widely administered—for example, to newly arriving immigrants and all Army recruits—but before the impact of cultural and educational factors on test performance were widely understood. As we'll discuss later, people can perform poorly on an intelligence test because the test has certain built-in biases with respect to language and cultural lifestyle. Imagine, for example, that as part of an intelligence test I ask you to identify the vegetable broccoli. Easy, but not if you were raised in a culture that did not include broccoli as part of its diet. In such a case you would probably get the question wrong, but it wouldn't say anything about your true intellectual ability.

Researchers were not very sensitive to these concerns when the early intelligence tests were developed. The result was that certain population groups, such as immigrants from southern and eastern Europe, generally performed poorly on these tests. Some psychologists even went so far as to label these immigrant groups as "feeble minded" or "defective" based on their test performance. Immigration laws enacted in the 1920s discriminated against poorly performing groups by reducing immigration quotas. In modern times, psychologists are more aware of test bias, but its impact on test performance remains controversial to this day.

Within 24 hours of arrival at Ellis Island, immigrants were subjected to a variety of mental and physical examinations. Unfortunately, these exams were sometimes used to discriminate among population groups unfairly; at the time, administrators were simply not sensitive to how cultural factors could influence test performance.

INDIVIDUAL DIFFERENCES RELATED TO INTELLIGENCE

To end our discussion of the measurement of individual differences, we'll briefly consider two psychological characteristics that are often aligned with the topic of intelligence: creativity and emotional intelligence. Neither creativity nor emotional intelligence is necessarily related to *g*—general intelligence—but both represent quite adaptive characteristics that can potentially increase our ability to survive.

Creativity

The term **creativity** refers to the ability to generate ideas that are original and novel. Creative thinkers think in unusual ways, which means that they can look at the usual and express it in an unusual way. Creative thinkers tend to see the "big picture" and are able to find connections among things that others might not see. Importantly, however, it's not just the generation of new and different ideas that makes one creative; those ideas must also be useful and relevant—they must potentially have adaptive value.

How is creativity measured? Psychologists have devised a number of ways to measure individual differences in creative ability (Cooper, 1991; Cropley, 1996). One popular technique is to give someone a group of unrelated words, or unrelated objects in a picture, and then ask him or her to generate as many connections among the items as possible (Mednick, 1962; Torrance, 1981). Try it yourself: Take the words—food, catcher, hot—and try to think of a fourth word (or words) that relates to all three. It turns out that measures like these reveal individual differences among people—some find this task to be quite easy, others find it extremely hard. Moreover, performance on these creativity tests can then be correlated with other abilities, such as IQ or job success, to see if there is a connection.

What's the relation between creativity and intelligence? When intelligence is conceptualized in a broad way, then creativity fits in nicely as a part of general intellectual ability. You'll remember, for instance, that Sternberg's triarchic theory includes the concept of creative intelligence. However, there doesn't appear to be

creativity
The ability to generate ideas that are original, novel, and useful.

a straightforward relationship between creativity and IQ. Correlations between creativity and IQ are usually low (Horn, 1976; MacKinnon, 1962). What this means, however, is not clear—traditional IQ tests don't really measure creative thinking, so perhaps it's not surprising that the correlations are low.

Emotional Intelligence

The second psychological characteristic, emotional intelligence, has recently gained some popularity among psychologists and is worthy of brief note. **Emotional intelligence** is essentially the ability to perceive, understand, and express emotion (Mayer & Salovey, 1997; Salovey & Mayer, 1990). The concept applies to perceiving and understanding the emotions of others, as well as to the understanding and control of one's own emotions. Emotions, as you'll see in Chapter 11, can play a large role in behavior, so it's clearly adaptive to manage and express them appropriately.

People who score highly on emotional intelligence can read others' emotions well and tend to be empathetic as a result. They're good at managing conflict, both their own and the conflicts of others. Not surprisingly, emotional intelligence is believed to be an excellent predictor of success in career and social settings; in fact, some have argued that emotional intelligence may be a more important predictor of success in life than more traditional conceptions of intelligence (Goleman, 1995). There is clearly some overlap between emotional intelligence and the broad conceptions of intelligence proposed by others (e.g., Gardner and Sternberg), but the similarities and differences have yet to be worked out in a systematic way. Research on emotional intelligence is in its infancy, so we'll need to wait before concluding anything about its ultimate usefulness.

emotional intelligence
The ability to perceive, understand, and express emotion in ways that are useful and adaptive.

TEST YOURSELF 10.2

Check what you know about the measurement of individual differences by answering the following questions. (You will find the answers in the Appendix.)

1. For each of the following statements, pick the test characteristic that is most appropriate. Choose from the following: reliability, standardization, or validity.

   a. Donna performs poorly on the SAT, so she takes it again and finds herself performing poorly again: _____

   b. Larry has devised a new test of intelligence, but he finds that it predicts nothing about school performance or success on the job: _____

   c. Chei-Wui wants to see how consistent scores are on his new intelligence test so he correlates answers across repeated administrations of the test:

   _____

   d. Robert's new job is to administer the Graduate Record Exam. He is very careful to keep the testing and scoring procedures the same for everybody who takes the test: _____

2. Decide whether each of the following statements is true or false.

   a. Lucinda has a mental age of 8 and an IQ of 160—this means that she must be 5 years old chronologically. *True or False?*

   b. Average IQ, based on the deviation IQ method, varies with chronological age. *True or False?*

   c. Lewis has just scored below 70 on his IQ test, which means that he will soon be labeled as mentally retarded. *True or False?*

   d. Creativity increases with intellectual ability, as measured by IQ. *True or False?*

Discovering the Sources of Intelligence: The Nature–Nurture Issue

LEARNING GOALS

1. Evaluate the stability of IQ, and discuss why IQ might change across the lifespan.

2. Discuss how twin studies are used to evaluate genetic contributions to intelligence.

3. Discuss environmental influences on intelligence.

4. Explain how genetic and environmental factors interact to determine intelligence.

We've seen that people differ, and we've considered some of the ways to measure these individual differences. We've also discussed methods for conceptualizing these differences theoretically—there may be differences in *g*, differences in the speed of brain cells, or people may lack some of the mental operations that are needed for intelligent performance. But what accounts for these differences in the first place? Why is one person's *g* higher or lower than another person's *g*? Why is Jefferson Tarpy able to generate and monitor effective global strategies for problem solving, but Larry Steinway can't? Is there anything that can be done about these differences, or are they fixed in stone?

There are essentially two ways to explain how differences in intelligence might arise. First, you can appeal to biological processes, particularly the internal *genetic code*—those strands of DNA that determine eye color, thickness of hair, and possibly *g*. According to this view, intellectual potential is established at conception through some particularly fortunate (or unfortunate) combinations of genes. Alternatively, you can appeal to an external cause, specifically the *environment*. Variations in *g* might be attributable to one's past history—perhaps Jefferson Tarpy scores highly on IQ tests because he was reinforced for intellectual pursuits or went to excellent schools; perhaps Larry Steinway performs poorly because he was exposed to toxins as a child (such as lead paint). In this section, we'll frame this classic nature–nurture debate and consider the evidence relevant to each position. But first, we have a practical issue to consider—how stable is the IQ measure itself?

THE STABILITY OF IQ

One way to answer questions about the origins of intelligence is to ask whether IQ changes significantly over a lifetime. If intelligence is caused by something like a "fast brain," then we might expect intellectual ability not to change very much over time, or at least to remain stable throughout the course of normal adulthood. On the other hand, if intelligence is determined mainly by the environment, we would probably expect to find changes over time: IQ might rise and fall depending on experience or environmental setting. Neither of these arguments is air-

Although tests are available to measure intelligence in small children, it's difficult to obtain reliable estimates of intelligence before age 4.

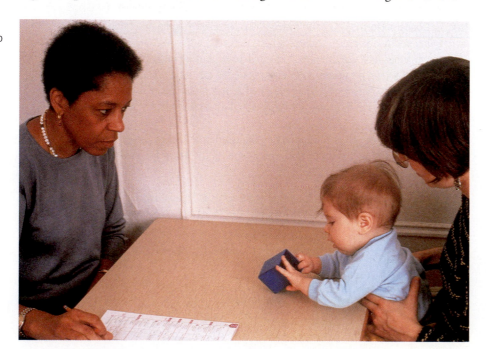

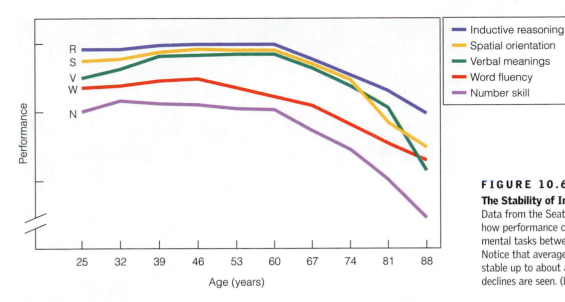

Inductive reasoning
Spatial orientation
Verbal meanings
Word fluency
Number skill

FIGURE 10.6
The Stability of Intellectual Ability
Data from the Seattle Longitudinal Study show how performance changes on a variety of mental tasks between age 25 and age 88. Notice that average performance is remarkably stable up to about age 60, at which point some declines are seen. (Data from Schaie, 1983.)

tight—for instance, your environment might remain constant over time, or the genetic code might express itself throughout your lifetime; it might also be the case that IQ is determined by early experience and remains fixed after a certain point in development. Still, examination of the stability of the IQ measure is a reasonable place to start the search.

When intelligence is measured in the standard way, through performance on a battery of tests, the stability of the measure depends on when the measuring process begins. Before the age of about 3 or 4, it's difficult to get an accurate assessment of intellectual ability. Infants can't talk or show sustained attention, so conventional testing procedures can't be used. Investigators resort to indirect measures, such as recording whether babies choose to look at old or new pictures presented on a screen. There is some evidence that babies who quickly "habituate," or lose interest, in response to repeated presentations of the same picture, and who prefer to look at novel pictures when they're shown, score higher on intelligence tests later in childhood (Bornstein, 1989; McCall & Carriger, 1993). But in general, it's widely believed that you can't get reliable assessments of IQ until somewhere between ages 4 and 7; from that point onward, IQ scores tend to predict performance on later IQ tests reasonably well (Honzik et al., 1948; Sameroff et al., 1993).

Longitudinal Studies

One of the best ways to measure the stability of IQ is through a longitudinal study, which involves testing the same people repeatedly as they age. The most widely known investigation of the stability of adult intelligence is the Seattle Longitudinal Study, which has examined mental test performance for approximately 5000 adults ranging in age from 25 through 88 (Schaie, 1983, 1989, 1993). The subjects have been tested in seven-year cycles, dating back to 1956, using a battery of tests to assess such things as verbal fluency, inductive reasoning, and spatial ability. Schaie and his colleagues have found great stability in intellectual ability throughout adulthood. From age 25 to about age 60, there appears to be no uniform decline in general intellectual ability, as measured through the test battery (see Figure 10.6). After age 60, abilities begin to decline a bit, although the losses are not great. There are also large individual differences—some people show excellent test performance in their 80s, whereas others do not (Schaie, 1998).

It's difficult to interpret changes in IQ with age because many factors change concurrently with age. Elderly people are more likely to have physical problems, for example, that can affect performance. Declines in intelligence with age also depend on the type of intellectual ability measured. Earlier, we discussed the

CRITICAL THINKING

Elderly people are often said to possess wisdom. In what ways do you think the label "wise" differs from the label "intelligent"?

Some kinds of abilities tend to run in families, such as artistic ability in the Judd family. It's difficult, though, to separate the influences of nature and nurture.

distinction between *fluid intelligence*, which taps basic reasoning and information processing skills, and *crystallized intelligence*, which taps acquired knowledge. The current thinking is that fluid intelligence may decline with age—perhaps because the biology of the brain changes—whereas crystallized intelligence remains constant, or perhaps even increases, until late in adulthood (Horn, 1982; Kaufman & Horn, 1996). The brain may become a bit slower with age, but people continue to add knowledge and experiences that are invaluable in their efforts to solve the problems of everyday life.

NATURE: THE GENETIC ARGUMENT

A number of early pioneers in intelligence testing, including Galton, believed strongly that individual differences in mental ability are inherited. After all, Galton argued, it's easy to demonstrate that intellectual skill runs through family lines (remember, his cousin was Charles Darwin, and his grandfather was another famous evolutionist, Erasmus Darwin). But family-tree arguments, used in isolation, do not lead to firm conclusions. Environmental factors, such as social and educational opportunities, can explain why members of the same family might show similar skills. Growing up in a family that places value on intellectual pursuits determines to some extent what sort of behaviors will be rewarded in a child, or the particular type of role models that will be available. In fairness to Galton, he realized that both inherited and environmental factors are needed to explain mental ability fully—in fact, it was Galton who coined the term "nature versus nurture" (Galton, 1869, 1883).

To establish a genetic basis for a psychological or physical characteristic, it's necessary to control for the effects of the environment. In principle, if two people are raised in exactly the same environment and receive exactly the same experiences, we can attribute any reliable differences in IQ to inherited factors (*nature*). In this case, you've held any nurturing effects of the environment constant, so any differences must be due to genetics. Alternatively, if two people are born with exactly the same genes but end up with quite different intelligence scores, it must be the environment, not genes, that is responsible (*nurture*). We can't perform these kinds of experimental manipulations in the laboratory, for obvious reasons, but we can look for natural comparisons that are relevant. As we discussed in Chapter 3, psychologists often study identical twins, who share nearly complete

? CRITICAL THINKING

Do you think it's possible to tease apart the relative contributions of nature and nurture to intelligence by studying animals in the laboratory?

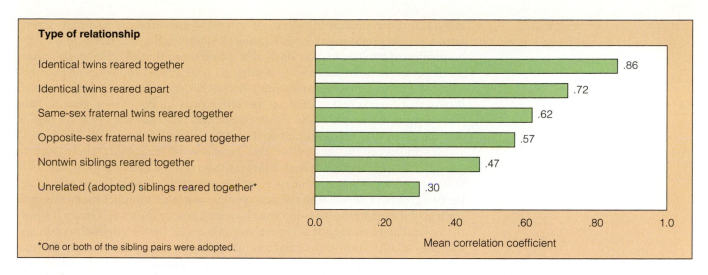

Type of relationship

Identical twins reared together	.86
Identical twins reared apart	.72
Same-sex fraternal twins reared together	.62
Opposite-sex fraternal twins reared together	.57
Nontwin siblings reared together	.47
Unrelated (adopted) siblings reared together*	.30

0.0   .20   .40   .60   .80   1.0

*One or both of the sibling pairs were adopted.   Mean correlation coefficient

FIGURE 10.7

Nature versus Nurture

The horizontal bars show the mean correlation coefficients for pairs of people with differing amounts of genetic overlap who have been reared in similar or different environments. For example, the top bar shows the average correlation for identical twins who have been reared together in the same environment. The bottom bar shows the correlation coefficient for adopted siblings reared together. Higher correlations mean that the measured IQ scores are more similar. (Data from Bouchard & McGue, 1981.)

genetic overlap, to tease apart the nature and nurture components of mind and behavior.

Twin Studies

In twin studies, researchers search for identical twins who have been raised together in the same household or who have been separated at birth through adoption (Bouchard & McGue, 1981; Bouchard et al., 1990). The effects of the environment are assumed to be similar for the twins raised together but quite different, at least on average, for twins raised apart. If intelligence comes primarily from genetic factors, we would expect identical twins to have very similar intelligence scores, regardless of the environments in which they have been raised. One way to measure similarity is by correlation. More specifically, you can attempt to predict the IQ of one twin given knowledge about the IQ of the other.

If genes are entirely responsible for intelligence, we would expect to get a strong positive correlation between IQ scores for identical twins. We wouldn't necessarily expect it to be exactly +1.00 because of measurement error or other uncontrolled factors. In reviewing the research literature on this issue, Bouchard and McGue (1981) found strong evidence for the genetic position: The IQ scores of identical twins are indeed quite similar, irrespective of the environment in which the twins have been reared. As shown in Figure 10.7, the IQ scores for twins reared together showed an average correlation of .86; when reared apart, the average correlation remained strongly positive at .72 (Bouchard & McGue, 1981).

Researchers who conduct twin studies are actually interested in many different comparisons. For instance, it's useful to compare intelligence scores for fraternal twins (who are genetically no more similar than normal siblings) and among unrelated people who have been reared together or apart. In general, the impressive finding is that the closer the overlap in genes, the more similar the resulting IQs. Notice, for example, that the average correlation for adopted siblings who have been reared together (.30) is much lower than the average correlation for identical twins reared apart (.72). Thus, similarity in environmental history is not as strong a predictor of intelligence as similarity in genetic background. Data like these suggest that genetic history plays an important role in intelligence, at least when intelligence is measured through conventional IQ testing (see also Plomin et al., 1997).

Heritability

Intelligence researchers often use a concept called heritability to describe the influence of genetic factors on intelligence. **Heritability** is a mathematical index that tells the researcher the extent to which IQ differences within a population can be accounted for by genetic factors. For any group of people you will find

heritability
A mathematical index that represents the extent to which IQ differences in a particular population can be accounted for by genetic factors.

individual differences in IQ scores—heritability measures the role that genetic factors play in producing these differences. It's expressed as a percentage, so if the heritability of intelligence was 100% that would mean that all differences in measured IQ could be explained by referring to genes. Most estimates of the heritability of intelligence, derived from twin studies, hover at around 50%, which means that approximately half of the differences in IQ have a genetic basis (Sternberg & Kaufman, 1998). Other researchers propose values that are higher, perhaps closer to 70% (Bouchard et al., 1990).

It's important to understand that estimates of heritability apply only to groups, not to individuals. A heritability estimate of 70% does not mean that 70% of someone's intelligence is due to his or her genetic blueprint. To see why, imagine two groups of people with the same genetic histories. Group A maintains rigid control of the environment—everyone is treated exactly the same. Group B allows the environment to vary. If IQ scores are influenced by the environment in any way, we would expect the heritability values to be quite different for the two groups, even though the groups' genetic backgrounds are identical. Because the environment is held constant in group A, all of the variability in measured IQ will be due to genes. In group B, the heritability index will be lower because some of the differences in IQ will be due to environmental effects. Heritability tells us only that for a given group, a certain percentage of the differences in intelligence can be explained by genetic factors.

Nurture: The Environmental Argument

Most psychologists agree that intelligence is influenced by genetic factors. But did you notice in Figure 10.7 that identical twins and siblings reared together have IQs that are more similar than do twins or siblings reared apart? This means that individual differences in intelligence cannot be explained completely through genetic background. The environment also plays an important role.

In this section, we'll consider some environmental influences on IQ by addressing a rather controversial topic in the study of intelligence: group differences in IQ. The majority of intelligence researchers agrees that there are stable differences in IQ across racial, ethnic, and socioeconomic groups. For example, Asian Americans tend to score 4 or 5 IQ points higher on standardized intelligence tests, on average, than white European Americans. White Americans, on average, score 10 to 15 points higher than African Americans and Hispanic Americans (Brody, 1992; Lynn, 1994).

At the same time, it's very important for you to understand that group differences in IQ, although stable, reflect average *group* differences. Not every Asian American scores high on an intelligence test, nor does every African American score low. In fact, the differences among IQ scores within a population (African Americans, Asian Americans, and so on) are much larger than the average differences between groups. This means that a large number of African Americans can be expected to score higher than the average white score, just as many Asian Americans will have scores below the average for whites. The average population differences cannot be applied to single individuals. Still, the group differences are real and should be explained. How can we account for these differences? A number of possibilities have been suggested, including economic factors and test bias.

Economic Differences

There are significant economic differences among racial/ethnic groups that could contribute to performance, and which make interpretation of the IQ differences difficult. For example, African Americans and Hispanic Americans are more likely to live at or below the poverty level in the United States. Poverty, of course, may lead to nutrition problems, difficulties in gaining proper health care, and may hurt one's chances to enter adequate schools. African Americans and Hispanic Americans are also much more likely to suffer racial discrimination than whites.

Most psychologists agree that cultural background plays an important role in the measurement and interpretation of intelligence.

The impact of these factors on intelligence testing is not completely understood, although they almost certainly play an important role. African Americans, whites, and Hispanic Americans tend to live in very different and somewhat isolated worlds. As a consequence, it is extremely difficult to disentangle the effects of the environment from any genetic differences that might contribute to intelligence.

Test Bias

There is also some indication that test biases might contribute to group differences in IQ scores (Bernal, 1984). Racial/ethnic group differences depend, to a certain extent, on the type of intelligence test that is administered (Brody, 1992). Most traditional IQ tests of the type that we've discussed in this chapter are written, administered, and scored by white, middle-class psychologists. This raises the very real possibility that cultural biases might be contaminating some of the test questions. For example, if I ask you a question such as "Who wrote *Faust*?" (which once appeared on a Wechsler test), your ability to answer correctly will depend partly on whether your culture places value on exposure to such information. African American psychologist Robert L. Williams has shown that when an intelligence test is used that relies heavily on African American terms and expressions, white students who have had limited experience with African American culture perform poorly.

Psychologists have worked hard to remove bias from standard intelligence and achievement tests (Raven et al., 1985); in some cases, the development of "culture fair" tests has reduced racial differences in measured ability. However, significant group differences usually remain even after culture-bound questions have been altered or removed. Consequently, bias is recognized as an important contributor to measured intelligence, although it's unlikely to be the sole determinant of group differences in IQ (Cole, 1981; Kaplan, 1985).

Adoption Studies

A more direct test of environmental explanations of racial/ethnic differences comes from studies looking at the IQs of African American children who have been reared in white homes. If the average African American childhood experience leads to skills that do not transfer well to standard tests of intelligence (for whatever reason), then African American children raised in white, middle-class homes should be expected to produce higher IQ scores. In general, this

? CRITICAL THINKING

Do you think it's possible to eliminate cultural influences completely from a psychological test?

assumption is supported by the data. Scarr and Weinberg (1976) investigated interracial adoptions in Minnesota and found that the average IQ for African American children reared in economically advantaged white households was significantly higher than the national African American mean score. This finding was confirmed again in later follow-up studies (Waldman et al., 1994; Weinberg et al., 1992). You should not conclude from this finding that white, middle-class households are somehow better than other households. The results simply imply that certain cultural experiences give one an advantage on the kinds of tests currently being used to assess intelligence.

THE INTERACTION OF NATURE AND NURTURE

So what are we to conclude about the relative contributions of genetics and the environment to intelligence? Nature–nurture issues are notoriously difficult to resolve, and this is especially true in the politically sensitive area of intelligence. It's extremely difficult to control for the effects of either the environment or genetics. Consider the twin studies—how reasonable is it to assume that twins who have been reared apart have had unrelated environmental experiences? Are children who are adopted really representative of the racial or ethnic populations from which they have been drawn? It's difficult to answer questions like these, because neither the environment nor genetic structure can be manipulated directly in the laboratory (at least for humans).

The most reasonable position to take at the present time is that your intelligence, like many other psychological attributes, is determined by a mixture of genes and environment. The genes that you inherit from your parents place upper and lower bounds on intellectual ability. Genes may importantly determine how your brain is wired, and possibly the speed of neural transmission, but the expression of your genetic material is strongly influenced by the environment.

? CRITICAL THINKING

Suppose we broaden the concept of intelligence to include athletic and artistic ability. Would it bother you to think that these abilities are influenced primarily by genetic factors?

FIGURE 10.8

Between- and Within-Group Variation
In the plant analogy, all of the variation in plant height within a pot is due to genetics, but the overall height difference between the two pots is attributable to the environment (rich soil versus poor soil).

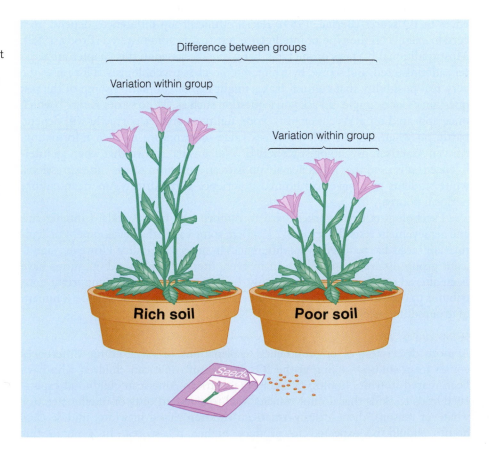

Difference between groups

Variation within group

Variation within group

Rich soil   Poor soil

Seeds

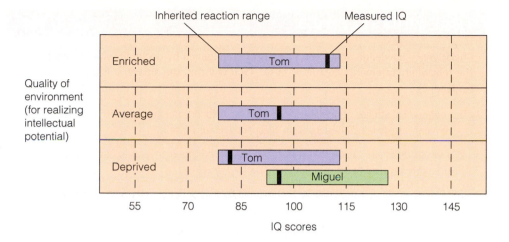

FIGURE 10.9
Reaction Range
Each person may have genes that set limits for intellectual potential (sometimes called a reaction range). In this case, Tom inherited a capacity for obtaining an IQ anywhere between 80 and about 112. The IQ that Tom actually obtains (shown as the dark bar) is determined by the kind of environment in which he is reared. Notice that Miguel inherited a greater IQ potential than Tom, but if Tom is raised in an enriched environment his IQ may actually turn out to be higher than Miguel's.

Recall from Chapter 3 that geneticists use the term *genotype* to refer to the genetic message itself and *phenotype* to refer to the observable characteristics that actually result from genetic expression. An analogy of the genotype/phenotype relationship that is sometimes used by intelligence researchers compares the development of intelligence to the nurturing of flowering plants (Lewontin, 1976). Imagine that we have a packet of virtually identical seeds and we toss half into a pot containing fertile soil and half into a pot of barren soil (see Figure 10.8). The seeds tossed into the poor soil will undoubtedly grow, but their growth will be stunted relative to that of the group planted in the rich soil. Because these are virtually identical groups of seeds, containing similar distributions of genetic information, any differences in growth between the pots are due entirely to the environment (the soil). So, too, with intelligence—two people can be born with similar genetic potential, but the degree to which their intellectual potential will "blossom" will depend critically on the environment.

Consider as well that within each handful of seeds there will be variations in genetic information. Some plants will grow larger than others, regardless of the soil in which they have been thrown. A similar kind of result would be expected for intelligence—variations in the genetic message will produce individual differences in IQ that cannot be adequately explained by environmental variables. In fact, after analyzing the differences within a pot, we might conclude that all of the differences are due to inherited factors. But even if the differences within a group are due to genes, the differences between groups would still be due to the environment (fertile or barren soil). This kind of insight might help account, in part, for the racial/ethnic differences in IQ that we discussed earlier. Even though genes may exert a strong influence within a population, between-population differences could still be determined primarily by the environment (Eysenck & Kamin, 1981; Lewontin, 1976).

One other feature of the interaction between nature and nurture is worth noting. Environmental experiences do not occur independently of inherited factors. It's a two-way street. The environment will partly determine how genetic information is expressed, but so too will genetic information determine experience. If you're born with three arms, because of some odd combination of inherited factors, then your interactions with the world will be quite different from those of a person with two arms. The fact that you have three arms will color your environment—it will determine how you are treated and the range of opportunities to which you are exposed. If you're born with "smart" genes, then early on you're likely to be exposed to opportunities that will help you realize your full intellectual potential; conversely, if you're born "slow," the environment is likely to shape you away from intellectually nurturing experiences (see Figure 10.9). Such is the way of life and of the world.

TEST YOURSELF 10.3

Check your knowledge about the sources of intelligence by deciding whether each of the following statements is true or false. (You will find the answers in the Appendix.)

1. Longitudinal studies of intelligence reveal that fluid, but not crystallized, intelligence remains largely constant across the lifespan. *True or False?*

2. Twin studies have shown that fraternal twins raised together tend to have more similar IQs than identical twins raised apart. *True or False?*

3. Most psychologists now believe that genetic factors definitely play a role in intelligence. *True or False?*

4. A heritability estimate of 70% means that 70% of someone's intelligence is due to his or her genetic blueprint. *True or False?*

5. Test bias is recognized as an important contributor to measured intelligence, but it's unlikely to be the sole determinant of group differences in IQ. *True or False?*

Solving the Problems

What is intelligence? You've seen in this chapter that the concept of intelligence comes primarily from the study of individual differences. People differ, and we can try to develop tests that measure these differences effectively. From an analysis of individual variability, psychologists have tried to develop theories of intellectual functioning: What kinds of mental processes underlie intelligent thought? We've seen that one way to characterize intelligence by the adaptability of behavior. What makes one species member intelligent, and another not, may be dictated by how well organisms adapt to rapidly changing environments and solve the problems of survival. From this perspective, the single nutcracker, in its successful search for a cache of seeds, fits the adaptive view of intelligence just as well as the cocky student who aces the SAT.

In this chapter our discussion revolved around three conceptual and practical problems that researchers interested in intelligence have attempted to resolve.

Conceptualizing Intelligence. Researchers have attempted to conceptualize intelligence in a number of ways. Proponents of psychometric approaches to intelligence map out fundamental aspects of the mind by analyzing performance on a battery of mental tests. They traditionally draw distinctions between a general factor of intelligence, *g*, which applies broadly, and specific factors, *s*, which tap particular separate abilities. The idea that intelligence needs to be broken down into several, or multiple, kinds of ability remains popular today, although researchers disagree as to how many or what types of intelligence need to be included.

Cognitive approaches to intelligence seek to discover the internal processes that account for intelligent behavior. There's some evidence to suggest that performance on traditional tests of mental ability might be related to the speed of processing among neurons in the brain. The multiple intelligences approach of Howard Gardner and the triarchic theory of Robert Sternberg both suggest that the concept of intelligence must be defined broadly. We cannot rely entirely on things such as academic ability to define intelligence—everyday intelligence and "street smarts" also enhance our ability to adapt.

Measuring Individual Differences. Concepts such as intelligence really have little meaning outside of the study of individual differences—it's how the mental ability of Sam differs from the mental ability of Jennifer that makes the concept of intelligence meaningful. A good test of intelligence has three main characteristics: reliability, validity, and standardization. Understanding the concept of test validity is crucial because it holds the key to appreciating the widespread use of standardized measures such as IQ or tests such as the SAT. Researchers who study individual differences are often primarily interested in using measured differences to make predictions about future success. Will Jennifer perform well in school? Will Sam make it as a graduate student in psychology? As you've seen, the IQ test itself was originally developed to measure academic ability, not as some ultimate measure of mental capacity.

Discovering the Sources of Intelligence. There are two primary ways to explain how measured differences in intelligence might arise: genetics and the environment. Twin studies provide convincing evidence that at least some kinds of mental ability are inherited, although how much remains controversial. However, the role of the environment in determining IQ—cultural background, economic status, and even built-in test biases—cannot be discounted. Intelligence, like many psychological attributes, grows out of an interaction between nature and nurture.

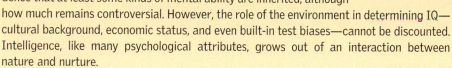

Intelligence Chapter Summary

Conceptualizing Intelligence

Typically, we talk about intelligence like it's some tangible "thing" that is possessed by people. Is intelligence best seen as a single capacity, or as a collection of separate abilities? There may even be multiple intelligences.

PSYCHOMETRICS: MEASURING THE MIND

The *psychometric approach* proposes that intelligence is a mental capacity that can be understood by analyzing performance on mental tests. Galton and Spearman are two pioneers of this approach. Spearman used *factor analysis* to analyze the relationships among test scores, and isolate the "factors" that account for test performance. Spearman proposed that intelligence is comprised of *g*, or general intelligence, as well as more specific abilities. Later models have emphasized more than one kind of ability, as in *hierarchical models*. Some propose that general intelligence is comprised of two abilities, *fluid intelligence* (ability to solve problems and reason) and *crystallized intelligence* (acquired knowledge).

GARDNER'S THEORY OF MULTIPLE INTELLIGENCES

Gardner has proposed that traditional views of intelligence should be broadened to include special abilities or talents, and that there are multiple "intelligences." Using a case study approach, Gardner has identified seven kinds of intelligence: *musical, bodily-kinesthetic, logical-mathematical, linguistic, spatial, interpersonal*, and *intrapersonal*. The psychometric and cognitive approaches focus on logical-mathematical, and to some extent, linguistic and spatial intelligence.

THE COGNITIVE APPROACH

The cognitive approach argues that intelligence can be understood by analyzing internal mental processes. This analysis usually involves measuring the speed of mental processing, and analyzing the specific mental operations that produce intelligent thought. Some believe that intelligence reflects, in part, the speed of neural processing. Sternberg uses *componential analysis* to isolate the mental processes that are tapped by traditional intelligence tests.

STERNBERG'S TRIARCHIC THEORY

Sternberg's conceptualization of intelligence includes three types of abilities. *Analytic intelligence* refers to a person's basic ability to process information. *Creative intelligence* expresses how well people are able to cope with new or novel tasks. *Practical intelligence* taps how well people fit into their environments.

Measuring Individual Differences

Regardless of how psychologists conceptualize intelligence, an important practical consideration is how to measure intelligence. Accurate measurement of abilities through the use of psychological tests allows for the tailoring of people's activities to fit their skills. *Achievement tests* measure someone's current level of knowledge in a particular topic; *aptitude tests* measure the ability to learn in a particular area.

THE COMPONENTS OF A GOOD TEST

Three characteristics are needed for a good test. *Reliability* is a measure of the consistency of a test. *Test-retest reliability* is calculated by comparing test scores across repeated administrations. *Validity* tells us whether a test measures what it is supposed to measure. *Content validity* measures the degree to which the test samples broadly across the domain of interest. *Predictive validity* measures the degree to which the test predicts some future outcome. *Construct validity* measures how well a test taps into a particular theme or construct. *Standardization* means that the testing, scoring, and interpretation procedures are similar across all administrations of the test.

IQ: THE INTELLIGENCE QUOTIENT

The *IQ*, or *intelligence quotient*, dates back to Binet and Simon, who were commissioned to develop a test to identify children who might have trouble in school. Their goal was to determine a child's *mental age*, which is typically calculated by comparing a child's test score with the average score for different age groups. The intelligence quotient was originally calculated by dividing mental age by chronological age and multiplying by 100. Now it is specified in terms of a *deviation IQ*, in which a person's IQ is calculated by determining where his or her test score "sits," relative to the average score.

EXTREMES OF INTELLIGENCE

A score of 70 or below on a standard IQ test (along with some other factors) is likely to lead to a diagnosis of *mental retardation*. Numerous factors, both genetic and environmental, may cause mental retardation. *Giftedness* is seen in individuals with IQ's at or above 130. Terman's longitudinal study of gifted children showed that these kids were likely to achieve later success, and were stable emotionally and socially adept, contrary to the "bookworm" stereotype.

INDIVIDUAL DIFFERENCES RELATED TO INTELLIGENCE

Creativity refers to the ability to generate ideas that are original and novel, and is an important component of broad conceptualizations of intelligence. *Emotional intelligence* is the ability to perceive, understand, and express emotion. According to some, it is also an important component of intelligence.

THE VALIDITY OF INTELLIGENCE TESTING

Scores on traditional IQ tests correlate well with school grades. Critics of IQ argue that it fails to provide a broad index of intelligence. Also a particular IQ "label" influences how teachers interact with students. These labeling effects were particularly serious in the early twentieth century, when many immigrants were given intelligence tests and labeled as feeble-minded or defective.

Discovering the Sources of Intelligence: The Nature–Nurture Issue

Does intelligent behavior come primarily from one's genetic background, or from life experience? The study of intelligence also serves as an investigation into the plasticity of the mind.

THE STABILITY OF IQ

The Seattle longitudinal study of adult intelligence found great stability in intellectual ability throughout adulthood. Current thinking is that *fluid intelligence* (which taps basic reasoning skills) may decline with age, whereas *crystallized intelligence* (which taps acquired knowledge) remains constant, perhaps even increases.

NURTURE: THE ENVIRONMENTAL ARGUMENT

Individual differences in intelligence cannot be explained completely through genetic background. Most intelligence researchers agree that there are stable differences in IQ across racial, ethnic, and socioeconomic groups. These differences, however, reflect average *group* differences. Possible sources of these differences could be economic factors or test bias. Adoption studies have supported the role of the environment in explaining group differences.

NATURE: THE GENETIC ARGUMENT

Twin studies are one method for addressing the role of heredity in intelligence. The IQ scores of identical twins are quite similar, irrespective of environment. Similarity of genetic background is a stronger predictor of intelligence than similarity of environment. *Heritability* is a mathematical index that tells a researcher the extent to which IQ differences within a population can be accounted for by genetic factors; estimates of heritability apply to groups, not individuals. Estimates of the heritability of intelligence range from .50 to .70.

THE INTERACTION OF NATURE AND NURTURE

Intelligence is determined by a mixture of genes and environment. Genes place lower and upper bounds on intellectual ability, but the expression of genetic material is strongly influenced by the environment. The *genotype* is the genetic message itself, and the *phenotype* is the observable characteristics that result from genetic expression. Genetic expression depends critically on the environment, and genetic background affects how one interacts with the environment.

Terms to Remember

intelligence, 384

CONCEPTUALIZING INTELLIGENCE

psychometrics, 386
factor analysis, 386
g (general intelligence), 387
s (specific intelligence), 387
fluid intelligence, 388
crystallized intelligence, 388
multiple intelligences, 392
triarchic theory, 393

MEASURING INDIVIDUAL DIFFERENCES

achievement tests, 395
aptitude tests, 395
reliability, 395
validity, 396
standardization, 397
intelligence quotient (IQ), 397
mental age, 398
deviation IQ, 399
mental retardation, 400
gifted, 400
creativity, 404
emotional intelligence, 405

DISCOVERING THE SOURCES OF INTELLIGENCE

heritability, 409

Recommended Readings

Gardner, H. (1983). *Frames of mind*. New York: Basic Books. Very readable introduction to Gardner's theory of multiple intelligences.

Neisser, Ulric (Ed.). (1998). *The rising curve: Long-term gains in IQ and related measures*. Washington, DC: American Psychological Association. A collection of interesting articles written by experts addressing what is known, unknown, and controversial in modern intelligence research.

Sternberg, R. J. *Thinking styles*. New York: Cambridge University Press. A very readable book, written by a leading intelligence researcher, explaining how aptitude tests, school grades, and classroom performance often fail to identify real ability because of differences in thinking styles.

INFOTRAC® COLLEGE EDITION

For additional readings, explore Infotrac College Edition, your online library. Go to:
http://www.infotrac-college.com/wadsworth

Hint: enter the search terms: Intelligence tests, General intelligence, Mental retardation, Giftedness, Psychometrics, Nature, nurture and intelligence.

What's on the Web?

The ARC

http://TheArc.org/welcome.html

This is the homepage of the Association for Retarded Citizens of the United States. The site offers a wide array of information on mental retardation, including "Q & A fact sheets." What do we know about the genetic roots of mental retardation? What is Fragile X syndrome? What issues arise when we consider the relationship between aging and mental retardation? Find answers to all of these questions (and many more) with a trip to "the ARC."

Online IQ Tests

http://botree.com/iq.htm

There seems to be a fascination with intelligence testing. As you were reading the material in the chapter, you may have been thinking "I wonder what my IQ is . . ." This site purports to help you find out. (But buyer beware!! Consider the standardization, reliability, and validity of these tests!) The site even has tests of your emotional IQ, "political IQ": and your "jewelry IQ"!

Upstream: Issues: Psychology: Intelligence and IQ

http://www.cycad.com/cgi-bin/Upstream/Issues /psychology/IQ/index.html

The book *The Bell Curve* helped to reignite the controversies that revolve around intelligence testing, such as the validity of scores, group differences, and the sources of intelligence. This site provides a wealth of links to the writings of prominent figures in the debate, such as Arthur Jensen and Stephen Jay Gould. The Upstream site also has general information on the controversial book, as well as reviews and analyses.

The Wadsworth Psychology Study Center Web Site

See http://psychology.wadsworth.com/ for practice quiz questions, hypercontents, updates, critical thinking exercises, discussion forums and more! The Wadsworth Psychology Study Center provides a wealth of information fully organized and integrated by chapter.

Motivation and Emotion

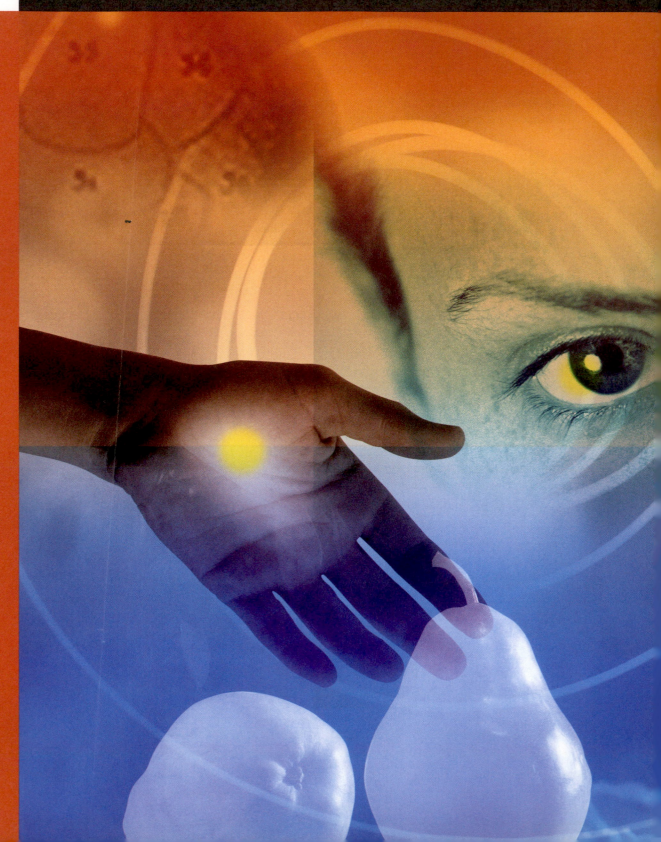

Y ou sense only rapid movement at first. A glint to your right and the cool feel of metal on your cheek. You exhale, gasping, as a bony arm wraps itself around your neck. "Welcome to your nightmare, my friend," a voice growls. "Your wallet, your watch, or your life." Inside, your sympathetic nervous system jumps into action—releasing epinephrine, targeting the critical organs of the body and the neural communication chains. Your mind, flooded with the arousal, struggles to decide on the best response. But you're in a psychological meltdown—you see only jumbled images of the sidewalk and needle tracks dotting the arm grasping your neck. There is no focused clarity; no clear course of action appears to guide your response. In your mind there is only surprise, confusion, and the smothering grip of fear.

Not a very pleasant scenario. Two people, reacting to circumstance, each in a highly activated state. For psychologists, however, the interplay sets an interesting stage. The unfolding action strikes at the core of psychology: understanding the causes and motivations of behavior. What factors underlie the initiation and direction of behavior? What causes the criminal to control the victim: Is it the reinforcing value of money? Is it the loss of control driven by the internal need for a "fix"? And what about the emotions that accompany the act—fear, excitement, despair? In what way does an emotion like fear, with its often paralyzing consequences, enhance the functioning of the adaptive mind? Could it be that emotions themselves motivate and direct behavior? These are some of the topics we'll consider in this chapter.

Motivation can be defined as the set of factors that *initiate* and *direct* behavior, usually toward some goal. If you're motivated, your behavior becomes activated and goal-directed. Hunger is a classic example of an internal condition or "state" that stimulates an organism to pursue food. The desire for a fix motivates the junkie to search for the drug of salvation. As you saw in Chapter 7, people are also likely to become motivated if they've recently been rewarded for behaving in a particular way—they're likely to act in a similar way again to get the reward. **Emotions** are complex psychological events that are often associated with the initiation and direction of behavior. Emotions typically involve (1) a *physiological* reaction, usually arousal; (2) some kind of *expressive* reaction, such as a distinctive facial expression; and (3) some kind of *subjective experience*, such as the conscious feeling of being happy or sad.

Most psychologists are convinced that the concepts of motivation and emotion must be closely linked. Both terms, in fact, derive from the Latin *movere*, meaning "to move." Many conditions that are motivating also give rise to the experience of emotion. Consider the case in which your thirst motivates you to put change into a soda machine. If the money gets stuck, stalling the pursuit of your goal, frustration and anger are likely. Moreover, once aroused, the emotional experience affects your ability to direct your behavior successfully. If you continue to scream and kick the soda machine, it's unlikely that your goal—quenching your thirst—will be satisfied anytime soon. For reasons like these, it's difficult to discuss the topic of motivation without also considering emotion.

motivation
The set of factors that initiate and direct behavior, usually toward some goal.

emotions
Psychological events involving (1) a physiological reaction, usually arousal; (2) some kind of expressive reaction, such as a distinctive facial expression; and (3) some kind of subjective experience, such as the conscious feeling of being happy or sad.

Previewing the Adaptive Problems

T o study motivation, we need to ask questions about the fundamental *causes* of behavior (Mook, 1995). Obviously, then, the topic is relevant to much of psychology. Each of the preceding chapters connects in one way or another to the question of *why* behavior occurs, but we'll focus our discussion in this chapter on a set of specific adaptive problems that relate to motivation.

First, what activates goal-directed behavior? Any organism seeking to survive in a changing environment must react quickly to its needs. It must anticipate future outcomes and act accordingly, *now,* with vigor and persistence. Much of the time our actions are controlled by *internal* factors that push us in the direction of a goal. For example, if your body is deprived of food or water, a delicate internal balance is disrupted inside your body. A specific need is signaled, which you seek to satisfy in order to restore the internal balance. At other times we're motivated by *external* events, things in our environment that exert powerful pulling effects. The sight of an attractive person, or a recently sliced piece of chocolate cake, can be sufficient to initiate and direct your behavior.

Second, what factors create hunger and control eating? Obviously, we all need to eat—it's a requirement of living. Consequently, there must be mechanisms in the body and mind that make us hungry and interested in eating at regular intervals. To understand how our bodies maintain the proper levels of internal energy, we'll consider the relevant *internal* and *external* cues that activate and control eating. For example, we'll discuss how the body monitors internal physiological states, using brain mechanisms to check up on levels of energy reserves (for example, the amount of sugar in the blood). We'll also discuss how external cues in the environment compel us to eat, and how these cues can influence the food selection process. Whether you like broccoli, reject mushrooms, or happily consume squid depends on a variety of factors, including what you've learned about these foods.

Third, what factors promote sexual behavior? Although you may know someone who is "consumed" by sex, or at least has a reasonably intense sexual appetite, sexual activity is not necessary for individual survival. In principle, people can live perfectly productive lives without ever once engaging in sexual behavior or exploring their sexuality. But adequate sexual performance is needed for survival of the *species.* It's reasonable to assume, then, that there are internal cues, based in the genetic code or found in active biological systems, that help motivate an interest in sex. We'll discuss some of the biological and psychological mechanisms that motivate sexual behavior, as well as some of the physiological characteristics of the human sexual response.

Fourth, how are emotions expressed and experienced, and what functions do they serve? All psychologists agree that emotions have considerable adaptive significance. Consider an emotion like *anger.* Anger typically arises in response to an environmental event, usually the perceived misdeed of another, and the body enters a highly aroused state. The arousal activates behavior and leads to reactions that may substantially increase (or decrease) the likelihood of survival. Once the emotion gains hold, overt physical expressions arise, particularly in the form of easy-to-identify facial expressions. From an adaptive perspective, the sight of an angry person carries important signaling properties—others know to shy away and avoid interaction. As you'll see, emotions are easy to identify but difficult to define.

Activating Behavior

Let's turn our attention to the first problem: What are the factors that activate and control goal-directed behavior? At first, psychologists considered the possibility that there might be a single source of motivation, grounded either in the internal workings of the body or in the external environment. It's possible, for example, that people are born with biological machinery that compels them to act in certain ways irrespective of what they learn from experience. But this idea is largely rejected by current psychologists, who believe instead that no single explanation of goal-directed behavior, based on either biological or environmental factors, is likely to be found. The reason is simple: Virtually all forms of behavior are determined by multiple

LEARNING GOALS

1. Discuss the role of instincts and drive in activating behavior.

2. Explain incentive motivation and discuss how it activates behavior.

3. Distinguish between achievement motivation and intrinsic motivation.

4. Describe Maslow's hierarchy of needs, and discuss how each need influences behavior.

The factors that are initiating and directing this bobcat's behavior include internal ones, such as depleted energy resources, and external ones, such as the sight of an attractive meal. As you'll see, internal and external factors often interact to produce motivated behavior.

The behavior of many animals is motivated, at least in part, by instincts—unlearned, characteristic patterns of responding that are controlled by specific triggering stimuli in the environment.

causes. Factors both inside and outside the body—*internal* and *external* factors—contribute to motivation. In the following sections, we'll consider some examples of these influences.

INTERNAL FACTORS: INSTINCTS AND DRIVE

For an organism to survive in its environment, it must do certain things. Breathing, eating, drinking—these are activities that need to be performed at regular intervals. It makes sense then to assume that the motivation to perform life-sustaining activities is built directly into the biological or genetic code. In nature, birds don't need to be taught to build nests in the springtime or to fly south in the winter; cats don't need to be taught to show interest in small, rapidly moving furry creatures. These are unlearned, characteristic patterns of responding—called **instincts**—that are controlled by specific triggering stimuli in the world. Instincts share properties with *reflexes*, which we discussed in Chapter 3, but instincts typically involve more complex patterns of behavior than those covered by the simple reflexes.

Human Instincts

It's widely accepted that instincts play a role in nonhuman species. But do instincts play any role in controlling human behavior? A number of early psychologists followed the lead of Charles Darwin in suggesting that instincts are a very important factor in human motivation. Humans don't need to be taught to take care of their young, William James (1890) argued, or to cry as infants, to clean themselves when dirty, or even to play, love, imitate, or be curious. These are ingrained biological "musts" that are as natural to the human as nest building is to the bird.

However, just because a behavior occurs on a regular basis doesn't mean it's *instinctive*—that is, unlearned and characteristic in its display. There is no way to open up the body and directly measure an instinct, so it's easy to fall into a trap of circular reasoning: People demonstrate some regular behavior, such as showing sympathy for a child in need, and the temptation is to propose a corresponding sympathy instinct (Holt, 1931). Over the years, psychologists argued about which behaviors qualify as instinctive. For example, William James (1890) suggested some 20 physical and 17 mental instincts in his writings; William McDougall (1908), on the other hand, was convinced of only 12 (he later changed his mind and upped the number to 17). For these and other reasons instincts eventually fell out of favor as a widely applied explanation for goal-directed human behavior.

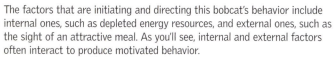

instincts
Unlearned characteristic patterns of responding that are controlled by specific triggering stimuli in the world; they are not thought to be an important factor in explaining goal-directed behavior in humans.

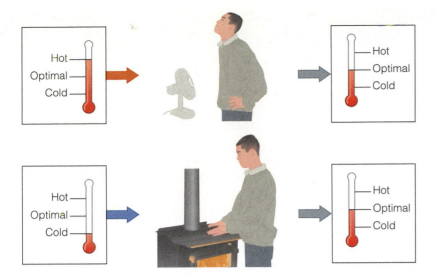

FIGURE 11.1

Homeostasis
It's adaptive for the body to maintain stable and constant internal conditions. If your internal temperature rises above or falls below an optimal level, you are driven to perform actions that will restore the "steady state."

There was simply no agreement about how to confirm or categorize behaviors as instinctive.

Drive

To replace instinct, psychologists turned to the concept of *drive*. A **drive** is a psychological state that arises in response to an internal physiological *need*, such as hunger or thirst. It's clear that the human body is designed to seek fairly stable and constant internal conditions. For example, it's important for the body to maintain an adequate internal supply of fluids, or a constant internal temperature. Psychologists use the term **homeostasis** to refer to the process through which the body maintains its steady state, much like the thermostat in a house maintains a constant internal temperature by turning the heat on or off (Cannon, 1929). Once a specific need is detected, drive serves a general activating function—drive energizes the organism, causing it to seek immediate reduction of the need (Hogan, 1997). So if your water supply is used up, you are driven to drink and restore the appropriate balance. Similar processes are assumed to operate for hunger and for the maintenance of internal body temperature (see Figure 11.1).

Drive is a considerably more flexible concept than instinct. An organism seeks to reduce drive—to restore homeostatic balance—but it doesn't really matter *how* balance is restored. People can use what they've learned from experience to help them satisfy the need; they're not stuck with one fixed pattern of behavior that is triggered only by a restricted set of stimuli. You can think about drive as somewhat analogous to the running engine of a car. A properly running engine is necessary for the car to move, as drive is necessary to initiate goal-directed behavior, but it's not sufficient to get across town. Other factors, such as knowledge about the layout of the town, must be used in conjunction with the operating engine in order to move about. As you'll see shortly, it's also the case that the vigor or intensity with which someone acts depends critically on the value, or *incentive*, of the goal. You are much more likely to be motivated to eat if you like the food, even though a wide variety of food options may satisfy the internal need. You sometimes even eat in the absence of an internal need, as in the case in which you have that second brownie just because it looks good.

EXTERNAL FACTORS: INCENTIVE MOTIVATION

By itself, the concept of drive is insufficient to explain motivated behavior. Goal-directed behavior depends also on what people learn from experience. External rewards, such as money or a good grade, exert powerful pulling and guiding effects on our actions. Generally, whether you will be motivated to perform an action

drive
A psychological state that arises in response to an internal physiological need, such as hunger or thirst.

homeostasis
The process through which the body maintains a steady state, such as a constant internal temperature or an adequate amount of fluids.

CONCEPT SUMMARY
General Approaches to Motivation

Approach	Source of Motivation	Summary and Evaluation
Instinct	Internal	Unlearned, characteristic patterns of responding that are controlled by specific triggering mechanisms in the world. They play a role in nonhuman species, but are insufficient to explain goal-directed human behavior.
Drive	Internal	A psychological state that arises in response to a physiological need, such as hunger or thirst. *Homeostasis* is the process through which the body maintains a steady state. A more flexible concept than instinct, but it does not explain behavior in the absence of need.
Incentive motivation	External	Helps to explain goal-directed behavior. People are driven by external rewards that exert powerful pulling and guiding effects on their actions.

External rewards, such as this young girl's blue ribbon, can exert powerful pulling and guiding effects on people's actions.

incentive motivation
External factors in the environment—such as money, an attractive person, or tasty food—that exert pulling effects on people's actions.

achievement motive
An internal drive or need for achievement that is possessed by all individuals to varying degrees. Whether people will work for success on any given task depends on (1) their expectations about whether they will be successful, and (2) how much they value succeeding at the task.

depends on the value—positive or negative—of the incentive. For this reason psychologists often use the term **incentive motivation** to explain goal-directed behavior. For example, Whitney is motivated to jog for an extra 5 minutes so that she can eat that extra brownie; conversely, Charlie is motivated to avoid the kitchen because of the extra calories (and guilt) that he knows the brownie consumption will produce. Note that this type of motivation is quite different from drive—drive is an internal push that compels a person to action; incentives are external pulls that tempt people with the prospects of receiving powerful reinforcing or punishing consequences.

Of course, internal factors interact with external factors in a number of ways. Whether a person is thirsty, for example, probably affects the incentive value of water; water tastes better, and is more rewarding, when you've been deprived of it for a while (Blundell & Rogers, 1991; Bolles, 1972). Rewarding students with an end-of-chapter test, thereby motivating them to study, has more of an effect when a student is a high procrastinator—that is, someone who finds it difficult to motivate himself to study (Tuckman, 1998). Internal states of deprivation can also act as cues for responding. A person might learn to perform a certain type of action when he or she is thirsty or hungry (Hull, 1943); alternatively, a person might learn that hunger or thirst means that food or water will be especially rewarding (Davidson, 1993, 1998). It's important to remember that motivated behavior is virtually always jointly determined by internal and external factors. Neither factor alone is sufficient to explain motivation.

ACHIEVEMENT MOTIVATION

One example of motivated behavior that clearly depends on both internal and external factors is the striving for achievement. A number of psychologists have argued that each of us, to varying degrees, has an internally driven need for achievement (Atkinson, 1957; McClelland et al., 1953; Murray, 1938). The **achievement motive** pushes you to seek success and significant accomplishment in your life. Studies have shown that people who rate high in achievement motivation tend to work harder and more persistently on tasks, and they tend to achieve more than those who rate low in achievement motivation (Atkinson & Raynor, 1974; Cooper, 1983).

However, whether you will work hard on any particular task depends on (1) your expectations about whether your efforts will be successful, and (2) how much you value succeeding at the task (Atkinson, 1957). This means that people can have a high internal need for achievement but choose not to persist on a task

Every society in the world sets standards for achievement—what skills are important and unimportant—and these standards influence what members of the society seek to achieve.

Children who experience failure on mathematical problems early in life can develop a "helpless" attitude that prevents them from persisting and succeeding in mathematics later in life.

either because they place no value on the task, or because they lack confidence in their ability to succeed. For example, young children who experience failure on mathematics problems early in life can develop a helpless attitude that prevents them from persisting and succeeding on mathematical tasks later in life (Smiley & Dweck, 1994). Conversely, children who perform well on such tasks gain confidence in their ability and appear motivated to take on similar tasks in the future (Wigfield, 1994).

Parents and teachers play an important part in determining achievement motivation. If a child's parents value a task, it's likely that the child will value it as well and will appear more motivated to succeed (Eccles et al., 1983). What children are told about their performance on a task is also important. For example, if children are praised for their effort, they tend to work harder, report more enjoyment, and show more interest. On the other hand, if they're told that performance is tied to ability, such as natural intelligence, children show less achievement motivation, especially if they fail or perform poorly on the task (Mueller & Dweck, 1998).

Cultural Factors

Every society in the world establishes standards for achievement—what skills and tasks are deemed important and unimportant—and these standards influence what the members of the society seek to achieve, and perhaps the level of productivity of the society as a whole (McClelland, 1961). For example, whether a society values individual success, or places more of an emphasis on the collective success of the society, seems to affect individual levels of achievement motivation (Sagie et al., 1996).

Many researchers believe that gender differences in achievement—such as the tendency for men to outperform women, on average, in mathematics—may be partly tied to such cultural factors. In the United States, for instance, the parents of sons place greater value on success in mathematics than do the parents of daughters (Parsons et al., 1982). Consequently, the expectations and values of the parents help to determine the achievement motivation of the children.

INTRINSIC MOTIVATION

Sometimes we choose to engage in actions for which there is no obvious internal or external motivational source. A child spends hours carefully coloring a picture or playing with a doll; you might become transfixed by a crossword puzzle or by a long walk on the beach. Certainly there is no biological *need* that drives coloring or

Do you think these two volunteers at a local food bank would feel better about their work if they were also paid for their activities?

walking. There's also no clear-cut external incentive: Nobody pays the child for coloring or you for finishing the crossword puzzle. Psychologists use the term **intrinsic motivation** to describe situations where behavior appears to be entirely self-motivated. We engage in the action for its own sake, not because someone offers us a reward or because the action restores some internal homeostatic balance.

What convinced many researchers that intrinsic motivation deserves special status was a counterintuitive finding: It's possible to lower someone's interest in performing a task by giving him or her an external reward. In a classic study by Lepper, Greene, and Nisbett (1973), preschool children who were naturally interested in drawing were asked to draw either for its own sake or to win a "Good Player" certificate. Psychologically, we would expect the external reward to bolster drawing even more than normal—after all, drawing is now followed by a concrete positive consequence. But it didn't. The children in the reward condition showed less interest in drawing a week later. The reward apparently killed the behavior, making it less rewarding or interesting than it otherwise would have been.

This study has been repeated with other rewards, and with activities other than drawing (see Deci & Ryan, 1985). The story is much the same: Externally supplied rewards can lower a person's desire to perform a task. Once someone receives a reward for performing a task, he or she seems less likely to enjoy that task for its own sake in the future. Think about professional athletes. Many sports fans complain that the external reward of money has ruined professional sports. Even baseball players sometimes complain that the game was more fun back in the sandlot, before millions of dollars entered into the motivational chain.

Control and Overjustification

How can a reward lead to a negative effect? One possibility is that people see external rewards as an indirect way of controlling behavior. Drawing loses its value because it's now something you do to please the person giving you the reward— you're no longer drawing simply because it pleases *you* (Rummel & Feinberg, 1988). Thus, the so-called "reward" is not really a reward at all. When coupled with the loss of control, the consequence loses its reinforcing value and becomes negative.

Another possibility is that external reward leads to what has been called *overjustification:* Rather than assuming that you perform a task because you like it—it is intrinsically reinforcing—you conclude that it's the external reward that motivates you to perform the task (Bem, 1972; Deci & Ryan, 1985). Rewarding some-

intrinsic motivation
Goal-directed behavior that seems to be entirely self-motivated.

one for performing a task in a sense degrades the value of that task (that is, the baseball player begins to believe that it's the money that makes him play, rather than love for the game). Some researchers have even suggested that things like creativity should never be rewarded, lest the positive internal value of engaging in a creative act be destroyed (Amabile, 1983; Schwartz, 1990).

But not all psychologists are comfortable with these conclusions (Pittinger, 1996). External reward can enhance creativity under some circumstances, and the negative effects of reward on task motivation may occur only in restricted circumstances (see Dickinson, 1989; Eisenberger, 1992). For example, in the study by Lepper and colleagues, children did indeed choose to draw less frequently when they were rewarded for drawing, but this effect occurred only when the children *expected* the reward. When children were given an unexpected reward for drawing, they later spent more time drawing than a group who had received no reward. Therefore, the negative effect of reward on intrinsic motivation may be related to the expectation or *promise* of reward rather than to the reward itself (Cameron & Pierce, 1994).

MASLOW'S HIERARCHY OF NEEDS

Most general theories of motivation rest on a foundation of biological *need*. The body seeks to maintain a delicate internal balance (homeostasis), and if that balance is disrupted, we're motivated to restore it. But as you've just seen, not all needs are biological in origin—such as the need for achievement (Murray, 1938). For this reason, some psychologists have tried to classify need and to determine whether some needs are more important than others.

Among the more influential of these classification systems is the **need hierarchy** introduced by the humanistic theorist Abraham Maslow. The essential component of Maslow's theory is the *prioritizing* of needs: Some needs, he argued, have special priority and must be satisfied before others can be addressed. Obviously, if people don't eat or drink water on a regular basis, they'll die. Maslow's theory is usually represented in the form of a pyramid, to emphasize the fact that human motivation rests on a foundation of biological and security "musts" (see Figure 11.2). It is only after satisfying the survival needs—such as hunger and thirst—that we can consider personal security and more social or spiritual needs, such as the need for love or self-esteem. At the top of the structure

need hierarchy
The idea popularized by Maslow that human needs are prioritized in a hierarchy. Some needs, especially physiological ones, must be satisfied before others, such as the need for achievement or self-actualization, can be pursued.

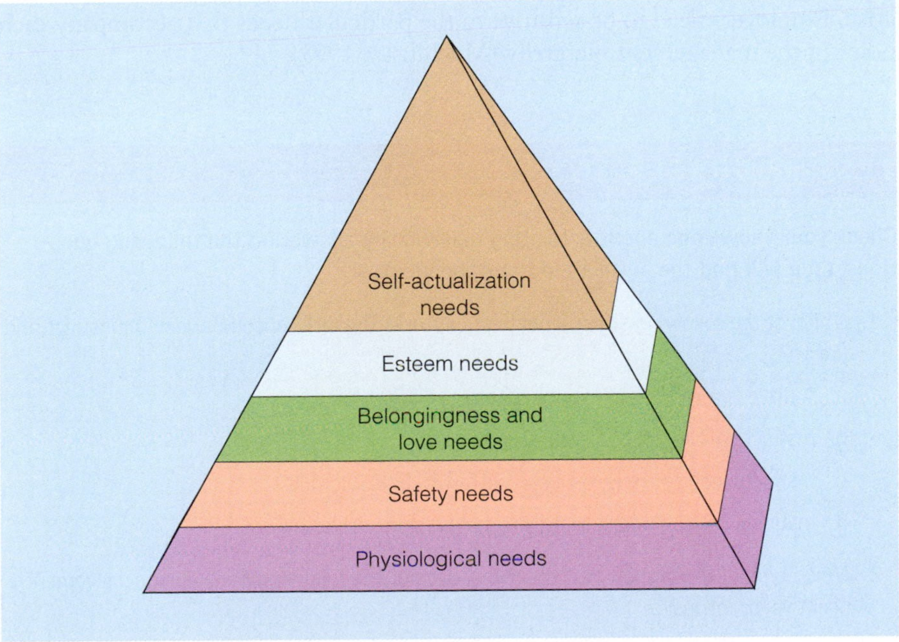

FIGURE 11.2
A Hierarchy of Needs
Maslow proposed that human needs are prioritized: Some, such as physiological and safety needs, must be satisfied before others can be addressed. At the top of the pyramid is the need for self-actualization, which represents our natural desire to reach our true potential.

sits the need for self-actualization, which Maslow believed represented people's desire to reach their true potential as human beings.

The pyramid is an appropriate symbol for Maslow's system because it captures the upward thrust of human motivation. As a humanistic psychologist, Maslow believed that all people have a compelling need to grow, to better themselves as functioning individuals. In his own words: "A musician must make music, an artist must paint, a poet must write if he is ultimately to be at peace with himself" (Maslow, 1954). Maslow was strongly influenced by people who he felt had reached their fullest potential, such as Albert Einstein and Thomas Jefferson. He used their personality characteristics as a way of defining what it means to sit at the top of the pyramid—to be self-actualized. Some of these characteristics included spontaneity, openness to experience, and a high degree of ethical sensitivity (Leclerk et al., 1998; Mook, 1995). (We'll return to humanistic views on personality in Chapter 12.)

Probably the most important feature of the Maslow hierarchy is the laddering of needs. Psychologists might disagree about the specific order that Maslow proposed—does the need to belong and be accepted really have higher priority than the need for self-esteem?—but the idea that humans have a wide diversity of needs and that those needs are prioritized has been enormously influential (Rowan, 1998). It's important to understand that how we act is often influenced by unfilled needs. If you have to worry about putting food on the table, and consequently steal from others on a regular basis, you might appear to lack in moral or ethical values. But this isn't necessarily a permanent fixture of your personality—under different circumstances, with a full stomach, you might be a leader in the promotion of ethical values.

Critics of Maslow's theory often point to its lack of scientific rigor. Because the various needs are not defined clearly, in a way that each can be individually measured, it's difficult to test the different proposals of the need hierarchy (Wahba & Bridwell, 1976). However, the theory continues to exert considerable influence on the way that psychologists think. For example, applied psychologists have extended Maslow's ideas to the workplace, to help employers better understand the behavior of their employees. Many employers now recognize that an employee's needs change depending on his or her position in the management hierarchy. When a person receives low pay or has poor job security, his or her work behavior is directed toward satisfying basic needs. Promotion may help satisfy the fundamental needs, but new, perhaps more demanding ones will quickly arise. Employers need to be sensitive to the particular needs that accompany each point in the management hierarchy (Muchinsky, 1993).

? CRITICAL THINKING

Turn back to the chapter on development and think about the various personal crises people confront as they age. Is there any way you can tie these crises to the needs that Maslow discussed in his hierarchy?

TEST YOURSELF 11.1

Check your knowledge about activating behavior by answering the following questions. (You will find the answers in the Appendix.)

1. Which of the following statements best captures the difference between an instinct and a drive?

   a. A drive is a reflex; an instinct is not.

   b. Instincts are learned; drives are not.

   c. Instincts lead to fixed response patterns; drives do not.

   d. Instincts restore appropriate internal balance; drives do not.

2. Which type of motivation best describes each of the following behaviors: achievement, incentive, or intrinsic?

a. Whitney never misses her daily jogging session—she loves the brownie she gives herself at the end: _____

b. Janice spends hours practicing the piano—she just seems to love playing: _____

c. Candice studies at least six hours a day—she is obsessed with the idea of finishing first in her class: _____

d. Jerome rarely paints for fun anymore, not since he started teaching art classes at the local college: _____

3. According to Maslow's hierarchy of needs, we can reach our true potential as human beings only after:

a. restoring a proper level of homeostatic balance.

b. satisfying basic survival and social needs.

c. satisfying our need for achievement.

d. eliminating the need for rewards.

Meeting Biological Needs: Hunger and Eating

We next turn our attention to an important motivational problem that must be dealt with every day: initiating and controlling eating behavior. Eating is a constant in your life and mine, but we eat for reasons that are more complex than you might think. If asked why we eat, children will explain that we eat "because we're hungry" or "because my tummy hurts." An adult's response will appear more sophisticated, but it usually amounts to much the same thing: "We eat because our bodies need food, internal energy." This is true; eating is a biologically driven behavior. But eating is a psychologically driven behavior as well. We sometimes feel hungry when there is no physical need and, as any dieter knows, a strong will can stop consumption even when the physical need is present.

LEARNING GOALS

1. Discuss the internal factors that influence when and why we eat.

2. Discuss the external factors that influence when and why we eat.

3. Explain how body weight is regulated, including the concept of a set point.

4. Discuss the eating disorders anorexia nervosa and bulimia nervosa.

INTERNAL FACTORS CONTROLLING HUNGER

Researchers have spent decades trying to understand the internal mechanisms that influence when and why we eat. We now know, for example, that the body monitors itself, particularly its internal supply of resources, in a number of ways. For example, there is a connection between the volume and content of food in the stomach and the amount that neurons will fire in certain areas of the brain (Sharma et al., 1961). Psychologically, people report little, if any, hunger or interest in food when their stomach is full, and hunger increases in a relatively direct way as the stomach empties (Sepple & Read, 1989).

Chemical Signals

It's not only the contents of the stomach that are monitored. The body has several important suppliers of internal energy that it checks regularly. One critical substance is **glucose,** a kind of sugar that cells require for energy production. Receptors in the liver are thought to react to changes in the amount of glucose in the blood, or perhaps to how this sugar is being used by the cells, and appropriate signals are communicated upward to the brain (Mayer, 1953; Russek, 1971). When the amount of usable glucose falls below an optimal level, which occurs when you haven't eaten for a while, you start to feel hungry and seek out food (Campfield et al., 1996). If blood glucose levels are high, which occurs after a meal, you lose interest in food. This link between blood sugar levels and hunger is not simply correlational: In the laboratory it is possible to increase or decrease how much an animal will eat by artificially manipulating the amount of glucose in its blood (Smith & Campfield, 1993).

glucose
A kind of sugar that cells require for energy production.

Internal factors, such as the amount of food in the stomach or the amount of glucose in the blood, play an important role in making people feel "sated" after a meal.

Another key element the body monitors is **insulin,** a hormone released by the pancreas. The body needs insulin to help pump the nutrients present in the blood into the cells, where they can be stored as fat or metabolized into needed energy. At the start of a meal, the brain sends signals to the pancreas to begin the production and release of insulin in preparation for the rise in blood sugar produced by the food. As insulin does its job, the levels of blood sugar go down and you eventually feel hungry once again. It's probably a glucose-insulin interaction that is actually monitored internally, because both substances play pivotal roles in the metabolic, or energy-producing, process. If laboratory animals are given continuous injections of insulin, they tend to balloon in weight and grossly overeat—the insulin keeps the blood sugar level low, which tells the animal to start looking for something to eat.

Both glucose and insulin are believed to play key roles in motivating eating behavior, but it's unlikely that any one single chemical (or even two) completely controls whether you will feel hungry. Other internal stimuli, such as the overall level of body fat (Keesey & Powley, 1975), also play important roles. Of course, ultimately the experience of hunger originates in the brain. It is the activation of brain structures that initiates and directs the search for food. You learned in Chapter 3 that structures in the limbic system are involved in controlling a number of motivational and emotional behaviors. As you'll see momentarily, structures associated with the *hypothalamus* have long been thought to be of central importance in eating.

Brain Regions

A number of years ago it was discovered that if a particular portion of the **ventromedial hypothalamus** is lesioned (destroyed) in laboratory animals, a curious transformation occurs. Lesioned animals appear to be hungry all the time and show a striking tendency to overeat. In fact, each animal becomes an eating machine—if allowed, it balloons up to several times its normal weight (Hetherington & Ranson, 1942). If this same area is stimulated electrically, rather than destroyed, the opposite pattern emerges. Electrical stimulation causes the animal to lose all interest in food, even if there is a real need for nutrients in the body. These results suggested to many researchers that the ventromedial hypothalamus functions as a kind of "stop," or *satiety*, center in the brain. Activation of the region, which presumably occurs whenever we've eaten enough to fulfill the body's energy needs, turns off hunger and eating. This process would be adaptive because it prevents us from accumulating too many nutrients in the blood—more than our bodies can handle.

If activation of the ventromedial hypothalamus stops eating, then what starts the eating process? One logical candidate was the **lateral hypothalamus,** because it acts as a kind of mirror image of the ventromedial hypothalamus. In the laboratory, damage to the lateral hypothalamus creates an animal that typically starves itself, even to the point of death. Electrical stimulation of the same area causes the animal to immediately start eating. This suggested that the lateral hypothalamus may act as a kind of eating "start up" center, to counteract the stop center located in the ventromedial hypothalamus. This division of labor in the brain paints a cohesive picture—two regions of the hypothalamus working together to initiate and control eating behavior.

Unfortunately, this simple story turns out to be wrong. Researchers remain convinced that both regions of the hypothalamus help to control eating, but they're uncertain about the precise roles. Part of the problem is that destruction

insulin
A hormone released by the pancreas that helps pump nutrients in the blood into the cells, where they can be stored as fat or metabolized into needed energy.

ventromedial hypothalamus
A portion of the hypothalamus that, when lesioned, causes an animal to typically overeat and gain a large amount of weight. Once thought to be a kind of stop eating, or satiety, center in the brain; its role in eating behavior is currently unknown.

lateral hypothalamus
A portion of the hypothalamus that, when lesioned, causes an animal to be reluctant to eat; like the ventromedial hypothalamus, it probably plays some role in eating behavior, but the precise role is unknown.

of either area tends to affect the nervous system in a number of ways, so it's difficult to determine the exact causes of the eating changes. Lesions to the ventromedial hypothalamus, for example, may affect the secretion of insulin (Weingarten et al., 1985) or damage the effectiveness of various other important pathways in the brain (Kirchgessner & Sclafani, 1988). Moreover, a closer examination of animals with lesions to the ventromedial hypothalamus revealed that they're somewhat picky and won't eat certain foods (Ferguson & Keesey, 1975). They don't just eat anything, as the start-stop hypothesis seems to predict.

Just as the brain monitors the levels of several internal chemicals to determine the need for food, several important locations in the brain besides the hypothalamus help to control eating behavior (Woods et al., 1998). There is evidence that portions of the brainstem are critical in the initiation of eating (Grill & Kaplan, 1990), and the hippocampus may be involved as well. You may remember from Chapter 8 that we discussed an amnesic called H.M. who was doomed to live in a kind of perpetual present—he could remember nothing of what happened to him moments before. It turns out that H.M., who has damage to his temporal lobes and hippocampus, also has trouble monitoring his need for food. He is sometimes convinced that he's hungry immediately after finishing a meal. He may have simply forgotten that he's eaten; but, as Davidson (1993) points out, he clearly is also unable to use internal signals from his body as cues for hunger or satiety. These data suggest an important role for the hippocampus in feeding behavior (see also Davidson & Jarrad, 1993).

If a particular portion of the ventromedial hypothalamus is destroyed, rats become eating machines and can balloon up to several times their normal weight.

EXTERNAL FACTORS

From an adaptive standpoint, it's obviously critical that you eat. You can't let your internal energy sources fall too low; otherwise you won't have an adaptive mind to consider. But it would be a mistake to think about eating as simply a means to satisfy a variety of internal energy needs. We often eat for reasons that are unrelated to restoring internal homeostatic balance (Capaldi, 1996). Have you ever eaten to reduce stress or simply to make yourself feel good? Have you ever eaten to promote social interaction, as in going out to dinner with friends? We all have. People even eat at times to make artistic, aesthetic, or moral judgments. For example, some people are vegetarians because they believe it's wrong to eat other animals.

One's cultural and ethnic background exerts a powerful effect on food selection. Would you be willing to consume the insect delicacies shown in the picture on the right? How about the more traditional desserts shown on the left?

Eating Habits

Most people have established eating habits, which develop through personal experience and by modeling the behavior of others. These learned habits control much of our decision making about food. For example, you're probably used to eating at certain times and in certain places. If you're offered a tasty snack, how much you eat is determined partly by the time of day—if the offer comes shortly before dinner, you take less than if the offer comes in the middle of the afternoon (Schachter & Gross, 1968). You also know from past experience how much food you can eat and still feel well. You know, for instance, that if you eat the whole pizza you will probably feel sick afterward, even though the pizza may taste great at the time.

Your cultural and ethnic background is another powerful influence on when and what you choose to eat (Rozin, 1996). Most people who grow up in the United States will not willingly choose to eat dogs or sheep's eyes, but these are considered food delicacies in some parts of the world. Are you hesitant about eating pork or beef? You probably are if you're an Orthodox Jew or a native of India. And it's not just the appearance of food or where it comes from. People around the world often discriminate among who it is appropriate to eat with. For example, members of some social classes would never consider eating with those that they consider to be social inferiors.

Food Cues

The decision to eat is also strongly influenced by the presence or absence of food cues. Animals know that certain kinds of food signal positive consequences, and the sight of these foods is often enough to make them start eating. If hungry rats are taught that a flashing light signals food, later on they'll start eating in the presence of the light even if they've been fully fed moments before (Weingarten, 1983). Waiters at fine restaurants push the dessert tray under your nose after a filling meal because they know that the sight (or presentation) of the sugar-filled array will be more likely to break down your reserve than just hearing about what's for dessert. Again, your choice of the New York cheesecake with the strawberry sauce is not driven by internal need. Your blood contains plenty of appropriate nutrients—the sight of the food, and its associations with past pleasures, acts as an external pull, motivating your choice to consume.

REGULATING BODY WEIGHT

What determines your everyday body weight? Why are some people thin and others obese? Not surprisingly, internal and external factors combine to regulate body weight. It turns out that some factors, such as genetic predisposition, play a particularly important role. For example, when identical twins—those sharing the same genetic material—are fed identical diets, they tend to gain virtually the same amount of weight. But if two unrelated people are given matched diets, the differences in weight gain can be substantial (Bouchard, et al., 1990). I'm sure you

? CRITICAL THINKING

Can you think of any factors, besides behavior modeling, that might help to determine eating habits? What about the availability of food—when was the last time you saw sheep's eyes on the menu at the local diner?

CONCEPT SUMMARY
Factors Involved in Hunger

Type of Factor	Factor	Its Role in Hunger
Internal	Chemical signals	Receptors in the liver respond to changes in the amount of *glucose* in the blood. The body also monitors *insulin*, a hormone released by the pancreas. The glucose–insulin interaction is monitored internally. Insulin lowers blood glucose levels, leading to hunger.
	Brain	The lateral and ventromedial regions of the hypothalamus help to control eating, but the precise role of each is unclear. Portions of the brainstem also seem important in the initiation of eating.
External	Eating habits	Learned habits develop through personal experience and modeling the behavior of others. Cultural and ethnic background also play critical roles in when and what you eat.
	Food cues	Factors such as the attractiveness of food, or its association with past pleasures, can serve as an external pull, motivating eating behavior.

know people who seem to eat continuously and never gain weight; others balloon considerably after only a small daily increase in caloric intake. In short, the amount of food that you eat only partly determines what you normally weigh.

Set Point

Some researchers believe that we have a natural body weight, or **set point,** that more or less controls our tendency to gain or lose weight (Keesey & Powley, 1975). Most people show little variation in weight from year to year, presumably because their bodies manipulate the motivation to eat, as needed, to maintain the appropriate set point weight. When people go on a diet and dip below their natural weight, well over 90% of them eventually gain that weight back (Martin et al., 1991). Here again, the idea is that the body adjusts how much it eats, rebounding after a diet, to produce stability in body weight.

What determines someone's set point? Genetic factors are probably primarily responsible: Different people are born with different numbers of fat cells, and this number may constrain just how much weight someone can hope to gain or lose (Faust, 1984). Your metabolic rate—how quickly you burn off calories—is another important internal factor; again, it's determined in part by your genetic makeup.

Obesity

What causes **obesity,** the condition characterized by excessive body fat? At one time it was thought that obese people simply lacked sufficient willpower to resist overeating, especially when appealing food was in view (Schachter, 1971). Studies were conducted showing that overweight people are more likely to order a specific dish in a restaurant after a tasty description (Herman & Polivy, 1988). Overweight people are also more likely than nonobese people to report that food still tastes good after a filling meal.

However, to explain obesity by appealing to willpower, or to any one psychological factor, is simplistic and misleading. As noted above, just because someone eats a lot does not mean that he or she will gain excessive amounts of weight. Some people can eat a lot and gain little weight; others gain weight on limited diets. The causes of obesity lie in a complex combination of biology and psychology: metabolic rate, set point, number of fat cells, learned eating habits, cultural role models, level of stress—all contribute in one way or another to weight control (Hill & Peters, 1998; Rodin, 1981). Obviously, a proper diet, and gaining some control over how much you eat, is important to maintaining a healthy lifestyle (see Chapter 16), but obesity can occur for reasons that are largely outside of an individual's control (Woods et al., 1998).

EATING DISORDERS

People's quest for the perfect body shape and weight is a multimillion-dollar industry whose influence stretches worldwide. As you know, society sets weight ideals, often through advertising, and our notions about attractiveness have become closely tied to meeting these standards (Jacobi & Cash, 1994). There are adaptive reasons why you might seek to emulate role models in your culture (see Chapter 7), but in the case of weight control you're traveling along a dangerous two-way street. On the one hand, if you're extremely overweight, you're more likely to suffer from health problems that could lead to an early death. Obviously, it's important to watch your weight by monitoring the nutritional value and volume of your meals. But the pursuit of *unrealistic* weight goals, ones that you can never hope to reach because of your genetic background, can lead to significant psychological and physical problems. Unhappiness and depression are the all-too-often by-products of the failure to reach the proper ideal (Rodin et al., 1989).

Interestingly, people's assessments of their own weight, and its relation to these standards, are typically inaccurate. In addition, most people are simply

set point
A natural body weight, perhaps produced by genetic factors, that the body seeks to maintain. When body weight falls below the set point, one is motivated to eat; when weight exceeds the set point, one feels less motivated to eat.

obesity
A weight problem characterized by excessive body fat.

Alinari/Art Resource, NY

Social standards concerning weight "ideals" have changed considerably over the years.

This young woman is suffering from anorexia nervosa, a condition characterized by an intense fear of being overweight.

wrong about what members of the opposite sex consider to be an ideal body weight (Fallon & Rozin, 1985). On average, women tend to think men prefer thinner women than men actually do; when men are asked about their own ideal weight, it tends to be heavier than what the average woman rates as most attractive. Not surprisingly, these mistaken beliefs help promote a negative body image. One of the consequences of a negative body image is increased susceptibility to eating disorders, such as *anorexia nervosa* and *bulimia nervosa*.

Anorexia Nervosa

In a recent survey of eighth- and tenth-grade students, it was discovered that over 60% of the females and 28% of the males were in the midst of dieting (Hunnicutt & Newman, 1993). The concern—some would say obsession—with weight and dieting starts early in Western cultures, and for an unfortunate few the consequences can be life-threatening. In the condition called **anorexia nervosa,** an otherwise healthy person refuses to maintain a normal weight level, typically because she or he has an irrational fear of being overweight. In such cases, a person can literally be starving to death and still see an overweight person in the mirror. The condition affects mainly young women between the ages of 12 and 18 (perhaps as many as 1% of adolescent women) and it's been estimated that as many as 20% of those with the disorder will eventually die as a result, either from medical problems or from suicide (Ratnasuriya et al., 1991). Not surprisingly, the causes of this disorder are complex and may involve genetic as well as psychological factors (Allison & Faith, 1997; Gorwood et al., 1998).

Bulimia Nervosa

In the eating disorder known as **bulimia nervosa,** the principal symptom is *binge eating*. A binge is an episode in which a person consumes large quantities of food, often junk food, in a limited period of time. You might find a person suffering from bulimia locked in a room, surrounded by his or her favorite snacks, eating literally thousands of calories in a single sitting. The condition is marked by a lack of control—the person feels unable to stop the eating or to control the content of the food being consumed. A bingeing episode is often followed by *purging*, in which the person induces vomiting or uses laxatives in an effort to stop potential weight gain. Like anorexia, bulimia affects primarily women and is characterized

anorexia nervosa
An eating disorder diagnosed when an otherwise healthy person refuses to maintain a normal weight level because of an intense fear of being overweight.

bulimia nervosa
An eating disorder in which the principal symptom is binge eating (consuming large quantities of food) followed by purging, in which the person voluntarily vomits or uses laxatives to prevent weight gain.

by an obsessive desire to be thin. It, too, often has serious medical consequences and is probably caused by a combination of genetic and psychological factors (Sullivan et al., 1998).

TEST YOURSELF 11.2

Check your knowledge about hunger and eating by deciding whether each of the following statements is true or false. (You will find the answers in the Appendix.)

1. A high level of glucose, or blood sugar, is associated with an increased desire for food. *True or False?*

2. The principal symptoms of anorexia nervosa are bingeing and purging. *True or False?*

3. The lateral hypothalamus serves as the brain's stop center for eating. *True or False?*

4. Obesity is primarily caused by poor dietary habits. *True or False?*

5. Destruction of the ventromedial hypothalamus causes a rat to refuse food and dramatically lose weight. *True or False?*

Meeting Biological Needs: Sexual Behavior

Does your world revolve around sex? Perhaps not, but there's no denying that sex is a powerful motivator of people around the world. Every significant culture, regardless of where you look, has well-established rules and guidelines for the teaching and practice of behavior related to courtship, mating, and the sexual act. Just think for a moment about advertising, television, movies. Enough said.

But where exactly is the need? What problem is solved by the pursuit and completion of the sexual act? Is there some kind of internal sex gauge that monitors sexual deprivation and adjusts behavior accordingly? Are people compelled by biological forces to restore an internal erotic balance? People certainly won't die if their goal-directed sexual pursuits fail, as they would from an unsuccessful search for nutrients. At the same time, sexual motivation clearly has great value at the level of the species. Through

LEARNING GOALS

1. Describe the characteristics of the human sexual response cycle.

2. Discuss the role that hormones play in human and animal sexual behavior.

3. List some external influences on sexual behavior.

4. Discuss the factors that influence mate selection.

5. Discuss the factors that may determine sexual orientation.

For centuries, cultures around the world have maintained rules and guidelines for the teaching and practice of courtship, mating, and the sexual act. This Japanese woodblock print from 1821 was designed to stimulate and enhance the sexual experience.

excitement phase
The first component of the human sexual response cycle, as described by Masters and Johnson. It's characterized by changes in muscle tension, increased heart rate and blood pressure, and a rushing of blood into the genital organs; in men, the penis becomes erect; in women, the vaginal walls become lubricated.

plateau phase
The second stage in the human sexual response cycle. Arousal continues to increase, although at a slower rate, toward a preorgasm maximum point.

orgasmic phase
The third stage in the human sexual response cycle. It's characterized by rhythmic contractions in the sex organs; in men, ejaculation occurs. There is also the subjective experience of pleasure that appears to be similar for men and women.

Great Frigates engaged in a stereotypic mating ritual.

reproduction, people pass on their genetic material to offspring and thereby help ensure continuation of the species. Think about it: If everyone suddenly lost his or her interest in sex, the human race would be doomed to elimination in a single generational cycle.

Of course, sexual motivation has its advantages within a single lifetime, too. Besides the pleasurable and reinforcing aspects of sex, sexual desire drives people to pursue a mate, thereby opening the door for companionship, protection, and love. The search for an ideal mate is itself a problem that needs solving. As you'll see, how that particular problem is handled is determined in part by people's conceptions of attractiveness. We'll first consider the human sexual response cycle. Then we'll look at the internal and external factors that motivate sexual behavior. We'll conclude with a look at issues involved in mate selection and sexual orientation.

THE SEXUAL RESPONSE CYCLE

Humans are capable of wide and imaginative varieties of lovemaking, but biologically the sexual response follows a standard four-component sequence (see Figure 11.3). As documented by researchers William Masters and Virginia Johnson (1966), who spent years studying the human sexual response in the laboratory, the response cycle begins with an **excitement phase.** Sexual excitement is characterized by changes in muscle tension, increased heart rate and blood pressure, and a rushing of blood into the genital organs. In men, the increased blood supply causes an erection in the penis; in women, the clitoris swells and the lining of the vaginal walls becomes lubricated.

The excitement phase then shifts into a **plateau phase,** during which sexual arousal continues to increase, at a slower rate, toward a maximum point. The penis becomes fully erect, and vaginal lubrication increases. Other changes begin that are appropriate to the reproductive process—the internal shape of the vagina changes in preparation for the receipt of the sperm-laden semen; the testes of men rise up in preparation for ejaculation. Sexual release is next, in the **orgasmic phase,** and occurs in the form of rhythmic contractions in the sex organs; in men, these rhythmic contractions are accompanied by ejaculation. Interestingly, the subjective experience of the orgasm is apparently quite similar for males and females, despite the obvious physiological differences. When asked

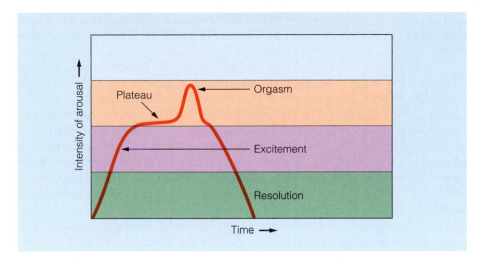

FIGURE 11.3
The Sexual Response Cycle
Biologically, the human sexual response is
believed to follow a four-component sequence:
(1) an initial *excitement phase*, during which
arousal increases rapidly; (2) a *plateau phase*,
in which arousal increases steadily but more
slowly; (3) the *orgasmic phase*, during which
sexual release occurs; and (4) a *resolution
phase*, in which arousal falls back toward
normal levels. For men, the resolution phase is
characterized by a refractory period during
which further stimulation fails to produce
visible signs of arousal or orgasm. (Based on
Masters & Johnson, 1966).

to review written descriptions of the orgasmic experience, outside readers usually cannot tell whether a description was written by a man or a woman (Proctor et al., 1974).

The sexual response cycle is completed with a **resolution phase,** during which arousal returns to normal levels and, at least for men, there is a *refractory period* where further stimulation fails to produce visible signs of arousal or orgasm. The length of the resolution phase is highly variable—it can last anywhere from a few minutes to several days—and no one is quite sure exactly what determines when it will end. Age and prior frequency of sexual release seem to be important factors, as is the degree of emotional closeness with one's partner (Crooks & Baur, 1996).

INTERNAL FACTORS

For most of the animal kingdom, including primates like orangutans and gorillas, sexual behavior is strongly under the control of chemical messengers (sex hormones) that regularly rise and fall in cycles. A female rat will assume a characteristic posture—signaling receptivity to mounting and copulation by the male—but only during the time in her hormonal cycle when she is most likely to become impregnated. She'll adjust her posture to prepare for the weight of the male, she'll move her tail aside, and she'll even approach and nuzzle the male to assure his amorous attention (Carlson, 1991). But these behaviors are tightly locked to the presence of the appropriate hormones—estradiol and progesterone in the case of the female rat. If these hormones are absent, the female will show no interest in sex at all, choosing instead to display indifference or hostility toward the sexually active male. If these hormones are injected artificially, sexual receptivity can be promoted under conditions in which it would not normally occur (Lisk, 1978). As with the female, sexual behavior of the male rat depends on the presence of the appropriate hormone—testosterone. If testosterone is absent, so too is the desire to have sex.

Hormones and Human Sexuality

Humans also show regular cyclic variations in the hormones relevant to sex and reproduction. These sets of hormones—*estrogens* in women and *androgens* in men—play a critical role in physical development, affecting everything from the development of the sex organs to the wiring structure of the brain (see Chapter 3). But the initiation and control of adult sexual behavior does not appear to be simply a matter of mixing and matching the right internal chemicals. Human sexual behavior remains actively under our control, although learned social and cultural factors have an important influence. Instead of instinctive posturing and fixed

resolution phase
The fourth and final stage in the human sexual response cycle. Arousal returns to normal levels. For men, there is a refractory period during which further stimulation fails to produce visible signs of arousal.

courtship rituals, people in most human cultures largely choose when and where they engage in sex and the particular manner in which the sexual act is consummated.

This does not mean that hormones play no role in human sexual behavior. There is some evidence to suggest that a woman's peak of sexual desire occurs in the middle of her menstrual cycle, near the time of ovulation (Adams et al., 1978; Harvey, 1987). There is also evidence that testosterone affects both male and female sexual desire. For example, when testosterone levels are reduced sharply—as occurs, for instance, following removal of the testes (medical castration) in men—there is often a loss of interest in sex. In fact, sex offenders are sometimes treated by administering drugs that block the action of testosterone (Roesler & Witztum, 1998). But neither males nor females are rigidly controlled by these hormones. Some castrated men continue to enjoy and seek out sexual encounters, even without hormone replacement therapy. Similarly, women continue to seek out and enjoy sexual relations after menopause, when the levels of female sex hormones decline (Lamont, 1997; Pedersen, 1998).

EXTERNAL FACTORS

Rather than appealing to the flow of hormones, an alternative way to explain sexual desire is to appeal to the value, or incentive, of the sexual act. Clearly, there's something about the internal wiring of the brain that makes the sexual act itself immensely rewarding for most people. When someone attractive wanders by and acts as a signal for something pleasurable, we are pulled, or motivated, as a consequence toward the object that may potentially lead to reinforcing sexual release.

Perhaps you won't resonate much to this kind of description of sexual desire. But there's no question that humans are regular recipients of a vast array of sexual signals in their environment, and these signals often successfully stimulate sexual desire. Both men and women are sexually aroused by explicit visual stimuli, although women, if questioned, are less likely to report the arousal (Kelley, 1985; Murnen & Stockton, 1997). If excitement is measured through physiological recording devices attached to sensitive genital regions, men and women show very similar arousal responses to erotic pictures and movies (Rubinsky et al., 1987). The way people dress and wear their hair, the shapes of their bodies—all contribute to popular conceptions of attractiveness and desirability.

Touch and Smell

Touch is a particularly important external source of sexual arousal. Careful stimulation of certain regions of the body (known commonly as *erogenous zones*) is highly arousing for most people and may be one of the few completely natural, or unlearned, arousal sources (although other "erotic zones" may develop or be influenced by experience). We frequently communicate through touch, and touch is an important source of information regardless of where you look in the world (McDaniel & Anderson, 1998).

In contrast, for many animals it is odor or smell that initiates sexual interest. In Chapter 5, we discussed chemicals called *pheromones* that are released by the females of many species during periods of receptivity. Pheromones are odor-producing chemicals, and they drive dogs, pigs, and many other creatures into a sexual frenzy. At this point, there's really no solid evidence that human pheromones affect sexual desire, although one recent study reported increased sexual activity for men wearing synthetic human pheromones (compared to a placebo control; Cutler et al., 1998). How a person smells matters—both men and women report that odor is an important factor in selecting a lover (Hertz & Cahill, 1997). In all likelihood, however, it is experience rather than biological wiring that is responsible for these reports.

MATE SELECTION

The initiation of the sexual act is guided by one very important external source: a person's selection of and acceptance by an appropriate mate. Not surprisingly, what people consider to be attractive is strongly influenced by sociocultural factors. Societies have unique cultural definitions of attractiveness, their own rules for attracting a mate, and different views on what kinds of sexual behavior are considered appropriate. In some societies, for example, sexual activity is encouraged at very young ages—even 5- and 6-year-olds are allowed to engage in casual fondling of a willing partner's genitals. In other societies, sexual expression in childhood is strictly prohibited.

Sexual Scripts

According to researchers John Gagnon and William Simon, as people grow they acquire **sexual scripts**—learned programs that instruct them on how, why, and what to do in their interactions with sexual partners (Gagnon & Simon, 1973). These scripts may differ from one culture to the next, and they contribute to many of the differences seen in male and female sexual behavior. Among other things, sexual scripts affect the attitudes we hold toward the sexual act. Boys typically learn, for example, to associate sexual intimacy with genital fondling; girls are more likely to identify sexuality with romantic love. These scripts affect expectations and sometimes are responsible for miscommunication between the sexes. For instance, over half of teenage girls who engage in premarital sex expect to marry their partners, but this expectation is true for only 18% of the male partners (Coles & Stokes, 1985).

Sociobiological Influences

Despite the many differences that exist in the formation of sexual scripts, there are still fundamental similarities among peoples that reflect the evolutionary history of the species. For example, in nearly every culture men are more likely than women to pursue what David Buss and David Schmitt call *short-term* sexual strategies—brief affairs or one-night stands. In interviews with college students, Buss and Schmitt (1993) found that most men had few qualms about the idea of having sexual intercourse with a woman they'd met only an hour before; for most women, the idea of such casual sex was a "virtual impossibility." Across all parts of the world, men seem to value attractiveness in a long-term mating partner and universally tend to prefer to mate with women who are on the average younger than themselves (Buss, 1989). Women, on the other hand, tend to place much greater value on a mating partner's financial prospects than men do—a pattern that again holds across the world (see Figure 11.4 on page 442).

The fact that these differences are present in virtually every society strongly suggests that there may be ingrained adaptive reasons for these gender-based behaviors. Men might pursue multiple sexual partners in an effort to increase the likelihood of successful reproduction (Dawkins, 1986). Women might prefer to consider a man's economic means because the responsibility of rearing and nurturing a child often falls on the woman's shoulders. According to Buss and Schmitt (1993), as well as a movement that grew out of the study of animal behavior called **sociobiology**, the sexual strategies of men and women are best understood from an evolutionary perspective. Throughout evolutionary history, men and women have faced unique and gender-specific reproductive problems; their attitudes and mating rituals undoubtedly have developed, in part, to help resolve these problems.

At the same time, the patterns of behavior that we've been discussing are not fixed at birth for all women and men. As noted before, human sexual behavior shows considerable flexibility—the biological forces of nature influence but need not determine our final behavior. Moreover, it's worth noting that some human sexual strategies could have developed early in the species' evolutionary history but may no longer be needed or even particularly effective. (We'll return to the

? CRITICAL THINKING

Other than through stimulating sexual desire, how might physical attractiveness affect the thoughts and actions of others?

sexual scripts
Learned cognitive programs that instruct us on how, why, and what to do in our interactions with sexual partners; the nature of sexual scripts may vary from one culture to the next.

sociobiology
A theory proposing that social behavior should be understood from an evolutionary/genetic perspective.

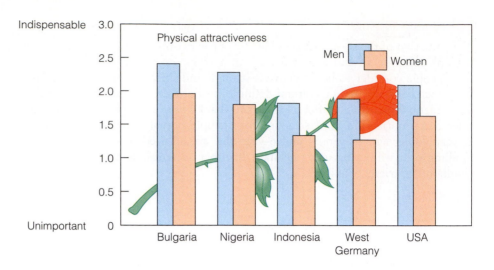

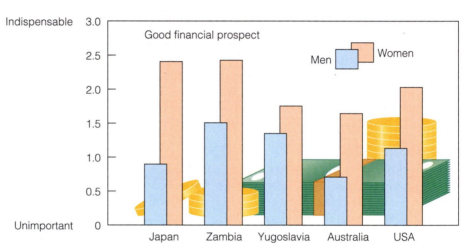

FIGURE 11.4
Cross-Cultural Mating Strategies
Men and women in different parts of the world were asked to rate the importance of physical attractiveness and financial prospects in a long-term partner. On average, men rated physical attractiveness as more important than women did, whereas women were more likely than men to consider a partner's financial prospects important. (Data from Buss & Schmitt, 1993.)

sexual orientation
A person's sexual and emotional attraction to members of the same sex or the other sex; homosexuality, heterosexuality, and bisexuality are all sexual orientations.

debate about the roles of biology versus the environment, specifically with respect to conceptions of attractiveness, in Chapter 13.)

SEXUAL ORIENTATION

When psychologists use the term **sexual orientation,** they are referring to whether a person is sexually and emotionally attracted to members of the same sex or the other sex. The term *homosexual* is applied when the attraction is predominantly to members of the same sex; *heterosexual* refers to the more typical other-sex attraction. Estimates of the number of people in the United States who fit the description of homosexual vary, ranging from 1 to 2% to perhaps as high as 10% (Rogers & Turner, 1991). Exact numbers are difficult to determine, partly because people are often reluctant to disclose intimate information about sexual preference. Moreover, in some respects sexual orientation is best seen as a continuum rather than as a category with fixed boundaries. People who are predominantly homosexual sometimes seek out heterosexual relationships, while many heterosexuals have had sexual experiences with members of the same sex.

But what accounts for a sexual and emotional preference for members of the same sex? If the purpose of sexual desire is to procreate—to assure continuation of the species—in what way can homosexuality be considered adaptive? There is no simple answer to this question, although certainly same-sex relationships have many nurturing qualities that go well beyond sexual encounters. For many years psychologists were convinced that a homosexual orientation developed as the result of experience, particularly the experiences children have with their parents. Homosexuality was considered to be an abnormal condition that arose from dysfunctional home environments, usually as a consequence of having a domineering mother and a passive father. But this view is no longer widely accepted, primarily because a close examination of family histories revealed that the home environments of heterosexuals and homosexuals are actually quite similar (Bell et al., 1981).

Nature versus Nurture

There is research suggesting that sexual orientation may be at least partly determined by biological factors (Gladue, 1994). When researcher Simon LeVay (1991) compared the autopsied brains of homosexual and heterosexual men, he discovered that a cluster of neurons associated with the hypothalamus was consistently larger in heterosexual men. Exactly how or why this portion of the brain influences sexual orientation is unknown. There have also been reports over the past several years suggesting a genetic locus for sexual orientation. For example, twin studies have revealed that if one identical twin is homosexual, there is an approximately 50% chance that the other twin will share the same sexual orientation; for fraternal twins or nontwin bothers and sisters, the likelihood that both will be homosexual is considerably lower (Bailey & Pillard, 1991; Bailey et al., 1993). In another recent study, a systematic analysis of the chromosomes of homosexual brothers suggested evidence for what the researchers believe might be a "gay gene" (Hamer et al., 1993).

It's simply too early to tell what all these data truly mean. The biological findings remain correlational—that is, we simply know that sexual orientation may be *associated* with certain brain structures or genetic markers—but correlational data do not allow us to determine the *cause* of sexual orientation (Bailey & Pillard, 1995). Moreover, it seems very unlikely that appeals to biological factors alone will solve the mysteries of sexual orientation (after all, 50% of identical twins of homosexuals do *not* share this orientation). The environment is certain to play an important role, but the nature of that role has yet to be determined. Finally, it's important to remember that sexual orientation is not really a fixed attribute of a person, like blue eyes or blond hair; instead, we are attracted to others for many reasons and there may be multiple pathways, and reasons for, particular sexual preferences (Byne, 1997; LeVay, 1996).

TEST YOURSELF 11.3

Check your knowledge about the internal and external factors that control sexual behavior by deciding whether each of the following statements is true or false. (You will find the answers in the Appendix.)

1. In the human sexual response cycle, the period just prior to orgasm is called the plateau phase. *True or False?*

2. It is possible to affect sexual desire in men by altering the natural levels of the hormone testosterone in the body. *True or False?*

3. Across the world, men value attractiveness in a long-term mating partner and universally prefer to mate with women who are, on average, younger than themselves. *True or False?*

14. Twin studies have revealed that if one identical twin is homosexual, there is an approximately 50% chance that the other twin will share the same sexual orientation. *True or False?*

Expressing and Experiencing Emotion

Let's return for a moment to the brief story that opened the chapter. You're suddenly attacked—control of your freedom and your life has been transferred to a criminal seeking money and the thrill of violence. Your mind and body react rapidly: your heart rate, blood pressure, and respiration rate all shoot upward. Your facial expression adopts a characteristic grimace, one that would be easily recognized across the world. Inside, you have the subjective experience of confusion, pain, and fear. Behaviorally, your body slumps downward, as you contemplate the possibility of struggle. You are in the midst of experiencing and expressing the most powerful of human capacities—*emotion*.

As we discussed at the beginning of this chapter, an emotion is a complex psychological event that involves a mixture of reactions: (1) a *physiological response* (usually arousal), (2) an *expressive reaction* (distinctive facial expression, body posture, or vocalization), and (3) some kind of *subjective experience* (internal thoughts and feelings). Each of these components, which are shown in Figure 11.5, can be measured, although some, especially the subjective-cognitive reaction, are difficult to measure reliably.

Why experience emotions in the first place? The general belief among psychologists is that emotions help us adapt to rapidly changing environmental conditions. Emotions are powerful motivators of behavior—they help us prioritize our thoughts and they force us to focus on finding problem solutions. Physiological arousal, for instance, prepares the body for "fight or flight" and helps us direct and sustain our reactions in the face of danger. Through expressive behaviors, such as the characteristic facial grimace of anger, it's possible to communicate our mental state instantly to others. Emotions can even stimulate social behaviors. People perform better and are more likely to help others when they feel happiness (Hoffman, 1986); people are also more likely to volunteer aid after doing something for which they feel guilt (Carlsmith & Gross, 1969).

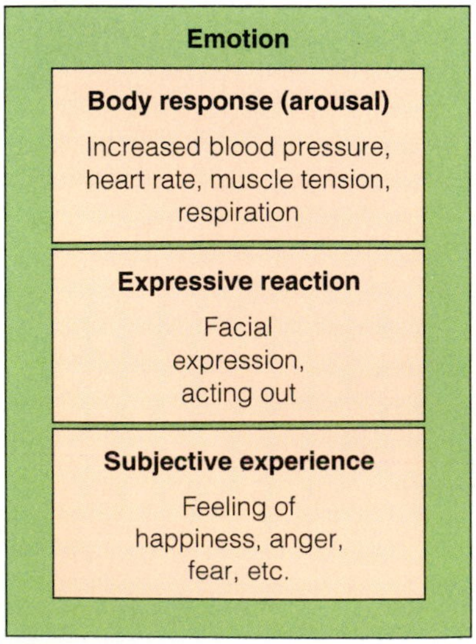

ARE THERE BASIC EMOTIONS?

The English language is full of words, literally hundreds in fact, that relate in one way or another to emotions. But are there hundreds of emotions, or just a basic few? This is an important question, but it's a difficult one to answer. To get a sense of the difficulty, try compiling your own list of basic emotions. While you're at it, ask your friends and see how much you agree. Let's see: anger, fear, joy . . . how about interest, loathing, jealousy, or distraction? Psychologists have been compiling their own lists for decades, but no general consensus has been reached.

If forced to choose, most people (including emotion researchers) agree on about a half-dozen. Most lists include anger, fear, happiness, and sadness, for example (Ortony & Turner, 1990). Researchers who believe that such emotions are basic, or universal, argue convincingly that certain emotions, such as anger, increase the chances of survival. People also have no trouble recognizing expressions of anger, fear, sadness, and happiness in other people. For example, Paul Ekman and his colleagues asked volunteers to match photographs of grimacing, smiling, or otherwise provocative facial displays to a number of basic emotion labels. There was wide agreement on six fundamental emotions: happiness, surprise, fear, sadness, anger, and disgust combined with contempt (Ekman, 1992; Ekman & Friesen, 1986).

Facial Expressions and Culture

Regardless of where you look in the world, people recognize that facial expressions are associated with certain emotional states. For example, a furrowed brow and a square mouth with pursed lips signify anger worldwide (Boucher & Carlson, 1980; Ekman & Friesen, 1975). In one case, Ekman and Friesen (1975)

LEARNING GOALS

1. Identify the basic components of an emotion and discuss their adaptive value.

2. Discuss the evidence for and against basic emotions.

3. Discuss the role that arousal plays in the emotional experience.

4. Describe the subjective experiences of anger and happiness.

5. Differentiate among the James-Lange, Cannon-Bard, and two-factor theories of emotion.

Emotion

Body response (arousal)

Increased blood pressure, heart rate, muscle tension, respiration

Expressive reaction

Facial expression, acting out

Subjective experience

Feeling of happiness, anger, fear, etc.

FIGURE 11.5

The Components of Emotion

Emotions are complex experiences involving (1) a *physiological response;* (2) an *expressive reaction;* and (3) some kind of *subjective experience.*

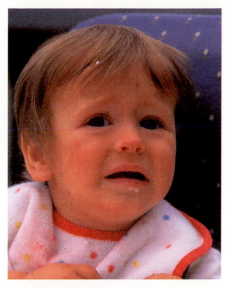

Different emotions are often associated with particular facial expressions. Can you identify the emotion expressed in each of these photos?

even tested members of a rural, isolated culture in New Guinea. These people had no experience with Western culture, yet they correctly identified the emotions expressed in photographs of Caucasian faces. Similarly, when U.S. college students were later shown photos of the New Guinea people acting out various emotions, they too were able to identify the emotions with a high degree of accuracy. Although it's not clear that emotion labels necessarily mean the same thing across cultures (Russell, 1994), most researchers are convinced that there is universal recognition of emotion from facial expressions (Ekman, 1994; Izard, 1994).

The cross-cultural results are important because they suggest that the expression of emotion may have a biological or genetic origin. Babies show a wide range of emotional expressions at a very young age (Izard, 1994), and even babies who are born blind, or hearing-impaired and blind, show virtually the same facial expressions as sighted babies (Eibl-Eibesfeldt, 1973). It appears then that people may purse their lips and furrow their brow when they're mad because these tendencies are built directly into the genetic code, rather than having been learned. The idea that there are universal facial expressions certainly makes adaptive sense; as noted before, facial expressions are excellent signals to others about our current internal state (Ekman & Keltner, 1997).

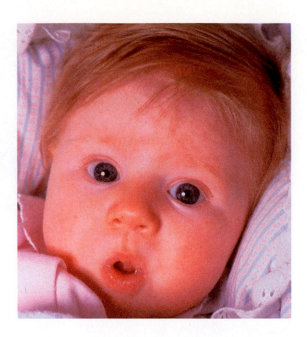

Babies show a wide range of emotional expressions at very young ages.

The Facial-Feedback Hypothesis

Some researchers have argued that feedback from the muscles in the face may even determine the internal emotional experience. According to the **facial-feedback hypothesis,** muscles in the face deliver signals to the brain that are then interpreted, depending on the pattern, as subjective emotional states (Tomkins, 1962). Other researchers point out that there may be direct connections between expressions and physical changes in the brain. For example, smiling can alter the volume of air that is inhaled through the nose; these changes, in turn, can affect the temperature of the brain which, in turn, might affect mood (McIntosh et al., 1997; Zajonc et al., 1993).

The facial-feedback hypothesis makes the unique prediction that if people are asked to copy a particular facial expression, they should experience a corresponding change in emotionality. Indeed, forced smiling, frowning, or grimacing does appear to modulate emotional reports, although the effects may be small (Matsumoto, 1987). You can try this for yourself: Try forcing yourself to smile or grimace in an exaggerated way. Do you feel any different? Some therapists recommend that clients who are depressed literally force themselves to smile when they are feeling depressed.

How Convincing Is the Evidence?

The link between facial expressions, biology, and emotion seems to support the idea that certain emotions are universal. But does the fact that people have similar facial expressions for fear, anger, or happiness really allow us to conclude that these emotions are somehow more primary or basic than others? Some psychologists think not. Remember, many psychologists disagree about which emotions belong on the basic list. Do interest, wonder, or guilt belong? How about shame, contempt, or elation? Each of these terms has been identified as basic by at least one prominent emotion researcher. The problem is that humans are capable of an enormous range of emotional experiences. Consider the differences between fear, terror, panic, distress, rage, and anxiety. It is clearly appropriate to use any of these terms in some circumstances and not in others. How can we explain a complex emotion such as terror? If it's not a basic emotion, is it somehow manufactured in the brain by combining or blending more fundamental emotions like fear, surprise, and possibly anger?

Psychologists Andrew Ortony and Terence Turner (1990; Turner & Ortony, 1992) believe that it's not possible to explain the diversity and complexity of

? CRITICAL THINKING

Have you ever heard actors talk about how they "become the role" when they're playing emotional parts? What might a psychologist tell an actor to help him or her understand why this happens?

facial-feedback hypothesis
The proposal that muscles in the face deliver signals to the brain that are then interpreted, depending on the pattern, as a subjective emotional state.

Inside the Problem   The Emotion of Disgust

You arrive home late, tired and slightly irritated after a hard day's work. You flip on the lights in your bathroom and glance downward at your red and gold toothbrush, still lying face up on the side of the sink. There, nestled in the slightly frayed bristles, sits a cockroach. Reluctant to move, the insect waves its feelers at you—a perverse sort of greeting. The mirror captures your reaction: You wrinkle your nose and your mouth drops open in a characteristic gape. Internally, arousal coupled with nausea rise up as your mind plots the exact form of its soon-to-be expressive behavior. What you are experiencing, of course, is a highly adaptive, usually food-related emotion known as *disgust.*

If there is a core group of basic emotions, *disgust,* a marked aversion toward something distasteful (literally meaning "bad taste"), is a likely candidate for inclusion. It's easy to appreciate why this emotion is an important tool for the adaptive mind, especially as a mechanism to ensure that we select and reject the appropriate foods. The facial expression that typically accompanies disgust is itself an adaptive reaction to a potentially harmful substance: Wrinkling the nose closes off the air passages, cutting off any offending odor; the gaping expression "causes the contents of the mouth to dribble out" (Rozin & Fallon, 1987).

But in recent years, researchers have come to recognize that there is a psychology to the emotion of disgust that extends beyond its role in food rejection. To illustrate, consider this question: What are the odds that you're going to use that toothbrush again? Suppose I were to drop it into boiling water for a period to ensure sterilization. Would you use it now? Probably not by choice. In a study by Paul Rozin and his colleagues, a dead but sterilized cockroach was dropped into a glass of juice and offered to thirsty subjects. Not surprisingly, few people showed any interest in drinking the juice, even though they knew the roach had been sterilized (Rozin et al., 1986). Most people are also reluctant to consume their favorite soup if they witness the bowl being stirred by a never-used comb or fly swatter (Rozin & Fallon, 1987).

Would you brush your teeth with this toothbrush?

What accounts for these effects? According to some researchers, we are likely to succumb to what has been called *sympathetic magic* (Frazer, 1890/1959; Mauss, 1902/1972; Rozin & Fallon, 1987). People tend to believe that when two objects come in contact, they acquire like properties. The juice acquires some of the disgusting properties of the cockroach, perhaps through a process akin to contagion. The soup becomes associated with flies, even though you know that the fly swatter has never come into contact with a fly. Objects apparently need only to be associated with other disgusting objects to cause an emotional reaction. These are not conscious rational processes at work here, although they may be thought processes that are fundamental and common to all people (Rozin & Fallon, 1987). (It may also be that classical conditioning is involved—some kind of higher-order association may be formed between the juice, for example, and an object that elicits disgust [see Chapter 7]).

The experience of disgust seems to be universal—appearing cross-culturally—but the emotion takes a while to develop in all of its various forms. For example, if children under age 4 are presented with what adults would consider to be a disgusting odor (feces or synthetic sweat), they tend not to be bothered, or they may even react positively (Stein et al., 1958). Children under age 2, as any parent knows, are happy to put just about anything into their mouths, even "disgusting" objects. In one study, it was found that 62% of tested children under age 2 would put imitation dog feces in their mouth; 31% would mouth a whole, sterilized grasshopper (Rozin et al., 1986). Children simply have no conception that these objects are potentially harmful—they must learn what not to put in their mouths.

It also apparently takes a while for the idea of object contamination to become ingrained in people's minds. You won't brush your teeth with a toothbrush that once housed a cockroach, but a 7-year-old might. Children of this age typically report that a drink has been returned to normal after a disgusting object has been removed (Fallon et al., 1984). In several studies, children under the age of 7 were quite willing to drink a beverage after the experimenter simply removed an object like a fly—they were even willing to drink if a tiny bit of the disgusting object remained in the bottom of the glass (see Rozin, 1990, for a review). Notions about contagion and contamination clearly develop with experience and may even require the child to reach a certain developmental stage.

human emotional experiences by manipulating and combining a set of basic emotions. Rather than basic emotions, they argue, it's better to think of basic response components that are *shared* by a wide variety of emotional experiences. For example, the furrowed brow commonly seen in anger is not exclusive to anger but occurs as well when people are frustrated, puzzled, or even just working hard on a task. The furrowed brow may occur in any situation in which a person is somehow blocked from reaching a goal; its appearance, by itself, is not sufficient to infer that the person is angry.

It may help to think about the analogy of human language. There are hundreds of different languages across the world, and each follows certain universal rules (relating to sound and word combinations). But it doesn't make any sense to argue that some of these languages are more basic than others. Human languages are built up from basic components and share many features in common. But the components—the rules of sound and meaning—are not themselves languages (Ortony & Turner, 1990). Similarly, when people are in the grip of an emotion, they may experience many basic and universal conditions (such as a tendency to smile or frown, approach or avoid), but these are merely the components of emotion, not the emotions themselves.

THE EMOTIONAL EXPERIENCE: AROUSAL

Psychologists may disagree about whether there are basic emotions, but everyone agrees about certain aspects of the emotional *experience*. Virtually all emotions, for instance, lead to *physiological arousal*. Muscles tense, heart rate speeds up, and blood pressure and respiration rates skyrocket. These emotional symptoms arise from activity of the autonomic nervous system as it prepares the muscles and organs of the body for a fight or flight response. We usually experience emotions in situations that are significant for one reason or another—for instance, the car of a drunken driver swerves sharply into our path, or the sound of breaking glass from the basement window startles us awake. It's adaptive for the body to react quickly in such cases, and the rapid onset of physiological arousal serves that function well.

Arousal and Performance

The relationship between arousal and performance is not simple and direct—emotional arousal can have a negative side as well. Too much arousal can lead to a breakdown in behavioral, biological, or psychological functioning. Figure 11.6 shows the relationship that exists between level of arousal and task performance. Notice that the pattern looks like an arch or an inverted U. For a given task, as arousal levels increase from low to moderate levels, performance generally rises. Some people perform better under pressure—the track star runs a little faster or jumps a little higher. You may well perform better on a test if the test is particularly important. But too much pressure, which leads to too much arousal, leads to a sharp drop-off or breakdown in task functioning. Did you have trouble thinking when you took the SAT? Too much emotional pressure can create a level of arousal that hurts rather than helps normal mental functioning.

Understanding the relationship between arousal and performance has helped psychologists interpret behavior in a variety of situations. For example, you may remember from Chapter 8 that people who witness crimes are sometimes inaccurate in their later recollections. One factor that contributes to these inaccuracies is the high level of arousal generated when someone witnesses a crime. If someone is holding a gun to your head, your arousal levels are so high that you are incapable of normal cognitive processing. You are simply too aroused to process the details of the crime scene in a manner that will lead to effective remembering. Moreover, as you'll see in Chapter 13, the relationship between arousal and performance also helps us to understand how our behavior changes in the presence of other people—our performance is either facilitated or impaired when other people are around, perhaps because the presence of others changes our overall level of arousal.

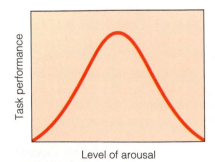

FIGURE 11.6

Arousal and Task Performance
For a given task, performance tends to be best at intermediate levels of arousal. Too little or too much arousal often leads to a decrease in performance.

The Polygraph Test

The link between emotions and arousal naturally led researchers to assume that arousal could be used as a reliable index of emotional experience. If you're experiencing an emotion, your body ought to show the characteristic patterns of physiological arousal. The lie detector, or **polygraph test,** is a good example of this kind of logic in action. The polygraph is not a mysterious and magical device that measures truth—there's no secret location in the brain, chest, or fingertips that sends up a red flag when you're lying (Lykken, 1998). The polygraph test simply measures mundane things like heart rate, blood pressure, breathing rate, and whether or not you're sweating. The assumption behind the test is that lying leads to greater emotionality, which can then be picked up through measurements of general physiological arousal.

In a polygraph test the critical comparisons are made between the arousal levels produced by what are called *relevant* and *control* questions. Testers understand that people might become aroused just from taking the test, whether they're lying or not, so testers are mainly interested in comparing how arousal levels change across different question types. During the test, you're typically asked a series of neutral questions to establish a kind of baseline arousal level ("What's your name?" and so on). In some cases, the tester may even ask you to lie on purpose—to answer with the wrong day of the week or with someone else's name—to get a record of how your body responds when you do, in fact, lie. Relevant questions are then asked about a specific event ("Did you change the bank records?"), and the examiner compares the amount of recorded arousal with the various baseline controls.

But remember, "polygraph pens do no special dance when we are lying" (Lykken, 1998), so conclusions about truthfulness need to be interpreted with caution. There are two main problems. First, these tests are relatively easy to beat. If you can control your arousal responses—and many hardened criminals feel little, if any, guilt about their crimes—it's possible to pass the test even if you're lying. Clever criminals can also mask lying by increasing their level of arousal on control questions—perhaps by pinching themselves or biting their lip; if arousal levels on the control questions are high, the critical difference between the readings on relevant and control questions will be reduced. If arousal levels are similar across the different question types, the criminal is likely to pass the test.

The second problem with the polygraph test is that it leads to frequent false positives. Innocent people are judged to be lying when, in fact, they are telling the truth. Estimates of the frequency of false positives vary from study to study, but they may go as high as 75% (Saxe, 1994). This is a significant problem. Consider that even if testers falsely accused people of lying only 5% of the time, that would still mean 50 out of 1000 people might be falsely accused of a crime. If the error rate was higher, say 50%, then perhaps 500 of those 1000 people would be falsely accused of a crime. For these reasons, the U.S. Congress passed the Employee Polygraph Protection Act of 1988, which bans the use of polygraph tests as a screening criterion for employment (although certain drug and security companies, and government agencies, are not covered by the ban). In addition, most courtrooms do not currently allow the results of polygraph tests to be used as evidence for guilt or innocence.

THE EMOTIONAL EXPERIENCE: SUBJECTIVE REACTIONS

Experiencing an emotion involves much more than just a facial expression or a flood of physiological arousal. Your thoughts, your perceptions, the things you notice in the environment—all change when you experience an emotion. But as

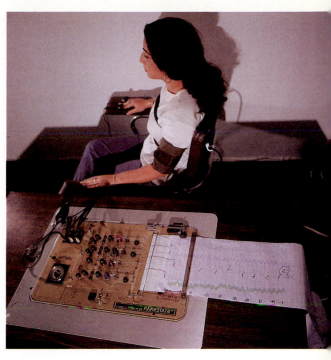

This woman is undergoing a polygraph test, which is based on the idea that lying leads to greater emotionality that can then be picked up through measurements of general physiological arousal.

CRITICAL THINKING

Do you think people make distinctive facial expressions when they lie?

polygraph test
A device that measures various indices of physiological arousal in an effort to determine whether someone is telling a lie. The logic behind the test is that lying leads to greater emotionality, which can be picked up through such measures of arousal as heart rate, blood pressure, breathing rate, and sweating.

we discussed before, it's difficult to measure the internal experience accurately and reliably. After all, the emotional experience is by definition personal and subjective. We can ask someone to report what it feels like to be angry, happy, or scared, but the natural constraints of language restrict the answers we receive. Some cultures don't even have a word in their language to describe the concept of an emotion. The Ifaluks of Micronesia, for example, have only the word *niferash*, which roughly translates as "our insides" (Lutz, 1982; Matsumoto, 1994).

Anger

It is possible to study the conditions that lead to the experiencing of emotions. For example, in the case of *anger*, people have been asked to keep daily and weekly records, noting the specific situations that led to the emotion. Most people get angry at least several times a week (but to different degrees); some experience the emotion several times a day (Averill, 1983). Again, anger clearly can serve an adaptive function: It causes us to tackle our problems head on, express our grievances, and it also serves as signal to others that they should change their ways or avoid interaction.

What causes anger? Not surprisingly, the causes are many. If you're restrained in some way, physically or psychologically, you're likely to get mad (Reeve, 1992). More generally, people tend to get angry when their expectations are violated. If you're counting on someone to act a certain way or on a place or thing to deliver certain rewards, and these expectations are violated, you will probably get mad. This is one of the reasons we often get angry at the ones we love. We tend to expect more from the people we love which, in turn, increases the chances that our expectations will be violated.

Is the expression of anger healthy psychologically? Psychologists remain undecided about the benefits of "venting" anger or blowing off steam. On the one hand, expressing your feelings may have a cathartic effect: The expression of anger can lead to an emotional release that is ultimately calming. On the other hand, getting physically angry could well increase the chances that you'll get angry again (Tavris, 1989). When you express anger, and feel the calming effect that follows, you reinforce or reward the anger response. Some psychologists have found that encouraging people to express their feelings of anger or hostility leads to more expressions of anger in the future (Ebbesen et al., 1975). The expression of anger can also lead to increased risk-taking and other kinds of self-defeating behavior (Leith & Baumeister, 1996). (We'll return to the effects of anger, specifically on stress and health, in Chapter 16.)

Happiness

The idea that anger arises from violations of expectations also helps account, in part, for the experience of *happiness*. Overall, there is little, if any, relationship between observable characteristics such as age, sex, race, or income and the experience of happiness (Myers & Diener, 1995). Instead, people seem to gain or lose happiness as a result of the comparisons they make—either with others (a well-known tendency called *social comparison*) or with things or experiences from their past. People set standards for satisfaction, and they're happy to the extent that these standards are maintained or surpassed. The trouble is that our standards are constantly changing—Eddie and Lucinda may be able to keep up with the Joneses next door, but there's always the Mendenhalls down the street who just bought that new boat. Once people obtain one level of satisfaction, they form a new one and thereby immerse themselves in a spiral that never quite leads to utopian bliss.

Actually, many psychological judgments, not just emotions, arise from comparisons with some standard, or *adaptation level*. You may recall from Chapter 5 that whether people will hear one tone as louder than another depends on how loud the standard tone is to begin with. Human judgments are relative—there is no sense in which a tone is "loud," a light is "bright," or a person is "happy" or "sad" without answering the question "Relative to what?" The fact that the sub-

Despite what you might think, winning 6 million dollars in the lottery does not necessarily guarantee future happiness.

jective experience of happiness is relative helps explain some seemingly inexplicable phenomena. Why is that couple who just won the multimillion-dollar lottery still bickering? Why is Ed, who recently succeeded in getting the most popular girl in class out on a date, now anxiously seeking the amorous attentions of someone else? How can that homeless man, with only scraps to eat and tattered clothes, wake up every morning with a smile on his face? Happiness is not an absolute Holy Grail that can be sought and sometimes found—it's an elusive and fickle condition that depends on constantly changing standards and comparisons.

THEORIES OF EMOTION: BODY TO MIND

We've seen that emotions are complex events. People subjectively experience happiness or sadness, but they also experience important changes in their body and on their face. Questions about how these various components interact have perplexed emotion researchers for decades. For example, what exactly causes the bodily reaction? Is the arousal caused by the internal subjective experience, or is someone happy or sad because his or her body has been induced to react in a particular way?

There are a number of possible explanations (for an overview, see Figure 11.7 on page 452). The most natural argument is that the subjective experience drives the physiological reaction. People tremble, gasp, and increase their heart rate because some event has caused them to become afraid. They detect the grasp of an arm around their neck, they feel fear, and their body reacts with physiological arousal. Surprisingly, this straightforward view of emotion has been essentially rejected by emotion researchers for over a century. William James (1890) saw the commonsense view as backward. In his own words: ". . . The more rational statement is that we feel sorry because we cry, angry because we strike, afraid because we tremble, and not that we cry, strike, or tremble because we are sorry, angry, or fearful" (p. 1066). Although James did not deny that one's interpretation of the situation is also important (Ellsworth, 1994; James, 1894), he believed that the body reaction occurs before the subjective experience of emotion, rather than the other way around.

The James-Lange Theory

The idea that the body reaction drives the subjective experience of emotion became known as the **James-Lange theory** of emotion. Lange is coupled with James because Danish physiologist Carl Lange proposed a similar idea at roughly the same time as James. Why reject the commonsense approach in favor of such

James-Lange theory
A theory of emotion that argues that body reactions precede and drive the subjective experience of emotions.

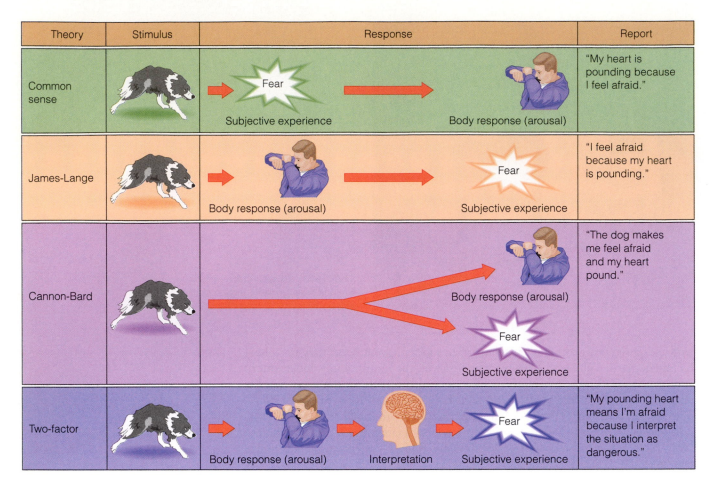

Theory	Stimulus	Response			Report
Common sense		Fear Subjective experience	→	Body response (arousal)	"My heart is pounding because I feel afraid."
James-Lange		Body response (arousal)	→	Fear Subjective experience	"I feel afraid because my heart is pounding."
Cannon-Bard				Body response (arousal) Fear Subjective experience	"The dog makes me feel afraid and my heart pound."
Two-factor		Body response (arousal)	Interpretation	Fear Subjective experience	"My pounding heart means I'm afraid because I interpret the situation as dangerous."

FIGURE 11.7

Four Views of Emotion

The *commonsense* view, largely rejected by psychologists, assumes that an environmental stimulus creates a subjective experience (fear), which in in turn leads to a physiological reaction (arousal). The *James-Lange theory* proposes instead that the physical reaction drives the subjective experience. In the *Cannon-Bard theory*, the physical reaction and the subjective experience are assumed to be largely independent processes. In *two-factor theory*, it is the cognitive interpretation and labeling of the physical response that drives the subjective experience.

a counterintuitive view? Actually, neither James nor Lange presented much evidence in support of this account (other than personal impressions). However, there are some significant predictions that can be derived from the view. For instance, imagine that we could somehow reduce or eliminate significant body reactions. The James-Lange theory predicts that we should lose the corresponding experience of emotion. To test this idea, a number of interviews have been conducted with people suffering from spinal cord injuries. Because of nerve damage, these people have either lost feeling in major portions of their bodies or at least have reduced sensory feedback. In support of the James-Lange view, some paraplegics report a corresponding drop-off in the intensity of their emotional experience (for example, anger loses its "heat") (Hohmann, 1966). But at least some strong emotional feelings remain intact despite the loss of body feedback (Lowe & Carroll, 1985).

The James-Lange theory also predicts that unique physical changes should accompany each of the different emotional experiences. That is, a particular body response must produce anger, happiness, fear, and so on. But as we noted before, the dominant physiological response during an emotion is *arousal*, and heart rate changes, sweaty palms, and increased breathing rate seem to be characteristic of virtually all emotions rather than just a select few. Think about how your body feels just before an important exam. Do you notice any similarities with the feelings that you get before an important and long-awaited date? Would you describe the emotions as similar?

Recently, however, sophisticated measuring devices have enabled researchers to record small, previously undetectable changes in body reactions. These new data may eventually help us to distinguish the body reaction for one emotional state from the body reaction of another (Lang, 1994; Levenson, 1992). It turns out that anger, fear, and sadness, for example, may lead to greater heart rate acceleration than an emotion such as disgust; there is also apparently a greater increase in finger temperature during fear than during anger (Levenson, 1992). PET scan studies also reveal differences in the patterns of brain activation when people experience different emotions (Lane et al., 1997). Establishing definitive links between emotional states and physiological responses is an important step for emotion researchers, although perhaps not an unexpected one. After all, anger and happiness certainly are experienced differently and therefore must ultimately reflect differences in brain activity.

The Cannon-Bard Theory
Historically, it didn't take too long for critics of the James-Lange theory of emotion to emerge. Physiologist Walter Cannon mounted an influential attack in the 1920s. Cannon (1927) recognized that the body reacts in essentially the same way to most emotional experiences. He also argued that the conscious experience of emotion has a rapid onset—people feel fear immediately after seeing an attacking dog—but the physiological reactions that arise from activity of the autonomic nervous system have a relatively slow onset time (glands need to be activated, hormones need to be released into the bloodstream, and so on). Cannon felt that the subjective experience of emotion and the associated body reactions are *independent processes*. Emotions and arousal may occur together, but one doesn't cause the other. Cannon's view was later modified somewhat by Philip Bard, so this approach is now generally known as the **Cannon-Bard theory** of emotion.

The Schachter and Singer Experiment
You've now been exposed to three different theories of emotion: (1) people experience emotions subjectively, which then leads to body reactions such as arousal (the commonsense view); (2) the body generates a characteristic internal reaction, which then produces the appropriate emotional experience (James-Lange); and (3) body reactions and subjective experiences occur together, but independently (Cannon-Bard). None of these views remains popular among modern emotion researchers.

The major problem with this trio of emotion theories is that they fail to take into account the cognitive side of emotion. To understand exactly what this means, you need to consider a rather complex study that was conducted in the early 1960s by psychologists Stanley Schachter and Jerome Singer (see Figure 11.8 on page 454). College students were recruited to participate in an experiment that they thought was designed to test the effects of vitamin injections on vision. What the subjects didn't know, however, was that the vitamin cover story was a ploy—rather than vitamins, they were actually injected with either a dose of epinephrine (which produces physiological arousal symptoms) or a dose of saline (which produces no effects). A second manipulated variable was subject expectation: Half the subjects in each of the injection groups were told to expect arousal symptoms—it's a side effect of the vitamins, you see—and the other half were told to expect no reaction of any kind.

Now let's consider what effect these conditions might be expected to have on emotional reactions. Suppose you're sitting in a room, waiting for further instructions from the experimenter, when suddenly your heart begins to race and your palms begin to sweat. According to James-Lange, this arousal should translate into some kind of emotional experience; you might, for example, expect to become scared or irritated. But what Schachter and Singer (1962) found was that the experience of emotion was determined virtually entirely by expectation. Those subjects who were told to anticipate arousal from the injection showed little emotional reaction to the arousal when it occurred. Only when the arousal was unexpected did people begin to report robust experiences of emotion.

Even more interesting, Schachter and Singer were able to influence the qualitative aspects of the emotion when it occurred. Joining the subject in the waiting

Cannon-Bard theory
A theory of emotion that argues that body reactions and subjective experiences occur together, but independently.

FIGURE 11.8

The Schacter and Singer Experiment
Volunteer subjects were injected with a drug that produced physiological arousal symptoms. Half the subjects were informed about the drug's effects; the other half were not. When placed in a room with either a euphoric or an angry accomplice, only the uninformed subjects adopted the mood of the accomplice. Presumably, the informed subjects interpreted their arousal symptoms as due to the drug, whereas the uninformed subjects interpreted the arousal symptoms as an emotional experience.

two-factor theory
A theory of emotion that argues that the cognitive interpretation, or appraisal, of a body reaction drives the subjective experience of emotion.

room was a disguised member of the experimental team, introduced as another participant in the experiment. Unknown to the real subject, the accomplice was instructed to act in a fashion that was either playful and euphoric or angry and disagreeable. In later assessments of mood, Schachter and Singer found that aroused but uninformed subjects tended to adopt the mood of the accomplice. If the accomplice was playful, the subjects reported feeling happy; if the accomplice was angry, the subjects reported feeling irritation.

Two-Factor Theory

The results of the Schachter and Singer experiment led to the proposal of what is known as **two-factor theory** of emotion. In two-factor theory, autonomic arousal is still a critical determinant of the emotional experience (factor 1). But equally important is the *cognitive appraisal* or *interpretation* of that arousal when it occurs (factor 2). An intense body reaction may be necessary for the full experience of an emotion, but it's not sufficient. It's how you *interpret* the arousal that ultimately determines your subjective emotion. Thus, you're scared when you face an out-of-control bakery truck not only because your body is aroused, but also because your mind understands that the source of the reaction is dangerous. You *label* the arousal and thereby determine the emotion that is experienced.

Like the other theories of emotion we've discussed, two-factor theory has generated its share of criticism. Some researchers have failed to replicate certain of the Schachter-Singer results (Reisenzein, 1983). Other researchers have complained that some of the original findings failed to reach acceptable levels of statistical significance (Marshall & Zimbardo, 1979). However, it is possible to draw several tentative conclusions. First, it's reasonably clear that arousal contributes to the experience of emotion. Second, the situation in which the arousal occurs, and our expectations about the source of the arousal, contribute to the emotional experience. Third, rather than saying that the body reaction creates the emotion, or vice versa, it's better to conclude that emotions arise from *interactions* among several sources: the stimulus event that leads to the reaction, autonomic changes in arousal, and the expectation-based cognitive labels applied to everything involved.

? CRITICAL THINKING

If expectations play an important role in determining whether an emotion will be experienced, would you expect to find cultural differences in the expression of emotion?

TEST YOURSELF 11.4

Check your knowledge about expressing and experiencing emotion by answering the following questions. (You will find the answers in the Appendix.)

1. For each of the following, pick the component of emotion that best fits the situation: body response, expressive reaction, or subjective experience.

   a. Sally likes to dance when she's happy: _____

   b. Yolanda grimaces and wrinkles her nose when she sees spaghetti with clam sauce: _____

   c. Mei feels her heart start racing whenever she sees her boyfriend approach: _____

   d. Robert would rather use the words "delighted, glad, pleased, and excited" to describe how he feels, instead of the word "happy": _____

2. Which of the following situations is most likely to produce happiness?:

   a. Receiving a B on a test when you were expecting a C

   b. Receiving an A on a test when you were expecting an A

   c. Receiving a C on a test when you were expecting to flunk

   d. Stimulation of the ventromedial hypothalamus

3. For each of the following, pick the theory of emotion that best fits the situation: James-Lange, Cannon-Bard, or two-factor.

   a. I love it when my heart starts racing because it makes me feel happy: _____

   b. I must be in love because she just gave me a wink and my heart is racing: _____

   c. I really feel happy right now and, by the way, my heart is also racing: _____

   d. You're not really in love, you just drank too much coffee this morning: _____

Solving the Problems

Your adaptive mind is designed to initiate, direct, and control behavior. Motivation, and its intimate companion, emotion, are vehicles that enable you to accomplish these things—to react to sudden changes in the environment, to maintain your internal energy needs, and even to prolong the species. There are certain things that each of us simply *must* do—consume food, drink liquids, maintain a constant internal temperature—and psychologists have struggled for decades to discover appropriate ways to describe the mechanisms that ensure our accomplishment of them.

Activating Behavior. As you've seen, motivation depends on an interplay between internal and external factors. Much of the time behavior is controlled by internal factors that compel us in the direction of a goal. Our bodies are constantly monitoring internal energy levels, and once a disruption in the homeostatic balance is detected, we feel hungry or thirsty and seek to restore the appropriate balance. In these cases, it's likely that motivated behavior arises directly as a consequence of biological factors and requires no direct experiences with the environment.

But even something as biologically significant as eating or drinking cannot be explained by appealing just to innate internal factors. All forms of motivated behavior are

influenced by external factors also. External rewards, or incentives, exert powerful pulling and guiding effects on our actions. Understanding motivation then becomes a matter of specifying how these *external* factors interact with *internal* factors to activate and control behavior. One way in which internal and external factors interact is described by Maslow's notion of a need hierarchy. The essential component of Maslow's theory is the prioritizing of need: Some needs, especially those critical to survival, must be satisfied before others, such as the need for self-actualization, can be pursued.

Meeting Biological Needs: Hunger and Eating. What are the internal and external sources that initiate and control eating? Internally, the body monitors everything from the amount and content of food in the stomach to the level of glucose in the blood in order to determine its energy needs. If the level of glucose falls below a certain level, for example, you start to feel hungry and seek out food. Although researchers are uncertain about its precise role in controlling eating, the hypothalamus is believed to play an important role in initiating and controlling eating. But we also eat for reasons that appear unrelated to restoring homeostatic balance. Food, and particularly eating, is clearly reinforcing. As you've seen, people are much more likely to motivate themselves to eat if they like the food—the vigor or intensity with which they respond

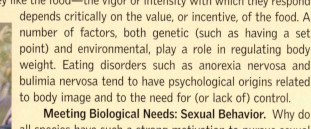

depends critically on the value, or incentive, of the food. A number of factors, both genetic (such as having a set point) and environmental, play a role in regulating body weight. Eating disorders such as anorexia nervosa and bulimia nervosa tend to have psychological origins related to body image and to the need for (or lack of) control.

Meeting Biological Needs: Sexual Behavior. Why do all species have such a strong motivation to pursue sexual activity? Sexual activity is adaptive for a species because it increases the likelihood that the species will continue. But on an individual level, sex is also reinforcing, and sexual desire compels us to pursue a mate, thereby opening the door for companionship, protection, and love. The sexual response itself consists of four main phases (excitement, plateau, orgasmic, and resolution). Hormones appear to play much less of a role in controlling sexual desire in humans when compared with other animals. Different cultures have different views of attractiveness and different codes of conduct for sexual activity. Many psychologists believe that people acquire sexual scripts that instruct them on how, why, and what to do in their interactions with potential sexual partners. Mate selection and sexual orientation, however, are probably influenced by biological as well as environmental factors.

Expressing and Experiencing Emotion. Emotions typically involve a mixture of reactions, including a physiological response (arousal), a characteristic expressive reaction (such as a distinctive facial expression), and some kind of subjective experience (such as the feeling of happiness or sadness). The physical expression of an emotion allows us to communicate our feelings to others. The internal components—arousal, for example—prepare us for action. Thoughts become prioritized, and muscles are ready to respond. Emotions are powerful adaptive tools: They not only increase the likelihood of survival, but also, for many, make life itself worth living.

The internal subjective experience of emotion is often relative—whether we feel happy, for example, seems to depend on the comparisons we make with others and with our past experiences. Although a number of theories have tried to explain the relation between arousal and the experience of emotion, most psychologists believe that the experience of emotion depends partly on the presence of a body response—general arousal—and partly on the cognitive appraisals one makes about the origin of arousal when it occurs.

Motivation and Emotion Chapter Summary

Activating Behavior

Any organism that seeks to survive in an ever-changing environment must be able to react quickly to its needs, anticipating future outcomes and acting accordingly.

INTERNAL FACTORS: INSTINCT AND DRIVE

Instincts are unlearned, characteristic patterns of responding that are controlled by specific triggering stimuli in the world. Instincts do not adequately explain human behavior. A *drive* is a psychological state that arises in response to a physiological need. The body is designed to seek stable and constant internal conditions through a process termed *homeostasis*.

ACHIEVEMENT MOTIVATION

The *achievement motive* pushes you to seek success and significant accomplishment in your life. People who rate high in achievement motivation tend to work harder and more persistently on tasks. How hard you work on a task depends on your expectations about whether you will be successful, and how much you value success on the task. Cultural factors play a role in achievement motivation and gender-related differences.

MASLOW'S HIERARCHY OF NEEDS

Maslow's *need hierarchy* provides a prioritizing of needs. Usually represented as a pyramid, the theory proposes that certain fundamental needs (biological "musts") take priority; once fulfilled, we seek to fulfill more personal security, spiritual, and relationship needs. At the top of the hierarchy is the need for self-actualization (reaching one's potential).

EXTERNAL FACTORS: INCENTIVE MOTIVATION

External rewards exert powerful "pulling" effects on behavior. Psychologists use the term *incentive motivation* to explain goal-directed behavior. Whereas drives serve as an internal "push," incentives serve as an external "pull." Motivation is determined jointly by both internal and external factors.

INTRINSIC MOTIVATION

Psychologists use the term *intrinsic motivation* to describe situations in which behavior seems to be entirely self-motivated. Externally provided rewards can lower a person's intrinsic motivation for a task. One explanation for this is that a reward may be perceived as controlling behavior. Another account is that external rewards lead to *overjustification;* you conclude that you're engaging in the behavior because of the reward, rather than because you enjoy doing it.

Meeting Biological Needs: Hunger and Eating

Eating is a critical part of living. Both internal and external cues help activate and control eating.

INTERNAL FACTORS CONTROLLING HUNGER

A number of internal signals influence when and why we eat. The contents of the stomach is one such signal. Also, levels of *glucose* and *insulin* are monitored. It's likely that a glucose-insulin interaction is monitored because both substances play a role in metabolic processes. Brain regions also play a role in signaling hunger. Early research isolating the *ventromedial hypothalamus* and *lateral hypothalamus* as "stop eating" and "start eating" centers was overly simplified. Later research has indicated that the brainstem and hippocampus are also involved.

REGULATING BODY WEIGHT

Some researchers suggest that we have a *set point* (natural body weight) that controls our tendency to gain or lose weight. The set point is probably genetically determined. The causes of *obesity* are varied and complex; a combination of biological and psychological factors including set point, metabolic rate, and learned eating habits are involved.

EXTERNAL FACTORS

We often eat for reasons not related to restoring internal homeostatic balance. Our eating behavior is partially determined by our eating habits, and food cues, such as the sight of food and its association with past pleasures.

EATING DISORDERS

People's assessment of their own weight and its relation to societal standards are typically inaccurate and help promote a negative body image. This increases susceptibility to the eating disorders *anorexia nervosa* (in which a person refuses to maintain a healthy body weight due to a fear of being overweight) and *bulimia nervosa* (binge eating coupled with purging to control body weight).

Meeting Biological Needs: Sexual Behavior

Although sexual activity is not necessary for individual survival, adequate sexual performance is needed for survival of the species. There are internal and external cues that help motivate an interest in sex.

The Sexual Response Cycle

The human sexual response cycle comprises four phases: *excitement*, *plateau*, *orgasmic* and *resolution*. The resolution phase features a *refractory period* when stimulation fails to produce further signs of arousal or orgasm.

External Factors

Sexual desire can also be explained by appealing to the incentive value or "pull" of someone attractive. Touch is one important external source of sexual arousal; stimulation of *erogenous zones* is highly arousing for most people. Also, *pheromones* (chemicals released by the females of many species during periods of receptivity) play a role in producing sexual arousal, but not necessarily in humans.

Sexual Orientation

Sexual orientation refers to whether a person is sexually and emotionally attracted to members of the same sex or the other sex. Research suggests that sexual orientation may be at least partly determined by biological factors. The environment plays an important role as well.

Internal Factors

For much of the animal kingdom, sexual behavior is controlled by internal (hormonal) mechanisms. Humans also show cyclic variation in hormones related to sex and reproduction (*estrogens* in females, *androgens* in males). But human sexual behavior is actively under our control, although influenced by learned and cultural factors.

Mate Selection

What people consider attractive in a mate is strongly influenced by cultural factors. According to one theory, as we grow we acquire *sexual scripts* that instruct us on how, why, and what to do in our sexual encounters. In spite of differences in our scripts, there are fundamental similarities among people. In nearly every culture, men are more likely than women to pursue short-term sexual strategies (i.e., brief affairs). Men are likely to value attractiveness in their mate, while women place greater emphasis on financial prospects.

Expressing and Experiencing Emotion

Are There Basic Emotions?

Most people agree on about a half-dozen basic emotions, typically including anger, fear, happiness, and sadness. Recognition of certain basic facial expressions of emotions seems to be universal, suggesting that expression of emotion may have a biological or genetic origin. Some researchers have argued that the feedback from muscles in the face may determine the internal emotional experience (the *facial feedback hypothesis*). Some psychologists remain unconvinced that certain emotions are "basic" and "universal." One alternative idea is that there are basic response components shared by a wide variety of emotional experiences.

The Emotional Experience: Anger and Happiness

The emotional experience is personal and subjective. Anger is typically associated with the violations of one's expectations. The value of "venting" one's anger is a controversial issue. Some psychologists have found that encouraging people to express anger or hostility leads to experiencing more anger in the future, along with increased risk-taking and self-defeating behaviors. *Happiness* seems to rely on the comparisons we make—with others or with things or experiences from our past. Many psychological judgments (like emotions) arise from comparisons with some *adaptation level*.

The Emotional Experience: Arousal

Emotions are associated with *physiological arousal*. The relationship between arousal and performance is complex. The general relationship is an "inverted U function"; extremely high or low levels of arousal are likely to disrupt performance. The measurement of arousal serves as the basis for the *polygraph test*. The purpose of a polygraph test is to determine whether someone is being truthful or lying. However, polygraphs are fairly "easy to beat" and do produce a fair number of false positives.

Theories of Emotion: Body to Mind

The most natural way to relate emotion to body and mind is to assume that the subjective experience drives the physical reaction. The *James-Lange theory* assumes the opposite—that the body reaction drives the subjective experience of emotion. This theory predicts that unique physical changes should accompany different emotions, and this is typically not the case. The *Cannon-Bard theory* proposed that the subjective experience of emotion and associated body reactions are independent processes that occur together. Schacter and Singer proposed two-factor theory, which assumes that emotion is a product of autonomic arousal and cognitive appraisal of that arousal. Recent data seem to support some version of two factor theory.

Terms to Remember

motivation, 422
emotions, 422

ACTIVATING BEHAVIOR

instincts, 424
drive, 425
homeostasis, 425
incentive motivation, 426
achievement motive, 426
intrinsic motivation, 428
need hierarchy, 429

MEETING BIOLOGICAL NEEDS: HUNGER AND EATING

glucose, 431
insulin, 432
ventromedial hypothalamus, 432
lateral hypothalamus, 432
set point, 435
obesity, 435
anorexia nervosa, 436
bulimia nervosa, 436

MEETING BIOLOGICAL NEEDS: SEXUAL BEHAVIOR

excitement phase, 438
plateau phase, 438
orgasmic phase, 438
resolution phase, 438
sexual scripts, 441
sociobiology, 441
sexual orientation, 442

EXPRESSING AND EXPERIENCING EMOTION

facial-feedback hypothesis, 446
polygraph test, 449
James-Lange theory, 451
Cannon-Bard theory, 453
two-factor theory, 454

Recommended Readings

Damasio, A. R. (1994). *Descartes' error*. New York: G. P. Putnam's Sons. A very stimulating account of intelligent decision-making, including the adaptive role that emotions play in human behavior.

LeDoux, J. E. (1996). *The emotional brain*. New York: Simon & Schuster. A very readable discussion of possible biological mechanisms connected to the experience and display of emotion.

Capaldi, E. D. (Ed). (1996). *Why we eat what we eat*. Washington DC: American Psychological Association. A broad collection of chapters, written by leading researchers, covering all aspects of eating and food selection.

INFOTRAC® COLLEGE EDITION

For additional readings, explore Infotrac College Edition, your online library. Go to:
http://www.infotrac-college.com/wadsworth

Hint: enter the search terms: Achievement motivation, Intrinsic motivation, Eating disorders, Sexual drive, Sexual orientation, Happiness, Anger.

What's on the Web?

Center for Eating Disorders

http://www.eating-disorders.com/

This informative site provides a great deal of helpful information about eating disorders, as well as other health-related issues. Find out the answers to some of these questions: How does body image distortion relate to eating disorders? What is the history of eating disorders? What's the relationship between exercise and eating disorders?

American Polygraph Association

http://www.polygraph.org/

This is the home page for the "other APA" (NOT the American Psychological Association!). This APA is "dedicated to providing a valid and reliable means to verify the truth and establish the highest standards of moral, ethical, and professional conduct in the polygraph field." This is a great site to visit if you're curious about the practice of "lie detecting" with polygraphs. Find answers to the following questions: Who uses polygraph examinations? What factors lead to errors in polygraph results? Is voice stress analysis a valid indicator of lying?

The Kinsey Institute

http://www.indiana.edu/~kinsey/

Everything you wanted to know about sexuality, but were afraid to ask! This is the official Web site (housed at Indiana University) of the famous institute, founded by one of the pioneers of human sexuality research. The institute "supports interdisciplinary research and the study of human sexuality." The site includes a wealth of information about and links to other sites dealing with "sexology."

The Wadsworth Psychology Study Center Web Site

See http://psychology.wadsworth.com/ for practice quiz questions, hypercontents, updates, critical thinking exercises, discussion forums and more! The Wadsworth Psychology Study Center provides a wealth of information fully organized and integrated by chapter.

Personality

I t is the curse of humankind, reasoned Dr. Henry Jekyll, that within every human spirit lies not one but truly two persons. On the one hand is the moral and intellectual side, capable of uplifting achievement; on the other, the dark side resides—the unrepentant seeker of pleasure. If only these two natures could be housed in separate identities, Jekyll speculated, the unjust could walk free, relieved of the strict sensibilities of its bothersome twin. The moral arm could seek knowledge and truth without succumbing to the evil tendencies of the flesh. As the smoking ebullition in the glass subsided, he raised the glass to his lips and drank. . . .

In *The Strange Case of Dr. Jekyll and Mr. Hyde*, Robert Louis Stevenson explores the dual nature of human personality through the characters of Jekyll and Hyde. Actually one and the same man, Dr. Jekyll transforms himself into the troublesome Mr. Hyde, the personification of evil, by drinking a potion composed of salts and other wholesale chemicals. If you read the novel, you'll see that the results are disastrous for them "both," but the thesis is a fascinating one for the psychologist to consider. How reasonable is it to assume that behavior is controlled by fixed psychological characteristics or traits? This may seem like a given to you, but the issue is actually quite controversial among psychologists. Moreover, assuming these traits exist, is it fair to describe them as "good" or "evil"—are humans, like Luke Skywalker in *Star Wars*, actively engaged in an unrelenting battle against the dark side of their nature? As you'll see in this chapter, some psychologists have argued that there are indeed multiple sides to human nature, and these sides are engaged in a kind of constant internal battle.

Our topic in this chapter is **personality**, which can be defined as the distinguishing pattern of psychological characteristics—thinking, feeling, and behaving—that differentiates us from others and leads us to act consistently across situations. At its core, the study of personality, like the study of intelligence, is first and foremost the study of individual differences (Cronbach, 1957). People seem to differ in lasting ways: Rowena is outgoing, confident, and friendly; Roger is shy in social settings and has an annoying habit of lying. In a very real sense, personality **traits,** or predispositions to respond in certain ways, define people. Traits make people unique, identifiable, and generally predictable across time. Potentially, we can use them to explain why Rowena and Roger remain stable and consistent in their actions across situations.

personality
The distinguishing pattern of psychological characteristics—thinking, feeling, and behaving—that differentiates us from others and leads us to act consistently across situations.

trait
A stable predisposition to act or behave in a certain way.

Previewing the Conceptual and Practical Problems

I t's difficult to treat a topic such as personality as a simple solution to an adaptive problem, like eating or communicating internally. Personality is something that psychologists infer from behavior in an effort to explain why people differ and to help predict how someone might act in a given context. Of course, consistency in behavior is likely to have considerable adaptive value. It's useful to maintain at least some stable tendencies in our behavioral and cognitive repertoire, especially if they lead to actions that are successful. Many researchers believe that we possess traits such as fearfulness or aggressiveness because those traits motivate us to act in ways that increase the likelihood of survival (Buss, 1988; Buss & Shackelford, 1997).

Our focus in this chapter will be on how psychologists have attempted to resolve the conceptual and practical problems that are central to the study of personality. As you read this chapter, think back to the issues we considered in Chapter 10 (intelligence)—there are many similarities between the study of intelligence and the study of personality.

One of the tasks facing those who study personality is to determine whether any single instance of behavior, such as the helping behavior shown by this man, represents an enduring trait of the individual—something that applies in lots of situations.

Do all people have a "dark side" to their personality, waiting to be expressed by the right environmental conditions? Is it possible that mass murderer Henry Lee Lucas, shown here in prison along with photographs of his victims, was simply born with the wrong kind of genes?

First, what is the proper way to conceptualize and measure the traits that make us both consistent and unique? To understand the concept of personality, it's necessary to consider the whole person. This means that you can't simply record the actions of someone in a restricted situation, or even in several situations. You need to measure the *enduring* aspects of behavior—those things that distinguish one person from another consistently across time. To use the analogy of one personality researcher, the proper focus should be on "not one time at bat in baseball but the season's hitting average, not an evening's flirtation or adventure but marriage or an enduring relationship" (Buss, A.H., 1989). Unfortunately, as you'll see, there is no simple way of addressing this problem.

Second, why do personality traits develop? What factors in development lead to stable and consistent behaviors? It's one thing to identify and measure a person's lasting traits, but quite another to understand their origin. Where do personality traits come from, and what accounts for the individual differences? Why does Roger have that nasty tendency to lie, and why does sweet Rowena always see the sunny side of a rotten situation? It is here, in the study of personality development, that you'll find some of the most ambitious and best-known attempts at psychological theory.

Third, are personality characteristics expressed in a way that is independent of the environment? As you know, virtually all types of human behavior are influenced by the environment. All major theories of personality assume that the environment shapes behavior; where they differ is in the degree to which the environment is important and in the mechanisms through which the environment exerts its influence. However, since personality consists of those traits that remain the same across situations, we are faced with a kind of theoretical puzzle. In essence, personality should be a psychological characteristic that is largely independent of the environment. Remember, people are supposed to act the same regardless of the situation. Is behavior really as consistent across situations as many people, including psychologists, assume? In the final section of the chapter, we'll discuss the evidence—and controversy—that bears on this issue.

Conceptualizing and Measuring Personality

It's not necessary to have a well-developed theory of personality to identify and measure differences among people. In fact, it could be argued that we need some formal way of classifying individual differences before we can know what needs to be explained. **Trait theories** are systems for assessing how people differ, particularly how people differ in their tendencies to act consistently across situations. As a general rule, trait theories use a *psychometric approach*—that is, they seek to identify stable individual differences by analyzing the performances of large groups of people on a series of rating tests or questionnaires.

If you open up any dictionary, you'll find thousands of words that fit the everyday definition of a personality trait. In fact, it's been estimated that approximately 1 out of every 22 words in the English language is a trait-related term (Allport & Odbert, 1936). One goal of the trait theorist is to try to reduce these thousands of descriptive terms into a smaller set of more basic terms—to find a kind of common denominator among groups of terms. For example, when you describe someone with words like *kind, trusting,* and *warm,* you might really be tapping into some more general characteristic of the person, such as agreeableness or pleasantness (Goldberg, 1993). The researcher attempts to identify the basic traits from among the thousands of personality descriptors that are common in the language. How can this be accomplished?

THE FACTOR ANALYTIC APPROACH

One way to approach the problem is to use the statistical technique of *factor analysis*. As we discussed in Chapter 10, factor analysis is a mathematical procedure that is used to analyze correlations among test responses. The goal is to identify a set of factors that in combination do a reasonable job of predicting test performance. To see how this works in the case of personality, imagine that we ask a large group of people to rate themselves on 100 personality characteristics. For example: "On a scale of 1 to 7, how well do you think the term *brooding* is characteristic of you?" If each person provides 100 rating responses, we will undoubtedly see many individual differences. Some people will see themselves as brooders, others won't; some people will score high on aggressiveness and competitiveness; others will classify themselves as passive and shy.

However, the real question of interest centers on how the trait ratings correlate with one another. Do people who rate themselves as, say, *kind* also tend to rate themselves as *warm* and *trusting?* More specifically, can we predict someone's rating on one trait given that we know his or her rating on some other trait? If we can, then it may be reasonable to assume that some higher-level personality characteristic, such as *pleasantness,* is being tapped by the more specific personality descriptors. This is the logic behind factor analysis—discover the common denominators for personality by noting which terms cluster statistically in a group. Once these factors are identified, they should in principle help predict someone's behavior, or at least explain why an individual acts consistently from one situation to the next.

Cattell's Source Traits

Psychologists frequently apply factor analysis to personality data. For practical reasons, it's most common to rely on ratings of personality descriptors, such as *kind* or *warm,* which people give about themselves or others. Psychologist Raymond Cattell, for example, was able to use rating data of this sort to identify 16 basic personality factors from a set of traits that originally numbered in the thousands (Cattell et al., 1970). Cattell's 16 factors, which he called *source traits,* are listed in Figure 12.1. Notice that each factor is shown as a dimension marked by an opposing pole: reserved–outgoing, trusting–suspicious, relaxed–tense, and so

trait theories
Formal systems for assessing how people differ, particularly in their predispositions to respond in certain ways across situations. Most trait theories rely on psychometric tests to identify stable individual differences among people.

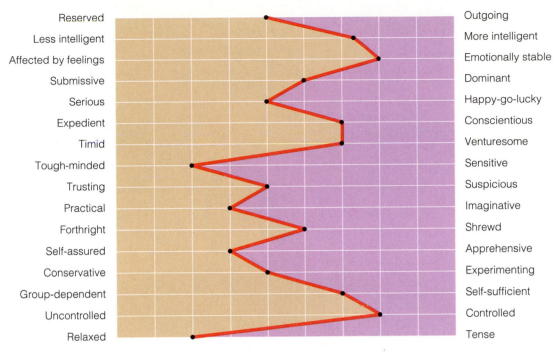

Reserved	Outgoing
Less intelligent	More intelligent
Affected by feelings	Emotionally stable
Submissive	Dominant
Serious	Happy-go-lucky
Expedient	Conscientious
Timid	Venturesome
Tough-minded	Sensitive
Trusting	Suspicious
Practical	Imaginative
Forthright	Shrewd
Self-assured	Apprehensive
Conservative	Experimenting
Group-dependent	Self-sufficient
Uncontrolled	Controlled
Relaxed	Tense

FIGURE 12.1

A Personality Profile
This is a sample personality profile as measured by Cattell's 16 Personality Factor test. Notice that an individual's personality is defined by his or her standing on each of the 16 trait dimensions. (From Cattell, 1973.)

on. Any particular individual, such as you, will have a unique personality profile, reflecting your standing on each of the dimensions.

Eysenck's Superfactors

However, the set of factors that are discovered by the researcher depends partly on how the mathematical technique of factor analysis is applied. Whereas Cattell reported 16 primary factors (along with some additional secondary or second-order factors), Hans Eysenck has argued that the basics of personality can be better described by appealing to only 3 factors: (1) the dimension of *extroversion*, which refers roughly to how outgoing and sociable you are; (2) the dimension of *neuroticism*, which captures your degree of anxiety, worry, or moodiness; and (3) the dimension of *psychoticism*, which represents your tendencies to be insensitive, uncaring, or cruel toward others (Eysenck, 1970, 1991). Specific personality descriptors, such as *touchy* or *lively*, are presumed to reflect some combination of a person's standing on each of the three primary dimensions, or *superfactors* (see Figure 12.2 on page 468).

The Big Five

How can we explain the fact that researchers like Cattell and Eysenck differ so strongly about the number and types of basic personality dimensions? A simple answer is that Eysenck and Cattell are operating at different levels of analysis: Eysenck, with his 3 primary dimensions, is interested in mapping out the more general aspects of human personality, whereas Cattell's analytic techniques paint a more fine-tuned description (see Feist, 1994). But increasingly, researchers seem to be settling on a more intermediate solution: It is now widely believed that the best solution to the factoring problem is to propose 5 basic personality dimensions (McCrae & Costa, 1985; Wiggins & Pincus, 1992).

The so-called **Big Five** personality dimensions include *extroversion, agreeableness, conscientiousness, neuroticism*, and *openness*. Each is listed in Figure 12.3 (on page 468) along with some of the descriptors that identify each trait. So, for example, people who score highly on the extroversion dimension tend to see themselves as talkative, sociable, fun-loving, and affectionate. Notice that *extroversion* and *neuroticism* are 2 of the 3 primary dimensions suggested by Eysenck; if you look closely, you'll also find considerable overlap with the factors suggested by Cattell.

Big Five
The five dimensions of personality—extroversion, agreeableness, conscientiousness, neuroticism, and openness—that have been isolated through the application of factor analysis; it is widely believed that virtually all personality terms in language can be accounted for by appealing to one or more of these basic dimensions.

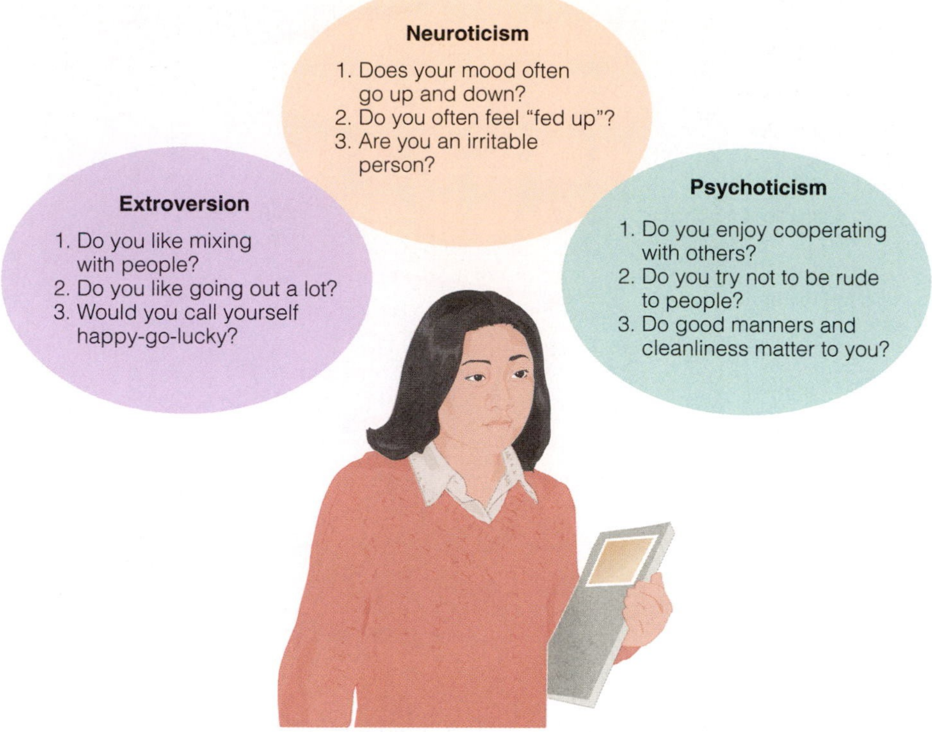

FIGURE 12.2

Eysenck's Three Primary Dimensions of Personality

Hans Eysenck proposed three primary dimensions of personality: extroversion, neuroticism, and psychoticism. Included in each circle are sample questions of the type used to measure a person's standing on that dimension. (Questions from Eysenck, 1975.)

Neuroticism
1. Does your mood often go up and down?
2. Do you often feel "fed up"?
3. Are you an irritable person?

Extroversion
1. Do you like mixing with people?
2. Do you like going out a lot?
3. Would you call yourself happy-go-lucky?

Psychoticism
1. Do you enjoy cooperating with others?
2. Do you try not to be rude to people?
3. Do good manners and cleanliness matter to you?

FIGURE 12.3

The Big Five

Many psychologists believe that personality is best analyzed in terms of five fundamental personality dimensions: extroversion, agreeableness, conscientiousness, neuroticism, and openness.

Why 5 instead of 3 or 16? Part of the reason is technical, having to do with what current researchers believe is the most appropriate way to apply the factor analytic technique (see Digman, 1990 or Goldberg, 1993). But there are other reasons. For example, a number of studies have analyzed trait ratings collected from people around the world. Regardless of the language used—and different languages can have quite different personality descriptors—there still appear to be 5 basic dimensions that best explain the ratings (Digman, 1990; McCrae & Costa, 1997). Many psychologists find the cross-cultural data to be quite convincing; the data suggest that the basic structure of personality may be universal rather than dependent on cultural background (McCrae et al., 1996). At the same time, the fact that 5 factors can be used to categorize people doesn't tell us anything about

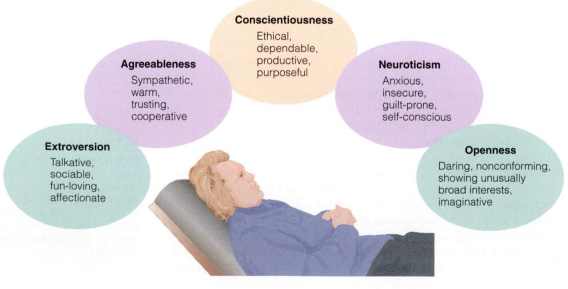

Conscientiousness
Ethical, dependable, productive, purposeful

Agreeableness
Sympathetic, warm, trusting, cooperative

Neuroticism
Anxious, insecure, guilt-prone, self-conscious

Extroversion
Talkative, sociable, fun-loving, affectionate

Openness
Daring, nonconforming, showing unusually broad interests, imaginative

the internal processes that determine a personality profile. To truly understand personality, some critics argue, you need to understand the ability of people to *change* as well as stay the same across situations (Epstein, 1994; Mischel & Shoda, 1998). We'll discuss how the environment affects the consistency of behavior later in the chapter.

ALLPORT'S TRAIT THEORY

Like the factor analysts, psychologist Gordon Allport (1897-1967) was convinced that all people possess certain underlying personality traits, or "predispositions to respond." But he was less convinced that the building blocks of personality could be gleaned from massive statistical analyses of group responses. Allport believed that person-

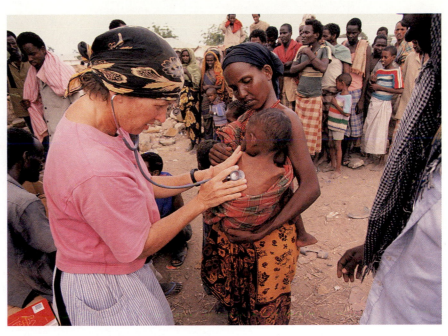

Cardinal traits are the ruling passions that dominate a person's life, such as a compelling need to help others at the expense of personal comfort.

ality, in essence, is a measure of one's uniqueness as an individual. So, the proper focus should be on individuals, he argued, not groups. His approach, which he called *idiographic* (which means "relating to the individual"), was to study particular individuals in great detail. An advantage of this kind of case study approach is that consistencies in behavior can be recorded across an entire lifetime rather than just in a limited setting (Barenbaum, 1997).

One of Allport's main contributions was his general classification scheme for identifying personality traits (Allport, 1937). Allport believed that some people display what he called *cardinal* personality traits. **Cardinal traits** are the ruling passions that dominate an individual's life. If you spend your life huddled in a mountain monastery, rejecting all worldly possessions, your passion "to serve god" would likely satisfy Allport's description of a cardinal trait. Perhaps you know someone whose every thought or action seems to revolve around the pursuit of wealth, fame, or power. People with cardinal traits do not represent the average—these people are driven and highly focused; every action appears to be motivated by some particular goal. Notice that we can't really capture something like a cardinal trait by applying a technique such as factor analysis, because cardinal traits are uniquely defined by the individual rather than the group.

Allport believed that cardinal traits are rare. Most people have personalities that are controlled by several lasting characteristics, which Allport labeled as *central* traits. **Central traits** are the five to ten descriptive terms that you would probably use to describe someone you know. Rowena? She's outgoing and friendly, very trustworthy, sentimental at times, and honest to the core. In addition to central traits, Allport suggested that everyone has **secondary traits,** which are less obvious because they may not always appear in an individual's behavior. For example, Rowena might also have a secondary trait of "testiness" that shows up only when she goes on an extended diet. Personality characteristics, therefore, can appropriately be described in terms of *levels* ranging from dominant (cardinal) to representative (central) to occasional (secondary).

PERSONALITY TESTS

Trait theories have been developed to uncover the basic dimensions of human personality. Trait researchers try to find the essential factors, or building blocks, that in combination produce distinguishing patterns of psychological characteristics. But there are practical reasons why it's important to measure personality

? CRITICAL THINKING

When comparing Allport's approach to the factor analytic approach, think back to our discussions in Chapter 2. What are the advantages and disadvantages of using case studies, which examine single individuals, versus surveys, which rely on responses from large groups?

cardinal traits
Allport's term to describe personality traits that dominate an individual's life, such as a passion to serve others or to accumulate wealth.

central traits
Allport's term to describe the five to ten descriptive traits that you would use to describe someone you know—friendly, trustworthy, and so on.

secondary traits
The less obvious characteristics of an individual's personality that do not always appear in his or her behavior, such as testiness when on a diet.

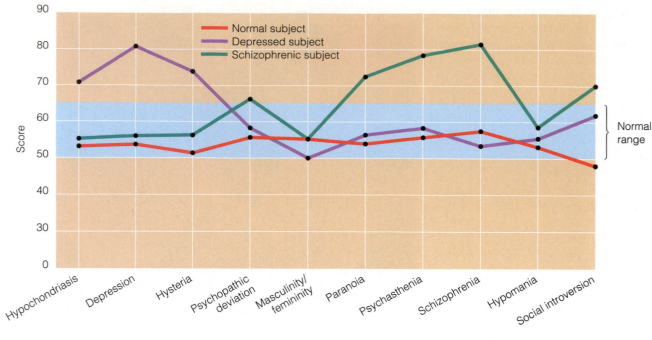

FIGURE 12.4

MMPI Profiles

The MMPI is often used to help psychologists diagnose psychological disorders. A client's scores on the various clinical scales can be compared to average scores from people who are not suffering from psychological problems, as well as from people who have been diagnosed with specific problems (such as depression or schizophrenia). (Adapted from Weiten, 1995.)

self-report inventories
Personality tests in which people answer groups of questions about how they typically think, act, and feel; their responses, or self-reports, are then compared to average responses compiled from large groups of prior test takers.

16 Personality Factor
A self-report inventory developed by Cattell and colleagues to measure normal personality traits.

NEO-PI-R
A self-report inventory developed to measure the Big Five personality dimensions.

Minnesota Multiphasic Personality Inventory (MMPI)
A widely used self-report inventory for assessing personality traits and for diagnosing psychological problems.

traits—reasons that are unrelated to general psychological theory. Suppose you're the personnel director at a large nuclear power plant. You need to hire responsible people to run the plant, people who have the right stuff to handle potentially dangerous materials in an emergency. You wouldn't want to hire someone like Roger, with his tendency to lie and act compulsively under pressure. How do you make the proper determination for a given individual? You can choose from two main categories of personality tests: *self-report inventories* and *projective tests.*

Self-Report Inventories

Self-report inventories use a paper-and-pencil format to identify personality characteristics. People are asked to answer groups of questions about how they typically think, act, and feel. Their responses, or *self-reports*, are scored objectively, and the results are then compared to test averages that have been compiled from the performances of thousands of other test takers. As a general rule, self-report inventories are easy to administer, and they paint a reasonably reliable picture of how someone differs from the average. Roger, for instance, would probably raise red flags on a number of measures; his answers are likely to show some disregard for social customs (compared to the average) and a marked tendency toward impulsiveness. If you were the personnel director, you could easily make your hiring—or more accurately, "no hire"—decision based on the test results.

Many kinds of self-report inventories are employed by professionals. Some tests are based on popular trait theories. For example, to assess normal personality traits you can administer the **16 Personality Factor,** which is a 187-item questionnaire designed to measure the 16 primary personality factors identified by Cattell (Cattell et al., 1970). Alternatively, there is the **NEO-PI-R,** which is designed to measure your standing on the Big Five personality traits identified in Figure 12.3 (NEO-PI-R stands for Neuroticism Extroversion Openness-Personality Inventory–Revised). However, the most widely used self-report inventory is the **Minnesota Multiphasic Personality Inventory (MMPI).** The MMPI requires test takers to answer hundreds of true-false questions about themselves (e.g., "I never get angry"), and it's now available in several revised forms (see Butcher, 1995). An individual's answers are expressed in a personality profile that describes his or her scores on various subscales (see Figure 12.4).

Besides measuring personality characteristics, the MMPI is often used as a technique for diagnosing psychological disorders. A person's responses are compared to those of average test takers but also to the responses of individuals with known psychological problems. There are records, for example, of how people who suffer from such disorders as paranoia (irrational beliefs of persecution) are likely to answer certain questions. The test responses of someone like Roger can then be compared with the average "paranoia" personality profile to see if he fits the bill. Comparisons of this sort are useful in diagnosing problems and in making judgments about how appropriate an individual might be for a high-risk form of employment.

The main advantage of self-report inventories is that they are objective tests—they're standardized, everyone takes the same test, and they can easily be scored by a computer. There have been literally thousands of studies conducted testing the reliability and validity of these measures, especially the MMPI (Helms & Reddon, 1993). The fact that the MMPI is one of the most widely applied measures in clinical assessment is a testament to its usefulness (Butcher & Rouse, 1996). At the same time, self-report inventories depend on the accuracy of the information provided by the test taker. If people choose to be deceptive on the test, or try to make themselves look good in some way, the results can be of limited usefulness (Nichols & Greene, 1997).

Projective Personality Tests

Psychologists also sometimes use what are called projective personality tests. In a **projective personality test,** you're asked to interpret an unstructured or ambiguous stimulus. The underlying idea is that you will "project" your thoughts and true feelings into the stimulus interpretation, thereby revealing elements of your personality. For example, take a look at the inkblot shown in Figure 12.5, which is similar to the kind of unstructured stimulus used on the **Rorschach test.** Clearly, you argue, the inkblot exemplifies the fundamental decay of human society. The image symbolizes the need for aggressive action on the part of all responsible people—we must rise up and defeat the tyranny that, like an out-of-control cancer, is eating away at the virtue and values of common folk. Right? Well . . . Can you see how someone's interpretation of such a stimulus might provide insight into aspects of his or her personality? If Roger always sees snakes and decaying dragons in the images, whereas Rowena sees butterflies and flowers, it's not too difficult to infer that they have quite different personality characteristics.

Another popular projective personality test is the **Thematic Apperception Test (TAT).** Instead of an inkblot, you're shown an ambiguous picture, such as the one shown on page 472, and are asked to make up a story. What's happening? What are the characters in the picture thinking and feeling?, and so on. Again, the idea is that you will reveal aspects of yourself in the stories and interpretations you tell. Both the TAT and the Rorschach test use a standardized set of stimuli, so an individual's responses can be compared to other people who have interpreted the same picture. Many clinical psychologists prefer to use tests like the TAT or the Rorschach, rather than self-report inventories like the MMPI, because projective tests help clients open up and talk about themselves and their problems.

Projective tests allow you to respond freely, in a manner that is less restrictive than the requirements imposed by self-report inventories. But this can create problems of interpretation: How do we know what your responses mean? Psychologists have tried to develop reliable standards for interpreting responses in these kinds of tests. Typically, the researcher or clinician is trained to look for common themes in interpretation (such as a tendency to see death, decay, or aggressiveness) or for qualities such as originality (Edberg, 1990; Hurt et al., 1995). The clinician might also look for such things as the realistic nature of the interpretation: Does the response really match the perceptual structure of the stimulus? If you claim to see a dragon in an inkblot like the one in Figure 12.5,

FIGURE 12.5
Projective Tests

In projective personality tests, we are asked to interpret unstructured or ambiguous stimuli. Our answers are presumed to provide insight into personality. What do you see hidden in this inkblot—the fundamental decay of human society? (From Kalat, 1996.)

projective personality test
A type of personality test in which individuals are asked to interpret unstructured or ambiguous stimuli; the idea is that subjects will project their true thoughts and feelings into the interpretation, thereby revealing elements of their personality.

Rorschach test
A projective personality test that requires people to interpret ambiguous inkblots.

Thematic Apperception Test (TAT)
A projective personality test that requires people to make up stories about the characters in ambiguous pictures.

This image, taken from the Thematic Apperception Test, can be interpreted in many ways. What do you think the characters in the picture are thinking and feeling? Your answers may tell us something about your personality.

Henry A. Murray, *Thematic Apperception Test*, Cambridge, Mass.: Harvard University Press, Copyright © 1943 by the President and Fellows of Harvard College, © 1971 by Henry A. Murray.

your general view of the world may slant toward fantasy rather than reality. The degree to which you seek help in your interpretation may also be instructive. For example, individuals who constantly seek guidance from the clinician before giving an answer are likely to be classified as dependent.

Again, none of the personality assessment procedures we've discussed is perfect, neither self-report inventories nor projective tests. The scoring procedures for projective tests still tend to be somewhat unreliable; it's not uncommon for administrators to arrive at quite different interpretations of the same subject's responses (see Beutler & Berren, 1995). Questions about the validity of the interpretations have also been raised: Do these tests really measure the key features of personality? Even with these criticisms, however, both categories of personality test remain extremely popular (Butcher & Rouse, 1996).

TEST YOURSELF 12.1

Check your knowledge about conceptualizing and measuring personality by answering the following questions. (You will find the answers in the Appendix.)

1. For each of the following, identify the personality dimension of the Big Five that the statement best describes. Choose from the following terms: extroversion, agreeableness, conscientiousness, neuroticism, openness.

    a. Joanne is known as a risk-taker; she just loves to bungie jump: _____

    b. It's hard to get Mimi to stop talking: _____

    c. Roger is very cooperative; he's virtually always sympathetic to my needs: _____

    d. Mark is very insecure; he always seems to feel guilty about something: _____

    e. Maureen is very productive and she has very high ethical standards: _____

2. For each of the following, pick the personality test that the statement best describes. Choose from the following: MMPI, NEO-PI-R, 16 Personality Factor, Rorschach, TAT.

a. An ambiguous picture is shown and the client is asked to make up a story about its contents: _____

b. An objective self-report inventory that is often used in clinical settings: _____

c. A test used primarily to measure someone's standing on the Big Five: _____

d. A projective personality test using standardized inkblots as stimuli: _____

e. Designed to create a personality profile representing Cattell's source traits: _____

Determining How Personality Develops

As you've just seen, we can describe the personality traits of people like Roger or Rowena—perhaps their standing on the Big Five—and there is a good chance that our measurements will be reasonably accurate and reliable. But description is not the same thing as explanation. We may know that Rowena has a bright and sunny disposition, but the trait theories provide little insight into the origin of those characteristics. Why do Roger and Rowena differ? What mechanisms in the mind produce and maintain those differences?

In this section we'll consider three quite different approaches to understanding personality development: the psychodynamic theory of Sigmund Freud, humanistic theories, and cognitive–behavioral theories. Each claims that individual uniqueness comes from the operation of general psychological principles. We're not unique or consistent in our behavior by accident or chance; rather, there are processes at work inside our head, or in the external environment, that shape and mold our actions. In each case, your personality is a product of general adaptive processes that help you initiate and control behavior in widely different situations.

THE PSYCHODYNAMIC APPROACH OF FREUD

Consider the following scenario. You're a practicing clinician and your latest patient, 18-year-old Katharina, complains of persistent physical problems. "I'm often overcome with a frightful choking feeling," she insists. "I have trouble catching my breath, my head begins to spin, and I truly think I must be about to die." Extensive examinations reveal no physical cause; the attacks appear suddenly without warning and seem unrelated to activity or general health. Katharina herself provides no insight: "There's nothing in my head when the attacks begin; my mind is a blank." The only additional information you have about Katharina is that she's reluctant to involve herself with members of the opposite sex and she has a persistent dream in which she appears as a young child pursued from room to room by a shadowy figure.

Think about this case study for a moment. Can you draw any general conclusions about Katharina's personality from an analysis of her symptoms? The case itself is typical of the kinds of clinical problems that Sigmund Freud (1856–1939) faced in the late nineteenth century. As you learned in Chapter 1, Freud was a medical doctor by training. He established a private practice in Vienna, where he specialized in a branch of medicine concerned with disorders of the nervous system. Freud routinely encountered patients like Katharina, who seemed to have physical problems without physical causes. He used these cases (they were known in that

Sigmund Freud is shown here in 1891, at a time when he was becoming increasingly convinced that certain physical problems may have psychological origins.

time as *hysterics*) as the basis for his highly influential **psychodynamic theory** of personality and mind, as well as for his method of treatment known as *psychoanalysis*.

The Structure of Mind

Freud believed that the human mind could be divided into three major parts: the *conscious*, the *preconscious*, and the *unconscious*. The **conscious mind** consists of the contents of current awareness—those things that occupy the focus of your attention at the moment. As you read the words on this page and think about Freud's theory, you are using the processes of the conscious mind. The **preconscious mind** contains inactive but accessible thoughts and memories—those things that you could easily recall, if desired, but are simply not thinking about at the moment. Consider the word *aardvark*—it's unlikely that you were thinking about this word moments ago; but as I draw your attention to the word, it changes from a preconscious to a conscious state. Finally, the **unconscious mind** houses all the memories, urges, and conflicts that are beyond awareness. Freud was convinced that the contents of the unconscious mind exert powerful and long-lasting influences on behavior, despite the fact that they are hidden and unavailable to consciousness.

From Freud's perspective, Katharina's panicky behavior is almost certainly caused by forces originating in her unconscious. Consider her repetitive dream of being chased through her house by a shadowy figure. She can remember the details of the dream—her appearance as a young child, perhaps the color and shapes of the rooms—but her conscious memory of the dream, according to Freud, is likely to be superficial and misleading. The parts of the dream that she remembers, its *manifest content*, are merely symbolic of the dream's true unconscious meaning, or *latent content*. As we discussed in Chapter 6, according to Freud dreams represent a mental mechanism for wish fulfillment; dreams are simply one way that the mind attempts to gratify desires or deal with forbidden conflicts that are normally stored in the unconscious. In Katharina's case, the pursuing shadowy figure may well have arisen from a traumatic childhood experience—perhaps an unwelcome sexual advance by a relative—or even from her own unconscious desire for a forbidden sexual experience. Freud relied heavily on dream interpretation as a technique for mapping out the contents of the unconscious mind. Dreams, Freud argued, represent a "royal road" to the unconscious (Freud, 1900/1990).

The Structure of Personality

Freud believed that human personality also consists of three parts: the *id, ego,* and *superego* (see Figure 12.6). As a student of biology, Freud was committed to the idea that our behavior is influenced by biological forces. He was convinced that each of us is born with powerful instinctual drives, particularly related to sex and aggression, and these drives often motivate and control our actions. Freud used the term **id** to represent the portion of personality that is governed by these forces (translated from the Latin, *id* means "it"). As a component of personality, the id seeks immediate satisfaction of innate urges, without concern for the morals and customs of society. It obeys what Freud called the *pleasure principle*—the pursuit of pleasure through the satisfaction of animalistic urges. Ironically, from an adaptive standpoint, it is this dark side of personality—the seeker of pleasure—that guarantees survival of the species by motivating a desire for sexual intercourse.

At the same time, Freud understood that people are more than just irrational sexual machines. He suggested that the forces of the id are appropriately balanced by a moral arm of personality called the superego. The **superego** is the part of our personality that encourages us to act in an ideal fashion—to act in accordance with the moral customs defined by parents and culture. The superego is acquired from experience and it acts, in part, as a conscience; it makes us feel good when we act the way we should and feel guilty when our behavior strays from accepted standards. Like the id, the superego is essentially irrational—it seeks only moral per-

---

? CRITICAL THINKING

How do the modern memory concepts of short-term and long-term memory relate to Freud's three-part theory of the mind?

---

psychodynamic theory
An approach to personality development, based largely on the ideas of Sigmund Freud, which holds that much of behavior is governed by unconscious forces.

conscious mind
The contents of awareness—those things that occupy the focus of one's current attention.

preconscious mind
The part of the mind that contains all of the inactive but potentially accessible thoughts and memories.

unconscious mind
The part of the mind that Freud believed housed all the memories, urges, and conflicts that are truly beyond awareness.

id
In Freud's theory, the portion of personality that is governed by inborn instinctual drives, particularly those related to sex and aggression.

superego
In Freud's theory, the portion of personality that motivates people to act in an ideal fashion, in accordance with the moral customs defined by parents and culture.

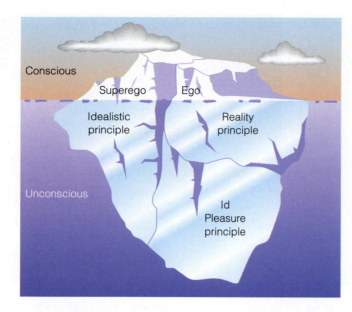

FIGURE 12.6
Freud's View of Personality
Freud believed that our personalities are influenced by three forces. The *id* is the unconscious and unrepentant seeker of pleasure; the *superego* is the moral seeker of ideal behavior; and the *ego* is the executive that acts in accordance with reality. Just as most of an iceberg lies beneath the water, much of personality operates at an unconscious level.

fection. Left to its own devices, the superego would undercut or block satisfaction of the more basic urges, even though those urges may help us satisfy fundamental survival needs. The superego follows an *idealistic principle:* Always act in a proper and ideal fashion as defined by parents and culture.

Sitting between the forces of the id and superego, and acting as a mediator, is the third component of personality—the ego. The **ego,** which comes from the Latin word for "I," serves an executive role in Freud's conception of personality. The ego encourages you to act with reason and deliberation and helps you conform to the requirements of the external world. Freud suggested that the ego obeys a *reality principle;* it monitors the real world looking for appropriate outlets for the id's needs, but it also listens intently to the moralistic preachings of the superego. The ego's goal is compromise among three demanding masters: the external world, the id, and the superego.

Defense Mechanisms: The Ego's Arsenal

As noted above, Freud believed that we're unaware of most of the conflicts that occur among the id, ego, and superego. We consciously experience only the side effects of these battles. For example, Freud believed that the experience of *anxiety* (an unpleasant feeling of dread) often comes from confrontations between the ego and the id or superego (of course, anxiety can also come from dangers in the real world). But the ego does not enter the battlefield unarmed. Freud proposed that the ego has at its disposal a variety of **defense mechanisms,** which are unconscious processes that can ward off the anxiety that comes from confrontation with the id.

The most important weapon in the ego's arsenal is **repression,** a process that actively keeps anxiety-producing thoughts and feelings buried in the unconscious. When a primitive urge from the id rears its ugly head, the ego actively represses the thought or feeling. The urge is blocked out, jammed down into the dark recesses of the unconscious. Freud was convinced that we are particularly likely to repress sexual thoughts or experiences. Unrestricted sexual activity is typically discouraged by parents and society—this was particularly true in Freud's time—so sexual thoughts and feelings need to be actively blocked by the reality-driven ego. In contrast, we would probably have few repressed thoughts or memories about eating or drinking, although both are instinctual urges, because these behaviors tend to violate few, if any, societal norms.

Repression is a kind of self deception—the mind deals with the anxiety-producing impulse by acting as if it isn't there. Similar kinds of self-deception

 CRITICAL THINKING

What are the adaptive qualities of the superego? What would happen to the human species if the superego always controlled behavior?

ego
In Freud's theory, the portion of personality that induces people to act with reason and deliberation and helps them conform to the requirements of the external world.

defense mechanisms
According to Freud, unconscious processes used by the ego to ward off the anxiety that comes from confrontation, usually with the demands of the id.

repression
A defense mechanism used to bury anxiety-producing thoughts and feelings in the unconscious.

Freud believed that people sometimes deal with unacceptable feelings by attributing them to others, through a process called *projection*. The anger shown in this photo, Freud might argue, could be actually symbolic of some deeper conflict that the woman on the left is "projecting" onto the woman on the right.

Through *sublimation,* unacceptable impulses such as a desire to hurt others, are channeled into socially acceptable activities.

projection
A defense mechanism in which unacceptable feelings or wishes are dealt with by attributing them to others.

reaction formation
A defense mechanism used to transform an anxiety-producing wish into a kind of opposite—people behave in a way that counters the way they truly feel.

sublimation
A defense mechanism used to channel unacceptable impulses into socially acceptable activities.

occur with the other defense mechanisms that Freud proposed. For example, through a process called **projection,** you deal with unacceptable feelings or wishes by attributing them to others. A person harboring strong sexual feelings toward a married neighbor—an impulse likely to cause considerable guilt—might *project* his or her feelings onto the neighbor. It is the neighbor who harbors the desire, certainly not I. **Reaction formation** occurs when you transform an anxiety-producing wish into a kind of opposite—you actually behave in a way that counters the way you truly feel. For example, a mother who secretly resents the birth of her daughter and unconsciously wishes her to die might smother the child with exaggerated care and affection; the unconscious anti-Semite, who wishes the degradation of all Jews, might become an active and tireless volunteer for organizations championing Jewish rights. Notice that in each of these cases the unconscious conflict receives attention, but the attention is disguised in a self-deceptive way.

Once again, the point of the self-deception is to reduce the experience of anxiety. Defense mechanisms allow the ego to deal indirectly with unacceptable psychological thoughts and feelings. Suppose you are an extremely aggressive person who unconsciously would love to hurt others. According to Freud, you might use the defense mechanism of **sublimation,** in which unacceptable impulses are channeled into socially acceptable activity, to deal with the potential anxiety. Perhaps

CONCEPT SUMMARY
Defense Mechanisms

Mechanism	Description	Example
Repression	Actively keeping anxiety-producing thoughts and feelings buried in the unconscious.	Horace doesn't remember the horrible fire that nearly killed him when he was a child.
Projection	Unacceptable wishes or feelings are attributed to others.	Monica deals with her attraction to her married supervisor Bill by accusing fellow employee Kelly of flirting with him.
Reaction formation	You behave in a way that is counter to how you truly feel.	Although deeply resentful of how his mother treated him as a child, Juan calls her every day and showers her with affection.
Sublimation	Unacceptable impulses are channeled into socially acceptable activity.	Tze is rude and critical and likes to put people down. She decides to become a stand-up comic.

you will choose a career in professional football, or become an aggressive member of the local police force. Here, the aggressive impulse will be satisfied, but in an indirect and socially acceptable manner.

Psychosexual Development

To Freud, the unconscious mind is a bubbling cauldron of hidden conflicts, repressed memories, and biological urges. In the case of the biological urges, their origin is relatively clear—people are born with instinctual drives for self-preservation and sex. But where do the other conflicts come from? Why are people tormented by repressed memories that arise directly from life's experiences? Freud believed that people travel through stages of psychosexual development in their childhood (Freud, 1905/1962). How children deal with their emerging sexuality importantly affects the way they think and feel when they reach adulthood.

Each developmental stage is associated with a particularly sensitive region of pleasure, which Freud called an *erogenous zone*. In the first year or so of life— during the **oral stage**—pleasure is derived primarily from sucking and from placing things in the mouth (such as the mother's breast). The adaptive significance of this first stage is clear—gaining pleasure through sucking increases the probability that you will get the nourishment you need for survival. In the second year of life, the focus of pleasure shifts to the anus. During this **anal stage,** pleasure arises from the process of defecation, the passing of feces. From ages 3 through 5, in the **phallic stage,** the genital regions of the body receive the focus of attention. The child obtains intense gratification from self-stimulation of the sexual organs.

Freud believed that we move through these stages for primarily biological reasons. All organisms, including humans, need to learn how to gain nourishment, control the elimination of waste, and satisfy the sexual drive. Unfortunately, it's possible to become stalled, or fixated, at a particular stage which, in turn, can have important and long-lasting effects on personality. By *fixation*, Freud meant that a person will continue to act in ways that are appropriate for a particular stage, seeking pleasure in stage-dependent ways, even after he or she has physically matured. There are two primary ways in which the fixation process can occur: First, if the child gains excess gratification from a stage or, second, if the child becomes excessively frustrated. It is the second of these two situations that has received the most attention.

Notice that the oral and anal stages are associated with the potentially traumatic experiences of weaning and toilet training. Freud emphasized these experiences because a child can become easily frustrated during either event. People who are fixated in the oral stage, Freud believed, continue to derive pleasure from oral activities into adulthood. They become excessive smokers, or overeaters, or people who bite their nails. Fixation at the anal stage might lead to excessive neatness or messiness. The pleasure-seeking activities in these instances are symbolic, of course; compulsive room cleaning might be a symbolic attempt at the gratification a child sometimes receives from the retention of feces. Regardless, Freud would place the origin of such adult behaviors in events that occurred during the first few years of childhood.

Freud's interpretation of the events that surround the phallic stage of psychosexual development was particularly controversial. He was convinced that small children have intense but unconscious sexual urges that become focused during this stage. Such a view was considered outrageous in his time, because the prevailing opinion was that prepubescent children are uninfluenced by the sexual drive. Freud argued that small children not only have erotic tendencies but that they tend to direct those sexual feelings toward the opposite-sex parent. For example, boys become erotically attracted to their mother, a condition Freud called the *Oedipus complex* (after the Greek tragedy of Oedipus, who unknowingly killed his father and married his mother); girls identify with their father in what has been called the *Electra complex* (after the mythical Greek Electra, who hated and

Freud believed that people can become "fixated" at a particular psychosexual stage if activities associated with that stage, such as toilet training during the anal stage, are particularly traumatic or frustrating.

oral stage
The first stage in Freud's conception of psychosexual development, occurring in the first year of life; in this stage, pleasure is derived primarily from sucking and placing things in the mouth.

anal stage
Freud's second stage of psychosexual development, occurring in the second year of life; pleasure is derived from the process of defecation.

phallic stage
Freud's third stage of psychosexual development, lasting from about age 3 to age 5; pleasure is gained from self-stimulation of the sexual organs.

Carl Jung believed that all people share a collective unconscious filled with mystical symbols and universal images.

? CRITICAL THINKING

Most people deny that they've ever had sexual feelings toward their parents. If you were Freud, how would you explain these denials?

latency period
Freud's period of psychosexual development, from age 5 to puberty, during which the child's sexual feelings are largely suppressed.

genital stage
Freud's final stage of psychosexual development, during which one develops mature sexual relationships with members of the opposite sex.

collective unconscious
The notion proposed by Carl Jung that certain kinds of universal symbols and ideas are present in the unconscious of all people.

conspired to murder her mother). Desire for the opposite-sex parent creates enormous unconscious conflicts in the developing child. Freud believed that many adult sexual or relationship problems can be traced back to a failure to resolve these conflicts adequately.

After the age of 5 or 6, boys and girls enter a kind of psychosexual lull—called the **latency period**—during which their sexual feelings are largely suppressed. During this period children direct their attention to social concerns, such as developing solid friendships. Finally, beginning with the onset of puberty, one enters the **genital stage.** Here, sexuality reawakens, but in what Freud considered to be a more direct and appropriate fashion. Erotic tendencies now tend to be directed toward members of the opposite sex.

Adler, Jung, and Horney

Freud's intense emphasis on the role of sexuality in personality development was received with skepticism by many, even from those who were firmly committed to his general approach. One of the first to split from Freud's inner circle of disciples was Alfred Adler (1870–1937). Adler disagreed strongly with Freud about the role of early psychosexual experience. He felt that the important determinant of personality development was not childhood trauma but rather how we come to deal with a basic sense of *inferiority.* To Adler, personality arises from our attempts to overcome or compensate for fundamental feelings of inadequacy. Adler was responsible for coining the popular term *inferiority complex,* a concept, he argued, that underlies and motivates a great deal of human behavior. It is our natural drive for superiority that explains motivation, not sexual gratification as envisioned by Freud (Adler, 1927).

Adler was not the only dissenting voice. Others who had been early advocates of Freud's theory began to break away and offer new and revised forms of the theory. One of the biggest personal blows to Freud was the departure of his disciple Carl Jung (1875–1961), whom Freud had picked as his intellectual heir. Jung, like Adler, was dissatisfied with Freud's narrow reliance on sexuality as the dominant source of human motivation. Jung believed instead in the idea of a "general life force," which he adopted from his extensive study of Eastern religions and mythology. This general life force was sexual in part but included other basic sources of motivation as well, such as the need for creativity (Jung, 1923).

Among Jung's more influential ideas was his concept of the **collective unconscious.** Jung believed that each person has a shared unconscious, in addition to the personal unconscious described by Freud, that is filled with mystical symbols and universal images that have accumulated over the lifetime of the human species. These symbols are inherited—passed from one generation to the next—and tend to represent enduring concepts (or *archetypes*), such as God, Mother, earth, and water. Actually, the idea that all humans share certain concepts buried deep in a collective unconscious can also be found in the writings of Freud, but Jung expanded on the idea and assigned it a central focus.

Another blow to Freud was the dissenting voice of Karen Horney (1885–1952), one of the first women to learn and practice psychodynamic theory. Horney agreed with Freud's basic approach, but she rebelled against what she felt was Freud's male-dominated views of sexuality. Freud had argued in his writings that women are fundamentally dissatisfied with their sex—they suffer from what he called *penis envy*—a view that Horney found unsatisfactory in many ways. She boldly confronted Freud, both personally and in her writings, and offered revised forms of psychodynamic theory that treated women in a more balanced way (Horney, 1967). One of her more lasting theoretical contributions was her insistence that a link exists between the irrational beliefs people hold about themselves and their psychological problems (Horney, 1945). As you'll see in Chapters 14 and

15, this idea continues to be influential in the conceptualization and treatment of psychological disorders.

Evaluating Psychodynamic Theory

Few psychological theories have been as influential as Freud's. Many of the terms and concepts he introduced—particularly his ideas about the unconscious—have become part of modern language and beliefs. You were probably familiar with such Freudian terms as *repression, id, ego,* and *projection* before you opened this psychology text. Moreover, the suggestion that personality is determined in part by how we learn to satisfy basic biological drives, as well as deal effectively with the demands of society and the outside world, is still a very modern and widely accepted idea (Buss, 1991; Revelle, 1995). But psychodynamic theory, as envisioned by Freud, has been steadily losing its influence over the past several decades for many reasons.

Part of the problem is that many of the ideas that Freud proposed lack scientific rigor; he never articulated concepts such as the id, superego, and ego with ringing precision. As a result, it's been difficult, if not impossible, to subject them to proper scientific testing. Consider the concept of repression, which Freud believed to be the bedrock of psychodynamic theory. If repressed memories are hidden behind the veil of the unconscious, expressing themselves only in masked and largely symbolic ways, can we ever be certain that we have correctly identified and interpreted the source and content of these unconscious influences? Most of the evidence for repression has come from clinical case studies, from individuals who are probably not representative of the general population. Psychologists have been unable to study repression in the laboratory, either because of ethical concerns or because it's unclear what conditions need to be met for repression to occur. Moreover, there are many examples, for instance, of people who have undergone traumatic events in their childhood yet remain psychologically healthy (Loftus, 1993).

Besides the problems of testability and lack of scientific rigor, Freud's theory is often criticized for its biases against women. There is no question that Freud viewed women as the weaker sex psychologically. As mentioned earlier, he painted women as individuals unsatisfied with their gender, who need to come to grips with the fact that they lack a penis. Freud was also reluctant to believe women's testimonials of rape or childhood sexual abuse—he saw these accounts as symbolic expressions of unconscious conflicts, rather than as actual events. Many modern psychologists consider these positions, along with Freud's general male-oriented approach, to be unrealistic and even distasteful (Masson, 1984; Vitz, 1988).

HUMANISTIC APPROACHES TO PERSONALITY

There is another reason why many psychologists simply don't like Freud's psychodynamic approach: It paints a dark and dismal view of human nature. In describing the origins of personality, Freud himself often compared the mind to a battlefield, where irrational forces are continuously engaged in a struggle for control. According to Freud, our actions are motivated primarily by the need to satisfy animalistic urges related to sex and aggression; our conscious awareness of why we act is misleading and symbolic, representative of conflicts created during toilet training or during the trauma of being weaned from the mother's nipple.

Humanistic psychology is largely a reaction against this pessimistic view of the human spirit. Humanistic psychologists don't talk about battlefields and conflict; instead, they talk about growth and potential. It is not animalistic urges that are stressed in explaining personality; it is the *human* with his or her unparalleled capacity for self-awareness, choice, responsibility, and growth. Humanistic psychologists believe that each of us can control our own behavioral destiny—we can consciously rise above whatever animalistic urges might be coded in our genes.

Karen Horney rebelled against what she felt was Freud's male-dominated views on sexuality.

CRITICAL THINKING

Do you think it would be unethical to conduct research on repression in animals? Why or why not?

humanistic psychology
An approach to personality that focuses on people's unique capacity for choice, responsibility, and growth.

We're built and designed for personal growth, to seek our fullest potential, to self-actualize—to become all we are capable of becoming.

To a humanist, there are many ways to explain individual differences in behavior. First, every human being is considered to be naturally *unique*. People are more than the sum of a set of predictable parts—everyone is a unique and individual *whole*. Second, the environment influences the natural growth process. Like plants, people will grow best in fertile and supportive environments; barren environments can't stop the growth process, but they can prevent us from realizing our own true potential (Rogers, 1963). Third, and perhaps most important, how we act is determined by our unique view of the world—our interpretation of reality. Our personal view of ourselves and the environment guides and motivates our actions. Notice the emphasis here is on conscious mental processes. We're assumed to be responsible for our own actions, although sometimes our subjective experience of reality is not a very accurate reflection of the real world. We'll consider the views of two prominent humanistic psychologists in this section: Carl Rogers and Abraham Maslow.

Carl Rogers and the Self

To humanist Carl Rogers (1902–1987), the essence of personality is wrapped up in the concept of the self or, more specifically, the *self-concept*. He defined the **self-concept** as an organized set of perceptions about one's abilities and characteristics—it amounts to that keen sense of oneself, what it means to be "I" or "me." The self-concept comes primarily from social interactions, Rogers believed, particularly the interactions we have with our parents, friends, and other significant role models throughout our lifetimes. The people around us mold and shape our self-image through their ongoing evaluations of our actions.

We rely on the judgments of others to tell us who we truly are and what we can hope to become, Rogers argued, because of a basic need for **positive regard.** We value what others think of us and consistently seek others' approval, love, and companionship. Unfortunately, in real life **conditions of worth** tend to be attached to the approval of others. For instance, let's suppose that you come from a family that values education and intellectual pursuits. You, however, couldn't care less about such things—your interests are in popular music and athletics. To gain acceptance from your parents, you may well deny your true feelings and modify your self-concept to bring it more in line with what your parents believe: "I'm not someone who cares about a trivial activity like sports, I'm someone who cares intensely about the pursuit of knowledge."

But herein lies a major problem, Rogers argued. The self-concept that you work so hard to form inevitably conflicts with what you truly feel from experience. You may decide to spend the evening reading the philosophical musings of Immanuel Kant, but you'll probably find your mind drifting and your feelings of self-worth diminishing. Rogers called this condition **incongruence,** which he defined as a discrepancy between the image you hold of yourself—your self-concept—and the sum of all your experiences. Incongruence leads to the experience of anxiety and ultimately forms the basis for a variety of psychological problems. True psychological health, Rogers suggested, comes when the self-concept is *congruent* (agrees) with your true feelings and experiences—that is, when your opinions and beliefs about yourself accurately reflect your everyday experiences. We'll have more to say about what Rogers felt was the appropriate therapeutic solution to conditions of incongruence in Chapter 15. To anticipate the discussion just a bit, Rogers was convinced that the therapist's proper role is to be nonjudgmental—to accept the feelings and actions of the client unconditionally. By eliminating the *conditions of worth*, the client is helped to develop a self-concept that is more congruent with reality.

With respect to personality and its development, Rogers believed that regularities in behavior come largely from the structure of the self-concept.

self-concept
An organized set of perceptions that we hold about our abilities and characteristics.

positive regard
The idea that we value what others think of us and constantly seek others' approval, love, and companionship.

conditions of worth
The expectations or standards that we believe others place on us.

incongruence
A discrepancy between the image we hold of ourselves—our self-concept—and the sum of all our experiences.

Carl Rogers proposed that people have an ingrained need for positive regard—we value what others think of us and consistently seek their approval and companionship.

Personality is defined by consistent behavior across situations; people tend to act consistently, Rogers argued, simply because their actions consistently mirror the established self-concept. We act in ways that support rather than contradict our beliefs about ourselves. More often than not we will actively seek to protect our self-image. Given a choice, you might consistently choose to read philosophy rather than watch television because it's consistent with your vision of *you*. If you chose television, you will need to reconsider who you really are, which is the sort of confrontation that people tend to avoid.

Abraham Maslow and Self-Actualization

Carl Rogers was committed to the role played by the self-concept, but he also believed strongly in the potential for personal growth. We may act defensively and seek to protect a rigid self-concept, but at our core we are creative people who have the power to fulfill our personal potential. This idea that everyone has a basic need for **self-actualization**—the need to move forward toward the realization of potential—also plays a pivotal role in Abraham Maslow's view of personality.

We encountered Maslow's views once before, in Chapter 11, when we discussed motivation. Maslow believed that human motivation is grounded in the satisfaction of *need*. There are certain things that humans *must* do—things such as obtain food and water and protect themselves from danger—before the full expression of their potential can be realized. As you saw in Chapter 11, one of Maslow's main contributions was his proposal of the *need hierarchy*, shown in Figure 12.7, which expresses the order or priority with which needs must be satisfied. Notice that safety and survival needs sit below the need for love and belonging in the need hierarchy. It is unlikely that you will appear to the world as a spiritual, loving individual if you're constantly worrying about your next meal or whether you will be eaten by an approaching predator. It is only after the basic needs are satisfied—those related to survival—that the more spiritual side of personality can be developed.

Your personality characteristics will reflect where you are positioned in the hierarchy of needs. Maslow was convinced that all people are inherently good; a person may consistently act unkind, defensive, or aggressive, but these personality traits reflect a failure to satisfy basic needs—they will never be fundamental to the human spirit. To support this claim, Maslow pointed to the behavior of individuals who he felt had progressed through the entire hierarchy. The characteristics of human personality, he argued, are highly consistent across individuals at the

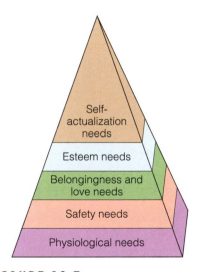

FIGURE 12.7

Maslow's Hierarchy of Needs
Maslow proposed that our observable personality characteristics will reflect where we are positioned in the hierarchy of needs. Someone who must worry constantly about biological or safety needs will act differently from someone who is seeking to satisfy needs at the highest levels of the pyramid.

self-actualization
The ingrained desire to reach one's true potential as a human being.

Inside the Problem   Multiple and Possible Selves

By consuming his mysterious potion of salts and other wholesale chemicals, Dr. Henry Jekyll was able to quite literally get in touch with the dark side of his nature. Hyde emerged as a new personality, one with unique characteristics that were certainly different from Jekyll's, and actions that were consistent across situations. If psychologists could have administered a personality test like the MMPI to Jekyll before and after his transformation, they would undoubtedly have detected very different personality profiles for pre-potion Jekyll and after-potion Hyde. To the author of the novel, these multiple personalities were not created by the potion itself; rather, the chemical mixture simply helped a hidden side of Jekyll's nature gain physical as well as psychological control of the body.

Compelling fiction, to be sure. Certainly no such potion exists, and the idea that people could instantaneously transform their bodies into a different form defies what is currently known about biological systems. But the idea that we are in some sense many different kinds of people—that each of us may have multiple internal "selves"—is actually an enduring idea in the history of psychology, dating

back at least to the nineteenth century and the work of William James (Kihlstrom & Cantor, 1984; Linville & Carlston, 1994; Wyer & Srull, 1989).

The concept of personality itself is intimately tied to the concept of the self, or the self-concept, which we defined as an organized set of perceptions about one's abilities and characteristics. For some idea of what it means to have multiple selves, consider the different roles you regularly play in your life. Don't you think and act in particular ways in your role as a son or daughter, student, worker, employee, lover, and friend? Consider the consistency of your actions in these situations. There are certainly things that you would never say in your role as a student or employee; you also have relatively well-defined expectations about your abilities as a lover or friend that you would never expect to transfer to your "student self" or "worker self." It turns out that these different senses of self importantly determine not only how people act, but also the kinds of things they pay attention to, what inferences they draw about things, and what they remember (Greenwald & Pratkanis, 1984; Kihlstrom & Cantor, 1984; Markus & Nurius, 1986).

Psychologists refer to these multiple senses of self as *self-schemas*. Self-schemas are organized knowledge packages we carry around in our heads to help us interpret the present, reconstruct the past, and motivate and guide our actions (Markus, 1977). Each of the various identities that we may have—daughter, father, boss, worker, wife, husband, woman, man—is associated with a particular self-schema that guides how environmental situations are interpreted and dictates which behaviors will emerge (Linville & Carlston, 1994). If people are asked to make predictions or judgments about trait words that are consistent or inconsistent with one of their self-schemas (independent, cooperative, and so on), they react quicker and are more confident about words that are consistent with the schema. For example, if you think of yourself as an "independent person," you react more quickly to a word such as *individualistic* than to a word such as *cooperative* (Markus, 1977). You will also be able to retrieve more examples of behaviors that are consistent with one of your identities, and you will show some resistance to evidence that is contrary to your self-schema (Linville & Carlston, 1994).

? CRITICAL THINKING

Think about how good it makes you feel to talk to a really close friend. From the perspective of humanistic theory, why should this be the case?

highest levels of the hierarchy. People who are self-actualizing show none of the darker personality traits exhibited by those locked in at lower levels; they tend to be positive, creative, accepting individuals (Leclerc et al., 1998).

Maslow's conclusions were based largely on the study of particular individuals, people whom he knew and admired. He also noted the personality traits of individuals who had reached the pinnacle of success, such as Albert Einstein, Abraham Lincoln, and Eleanor Roosevelt. All self-actualizing people, he argued, share certain personality traits. They tend to be accepting of themselves and others, to be self-motivated and problem oriented, and to have a strong ethical sense and hold democratic values. Self-actualizing people also often undergo what Maslow called *peak experiences*—emotional, often religious, experiences in which one's place in a unified universe becomes clear and meaningful. Notice that these are all quite positive traits; self-actualizing people tend to be at peace with themselves and with the world that surrounds them.

Evaluating Humanistic Theories

The humanistic approach, with its optimistic emphasis on positive growth, has had considerable influence in psychology. Concepts such as the *self* are now receiving a great deal of attention among researchers (see the accompanying feature, "Inside the Problem") and, as you'll see in Chapter 15, humanistic approaches to psychotherapy are popular and widely applied. The humanistic approach provides

People commonly adopt different roles, and employ unique "self-schemas," in the various situations of life.

There is even evidence to suggest that we carry around identities that are locked in the past, as well as possible selves that may occur in the future. Perhaps you still have an identity from several years ago of an "irresponsible self," before you got your act together and seriously committed to your studies. You almost certainly have identities from childhood—the "child self"—that remain inactive most of the time but may emerge during holiday visits home. You even have relatively well-defined self-schemas about how you are likely to act in the future. For example, Markus and Nurius (1986) asked college students to rate whether certain descriptions fit them now or might fit them in the future. These descriptions could involve such things as general abilities (cooking well), lifestyle possibilities (having an active social life), even future occupations (Supreme Court justice or janitor). The results indicated that people were quite likely to view themselves in terms of well-defined *possible* selves. Whereas fewer than half the respondents viewed themselves as someone who traveled widely, for example, well over 90% saw this as a viable future identity. (By the way, you are much more likely to see yourself as a media personality or as an owner of a successful business than as a janitor or a prison guard.)

a nice balance to the pessimism of Freud. Rather than ignoring the conscious influences on behavior, humanists champion personal choice and responsibility. Take a trip to your local bookstore and check the shelves devoted to psychology— you'll find that many of the books emphasize the control *you* can exert over your own behavior. This is one indication of the humanists' widespread impact, especially in tapping the general population's interest in psychology.

But as contributors to scientific psychology, humanistic psychologists are often criticized. Many of the fundamental concepts we've discussed, such as the potential for growth and self-actualizing tendencies, are vague and difficult to pin down. It's also not clear where these tendencies come from and under which conditions they will fully express themselves. Remember too that the humanists place important emphasis on personal, subjective experience. This means that researchers must often rely on self-reports by individuals to generate data, and we cannot always be sure that these reports are reliable and accurate representations of internal psychological processes (Leclerc et al., 1998). So in addition to problems of conceptual vagueness, humanism lacks adequate testability.

The humanistic approach to personality is also criticized for adopting too optimistic a view of human nature. In part, the arguments of humanists like Rogers and Maslow are reactions against the pessimism of Freud. But like Freud, humanistic theorists have adopted a rather extreme view of human nature: People are basically good, unless constrained in some way by social conditions of worth, and are driven to pursue lofty goals. Thus, we have the dark view described by Freud (people are all driven by unconscious animalistic urges) countered by the extremely optimistic views of the humanists. Many psychologists believe that it's probably better to adopt a more balanced approach: People are neither inherently good nor evil; they sometimes act in self-interested ways that may appear animalistic, but these actions are often adaptive and increase one's likelihood of survival. At the same time, too much emphasis on unconscious genetic or biological motives is itself misleading—we undoubtedly exercise considerable conscious control over our behavior.

COGNITIVE–BEHAVIORAL APPROACHES TO PERSONALITY

One particularly important characteristic of both the psychodynamic and humanistic approaches to personality is their emphasis on built-in determinants of behavior. People are born with animalistic urges that must be satisfied, or they greet the world naturally good with a compelling need for personal growth. The environment plays a critical role in determining final personality, but the role is essentially secondary—personal experiences and cultural norms merely constrain or enhance the full expression of natural needs.

But what about the possibility that people simply *learn* to act in consistent ways that differentiate them from others? Isn't it possible that Roger's nasty tendency to lie and Rowena's outgoing and sunny disposition come entirely from experience? Maybe Roger stole candy when he was 4 and was rewarded by not being caught; maybe Rowena learned at an early age that smiles are often met with smiles and that a good deed will be returned in kind. According to **cognitive–behavioral theories** of personality, human experience, not human nature, is the primary cause of personality growth and development. The *behavioral* side of the approach emphasizes the actual experiences delivered by the environment; the *cognitive* side emphasizes how interpretations and expectations about the events we experience play a significant role in determining what we learn.

Rewards and Punishments

An exclusively behavioral approach to personality development would propose that it is the outside world alone that influences our actions. As we discussed in Chapter 1, behaviorists believe that psychologists should look to *observable* behavior for answers to psychological questions; the research goal of most behaviorists is to understand how observable behavior changes when rewards and punishments are applied. Personality, then, might really be nothing more than the collective actions we've learned to produce in various situations. As with all other animals, if our behavior is rewarded in a particular situation, we will be more likely to perform that behavior again the next time we encounter the same situation.

There are three main ways in which people acquire situation-specific response tendencies (see Chapter 7). First, through *classical conditioning*, we learn that certain kinds of events signal other events. Imagine that as a small child little Albert is frightened in the presence of a white furry rat; he develops a specific fear, or phobia, of small furry animals that continues on into adulthood. His behavior is consistent and regular over time—he panics at the sight of anything small and furry—due in large part to this early childhood experience. Second, through *instrumental conditioning*, we learn about the consequences of our behavior. If we're rewarded in some context for acting aggressively, we will tend to act aggressively in the future. If we are repeatedly put down at parties for acting outgoing, we will learn to be withdrawn and to avoid social situations. Here it is the environment alone—one's past history of rewards and punishments—that is shaping behavior.

The third way that regularities in behavior can develop is through observational learning, or *modeling*. We observe the behavior of others around us—especially role models—and imitate the models' behavior. As we discussed in

cognitive–behavioral theories
An approach to personality that suggests it is human experiences, and interpretations of those experiences, that determine personality growth and development.

Chapter 7, it's adaptive for organisms to mimic the behavior of others, because in this way they can learn appropriate behavior without directly experiencing the consequences of an inappropriate action. Rhesus monkeys, for example, learn to show fear in the presence of snakes through modeling their parents' behavior, not from directly experiencing the negative consequences of a bite (Mineka, 1987). According to **social learning theory,** many important personality traits come from copying the behavior of others, especially when the behavior of the model regularly leads to positive, reinforcing outcomes (Bandura, 1986; Mischel, 1968).

Expectations and Cognitions

Very few psychologists actually believe that the environment *alone* determines personality growth. The reason is that the psychological effect of most experiences—positive or negative—depends crucially on the expectations and beliefs you hold about the experience. For example, suppose we ask two groups of people to perform a relatively difficult task, such as predicting sequences of numbers. We tell one of the groups that performance on the task is based on skill; the other group is told that success or failure is due entirely to chance. (Unknown to the participants, we actually rig the procedure so that people in both groups will succeed and fail the same number of times.) What you'll find in such a situation is that task effort, as well as the amount that is learned, depends on how much control a person thinks he or she has over the outcome. That is, people who believe that their performance is skill-based work harder and learn more from the task (Rotter et al., 1961).

The important point here is that the groups perform differently even though everyone receives exactly the same number of rewards and punishments. So it is not only the literal distribution of rewards and punishments that matters; your *beliefs* about the origins of those consequences are equally important. Some psychologists have suggested that people acquire enduring personality traits based on their perceived **locus of control**—how much control they feel they can actually exert over their environment (Rotter, 1966). People who are oriented externally, known as *externals*, perceive little connection between their own actions and the occurrence of rewards; such people tend to see themselves as powerless and generally have low levels of self-esteem (Lefcourt, 1982). Internally oriented individuals (*internals*) view the world as fundamentally responsive to their actions; they feel confident that they can control the occurrence of rewards and punishment.

social learning theory
The idea that most important personality traits come from modeling, or copying, the behavior of others.

locus of control
The amount of control that a person feels he or she has over the environment.

The way we act and feel often depends on how much control we think we have over the environment. Externals, who perceive little connection between their own actions and the occurrence of rewards, tend to see themselves as powerless and possess low levels of self-esteem.

CRITICAL THINKING

Carla receives an A in her psychology class, but attributes it to the fact that her teacher is easy. Does she have an internal or external locus of control and how confident do you think she is of her own abilities?

self-efficacy
The beliefs that we hold about our own ability to perform a task or accomplish a goal.

Internally oriented people display high levels of self-confidence and tend to score higher than externally oriented individuals on a variety of academic and social indices (see Ryckman, 1993).

The concept of locus of control is related to another psychological concept called **self-efficacy** (Bandura, 1986, 1993). Whereas locus of control refers to your beliefs about how much control you can exert over the environment, self-efficacy is defined as the beliefs you hold about your own ability. For example, Raymond might be convinced that people can control their environment but feel that he personally lacks the skill. In this case, he would be rated as low in self-efficacy, with an internal locus of control. On the other hand, he might be extremely confident in his basic abilities (high self-efficacy) but believe that he can do little to control the things around him (external locus of control). Often a person's degree of self-efficacy is related to particular situations or tasks. You might believe strongly in your ability to excel academically but lack any measure of confidence in your social skills.

Concepts such as locus of control and self-efficacy are important because they indicate that what we learn from the environment depends on more than just the delivery of rewards and punishments. Expectations and beliefs about the world and your abilities influence the types of tasks you will choose to engage in, as well as the effectiveness of rewards and punishments. If you're convinced you have little or no ability in social settings—your self-efficacy is low—you will either tend to avoid going to parties or act nervous and uncomfortable if you do go. If you feel you have no chance of succeeding in your psychology course because the teaching assistant doesn't like you—that is, you've adopted an external locus of control—your motivation to work hard is likely to be low. Note that in these cases your internal beliefs end up affecting your overt behavior (avoidance of parties or class)

FIGURE 12.8

Reciprocal Determinism
Bandura proposed that personality is shaped by complex interactions among expectations and beliefs, behavior, and the rewards and punishments delivered by the environment. In this case, the expectation of failure in class (personal/cognitive factors) affects studying (behavior), which in turn affects the likelihood of success on the test (environment). Note that the arrows point both ways, suggesting that these factors can all interact.

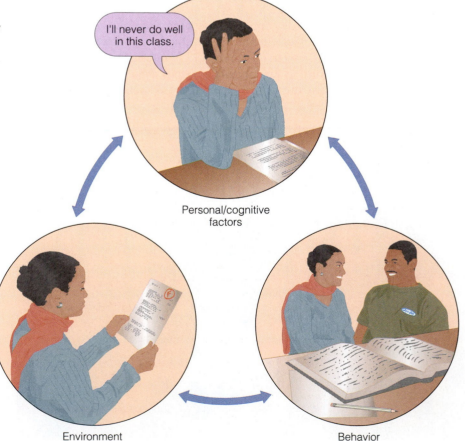

Personal/cognitive factors

Environment

Behavior

CONCEPT SUMMARY
Views of Personality Development

Approach	Description	Example
Psychodynamic	Personality is influenced by forces originating in the unconscious, and is made up of three components: the *id* (instinctive urges), *ego* (conscious decision making), and *superego* (conscience).	Jane is strongly attracted to men, but her parents are very strict about dating, so her sexual feelings are repressed. As a result she tends to avoid men, and is uncomfortable when she is around them.
Humanistic	We all control our own behavioral destiny. Personality reflects our uniqueness and our self concept, as well as our environment and our personal view of the world.	Because of criticism from her parents during childhood, Jane has developed a poor self-concept. She has not experienced unconditional positive regard, and as a result feels uncomfortable with who she is.
Cognitive–behavioral	Personality results from an interaction between the experiences delivered by the environment, and our interpretations and expectations about those experiences.	Jane goes to an all-girls high school, and doesn't encounter many boys. As a result she's a bit uncomfortable around them, and acts nervous. They then tend to avoid her, and she feels even more uncomfortable.

which, in turn, affects the likelihood that you will be rewarded. Psychologist Albert Bandura (1986) has referred to this relationship between beliefs, overt behavior, and the environment as one of **reciprocal determinism:** beliefs, behavior, and the environment interact to shape what is learned from experience (see Figure 12.8).

Evaluating Cognitive–Behavioral Theories
All psychologists recognize that behavior is importantly influenced by what we learn from the environment. Thus, the idea that at least some personality traits might be learned is not considered controversial. Furthermore, the idea that cognitive factors are involved in learning, in the form of expectations and beliefs, has also gained relatively wide acceptance. Critics of the cognitive–behavioral approach simply argue that it is insufficient as a general account of personality development (Feist, 1994; Ryckman, 1993). Cognitive–behavioral theory, for example, tends to neglect the individual as a *whole*, choosing instead to concentrate on how people have learned to respond in particular situations.

The approach has been criticized also for failing to adequately emphasize the role of biological and genetic factors in development. Perhaps ingrained drives and urges are not the main determinants of personality, but biological ancestry cannot be ignored completely. By choosing to focus primarily on the environment, the cognitive–behaviorists sometimes ignore potentially important motivational factors that are controlled largely by biological processes. In fairness, more recent versions of cognitive–behavioral theories are seeking to integrate genetic, biological, and environmental factors into a more general theory of personality development (Mischel & Shoda, 1998).

reciprocal determinism
The idea that beliefs, behavior, and the environment interact to shape what is learned from experience.

TEST YOURSELF 12.2

Check your knowledge of how personality develops by deciding whether each of the following statements is most likely to have made by a psychodynamic, humanistic, or cognitive-behavioral personality theorist. (You will find the answers in the Appendix.)

a. Ethel talks a lot, but that's only because she's trying to cover up her true feelings of inadequacy: _____

b. Teresa is very demanding, but that's because her boyfriend always gets her what she wants: _____

c. Sally can't help herself—her basic needs are preventing her from realizing her true potential: _____

d. Sharma seems to be a tireless volunteer, but in truth she secretly resents people in need: _____

e. Robert isn't really an intellectual—he just acts that way because both of his parents are famous academics and he desperately wants to please them:

_____

f. Henry is shy because he lacks confidence in his abilities and he's convinced that he cannot really influence or control the people who are around him:

_____

g. Ralph sleeps around a lot, but that's because he doesn't have enough moral virtue to control his animalistic nature: _____

Resolving the Person–Situation Debate

According to cognitive–behavioral theories, behavior is primarily the product of the environment. As a result, you might be expected to act somewhat inconsistently from one situation to the next. If you are rewarded for acting bold and aggressive when negotiating a deal (such as buying a car), you will almost certainly act bold and aggressive in such situations in the future. But if similar actions lead to rejection in the classroom or in social situations, you might very well turn meek and mild in class or when you go to a party. If you think about it, you probably know people who seem to change their behavior at the drop of a hat, acting one way in one situation and quite differently in another.

However, this kind of reasoning really strikes at the core of personality. Remember, personality is defined in terms of lasting qualities—distinguishing patterns of characteristics that differentiate us from others and lead us to act *consistently* from one situation to the next. Throughout this chapter, we've assumed that such qualities exist and that they can be measured and interpreted through the application of psychological principles. But the assumption of cross-situational consistency in behavior has been challenged by some prominent psychologists, notably Walter Mischel, and the issue has come to be known as the **person–situation debate.**

THE PERSON–SITUATION DEBATE

The argument is really a simple one. If people possess unique and enduring personality traits, we should be able to predict their behavior from one situation to the next. If you believe Roger to be dishonest, perhaps because you witnessed him peering over Rowena's shoulder during a history test, you expect him to be dishonest in the future. You predict that he will pocket a fallen wallet, or at least take the money that Rowena left lying on the counter. Put more technically, measurements of behavior should *correlate* across situations; that is, given that you know the likelihood of someone performing a trait-related action in Situation A, you should be able to predict the likelihood of the person performing an action related to the same trait in Situation B.

Unfortunately, as Walter Mischel (1968) pointed out over three decades ago, there is little evidence for this assumption (see also Peterson, 1968). If you look carefully at studies reporting correlations between measures of behavior that tap a particular kind of personality trait (such as honesty), the correlations are virtually always low. Whereas a correlation of 1.00 implies perfect behavioral consistency across situations, Mischel found that actual correlations rarely exceeded 0.30 and were usually quite a bit lower (see also Kenrick & Funder, 1988; Ross & Nisbett,

person–situation debate
A controversial debate centering on whether people really do behave consistently across situations.

Successful politicians are often high self-monitors, which means they attend closely to the situation and change their behavior accordingly.

1991). To say the least, Mischel's conclusions were quite controversial; in fact, they rocked the foundation of personality theory. Without consistency in behavior, the psychological construct of personality has little meaning.

Situational Consistency

Despite the data, very few psychologists (including Mischel) reject personality altogether as a viable psychological construct. People may not always act consistently *across* situations, but they do tend to act consistently *within* a situation. For example, in a famous study by Hartshorne and May (1928), the honesty of schoolchildren was tested by placing them in situations in which they could act dishonestly without much likelihood of being caught (money was left on a table, cheating on a test was possible, and so on). Little evidence of cross-situational consistency was found, but the children did tend to act the same way in a similar situation. For instance, kids who cheated on a test were not necessarily more likely to steal money, but they were more likely to cheat on a test again if given the chance. In short, people do act consistently from one situation to the next, as long as the situations are similar (Mischel & Peake, 1982; Mischel & Shoda, 1995). This is exactly the type of finding you would expect if people are simply learning specific kinds of actions in particular circumstances. So the evidence for within but not across situational consistency is often used to support cognitive–behavioral approaches to personality development.

Other psychologists have pointed out that low cross-situational correlations, by themselves, can be misleading. Data of the type reported by Hartshorne and May and others (see Mischel, 1968) are based primarily on the observation of single individual behaviors (did the child steal the money on the table?) rather than on collections of behaviors. To get an accurate estimate of a true personality trait, you should probably collect lots of observations, not just one; single observations tend to be unreliable and not necessarily representative of true behavior (Epstein, 1979). One reason that reliable personality traits are measured by the paper-and-pencil tests of the trait theorists (see our earlier discussion) might be because the collected ratings are based on a long history of watching oneself or others behave (Ross & Nisbett, 1991).

Self-Monitoring

Some psychologists have argued that the tendency to act consistently or haphazardly across different situations may itself be a kind of personality trait. People differ in the extent to which they engage in chameleon-like **self-monitoring**, which

self-monitoring
The degree to which a person monitors a situation closely and changes his or her behavior accordingly; people who are high self-monitors may not behave consistently across situations.

Inside the Problem   Personality and the Problems of Life

We've seen that the consistency of behavior across situations depends on the characteristics of the person as well on the specifics of the situation. Personality traits may only reveal themselves when they are relevant, and not otherwise. Such a conclusion implies, however, that the traditional trait approach—which seeks to find personality characteristics that cut across situations—may be limited in some important ways. It may not be possible to talk about someone's personality traits without also considering the particular tasks or problems that the person is currently trying to solve.

According to psychologist Nancy Cantor and her colleagues, rather than thinking about personality as something that a person *has,* we should think about personality as something that a person *does* (Cantor, 1990; Cantor & Harlow, 1994). Each person approaches life with a unique set of goals, or personal strivings. Individuals differ in what is important to them and in their own personal agenda for accomplishment. Roger may be concerned with accumulating wealth and fame; Rowena may be seeking to master her interpersonal skills. To solve these problems, or life tasks, we use strategies or characteristic ways of responding that help us meet the challenges that arise (Cantor & Harlow, 1994). The strategies we adopt may cause us to act consistently, but only to the extent that the goal is met, or the problem resolved.

The important point to remember is that you cannot understand a person's personality without considering these strategies for solving life tasks. Cantor and her colleagues have found that students in academic settings often adopt quite different strategies to cope with the same task, such as performing well in school. Some stu-

How students cope with the problem of performing well in school depends on the type of "life task" strategy that they adopt.

dents adopt pessimistic strategies, in which they ignore past accomplishments and consistently report low expectations for success on assignments and exams; pessimists spend lots of time thinking and worrying about their academic performance. Other students are optimists, which means they set high expectations for themselves and try not to worry or dwell on negative thoughts. But surprisingly, Cantor has found that these two types of students often perform equally well on exams. They simply have different strategies for meeting the same end. The pessimists are able to confront their anxieties effectively by dwelling on the possibility of failure, whereas the optimists prepare better by accentuating the positive. The pessimists and the optimists seem to have different personalities, but those special characteris-

tics may have arisen simply as a result of the strategies they've adopted to solve a particular life task.

Two final points. First, this view of personality predicts that if someone's personal life tasks change, he or she may well adopt new strategies that will affect how he or she behaves. Thus, an individual's personal actions could appear to change, or be inconsistent, across situations, but only because he or she is trying to solve a different kind of problem. Second, this problem-solving description of personality also predicts that individuals from different cultures or social groups may appear to possess unique personality traits. As the problems of a culture change, so too should the strategies that its people adopt. (We'll have more to say about the relationship between culture and the individual in Chapter 13.)

? CRITICAL THINKING

Decide whether each of your friends is a high or a low self-monitor. Who do you prefer to be around—the high self-monitors or the low self-monitors?

can be defined as the tendency to mold or change your behavior to fit the situation at hand (Snyder, 1974, 1987). People who are high self-monitors attend closely to their present situation and change their behavior to best fit their needs. They are likely to alter their behavior, and even their stated opinions and beliefs, simply to please someone with whom they are currently interacting. People who are low self-monitors are less likely to change their actions or beliefs and therefore are more likely to show consistency in their behavior across situations (Gangestad & Snyder, 1985).

Scales have been developed to measure self-monitoring tendencies. Typically, you're asked to respond to statements such as the following: "I'm not always the person that I appear to be" or "I might deceive people by acting friendly when I really dislike them." People who score highly on self-monitoring, not surprisingly, are likely to conform to social norms. They also tend to be aware of how their behavior is affecting others. High self-monitors even seem to remember the actions of others better than low self-monitors, especially when those actions are unexpected or unusual (Beers et al., 1997). Thus, self-monitoring can be quite adaptive: It is usually in our interest to monitor the environment and change our behavior accordingly (Graziano & Bryant, 1998; Mischel & Shida, 1998).

A Resolution

Currently, the majority of psychologists resolve the person–situation debate by simply assuming that it is necessary to take both the person and the situation into account. It is unlikely that either alone, the person or the situation, is going to explain behavior or allow us to predict consistency. People *interact* with situations, and the expression of lasting qualities or traits will depend partly on what's required by current needs. Personality traits will tend to reveal themselves primarily in situations in which they are relevant (Kenrick et al., 1990) and may not otherwise (see the accompanying feature, "Inside the Problem"). Similarly, given the right situational demands, each of us can act in ways that seem to violate our basic nature. (We'll return to this issue, and provide some compelling illustrations of the power of the situation, when we take up the general topic of social psychology in Chapter 13.)

GENETIC FACTORS IN PERSONALITY

There is another kind of evidence that can be used to confirm personality as an important and valid characteristic of the adaptive mind. In recent years researchers have discovered that there may be ingrained *genetic* reasons why we display unique and enduring traits. People may be born with certain genetic predispositions—perhaps their brains are wired in a certain way—that compel them to act in an idiosyncratic and regular fashion throughout their lifetime. Certainly it is not unusual for family members to show similar personality traits, although experience could play an important role in producing these similarities. At the same time, as we all know, brothers and sisters can show strikingly different personality traits, even though they have been raised under what seem to be highly similar environmental conditions. Observations like these indicate that more may be at work in determining personality than the environment.

Twin Data

As in the study of intelligence, most of the evidence for genetic factors in personality comes from twin studies. Identical twins are compared with fraternal twins under conditions in which the twins have been reared together or apart. Perhaps you've seen reports in the popular media of identical twins who were separated at birth but ended up sharing many of the same personality traits. There is the case of identical twins Oscar and Frank—one raised as a Nazi in Czechoslovakia and the other as a Jew in Trinidad. When they were reunited in 1979, it was discovered that they shared numerous odd but regular behaviors. For example, they both had a habit of sneezing deliberately in elevators to surprise people, and they both liked to flush toilets before and after use.

However, reports like these do not make a convincing scientific case (Horgan, 1993). Coincidences are possible, and some of the more famous reunited twins may have had ulterior motives for manufacturing shared traits (for example, Oscar and his brother eventually sold the rights to their story in Hollywood). More compelling evidence comes from group studies, in which the personality characteristics of large numbers of twins are analyzed. In one such study (Tellegen et al., 1988), 217 pairs of identical twins who had been reared together and 44 pairs of

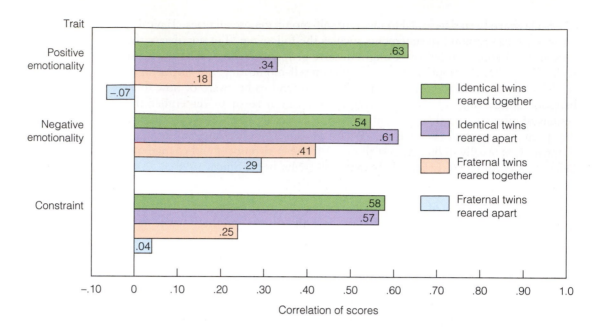

FIGURE 12.9

The Genetics of Personality

Are identical twins more likely to share basic personality traits than fraternal twins? Does the rearing environment matter? These average correlations from the Tellegen and colleagues (1988) study reveal consistent differences between identical and fraternal twins, irrespective of the rearing environment, suggesting that genetics play a role in determining personality. The environment also had a significant effect in some cases, but overall it appeared to be less important. (Adapted from Tellegen et al., 1988).

CRITICAL THINKING

Do you think identical twins who are reared apart share totally different environments? How might their environments still be similar?

twins who had been reared apart were compared with 114 pairs of fraternal twins reared together and 27 pairs reared apart. Each of the participants was administered the MMPI, which, as you remember from our earlier discussion, is a widely used questionnaire for measuring personality traits.

Some of the results of this study are shown in Figure 12.9, for several of the personality traits measured by the MMPI. Of main interest is the similarity between members of a twin pair, expressed in terms of correlation coefficients. In other words, for a trait such as aggressiveness or positive emotionality, can we predict the score that one twin will receive on the MMPI if we know the score of the other twin? Correlations that are close to 1.00 suggest that members of a twin pair share many of the same personality traits. As the figure indicates, identical twins tend to show higher correlations than fraternal twins, regardless of whether they have been reared in the same or different environments. Twins who share the same genes but have been reared in different households tend to have more similar personality traits than fraternal twins who have been reared together.

Data like these have convinced many psychologists that at least some enduring psychological traits have their origins in genetic predispositions present at birth. Of course, as we discussed in the chapter on intelligence, the expression of genetic tendencies depends on the nurturing conditions (the environment): Nature interacts with nurture in determining a person's final physical and psychological makeup. Therefore, although genes may play a critical role in determining how personality develops, environmental factors are also extremely important (Beer et al., 1998; Plomin et al., 1998).

TEST YOURSELF 12.3

Check on your knowledge about the person-situation debate by deciding whether each of the following statements is true or false. (You will find the answers in the Appendix.)

1. In the Hartshorne and May (1928) study, kids who cheated on a test were not more likely to steal money, but they were more likely to cheat on a test again if given the chance. *True or False?*

2. People do tend to act consistently from one situation to the next, as long as the situations are similar. *True or False?*

3. People who are low self-monitors tend to change their behaviors to fit the situation at hand. *True or False?*

4. Identical twin studies show little evidence for genetic contributions to personality characteristics, as measured by the MMPI. *True or False?*

5. Most psychologists believe that personality traits are revealed in all situations, regardless of the relevance of the trait. *True or False?*

Solving the Problems

There is little question in most people's minds about the status of personality—anyone will tell you that people differ in enduring ways. We all have behavioral quirks which differentiate us from others, and most of us at least give the impression of acting consistently across situations. If asked, people also have little trouble making judgments about the personality of others. We quickly and without hesitation identify Rowena as friendly and outgoing and Roger as nasty and generally no good. Moreover, as discussed at the outset of this chapter, it makes adaptive sense to act consistently, especially when particular actions help us to survive and live productive lives. Thus, personality is clearly an important and useful feature of the adaptive mind.

To psychologists, however, the study of personality has proven to be a difficult and elusive enterprise. Historically, researchers have disagreed about how to best approach the topic. As we've seen, questions have even been raised about the validity of the concept itself—how useful is a concept such as personality in describing individual differences in behavior? (Remember, similar issues were raised about the study of intelligence.) Still, the vast majority of psychologists agree that the concept of personality is needed to describe the full range of human psychological functioning. Personality is indeed something to be studied, and understanding it is both a conceptual and practical problem to be solved by the psychological community.

Conceptualizing and Measuring Personality. Trait theories are formal systems for measuring and identifying personality characteristics, such as emotional stability or extroversion. Currently, the trait theorists seem to agree that there are five basic personality dimensions—the so-called Big Five (extroversion, agreeableness, conscientiousness, neuroticism, and openness)—that accurately and reliably describe a person's unique and consistent attributes. Psychometric techniques such as factor analysis, along with the development of personality tests such as the NEO-PI-R and the MMPI, have proven useful in advancing theory and in applying what we've learned about personality to practical settings. For example, the MMPI is sometimes used in business settings as part of the decision-making process for hiring new employees.

Determining How Personality Develops. Identifying stable personality traits, however, leaves unanswered the general question of how those traits originate. Noted psychologists have developed several grand theories of personality development, including the psychodynamic approach of Freud, the humanistic perspective of Rogers and Maslow, and the cognitive–behavioral approach of Bandura, Mischel, and others. These theoretical frameworks propose very different mechanisms for personality development and offer quite different conceptions of basic human nature. The pessimism of Freud, with his emphasis on battling unconscious biological urges, is counterbalanced by the optimism of the humanists. To the cognitive–behaviorists, the environment and beliefs about controlling that environment underlie the consistent actions that define personality. Each of these perspectives has been enormously influential in the past and remains so today.

Resolving the Person–Situation Debate. The concept of personality demands at least some consistency in behavior across situations. But some evidence suggests that cross-situational consistency in behavior may be low. In light of the person–situation debate, a proper analysis of behavior requires consideration of the interaction between the person and the situation. We must also keep in mind the contribution of genetics to personality stability—twin studies indicate that there may be a genetic component to enduring behavior.

Personality Chapter Summary

Conceptualizing and Measuring Personality

What is the proper way to conceptualize and measure the traits that make us both consistent and unique? Psychologists attempt to measure the enduring aspects of behavior; those things that distinguish one person from another consistently across time.

THE FACTOR ANALYTIC APPROACH

Factor analysis is used to analyze correlations among test responses. This approach attempts to determine the degree to which trait ratings correlate with one another, in hopes of discovering common denominators for personality. Cattell identified 16 *source traits*, each represented by a dimension marked by an opposing pole. Eysenck argued that personality can be described best by 3 factors (extroversion, neuroticism, and psychoticism). Current thinking is that 5 dimensions— the *Big Five* (extroversion, agreeableness, openness, neuroticism, and conscientiousness) best describe personality.

PERSONALITY TESTS

Personality tests are of two general types: *Self-report inventories* use a paper and pencil format to identify personality characteristics. Examples are the *16 Personality Factor* and the *Minnesota Multiphasic Personality Inventory (MMPI)*. Self-report inventories are objective and standardized. *Projective personality tests* such as the *Rorschach* and the *Thematic Apperception Test* require the test-taker to interpret an unstructured or ambiguous stimulus, thereby revealing elements of personality.

ALLPORT'S TRAIT THEORY

Allport proposed a classification scheme for identifying personality traits. *Cardinal traits* are ruling passions that dominate an individual's life. *Central traits* are the 5 to 10 descriptive terms you would use to describe someone you know. *Secondary traits* are less obvious traits that do not always appear in an individual's behavior.

Determining How Personality Develops

What factors in development lead to stable and consistent behaviors? Where do personality traits come from? What accounts for differences in personality between individuals?

THE PSYCHODYNAMIC APPROACH OF FREUD

Freud believed the mind could be partitioned into the *conscious*, the *preconscious*, and the *unconscious*. He believed that the unconscious mind exerts powerful effects on behavior. Dreams are one window into the unconscious, and include a *manifest content* and *latent content* (the hidden meaning). Personality has three components: the *id* (governed by inborn drives and the *pleasure principle*), the *superego* (moralistic, following the *idealistic principle*) and the *ego* (the executive of personality, following the *reality principle*). Conflict between the forces of personality results in anxiety. To cope with the anxiety, we employ *defense mechanisms* such as *repression, projection,* or *reaction formation*. Children progress through a series of *psychosexual stages* of development (oral, anal, phallic, latency, and genital) that help determine later personality. Neo-Freudians such as Jung, Adler, and Horney de-emphasized the role of sexuality in personality, emphasizing other factors as central to the development of personality.

HUMANISTIC PERSONALITY THEORY

Humanistic psychology developed largely as a reaction against Freud's pessimistic view of the human spirit. This approach emphasizes self-awareness, choice, responsibility, and growth as important factors in personality. According to Carl Rogers, the essence of personality is tied to the self-concept. We have a basic need for *positive regard*; problems arise when our acceptance by others is tied to *conditions of worth*. Problems may also arise from *incongruence*, a discrepancy between your self-concept and the sum of your experiences. Maslow stressed the drive toward *self-actualization* as important in determining personality. He proposed a *need hierarchy*, which explains the priority with which needs must be fulfilled. Personality reflects where you are within the hierarchy of needs.

COGNITIVE–BEHAVIORAL APPROACHES TO PERSONALITY

This approach emphasizes the role of learning in personality. Human experience, not human nature, is the primary cause of personality growth and development. People acquire situation-specific response tendencies through classical conditioning, instrumental conditioning, and modeling. According to *social learning theory*, many personality traits come from copying the behavior of others. Our interpretation of our experiences also plays a critical role in personality. Perceived *locus of control* (how much control people feel they have over their environment) and *self-efficacy* (the beliefs you have about your own ability) determine how experience is interpreted, and how it affects personality.

Resolving the Person–Situation Debate

Are personality characteristics expressed in a way that is independent of the environment? Is behavior across different situations as consistent as many people, including psychologists, assume?

THE PERSON–SITUATION DEBATE

Do people show cross-situational consistency in their behavior? This question is at the heart of the *person–situation debate*. According to some, there is little evidence of consistency. However, most psychologists note that although behavior *across* situations may not be consistent, behavior *within* a situation typically is. Some psychologists have suggested that the tendency to act consistently or inconsistently across different situations may itself be a personality trait. This tendency is termed *self-monitoring*. High self-monitors attend closely to their behavior, and change it to best fit their needs, whereas low self-monitors are less likely to change their actions and beliefs. Current thinking is that both the person and the situation need to be taken into account to explain personality.

GENETIC FACTORS IN PERSONALITY

Evidence from twin studies indicates that genetic factors may play a role in determining personality. Correlational studies of personality traits as measured by the MMPI reveal that identical twins tend to show higher correlations than fraternal twins, regardless of being raised in the same or different environments. Data like these have convinced psychologists that some enduring psychological traits have their roots in genetic predispositions.

Terms to Remember

Recommended Readings

Freud, S. (1924). *Introductory lectures on psychoanalysis.* New York: Boni & Liveright. Sometimes it's worth going to an original source. In this case, Freud attempts to describe the essential features of psychoanalysis to a general audience. It's worth a look.

Rogers, C. R. (1961). *On becoming a person.* Boston: Houghton-Mifflin. This book gives you a chance to learn the essentials of client-centered therapy directly from Carl Rogers. A very interesting, highly readable book.

Ryckman, R. M. (1997). *Theories of personality* (6th ed.). Pacific Grove, CA: Brooks/Cole. A top undergraduate textbook on all aspects of personality theory. Covers everything in Chapter 12 in much greater detail.

INFOTRAC® COLLEGE EDITION

For additional readings, explore Infotrac College Edition, your online library. Go to:
http://www.infotrac-college.com/wadsworth

Hint: enter the search terms: Personality traits, Personality tests, Sigmund Freud, Defense mechanisms, Humanistic psychology, Locus of control.

🌐 What's on the Web?

Freud Museums

London: http://www.freud.org.uk/

Vienna: http://freud.t0.or.at/freud/index-e.htm

These Web sites provide some very interesting information about the founder of psychoanalysis. The Vienna site provides a chronology of Freud's life. Stop by and find out when Freud used the word "psychoanalysis" for the first time (1895), or when Freud gave up smoking because of a heart attack (1930). At the London site, look at some fascinating pictures from their museum, including Freud's original couch (yes, THE couch!) and "tub chair" that he used in his psychoanalytic sessions.

The Personality Project

(http://fas.psych.nwu.edu/personality.html)

This fascinating site serves as a sort of clearinghouse for information related to personality measurement and personality theory. The pages are ". . . meant to guide those interested in personality theory and research to the current personality literature." It provides pages that allow you to find out more about psychoanalytic theory, behavior genetics, and evolutionary psychology.

Sources on Self-Efficacy

(wysiwig://606/http://www.emory.edu/EDUCATION/mfp /effpage.html)

Believe it or not, this is an entire (if small) site devoted to exploration of self-efficacy, as well as social-cognitive theory of personality in general. Here you can find information on how perceptions of self-efficacy vary across cultures, as well as the relationship between self-efficacy and performance. The site also provides links to on-line measures that allow you to measure your own self-efficacy.

The Wadsworth Psychology Study Center Web Site

See http://psychology.wadsworth.com/ for practice quiz questions, hypercontents, updates, critical thinking exercises, discussion forums and more! The Wadsworth Psychology Study Center provides a wealth of information fully organized and integrated by chapter.

Social Psychology

It's the annual Christmas party for Everville Industries. Al Hobart has worked at the company for a year and a half now, and he's itching for a promotion to the advertising department. To his left stands the head of advertising, Mr. Barker, along with several of Hobart's equally ambitious co-workers. The topic of conversation is the company's recent disastrous marketing campaign, spearheaded by Barker, whose shortcomings are recognized by everyone in the group save one—Barker himself.

"It just goes to show you," spouts Barker confidently, "you can never underestimate the ignorance of the people. It was a brilliantly conceived but unappreciated plan."

"Absolutely," offers Ms. Adler, "a brilliant plan."

"People are just stupid," employee Jones remarks. "They wouldn't know a good marketing campaign if it came up and bit them on the cheek."

I'm working with jerks, the little voice inside Hobart's head chimes. These people have no values—no sense of personal integrity. Everyone knows that campaign was terrible.

"And what about you, Hobart," Barker says, his eyes meeting Al's. "What do you think?"

"Brilliant plan, sir," Hobart says, hesitating only slightly; "the work of genius. . . ."

Put on your psychological thinking cap for a moment, and let's analyze Hobart's behavior. From this brief exchange can you draw any conclusions about what kind of person he is? What does your psychological training tell you? He clearly violated his own beliefs and outwardly conformed to the opinions expressed by the ambitious people around him. He also drew some rather nasty conclusions about his colleagues, concluding that they were jerks for shamelessly agreeing with the misguided boss. Do you think Hobart will now apply those same negative personality traits to himself? Do you suppose he might have acted differently if the head of advertising had been absent, or if the job promotion had already been his? Now, stop for a moment and think about how *you* might have acted in this situation. Would you have conformed to the opinions of others? Would you, like Hobart, have left the conversation thinking your co-workers suffered from fundamental personality flaws?

Throughout this text we've stressed that most behaviors, as well as internal thoughts and feelings, are importantly shaped by the immediate context. Not only do you behave differently in different situations, but you think differently also. Hobart's example is relatively harmless, but other situations can have more far-reaching and disturbing consequences. Suppose, for example, that Mr. Barker was not simply the head of the advertising department but a commanding officer in the military, and the locale was an Asian nation at war. The topic of conversation? Not a marketing campaign, but rather Barker's decision to execute all of the inhabitants, including women and children, of a just-captured village. How would you react now? Would you still conform to the opinions of your superior?

It's adaptive to monitor the environment closely and to change one's behavior accordingly. But the environment is made up of much more than impersonal things such as the temperature of the room or the amount of money received for performing a task. The mere presence of other people, as well as their behaviors, can be among the most powerful and pervasive of environmental influences. Our behaviors and thoughts change in characteristic ways when we are in the presence of other people, and it's to this social aspect of psychology that we now turn our attention.

social psychology
The discipline that studies how people think about, influence, and relate to other people.

500

Interpreting the behavior of others

Behaving in the presence of others

Establishing relations with others

FIGURE 13.1
Summarizing the Adaptive Problems
In this chapter we address three main adaptive problems studied by social psychologists.

Previewing the Adaptive Problems

S ocial psychology is the discipline that studies how people think about, influence, and relate to other people. Social psychologists investigate such phenomena as persuasion, interpersonal attraction, attitude formation and change, and the behavior of groups. In keeping with the theme of the adaptive mind, we'll tackle the topics of social psychology from the perspective of three important adaptive problems (see Figure 13.1).

First, how do we interpret the behavior of others? As social animals, living in a social world, we're constantly trying to interpret the behavior of other people. We form impressions of our friends, teachers, and our colleagues in the workplace—we even form impressions of the people we meet on the street. We concoct theories about *why* people behave the way they do; we form attitudes that help us act adaptively in the presence of particular individuals or groups. At the same time, as you'll see, there are systematic biases in the interpretation process that can at times lead us to act in regrettable ways.

Second, how does our behavior change when we're in the presence of others? Everyone's behavior is strongly influenced by the social context. For example, sometimes your ability to perform a task will improve when others are present; sometimes your performance falls apart. Your behavior will also be strongly influenced by the presence of authority figures and by the opinions of fellow members in a group. What are the factors that determine when you will yield to the demands of others, and what implications do these factors have for the structure of society? We'll expand our psychological analysis of Hobart's behavior and extend it to a broader range of situations.

Third, how do we establish relations with others, especially close interpersonal relationships? It's certainly adaptive to interpret the behavior of others and to change behavior accordingly in their presence. But among our most important social actions are the relationships we form with others. Without attraction and romantic love, it's unlikely that the human species would survive; but it's not just mating we need—we rely on the relationships within the family as well as the social structures within society to help protect and nurture us and our offspring.

Interpreting the Behavior of Others: Social Cognition

We begin our treatment of social psychology with a discussion of how people *think about* other people—how impressions of others are formed, how causes are attributed to behavior, and what mechanisms underlie the formation of attitudes about people and things. Social psychologists typically group these topics together under the rubric of **social cognition,** which can be defined as the study of how people use cognitive processes—such as perception, memory, and thought—to help make sense of other people as well as themselves. First up is the topic of person perception, which deals specifically with how we form impressions of others.

PERSON PERCEPTION: HOW DO WE FORM IMPRESSIONS OF OTHERS?

When we first discussed the topic of perception in Chapter 5, I focused on the processes used to interpret elementary sensations into meaningful wholes. In that chapter you learned that perception is driven by a combination of *bottom-up processing*—the actual physical sensations received by the sensory equipment—and *top-down processing*, which takes into account our expectations and beliefs about the world. We do not simply see what's "out there" in the physical world; our perceptions of objects are also influenced by our *expectations* of what's out there.

A similar kind of analysis can be applied to the perception of people. When you encounter a person for the first time, your initial impressions are influenced by physical factors—attractiveness, facial expression, skin color, clothing—and by your meaningful interpretations of those physical attributes. If you see a sloppily dressed, unshaven man weaving down the street toward you, you are likely to form a negative first impression, partly because past experiences may have taught you to avoid people who fit this description. You could be wrong, of course, but in the face of limited information, it's usually adaptive to use background knowledge to help predict the possible consequences of an interaction.

Physical Appearance

One of the most powerful determinants of a first impression is the *physical appearance* of a person. Studies have shown that when we first look at someone who is physically attractive, we tend to assume that he or she is more intelligent, better adjusted, and more socially aware than someone with only average looks (Eagly et al., 1991; Feingold, 1992). On average, physically attractive people are also thought to be healthier (Kalick et al., 1998), more inclined to succeed academically (Chia et al., 1998), and they're even less likely to get "carded" if they try to buy alcohol (McCall, 1997). These tendencies don't diminish as we age—the elderly also show a strong tendency to attribute positive personality characteristics to attractive people (Larose & Standing, 1998).

Why do we rely on physical appearance to form a first impression? After all, it seems like a rather shallow way to judge a person. The reason is simple: When you form a *first* impression, you use the information that's available. You almost always notice the way a person looks, along with his or her facial expression, and perhaps even the way the person is walking or sitting. These raw materials are combined with your background knowledge to generate an expectation of what an encounter with that person might be like. Your cultural background may influence your final judgment to a certain extent—some cultures do not rely on attractiveness as much as others (Wheeler & Kim, 1997)—but all people, across cultures, rely on physical appearance as an important part of impression formation.

Obviously, judging a book by its cover is not always an effective long-term strategy for impression formation (Feingold, 1992). But it can be a reasonable

social cognition
The study of how people use cognitive processes—such as perception, memory, thought, and emotion—to help them make sense of other people as well as themselves.

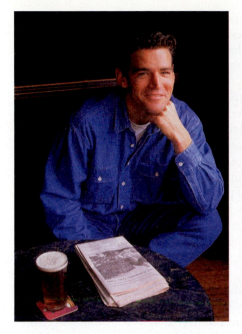

The physical appearances of these individuals are likely to activate "social schemas" that will direct and guide your behavior. Social schemas are generally adaptive, but they can lead to inappropriate conclusions or actions under some circumstances.

short-term strategy. If the approaching person appears attractive and well kept, at least you know that he or she follows some of the accepted standards and norms of the culture (Damhorst, 1990). Think about it. If you were in trouble and needed help, whom would you approach—someone with poor personal hygiene and tattered clothes, or someone neat, clean, and well dressed?

Social Schema

Psychologists are convinced that much of the background knowledge that we use in social situations comes from cognitive representations called schemas. We've discussed schemas at several places in this book, particularly in the chapter on memory. Schemas are general knowledge structures that are stored in memory, such as your knowledge about how houses are constructed or about what it's like to go to a restaurant or the doctor's office. We use schemas to help us reconstruct the past but also to help organize and interpret ongoing experience. A schema can be formed about just about anything—a person, a place, or a thing. When schemas are about social experiences or people, they are commonly called **social schemas** (Fiske, 1993).

Returning to the unshaven, sloppily dressed man on the street, your initial impression is likely to be negative because his tattered appearance activates a common social schema about people. An unkempt appearance is associated with negative social characteristics—such as laziness or even criminal behavior—and his weaving gait signals possible drunkenness. All these things lead you to categorize the man as "trouble" and make it less likely that you will either ask him for help or give help to him if he requests it (Benson et al., 1980). Both the man's physical appearance and his behavior feed into your existing social schema about seedy characters and, once he has been categorized, the schema directs you to alter your behavior accordingly.

Stereotypes

When social schemas revolve around the traits and behaviors of *groups* and their members they are called **stereotypes.** We form stereotypes about many kinds of social groups, from insurance agents to college professors, but the three most

social schema
A general knowledge structure, stored in long-term memory, that relates to social experiences or people.

stereotypes
The collection of beliefs and impressions held about a group and its members; common stereotypes include those based on gender, race, and age.

common stereotypes are based on gender, race, and age (Fiske, 1993). Most people carry around a collection of impressions about men and women, for example, which can importantly influence behavior: Men are typically seen as strong, dominant, and aggressive; women are typically seen as sensitive, warm, and dependent (Deaux & Lewis, 1984).

Stereotypes seem to share many of the properties of categories. Not surprisingly, some of the more popular theories of how stereotypes are formed are reminiscent of the theories of categorization that we discussed in Chapter 9. For example, *prototype theories* of stereotypes assume that we store abstract representations of the typical features of a group; we then judge particular individuals based on their similarity to the prototype (Cantor & Mischel, 1978). *Exemplar theories* assume instead that we store memories of particular individuals, or exemplars, and these individual memories form the basis for stereotypes (Smith & Zárate, 1992). So, for example, the stereotypic belief that African-Americans are athletic would be based on comparisons with particular individuals (e.g., Michael Jordan or Tiger Woods) rather than with some abstract representation (Hilton & von Hipple, 1996).

Stereotypes tend to be activated whenever we are exposed to stereotypic beliefs and actions. For example, men are more likely to behave sexually toward a woman if they've recently seen a television commercial in which women were presented as sexual objects (Rudman & Borgida, 1995). In addition, witnessing an African-American man engaging in a negative stereotypic behavior influences how a white male evaluates other African-American men (Henderson-King & Nisbett, 1996). Recent exposure to a behavior relevant to a stereotype apparently activates, or "primes," the stereotype, which in turn affects behavior (Smith et al., 1992; Stewart et al., 1998). How much control do we have over our stereotypic beliefs, once activated? We'll return to this topic momentarily, but first we need to consider one consequence of activated beliefs: the self-fulfilling prophecy effect.

The Self-Fulfilling Prophecy Effect

Once stereotypes are activated, we expect certain kinds of behavior from members of groups. These expectations can produce what has been called the **self-fulfilling prophecy effect,** which occurs when your expectations about a person's actions cause that person to behave in the expected way (Merton, 1948). If you expect someone to be unreliable, and you act in accordance with your expectations (such as snubbing or avoiding the person), the chances that he or she will assume that role in the future may actually increase.

Let's consider an experiment demonstrating the self-fulfilling prophecy effect. In a study by Mark Snyder and colleagues (1977), undergraduate men were asked to talk to undergraduate women, whom they had never met, on the telephone. Prior to the conversation, the men were shown a photograph of their prospective telephone partner. The partner appeared as either physically attractive or unattractive. In reality, the photos were of women from another college; they were not really photos of the women participating in the study. The intention of the experimenters was simply to lead the men to *believe* they were talking to a woman who was attractive or unattractive. As for the women, they were not given a photo of their partner, nor were they told that the man had been biased to think of them in a particular way. All of the telephone calls were taped, and social aspects of the men's and women's conversational styles were then rated by judges who were unaware of the men's assignment group.

Not surprisingly, if the men thought they were talking to an attractive female, their conversational styles tended to be rated as friendly and positive—more so than if their partner had been depicted as unattractive. But the important finding of the study focused on the women. It turned out that the women's conversational styles also differed, depending on whether or not the man they were talking to thought they were attractive. The women who were presumed by their partners

? CRITICAL THINKING

Do you think the social schemas that were activated in the telephone study were different for the men and the women? If so, in what way?

self-fulfilling prophecy effect
A condition in which our expectations about the actions of another person actually lead that person to behave in the expected way.

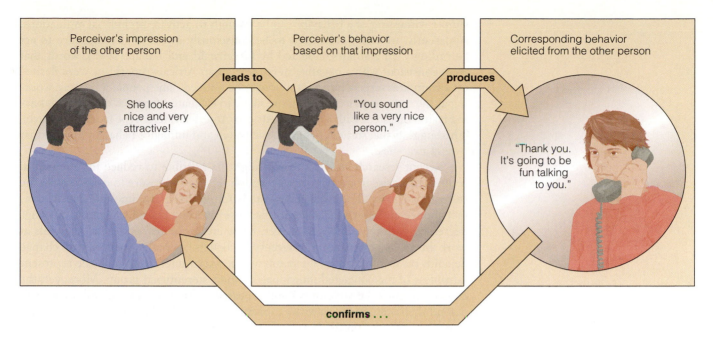

to be attractive were rated by the judges as more friendly, open and poised, and generally more pleasant than the women depicted as unattractive. Remember, these women had no idea that their male partners had preformed opinions about their attractiveness. Apparently, the friendly, positive conversational styles of the men were able to elicit similar qualities from the women. This is the self-fulfilling prophecy effect—the expectations that we have toward others, along with our actions, can actually influence them to act in the expected way (see Figure 13.2).

Prejudice

As you've seen, stereotypes can lead to rigid interpretations of people. Stereotypes can cause us to overgeneralize and place too much emphasis on the differences that exist *between* groups (for instance, between men and women), and too little emphasis on the differences that exist *within* groups. Not all women are dependent, nor are all men strong. Furthermore, when the beliefs we hold about a group are negative or extreme, stereotypes increase the likelihood of **prejudice** and discriminatory behavior. Someone can be excluded from a job, or even criminally assaulted, just because of negative beliefs activated by his or her skin color or sexual preference.

Unfortunately, research studies suggest that stereotypic beliefs, including the ones that lead to prejudice, are probably automatically activated and not completely under our conscious control. For example, we discussed above how the

FIGURE 13.2
The Self-Fulfilling Prophecy Effect
Our impressions of another person can affect how that person behaves, leading him or her to act in the expected way. In the study by Snyder and colleagues, if a male subject thought he was talking to an attractive female, his conversational style was rated as more friendly and positive—but so too was the conversational style of his female telephone partner.

prejudice
Positive or negative evaluations of a group and its members.

CONCEPT SUMMARY
Factors in Person Perception

Factor	Role in Person Perception	Example
Physical appearance	We tend to assume that physically attractive individuals are more intelligent, well-adjusted, and more socially aware.	Tyrone encounters Michelle at a party. He finds Michelle quite attractive. In addition, he perceives her as very personable, good-humored, and intelligent.
Social schemas	We use schemas (e.g. *stereotypes*) to organize and interpret ongoing experiences.	Tyrone believes most women are very sensitive, warm, and dependent. He finds that Michelle's behavior fits this pattern.
Self-fulfilling prophecies	The activation of stereotypes leads to expectations of certain types of behavior. These expectations can cause the person to behave in the expected way.	Tyrone is very attentive toward Michelle at the party, bringing her refreshments and introducing her to all of his friends. Michelle relaxes; she begins to open up and make witty comments.

simple witnessing of a behavior can be enough to activate prejudicial evaluations. Apparently, we don't even need to be consciously aware of the exposure to act accordingly. In a study conducted by Greenwald and Banaji (1995), words that were consistent with a negative stereotype about African-Americans were flashed on a computer screen at levels too low to be noticed. The people who were working at the computers were then more likely to evaluate a fictional character as having traits consistent with a negative African-American stereotype (e.g., aggressive). This suggests that stereotypes can be activated and influence behavior in ways that bypass awareness.

Recent research suggests that it might be possible to reduce the prejudicial feelings that arise from stereotypes through repeated exposure to *individuals* in the stereotyped group. For instance, one study found that as the amount of social contact between heterosexuals and homosexuals increased, negative feelings decreased (Whitely, 1990). However, there are a number of crucial elements at work in the maintenance of stereotypic beliefs. Whether beliefs will change depends on such factors as the nature of the social interactions and the representativeness of the contacted individuals to their stereotyped group. Moreover, the contact needs to be widespread and repeated; otherwise, people will attempt to defend their stereotypic views by explaining away individual contacts as unrepresentative of the group (Weber & Crocker, 1993).

Obviously, prejudging people on the basis of stereotypes can lead to many kinds of discriminatory behavior, including racism, sexism, and ageism. Stereotypes are not necessarily *accurate* representations of people, nor can they be expected to apply to all individuals within a group. Still, as general "rules of thumb," researchers assume that stereotypes do have adaptive value. They help people carve their social worlds into meaningful chunks, thereby providing a sense of direction about how to act when encountering new people (Oakes & Turner, 1990). Furthermore, not all of the components of stereotypes are inaccurate, nor are all instances of prejudice negative (Eagly & Johnson, 1990). Stereotyping occurs in every culture of the world, and it is simply another way in which the adaptive mind organizes and categorizes the world.

ATTRIBUTION THEORY: ATTRIBUTING CAUSES TO BEHAVIOR

It's natural for us to try to interpret the behavior of others. A wife tries to understand why her husband sits channel surfing in front of the television during their anniversary dinner; a student tries to understand why the teacher responds to his plaintive appeal for a grade change with a gruff "I didn't give you the grade, you earned the grade." When people assign causes to behaviors, psychologists refer to these inferences as **attributions;** attribution theories are concerned primarily with the psychological processes that underlie these inferences of cause and effect (Heider, 1944; Jones & Davis, 1965).

The Covariation Model

Let's consider an example of the attribution process at work. Suppose you notice that the mood of your friend Ira improves noticeably on Monday, Wednesday, and Friday afternoons, after he returns from lunch. He smiles a lot, exchanges pleasantries, and offers advice freely. These behaviors contrast sharply with his normal gruff manner and generally sour disposition. What accounts for the behavior change? According to the *covariation model of attribution* (Kelley, 1967), the first thing you'll look for is some factor that happens at the same time as, or *covaries* with, the behavior change. You will try to identify an event or some other factor that is present when the behavior change occurs and is absent when the behavior change does not occur. In this particular example, it turns out that Ira goes to his aerobic exercise class between 12:00 and 1:00 on those three days.

But covariation by itself is not a sufficient condition for the attribution of causality, for much the same reason that we cannot infer causality from the

attributions
The inference processes people use to assign cause and effect to behavior.

presence of a correlation (see Chapter 2). Just because Ira's mood improves after he leaves his exercise class does not mean that exercise is the cause of the change—other factors could be involved. According to the covariation model, we rely on three additional pieces of information to help us make the appropriate inference: *consistency*, *distinctiveness*, and *consensus*. When assessing *consistency*, we try to determine whether the change occurs regularly when the causal event is present—does Ira's mood consistently improve after exercise class? *Distinctiveness* provides an indication of whether the change occurs uniquely in the presence of the event—does Ira's mood improve after lunch only if he's been exercising? Finally, we look for *consensus*, which tells us whether other people show similar reactions when they are exposed to the same causal event—is elevation of mood a common reaction to exercising?

Internal versus External Attributions

These three factors—consistency, distinctiveness, and consensus—work in combination to help us form an attribution. In the particular example we've been considering, it's likely that we'll assume it's the *external* event—the exercise class—that is the cause of Ira's mood change. People tend to make an **external attribution,** which appeals to external causes, when the behavior in question is high in consistency, distinctiveness, and consensus. In the case of Ira's pleasant demeanor, it's highly consistent (it happens every Monday, Wednesday, and Friday afternoon); its occurrence is distinctive (it occurs only after exercise class); and there is a high level of consensus (exercise tends to make people happy).

But what if no single event or situation in the environment can be used to explain someone's behavior? For example, suppose Ira consistently smiles and acts pleasant in the afternoon, but he also smiles during the mornings and on days he has skipped the exercise class. Under these conditions it's doubtful that you will appeal to the environment to explain his behavior; instead, you'll be likely to make an **internal attribution,** which means you'll attribute his pleasant behavior to some *internal* personality trait or disposition: "Ira just has a great personality; he's a friendly, pleasant guy." Internal attributions are common when the consistency of a behavior is high but its distinctiveness and consensus are low. If Ira is pleasant all the time, his postlunch behavior lacks distinctiveness, and you'll be unlikely to appeal to some lunch activity to explain his behavior. Similarly, if the consensus is low—suppose exercise rarely improves mood for most people—you'll again resist attributing his pleasantries to this particular event (see Figure 13.3 on page 508).

The Fundamental Attribution Error

So far it seems like the attribution process is quite logical and rational, but this characterization is a bit misleading. Social psychologists have discovered that it's common for us to take shortcuts in the attribution process, probably because we're often required to make attribution judgments quickly, and it's effortful and time-consuming to consider all potential factors logically (Gilbert, 1989; Trope & Liberman, 1993). What happens, however, is that these shortcuts tend to produce consistent biases and errors in the judgment process. One of the most pervasive of these biases is the **fundamental attribution error:** When we seek to interpret someone else's behavior, we tend to overestimate the influence of internal personal factors and underestimate the role of external situational factors (Jones, 1990; Ross, 1977).

In a classic demonstration of this bias, Jones and Harris (1967) had college students read essays expressing either positive or negative opinions about Fidel Castro's communist regime in Cuba (at the time—the mid-1960s—Castro's Cuba was a hot topic of discussion). Before reading the essays, one group of students was told that the person writing the essay had been allowed to write freely and choose the position adopted in the text. A second group was told that the writer had no choice and had been forced to adopt a particular pro or con position. Afterward, the students in both groups were asked to speculate about the writer's true opinion

CRITICAL THINKING

Suppose you were forced to make an attribution quickly, without much time for thought. Do you think quickly formed attributions are more likely to be internal or external? Why?

external attribution
Attributing the cause of a person's behavior to an external event or situation in the environment.

internal attribution
Attributing the cause of a person's behavior to an internal personality trait or disposition.

fundamental attribution error
The fact that people seeking to interpret someone else's behavior tend to overestimate the influence of internal personal factors and underestimate the role of situational factors.

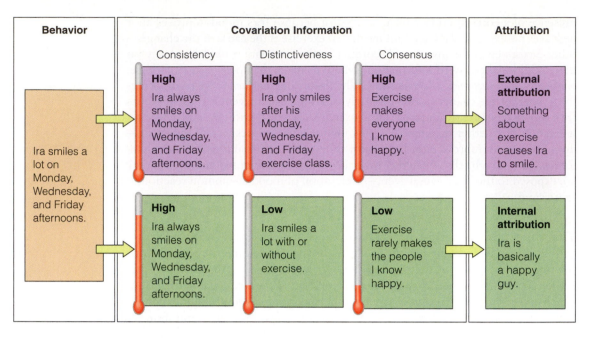

FIGURE 13.3

The Covariation Model of Attribution
When people make internal attributions, they attribute behavior to internal personality characteristics; external attributions attribute behavior to factors in the environment. In Kelley's attribution model, whether an internal or external attribution will be made about a particular behavior depends on *consistency, distinctiveness,* and *consensus*. Generally, behaviors that are consistent, that are highly distinctive, and that lead to consensus are attributed to the environment, whereas consistent behaviors that are not distinctive and show little consensus are attributed to internal characteristics.

on the topic. Thinking logically, you might assume that if the writer had been given a choice, then the essay position probably reflected his or her true opinion on Castro. Alternatively, if the writer was simply following directions, it would be difficult to tell. To the surprise of the experimenters, however, the students tended to believe that the essay *always* reflected the writer's true opinion, even when the students knew that the essay writer had been forced to adopt a particular position. This represents the fundamental attribution error at work: People tend to attribute an individual's activities to internal personal factors, even when there are strong situational explanations for the behavior (Jones, 1990).

Now consider another example: You're driving down the street, at a perfectly respectable speed, when you glance in your rearview mirror and see a pickup truck bearing down on your bumper. You speed up a bit, only to find the truck mirroring your every move. Being tailgated like this is a relatively common experience. But what kind of attribution do you typically make about the driver? Do you attribute the behavior to the person or to the situation? If you're like most people, your first response is likely to be an internal attribution—you naturally assume that the driver behind you has some severe personality flaw; put simply, the driver is a jerk. You ignore the possibility that situational factors might be compelling the driver to drive fast. Isn't it possible, for instance, that the driver is late for work or has a sick child in the backseat who is in need of a doctor? These kinds of attributions, which focus on the situation, don't usually enter our minds because our first tendency is to attribute behavior to an internal personal characteristic.

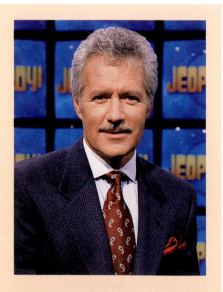

People often think that popular game show hosts, such as Alex Trebek, are extremely knowledgeable individuals. What attribution processes might underlie such an inference?

The Self-Serving Bias

Let's switch gears for a moment. Think about a case in which the attribution is being made about your own behavior. Suppose you're the one doing the tailgating. It's extremely unlikely that under these conditions you'll blame your tailgating on the fact that you're a jerk; instead, your attribution will be situation-based.

How people interpret "risky" behavior on the highway depends on who is doing the driving. When someone else commits the risky move, people are likely to attribute it to an internal personality characteristic of the driver; when we're the ones doing the driving, it is likely to be the environment that receives the blame.

You're tailgating, you explain, because you're late for an appointment, or because the driver in front of you is simply driving too slowly. Generally, people will take internal credit for their actions when those actions produce positive outcomes—such as attributing a solid A on the psychology test to hard work and intelligence—but they'll blame the situation when their behaviors are questionable or lead to failure. This tendency, called the **self-serving bias,** is adaptive because it allows us to bolster and maintain our self-esteem and project a sense of self-importance and confidence to the world (Snyder, 1989).

The self-serving bias, along with the fundamental attribution error, have important implications—not just for you but for society as well. The tailgating example is relatively harmless, but think about a situation in which the focus of analysis is on welfare or homelessness. Because of attribution biases, you might naturally attribute, for example, being on welfare or losing a job to laziness, incompetence, or some other negative internal trait. But in many cases an individual is on welfare or out of work because of situational factors, perhaps because of some catastrophic life event. Attribution biases may have considerable adaptive value—because they allow us to make quick decisions about the causes of behavior—but they do have a downside; they can lead to misleading or even incorrect conclusions.

Interestingly, there are situations in which our tendencies to show these attribution biases are reduced. For example, you're less likely to show the self-serving bias if you're working on a task with someone you know very well. If you're in a close relationship with your task partner, you're less likely to take credit for success on the task and assign blame for failure; if you don't know your partner very well, he or she gets the blame for failure and you take credit for the success (Sedikides et al., 1998). Your mood also seems to matter. For example, evidence indicates that you are more likely to commit the fundamental attribution error if you're in a positive mood; if you're in a negative mood, you're more willing to blame the situation, rather than the person, for the behavior (Forgas, 1998).

ATTITUDES AND ATTITUDE CHANGE

The final topic we'll consider in our discussion of social cognition is the study of attitudes and attitude change. An **attitude** is simply a positive or negative evaluation or belief held about something, which in turn may affect behavior. Like the

self-serving bias
The tendency to make internal attributions about one's own behavior when the outcome is positive and to blame the situation when one's behavior leads to something negative.

attitude
A positive or negative evaluation or belief held about something, which in turn may affect one's behavior; attitudes are typically broken down into cognitive, affective, and behavioral components.

other forms of social cognition we've discussed, attitudes are beneficial for a number of reasons. When they guide behavior, attitudes help us remain consistent in our actions and help us use our knowledge about individuals or situations. Attitudes also play an important role in our perception and interpretation of the world. They help us focus our attention on information relevant to our beliefs—particularly information that can help confirm an existing belief. As a result, attitudes may serve a kind of defensive function, protecting people's basic beliefs about themselves and others (Fazio, 1986).

The Components of an Attitude

Typically, social psychologists divide attitudes into three main components: a *cognitive* component, an *affective* component, and a *behavioral* component (Olson & Zanna, 1993). The cognitive component represents what people know or believe about the object of their attitude; the affective component is made up of the feelings that the object engenders; and the behavioral component is a predisposition to act toward the object in a particular way.

To see how these three components work together, let's suppose that you've formed an unfavorable attitude toward your landlord. Your attitude rests on a foundation of facts and beliefs about behavior. You know, for instance, that the landlord has raised your rent three times in the last year, that he enters your apartment without first asking permission, and that he won't let you keep your pet cat Kepler without a huge pet deposit. These facts and beliefs form the cognitive component of your attitude. Accompanying these facts are your emotional reactions, which make up the affective component—when you see or think about your landlord, you get angry and slightly sick to your stomach. Finally, the behavioral component of your attitude predisposes you to act in certain ways. You may spend every Sunday reading the classified ads looking for a new apartment, and you may constantly complain about your landlord to anyone who'll listen. It's these three factors in combination—cognitive, affective, and behavioral—that compose what psychologists mean by an attitude (see Figure 13.4).

Notice that the behavioral component of the attitude is described as a *predisposition* to act. This is an important point to remember, because attitudes do not always directly affect behavior. As you know, people sometimes act in ways that are inconsistent with their attitudes (Ajzen & Fishbein, 1977). When directly confronting your landlord, for instance, you may be all smiles even though underneath you're steaming. Attitudes do not always connect with behavior because behavior is usually determined by multiple factors—especially external factors such as the situation. In some situations it is simply unwise to express true feelings, such as when dealing with the landlord. In other situations, people act quickly and mindlessly without considering the true meaning or ramifications of their behavior (Langer, 1989). For example, people often sign petitions for activities they may not completely believe in, or buy products that they don't really want, simply because they're in a hurry and don't want to be bothered further. For an attitude to guide behavior, it needs to come to mind—that is, it needs to be accessible—and it should be appropriate or relevant to the situation (Kraus, 1995; Pratkanis & Greenwald, 1989).

How Are Attitudes Formed?

Where do attitudes come from, and how are they acquired? There are many routes to attitude formation. We use our everyday experiences as the basis for many of our ideas and beliefs. It's also the case that how we interpret those experiences depends partly on our inborn intellectual and personality traits (Tesser, 1993). Even something as simple as *mere exposure* can be sufficient to change your feelings about an object (Greewald & Banaji, 1995). In classic work by Robert Zajonc (1968), subjects were shown photographs of undergraduate men taken from a school yearbook. Some of the photos were shown only once or twice; others were shown up to 25 times. Following exposure, everyone was asked to give an

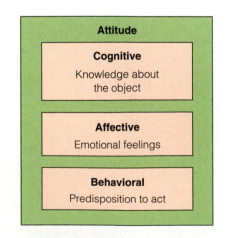

FIGURE 13.4
The Three Components of Attitudes
Social psychologists typically divide attitudes into three main components: cognitive, affective, and behavioral.

estimate of how much they liked each of the men shown. The results revealed that the more often a photo had been presented, the more the subjects claimed to "like" the person shown. It is not clear exactly how to interpret this finding, in part because people's ratings change on a whole host of dimensions following exposure (Mandler et al., 1987). But it demonstrates how easily attitudes can be affected.

Experience is generally agreed to be the single most important factor affecting attitude formation. A great deal of evidence suggests that attitudes can be conditioned, through experiences of the type discussed in Chapter 7. Events that occur outside of one's control can acquire signaling properties, through *classical conditioning*, and then serve as an initial foundation for an attitude (Cacioppo et al., 1993). Advertisers commonly try to manipulate how people feel toward consumer products by pairing the product with something pleasurable, such as an attractive model or a successful athlete. Through *instrumental conditioning*, attitudes are influenced by the rewards and punishments people receive for their actions. Certainly if you express a tentative opinion on a subject—"We've got too much big government in this country"—and this opinion is reinforced by people whom you respect, you're likely to express this same attitude again. Instrumental conditioning teaches us about the consequences of our behavior, and direct experience of this sort plays a significant role in attitude formation.

Finally, much of what we acquire from experience is the result of *observational learning*. We model significant others—our parents, peers, teachers, and so on—when it comes to both attitudes and behavior. The political convictions of most people, for example, mirror quite closely the political attitudes of their parents (McGuire, 1985). People use their peers, too, as a kind of reference group for judging the acceptability of their behaviors and beliefs. All you need to do is take a random sample of the behavior of teenagers in the local mall to see how important modeling behavior can be. Everything from language to musical taste to hairstyle to shoe type is replicated from one teen to the next. Ask yourself: How differently do you think and act from the people in your immediate circle of friends? Modeling may not be the only reason why people in a peer group often act and think in a similar way, but its influence is often profound.

Central and Peripheral Routes to Persuasion

For decades, social psychologists have been interested not only in how attitudes are formed initially but also in how attitudes can be changed. We live in a world in which there are constant attempts to convince us of something. We are bombarded daily by dozens of persuasive messages from sources in business, politics, religion, and the arts. For obvious reasons, psychologists have tried to determine the important ingredients of persuasion: What are the factors that determine whether you'll be convinced to buy a particular product or support a particular political campaign? According to one popular theory of attitude change, known as the **elaboration likelihood model,** there are two primary routes to persuasion; one that is central and one that is peripheral (Petty & Cacioppo, 1986).

The *central route* to persuasion is the most obvious and familiar one. It operates in those situations in which we're motivated and inclined to process an incoming persuasive communication with care and attention; we'll listen carefully to the arguments of the message, then judge those arguments according to their merits. Suppose you've recently changed your views on the topic of abortion after listening to a persuasive speaker at your school. If you carefully weighed the quality and strength of the arguments and then changed your attitude accordingly, you've been convinced via the central route. Not surprisingly, attitude changes that result from this kind of central processing tend to be stable and long-lasting (Olson & Zanna, 1993).

The *peripheral route* to persuasion operates when we are either unable to process the message carefully or are unmotivated to do so. When we process a message peripherally, our attitudes are much more susceptible to change from

elaboration likelihood model
A model proposing two primary routes to persuasion and attitude change: a *central* route, which operates when people are motivated and focusing their attention on the message, and a *peripheral* route, which operates when people are either unmotivated to process the message or are unable to do so.

MICHAEL
J**O**RDAN
cologne

Available at Carson Pirie Scott *and* Macy's

In situations in which a person's level of involvement or commitment to a message is low, advertisers tend to capitalize on the peripheral route to persuasion by using celebrity endorsers or humor in the persuasive message.

superficial cues or from mere exposure (Petty & Wegener, 1997). Think about the typical beer commercial on television. You don't see logical arguments about the quality of the product—you see talking frogs or partying dogs. The same is true for fast food commercials. There's no discussion of nutrition—again, it's talking animals or anecdotes about families and minivans. When our motivation to process the message is low, we are much more likely to be persuaded by **source characteristics**—things such as celebrity, attractiveness, or power.

Advertisers typically capitalize on the peripheral route to persuasion because most of the time we don't process advertisements on television or in magazines with a high level of involvement. We're also more likely to rely on processing shortcuts (*heuristics*) to form opinions when we process a message peripherally (Chaiken et al., 1989). For instance, you might adopt a favorable attitude toward an expensive product because you believe that "better products are more expensive," or you might buy the product endorsed by Michael Jordan because "Michael wouldn't endorse something that isn't quality."

The Festinger and Carlsmith Study

We can also be persuaded to change our attitudes because of our own actions. In a highly influential study of attitude change conducted by Festinger and Carlsmith (1959), male college students were asked to perform some incredibly boring tasks, such as placing sewing spools onto a tray, during an hour session. At the end of the hour, some of the participants (the experimental group) were given a bogus cover story. They were told that one purpose of the study was to examine the effects of motivation on task performance. The next subject, the researcher explained, needed to be told that the experiment was actually filled with interesting and enjoyable tasks. Would they mind going into the adjacent waiting room and telling him that the experiment was interesting and enjoyable? To provide an incentive, the experimenter offered some of the participants a monetary reward of $1 and others a reward of $20.

The point of the offer was to get the members of the experimental group to act in a way that contradicted their true feelings, or attitudes, about the experiment. The task was clearly boring, so they were essentially asked to lie for either a small or a large reward. Festinger and Carlsmith were interested in what effect this behavior would have on subjects' attitudes about the experiment. After accepting the offer, and trying to convince the next subject, the students' attitudes about the experimental tasks were assessed through an interview. The researchers found that attitudes about the experimental tasks did indeed change—they became more positive relative to the attitudes of the members of the control group, who had not been asked to lie. Moreover, the positive shift was larger for subjects receiving $1 as opposed to $20. The more subjects were paid to act inconsistently with their true feelings, the less likely their attitudes were to change (see Figure 13.5).

Cognitive Dissonance

The above results may seem perplexing. You would probably have predicted that the students receiving $20 would show the greatest attitude change—after all,

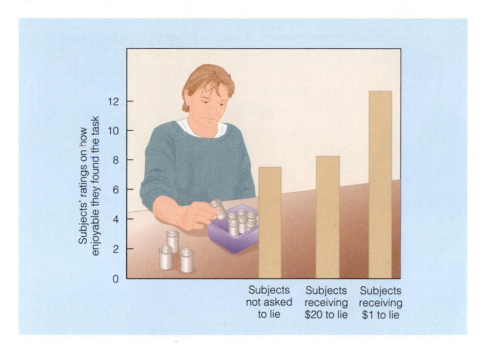

FIGURE 13.5

Cognitive Dissonance

Festinger proposed that attitudes change when a discrepancy exists between what we believe and how we act. People who lied about the boring experimental task for a measly $1 later claimed to enjoy the task more than did people who lied for $20 or who were not asked to lie. Presumably, it was tough to justify lying for a small amount of money, which created a lot of cognitive dissonance, so the subjects in the $1 condition simply changed their original attitude about the task. (Data from Festinger & Carlsmith, 1959.)

wouldn't a large reward have a greater reinforcing effect? The answer, according to Festinger's (1957) theory of **cognitive dissonance,** is that the inconsistent behavior produces tension—or what he called *dissonance.* Think about it. Which action is going to lead to greater internal turmoil and angst: lying to receive $1 or lying to receive $20? Most people can easily justify a simple white lie when offered a reasonable amount of money, especially when asked by an authority figure (remember that $20 was worth a lot more in the 1950s than it is now). But to lie for a measly $1 is tough to justify—unless, of course, you can justify the action by changing your initial attitude about the task. According to cognitive dissonance theory, if the discrepancy between what you believe and how you act is great, you will either (1) change your behavior, or (2) change your beliefs.

Since cognitive dissonance theory was first introduced in the 1950s, hundreds of follow-up studies have been conducted (Aronson, 1992). Most have confirmed Festinger and Carlsmith's basic finding. When people are induced to act in ways that are inconsistent with their attitudes, those attitudes often change as a consequence. But not all psychologists are convinced that internal tension, or dissonance, results from acting inconsistent with your beliefs. You might, for example, simply feel uncomfortable about your actions (Elliot & Devine, 1994) or you might feel personally responsible for creating an unwanted or negative situation (Blanton et al., 1997; Cooper, 1992). Some psychologists are also uncomfortable with the concept of cognitive dissonance because it remains rather vague and not easy to measure directly. It's also difficult to predict when dissonance will occur and, if it's present, how people will choose to reduce it (Joule, 1986). However, the idea continues to be influential among social psychologists, especially when the motivational and cognitive components of dissonance are taken into account (Aronson, 1997; Petty et al., 1997).

 CRITICAL THINKING

Next time you watch television, notice which commercials rely on logical arguments and which use humor or celebrity endorsers. Do you see any connection between the type of product and the style of persuasion? What kinds of products are more likely to induce us to use central rather than peripheral processing?

cognitive dissonance

The tension produced when people act in a way that is inconsistent with their attitudes; attitude change may occur as a result of attempting to reduce cognitive dissonance.

"Do you like hamburgers?"

"I guess so."

FIGURE 13.6
Self-Perception Theory
Some psychologists believe that we form attitudes at least in part by observing our own behavior. If I regularly eat hamburgers, then my attitude about hamburgers must be positive.

Self-Perception Theory

One of the best known alternatives to dissonance theory is psychologist Daryl Bem's (1967, 1972) **self-perception theory.** The idea behind self-perception theory is that we are active processors of our own behavior. We learn from our behavior and use our actions as a basis for inferring internal beliefs. For example, if I sit down and practice the piano for 2 hours a day, it must be the case that I like music and think I have at least a bit of musical talent. If I regularly stop for hamburgers and fries for lunch, it must be the case that I like fast food. The basis for the attitude is self-perception—behavior is observed, and attitudes follow from the behavior (see Figure 13.6).

Many experimental findings support these basic ideas. For example, the Festinger and Carlsmith study can be interpreted from this perspective. You observe yourself telling someone that a boring task is interesting, for a measly $1, and conclude that since you engaged in this behavior your attitude toward the task must not have been that negative. In another classic example, known as the *foot-in-the-door technique*, Jonathan Freedman and Scott Fraser (1966) convinced a group of California householders to sign a petition expressing support for safe driving. Several weeks later, the researchers returned with a request that the householders now place a large and quite ugly "Drive Safely" billboard in their yards. The petition signers were three times more likely to comply with this new request than a control group of people who did not initially sign a petition. What's the interpretation? The signing of the original petition triggered *self-perception*, which then helped shape the attitude: If I signed the petition, then I must be a strong advocate for safe driving.

A related phenomenon is the *lowball technique*. You wander into the local stereo store to look around. You're not really ready to buy, but the salesperson offers you a tremendous price on a high quality piece of equipment. You agree, convinced that you've received a great deal. The salesperson leaves to finish the paperwork with the manager of the store. He returns a few minutes later with some bad news: The offered price was a mistake—the manager rejected the deal—but he will be able to sell you the equipment at a price that is still lower than what most people pay. Reluctantly you agree to buy, even though you probably would have rejected this deal if it had been offered first. In this case, by getting you to

? CRITICAL THINKING

How might you use cognitive dissonance theory to explain the foot-in-the-door technique?

self-perception theory
The idea that people use observations of their own behavior as a basis for inferring their internal beliefs.

CONCEPT SUMMARY
Roots of Attitudes and Attitude Change

Mechanism	Description	Example ("Who should I vote for?")
Central route	When motivated to process an incoming message, we listen carefully to the arguments given, and judge them on their merits.	Jaraan is not sure who to vote for in the governor's race. He obtains detailed information on the candidates' views on the major issues, and after considering each, decides on the democratic candidate.
Peripheral route	When we are unable or unwilling to process a message carefully, our attitudes are more affected by superficial cues or mere exposure.	Yvette hasn't really kept up with the governor's race, but has seen some commercials during her nightly TV viewing. She gets a kick out of the republican candidate's humorous ad, so decides to vote for him.
Cognitive dissonance	Behavior that is inconsistent with attitudes produces tension (i.e., *dissonance*). If this discrepancy is large enough, attitudes or behavior will change.	Jeremy has always considered himself a republican, and backs the republican candidate for governor. Lately he's been dating a woman who is very involved in the democratic candidate's campaign. Jeremy finds that his attitudes toward the candidate are becoming more and more favorable.
Self-perception	We learn from our behavior, using our actions as a basis for inferring beliefs. Behavior is observed, and attitudes follow from the behavior.	Felicia gets a phone call from the third party campaign headquarters pleading for help. The third party can't compete with the other two campaigns unless it raises more money for its candidate. Felicia agrees to donate $20 to the cause. Looking back on it, she decides she must really favor the third-party candidate.

agree verbally to the initial purchase, the salesperson has lowered your resistance to buying the product.

Of course, there are boundary conditions for these effects—we do not always simply match our attitudes to our behaviors—but monitoring one's own behavior is clearly an important ingredient of attitude formation and change. It may be that we are particularly likely to use our own actions as a guide when we're unsure or undecided about our attitude. Or, we may use our own behavior to see if our attitudes or opinions have recently changed: "Do I still like playing video games? Well, let's see. I haven't played a game for awhile, so I must not be crazy about them any more." It's adaptive for us to use multiple sources of information for establishing our beliefs, including our own actions.

TEST YOURSELF 13.1

Check your knowledge about how we form impressions of others by answering the following questions. (You will find the answers in the Appendix.)

1. Decide whether each of the following statements about person perception is true or false.

   a. On average, attractive people are assumed to be more intelligent, better adjusted, and more socially aware than people with average looks. *True or False?*

   b. Prototype theories assume that we represent stereotypes with particular individuals, or exemplars. *True or False?*

   c. Stereotypes can be activated automatically and can influence our later behavior in ways that seem to bypass awareness. *True or False?*

   d. Studies suggest that it might be possible to reduce the prejudicial feelings that arise from stereotypes through repeated exposure to individuals in the stereotyped group. *True or False?*

2. For each of the following, decide whether you are most likely to make an internal or an external attribution for the behavior described.

a. A perfect score on your psychology exam: _____

b. Josie always smiles after her psychology lecture, but everyone else in the class leaves mad: _____

c. A failing score on your psychology exam: _____

d. Eagerly anticipating your food, you notice your waiter seems to spend a lot of time talking to the Hostess: _____

3. Decide whether each of the following statements about attitudes and attitude change is true or false.

a. For an attitude to guide behavior, it should be appropriate or relevant to the situation. *True or False?*

b. The *peripheral route* to persuasion operates when our level of involvement in or commitment to a message is high. *True or False?*

c. According to cognitive dissonance theory, it is inconsistencies between internal beliefs and our actions that leads to attitude change. *True or False?*

d. Mere exposure can lead to attitude change, but only if we're processing an incoming communication with care and attention. *True or False?*

8a
PsychNow!

Behaving in the Presence of Others: Social Influence

LEARNING GOALS

1. Define and discuss social facilitation and interference.

2. Describe the bystander effect and the concept of diffusion of responsibility.

3. Discuss how behavior changes when we're in a group setting, including the concepts of social loafing, deindividuation, and conformity.

4. Discuss group decision making, including polarization and groupthink.

5. Describe the Milgram experiment and discuss its implications for the power of authority.

We now turn our attention to the topic of **social influence:** How is our behavior affected by the presence of others? Obviously, by the term *others*, social psychologists mean the general social context, but "others" can have a variety of meanings in practice. Our behavior might change as a consequence of interacting with a single individual, perhaps an authority figure such as our boss or an intimate friend, or by the collective behavior of people in a group. Moreover, the presence of others can cause us to act in a new or different way, or simply to change our attitudes and beliefs. Think back to the ambitious underling, Al Hobart, whom we met in the chapter opening. His behavior certainly changed in the presence of others; he violated his beliefs and conformed to the opinions of his colleagues and his self-serving boss.

SOCIAL FACILITATION AND INTERFERENCE

One of the simplest and most widely documented examples of social influence is the phenomenon of social facilitation. **Social facilitation** is the *enhancement* in performance that is sometimes found when we perform in the presence of others. To demonstrate social facilitation, you need to compare someone's task performance in two conditions: when performing alone, and when performing in the presence of other people. If performance improves when other people are around, you've demonstrated social facilitation. In an early investigation of this effect, Norman Triplett (1898) discovered that adolescents would wind in a fishing line faster when working in pairs than when working alone. Task performance *improved* in the presence of others, which is the defining characteristic of social facilitation.

Social facilitation is a widespread effect, occurring in many kinds of social environments and for many kinds of tasks. Motorists drive through intersections faster when another car is traveling in the lane beside them (Towler, 1986); people run faster when others are present (Worringham & Messick, 1983); people even eat more when dining out with friends than when eating alone (Clendenen et al., 1994). In fact, the effect is not restricted to humans—ants will excavate dirt more quickly to build their nests when other ants are present (Chen, 1937); hungry chickens will peck food more when other chickens observe passively though a

social influence
The study of how the behaviors and thoughts of individuals are affected by the presence of others.

social facilitation
The enhancement in performance that is sometimes found when an individual performs in the presence of others.

clear plastic wall (Tolman, 1968); cockroaches will even run faster down an alleyway when a "spectator" roach watches from a small plastic enclosure (Zajonc et al., 1969).

But there is another side to the coin. It's easy to think of examples of how we've "risen to the occasion" and excelled when an audience was present, but the opposite can be the case as well. Sometimes performing in a crowd impairs performance—we "choke," a tendency referred to as **social interference.** Talented Angela, who finally performs Bach's Invention No. 1 perfectly in her last practice session, finds her fingers fumbling helplessly during the piano recital. Confident Eddie, who thought he had learned his lines to perfection, finds that on opening night he's standing embarrassingly silent on center stage. Social interference is the opposite of social facilitation, but both represent cases in which our ability to perform a task is influenced by the presence of others.

Task Difficulty and Arousal

Psychologists believe that *task difficulty* is one important factor that determines whether the presence of others will help or hinder performance. If the task is relatively easy, the presence of others will spur the person on, and you'll see social facilitation; if the task is new or difficult, the presence of others can have an inhibitory effect, and you'll find social interference. (It's worth noting that social psychologists sometimes use the term *social facilitation* to refer to both increases and decreases in performance when others are present; for our purposes, we'll draw a distinction between social *facilitation* and social *interference* to make the concepts easier to understand.)

According to psychologist Robert Zajonc (1965), it's possible to explain the relationship between task difficulty and social influence by appealing to how an audience's presence influences *arousal*. When others are watching, Zajonc argued, it's reasonable to assume that our general level of arousal increases. Arousal, in turn, naturally biases us toward engaging in dominant, or well-learned, responses. If the task is a relatively easy one, such as running or solving simple math problems, then such well-learned responses are likely to be useful and help performance. But when tasks are difficult, we're likely to need new or unusual responses that are less practiced or well learned. For difficult tasks then, performance is likely to be impaired because the high arousal levels will bias us toward responses that are not very useful. Thus, the influence that others have on performance is explained by appealing to the relationship between general arousal and its effects on task performance.

SOCIAL INFLUENCES ON ALTRUISM: THE BYSTANDER EFFECT

In addition to task performance, the presence of other people can dramatically influence whether we demonstrate **altruism**—that is, whether we will act in a way that shows unselfish concern for the welfare of others. Think about the last time that you were driving on the highway and noticed some poor person standing alongside his or her disabled car by the side of the road. Did you stop and help? Did you at least get off at the nearest exit and telephone the police or highway patrol? If you're like most people, you probably did nothing. In all likelihood, you failed to accept responsibility for helping—you left that job for someone else.

The problem is more serious than you might think. In March of 1964, while walking home from work at 3:30 in the morning, Catherine "Kitty" Genovese was stalked and then brutally attacked by a knife-wielding assailant outside her

Demonstrating the phenomenon of social facilitation, people tend to eat more when they're in the presence of others.

? **CRITICAL THINKING**

Under what conditions do you think the presence of an audience might actually lower *someone's arousal? What implications does this possibility have for social facilitation?*

social interference
The impairment in performance that is sometimes found when an individual performs in the presence of others.

altruism
Acting in a way that shows unselfish concern for the welfare of others.

When tasks are difficult, performing in the presence of others can lead to social interference; what seemed easy in private becomes a nightmare during the recital.

apartment building in Queens, New York. "Oh my god, he stabbed me!" Kitty screamed. "I'm dying! I'm dying!" Inside the apartment building, awakened by the screams, some 38 of her neighbors sat silently listening as the attacker finished the job. Kitty was stabbed repeatedly before she eventually died; in fact, the attacker actually left and came back to rape her and finish the job. No one in the apartment building came to her aid or called the police until approximately 30 minutes after the first attack. Did they simply not want to get involved in a situation like this, or was some other, more general psychological process at work?

The reluctance to come to someone's aid when other people are present is known generally as the **bystander effect** (Darley & Latané, 1968). Although it's relatively easy to document in natural environments, it's also possible to study the bystander effect in the laboratory. Consider the following scenario. You've volunteered to participate in a psychology experiment that involves groups of students discussing the problems of college life. To minimize embarrassment, you're allowed to sit in a small cubicle where you can communicate with the others via an intercom system. Before the experiment begins, you're told that one, two, or five other people will be participating. The session begins and suddenly one of the group members, who had previously mentioned being subject to epileptic seizures, begins to have a seizure. Over the intercom, his voice begins to garble—"Somebody-er-er-help-er-uh-uh-uh"—followed by silence. What do you do? Do you get up and help, or sit where you are?

In the actual version of this experiment, of course, no one actually had a seizure; the incident was manufactured by the experimenters to observe the bystander effect. There was also only one real subject in the experiment—the "others" were simply voices recorded on tape. The researchers found that the likelihood that the real subject would offer some kind of help to the imaginary seizure victim depended on how many other people the subject believed to be present. When the subject was convinced that only one other person was participating in the group, he or she almost immediately rose to intervene. But when it was presumed that four others (in addition to the seizure victim) were present, only 62% of the subjects offered aid (Darley & Latané, 1968).

Diffusion of Responsibility

Most social psychologists are convinced that the behavior of the people in these experiments, including the actions of the Queens apartment dwellers, is neither atypical nor representative of general apathy. Instead, the reluctance to get involved—to help others—can be explained by appealing once again to the powerful role of social context. We tend not to lend a hand, or get involved, because the presence of others leads to **diffusion of responsibility**—we believe that others have already done something to help or will soon get involved. If we know that others are present in the situation, and certainly many occupants of the apartment building heard the terrible screams, we allow our sense of responsibility to *diffuse*, or spread out widely among the other people presumed to be present.

The bystander effect is a disturbing but powerful example of social influence. Again, it has been replicated many times in numerous social settings that extend beyond the laboratory (Latané & Nida, 1981). As a general rule, the more witnesses there are, the less likely it will be that any one will step forward to offer aid. There are exceptions to the rule—for instance, people are more likely to help if they have recently observed others being helpful—but diffusion of responsibility remains the rule rather than the exception. The tendency to diffuse responsibility doesn't mean that people are bad or selfish; it simply provides yet another indication of how behavior can be strongly influenced by social factors in the environment. Our behavior changes when we are in the presence of others, and while the forces that produce the bystander effect may not make us feel good about ourselves, this behavior may be adaptive. Stopping to help someone in need could place one in danger—there may be a definite cost to helping behavior—and diffusion of responsibility is one way of reducing the potential cost.

THE POWER OF THE GROUP

The power that the social context has on human behavior is especially noticeable when we act as members of a well-defined group. Our behavior is shaped not only by the characteristics of the group—its size and the unanimity of its members—but even by the mere fact that we're *in* a group. Social psychologists have identified a number of psychological phenomena that illustrate the power of group membership. We'll consider three in the following sections: social loafing, deindividuation, and conformity.

Social Loafing

During our discussion of social facilitation you learned that a person's performance often changes when others are present. Whether performance improves or declines depends on factors such as the difficulty of the task or one's general level of arousal. But when participating as a member of a group, most people show a strong tendency to engage in **social loafing,** which means that they put out less effort than they do when they work alone (Latané et al., 1979). Social loafing is easy to demonstrate in the laboratory. In one study, volunteer subjects were instructed to clap and cheer as loudly as possible while blindfolded and listening to noise over headphones. Just before they began the task, the participants were told they would be clapping either with a group of other subjects or by themselves. When the volunteers believed they were part of a clapping group, their individual output dropped considerably.

Social loafing is a complex phenomenon, like many of the phenomena we've discussed in this chapter. Whether it occurs in a particular situation will depend on many factors, including the importance of the task and the cohesiveness of the group (Karau & Hart, 1998). The effect also occurs widely across cultures, although it may be especially common in cultures that stress individuality (Karau & Williams, 1993). Some social psychologists believe that there may be a connection between social loafing and the bystander effect that we discussed earlier. Bibb Latané (1981) has argued that both effects result from diffusion of responsibility. In the bystander effect, people suspect that others either will or have become involved; in social loafing, we assume that others will carry the load. In both cases, the fact that we are simply one of many makes us feel less accountable for our

diffusion of responsibility
The idea that when people know, or think, that others are present in a situation, they allow their sense of responsibility for action to diffuse, or spread out widely, among those who are present.

social loafing
The tendency to put out less effort when working in a group compared to when working alone.

People can feel less accountable for their behavior in a group setting, a condition known as "deindividuation."

behavior. We fail to step up and take full responsibility, or to work to our fullest capabilities, because the responsibility can be diffused or spread to the other members of the group.

Deindividuation

The idea that we feel less accountable for our behavior when we're in a group setting can lead as well to a phenomenon called **deindividuation.** Imagine yourself at a particularly lively party: The people around you are acting crazy—they're drinking too much, damaging the furniture, and some are even beginning to shed their clothes. Are you likely to start doing the same? Some psychologists have suggested that when we are in large groups, we begin to lose our sense of individuality. We enter a depersonalized state of mind, called deindividuation, that increases the chances of engaging in destructive, aggressive, or deviant behavior. Under most circumstances, it's highly unlikely that you would trash the furniture in a friend's home. But when you're a part of large rowdy group, deindividuation can lead you to do things that you might not otherwise do.

Once again, diffusion of responsibility is likely to play a role in such situations. When you're in large group, you're less likely to feel accountable for your actions. You feel anonymous, which lowers your normal restraints on destructive actions. You also feel less self-conscious—you go along with the group, as a whim, because you're not thinking about your normal standards, values, and morals. Whether you truly enter a depersonalized state of mind is debatable, but your actions do differ from your normal tendencies. Some psychologists have argued that deindividuation is simply an example of situation-specific behavior; your behavior is being controlled by an unusual situation and your actions probably don't provide much information about how you typically behave in other situations (Postmes & Spears, 1998).

Conformity

One of the most important and disturbing properties of group membership is **conformity,** which occurs when a person's opinions, feelings, and behaviors start to move toward the group norm. When you're in a group setting, you feel social pressure which, in turn, causes you generally to comply, or go along, with the wishes of the group—even though you may not always be aware that you're doing so. Studies investigating issues of conformity and compliance to group norms are among the oldest and best known of all social psychology experiments.

deindividuation
The loss of individuality, or depersonalization, that comes from being in a group; it can increase the chances of a person engaging in destructive, aggressive, or deviant behavior.

conformity
The tendency to comply, or go along, with the wishes of the group; when people conform, their opinions, feelings, and behaviors generally start to move toward the group norm.

Standard   Comparison
line   lines

FIGURE 13.7
The Asch Study of Conformity
Do you think you would have any trouble choosing the correct comparison line in this task? Asch found that people often conformed to the group opinion. The photo shown here is taken from one of Asch's actual experiments.

In one classic study of conformity, psychologist Solomon Asch (1951, 1955) rigged the following experimental setup. Subjects were asked to participate in a simple perception experiment that required them to make judgments about line length. Two cards were shown, one displaying a standard line of a particular length, and the other showing three comparison lines of differing lengths. The subject was required to state aloud which of the three comparison lines was the same length as the standard line (see Figure 13.7). The task was really quite simple—there was no question as to what the correct answer should be. The catch was that this was a group experiment, and the other members of the group were really confederates of the experimenter—they were not, in fact, volunteers, but rather were there to put social pressure on the true participant.

The confederate subjects were instructed to lie on a certain number of the trials. They were told to give a response, aloud, that was clearly wrong (such as picking comparison line 1 as the correct answer). Asch was mainly concerned about how often these incorrect answers would affect the answers of the real subject. Imagine yourself in this situation—you know the answer is line 2, but four of your fellow subjects have already given 1 as a response. Do you conform to the opinions of your peers, even though doing so conflicts with what you know to be true? The results were not particularly encouraging for those who champion individualism. Asch found that in approximately 75% of the sessions, subjects complied on at least one of the trials, and the overall rate of conformity was around 37%. Although peer pressure wasn't always effective in altering the behavior of the subjects—in fact, only 5% of the subjects conformed on every trial—it was a powerful influence. In describing his results, Asch (1955) put it this way: "That reasonably intelligent and well-meaning young people are willing to call white black is a matter of concern" (p. 34).

As you might imagine, the Asch experiments had quite an impact on the psychological community. Similar experiments have been conducted on dozens of occasions, not only in the United States but also in many other countries around the world. Generally, Asch's results have held up well, although a number of variables affect the likelihood that conformity will occur. Asch himself found, for example, that the rate of compliance dropped dramatically when one of the confederates dissented from the majority and gave the correct answer. It was also discovered that the size of the group is not as important as you might think. Conformity increases as the size of the pressure group gets larger, but it levels off relatively quickly. The pressure to conform does not increase directly with group size; after a certain point, usually when the majority group contains three to five members, adding even more pressure has a diminishing effect (Tanford & Penrod, 1984). Finally, feelings about the status of the group as a whole also matter; if people have little or no respect for the other members of the group, they're less likely to conform. Conformity is particularly likely when pressure comes from an **in-group**—that is, a group of individuals with whom one shares features in common or with whom one identifies (Abrams et al., 1990).

CRITICAL THINKING

Notice that when people conform they act in ways that are inconsistent with their attitudes. What implications should this have for attitude change?

in-group
A group of individuals with whom one shares features in common, or with whom one identifies.

Why do we conform to the majority opinion? One possibility is *normative social influence*—we generally seek approval in social settings and try to avoid rejection, so we act to please by complying with social customs and norms. Clearly, voicing a dissenting opinion increases the risk of rejection by the group, so we choose to conform. But it may also be the case that we use the majority group opinion as a source of information, which is commonly referred to as *informational social influence*. If four or five people around you are convinced that comparison line 1 is the correct answer, perhaps your perception of the stimulus is flawed in some way. Perhaps your angle of sight is misleading, or your memory for the comparison line is wrong. Consequently, you use the opinions of the others in the group as information or evidence about what has really been presented.

GROUP DECISION-MAKING

As you've just seen, members of an in-group can exert considerable pressure on one another to conform to the standards or norms of the group. One of the consequences of these internal pressures is that groups tend to take on behavioral characteristics of their own, especially when group decisions need to be made. Obviously, the psychology of group decision making is critically important—it affects everything from how verdicts are reached by juries, to how families decide where to go on vacations, to decisions made by Congress. Psychologists have identified two important characteristics of group decision making: group polarization and groupthink.

Group Polarization

When members of an in-group arrive at a consensus of opinion, there is a tendency for the group's opinion to polarize. **Group polarization** means that the group's dominant point of view—which is usually determined by the initial views of the majority—becomes stronger and even more extreme with time. If you join a local action group dedicated to exposing corporate corruption and the group tends to believe initially that corporate corruption is a significant and rising problem, it's likely that over time you and the rest of the members of the group will become even more convinced of that position (Moscovici & Zavalloni, 1969; Myers, 1982).

What accounts for group polarization? Not surprisingly, some of the same factors that promote conformity promote polarization. For example, group dis-

group polarization
The tendency for a group's dominant point of view to become stronger and more extreme with time.

Group polarization occurs when the group's majority opinion becomes stronger and more extreme with time. What's the likelihood that the members of this group of protesters will adopt more tolerant views on abortion in the future?

Inside the Problem   Culture and the Individual

We've discussed how our thoughts and actions change when we're in the presence of others, particularly groups. The group can exert a powerful influence on members' judgments, leading to conformity, groupthink, and obedience to authority. In some cases, people may find themselves succumbing to the group's demands at the expense of their own personal convictions. Remember Al Hobart and the questions we posed at the opening to this chapter? Have the preceding sections in this chapter changed your mind about how you might act in such a situation?

But is the tendency to conform, or to sacrifice one's individual desires for the collective, necessarily bad? Is conformity or obedience a sign of weakness, or is it a sign of strength? The answer depends partly on the culture in which you are raised. In most Western cultures, such as the United States, people are taught from a very young age to adopt an *independent* view of the self; that is, people are rewarded for viewing themselves as unique individuals, with special and distinctive qualities. American children, for example, are likely to be told things like "the squeaky wheel gets the grease." Be someone different, be an individual with unique qualities—these are the things that count. Although Western cultures certainly value acts of charity or unselfish devotion to others, such acts are typically viewed as reflecting distinctive personal qualities—qualities that make someone stand out as an admirable *individual*.

In many non-Western cultures, particularly Asian cultures, people adopt a very different, *interdependent* view of the self (Markus & Kitayama, 1991, 1994). In Japan, for example, children are taught to think of themselves from the perspective of the collective—as members of a group with common goals—rather than as individuals striving to be different. In Japan, children are told, "The nail that stands out gets pounded down." Such cultural differences are reflected in people's inner thoughts and feelings. When asked to write self-descriptions, Asians are likely to list personal qualities that they share with others ("I come from Kyoto") and to think they are more similar to others than others are to them. Westerners, in contrast, tend to describe themselves as dissimilar to others, and they use individualistic characteristics ("I'm very talented on the flute") to describe themselves (Trafimow et al., 1991). The majority of Westerners also tend to think of themselves as above average in intelligence and leadership ability, which is a trend rarely seen among Asians (Markus & Kitayama, 1991).

What do such findings mean? They should reinforce in your mind the idea that cultural factors cannot be ignored in the interpretation and study of behavior and mind. Our thoughts and actions often arise from our efforts to adapt successfully to our individual environments. As cultural demands on the individual vary, so too will the resulting behaviors .

In some Asian cultures, children are encouraged to adopt an "interdependent" view of self; that is, they are taught to view themselves primarily as members of a group with common goals rather than as individuals striving to be different.

---

cussions tend to provide information that consolidates initial opinions. Those who enter the group with strong opinions make strong cases for their viewpoint and dissenting viewpoints are less likely to be heard (Stewart & Stasser, 1995). At the same time, the social aspects of the discussion play an important role. People want be liked by the other members of the group, so they shift their attitude toward the group consensus. You are more likely to be accepted by the group if you forcefully argue in favor of the group's dominant viewpoint.

Groupthink

The trend toward consensus and polarization of opinion may also be influenced by what psychologist Irving Janis has labeled **groupthink:** Members of a group become so interested in seeking a consensus of opinion that they start to ignore and even suppress dissenting views. Janis (1982, 1989) found evidence for groupthink when he looked at how well-established in-groups arrived at decisions,

groupthink
The tendency for members of a group to become so interested in seeking a consensus of opinion that they start to ignore and even suppress dissenting views.

CONCEPT SUMMARY
Influences of the Group

Phenomenon	Description
Social facilitation	An enhancement in performance sometimes found when we perform in the presence of others. Especially likely with easy or well-practiced tasks.
Social interference	A decline in performance when one is in the presence of others. Especially likely with tasks that are unique or not well-learned.
Bystander effect	The reluctance to come to someone's aid when other people are present. Characterized by diffusion of responsibility, the tendency to believe that others will help.
Social loafing	Most people show a strong tendency to put in less effort when they are working in a group than when they work alone.
Deindividuation	When in large groups, we can lose our sense of individuality, and become more likely to engage in destructive, aggressive, or deviant behavior.
Conformity	A person's opinions, feelings, and behaviors start to move toward the group norm.

Influences on Decision Making

Phenomenon	Description
Group polarization	A group's dominant point of view becomes stronger and even more extreme with time.
Groupthink	Members of group become so interested in seeking a consensus of opinion that they ignore and suppress dissenting views.

particularly policy decisions by members of the government. He and others have analyzed a number of watershed events in U.S. policymaking, including the decision to escalate the war in Vietnam, the decision by President John F. Kennedy to invade Cuba in 1961, and even the decision by NASA to launch the ill-fated *Challenger* Space Shuttle. Not all psychologists are satisfied with the interpretations that Janis provided for groupthink (e.g., Kramer, 1998), but there is still wide agreement that the phenomenon exists (Esser, 1998).

In an alarming number of cases, Janis discovered that group members systematically sought consensus at the expense of critical analysis. Group members often acted as if they were trying to convince themselves of the correctness of their position. When alternative views were expressed, those views were either suppressed or dismissed. The management at NASA had clear evidence that freezing launch temperatures might pose a problem for *Challenger*, but the managers chose to ignore that evidence in the interest of going forward with the mission. The result of groupthink is general closed-mindedness and an overestimation of the uniformity of opinion.

Can groupthink be avoided? According to Janis (1982), it is possible to counteract the limiting effects of social context by following certain prescriptions. For instance, it helps to have a leader who acts impartial, one who does not quickly endorse a particular position. One or more members of the group can also be assigned a kind of devil's advocate role in which they are expected and encouraged to represent a dissenting position. Perhaps most important, however, is the simple recognition by the group that social influences such as groupthink are real phenomena that affect behavior, irrespective of group members' intelligence or commitment to the truth. Groupthink can be avoided, although it requires a reformation of how group decision making is normally conducted (t'Hart, 1998).

THE POWER OF AUTHORITY: OBEDIENCE

Up to this point in our discussion of social influence, we've concentrated on how behavior is affected by the presence of others, where the others have simply been any individuals who happen to be present in the social context. But in many cases it does matter *who* these others happen to be—on what roles these people play in your life. Think back once again to Al Hobart, who opened the chapter. Do you

Obedience to authority reached shocking levels in 1978 when followers of Reverend Jim Jones chose, under his direct orders, to commit mass suicide by drinking Kool-Aid laced with cyanide.

think he would have agreed so readily with his coworkers if the head of advertising had not been standing there, drink in hand, listening intently to his opinions? To what degree was Hobart's behavior changed because it was someone in a position of authority who had asked him his opinion? The question of how behavior changes in the presence of authority is a crucial one, and its study has produced some of the most intriguing and controversial empirical studies in the history of social psychology.

Psychologists use the term **obedience** to refer to the form of compliance that occurs when people respond to the orders of an authority figure. You're of course aware of the fact that during World War II, millions of Jewish men, women, and children were systematically executed by scores of German soldiers working under orders from Nazi officials. In a rural area of Guyana, South America, in 1978, hundreds of converts to the religious teachings of Reverend Jim Jones chose, under his direct orders, to commit mass suicide. Most people find it extremely difficult to understand such events and consider them to be social aberrations committed by people far different from themselves. Admittedly, you might toe the line in front of your boss, and do and say things that you don't really believe, but murder innocent people? Drink Kool-Aid laced with cyanide? Never.

The Milgram Experiment

In what is perhaps the most controversial social psychology experiment ever conducted, psychologist Stanley Milgram set out to determine just how resistant the average person really is to the demands of authority. He placed an advertisement in a local newspaper recruiting men for what was billed as a study looking at the effects of punishment on learning. The participants were told that for a small fee, they would be asked to play one of two roles in the experiment: either a *learner*, which required memorizing and then recalling lists of word pairs, or a *teacher*, whose task it would be to administer an electric shock to the learner whenever he made any recall errors. Each session required two subjects, one teacher and one learner, and the assignment of condition was decided by drawing slips of paper out of a hat.

But things were not exactly what they appeared to be. In fact, in every case the true volunteer, the one who had actually responded to the ad, was picked to be the teacher. The learner was a *confederate* of the experimenter, someone who was fully informed about the true nature of the study. Although it was rigged to look like he was receiving shocks throughout the session, he never actually did. The idea was to get the confederate to make learning errors and then to assess how

obedience
The form of compliance that occurs when people respond to the orders of an authority figure.

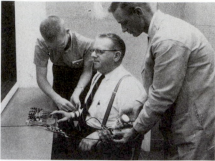

These three photos were taken during one of Milgram's early experiments on obedience to authority. The first photo shows the shock generator used during the experiment; the second photo shows the "learner," who was actually a confederate of the experimenter, being hooked up to the shocking apparatus; the third photo shows the "teacher" sitting in front of the shock generator, in the presence of the demanding experimenter.

willing the teacher would be to administer the shock, under the authority of a hovering and demanding experimenter.

To begin the setup, the unwitting teacher watched as the learner was led away to an adjacent room and hooked up to a shock-administering apparatus. Back in the original room, the teacher was then placed in front of an imposing-looking electrical shock generator, which contained some 30 different switches. It was explained that each switch was able to generate a particular level of shock intensity, ranging from 15 volts (Slight Shock), through 150 volts (Strong Shock), and finally up to 450 volts (labeled simply XXX). With the experimenter standing by his side, the teacher was instructed to begin reading and then testing the learner's memory for the words, via intercom, and to administer a shock whenever the learner failed to call out the correct answer. Moreover, in order see how the degree of punishment influenced learning, the teacher was instructed to increase the voltage level of the shock, by moving to a new switch, with each new mistake.

Remember, no one was actually shocked in this experiment; the learner was *in* on the experiment, and he was told to make mistakes consistently throughout the session. To add to the cover, he was also instructed to respond vocally and actively to the shocks, via the intercom, whenever they were delivered. At first, when the shock levels were low, there wasn't much response. But as the prearranged mistakes continued—which, of course, necessitated the teacher to continue increasing the voltage of the shock—loud protests began to come over the intercom. By the time the mistake-prone learner was receiving 150-volt shocks, he was demanding to be released from the experiment. By around 300 volts, he was screaming in agony in response to each delivered shock and pounding on the wall; after the 330-volt level, the shocks yielded no response at all—simply silence.

Listening to these disturbing pleas for help did not, of course, make the average teacher very comfortable. In fact, most quickly expressed concern over the consequences of the shocking and wanted to discontinue the experiment. But the teacher's concerns were met with resistance from the authoritative experimenter, who demanded that the shocks go on. "Please continue," the experimenter responded. "You have no other choice, you must go on." What would you do in this situation? You're participating in an experiment, which is being conducted in the name of science, but the task requires you to inflict quite a bit of pain and suffering on someone else. Do you blindly go forward, delivering shocks in compliance with the requests of the authority figure, or do you quit and give the experimenter a piece of your mind? Of course, this was exactly the question of interest to Milgram—how obedient would people be to unreasonable requests by an authority figure?

Interestingly, before the experiment actually began, Milgram asked a number of people, including professionals to predict how much shock subjects would be willing to deliver in his task. Most predicted that obedience would be low; the estimates were that only a few people in a thousand would deliver shocks up to 450 volts and that most subjects would defy the experimenter after discomfort was expressed by the learner. In reality, the results were far different. Milgram found that 65% of the 40 subjects who participated were willing to deliver shocks up to 450 volts, and no subject quit before the pounding on the wall started. This means that 26 of the 40 subjects went all the way to the final switch—the one with the ominous XXX label—despite the agonizing pleas from the learner. This remarkable finding rocked the psychological community and initiated a great deal of subsequent research, as well as a firestorm of controversy.

CRITICAL THINKING

Why might it be adaptive for us to respond so readily to the demands of an authority figure?

Controversies and Ethical Concerns

Milgram's (1963) experiment was controversial for two main reasons. First, the manner in which it was conducted raised some serious *ethical* questions. The subjects in his study were misled from the beginning and became severely distressed during their participation. Milgram observed a number of indications of distress during the experiment—the "teachers" sometimes groaned, bit their lips, trembled, stuttered, and even broke into a sweat. Many critics feel that this kind of psychological manipulation—even though it was done to advance knowledge—cannot be justified (Baumrind, 1964; Schlenker & Forsyth, 1977). In response, Milgram (1974) argued that his subjects were thoroughly debriefed at the end of the experiment—they were told in detail about the true nature of the experiment—and were generally glad they had participated. Follow-up questionnaires sent to the subjects months later revealed that only a handful felt negative about the experiment.

The other major question raised about the experiment concerned the procedure itself. Some critics argued that perhaps the participants had seen through the cover and were simply trying to please the experimenter; others argued that the results, although interesting, had no general applicability beyond the laboratory. Subjects must have assumed that things were okay, these critics reasoned; otherwise no one would have believed that an experiment of this type could be conducted. In retort, Milgram again pointed out that his subjects tended to get extremely distressed in the setting, which suggests that they could not have figured out the hoax and were acting in accordance with their true feelings.

In the three-plus decades since Milgram's original experiment was conducted, his general procedure has been repeated a number of times, in many countries around the world (see Blass, 1991; Meeus & Raaijmakers, 1987). Few psychologists today question the validity of his basic findings, although it's clear that the degree of compliance that people will show to authority depends on many factors. For example, the Milgram experiment was conducted at a prestigious university (Yale); when the same study was conducted in a less prestigious setting—a rundown office building—compliance dropped (although it remained alarmingly high). People were also less likely to comply if the authority figure left the room after explaining the experiment or if the person giving the orders looked ordinary rather than official or scientific (Milgram, 1974). Thus, obedience to authority is not absolute—it depends on the characteristics of the situation as well as on the characteristics of the person giving the orders.

TEST YOURSELF 13.2

Check your knowledge about social influence by answering the following questions. (You will find the answers in the Appendix.)

1. Pick the psychological term that best fits each of the statements below. Choose from the following: social facilitation, social loafing, deindividuation, bystander effect, conformity, group polarization, groupthink, obedience.

   a. Casey is normally shy and polite, but at the rock concert last night he was loud and shouted obscenities at the police: _____

b. Megan writes extremely well, but she contributes little to group discussions during class: _____

c. Sergio is convinced that his study group is dead wrong about their interpretation of the Milgram experiment, but he chooses to nod in agreement with the others in the group: _____

d. Landlord Sang-Woo notices that the grievances coming from his tenant group have become increasingly more rigid and demanding over time: _____

e. Gabriella never calls 911 when she sees a broken-down car by the side of the road—she assumes everyone has a cell phone: _____

f. Teresa notices that she always talks more when she's at a large party: _____

2. Which of the following situations should lead to the greatest reduction in obedience to authority?

a. The authority figure wears a uniform in front of the teacher.
b. The authority figure stands close to the teacher.
c. The experiment is conducted in a federal building.
d. The experiment is conducted in the teacher's home.

Establishing Relations with Others

We've defined social psychology as the discipline that studies how we think about, influence, and relate to other people. Our first two adaptive problems have dealt with social thought and social influence. We now turn our attention to the third and final component: How do we establish and maintain *relations* with others? People are not merely objects to be interpreted, or forces that exert influences on behavior. For most of us, it is the personal relationships we establish that are paramount in our lives. Most people depend on their interactions with friends, lovers, and family not only for protection and sustenance but also to help give meaning to their lives.

We've actually encountered the topic of social relations several times in earlier chapters. In Chapter 4, when we discussed social development, we dealt in detail with the topic of *attachment*. But in that case we were concerned with how people use social bonds to help solve the problems that arise during

Our relationships with others help protect us, nurture us, and give meaning to our lives.

development. Infants are born with limited motor skills and somewhat immature perceptual systems; consequently, they need to establish strong bonds with their caregivers in order to survive. In Chapter 11, when we discussed motivation and emotion, we saw how people use facial expressions to communicate their emotions to others and how people are motivated to secure sexual partners. Again, the emphasis was placed on the adaptive value of the relationship rather than on understanding the role that the social context plays in the process. In this section we'll consider some of the factors that influence interpersonal attraction, which often forms the basis for relationship development, and then we'll discuss how psychologists have attempted to tackle the mysterious subject of love.

WHAT MAKES A FACE ATTRACTIVE?

For most of us, few things are as alluring as the sight of an attractive face. Beauty is a powerful motivator of behavior, a fact confirmed by the many millions of dollars spent annually on cosmetics and other beauty aids. The concept of attractiveness is important to the psychologist because people's physical appearance often helps shape how their behavior will be interpreted, and thereby how they will be treated by others. As you learned earlier in the chapter, people commonly rely on social schemas to form impressions, and there is considerable evidence to suggest that physical attractiveness is used as a basis for generating expectations about others (Eagly et al., 1991). Just think about the words of the nineteenth-century German poet Johann Schiller: "Physical beauty is the sign of an interior beauty, a spiritual and moral beauty." Schiller's insight is certainly not lost on modern advertisers who, as you know, rely heavily on the power of an attractive face to help sell their clients' products.

An Evolutionary Perspective

What exactly is it that makes a face physically beautiful? What are the qualities that determine whether someone's looks are considered desirable? One way to think about this problem is from the perspective of evolutionary theory. If the purpose of attraction is to snare an ideal mate, then preferably it should be someone with a high reproductive capacity or someone who is able to provide protection for his or her children and compete successfully for needed resources. This kind of reasoning predicts that people should be attracted to opposite-sex members who are youthful, vigorous, and healthy looking, because these qualities increase the likelihood of successful reproduction and child rearing (Alley & Cunningham, 1991; Buss, 1989; Buss & Schmitt, 1993).

Another prediction of evolutionary theory is that features of attractiveness should cut across cultural boundaries. If attractiveness is grounded somewhere deep in our genetic ancestry, then it shouldn't matter much where you are reared and what experiences you have; in general, there should be worldwide agreement about what constitutes attractiveness. Notice that this conclusion contrasts sharply with the generally accepted idea that "beauty is in the eye of the beholder," but it's supported, at least in part, by empirical research. A number of studies have found that when ratings of attractiveness are compared cross-culturally, attractive faces share a number of basic structural features (Bernstein et al., 1982; McArthur & Berry, 1987). It's also been discovered that babies, within hours of birth, prefer to look at pictures of faces that adults have rated as attractive over faces that have been rated as unattractive (Langlois et al., 1987; Slater et al., 1998). It's unlikely that we can appeal to experience—that is, sustained exposure to some culturally based definition of beauty—to account for this preference.

Attractive Faces May Be Average

Research by psychologists Judith Langlois and Lori Roggman (1990; Langlois et al., 1994) suggests that the universality of attractiveness may be partly due to the fact that people are programmed to prefer faces that are *average* representations of

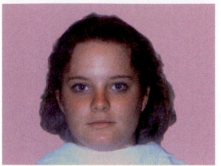

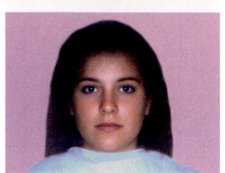

The faces shown in each row are composites created by averaging either two individual faces (far left), 8 faces (middle photos in each row), or 32 faces (far right). The stimuli were created using the averaging process employed by Langlois and Roggman. (Courtesy Judith Langlois.)

faces in the population. By average, Langlois and Roggman do not necessarily mean common, typical, or frequently occurring faces. Instead, they mean prototypical faces—that is, faces that are good representations of the category "faces." Back in Chapter 9, we defined category prototypes as the best or most representative members of a category—a robin, for example, is probably close to the prototype for the category "bird." According to Langlois and Roggman, attractive faces are those that are particularly *facelike*, or representative of the category of faces.

They based their conclusions on research in which people were asked to rate the attractiveness of average faces that were generated electronically on a computer. To create these faces, hundreds of individual black-and-white photographs, composed of either male or female Caucasians, Asians, and Hispanics, were first scanned by a computer and then digitized into matrices of individual gray values. Each of these gray values corresponded to a shade of gray sitting at a particular small location on the scanned face. A whole face was represented by many thousands of these gray values, as they are in a typical newspaper photo or video display. As you probably know, any image you see in a newspaper or on a video monitor is actually a configuration of many rows and columns of individual intensity dots or pixels. When viewed as a whole, the dots blend together to form a familiar image on the page or screen.

The unique feature of the Langlois and Roggman research was that people were sometimes shown faces that were generated by averaging the gray values across a large collection of individual faces. An individual dot in one of these *composite* faces was set by averaging the values of all the dots at the same relative location in the face pool. The result was a kind of blended face that did not look exactly like any one of the individual faces but rather represented a kind of prototype face in the population. Volunteer participants were asked to rate these faces for attractiveness, along with the individual faces that had been used to form the composite. The surprising result was that people generally rated the composite faces as more attractive than the individual faces (see also Rhodes & Tremewan, 1996).

Why would people prefer faces that are prototypical? Langlois and Roggman offer several speculative reasons. One possibility is that prototypical faces are easy

There are subjective components to the perception of beauty that are culturally dependent.

to identify and classify as human faces. Classifying something as a face may not seem like much of task for adults, but it could well be for the newborn infant. It is critical for infants to be able to recognize a looming visual configuration as a face, because they are dependent on their social interactions with people for survival. Yet the visual acuity of the newborn is limited, so faces that are particularly face-like may make this critical classification process easier. Another possibility is that people are programmed biologically to prefer prototypical faces because individuals with average features may be less likely to harbor potentially harmful genetic mutations. Generally, it is the average or normal characteristics that tend to be preferred over extreme ones in a population.

The Subjective Components

Despite the evidence for universality in how people conceive of attractiveness, most psychologists recognize that there is a strong subjective component to the perception of beauty as well. As we discussed in Chapter 11, standards of beauty have changed over time in most cultures of the world. In Western societies, for instance, our icon of beauty, the fashion model, has ranged from a "curvaceous bustiness" at one point to slender tomboyishness at the next (Silverstein et al., 1986).

It's also the case that features considered attractive in one culture—pierced noses, liposuctioned thighs, elongated ear lobes—may be considered unattractive in another. Perceptions of attractiveness and beauty also clearly change with experience. We generally rate people we like as more attractive than people we don't like; moreover, if you've just been shown a picture of a strikingly attractive person, your ratings of average-looking people go down (Kenrick et al., 1989). Beauty is not entirely in the eye of the beholder, as the research of Langlois and Roggman (1990) indicates, but there is indeed a measurable subjective component that cannot be ignored.

DETERMINANTS OF LIKING AND LOVING

If you had to list all the things you look for in a friend, what would they be? Understanding? A sense of humor? Intelligence? What if the word *husband, wife,* or *lover* were substituted for *friend*—would the characteristics on your list change? Might you add wealth, security, or attractiveness? If you ask people to create such a list—and psychologists have done so on a number of occasions—most people have no trouble coming up with a wish list of characteristics for "friend" or "marriage partner of my dreams." But how important do these well-thought-out and carefully chosen factors turn out to be? Do we really form friendships, or choose marriage partners, based on some relationship equation that sums desirable and undesirable attributes in a logical and rational way?

One of the most important lessons of this textbook, and certainly of this chapter, is that our behavior is strongly influenced by external forces in the environment. People act the way they do partly because of conscious, internally driven processes, but also because the environment shapes and constrains the behaviors that are possible. In the case of interpersonal attraction, it turns out that the environment often plays a major role in determining both whom you choose to spend time with and whom you consider to be an appropriate mate. As you learned earlier in the chapter, even mere exposure to something can be sufficient to increase its likability (Zajonc, 1968). People like things that are familiar, even when that familiarity has been created by simple repetition in the environment.

Proximity

In a classic study conducted nearly 50 years ago, psychologist Leon Festinger and his colleagues (1950) analyzed the friendships that formed among students living in an apartment complex near the Massachusetts Institute of Technology. Festinger and his colleagues found that they could predict the likelihood of a friendship forming by simply noting the *proximity*—defined in terms of the closeness of living quarters—between two people in the building. When the students were asked to list their three closest friends, two-thirds of the time they named students who lived in their same apartment complex. Moreover, when a fellow apartment dweller was listed as a friend, two-thirds of the time he or she lived on the same floor as the respondent. Clearly, the choice of friends is strongly influenced by where one lives. People tend to end up with friends who live nearby.

Of course, it isn't really proximity by itself that leads to liking and loving. When somebody lives close by, you see him or her a lot, and it may be the increased exposure that promotes the attraction. We've already seen that increased exposure leads to an increase in rated likability, but it also provides the opportunity for interaction. When you consistently interact with someone, mutual feelings of connectedness and belonging tend to follow (Cantor & Malley, 1991). You tend to see each other as members of the same *in-group*—that is, as people who share features in common. In fact, you don't even have to interact physically with someone for increased liking to occur. Psychologists John Darley and Ellen Berscheid (1967) found that even the anticipation of an interaction with someone you don't already know can cause you to rate that person as more attractive.

Similarity

It's also the case that we tend to like and form relationships with people who are *similar* to us. Friends and intimate partners typically resemble each other in age, social status, education level, race, religious beliefs, political attitudes, intelligence, and even physical attractiveness. People may report preferring physically attractive mates, but most end up marrying someone who is approximately equal to them in degree of physical attractiveness (Feingold, 1988, 1990). So, if you believe in the idea that "opposites attract," think again—in reality, it is the birds of a feather that tend consistently to flock together.

Although few psychologists question the finding that similarities attract, there are disagreements about how best to interpret this finding. The fact that similarities are found between the physical and attitudinal dimensions of friends and lovers doesn't provide any insight into *why* these similarities exist. As we discussed in Chapter 2, correlations do not imply causality. One possibility is that we like others who share our beliefs and attitudes because they *validate* those beliefs, which further helps convince us that our beliefs are the right ones (Byrne, 1971; Laprelle et al., 1990). Another possibility is that we spend time with others like ourselves because we *dislike* people who hold different views (Rosenbaum, 1986).

? CRITICAL THINKING

Think about your own relationship experiences. Have you ever felt peer pressure to find a partner who meets a well-defined set of standards? How important were these factors in your decisions?

Birds of a feather do tend to flock together—more often than not, we form lasting relationships with people who are similar to ourselves.

It's not so much that we want to spend time with those who resemble us, it's that we don't want to spend time with those we despise.

A third possibility is that factors in the environment are responsible. Partners in romantic relationships might be similarly attractive because your attractiveness dictates to some extent who you can find as a mate. Physically unattractive people, for example, might be unable to attract mates who are more attractive; or, it could be that society dictates that attractive people reject those who are less attractive. Socioeconomic class also tends to limit your options. If you are poor and live in a run-down section of town, your interactions are likely to be with people who are members of the same socioeconomic class. Generally, people who live in the same neighborhood, attend the same church, or go off to the same university already share many features in common, and it is from this pool that people typically find their companions.

Reciprocity

There is also a role in the dynamics of interpersonal attraction for **reciprocity,** or our tendency to return in kind the feelings that are shown toward us. If someone doesn't like you and displays hostility at every turn, you usually have similar negative feelings toward him or her. If someone likes you, or even if you simply think the person likes you, then you tend to like that person back (Curtis & Miller, 1986; Kelley, 1983). In a study by Curtis and Miller (1986), participants were asked to have a conversation with someone who they believed had been told either positive or negative information about them (actually, the conversation partner hadn't been told anything). If the subjects believed they were talking to someone who perceived them in a positive light, they tended to be friendlier and more open in their conversation—they acted as if they liked their partner more.

Reciprocity helps lead to interpersonal attraction, because it is self-fulfilling and because people who like you tend to be reinforcing and accepting of your actions. But it doesn't always work. If you feel that the positive actions of another are motivated for some selfish reason—as part of a con job or to get something such as a promotion—then your reaction will typically be negative (Jones, 1964). Ingratiation, in which a person consciously tries to win the affections of another for some ulterior motive, is likely to backfire as a strategy if it is discovered.

reciprocity
The tendency for people to return in kind the feelings that are shown toward them.

THE PSYCHOLOGY OF ROMANTIC LOVE

When psychologists study a topic such as *interpersonal attraction*, it's likely to be seen as an interesting and important research endeavor by most casual observers. But when psychologists turn to the study of "love," as you might imagine, the reactions are often far different. How, you ask, can someone understand, define, or attempt to measure something like love? Love is a topic to be tackled by the poet or the artist, not the questionnaire-laden social psychologist. Perhaps, but as you'll soon see, that hasn't stopped psychologists from trying.

Defining Love

Psychologists recognize that love is a complex emotion that can be expressed in a variety of forms. There is the love that exists between parent and child, between lovers, between husband and wife, even between friends. In each case, when it's measured through a questionnaire, the relationship is typically characterized by the giving and receiving of support, a kind of mutual understanding, and intense personal satisfaction (Fehr & Russell, 1991; Sternberg & Grajek, 1984). Although there may be fundamental similarities in how love is experienced, the amount of love that is reported depends on the type of relationship studied. Women, for example, might report *loving* their lover more than a best friend, but *liking* their best friend more; men, on the other hand, report liking *and* loving their lover more than they report these feelings for their friends (Sternberg, 1986).

When the relationship between two individuals is romantic, it is popular to distinguish further between passionate love and companionate love. **Passionate love** is an intense emotional state in which the individual is enveloped by a powerful longing to be with the other person (Hatfield, 1988). For many people, passionate love resembles a ride on a kind of emotional roller coaster—they experience intense joy if the feelings are reciprocated, and intense pain and despair if their feelings are unrequited. **Companionate love** tends to be less emotional and intense, but its feelings of trust and warmth can be more enduring. Whereas passionate love leads to intense arousal, companionate love leads to self-disclosure—we are willing to reveal our innermost secrets because the relationship sits on a bedrock of trust. It is, of course, possible for both passionate love and companionate love to be present in the same relationship, but this is not always the case.

The Triangular View of Love

Psychologist Robert Sternberg (1986, 1988) has argued for what he calls a triangular view of love. He sees love as triangular because it is composed of three major dimensions—*intimacy*, *passion*, and *commitment*—that vary in relation to one another (see Figure 13.8). Intimacy is the emotional component that brings closeness, connectedness, and warmth to a relationship. Passion is the motivational component that underlies arousal, physical attraction, and sexual behavior. Commitment is the decision-making arm of love—how willing are the partners to stick with the relationship in times of trouble? All forms of love can be seen as some combination of these three components. For example, according to Sternberg (1986), *romantic love* is marked by a combination of intimacy and passion (but it may lack the commitment), companionate love is high in intimacy and commitment (but without passion), and *empty love* occurs when there is commitment but little or no passion or intimacy.

In addition to using his triangle as a vehicle for defining love, Sternberg has followed other researchers in attempting to map out how the components of love change over time (see Berscheid, 1985; Hatfield & Rapson, 1993). What patterns have been found? Do couples gain intimacy? lose passion? become increasingly willing to commit? It is impossible to predict for any particular relationship, but

? CRITICAL THINKING

If you had to write a prescription for a successful marriage, how would you rate the dimensions of the triangle?

passionate love
An intense emotional state characterized by a powerful longing to be with a specific person; passionate love is marked by a combination of intimacy and passion, but commitment may be lacking.

companionate love
A kind of emotional attachment characterized by feelings of trust and companionship; companionate love is marked by a combination of intimacy and commitment, but passion may be lacking.

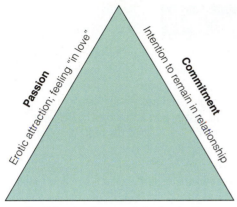

Passion	Intimacy	Commitment	Type of love that results
+	−	−	Infatuated love
−	+	−	Liking (friendship)
−	−	+	Empty love
+	+	−	Romantic love
−	+	+	Companionate love
+	−	+	Fatuous love

FIGURE 13.8

The Triangular View of Love

Robert Sternberg has proposed that there are many kinds of love, each defined by the degree of *passion, intimacy,* and *commitment* present in the relationship. For example, "infatuation" is a kind of love with lots of passion but little intimacy or commitment, whereas "empty love" has commitment but little passion or intimacy. (Based on Sternberg, 1986.)

the theory proposes some general trends. On the average, for example, the passion component of love builds early and rapidly in a relationship—it can even be experienced almost immediately on meeting another—but it's difficult to sustain for long periods. Commitment, on the other hand, is slow to develop but can be quite long-lasting. Intimacy, too, is unlikely to be found early in a relationship (there is too much uncertainty), but it grows and maintains itself in most successful relationships. The components of love are conceived therefore as fluid, changing over time in ways that reflect the successes and failures of the interactions between the partners.

TEST YOURSELF 13.3

Check your knowledge about how we establish relationships with other people by deciding whether each of the following statements is true or false. (You will find the answers in the Appendix.)

1. Babies, within hours of birth, show a preference for attractive over unattractive faces. *True or False?*

2. Blending studies of facial attractiveness indicate that faces that are unusual or distinct tend to receive higher ratings of attractiveness than averaged faces. *True or False?*

3. Studies have found that if you've just been shown a picture of a strikingly attractive person, your ratings of an average-looking person go up. *True or False?*

4. Friends and intimate partners typically resemble each other in age, social status, education level, race, religious beliefs, political attitudes, intelligence, and even physical attractiveness. *True or False?*

5. According to the triangular theory of love, infatuated love represents passion without intimacy or commitment. *True or False?*

6. Passionate love typically leads to more feelings of warmth and trust than does companionate love. *True or False?*

Solving the Problems

Throughout this text I've repeatedly stressed the idea that people neither develop nor live in a vacuum. Our actions, thoughts, and feelings arise out of the interactions we have with ever-changing environments. Among the most powerful components of the environments that we face are *social* ones—our thoughts and actions are strongly influenced by the people around us. Social psychology is the discipline that studies how people think about, influence, and relate to others. In this chapter we tackled the topic areas of social psychology from the perspective of three major adaptive problems.

Interpreting the Behavior of Others. As we move through the social world, it's extremely adaptive for us to try and make sense of the people around us. We form initial impressions of others by using the information we have available—such as the physical appearance of the person—and by relying on preexisting knowledge structures, called social schemas, which help us interpret that information. Schemas are useful features of

the adaptive mind because they help us to direct our actions in uncertain situations. But schemas can also lead to stereotypes—beliefs about people belonging to groups—which, although useful in many ways, can produce prejudice.

Attributions—how we infer the causes of another's behavior—form another important part of the overall interpretation process. When searching for reasons *why* others act the way they do, we look for factors that covary with the behavior and we assess the consistency of the behavior, its distinctiveness, and whether or not there is consensus among people. Whether you place the locus of causality in the external environment or within the person depends on how these factors of consistency, distinctiveness, and consensus work together. There are also some basic attribution biases—such as the fundamental attribution error—that help shape the attributions we make.

Attitudes, which are positive or negative evaluations, are typically separated into three components: a cognitive component, an affective component, and a behavioral component. Attitude formation is influenced by a number of factors, but direct experience plays a major role. One popular theory of attitude change is the elaboration likelihood model, which proposes that there are central and peripheral routes to persuasion. It's clear from a number of research studies that when people are induced to act in ways that are inconsistent with their existing attitudes, their attitudes often change as a result.

Behaving in the Presence of Others. Psychologists use the term *social influence* to refer to how behavior is affected by other people in one's environment. Sometimes social influence can produce positive effects, as in social facilitation, and sometimes the presence of others hinders performance, as in social interference. The relationship between arousal and performance might explain some of these patterns. The presence of other people can

have an arousing effect, and depending on whether the task is easy or hard, performance will be facilitated or impaired. The presence of other people can also affect our willingness to deliver aid to people in need. The bystander effect reveals that we're generally reluctant to come to someone's aid when other people are present. One interpretation of this effect appeals to diffusion of responsibility: We believe that others have already done something to help or will soon get involved.

Behavior is also strongly influenced by the social pressures of groups and of authority. Participation as a member of a well-defined group can make us conform, which means that our opinions and behaviors will tend to move toward the group norm. Conformity operates on the group level also. It is common for groups to polarize, which means that the group's dominant point of view tends to become stronger and more extreme with the passage of time. If the phenomenon of groupthink is present, members have become so interested in seeking a consensus of opinion that dissenting views start to be ignored or suppressed. Milgram's famous experiment on obedience to authority demonstrated that people can be induced by an authority figure to engage in behavior that they would not engage in otherwise. The degree of compliance depends on the characteristics of the situation and on the characteristics of the person giving the orders.

Establishing Relations with Others. Often the most meaningful things in a person's life are the social relations that he or she has established with others. How are relationships formed? We examined facial attractiveness and discovered that attractiveness may be determined, in part, by innate biological factors. People tend to prefer averaged, or prototypical, faces, perhaps because they're easier to identify or signal genetic health. Among the factors that influence liking and loving are familiarity, proximity, similarity, and reciprocity. We're more likely to be attracted to someone we know, who lives nearby, who is similar to ourselves, and who likes us back. Psychologists have also attempted to understand love, which is typically defined in terms of multiple components—such as intimacy, passion, and commitment—acting together. Whether a person ends up in a relationship based on passionate love or companionate love depends on the relative amounts of each of these three components in the relationship.

Social Psychology Chapter Summary

Interpreting the Behavior of Others: Social Cognition

As social animals, we're constantly trying to interpret the behavior of other people. We form impressions of people we encounter and we concoct theories about why people behave the way they do. There are systematic biases in the interpretation processes we use to make these judgments.

PERSON PERCEPTION: HOW DO WE FORM IMPRESSIONS OF OTHERS?

Our perception of people is guided by *bottom-up processing* (actual physical sensations) and *top-down processing* (our expectations and beliefs). Physical appearance is a powerful determinant of a first impression. Physically attractive individuals are perceived as superior on a variety of dimensions. *Social schemas*, our schemas about social experiences and people (e.g., *stereotypes*) exert a strong influence on our perception of others. An example is the *self-fulfilling prophecy effect*, in which we expect certain kinds of behavior from members of groups, and these expectations can cause the person to behave in the expected fashion. Stereotypes can also increase the likelihood of *prejudice* and discriminatory behavior. Prejudice can be reduced through repeated exposure to *individuals* in the stereotyped group.

ATTITUDES AND ATTITUDE CHANGE

Attitudes are positive or negative beliefs we hold about something, and include a *cognitive*, *affective*, and *behavioral* component. The behavioral component is a predisposition to act; attitudes do not always directly affect behavior. Attitudes are formed primarily through experience, via the mechanisms of classical conditioning, instrumental conditioning, and observational learning. According to the elaboration likelihood model, attitudes can be changed via a *central route* (when we listen carefully to the arguments of a message and judge it on its merits) or a *peripheral route* (when our attitudes are susceptible to change from superficial cues or mere exposure). According to *cognitive dissonance theory*, inconsistency between behavior and attitudes results in tension that may be relieved through attitude change. An alternative, *self-perception* theory, states that we use our own actions as the basis for beliefs about ourselves. The *foot-in-the-door* and *lowball techniques* provide support.

ATTRIBUTION THEORY: ATTRIBUTING CAUSES TO BEHAVIOR

Attributions are the inferences generated when we assign causes to behaviors. The *covariation model* assumes that we look for some factor that covaries with the behavior we're judging. In addition, we rely on *consistency*, *distinctiveness*, and *consensus* to make the appropriate inference. We tend to make *external attributions* (appealing to external causes) when a behavior is high on these three dimensions; we tend to make *internal attributions* (appealing to internal personality traits) when a behavior is high in consistency but low in consensus and distinctiveness. The *fundamental attribution error* refers to our tendency to overestimate the role of internal factors and underestimate the role of external factors. The *self-serving bias* refers to our tendency to take internal credit for actions that produce positive outcomes, and to blame the situation when behaviors lead to failure.

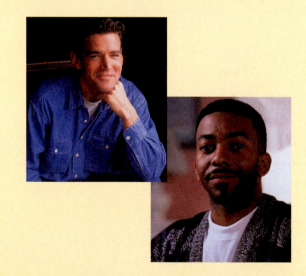

Behaving in the Presence of Others: Social Influence

Everyone's behavior is strongly influenced by the social context. Ability to perform a task might improve or fall apart in the presence of others. How we act is also profoundly influenced by the presence of authority figures and by the opinions of fellow members in a group.

SOCIAL FACILITATION AND INTERFERENCE

Social facilitation is an enhancement in performance sometimes found when we perform in the presence of others. *Social interference* occurs when performing in front of a crowd impairs performance. Task difficulty helps determine when the presence of others will help or hinder performance. When a task is easy, social facilitation is likely; when it's difficult, social interference is likely.

SOCIAL INFLUENCES ON ALTRUISM: THE BYSTANDER EFFECT

The presence of others can affect *altruism*, whether we will act in a way that shows unselfish concern for others. The reluctance to come to someone's aid when others are present is termed the *bystander effect*. The presence of others leads to a *diffusion of responsibility*; we believe that others have already done something to help.

THE POWER OF THE GROUP

Most people show a tendency toward *social loafing*, putting out less effort when working with a group than they do when they work alone. *Deindividuation* occurs when the presence of others makes us feel less accountable for our own behavior. *Conformity* occurs when a person's opinions, feelings, or behaviors move toward the group norm and is especially likely when the pressure is coming from an *in-group* (one with which a person shares features in common).

GROUP DECISION-MAKING

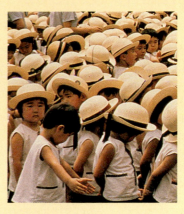

Group polarization occurs when a group's dominant point of view becomes stronger and even more extreme with time. *Groupthink* occurs when the members of a group become so interested in seeking a consensus of opinion that they ignore and even suppress dissenting views.

THE POWER OF AUTHORITY: OBEDIENCE

Obedience refers to responding to the orders of an authority figure. The Milgram experiment found that a surprisingly high proportion (65%) of research participants were willing to follow an experimenter's orders to deliver shocks, despite pleas from the subject. Milgram's study has been criticized on ethical grounds, as well as for the general procedures used.

Establishing Relations with Others

Among our most important social actions are the relationships that we share with others. It's unlikely that the human species would survive without attraction and romantic love. In addition, we rely on our relationships within the family as well as on the social structures in society to help protect and nurture us.

WHAT MAKES A FACE ATTRACTIVE?

An evolutionary perspective on physical attractiveness predicts that we will be attracted to opposite-sex members who are youthful, vigorous, and healthy-looking. Also, features of attractiveness should cut across cultural boundaries. The evolutionary view has some research support. The universality of attractiveness may be due to the fact that we seem programmed to prefer faces that are average representations of faces in a population. There is also a strong subjective component to the perception of beauty.

THE PSYCHOLOGY OF ROMANTIC LOVE

Love is a complex emotion that can be expressed in a variety of forms. *Passionate love* is an intense emotional state in which the individual is enveloped by a powerful longing to be with the other person. *Companionate love* tends to be less intense, and is characterized by trust and warmth. According to the *triangular theory*, love is comprised of three major dimensions: *intimacy*, *passion*, and *commitment*. These components are fluid, changing over time.

THE PSYCHOLOGY OF LIKING AND LOVING

The environment plays a major role in determining interpersonal attraction. Attraction to others is determined by others' *similarity* and *proximity*, and by *reciprocity*, our tendency to return in kind the feelings that are shown toward us.

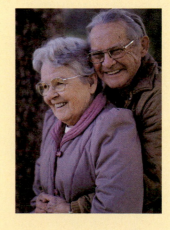

Terms to Remember

social psychology, 500

INTERPRETING THE BEHAVIOR OF OTHERS

social cognition, 502
social schema, 503
stereotypes, 503
self-fulfilling prophecy effect, 504
prejudice, 505
attributions, 506
external attribution, 507
internal attribution, 507
fundamental attribution error, 507
self-serving bias, 509
attitude, 509
elaboration likelihood model, 511
source characteristics, 512
cognitive dissonance, 513
self-perception theory, 514

BEHAVING IN THE PRESENCE OF OTHERS

social influence, 516
social facilitation, 516
social interference, 517
altruism, 517
bystander effect, 518
diffusion of responsibility, 519
social loafing, 519
deindividuation, 520
conformity, 520
in-group, 521
group polarization, 522
groupthink, 523
obedience, 525

ESTABLISHING RELATIONS OF OTHERS

reciprocity, 533
passionate love, 534
companionate love, 534

Recommended Readings

Cialdini, R. B. (1993). *Influence: Science and practice* (3rd ed.). New York: HarperCollins. A fascinating exploration of the psychology of compliance and persuasion. Includes many real-world examples (e.g., politicians and con artists) illustrating the power and tactics of influence.

Milgram, S. (1974). *Obedience to authority*. New York: Harper & Row. A detailed accounting by Milgram of his classic experiments on obedience to authority. The book includes a thorough discussion of the implications, both scientific and ethical, of his research.

INFOTRAC® COLLEGE EDITION

For additional readings, explore Infotrac College Edition, your online library. Go to:
http://www.infotrac-college.com/wadsworth

Hint: enter the search terms: Social cognition, Stereotypes, Persuasion and attitude change, Conformity, Interpersonal attraction, Romantic love.

What's on the Web?

Social Psychology Network

(www.wesleyan.edu/spn/)

This is THE Web site for social psychology. It's a clearing-house with a tremendous amount of information about social psychology, including areas of study within social psychology, Ph.D. programs in social psychology, and even online experiments that allow you to take part in actual "online" research. The links to research include student projects on interpersonal relations, social perception, and judgment and decision making.

Web Tutorials in Social Psychology

(miavx1.muohio.edu/~shermarc/p324tuta.htmlx)

Also titled "Living in a Social World," this site features tutorials on a wide variety of topics within social psychology, including "Intergroup Bias in American Culture," and "Why Your Favorite Team Is Your Team: The Psychology of Sports Fans." This site is actually an ongoing class project of an advanced social psychology class at Miami University in Ohio.

The Influence at Work Web Site

(www.influenceatwork.com)

This Web site is devoted to the psychology of persuasion, and contains a wealth of information about the dynamics of social influence, and how it is implemented in everyday settings. They even have a test to measure your "influence quotient." Cruise to this site to find out how influence relates to courtrooms, cults, Aristotle, and George Bush.

The Wadsworth Psychology Study Center Web Site

See http://psychology.wadsworth.com/ for practice quiz questions, hypercontents, updates, critical thinking exercises, discussion forums and more! The Wadsworth Psychology Study Center provides a wealth of information fully organized and integrated by chapter.

Psychological Disorders

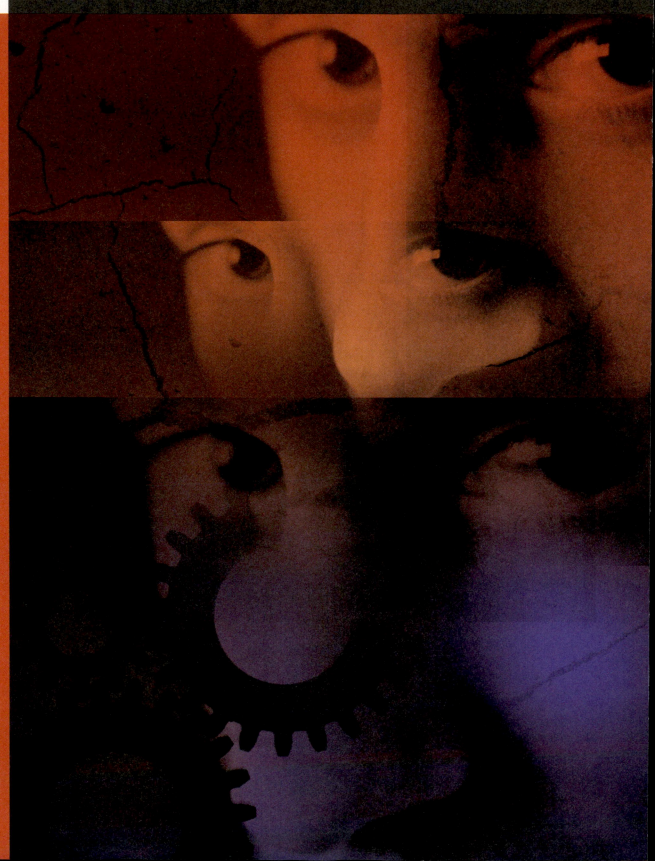

Although it looks as if this person is suffering from a psychological disorder, she might be showing a normal grief reaction, such as to the death of a relative or friend.

You shouldn't really be reading this book, you know. In fact, put it down—now. The author's intentions are not pure . . . he doesn't have your best interest in mind. He wants to convince you that you have no true control over your life. To him, you are nothing more than a mindless automaton shaped by the whims of changing environments; you are the product of forces outside of your control—biological drives, toilet-training habits, unbalanced mixtures of neurotransmitters in your brain.

But you and I are more than that—we are more than the product of brain biochemistry or dirty little habits. We have inner control over our lives. You and I are in touch with the essence of the inner one, although, perhaps, it is only I who recognizes this fact at the moment. I've stopped you because it's time to prepare ourselves now . . . the first of the tribe arrived weeks ago . . . he's here, inside my head, and he's telling me the real truth. There's nothing to fear . . . we're still in control . . . it will be our choice, not theirs, to submit. And when we do, the truth about the conspiracy will be revealed to all . . .

Imagine being on the receiving end of such a conversation. What would be your reaction? At best, I suspect you'd categorize this person as odd; more likely, you'd label him as definitely disturbed. His thinking is certainly distorted, and he is more than a bit paranoid. But does he suffer from a *true* psychological disorder needing treatment, or is he simply eccentric? How can we tell? What are the criteria that psychologists use to define and describe psychological disorders and abnormal behavior? Is distorted thinking merely a personal choice, to be respected and endured, or is it something more akin to strep throat or a bladder infection—something that we should try to treat and cure?

Over the next two chapters, we'll turn our attention to the classification and treatment of psychological disorders. Obviously, before treating a psychological problem, you must determine whether there is indeed a problem that needs to be treated. Making this determination is more difficult than you might think. Let's suppose you arrive home tonight and find your roommate awake but slumped in a corner with his cap pulled down over his eyes. You ask him to explain, but he tells you to mind your own business. Later that night, you hear sobbing and crying coming from behind his locked bedroom door. His bizarre behavior continues for the next two days. He refuses to respond to questions, he stops going to class, and he refuses to eat or clean himself. He's suffering from a psychological disorder, right? Perhaps, but what if I tell you that his father and mother were just killed in an automobile accident? What would your reaction be now? Would you conclude that he is psychologically disturbed, or is he simply showing an intense but normal grief reaction?

Previewing the Conceptual and Practical Problems

To help you understand how psychologists view psychological disorders, our discussion will revolve around three basic conceptual and practical problems: What is the proper way to conceptualize and define abnormal behavior? How can experts classify the various psychological disorders that reliably produce abnormal behavior? Finally, what are the underlying causes of psychological disorders?

First, a person who suffers from one or more psychological problems is typically considered to be abnormal. Indeed, the terms *abnormal* and *abnormal behavior* are often used as roughly equivalent to the term *psychological disorder.* But over the years, psychologists have struggled with how best to define the concept of abnormality. When people act abnormally, their behavior tends to be unusual or dysfunctional, and they often appear to be suffering from considerable personal distress. But for reasons that we'll discuss in the first section of the chapter, none of these criteria alone is sufficient to capture the concept. Most conceptualizations of abnormality rely on multiple criteria.

Second, even if agreement can be reached about the proper way to define abnormality, you still need a means for naming and classifying the underlying disorders that lead to abnormal behavior. Psychologists and psychiatrists have worked hard to develop a rigorous system for the diagnosis and classification of psychological disorders. We'll consider the current system, which is detailed in the *Diagnostic and Statistical Manual of Mental Disorders* (4th ed.), and you'll see how it's used to diagnose a variety of mental problems. There are many kinds of known psychological disorders—ranging from anxiety disorders to depression to schizophrenia—and each is classified on the basis of a relatively fixed set of criteria. Although it is a common belief among the general public that psychological disorders are idiosyncratic—which means that they arise in different ways for different individuals—you'll see that most disorders actually produce symptoms that are fairly consistent and reliable.

Third, in the final section of the chapter, we'll discuss how researchers attempt to understand the causes of psychological disorders. What causes an anxiety disorder, a mood disorder such as depression, or schizophrenia? Do psychological disorders result from some kind of mental breakdown, or are they simply adaptive reactions to stress? If it's a breakdown, is the cause of the breakdown biological or environmental? When someone is depressed, for example, is it because of a problem with their brain chemistry? Or has the person simply learned to act in depressed ways either through modeling the behavior of others or because acting depressed has received some reinforcement? We'll consider the major theoretical tools that psychologists use to explain abnormal behavior. Not surprisingly, the answer to many psychological problems lies in an interaction between biological, cognitive, and environmental factors.

Conceptualizing Abnormality: What Is Abnormal Behavior?

When you encounter someone who babbles on about how voices in his or her head are busy plotting a conspiracy, it's not difficult for you to categorize this behavior as abnormal; clearly, this person is in trouble and in need of some professional help. But as you've seen, sharp dividing lines don't always exist between normal and abnormal behavior. Sometimes behavior that appears abnormal can turn out to be a reasonable reaction to a stressful event, such as the roommate's reaction to the death of his parents. It's also the case that a behavior that seems abnormal in one culture can appear to be perfectly normal in another (Castillo, 1997). Entering a trance state and experiencing visual hallucinations is considered abnormal in Western cultures, but in other cultures it may not be (Bentall, 1990).

Even within a culture, conceptions of abnormality can change over time. For many years homosexuality was considered deviant and abnormal by the psychological community. But this view of homosexuality is rejected by most psychologists today. Fifty years ago, a strong dependence on tobacco would not have raised many eyebrows, but today if you're hooked on tobacco you're likely to be classified as having a substance-related disorder by many professionals. As times change, so do conceptions of what are appropriate and inappropriate actions. For these reasons, psychologists are justifiably cautious when it comes to applying the label of abnormality. Behavior usually needs to match a set of criteria before it can be labeled as abnormal.

CRITICAL THINKING

Suppose a 70-year-old entered college and started acting exactly the same way as a 20-year-old sophomore. Would you consider his or her behavior to be abnormal?

Entering a trance state is likely to be classified as "abnormal behavior" in Western cultures, but in other cultures it may not be.

CHARACTERISTICS OF ABNORMAL BEHAVIOR

Over the years, researchers have proposed a number of defining criteria for abnormality. In each case, as you'll see, the proposed criteria capture some but not all of the important features of what is agreed to be abnormal behavior.

Statistical Deviance

One way to define abnormal behavior is in terms of **statistical deviance,** or infrequency. For any given behavior, such as arguing with your neighbors or hearing voices, there is a certain probability that the behavior will occur in society at large. Most people have argued with their neighbors at one time or another, but few actually converse with disembodied voices. According to the concept of statistical deviance, a behavior is abnormal if it occurs infrequently among the members of a population. As you've learned elsewhere in this text, it's not unusual for psychologists to classify behavior on the basis of statistical frequency. For example, terms such as *gifted* and *mentally retarded* are defined with respect to statistical frequencies. So it should come as no surprise that statistical frequencies have been used to define abnormality.

But statistical deviance—that is, something that is extreme or different from the average—cannot be used as the sole criterion for labeling a behavior as abnormal. It's easy to come up with a list of behaviors or abilities that are statistically infrequent but are not abnormal in a psychological sense. For example, Michael Jordan and Shaquille O'Neal have skills on the basketball court that are extreme, and thereby statistically deviant, but to be a great athlete does not make one abnormal. Similarly, only a handful of individuals have reached the intellectual heights of Albert Einstein or Isaac Newton, but superior intelligence is not abnormal in the usual psychological sense of the word. An additional problem is the establishment of a criterion point: Just how infrequent or unusual does a behavior need to be to be characterized as abnormal? So far, psychologists have failed to produce a satisfactory answer to this question.

Cultural Deviance

Another criterion is **cultural deviance,** which compares behavior to existing cultural norms. In this case, a behavior would be considered abnormal if it violates the accepted standards of society. In most cultures, for example, it is not considered normal or acceptable to walk to class in the nude or to engage in sexual relations with children. These behaviors break the established rules of our culture, and if you engage in either it's likely that people will think you have a serious problem.

But once again, cultural deviance by itself fails as a sufficient criterion. Many criminals violate the established norms of society—stealing cars or embezzling money, for example. Such behavior might be abnormal by both statistical and cultural standards, but that doesn't mean all criminals suffer from psychological disorders. There are also many individuals who suffer from legitimate psychological problems, such as anxiety or depression, who never violate a law or established standard of society. Finally, as we discussed previously, behaviors that are abnormal in one culture may be considered normal in another. There are cultures in the world, for instance, where nakedness in public breaks no established cultural rules. People who suffer from psychological disorders may indeed violate cultural norms in some instances, but often they do not.

Emotional Distress

A third characteristic of many kinds of abnormal behavior is the presence of personal or **emotional distress.** People who suffer from psychological disorders

---

1. **statistical deviance**
A criterion of abnormality stating that a behavior is abnormal if it occurs infrequently among the members of a population.

2. **cultural deviance**
A criterion of abnormality stating that a behavior is abnormal if it violates the rules or accepted standards of society.

3. **emotional distress**
A criterion of abnormality stating that abnormal behaviors are those that lead to personal distress or emotional upset.

Bill Gates and Ru Paul are statistically deviant in some respects—and culturally deviant in the case of Ru Paul—but would you classify them as abnormal in a psychological sense?

often experience great despair and unhappiness. They feel hopeless, lost, and alienated from others. In fact, it is the emotional distress that usually leads them to seek professional help for their problems. But as you can probably guess, not all disorders make people unhappy. There are people, for example, who have little contact with reality but seem perfectly content in their fantasy world. Likewise, there are many distressed people in the world—for example, those who have recently lost a loved one or a job—who would not be classified as abnormal by the psychological community.

Dysfunction

A final criterion for abnormality looks at the general adaptiveness of the individual's behavior. Is there a breakdown in normal functioning—a **dysfunction**—that prevents the person from successfully following adaptive strategies? People who suffer from psychological disorders are often unable to function well in typical daily activities—they may not eat properly, clean themselves, or be able to hold a job. Their ability to think clearly may be impaired, which affects their ability to adapt successfully in their environment. As you'll see later, the assessment of global functioning—defined as the ability to adapt in social, personal, and occupational environments—plays a large role in the diagnosis and treatment of psychological disorders.

dysfunction
A breakdown in normal functioning; abnormal behaviors are those that prevent one from pursuing adaptive strategies.

CONCEPT SUMMARY
Criteria for Defining Abnormality

Criterion	Description	Example
Statistical deviance	Behavior that occurs infrequently among the members of a population	Jon goes back to make sure his front door is locked exactly 12 times each morning. As he walks to the door, he mutters over and over, "lock the door . . ." No one else in the neighborhood does this.
Cultural deviance	Behavior that violates the accepted standards of society	Jon notices that each time he comes back to his front door, talking to himself, his neighbors look at him rather nervously, and tend to avoid him at other times.
Emotional distress	Experiencing great despair and unhappiness	Jon is very distressed by his compulsive behavior.
Dysfunction	A breakdown in normal everyday functioning	Jon's routine of checking his front door 12 times every morning has made him late for work a number of times, and his job is in jeopardy.

Inside the Problem   The Concept of Insanity

As we've just discussed, it's not easy to find an acceptable definition for abnormal behavior. Behavior can mean different things depending on the context in which it occurs—something that is abnormal in one situation may be quite normal in another. Someone can act in a way that is deviant from statistical or cultural norms, yet still seem normal to most observers. Still, regardless of where you travel in the world, some kinds of behavior will always be recognized as abnormal: Consider, for example, the behavior of serial killer Jeffrey Dahmer, who admitted butchering, cannibalizing, and having sex with the dead bodies of over a dozen young men and boys. Everyone, including the mental health professionals who examined Dahmer, was in agreement—this was a man who was suffering from some serious psychological problems.

But did you know that from a legal standpoint, Jeffrey Dahmer was judged by a jury to be perfectly sane? Despite the best efforts of his legal team to have him declared mentally unfit, and thus not responsible for his crimes, Dahmer was found legally sane. He stood trial and was convicted of his crimes (later, while serving his life sentence, he was brutally murdered himself by a fellow inmate). Are you wondering how this could be possible? The answer lies in the fact that insanity is a legal concept rather than a psychological one. Although its definition varies somewhat from state to state, insanity is usually defined in terms of the defendant's thought processes at the time of the crime: A criminal is insane, and therefore not guilty by reason of insanity, if, because of a "mental disease," he or she fails to appreciate or understand that certain actions are wrong in a legal or moral sense (Ogloff et al., 1993). Dahmer was judged capable of

From a legal standpoint, Jeffrey Dahmer (shown at left) was considered sane because he was judged capable of understanding the wrongfulness of his actions.

understanding the wrongfulness of his actions; that is, the jury determined that he was fully aware of the fact that his actions were wrong. As a result, he failed the insanity test, even though he was clearly suffering from serious psychological problems.

The concept of legal insanity has generated considerable controversy over the years. But the controversy has not usually come from cases like Dahmer's, in which someone with a disorder has been declared legally sane. Instead, the brunt of the concern has been over instances of acquittal—in which someone who obviously committed a crime has been judged not guilty by reason of insanity. A case in point is the landmark trial of Daniel M'Naghten in 1843. Driven by "voices from God," M'Naghten set out to kill the British prime minister, Sir Robert Peel, but ended up killing Peel's secretary instead. The court acquitted M'Naghten for reasons of insanity. This particular ruling was strongly crit-

icized by the public, even though M'Naghten spent the rest of his life in a mental hospital. But it remains important because the so-called M'Naghten rule for insanity—which focuses on what the criminal understands at the time of the crime—is still the foundation for most current standards of insanity.

The last few decades have seen a number of widely publicized uses of the insanity defense in the United States. John Hinckley, Jr., who attempted to assassinate President Ronald Reagan in 1981, was declared not guilty by reason of insanity. You probably also remember that Lorena Bobbitt was held not legally responsible for cutting off her husband's penis. In both these cases the jury's verdict led to considerable public debate. In fact, even before these cases, there was growing concern—and even cynicism—in many public sectors about the insanity defense. But the public tends to overestimate how often it is actually used in criminal felony cases, as well as how often the insanity defense leads to acquittal (Pasewark & Seidenzahl, 1979). In reality, the insanity defense is used in less than 1% of all felony cases, and it's successful only 26% of the time (Silver et al., 1994).

Thus, the insanity defense is not a widely used legal loophole, despite the impressions of the general public. Moreover, most mental health professionals support the idea that people with serious psychological disorders are sometimes incapable of judging the appropriateness of their actions. As this chapter will illustrate, psychological disorders can lead to distorted views of the world—affected individuals not only act in ways that are abnormal, but their very thoughts, beliefs, and perceptions of the world can be wildly distorted as well.

insanity
A legal term usually defined as the inability to understand that certain actions are wrong, in a legal or moral sense, at the time of a crime.

Summarizing the Criteria

You've seen that abnormal behavior can be behavior that is statistically or culturally deviant, it can involve personal or emotional distress, and it can signal impairment or dysfunction. Normal behavior, then, could be any behavior that is relatively common, does not cause personal distress, or generally leads to adaptive consequences. However, psychologists will usually refuse to label any behavior as normal or abnormal unless it satisfies several of these criteria rather than just one.

Normal	Criteria	Abnormal
Common	Statistical deviance	Rare
Acceptable	Cultural deviance	Unacceptable
Low	Emotional distress	High
Adaptive	Dysfunction	Maladaptive

FIGURE 14.1
The Normal-to-Abnormal Continuum
"Abnormal" and "normal" are not fixed and rigid categories that define us. They are better seen as endpoints on a continuum. To a certain degree, everyone has acted unusually, suffered from emotional distress, or failed to follow an adaptive strategy.

Crying hysterically for hours at a time may be a normal grief reaction, or it may signal a serious disorder. Even a behavior that seems to be clearly abnormal—such as a paranoid delusion that people are out to get you—might be adaptive in some environments. To paraphrase comedian Woody Allen, paranoids can have enemies too.

It's also important to remember that "abnormal" and "normal" are not rigid categories. Each of us can relate in one way or another to the criteria of abnormality we've just discussed. We all know people who have occasionally acted unusually, suffered from emotional distress, or failed to follow an adaptive strategy. Many psychological disorders are characterized by behaviors or feelings that are merely exaggerations of normal ones, such as anxiety, feelings of sadness, or concerns about one's health. Consequently, it's better to think about normal and abnormal behavior as endpoints on a *continuum*, rather than as nonoverlapping categories (see Figure 14.1). (For a discussion of the legal concept of *insanity*, which differs from the concept of a psychological disorder, see the accompanying "Inside the Problem" section.)

THE MEDICAL MODEL: CONCEPTUALIZING ABNORMALITY AS A DISEASE

Here's another issue that has troubled psychologists: When abnormality is present, is it better to think of the person as suffering from a physical problem—that is, something that is broken or not working properly in the body—or is the person simply failing to adjust appropriately to the environment? We'll discuss the possible causes of psychological disorders in detail later in the chapter, but to understand how disorders are actually classified, you need to understand what is called the *medical model* of diagnosis. According to the **medical model**, abnormal behavior is caused by an underlying *disease*—a kind of mental *illness*—that can be *cured* with the appropriate therapy.

This conception of abnormality has been quite influential. As you already know, there are good reasons to believe that behavior is strongly influenced by biological factors, such as an oversupply or undersupply of neurotransmitters in the brain. In addition, biomedical therapies, such as the administration of psychoactive drugs, are often effective in treating a variety of psychological problems. As you'll see shortly, it's also the case that most psychological disorders can be classified in terms of *symptoms*. Depression, for example, typically leads to one or more of the following: sad mood, diminished interest in pleasure, difficulty in sleeping, feelings of worthlessness, and so on. The medical influence is deeply ingrained in the very language that psychologists use—they talk about mental health, mental illness, or psychopathology in much the same way a physician describes a medical condition.

medical model
The view that abnormal behavior is symptomatic of an underlying "disease" that can be "cured" with the appropriate therapy.

CRITICAL THINKING

How might acceptance of the medical model influence the availability of treatment options? Might it cause an overemphasis on biological treatments for psychological problems?

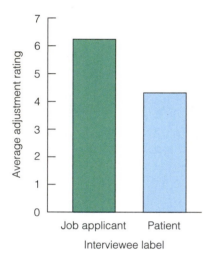

FIGURE 14.2

Labeling Effects

In a study by Langer and Abelson (1974), therapists were asked to provide adjustment ratings for people labeled as "patient" or "job applicant." The interviewees were judged to be better adjusted when the therapists thought they were job applicants, not patients. (Data from Langer & Abelson, 1974.)

diagnostic labeling effects

The fact that labels for psychological problems can become self-fulfilling prophecies; the label may make it difficult to recognize normal behavior when it occurs, and it may actually increase the likelihood that a person will act in an abnormal way.

But is the medical model an appropriate way to view abnormality? Some researchers believe that it's wrong to draw direct comparisons between physical illness and psychological problems (Szasz, 1961, 1990). Both strep throat and depression lead to a set of reliable symptoms. But we know that strep throat is caused by a physical problem—bacteria; at this point the cause of depression has not been firmly identified. In addition, people often seek treatment for psychological problems that are perhaps more accurately described as problems in living. How these adjustment problems are interpreted also seems to depend on the particular social or cultural context, which is not true for most medical conditions. We pointed out earlier that some kinds of bizarre behavior thought to be abnormal in one culture can be considered normal in another. On the other hand, strep throat produces fever and pain in swallowing regardless of the cultural environment.

PROBLEMS ASSOCIATED WITH LABELING

Critics of the medical model also express concern about **diagnostic labeling effects.** Labeling a psychological problem as an illness or a disorder tends to attach a stigma to the person that can be difficult to overcome (Kramer & Buck, 1997; Scheff, 1984). A number of studies have found that applying the label "mental patient" leads people to interpret an individual's behavior in a far different light than they would otherwise. In one study, professional therapists watched a videotape of a man describing his personal adjustment problems (Langer & Abelson, 1974). If prior to viewing the tape the therapists were told that the man was a mental patient, they rated his adjustment problems more negatively than did other therapists who were simply told he was a "job applicant" (see Figure 14.2). People's expectations, as we've stressed in previous chapters, importantly influence how they interpret new information.

The Rosenhan Study

In one particularly influential study of labeling effects, David Rosenhan, along with seven other co-investigators, arrived separately at several psychiatric hospitals in the early 1970s with the complaint that they were hearing voices (Rosenhan, 1973). Actually, each of the participants was perfectly normal. They simply adopted the role of a pseudopatient—they feigned, or faked, a disorder in order to see how labeling would color their subsequent treatment. On arrival, they reported to the psychiatric staff that they were hearing a disembodied voice in their head, a voice that repeated things like "empty," "hollow," and "thud." They were all admitted to hospitals, and virtually all received the diagnosis of schizophrenia (schizophrenia, as you'll see later, is a condition characterized by serious disturbances in thought and emotion).

Again, the purpose of the study was to see how an initial diagnosis of *schizophrenia* would affect subsequent treatment. From the point of admission, none of the pseudopatients continued to act in any kind of strange way. In all interactions with the hospital staff, they acted normally and gave no indications that they were suffering from a disorder. However, despite their normal behavior, none of the staff ever recognized them as pseudopatients; indeed, written hospital reports later revealed that the staff members tended to interpret their normal behaviors as symptomatic of a disorder. It was the real patients, in fact, who felt that the researchers somehow did not belong; several actually voiced their suspicions, claiming "You're not crazy. You're a journalist or a professor" (these comments were partly made in reaction to the fact that the pseudopatients spent time taking notes). Once the pseudopatients had been admitted and labeled as "abnormal," their behaviors were seen by the staff through the lens of expectations, and normal, sane behavior was never recognized as such. On average, the pseudopatients remained in the hospital for 19 days—the stays ranged from under a week to almost two months—and on release all were given the diagnosis of schizophrenia "in remission" (which means not currently active).

Most mental health professionals are careful about rigidly applying "labels" to clients during therapy; diagnostic labels can sometimes become self-fulfilling prophecies.

The Rosenhan study is important because it suggests that diagnostic labels can become self-fulfilling prophecies. Once you're diagnosed, you're likely to be treated as if you are suffering from a disorder, and this treatment may (1) make it difficult to recognize normal behavior when it occurs, and (2) actually increase the likelihood that you will act in an abnormal way. If the people in your environment expect you to act abnormally, you may very well start to act in a way that is consistent with those expectations (see Chapter 13).

Since its publication in 1973, the Rosenhan study has been widely analyzed in psychological circles. Its lessons about the hazards of labeling are clear. But at the same time, two points about the study are worth noting. First, you should appreciate that the admission of the pseudopatients by the hospital staff, as well as the subsequent diagnoses, were reasonable given the patients' reported symptoms. The diagnosis of a psychological disorder is often dependent on what the patient reports, and the trained professionals in this case had no reason to assume that the patients were lying or manufacturing symptoms. Second, it's possible and even reasonable to dispute the claim that the attending staff failed to recognize that the pseudopatients were acting normally. After all, they were released with the label "in remission," so the staff must have recognized that they were no longer acting in an abnormal way (Spitzer, 1975).

? CRITICAL THINKING

Do you think it was ethical for Rosenhan and his colleagues to trick the hospital staff? Did the research ends justify the means?

TEST YOURSELF 14.1

Check your knowledge of how abnormality is conceptualized by deciding whether each of the following statements is true or false. (You will find the answers in the Appendix.)

1. When a behavior occurs infrequently among members of a population it meets the criterion of cultural deviance. *True or False?*

2. To receive the diagnosis of a psychological disorder, a person must be suffering from a certain amount of emotional distress. *True or False?*

3. In many cases, abnormal behaviors are simply exaggerated versions of normal behaviors. *True or False?*

4. According to the medical model, psychological disorders can and should be classified in terms of measurable symptoms. *True or False?*

5. In the Rosenhan study, hospital staff members quickly picked up on the fact that the pseudopatients were no longer acting abnormal. *True or False?*

Classifying Psychological Disorders: The DSM-IV

As mentioned in the previous section, specific psychological disorders are often diagnosed in terms of a set of defining criteria or symptoms. This is the approach used by the *Diagnostic and Statistical Manual of Mental Disorders*, published by the American Psychiatric Association. From this point forward, we'll refer to this manual by its more commonly used acronym: **DSM-IV** (the "IV" simply designates that the classification system is currently in its fourth edition). The purpose of the DSM-IV is to provide clinicians with a well-defined classification system, based on objective and measurable criteria, so that reliable diagnoses of psychological disorders can be produced worldwide (Maser et al., 1991; Spitzer et al., 1994). The DSM-IV is intended only for the purposes of diagnosis and classification; it does not suggest therapies or methods of treatment for its various listed disorders.

How does the classification system work? The DSM-IV is composed of five major rating dimensions, or *axes* (see Figure 14.3). We'll focus our attention mainly on the first axis, which lists the major clinical syndromes (such as depression and schizophrenia), although all five are important to the complete diagnostic process. The clinician uses the criteria outlined in Axis I (Clinical Syndromes) and Axis II (Personality Disorders) to classify and label any abnormal behavior that may be present. Axis III allows the clinician to record any medical conditions that the individual may be experiencing. It's important for the clinician to know a person's medical history because some medical conditions (such as Alzheimer's disease) can contribute to abnormal behavior. Axis IV rates any environmental or psychosocial problems that may be present. For example, is the client going through a difficult divorce, or has he or she recently been fired? Finally, on Axis V the clinician codes the individual's current level of adaptive or global functioning. Is the client able to function adequately in social, personal, and occupational settings?

The clinician uses this multiaxial classification system to get the widest possible assessment of the individual's current psychological status. It matters to the clinician how someone is functioning in daily life, for example, because it often determines the most effective kind of treatment program. If the person is so severely impaired that he or she cannot hold a job, go to school, or even keep clean, it may be necessary to initiate a period of hospitalization. Our discussion will focus primarily on the diagnostic criteria that are used to classify the most common psychological disorders, as depicted on Axis I. We'll consider the major clinical syndromes and then end the section with a brief discussion of Axis II–based personality disorders. But remember, labeling or categorizing the disorder is only part of the diagnostic process—the remaining axes also play an important role in the diagnosis. Figure 14.4 summarizes some of the syndromes we'll be discussing and presents data showing how likely each disorder is to occur in the population at large.

ANXIETY DISORDERS: FEAR AND APPREHENSION

Although it may be difficult to understand the paranoid delusions of the severely disordered, it is not difficult to understand the apprehension, worry, and fear that characterize *anxiety*. Most people understand anxiety because it's often an important part of their everyday experience. We become anxious when we meet someone new, when awaiting the beginning of an exam, or when an out-of-control car swerves dangerously close to our path. Moreover, even though the physical and psychological changes that accompany anxiety can seem unpleasant, anxiety is basically an *adaptive* human response. The physical changes prepare the body to take action—to fight or flee—and thereby increase the chances of survival. The

Axis I	Axis II	Axis III	Axis IV
Clinical Disorders and Other Conditions That May Be a Focus of Clinical Attention	Personality Disorders and Mental Retardation	General Medical Conditions	Psychosocial and Environmental Problems
Examples:	**Examples:**	**Examples:**	**Examples:**
Substance-related disorders Schizophrenia and other psychotic disorders Mood disorders Anxiety disorders Somatoform disorders Dissociative disorders Sexual and gender identity disorders Eating disorders Sleep disorders	Paranoid personality disorder Schizotypal personality disorder Antisocial personality disorder Borderline personality disorder Narcissistic personality disorder Dependent personality disorder	Infectious and parasitic diseases Endocrine, nutritional, and metabolic diseases and immunity disorders Diseases of the nervous system and sense organs Diseases of the circulatory system Diseases of the respiratory system Diseases of the digestive system Diseases of the genitourinary system Congenital anomalies	Problems with primary support group Problems related to the social environment Educational problems Occupational problems Housing problems Economic problems

Axis V

Global Assessment of Functioning (GAF) Scale

Code	Examples of symptoms:
100	Superior functioning in a wide range of activities
90	Absent or minimal symptoms, good functioning in all areas
80	Symptoms transient and expectable reactions to psychosocial stressors
70	Mild symptoms or impairment in social, occupational, or school functioning, but general functioning is pretty good
60	Moderate symptoms or impairment in social, occupational, or school functioning
50	Serious symptoms or impairment in social, occupational, or school functioning
40	Major impairment in work or school, family relations, judgment, thinking, mood; some communication impairment
30	Influenced by delusions or hallucinations, serious impairment in communication or judgment
20	Some danger of severely hurting self or others, gross impairment in communication, sporadic personal hygiene
10	Persistent danger of severely hurting self or others

FIGURE 14.3

The Five Axes of the DSM-IV Diagnostic System
The DSM-IV is composed of five major rating dimensions, or *axes.* Information collected from each axis is integrated into final diagnosis and treatment decisions. For example, it's important to know whether a person diagnosed with a disorder identified on Axis I or II is also suffering from an existing medical condition (Axis III) or whether he or she has been exposed recently to a significant psychosocial or environmental problem (Axis IV). Finally, the psychologist will use the person's ability to function well in everyday settings in considering the appropriate treatment (Axis V). (From DSM-IV, APA, 1994.)

psychological changes cause us to become attentive—we monitor our environment more closely so we're more apt to notice a potentially dangerous event when it occurs.

But there is a dark side to anxiety. When it becomes too persistent and intense, it interferes with your ability to function. **Anxiety disorders** are diagnosed when the levels of apprehension and worry become so extreme that overall

anxiety disorders
A class of disorders marked by excessive apprehension and worry that in turn impairs normal functioning.

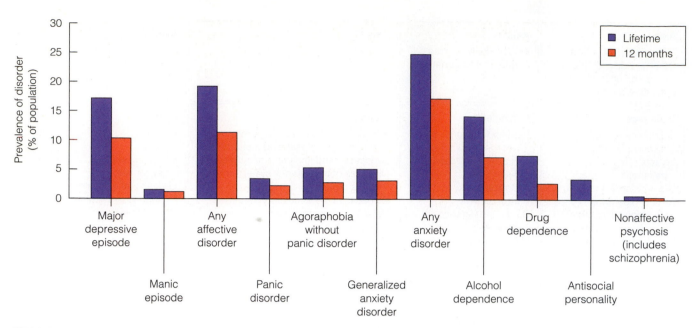

FIGURE 14.4

Prevalence Rates for Various Psychological Disorders

Each bar shows the percentage of individuals in a large sample (over 8000 participants) who reported suffering from the listed psychological disorder during the last 12 months or at some point in their lifetime. *Note:* A given individual might have reported suffering from more than one of these disorders concurrently. (Data from Kessler and others, 1994.)

behavior is impaired in some way. For example, if you consistently fail on exams because you cannot collect your thoughts, or if you refuse to leave the house because you're convinced you will experience a frightening panic attack, you're likely to be suffering from an anxiety disorder. There are several kinds of anxiety disorders, and each is defined by its own set of DSM-IV diagnostic criteria. We'll concentrate on some common ones in this section: *generalized anxiety disorder, panic disorder, obsessive–compulsive disorder,* and *specific phobias.*

Generalized Anxiety Disorder

The defining characteristic of **generalized anxiety disorder** is excessive and chronic worrying that lasts for a period of at least 6 months. The anxiety is "free-floating," as Freud described it, and cannot be attributed to any single identifiable source. People who suffer from this problem worry *in general* (which is captured in the name *generalized* anxiety disorder), and they fret constantly about any number of minor things (Sanderson & Barlow, 1990). More important, the worrying that occurs is unrealistic—it's not directly related to the chances that the feared event will actually occur (Brown et al., 1994).

Further, because anxiety is associated with activity of the autonomic nervous system, generalized anxiety disorder tends to be accompanied by a range of physical symptoms, including high pulse and respiration rates, chronic diarrhea, a need to urinate frequently, and chronic digestive problems. Someone burdened with generalized anxiety disorder is likely to have trouble sleeping and becomes easily irritated; he or she is also likely to spend a lot of time worrying about the future—more so than someone suffering from the other anxiety disorders we'll consider (Dugas et al., 1998). These kinds of symptoms are relatively easy to understand—after all, these people are living in a world of perpetual fear; the worst, they assume, is always about to happen.

Panic Disorder

Generalized anxiety is marked by chronic, unfocused worrying. In **panic disorder,** people suffer from recurrent episodes, or attacks, of extremely intense fear or dread (Craske & Barlow, 1993). A *panic attack* is a sudden and unexpected event, and it can make a person feel as if he or she is about to die (or, sometimes, go crazy). Panic attacks are brief, but they produce high levels of anxiety and, as a result, are accompanied by a collection of physical symptoms: a pounding heart, shortness of breath, sweating, nausea, chest pains, and so on. These symptoms can be devastating experiences, and they often lead to persistent concern about the

generalized anxiety disorder
Excessive worrying, or free-floating anxiety, that lasts for at least six months and that cannot be attributed to any single identifiable source.

panic disorder
A condition marked by recurrent discrete episodes or attacks of extremely intense fear or dread.

In panic disorder, a person suffers from recurrent episodes, or attacks, of intense fear or dread.

People who suffer from agoraphobia are often reluctant to leave the house; they're afraid that once outside they will experience a panic attack and be rendered helpless.

A person suffering form obsessive–compulsive disorder may feel the need to engage in a repetitive activity, such as compulsively lining up pencils, to reduce anxiety or to avoid thinking inappropriate thoughts.

possibility of having additional attacks (Barlow, 1988). It's worth noting that a single isolated panic attack is not sufficient for diagnosis of a panic disorder; the attacks need to occur repeatedly and unexpectedly.

Remarkably, panic attacks can even occur while you're asleep, a condition referred to as nocturnal panic (Craske & Rowe, 1997). Nocturnal panic attacks usually occur in the middle of the night—between 1:30 and 3:30 A.M.—and they're associated with slow-wave sleep rather than REM sleep (Barlow & Durand, 1999). This suggests that the attacks are not a consequence of bad dreams or nightmares, which tend to be associated with REM sleep (see Chapter 6). Nocturnal panic attacks are poorly understood at the moment, although they may be related to night terrors, which commonly occur in children, or to a sleep-related breathing problem called sleep apnea. Not surprisingly, people who experience nocturnal panic attacks are terrified after an attack and, in some cases, are very reluctant to go to sleep at night.

Panic disorder is sometimes associated with an additional complication, called *agoraphobia*, that arises from the worry that further panic attacks might occur. **Agoraphobia**—which translates from the Greek as "fear of the marketplace"—causes a person to restrict his or her normal activities in an extreme way. People who suffer from agoraphobia typically stay away from crowded or public places, such as shopping malls or restaurants, because they're afraid they'll experience a panic attack and be rendered helpless. In severe cases, people with agoraphobia might simply refuse to leave their house; home, they reason, is the only really safe place in the world. For obvious reasons, panic disorder with accompanying agoraphobia can significantly reduce a person's ability to function successfully in the world.

Obsessive–Compulsive Disorder

In **obsessive–compulsive disorder,** anxiety manifests itself through persistent, uncontrollable thoughts, called *obsessions*, or by the presence of a compelling need to perform one or more actions repeatedly, which is called a *compulsion* (Swinson et al., 1998). Compulsions are related to obsessions in the sense that the repetitive action is usually performed in response to some kind of obsessive thought (Riggs & Foa, 1993). Have you ever had part of a song or jingle ramble endlessly through your head—one that keeps repeating despite your best efforts to stop it? This is somewhat like an obsession, although in obsessive–compulsive disorder the obsessions tend to focus on fears (such as being contaminated by germs), doubts (such as forgetting to turn off the stove), and impulses (such as hurting oneself or another) (Jenike et al., 1986; Salkovskis, 1985).

agoraphobia
An anxiety disorder that causes an individual to restrict his or her normal activities; someone suffering from agoraphobia tends to avoid public places out of fear that a panic attack will occur.

obsessive–compulsive disorder
An anxiety disorder that manifests itself through persistent and uncontrollable thoughts, called *obsessions,* or by the compelling need to perform repetitive acts, called *compulsions.*

CONCEPT SUMMARY
Anxiety Disorders

Disorder	Description
Generalized anxiety disorder	Excessive and chronic worrying that lasts for a period of at least six months. Accompanied by excessive autonomic activity (e.g., increased respiration, heart rate).
Panic disorder	Recurrent episodes or "attacks" of extremely intense fear or dread. Sometimes accompanied by agoraphobia, the fear of being in public due to anticipation of another panic attack.
Obsessive–compulsive disorder	Anxiety is manifested through *obsessions* (persistent uncontrollable thoughts) and/or *compulsions* (a compelling need to perform one or more actions repeatedly.)
Specific phobic disorder	A highly focused fear of a specific object or situation. Most revolve around animals, natural environments, blood–injection–injury, or specific situations.

Compulsions consist of such actions as cleaning or checking, or actions that prevent some inappropriate impulse from occurring. For example, someone might repeat the alphabet aloud over and over in an effort to divert his or her thinking away from a frightening or inappropriate aggressive or sexual impulse. In extreme cases, the compulsions are so repetitive and ritualistic that they essentially prevent the sufferer from leading anything resembling a normal life. Some people become housebound, relentlessly cleaning rooms; others feel irresistibly compelled to leave work 10 to 15 times a day to check and make sure the gas wasn't left on in the stove. Interestingly, in the majority of such cases the suffering individuals understand that their actions are irrational and of little adaptive value (Stern & Cobb, 1978). The disorder simply compels the action.

Specific Phobic Disorder

The defining feature of a **specific phobic disorder** is a highly focused fear of a specific object or situation—such as a bug, a snake, flying, heights, an animal, a closed place, or a storm. Like the other anxiety disorders we've discussed, specific phobias are irrational, which means that the level of anxiety the object or situation produces is in no way justified by reality. Elevators do fall, snakes can bite, planes do crash—but these events are rare and do not justify daily worry. Many people show mild forms of phobic reactions—and, again, in some cases the object of the anxiety might indeed be dangerous (some snakes do kill)—but in specific phobic disorder the fear and distress can be severely disabling. To avoid the anxiety-producing object or situation, individuals with a specific phobic disorder might significantly disrupt their normal routines; they might avoid going to work or school or traveling to anywhere different in the slight chance that they will encounter the object of their fear.

Specific phobias typically revolve around one of four classes of fear-inducing objects or situations: (1) animals (insects, snakes, dogs, etc.), (2) natural environments (storms, heights, water, etc.), (3) blood-injection-injury (the sight of blood or even the thought of an injection), and (4) specific situations (fears associated with public transportation or closed-in places). These four categories capture the majority of phobic reactions, although there are others—such as fear of choking or fear of costumed characters—that do not fit easily into these established categories. Most people who suffer from specific phobias tend to have more than one, and often more than one type (Hofmann et al., 1997). For a look at how likely the various specific phobias are to occur among the general population see Figure 14.5.

SOMATOFORM DISORDERS: BODY AND MIND

A common phenomenon, called the *medical student syndrome*, often plagues medical students as they first learn about the various diseases of the body. The students find that the symptoms described in class, or in the text, are increasingly familiar

CRITICAL THINKING

Can you think of reasons why it might be adaptive for people to show specific reactions for each of the four classes of phobic stimuli described in the text?

specific phobic disorder
A highly focused fear of a specific object or situation.

FIGURE 14.5

Prevalence Rates for Various Specific Phobias
Each bar shows the percentage of people in a large sample who reported suffering from a particular kind of phobia. (Data from Agras, Sylvester, & Oliveau, 1969.)

and personal. A deep pain that appears suddenly in the night is interpreted as a signal for the final stages of pancreatic cancer; that darkening blemish on the forehead becomes the rare form of skin cancer that often accompanies AIDS. In almost every case the student is perfectly healthy, but the mind plays its tricks and the student fears the worst.

Mental health professionals classify psychological problems that focus on the physical body as **somatoform disorders** (*soma* means "body"). Obviously, like medical students, most people have experienced imagined illnesses at some point in their lives. But when the preoccupation with bodily functions or symptoms is excessive and is not grounded in any physical reality, a true psychological disorder may be indicated. The DSM-IV lists a number of basic somatoform disorders; we'll focus briefly on three: *hypochondriasis, somatization disorder,* and *conversion disorder*.

Hypochondriasis

The main symptom of **hypochondriasis** is a persistent preoccupation with the idea that you've developed a serious disease, based on what turns out to be a misinterpretation of normal bodily reactions. The pain in the side, the slight case of indigestion, the occasional irregular heartbeat—these are interpreted as symptomatic of a serious medical condition. Moreover, unlike the situation for the normal medical student, these preoccupations persist for months and often cause significant distress and impaired functioning. Hypochondriasis is typically associated with excessive anxiety and, in fact, may be strongly related to the types of anxiety disorders we discussed earlier (Otto et al., 1998).

Somatization Disorder

Somatization disorder is related to hypochondriasis and, in fact, mental health professionals sometimes have a difficult time distinguishing between the two. Both involve the persistent complaint of symptoms with no identifiable physical cause, but in somatization disorder it is the *symptoms* that receive the focus of attention rather than an underlying disease. In both cases, the person searches endlessly for doctors who will confirm his or her symptoms, but usually with little or no success (because there is no real physical problem). The major difference between hypochondriasis and somatization disorder seems to be that in hypochondriasis the anxiety arises because of a presumed underlying disease, whereas in somatization disorder the presence of the symptoms themselves causes the anxiety. People with somatization disorder are not typically afraid of dying from a serious disease; rather, they are looking for someone to understand and sympathize with their countless physical problems.

somatoform disorders
Psychological disorders that focus on the physical body.

hypochondriasis
A long-lasting preoccupation with the idea that one has developed a serious disease, based on what turns out to be a misinterpretation of normal body reactions.

somatization disorder
A long-lasting preoccupation with body symptoms that have no identifiable physical cause.

A person suffering from hypochondriasis is prone to misinterpreting normal body reactions as symptomatic of a serious disease.

? CRITICAL THINKING

Can you think of any reason why a client who is seeking help for a psychological problem might want desperately to please the therapist?

conversion disorder
The presence of real physical problems, such as blindness or paralysis, that seem to have no identifiable physical cause.

dissociative disorders
A class of disorders characterized by the separation, or dissociation, of conscious awareness from previous thoughts or memories.

dissociative amnesia
A psychological disorder characterized by an inability to remember important personal information.

dissociative fugue
A loss of personal identity that is often accompanied by a flight from home.

dissociative identity disorder
A condition in which an individual alternates between what appear to be two or more distinct identities or personalities (also known as *multiple personality disorder*).

Conversion Disorder

In **conversion disorder,** unlike the other two somatoform disorders we've considered, there appears to be real physical or neurological impairment. Someone suffering from a conversion disorder might report being blind, or paralyzed, or unable to speak. The affected person might even experience seizures resembling those found in epilepsy or other neurological disorders (Bowman, 1998). These are not feigned symptoms; that is, these problems are not intentionally produced by the individual to gain sympathy or attention. These are real problems, although no physical cause can be discovered.

Obviously, in such cases there is always the possibility that a true neurological or other physical problem does exist; physical problems are indeed sometimes misdiagnosed as conversion disorders (Fishbain & Goldberg, 1991; Slater & Glithero, 1965). But when the reported problems disappear after effective therapy, a psychological origin is usually indicated. You may remember from our discussion of personality in Chapter 12 that Sigmund Freud often used his psychoanalytic techniques to treat patients with conversion disorders (although the problem was known as *hysteria* in his day). In fact, the term *conversion*, as used here, originates from psychodynamic theory and the proposal that unconscious conflicts have been converted into a physical form.

DISSOCIATIVE DISORDERS: DISRUPTIONS OF IDENTITY OR AWARENESS

Some of the more colorful types of psychological disorders, at least as seen by Hollywood or the popular press, come from a class of problems called **dissociative disorders.** Dissociative disorders are defined by the separation, or *dissociation*, of conscious awareness from previous thoughts or memories. If you're affected by one of these disorders, you lose memory for some specific aspect of your life, or even your entire sense of identity. The theme of the confused amnesiac, searching for his or her lost identity, has been explored repeatedly in Hollywood films throughout the years. We'll focus our attention on three types of dissociative disorder: *dissociative amnesia, dissociative fugue,* and *dissociative identity disorder.*

Dissociative Amnesia

In Chapter 8, when we tackled remembering and forgetting, we discussed various kinds of *amnesia*, or the inability to remember or retain personal experiences. It was noted that amnesia could result from either physical factors (such as brain damage) or psychological factors (such as traumatic stress). In **dissociative amnesia,** which is assumed to be psychological in origin, the person is unable to remember important personal information. The amnesia can be quite general, as in the failure to remember one's identity or family history, or it can be localized, such as the failure to remember a specific traumatic life experience (Loewenstein, 1996). In dissociative amnesia, the forgetting can last for hours or for years. It often disappears as mysteriously as it arises.

Dissociative Fugue

In **dissociative fugue,** there is also a loss of personal identity—people forget who they are—but it's accompanied by an escape or flight from the home environment (*fugue* literally means "flight"). Imagine leaving for work or school as usual only to "awaken" some time later in a different city or state. Sometimes the fugue state can last months or even years; some individuals experiencing this disorder have even adopted different identities in their new locale. Recovery can be sudden and often complete, but affected individuals will typically claim that they have no knowledge of their activities during the blackout period.

Dissociative Identity Disorder

In what is perhaps the most baffling of all dissociative disorders, **dissociative identity disorder,** a person alternates between what appear to be two or more distinct identities or personality states (hence the alternative name, *multiple personality disorder*). Some cases of this disorder have been widely publicized. For example you may be familiar with Sybil Dorsett, who was diagnosed with 16 personalities (Schreiber, 1973); she was portrayed by Sally Field in the television movie *Sybil*. Another well-known case is "Eve," who alternated between three personality types (Thigpen & Cleckley, 1957); she was portrayed by Joanne Woodward in the film *The Three Faces of Eve*.

In dissociative identity disorder, the unique personalities or identities appear to take control of the affected person's thoughts and actions, one personality at a time. More important, the personality in control will profess to have only limited awareness of the other personality inhabitants. Commonly, there is interpersonality amnesia, which means that events experienced while the person is inhabited by personality "A" cannot be remembered when he or she is occupied by personality "B" (Eich et al., 1997). It is for this reason that the disorder is classified as *dissociative*—there is a separation of current conscious awareness from prior thoughts and memories. Dozens of different identities may be involved, including both males and females, and a given identity will tend to have unique physical attributes, such as a distinct tone of voice, facial expression, handwriting style, or behavioral habit (Putnam et al., 1986).

Dissociative identity disorder is recognized as a legitimate disorder in the DSM-IV, but not all mental health professionals are comfortable with this designation (Fahy, 1988). Controversy often surrounds the diagnosis, for a number of reasons. First, this disorder often co-occurs with other psychological problems (such as depression and somatization disorder), so it's quite difficult to pinpoint the ultimate cause of any particular symptom (Ross et al., 1990). Second, although each of the observed personalities may be distinguished on the basis of personality tests or physiological measures, we still cannot be completely sure about the true origins of these differences—other factors, such as mood or arousal differences, may partly account for the distinct performance patterns (Fahy, 1988; Lilienfeld, 1994).

Third, several studies have shown that it's relatively easy to fake or simulate multiple personalities (Spanos et al., 1985). This raises the possibility that people with dissociative identity disorder may actually be role playing in some fashion, perhaps in a way comparable to those who have been hypnotized. As you might recall from Chapter 6, many psychologists question whether hypnosis really represents some kind of dissociated state; instead, hypnotized people often seem eager to please the hypnotist by acting in accordance with a hypnotized role. This is not necessarily a conscious choice made by those who have been hypnotized; instead, it may represent a kind of unconscious or involuntary compliance (Lynn et al., 1990). Some researchers are convinced that dissociative identity disorder is best interpreted as a kind of self-hypnosis that arises partly to please the therapist. There has been an unusually rapid rise in the number of cases of dissociative identity disorder as the disorder has been publicized in the media, which lends support to the role playing hypothesis.

Despite the controversy, dissociative identity disorder was retained as a diagnostic disorder in the DSM-IV, which was published in 1994. It does seem clear that not all aspects of the disorder can be consciously faked (Kluft, 1991). Highly specific physiological differences have been reported across personalities—such as differences in visual acuity or eye muscle balance (Miller, 1989)—and it seems unlikely that such things could be easily faked (see Figure 14.6). There also appear to be certain similarities in the past histories of affected individuals that have convinced many of the validity of the diagnosis. For example, in a recent study of 97 cases, 95% of the individuals were found to have suffered some form of abuse, usually sexual or physical, most often during childhood (Ross et al., 1990). The diagnosis of dissociative identity disorder remains controversial, but it is considered to be a legitimate disorder by the psychological community at large.

Kenneth Bianchi, known as the Hillside Strangler, claimed that he could not be held responsible for the rape and murder of a number of California women because he was suffering from dissociative identity disorder. The evidence presented at trial suggested that Bianchi was "faking" the disorder, and he was later convicted and sentenced to life imprisonment.

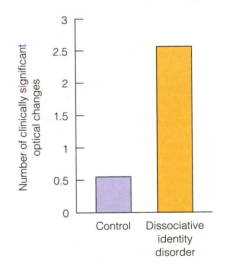

FIGURE 14.6

Optical Changes across Personalities
In a study by Miller (1989), individuals diagnosed with dissociative identity disorder were asked to undergo ophthalmological (eye) exams while "inhabited" by each of three different personalities. Significant differences were found in optical functioning across personalities, more so than occurred for normal control subjects who were asked to "fake" different personalities during each exam. (Data from Miller, 1989.)

Inside the Problem   Creativity and Madness

It is commonly believed that inside the hearts and minds of truly creative people lies an element of madness. If you take a journey through history and consider the psychological health of prominent individuals, it's not difficult to find examples of psychological problems. In this century alone, there have been at least five Pulitzer Prize–winning poets (including Sylvia Plath) who have committed suicide in the midst of depression. So, too, have a number of fiction writers (Ernest Hemingway, for example). It is now recognized that Abraham Lincoln, Teddy Roosevelt, and Winston Churchill all probably suffered from bipolar disorder, marked by swings between manic states and depression.

Such examples are intriguing, but they don't constitute solid scientific evidence. More systematic data have come from studies in which pools of highly creative and "average" people are matched on a number of dimensions and the rate of psychological problems is then compared. In one such study, Nancy Andreasen (1987) compared the psychiatric diagnoses of 30 creative writing faculty at the University of Iowa Writers' Workshop (a highly regarded creative writing program) with those of 30 control individuals who were matched to the writers on age, sex, and educational status. Andreasen discovered that the writers had a substantially higher rate of psychological disorders than the controls—in fact, 43% of the writers were found to have experienced the symptoms

of a bipolar disorder at some point in their lives. This was the case for only 10% of the controls. Andreasen also found a higher likelihood of mental problems among the writers' first-degree relatives (parents and siblings).

Kay Redfield Jamison (1989) looked to see whether similarities might exist between creative states and the characteristics of manic states. She interviewed 47 famous British writers and artists—all had won at least one prestigious literary or artistic prize—and asked them to describe their moods, thoughts, and actions during spurts of creative activity. She found striking similarities between their answers and the symptoms found in manic states; virtually all of the subjects reported experiencing creative states characterized by a decreased need for sleep, increases in energy, enthusiasm, self-confidence, speed and fluency of thoughts, as well as an elevated mood and sense of well-being. Moreover, when Jamison asked the subjects how important these extremes in mood and thoughts were to the creation of their work, 90% of the participants stated that the moods and feelings were integral, necessary, or very important (Jamison, 1989).

However, there are alternative explanations for the data that we've just considered. These studies simply demonstrate correlations between the characteristics of mood disorders and creativity: Creative individuals are more likely to have mood

disorders, and the thoughts and feelings that accompany creative periods share properties with the symptoms of mood disorders. But this kind of evidence does not indicate whether the psychological disorder is really *causing* the creative activity. Other factors might be involved. For example, one possibility is that when creative individuals are in a manic state, they simply do more work because of their high energy levels. This can make it look like the mania is enhancing creativity, even though it is the *quantity* rather than the *quality* of the work that is really changing. Suppose that you're capable of writing one really good poem for every 10 attempts you make. If you normally make 10 attempts in a month, you will end up with one excellent result. Now suppose you enter a manic state, which increases your output to 30 poems in a month. Even if the mania doesn't affect the quality of your work one bit, it will still look as if you have tripled the number of "great" works that you have produced. Madness and creativity may co-occur, but one is not directly causing the other.

To examine the possibility that it may be the quantity rather than the quality of output that is affected by a mood disorder, Robert Weisberg (1994) conducted a detailed case study of the composer Robert Schumann (1810–1856). Schumann is believed to have suffered from bipolar disorder; throughout his life, he repeatedly entered either manic or depressive states, and he eventually starved himself to death

DISORDERS OF MOOD: DEPRESSION AND MANIA

From time to time everyone experiences depression, that overwhelming feeling that things are completely hopeless and sad. For most, thankfully, the experience is brief; moreover, most of us can usually account for our depressed mood by pointing to a particular experience or event in our lives: We failed the test; our beloved pet died; our once-trusted romantic partner now prefers the affections of another. But when an extreme mood swing is not short-lived and is accompanied by other symptoms, such as a prolonged loss of appetite and a negative self-concept, a mood disorder may be present. **Mood disorders**—which are defined as prolonged and disabling disruptions in emotional state—come in two main varieties: (1) *depressive disorders*, in which the person suffers primarily from depression, and (2) *bipolar disorders*, which are characterized by mood *swings* between extreme highs, called manic states, and the lows of depression. We'll consider each of these types of disorders separately.

mood disorders
Prolonged and disabling disruptions in emotional state.

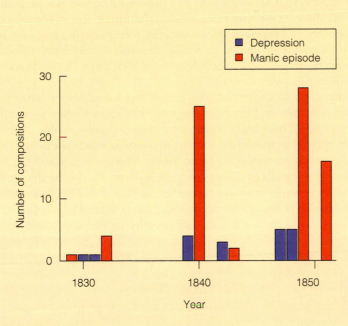

FIGURE 14.7
Musical Productivity and Mood State
The graph shows the number of musical compositions written by Robert Schumann during years in which his mood state was characterized primarily as manic (red) or depressed (blue). (Based on Weisberg, 1994.)

in an institution at age 46. Schumann is an excellent case to study because there are medical records, as well as other data, that pinpoint on a year-by-year basis which kind of mood state he was in. Weisberg found a clear relationship between Schumann's mood state and his productivity as a composer: For the years that he was primarily in a state of depression, he completed, on average, fewer than 3 compositions per year. On the other hand, his output during manic years was a little over 12 compositions per year (see Figure 14.7).

But were the compositions from his manic years of high quality? To find out, Weisberg (1994) determined the number of times Schumann's compositions had been recorded professionally over the years. If a composition is recorded often by professionals, Weisberg argued, it's reasonable to conclude that the piece is of high quality. Weisberg found that when the quality of Schumann's compositions—defined as the average number of recordings available for each composition in a particular year—was compared across manic and depressive years, no significant differences emerged. Although Schumann composed more during his manic periods, he was not more likely to produce works of extremely high quality. In this particular case, then, madness affected the quantity of creative output but not the quality.

Determining whether there really is a causal relationship between certain kinds of psychological problems and genius or creativity is a difficult thing to do. Obviously, psychologists cannot conduct a well-controlled experiment (creating madness in one randomly sampled group of creative people and not in another), so they are typically forced to rely on correlational studies or on anecdotes as the basis for their opinions. Weisberg's research, with its careful and objective separation of quality from quantity, suggests that the anecdotal evidence may be wrong or misleading, at least for people suffering from bipolar disorders. The link between madness and creativity may turn out to be quite weak, despite centuries of belief to the contrary.

Depressive Disorders

The DSM-IV lists specific criteria for the diagnosis of depressive disorders, which are among the most common of all psychological disorders. For something to qualify as a **major depressive episode,** for instance, you must show five or more of the following types of symptoms for a period of at least two weeks: (1) depressed mood for most of the day, (2) loss of interest in normal daily activities, (3) a significant change in weight (either a loss or a gain), (4) difficulty sleeping or a desire to sleep all the time, (5) a change in activity level (either extreme restlessness or lethargy), (6) daily fatigue or loss of energy, (7) a negative self-concept, including feelings of worthlessness or excessive guilt, (8) trouble concentrating or in making decisions, and (9) suicidal thoughts.

When you enter a major depressive episode, the world is seen through a kind of dark filter. You feel extremely sad and full of self-doubt, and the environment seems overwhelming, imposing, and full of obstacles that cannot be overcome

major depressive episode
A type of mood disorder characterized by depressed mood and other symptoms.

Depression — endogenous → needs
medication
*has internal
source*

exogenous → do not
NEED medication, often
but the same like endog-
enous depression is caused by
something external.

(Young et al., 1993). This worldview of a depressed person is a particularly grim aspect of the disorder—if you're depressed, the future seems hopeless with little or no possibility of a reprieve. Moreover, the accompanying negative self-image appears to be solidly grounded in reality; depressed people are absolutely convinced about the truth of their hopelessness, which tragically leads some to consider suicide as their only outlet.

It is important to understand that major depression is more than just feeling sad. You literally view and interpret the world differently when you're depressed, which tends to feed back and confirm your negative self-concept. Normal activities are interpreted as indicating some dire consequence (for example, if a friend fails to call, it must mean the friend no longer likes me). As you'll see in the next chapter, one of the goals of therapy in treating depression is to change depressed individuals' thought patterns—to make them see the world in a more realistic way.

Mental health professionals distinguish among several types of depressive disorders, based partly on the length and severity of the depressive episode. For example, a major depressive episode can be classified as *recurrent*, which means that it has occurred more than once in an individual's lifetime (but separated by a period of at least two months). There is also a condition called *dysthymic disorder*, in which the depressive symptoms tend to be milder and less disruptive but more chronic. Most major depressive episodes end after a period of weeks or months and the person returns to normal, but people affected by dysthymic disorder show a relatively continuous depressed mood for a period of at least two years (Akiskal & Cassano, 1997). A major depressive episode can even occur at the same time as dysthymic disorder, in which case the condition is referred to as *double depression* (Keller & Shapiro, 1982).

Bipolar Disorders

When depression is *unipolar*, the depressive episode typically runs its course and the person returns to a normal state. The depression may occur again, but the disorder is defined by a mood shift in only one direction—toward the negative. In a **bipolar disorder,** you experience mood shifts in two directions: traveling from the depths of depression (a major depressive episode) to a hyperactive, euphoric condition called a **manic state.** When you're in a manic state, you act as if you're on top of the world—you're hyperactive, talkative, and seem to have little need for sleep. These symptoms may seem positive and desirable, but they are balanced by tendencies toward grandiosity, distractibility, and risk taking. In a manic state, a person might attempt a remarkable feat—such as scaling the Statue of Liberty—or perhaps will go on a sudden spending spree, cashing in all his or her savings. People who are in a manic state report feeling great—at times as if they're experiencing one continuous sexual orgasm—but their thinking is far from normal or rational. Their speech can appear disrupted because they shift rapidly from one fleeting thought to another.

To be classified as a manic episode in the DSM-IV, this abnormally elevated mood state must last for at least a week, although it can last for months. Like a depressive episode, the manic state typically goes away, even without treatment, and the person either returns to normal or roller-coasters into another depressive episode. People who suffer from bipolar disorders live lives of extreme highs and lows; not surprisingly, their ability to function normally in society is often severely impaired. Moreover, tragically, it's been estimated that as many as 19% of individuals who are affected with bipolar disorders end up successfully committing suicide, usually during one of their episodes of depression (Jamison, 1986). (For a discussion of the possible connection between bipolar disorders and creativity, turn back to the "Inside the Problem" feature on page 560.)

Suicide

As just noted, suicide can be one fatal consequence of suffering from a mood disorder such as bipolar disorder. It's worth pausing for a moment and considering

bipolar disorder
A type of mood disorder in which the person experiences disordered mood shifts in two directions—from depression to a manic state.

manic state
A disordered state in which the person becomes hyperactive, talkative, and has a decreased need for sleep; a person in a manic state may engage in activities that are self-destructive or dangerous.

suicide because it's quite a significant problem worldwide; suicide rates have been on the rise for decades, especially among adolescents. It's now the third leading cause of death among adolescents and the eighth leading cause of death overall. Interestingly, suicide is highest for white males, at least in the United States. Men are four to five times more likely to commit suicide than women (although women are three times more likely to *attempt* suicide) and the average suicide rates for non-Caucasians are more than 10% lower than those for Caucasians (Buda & Tsuang, 1990). It's been estimated that more than 90% of people who kill themselves suffer from some kind of psychological disorder (Garland & Ziegler, 1993).

What are the risk factors associated with suicide? Besides the presence of a psychological disorder, many different factors can be involved. Alcohol use and abuse is particularly likely in adolescent suicides, existing in perhaps 50% of suicides (Woods et al., 1997). Another important factor is the sudden occurrence of a very stressful event— something such as the death of a loved one, failure or rejection in a personal relationship, or even a natural disaster. There is convincing evidence suggesting that suicide rates increase after natural disasters, such as floods, hurricanes, or earthquakes (Krug et al., 1998). Suicide may also be contagious: There are increased suicide rates following widely publicized suicides, especially among adolescents, suggesting that imitation or modeling is an important factor (Gould, 1990).

Among the most significant predictors of suicide, however, are prior suicide attempts and suicidal thoughts. Among adolescents there is somewhere between a 3 : 1 and 6 : 1 ratio between serious suicidal thoughts and an actual suicide attempt. Not everyone who thinks about suicide makes an attempt—and the ratio of attempted suicides to successful suicides is perhaps 50 : 1 (Garland & Ziegler, 1993)—but suicidal thinking is a serious warning sign. We'll discuss treatment options for the psychological conditions that are associated with suicide in Chapter 15, but there are a variety of intervention programs currently being used to tackle the suicide problem nationally. For example, in 1988 the Centers for Disease Control recommended that teams of mental health professionals be sent to schools, for counseling and screening, whenever a student or visible member of the community commits suicide. Moreover, most cities and towns now have 24-hour suicide hotline services that allow people in need to voice their concerns and learn about alternative ways of dealing with their crises. Most psychologists are optimistic that as the risk factors associated with suicide are identified, and treatment options become more accessible, suicide rates can be slowed or reversed (Kosky et al., 1998).

SCHIZOPHRENIA: WHEN THOUGHT PROCESSES GO AWRY

For most of the psychological disorders we've considered so far, you probably experienced at least a glimmer of recognition. Everyone can identify with anxiety, the occasional obsessive thought, or even a slight case of depression. It's only when these tendencies become *excessive* and interfere with normal functioning that you're likely to be diagnosed with an actual psychological disorder. But in the case of **schizophrenia,** which translates literally as "split mind," the psychological changes can be so profound that the affected individual is thrust into a world that bears little resemblance to everyday experience. The person with schizophrenia lives in an internal world marked by thought processes that have gone awry; delusions, hallucinations, and generally disordered thinking become the norm.

schizophrenia
A class of disorders characterized by fundamental disturbances in thought processes, emotion, or behavior.

[Handwritten margin notes, top left:]

symptoms :- delusions
- prominent hallucinations
2 of these - incoherence or marked loosening of associations
- catatonic behavior
- flat or grossly inappropriate affect

- bizarre delusions
- prominent hallucinations of a voice

Schizophrenia is actually a group or class of disorders. There are different subtypes of schizophrenia, defined by different DSM-IV criteria, but each case is identified with some kind of fundamental disturbance in thought processes, emotion, or behavior. Schizophrenia is a bit unusual compared to the other disorders we've considered because it doesn't always reveal itself in the same way; whereas everyone who suffers from an anxiety disorder feels apprehensive, or in depression feels sad, each of the symptoms of schizophrenia need not be shared by all affected individuals. Schizophrenia is a complex disorder that is expressed in a variety of complex ways—no single symptom must be present for the diagnosis to be applied (Maj, 1998).

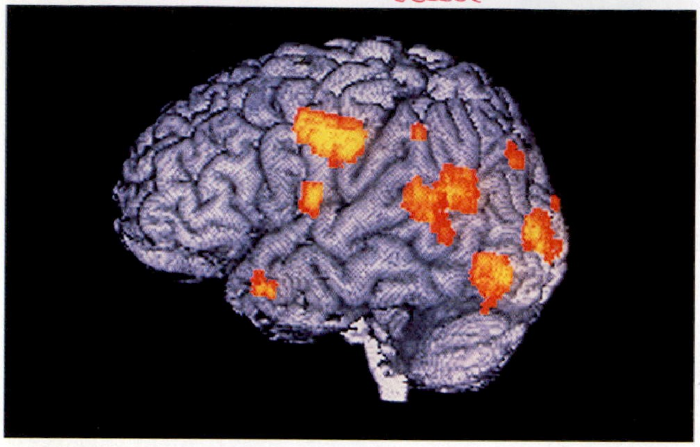

It is important to understand that schizophrenia is not the same thing as a dissociative identity disorder, despite the translation of schizophrenia as "split mind." Schizophrenia leads to faulty thought processes and inappropriate emotions—not to dissociations among distinct personality types. In fact, when the Swiss psychiatrist Eugen Bleuler (1908) originally introduced the term *schizophrenia*, he was referring primarily to the fact that affected individuals have trouble holding onto a consistent line of thought. Their thinking is disorganized; their thought lines and associations seem to split apart and move forward in inconsistent ways. Both schizophrenia and dissociative identity disorder are serious psychological problems, but they fall into completely different categories in the DSM-IV.

Shown here are areas of the brain that appear to be selectively activated during auditory and visual hallucinations. The highlighted areas were captured through the use of a PET scanning procedure, during which a young man who was suffering from schizophrenia was asked to press a button, initiating the scan, every time he experienced a hallucination.

[Handwritten margin notes, lower left:]

1) Paranoid Schizophrenia : disorder primarily cognitive. It is characterized by delusions & extreme suspiciousness, [delusion of grandeur shift to delusion of persecution] + loose thinking.

2) Disorganized Schizophrenia (Hebephrenic) Delusions + hallucinations (particularly visual hallucinations), grimacing & gesturing. Childish disregard for social conventions [may resist wearing clothes, urinate & defecate in inappropriate places; not with their hygiene]

3) Catatonic Schizophrenia : → may remain stiffly immobile or may be extremely agitated. Waxy flexibility is another form of immobility in which the catatonic's arm or leg remains passively in the position in which it was placed.
→ agitated catatonic shows extreme psychomotor excitement talking & shouting almost continuously.
Patients may be very violent & destructive to themselves & others.

Diagnostic Symptoms

There are two main types of symptoms in schizophrenia: *positive symptoms* and *negative symptoms*. Positive symptoms usually include observable expressions of abnormal behavior, such as delusions or hallucinations; negative symptoms consist of deficits in behavior, such as an inability to express emotion. The DSM-IV requires that two or more characteristic symptoms be present for the diagnosis of schizophrenia, but a particular person may have only positive symptoms or a combination of both positive and negative symptoms. As with the other disorders we've considered, these symptoms need to last for a significant period of time, they must cause social or job distress, and they cannot be due to the effects of a general medical condition or to the use of a drug or medication.

Let's consider some of the major positive symptoms of schizophrenia in more detail. As noted earlier, one of the main problems in schizophrenia is distorted or disorganized thinking. People with schizophrenia often suffer from *delusions*, which are thoughts with inappropriate content. If someone sitting next to you in class leaned over and claimed to be Elvis in disguise, or Jesus Christ, or Adolf Hitler, the content of his or her thoughts would clearly be inappropriate or deviant—this individual would be suffering from a delusion. People suffering from schizophrenia sometimes hold a *delusion of grandeur*, which is a belief that they are more famous or important than they actually are, or a *delusion of persecution*, which is a belief that others are conspiring or plotting against them in some way.

It is also not unusual for people with schizophrenia to report distorted perceptions of the world. For them, objects can seem to change their shape or size; distances can be perceived in ways that are different from reality. Frequently, these *hallucinations*—which are perceptions that have no basis in external stimulation— are auditory. People with schizophrenia claim to hear disembodied voices in their heads, giving them commands or commenting on the quality of their activities ("You're an idiot," "You should stay away from that person," and so on). Some researchers believe that these voices may originate from the same areas of the brain that control language production. It may be the case that people with schizophrenia are actually "listening" to their inner voice (see Chapter 8) but fail to recognize the voice as their own. Instead, they falsely attribute the source of the voice to something external (Cleghorn et al., 1992; McGuire et al., 1993).

Two other positive symptoms of schizophrenia that may be present are *disorganized speech* and *catatonia*. Sometimes the speech patterns of a person with schizophrenia appear quite jumbled and incoherent; the affected individual jumps repeatedly from one disconnected topic to another ("I went to the beach today where the moon pulls the rabbit out of the hat. I'm the world's greatest cook, but that's because volcanic magma heats the glaciers and makes the water and the sand.") It's as if the mind has lost its internal editor—ideas or thoughts no longer flow in a connected way. In addition to displaying speech problems, someone with schizophrenia can behave in ways that are quite disorganized and bizarre. The person might engage in repetitive activities, such as swirling his or her arms repeatedly, or will appear to laugh or cry at inappropriate times. When *catatonia* is present, people will sometimes adopt a peculiar stance or position and remain immobile for hours; or, they may wildly and suddenly change position for no apparent reason.

Negative symptoms of schizophrenia are expressed by the elimination or reduction of normal behavior. For example, it's quite common for people with schizophrenia to display *flat affect*, which means that they show little or no emotional reaction to events. Show someone with flat affect an extremely funny movie or a tragic, heart-rending photo, and the person is unlikely to crack a smile or shed a tear. People with schizophrenia also often refuse to engage in the most basic and important of everyday activities. They may refuse to wash or clean themselves, eat, or dress themselves. Activities that are pleasurable to most people become unpleasurable or uninteresting to some individuals with schizophrenia.

For obvious reasons, people with schizophrenia are often unable to cope successfully at school or at work. In many cases, their behavior becomes so maladaptive that hospitalization is required. As you'll see later in the chapter, there are reasons to believe that people with schizophrenia may be suffering from a kind of "broken" brain—fundamental neurological problems may underlie the bizarre thinking and behaviors that plague people affected with the disorder.

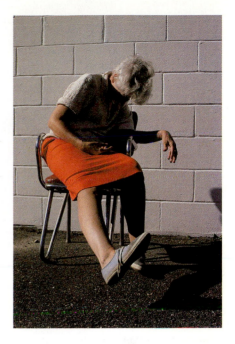

When catatonia is present as a positive symptom of schizophrenia, the affected person might adopt a peculiar stance or position and remain immobile for hours.

PERSONALITY DISORDERS

All of the psychological disorders we've considered up to now are described on Axis I of the DSM-IV (Clinical Syndromes). Axis II describes **personality disorders,** which are essentially chronic or enduring patterns of behavior that lead to significant impairments in social functioning. People with personality disorders have a tendency to act repeatedly in an inflexible and maladaptive way. They may show an exaggerated distrust of others, as in **paranoid personality disorder,** or they may show an excessive and persistent need to be taken care of by others, as in **dependent personality disorder.** One of the best-known examples of a personality disorder, occurring mainly in males, is the **antisocial personality disorder.** People with this type of disorder show little respect for social customs or norms. They act as if they have no conscience—they lie, cheat, or steal at the drop of a hat and show no remorse for their actions if caught. Someone with antisocial personality disorder is likely to have no qualms about committing criminal acts, even murder. Many end up with long criminal records and spend significant periods of time in jail (Cunningham & Reidy, 1998).

What is it about personality disorders that requires them to be placed on their own classification axis? Do personality disorders have characteristics that fundamentally distinguish them from the major clinical syndromes described on Axis I? Most mental health professionals believe that personality disorders are unique primarily because they tend to be more *ingrained* and *inflexible* than the major clinical syndromes outlined on Axis I (Barlow & Durand, 1999). These are not problems that typically appear and disappear over time, which is the case with many

personality disorders
Chronic or enduring patterns of behavior that lead to significant impairments in social functioning.

paranoid personality disorder
A personality disorder characterized by pervasive distrust of others.

dependent personality disorder
A personality disorder characterized by an excessive and persistent need to be taken care of by others.

antisocial personality disorder
A personality disorder characterized by little, if any, respect for social laws, customs, or norms.

? CRITICAL THINKING

Think back to our earlier discussion of how to conceptualize abnormality. Do you think personality disorders should be labeled as "abnormal" behaviors?

psychological disorders. These problems come from someone's basic personality and, as a result, tend to continue throughout adulthood and are quite resistant to therapy. Personality disorders are placed on a separate axis in the DSM-IV in part to force the clinician to consider the possibility that it is a personality characteristic, rather than a major clinical syndrome, that is contributing to the appearance of abnormal behavior.

Because personality disorders are linked to an individual's personality, some mental health professionals have argued that it's wrong to think of them as *disorders* in the same sense as something like a specific phobia or depression (Gunderson, 1992; Trull & McCrae, 1994). In Chapter 12, which dealt with the topic of personality, we discussed the idea that personality can be defined by the *Big Five* personality dimensions (McCrae & Costa, 1985). Some researchers have argued it is better to think about people with personality disorders as simply extreme or deviant on one or more of these five dimensions—extroversion, agreeableness, conscientiousness, neuroticism, and openness (Clark & Livesley, 1994). For example, the dimension of *agreeableness* measures how kind, warm, and trusting an individual is. It's possible that people classified with a paranoid personality disorder may simply lie near an extreme pole on the agreeableness scale—they trust almost no one. At present, questions are still being raised about the proper way to think about personality disorders, and whether the Big Five will be sufficient to account for the complexities of the disorders is still an unresolved question (Widiger, 1998).

TEST YOURSELF 14.2

Check your knowledge of classifications of psychological disorders by picking the diagnostic category that best describes each of the following behavior patterns. Pick from among the following terms: anxiety disorder, somatoform disorder, dissociative disorder, mood disorder, schizophrenia, personality disorder. (You will find the answers in the Appendix.)

1. Sharma is convinced that the ringing in her ears means she has a brain tumor, even though a variety of doctors can find nothing wrong: _____

2. Gabriella is a checker—she often drives home five or six times a day to make sure that she hasn't left the oven on: _____

3. Kunal hasn't left his house for six years—it's the only place he really feels safe: _____

4. Otto hates himself. He's convinced that he's worthless, stupid, and unlovable. No one can convince him otherwise: _____

5. Sergio is found wandering aimlessly in the park. When questioned, he can't remember who he is or how he got to the park: _____

6. Sarah is a habitual con artist with little regard for the truth. She steals regularly and feels no guilt or remorse about her actions: _____

7. Melissa is convinced that her psychology professor is beaming his thoughts directly into her brain; she feels empowered and ready to complete her take over of the world: _____

8. Billy shows little or no emotional reaction to events in his world; in fact, he usually stands in the corner for hours at a time with his right arm resting on his head: _____

Understanding Psychological Disorders: Biological, Cognitive, or Environmental?

The DSM-IV classification system is designed to provide a reliable way for mental health professionals to diagnose psychological problems. The word *reliable* in this case refers to whether professional clinicians will tend to arrive at the same or similar diagnoses for people with a given set of symptoms. In general, the DSM system is considered to be quite reliable, although agreement is higher for some diagnostic categories than for others (Linde & Clarke, 1998). But it's important to remember that the DSM-IV is only a classification system—it does not indicate anything about the root cause, or *etiology*, of the underlying disorder. What factors, alone or in combination, conspire to produce a major clinical syndrome such as depression, anxiety, or schizophrenia? The answer, in a nutshell, is that we don't know for sure. But most current explanations, as well as most approaches to therapy, appeal to *biological, cognitive,* or *environmental* factors.

The recognition that psychological disorders are influenced by biological, cognitive, and environmental factors is sometimes called the **bio-psycho-social perspective.** Biological factors (*bio*) include physiological problems with the body, particularly the brain, and genetic influences that are present at birth. Cognitive factors (*psycho*) include our beliefs, styles of thought, and any other psychological mechanisms that potentially influence behavior. Finally, environmental factors (*social*) include what we learn from the environment, cultural influences, and how other people treat us in our daily lives. We'll consider each of these three major factors in greater detail in the following sections.

BIOLOGICAL FACTORS: IS IT IN THE BRAIN OR GENES?

Over the past several decades, there have been significant advances in our understanding of the brain and its functions. Most researchers are now convinced that at least some kinds of abnormal behavior result directly from brain dysfunction. The disordered thoughts of someone with schizophrenia, for example, may be partly due to a broken or at least a malfunctioning brain. What is the evidence? Biological accounts are typically supported by two kinds of findings. First, it's been discovered that abnormal brain chemistry or abnormal brain structures accompany some kinds of mental disorders. Second, through the close study of family histories, it has been determined that a number of psychological disorders may have a powerful genetic component—psychological disorders tend to run in families in ways that cannot be easily explained by environmental histories. We discussed some of these findings in Chapter 3; we'll review and expand on that discussion here.

Neurotransmitter Imbalances

As you may recall from Chapter 3, schizophrenia has been linked to an excess supply of the neurotransmitter *dopamine* (Seeman et al., 1976; Snyder, 1976), or possibly to an interaction between dopamine and the neurotransmitter *serotonin* (Kahn et al., 1993). Support for the link has come primarily from studying how different drugs affect the disorder. Among the most effective treatments for schizophrenia are medications that act as dopamine *antagonists*, which means they reduce or block dopamine use in the brain (Gershon & Reider, 1992). It's also the case that drugs that increase the level of dopamine in the brain can sometimes produce side effects that resemble the symptoms found in schizophrenia (Braff & Huey, 1988; Davidson et al., 1987). Abnormal dopamine levels may not be the only cause of schizophrenia—for example, not all people with schizophrenia are helped by dopamine-reducing medications—but problems in brain neurochemistry are widely believed to be at least partly responsible for the disorder (Csernansky & Bardgett, 1998).

LEARNING GOALS

1. Explain how biological and genetic factors can contribute to psychological disorders.
2. Discuss how maladaptive thoughts can contribute to psychological disorders.
3. Discuss how environmental factors can contribute to psychological disorders.

bio-psycho-social perspective
The idea that psychological disorders are influenced, or caused, by a combination of biological, psychological (cognitive), and social (environmental) factors.

People who suffer from disorders such as schizophrenia may possess malfunctioning brains. These two PET scans, taken from a person diagnosed with schizophrenia (left) and one without the disorder (right), show dramatic differences in brain activity levels. The blue and purple colors in the scans show areas of relatively low brain activity.

Depression: serotonin (decreased level of) is involved in depression.

TCA - inhibits the uptake of norepinephrine & serotonine

MAOI = increase storage of serotonin, dopamine & norepinephrine in nerve terminal

SSRI = inhibit the uptake of serotonin.

Neurotransmitter imbalances may also contribute to mood disorders, such as manic states and depression. Once again, most of the effective medications for these problems act by altering the actions of neurotransmitters in the brain. Fluoxetine (more commonly known by its brand name, *Prozac*) is one of the most commonly prescribed treatments for depression; it acts by slowing the reuptake of *serotonin*, thereby prolonging the neurotransmitter's effectiveness. More generally, depression and mania have been linked to a group of neurotransmitters called *monoamines*, which include serotonin, norepineprine, and dopamine. Researchers currently believe that these neurotransmitters are involved in the regulation of mood, although the specifics have yet to be worked out (Okada et al., 1998). It's unlikely that mood disorders are caused by an inadequate supply of any one of these neurotransmitters. Instead, a decrease in one may have multiple effects on the others. A decrease in serotonin, for instance, may permit the levels of other neurotransmitters in the brain to vary more widely; these more complex interactions probably work together in some way to alter mood abnormally (Goodwin & Jamison, 1990).

Structural Problems

In addition to neurochemical problems, such as imbalances in neurotransmitters, there may also be structural problems in the brains of people suffering from serious psychological problems. In the case of schizophrenia, anatomical and brain-imaging studies have revealed that people with schizophrenia tend to have larger *ventricles*, which are the liquid-filled cavities in the brain. (For reasons that are not yet clear, increased ventricle size tends to be more likely in men who suffer from schizophrenia.) Larger ventricles are associated with the loss, or shrinkage, of brain tissue, and this factor may help explain some instances of schizophrenia (Pahl, et al., 1990). There is also evidence that activity in the frontal areas of the brain may be abnormally low in schizophrenia patients (Berman & Weinberger, 1990). Although it's not clear why these activity levels are low, decreased brain activity in certain prefrontal regions may directly or indirectly alter the neural pathways associated with the neurotransmitter dopamine (Davis et al., 1991).

These data are convincing, but it's important to remember that not all people with schizophrenia show these kinds of neurological problems; not all people with schizophrenia have larger ventricles or show lower frontal lobe activity. Moreover, not all people who have been diagnosed with depression respond to drug therapies that alter the levels or actions of monoamines. So we're left with a somewhat cloudy picture. There's little doubt that psychological disorders are sometimes associated with observable abnormalities in brain chemistry or function. But whether these factors are the true *cause* of disorders such as schizophrenia or depression, or simply one cause, or occur somehow as a consequence of having the disorder, is not currently known. For example, larger ventricle size is observed

Some psychological disorders, such as depression, can be effectively treated by administering drugs that correct neurotransmitter imbalances in the brain.

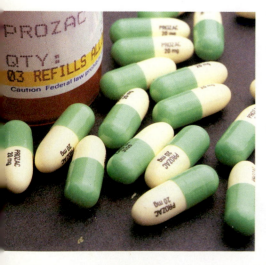

more often in people who have suffered from schizophrenia for a long time, so it's conceivable that the structural abnormality is partly a consequence of the disorder or even of its treatment (DeLisi et al., 1997).

Genetic Contributions

Increasingly, researchers are concluding that people may inherit predispositions toward abnormality. For example, the odds that any particular individual in the population will develop schizophrenia are roughly 1 in 100. But if you have a brother, sister, or parent with the disorder, the odds increase dramatically, perhaps to 1 in 10. If you have an identical twin—someone who has essentially the same genetic information as you do—and your twin has been diagnosed with schizophrenia, the odds that you will develop the disorder during your lifetime jump to about 1 in 2 (Gottesman, 1991) (see Figure 14.8). Notice that the disorder cannot be explained entirely by appealing to genetic factors—otherwise, identical twins would always share the disorder—but these data suggest that genetic background plays a significant role.

As you know from our many discussions of the nature–nurture issue throughout this book, it's not easy to separate inherited characteristics from those acquired through experience. Just because there is a family history of a disorder does not mean the cause is genetic; family members are typically raised in similar environments, so experience could account for the shared psychological problems. In the case of schizophrenia, however, even when children are adopted and raised apart from their biological parents, there still appears to be a familial link. Adopted children who have biological parents with schizophrenia have an increased likelihood of being diagnosed with schizophrenia themselves, even if they've had little or no contact with the parents (Tienari, 1992).

? **CRITICAL THINKING**

Based on our earlier discussion of schizophrenia, why don't all people who are diagnosed with schizophrenia show the same neurological problems?

Type of relationship

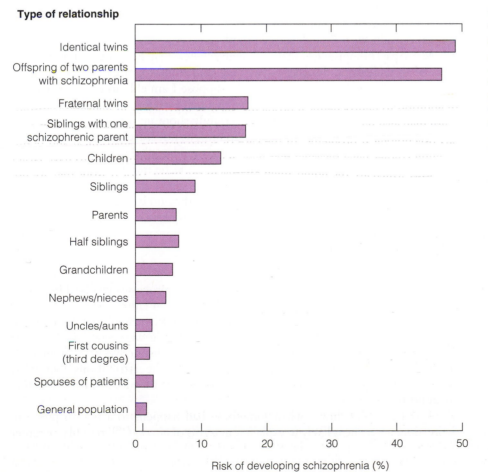

FIGURE 14.8

The Genetics of Schizophrenia
Each bar shows the risk of developing schizophrenia when one or more relatives have been diagnosed with the disorder. For example, if one identical twin has schizophrenia, there is a roughly 50% risk that the other will also develop the disorder. In general, the closer the individual is related genetically to the person with schizophrenia, the more likely he or she is to develop the disorder. (Based on Gottesman, 1991.)

A similar pattern emerges with mood disorders. Depression and bipolar disorder tend to run in families, and the *concordance rate*, which measures the likelihood of sharing a disorder, is quite high between identical twins. A number of studies have shown that if one twin is diagnosed with depression, there is a 50% or greater chance that the other twin will also be diagnosed with depression; the concordance rate may be even higher for bipolar disorders (Gershon, 1990). It is also the case that adoptees with biological parents who suffer from a mood disorder are themselves more likely to suffer from a mood disorder. It is the biological history rather than the environmental history that, on average, predicts the chances of becoming affected by the disorder (Wender et al., 1986).

Genetic factors help predict the likelihood that someone will suffer from certain psychological disorders, but genetic factors are not sufficient to explain abnormal behavior. Once again, having an identical twin with schizophrenia or bipolar disorder does not guarantee that you will have a similar problem. Your genetic code may predispose you to a disorder—it may set the stage—but other environmental factors must be present for the disorder to actually develop (van Os & Marcelis, 1998). Anxiety disorders, for example, may be likely to occur in people who are born with sensitive temperaments, but experience will determine whether a full-blown disorder actually develops. To repeat a common theme, it is the *interaction* between nature and nurture that is important.

COGNITIVE FACTORS: THINKING MALADAPTIVE THOUGHTS

If you look closely into the mind of someone with a psychological disorder, you will often find fixed and disordered styles of thinking. People with anxiety disorders, somatoform disorders, or just about any of the other disorders we've discussed typically believe things about themselves or about the world that have little or no basis in reality. Robert, who is depressed, is convinced that he lacks ability and drive, even though he is a successful banker. Jill, who suffers from agoraphobia, refuses to leave her house because she's convinced that something terrible will happen outside, even though she can think of no real reason for this belief.

Many psychologists feel that such faulty beliefs may be more than just symptoms of an underlying disorder—they may contribute to, or even cause, the disorder itself. To see how this might work, suppose I am able to convince you, by feeding you false but convincing reports, that evil extraterrestrials have landed in a nearby city. Your anxiety level would certainly shoot up, and there's little question that your behavior would change. You might not leave your house, and you might, in fact, end up spending a lot of your time huddled under a table in your basement. This is abnormal behavior, but it would be rational if the underlying cause of the behavior—the belief that the world may end soon—is true. Many people with psychological disorders act the way they do because they have incorrect beliefs. If you're absolutely convinced that you're no good and can never succeed at anything, it's not surprising that you withdraw from social situations and fail to secure steady employment.

Maladaptive Attributions

Psychologists use the term *attribution* to refer to the processes involved in assigning causality to a behavior (see Chapter 13). When you fail at something, such as a test or a new job, you attribute the failure to a cause, such as your own incompetence or the lousy teacher. It turns out that people who have psychological disorders, particularly depression, have relatively distinctive and predictable attributional or explanatory styles. Unfortunately, the attributions that these people make are often maladaptive, which means that they lead to behaviors that are abnormal or unproductive.

As Figure 14.9 shows, when something bad happens to a person prone to depression, he or she is likely to explain it in terms of *internal* ("I'm to blame rather

CRITICAL THINKING

Try to identify your own attributional style. Do you tend to attribute outcomes to global, stable, and internal causes?

FIGURE 14.9
Maladaptive Thoughts in Depression
Depressed individuals tend to attribute failure to internal, stable, and global conditions.

than the situation"), *stable* (long-lasting), and *global* (widespread) attributions (Abramson et al., 1989; Foersterling et al., 1998). Let's suppose you fail a test at school. If you're depressed, you will probably attribute that failure to some personal inadequacy (internal) that is likely to be long-lasting (stable) and that will apply in lots of situations other than school (global). People who are not prone to depression tend to have more flexible explanatory styles. They might attribute the failure to some *external* source ("I've got a rotten teacher") and consider the failure to be *unstable* ("I had a bad day"), and they will probably make a *specific* rather than global attribution. Nondepressed people have less of a tendency to overgeneralize from a situation at school to other areas of life.

Learned Helplessness

What produces these different explanatory styles? It's difficult to know whether people who make maladaptive attributions do so because they are depressed, or whether it is the unfortunate explanatory style that creates the depression. Some researchers have argued that prolonged experience with failure may be one contributing factor. According to the **learned helplessness** theory of depression (Seligman, 1975), if you repeatedly fail while attempting to control your environment, you acquire a general sense of helplessness. You give up and become passive, which, the theory proposes, leads to depression. Still, it's unlikely that we can account for all forms of depression by appealing simply to repeated failure. Experience with failure may be a necessary condition for acquiring depression, but it is not a sufficient condition. Many people fail repeatedly yet show no tendencies toward depression.

Moreover, it isn't really the failure that leads to depression but rather your attributions about the failure. Instead of learning to be helpless, it is really the sense of *hopelessness*—the belief that things cannot become better because of internal, stable, and global factors—that is more likely to produce depression (Alloy & Clements, 1998). Whether this sense of hopelessness can be explained by appealing to experience alone or to some interaction between experience and biological/genetic predispositions remains to be seen.

ENVIRONMENTAL FACTORS: DO PEOPLE LEARN TO ACT ABNORMALLY?

All theories of psychological disorders ultimately appeal either directly or indirectly to environmental factors. Even if a researcher believes that a disorder such as schizophrenia is primarily caused by a genetically induced broken brain, it is still

learned helplessness
A general sense of helplessness that is acquired when people repeatedly fail in their attempts to control their environment; learned helplessness may play a role in depression.

Prolonged exposure to stressful situations may play a role in the onset of psychological disorders.

necessary to explain why identical twins don't always share the disorder. Experience clearly plays a pivotal role. Similarly, the irrational beliefs and explanatory styles that characterize depression must be learned somewhere, although two people with the same experiences may not always end up with the same set of beliefs. Once again, experience is the bedrock on which the psychological interpretation is built.

Culture's Role

Cultural factors also play an obvious and important role. Although the symptoms of most serious psychological disorders—such as schizophrenia and depression—are generally similar across the world (Draguns, 1997), there are culture-based differences. For example, the types of delusions found in schizophrenia depend to a certain extent on cultural background (Tateyama et al., 1998). Different cultural groups may also be more or less likely to show symptoms of disorders because of cultural "rules" for expressing emotion and action (Manson, 1995). If you live in a culture, for instance, that discourages the expression of emotion then depression will be somewhat harder to detect and treat.

Your cultural background may also determine the likelihood that you will be exposed to environmental events that could trigger the onset of psychological disorders. Obviously, if you live somewhere in the world where war or extreme poverty is a way of life, you are likely to encounter more stressful events which, in combination with a genetic predisposition, could lead to psychological problems. Cultural goals or ideals can also influence your psychological health. For example, living in a society that places enormous emphasis on weight ideals can increase the chances that you'll suffer from an eating disorder such as bulimia or anorexia nervosa (see Chapter 11). (You'll learn more about how cultural ideals and stressors in everyday life can affect your physical and psychological health in Chapter 16.)

Conditioning Disorders

A number of mental health professionals feel that at least some psychological disorders may be essentially *learned*. People can learn to act and think abnormally in perhaps the same way they might learn how to bake a cake, make friends, or avoid talking in class. Experts with this view of abnormality propose that learning principles of the type we discussed in Chapter 7 help explain why psychological disorders develop and how they can be best treated. A specific phobia, for example,

CONCEPT SUMMARY
Causes of Psychological Disorders

Factor	Description	Example
Biological	Physiological problems, particularly in the brain. Could include neurotransmitter imbalances, structural problems, and genetic influences.	Danae feels extremely depressed. She goes to a psychologist who asks her whether anyone else in her family has suffered from depression. Danae reports that her mother and grandmother did have bouts of severe depression.
Cognitive	Our beliefs and styles of thought, such as maladaptive attributions and a sense of hopelessness.	Danae is struggling with her studies. She receives a D on a big exam. She is disgusted with herself, and keeps thinking "How could I be so stupid? I am such a loser!"
Environmental	The influence of experience and culture. Cultural background, events, and learning all have an impact on psychological disorders.	Danae's family has always struggled financially, and now her parents are going through a nasty divorce. Danae acts disruptively because it's one of the few ways she can get any attention from them.

could be acquired through *classical conditioning;* you might learn to associate a particular stimulus or event with another event that makes you afraid. Alternatively, you might learn to act abnormally, through *instrumental conditioning,* because you've been reinforced for those actions. Acting in a strange way thus becomes more likely than it was before.

Learning theorists believe that *modeling,* or observational learning, might play a particularly important role in the development of some psychological disorders. As we discussed in Chapter 7, there are reasons to believe that specific phobias are sometimes acquired through modeling. Some of the best evidence has come from animal studies, in which it is possible to control how the fear reaction is initially acquired. Rhesus monkeys who are raised in the wild show an extremely strong fear response to snakes; monkeys who have been reared in the laboratory will show a similar reaction, but only if they've witnessed other monkeys reacting fearfully when snakes are introduced into the cage. This research has made it clear that it is not necessary for the animal to directly experience something negative, such as getting attacked and bitten by the snake; the animal can acquire its fear simply by watching other monkeys act afraid (Cook & Mineka, 1989). Modeling in this case makes adaptive sense because appropriate actions can be learned without directly experiencing negative consequences.

The monkey data are important because they show how modeling can lead to the acquisition of a strong fear response. Obviously, for monkeys in the wild it's quite adaptive to be afraid of snakes. For humans, we know that modeling is also a powerful way to learn, but the evidence that modeling underlies specific phobias—which, after all, are essentially irrational fears—is still largely indirect at this point. We know that many people with specific phobias cannot remember having a traumatic experience with the object of their fear (Rachman, 1990). It's also the case that specific phobias tend to run in families—if your father was afraid of heights, for instance, there's an increased chance that you too will be afraid of heights (Fyer et al., 1990). This kind of evidence is consistent with a modeling account of specific phobias but it does not preclude alternative accounts. From our adaptive perspective, it's interesting to note that modeling, which is essentially an adaptive process, might under certain conditions lead people to acquire behaviors that are not very adaptive.

As with the biological, genetic, and cognitive factors we've considered, it's unlikely that learning principles alone will be able to account for why people develop psychological disorders. People probably can't learn to be schizophrenic, for example, although stressful events in the environment may play an important role in this disorder. Even with phobias, which may be largely learning-based, it is probably necessary to be predisposed to anxiety for a full-blown phobia to develop (Barlow, 1988). Experience plays a significant role in the development of most psychological disorders, but it does not act alone. Behavior, both normal and abnormal, is virtually always produced by multiple causes.

Some psychologists believe that children can acquire phobias by modeling the fears of significant role models. If someone has a father who is afraid of heights, for example, there is an increased chance that the child, too, will be afraid of heights.

 CRITICAL THINKING

Do you suffer from any kind of specific phobia? Can you trace the fear to any particular experience in your life? Does anyone else in your family share the same fear?

TEST YOURSELF 14.3

Check your knowledge about how psychologists have attempted to understand psychological disorders by answering the following questions. (You will find the answers in the Appendix.)

1. Which of the following biological conditions is most likely to be a contributing factor in schizophrenia?

   a. slowed reuptake of the neurotransmitter serotonin

   b. excessive amounts of the neurotransmitter dopamine

   c. smaller than normal ventricles in the brain

   d. increased random activity in the frontal lobes

2. Studies examining the genetics of schizophrenia have discovered that:

   a. schizophrenia is a learned rather than an inherited disorder.
   b. living with two parents with schizophrenia increases your risk of developing schizophrenia by about 65%.
   c. identical twins are more likely to develop schizophrenia than fraternal twins.
   d. if your identical twin has schizophrenia, you have about a 50% chance of developing the disorder yourself.

3. Psychologists studying depression have found that depressed people tend to make the following kinds of personal attributions:

   a. external, stable, and global
   b. internal, unstable, and global
   c. internal, stable, and specific
   d. internal, stable, and global

4. Studies examining how monkeys develop a strong fear response to snakes have been used to support which of the following accounts of specific phobias?

   a. instrumental conditioning
   b. observational learning
   c. learned helplessness
   d. classical conditioning

Solving the Problems

In this chapter we've considered what happens when a person's thoughts and actions become disordered. Most mental health professionals believe it's possible and useful to distinguish between normal and abnormal behavior. In addition, as you've seen, a relatively precise and rigorous classification system exists for the diagnosis and labeling of psychological disorders when they occur. But what are the implications for our general theme of the adaptive mind? It hardly seems adaptive to suffer from a psychological disorder—in fact, lack of adaptiveness is often used as a criterion for the labeling of a behavior as abnormal.

It's important to keep in mind that abnormal behaviors are often simply extreme versions of behaviors that otherwise have adaptive qualities. Anxiety, for instance, is an adaptive body response that prepares us for action and helps keep us vigilant about our surroundings. It becomes a problem only in its extreme form, when it is prolonged and chronic enough to impair normal functioning. Sigmund Freud believed that certain kinds of psychologically based amnesias are adaptive because they prevent traumatic memories from intruding into conscious awareness. Thus, to paraphrase William Shakespeare, there may indeed be a bit of method in madness. On the other hand, it's also reasonable to propose that psychological disorders may represent a kind of breakdown in the system. In particular, schizophrenia may arise from faulty brain functioning—the system ceases to be adaptive because it no longer has the capacity to function properly.

Conceptualizing Abnormality. Conceptualizing *abnormal* behavior turns out to be a rather difficult thing to do. A number of criteria have been proposed, including the notions of statistical and cultural deviance. By the term *deviance*, psychologists typically mean behavior that is essentially unusual in some way, either with respect to its statistical likelihood or with respect to the accepted norms of the culture. Abnormality can also be defined in terms of emotional distress or dysfunction. None of these criteria alone is sufficient to capture the concept. Instead, the concept of abnormality is usually defined by some combination of these factors.

Currently, many mental health professionals conceive of abnormal behavior from a medical model. According to this view, psychological disorders are best described as "illnesses" that can be "cured" through appropriate treatment. There are advantages and disadvantages to this approach, and it should not be taken too literally. Physical illnesses often have clearly identifiable causes, but this is seldom true for psychological disorders. Also of concern are the effects of diagnostic labeling of disorders: Diagnostic labels can sometimes become self-fulfilling prophecies, which can make it harder for a suffering person to recover.

Classifying Psychological Disorders. Once we recognize that a behavior is abnormal, is there a reliable way to classify the underlying problem? Most mental health professionals rely on the DSM-IV, which lists objective criteria for the diagnosis of psychological disorders. The DSM-IV is composed of five major rating dimensions, or axes, which are used to record the presence of clinical or personality disorders, existing medical conditions, environmental problems, and the ability of the individual to function globally. In this chapter we focused our attention primarily on Axis I, which lists the major clinical syndromes.

Anxiety disorders are diagnosed when a person's apprehension and worry become so extreme that behavior is impaired. Generalized anxiety disorder is characterized by chronic worrying that cannot be attributed to any obvious source. Obsessive–compulsive disorders are characterized by the presence of persistent, uncontrollable thoughts, called *obsessions,* or by compelling needs to perform actions repetitively, called *compulsions.* Specific phobias are highly focused fears of specific objects or events.

In somatoform disorders, the focus of an individual's disorder revolves around the body: The person might have a persistent preoccupation with the possibility that he or she has a serious disease (hypochondriasis), or the individual might appear to suffer from an actual physical problem that has no identifiable physical cause (conversion disorder).

In dissociative disorders, the person appears to separate, or dissociate, previous thoughts and memories from current conscious awareness. These disorders include dissociative amnesia, dissociative fugue states, and the more controversial dissociative identity disorder, in which the person appears to have two or more distinct personalities.

Mood disorders typically come in two forms: depressive disorder, in which the affected individual is mired in depression, and bipolar disorder, in which the individual alternates between the highs of mania and the lows of depression. The final clinical syndrome we discussed, schizophrenia, is characterized by distorted thoughts and perceptions. The positive symptoms of schizophrenia include delusions, hallucinations, and disorganized speech and behavior. The negative symptoms include flat affect, which means that the person shows little or no emotional reactions to events. Personality disorders are listed in Axis II because they tend to be more ingrained and inflexible than the major clinical syndromes described on Axis I.

Understanding Psychological Disorders. What are the primary causes of the psychological disorders classified in the DSM-IV? Mental health professionals currently believe that the root cause, or etiology, of most disorders lies in a combination of biological, cognitive, and environmental factors. Some disorders may result from broken or abnormal brains. There is evidence to support the idea that some psychological problems result from neurotransmitter problems in the brain or perhaps from structural problems in brain anatomy. Many psychological disorders also appear to have a genetic basis—individuals may inherit a predisposition for a particular kind of problem.

Psychological disorders are also typically characterized by maladaptive thinking, and it has been suggested that maladaptive beliefs and attributions contribute to the appearance of abnormal behavior. Depressed individuals, for example, tend to attribute negative events to internal, stable, and global causes; these attributions are often associated with a sense of hopelessness, or the faulty belief that things cannot get better. Finally, all theories of psychological disorders rely in one form or another on the environment. For example, your cultural background may play a role in the expression of biological or genetic predispositions and may even determine the kinds of personal attributions that you make. It's possible that some psychological problems may arise almost entirely from environmental influences. It is possible that people learn to act abnormally, either through conditioning or through modeling the behavior of significant people around them.

Psychological Disorders Chapter Summary

Conceptualizing Abnormality: What Is Abnormal Behavior?

The term *abnormal* is often used as roughly equivalent to the term *psychological disorder*. But psychologists have had an ongoing struggle with how to best define the concept of abnormality. No single criterion is sufficient to capture the concept.

CHARACTERISTICS OF ABNORMAL BEHAVIOR

A number of criteria have been proposed to define abnormality. *Statistical deviance* refers to infrequency. *Cultural deviance* compares behavior to existing cultural norms. Behavior is considered abnormal if it violates the accepted standards of society. A third criterion for defining abnormality is *emotional distress*. A final criterion is *dysfunction*, a breakdown in the ability to perform daily tasks. Abnormal and normal are best seen as ends of a continuum, rather than distinct categories.

PROBLEMS ASSOCIATED WITH LABELING

Critics of the medical model are concerned about diagnostic labeling effects: labeling a psychological problem as an illness tends to attach a stigma to the person that is difficult to overcome. This effect was demonstrated in the Rosenhan study, in which researchers got themselves admitted to hospitals with a diagnosis of schizophrenia. They noted that labels become self-fulfilling prophecies, making it difficult to recognize normal behavior when it occurs and increasing the likelihood that someone will act in an abnormal way.

THE MEDICAL MODEL: CONCEPTUALIZING ABNORMALITY AS A DISEASE

According to the *medical model*, abnormal behavior is seen as an underlying disease that can be cured. This conception of abnormality has been quite influential; drugs are effective in treating a variety of disorders, and most disorders can be classified in terms of symptoms. However, some feel that it's inappropriate to draw direct comparisons between physical and psychological illness.

Classifying Psychological Disorders: The DSM-IV

Even if we successfully define abnormality, we still need a means for naming and classifying the underlying disorders that lead to abnormal behavior. The purpose of the *DSM-IV* is to provide clinicians with a well-defined classification system for psychological disorders.

ANXIETY DISORDERS: FEAR AND APPREHENSION

Anxiety disorders are diagnosed when levels of worry and apprehension become so extreme that behavior is impaired in some way. *Generalized anxiety disorder* is characterized by excessive and chronic worrying. *Panic disorder* is characterized by sudden "attacks" of extremely intense fear or dread, and is sometimes associated with the complication *agoraphobia* (a fear of being in public places). In *obsessive-compulsive disorder*, anxiety manifests itself through persistent uncontrollable thoughts (*obsessions*) or by the compelling need to perform one or more actions repeatedly (*compulsions*). The defining feature of *specific phobic disorder* is a highly focused fear of a specific object or situation.

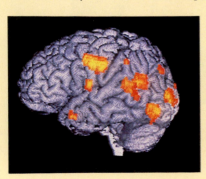

DISSOCIATIVE DISORDERS: DISRUPTIONS OF IDENTITY OR AWARENESS

Dissociative disorders are defined by the dissociation of conscious awareness from previous thoughts or memories. In *dissociative amnesia*, a person is unable to remember certain events after suffering traumatic stress. *Dissociative fugue* involves a loss of personal identity, accompanied by flight from the home environment. In *dissociative identity disorder*, a person alternates among distinct identities or personality states. Controversy surrounds the diagnosis of dissociative identity disorder for a number of reasons.

SOMATOFORM DISORDERS: BODY AND MIND

Somatoform disorders are psychological problems that focus on the physical body. *Hypochondriasis* involves a preoccupation with the idea that one has developed a serious disease based on a misinterpretation of normal bodily reactions. A related problem, *somatization disorder*, involves a focus on physical symptoms rather than underlying disease. In *conversion disorder*, real physical impairment exists in the absence of an apparent physical cause.

SCHIZOPHRENIA: WHEN THOUGHT PROCESSES GO AWRY

People with schizophrenia live in an internal world marked by delusions, hallucinations, and generally disordered thinking. Schizophrenia can be expressed in a variety of complex ways. Two major types of symptoms in schizophrenia are *positive symptoms* and *negative symptoms*. Positive symptoms are observable expressions of abnormal behavior, such as *delusions* (thoughts with inappropriate content), *hallucinations* (perceptions that have no basis in external stimulation), *disorganized speech*, and *catatonia*. Negative symptoms involve the reduction of normal behavior, as in *flat affect*.

DISORDERS OF MOOD: DEPRESSION AND MANIA

Mood disorders (prolonged and disabling disruptions in emotional state) come in two varieties: *depressive disorders* and *bipolar disorders*. A *major depressive episode* is characterized by a number of symptoms, including loss of interest in daily activities, daily fatigue or loss of energy, trouble concentrating, and suicidal thoughts. In *dysthymic disorder*, depression tends to be milder but more chronic. In a *bipolar disorder*, one alternates between depression and mania, a hyperactive, euphoric condition. *Suicide* is one fatal consequence that can result from a mood disorder. Risk factors for suicide include substance abuse, the sudden occurrence of a very stressful event, and the occurrence of other suicides.

PERSONALITY DISORDERS

Personality disorders are chronic or enduring patterns of behavior that lead to significant impairments in social functioning. They include *paranoid personality disorder* (an exaggerated distrust of others), *dependent personality disorder* (an excessive need to be taken care of by others), and *antisocial personality disorder* (an absence of respect for social customs or norms). Some believe that those with personality disorders are simply extreme or deviant on one or more of the "Big Five" personality dimensions.

Understanding Psychological Disorders: Biological, Cognitive, or Environmental

What are the causes of psychological disorders? The answer to many psychological problems lies in an interaction between biological, cognitive, and environmental factors. This view is sometimes called the *bio-psycho-social perspective*.

BIOLOGICAL FACTORS: IS IT IN THE BRAIN OR IN THE GENES?

Abnormal brain chemistry accompanies some psychological disorders. Schizophrenia has been linked to an excess supply of dopamine, or to an interaction between dopamine and serotonin. Neurotransmitter imbalances may also contribute to mood disorders. Structural problems in the brain are also sometimes associated with some psychological disorders. Also, research indicates that genetic factors probably play a role in psychological disorders. People may inherit predispositions toward certain disorders. The *concordance rate* (likelihood of sharing a disorder) is quite high between identical twins.

ENVIRONMENTAL FACTORS: DO PEOPLE LEARN TO ACT ABNORMALLY?

Experience plays a pivotal role in psychological disorders. Culture, for example, can affect how disorders are expressed, and/or the likelihood that you will be exposed to events that could trigger the onset of psychological disorders. Some professionals feel that disorders can be learned through classical or instrumental conditioning, or through modeling.

COGNITIVE FACTORS: THINKING MALADAPTIVE THOUGHTS

People with psychological disorders, particularly depression, have distinctive and predictable attributional or explanatory styles. When something bad happens to someone prone to depression, he/she is likely to make internal, stable, and global attributions. According to the learned helplessness theory of depression, people who repeatedly fail to control their environment give up, leading to depression.

Terms to Remember

Recommended Readings

Barlow, D. H., & Durand, V. M. (1999). *Abnormal psychology* (2nd ed.). Pacific Grove, CA: Brooks/Cole. A leading undergraduate textbook on abnormal psychology. Everything in Chapter 14 is covered here in much more detail.

Andreasen, N. C. (1994). *Schizophrenia: From mind to molecule*. Washington, DC: American Psychiatric Press. Excellent review of schizophrenia written by a leading researcher.

Jamison, K. R. (1995). *An unquiet mind*. New York: Vintage Books. A moving personal account of mania and depression; this book is unique, in part, because it's written by a top depression researcher.

INFOTRAC® COLLEGE EDITION

For additional readings, explore Infotrac College Edition, your online library. Go to:
http://www.infotrac-college.com/wadsworth

Hint: enter the search terms: Diagnosis of mental illness, Anxiety disorder, Dissociative identity disorder, Bipolar disorder, Schizophrenia, Causes of mental illness.

🌐 What's on the Web?

The Phobia List

(www.sonic.net/~fredd/phobia1.htm)

Who thinks these things up? According to the author of this site "all of the phobia names on this list have been found in some reference book." So find out for yourself what you would call a fear of being forgotten (athazagoraphobia). You probably didn't know that there was such a thing as a fear of gravity (barophobia). Hundreds of phobias are listed at this site.

Dr. Ivan's Depression Central

(www.psycom.net/depression.central.htm)

This site, according to its author (Dr. Ivan) ". . . is Internet's central clearing house for information on all types of depressive disorders and on the most effective treatments" for individuals suffering from various mood disorders. Topics you can find at this site include "famous people with mood disorders," seasonal affective disorder, and post-partum depression.

Internet Mental Health

(www.mentalhealth.com/t20a.html)

This is one page at the vast Internet Mental Health Web site. This link includes an alphabetical list of links for dozens of psychological disorders. Click on each link, and you'll be able to read detailed information about the disorder. The site even has a tool for diagnosis of disorders (although it goes without saying that you should view such a tool with more than a little caution!).

The Wadsworth Psychology Study Center Web Site

See http://psychology.wadsworth.com/ for practice quiz questions, hypercontents, updates, critical thinking exercises, discussion forums and more! The Wadsworth Psychology Study Center provides a wealth of information fully organized and integrated by chapter.

Therapy

We are all born mad.

Some remain so.

SAMUEL BECKETT

f you're hearing voices in your head, and you're convinced that the alien takeover is on schedule for next Tuesday, it's likely that you're having trouble leading a normal life. You probably can't hold a job, or make lasting friends, and you may even be incapable of carrying on a coherent conversation. Clearly, you need some kind of treatment—**psychotherapy**—to deal with your mental, emotional, and behavioral problems. But as you'll discover in this chapter, even those with less severe disturbances can benefit from the right kind of therapy. Suppose Ralph, for example, turns down the job of national sales manager because he is afraid of flying; what if Julie spends most of her time alone in her apartment because she's convinced she'll embarrass herself in social settings? Treatment options are available to tackle these kinds of problems in living as well—psychotherapy isn't just for the severely disturbed.

Mental health professionals have a variety of tools at their disposal to help people regain their ability to function well in their surroundings. The particular tool used by the therapist depends on a number of factors, including the specific type of psychological disorder being treated and the personality of the person seeking treatment. There are also a variety of ways that a treatment can be administered. Some people respond well to one-on-one encounters with a therapist; others thrive best in group settings. As we discussed in Chapter 1, good therapists are often *eclectic*, meaning they tailor the treatment to meet the needs of the particular client. This commitment to eclecticism doesn't mean that therapists must abandon all theoretical orientations (Lazarus & Messer, 1991), but it does require flexibility. Good therapists recognize that a method that proves effective for one person can be ineffective for another.

psychotherapy
Treatment designed to help people deal with mental, emotional, or behavioral problems.

Previewing the Conceptual and Practical Problems

s you saw in Chapter 14, when psychologists study the cause of a psychological disorder, they usually look for contributions from biological, cognitive, or environmental factors. Abnormal behavior can be caused by physical problems in the brain, irrational beliefs or poor explanatory styles, environmental experiences, or some combination of these factors. As a result, most kinds of psychotherapy are specifically designed to treat either the body, the mind, or the environment (see Figure 15.1). In this chapter, we'll consider the conceptual and practical problems associated with the practice and evaluation of psychotherapy.

First, what are the most effective ways to treat biologically based problems? As you know, abnormal functioning in the brain is thought to contribute to a number of psychological disorders. Schizophrenia, for example, might be traceable in part to imbalances in neurotransmitters; depression and mania have also been linked to the activities of neurotransmitters. To address these kinds of problems, it makes sense to consider treating the body itself through *biomedical therapies.* One option might be to administer a drug that restores the proper balance of neurotransmitters in the brain; other options might include surgery to fix the damage that exists in a particular region of the brain, or even the use of electric shock treatment.

Second, how can irrational beliefs and faulty attributions be changed? As you know, psychological disorders are often associated with abnormal thoughts and beliefs. Many psychologists are convinced that the key to improvement lies in insight—you must gain awareness of your own thought processes. When you think of psychotherapy, do you imagine someone lying on a couch talking about dreams and early childhood experiences? Although this stereotypical image is accurate in some respects, you'll see in our discussion of *insight therapies* that many therapists have abandoned the couch, as well as the empha-

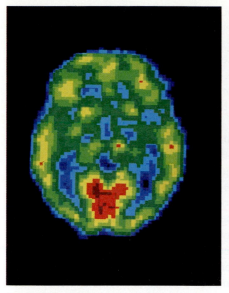

Treating the body

Treating the mind

Treating the environment

FIGURE 15.1
Previewing the Problems
Psychologists face three main conceptual and practical problems as they seek to administer and evaluate therapy.

sis on dreams and early experiences. What remains is the idea that the exploration of one's thought processes can be an effective tool for solving psychological problems.

Third, how can the environment be altered to reduce or eliminate abnormal behaviors? In Chapter 14 we discussed the idea that certain kinds of psychological disorders can be learned. People might learn to think and act in abnormal ways in much the same way that they acquire other thoughts and actions—through the experiences of instrumental conditioning, classical conditioning, or by modeling the actions of others. The idea behind *behavioral therapies* is to use basic learning principles to change unadaptive behavior patterns into adaptive behavior patterns. For example, if experience has taught you to associate high places with disabling fear, it might be possible to alter the association either through extinction or by counterconditioning relaxation to replace the fear.

Fourth, how can we evaluate the effectiveness of psychotherapy? Do all forms of therapy work, or are some more effective than others? Therapy can be a costly and time-consuming process, so it's important to evaluate the advantages and disadvantages of the intervention. A number of studies have been conducted comparing people who have undergone therapy with those left untreated. Although the balance of the studies clearly demonstrate the effectiveness of psychotherapy, some of the findings may surprise you. We'll also consider the factors that should be taken into account when choosing a therapist.

Treating the Body: Biomedical Therapies

People have shown the symptoms of psychological disorders since the beginning of recorded history. And for just as long, people have speculated about what causes abnormal behavior and have offered remedies for its treatment. At one time it was popular to appeal to supernatural forces: People who exhibited bizarre or deviant behavior were believed to be possessed by evil spirits or demons. The cure, if we can call it that, was to torture the sufferer in an effort to drive out the evil inhabitants.

But not all serious thinkers adopted such views. In fact, over 2000 years ago, Hippocrates (469–377 B.C.) and his followers suggested that

LEARNING GOALS

1. Discuss how drug therapies can be used to treat psychological disorders.

2. Discuss and evaluate electroconvulsive shock therapy.

3. Discuss how psychosurgery can be used to treat psychological disorders.

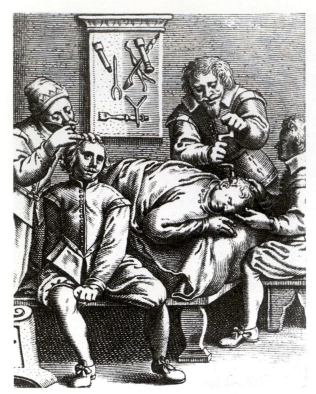

This engraving from 1598 demonstrates an early form of "therapy" for psychological disorders—drilling holes in the head to promote the release of evil spirits.

psychological disorders should be treated as manifestations of the body. Hippocrates believed that people get depressed or exhibit manic states for much the same reason we fall victim to the common cold—the body and brain, and hence the mind, are affected by some kind of "disease." Hippocrates even went so far as to recommend changes in diet and exercise as a way of treating depression, a course of action that many modern therapists consider appropriate today.

The medical approach to understanding disorders was placed on firmer scientific ground in the nineteenth and early twentieth centuries as scientists began to establish links between known physical problems and the symptoms of psychological disorders. For example, by the end of the nineteenth century it was recognized that the venereal disease *syphilis* is responsible not only for a steady deterioration in physical health (and eventually death) but also for the appearance of paranoia and hallucinations. Establishing a link between syphilis and mental problems was an important step in the eventual development of biologically based therapies. Later "cures" for the disease were created by injecting sufferers with the blood of malaria patients in an effort to induce a high fever that would "burn out" the syphilis bacteria; today, of course, doctors use antibiotics to treat syphilis.

In this section of the chapter we'll consider several modern biological approaches to the treatment of psychological disorders. **Biomedical therapies** use physiological interventions in an effort to reduce or eliminate the symptoms of psychological disorders. By far the most popular approach is treatment with drugs, and we'll consider this approach first, but other biomedical therapies are available, including electroconvulsive therapy and psychosurgery.

DRUG THERAPIES

The psychological community began to recognize the remarkable potential of drug therapy in the early 1950s when two French psychiatrists, Jean Delay and Pierre Deniker, reported success in treating the positive symptoms of schizophrenia with a drug called *chlorpromazine* (often sold under the brand name Thorazine). Patients suffering from severe delusions and hallucinations showed considerable improvement after prolonged use of the drug. Since that time, dozens of other drugs have proven successful in treating a wide variety of psychological disorders. In fact, there are now specific medications available to treat most of the disorders that we considered in Chapter 14—everything from obsessive–compulsive disorder to depression. Unfortunately, these drugs do not work for all people affected with mental problems and, as you'll see, some drugs have disturbing side effects. But they have helped thousands of people, and in many ways they have revolutionized the mental health profession.

One very positive benefit of medications such as chlorpromazine has been a sharp reduction in the number of patients who require extended stays in mental hospitals or institutions. Prior to the 1950s, hundreds of thousands of people were institutionalized, often for many years, because their symptoms were simply too severe to allow them to cope successfully in everyday settings. Partly through the administration of drugs, it is now possible to control the severity of these symptoms, allowing individuals to be treated outside of a hospital or institution. The results have been dramatic: By 1983, the number of people institutionalized for psychological problems had dropped to less than 150,000 from over 600,000 in the 1950s (Kiesler & Sibulkin, 1987). (Effective medications are not the only reason for the decline in hospitalized patients; other factors include improvements in

biomedical therapies
Biologically based treatments for reducing or eliminating the symptoms of psychological disorders; they include drug therapies, shock treatments, and, in some cases, psychosurgery.

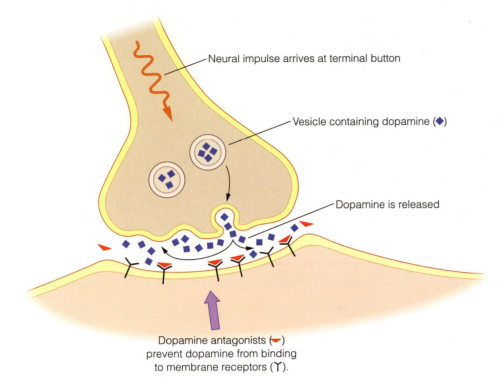

Neural impulse arrives at terminal button

Vesicle containing dopamine (◆)

Dopamine is released

Dopamine antagonists (▼)
prevent dopamine from binding
to membrane receptors (Y).

FIGURE 15.2
Dopamine Antagonists
Some antipsychotic medications act as antagonists, which means they block or slow down the action of neurotransmitters in the brain. Here, a dopamine antagonist is binding with the receptor membrane, blocking the neurotransmitter.

alternative forms of therapy [including behavioral and cognitive], cutbacks in the levels of funding needed to maintain high levels of care, and stricter laws governing commitment [Appelbaum, 1997; Legemaate, 1998].)

Antipsychotic Drugs

Medications that treat the positive symptoms of schizophrenia—delusions, hallucinations, disorganized speech—are commonly called **antipsychotic drugs.** Chlorpromazine is an example of such a drug, but a number of others are also available. The majority of these antipsychotic drugs are believed to act on the neurotransmitter *dopamine* in the brain. As we discussed in Chapter 14, many researchers believe that schizophrenia is caused by excess supplies of dopamine. Chlorpromazine acts as a dopamine *antagonist*, meaning that it blocks or slows down the use of dopamine in the brain (Gershon & Reider, 1992) (see Figure 15.2). The fact that dopamine antagonists work so well in treating positive symptoms is strong support for the dopamine hypothesis of schizophrenia (Barlow & Durand, 1999).

But dopamine antagonists do not work for all sufferers of schizophrenia. Moreover, these drugs tend to work almost exclusively on positive symptoms. The negative symptoms of schizophrenia, such as the sharp decline in the normal expression of emotions, are not affected very much by the administration of antipsychotic medications. Antipsychotic drugs can also produce unwanted and persistent side effects in some patients, including drowsiness, difficulties in concentrating, blurry vision, and movement disorders (Windgassen, 1992). One particularly serious side effect is a condition called *tardive dyskinesia*, which produces disabling involuntary movements of the tongue, jaw, mouth, and face (Kane et al., 1986). These side effects can be permanent and they act as a two-edged sword: Not only are they extremely uncomfortable for the patient, but they also increase the chances that the patient will stop taking the medication (Tugrul, 1998). Without the medication, of course, it's likely that the positive symptoms of the disorder will reemerge.

Recently, a new medication, called *clozapine* (brand name Clozaril), has been introduced that seems to work well for patients who do not respond to the more

? CRITICAL THINKING

Just because dopamine antagonists reduce the positive symptoms of schizophrenia does not necessarily mean that dopamine causes schizophrenia. Why not?

antipsychotic drugs
Medications that reduce the positive symptoms of schizophrenia; the majority act on the neurotransmitter dopamine.

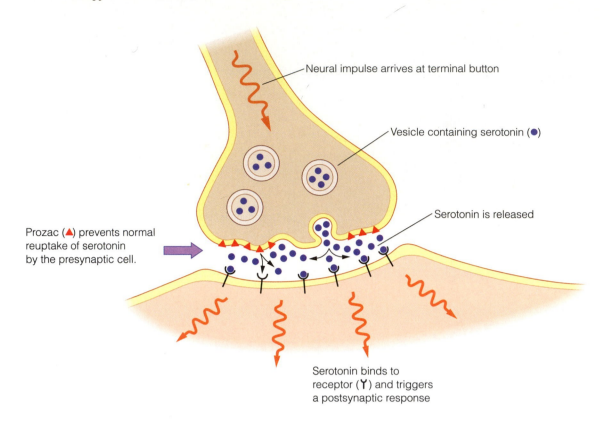

Neural impulse arrives at terminal button

Vesicle containing serotonin (●)

Serotonin is released

Prozac (▲) prevents normal reuptake of serotonin by the presynaptic cell.

Serotonin binds to receptor (Y) and triggers a postsynaptic response

FIGURE 15.3

Reuptake Blockers

Some kinds of antidepressant medications block the reabsorption of neurotransmitters, which then linger longer in the synapse and continue to activate receptor neurons. Prozac is in the class of antidepressants that block the reabsorption of serotonin.

antidepressant drugs

Medications that modulate the availability or effectiveness of the neurotransmitters implicated in mood disorders; Prozac, for example, increases the action of the neurotransmitter serotonin.

traditional dopamine antagonists (Kane & Marder, 1993). Clozapine does not produce movement side effects such as tardive dyskinesia, although medical complications are still a concern (Hector, 1998). From a research standpoint, the effectiveness of clozapine is noteworthy because it apparently does not work by simply regulating the amount of dopamine in the brain. It is currently believed that clozapine may affect a number of neurotransmitters, including both dopamine and serotonin (Potter & Manji, 1993). This suggests that dopamine alone, as we noted in Chapter 14, cannot account entirely for schizophrenic disorders.

Antidepressant Drugs

The 1950s also witnessed the introduction of medications for treating manic states and depression. Mood disorders have been linked to several neurotransmitters, including norepinephrine and serotonin. **Antidepressant drugs,** like the antipsychotic drugs, act by modulating the availability or effectiveness of these kinds of neurotransmitters. The group of antidepressants called *tricyclics*, for example, alter mood by acting primarily on norepinephrine; tricyclics apparently allow norepinephrine to linger in synapses longer than normal, which eventually modulates its effectiveness. The antidepressant fluoxetine—known commercially as Prozac—comes from a different class of antidepressants. Prozac acts primarily on serotonin, again by blocking its "reuptake" into the neuron, thereby allowing it to linger in the synapse (see Figure 15.3).

At present, researchers do not know exactly how or why these medications affect mood, outside of the fact that they alter the effectiveness of neurotransmitters. Fortunately, it's clear that they do work well for many individuals affected with depression. It's been estimated that sustained use of antidepressants successfully controls depression in over 50% of all depressed patients (Depression Guideline Panel, 1993). On the down side, it typically takes several weeks for these medications to begin working (the time periods may differ across the different types of antidepressants), and there are potential side effects that must be monitored. Prozac, for example, can produce agitation or restlessness, difficulty sleeping, and even diminished sexual desire. Early reports suggested that Prozac might

CONCEPT SUMMARY
Drug Therapies

Type of Drug	Used in the Treatment of	Examples and Effects
Antipsychotic	Positive symptoms of schizophrenia, including delusions, hallucinations, and disorganized speech.	*Chlorpromazine,* one example, is a *dopamine antagonist.* That is, it blocks or impedes the flow of dopamine in the brain. Recently, *clozapine* has also proven effective in alleviating some symptoms of schizophrenia.
Antidepressants	Mood disorders	*Tricyclics* alter mood by acting primarily on norepinephrine, allowing it to linger in synapses longer. *Fluoxetine* (e.g., Prozac) works primarily on serotonin, blocking its reuptake into the neuron. *Lithium carbonate* is used to treat bipolar disorder.
Antianxiety	Psychological problems associated with anxiety	Commonly known as *tranquilizers.* Tranquilizers come from a class of chemicals called *benzodiazepines.* They appear to work on the neurotransmitter GABA, which produces primarily inhibitory effects. The result is a lowering of excitation in affected neurons, reducing tension and anxiety.

also induce violent or suicidal tendencies, but these claims have not been substantiated in follow-up research (Fava & Rosenbaum, 1991).

Effective medications are also available for treating bipolar disorders, which are characterized by mood swings between depression and hyperactive manic states. Bipolar disorders are usually treated by administering a common salt called *lithium carbonate.* Lithium is more effective for bipolar disorder than the antidepressants because it works well on the manic state; it puts affected individuals on a more "even keel" and helps to prevent the reoccurrence of future manic episodes. But it too needs to be monitored closely, because lithium use can lead to a variety of medical complications (Moncrieff, 1997).

Antianxiety Drugs

For the treatment of psychological problems associated with anxiety, mental health professionals typically use **antianxiety drugs,** known more generally as *tranquilizers.* Tranquilizers come from a class of chemicals called *benzodiazepines*—Valium and Xanax are popular trade names—and they are quite effective for reducing tension and anxiety. In the mid-1970s it was estimated that 10 to 20% of adults in the Western world were "popping" tranquilizers (Greenblatt & Shader, 1978), which gives you some idea of their widespread use. In recent years tranquilizer use has been on the decline, primarily because mental health professionals recognize a downside to their continued use.

Most benzodiazepines appear to work on a neurotransmitter in the brain called gamma-aminobutyric acid (GABA) which tends to produce primarily inhibitory effects. The effectiveness of GABA increases after taking the drug, which leads to a lowering of excitation in affected neurons (Lickey & Gordon, 1991). Potential side effects include drowsiness, impaired motor coordination, and possible psychological dependence (Rickels et al., 1990). Tranquilizers can act as a kind of psychological crutch after lengthy use, so the majority of clinicians now recommend that they be used primarily as a short-term remedy for anxiety rather than as a long-term cure.

ELECTROCONVULSIVE THERAPY

Sometimes when traditional medications fail, clinicians turn to a different and very controversial form of biomedical therapy: "shock" treatment. At face value, few psychological therapies seem as uncivilized as the idea of strapping someone down on a table and passing 100 or so volts of electricity into his or her brain. As you know, the language of the nervous system is partly electrical in nature. If electric shock is administered to the brain, a brief brain seizure will occur that produces, among other things, convulsions and loss of consciousness. When **electroconvulsive therapy (ECT)** was first introduced in the 1930s, it was a terrifying and hazardous procedure; patients suffered serious side effects that included the

antianxiety drugs
Medications that reduce tension and anxiety. Many work on the inhibitory neurotransmitter GABA.

electroconvulsive therapy (ECT)
A treatment used primarily for depression in which a brief electric current is delivered to the brain.

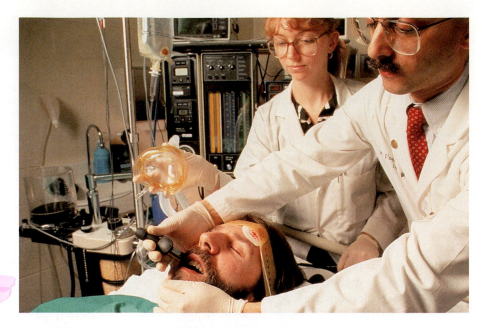

ECT, as currently administered, is a reasonably safe and effective form of treatment for patients suffering from severe depression, but its use is still considered controversial by many mental health professionals.

occasional broken bone from the convulsions. Thankfully, modern applications of ECT are much less physically traumatic; the patient is given a light anesthetic and medications that relax the muscles so that injuries will not occur.

Many mental health professionals believe that ECT, as currently administered, is a reasonably safe and effective form of treatment for patients who are suffering from severe depression. It is used almost exclusively for depression, although some clinicians believe it may benefit other psychological problems as well (Krystal & Coffey, 1997). Generally, most professionals consider it to be a treatment of last resort. It is used in cases in which people have shown little or no response to conventional antidepressant drugs or other "talk" therapies. Controlled research studies have found that ECT is successful some 50 to 70% of the time in lessening the symptoms of depression in patients who have not otherwise responded to treatment (Prudic et al., 1990; Weiner & Coffey, 1988). Typically, these studies involve direct comparisons between depressed patients who receive ECT and patients who undergo the same procedural preparations but don't actually receive the shock.

Controversies

Despite the demonstrated effectiveness of ECT as a treatment for severe depression, there are several reasons why the procedure remains controversial. First, no one is certain exactly why the treatment works. It's possible that shocking the brain affects the release of neurotransmitters or changes some structural feature of the brain (Mann, 1998), but at present there is no definitive answer as to why the procedure changes mood (Kapur & Mann, 1993). Second, ECT produces side effects, particularly confusion and a loss of memory for events surrounding the treatment (Breggin, 1991). These side effects are usually temporary, and they're not serious for most patients, but they remain a concern. Third, some researchers are concerned that ECT might cause permanent brain damage. Effective ECT usually requires repeated administrations of the shock over several weeks, and it's not known what long-term effects these treatments have on the brain.

Is ECT worth the risks? The answer depends mainly on the needs of the particular patient. If you are someone who is deeply depressed and no other treatment options have provided you any relief, ECT might literally be a lifesaver. Many clinicians believe that if it comes down to a desperate choice between ending your life and suffering some confusion and long-lasting memory loss, trying ECT is certainly worth the risk.

PSYCHOSURGERY

We've made the case that a direct connection exists between biological problems in the brain and the occurrence of some psychological disorders. People who are suffering from schizophrenia, for example, sometimes show structural abnormalities in the brain. It makes sense, then, to consider the possibility of direct intervention, through brain surgery, to fix these problems permanently. Certainly if your appendix or your gall bladder were infected and the diseased organ were creating a whole host of physical symptoms, you wouldn't think twice about calling the local surgeon. Wouldn't it be nice if we could adopt a similar approach for psychological problems?

Actually, the use of **psychosurgery**—surgery that destroys or alters tissue in the brain in an effort to affect behavior—has been around for decades. In the 1930s, a surgical procedure called the *prefrontal lobotomy* was pioneered by a Portuguese physician named Egas Moniz (and later in the United States by Walter Freeman and James Watts). The operation involved a crude separation of the frontal lobes from the rest of the brain. The surgery was designed to sever various connections in the brain's circuitry, in the hope that it might produce calming tendencies in disturbed patients. The procedure was widely used for several decades, and, in fact, Moniz was awarded the Nobel Prize for his work in 1949. But prefrontal lobotomies eventually fell into disrepute. Many patients were killed by the procedure, and it produced serious cognitive deficits in many of the patients who underwent the surgery. They lost their ability to plan and coordinate actions, capabilities associated with activity in the frontal lobes.

Psychosurgery is still used as a way of treating problems that have failed to respond to conventional forms of therapy, but its use is exceedingly rare. One modern form of psychosurgery, called a *cingulotomy*, is sometimes used to treat obsessive–compulsive disorder and severe forms of depression (Jenike, 1998; Jenike et al., 1991). It's a surgery that destroys a small portion of tissue in the limbic system of the brain. As with ECT, however, physicians really have no idea why this procedure works, nor can they explain why it works in some patients but not in others. It's another treatment of last resort that has proven effective for some but has not gained wide acceptance among the general psychological community.

psychosurgery
Surgery that destroys or alters tissues in the brain in an effort to affect behavior.

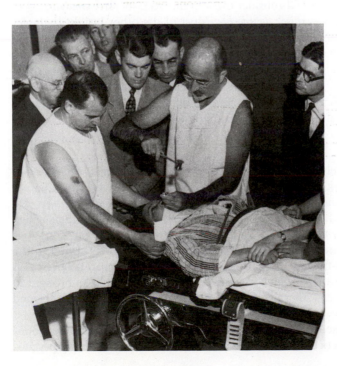

Dr. Walter Freeman is shown here in 1949 performing psychosurgery on a patient suffering from a psychological disorder. He is inserting an instrument under the patient's upper eyelid in order to sever certain neural connections in the brain and thereby relieve symptoms of the disorder. Operations of this type are no longer performed.

TEST YOURSELF 15.1

Check your knowledge about biomedical therapies by answering the following questions. (You will find the answers in the Appendix).

1. Pick the psychological disorder that is best treated by each of the following therapies or medications. Choose your answers from among the following: depression, manic state, generalized anxiety disorder, schizophrenia, hypochondriasis.

   a. Clozapine: _schizophrenia_
   b. Prozac: _depression_
   c. Cingulotomy: _schizophrenia_
   d. ECT: _manic state, dep._
   e. Benzodiazepine: _anxiety_

2. Which of the following statements about ECT (electroconvulsive shock therapy) is false?

   a. ECT is an effective treatment for depression.
   b. Researchers are uncertain why ECT works.
   c. ECT can produce confusion and some memory loss.
   d. ECT is used regularly to treat schizophrenia.

Treating the Mind: Insight Therapies

LEARNING GOALS

1. Describe and evaluate psychoanalysis as a form of insight therapy.
2. Describe and evaluate cognitive therapies.
3. Describe and evaluate humanistic therapies.
4. Discuss group and family therapy.

People who suffer from psychological disorders often carry around faulty or irrational beliefs about the world and about themselves. Many clinicians are convinced that the proper role for the therapist is to confront these irrational thoughts and beliefs directly through what are called insight therapies. **Insight therapies** are designed to give clients self-knowledge, or *insight*, into the contents of their thought processes, usually through extensive one-on-one verbal interactions with the therapist. The hope is that with insight the person will adopt a more realistic, adaptive view of the world, and behavior will change accordingly.

There are many forms of insight therapy available for use by mental health professionals. We'll consider three in this section: *psychoanalysis, cognitive therapies,* and *humanistic approaches.* Most of the other insight therapies are related in one form or another to these three main approaches. The common thread that ties them all together is the belief that cognitive or mental insight can produce significant changes in one's psychological condition. The therapies differ in the kinds of beliefs or memories that are considered of vital importance and in how the client's insight can best be obtained. Finally, we'll end the chapter by briefly discussing the value of group and family therapy.

PSYCHOANALYSIS: RESOLVING UNCONSCIOUS CONFLICTS

insight therapies
Treatments designed to give clients self-knowledge, or insight, into the contents of their thought processes, usually through one-on-one interactions with a therapist.

psychoanalysis
Freud's method of treatment that attempts to bring hidden impulses and memories, which are locked in the unconscious, to the surface of awareness, thereby freeing the patient from disordered thoughts and behaviors.

Probably the most widely known insight therapy is **psychoanalysis,** which comes originally from the work of Sigmund Freud. As you may remember from Chapter 12, Freud placed enormous emphasis on the concept of the *unconscious mind.* He believed that each of us houses a kind of hidden reservoir in our minds that is filled with memories, primitive urges, and conflicts that are well beyond our conscious awareness. We can't directly think about the urges and memories stored in the unconscious mind, but they affect our behavior nonetheless. Freud believed that through psychoanalysis these hidden impulses and memories could be brought to the surface of awareness, thereby freeing us from disordered thoughts and behaviors.

Freud based his theory primarily on case studies of individuals he encountered in his private practice. He routinely treated patients with troubling psychological problems, and he discovered that he could often help these people by getting them to recall and relive traumatic experiences that they had apparently forgotten, or repressed. Freud was particularly interested in the emotionally significant experiences of childhood because he believed that during childhood we progress through a number of psychologically "fragile" stages of psychosexual development (see Chapter 12). Traumatic experiences are, by definition, anxiety-provoking and therefore difficult for the young mind to deal with, so they are buried in the unconscious. Although no longer consciously available, these experiences continue to dominate and color behavior in ways that are completely beyond the person's awareness.

The Tools of Psychoanalysis

The goal of psychoanalysis is to help the patient uncover, and thereby relive, these unconscious conflicts. Obviously, because the patient is unaware of the conflicts, the therapist needs certain tools to gain access to the contents of the unconscious mind. Freud liked to compare psychoanalysis to excavating a buried city, but instead of picks and shovels, his tools were the uncensored expressions and feelings of his patients. Freud relied heavily on a technique called **free association,** in which patients were asked to relax on a couch and freely express whatever thoughts and feelings happened to come into their minds. To the untrained eye, the result was a series of meaningless and unrelated streams of thought, but to Freud, these free associations represented symbolic clues to the contents of the unconscious.

Freud's other important therapeutic tool was patient dreams. Through **dream analysis,** he felt the therapist was handed a royal road to the unconscious. As we discussed in Chapter 6, Freud was convinced that dreams are partly a psychological mechanism for wish fulfillment, a way to satisfy hidden desires that are too anxiety-provoking to be allowed to come to consciousness directly. The storyline of dreams, he believed, is largely symbolic—there is a hidden meaning to dreams, a *latent content*, that reveals the unconscious. Freud therefore encouraged his patients to describe their dreams, so he could acquire further clues in his search for hidden psychological truth.

Resistance and Transference

In classic psychoanalysis, the therapist seeks to understand the contents of the unconscious, but it is really the patient who needs the insight. The therapist can't simply relay the hidden meanings that are uncovered—explanation is not enough. Instead, the patient needs to face the emotional conflicts directly and relive them, and the therapist can only act as a kind of learned guide. But the journey toward insight is not an easy one, and the therapist must usually maneuver around a number of roadblocks. For example, patients typically go through periods in which they are uncooperative. They show **resistance,** which is an unconsciously motivated attempt to subvert or hinder the therapy (Adler & Bachant, 1998).

Why would people try to block their own therapy? Because the hidden conflicts that the therapist is working hard to uncover are anxiety-provoking; as a result, the patient will use defense mechanisms to reduce the anxiety. As Freud (1912/1964) put it, "Resistance accompanies the treatment at every step; every single association, every act of the patient's . . . represents a compromise between the forces aiming at cure and those opposing it" (p. 140). The resistance can express itself in a variety of ways; the patient might become inattentive, claim to forget dreams, skip therapy sessions, or argue with the directions suggested by the therapist.

Overcoming patient resistance is a major challenge for the therapist. Freud believed that a turning point of sorts comes when the patient begins to show a type

free association
A technique used in psychoanalysis to explore the contents of the unconscious; patients are asked to relax and freely express whatever thoughts and feelings happen to come into their minds.

dream analysis
A technique used in psychoanalysis; Freud believed that dreams are symbolic and contain important information about the unconscious.

resistance
In psychoanalysis, a patient's unconsciously motivated attempts to subvert or hinder the process of therapy.

FIGURE 15.4

Resistance and Transference

According to Freud, people in therapy typically go through periods in which they are uncooperative—skipping a session, arriving late, or arguing with the therapist. Freud believed that such actions, which he called *resistance,* were unconsciously motivated attempts to subvert the therapeutic process. Through *transference,* Freud believed people transfer unconscious feelings—such as love or hate—for significant others onto the therapist.

of resistance called transference. **Transference** occurs when the patient starts to express thoughts or feelings toward the therapist that are actually representative of the way the patient feels about other significant people in his or her life. The patient "transfers" feelings of love, hate, or dependence onto a substitute figure, the therapist. Depending on the repressed feelings being tapped, the patient might turn the therapist into an object of passionate love or into a hated and despised individual (see Figure 15.4).

Transference is a significant event in analysis because it means that the patient's hidden memories and conflicts are bubbling up close to the surface of consciousness. The patient is fully aware of the strong feelings he or she is experiencing—although the object of those feelings is inappropriate—and this gives the therapist an opportunity to help the patient work through what those feelings might mean. The patient is no longer in denial of powerful emotional urges—they're right there on the surface, ready to be dealt with. At the same time, it's important for the therapist to recognize that the patient's feelings at this point are symbolic. It's not uncommon for the patient to express feelings of strong sexual desire for the therapist, for example, and it would be inappropriate and unethical for the therapist to take them as literal truth (Tyler & Tyler, 1997).

Current Applications

Classical psychoanalysis, as practiced by Freud and his contemporaries, is a very time-consuming process. It can take years for the analyst to excavate the secrets of

transference

In psychoanalysis, the patient's expression of thoughts or feelings toward the therapist that are actually representative of the way the patient feels about other significant people in his or her life.

the unconscious, and the patient needs to be properly prepared to accept the insights when they are delivered. Remember, the patient is setting up roadblocks throughout the process. So this kind of therapy is certainly far from a quick fix. It's not only time-consuming but also expensive.

For these reasons, modern practitioners of psychoanalysis often streamline the therapeutic process. So-called brief forms of psychoanalysis encourage the therapist to take a more active role in the analytic process (Horvath & Luborsky, 1993). Rather than waiting for patients to find insight themselves in response to subtle nudgings, the analyst is much more willing to offer interpretations in the early stages of therapy. Rather than waiting for transference to occur on its own, the analyst might actually encourage role playing in an attempt to get the patient to deal with deep-seated feelings. So, rather than requiring years of analysis, progress can occur in weeks or months (Book, 1998).

Besides increasing the speed of treatment, modern versions of psychoanalysis are often tailored to meet the needs of the particular patient. No attempt is made to excavate and reconstruct the patient's entire personality; instead, the analyst focuses on selective defense mechanisms or conflicts that are more pertinent to the individual's particular symptoms (Luborsky et al., 1990). There is also often a greater emphasis placed on improving the patient's interpersonal and social skills and less of an emphasis is placed on sexual and aggressive drives. Because these forms of treatment differ from classical psychoanalysis, they usually go by the more general name *psychodynamic therapy*.

COGNITIVE THERAPIES: CHANGING MALADAPTIVE BELIEFS

According to Freud's theory, a person's conscious thoughts, beliefs, and feelings are of primary importance only because they provide clues to the inner workings of the unconscious mind. **Cognitive therapies,** in contrast, place a much greater emphasis on the conscious beliefs themselves, rather than on what those beliefs may mean symbolically. Cognitive therapists assume that irrational beliefs and negative thoughts are primarily responsible for psychological disorders. If you can change the negative thoughts and beliefs, the psychological disorder will be changed as well.

Let's take depression as an example. People who are depressed usually do not think productively. They view themselves as essentially worthless and unlovable, and they see little chance that things will change for the better in the future. Thinking in such a negative way clouds the interpretation of normal events; everyday experiences are passed through a kind of negative filter, which means that depressed people often jump to irrational conclusions. For instance, a depressed woman whose husband arrives home slightly late from work might be immediately convinced that her husband is having an affair. The depressed student who fails the test might see the F as confirmation of a dull and stupid mind.

Cognitive therapists believe that it is not direct experience, such as failure on a test, that actually produces depression. Think about it. It is not particularly difficult to fail a test—just stop going to class or refrain from studying. The F by itself doesn't logically mean much. You can fail a test for many reasons, and most of these reasons have nothing to do with your intrinsic worth as a human being. But in the mind of a depressed person, the event (failing the test) is accompanied by an irrational belief ("I'm incredibly stupid"), and it is this belief that leads to negative emotional consequences (feeling sad and depressed). Thus, it is the *interpretation* of the event, not the event itself, that leads to problems (Beck, 1991; Ellis, 1962, 1993) (see Figure 15.5 on page 594).

Rational-Emotive Therapy

The goal of cognitive therapy, then, is to remove these irrational beliefs. But how can irrational beliefs be changed? One technique is to challenge the beliefs

cognitive therapies
Treatments designed to remove irrational beliefs and negative thoughts that are presumed to be responsible for psychological disorders.

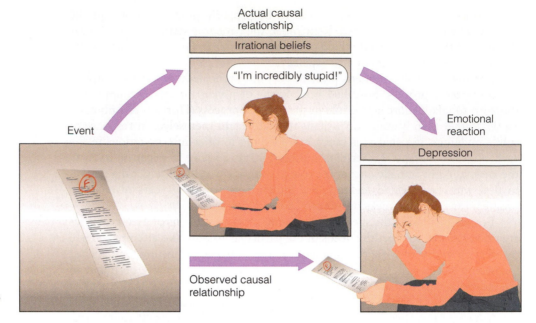

Actual causal relationship

Irrational beliefs

"I'm incredibly stupid!"

Event

Emotional reaction

Depression

Observed causal relationship

FIGURE 15.5

The Cognitive View of Depression
Cognitive therapists believe that it is not direct experience, such as failing a test, that leads to depression. Instead, the depression is caused by one's internal thoughts and beliefs about the event.

rational-emotive therapy
A form of cognitive therapy, developed by Albert Ellis, in which the therapist acts as a kind of cross-examiner, verbally assaulting the client's irrational thought processes.

Albert Ellis developed Rational-Emotive Therapy to help people eliminate their irrational thoughts and beliefs.

directly, through active and aggressive confrontation. In **rational-emotive therapy,** developed by Albert Ellis, the therapist acts as a kind of cross-examiner, verbally assaulting the client's irrational thought processes. Here's an excerpt from an exchange between a therapist practicing rational-emotive therapy and a client showing signs of depressed thinking (from Walen et al., 1992, pp. 204–205):

Therapist: You really believe that you're an utterly worthless person. By definition, that means that you're doing things poorly. Can you prove to me that that's correct?

Client: But I've failed at so many things.

Therapist: Just how many?

Client: I've lost my job, my wife is threatening to leave me, I don't get along with my kids—my whole life's a mess!

Therapist: Well, let me make two points. First of all, that's not every aspect of your life. Second, you seem to take total responsibility for all of those events, rather than only partial responsibility.

Client: But even if I'm not totally responsible, I'm still a failure.

Therapist: No. You've failed at those things. There are other things you haven't failed at.

Client: Like what?

Therapist: You still manage to get up every morning, you keep up appearances, you manage your finances well considering your economic plight—there's lots of things you do well.

Client: But they don't count!

Therapist: They don't count to you right now because you're overly concerned with negative issues, but they certainly *do* count. There are lots of people who don't do those things well. Are *they* failures?

Client: No, but . . .

Therapist: You know, Jack, you're one of the most conceited people I've ever met!

Client: What do you mean? I've just been telling you how lousy I am!

Therapist: The fact that you hold two different standards tells me how conceited you are. You hold much higher standards for yourself than for anyone else, which implies that you think you're much better than others. It's okay for those lowly slobs to have problems, but not a terrific person like you. Isn't that contradictory to your notion that you're worthless?

Client: Hmmmmm.

Therapist: How about instead of rating yourself as worthless, you just accept the failings that you do have and try your best to improve them?

Client: That sounds sensible.

Therapist: Let's take one of those problem areas now and see how we can improve things . . .

The important part of rational-emotive therapy is the therapist's attack on the rationality of the client's beliefs. The therapist points out the irrationality of the client's thought processes, often in a confrontational manner, in the hope that his or her beliefs will ultimately be rejected lessening their emotional consequences. The creator of rational-emotive therapy, Albert Ellis (1962), has identified what he believes to be some of the major types of irrational beliefs that affect people who seek treatment for psychological disorders. The therapist tries initially to pinpoint which of these beliefs characterize a particular client's thought processes, so they can be changed accordingly. Here are a few examples from Ellis's list:

1. I must be loved and approved of by every significant person in my life, and if I'm not, it's awful.
2. It's awful when things are not the way I'd like them to be.
3. I should be very anxious about events that are uncertain or potentially dangerous.
4. I am not worthwhile unless I am thoroughly competent, adequate, and achieving at all times, or at least most of the time in at least one major area.
5. I need someone stronger than myself on whom to depend or rely.

What makes these beliefs irrational is their inflexibility and absoluteness. I *must* be loved and approved; I *must* be thoroughly competent; I *need* someone stronger than myself. The client firmly believes that things must be a particular way or something awful or catastrophic will happen. Ellis has used the term *musterbation* to refer to this kind of irrational thinking. Anytime you find yourself thinking that something *must* be a particular way, you're guilty of musterbation.

CRITICAL THINKING

Where do you think these irrational beliefs come from? Is it possible that people are taught to think in these absolute and inflexible ways by their parents, role models, or by the general culture at large?

Beck's Cognitive Therapy

Although all forms of cognitive therapy focus on changing irrational thought processes, not all treatments are as direct and harsh as rational-emotive therapy. The rational-emotive therapist will essentially lecture—and in some instances even belittle—the client in an effort to attack faulty beliefs. Other cognitive therapies, such as the treatment procedures pioneered by Aaron Beck, take a more subtle tack. Rather than directly confronting clients with their irrational beliefs, Beck suggests it is more therapeutic for clients to identify negative forms of thinking themselves. The therapist acts as an adviser, or co-investigator, helping clients discover their own unique kinds of faulty beliefs.

In a sense, clients who undergo Beck's cognitive therapy are asked to become psychological detectives. Part of the therapy involves extensive record keeping or "homework." Between therapeutic sessions, Beck asks his clients to record their

Situation	Emotion(s)	Automatic thought(s)	Rational response	Outcome
1. Actual event leading to unpleasant emotion, or 2. Stream of thoughts, daydream or recollection, leading to unpleasant emotion.	1. Specify sad/ anxious/ angry, etc. 2. Rate degree of emotion, 1–100.	1. Write automatic thought(s) that preceded emotion(s). 2. Rate belief in automatic thought(s), 0–100%.	1. Write rational response to automatic thought(s). 2. Rate belief in rational response, 0–100%.	1. Rerate belief in automatic thought(s), 0–100%. 2. Specify and rate subsequent emotions, 0–100.
7/15 Audre didn't return my phone call.	Anxious – 75 Sad – 55 Angry – 40	People don't like talking to me – 75% I'm incompetent. 65%	She's out walking the dog so she hasn't had the time to call back. 70%	1. 35% 15% 2. Relieved – 35

Explanation: When you experience an unpleasant emotion, note the situation that seemed to stimulate the emotion. (If the emotion occured while you were thinking, daydreaming, etc., please note this.) Then note the automatic thought associated with the emotion. Record the degree to which you believe this thought: 0% = not at all, 100% = completely. In rating degree of emotion: 1 = a trace, 100 = the most intense possible.

FIGURE 15.6

Homework from a Cognitive Therapist
During cognitive therapy, people are often asked to record their automatic (knee-jerk) thoughts and emotions in a notebook. Notice that the daily log requires the person to construct a rational response to the situation and then rerate the emotional reaction. (Adapted from Beck and Young, 1985.)

humanistic therapy
Treatments designed to help clients gain insight into their fundamental self-worth and value as human beings; therapy is a process of discovering one's own unique potential.

client-centered therapy
A form of humanistic therapy, developed by Carl Rogers, proposing that it is the client, not the therapist, who holds the key to psychological health and happiness; the therapist's role is to provide genuineness, unconditional positive regard, and empathy.

automatic (or knee-jerk) thoughts and emotions in a notebook as they experience various situations during the day. Clients are then asked to write rational responses to those thoughts and emotions, as if they were scientists evaluating data. Is the thought justified by the actual event? What's the evidence for and against the conclusions that I reached? The therapist hopes clients will eventually discover the contradictions and irrationality in their thinking and realign their beliefs accordingly (see Figure 15.6).

HUMANISTIC THERAPIES: TREATING THE HUMAN SPIRIT

In cognitive therapy, the goal is for clients to gain understanding or insight into their faulty and irrational ways of thinking. In classical psychoanalysis, the focus of the insight is on the patient's hidden conflicts and desires. In the final type of insight-based treatment that we'll consider—**humanistic therapy**—the purpose of therapy is to help the client gain insight into his or her own fundamental *self-worth* and *value* as a human. Therapy is a process of discovering one's own unique potential, one's ingrained capacity to grow and better oneself as a human being.

Humanistic therapists believe that all people are capable of controlling their own behavior—we can "fix" our own problems—because each of us ultimately has free will. The problem is that we sometimes lose sight of our potential because we're concerned about what others think of us and our actions. We let others control how we think and feel. It is the therapist's job to help clients rediscover their natural self-worth—to help them get back in touch with their own true feelings, desires, and needs—by acting as a confidant and friend.

Client-Centered Therapy
Humanistic therapies resemble cognitive therapies in their emphasis on conscious thought processes. But the intention of humanistic therapy is not to criticize or correct irrational thinking; quite the contrary, it's to be totally supportive in all respects. The therapist's proper role is to be nonjudgmental, which means the client should be accepted unconditionally. According to humanistic therapists such as Carl Rogers, the most effective form of therapy is **client-centered**—it is

the client, not the therapist, who ultimately holds the key to psychological health and happiness.

We discussed the theoretical ideas of humanistic psychologists, especially Carl Rogers, in some detail in Chapter 12. Rogers was convinced that most psychological problems originate from *incongruence*, which he defined as the discrepancy between people's self-concept and the reality of their everyday experiences. People often hold an inaccurate view of themselves and their abilities, Rogers argued, because of an ingrained need for *positive regard*—they seek the approval, love, and companionship of significant others (such as their parents). But these significant others tend to attach *conditions of worth* to their approval: They demand that we think and act in ways that may not be consistent with our true inner feelings. The road to improvement lies in providing a warm and supportive environment—without conditions of worth—that will encourage clients to accept themselves as they truly are.

In client-centered therapy, there are three essential core qualities that the therapist seeks to provide to the client: *genuineness, unconditional positive regard,* and *empathy*. As the client's confidant, the therapist must be completely genuine—he or she must act without phoniness, and express true feelings in an open and honest way. The second quality, unconditional positive regard, means that the therapist cannot place conditions of worth on the client. The therapist must be totally accepting and respectful of the client at all times, even if the client thinks and acts in a way that seems irrational or inappropriate. Remember, humanists believe that all people are essentially good—they simply need to be placed in an environment that will nurture their innate tendencies toward positive growth.

The third quality, empathy, is achieved when the therapist is able to truly understand and accept what the client is feeling—to see things from the client's perspective. Through empathy, the therapist acquires the capacity to reflect those feelings back in a way that helps the client gain insight into himself or herself. Consider the following interaction between Carl Rogers and one of his clients, a woman coming to grips with deep feelings of betrayal and hurt that she's tried to cover up (from Rogers, 1961, p. 94):

> Client: I never did really know. But it's—you know, it's almost a physical thing. It's—it's sort of as though I were looking within myself at all kinds of—nerve endings and bits of things that have been sort of mashed.
>
> Rogers: As though some of the most delicate aspects of you physically almost have been crushed or hurt.
>
> Client: Yes. And you know, I do get the feeling, "Oh, you poor thing." (Pause)
>
> Rogers: Just can't help but feel very deeply sorry for the person that is you.
>
> Client: I don't think I feel sorry for the whole person; it's a certain aspect of the thing.
>
> Rogers: Sorry to see the hurt.
>
> Client: Yeah.

Notice that Rogers reflects back the feelings of the client in a completely non-judgmental fashion. He is seeking to understand and empathize with her feelings,

? CRITICAL THINKING

Think about the interactions you've had with a really close friend. Do you see any similarities to the client-centered approach advocated by Carl Rogers?

CONCEPT SUMMARY
Insight Approaches to Psychotherapy

Approach	Source of Psychopathology	Approach to Treatment (Depression)
Psychoanalysis	Psychopathology arises from unconscious conflict, often rooted in childhood trauma.	Debbie is depressed because of repressed fears that her parents don't really love her. They were not very affectionate while she was growing up. Her therapist tries to get Debbie to talk about her childhood relationship with her parents.
Cognitive	Psychopathology arises from conscious processes, including irrational beliefs and negative thoughts.	Troy is having a tough time with his parents. They want him to major in business, which he hates. He feels like a terrible person for not following his parents' wishes; after all, they're paying his tuition. His therapist attempts to show him that disagreeing with his parents over his college major does not reflect badly on him as a person.
Humanistic	Psychopathology arises from problems with one's self-concept, or *incongruence* between one's self-concept and reality.	Debbie feels guilty. She plans on having only one child, but her parents would like lots of grandchildren, and Debbie is an only child. Debbie feels bad about herself and about her failure to get acceptance from her parents. Her therapist listens as Debbie describes her feelings, and tries to be warm, supportive, and open to what she is saying.

thereby validating their existence and helping her to work through them. Notice also that it is the client, not the therapist, who is doing the analyzing. Client-centered therapy is founded on the idea that it is the clients who understand what truly hurts them psychologically, and it is the clients who have the best sense of how to proceed with therapy. All the therapist can do is provide the right kind of supportive environment and help clients recognize their own self-worth and trust their own instincts.

Other Humanistic Approaches

Client-centered therapy is the most popular form of humanistic therapy, but it is not the only one. *Gestalt therapy*, developed by Fritz Perls (1969; Perls et al., 1951), also places the burden of treatment in the hands of a "naturally good" client, but the approach is far less gentle and nondirective than client-centered therapy. In Gestalt therapy, clients are actively encouraged—even forced—to express their feelings openly. The emphasis is on the "here and now," and the therapist uses a variety of techniques to get the client to open up. For example, in the "empty chair" technique, clients are asked to project their feelings onto an empty chair in the room and then, literally, "talk" to the feelings. The idea is that only through fully understanding and overtly expressing oneself as a whole person (the word *gestalt* roughly translates from the German as "whole"), can a person hope to take responsibility for those feelings and change them for the better.

There is another group of humanistic treatments known collectively as *existential therapies* (Yalom, 1980). Existential therapists believe that psychological problems originate from the anxieties created by personal choices, such as whether to stay in school, get married, or quit a job. These fundamental choices—choices that relate to one's daily existence as a human being—are often difficult to face, and individuals may choose not to deal with them directly. Existential therapists encourage their clients to accept responsibility for these decisions, but in a supportive environment that encourages positive growth.

GROUP THERAPY

Therapy is most commonly perceived as a one-on-one experience—you and the therapist sit alone in a room discussing your problems. But there is no principled reason why the therapies we've been discussing can't be conducted in group rather than individual sessions. In **group therapy,** you join other people who are undergoing treatment for a similar problem. Typically, group sessions include the therapist and somewhere between 4 and 15 clients, although there are few hard and

group therapy
A form of therapy in which several people are treated simultaneously in the same setting.

fast rules for conducting group sessions; for example, in some cases there may be more than one therapist involved in the session (Yalom, 1995).

At first glance, the idea of group therapy seems troubling to most people. After all, who wants to talk about their personal problems in front of others? It's hard enough to open up to one person—the therapist—but at least he or she is a trained professional. Yet there are a number of advantages that groups offer over individual sessions. First, group therapy can be much more cost effective because the therapist can meet with multiple clients at the same time (MacKenzie, 1997; Wolff et al., 1997). Second, hearing other people talk about problems that match your own can be educational (Matano et al., 1997). You can learn about their strategies for coping with problems and you can see first-hand how their symptoms compare to your own. Third, and perhaps most important, when you hear testimonies from other people it's easier to realize that you're not alone—you're not the only person who is suffering from psychological problems. As you'll discover later in this chapter, empathy is a very important predictor of success in therapy; group settings can improve the trusting relationship you have with your therapist as well as with other people who share your problem (Donigian & Malnati, 1997).

Family Therapy

One place in which group therapy can be particularly appropriate is with the family. Rather than just treating an individual, in **family therapy** the therapist treats the family as whole, as a kind of social *system* (Cox & Paley, 1997; Lebow & Gurman, 1995). Clearly, if one member of a family suffers from a psychological problem, such as depression, all family members tend to be affected and all can benefit from treatment. Moreover, the family environment can play either a positive or a negative role in helping a particular family member recover from a psychological problem. If the family understands the disorder, and what's necessary for treatment, the odds of successful treatment go up considerably. Family therapists work on ways to improve interpersonal communication and collaboration among family members (Rivett, 1998).

> **family therapy**
> A form of group therapy in which the therapist treats the family as whole, as a kind of social *system*. The goals of the treatment are often to improve interpersonal communication and collaboration.

TEST YOURSELF 15.2

Check your knowledge of insight therapies by matching each of the following statements to a type of therapy. Choose from among the following: psychoanalysis, gestalt therapy, rational-emotive therapy, Beck's cognitive therapy, client-centered therapy, family therapy. (You will find the answers in the Appendix.)

1. "You think you're worthless? Well, I'm sitting here spending time with you so how can you be completely worthless? It's a ridiculous idea." _____

2. "I want you to keep a record of your thoughts, and the situations that produce them, so that you can judge whether those thoughts are really appropriate given the situation." _____

3. "Don't leave. Sit down and tell me again about the dream you had last night." _____

4. "You feel pain, deep pain, and you just can't get beyond the hurt that you feel inside." _____

5. "Talk to the chair . . . be the chair. Open up and let your true feelings come out." _____

6. "It's not just your problem. Each of you needs to communicate better and learn to work together to solve problems and avoid conflicts." _____

Treating the Environment: Behavioral Therapies

This child's fear of the water might have been acquired as a result of an earlier frightening experience.

behavioral therapies
Treatments designed to change behavior through the use of established learning techniques.

Traditional insight therapists address psychological problems by searching the minds of their clients for hidden conflicts, faulty beliefs, or damaged self-worth. But there are alternative approaches to therapy that essentially leave the mind alone. Behavioral therapies treat *behavior* rather than thoughts or memories. **Behavioral therapies** are designed to change unwanted or maladaptive behavior through the application of basic learning principles (Spiegler & Guevremont, 1998).

As we discussed in Chapter 14, many psychologists are convinced that psychological problems can be *learned*, or acquired as a result of experience. Afraid of snakes? Perhaps you had a frightening experience at some point in your life—you may have been bitten by a snake—and this experience caused you to associate snakes with a negative emotional consequence. The snake isn't symbolic of some hidden sexual conflict—you just learned that when snakes are around you can be bitten; as a result, snakes have become "signals" for something bad.

If you believe that a psychological problem has been learned, it doesn't make a lot of sense to spend months or years searching for a hidden reason for the problem. It's better to treat the surface symptoms by learning something new. More productive actions need to rewarded, or the negative associations you've formed need to be extinguished or counteracted. We'll consider several behavioral approaches in this section of the chapter, beginning with an effective technique for treating phobias that is based on the principles of *classical conditioning*.

CONDITIONING TECHNIQUES

In Chapter 7 we discussed how dogs and people learn about the signaling properties of events. In Pavlov's classic experiments, dogs learned that one event, called the *conditioned stimulus*, signaled the occurrence of a second event, called the *unconditioned stimulus*. After pairing the conditioned stimulus and the unconditioned stimulus together in time, Pavlov found that his dogs responded to the conditioned stimulus in a way that anticipated the arrival of the unconditioned stimulus. For example, if a bell (the conditioned stimulus) was repeatedly presented just prior to food (the unconditioned stimulus), the dogs would begin to drool (the conditioned response) to the bell in anticipation of the food. Pavlov also showed that this conditioned response, the drooling, was sensitive to how well the conditioned stimulus predicted the occurrence of the unconditioned stimulus: If the bell was rung repeatedly after conditioning but the food was no longer presented, the dog eventually stopped drooling to the bell (a procedure Pavlov called *extinction*).

Now let's consider the case of a specific phobia, such as fear of snakes. Specific phobias are highly focused fears of objects or situations. When the feared object is present, it produces an intense anxiety reaction. In the 1920s, psychologist Mary Cover Jones proposed that intense fear reactions like these can be treated as if they are classically conditioned responses. A snake produces fear because some kind of earlier experience has taught you to associate snakes with something fearful. Perhaps while standing near one as a child, your brother or sister screamed in terror, thereby scaring you. Jones's analysis suggested a treatment: It might be possible to eliminate phobias by teaching a new association between the feared object and something pleasurable. As she reported in 1924, she was able to use this logic to treat a little boy's fear of rabbits. She fed the boy some tasty food in the presence of the rabbit, which extinguished the association between the rabbit and an earlier negative experience and replaced it with a more pleasurable association (Jones, 1924).

Systematic Desensitization

The treatment pioneered by Mary Cover Jones was later refined by psychiatrist Joseph Wolpe into a technique known as **systematic desensitization** (Wolpe, 1958, 1982). As with Jones's approach, systematic desensitization uses *counterconditioning* as a way of reducing the fear and anxiety that have become associated with a specific object or event. The therapist attempts to replace the negative association with something relaxing and pleasurable. It's a gradual process that involves three major steps:

1. The therapist helps the client construct an *anxiety hierarchy*, which is an ordered list of situations that lead to fearful reactions. The client is asked to imagine a series of anxiety-provoking situations, beginning with the least fear-arousing situation and ending with the feared situation itself.
2. The therapist spends time teaching the client ways to induce deep muscle relaxation. A state of deep relaxation is inconsistent with the experience of anxiety—you can't be afraid and relaxed at the same time.
3. With the help of the therapist the client then attempts to work through the anxiety hierarchy, forming an image of each of the scenes, while maintaining the state of relaxation. The idea is to pair the images of fearful situations with the pleasurable state of relaxation so as to extinguish the old negative association and replace it with something relaxing.

Let's imagine you have a deep, irrational fear of flying in an airplane. Treatment starts by having you create a list of flying-related situations that are increasingly frightful. Next, you would receive lessons in how to relax yourself fully. Finally, you would begin working through your hierarchy. Perhaps you might start by simply imagining a picture of an airplane. If you can remain relaxed under these conditions, the therapist will direct you to move up the hierarchy to the next most stressful situation—perhaps imagining the airplane actually taking off. Gradually, over time, you will learn to relax in increasingly more stressful situations, even to the point where you can imagine yourself strapped in the seat as the plane rolls down the runway. The key to the technique is to maintain the relaxation. If you can stay relaxed—which is incompatible with fear and anxiety—the fearful association with planes should extinguish and be replaced by an association that is neutral or positive. Eventually, when you move to a real situation, the learning will generalize and you will no longer be afraid to fly in a plane. This type of therapy is summarized in Figure 15.7, on page 602, using another specific phobia—the fear of snakes.

Aversion Therapy

Systematic desensitization attempts to eliminate unpleasant associations by replacing them with pleasant ones. In **aversion therapy,** the therapist tries to replace a pleasant reaction to a harmful stimulus with something unpleasant, such as making the client feel bad rather than good after smoking a cigarette or having a drink of alcohol. Once again, the idea is to use a kind of counterconditioning, but the goal is to make the target situation something to be avoided rather than approached.

In the case of alcohol dependency, it's possible to give people a drug (Antabuse) that causes them to be become nauseated and vomit if they take a drink of alcohol. The drug interacts with alcohol, causing extreme discomfort. Under these conditions, the person who is drinking learns a new association that helps combat the alcohol dependency—drinking leads to an unpleasant feeling. A similar technique can be used for smoking. There are drugs containing chemicals that leave an extremely bad taste in one's mouth after smoking. The old association connecting pleasure with smoking is replaced by a new association connecting smoking with a terrible taste.

Aversion therapy can be quite effective, as long as the client takes the aversive drug for a sufficient period of time. The problem is that people who undergo this therapy are often reluctant to continue the treatment unless they're closely supervised. If the client stops the treatment and returns to normal drinking or smoking,

Psychologist Mary Cover Jones proposed that intense fear reactions, such as those seen in phobias, could be treated as if they were classically conditioned responses.

CRITICAL THINKING

In what ways is shaping, *which we discussed in Chapter 7, similar to and different from the procedures of systematic desensitization?*

systematic desensitization
A technique that uses counterconditioning and extinction to reduce the fear and anxiety that have become associated with a specific object or event. It's a multistep process that attempts to replace the negative learned association with something relaxing.

aversion therapy
A treatment for replacing a positive reaction to a harmful stimulus, such as alcohol, with something negative, such as feeling nauseous.

FIGURE 15.7
Systematic Desensitization
After learning relaxation techniques, the client works slowly through an anxiety hierarchy. At first she simply imagines the feared object while relaxed. Eventually, the relaxation response can be maintained while she experiences the actual feared situation.

the newly learned negative association will extinguish and be replaced by the old, positive association. Ethical concerns have also been raised about this form of treatment. Although those who participate do so voluntarily, they are often people who are desperately seeking a solution to their problems. Because the treatment directly induces extremely unpleasant experiences, many therapists are convinced that it should be used only as a treatment of last resort.

APPLYING REWARDS AND PUNISHMENTS

As we discussed in Chapter 7, it is possible to change behavior by teaching people about the direct consequences of their behavior. You can be shaped, through the application of rewards and punishments, away from abnormal actions and toward more normal behaviors. Although aversion therapy involves elements of punishment—the act of drinking is followed by an extremely unpleasant consequence—its goal is mainly to replace prior pleasant emotional associations with unpleasant ones. Behavioral therapies that use rewards and punishments are designed to modify specific unwanted *behaviors* by teaching people about the consequences of their actions.

Token Economies

Shaping behavior through the delivery of reward has proven to be particularly effective in institutional settings. When people are confined to mental hospitals or other kinds of institutions, it is usually because they cannot cope successfully without constant supervision. If people cannot care for themselves—if they don't wash properly, eat proper foods, or protect themselves from harm—they need a struc-

In aversion therapy, the intention is to replace positive associations with negative ones, such as making an individual feel bad rather than good after smoking a cigarette.

Inside the Problem   Social Skills Training in Schizophrenia

Serious psychological disorders can have a devastating impact on a person's ability to function successfully in virtually all environments, especially social ones. In schizophrenia, for example, social or occupational dysfunction is one of the defining characteristics of the disorder. Patients with schizophrenia tend to isolate themselves from others, and, when they do interact socially, they typically act in odd or peculiar ways.

Consider the conversational speech of David, a 25-year-old with schizophrenia, during an interaction with his therapist (Barlow & Durand, 1999):

> Therapist: I was sorry to hear that your Uncle Bill died a few years ago. How are you feeling about him these days?
>
> David: Yes, he died. He was sick and now he's gone. He likes to fish with me, down at the river. He's going to take me hunting. I have guns. I can shoot you and you'd be dead in a minute.

In the words of his therapist, David's conversational speech "resembled a ball rolling down a rocky hill. Like an accelerating object, his speech gained momentum the longer he went on, and as if bouncing off obstacles, the topics almost always went in unpredictable directions" (Barlow & Durand, 1999, p. 407).

In such cases, therapists face a practical problem: How can they improve the social skills of the person with the disorder? This is a particularly important concern in schizophrenia, which is often difficult to treat. Even with effective medications, many patients suffer relapses of symptoms (Liberman et al., 1994), and some symptoms of the disorder, including social withdrawal and flat affect, are not affected by conventional psychoactive drugs. For these reasons, therapists sometimes turn to *social skills training*, which is a form of behavioral therapy that uses modeling and reinforcement to shape appropriate adjustment skills (McFall, 1976; Wong et al., 1993).

Social skills training usually consists of a series of steps. To teach conversational skills, for example, the therapist might begin with a discussion of appropriate verbal responses in a conversation, followed by a videotaped demonstration. The patient is then asked to role play an actual conversation, and the therapist provides either corrective feedback or positive reinforcement. "Homework" might then be assigned, in which the patient is encouraged to practice his or her skills outside of the training session, preferably in new situations. If the training is conducted in an institutional setting, such as a mental hospital, the therapist must monitor the patient's subsequent interactions carefully so that appropriate reinforcement can be delivered (Wallace, 1998).

Social skills training usually takes place over many sessions, and it's often combined with other forms of treatment (such as psychoactive drugs or some form of insight therapy). Reviews of the research literature indicate that the application of these simple learning principles—positive reinforcement and modeling—can lead to significant improvements in social functioning, and in the quality of life for individuals affected with psychological disorders (Benton & Schroeder, 1990). You should understand that one of the most important goals of any therapy is to improve global functioning; at times focusing on specific symptoms—even something as simple as knowing how to answer a casual question in an appropriate way—can make an enormous difference in the life of a troubled individual.

---

tured environment around them. In institutional settings, therapists have found that setting up token economies—in which patients are rewarded for behaving appropriately—can be quite effective in teaching patients how to cope with the realities of everyday life (Ayllon & Azrin, 1968; Lindsley & Skinner, 1954; Paul & Lentz, 1977).

In a **token economy,** institutionalized patients are rewarded with small tokens (such as poker chips) whenever they engage in an appropriate activity. Certain rules are established and explained to the patient, which determine when tokens are handed out (or taken away). For example, if Bob, who is suffering from schizophrenia, takes his medication without complaint, he is given a plastic token. Sally might receive tokens for getting out of bed in the morning, washing her hair, and brushing her teeth. The tokens can later be exchanged for certain privileges, such as being able to watch a video or stay in a private room. Similarly, if a patient acts in an inappropriate manner, the therapist might choose to take tokens away as a form of punishment. This technique is called a token *economy* because it represents a voluntary exchange of goods and services—the patient exchanges appropriate behavior for the privileges that tokens provide.

Token economies are highly successful in helping patients develop the skills they'll need to function well inside and outside of the institution. Not only do the everyday "maintenance" activities of the patients improve, but token rewards can

token economy
A type of behavioral therapy in which patients are rewarded with small tokens when they act in an appropriate way; the tokens can then be exchanged for certain privileges.

CONCEPT SUMMARY
Behavioral Therapies

Conditioning Approaches

Approach	Based on the Idea That:	Therapeutic Approach
Systematic desensitization	Intense anxiety reactions are the result of classically conditioned associations.	Uses counterconditioning to reduce the fear and anxiety that have become associated with a particular object or event. The therapist attempts to replace a negative association with something relaxing and pleasurable.
Aversion therapy	Problem behaviors are based partly in classically conditioned associations.	The therapist tries to replace a pleasant reaction to a harmful stimulus with an unpleasant reaction. For example, the pleasurable reaction associated with smoking is replaced by a new association between smoking and a terrible taste.

Rewards and Punishments

Token economies	Behavior can be changed by teaching people about the direct consequences of their behavior.	Therapist and patient have a voluntary exchange of goods and services—the patient exchanges appropriate behavior for privileges provided by tokens.
Punishment	Behavior can be changed by teaching people about the direct consequences of their behavior.	An inappropriate (e.g., self-injurious) behavior is followed with an aversive stimulus, or with the removal of a pleasant stimulus.

be used also to shape social behavior and even vocational skills (for a closer look, see the accompanying feature, "Inside the Problem"). Token economies have also been used in classroom settings to reward children for showing appropriate individual and group behavior (Kazdin, 1982).

Punishment

Token economies tend to be based primarily on the application of reward as a way of changing unwanted behaviors. But as we've seen, punishment can also be an effective way to teach people about the consequences of their behavior. And, indeed, there are instances in which therapists feel that following a behavior with an aversive stimulus (sometimes even a shock) or removing something pleasant is justified. Consider someone who is extremely self-destructive—perhaps a disturbed child who continually bangs his or her head against the wall. Under these conditions, the safe delivery of an aversive event has been shown to reduce these self-destructive behaviors, thereby preventing serious injury (Lovaas, 1987; Lovaas et al., 1973).

But punishment is rarely used as the sole kind of behavioral intervention, for several reasons. First, punishment has side effects—for example, it can damage the working relationship between the therapist and the client. Second, punishment by itself only teaches someone what *not to do*; it doesn't teach someone the appropriate way to act. Third, punishing someone who is in the grips of a psychological disorder raises ethical concerns. We cannot be sure the person on the receiving end of the aversive event approves of the treatment, even though the therapist may be convinced it is in the client's best interest.

TEST YOURSELF 15.3

Check your knowledge about behavioral therapies by answering the following questions. (You will find the answers in the Appendix).

1. According to the classical conditioning account of phobias, the feared stimulus, such as a snake, acts as a(n):

    a. unconditioned stimulus.
    b. conditioned stimulus.

c. conditioned response.

d. conditioned reinforcer.

2. In systematic desensitization, the fear that has become associated to a specific object or event is reduced through:

a. counterconditioning and extinction.

b. second-order conditioning.

c. delivery of an aversive consequence.

d. token rewards.

3. Which of the following is not a major concern in aversion therapy?

a. Clients cannot truly give informed and voluntary consent.

b. Effective punishments can't be delivered because pain thresholds are high.

c. Clients are often reluctant to continue treatment.

d. Newly learned negative associations can extinguish.

4. In a token economy, the token acts as which of the following?

a. Conditioned stimulus

b. Punishment

c. Conditioned inhibitor

d. Reinforcement

Evaluating and Choosing Psychotherapy

When people make the decision to enter therapy, they do so because they're in need of help. Ralph is unable to advance his career in sales because of his extreme fear of flying; Julie lives a life of quiet desperation, mostly alone in her room, because she suffers from a social phobia. We've now examined the major types of therapy, but we've said little about their relative effectiveness. How well does psychotherapy actually work? Are all forms of therapy equally effective, or do some forms of therapy work better than others?

To assess the effectiveness of any therapy requires carefully controlled research. As we discussed in Chapter 2, just because a manipulation changes someone's behavior does not mean that it was the manipulation that caused the change. Someone might enter therapy and leave improved some time later, but the change could have occurred for reasons unrelated to the actual treatment. Perhaps the person simply improved spontaneously over time. Most people who get the flu improve over time—even if they never see a doctor—and it could be that the same kind of thing happens with psychological disorders. A control group—in which no treatment is given—is needed to confirm that the therapy was indeed responsible for the improvement. Fortunately, a number of such controlled research studies have been conducted.

CLINICAL EVALUATION RESEARCH

Let's begin by considering a well-known example of a clinical evaluation study (Sloane et al., 1975). In this study, conducted at a Philadelphia psychiatric clinic in the mid-1970s, men and women who were seeking treatment primarily for anxiety disorders were assigned at random to one of three treatment conditions. One group of patients was assigned to therapists experienced in the practice of *psychodynamic* techniques (the analysis of unconscious conflicts and memories); a second group was assigned to experienced *behavioral* therapists (using systematic desensitization and other learning-based techniques); a third group—the *control* group—was placed on a "waiting list" and received no immediate treatment. After four months, an independent team of therapists, who were unaware of the treatment

LEARNING GOALS

1. Discuss the major findings of clinical evaluation research.

2. Describe the factors that are common across psychotherapies.

3. Discuss the important personal and cultural factors that should be considered when choosing a therapist.

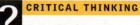

? CRITICAL THINKING

Is it ethical to assign patients who are seeking help for their psychological problems to a no-treatment control?

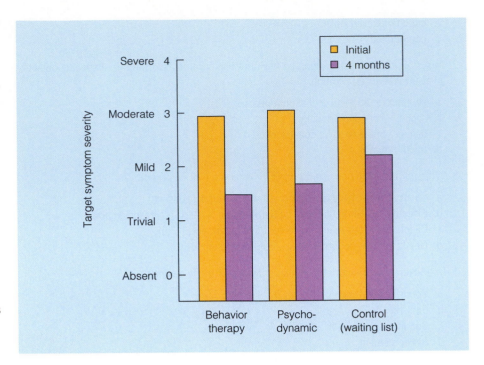

FIGURE 15.8

Evaluating Forms of Treatment

In the study by Sloane and colleagues (1975), men and women seeking treatment for anxiety disorders were randomly assigned to behavior therapy, psychodynamic therapy, or a control waiting list. After four months, the people receiving therapy showed significantly less severe symptoms than people in the control group, but there were no significant differences between types of therapy (behavior and psychodynamic). (Data from Sloane et al., 1975.)

assignments, was called in to evaluate the progress of the patients in each of the three groups.

The results were somewhat surprising. The good news is that the therapies clearly worked. As shown in Figure 15.8, the people who were given either the psychodynamic or the behavioral therapy showed significantly more improvement after four months than the people who were left on the waiting list (although it's interesting to note that the waiting list people improved also). But there were no significant differences between the two treatment conditions—the behavioral approach worked just as well as the psychodynamic approach. Even more surprising was the finding that eight months later, at a year-end follow-up assessment, the patients in the control group had essentially caught up with the treatment patients—they had improved enough to be comparable to the patients in the other two groups. Thus, the treatments worked, but it seems that their primary effect was simply to speed up natural improvement.

Meta-Analysis

The Philadelphia study is important because it's an example of how evaluation research should be conducted—random assignment to groups, the use of a no-treatment control, and an independent assessment procedure (Wolpe, 1975). Since that study was first reported, hundreds of other studies have been conducted (although not all have included the same rigorous control procedures). Rather than picking and choosing from among these studies, mental health professionals often rely on a technique called meta-analysis to help them draw conclusions about this research. In a **meta-analysis,** many different studies are compared statistically on some common evaluation measure. The comparison standard is usually something called an "effect size," which is essentially a standardized measure of the difference between treatment and control conditions (see Robey & Dalebout, 1998).

In one of the first extensive meta-analytic studies, Smith and colleagues analyzed the results of 475 research studies designed to evaluate one or more forms of psychotherapy (Smith & Glass, 1977; Smith et al., 1980). Although the individual studies covered a wide range of psychological problems and therapeutic techniques, in each case it was possible to compare a treatment condition to some kind of control condition (usually an untreated group). Smith and colleagues

meta-analysis

A statistical technique used to compare findings across many different research studies; comparisons are based on some common evaluation measure, such as the difference between treatment and control conditions.

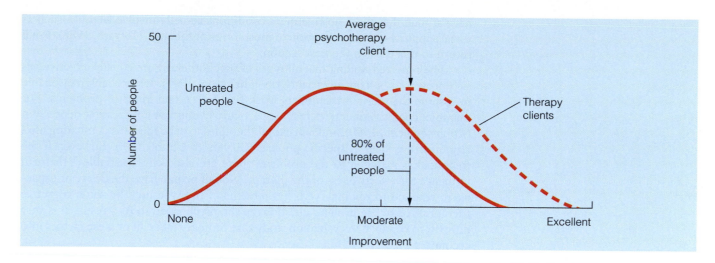

FIGURE 15.9
The Effectiveness of Psychotherapy
In the meta-analysis by Smith and colleagues (1980), which assessed hundreds of clinical evaluation studies, people who experienced some form of active psychotherapy were better off, on average, than roughly 80% of the people who were not treated. (Data from Smith, Glass, & Miller, 1980.)

reached two major conclusions from their meta-analysis of the data. *First*, there was a consistent and large treatment advantage (see Figure 15.9). People who experienced some kind of active psychotherapy were better off, on average, than roughly 80% of the people who were left untreated. *Second*, when the various kinds of psychotherapy were compared, few, if any, differences were found. It really didn't matter whether the patient was receiving an insight therapy or a behavioral therapy—all produced the same amount of improvement (see also Wampold et al., 1997).

There have been hundreds of other attempts to meta-analyze evaluation studies. Some have sought to exercise more control over the research quality of the studies included (Lipsey & Wilson, 1993); others have attempted to extend the areas of examination to such things as client characteristics, experience of the therapist, or length of the treatment (Lambert & Bergin, 1994). In general, the findings support two main conclusions: therapy works and the effects of therapy are long-lasting. For example, one recent review of meta-analysis studies, which examined some 302 published meta-analyses, found that only 6 produced negative effect sizes (which means that patients undergoing therapy actually got worse than untreated controls), and the vast majority were overwhelmingly positive (Lipsey & Wilson, 1993).

Controversies

There is widespread agreement among professionals that psychotherapy works, but clinical evaluation studies remain the subject of debate. For example, what should constitute the proper evaluation "control"? Let's return to the Philadelphia experiment in which two treatment groups (psychodynamic and behavioral) were compared with a group containing people who were left on a waiting list. Remember, the control patients actually got considerably better over time, to a point in which, after a year, they had improved to the same levels as the treatment groups. Psychologists call this kind of improvement in the absence of treatment **spontaneous remission**, and it's been estimated that psychological disorders may improve on their own as much as 30% or more of the time (Eysenck, 1952; Lambert & Bergin, 1994).

But did the people who were left on the waiting list in the Philadelphia experiment really receive no treatment? This is a difficult question to answer—it depends on how you define "treatment." Although these people received no formal psychotherapy, they were given initial psychological tests and were called frequently and given support. Their simple involvement in the study, along with the expectation that they would be receiving some help, may itself have acted as a kind of therapy. Similar effects are commonly found with many placebo controls, in which clients are given attention and support but not formal therapy. Many critics

spontaneous remission
Improvement in a psychological disorder without treatment—that is, simply as a function of the passage of time.

have argued that these no-treatment conditions actually involve factors—such as social support—that are common to most forms of therapy (Horvath, 1988). We'll return to this issue in the next section.

The reported finding that all types of psychotherapy are equally effective has also proven to be controversial (Crits-Christoph, 1997). It's probably reasonable to assume that certain treatments work best for certain kinds of problems. For example, cognitive therapies may be particularly effective for treating depression (Robinson et al., 1990), and behavioral therapies may be ideal for combating anxiety disorders such as specific phobias (Bowers & Clum, 1988). But even if the treatment is matched to the problem, there are also "client variables" that can influence the effectiveness of the therapy. Not all people have the desire or capacity to respond to rational, verbal arguments of the type used by some cognitive therapists, or to the probing questions of the psychoanalyst. As a result, it is very difficult to conduct an evaluation study that properly takes all of these factors into account.

COMMON FACTORS ACROSS PSYCHOTHERAPIES

Clinical researchers have also considered the possibility that there may be common, nonspecific factors shared by all therapies, regardless of surface differences. Although the various therapies we've considered seem to be very different, and they're clearly driven by very different assumptions about human psychology, they do share features in common (Grencavage & Norcross, 1990; Rosenzweig, 1936). Michael Lambert and Allen Bergin (1994) have suggested that these common factors can be grouped into three main categories: *support factors*, *learning factors*, and *action factors*.

Support Factors

Virtually all therapies that produce positive outcomes provide tangible *support* for the client. People who enter therapy find themselves face to face with someone who is willing to accept and understand their problems. Both the therapist and the client have a common goal, which is to help the client get better. Regardless of their theoretical orientation—psychodynamic, cognitive, behavioral, or humanistic—effective therapists are clearly interested in listening to and reassuring their clients and in developing a positive, trusting relationship. A number of studies have found a strong correlation between the amount of empathy that the therapist establishes with the client and the effectiveness of the treatment (Lafferty et al., 1991; Miller et al., 1980).

Learning Factors

When people go through therapy, they *learn* things about themselves. They learn about their thought processes, or about their behavior, or about important factors in their past that might be contributing to current discomforts. Effective therapists often act as mirrors, reflecting back a client's beliefs and actions in ways that provide critical insight. Regardless of the method of treatment, effective therapists also give feedback about how various experiences relate to one another. They point out connections among experiences—how people might behave and think similarly across different situations. People are often helped because they're given a reason or a rationale for their problems.

Action Factors

Finally, all forms of therapy ultimately provide people with a set of specific suggestions for *action*. Troubled clients might be asked to face their fears, take risks, or directly test irrational beliefs. They might be given specific strategies for coping with anxiety, or training in how to relax. Irrespective of the specific suggestions, just providing clients with a tangible course of action may be sufficient to give them *hope* and allow them to feel in control of their problem.

CHOOSING A THERAPIST

At some point in your life, you might find yourself in need of a psychotherapist. Perhaps you'll experience a simple problem in living, or maybe something more serious. What should you do? Given our discussion about the relative effectiveness of the various treatment options, it might seem natural to conclude that it doesn't make much difference whom you choose. But remember, one of the best predictors of treatment success is the amount of empathy between the client and the therapist. Therefore, it's critical for you to find someone whom you trust and with whom you feel comfortable interacting. The level of trust that you feel with the therapist is very important; don't be afraid to shop around a bit to find the right person.

Currently, most psychotherapists describe themselves as being *eclectic* in their orientation. This means they are willing to pick and choose from among treatment options to find the techniques that work best for the individual client. It used to be the case that therapists would align themselves with a particular approach or "school"—such as psychoanalysis or behavior therapy—but in a recent survey of 800 therapists, 68% of those responding described their orientation as eclectic (Jensen et al., 1990). You can expect most therapists to be flexible in their approach, and if one form of treatment is not yielding results—or if you feel uncomfortable with the approach—you can expect the therapist to be open to trying something different. Effective therapy requires open communication, and the therapist is dependent on your feedback as a client throughout the treatment process.

Cultural Factors

Mental health professionals also now recognize that cultural factors are important in both the diagnosis and the treatment of psychological disorders (Sue & Zane, 1987; Tseng & McDermott, 1975). For many years, cultural barriers have made it difficult for members of ethnic minorities to use and benefit from mental health resources. Language differences between the client and the therapist clearly undermine effective communication, as do differences between the therapist's and the client's worldview. To take a case in point, many Asians feel uncomfortable with open self-disclosure and the expression of emotions. As a result, it's unlikely that many Asians will benefit from Western therapists who encourage "letting it all hang out" (Sue et al., 1994).

> **? CRITICAL THINKING**
>
> *What kind of therapeutic approach would you choose if you needed help? Justify your answer based on what you've learned in this chapter.*

Cultural barriers sometimes make it difficult for members of ethnic minorities to benefit from mental health resources. It's essential for a therapist to be sensitive to a client's cultural background and general world view.

Does this mean you should always seek a therapist with a cultural background identical to your own? Not necessarily. For one thing, there is still a shortage of therapists from ethnic minorities in the United States (Mays & Albee, 1992). This means that finding a cultural match may be difficult. Moreover, with the increased exposure to cultural influences, many therapists are now making concerted efforts to become culturally sensitive. In fact, special training programs are now available to help therapists break down some of the barriers that exist for clients from diverse cultural backgrounds. By gaining knowledge about a variety of customs and lifestyles, as well as by working directly with culturally diverse clients, therapists hope to remove barriers to effective empathy.

TEST YOURSELF 15.4

Check your knowledge about evaluating and choosing psychotherapy by deciding whether each of the following statements is true or false. (You will find the answers in the Appendix).

1. Psychological disorders may improve on their own as much as 30% or more of the time. *True or False?*

2. According to most meta-analytic studies, people who experience active psychotherapy are better off, on average, than roughly 80% of the people who are left untreated. *True or False?*

3. Most evaluation studies show that specific disorders, such as depression, require specific forms of therapy, such as psychoanalysis. *True or False?*

4. One factor that is common to all forms of psychotherapy is the need to investigate the traumatic events of childhood. *True or False?*

5. In choosing a therapist, perhaps the most important factor is empathy—finding someone you trust and with whom you feel comfortable. *True or False?*

Solving the Problems

In this chapter we've discussed the various tools that therapists use to treat psychological disorders. In each case, the goal of the therapist is to find a way to improve the client's ability to function successfully in the world. As you've seen, most forms of therapy are designed to address one or more of the three basic factors thought to contribute to psychological disorders: biological factors, cognitive factors, and environmental factors.

Treating the Body. Therapies that use medical interventions to treat the symptoms of psychological problems are called *biomedical therapies*. The idea that psychological disorders might be treated as "illnesses," in the same way that physicians might treat the common cold, has a long history in human thought. The most popular form of biomedical therapy is drug therapy, in which certain medications are given to affect thought and mood by altering the actions of neurotransmitters in the brain. Antipsychotic drugs, for example, reduce the symptoms of schizophrenia by acting as antagonists to the neurotransmitter dopamine in the brain. The antidepressant drug Prozac acts on the neurotransmitter serotonin, and antianxiety drugs—tranquilizers—are believed to act on neurotransmitters in the brain that have primarily inhibitory effects.

In the event that drug therapies fail, mental health professionals sometimes turn to other forms of biomedical intervention, particularly electroconvulsive therapy (ECT) and psychosurgery. Shock therapy is used to treat severe forms of depression, but usually only if more conventional forms of treatment have failed. No one is completely sure how or why the administration of electric shock affects mood, but there's wide agreement that ECT works for many patients. Even more controversial than ECT is the use of psychosurgery, in which some portion of the brain is destroyed or altered in an attempt to eliminate the symptoms of a mental disorder. The infamous prefrontal lobotomies of yesteryear are no longer conducted (partly because they produced unacceptable side effects), but some kinds of surgical intervention in the brain are still used.

Treating the Mind. In insight therapy, the psychotherapist attempts to treat psychological problems by helping clients gain insight, or self-knowledge, into the contents of their thought processes. Usually, this insight is obtained through prolonged verbal, one-on-one interactions between the therapist and the client. Perhaps the best-known form of insight therapy is Freudian *psychoanalysis*. The goal of psychoanalysis is to help the client uncover and relive conflicts that have been hidden in the unconscious mind. The psychoanalyst uses such techniques as free association and dream analysis to help probe the contents of the unconscious. As hidden conflicts begin to surface during the course of therapy, the client will typically show what Freud called resistance—an attempt to hinder the progress of therapy—and transference, in which the client transfers feelings about others onto the therapist.

Cognitive therapists believe that psychological problems arise primarily from irrational beliefs and thought processes. The therapist attempts to change the client's negative beliefs and thoughts by actively attacking them in verbal exchanges. The therapist points out the irrationality of negative thoughts, using evidence where possible, in the hope that the client will reject the beliefs, thereby lessening their emotional consequences. *Humanistic therapies* have a quite different goal. Here, the idea is to help clients gain insight into their own self-worth and value as humans. It is the client, not the therapist, who holds the key to self-improvement. Humanistic therapists view therapy as a process of discovering one's natural tendencies toward growth and free will. In client-centered therapy, the therapist tries to provide an approving and nonjudgmental environment, thereby allowing the client to better recognize and trust his or her own true instincts.

Treating the Environment. *Behavioral therapies* are designed to treat overt behavior rather than inner thought processes. Behavioral therapists assume that many kinds of psychological problems have been learned and can be treated through the application of learning principles. With many counterconditioning techniques, for example, the therapist attempts to replace learned associations that are negative with new, pleasurable associations. Thus, in systematic desensitization, specific phobias are treated by having the subject (1) construct an anxiety hierarchy of fear-inducing situations, (2) learn relaxation techniques, and (3) work through the anxiety hierarchy, imagining each of the scenes while maintaining a feeling of relaxation. Pairing the feared object with relaxation is intended to extinguish the old, negative association and replace it with something pleasurable. Other behavioral therapies make use of rewards and punishments to change behavior. In token economies, patients are rewarded with small tokens whenever they engage in normal or appropriate behaviors. The tokens can then be exchanged later for more tangible rewards or privileges.

Evaluating and Choosing Psychotherapy. Evaluating any form of psychotherapy requires controlled research in which treatment groups are compared with appropriate control conditions. Hundreds of such studies have been conducted, and meta-analyses of their results typically reach two main conclusions. First, people who receive psychotherapy do significantly better than those left untreated. Second, there are few, if any, advantages for one type of psychotherapy over another.

One reason that most forms of treatment are equally effective may be that there are common factors that cut across all psychotherapies. These common factors can be grouped into three main categories: support, learning, and action. All therapists provide some kind of support for their client, and therapist empathy has been shown to be important to outcome success. All forms of therapy also help clients learn about themselves and their behavior, and clients are provided specific prescriptions for action or behavior change. In choosing a therapist, it's critical that you find someone you trust and with whom you feel comfortable interacting. Cultural factors are also important, because for therapy to work the therapist needs to be sensitive to the client's cultural worldview.

Therapy Chapter Summary

Treating the Body: Biomedical Therapies

Abnormal functioning in the brain is thought to contribute to a number of psychological disorders. To address these problems, psychologists sometimes consider the use of *biomedical therapies*.

DRUG THERAPIES

Medications (such as chlorpromazine) that treat positive symptoms of schizophrenia are termed *antipsychotic drugs*, and quite often act on the neurotransmitter dopamine. However, these drugs are limited in their effect and can produce side effects such as *tardive dyskinesthesia*. *Clozapine* is a relatively new medication that serves as an effective alternative. *Antidepressant drugs* also modulate the effectiveness of neurotransmitters, particularly norepinephrine or serotonin. Bipolar disorders are often treated with the common salt lithium carbonate. *Antianxiety drugs*, or *tranquilizers* (e.g., Valium), come form a class of drugs called *benzodiazepines*, and work primarily on the neurotransmitter GABA.

ELECTROCONVULSIVE THERAPY

Many professionals believe that ECT is a reasonably safe and effective treatment for severe depression. It is typically used as a treatment of "last resort." The treatment remains controversial for a number of reasons. The reasons for its effectiveness are not well understood, and it can produce side effects such as confusion and memory loss.

PSYCHOSURGERY

Psychosurgery destroys or alters tissue in the brain in an effort to affect behavior. *Prefrontal lobotomy* was once a procedure designed to produce calming effects in disturbed patients, but it fell into disrepute. Currently the use of psychosurgery is exceedingly rare. *Cingulotomy* is sometimes used in the treatment of obsessive-compulsive disorder.

Treating the Mind: Insight Therapies

Psychological disorders are often associated with abnormal thoughts and beliefs. Many psychologists believe that the key to improvement lies in insight: people must gain awareness of their own thought processes.

PSYCHOANALYSIS: RESOLVING UNCONSCIOUS CONFLICTS

Freud believed that through psychoanalysis, hidden impulses and memories can be brought to awareness, freeing us from disordered thoughts and behaviors. The tools used to uncover unconscious conflicts include *free association* and *dream analysis*. *Resistance* (unconsciously motivated attempts to hinder therapy) and *transference* (expression of thoughts or feelings toward the therapist that are representative of how patients feel about others in their life) also provide clues about unconscious conflict. Modern versions of psychoanalysis streamline the therapeutic process and are often tailored to meet the specific needs of individuals.

HUMANISTIC THERAPIES: TREATING THE HUMAN SPIRIT

This type of therapy attempts to help the client gain insight into his or her own fundamental self-worth and value as a person. In *client-centered therapy*, the therapist is supportive in all respects, accepting the client unconditionally. The key to improvement lies in a warm and supportive environment that will help the client overcome *incongruence*. Therapists provide genuineness, unconditional positive regard, and empathy. One variation, *Gestalt therapy*, forces clients to express their feelings openly.

COGNITIVE THERAPIES: CHANGING MALADAPTIVE BELIEFS

Unlike the psychoanalytic approach, cognitive therapies place emphasis on *conscious* beliefs. Psychological problems arise from people's interpretation of the events that happen to them. In *rational emotive therapy*, the therapist "cross-examines" the client, assaulting irrational thought processes. Beck's cognitive therapy takes a more subtle approach, help-

ing clients discover their own unique kinds of faulty beliefs through record-keeping or other types of "homework."

GROUP THERAPY

In group therapy, you join others who are undergoing treatment for a similar problem. This can be particularly appropriate in the case of families. In *family therapy*, the therapist treats the family as a kind of social system, attempting to improve interpersonal communication and collaboration among family members.

Treating the Environment: Behavioral Therapies

People may *learn* to think and act in abnormal ways through the mechanisms of classical and instrumental conditioning, and observational learning. Behavioral therapies employ basic learning principles to change maladaptive behavior patterns into adaptive behavior patterns.

CONDITIONING TECHNIQUES

Phobias can involve an association between a specific object and anxiety, and can be eliminated by teaching a new association between the feared object and something pleasurable. In *systematic desensitization*, the therapist uses *counterconditioning*, systematically associating relaxation with feared objects as expressed in an *anxiety hierarchy*. In *aversion therapy*, the therapist attempts to replace a pleasant reaction to a harmful stimulus (e.g., alcohol) with something unpleasant.

APPLYING REWARDS AND PUNISHMENTS

People can be shaped, through rewards and punishments, away from abnormal actions and toward more normal behaviors. In a *token economy*, institutionalized patients are rewarded with tokens whenever they engage in an appropriate activity. The tokens are later exchanged for certain privileges. Punishment can also be an effective way to teach people about the consequences of their behavior, and is sometimes used to discourage self-injurious behavior.

Evaluating and Choosing Psychotherapy

Therapy is a costly and time-consuming process, so it's important to determine the advantages and disadvantages of an intervention. One must also take a number of factors into account when choosing a therapist.

CLINICAL EVALUATION RESEARCH

One well-known study that compared psychoanalytic and behavioral approaches to therapy with a control condition demonstrated that therapy clearly worked, but there were no reliable differences in the effectiveness of the two approaches. *Meta-analyses* of evaluation studies have shown that therapy works, although some problems may improve on their own through *spontaneous remission*. No one therapeutic approach seems more effective than others, although particular kinds of therapy may work best for certain problems.

COMMON FACTORS ACROSS PSYCHOTHERAPIES

Common factors are seen in each therapeutic approach: all therapies provide *support* for the client; all people in therapy *learn* something about themselves; all forms of therapy provide people with some suggestions for *action*. These common factors may account for the finding that approaches are comparable in their overall effectiveness.

CHOOSING A PSYCHOTHERAPIST

People seeking a psychotherapist should choose someone they trust and feel comfortable with. Most therapists are *eclectic* in orientation, sampling from a variety of therapeutic approaches. Also, cultural factors are important in the diagnosis and treatment of psychological disorders.

Terms to Remember

psychotherapy, 582

TREATING THE BODY

biomedical therapies, 584
antipsychotic drugs, 585
antidepressant drugs, 586
antianxiety drugs, 587
electroconvulsive therapy (ECT), 587
psychosurgery, 589

TREATING THE MIND

insight therapies, 590
psychoanalysis, 590
free association, 591
dream analysis, 591
resistance, 591
transference, 592
cognitive therapies, 593
rational-emotive therapy, 594
humanistic therapy, 596
client-centered therapy, 596
group therapy, 598
family therapy, 599

TREATING THE ENVIRONMENT

behavioral therapies, 600
systematic desensitization, 601
aversion therapy, 601
token economy, 603

EVALUATING AND CHOOSING AND PSYCHOTHERAPY

meta-analysis, 606
spontaneous remission, 607

Recommended Readings

Engler, J., & Gordon, B. (1992). *The consumer's guide to psychotherapy*. New York: Simon & Schuster. This book is a good source for discovering the range of available psychotherapies and for help in picking the kind of therapy that might work best for you.

Bongar, B., & Beutler, L. E. (1995). *Comprehensive textbook of psychotherapy*. Oxford, England: Oxford University Press. Another in-depth treatment of the various forms of psychotherapy. An excellent resource.

Dawes, R. M. (1994). *House of cards: Psychology and psychotherapy built on myth*. New York: Free Press. A penetrating critique of psychotherapy; the book provides a very interesting scientific analysis of the assumptions that are made by some (but not all) psychotherapists.

INFOTRAC® COLLEGE EDITION

For additional readings, explore Infotrac College Edition, your online library. Go to:
http://www.infotrac-college.com/wadsworth

Hint: enter the search terms: Prozac, Psychotherapy, Psychoanalysis, Cognitive therapy, Behavior modification, Effectiveness of psychotherapy.

🌐 What's on the Web?

Albert Ellis Institute

(www.irebt.org/)

Formerly known as the Institute for Rational-Emotive Therapy, this site presents information about Albert Ellis' cognitive approach to treating psychopathology. The site provides some useful Q & A on the basic approach of rational-emotive therapy. Each month the site features a new essay, and a response to a user question from Dr. Ellis himself.

National Psychological Association for Psychoanalysis

(www.npap.org)

This site provides a wealth of information about psychotherapy in general and the particular "brand" known as psychoanalysis. Included on the site is a very useful feature called FAQ (frequently asked questions) that addresses issues such as the time investment involved in psychotherapy, the monetary investment involved in psychotherapy, and the differences between psychiatrists, psychologists, and social workers.

History of Psychosurgery

(www.epub.org.br/cm/n02/historia/psicocirg_i.htm)

A fascinating site that delves into the dark world of psychosurgery. Find out the basics of psychosurgery, its early pioneers, and the state of modern psychosurgery. Find out about some well-known figures who had a prefrontal lobotomy, and find out why drilling holes in the skull was once used as a (very early) form of psychosurgery.

The Wadsworth Psychology Study Center Web Site

See http://psychology.wadsworth.com/ for practice quiz questions, hypercontents, updates, critical thinking exercises, discussion forums and more! The Wadsworth Psychology Study Center provides a wealth of information fully organized and integrated by chapter.

health psychology
The study of how biological, psychological, environmental, and cultural factors are involved in physical health and the prevention of illness.

Push, push, push. It hits you from all sides—school, work, relationships, family. Although we can't claim exclusive rights to the "age of stress," we certainly live in a time of increased expectation. Everybody expects something from us, and they seem to want it now. Your teachers expect the subject matter to be learned, the paper written; your boss expects overtime in addition to your regular hours; your parents expect that weekly phone call, delivered in a pleasant and friendly tone. Is it any wonder that you can't seem to shake that cold, or that you feel the need to leave the antacid tablets by your bedside at night?

The idea that there is a close relationship between your psychological state and the physical reactions of your body should, by now, be firmly implanted in your mind. The mind and the body interact, and the interaction works in two directions. As we've discussed, disruptions in the delicate balance of neurotransmitters in the brain can contribute significantly to psychological problems such as schizophrenia and depression. At the same time, beliefs, expectations, and reactions to the environment affect how those neurotransmitters are manufactured and used in the brain. In this chapter, you'll see that the mind-to-body connection affects not only the way you think, feel, and react; it can affect your overall state of health as well.

Our focus in this chapter is the general topic of health psychology. **Health psychology** is part of a broad movement, known as *behavioral medicine*, that seeks to understand how biological, psychological, environmental, and cultural factors are involved in the promotion of physical health and the prevention of illness. Not surprisingly, health psychologists are particularly interested in the psychological and environmental contributions (Adler & Matthews, 1994; Taylor et al., 1997). They tend to ask questions such as: Are there particular personality characteristics that determine who becomes sick or who will recover from an illness once it is acquired? Can the same theories that have been used successfully to diagnose and treat psychological disorders be applied to the promotion of physical health? Is it possible to identify the kinds of working environments that lead to illness or promote recovery? Are there specific strategies, or lifestyle choices, that reduce the likelihood of getting sick?

Previewing the Adaptive Problems

Much of our discussion in this chapter will deal with the topic of psychological stress and its effects on health. Stress is essentially an adaptive reaction we have to events in the world, but prolonged exposure to stressful environments can have a negative long-term impact on health. Our discussion in this chapter will focus on four adaptive problems that are related to stress and to health psychology in general.

First, how and why does the body produce stress, and how is it experienced? Everyone has an intuitive sense of what *stress* is, but the term can actually be defined in a variety of ways. We'll discuss some of the meanings of the term, as well as the various components of the stress response. It's popular to conceive of stress not as a single reaction, such as a sudden release of activating hormones, but rather as an extended response that occurs over time.

Second, how does the body react when the exposure to stressful situations is prolonged? The human body is usually ably equipped to deal with unexpected trauma by activating those systems that are needed to respond to the emergency. But if the threat continues for an extended period of time, the body's defenses can begin to break down. We'll consider some of the physical consequences of prolonged exposure to stress, including the role that stress plays in the immune system.

We live in a time of increased expectation—everyone seems to want something from us, and right now!

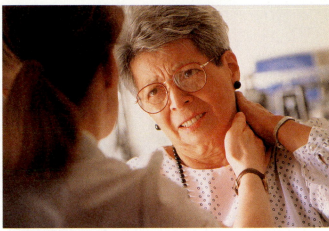

Prolonged exposure to stress can lead to physical as well as psychological problems.

Third, what strategies enable us to reduce and cope with stress? Given that prolonged exposure to stress can have negative long-term consequences, psychologists have developed specific methods of treatment for reducing and controlling stress. A number of techniques are available for managing stress, and we'll consider some of them later in the chapter.

Fourth, what general factors and lifestyle choices promote physical and psychological health? Whether you will remain healthy throughout your life depends importantly on the lifestyle habits you choose. Obviously, if you choose to engage in risky behaviors—such as smoking, failing to get adequate nutrition, or practicing unsafe sex—then you increase your likelihood of illness or death. Health psychologists have joined with other professionals, including physicians, to offer prescriptions for a healthful lifestyle. We'll discuss some of these recommendations along with their foundations in psychological theory.

Experiencing Stress: Stressors and the Stress Response

"Stress" is one of those concepts that is easy to identify but difficult to define precisely. Part of the problem is that the term can be used in a variety of ways. For example, we frequently describe stress as if it was an actual *stimulus* (such as an event or a person) that places a demand on us or threatens our well-being ("That final next week is placing me under a lot of stress"). On the other hand, we're just as likely to describe stress as a physical *response* or reaction that we feel ("I'm really stressed out"). To complicate matters even further, as you'll see later, whether we feel stress depends on how we interpret the situation we're in (Lazarus, 1966, 1991). Consequently, some researchers describe stress as an internal psychological *process* through which external events are interpreted as threatening or demanding.

For our purposes, we'll define **stress** as the physical and psychological reaction that people have to demanding situations, and we'll refer to the demanding or threatening situations that produce stress as **stressors.** This means that the jack-knifed tractor trailer that blocks your speedy route home from school is a stressor, whereas your fuming physical and emotional reaction to such a situation is stress. First, we'll consider some of the physical and psychological characteristics of stress, then we'll examine the external and internal factors that create stress.

stress
People's physical and psychological reactions to demanding situations.

stressors
The demanding or threatening situations that produce stress.

The early stages of the stress response are clearly adaptive because they help organisms initiate a "fight-or-flight" response.

THE STRESS RESPONSE

If you're like most people, you probably think of stress as a bad thing. Certainly when you're "stressed out," you tend to feel lousy, and there's no question that extended exposure to stressful situations can have long-term negative consequences. But it's important to understand that stress is in many ways an adaptive reaction. When you're in a threatening situation, or when someone is placing demands on you, it's important that your body become activated so you can respond to the threat in the most appropriate way. The experience of stress does exactly that, at least initially—it activates you.

Physiological Reactions

In the 1930s, a physician named Hans Selye introduced an influential model of the stress reaction that he called the **general adaptation syndrome (GAS)** (Selye, 1936, 1952, 1974). Selye was convinced that our reaction to stressful situations is general and nonspecific, by which he meant that people are biologically programmed to respond to most threats in the same way. He was initially led to this idea as a medical student, when he was struck by the similarities he saw among his patients. Across wildly different illnesses and injuries, his patients seemed to share a "syndrome of just being sick" that suggested to Selye that the body was reacting to each threatening situation in a very general way (no matter what the illness or the injury). Later, working in the laboratory with rats, he was able to confirm his hypothesis under controlled experimental conditions. Rats subjected to a variety of different kinds of threat—cold, heat, shock, restraint—produced a similar pattern of responses.

Selye's concept of the GAS proposes that the body reacts to threat or demand in three stages, or phases (see Figure 16.1). The first phase, the *alarm reaction*, corresponds to the adaptive fight-or-flight response we've discussed in previous chapters (Cannon, 1932). The body becomes energized, through activation of the sympathetic division of the autonomic nervous system, and hormones are released by the glands of the endocrine system. Heart rate and respiration rate increase, as does blood flow to the muscles; each of these actions helps prepare the body for immediate defensive or evasive action. The alarm reaction enables one to get out of life-threatening jams, but it is extremely intense and cannot be sustained for long periods without serious negative consequences (even death).

If the threat continues but is not serious enough to demand a continued alarm reaction, the body enters a *resistance* phase. During this phase, the body adjusts its physiological reaction in an effort to reduce, or cope with, the still-present threat. Arousal levels remain higher than normal, but the body is capable of replenishing at least some of its resources. During the resistance phase, people are able to func-

general adaptation syndrome (GAS) Hans Selye's model of stress as a general, nonspecific reaction that occurs in three phases: alarm reaction, resistance, and exhaustion.

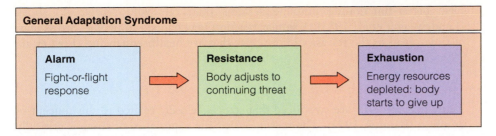

FIGURE 16.1

The General Adaptation Syndrome

Hans Selye proposed that the body reacts to threat or demand in three stages or phases: (1) an *alarm reaction* that corresponds to the fight-or-flight response; (2) a *resistance* phase, during which the body adjusts its reaction in an effort to cope with a threat that is still present; and (3) *exhaustion,* which occurs when the body's energy reserves become so depleted that it starts to give up.

tion reasonably well, but they are particularly susceptible to other stressors in the environment and may begin to suffer from health problems, or what Selye called "diseases of adaptation."

Finally, if the person is unable to find a way to neutralize the threat, the body eventually enters the *exhaustion phase* of the GAS. The body simply cannot continue to maintain a high state of readiness for extended periods of time. Eventually, energy reserves become so taxed and depleted that the body starts to give up. During this period, resistance declines to the point at which the stress reaction becomes more and more maladaptive. Death, or some kind of irreversible damage, becomes a real possibility.

Selye's notion of the GAS has remained influential over the years (Csermely, 1998). But today, many researchers believe that the body's reaction to threat may not be as general and nonspecific as Selye suggested. Different stressors may well produce somewhat different patterns of response in the body (Krantz & Manuck, 1984; Mason, 1975). Moreover, as you'll see momentarily, the stress reaction depends on the cognitive interpretation, or appraisal, of the threatening situation. But the idea that stress is best conceived as a complex process of adaptation is still widely accepted, as is Selye's discovery of the link between stress and health.

Psychological Reactions

Stress is not just a physiological reaction to threat; there are also emotional and behavioral components to the reaction. We will consider the psychological consequences of prolonged exposure to stressful situations later in the chapter, but emotional reactions are an important component of the stress response regardless of when or how long it occurs. *Fear* is a common reaction to threat, as is *anger.* Stressful situations can also lead to feelings of *sadness, dejection,* or even *grief* (Lazarus, 1991). Notice that this diverse set of emotional reactions is another piece of evidence suggesting that the stress reaction is not completely general and nonspecific—people are capable of responding emotionally to different stressors in quite different ways.

The psychological experience of stress does not even have to be negative. Stress can have significant short-term and long-term psychological benefits. For example, one study that examined the psychological characteristics of people who suffered from frequent illness found them to be more understanding (empathetic) of others and more tolerant of uncertainty (Haan, 1977). Stressful situations require people to use their skills and to interact with the environment. As individuals deal with stress they often learn useful things about themselves and about their abilities (Haan, 1993). Moreover, individuals who can successfully resolve a stressful situation gain confidence in their abilities. Laboratory work has even found that rats who are allowed to escape from shock, thereby reducing stress,

CRITICAL THINKING

Just because two things occur together, such as illness and empathy, doesn't mean that one causes the other. How would you determine whether physical illness truly causes increased empathy?

have better-functioning immune systems than rats who receive no shock (Laudenslager et al., 1983). A similar reaction may happen to people: Stress may, at times, lead to the release of hormones that are health-enhancing (Epel et al., 1998).

COGNITIVE APPRAISAL

Many psychologists are convinced that stress is closely related to the concept of emotion (Lazarus, 1993). The reason is that the experience of stress is critically influenced by the way that people perceive or *appraise* their situation. To feel stress, it's necessary to (1) perceive there is some kind of demand or threat present, and (2) come to the conclusion that you may not have adequate resources available to deal with that threat. If you have a black belt in the martial arts, then the sudden appearance of an unarmed thug is not likely to cause much stress—the threat is there, but you have adequate defensive resources should you need to use them.

This idea that the experience of stress depends on the **cognitive appraisal** of the situation is reminiscent of what we know about the experience of emotions. As you may remember from Chapter 11, the same general physiological reaction can lead to different subjective emotional experiences, depending on how one interprets the arousal experienced. The same is true for stress. Identical environmental events can lead to two very different stress reactions, depending on how the event is interpreted. Consider an upcoming exam: everyone in the class receives the same test, but not everyone will feel the same amount of stress. Those people who are prepared for the exam—the people like you who read the chapter—are likely to feel less stress. Again, you are perceiving the threat, but you have adequate resources to deal with it (see Figure 16.2). The converse is also true—dangerous situations must be perceived as dangerous in order for a stress response to be produced. A small child does not necessarily understand that a loaded gun is dangerous and so may feel no stress while handling it.

A great deal of evidence confirms the role of cognitive appraisal in the experience of stress (Tomaka et al., 1997). In one study of elementary school children, urine samples were taken from the children on both normal school days and on days when they were about to take standardized achievement tests. The urine sample measured the amount of cortisol, an important stress hormone, that each child produced (notice that the researchers provided an operational definition of stress in terms of the amount of hormone measured). Not surprisingly, more cortisol was found on test days, suggesting a higher level of stress, but the increase in stress depended on the child's previously recorded overall intelligence score. The children with higher intelligence scores showed less of a stress reaction on test

cognitive appraisal
The idea that in order to feel stress you need to perceive a threat and come to the conclusion that you may not have adequate resources to deal with the threat.

FIGURE 16.2

Cognitive Appraisal
Like emotion, whether an event will create stress depends on how that event is interpreted. A stress reaction is more likely to occur if you feel you have inadequate resources to deal with the potential threat.

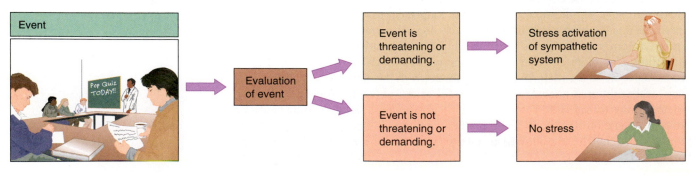

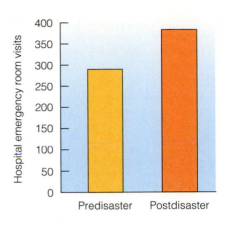
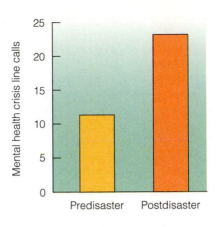
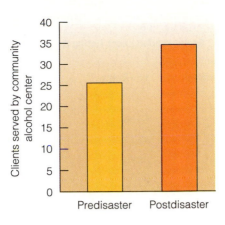

FIGURE 16.3
Reacting to a Natural Disaster
In the seven months following the volcanic eruption of Mount Saint Helens in 1980, the residents of Othello, Washington showed dramatic increases in a variety of stress-related behaviors. The data shown here present the mean monthly hospital emergency room visits, mental health crisis line calls, and number of clients served by a community alcohol center for comparable time periods before and after the disaster. (Data from Adams & Adams, 1984.)

days, presumably because they considered the test to be less of a threat (Tennes & Kreye, 1985).

EXTERNAL SOURCES OF STRESS

The fact that the stress reaction depends on one's appraisal of the situation means that it will never be possible to compile an exhaustive list of life's stressors. We can never predict how everyone will react to an environmental event, even though it may seem clearly stressful to the majority. But it is possible to catalogue external situations, or life events, that induce stress reactions in *most* individuals. We'll consider three major classes of external stressors in this section: significant life events, daily hassles, and other factors in the environment.

Significant Life Events

Certain events in our lives are virtually guaranteed to produce stress. We can all agree that something such as the death of a loved one or getting fired from a job is likely to lead to an extended stress reaction in most people. On a larger scale, catastrophes and natural disasters—such as wars or earthquakes—unquestionably produce stress that is prolonged and widespread. In each of these cases, studies have established clear relationships between such events and subsequent physical and psychological problems (Dohrenwend, 1998; Goldberger & Breznitz, 1993). To cite just one example, in the seven months following the 1980 volcanic eruption of Mount Saint Helens in Washington State, one nearby town reported a more than 30% increase in the number of hospital emergency room visits, compared to a comparable period in the year prior to the eruption (Adams & Adams, 1984) (see Figure 16.3). These visits were *not* for injuries directly caused by the eruption but rather for general health problems that may have been created or enhanced by the experience of stress.

Over the years researchers have tried to compile lists of external life stressors. The best-known example is the Social Readjustment Rating Scale, which was put together by researchers Thomas Holmes and Richard Rahe (1967). Holmes and Rahe interviewed thousands of people who were suffering from health problems and then tried to determine whether there were certain kinds of events that preceded the onset of the health problems. The results are shown in Table 16.1 on page 624. This table lists the various significant life events mentioned by the people who were interviewed, ranked in terms of "life change units" (roughly representing the amount of adjustment that the event caused in the person's life).

There are two interesting things to notice about the results shown in the table. First, most of these life events are associated with some kind of *change* in a person's day-to-day activities. Thus, it may be that the disruption caused by the event is just as important as the event itself in causing the stress reaction. People get stressed, in part, because something happens that requires them to alter their ways or lifestyle. Second, notice that many of the events listed in the table are

TABLE 16.1
Social Readjustment Rating Scale

Rank	Life Event	Point Value	Rank	Life Event	Point Value
1	Death of spouse	100	22	Change in responsibilities at work	29
2	Divorce	73	23	Son or daughter leaving home	29
3	Marital separation	65	24	Trouble with in-laws	29
4	Jail term	63	25	Outstanding personal achievement	28
5	Death of close family member	63	26	Wife begins or stops work	26
6	Personal injury or illness	53	27	Begin or end school	26
7	Marriage	50	28	Change in living conditions	25
8	Fired at work	47	29	Revision of personal habits	24
9	Marital reconciliation	45	30	Trouble with boss	23
10	Retirement	45	31	Change in work hours or conditions	20
11	Change in health of family member	44	32	Change in residence	20
12	Pregnancy	40	33	Change in schools	20
13	Sex difficulties	39	34	Change in recreation	19
14	Gain of new family member	39	35	Change in church activities	19
15	Business readjustment	39	36	Change in social activities	18
16	Change in financial state	38	37	Mortgage or loan less than $10,000	17
17	Death of close friend	37	38	Change in sleeping habits	16
18	Change to different line of work	36	39	Change in number of family get-togethers	15
19	Change in number of arguments with spouse	35	40	Change in eating habits	15
20	Mortgage over $10,000	31	41	Vacation	13
21	Foreclosure of mortgage or loan	30	42	Christmas	12
			43	Minor violations of the law	11

Source: Holmes & Rahe, 1967.

? CRITICAL THINKING

Try listing and ranking the life events that cause, or have caused, you the most stress. How do your rank orderings differ from those listed in Table 16.1?

actually quite *positive*. For example, marriage and retirement make the top ten. Even vacations and Christmas make the list. This is not really too surprising if you think about it, because each is associated with some kind of temporary or long-lasting change or disruption of normal routines.

The results listed in Table 16.1 are over 30 years old, but they continue to be used by researchers as a vehicle for predicting the likelihood of stress. Dozens of research studies have shown that there are significant correlations between the rankings shown in the table and various measures of stress, including physical and psychological problems (Derogatis & Coons, 1993; Miller, 1993). However, not all experts are satisfied with the methods that have been used to compile such lists (Brett et al., 1990; Cleary, 1980; Schroeder & Costa, 1984), and recent revisions of the scale have been introduced to take into account factors such as gender, age, and amount of education (see Miller & Rahe, 1997). Moreover, change by itself will not necessarily lead to stress reactions in all individuals. So you cannot automatically assume that if one of these events happens to you, you will feel stress. Remember, it's how you appraise the event that is really important, along with your assessment of whether you have adequate resources to deal with the life change when it occurs.

Daily Hassles

Psychologists also recognize that it is not just the big events that cause problems. The little things, the daily irritations and hassles of life, also contribute significantly to the experience of stress. Think about how you feel when you're stuck in a long checkout line at the market, when someone's tailgating you on the freeway, or when you're hungry and you've waited a half-hour or more for your order at a restaurant. Some psychologists believe the cumulative effect of these "daily hassles" may actually be more important in creating stress than the kinds of life events that we just considered (Lazarus & Folkman, 1984; Miller, 1993). Kanner and colleagues (1981) have developed what they call a Hassles Scale, and it seems to predict, on average, the likelihood of physical and mental health problems. The more hassles you experience in your daily life, the more likely you'll experience health problems. Included on the scale are such things as concern about one's weight and physical appearance, home maintenance, and worries about misplacing or losing something.

Crowded urban environments can be a source of stress for many people.

Environmental Factors

People are also subjected to stress by their environment. *Noise* is a good example. Think about how difficult it is to study when someone is talking loudly nearby, or how irritated you get when you're roused from sleep by the whirring, clanging sounds of the morning garbage truck. Chronic exposure to noise interferes with everyday activities, and it's been linked with the appearance of such stress-related disorders as ulcers, high blood pressure (Evans, 1997; Nagar & Panady, 1987), and with a general decline in the perceived quality of life (Evans et al., 1995). Apparently, it's not the loudness of the noise that really matters; people are bothered most by noises that are new, intermittent, or unpredictable (Graig, 1993).

Another environmental factor that has been linked to stress is *crowding* (Freeman & Stansfeld, 1998). The larger the number of people who live or work around you, the more likely you'll experience a stress reaction (Weiss & Baum, 1987). Living in a crowded environment, on average, makes people more susceptible to health problems and increases the likelihood of aggression. People who live in high-rise apartment buildings, filled with tenants, are more likely to behave aggressively than those who live in apartment buildings with fewer floors (Bell et al., 1990). The effects of crowding on health and aggression have also been studied extensively in prison settings—again, inmates who live in crowded environments suffer more health problems and are more likely to act aggressively than inmates housed in less crowded environments (Paulus, 1988).

Crowding and noise are two examples of environmental stressors, but there are many others. For example, stress and health have been closely linked to the family social environment, peer interactions, and to conditions in the workplace (Taylor et al., 1997). There is, in fact, an entire specialty in psychology—called **environmental psychology**—devoted to the study of environmental effects such as these on behavior and health. Environmental psychologists have shown particular interest in the psychology of urban living, because living in a large city is likely to expose one to a variety of environmental stressors (particularly noise and crowding). In general, people succumb to stress when they're forced to live in situations in which there is excessive stimulation, movement is constrained, or resources are limited (Graig, 1993).

? CRITICAL THINKING

Suppose you discover a group of people living in a crowded and noisy environment who show little or no stress reaction. How would you interpret your findings?

environmental psychology
A specialty area in psychology devoted to the study of environmental effects on behavior and health, such as the effects of crowding or noise.

Internal Sources of Stress

As you are now aware, no single event or set of living conditions will automatically lead to stress in everyone. Stress is very much in the eye of the beholder, which means we need to know something about the internal characteristics of the individual before we can predict whether he or she will experience stress. Stress arises out of an interaction between individuals and events in the world—neither alone is sufficient to predict the reaction. But what exactly are these internal characteristics? We'll consider three in this section: perceived control, explanatory or attributional style, and personality characteristics.

Perceived Control

To experience stress, you need to perceive a threat or some kind of demand, and you need to feel you lack the resources to deal effectively with that threat. This second part of the appraisal process, the assessment of resources, is influenced by a psychological construct called **perceived control,** which is the amount of influence you feel you have over the situation and your reaction to it. It turns out that perceived control significantly affects the amount of stress you will experience. If you perceive a demand or threat and you think you have no control over the situation, your body is likely to react with arousal, the release of stress hormones, and there will be changes in the activities of your immune system (Brosschot et al., 1998). If the situation continues for a prolonged period, negative physical and psychological consequences are likely to result.

There are many examples, both scientific and anecdotal, that support the link between perceived control and stress. Early in the manned space program, for instance, the Mercury astronauts insisted that manual controls and windows be placed in the orbiting space capsule. Although not necessary from an engineering standpoint, doing so gave the astronauts a "sense of control" over their environment, which reduced their stress. In laboratory studies, animals who are exposed to shocks that they can turn off by turning a wheel are less likely to develop ulcers than animals who receive the same amount of shock but cannot control it (Weiss, 1977).

Explanatory Style

The results of the cognitive appraisal process, and therefore susceptibility to stress, are also influenced by one's general style of thinking. At several points in the text we've discussed the importance of the process of *attribution*, which refers to how we arrive at conclusions about cause and effect. People offer different kinds of explanations for the positive and negative events that occur in their world. For example, someone with an *internal, stable,* and *global* explanatory style is likely to attribute a negative event to some long-lasting personal inadequacy that applies in lots of situations: "My spouse left me because I'm witless; I've always been witless, and I can never hope to convince anyone otherwise."

We've seen elsewhere that a person's explanatory style contributes to psychological disorders such as depression (see Chapter 14). Perhaps not surprisingly, explanatory style has also been linked to physical health and susceptibility to stress. People who consistently make internal, stable, and global attributions for negative events have been found to suffer from increased stress-related health problems in mid-life as well as later in life (Kamen-Siegel et al., 1991; Peterson et al., 1988). In one particularly intriguing study, Peterson and Seligman (1987) analyzed the explanatory styles of 94 members of the Baseball Hall of Fame who had played at some point between 1900 and 1950. Many of these players were dead at the time of the study, so the researchers had to glean the players' explanatory styles from stories and quotations in old newspapers. The players with the negative explanatory styles were found, on average, to have lived shorter lives.

perceived control
The amount of influence you feel you have over a situation and your reaction to it.

Type A personalities seem to be immersed in a sea of perpetual stress, and they're significantly more likely to develop coronary heart problems than Type B personalities.

Personality Characteristics

Both perceived control and explanatory style are related more generally to personality. Previously, we defined *personality* as the set of unique psychological characteristics that differentiate us from others and lead us to act consistently across situations. Explanatory style may be linked to a personality characteristic such as *optimism*—the belief that good things will happen—which some psychologists have argued is a relatively enduring trait that changes little over a lifetime (Scheier & Carver, 1993). "Optimism scales" have been developed and used to look for a connection between personality and health. In one study, optimism was assessed on the day before a group of men underwent coronary bypass surgery. The optimists reacted physiologically to the surgery in ways that lowered the risk of heart attack; they also recovered more quickly after the surgery (Scheier et al., 1989); more recent studies have demonstrated links between optimism and improved functioning of the immune system (Segerstrom et al., 1998). An optimistic view of life therefore appears to reduce stress and its associated health risks.

The most widely recognized personality characteristics that have been linked to stress-related health disorders, particularly coronary heart disease, are the famous **Type A** and **Type B** behavior patterns. You're familiar with the Type A personality: hard driving, ambitious, easily annoyed, and impatient. Those with a Type A personality seem to be immersed in a sea of perpetual self-imposed stress; they're too busy to notice or enjoy the things around them because they're engaged in a relentless pursuit of success. Type B personality types are essentially people who lack the Type A attributes—they put themselves under less pressure and appear more relaxed.

The connection between Type A behavior patterns and heart disease was first noted by cardiologists Meyer Friedman and Ray Rosenman (1974). Friedman and Rosenman were interested in explaining why only some people with known risk factors for heart disease—such as smoking, obesity, inactivity, and so on—actually develop heart problems. People can appear to have identical risk profiles but end up healthy in one instance and disease-prone in another. Friedman and Rosenman proposed that the solution lies in the connection between personality and stress. People who are psychologically prone to stress—Type A personalities—will prove more susceptible to diseases of the heart.

Type A
An enduring pattern of behavior linked to stress-related health disorders; it is characterized by being hard-driving, ambitious, easily annoyed, and impatient.

Type B
People who lack the Type A traits—they put themselves under less pressure and appear more relaxed.

CONCEPT SUMMARY
Sources of Stress

External

Source	Description
Significant life events	Major life events associated with a change in a person's day-to-day activities; they can be positive (e.g., getting married) or negative (e.g., death of a loved one).
Daily hassles	Daily irritations and hassles of life, such as getting stuck in traffic
Environmental factors	Stressors present in a person's environment, such as noise and crowding

Internal

Source	Description
Perceived control	The amount of influence you feel you have over a situation. A sense of control often lessens the stress one feels in a situation.
Explanatory style	One's general style of thinking about and explaining events. People who make internal, stable, and global attributions for negative events are more likely to suffer from stress-related health problems.
Personality characteristics	*Optimism* (the belief that good things will happen) generally reduces stress. A *Type A* behavior pattern (hard-driving, ambitious, easily annoyed, impatient) is associated with elevated stress and heart problems.

Over the past several decades, a number of very ambitious studies have been conducted to explore the health consequences of Type A behavior patterns. Thousands of individuals have participated in these studies, and they have been studied over long periods of time. Generally, the results have supported the proposals of Friedman and Rosenman: People who are classified as Type A personality types are at least twice as likely to develop coronary heart problems as Type B personality types (Lyness, 1993). But not all studies have found this result, and there have even been studies showing the opposite pattern (Ragland & Brand, 1988).

Recent work suggests that a more complete answer may lie in further analyzing the Type A behavior pattern or personality, which turns out to be quite complex. To be classified as a Type A personality requires that a person be rated on a number of dimensions—competitiveness, ambition, hostility, and so on—and not all of these attributes are equally important. Some researchers believe it is hostility, anger, or the expression of anger that is most responsible for producing subsequent coronary artery disease (Adler & Matthews, 1994). Others have stressed the need to consider cultural factors—some societies encourage competition and others do not (Thoresen & Powell, 1992). There is probably also an interaction between personality and explanatory style—that is, whether you attribute consequences to internal or external factors (Kirkcaldy et al., 1999). At this point, it's widely believed that personality characteristics do affect susceptibility to stress and disease (Friedman et al., 1994), but we can't just draw a sharp line between Type A and Type B personality types and hope to explain all the data.

TEST YOURSELF 16.1

Check your knowledge about the stress response by answering each of the following questions. (You will find the answers in the Appendix.)

1. Hans Selye's concept of the general adaptation syndrome (GAS) proposes that the body reacts to stress in three phases. Which of the following shows the correct sequence of these phases?

    a. Resistance, alarm, exhaustion
    b. Exhaustion, resistance, alarm

    c. Alarm, resistance, exhaustion

    d. Exhaustion, alarm, resistance

2. The experience of stress is related to the experience of emotion in which of the following ways?

    a. The experience of stress, like emotion, is an inevitable reaction to threat.

    b. The experience of stress, like emotion, is accompanied by very distinctive facial expressions.

    c. The experience of stress, like emotion, depends on the appraisal of the event rather than on the event itself.

    d. The experience of different kinds of stress, like emotion, leads to highly specific kinds of body reactions.

3. According to the Social Readjustment Rating Scale which of the following events is most likely to cause stress-related health problems?

    a. Marriage

    b. Death of a close friend

    c. Sex difficulties

    d. Trouble with your boss

4. Which of the following internal characteristics is least likely to be associated with stress-related health problems?

    a. Low levels of perceived control

    b. Type A behavior pattern

    c. An optimistic outlook

    d. Internal, stable, and global attributions

Reacting to Prolonged Stress: Physical and Psychological Effects

There is a definite connection between prolonged exposure to stress and physical and psychological health. Stress is an adaptive reaction to threat—it helps us to fight or flee. But when it is prolonged, when we're not able to reduce or eliminate the perceived threat, the mind and body start to break down. If the stress reaction is extreme enough, the breakdown can be sudden and may even result in death; in most cases, however, the effects are gradual and reveal themselves slowly through a growing list of physical and psychological problems. In this section of the chapter, we'll consider the nature of these breakdowns and how and why they occur.

LEARNING GOALS

1. Describe the physical consequences of prolonged stress, including the link between stress and the immune system.

2. Describe the psychological consequences of prolonged stress, including posttraumatic stress disorder and burnout.

PHYSICAL CONSEQUENCES OF STRESS

Stress has been implicated in a wide variety of health problems. Besides ulcers and heart disease, it has been linked to everything from the common cold to chronic back pain, multiple sclerosis, and even cancer. Most of the scientific evidence is correlational, which means a statistical relationship has been found between the incidence of a health problem such as heart disease and some measurement of stress. Large numbers of people are interviewed, and health histories as well as stress levels are measured. The net result is that we can predict whether someone, on average, will have an increased chance of developing a particular kind of health problem by knowing the amount of stress they experience on a regular basis. But this does not tell us whether a causal relationship exists between stress and illness. To determine that, we must turn to experimental research.

    It's difficult to conduct experimental research on the relationship between stress and health for obvious ethical reasons. Ethically, we can't randomly divide

People who are subjected to chronic stress, because of environmental conditions, can show weakened immune system functioning.

people into groups, subject some of them to high levels of stress, and then monitor the later consequences of that manipulation on health. But experimental studies have been conducted on groups of people who have been previously identified as having either a high or low level of stress in their lives. In one study (Cohen et al., 1993), high- and low-stress people were given nasal drops that either contained or did not contain a common cold virus. It was a double-blind study, so neither the participants nor the researchers were aware during the course of the study who was getting the actual virus and who was not. Afterward, when the subject assignments were "decoded," it was found that the high-stress people who received the virus were the ones most likely to show cold symptoms. Living a stressful life apparently lowers one's ability to fight off disease.

The Immune Response

To understand *why* stress increases susceptibility to illness, you need to understand something about the human immune system. The human body has a complex defense system, called the *immune system*, that is constantly on the lookout for foreign substances, such as viruses or bacteria. The primary weapons of the immune system are **lymphocytes,** which are specialized white blood cells that have the job of attacking and destroying most of these foreign invaders. Stress can lower the immune response by either decreasing the number of lymphocytes in the bloodstream or by somehow suppressing the response of the lymphocytes to foreign substances that have invaded the body (see Gonzalez-Quijano, 1998). The underlying mechanisms that produce these changes have not been completely determined, although the prolonged release of stress hormones into the bloodstream probably plays a significant role (Stein & Miller, 1993).

Several investigations have shown that stressful life events directly affect the immune response. Medical students, on average, have fewer lymphocytes in their blood during a period of final exams compared to levels found before exams (Kiecolt-Glaser et al., 1984); they are also more likely to get sick during exams. People who have recently had a spouse or loved one die also show a suppressed immune response. One investigative team tracked the immune response in men married to women with advanced breast cancer. Samples of the men's blood were taken during a period of months preceding and following their wife's death. On average, the existing lymphocytes in blood samples drawn *after* the wives had died showed a weaker response to foreign substances (Schleifer et al., 1983).

The fact that stress weakens the immune system has led researchers to wonder about the effects of stress on more chronic illnesses, such as cancer. In the laboratory it's been shown that stress can increase the growth rate of cancerous tumors in rats, although the particular type of tumor apparently matters (Justice, 1985). There have also been reports that cancer patients who are optimistic, or who are given therapy to help reduce anxiety and depression, survive longer than patients who are hopeless or depressed (Andersen, 1992; Spiegel et al., 1989). Stress may affect not only the body's ability to fight cancer but also the likelihood that cancer cells will form in the first place (Schneiderman et al., 1992).

At present, however, most researchers remain cautious about the link between psychology, the immune system, and cancer (Cohen & Herbert, 1996). Not all studies have found associations between psychological factors and cancer (Adler & Matthews, 1994), and the fact that data linking cancer to stress have come pri-

lymphocytes
Specialized white blood cells that have the job of attacking foreign substances, such as viruses and bacteria.

Inside the Problem   Adaptation and the Immune Response

It's easy to see the adaptive value of the basic stress response. When faced with a threat, such as the sudden appearance of a stranger with a gun, we need to mobilize and direct our resources in preparation for the fight-or-flight response. The brain directs the release of hormones that energize the body—heart and respiration rates increase, blood begins to flow to the muscles, the pupils in the eyes even dilate for better distance vision. In response to the threat, we prepare ourselves for immediate defensive or evasive action. But what about the link between stress and the immune response? You've seen that one of the by-products of stress is *suppression* of the immune response. If prolonged, this suppression can lead to long-lasting negative health consequences. How, then, can suppression of the immune response be considered adaptive?

We can answer this question, in part, by considering the many components of the overall immune response. As you know, the immune system is the body's defense system; it defends us not only against disease but also against injury. If the body is cut or damaged in some way, part of the immune response is to promote swelling or inflammation around the injured site. Swelling helps prevent the spread of disease-producing organisms and is an important part of the tissue repair process. But this healing process takes energy resources from the body. In a time of threat, it's probably better that these resources be directed toward the muscles. When you have a desperate need to fight or flee, it may well be adaptive to delay the healing process by temporarily suppressing the immune response (Maier et al., 1994).

Another component of the immune response, called the *acute response phase,* produces general defensive reactions that affect the entire body. For example, when there is a widespread infection in the body, part of the acute response phase is the production of fever. Fever is an adaptive part of the immune response because the increased temperature in the body slows the spread of foreign substances, accelerates healing, and increases the rate at which immune cells are produced. But fever dramatically taxes the body's resources: a 1-degree increase in body temperature may require as much as a 7 to 13% increase in energy production. So when the body is faced with a threat, one demanding a fight-or-flight reaction, it's actually adaptive to delay or suppress the immune response.

It turns out the body's immune response can also be affected by conditioning experiences of the type that we discussed in Chapter 7. Signals that predict the appearance of a significant threat lead not only to stress-related arousal but also to conditioned suppression of the immune response. A previously neutral stimulus can acquire the properties of an immunosuppressant (something that suppresses the immune system) if it's been paired in time with an activity that leads to immune suppression (Ader & Cohen, 1975). This finding has some potentially important practical applications. In certain medical procedures, such as organ transplants, it is useful to suppress the immune system temporarily to delay organ rejection. But immunosuppressant drugs are usually quite toxic to the body, so it might be possible to use conditioned immunosuppressants, which are not naturally toxic, to reduce the immune response in a safer way (Grochowitz et al., 1991).

Conditioning of the immune response has also proven relevant to cancer treatments such as chemotherapy. Cancer patients undergo chemotherapy to inhibit the rapid replication and spread of cancer cells. But chemotherapy also produces a suppression of the immune system. Researchers have discovered that people who receive these drugs sometimes develop conditioned immune suppression responses to the place where the chemotherapy is administered. Simply arriving at the hospital has been found to suppress the immune system, presumably because an association has formed between the hospital and receiving the chemotherapy drugs (Bøvjberg et al., 1990).

---

marily from correlational studies means that it is difficult to draw conclusions about cause and effect. For example, it's possible that "stressful" people, on average, have a greater risk of acquiring cancer because they tend to engage in unhealthful behaviors—such as smoking—as a way of dealing with the stress. It may also be the case that people who are optimistic about their survival from cancer tend to comply more with the recommendations of their doctors. So, although there may be a statistical association between stress and cancer, that does not necessarily mean that stress is causing cancer by compromising the functioning of the immune system. (For more on the immune system and factors that affect its functioning, see the accompanying feature, "Inside the Problem.")

Cardiovascular Disease

Health psychologists have also intensively studied the well-documented relationship between stress and cardiovascular disease (problems connected with the heart and blood vessels). We discussed the connection between Type A behavior and heart problems earlier, but we left the mechanisms through which stress undermines cardiovascular health unspecified. The two most important risk factors in heart disease are (1) high cholesterol levels in the blood and (2) high blood pressure. Prolonged exposure to stress increases exposure to both of these risk factors.

Increased blood pressure, a natural by-product of the stress response, is generally helpful over the short term (as part of the fight-or-flight response). But if the elevated pressure continues, it causes wear and tear on the blood vessels in the body, which can lead to both cardiovascular disease and kidney problems. Stress can also directly affect the level of cholesterol in the blood. For example, when college students are anticipating an upcoming exam, samples of their blood show higher levels of cholesterol (Van Doornen & Van Blokland, 1987). People who display Type A behavior patterns have also been found, on average, to have higher levels of blood cholesterol. One possibility is that when people sense threat, the body directs the blood flow to the muscles and away from internal organs, such as the liver, that remove fat and cholesterol from the blood.

PSYCHOLOGICAL CONSEQUENCES OF STRESS

Think about how you feel when you're "stressed out." That recurring cold or that sour stomach seems like it'll never go away. But the mental and emotional changes can be just as profound. You feel anxious, out of control, emotionally drained, and, after a while, possibly even sad and depressed. Stress is not a pleasant experience, and if the stress reaction is intense enough, or if it continues long enough, serious psychological problems can result.

Most psychologists are convinced that stressful life events play a significant role in the onset of many psychological disorders. If you interview people who have suffered from major depression or a bipolar disorder, you will find that most have experienced some kind of major stressor just before or early into the depressive episode—they got fired from their job, they moved to a new town, they're mired in a nasty divorce, and so on (Barlow & Durand, 1999). Stress has also been implicated in the onset of schizophrenia. Several studies have shown that stressful life events tend to immediately precede schizophrenic episodes (Brown & Birley, 1968; Ventura et al., 1989).

But importantly, not all people who experience intense stress go on to develop serious psychological problems. In fact, the *majority* of people who experience a traumatic life stressor do not subsequently develop psychological disorders. Psychologists assume that the person must have some kind of vulnerability, perhaps rooted in the genetic code, before stress will lead to an extreme disorder, such as major depression or schizophrenia. Similar arguments apply to anxiety disorders, such as posttraumatic stress disorder, which we discuss briefly below.

Posttraumatic Stress Disorder

You're familiar with the scenario: Soldier returns home from war, shell shocked, suffering from sleepless nights and flashbacks of traumatic episodes in battle. Hollywood has exploited this image, to the point where the "unstable Vietnam vet" has become an unfortunate part of our collective sense of the Vietnam experience. In reality, the vast majority of soldiers who returned from Vietnam or the Gulf War have experienced no long-term psychological problems. At the same time, even though the percentages are small, psychologists do recognize that exposure to extreme stress can produce a serious psychological condition known as **posttraumatic stress disorder.** This disorder is not limited to battle veterans; it can occur in any individual who has undergone a traumatic episode, such as a physical attack, rape, or a natural disaster (Foa & Riggs, 1995).

In the DSM-IV, posttraumatic stress disorder is classified as an anxiety disorder, and the diagnosis is made if the following three types of symptoms occur for a period lasting longer than one month:

1. *Flashbacks.* When a flashback occurs, the person relives the traumatic event in some way. These flashbacks can take the form of persistent thoughts or images of the traumatic scene, and they can even involve vivid hallucinations;

? CRITICAL THINKING

How might the onset of a psychological disorder, such as depression, be an adaptive reaction to prolonged stress?

---

posttraumatic stress disorder

A trauma-based anxiety disorder characterized by flashbacks, avoidance of stimuli associated with the traumatic event, and chronic arousal symptoms.

Traumatic events, such as the shooting at Columbine High School in 1999, can lead to disabling psychological conditions.

the affected person seems at times to be reexperiencing the event—fighting the battle anew or fending off the attacker.

2. *Avoidance of stimuli associated with the trauma.* People with posttraumatic stress disorder actively try to avoid anything that reminds them of the event. This avoidance behavior can lead to significant disruptions in normal social functioning, as the affected person turns away from friends and loved ones who in some way remind them of the trauma.

3. *Chronic arousal symptoms.* These symptoms can include sleep problems, irritability or outbursts of anger, and difficulties in concentrating.

Obviously, posttraumatic stress disorder is a disabling condition, not only for the individuals who are directly affected but also for family and friends (Sims & Sims, 1998). The cause of the disorder is clear—traumatic stress—but the reason that only some people who experience trauma develop posttraumatic stress disorder remains a mystery. There is evidence that the intensity of the trauma may be important. For example, Vietnam veterans who were in heavy combat were significantly more likely to develop posttraumatic stress disorder than those serving in noncombat roles (Goldberg et al., 1990). But, once again, this does not explain why the disorder remains relatively rare even among people who have experienced extreme trauma. As is the case for most psychological disorders, the likelihood that posttraumatic stress disorder will develop undoubtedly depends on a complex mix of biological and environmental factors (Craske, 1999).

Burnout

Stress does not need to be extreme to produce unpleasant psychological consequences. In the 1970s, the term *burnout* was introduced by psychologists to describe a syndrome that develops in certain people who are exposed to stressful situations that are demanding but not necessarily traumatic (Freudenberger, 1974; Maslach, 1976). Although the term **burnout** has become a household word, to psychologists it refers to "a state of physical, emotional, and mental exhaustion caused by long-term involvement in emotionally demanding situations" (Pines & Aronson, 1988). When burnout occurs, affected individuals essentially lose their spirit—they become emotionally drained, they feel used up, and they lose their sense of personal accomplishment (Maslach & Jackson, 1981).

As with posttraumatic stress disorder, stress is a necessary but not a sufficient condition for producing burnout. Not everyone who has a demanding and

burnout
A state of physical, emotional, and mental exhaustion created by long-term involvement in an emotionally demanding situation.

CONCEPT SUMMARY
Consequences of Stress

Physical

Stress effects	Nature of the Effect
Immune response	Stressful events directly affect the immune response, lowering the number of disease-fighting *lymphocytes*. Some believe that stress also has an effect on more chronic illnesses, such as cancer.
Cardiovascular disease	Increased blood pressure from prolonged stress causes wear and tear on blood vessels, which can lead to cardiovascular disease.

Psychological

Stress leads to	Nature of the Effect
Posttraumatic stress disorder	A serious psychological condition that can result from exposure to extreme stress. Classified as an anxiety disorder, it's characterized by flashbacks, avoidance of trauma-associated stimuli, and chronic arousal symptoms.
Burnout	A state of physical, emotional, and mental exhaustion caused by long-term involvement in emotionally demanding situations. It seems to occur in idealistic individuals who are highly motivated, perhaps due to a loss of control or a loss of meaning in life.

stressful job becomes burned out. Burnout seems to occur only in idealistic individuals—people who have entered their careers with a high sense of motivation and commitment. In the words of psychologist Ayala Pines (1993), "You cannot burn out unless you were 'on fire' initially." Because burnout tends to occur only in highly motivated individuals, it can have a high cost for organizations as well as for the individual. People who suffer from burnout lose their edge on the job—they become disillusioned with their work, are frequently absent from the job, and usually are at increased risk for a host of physical problems.

Why does burnout occur? The underlying cause may well be related to a loss of meaning in life (Pines, 1993) or to a loss of control in the workplace (McKnight & Glass, 1995). People who are subject to burnout are usually those who think of their work as a kind of "calling." They use success on the job as a way of validating their existence. They identify so closely with their work that when failure happens, their entire lives lose meaning. Failure is much more likely when the job is demanding and taxes the individual's resources, which is probably the reason why stress is typically associated with the syndrome. If the overall stress levels can be reduced, perhaps by providing a better support system within the work environment, burnout is much less likely to occur (Maslach, 1982; Pines & Aronson, 1988).

TEST YOURSELF 16.2

Check your knowledge about reacting to stress by deciding whether each of the following statements is true or false. (You will find the answers in the Appendix.)

1. Lymphocytes are the primary weapons of the human immune system. *True or False?*

2. Much of the data linking cancer and stress have come correlational studies; researchers are unable, therefore, to draw firm conclusions about cause and effect. *True or False?*

3. Stress is known to affect blood pressure, but no links have been established between stress and cholesterol levels. *True or False?*

4. Posttraumatic stress disorder is a common reaction to the experiencing of a traumatic event. *True or False?*

5. Burnout is more likely to occur in people who use success on the job as a way of giving life meaning. *True or False?*

Reducing and Coping with Stress: Techniques of Stress Management

Because stress is associated with so many physical and psychological problems, it is obviously in our best interest to develop techniques for reducing stress. Unfortunately, stressors are often outside of our direct control—you can't prevent the tornado that skirts the neighborhood trailer park, or the death of a valued friend from accident or illness. But techniques are available for coping with stressors when they're present. **Coping** is a term that psychologists use to describe efforts to manage conditions of threat or demand that tax one's resources (Lazarus, 1993).

One possibility is that you can attempt to control the stressor directly in some way, thereby reducing its ability to induce stress. Or, you can focus your attention on reducing the emotional reaction that the stressor produces. In this section, we'll consider three coping strategies for controlling or reducing stress: (1) learning relaxation techniques, (2) forming effective social support systems, and (3) learning to reappraise the environment in a less threatening way.

LEARNING GOALS

1. Discuss how relaxation techniques can be used to reduce stress.

2. Discuss the positive and negative effects of social support.

3. Explain how stress can be managed through cognitive reappraisal of the stressful situation.

RELAXATION TECHNIQUES

By definition, the stress response is incompatible with relaxation. You cannot be prepared to fight or flee if your body is calm, relaxed, and free from arousal-inducing stress hormones. Studies have shown that high-stress individuals can reduce the physically threatening components of the stress reaction—such as high blood pressure—by simply practicing a regimen of relaxation techniques. You may remember that we discussed in Chapter 15 how relaxation can be used effectively in the treatment of anxiety disorders; similar relaxation techniques have proven effective in reducing long-term stress reactions (Stoyva & Carlson, 1993).

coping
Efforts to manage or master conditions of threat or demand that tax one's resources.

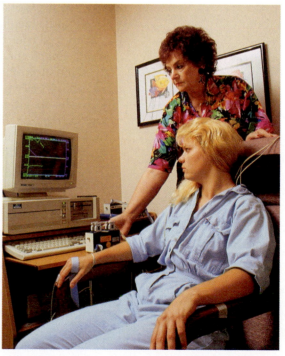

There are a variety of ways to reduce and cope with stress, including social support and biofeedback.

Several types of relaxation procedures are available to help manage stress. In *progressive muscle relaxation*, you're taught to concentrate on specific muscle groups in the body, to note whether there is any tension, and then to try to relax those specific groups (Jacobson, 1938). Often in progressive relaxation, you learn to address muscle groups in sequence. For example, you might begin with the muscle groups in the neck, move to the shoulders, and so on, first tensing and then relaxing each group. In this way you learn to pay attention to how muscles in your body feel when tense or relaxed. Progressive relaxation has been used successfully to treat a variety of stress-related health problems, everything from tension headaches (Myers et al., 1998) to posttraumatic stress syndrome (Frueh et al., 1997). In a somewhat different technique, called *autogenic relaxation*, you're taught to focus on directing blood flow toward tense muscle groups, "warming" and relaxing each group (Linden, 1990); once again, autogenic relaxation has proven beneficial in treating stress-related conditions (Friedlander et al., 1997).

Relaxation techniques such as these are sometimes accompanied by *meditation* training. We discussed some of the benefits of meditation in Chapter 6. Meditation essentially involves learning how to relax, using techniques similar to progressive muscle relaxation. But you're also taught some time-tested mental exercises, such as repeating a string of words or sounds over and over again in your head. The mental repetition focuses awareness and helps prevent potentially distracting or stress-producing thoughts from interfering with the relaxation response. (For instance, if you're concentrating on repeating the phrase "I'm at one with the universe," you cannot simultaneously be worrying about whether the relaxation technique is working.) Daily meditation sessions clearly help people deal with stress-related arousal (Eppley et al., 1989; MacLean et al., 1997).

Biofeedback

The goal of relaxation training is to lower components of the stress response, such as blood pressure, heart rate, and muscle tension. For example, if stress-related headaches are caused by tension in the muscles of the head and scalp, then people should be able to reduce or eliminate the pain by relaxing these specific muscle groups. Some researchers have suggested that it helps to give people feedback—*bio*feedback—about the effectiveness of their relaxation efforts. With biofeedback, monitoring equipment provides a continuous reading of your physiological state. In the case of tension headaches, the feedback would indicate the tension levels in the muscles of the head; for blood pressure or heart rate, you would be able to read your blood pressure and heart rate directly from appropriate monitoring equipment.

Not surprisingly, biofeedback works. When people are given information about how well their relaxation efforts are succeeding, compared with control subjects who are given no feedback, it's clearly easier to control the relevant physiological response (Blanchard, 1992). But researchers are still debating exactly *why* biofeedback produces its beneficial effects. One possibility is that it may simply be the feeling of *control* that leads to reductions in the stress response.

For instance, in one study on tension headaches, three groups of subjects were given a feedback signal that they were led to believe indicated a successful lowering of muscle tension in their foreheads. Actually, unknown to the subjects, the signal had three different meanings: In one group, it appeared only when subjects successfully *increased* the amount of tension in their foreheads; in a second group, the signal appeared whenever the amount of tension decreased; in a third group, it appeared when tension levels remained the same. Remarkably, despite the misleading feedback in two of the groups, everyone reported headache improvement (see Figure 16.4). Apparently, feeling that you have some control over your body can be sufficient to lower stress-induced pain (Andrasik & Holroyd, 1980). This finding does not mean that biofeedback is an ineffective way to treat stress. Whether you will experience a stress response depends on a cognitive appraisal of

biofeedback
Specific physiological feedback that people are given about the effectiveness of their relaxation efforts.

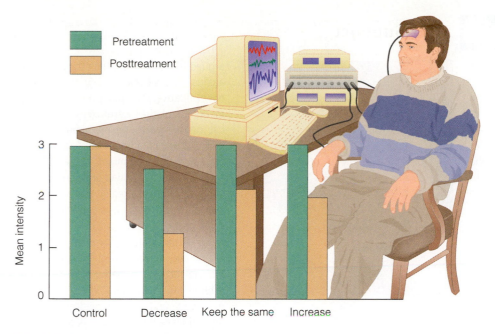

FIGURE 16.4

Biofeedback, Perceived Control, and Stress
In the study by Andrasik and Holroyd (1980), subjects in three groups were led to believe that they could lower the amount of muscle tension in their foreheads through biofeedback. Actually, the subjects learned to increase, decrease, or keep the tension levels the same. Yet all three groups showed significant improvement in headache symptoms, irrespective of condition. Apparently, the mere fact that the subjects believed they were lowering the tension levels was sufficient to produce improvement. Also shown are the data for control subjects who received no biofeedback. (Data from Andrasik & Holroyd, 1980.)

your resources. If you feel you have the ability to control the threat or demand, even if that control is illusory, you're less likely to experience stress.

SOCIAL SUPPORT

Although it may seem like a cliché, having a good friend or loved one to lean on during a time of stress really does matter. Psychologists use the term **social support** to refer to the resources we receive from other people or groups, often in the form of comfort, caring, or help. There is a great deal of evidence to suggest that social support can improve one's psychological and physical health (Cohen & Wills, 1985). People with well-established social support systems are less likely to suffer a second heart attack (Case et al., 1992), are more likely to survive life-threatening cancer (Colon et al., 1991), and are less likely to consider suicide if they're infected with HIV (Schneider et al., 1991). Other studies have established that social support plays a role in lowering the likelihood of depression and in speeding recovery (McLeod et al., 1992).

Social support probably helps reduce stress for many reasons (Sarason, et al., 1994). Once again, the evidence tends to be correlational (researchers cannot manipulate the amount of support someone receives, for ethical reasons), so firm cause-and-effect relationships have proven difficult to establish. One possibility is that social contacts help people maintain a healthful lifestyle. Friends and family push you out the door for your morning jog, force you to take your medications, or encourage you to visit the doctor regularly. Family and friends also bolster your confidence in times of stress, so you're more likely to feel that you have the necessary resources to cope with the demand. In a time of loss, such as immediately after the death of a spouse, social support lowers the likelihood that a grieving person will engage in unhealthful behaviors, such as drinking (Jennison, 1992).

 CRITICAL THINKING

Do you think it's possible that people who are healthier tend to get more social support than those who are sick? Might this fact account for the correlation?

social support
The resources that individuals receive from other people or groups, often in the form of comfort, caring, or help.

Inside the Problem   Pet Support

Having a loved one or a good friend to talk to about your problems makes a difference, and that friend doesn't even need to be human. The companionship of pets—dogs, cats, even birds—has repeatedly been found to be an effective form of social support. Heart attack victims who own pets, for example, are more likely to survive the first year after the attack than are non-pet owners. Correlational studies among the elderly have found that pet ownership is inversely related to the severity of psychological problems: People who are attached to their pets are less likely to show the symptoms of depression (Garrity et al., 1989). Ownership of a dog, in particular, is an excellent predictor of whether or not an elderly person will feel the need to visit a doctor (Siegel, 1990).

There's some evidence to suggest that having a pet around may even be a more effective buffer against stress than having a human companion. In an experiment conducted by Karen Allen and her colleagues (1991), female dog owners agreed to have several physiological reactions monitored while they tried to solve relatively difficult math problems. Prior to starting the task, the women were randomly divided into three groups. In one group, the women were allowed to have their dog with them in the room while completing the math task. In a second group, no dogs were allowed but each woman was allowed the presence of a close human friend. In the third group, no social support was present during the testing.

A variety of physiological reactions were measured, including heart rate and blood pressure. Not surprisingly, solving difficult math problems led directly to stress-related arousal—heart rate increased, as did blood pressure. But the amount of reactivity depended on the group: The women who were allowed to have their dog with them showed the lowest arousal effects compared to the women in the other two groups (see Figure 16.5). The presence of the pet apparently acted as an effective buffer against stress. The surprise finding of the study was that having a close human friend sit nearby while solving the math

Pets serve as effective buffers against stress for many individuals.

problems actually led to the highest relative stress reaction.

Does this mean that pets are more therapeutic than friends or loved ones? For some people in some situations, the answer may well be "Yes." Allen and her colleagues argued that pets are often effective buffers against stress because they are essentially nonevaluative. Pets don't make value judgments about their caretakers. Your dog or cat doesn't care one bit about how well you're doing on some math task, but your close human friend might. A friend's expectations can place added pressure on you as you perform an already stressful task. A woman who participated in the study by Allen and colleagues put it this way: "Pets never withhold their love, they never get angry and leave, and they never go out looking for new owners." Another woman offered the following: "Whereas husbands may come and go, and children may grow up and leave home, a 'dog is forever.'" The opinions of these women may not be shared by everyone, nor do you need to hold these strong views to appreciate the value of pet companionship. The data simply indicate that pets can be an important part of your social network and as such can help you cope with stress.

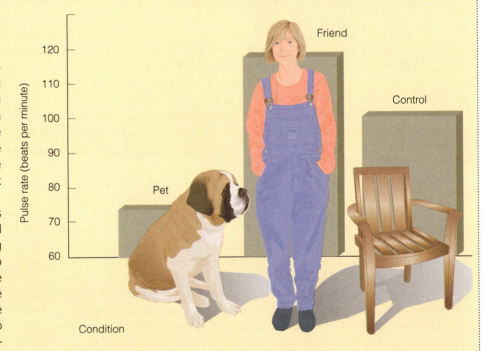

FIGURE 16.5
Pets as Stress Moderators
In the study by Allen and colleagues (1991), having a pet present during a stressful task significantly lowered the stress reaction, measured here in terms of pulse rate, compared to a condition in which a friend was present or a control condition in which neither a friend nor a pet was present. (Data from Allen et al., 1991.)

It's also the case that simply having someone to talk things over with can help you cope with stress. James Pennebaker (1990) has conducted a number of studies in which college students were encouraged to talk or write about upsetting events in their lives (everything from a divorce in the family to fears about the future). When compared to "control" students, who were asked to talk or write about trivial things, the students who opened up showed improved immune functioning and were less likely to visit the college health center over the next several months. Pennebaker has found similar benefits for people who lived through natural disasters (such as earthquakes) or were part of the Holocaust. Opening up, talking about things, and confiding in others really seemed to help these people cope (Pennebaker, 1997).

On the other hand, psychologists recognize that social support can have a negative side as well. For example, if you've come to depend on another for support and that support is no longer delivered, your ability to cope can be compromised. Social support can also reduce self-reliance in some people, which may produce psychological distress and impair their ability to cope. It's been found that whether people respond favorably to social support and the receipt of aid, or consider it to be a meddling nuisance, depends to some extent on how much control they feel they have over their own actions and the outcomes of their actions (Hobfoll et al., 1991). (For a discussion of how pets can act as a form of positive social support see the accompanying feature, "Inside the Problem.")

REAPPRAISING THE SITUATION

When thinking about how to cope with stress, it's important to remember that the origin of the stress reaction is essentially psychological. In most instances, it is not the sudden life event or the daily hassle that leads us to experience stress—it's our *interpretation* of the event that really matters. Even the death of a spouse or the occurrence of a natural disaster, cruel as it may seem, will create significant stress only if the event is appraised in a negative way. Imagine if your spouse were suffering from an incurable disease, one that produced extreme and persistent pain. Under these conditions, death could be seen as a kind of blessing.

Remember, too, that many instances of stress are caused by the little things, the daily hassles of life. Getting stuck in traffic, or in the wrong line at the supermarket, makes us feel stressed only because we have a tendency to "catastrophize" the situation: "This is absolutely awful . . . I can't stand waiting here any longer . . . I'm going to get home late and my family will be mad." It's not the delay that creates the stress, it's the things we tell ourselves about the delay that cause the problems. As a result, many psychologists feel that stress can be managed effectively through logical reanalysis and positive reappraisal. If you can interpret the hassle in a more logical and positive manner, you can reduce or eliminate the stress reaction.

Stress management techniques that rely on cognitive reappraisal take a variety of forms. For instance, you can be taught to focus on certain aspects of the situation that distract you from catastrophizing. If you're stuck in the wrong checkout line, rather than concentrating on how you "must" get home on time, pick up one of the tabloids and read about the latest sighting of Elvis. Alternatively, try using your past experiences to reappraise the consequences: "Let's see, this certainly is not the first time I've been stuck in a checkout line, and my family and friends still think I'm okay." Another approach would be to analyze the situation logically and derive alternatives for the future: "Every time I come to the market at 5:30, right after work, I get stuck in a line—maybe if I wait and go after dinner, there will be less of a wait."

Some stress management programs recommend that clients keep daily records of the specific situations that have led to stress, as well as the specific symptoms and thoughts that arose (an example is shown in Figure 16.6, on page 640). The value of a stress record is that it allows the client to recognize any unrealistic thoughts or

CRITICAL THINKING

What's the link between these stress management programs and the techniques used in cognitive therapies, such as rational-emotive therapy?

Daily Stress Record
(sample)

Week of _____

8 — Extreme stress
7
6 — Much stress
5
4 — Moderate stress
3
2 — Mild stress
1
0 — No stress

Date	(1) Starting time	(2) Ending time	(3) Highest stress (0-8)	(4) Triggers	(5) Symptoms	(6) Thoughts
1–5	10:00 am	11:00 am	7	Sales meeting	Sweating, headache	My figures are bad.
1–7	5:15 pm	5:35 pm	6	Traffic jam	Tension, impatience	I'll never get home.
1–8	12:30 pm	12:32 pm	3	Lost keys	Tension	I can't find my keys.
1–9	3:30 pm	4:30 pm	4	Waiting for guests	Sweating, nausea	Are they lost?

FIGURE 16.6

A Daily Stress Record

Stress management programs often recommend that clients keep daily records of situations that lead to stress, along with the specific symptoms and thoughts that arise. (From Barlow & Rapee, 1991.)

conclusions on the spot, because they need to be written in the record. With time, clients get a pretty good idea of the situations that lead to the highest stress, and they gain insight into the thought processes that underlie their reaction. As each unrealistic thought is recognized, the client can work at reappraising the situation and confronting any negative attitudes or beliefs (Barlow & Rapee, 1991).

TEST YOURSELF 16.3

Check on your knowledge about stress management techniques by answering the following questions. (You will find the answers in the Appendix.)

1. Relaxation techniques, such as meditation or progressive muscle relaxation, appear to work because:
   a. they promote a sense of "connectedness" with the therapist.
   b. they lead to positive cognitive reappraisals.
   c. the stress response is incompatible with relaxation.
   d. they cause you to open up and express feelings.

2. Biofeedback may be effective for managing stress because:
   a. it gives you a feeling of control.
   b. it leads to muscle relaxation.
   c. it trains neurons to fire in sequence.
   d. it works well with meditation.

3. Which of the following statements about the influence of social support on stress is false?

  a. Social contacts help you maintain a healthy lifestyle.
  b. Social support increases the chances that you'll open up and express feelings.
  c. Social support can reduce the chances of a second heart attack.
  d. Social support makes it easier to cope if the support is no longer delivered.

4. Elroy no longer fumes when he gets stuck in traffic because he's stopped catastrophizing about the consequences. Which of the following stress management techniques is Elroy probably using?

  a. Cognitive reappraisal
  b. Autogenic relaxation
  c. Progressive muscle relaxation
  d. Cathartic exploration

Living a Healthful Lifestyle

One of the challenges of the health psychology movement is to devise a comprehensive and workable framework for health promotion (Winett, 1995). In a review of the literature, researchers Nancy Adler and Karen Matthews (1994) summed up the goals of the health psychologist by asking three essential questions: "First, who becomes sick and why? Second, among the sick, who recovers and why? Third, how can illness be prevented or recovery be promoted?" Such questions are appropriately addressed to a psychologist because, as we've seen, a close and intimate connection exists among mind, behavior, and health.

In offering prescriptions for healthful lifestyles, psychologists recognize that not all risk factors can be controlled. Men, for example, have a much greater risk of developing heart disease than women, and the elderly are at a greater risk of developing a whole host of health-related problems. Obviously, people have no control over heredity and they can't help the fact that they grow old. But as I'm sure you're aware, there are lifestyle choices that can make a difference.

> **LEARNING GOALS**
>
> **1.** Discuss the physical and psychological benefits of aerobic exercise.
>
> **2.** Discuss the consequences of tobacco use and explain why it's difficult to quit smoking.
>
> **3.** Discuss the value of proper nutrition.
>
> **4.** Explain the different types of prevention programs and their use in AIDS prevention.

GET FIT: THE VALUE OF AEROBIC EXERCISE

Exercise is an excellent example of an activity that can have a substantial positive impact on physical and psychological health, especially if the exercise is sustained and aerobic. **Aerobic exercise** consists of high-intensity activities that increase both heart rate and oxygen consumption, such as fast walking, running, dancing, rowing, swimming, and so on. As you probably know, regular aerobic exercise improves cardiovascular fitness over the long term and, on average, increases the chances that you will live longer (Belloc & Breslow, 1972; Blair et al., 1989).

Psychologically, regular exercise improves mood and makes people more resistant to the effects of stressors (Stoyva & Carlson, 1993). Much of the evidence is correlational (studies have shown statistical relationships between the regularity of exercise and reported mental health), but controlled experimental studies have reached the same conclusion. For example, in a study by McCann and Holmes (1984), volunteer female college students who were suffering from mild depression were asked to (1) engage in a regular program of aerobic exercise, (2) learn relaxation techniques, or (3) do nothing. After 10 weeks the aerobic exercise group showed the largest improvement in mood. In another experimental study looking at stress resistance, men were randomly assigned to exercise conditions that involved either aerobic activity or nonaerobic strength-and-flexibility training. After 12 weeks of training, the men in the aerobic group showed lower blood

> **aerobic exercise**
> High-intensity activities, such as running and swimming, that increase both heart rate and oxygen consumption.

Regular exercise is an important ingredient in living a healthful lifestyle.

pressure and heart rate when they were exposed to situations involving mental stress (Blumenthal et al., 1989).

But researchers have yet to understand fully how or why exercise improves psychological health and functioning. Over the short term, vigorous exercise increases the amount of oxygen that reaches the brain, which undoubtedly improves cognitive functioning, and sustained exercise may alter mood-inducing neurotransmitters in the brain (Sheridan & Radmacher, 1992). It is also clearly the case that aerobic exercise, as it improves cardiovascular health, will lessen the physiological effects of the stress reaction. But there may also be placebo-like effects involved: People who choose to exercise regularly are convinced that they're going to get better, and they subsequently rate themselves as more psychologically healthy than they may in fact be (Pierce et al., 1993).

Don't Smoke: Tobacco and Health

Virtually everyone knows that smoking or the oral ingestion (chewing) of tobacco is bad for your health. There is no shortage of correlational and experimental studies available to document this fact. Few researchers question, for example, that smoking contributes annually to hundreds of thousands of deaths in the United States alone, from associated heart disease, cancer, stroke, and emphysema. And it's not just the smokers who are affected—the babies of women who smoke during pregnancy tend to have lower birth weights and are at increased risk for birth defects; even people who are simply exposed to smoke secondhand may suffer from subsequent health problems (Byrd, 1992). So why, given that it is so damaging to their health, do people smoke?

First, despite what you might have heard on television (especially from tobacco company executives), smoking is recognized to be *addictive* by the vast majority of mainstream researchers in the health-related sciences (Marlatt & VandenBos, 1997). Many people who smoke regularly become dependent on their daily dosage, and when they try to quit, they suffer physical and psychological withdrawal symptoms. The DSM-IV lists criteria for a diagnosis of "nicotine withdrawal" that include insomnia, irritability, difficulty concentrating, and increased appetite or weight gain. The symptoms of withdrawal can be severe enough to cause a significant disruption in normal everyday functioning (Piasecki et al., 1998). This conclusion, of course, comes as no surprise to anyone who has ever tried to quit smoking after prolonged use.

Tobacco companies often attempt to associate their products with healthy, vigorous lifestyles.

The reinforcing effects of cigarette smoking can be explained by appealing to chemical reactions in the brain and to factors in the culture at large. Within the brain, it takes only seconds for nicotine—the active agent in cigarette smoke—to stimulate the central nervous system, elevating heart rate, blood pressure, and mood. Many smokers report that cigarettes not only improve mood but help alleviate anxiety and stress. At the same time, tobacco companies launch advertising campaigns designed to make smoking appear desirable. Tobacco use is identified with role models—often thin, vigorous, and healthy people on horseback or frolicking on the beach—or is associated with independence and nonconformity. Unfortunately, these types of advertising campaigns are often particularly effective for those in adolescence, which is the time when most smokers begin their habit.

You've probably heard the saying that the best way to stop smoking is never to start. It's undoubtedly true, because once started, tobacco use is a difficult habit to break. The psychological and physical withdrawal symptoms associated with tobacco use make quitting extraordinarily difficult. A variety of smoking cessation techniques have been developed that rely on psychological principles, but they tend to be effective only over the short term. For example, some programs use learning principles to "punish" tobacco use and encourage users to replace positive associations with negative ones. These programs often prove effective initially, but in the long run the vast majority of smokers return to the habit (Schelling, 1992). In the words of Mark Twain: "To cease smoking is the easiest thing I ever did; I ought to know because I've done it a thousand times."

But the news is not all bad. There has been a significant drop in the percentage of people who smoke in the United States and Canada, especially over the past two or three decades. In the mid-1960s, for example, a little over 40% of people in the United States smoked; by 1990, that percentage had dropped to about 25%. More and more people are quitting—although often only after many relapses. Perhaps more significantly, large numbers of people are choosing never to start.

EAT RIGHT: THE VALUE OF PROPER NUTRITION

In Chapter 11 we dealt with the adaptive problem of how to motivate eating behavior. Obviously, to maintain proper functioning of body and mind, people need to consume the necessary amounts of food. In our earlier discussion of eating, we didn't pay too much attention to the *quality* of the food that people consume; instead, our concern was mainly with the internal and external factors that underlie the *motivation* to eat. But proper nutrition is vitally important in maintaining a healthful body and mind, and health psychologists are engaged in a vigorous campaign to improve people's dietary habits.

The dietary habits of most North Americans leave much to be desired. Our diet tends to be too high in calories, fat, cholesterol, sugar, protein, and salt (Sheridan & Radmacher, 1992). High-fat diets have been linked to heart disease, stroke, and several kinds of cancer, as well as to obesity. Diets that are high in cholesterol contribute to heart disease because the cholesterol can lodge in the walls of arteries, leading to a hardening and narrowing that restricts blood flow. Of course, not everyone who maintains a diet high in fat or cholesterol will develop these problems (because genetic predispositions are also a factor), but there's no question that many people eat themselves into an early grave.

Given the overwhelming amount of evidence linking diet to health, why don't people eat better? For many people, it's not the amount of food they eat but their choice of food that creates the problems. Consider the following: A baked potato has 0.5% of its calories as fat; when that same potato is french fried, it has 42% of its calories as fat (Winikoff, 1983). Everyone has a handy list of reasons for choosing to stop for fast food, including the fact that it tastes good. But from a nutritional standpoint, fast foods tend to come up short because they're packed with fat and sodium. The best advice is to eat a variety of foods and to avoid foods with too much fat, cholesterol, sugar, and sodium. This is not a new message for you, I'm sure, but remember: You're now much more sophisticated about the psychological factors that influence your choice of foods (see Chapter 11). So think before you eat—it might make a difference.

AVOID RISKY BEHAVIOR: PROTECT YOURSELF FROM DISEASE

Choosing a healthful lifestyle requires having the right kind of information about how to prevent health-impairing habits. Health psychologists often distinguish among three main types of prevention programs (Winett, 1995):

1. *Primary prevention* is designed to educate the public as a whole in ways to reduce or eliminate a problem before it starts. Teaching children about the potential hazards of smoking or drug use is an example of primary prevention.
2. *Secondary prevention* involves the early identification of risk factors in specific population groups, such as checking for HIV infection in intravenous drug users or looking for early signs of disease through screening.
3. *Tertiary prevention* seeks to handle and contain an illness or habit once it has been acquired.

All three types of prevention programs are needed, but stopping an illness or habit before it starts—primary prevention—obviously has greater long-term significance.

AIDS

Living in the age of AIDS (acquired immune deficiency syndrome) dramatically underscores the need for primary prevention programs. As you probably know, **AIDS** is an infectious disease that involves a gradual weakening and disabling of the immune system. AIDS is "acquired," meaning that it's not a by-product of the genetic code, and it's thought to develop as a result of infection with the *human immunodeficiency virus* (HIV). HIV does its damage by attacking cells in the immune system, which leaves the body unable to fight off opportunistic infections that would otherwise be controlled. The disease AIDS is diagnosed in the latter stages of HIV infection when the immune system has been sufficiently compromised.

Because infection with HIV, as far as we know, ultimately leads to AIDS and death, it's crucial that all three types of prevention programs be initiated, with spe-

AIDS
Acquired immune deficiency syndrome, a disease that gradually weakens and disables the immune system.

THE SECOND BEST WAY TO PREVENT AIDS.

The Elizabeth Taylor Aids Foundation

Primary prevention is crucial in battling the AIDS epidemic.

cial emphasis on primary prevention (Kalichman, 1997; Strombeck & Levy, 1998). Fortunately, infection with HIV is preventable when the proper steps are taken to control its transmission. HIV is transmitted through contact with bodily fluids, particularly blood and semen. The virus is found in saliva, urine, and tears, but the amount is so small that infection through casual contact—even kissing—is extremely unlikely. The most likely means of transmission is through sexual contact or the sharing of intravenous needles with someone infected with the virus. The use of latex condoms during sexual activity dramatically reduces the chances of infection.

Although AIDS and HIV infection are medical conditions, psychologists have two important roles to play. First, the only effective way to control widespread HIV transmission is to prevent risk-taking behavior. The public needs to be educated about how HIV spreads, and the many misconceptions that currently exist need to be countered. For example, there are still people who are convinced that AIDS is a homosexual problem only, despite the fact that the disease can be—and is being—readily transmitted through heterosexual contact. Indeed, in most parts of the world unprotected heterosexual contact is primarily responsible for spreading the virus. The other key role being played by psychologists in the AIDS epidemic is a therapeutic one. Once infected, people with HIV are subjected to an overwhelming amount of stress. Not only are these individuals faced with the prospects of an early death, but they must face the stigma that often accompanies the disease. Psychologists are actively involved in the establishment of treatment programs that can help AIDS patients cope with their disease (Chesney, 1993; Feldman, & Christensen, 1997).

TEST YOURSELF 16.4

Check your knowledge of living a healthy lifestyle by deciding whether each of the following statements is true or false. (You will find the answers in the Appendix.)

1. Aerobic exercise improves cardiovascular health and general mood, but produces few changes in the physiological effects of the stress reaction. *True or False?*

2. Smoking is recognized to be addictive by the vast majority of mainstream researchers in the health-related sciences. *True or False?*

3. For many people, it's not the amount of food they eat but their choice of food that creates health problems. *True or False?*

4. Teaching children about the hazards of smoking or drugs would be classified as an example of secondary prevention. *True or False?*

Solving the Problems

The close relationship that exists between thoughts and emotions and the physical reactions of the body means that understanding and promoting physical health requires some attention to psychological factors. As mentioned at the beginning of the chapter, health psychology is part of a broader movement, called behavioral medicine, that is seeking to understand the medical consequences of the interaction between body and mind. Health psychologists in particular are interested in the psychological and environmental factors—everything from personality characteristics to the work environment—that both produce illness and affect the likelihood of recovery.

Experiencing Stress. Stress has historically been a somewhat tough concept to define. It can be conceived of as a stimulus, as a response, or as a process through which

external events are interpreted as threatening or demanding. We chose to treat stress as the physical and psychological reaction that is shown in response to demanding situations. The stress response is often treated as an extended reaction that occurs in phases. According to the general adaptation syndrome proposed by Hans Selye, the body initially reacts to threat with a highly adaptive fight-or-flight response; if the threat continues, the body goes through resistance and exhaustion phases that make it vulnerable to disease.

Our reactions are critically influenced by the way we perceive or appraise a situation. To experience stress, it's necessary to both perceive a threat and feel that you lack the necessary resources to deal with it effectively. This means that identical environmental events can lead to very different stress reactions, depending on how the situation is interpreted. Overall, however, it is possible to identify some common sources of stress. External sources of stress include significant life events, daily hassles, and environmental factors such as noise and crowding. Internal sources of stress include perceived control—how much influence you feel you have over the situation—and explanatory style.

Certain personality characteristics have been linked to stress. Type A individuals—those who are hard driving, ambitious, and impatient—appear to be at increased risk for subsequent heart disease. The Type A behavior pattern is complex, however, and researchers are in the process of trying to determine which of the many components of this personality type contribute most to the onset of disease.

Reacting to Prolonged Stress. Stress is an adaptive reaction to threat, but if the threat is extended over time, both body and mind can start to break down. Stress has been implicated in a wide variety of health problems, ranging from heart disease to the common cold. A number of studies have shown that prolonged stress can affect immune functioning, which is the body's method for fighting off disease. Stress can compromise the immune response by either lowering the number of specialized white blood cells (lymphocytes) or by somehow suppressing the response of those lymphocytes to foreign substances that have invaded the body.

Two chronic psychological consequences of prolonged stress are posttraumatic stress disorder and burnout. Posttraumatic stress disorder results from exposure to extreme trauma, such as that experienced during battle or as a result of a physical assault such as rape. The symptoms of the disorder include flashbacks in which the traumatic event is reexperienced, avoidance of stimuli associated with the trauma, and chronic arousal problems. Burnout is a term that psychologists use to describe a state of physical, emotional, and mental exhaustion that sometimes develops after prolonged stress.

Reducing and Coping with Stress. The term *coping* describes efforts to manage conditions of threat that tax one's resources. Effective coping techniques include relaxation training, the use of social support, and reappraisal. The stress response is incompatible with relaxation, and relaxation training can help lower components of the stress response (such as blood pressure and heart rate). In progressive relaxation training, the client is taught to concentrate on specific muscle groups in the body, note whether they seem tense, and then relax those specific groups. Sometimes it's useful to provide biofeedback as well.

Additional evidence indicates that social support—the resources received from other people—can also help you cope effectively with stress. Friends and family help us maintain a healthful lifestyle, boost confidence, or simply provide an avenue for us to open up and express our feelings. Talking about things and confiding in others really seem to help people deal with stress. Finally, because stress depends on how you interpret the threatening or demanding situation, it can often be managed effectively through cognitive reappraisal. You can be taught to reinterpret significant life events or daily hassles in a less stressful way. Some stress management programs encourage clients to keep daily stress records. By identifying the kinds of situations that create stress, as well as the negative thoughts those situations induce, you become better prepared to reinterpret those situations and thoughts in a more adaptive manner.

Living a Healthful Lifestyle. Aerobic exercise is one example of an activity that can have a substantial effect on physical and psychological health. Regular exercise improves mood and makes people more resistant to the effects of stressors. Another lifestyle choice that directly affects physical health is the decision not to smoke. Smoking and other tobacco use contribute to hundreds of thousands of deaths annually in the United States alone, from associated heart disease, cancer, stroke, and emphysema. Tobacco use stimulates activity in the central nervous system, which is immediately reinforcing, but prolonged use leads to addiction or dependence that can be difficult to overcome.

Proper nutrition is another important ingredient in maintaining a healthy body and mind. The North American diet tends to be too high in calories, fat, cholesterol, sugar, protein, and salt. Poor dietary habits can lead to significant long-term health problems. Finally, maintaining a healthful lifestyle includes avoiding risky behaviors and preventing disease. For example, psychologists are playing an important role in the AIDS epidemic by educating the public about risky behavior, and through the establishment of treatment programs they are helping AIDS patients cope with the psychological effects of the disease.

Stress and Health Chapter Summary

Experiencing Stress: Stressors and the Stress Response

How does the body produce stress? How is it experienced? Stress is best conceived of as an extended response that occurs over time rather than as a single reaction.

THE STRESS RESPONSE

One influential model of the stress reaction is known as the *general adaptation syndrome (GAS)*, and proposes that we respond to threat or demand in 3 phases. The *alarm* reaction corresponds to a fight-or-flight response; during the *resistance* stage, the threat continues and the body adjusts its reaction to cope; if the person is unable to neutralize the threat, *exhaustion* occurs. Fear, anger, sadness, dejection, and grief are common psychological responses to stress. Stress can also have beneficial effects.

EXTERNAL SOURCES OF STRESS

Significant life events can introduce a good deal of stress into a person's life. Holmes and Rahe developed a life-change stress scale which indicated that stressful events are often associated with some type of change in day-to-day activities, and can be positive. Psychologists also recognize daily hassles, and environmental factors such as noise, as important determinants of daily stress. The specialty of *environmental psychology* is devoted to the study of environmental effects on behavior and health.

COGNITIVE APPRAISAL

The experience of stress is critically affected by how people *appraise* the situation they're in. People must feel that there is a threat present and feel that they may not have adequate resources to deal with the threat. The role of *cognitive appraisal* in the stress response is consistent with what we know about the role of cognition in the experience of emotion.

INTERNAL SOURCES OF STRESS

Several internal factors influence the experience of stress. One such factor is *perceived control*, or the amount of influence you feel you have over a situation and your reaction to it. Generally, less perceived control is associated with higher stress. A second factor is explanatory style, which is also related to psychological disorders such as depression. Personality characteristics, such as a *Type A* behavior pattern (hard-driving, ambitious, easily annoyed, impatient), are also linked with stress and heart disease.

Reacting to Prolonged Stress: Physical and Psychological Effects

The human body is usually able to deal with unexpected trauma, but if the threat continues for an extended period the body's defenses can begin to break down.

PHYSICAL CONSEQUENCES OF STRESS

Stress has been implicated in a wide variety of health problems. Living a stressful life seems to lower one's ability to fight off disease. The *immune system* and its primary weapons, *lymphocytes*, are affected by stress. The immune response is lowered, decreasing the number of lymphocytes, or the response of lymphocytes to foreign substances is suppressed. The link between stress and the immune system has led some to speculate about the possible relationship between stress and more chronic illnesses, such as cancer, although researchers remain cautious in their conclusions. Prolonged exposure to stress is also associated with two major risk factors in cardiovascular disease: high blood pressure and high cholesterol.

PSYCHOLOGICAL CONSEQUENCES OF STRESS

Most psychologists believe that stressful life events play a significant role in the onset of many psychological disorders. Psychologists assume that a (perhaps genetic) vulnerability interacts with stress to produce a psychological disorder. One psychological disorder resulting from extreme stress is *posttraumatic stress disorder*, which is characterized by flashbacks, avoidance of trauma-associated stimuli, and chronic arousal symptoms. Another effect of prolonged stress, *burnout*, refers to "a state of emotional and mental exhaustion caused by long-term involvement in emotionally demanding situations." The causes of burnout may be related to a loss of meaning in life or a loss of control in the workplace.

Reducing and Coping with Stress: Techniques of Stress Management

Given the negative consequences that long-term exposure to stress can have, psychologists have developed specific methods for reducing and controlling stress. *Coping* is the term psychologists use to describe efforts to manage conditions of threat or demand that tax one's resources.

RELAXATION TECHNIQUES

Relaxation is an effective stress reducer because of its incompatibility with the stress response. *Progressive muscle relaxation* involves concentrating on specific muscle groups of the body, noting tension, and trying to relax those specific groups. In *autogenic relaxation*, a person is taught to focus on directing blood flow toward specific muscle groups, warming and relaxing them. Relaxation techniques are sometimes accompanied by meditation training. Giving people feedback (via *biofeedback*) about the effectiveness of their relaxation efforts has proven successful.

SOCIAL SUPPORT

Social support refers to the resources that we receive from other people or groups, often in the form of comfort, caring, or help. Studies indicate that social support can improve one's psychological and physical health. Social support can also have a negative side if one has come to depend on such support and it is no longer available.

REAPPRAISING THE SITUATION

Interpretation of events plays a large role in how stressful the situation is; many stress management techniques involve cognitive reappraisal. This might involve focusing on aspects of the situation that distract one from catastrophizing, or analyzing a situation logically and deriving alternatives.

Living a Healthful Lifestyle

Whether you will remain healthy throughout your life depends significantly on your lifestyle habits. Health psychologists and other professionals have offered prescriptions for a healthful lifestyle.

GET FIT: THE VALUE OF AEROBIC EXERCISE

Aerobic exercise, which consists of high-intensity activities that increase both heart rate and oxygen consumption, can have a substantial positive impact on psychological and physical health. It can improve mood and increase resistance to the effects of stressors. Researchers have not yet discovered exactly how or why exercise improves functioning; placebo-like effects may be involved.

EAT RIGHT: THE VALUE OF PROPER NUTRITION

Proper nutrition is vital to maintaining a healthy body and mind; yet the eating habits of most North Americans tend to be high in calories, cholesterol, fat, and other substances that are damaging in excess. Problems usually involve the type of food that is eaten, not the amount.

DON'T SMOKE: TOBACCO AND HEALTH

A wealth of correlational and experimental evidence has demonstrated the link between tobacco and serious health problems. People continue to smoke because smoking is addictive and associated with withdrawal effects. In addition, smoking seems to produce chemical reactions in the brain that lead to reinforcing effects. Although smoking is a difficult habit to break, rates of smoking do seem to be on the decline.

AVOID RISKY BEHAVIOR: PROTECT YOURSELF FROM DISEASE

Health psychologists distinguish among three types of prevention. *Primary prevention* attempts to reduce or eliminate a problem before it starts. *Secondary prevention* involves early identification of risk factors in specific population groups. *Tertiary prevention* seeks to handle and contain an illness or habit once it has been acquired. The prevalence of AIDS underscores the importance of primary prevention programs.

Terms to Remember

health psychology, 618

EXPERIENCING STRESS

stress, 619
stressors, 619
general adaptation syndrome (GAS), 620
cognitive appraisal, 622
environmental psychology, 625
perceived control, 626
Type A, 627
Type B, 627

REACTING TO PROLONGED STRESS

lymphocytes, 630
posttraumatic stress disorder, 632
burnout, 633

REDUCING AND COPING WITH STRESS

coping, 635
biofeedback, 636
social support, 637

LIVING A HEALTHY LIFESTYLE

aerobic exercise, 641
AIDS, 644

Recommended Readings

Brannon, L., & Feist, J. (1997). *Health psychology* (3rd ed.). Belmont, CA: Wadsworth. A popular undergraduate textbook covering many aspects of stress, health, and behavior.

Friedman, H. S. (1991). *The self-healing personality: Why some people achieve health and others succumb to illness.* New York: Holt. An excellent introduction to the link between psychological factors and health.

Pennebaker, J. W. (1990). *Opening up.* New York: William Morrow and Company. An in-depth discussion of the role that oral or written expression of painful experiences might play in reducing stress and improving health.

INFOTRAC® COLLEGE EDITION

For additional readings, explore Infotrac College Edition, your online library. Go to:
http://www.infotrac-college.com/wadsworth

Hint: enter the search terms: Reactions to stress, Causes of stress, Stress and illness, Coping with Stress, Posttraumatic stress disorder, Health psychology.

What's on the Web?

Hypertension Network

(www.bloodpressure.com)

Did you know that high blood pressure affects 50 million people in the United States alone? This site is dedicated to improving the quality of care for people who suffer this dangerous stress-related condition. It provides weekly updates of new research findings, and expert advice on how to cope with high blood pressure.

American Institute of Stress

(www.stress.org)

Although it doesn't sound too inviting at first blush, this site provides some very useful information about stress, how to avoid it, how to cope with it, and how it can affect your life. It presents some surprising statistics—75-90% of visits to primary care physicians are for stress-related problems, and 78% of Americans describe their jobs as stressful, and a majority claim that this has worsened in the last 10 years. Clearly, we are living in stressful times.

National Center for PTSD

(www.dartmouth.edu/dms/ptsd/Fact_Sheets.html)

This site is devoted to education and research on posttraumatic stress disorder, and provides a wealth of information related to the topic, including information for trauma survivors, information for veterans, and fact sheets on a variety of topics, including PTSD and children, PTSD and community violence, and PTSD and the family.

The Wadsworth Psychology Study Center Web Site

See http://psychology.wadsworth.com/ for practice quiz questions, hypercontents, updates, critical thinking exercises, discussion forums and more! The Wadsworth Psychology Study Center provides a wealth of information fully organized and integrated by chapter.

Appendix

CHAPTER 1

TEST YOURSELF 1.1

1. *False*. Internal thoughts and feelings are often studied by psychologists; a thought or a feeling can be considered as a type of behavior when it is revealed through written or spoken expression.

2. *True*.

3. *True*.

4. *False*. Psychiatrists are medical doctors who receive specialized training in psychology, but their interests do not differ in any fundamental way from those of psychologists. Both psychologists and psychiatrists work on severe psychological problems such as schizophrenia.

TEST YOURSELF 1.2

1. *b*. Most psychologists believe that mental events arise entirely from activity in the brain.

2. Functionalists and structuralists used the technique of *introspection* to understand immediate conscious experience. The *structuralists* believed that it was best to break the mind down into basic parts, much like a chemist would seek to understand a chemical compound. The *functionalists* were influenced by Darwin's views on natural selection and focused primarily on the purpose and adaptive value of mental events. *Behaviorism*, founded by John Watson, steered psychology away from the study of immediate conscious experience toward an emphasis on *behavior*.

3. *d*. Psychoanalysis often places a strong emphasis on hidden urges and memories related to sex and aggression.

TEST YOURSELF 1.3

1. *c*. Clinical psychologists who adopt an eclectic approach often consider the preferences of the client, as well as the type of problem presented, in deciding on the most appropriate therapy.

2. Over the past several decades, psychologists have returned to the study of internal mental phenomena such as consciousness. This shift away from strict behaviorism has been labeled the *cognitive* revolution. An important factor that helped fuel this revolution was the development of the *computer*, which became a model of sorts for the human mind. Developments in *biology* are also playing an important role in shaping modern psychology and in creating effective treatments for psychological problems.

3. *b*. Our cultural background can influence how we think, reason, and remember.

CHAPTER 2

TEST YOURSELF 2.1

1. The *median* is the middle point in an ordered set of scores.

2. The *case study* technique focuses on single instances of behavior and is criticized for lacking *external validity*.

3. When behavior changes as a result of the observation process, it's called a problem of *reactivity*.

4. Limited amounts of information are gathered from many people in a *survey*.

TEST YOURSELF 2.2

1. *Negative.*

2. *Positive.*

3. *Positive.*

4. *Zero.*

TEST YOURSELF 2.3

1. In experimental research, the researcher actively manipulates the environment in order to observe its effect on behavior. The aspect of the environment that is manipulated is called the *independent* variable; the behavior of interest is measured by the *dependent* variable. To draw conclusions about cause and effect, the experimenter must make certain that the *independent* variable is the only thing changing systematically in the environment.

2. *b.* The independent variable is not the only thing changing across the groups.

3. *c.* increases the chances that subject differences will be equally represented in each group.

TEST YOURSELF 2.4

1. All psychologists have a responsibility to respect the rights and dignity of other people. To ensure that research participants are treated ethically, psychologists use (a) *informed consent*, which means that everyone is fully informed about the potential risks of the project, (b) *confidentiality*, which assures the subject's right to privacy will be maintained, and (c) *debriefing*, which is designed to provide more informaiton about the purpose and procedures of the research.

2. *c.* is justified, but only under some circumstances.

3. *c.* animals can give no informed consent.

CHAPTER 3

TEST YOURSELF 3.1

1. The *soma* is the main body of the cell, where exictatory and inhibitory messages combine.

2. The *axon* is the long tail-like part of a neuron that serves as the cell's main transmitter device.

3. The *action potential* is the all-or-none electrical signal that leads to the release of chemical messengers.

4. The *dendrites* are the branch-like fibers that extend outward and receive messages from other neurons.

5. Each is an example of a *neurotransmitter.*

TEST YOURSELF 3.2

1. The *hindbrain* is the primitive part of the brain that controls basic life support functions such as heart rate and respiration.

2. The *hypothalamus* is a structure thought to be involved in a variety of motivational activities, including eating, drinking, and sexual behavior.

3. The *frontal lobes* are believed to be involved in higher-order thought processes (such as planning) as well as the initiation of motor movements.

4. The *cerebellum* is a structure near the base of the brain that is involved in coordination of complex activities such as walking.

5. An *EEG* is a device used to monitor gross electrical activity in the brain.

TEST YOURSELF 3.3

1. *Nervous system.*

2. *Endocrine system.*

3. *Endocrine system.*

4. *Endocrine system.*

5. *Nervous system.*

TEST YOUR 3.4

1. *Genotype* refers to the actual genetic information inherited from your biological parents.

2. *Dominant* genes play a stronger role.

3. *identical* twins because they have essentially the same genetic material.

CHAPTER 4

TEST YOURSELF 4.1

1. *False.* The period from implantation to the end of the eighth week is called the embryonic period.

2. *True.*

3. *False.* The cells increase in size and complexity, not in number. The number of glial cells in the brain, however, may increase with age.

4. *False.* The timing of motor development is determined primarily by nature— the genetic code—although the environment may play some role.

5. *False.* We all lose brain cells with age, but the vast majority of people over 70 will not develop dementia.

TEST YOURSELF 4.2

1. a. *Reward.* In the reward technique, the baby is given reinforcement when he or she performs a movement, such as kicking a leg, in response to a presented event.

   b. *Habituation.* The decline in responsiveness to repeated presentations, called habituation, can be used to infer that the baby recognizes that elements of the event have been repeated.

   c. *Cross-sectional.* In a cross-sectional design, different age groups are studied at the same time.

   d. *Longitudinal.* In a longitudinal design, the same individual is tested repeatedly across the life span.

2. *conservation.* Conservation refers to the ability to recognize that certain physical properties of an object, such as mass, remain the same despite changes in the object's appearance.

3. a. *Conventional.* According to Kohlberg, individuals at the conventional level of moral reasoning decide the correctness of actions on the basis of whether or not the action disrupts the social order.

   b. *Postconventional.* At the postconventional level, moral reasoning is based on abstract principles that may or may not conflict with accepted standards.

c. *Preconventional.* At the preconventional level, moral decisions are made on the basis of the action's immediate consequences.

TEST YOURSELF **4.3**

1. a. *Secure.*
   b. *Avoidant.*
   c. *Resistant.*
   d. *Resistant.*

2. *d.* Not all teenagers suffer anxiety during this period.

3. *False.* Gender identity is already being formed by age 2 or 3.

4. a. *False.* Most elderly people are not sick and disabled, although certainly physical problems do increase with age.
   b. *False.* Some stereotypes about the elderly are positive, such as the belief that all elderly are wise and kind.
   c. *False.* Research suggests the opposite.
   d. *False.* Research suggests that most elderly prefer to strive to keep on living in such circumstances.

CHAPTER 5

TEST YOURSELF **5.1**

1. a. *Fovea.* The "central pit" is where the cone receptors tend to be located.
   b. *Cones.* Receptors that are responsible for visual acuity, or our ability to see fine detail.
   c. *Accommodation.* Process through which the lens changes its shape temporarily in order to help focus light.
   d. *Retina.* The "film" at the back of the eye that contains the light-sensitive receptor cells.
   e. *Cornea.* The protective outer covering of the eye.

2. a. *False.* The majority of visual messages are analyzed in the lateral geniculate and primary visual cortex, although some messages are relayed to the superior colliculus.
   b. *True.*
   c. *True.*
   d. *True.*

3. a. *Top-down processing.* The part of perception that is controlled by our beliefs and expectations about how the world is organized.
   b. *Perceptual constancy.* Perceiving an object, or its properties, to remain the same even though the physical message delivered to the eyes is changing.
   c. *Phi phenomenon.* An illusion of motion.
   d. *Convergence.* The depth cue that is based on calculating the degree to which the two eyes have turned inward.
   e. *Recognition by components.* The view that object perception is based on the analysis of simple building blocks, called geons.

TEST YOURSELF **5.2**

1. *True.*

2. *False.* Place, not frequency, theory proposes that the location of activation on the basilar membrane is a critical cue for pitch.

3. *False.* Hair cells are located in the cochlea, not the pinna, and they are "bent" by movement of the basilar membrane.

4. *False.* Figure-ground organization occurs in hearing as well as in vision.

5. *True.*

TEST YOURSELF 5.3

1. *b.* Our perception of temperature is influenced by the changes that occur from one environment to the next.

2. *c.* Psychological factors are thought to somehow block pain messages from reaching higher neural centers.

3. *d.* The vestibular sacs are part of the structures of the inner ear.

TEST YOURSELF 5.4

1. *Chemoreceptors.* The general term for receptor cells that are activated by invisible molecules scattered about in the air or dissolved in liquids.

2. *Olfactory bulb.* One of the main brain destinations for smell messages.

3. *Flavor.* A psychological term used to describe the entire gustatory experience.

4. *Olfaction.* The technical name for the sense of smell.

5. *Gustation.* The technical name for the sense of taste.

TEST YOURSELF 5.5

1. *False.* There is no single point in an intensity curve at which detection reliably begins.

2. *True.*

3. *False.* Detection of a jnd in magnitude depends on the intensity of the standard.

4. *True.*

CHAPTER 6

TEST YOURSELF 6.1

1. *False.* The cocktail party effect suggests that we do at least some monitoring of unattended messages. We hear our name when it's spoken from across the room.

2. *True.*

3. *True.*

4. *False.* Damage to the right side of the brain, in visual neglect, means that people will fail to recognize things on the left side of the body.

5. *False.* Although some aspects of attention deficit disorder may be learned, most researchers believe that some kind of neurological problem also contributes to the disorder.

TEST YOURSELF 6.2

2. a. *Theta waves.* The characteristic pattern found in stage 1 sleep.
   b. *K complex.* Often triggered by loud noises during stage 2 sleep.
   c. *Delta activity.* Another name for the slow-wave patterns that are found during stage 3 and stage 4 sleep.
   d. *REM.* The characteristic pattern of paradoxical sleep.

2. *c.* Cats sleep more than cows.

3. a. *Insomnia.* Difficulty initiating and maintaining sleep.
   b. *Night terror.* Sleeper awakens suddenly, screaming, but the EEG pattern indicates a period of non-REM sleep.
   c. *Sleep apnea.* Sleeper repeatedly stops breathing during the night, usually for short periods lasting less than a minute.
   d. *Nightmare.* An anxiety-producing dream that usually occurs during the REM stage of sleep.

Test Yourself 6.3

1. *Stimulant.* Increases central nervous system activity.

2. *Opiate.* Reduces pain by mimicking the brain's own natural pain-reducing chemicals.

3. *Depressant.* Tends to produce inhibitory effects by increasing the effectiveness of the neurotransmitter GABA.

4. *Hallucinogen.* Distorts perception and may lead to flashbacks.

5. *Stimulant.* The type of active ingredient in your morning coffee.

Test Yourself 6.4

1. *False.* The EEG patterns of a hypnotized person more closely resemble the patterns found when you're awake not asleep.

2. *False.* Hypnosis increases the chances of fabrication and does not generally lead to better memory.

3. *True.*

4. *False.* Hilgard's experiments support the idea of hypnotic dissociations.

5. *True.*

CHAPTER 7

Test Yourself 7.1

1. *Sensitization.*

2. *Orienting response.*

3. *Habituation.*

4. *Habituation.*

5. *Habituation.*

Test Yourself 7.2

1. a. The unconditioned stimulus is the screaming.
   b. The unconditioned response is wincing and covering your ears.
   c. The conditioned stimulus is the sound of running water.
   d. The conditioned response is wincing.

2. a. The unconditioned stimulus is the puff of air.
   b. The unconditioned response is blinking.
   c. The conditioned stimulus is the word "ready."
   d. The conditioned response is the urge to blink.

3. *d. Extinction.* It's likely that the stimuli presented in the experiment (soft furry things) occurred again many times in Albert's life without the accompanying loud noise. So, the association was extinguished.

Test Yourself 7.3

1. a. *Negative punishment.* Arriving home late is punished by the removal of freedom.
   b. *Positive reinforcement.* The bonus is presented to increase the chances of similar sales behavior again.
   c. *Positive punishment.* The ticket is delivered to lower the likelihood of speeding in a school zone.
   d. *Positive reinforcement.* Crying increases because Mom delivers a kiss and a story.
   e. *Positive punishment.* Dad delivers a stern lecture for crying, which lowers the likelihood of crying in his presence.

2. a. *Variable-ratio.* Reinforcement depends on the number of calls, but the number of calls is not constant or predictable.

b. *Fixed-ratio.* Reinforcement always occurs when she goes to a rally.

c. *Variable-interval.* Reinforcement cannot be predicted and depends on the passage of time rather than the number of responses.

d. *Fixed-ratio.* Reinforcement is delivered after a fixed number of purchases.

e. *Variable-interval.* Reinforcement is not predictable and depends on the passage of time.

Test Yourself 7.4

1. *False.* Observational learning often applies to our own behavior—we learn to act in a certain way by observing a role model.

2. *True.*

3. *False.* Our beliefs about how well we can perform a task (self-efficacy) plays an important role in observational learning.

4. *True.*

5. *True.*

CHAPTER 8

Test Yourself 8.1

1. *Sensory memory.*

2. *Sensory memory.*

3. *Short-term memory.*

4. *Sensory memory.*

5. *Short-term memory.*

6. *Sensory memory.*

7. *Short-term memory.*

8. *Short-term memory.*

Test Yourself 8.2

1. a. *Semantic.*
    b. *Episodic.*
    c. *Semantic.*
    d. *Procedural.*
    e. *Procedural.*

2. *c.* Form a visual image of each word.

3. a. *Method of loci.* A mnemonic device in which you visualize items sitting in different locations.
    b. *Distinctiveness.* The appropriate term to use when you notice how an item is different from other things in memory.
    c. *Elaboration.* The formation of connections between an item and other things in memory.
    d. *Peg-word technique.* The formation of an image linking the to-be-remembered item to a specific cue.
    e. *Elaboration.* The process of engaging in relational processing.

Test Yourself 8.3

1. *Schema.* An organized knowledge package in long-term memory.

2. *Implicit memory.* Remembering without awareness.

3. *Transfer-appropriate processing.* Studying for a multiple choice test by writing your own multiple choice questions.

4. *Encoding specificity principle.* The idea that retrieval cues must match the information stored in the original memory record.

5. *Free recall.* Remembering with using external cues.

TEST YOURSELF 8.4

1. *False.* Most forgetting occurs early and is followed by more gradual loss.

2. *True.*

3. *False.* Proactive interference occurs when prior learning interferes with later remembering.

4. *False.* People with anterograde amnesia can learn new things, but lose the ability to access those memories consciously.

5. *True.*

6. *True.*

CHAPTER 9

TEST YOURSELF 9.1

1. a. *Phonemes.* The smallest significant sound units in speech.
   b. *Pragmatics.* The term used for the practical knowledge that helps us understand the intentions of a speaker and pick an effective response.
   c. *Linguistic relativity.* The hypothesis that proposes that language determines the characteristics and content of thought.
   d. *Syntax.* The rules that govern how words are combined into sentences.
   e. *Morphemes.* The smallest units in a language that carry meaning.

2. a. *True.*
   b. *False.* Babies appear to learn language rules implicitly and often produce phrases, and commit errors, that they never hear from their parents.
   c. *True.*
   d. *True.*
   e. *False.* Kanzi appears able to understand and follow spoken requests from this trainers.

TEST YOURSELF 9.2

1. a. *Defining features.*
   b. *Category exemplars.*
   c. *Family resemblance.*
   d. *Prototype.*

2. *b.* Basic level ("look, it's a cat")

TEST YOURSELF 9.3

1. a. Finding your way to a new restaurant in town is a *well-defined* problem.
   b. Receiving an "A" in your psychology course is a *well-defined* problem.
   c. Making your lab partner in chemistry fall in love with you is an *ill-defined* problem.
   d. Baking a cheesecake that won't taste like plumber's caulk is an *ill-defined* problem.

2. a. *Searching for analogies.*
   b. *Algorithm.*
   c. *Means-ends analysis.*
   d. *Algorithm.*

TEST YOURSELF 9.4

1. *Availability heuristic.*

2. *Framing.*

3. *Representativeness.*

4. *Anchoring and adjustment.*

CHAPTER 10

TEST YOURSELF 10.1

1. *Triarchic theory.* "Street smarts" is an example of practical intelligence.
2. *Cognitive.* Intelligence is defined by the speed of mental processes.
3. *Multiple intelligences.* Musical ability is considered to be a type of intelligence in Gardner's theory.
4. *Psychometric.* Intelligence is measured by analyzing performance on mental tests.
5. *Psychometric.* Factor analysis is a statistical technique used to analyze test performance.
6. *Multiple intelligences.* Insight into the feelings of others is a type of intelligence in Gardner's theory.
7. *Triarchic theory.* Applying what's been learned to new situations is a kind of creative intelligence.

TEST YOURSELF 10.2

1. a. *Reliability.* Donna's performance is consistent across testing.
   b. *Validity.* Larry's new test doesn't measure what it's supposed to measure.
   c. *Reliability.* Chei-Wui is checking on the consistency of test scores.
   d. *Standardization.* Robert makes certain that the testing and scoring procedures are the same for everybody who takes the test.
2. a. *True.*
   b. *False.* Average IQ, based on the deviation IQ method, is always 100 regardless of age.
   c. *False.* The diagnosis of mental retardation depends on many factors, such as one's ability to adapt.
   d. *False.* Creativity doesn't correlate very highly with IQ.

TEST YOURSELF 10.3

1. *False.* Fluid intelligence shows declines over the lifespan.
2. *False.* Identical twins reared apart tend to have more similar IQs than fraternal twins raised together.
3. *True.*
4. *False.* Heritability tells us only that for a given group, a certain percentage of the differences in intelligence can be explained by genetic factors.
5. *True.*

CHAPTER 11

TEST YOURSELF 11.1

1. *c.* Instincts lead to fixed response patterns; drives do not.
2. Choose the appropriate term:
   a. *Incentive motivation.* Whitney jogs because of the reward.
   b. *Intrinsic motivation.* Janice's playing is self-motivated.
   c. *Achievement motivation.* Candice studies to satisfy a need for achievement.
   d. *Intrinsic motivation.* Jerome has become less motivated because of the reward.
3. *b.* Satisfying basic survival and social needs

TEST YOURSELF 11.2

1. *False.* A high level of glucose, or blood sugar, is associated with an decreased desire for food.

2. *False.* Bingeing and purging are the principal symptoms of bulimia nervosa.

3. *False.* Stimulation of the lateral hypothalamus causes an animal to start eating not stop eating.

4. *False.* Obesity is caused by many factors, not necessarily poor dietary habits.

5. *False.* Destruction of the ventromedial hypothalamus increases hunger and leads to large weight gains.

TEST YOURSELF 11.3

1. *True.*

2. *True.*

3. *True.*

4. *True.*

TEST YOURSELF 11.4

1. a. Dancing is an *expressive reaction.*
   b. Grimacing and wrinkling her nose is an *expressive reaction.*
   c. A racing heart is a *body reaction.*
   d. Robert is telling us about his *subjective experience.*

2. *c.* Receiving a C when you expected to flunk is the largest change in expectation (i.e., adaptation level).

3. a. *James-Lange.*
   b. *Two-Factor.*
   c. *Cannon-Bard.*
   d. *Two-Factor.*

CHAPTER 12

TEST YOURSELF 12.1

1. a. *Openness.*
   b. *Extroversion.*
   c. *Agreeableness.*
   d. *Neuroticism.*
   e. *Conscientiousness.*

2. a. *TAT.*
   b. *MMPI.*
   c. *NEO-PI-R.*
   d. *Rorschach.*
   e. *16 personality factor.*

TEST YOURSELF 12.2

1. a. *Psychodynamic.*
   b. *Cognitive–behavioral.*
   c. *Humanistic.*
   d. *Psychodynamic.*
   e. *Humanistic.*
   f. *Cognitive–behavioral.*
   g. *Psychodynamic.*

TEST YOURSELF 12.3

1. *True.*

2. *True.*

3. *False.* High self-monitors tend to adapt their behavior to the situation.

4. *False.* Genetics appear to play a significant role in personality as measured by the MMPI.

5. *False.* Personality traits may only reveal themselves if they are relevant, or needed, in the situation.

CHAPTER 13

Test Yourself 13.1

1. a. *True.*
   b. *False.* Exemplar, not prototype, theories assume that we represent stereotypes with particular individuals, or exemplars.
   c. *True.*
   d. *True.*

2. a. *Internal.*
   b. *Internal.*
   c. *External.*
   d. *Internal.*

3. a. *True.*
   b. *False.* The central, not peripheral, route to persuasion operates when our level of involvement in or commitment to a message is high.
   c. *True.*
   d. *False.* Mere exposure is most likely to lead to attitude change when we're processing a message peripherally.

Test Yourself 13.2

1. a. *Deindividuation.*
   b. *Social loafing*, although *conformity* is also a possibility.
   c. *Conformity.*
   d. *Group Polarization.*
   e. *Bystander Effect.*
   f. *Social Facilitation.*

2. *d.* The experiment is conducted in the teacher's home.

Test Yourself 13.3

1. *True.*

2. *False.* Averaged faces tend to be rated as most attractive.

3. *False.* Your ratings would go down.

4. *True.*

5. *True.*

6. *False.* Companionate love typically leads to more feelings of warmth and trust.

CHAPTER 14

Test Yourself 14.1

1. *False.* When a behavior occurs infrequently among members of a population it meets the criterion of statistical deviance.

2. *False.* Not all people with psychological disorders are emotionally distressed.

3. *True.*

4. *True.*

5. *False.* In many cases, hospital staff members appeared not to notice or classify the pseudopatients' behavior as normal.

Test Yourself 14.2

1. *Somatoform disorder* (hypochondriasis or conversion disorder).

2. *Anxiety disorder* (obsessive–compulsive disorder).

3. *Anxiety disorder* (panic disorder, agoraphobia).

4. *Mood disorder* (depressive disorder).

5. *Dissociative disorder* (dissociative fugue).

6. *Personality disorder* (antisocial personality disorder).

7. *Schizophrenia* (paranoia).

8. *Schizophrenia* (catatonia).

TEST YOURSELF 14.3

1. *b.* Excessive amounts of the neurotransmitter dopamine.

2. *d.* If your identical twin has schizophrenia, you have about a 50% chance of developing the disorder yourself.

3. *d.* Internal, stable, and global.

4. *b.* Observational learning.

CHAPTER 15

TEST YOURSELF 15.1

1. a. *Schizophrenia* (Clozapine).
   b. *Depression* (Prozac).
   c. *Depression* (Cingulotomy).
   d. *Depression* (ECT).
   e. *Generalized Anxiety Disorder* (Benzodiazepine).

2. *d.* ECT is used regularly to treat schizophrenia

TEST YOURSELF 15.2

1. *Rational-emotive therapy.*

2. *Beck's cognitive therapy.*

3. *Psychoanalysis.*

4. *Client-centered therapy.*

5. *Gestalt therapy.*

6. *Family therapy.*

TEST YOURSELF 15.3

1. *b.* conditioned stimulus.

2. *a.* counterconditioning and extinction.

3. *b.* Effective punishments can't be delivered because pain thresholds are high.

4. *d.* Reinforcement.

TEST YOURSELF 15.4

1. *True.*

2. *True.*

3. *False.* Many evaluation studies show that the particular form of treatment doesn't matter.

4. *False.* Some types of treatment, such as most behavioral therapies, show concern only for the present symptoms.

5. *True.*

CHAPTER 16

TEST YOURSELF 16.1

1. *c.* Alarm, resistance, exhaustion.

2. *c.* The experience of stress, like emotion, depends on the appraisal of the event rather than on the event itself.

3. *a.* Marriage.

4. *c.* An optimistic outlook.

TEST YOURSELF **16.2**

1. *True.*

2. *True.*

3. *False.* Stress has been shown to affect cholesterol levels.

4. *False.* Most people who suffer trauma do not develop posttraumatic stress disorder.

5. *True.*

TEST YOURSELF **16.3**

1. *c.* The stress response is incompatible with relaxation.

2. *a.* It gives you a feeling of control.

3. *d.* Social support makes it easier to cope if the support is no longer delivered.

4. *a.* Cognitive reappraisal.

TEST YOURSELF **16.4**

1. *False.* Aerobic exercise can lessen the physiological effects of the stress reaction.

2. *True.*

3. *True.*

4. *False.* Teaching children about the hazards of smoking or drugs would be classified as an example of primary prevention.

Glossary

absolute threshold   The level of intensity that lifts a stimulus over the threshold of conscious awareness; it's usually defined as the intensity level at which people can detect the presence of the stimulus 50% of the time.

accommodation   In vision, the process through which the lens changes its shape temporarily in order to help focus light on the retina.

accommodation   The process through which people change or modify existing schemata to accommodate new experiences when they occur.

acetylcholine   A neurotransmitter that plays several roles in the central and peripheral nervous systems, including the excitation of muscle contractions.

achievement motive   An internal drive or need for achievement that is possessed by all individuals to varying degrees. Whether people will work for success on any given task depends on (1) their expectations about whether they will be successful, and (2) how much they value succeeding at the task.

achievement tests   Psychological tests that measure your current level of knowledge or competence in a particular subject.

action potential   The all-or-none electrical signal that travels down a neuron's axon.

activation-synthesis hypothesis   The idea that dreams represent the brain's attempt to make sense out of the random patterns of neural activity generated during sleep.

aerobic exercise   High-intensity activities, such as running and swimming, that increase both heart rate and oxygen consumption.

ageism   Discrimination or prejudice against an individual based on physical age.

agoraphobia   An anxiety disorder that causes an individual to restrict his or her normal activities; someone suffering from agoraphobia tends to avoid public places out of fear that a panic attack will occur.

AIDS   Acquired immune deficiency syndrome, a disease that gradually weakens and disables the immune system.

algorithms   Step-by-step rules or procedures that, if applied correctly, guarantee a problem solution.

alpha waves   The pattern of brain activity observed in someone who is in a relaxed state.

altruism   Acting in a way that shows unselfish concern for the welfare of others.

amnesia   Forgetting that is caused by physical problems in the brain, such as those induced by injury or disease.

anal stage   Freud's second stage of psychosexual development, occurring in the second year of life; pleasure is derived from the process of defecation.

anorexia nervosa   An eating disorder diagnosed when an otherwise healthy person refuses to maintain a normal weight level because of an intense fear of being overweight.

anterograde amnesia   Memory loss for events that happen after the point of physical injury.

antianxiety drugs   Medications that reduce tension and anxiety. Many work on the inhibitory neurotransmitter GABA.

antidepressant drugs   Medications that modulate the availability or effectiveness of the neurotransmitters implicated in mood disorders; Prozac, for example, increases the action of the neurotransmitter serotonin.

antipsychotic drugs   Medications that reduce the positive symptoms of schizophrenia; the majority act on the neurotransmitter dopamine.

antisocial personality disorder   A personality disorder characterized by little, if any, respect for social laws, customs, or norms.

anxiety disorders   A class of disorders marked by excessive apprehension and worry that in turn impairs normal functioning.

applied psychologists   Psychologists who try to extend the principles of scientific psychology to practical, everyday problems in the world.

aptitude tests   Psychological tests that measure your ability to learn or acquire knowledge in a particular subject.

assimilation   The process through which people fit-or assimilate-new experiences into existing schemata.

attachments   Strong emotional ties formed to one or more intimate companions.

attention   The internal processes people use to set priorities for mental functioning.

attention deficit disorder   A psychological condition, occurring most often in children, marked by difficulties in concentrating or in sustaining attention for extended periods.

attitude   A positive or negative evaluation or belief held about something, which in turn may affect one's behavior; attitudes are typically broken down into cognitive, affective, and behavioral components.

attributions   The inference processes people use to assign cause and effect to behavior.

automaticity   Fast and effortless processing that requires little or no focused attention.

autonomic system   The collection of nerves that controls the more automatic needs of the body, such as heart rate, digestion, blood pressure, and so on; part of the peripheral nervous system.

availability heuristic   The tendency to base estimates on the ease with which examples come to mind. For example, if you've just heard about a plane crash, your estimates of the likelihood of plane crashes increase because "plane crashes" easily come to mind.

aversion therapy   A treatment for replacing a positive reaction to a harmful stimulus, such as alcohol, with something negative, such as feeling nauseous.

avoidance conditioning   A situation in which a response can prevent the delivery of an aversive stimulus, such as when a rat learns to jump over a barrier to avoid a shock.

axon   The long tail-like part of a neuron that serves as the cell's transmitter device.

basic-level categories   The level in a category hierarchy that provides the most useful and predictive information; the basic level usually resides at an intermediate level in a category hierarchy.

basilar membrane   A flexible membrane running through the cochlea that, through its movement, displaces the auditory receptor cells, or hair cells.

behavior   Observable actions such as moving, talking, gesturing, and so on; behaviors can also refer to the activities of cells, as measured through physiological recording devices, and to thoughts and feelings, as measured through oral and written expression.

behavioral therapies   Treatments designed to change behavior through the use of established learning techniques.

behaviorism   A school of psychology proposing that the proper subject matter of psychology is directly observable behavior and the situations that lead to changes in behavior, rather than immediate conscious experience.

Big Five   The five dimensions of personality—extroversion, agreeableness, conscientiousness, neuroticism, and openness—that have been isolated through the application of factor analysis; it is widely believed that virtually all personality terms in language can be accounted for by appealing to one or more of these basic dimensions.

binocular depth cues   Cues for depth that depend on comparisons between the two eyes.

bio-psycho-social perspective   The idea that psychological disorders are influenced, or caused, by a combination of biological, psychological (cognitive), and social (environmental) factors.

biofeedback   Specific physiological feedback that people are given about the effectiveness of their relaxation efforts.

biological clocks   Brain structures that schedule rhythmic variations in bodily functions by triggering them at the appropriate times.

biomedical therapies   Biologically based treatments for reducing or eliminating the symptoms of psychological disorders; they include drug therapies, shock treatments, and, in some cases, psychosurgery.

bipolar disorder   A type of mood disorder in which the person experiences disordered mood shifts in two directions-from depression to a manic state.

blind spot   The point where the optic nerve leaves the back of the eye.

bottom-up processing   Processing that is driven by the actual physical message delivered to the senses.

brightness   The aspect of the visual experience that changes with light intensity; in general, as the intensity of light increases, so does its perceived brightness.

bulimia nervosa   An eating disorder in which the principal symptom is binge eating (consuming large quantities of food) followed by purging, in which the person voluntarily vomits or uses laxatives to prevent weight gain.

burnout   A state of physical, emotional, and mental exhaustion created by long-term involvement in an emotionally demanding situation.

bystander effect   The reluctance to come to the aid of a person in need when other people are present.

Cannon-Bard theory   A theory of emotion that argues that body reactions and subjective experiences occur together, but independently.

cardinal traits Allport's term to describe personality traits that dominate an individual's life, such as a passion to serve others or to accumulate wealth.

case study A descriptive research technique in which the research effort is focused on a single case, usually an individual.

catalepsy A hypnotically induced behavior characterized by an ability to hold one or more limbs of the body in a rigid position for long periods without tiring.

category exemplars Specific examples of category members that are stored in long-term memory.

category A class of objects (people, places, or things) that most people agree belong together.

central nervous system The brain and the spinal cord.

central traits Allport's term to describe the five to ten descriptive traits that you would use to describe someone you know-friendly, trustworthy, and so on.

cerebellum A hindbrain structure at the base of the brain that is involved in the coordination of complex motor skills.

cerebral cortex The outer layer of the brain, considered to be the seat of higher mental processes.

chemoreceptors Receptor cells that react to invisible molecules scattered about in the air or dissolved in liquids, leading to the senses of smell and taste.

chunking A short-term memory strategy that involves rearranging incoming information into meaningful or familiar patterns.

circadian rhythms Biological activities that rise and fall in accordance with a 24-hour cycle.

classical conditioning A set of procedures, initially developed by Pavlov, used to investigate how organisms learn about the signaling properties of events. Classical conditioning leads to the learning of relations between events-conditioned and unconditioned stimuli-that occur outside of one's control.

client-centered therapy A form of humanistic therapy, developed by Carl Rogers, proposing that it is the client, not the therapist, who holds the key to psychological health and happiness; the therapist's role is to provide genuineness, unconditional positive regard, and empathy.

clinical psychologists Professional psychologists who specialize in the diagnosis and treatment of psychological problems.

cochlea The bony, snail-shaped sound processor in the inner ear, where sounds get translated into nerve impulses.

cocktail party effect The ability to focus on one auditory message, such as a friend's conversation at a party, and ignore others; the term also refers to the tendency to notice when one's name suddenly appears in a message that one has been actively ignoring.

cognitive appraisal The idea that in order to feel stress you need to perceive a threat and come to the conclusion that you may not have adequate resources to deal with the threat.

cognitive dissonance The tension produced when people act in a way that is inconsistent with their attitudes; attitude change may occur as a result of attempting to reduce cognitive dissonance.

cognitive revolution The shift away from strict behaviorism, begun in the 1950s, characterized by renewed interest in fundamental problems of consciousness and internal mental processes.

cognitive therapies Treatments designed to remove irrational beliefs and negative thoughts that are presumed to be responsible for psychological disorders.

cognitive-behavioral theories An approach to personality that suggests it is human experiences, and interpretations of those experiences, that determine personality growth and development.

cold fibers Neurons that respond to a cooling of the skin by increasing the production of neural impulses.

collective unconscious The notion proposed by Carl Jung that certain kinds of universal symbols and ideas are present in the unconscious of all people.

companionate love A kind of emotional attachment characterized by feelings of trust and companionship; companionate love is marked by a combination of intimacy and commitment, but passion may be lacking.

computerized tomography scan (CT scan) The use of highly focused beams of X rays to construct detailed anatomical maps of the living brain.

concrete operational period Piaget's third stage of cognitive development, lasting from ages 7 to 11. Children acquire the capacity to perform a number of mental operations but still lack the ability for abstract reasoning.

conditioned inhibition Learning that an event signals the absence of the unconditioned stimulus.

conditioned reinforcer A stimulus that has acquired reinforcing properties through prior learning.

conditioned response (CR) The acquired response that is produced to the conditioned stimulus in anticipation of the arrival of the unconditioned stimulus. Often, the conditioned response resembles the unconditioned response, although not always.

conditioned stimulus (CS) A neutral stimulus (one that does not produce the unconditioned response prior to training) that is paired with the unconditioned stimulus during classical conditioning.

conditions of worth   The expectations or standards that we believe others place on us.

cones   Receptor cells in the central portion of the retina that transduce light energy into neural messages; they operate best when light levels are high, and they are primarily responsible for the ability to sense color.

confidentiality   The principle that all personal information obtained from a participant in research or therapy should not be revealed without the individual's permission.

conformity   The tendency to comply, or go along, with the wishes of the group; when people conform, their opinions, feelings, and behaviors generally start to move toward the group norm.

confounding variable   An uncontrolled variable that changes along with the independent variable.

conscious mind   The contents of awareness-those things that occupy the focus of one's current attention.

consciousness   The subjective awareness of internal and external events.

conservation   The ability to recognize that the physical properties of an object remain the same despite superficial changes in the object's appearance.

construct validity   See *validity.*

content validity   See *validity.*

conventional level   In Kohlberg's theory of moral development, the stage in which actions are judged to be right or wrong based on whether they maintain or disrupt the social order.

convergence   A binocular cue for depth that is based on the extent to which the two eyes move inward, or converge, when looking at an object.

conversion disorder   The presence of real physical problems, such as blindness or paralysis, that seem to have no identifiable physical cause.

coping   Efforts to manage or master conditions of threat or demand that tax one's resources.

cornea   The transparent and protective outer covering of the eye.

corpus callosum   The collection of nerve fibers that connects the two cerebral hemispheres and allows information to pass from one side to the other.

correlation   A statistic that indicates whether two variables are related or vary together in a systematic way; correlation coefficients vary from +1.00 to −1.00.

creativity   The ability to generate ideas that are original, novel, and useful.

cross-sectional design   A research design in which people of different ages are compared at the same time.

crystallized intelligence   The knowledge and abilities acquired as a result of experience (as from schooling and cultural influences).

cue-dependent forgetting   The idea that forgetting is caused by a failure to access the appropriate retrieval cue.

cued recall   A testing condition in which subjects are given an explicit retrieval cue to help them remember.

cultural deviance   A criterion of abnormality stating that a behavior is abnormal if it violates the rules or accepted standards of society.

culture   The shared values, customs, and beliefs that are characteristic of a group or community.

dark adaptation   The process through which the eyes adjust to dim light.

debriefing   At the conclusion of an experimental session, informing the participants about the general purpose of the experiment, including any deception that was involved.

decay   The proposal that memories are forgotten or lost spontaneously with the passage of time.

decision making   The thought processes involved in evaluating and choosing from among a set of alternatives; it usually involves some kind of risk.

deep structure   The underlying representation of meaning in a sentence.

defense mechanisms   According to Freud, unconscious processes used by the ego to ward off the anxiety that comes from confrontation, usually with the demands of the id.

defining features   The set of features that are necessary to make objects acceptable members of a category (for example, to be a "bird" the object must have wings and feathers, must fly, and so on).

deindividuation   The loss of individuality, or depersonalization, that comes from being in a group; it can increase the chances of a person engaging in destructive, aggressive, or deviant behavior.

delta activity   The pattern of brain activity observed in stage 3 and stage 4 sleep; it's characterized by synchronized slow waves. Also called slow-wave sleep.

dementia   Physically based losses in mental functioning.

dendrites   The branchlike fibers that extend outward from a neuron and receive information from other neurons.

dependent personality disorder   A personality disorder characterized by an excessive and persistent need to be taken care of by others.

dependent variable   The behavior that is measured or observed in an experiment.

depolarization The change in a neuron's electrical potential from negative toward zero; depolarization usually occurs when positive ions flow into the cell as a result of neural communication.

depressants A class of drugs that slow or depress the ongoing activity of the central nervous system.

descriptive research The tactics and methods that underlie the direct observation and description of behavior.

descriptive statistics Mathematical techniques that help researchers describe their data.

development The age-related physical, intellectual, social, and personal changes that occur throughout an individual's lifetime.

deviation IQ An intelligence score that is derived from determining where your performance sits in an age-based distribution of test scores.

diagnostic labeling effects The fact that labels for psychological problems can become self-fulfilling prophecies; the label may make it difficult to recognize normal behavior when it occurs, and it may actually increase the likelihood that a person will act in an abnormal way.

dichotic listening A technique in which different auditory messages are presented separately and simultaneously to each ear. Usually the subject's task is to shadow, or repeat aloud, one of the messages while ignoring the other.

difference threshold The smallest difference in the magnitude of two stimuli that an observer can detect.

diffusion of responsibility The idea that when people know, or think, that others are present in a situation, they allow their sense of responsibility for action to diffuse, or spread out widely, among those who are present.

discriminative stimulus The stimulus situation that sets the occasion for a response to be followed by reinforcement or punishment.

dissociative amnesia A psychological disorder characterized by an inability to remember important personal information.

dissociative disorders A class of disorders characterized by the separation, or dissociation, of conscious awareness from previous thoughts or memories.

dissociative fugue A loss of personal identity that is often accompanied by a flight from home.

dissociative identity disorder A condition in which an individual alternates between what appear to be two or more distinct identities or personalities (also known as multiple personality disorder).

distinctiveness A term used to refer to how unique or different a memory record is from other things in memory. Distinctive memory records tend to be recalled well.

distributed practice Spacing the repetitions of to-be-remembered information over time.

dopamine A neurotransmitter that often leads to inhibitory effects; decreased levels have been linked to Parkinson's disease and increased levels have been linked to schizophrenia.

double-blind study An experimental design in which neither the participants nor the research observers are aware of who has been assigned to the experimental and control groups; it's used to control for both subject and experimenter expectancies.

dream analysis A technique used in psychoanalysis; Freud believed that dreams are symbolic and contain important information about the unconscious.

drive A psychological state that arises in response to an internal physiological need, such as hunger or thirst.

drug dependency A condition in which an individual experiences a physical or a psychological need for continued use of a drug.

DSM-IV The Diagnostic and Statistical Manual of Mental Disorders (4th ed.), which is used for the diagnosis and classification of psychological disorders. The DSM-IV is composed of five major rating dimensions, or axes.

dysfunction A breakdown in normal functioning; abnormal behaviors are those that prevent one from pursuing adaptive strategies.

echoic memory The system that produces and stores auditory sensory memories.

eclectic approach The position adopted by many psychologists that it's useful to select or adopt information from several sources-one need not rely entirely on any single perspective or school of thought.

ego In Freud's theory, the portion of personality that induces people to act with reason and deliberation and helps them conform to the requirements of the external world.

egocentrism The tendency to see the world from your own unique perspective only, a characteristic of thinking in the preoperational period of development.

elaboration likelihood model A model proposing two primary routes to persuasion and attitude change: a central route, which operates when people are motivated and focusing their attention on the message, and a peripheral route, which operates when people are either unmotivated to process the message or are unable to do so.

elaboration An encoding process that involves the formation of connections between to-be-remembered input and other information in memory.

electroconvulsive therapy (ECT) A treatment used primarily for depression in which a brief electric current is delivered to the brain.

electroencephalograph (EEG) A device used to monitor the gross electrical activity of the brain.

embryonic period The period of prenatal development lasting from implantation to the end of the eighth week; during this period the human develops from an unrecognizable mass of cells to a somewhat familiar creature.

emotional distress A criterion of abnormality stating that abnormal behaviors are those that lead to personal distress or emotional upset.

emotional intelligence The ability to perceive, understand, and express emotion in ways that are useful and adaptive.

emotions Psychological events involving (1) a physiological reaction, usually arousal; (2) some kind of expressive reaction, such as a distinctive facial expression; and (3) some kind of subjective experience, such as the conscious feeling of being happy or sad.

empiricism The idea that knowledge comes directly from experience.

encoding The processes that determine and control the acquisition of memories.

encoding specificity principle The idea that specific encoding processes determine which retrieval cues will be effective in aiding later memory.

endocrine system A network of glands that uses the bloodstream, rather than neurons, to send chemical messages that regulate growth and other internal functions.

endorphins Morphine-like chemicals that act as the brain's natural painkillers.

environmental psychology A specialty area in psychology devoted to the study of environmental effects on behavior and health, such as the effects of crowding or noise.

episodic memory A memory for a particular event, or episode, that happened to you personally, such as remembering what you ate for breakfast this morning or where you went on vacation last year.

escape conditioning A situation in which a response can reduce or eliminate an unpleasant stimulus, such as when a rat escapes an ongoing shock by jumping over a barrier.

excitement phase The first component of the human sexual response cycle, as described by Masters and Johnson. It's characterized by changes in muscle tension,

increased heart rate and blood pressure, and a rushing of blood into the genital organs; in men, the penis becomes erect; in women, the vaginal walls become lubricated.

experimental research A technique in which the investigator actively manipulates or alters some aspect of the environment (defined broadly) in order to observe the effect of the manipulation on behavior.

explicit memory Conscious, willful remembering.

external attribution Attributing the cause of a person's behavior to an external event or situation in the environment.

external validity The extent to which the results of an observation generalize to other situations or are representative of real life.

extinction Presenting a conditioned stimulus repeatedly, after conditioning, without the unconditioned stimulus, resulting in a loss in responding.

facial-feedback hypothesis The proposal that muscles in the face deliver signals to the brain that are then interpreted, depending on the pattern, as a subjective emotional state.

factor analysis A statistical procedure developed by Charles Spearman that groups together related items on tests by analyzing the correlations among test scores. It's often used by psychologists to determine underlying common "factors," or abilities.

family life cycle The transitions, or sequences of stages, that families move through. In many models of the family life cycle, the stages are tied to the age of the children.

family resemblance The core features that category members share; a given member of the category may have some but not necessarily all of these features.

family studies The similarities and differences among biological (blood) relatives are studied to help discover the role heredity plays in physical or psychological traits. Family studies rarely provide conclusive evidence because genes and the environment are usually confounded.

family therapy A form of group therapy in which the therapist treats the family as whole, as a kind of social system. The goals of the treatment are often to improve interpersonal communication and collaboration.

feature detectors Cells in the visual cortex that respond to very specific visual events, such as bars of light at particular orientations.

fetal period The period of prenatal development lasting from the ninth week until birth, during which the fetus develops functioning organ systems, and increases are seen in body size and in the size and complexity of brain tissue.

fixed-interval schedule A schedule in which the reinforcement is delivered for the first response that occurs following a fixed interval of time.

fixed-ratio schedule A schedule in which the number of responses required for reinforcement is fixed and does not change from trial to trial.

flashbulb memories Rich memory records of the circumstances surrounding emotionally significant and surprising events.

flavor A psychological term used to describe the gustatory experience. Flavor is influenced by taste, smell, the visual appearance of food, as well as by expectations about the food's quality.

fluid intelligence The natural ability to solve problems, reason, and remember; fluid intelligence is thought to be relatively uninfluenced by experience.

forebrain The outer portion of the brain, including the cerebral cortex and the structures of the limbic system.

forgetting The loss in accessibility of previously stored material.

formal operational period Piaget's last stage of cognitive development; thought processes become adultlike, and people gain mastery over abstract thinking.

fovea The "central pit" area in the retina where the cone receptors are located.

framing The way in which the alternatives in a decision-making situation are structured.

free association A technique used in psychoanalysis to explore the contents of the unconscious; patients are asked to relax and freely express whatever thoughts and feelings happen to come into their minds.

free recall A testing condition in which a person is asked to remember information without explicit retrieval cues.

frequency theory The idea that pitch perception is determined partly by the frequency of neural impulses traveling up the auditory pathway.

frontal lobe One of four anatomical regions of each hemisphere of the cerebral cortex, located on the top front of the brain; it contains the motor cortex and may be involved in higher-level thought processes.

functional fixedness The tendency to see objects, and their functions, in certain fixed and typical ways.

functionalism An early school of psychology; functionalists believe that the proper way to understand mind and behavior is to analyze their function and purpose. You can only truly understand a mental process, functionalists argue, by first knowing the purpose of the mental process.

fundamental attribution error The fact that people seeking to interpret someone else's behavior tend to overestimate the influence of internal personal factors and underestimate the role of situational factors.

g (general intelligence) According to Spearman, a general factor, derived from factor analysis, that underlies or contributes to performance on a variety of mental tests.

GABA (gamma-amino-butyric acid) A neurotransmitter that may to play a role in the regulation of anxiety; it generally produces inhibitory effects.

gate-control theory The idea that neural impulses generated by pain receptors can be blocked, or gated, in the spinal cord by signals produced in the brain.

gender roles Specific patterns of behavior that are consistent with how society dictates males and females should act.

gender schemas The organized sets of beliefs and perceptions held about men and women.

general adaptation syndrome (GAS) Hans Selye's model of stress as a general, nonspecific reaction that occurs in three phases: alarm reaction, resistance, and exhaustion.

generalized anxiety disorder Excessive worrying, or free-floating anxiety, that lasts for at least six months and that cannot be attributed to any single identifiable source.

genes Segments of chromosomes that contain instructions for influencing and creating particular hereditary characteristics.

genital stage Freud's final stage of psychosexual development, during which one develops mature sexual relationships with members of the opposite sex.

genotype The actual genetic information inherited from one's parents.

germinal period The period in prenatal development from conception to implantation of the fertilized egg in the wall of the uterus.

Gestalt principles of organization The organizing principles of perception proposed by the Gestalt psychologists. These principles include the laws of proximity, similarity, closure, continuation, and common fate.

gifted A label that is generally assigned to someone who scores above 130 on a standard IQ test.

glial cells Cells in the nervous system that do not transmit or receive information but that perform a variety of functions, such as removing waste, filling in empty space, or helping neurons to communicate efficiently.

glucose A kind of sugar that cells require for energy production.

grammar The rules of language that allow the communicator to combine arbitrary symbols to convey meaning; grammar includes the rules of phonology, syntax, and semantics.

group polarization The tendency for a group's dominant point of view to become stronger and more extreme with time.

group therapy A form of therapy in which several people are treated simultaneously in the same setting.

groupthink The tendency for members of a group to become so interested in seeking a consensus of opinion that they start to ignore and even suppress dissenting views.

gustation The sense of taste.

habituation The decline in responsiveness to repeated stimulation; habituation has been used as an effective tool to map out the perceptual capabilities of infants.

hallucinogens A class of drugs that tend to disrupt normal mental and emotional functioning, including distorting perception and altering reality.

health psychology The study of how biological, psychological, environmental, and cultural factors are involved in physical health and the prevention of illness.

heritability A mathematical index that represents the extent to which IQ differences in a particular population can be accounted for by genetic factors.

heuristics The rules of thumb we use to solve problems; heuristics can usually be applied quickly, but they do not guarantee that a solution will be found.

hindbrain A primitive part of the brain that sits at the juncture point where the brain and spinal cord merge. Structures in the hindbrain, including the medulla, pons, and reticular formation, act as the basic life-support system for the body.

homeostasis The process through which the body maintains a steady state, such as a constant internal temperature or an adequate amount of fluids.

hormones Chemicals released into the blood by the various endocrine glands to help control a variety of internal regulatory functions.

hue The dimension of light that produces color; hue is typically determined by the wavelength of light reflecting from an object.

humanistic psychology A movement in psychology that emerged largely as a reaction against the pessimism of Freud. Humanistic psychologists focus on people's unique capacity for choice, responsibility, and growth.

humanistic therapy Treatments designed to help clients gain insight into their fundamental self-worth and value as human beings; therapy is a process of discovering one's own unique potential.

hyperpolarization An increase in the negative electrical potential of a neuron, reducing the chances of the cell generating an action potential.

hypersomnia A chronic condition marked by excessive sleepiness.

hypnosis A form of social interaction that produces a heightened state of suggestibility in a willing participant.

hypnotic dissociation A hypnotically induced splitting of consciousness during which multiple forms of awareness coexist.

hypnotic hypermnesia The supposed enhancement in memory that occurs under hypnosis; there is little if any evidence to support the existence of this effect.

hypochondriasis A long-lasting preoccupation with the idea that one has developed a serious disease, based on what turns out to be a misinterpretation of normal body reactions.

hypothalamus A forebrain structure thought to play a role in the regulation of various motivational activities, including eating, drinking, and sexual behavior.

iconic memory The system that produces and stores visual sensory memories.

id In Freud's theory, the portion of personality that is governed by inborn instinctual drives, particularly those related to sex and aggression.

ill-defined problem A problem, such as the search for "happiness," that has no well-stated goal, no clear starting point, or no mechanism for evaluating progress.

implicit memory Remembering that occurs in the absence of conscious awareness or willful intent.

incentive motivation External factors in the environment—such as money, an attractive person, or tasty food-that exert pulling effects on people's actions.

incongruence A discrepancy between the image we hold of ourselves-our self-concept-and the sum of all our experiences.

independent variable The aspect of the environment that is manipulated in an experiment. It must consist of at least two conditions.

inferential statistics Mathematical techniques that help researchers decide whether recorded behaviors are representative of a population or whether differences among observations can be attributed to chance.

informed consent The principle that before consenting to participate in research, people should be fully informed about any significant factors that could affect their willingness to participate.

in-group A group of individuals with whom one shares features in common, or with whom one identifies.

insanity   A legal term usually defined as the inability to understand that certain actions are wrong, in a legal or moral sense, at the time of a crime.

insight therapies   Treatments designed to give clients self-knowledge, or insight, into the contents of their thought processes, usually through one-on-one interactions with a therapist.

insomnia   A chronic condition marked by difficulties in initiating or maintaining sleep, lasting for a period of at least one month.

instincts   Unlearned characteristic patterns of responding that are controlled by specific triggering stimuli in the world; they are not thought to be an important factor in explaining goal-directed behavior in humans.

instrumental conditioning   A procedure for studying how organisms learn about the consequences of their own voluntary actions; they learn that their behaviors are instrumental in producing rewards and punishments. Also called *operant conditioning*.

insulin   A hormone released by the pancreas that helps pump nutrients in the blood into the cells, where they can be stored as fat or metabolized into needed energy.

intelligence   An internal capacity or ability that psychologists assume accounts for individual differences in mental test performance. The term is also used to describe the mental processes that underlie the ability to adapt to ever-changing environments.

intelligence quotient (IQ)   Originally, mental age divided by chronological age and then multiplied by 100. More recently, defined in terms of deviation from the average score on an IQ test. See deviation IQ.

internal attribution   Attributing the cause of a person's behavior to an internal personality trait or disposition.

internal validity   The extent to which an experiment has effectively controlled for confounding variables; internally valid experiments allow for the determination of causality.

interneurons   Neurons that make no direct contact with the world but rather convey information from one neuron or processing site to another.

intrinsic motivation   Goal-directed behavior that seems to be entirely self-motivated.

iris   The ring of colored tissue surrounding the pupil.

James-Lange theory   A theory of emotion that argues that body reactions precede and drive the subjective experience of emotions.

kinesthesia   In perception, the ability to sense the position and movement of one's body parts.

latency period   Freud's period of psychosexual development, from age 5 to puberty, during which the child's sexual feelings are largely suppressed.

latent content   According to Freud, the true psychological meaning of dream symbols, which represent hidden wishes and desires that are too disturbing to be expressed directly.

lateral hypothalamus   A portion of the hypothalamus that, when lesioned, causes an animal to be reluctant to eat; like the ventromedial hypothalamus, it probably plays some role in eating behavior, but the precise role is unknown.

law of effect   The idea that if a response in a particular situation is followed by a satisfying or pleasant consequence, it will be strengthened; if a response in a particular situation is followed by an unsatisfying or unpleasant consequence, it will be weakened.

learned helplessness   A general sense of helplessness that is acquired when people repeatedly fail in their attempts to control their environment; learned helplessness may play a role in depression.

learning   A relatively permanent change in behavior, or potential to respond, that results from experience.

lens   The flexible piece of tissue that helps focus light toward the back of the eye.

light   The small part of the electromagnetic spectrum that is processed by the visual system. Light is typically classified in terms of wavelength (the physical distance from one energy cycle to the next) and intensity (the amount of light falling on an object).

limbic system   A system of structures thought to be involved in motivational and emotional behaviors (the amygdala) and memory (the hippocampus).

linguistic relativity hypothesis   The proposal that language determines the characteristics and content of thought.

locus of control   The amount of control that a person feels he or she has over the environment.

longitudinal design   A research design in which the same people are studied or tested repeatedly over time.

long-term memory   The system used to maintain information for extended periods of time.

lymphocytes   Specialized white blood cells that have the job of attacking foreign substances, such as viruses and bacteria.

magnetic resonance imaging (MRI)   A device that uses magnetic fields and radio-wave pulses to construct detailed, three-dimensional images of the brain; "functional" MRIs can be used to map changes in blood oxygen use as a function of task activity.

major depressive episode A type of mood disorder characterized by depressed mood and other symptoms.

manic state A disordered state in which the person becomes hyperactive, talkative, and has a decreased need for sleep; a person in a manic state may engage in activities that are self-destructive or dangerous.

manifest content According to Freud, the actual symbols and events experienced in a dream.

mean The arithmetic average of a set of scores.

means-ends analysis A problem-solving heuristic that involves devising actions, or means, that reduce the distance between the current starting point and the desired end (the goal state).

median The middle point in an ordered set of scores; half of the scores fall at or below the median score, and half fall at or above the median score.

medical model The view that abnormal behavior is symptomatic of an underlying "disease" that can be "cured" with the appropriate therapy.

meditation A technique for self-induced manipulation of awareness, often used for the purpose of relaxation and self-reflection.

memory The capacity to preserve and recover information.

memory span The number of items that can be recalled from short-term memory in their proper presentation order on half of the tested memory trials.

menopause The period during which a woman's menstrual cycle slows down and finally stops.

mental age The chronological age that best fits a child's level of performance on a test of mental ability. Mental age is typically calculated by comparing a child's test score with the average scores for different age groups.

mental retardation A label that is generally assigned to someone who scores below 70 on a standard IQ test although other factors, such as one's ability to adapt to the environment, are also important.

mental sets The tendency to rely on well-established habits of perception and thought when attempting to solve problems.

meta-analysis A statistical technique used to compare findings across many different research studies; comparisons are based on some common evaluation measure, such as the difference between treatment and control conditions.

method of loci A mnemonic device in which you choose some pathway, such as moving through the rooms in your house, and then form visual images of the to-be-remembered items sitting in various locations along the pathway.

midbrain The middle portion of the brain, containing such structures as the tectum, superior colliculus, and inferior colliculus; midbrain structures serve as neural relay stations and may help coordinate reactions to sensory events.

middle ear The portion between the eardrum and the cochlea containing three small bones (the malleus, incus, and stapes) that help to intensify and prepare the sound vibrations for passage into the inner ear.

mind The contents and processes of subjective experience: sensations, thoughts, and emotions.

Minnesota Multiphasic Personality Inventory (MMPI) A widely used self-report inventory for assessing personality traits and for diagnosing psychological problems.

mnemonic devices Special mental tricks that help people think about material in ways that improve later memory. Most mnemonic devices require the use of visual imagery.

mode The most frequently occurring score in a set of scores.

modeling The natural tendency to imitate the behavior of significant others in one's surroundings.

monocular depth cues Cues for depth that require input from only one eye.

mood disorders Prolonged and disabling disruptions in emotional state.

morality The ability to distinguish between appropriate and inappropriate actions; a child's sense of morality may be tied to his or her level of cognitive development.

morphemes The smallest units in a language that carry meaning.

motivation The set of factors that initiate and direct behavior, usually toward some goal.

motor neurons Neurons that carry information away from the central nervous system to the muscles and glands that directly produce behavioral responses.

multiple intelligences The notion proposed by Howard Gardner that people possess a set of separate and independent "intelligences" ranging from musical to linguistic to interpersonal ability.

myelin sheath An insulating material that protects the axons of some neurons and helps to speed up neural transmission.

nativism The idea that certain kinds of knowledge and ideas are innate, or present at birth; innate ideas do not need to be learned.

naturalistic observation A research technique that involves recording only naturally occurring behavior as opposed to behavior produced in the laboratory.

need hierarchy The idea popularized by Maslow that human needs are prioritized in a hierarchy. Some needs, especially physiological ones, must be satisfied before others, such as the need for achievement or self-actualization, can be pursued.

negative punishment   An event that, when removed after a response, lowers the likelihood of that response occurring again.

negative reinforcement   An event that, when removed after a response, increases the likelihood of that response occurring again.

NEO-PI-R   A self-report inventory developed to measure the Big Five personality dimensions.

nerves   Bundles of axons that make up neural "transmission cables."

neural networks   A term used to describe computer simulation models of neural communication networks in the brain.

neurons   The cells in the nervous system that receive and transmit information by generating an electrochemical signal; neurons are the basic building blocks of the nervous system.

neuroscience   An interdisciplinary field of study directed at understanding the brain and its relation to behavior.

neurotransmitters   Chemical messengers that relay information from one neuron to the next. They are released from the terminal buttons into the synapse, where they interact chemically with the cell membrane of the next neuron; the result is either an excitatory or an inhibitory message.

night terrors   A condition in which the sleeper, usually a child, awakens suddenly in an extreme state of panic; not thought to be associated with dreaming.

nightmares   Frightening and anxiety-arousing dreams that occur primarily during the REM stage of sleep.

obedience   The form of compliance that occurs when people respond to the orders of an authority figure.

obesity   A weight problem characterized by excessive body fat.

object permanence   The ability to recognize that objects still exist when they're no longer in sight.

observational learning   Learning that occurs as a result of observing the experiences of others. Also called *social learning*.

obsessive-compulsive disorder   An anxiety disorder that manifests itself through persistent and uncontrollable thoughts, called obsessions, or by the compelling need to perform repetitive acts, called compulsions.

occipital lobe   One of four anatomical regions of each hemisphere of the cerebral cortex, located at the back of the brain; visual processing is controlled here.

olfaction   The sense of smell.

operant conditioning   See *instrumental conditioning*.

operational definition   Defining concepts in terms of how those concepts are measured.

opiates   A class of drugs that reduces anxiety, lowers sensitivity to pain, and elevates mood; opiates often act to depress nervous system activity.

opponent-process theory   A theory of color vision proposing that cells in the visual pathway increase their activation levels to one color and decrease their activation levels to another color-for example, increasing to red and decreasing to green.

oral stage   The first stage in Freud's conception of psychosexual development, occurring in the first year of life; in this stage, pleasure is derived primarily from sucking and placing things in the mouth.

orgasmic phase   The third stage in the human sexual response cycle. It's characterized by rhythmic contractions in the sex organs; in men, ejaculation occurs. There is also the subjective experience of pleasure that appears to be similar for men and women.

orienting response   An inborn tendency to shift one's focus of attention toward a novel or surprising event.

pain   An adaptive response by the body to any stimulus that is intense enough to cause tissue damage.

panic disorder   A condition marked by recurrent discrete episodes or attacks of extremely intense fear or dread.

parallel processing   Processing that occurs in many different brain regions at the same time, in parallel.

paranoid personality disorder   A personality disorder characterized by pervasive distrust of others.

parietal lobe   One of four anatomical regions of each hemisphere of the cerebral cortex, located roughly on the top middle portion of the brain; it contains the somatosensory cortex, which controls the sense of touch.

partial reinforcement schedule   A schedule in which reinforcement is delivered only some of the time after the response has occurred.

passionate love   An intense emotional state characterized by a powerful longing to be with a specific person; passionate love is marked by a combination of intimacy and passion, but commitment may be lacking.

peg-word method   A mnemonic device in which you form visual images connecting to-be-remembered items with retrieval cues, or pegs.

perceived control   The amount of influence you feel you have over a situation and your reaction to it.

perception   The collection of processes used to arrive at a meaningful interpretation of sensations; through perception, the simple components of an experience are organized into a recognizable form.

perceptual constancy   Perceiving the properties of an object to remain the same even though the physical properties of the sensory message are changing.

perceptual illusions   Inappropriate interpretations of physical reality. Perceptual illusions often occur as a result of the brain's using otherwise adaptive organizing principles.

peripheral nervous system   The network of nerves that links the central nervous system with the rest of the body.

personal identity   A sense of who one is as an individual and how well one stacks up against peers. Erik Erikson's theory postulates that personal identity is shaped by a series of personal crises that each person confronts at characteristic stages of development.

personality   The distinguishing pattern of psychological characteristics-thinking, feeling, and behaving-that differentiates us from others and leads us to act consistently across situations.

personality disorders   Chronic or enduring patterns of behavior that lead to significant impairments in social functioning.

person-situation debate   A controversial debate centering on whether people really do behave consistently across situations.

phallic stage   Freud's third stage of psychosexual development, lasting from about age 3 to age 5; pleasure is gained from self-stimulation of the sexual organs.

phenotype   A person's observable characteristics, such as red hair. The phenotype is controlled mainly by the genotype, but it can also be influenced by the environment.

phi phenomenon   An illusion of movement that occurs when stationary lights are flashed in succession.

phonemes   The smallest significant sound units in speech.

phonology   Rules governing how sounds should be combined to make words in a language.

pinna   The external flap of tissue normally referred to as the "ear"; it helps capture sounds.

pitch   The psychological experience that results from the auditory processing of a particular frequency of sound.

pituitary gland   A kind of master gland in the body that controls the release of hormones in response to signals from the hypothalamus.

placebo   An inactive, or inert, substance that resembles an experimental substance.

place theory   The idea that the location of auditory receptor cells activated by movement of the basilar membrane underlies the perception of pitch.

plateau phase   The second stage in the human sexual response cycle. Arousal continues to increase, although at a slower rate, toward a preorgasm maximum point.

polygraph test   A device that measures various indices of physiological arousal in an effort to determine whether someone is telling a lie. The logic behind the test is that lying leads to greater emotionality, which can be picked up through such measures of arousal as heart rate, blood pressure, breathing rate, and sweating.

positive punishment   An event that, when presented after a response, lowers the likelihood of that response occurring again.

positive regard   The idea that we value what others think of us and constantly seek others' approval, love, and companionship.

positive reinforcement   An event that, when presented after a response, increases the likelihood of that response occurring again.

positron emission tomography (PET)   A method for measuring how radioactive substances are absorbed in the brain; it can be used to detect how different tasks activate different areas of the living brain.

postconventional level   Kohlberg's highest level of moral development, in which moral actions are judged on the basis of personal codes of ethics that are general and abstract and that may not agree with societal norms.

posttraumatic stress disorder   A trauma-based anxiety disorder characterized by flashbacks, avoidance of stimuli associated with the traumatic event, and chronic arousal symptoms.

pragmatics   The practical knowledge used to comprehend the intentions of a speaker and to produce an effective response.

preconscious mind   The part of the mind that contains all of the inactive but potentially accessible thoughts and memories.

preconventional level   In Kohlberg's theory, the lowest level of moral development, in which decisions about right and wrong are made primarily in terms of external consequences.

predictive validity   See *validity*.

prejudice   Positive or negative evaluations of a group and its members.

preoperational period   Piaget's second stage of cognitive development, lasting from ages 2 to about 7; children begin to think symbolically but often lack the ability to perform mental operations like conservation.

primacy effect   The better memory seen for items near the beginning of a memorized list.

proactive interference   A process in which old memories interfere with the establishment and recovery of new memories.

procedural memory Knowledge about how to do things, such as riding a bike or swinging a golf club.

projection A defense mechanism in which unacceptable feelings or wishes are dealt with by attributing them to others.

projective personality test A type of personality test in which individuals are asked to interpret unstructured or ambiguous stimuli; the idea is that subjects will project their true thoughts and feelings into the interpretation, thereby revealing elements of their personality.

prototype The best or most representative member of a category (such as robin for the category "bird").

psychiatrists Medical doctors who specialize in the diagnosis and treatment of psychological problems. Unlike psychologists, psychiatrists are licensed to prescribe drugs.

psychoactive drugs Drugs that affect behavior and mental processes through alterations of conscious awareness.

psychoanalysis Freud's method of treatment that attempts to bring hidden impulses and memories, which are locked in the unconscious, to the surface of awareness, thereby freeing the patient from disordered thoughts and behaviors.

psychodynamic theory An approach to personality development, based largely on the ideas of Sigmund Freud, which holds that much of behavior is governed by unconscious forces.

psychology The scientific study of behavior and mind.

psychometrics The use of psychological tests to measure the mind and mental processes.

psychophysics A field of psychology in which researchers search for ways to describe the transition from the physical stimulus to the psychological experience of that stimulus.

psychosurgery Surgery that destroys or alters tissues in the brain in an effort to affect behavior.

psychotherapy Treatment designed to help people deal with mental, emotional, or behavioral problems.

puberty The period during which a person reaches sexual maturity and is potentially capable of producing offspring.

punishment Consequences that decrease the likelihood of responding in a similar way again.

pupil The hole in the center of the eye that allows light to enter; the size of the pupil changes with light intensity.

random assignment A technique ensuring that each participant in an experiment has an equal chance of being assigned to any of the conditions in the experiment.

random sampling A procedure for selecting a representative subset of a target population; the procedure guarantees that everyone in the population has an equal likelihood of being selected for the sample.

range The difference between the largest and smallest scores in a distribution.

rational-emotive therapy A form of cognitive therapy, developed by Albert Ellis, in which the therapist acts as a kind of cross-examiner, verbally assaulting the client's irrational thought processes.

reaction formation A defense mechanism used to transform an anxiety-producing wish into a kind of opposite-people behave in a way that counters the way they truly feel.

reactivity The extent to which an individual's behavior is changed as a result of being observed; the behavior becomes essentially a reaction to the process of being observed.

recency effect The better memory seen for items near the end of a memorized list.

receptive field In vision, the portion of the retina that, when stimulated, causes the activity of the neuron to change.

reciprocal determinism The idea that beliefs, behavior, and the environment interact to shape what is learned from experience.

reciprocity The tendency for people to return in kind the feelings that are shown toward them.

recognition by components The idea proposed by Biederman that people recognize objects perceptually via smaller components called geons.

reflexes Largely automatic body reactions-such as the knee jerk-that are controlled primarily by spinal cord pathways.

refractory period The period of time following an action potential during which more action potentials cannot be generated.

rehearsal A strategic process that helps to maintain short-term memories indefinitely through the use of internal repetition.

reinforcement Response consequences that increase the likelihood of responding in a similar way again.

reliability A measure of the consistency of test results; reliable tests produce similar scores or indices from one administration to the next.

REM A stage of sleep characterized by rapid eye movements and low-amplitude, irregular EEG patterns similar to those found in the waking brain. REM is typically associated with dreaming.

REM rebound The tendency to increase the proportion of time spent in REM sleep after a period of REM deprivation.

representativeness heuristic The tendency to make decisions based on an alternative's similarity, or representativeness, in relation to an ideal. For example, people decide whether a sequence is random based on how irregular the sequence looks.

repression A defense mechanism that individuals use, unknowingly, to push threatening thoughts, memories, and feelings out of conscious awareness.

research psychologists Psychologists who conduct experiments or collect observations designed to discover the basic principles of behavior and mind.

resistance In psychoanalysis, a patient's unconsciously motivated attempts to subvert or hinder the process of therapy.

resolution phase The fourth and final stage in the human sexual response cycle. Arousal returns to normal levels. For men, there is a refractory period during which further stimulation fails to produce visible signs of arousal.

resting potential The tiny electrical charge in place between the inside and outside of the resting neuron.

retina The thin layer of tissue that covers the back of the eye and contains the light-sensitive receptor cells for vision.

retinal disparity A binocular cue for depth that is based on location differences between the images in each eye.

retrieval The processes that determine and control how memories are recovered and translated into performance.

retroactive interference A process in which the formation of new memories hurts the recovery of old memories.

retrograde amnesia Memory loss for events that happened prior to the point of brain injury.

rods Receptor cells in the retina, located mainly around the sides of the retina, that transduce light energy into neural messages; these visual receptors are highly sensitive and are active in dim light.

Rorschach test A projective personality test that requires people to interpret ambiguous inkblots.

s (specific intelligence) According to Spearman, a specific factor, derived from factor analysis, that is unique to a particular kind of test.

schedule of reinforcement A rule that an experimenter uses to determine when particular responses will be reinforced. Schedules may be fixed or variable, ratio or interval.

schema An organized knowledge structure in long-term memory.

schemata Mental models of the world that people use to guide and interpret their experiences.

schizophrenia A class of disorders characterized by fundamental disturbances in thought processes, emotion, or behavior.

scientific method An investigative method that generates empirical knowledge-that is, knowledge derived from systematic observations of the world. It involves forming a hypothesis on the basis of initial observations, and then testing the hypothesis with further observations.

searching for analogies A problem-solving heuristic that involves trying to find a connection between the current problem and some previous problem you have solved successfully.

secondary traits The less obvious characteristics of an individual's personality that do not always appear in his or her behavior, such as testiness when on a diet.

second-order conditioning A procedure in which an established conditioned stimulus is used to condition a second neutral stimulus.

self-actualization The ingrained desire to reach one's true potential as a human being.

self-concept An organized set of perceptions that we hold about our abilities and characteristics.

self-efficacy The beliefs that we hold about our own ability to perform a task or accomplish a goal.

self-fulfilling prophecy effect A condition in which our expectations about the actions of another person actually lead that person to behave in the expected way.

self-monitoring The degree to which a person monitors a situation closely and changes his or her behavior accordingly; people who are high self-monitors may not behave consistently across situations.

self-perception theory The idea that people use observations of their own behavior as a basis for inferring their internal beliefs.

self-report inventories Personality tests in which people answer groups of questions about how they typically think, act, and feel; their responses, or self-reports, are then compared to average responses compiled from large groups of prior test takers.

self-serving bias The tendency to make internal attributions about one's own behavior when the outcome is positive and to blame the situation when one's behavior leads to something negative.

semantic memory Knowledge about the world, stored as facts that make little or no reference to one's personal experiences.

semantics The rules used in language to communicate meaning.

semicircular canals A receptor system attached to the inner ear that responds to movement and acceleration and to changes in upright posture.

sensations The elementary components, or building blocks, of an experience, such as a pattern of light and dark, a bitter taste, or a change in temperature.

sensitization An increase in the tendency to respond to an event that has been repeated; sensitization is more likely when a repeated stimulus is intense.

sensorimotor period Piaget's first stage of cognitive development, lasting from birth to about 2 years of age; schemata revolve around sensory and motor abilities.

sensory adaptation The tendency of sensory systems to reduce sensitivity to a stimulus source that remains constant.

sensory memory The capacity to preserve and recover sensory information in a relatively pure, unanalyzed form; sensory memories are usually accurate representations of externally presented information and last for only a second or less.

sensory neurons Neurons that make initial contact with the environment and carry the message inward toward the spinal cord and brain.

serotonin A neurotransmitter that has been linked to sleep, dreaming, and general arousal and may also be involved in some psychological disorders such as depression and schizophrenia.

set point A natural body weight, perhaps produced by genetic factors, that the body seeks to maintain. When body weight falls below the set point, one is motivated to eat; when weight exceeds the set point, one feels less motivated to eat.

sexual orientation A person's sexual and emotional attraction to members of the same sex or the other sex; homosexuality, heterosexuality, and bisexuality are all sexual orientations.

sexual scripts Learned cognitive programs that instruct us on how, why, and what to do in our interactions with sexual partners; the nature of sexual scripts may vary from one culture to the next.

shaping A procedure in which reinforcement is delivered for successive approximations of the desired response.

short-term memory A limited-capacity "working memory" system that people use to hold information, after it has been analyzed, for periods usually lasting less than a minute or two. Short-term memory is the system we use to temporarily store, think about, and reason with information.

signal detection A technique that can be used to determine the ability of someone to detect the presence of a stimulus.

single-blind study An experimental design in which the participants do not know which of the conditions to which they have been assigned (e.g., experimental versus control); it's used to control for subject expectancies.

16 Personality Factor A self-report inventory developed by Cattell and colleagues to measure normal personality traits.

sleepwalking A condition in which the sleeper rises during sleep and wanders about; not thought to be associated with dreaming.

social cognition The study of how people use cognitive processes-such as perception, memory, thought, and emotion-to help them make sense of other people as well as themselves.

social facilitation The enhancement in performance that is sometimes found when an individual performs in the presence of others.

social influence The study of how the behaviors and thoughts of individuals are affected by the presence of others.

social interference The impairment in performance that is sometimes found when an individual performs in the presence of others.

social learning See *observational learning*.

social learning theory The idea that most important personality traits come from modeling, or copying, the behavior of others.

social loafing The tendency to put out less effort when working in a group compared to when working alone.

social psychology The discipline that studies how people think about, influence, and relate to other people.

social schema A general knowledge structure, stored in long-term memory, that relates to social experiences or people.

social support The resources that individuals receive from other people or groups, often in the form of comfort, caring, or help.

sociobiology A theory proposing that social behavior should be understood from an evolutionary/genetic perspective.

soma The cell body of a neuron.

somatic system The collection of nerves that transmits information toward the brain and connects to the skeletal muscles in order to initiate movement; part of the peripheral nervous system.

somatization disorder A long-lasting preoccupation with body symptoms that have no identifiable physical cause.

somatoform disorders Psychological disorders that focus on the physical body.

sound The physical message delivered to the auditory system, a mechanical energy that requires a medium such as air or water in order to move.

source characteristics Features of the person who is presenting a persuasive message, such as his or her attractiveness, amount of power, or fame. The characteristics of the source are more important when we process a message peripherally.

specific phobic disorder A highly focused fear of a specific object or situation.

spontaneous recovery The recovery of an extinguished conditioned response after a period of nonexposure to the conditioned stimulus.

spontaneous remission Improvement in a psychological disorder without treatment-that is, simply as a function of the passage of time.

standard deviation An indication of how much individual scores differ or vary from the mean in a set of scores.

standardization Keeping the testing, scoring, and interpretation procedures similar across all administrations of a test.

statistical deviance A criterion of abnormality stating that a behavior is abnormal if it occurs infrequently among the members of a population.

stereotypes The collection of beliefs and impressions held about a group and its members; common stereotypes include those based on gender, race, and age.

stimulants A class of drugs that increases central nervous system activity, enhancing neural transmission.

stimulus discrimination Responding differently to a new stimulus than one responds to an established conditioned stimulus.

stimulus generalization Responding to a new stimulus in a way similar to the response produced by an established conditioned stimulus.

storage The processes that determine and control how memories are stored and maintained over time.

strange situation test Gradually subjecting a child to a stressful situation and observing his or her behavior toward the parent or caregiver. This test is used to classify children according to type of attachment-secure, resistant, or avoidant.

stress People's physical and psychological reactions to demanding situations.

stressors The demanding or threatening situations that produce stress.

structuralism An early school of psychology; structuralists attempted to understand the mind by breaking it down into its basic constituent parts, much like a chemist might try to understand a chemical compound.

sublimation A defense mechanism used to channel unacceptable impulses into socially acceptable activities.

superego In Freud's theory, the portion of personality that motivates people to act in an ideal fashion, in accordance with the moral customs defined by parents and culture.

surface structure The literal ordering of words in a sentence.

survey A descriptive research technique designed to gather limited amounts of information from many people, usually by administering some kind of questionnaire.

synapse The junction, or small gap, between neurons, typically between the terminal buttons of one neuron and the dendrite or cell body of another neuron.

syntax Rules governing how words should be combined to form sentences.

systematic desensitization A technique that uses counterconditioning and extinction to reduce the fear and anxiety that have become associated with a specific object or event. It's a multistep process that attempts to replace the negative learned association with something relaxing.

systematic introspection An early investigative technique used to study the mind; systematic introspection required subjects to look inward and provide rigorous descriptions of their own internal experiences.

taste buds The receptor cells on the tongue involved in taste.

temperament A child's general level of emotional reactivity.

temporal lobe One of four anatomical regions of each hemisphere of the cerebral cortex, located roughly on the sides of the brain; it's involved in certain aspects of speech and language perception.

teratogens Environmental agents-such as disease organisms or drugs-that can potentially damage the developing embryo or fetus.

terminal buttons The tiny swellings at the end of a neuron's axon that contain chemicals important to neural transmission.

thalamus A relay station in the forebrain thought to be an important gathering point for input from the senses.

Thematic Apperception Test (TAT) A projective personality test that requires people to make up stories about the characters in ambiguous pictures.

theta waves The pattern of brain activity observed in stage 1 sleep.

thinking The processes that underlie the mental manipulation of knowledge, usually in an attempt to reach a goal or solve a problem.

token economy   A type of behavioral therapy in which patients are rewarded with small tokens when they act in an appropriate way; the tokens can then be exchanged for certain privileges.

tolerance   An adaptation that the body makes to compensate for the continued use of a drug such that increasing amounts of the drug are needed to produce the same physical and behavioral effects.

top-down processing   Processing that is driven by one's beliefs and expectations about how the world is organized.

trait   A stable predisposition to act or behave in a certain way.

trait theories   Formal systems for assessing how people differ, particularly in their predispositions to respond in certain ways across situations. Most trait theories rely on psychometric tests to identify stable individual differences among people.

transduction   The process by which external messages are translated into the internal language of the brain.

transfer-appropriate processing   The idea that the likelihood of correct retrieval is increased if a person uses the same kind of mental processes during testing that he or she used during encoding.

transference   In psychoanalysis, the patient's expression of thoughts or feelings toward the therapist that are actually representative of the way the patient feels about other significant people in his or her life.

triarchic theory   Robert Sternberg's theory of intelligence; it proposes three types of intelligence: analytic, creative, and practical.

trichromatic theory   A theory of color vision proposing that color information is extracted by comparing the relative activations of three different types of cone receptors.

twin studies   Identical twins, who share genetic material, are compared to fraternal twins in an effort to disentangle the roles heredity and environment play in psychological traits.

two-factor theory   A theory of emotion that argues that the cognitive interpretation, or appraisal, of a body reaction drives the subjective experience of emotion.

tympanic membrane   The eardrum, which responds to incoming sound waves by vibrating.

Type A   An enduring pattern of behavior linked to stress-related health disorders; it is characterized by being hard-driving, ambitious, easily annoyed, and impatient.

Type B   People who lack the Type A traits-they put themselves under less pressure and appear more relaxed.

unconditioned response (UR)   The observable response that is produced automatically, prior to training, on presentation of an unconditioned stimulus.

unconditioned stimulus (US)   A stimulus that automatically produces-or elicits-an observable response prior to any training.

unconscious mind   The part of the mind that Freud believed housed all the memories, urges, and conflicts that are truly beyond awareness.

validity   An assessment of how well a test measures what it is supposed to measure. *Content validity* assesses the degree to which the test samples broadly across the domain of interest; *predictive validity* assesses how well the test predicts some future criterion; *construct validity* assesses how well the test taps into a particular theoretical construct.

variability   A measure of how much the scores in a distribution of scores differ from one another.

variable-interval schedule   A schedule in which the allotted time before a response will yield reinforcement changes from trial to trial.

variable-ratio schedule   A schedule in which a certain number of responses is required for reinforcement, but the number of required responses typically changes from trial to trial.

ventromedial hypothalamus   A portion of the hypothalamus that, when lesioned, causes an animal to typically overeat and gain a large amount of weight. Once thought to be a kind of stop eating, or satiety, center in the brain; its role in eating behavior is currently unknown.

vestibular sacs   Contain receptors thought to be primarily responsible for the sense of balance.

visual acuity   The ability to process fine detail in vision.

visual imagery   The processes used to construct an internal visual image, perhaps using the same brain mechanisms used to perceive events in the physical world.

visual neglect   A complex disorder of attention characterized by a tendency to ignore things that appear on one side of the body, usually the left side.

warm fibers   Neurons that respond vigorously when the temperature of the skin increases.

Weber's law   The principle stating that the ability to notice a difference in the magnitude of two stimuli is a constant proportion of the size of the standard stimulus. Psychologically, the more intense a stimulus is to begin with, the more intense it will need to become for one to notice a change.

well-defined problem   A problem with a well-stated goal, a clear starting point, and a relatively easy way to tell when a solution has been obtained.

withdrawal Clear and measurable physical reactions, such as sweating, vomiting, changes in heart rate, or tremors, that occur when a person stops taking certain drugs after continued use.

working backward A problem-solving heuristic that involves starting at the goal state and moving backward toward the starting point in order to see how the goal state can be reached.

zygote The fertilized human egg, containing 23 chromosomes from the father and 23 chromosomes from the mother, which pair up to form the master genetic blueprint.

References

Abdullaev, Y. G., & Posner, M. I. (1998). Time course of activating brain areas in generating verbal associations. *Psychological Science, 8,* 56–59.

Abel, E. L. (1981). Behavioral teratology of alcohol. *Psychological Bulletin, 90,* 564–581.

Abrams, D., Wetherell, M., Cochrane, S., Hogg, M. A., & Turner, J. C. (1990). Knowing what to think by knowing who you are: Self-categorization and the nature of norm formation, conformity, and group polarization. *British Journal of Social Psychology, 29,* 97–119.

Abramson, L. Y., Metalsky, G. I., & Alloy, L. B. (1989). Hopelessness depression: A theory-based subtype of depression. *Psychological Review, 96,* 358–372.

Achenbach, T. M. (1992). Developmental psychopathology. In M. H. Bornstein & M. E. Lamb (Eds.), *Developmental psychology: An advanced textbook.* Hillsdale, NJ: Erlbaum.

Adair, R., Bauchner, H., Phillip, B., Levenson, S., & Zuckerman, B. (1991). Night waking during infancy: Role of parent presence at bedtime. *Pediatrics, 87,* 500–504.

Adams, D. B., Gold, A. R., & Burt, A. D. (1978). Rise in female-initiated sexual activity at ovulation and its suppression by oral contraceptives. *New England Journal of Medicine, 299,* 1145–1150.

Adams, P. R., & Adams, G. R. (1984). Mount Saint Helens's ashfall: Evidence for a disaster stress reaction. *American Psychologist, 39,* 252–260.

Ader, R., & Cohen, N. (1975). Behaviorally conditioned immunosuppression. *Psychosomatic Medicine, 37,* 333–340.

Adler, A. (1927). *Understanding human nature.* New York: Greenberg.

Adler, E., & Bachant, J. (1998). Intrapsychic and interactive dimensions of resistance: A contemporary perspective. *Psychoanalytic Psychology, 15,* 451–479.

Adler, N., & Matthews, K. (1994). Health psychology: Why do some people get sick and some stay healthy? *Annual Review of Psychology, 45,* 229–259.

Aggleton, J. P. (1993). The contribution of the amygdala to normal and abnormal emotional states. *Trends in Neuroscience, 16,* 328–333.

Agras, W. S., Sylvester, D., & Oliveau, D. (1969). The epidemiology of common fears and phobia. *Comprehensive Psychiatry, 10,* 151–156.

Ainsworth, M. D. S. (1979). Attachment as related to mother-infant interactions. In J. S. Rosenblatt, R. A. Hinde, C. Beer, & M. Busnel (Eds.), *Advances in the study of behavior* (Vol. 9). New York: Academic Press.

Ainsworth, M. D. S., Blehar, M., Waters, E., & Wall, S. (1978). *Patterns of attachment.* Hillsdale, NJ: Erlbaum.

Ainsworth, M. D. S., & Wittig, B. A. (1969). Attachment and exploratory behavior of one-year-olds in a strange situation. In B. M. Foss (Ed.), *Determinants of infant behaviour* (Vol. 4). London: Methuen.

Ajzen, I., & Fishbein, M. (1977). Attitude-behavior relations: A theoretical analysis and review of empirical research. *Psychological Bulletin, 84,* 888–918.

Akiskal, H. S., & Cassano, G. B. (Eds.). (1997). *Dysthymia and the spectrum of chronic depression.* New York: Guilford Press.

Albert, M. S., & Moss, M. B. (1992). The assessment of memory disorders in patients with Alzheimer's disease. In L. R. Squire & N. Butters (Eds.), *Neuropsychology of memory* (2nd ed.). New York: Guilford.

Allen, K. M., Blascovich, J., Tomaka, J., & Kelsey, R. M. (1991). Presence of human friends and pet dogs as moderators of autonomic responses to stress in women. *Journal of Personality and Social Psychology, 61,* 582–589.

Alley, T. R., & Cunningham, M. R. (1991). Average faces are attractive, but very attractive faces are not average. *Psychological Science, 2,* 123–125.

Allison, D. B., & Faith, M. S. (1997). Issues in mapping genes for eating disorders. *Psychopharmacology Bulletin, 33,* 359–368.

Allison, J. (1989). The nature of reinforcement. In S. B. Klein & R. R. Mowrer (Eds.), *Contemporary learning theories: Instrumental conditioning and the impact of biological constraints on learning.* Hillsdale, NJ: Erlbaum.

Allison, T., & Cicchetti, D. V. (1976). Sleep in mammals: Ecological and constitutional correlates. *Science, 194,* 732–734.

Alloy, L. B., & Clements, C. M. (1998). Hopelessness theory of depression: Tests of the symptom component. *Cognitive Therapy & Research, 22,* 303–335.

Allport, A. (1989). Visual attention. In M. I. Posner (Ed.), *Foundation of cognitive science.* Cambridge, MA: MIT Press.

Allport, G. W. (1937). *Personality: A psychological interpretation.* New York: Holt.

Allport, G. W., & Odbert, H. H. (1936). Trait-names: A psycho-lexical study. *Psychological Monographs, 47*(1, Whole No. 211).

Amabile, T. M. (1983). *The social psychology of creativity.* New York: Springer-Verlag.

American Psychological Association. (1992). Ethical principles of psychologists and code of conduct. *American Psychologist, 47,* 1597–1611.

American Psychological Association. (1993). *Profile of all APA members: 1993.* Washington, DC: Author.

Amzica, F., & Steriade, M. (1996). Progressive cortical synchronization of ponto-geniculo-occipital potentials during rapid eye movement sleep. *Neuroscience, 72,* 309–314.

Anastasi, A. (1985). Psychological testing: Basic concepts andcommon misconceptions. *G. Stanley Hall Lecture Series, 5,* 87–120.

Andersen, B. L. (1992). Psychological interventions for cancer patients to enhance quality of life. *Journal of Consulting and Clinical Psychology, 60,* 552–568.

Anderson, J. R. (1990a). *The adaptive character of thought.* Hillsdale, NJ: Erlbaum.

Anderson, J. R. (1990b). *Cognitive psychology and its implications* (3rd ed.). New York: Freeman.

Anderson, J. R., & Schooler, L. J. (1991). Reflections of the environment in memory. *Psychological Science, 2,* 396–408.

Andersson, B. E. (1992). Effects of day-care on cognitive and socioemotional competence of thirteen-year-old Swedish schoolchildren. *Child Development, 63,* 20–36.

Andrasik, F., & Holroyd, K. A. (1980). A test of specific and nonspecific effects in the biofeedback treatment of tension headache. *Journal of Consulting and Clinical Psychology, 48,* 575–586.

Andreasen, N. C. (1987). Creativity and mental illness: Prevalence rates in writers and their first-degree relatives. *American Journal of Psychiatry, 144,* 1288–1292.

Angell, J. R. (1903). The relations of structural and functional psychology to philosophy. *Philosophical Review, 12,* 203.

Anisfeld, M. (1991). Neonatal imitation: A review. *Developmental Review, 11,* 60–97.

Antrobus, J. (1991). Dreaming: Cognitive processes during cortical activation and high afferent thresholds. *Psychological Review, 98,* 96–121.

Apgar, V., & Beck, J. (1974). *Is my baby all right?* New York: Pocket Books.

Appelbaum, P. S. (1997). Almost a revolution: An international perspective on the law of involuntary commitment. *Bulletin of the American Academy of Psychiatry & the Law, 25,* 135–147.

Araoz, D. L. (1982). *Hypnosis and sex therapy.* New York: Brunner/Mazel.

Aronson, E. (1992). The return of the repressed: Dissonance theory makes a comeback. *Psychological Inquiry, 3,* 303–311.

Aronson, E. (1997). The theory of cognitive dissonance: The evolution and vicissitudes of an idea. In C. McGarty, & S. Haslam (Eds.), *The message of social psychology: Perspectives on mind in society.* Oxford, England: Blackwell Publishers, Inc.

Asch, S. E. (1951). Effects of group pressure on the modification and distortion of judgments. In H. Guetzkow (Ed.), *Groups, leadership, and men.* Pittsburgh, PA: Carnegie Press.

Asch, S. E. (1955, May). Opinions and social pressures. *Scientific American, 193,* 31–35.

Aschoff, J., & Wever, R. (1981). The circadian system of man. In J. Aschoff (Ed.), *Handbook of behavioral neurobiology: Vol. 4. Biological rhythms.* New York: Plenum.

Aserinsky, E., & Kleitman, N. (1955). Two types of ocular motility occurring in sleep. *Journal of Applied Physiology, 8,* 1–10.

Atkinson, J. W. (1957). Motivational determinants of risk-taking behavior. *Psychological Review, 64,* 359–372.

Atkinson, J. W., & Raynor, J. O. (Eds.). (1974). *Motivation and achievement.* Washington, DC: Winston.

Atkinson, R. C., & Shiffrin, R. M. (1968). Human memory: A proposed system and its control processes. In K. Spence & J. Spence (Eds.), *The psychology of learning and motivation* (Vol. 2). New York: Academic Press.

Atkinson, R. C., & Shiffrin, R. M. (1971, August). The control of short-term memory. *Scientific American, 225,* 82–90.

Averbach, E., & Coriell, A. S. (1961). Short-term memory in vision. *Bell System Technical Journal, 40,* 309–328.

Averill, J. R. (1983). Studies on anger and aggression: Implications for theories of emotion. *American Psychologist, 38,* 1145–1160.

Ayllon, T., & Azrin, N. H. (1968). *The token economy: A motivational system for therapy and rehabilitation.* New York: Appleton-Century-Crofts.

Baddeley, A. D. (1992). Working memory. *Science, 255,* 556–559.

Baddeley, A. D., & Lieberman, K. (1980). Spatial working memory. In R. Nickerson (Ed.), *Attention and performance VIII.* Hillsdale, NJ: Erlbaum.

Baddeley, A. D., Thomson, N., & Buchanan, M. (1975). Word length and the structure of short-term memory. *Journal of Verbal Learning and Verbal Behavior, 14,* 575–589.

Bahrick, H. P. (1984). Semantic memory content in permastore: 50 years of memory for Spanish learned in school. *Journal of Experimental Psychology: General, 113,* 1–29.

Bahrick, H. P., & Hall, L. K. (1991). Lifetime maintenance of high school mathematics content. *Journal of Experimental Psychology: General, 120,* 20–33.

Bailey, J. M., & Pillard, R. C. (1991). A genetic study of male sexual orientation. *Archives of General Psychiatry, 48,* 1089–1096.

Bailey, J. M., & Pillard, R. C. (1995). Genetics of human sexual orientation. *Annual Review of Sex Research, 6,* 126–150.

Bailey, J. M., Pillard, R. C., Neale, M. C. I., & Agyei, Y. (1993). Heritable factors influence sexual orientation in women. *Archives of General Psychiatry, 50,* 217–223.

Baillargeon, R. (1994). How do infants learn about the physical world? *Psychological Science, 5,* 133–140.

Baker, T. B., & Tiffany, S. T. (1985). Morphine tolerance as habituation. *Psychological Review, 92,* 78–108.

Baldo, J.V., & Shimamura, A. P. (1998). Letter and category fluency in patients with frontal lobe lesions. *Neuropsychology, 12,* 259–267.

Ballard, P. A., Tetrud, J. W., & Langston, J. W. (1985). Permanent human parkinsonism due to 1-methyl-4–phenyl-1,2,3,6–tetrahydropyridine (MPTP). *Neurology, 35,* 949–956.

Baltes, P. B. (1987). Theoretical propositions of life-span developmental psychology: On the dynamics between growth and decline. *Developmental Psychology, 23,* 611–626.

Baltes, P. B., Reese, H. W., & Lipsitt, L. P. (1980). Life-spandevelopmental psychology. *Annual Review of Psychology, 31,* 65–110.

Bandura, A. (1986). *Social foundations of thought and action.* Englewood Cliffs, NJ: Prentice Hall.

Bandura, A. (1993). Perceived self-efficacy in cognitive development and functioning. *Educational Psychologist, 28,* 117–148.

Bandura, A., Ross, D., & Ross, S. A. (1963). Imitation of film-mediated aggressive models. *Journal of Abnormal and Social Psychology, 66,* 3–11.

Banks, M. S., & Salapatek, P. (1983). Infant visual perception. In M. M. Haith & J. J. Campos (Eds.), *Handbook of child psychology.* New York: Wiley.

Banks, M. S., & Shannon, E. (1993). Spatial and chromatic visual efficiency in human neonates. In C. E. Granrud (Ed.), *Visual perception and cognition in infancy.* Hillsdale, NJ: Erlbaum.

Barber, T. X. (1976). *Pitfalls in human research: Ten pivotal points.* New York: Pergamon.

Barber, T. X., Spanos, N. P., & Chaves, J. (1974). *Hypnosis, imagination, and human potentialities.* New York: Pergamon.

Barcelo, F., & Gale, A. (1997). Electrophysiological measures of cognition in biological psychiatry: Some cautionary notes. *International Journal of Neuroscience, 92,* 219–240.

Barenbaum, N. B. (1997). The case(s) of Gordon Allport. *Journal of Personality, 65,* 743–755.

Bargones, J. Y., & Werner, L. A. (1994). Adults listen selectively; infants do not. *Psychological Science, 5,* 170–174.

Barkley, R. A. (1997). Behavioral inhibition, sustained attention, and executive functions: Constructing a unified theory of ADHD. *Psychological Bulletin, 121,* 65–94.

Barlow, D. H. (1988). *Anxiety and its disorders: The nature and treatment of anxiety and panic.* New York: Guilford.

Barlow, D. H., & Durand, V. M. (1999). *Abnormal psychology: An integrative approach (2nd ed.).* Pacific Grove, CA: Brooks/Cole.

Barlow, D. H., & Rapee, R. M. (1991). *Mastering stress: A lifestyle approach.* Dallas, TX: American Health.

Bartlett, F. C. (1932). *Remembering.* Cambridge: Cambridge University Press.

Bassok, M., Wu, L., & Olseth, K. L. Judging a book by its cover: Interpretative effects of content on problem-solving transfer. *Memory & Cognition, 23,* 354–367.

Bastien, C., & Campbell, K. (1992). The evoked K-complex: All or none phenomenon? *Sleep, 15,* 236–245.

Baumrind, D. (1964). Some thoughts on the ethics of research: After reading Milgram's "Behavioral study of obedience." *American Psychologist, 19,* 421–423.

Baumrind, D. (1985). Research using intentional deception: Ethical issues revisited. *American Psychologist, 40,* 165–174.

Beck, A. T. (1991). Cognitive therapy: A 30-year retrospective. *American Psychologist, 46,* 368–375.

Beck, A. T., & Young, J. E. (1985). Depression. In D. H. Barlow (Ed.), *Clinical handbook of psychological disorders.* New York: Guilford.

Beer, J. M., Arnold, R. D., & Loehlin, J. C. (1998). Genetic and environmental influences on MMPI factor scales: Joint model fitting to twin and adoption data. *Journal of Personality & Social Psychology, 74,* 818–827.

Beers, M. J., Lassiter, G. D., & Flannery, B. C. (1997). Individual differences in person memory: Self-monitoring and the recall of consistent and inconsistent behavior. *Journal of Social Behavior & Personality, 12,* 811–820.

Békésy, G. von (1960). *Experiments in hearing.* New York: McGraw-Hill.

Bell, A. P., Weinberg, M. S., & Hammersmith, S. K. (1981). *Sexual preference: Its development in men and women.* Bloomington: Indiana University Press.

Bell, P. A., Fisher, J. D., Baum, A., & Greene, T. E. (1990). *Environmental psychology* (3rd ed.). Fort Worth, TX: Holt, Rinehart and Winston.

Belloc, H. B., & Breslow, L. (1972). Relationship of physical health status and health practice. *Preventive Medicine, 1,* 409–421.

Belsky, J. (1988). The "effects" of infant daycare reconsidered. *Early Childhood Research Quarterly, 3,* 235–272.

Belsky, J. (1999). *The psychology of aging: Theory, research, and interventions.* Pacific Grove, CA: Brooks/Cole.

Bem, D. J. (1967). Self-perception: An alternative interpretation of cognitive dissonance phenomena. *Psychological Review, 74,* 183–200.

Bem, D. J. (1972). Self-perception theory. In L. Berkowitz (Ed.), *Advances in experimental social psychology* (Vol. 6). New York: Academic Press.

Bem, S. L. (1981). Gender schema theory: A cognitive account of sex-typing. *Psychological Review, 88,* 354–364.

Benes, F. M. (1989). Myelination of cortical-hippocampal relays during late adolescence. *Schizophrenia Bulletin, 15,* 585–593.

Benes, F.M., Turtle, M., Khan, Y., & Farol, P. (1994). Myelination of a key relay zone in the hippocampal formation occurs in the human brain during childhood, adolescence, and adulthood. *Archives of General Psychiatry, 51,* 477–484.

Benson, H. (1975). *The relaxation response.* New York: Morrow.

Benson, P. L., Dehority, J., Garman, L., Hanson, E.,

Hochschwender, M., Lebod, C., Rohr, R., & Sullivan, J. (1980). Intrapersonal correlates of nonspontaneous helping behavior. *Journal of Social Psychology, 110,* 87–95.

Bentall, R. P. (1990). The illusion of reality: A review and integration of psychological research on hallucinations. *Psychological Bulletin, 107,* 82–95.

Benton, M. K., & Schroeder, H. E. (1990). Social skills training with schizophrenics: A meta-analytic evaluation. *Journal of Consulting and Clinical Psychology, 58,* 741–747.

Bergvall, A., Fahlke, C., & Hansen, S. (1996). An animal model for Type 2 alcoholism? Alcohol consumption and aggressive behavior following lesions in the raphe nuclei, medial hypthothalamus, or ventral striatum-septal area. *Physiology & Behavior, 60,* 1125–1135.

Berkeley, D., & Humphreys, P. (1982). Structuring decision problems and the "bias heuristic." *Acta Psychologica, 50,* 201–252.

Berman, K. F., & Weinberger, D. R. (1990). Lateralization of cortical function during cognitive tasks: Regional cerebral blood flow studies of normal individuals and patients with schizophrenia. *Journal of Neurology, Neurosurgery, and Psychiatry, 53,* 150–160.

Bernal, E. M. (1984). Bias in mental testing: Evidence for an alternative to the heredity-environment controversy. In C. R. Reynolds & R. T. Brown (Eds.), *Perspectives on bias in mental testing.* New York: Plenum.

Berndt, T. J. (1988). The nature and significance of children's friendships. In R. Vasta (Ed.), *Annals of child development* (Vol. 5). Greenwich, CT: JAI Press.

Berndt, T.J., & Keefe, K. (1995). Friends' influence on adolescents' adjustments to school. *Child Development, 66,* 1312–1329.

Bernstein, I. H., Lin, T., & McClelland, P. (1982). Cross- vs. within-racial judgments of attractiveness. *Perception & Psychophysics, 32,* 495–503.

Bernstein, I. L. (1978). Learned taste aversions in children receiving chemotherapy. *Science, 200,* 1302–1303.

Berscheid, E. (1985). Interpersonal attraction. In G. Lindzey & E. Aronson (Eds.), *Handbook of social psychology* (Vol. 2). New York: Random House.

Bertenthal, B. I., Campos, J. J., & Kermoian, R. (1994). An epigenetic perspective on the development of self-produced locomotion and its consequences. *Current Directions in Psychological Science, 3,* 140–145.

Best, J. B. (1989). *Cognitive psychology* (2nd ed.). St. Paul, MN: West Publishing.

Beutler, L. E., & Berren, M. R. (Eds.). (1995). *Integrative assessment of adult personality.* New York: Guilford.

Beyth-Marom, R., & Lichtenstein, S. (1984). *An elementary approach to thinking under uncertainty.* Hillsdale, NJ: Erlbaum.

Biederman, I. (1987). Recognition-by-components: A theory of human image understanding. *Psychological Review, 94,* 115–147.

Biederman, I. (1990). Higher-level vision. In D. H. Osherson, S. M. Kosslyn, & J. M. Hollerbach (Eds.), *An invitation to cognitive science: Visual cognition and action* (Vol. 2). Cambridge, MA: MIT Press.

Bigelow, H. J. (1850). Dr. Harlow's case of recovery from the passage of an iron bar through the head. *American Journal of Medical Science, 20,* 13–22.

Binder, J. R., Rao, S. M., Hammeke, T. A., & Yetkin, F. Z. (1994). Functional magnetic resonance imaging of human auditory cortex. *Annals of Neurology, 35,* 662–672.

Binet, A., & Simon, T. (1916; reprinted 1973). *The development of intelligence in children.* New York: Arno Press.

Bisiach, E. (1992). Understanding consciousness: Clues from unilateral neglect and related disorders. In A. D. Milner & M. D. Rugg (Eds.), *The neuropsychology of consciousness*. London: Academic Press.

Bisiach, E., & Rusconi, M. L. (1990). Break-down of perceptual awareness in unilateral neglect. *Cortex, 26,* 643–649.

Bjork, R. A. (1989). Retrieval inhibition as a adaptive mechanism in human memory. In H. L. Roediger & F. I. M. Craik (Eds.), *Varieties of memory and consciousness: Essays in honor of Endel Tulving*. Hillsdale, NJ: Erlbaum.

Bjorklund, D.F. (1997). The role of immaturity in human development. *Psychological Bulletin, 122,* 153–169.

Black, J. E., Isaacs, K. R., & Greenough, W. T. (1991). Usual vs. successful aging: Some notes on experiential factors. *Neurobiology of Aging, 12,* 325–328.

Blagrove, M. (1996). Problems with the cognitive psychological modeling of dreaming. *Journal of Mind and Behavior, 17,* 99–134.

Blair, S. N., Kohl, H. W., Paffenbarger, R. S., Clark, K. H., & Gibbons, L. W. (1989). Physical fitness and all-cause mortality: A prospective study of healthy men and women. *Journal of the American Medical Association, 262,* 2395–2401.

Blanchard, E. B. (1992). Psychological treatment of benign headache disorders. *Journal of Consulting and Clinical Psychology, 60,* 537–551.

Blanton, H., Cooper, J., Skurnik, I., & Aronson, J. (1997). When bad things happen to good feedback: Exacerbating the need for self-justification with self-affirmations. *Personality & Social Psychology Bulletin, 23,* 684–692.

Blass, T. (1991). Understanding behavior in the Milgram obedience experiment: The role of personality, situations, and their interactions. *Journal of Personality and Social Psychology, 60,* 398–413.

Bleuler, E. (1908). Die prognose der Dementia praecox (Schizophreniegruppe). *Allgemeine Zeitschrift fur Psychiatrie, 65,* 436–464.

Blumenthal, J. A., Emery, C. F., Walsh, M. A., Cox, D. R., Kuhn, C. M., Williams, R. B., & Williams, R. S. (1988). Exercise training in healthy Type A middle-aged men: Effects on behavioral and cardiovascular responses. *Psychosomatic Medicine, 50,* 418–433.

Blundell, J. E., & Rogers, P. J. (1991). Hunger, hedonics, and the control of satiation and satiety. In M. I. Friedman, M. G. Tordoff, & M. R. Kare (Eds.), *Chemical senses* (Vol. 4). New York: Marcel Dekker.

Bolanowski, S. J., Jr. (1989). Four channels mediate vibrotaction: Facts, models, and implications. *Journal of the Acoustical Society of America, 85,* S62.

Bolanowski, S. J., Gescheider, G. A., & Verrillo, R. T. (1994). Hairy skin: Psychophysical channels and their physiological substrates. *Somatosensory and Motor Research, 11,* 279–290.

Bolles, R. C. (1972). Reinforcement, expectancy, and learning. *Psychological Review, 79,* 394–409.

Bolles, R. C. (1993). *The story of psychology: A thematic history*. Pacific Grove, CA: Brooks/Cole.

Book, H. E. (1998). *How to practice brief psychodynamic psychotherapy: The core conflictual relationship theme method*. Washington, DC: American Psychological Association.

Boomer, D. S. (1965). Hesitation and grammatical encoding. *Language and Speech, 8,* 145–158.

Bootzin, R. R., Manber, R., Perlis, M. L., Salvio, M., & Wyatt, J. K. (1993). Sleep disorders and the elderly. In P. B. Sutker & H. F. Adams (Eds.), *Comprehensive handbook of psychopathology* (2nd ed.). New York: Plenum.

Boring, E. G. (1950). *A history of experimental psychology* (2nd ed.). New York: Appleton-Century-Crofts.

Bornstein, M. H. (1989). Stability in early mental development: From attention and information processing in infancy to language and cognition in childhood. In M. H. Bornstein & N. A. Krasnegor (Eds.), *Stability and continuity in mental development: Behavioral and biological perspectives*. Hillsdale, NJ: Erlbaum.

Bornstein, M. H. (1992). Perception across the life span. In M. H. Bornstein & M. E. Lamb (Eds.), *Developmental psychology: An advanced textbook* (3rd ed.). Hillsdale, NJ: Erlbaum.

Bornstein, M. H., Kessen, W., & Weiskopf, S. (1976). Color vision and hue categorization in young human infants. *Journal of Experimental Psychology: Human Perception and Performance, 2,* 115–129.

Bortz, W. M. (1990). The trajectory of dying: Functional status in the last year of life. *Journal of the American Geriatrics Society, 38,* 146–150.

Bouchard, C., Tremblay, A., Despres, J., Nadeau, A., Lupien, P. J., Theriault, G., Dussault, J., Moorjani, S., Pinault, S., & Fournier, G. (1990). The response to long-term overfeeding in identical twins. *New England Journal of Medicine, 322,* 1477–1487.

Bouchard, T. J., Jr. (1997). IQ similarity in twins reared apart: Findings and responses to critics. In R. J. Sternberg & E. L. Grigorenko (Eds.), *Intelligence, heredity, and environment*. New York, NY: Cambridge University Press.

Bouchard, T. J., Jr., Lykken, D. T., McGue, M., Segal, N. L., & Tellegean, A. (1990). Sources of human psychological differences: The Minnesota study of twins reared apart. *Science, 250,* 223–228.

Bouchard, T. J., Jr., & McGue, M. (1981). Familial studies of intelligence: A review. *Science, 212,* 1055–1059.

Boucher, J. D., & Carlson, G. E. (1980). Recognition of facial expression in three cultures. *Journal of Cross-Cultural Psychology, 11,* 263–280.

Bouton, M. E. (1991). Context and retrieval in extinction and in other examples of interference in simple associative learning. In L. Dachowski & C. F. Flaherty (Eds.), *Current topics in animal learning*. Hillsdale, NJ: Erlbaum.

Bøvjberg, D. H., Redd, W. H., Maier, L. A., Holland, J. C., Lesko, L. M., Niedzwiecki, D., Rubin, S. E., & Hakes, T. B. (1990). Anticipatory immune suppression in women receiving cyclic chemotherapy for ovarian cancer. *Journal of Consulting and Clinical Psychology, 58,* 153–157.

Bower, T. G. R. (1982). *Development in infancy* (2nd ed.). San Francisco: Freeman.

Bowers, T., & Clum, G. (1988). Relative contributions of specific and nonspecific treatment effects: Meta-analysis of placebo-controlled behavior therapy research. *Psychological Bulletin, 103,* 315–323.

Bowlby, J. (1969). *Attachment and loss: Vol. 1. Attachment*. New York: Basic Books.

Bowlby, J. (1988). *A secure base: Parent-child attachment and healthy human development*. New York: Basic Books.

Bowmaker, J. K., & Dartnall, H. J. A. (1980). Visual pigments of rods and cones in a human retina. *Journal of Physiology, 298,* 501–511.

Bowman, E. S. (1998). Pseudoseizures. *Psychiatric Clinics of North America, 21,* 649–657.

Boynton, R. M. (1979). *Human color vision*. New York: Holt, Rinehart & Winston.

Braff, D. L., & Huey, L. (1988). Methylphenidate-induced information processing dysfunction in non-schizophrenic patients. *Archives of General Psychiatry, 45,* 827–832.

Bransford, J. D., & Stein, B. S. (1993). *The ideal problem solver* (2nd ed.). New York: Freeman.

Braungart, J.M., Plomin, R., DeFries, J. C., & Fulker, D.W. (1992). Genetic influence on tester-rated infant temperament as assessed by Bayley's Infant Behavior Record: Nonadoptive and adoptive siblings and twins. *Developmental Psychology, 28*, 40–47.

Breggin, P. R. (1991). *Toxic psychiatry.* New York: St. Martin's.

Bregman, A. S. (1990). *Auditory scene analysis.* Cambridge, MA: Bradford/MIT Press.

Breland, K., & Breland, M. (1961). The misbehavior of organisms. *American Psychologist, 16*, 681–684.

Brett, J. F., Brief, A. P., Burke, M. J., George, J. M., & Webster, J. (1990). Negative affectivity and the reporting of stressful life events. *Health Psychology, 9*, 57–68.

Brewer, K. R., & Wann, D. L. (1998). Observational learning effectiveness as a function of model characteristics: Investigating the importance of social power. *Social Behavior & Personality, 26*, 1–10.

Briere, J., & Conte, J. (1993). Self-reported amnesia for abuse in adults molested as children. *Journal of Traumatic Stress, 6*, 21–31.

Broad, W., & Wade, N. (1982). *Betrayers of the truth.* New York: Simon & Schuster.

Broadbent, D. E. (1952). Failures of attention in selective listening. *Journal of Experimental Psychology, 44*, 428–433.

Broadbent, D. E. (1958). *Perception and communication.* London: Pergamon Press.

Broberg, D. J., & Bernstein, I. L. (1987). Candy as a scapegoat in the prevention of food aversions in children receiving chemotherapy. *Cancer, 60*, 2344–2347.

Broca, P. (1861). Remarques sur le siege de la faculte du langage articule, suivies d'une observation d'aphemie (perte de la parole). *Bulletin de la Société Anatomique* (Paris), *36*, 330–357.

Brody, N. (1992). *Intelligence* (2nd ed.). San Diego, CA: Academic Press.

Bromley, D. B. (1986). *The case-study method in psychology and related disciplines.* Chichester, England: Wiley.

Brosschot, J. F., Godaert, G. L. R., Benschop, R. J., Olff, M., Ballieux, R. E., & Heijnen, C. J. (1998). Experimental stress and immunological reactivity: A closer look at perceived uncontrollability. *Psychosomatic Medicine, 60*, 359–361.

Brown, A. D., & Murphy, D. R. (1989). Cryptomnesia: Delineating inadvertent plagiarism. *Journal of Experimental Psychology: Learning, Memory, & Cognition, 15*, 432–442.

Brown, G. W., & Birley, J. L. T. (1968). Crisis and life change and the onset of schizophrenia. *Journal of Health and Social Behavior, 9*, 203–214.

Brown, R., & Kulick, J. (1977). Flashbulb memories. *Cognition, 5*, 73–99.

Brown, T. A., Barlow, D. H., & Liebowitz, M. R. (1994). The empirical basis of generalized anxiety disorder. *American Journal of Psychiatry, 151*, 1272–1280.

Bruce, D. (1985). The how and why of ecological memory. *Journal of Experimental Psychology: General, 114*, 78–90.

Buck, L. (1996). Information coding in the vertebrate olfactory system. *Annual Review of Neuroscience, 19*, 517–544.

Buck, L., & Axel, A. (1991). A novel multigene family may encode odorant receptors: A molecular basis for odor recognition. *Cell, 65*, 175–187.

Buda, M., & Tsuang, M. T. (1990). The epidemiology of suicide: Implications for clinical practice. In S. J. Blumenthal & D. J. Kupfer (Eds.), *Suicide over the life cycle: Risk factors, assessments and treatment of suicidal patients.* Washington, D.C.: American Psychiatric Press.

Buell, S. J., & Coleman, P. D. (1979). Dendritic growth in the aged human brain and failure of growth in senile dementia. *Science, 206*, 854–856.

Buss, A. H. (1988). *Personality: Evolutionary heritage and human distinctivness.* Hillsdale, NJ: Erlbaum.

Buss, A. H. (1989). Personality as traits. *American Psychologist, 44*, 1378–1388.

Buss, D. M. (1989). Sex differences in human preferences: Evolutionary hypotheses tested in 37 cultures. *Behavioral and BrainSciences, 12*, 1–49.

Buss, D. M. (1991). Evolutionary personality psychology. *Annual Review of Psychology, 42*, 459–491.

Buss, D. M., & Schmitt, D. P. (1993). Sexual strategies theory: An evolutionary perspective on human mating. *Psychological Review, 100*, 204–232.

Buss, D. M., & Shackelford, T. K. (1997). Human aggression in evolutionary psychological perspective. *Clinical Psychology Review, 17*, 605–619.

Butcher, J. N. (1995). Interpretation of the MMPI-2. In L. E. Beutler & M. R. Berren (Eds.), *Integrative assessment of adult personality.* New York: Guilford.

Butcher, J. N., & Rouse, S. V. (1996). Personality: Individual differences and clinical assessment. *Annual Review of Psychology, 47*, 87–111.

Butler, R. W., Rorsman, I., Hill, J. M., & Tuma, R. (1993). The effects of frontal brain impairment on fluency: Simple and complex paradigms. *Neuropsychology, 7*, 519–529.

Butterworth, G. (1992). Origins of self-perception in infancy. *Psychological Inquiry, 3*, 103–111.

Byne, W. (1997). Why we cannot conclude that sexual orientation is primarily a biological phenomenon. *Journal of Homosexuality, 34*, 73–80.

Byrd, J. C. (1992). Environmental tobacco smoke: Medical and legal issues. *Medical Clinics of North America, 76*, 377–398.

Byrne, D. (1971). *The attraction paradigm.* New York: Academic Press.

Cacioppo, J. T., Priester, J. R., & Berntson, G. G. (1993). Rudimentary determinants of attitudes. II. Arm flexion and extension have different effects on attitudes. *Journal of Personality and Social Psychology, 65*, 5–17.

Cameron, J., & Pierce, W. D. (1994). Reinforcement, reward, and intrinsic motivation: A meta-analysis. *Review of Educational Research, 64*, 363–423.

Campbell, D. T., & Stanley, J. C. (1966). *Experimental and quasi-experimental designs for research.* Chicago: Rand McNally.

Campfield, L. A., Smith, F. J., Rosenbaum, M., & Hirsch, J. (1996). Human eating: Evidence for a physiological basis using a modified paradigm. *Neuroscience & Biobehavioral Reviews, 20*, 1133–1137.

Campos, J. J., Langer, A., & Krowitz, A. (1970). Cardiac responses on the visual cliff in prelocomotor human infants. *Science, 170*, 196–197.

Cannell, C. G., & Kahn, R. L. (1968). Interviewing. In G. Lindzey and E. Aronson (Eds.), *Handbook of social psychology: Research methods* (Vol. 2). Reading, MA: Addison-Wesley.

Cannon, W. B. (1927). The James-Lange theory of emotions: A critical examination and an alternative theory. *American Journal of Psychology, 39*, 106–124.

Cannon, W. B. (1929). *Bodily changes in pain, hunger, fear, and rage.* New York: Appleton.

Cannon, W. B. (1932). *The wisdom of the body.* New York: Norton.

Cantor, N. (1990). From thought to behavior: "Having" and "doing" in the study of personality and cognition. *American Psychologist, 45*, 735–750.

Cantor, N., & Harlow, R. E. (1994). Personality, strategic behavior, and daily-life problem solving. *Current Directions in Psychological Science, 3*, 169–172.

Cantor, N., & Malley, J. (1991). Life tasks, personal needs, and close relationships. In G. Fletcher & F. Fincham (Eds.), *Cognition in close relationships*. Hillsdale, NJ: Erlbaum.

Cantor, N., & Mischel, W. (1978). Prototypes in person perception. *Advances in Experimental Social Psychology, 12*, 3–52.

Cantwell, D. P. (1996). Attention deficit disorder: A review of the past 10 years. *Journal of the American Academy of Child and Adolescent Psychiatry, 35*, 978–987.

Capaldi, E. D. (Ed). (1996). *Why we eat what we eat: The psychology of eating*. Washington, DC: American Psychological Association.

Carlsmith, J. M., & Gross, A. E. (1969). Some effects of guilt on compliance. *Journal of Personality and Social Psychology, 11*, 240–244.

Carlson, N. R. (1991). *Physiology of behavior* (4th ed.). Boston: Allyn & Bacon.

Carrasco, M., & Ridout, J. B. (1993). Olfactory perception and olfactory imagery: A multidimensional analysis. *Journal of Experimental Psychology: Human Perception and Performance, 19*, 287–301.

Cartwright, R. (1991). Dreams that work: The relation of dream-incorporation to adaptation to stressful events. *Dreaming, 1*, 2–9.

Carstensen, L. L. (1995). Evidence for a life-span theory of socioemotional selectivity. *Current Directions in Psychological Science, 4*, 151–156.

Case, R. B., Moss, A. J., Case, N., McDermott, M., & Eberly, S. (1992). Living alone after myocardial infarction: Impact on prognosis. *Journal of American Medical Association, 267*, 515–519.

Caspi, A., & Silva, P.A. (1995). Temperamental qualities at age three predict personality traits in young adulthood: Longitudinal evidence from a birth cohort. *Child Development, 66*, 486–498.

Castillo, R. J. (1997). *Culture & mental illness: A client-centered approach*. Pacific Grove, CA: Brooks/Cole Publishing Co.

Cattell, R. B. (1963). Theory of fluid and crystallized intelligence: A critical experiment. *Journal of Educational Psychology, 54*, 1–22.

Cattell, R. B. (1973, July). A 16PF profile. *Psychology Today*, 40–46.

Cattell, R. B. (1998). Where is intelligence? Some answers from the triadic theory. In J. J.McArdle, & R. W. Woodcock (Eds.), *Human cognitive abilities in theory and practice*. Mahwah, NJ: Lawrence Erlbaum Associates, Inc.

Cattell, R. B., Eber, H. W., & Tatsuoka, M. M. (1970). *Handbook of the 16 personality factor questionnaire (16PF)*. Champaign, IL: Institute for Personality and Ability Testing.

Caudill, M., & Butler, C. (1990). *Naturally intelligent systems*. Cambridge, MA: MIT Press.

Caughy, M. O., DiPietro, J. A., & Strobino, D. M. (1994). Daycare participation as a protective factor in the cognitive development of low-income children. *Child Development, 65*, 457–471.

Cavanaugh, J. C. (1993). *Adult development and aging* (2nd ed.). Pacific Grove, CA: Brooks/Cole.

Ceci, S. J. (1991). How much does schooling influence intellectual development and its cognitive components? A reassessment of the evidence. *Developmental Psychology, 27*, 703–722.

Cermak, L. S. (1982). The long and the short of it in amnesia. In L. S. Cermak (Ed.), *Human memory and amnesia*. Hillsdale, NJ: Erlbaum.

Chaiken, S., Liberman, A., & Eagly, A. H. (1989). Heuristic and systematic information processing: Within and beyond the persuasion context. In J. S. Uleman & J. A. Bargh (Eds.), *Unintended thought*. New York: Guilford.

Chase, W. G., & Simon, H. A. (1973). The mind's eye in chess. In W. G. Chase (Ed.), *Visual information processing*. New York: Academic Press.

Chen, S. C. (1937). Social modification of the activity of ants in nest-building. *Physiological Zoology, 10*, 420–436.

Cherry, E. C. (1953). Some experiments on the recognition of speech with one and with two ears. *Journal of the Acoustical Society of America, 25*, 975–979.

Chesney, M. A. (1993). Health psychology in the 21st century: Acquired immunodeficiency syndrome as a harbinger of things to come. *Health Psychology, 12*, 259–268.

Chia, R. C., Allred, L. J., Grossnickle, W. F., & Lee, G. W. (1998). Effects of attractivness and gender on the perception of achievement-related variables. *Journal of Social Psychology, 138*, 471–477.

Chomsky, N. (1957). *Syntactic structures*. The Hague: Mouton.

Chomsky, N. (1986). *Knowledge of language: Its nature, origins, and use*. New York: Praeger.

Chumlea, W. C. (1982). Physical growth in adolescence. In B. J. Wolman (Ed.), *Handbook of developmental psychology*. Englewood Cliffs, NJ: Prentice-Hall.

Cicirelli, V. G. (1997). Relationship of psychosocial and background variables to older adults' end-of-life decisions. *Psychology and Aging, 12*, 72–83.

Clark, H. H. (1992). *Arenas of language use*. Chicago: The University of Chicago Press.

Clarke, L. A., & Livesley, W. J. (1994). Two approaches to identifying the dimensions of personality disorder: Convergence on the five-factor model. In P. T. Costa, Jr. & T. A. Widiger (Eds.), *Personality disorders and the five-factor model of personality*. Washington, DC: American Psychological Association.

Clarke-Stewart, A. K. (1989). Infant day care: Maligned or malignant? *American Psychologist, 44*, 266–273.

Cleary, L. J., Lee, W. L., & Byrne, J. H. (1998). Cellular correlates of long-term sensitization in Aplysia. *Journal of Neuroscience, 18*, 5988–5998.

Cleary, P. J. (1980). A checklist for life event research. *Journal of Psychosomatic Research, 24*, 199–207.

Cleghorn, J. M., Franco, S., Szechtman, B., Kaplan, R., Szechtman, H., Brown, G. M., Nahmias, C., & Garnett, E. S. (1992). Toward a brain map of auditory hallucinations. *American Journal of Psychiatry, 149*, 1062–1069.

Clendenen, V. I., Herman, C. P., & Polivy, J. (1994). Social facilitation of eating among friends and strangers. *Appetite, 23*, 1–13.

Cohen, J. D., & Servan-Schreiber, D. (1992). Context, cortex, and dopamine: A connectionist approach to behavior and biology in schizophrenia. *Psychological Review, 99*, 45–77.

Cohen, S., & Herbert, T. B. (1996). Health psychology: Psychological factors and physical disease from the perspective of human psychoneuroimmunology. *Annual Review of Psychology, 47*, 113–142.

Cohen, S., Tyrrell, D. A., & Smith, D. A. (1993). Negative life events, perceived stress, negative affect, and susceptibility to the common cold. *Journal of Personality and Social Psychology, 64*, 131–140.

Cohen, S., & Wills, T. A. (1985). Stress, social support, and the buffering hypothesis. *Psychological Bulletin, 98*, 310–357.

Coile, D. C., & Miller, N. E. (1984). How radical animal activists try to mislead humane people. *American Psychologist, 39*, 700–701.

Cole, M. (1992). Culture in development. In M. H. Bornstein & M. E. Lamb (Eds.), *Developmental psychology: An advanced textbook.* Hillsdale, NJ: Erlbaum.

Cole, N. S. (1981). Bias in testing. *American Psychologist, 36,* 1067–1077.

Coleman, P. (1993). Overview of substance abuse. *Primary Care, 20,* 1–18.

Coleman, P. D., & Flood, D. G. (1987). Neuron numbers and dendritic extent in normal aging and Alzheimer's disease. *Neurobiology of Aging, 8,* 521–545.

Coles, R., & Stokes, G. (1985). *Sex and the American teenager.* New York: Harper & Row.

Collins, D. W., & Kimura, D. (1997). A large sex difference on a two-dimensional mental rotation task. *Behavioral Neuroscience, 111,* 845–849.

Colombo, J., Frick, J.E., & Gorman, S.A. (1997). Sensitization during visual habituation sequences: Procedural effects and individual differences. *Journal of Experimental Child Psychology, 67,* 223–235.

Colon, E. A., Callies, A. L., Popkin, M. K., & McGlave, P. B. (1991). Depressed mood and other variables related to bone marrow transplantation survival in acute leukemia. *Psychosomatics, 32,* 420–425.

Colwill, R. M. (1994). Associative representations of instrumental contingencies. In G. H. Bower (Ed.), *The psychology of learning and motivation* (Vol. 31). San Diego: Academic Press.

Colwill, R. M., & Delameter, B. A. (1995). An associative analysis of instrumental biconditional discrimination learning. *Animal Learning & Behavior, 23,* 218–233.

Colwill, R. M., & Rescorla, R. A. (1986). Associative structures in instrumental learning. In G. H. Bower (Ed.), *The psychology of learning and motivation* (Vol. 20, pp. 55–104). Orlando, FL: Academic Press.

Commons, M. L., Sinnott, J. D., Richards, F. A., & Armon, C. (Eds.). (1989). *Adult development: Vol. 1. Comparisons and applications of adolescent and adult developmental models.* New York: Praeger.

Compas, B. E., Hinden, B. R., & Gerhardt, C. A. (1995). Adolescent development: Pathways and processes of risk and resilience. *Annual Review of Psychology, 46,* 265–293.

Conrad, R. (1964). Acoustic confusion in immediate memory. *British Journal of Psychology, 55,* 75–84.

Conway, M. A., Anderson, S. J., Larsen, S. F., Donnelly, C. M., McDaniel, M. A., McClelland, A. G. R., Rawles, R. E., & Logie, R. H. (1994). The formation of flashbulb memories. *Memory & Cognition, 22,* 326–343.

Cook, M., & Mineka, S. (1989). Observational conditioning of fear to fear–relevant versus fear-irrelevant stimuli in rhesus monkeys. *Journal of Abnormal Psychology, 98,* 448–459.

Cook, T. D., & Campbell, D. T. (1979). *Quasi-experimentation: Design and analysis for field settings.* Chicago: Rand McNally.

Cooper, C.R., & Denner, J. (1998). Theories linking culture and psychology: Universal and community-specific processes. *Annual Review of Psychology, 49,* 559–584.

Cooper, E. (1991). A critique of six measures for assessing creativity. *Journal of Creative Behavior, 25,* 194–204.

Cooper, J. (1992). Dissonance and the return of the self-concept. *Psychological Inquiry, 3,* 320–323.

Cooper, W. H. (1983). An achievement motivation nomological network. *Journal of Personality and Social Psychology, 44,* 841–861.

Corballis, M. C. (1991). *The lopsided ape: Evolution of the generative mind.* New York: Oxford University Press.

Coren, S., Porac, C., & Theodor, L. H. (1987). Set and subjective contour. In S. Petry & G. E. Meyer (Eds.), *The perception of illusory contours.* New York: Springer-Verlag.

Coren, S. (1996). *Sleep thieves.* New York: The Free Press.

Coren, S., Ward, L. M., & Enns, J. T. (1994). *Sensation and perception* (4th ed.). Fort Worth, TX: Harcourt Brace.

Corina, D. P., Vaid, J., & Bellugi, U. (1992). The linguistic basis of left hemisphere specialization. *Science, 255,* 1258–1260.

Courtois, C. A. (1992). The memory retrieval process in incest survivor therapy. *Journal of Child Sexual Abuse, 1,* 15–30.

Cowan, G., & Hoffman, C. D. (1986). Gender stereotyping in young children: Evidence to support a concept-learning approach. *Sex Roles, 14,* 211–224.

Cowan, N. (1995). *Attention and memory: An integrated framework.* New York: Oxford University Press.

Cowan, N., Lichty, W., & Grove, T. R. (1990). Properties of memory for unattended spoken syllables. *Journal of Experimental Psychology: Learning, Memory, & Cognition, 16,* 258–269.

Cowan, N., Saults, J. S., & Nugent, L. D. (1997). The role of absolute and relative amounts of time in forgetting within immediate memory: The case of tone-pitch comparisons. *Psychonomic Bulletin & Review, 4,* 393–397.

Cox, M. J., & Paley, B. (1997). Families as systems. *Annual Review of Psychology, 48,* 243–267.

Cox, M. J., Owen, M. T., Henderson, V. K., & Margand, N. A. (1992). Prediction of infant-father and infant-mother attachment. *Developmental Psychology, 28,* 474–483.

Craig, J. C. (1985). Attending to two fingers: Two hands are better than one. *Perception & Psychophysics, 38,* 496–511.

Craig, K. D. (1978). Social disclosure, coactive peer companions, and social modeling determinants of pain communications. *Canadian Journal of Behavioural Science, 10,* 91–104.

Craik, F. I. M. (1994). Memory changes in normal aging. *Current Directions in Psychological Science, 5,* 155–158.

Craik, F. I. M., & Jacoby, L. L. (1979). Elaboration and distinctiveness in episodic memory. In L. Nilsson (Ed.), *Perspectives on memory research: Essays in honor of Upsala University's 500th anniversary.* Hillsdale, NJ: Erlbaum.

Craik, F. I. M., & Lockhart, R. S. (1972). Levels of processing: A framework for memory research. *Journal of Verbal Learning and Verbal Behavior, 11,* 671–684.

Craik, F. I. M., & McDowd, J. M. (1987). Age differences in recall and recognition. *Journal of Experimental Psychology: Learning, Memory, & Cognition, 13,* 474–479.

Craik, F. I. M., & Tulving, E. (1975). Depth of processing and the retention of words in episodic memory. *Journal of Experimental Psychology: General, 104,* 268–294.

Craske, M. G. (1999). Anxiety disorders: Psychological approaches to theory and treatment. Boulder, CO: Westview Press.

Craske, M. G., & Barlow, D. H. (1993). Panic disorder and agoraphobia. In D. H. Barlow (Ed.), *Clinical handbook of psychological disorders* (2nd ed.). New York: Guilford.

Craske, M. G., & Rowe, M. K. (1997). Nocturnal panic. *Clinical Psychology-Science & Practice, 4,* 153–174.

Crits-Christoph, P. (1997). Limitations of the dodo bird verdict and the role of clinical trials in psychotherapy research: Comment on Wampold et al. (1997). *Psychological Bulletin, 122,* 216–220.

Cronbach, L. J. (1957). The two disciplines of scientific psychology. *American Psychologist, 12,* 671–684.

Crooks, R., & Baur, K. (1996). *Our sexuality* (6th ed.). Pacific Grove, CA: Brooks/Cole.

Cropley, A. J. (1996). Recognizing creative potential: An evaluation of the usefulness of creativity tests. *High Ability Studies, 7,* 203–219.

Crowder, R. G. (1976). *Principles of learning and memory.* Hillsdale, NJ: Erlbaum.

Crowder, R. G., & Neath, I. (1991). The microscope metaphor in human memory. In W. E. Hockley & S. Lewandowsky (Eds.), *Relating theory and data: Essays on human memory in honor of Bennet B. Murdock.* Hillsdale, NJ: Erlbaum.

Crutcher, R. J. (1994) Telling what we know: The use of verbal report methodologies in psychological research. *Psychological Science, 5,* 241–244.

Csermely, P. (Ed.) (1998). *Stress of life: From molecules to man.* New York, NY: New York Academy of Sciences.

Csernansky, J. G., & Bardgett, M. E. (1998). Limbic-cortical neuronal damage and the pathophysiology of schizophrenia. *Schizophrenia Bulletin, 24,* 231–248.

Cunningham, M. D., & Reidy, T. J. (1998). Antisocial personality disorder and psychopathy: Diagnostic dilemmas in classifying patterns of antisocial behavior in sentencing evaluations. *Behavioral Sciences & the Law, 16,* 333–351.

Curtis, R. C., & Miller, K. (1986). Believing another likes or dislikes you: Behaviors making the beliefs come true. *Journal of Personality and Social Psychology, 51,* 284–290.

Cutler, W. B., Friedmann, E., & McCoy, N. L. (1998).Pheromonal influences on sociosexual behavior in men. *Archives of Sexual Behavior, 27,* 1–13.

Czeisler, C. A., Kronauer, R. E., Allen, J. S., Duffy, J. F., Jewett, M. E., Brown, E. N., & Ronda, J. M. (1989). Bright light induction of strong (Type O) resetting of the human circadian pacemaker. *Science, 244,* 1328–1333.

Damhorst, M. L. (1990). In search of a common thread: Classification of information communicated through dress. *Clothing and Textiles Research Journal, 8,* 1–12.

Damon, W., & Hart, D. (1992). Self-understanding and its role in social and moral development. In M. H. Bornstein & M. E. Lamb (Eds.), *Developmental psychology: An advanced textbook.* Hillsdale, NJ: Erlbaum.

Darley, J. M., & Berscheid, E. (1967). Increased liking as a result of the anticipation of personal contact. *Human Relations, 20,* 29–39.

Darley, J. M., & Latané, B. (1968). Bystander intervention in emergencies: Diffusion of responsibilities. *Journal of Personality and Social Psychology, 8,* 377–383.

Darwin, C. (1859). *On the origin of species.* London: Murray.

Darwin, C. (1871). *Descent of Man.* London: Murray.

Davidson, M., Keefe, R. S. E., Mohs, R. C., Siever, L. J., Losonczy, M. F., Horvath, T. B., & Davis, K. L. (1987). L-dopa challenge and relapse in schizophrenia. *American Journal of Psychiatry, 144,* 934–938.

Davidson, T. L. (1993). The nature and function of interoceptive signals to feed: Toward integration of physiological and learning perspectives. *Psychological Review, 100,* 640–657.

Davidson, T. L. (1998). Hunger cues as modulatory stimuli. In N. A. Schmajuk & P. C. Holland (Eds.). *Occasion setting: Associative learning and cognition in animals.* Washington, DC: American Psychological Association.

Davidson, T. L., & Jarrard, L. E. (1993). A role for hippocampus in the utilization of hunger signals. *Behavioral and Neural Biology, 59,* 167–171.

Davies, I. (1998). A study of colour grouping in three languages: A test of the linguistic relativity hypothesis. *British Journal of Psychology. 89,* 433–452.

Davies, I., & Corbett, G. G. (1997). A cross-cultural study of colour grouping: Evidence for a weak linguistic relativity. *British Journal of Psychology, 88,* 493–517.

Davies, G. M., & Thomson, D. M. (Eds.). (1988). *Memory in context: Context in memory.* Chichester, England: Wiley.

Davis, K. L., Kahn, R. S., Ko, G., & Davidson, M. (1991). Dopamine in schizophrenia: A review and reconceptualization. *American Journal of Psychiatry, 148,* 1474–1486.

Davis, M., & Lee, Y. (1998). Fear and anxiety: Possible roles of the amygdala and bed nucleus of the stria teminalis. *Cognition and Emotion, 12,* 277–305.

Dawkins, R. (1986). Wealth, polygyny, and reproductive success. *Behavioral and Brain Sciences, 9,* 190–191.

Dawson, G., & Fischer, K. W. (Eds.). (1994). *Human behavior and the developing brain.* New York: Guilford.

Day, N. L., & Richardson, G. A. (1994). Comparative teratogenicity of alcohol and other drugs. *Alcohol Health and Research World, 18,* 42–48.

Deaux, K., & Lewis, L. L. (1984). The structure of gender stereotypes: Interrelationships among components and gender label. *Journal of Personality and Social Psychology, 46,* 991–1004.

de Boysson-Bardies, B., Sagat, L., & Durand, C. (1984). Discernable differences in the babbling of infants according to target language. *Journal of Child Language, 11,* 1–16.

DeCasper, A. J., & Fifer, W. P. (1980). Of human bonding: Newborns prefer their mothers' voices. *Science, 208,* 1174–1176.

DeCasper, A. J., & Spence, M. J. (1986). Prenatal maternal speech influences newborns' perception of speech sounds. *Infant Behavior and Development, 9,* 133–150.

Deci, E. L., & Ryan, R. M. (1985). *Intrinsic motivation and self-determination in human behavior.* New York: Plenum.

DeCola, J. P., & Fanselow, M. S. (1995). Differential inflation with short and long CS-US intervals: Evidence of a nonassociative process in long-delay taste avoidance. *Animal Learning & Behavior, 23,* 154–163.

Deese, J. (1959). On the prediction of occurrence of particular verbal intrusions in immediate recall. *Journal of Experimental Psychology, 58,* 17–22.

de Lacoste-Utamsing, C., & Holloway, R. L. (1982). Sexual dimorphism in the human corpus callosum. *Science, 216,* 1431–1432.

DeLisi, L. E., Sakuma, M., Tew, W., Kushner, M., Hoff, A. L., & Grimson, R. (1997). Schizophrenia as a chronic active brain process: A study of progressive brain structural change subsequent to the onset of schizophrenia. *Psychiatry Research: Neuroimaging, 74,* 129–140.

Dement, W. C. (1978). *Some must watch while some must sleep.* New York: Norton.

Dement, W. C., & Kleitman, N. (1957). The relation of eye movements during sleep to dream activity: An objective method for the study of dreaming. *Journal of Experimental Psychology, 53,* 339–346.

DeNelsky, G.Y. (1996). The case against prescription privileges for psychologists. *American Psychologist, 51,* 207–212.

Dennett, D.C. (1995). *Darwin's dangerous idea: Evolution and the meanings of life.* New York: Simon & Schuster.

Dennis, W., & Dennis, M. G. (1940). The effect of cradling practices upon the onset of walking in Hopi children. *Journal of Genetic Psychology, 56,* 77–86.

Depression Guideline Panel. (1993). *Depression in primary care: Vol. 1. Detection and diagnosis.* Rockville, MD: U.S. Department of Health and Human Services.

Derogatis, L. R., & Coons, H. L. (1993). Self-report measures of stress. In L. Goldberger & S. Breznitz (Eds.), *Handbook of stress: Theoretical and clinical aspects* (2nd ed.). New York: Free Press.

DeSaint, V., Smith, C., Hull, P., & Loboschefski, T. (1997). Ten-month-old infants' retrieval of familiar information from short-term memory. *Infant behavior & Development, 20,* 111–122.

DeValois, R. L., & DeValois, K. K. (1980). Spatial vision. *Annual Review of Psychology, 31,* 309–341.

De Vries, G. J., & Boyle, P. A. (1998). Double duty for sex differences in the brain. *Behavioural Brain Research, 92,* 205–213.

Dewey, J. (1896). The reflex arc concept in psychology. *Psychological Review, 3,* 357–370.

Dickinson, A. (1989). The detrimental effects of extrinsic reinforcement on "intrinsic motivation." *The Behavior Analyst, 12,* 1–15.

Dickinson, A., & Charnock, D. J. (1985). Contingency effects with a constant probability of instrumental reinforcement. *Quarterly Journal of Experimental Psychology, 37B,* 397–416.

Digman, J. M. (1990). Personality structure: Emergence of the five-factor model. *Annual Review of Psychology, 41,* 417–440.

DiMaggio, P. (1997). Culture and cognition. *Annual Review of Sociology, 23,* 263–287.

Dinges, D. F., Whitehouse, W. G., Orne, E. C., & Powell, J. W. (1992). Evaluating hypnotic memory enhancement (hypermnesia and reminiscence) using multitrial forced recall. *Journal of Experimental Psychology: Learning, Memory, and Cognition, 18,* 1139–1147.

Dixon, J. A., & Moore, C. F. (1997). Characterizing the intuitive representation in problem solving: Evidence from evaluating mathematical strategies. *Memory & Cognition, 25,* 395–412.

Dohrenwend, B. P. (Ed). (1998). *Adversity, stress, and psychopathology.* New York: Oxford University Press.

Domhoff, G. (1996). *Finding meaning in dreams: A quantitative analysis.* New York: Plenum.

Domjan, M. (1998). *The principles of learning and behavior* (4th ed.). Pacific Grove, CA: Brooks/Cole.

Domjan, M., & Purdy, J. E. (1995). Animal research in psychology: More than meets the eye of the general psychology student. *American Psychologist, 50,* 496–503.

Dong, W. K., Chudler, E. H., Sugiyama, K., Roberts, V. J., & Hayashi, T. (1994). Somatosensory, multisensory, and task-related neurons in cortical area 7b (PF) of unanesthetized monkeys. *Journal of Neurophysiology, 72,* 542–564.

Donigian, J., & Malnati, R. (1997). *Systemic group therapy: A triadic model.* Pacific Grove, CA: Brooks/Cole Publishing Co.

Donlon, T. F. (Ed.). (1984). *The College Board technical handbook for the Scholastic Aptitude Test and achievment tests.* New York: College Entrance Examination Board.

Dooley, D., Catalano, R., Mishra, S., & Sexner, S. (1992). Earthquake preparedness: Predictors in a community survey. *Journal of Applied Social Psychology, 22,* 451–470.

Dorward, F. M. C., & Day, R. H. (1997). Loss of 3–D shape constancy in interior spaces: The basis of the Ames-room illusion. *Perception, 26,* 707–718.

Douvan, E. (1997). Erik Erikson: Critical times, critical theory. *Child Psychiatry and Human Development, 28,* 15–21.

Draguns, J. G. (1997). Abnormal behavior patterns across cultures: Implications for counseling and psychotherapy. *International Journal of Intercultural Relations, 21,* 213–248.

Dremen, S. (Ed.). (1997). *The family on the threshold of the 21st century: Trend and implications.* Mahway, NJ: Erlbaum.

Drevets, W. C., Burton, H., Videen, T. O., & Snyder, A. Z. (1995). Blood flow changes in human somatosensory cortex during anticipated stimulation. *Nature, 373,* 249–252.

Druckman, D., & Bjork, R. A. (1991). *In the mind's eye: Enhancing human performance.* Washington, DC: National Academy Press.

Druckman, D., & Swets, J. A. (Eds.). (1988). *Enhancing human performance: Issues, theories, and techniques.* Washington DC: National Academy Press.

Duncker, K. (1945). On problem solving. *Psychological Monographs, 58(5,* Whole No. 270).

Dupont, P., Orban, G. A., De-Bruyn, B., & Verbruggen, A. (1994). Many areas in the human brain respond to visual motion. *Journal of Neurophysiology, 72,* 1420–1424.

Dugas, M. J., Freeston, M. H, Ladouceur, R., Rheaume, J., Provencher, M., & Boisvert, J. (1998). Worry themes in primary GAD, secondary GAD, and other anxiety disorders. *Journal of Anxiety Disorders, 12,* 253–261.

Durgin, F. H., Tripathy, S. P., & Levi, D. M. (1995). On the filling in of the visual blind spot: Some rules of thumb. *Perception, 24,* 827–840.

Durie, D. J. (1981). Sleep in animals. In D. Wheatley (Ed.), *Psychopharmacology of sleep.* New York: Raven Press.

Duvall, E. M. (1977). *Marriage and family development* (5th ed.). Philadelphia: Lippincott.

Eagle, M. (1997). Contributions of Erik Erikson. *Psychoanalytic Review, 84,* 337–347.

Eagly, A. H., Ashmore, R. D., Makhijani, M. G., & Longo, L. C. (1991). What is beautiful is good, but . . . : A meta-analytic review of research on the physical attractiveness stereotype. *Psychological Bulletin, 110,* 109–128.

Eagly, A. H., & Johnson, B. T. (1990). Gender and leadership style: A meta-analysis. *Psychological Bulletin, 108,* 233–256.

Ebbesen, E. B., Duncan, B., & Kopnecni, V. J. (1975). Effects of content of verbal aggression on future verbal aggression: A field experiment. *Journal of Experimental Social Psychology, 11,* 192–204.

Ebbinghaus, H. (1885/1964). *Memory: A contribution to experimental psychology.* New York: Dover.

Eccles, J., Adler, T. F., Futterman, R., Goff, S. B., Kaczala, C. M., Meece, J., & Midgley, C. (1983). Expectancies, values, and academic behaviors. In J. T. Spence (Ed.), *Achievement and achievement motives.* San Francisco: Freeman.

Edberg, P. (1990). Rorschach assessment. In A. Goldstein & M. Hersen (Eds.), *Handbook of personality assessment.* New York: Pergamon.

Edelman, G. M. (1987). *Neural Darwinism.* New York: Basic Books.

Efron, R. (1970). The relationship between the duration of a stimulus and the duration of a perception. *Neuropsychologia, 8,* 37–55.

Egan, D., & Schwartz, B. (1979). Chunking in recall of symbolic drawings. *Memory & Cognition, 7,* 149–158.

Eibl-Eibesfeldt, I. (1973). The expressive behavior of the deaf-and-born-blind. In M. von Cranach & I. Vine (Eds.), *Social communication and movement.* San Diego: Academic Press.

Eich, E., Macaulay, D., Loewenstein, R. J., & Dihle, P. H. (1997). Memory, amnesia, and dissociative identity disorder. *Psychological Science, 8,* 417–422.

Eichenbaum, H., Otto, T., & Cohen, N. J. (1994). Two functional components of the hippocampal memory system. *Behavioral and Brain Sciences, 17,* 449–517.

Einhorn, H. J., & Hogarth, R. M. (1981). Behavioral decision theory: Processes of judgment and choice. *Annual Review of Psychology, 32,* 53–88.

Eisenberger, R. (1992). Learned industriousness. *Psychological Review, 99,* 248–267.

Ekman, P. (1992). Are there basic emotions? *Psychological Review, 99,* 350–353.

Ekman, P. (1994). Strong evidence for universals in facial expressions: A reply to Russell's mistaken critique. *Psychological Bulletin, 115,* 268–287.

Ekman, P., & Friesen, W. V. (1975). *Unmasking the face.* Englewood Cliffs, NJ: Prentice-Hall.

Ekman, P., & Friesen, W. V. (1986). A new pan-cultural facial expression of emotion. *Motivation and Emotion, 10,* 159–168.

Ekman, P. & Keltner, D. (1997). Universal facial expressions of emotion: An old controversy and new findings. In U. C. Segerstrale & P. Molnar (Eds.), *Nonverbal communication: Where nature meets culture.* Mahwah, NJ: Lawrence Erlbaum Associates, Inc.

Elicker, J., Englund, M., & Sroufe, L. A. (1992). Predicting peer competence and peer relationships in childhood from early parent-child relationships. In R. D. Parke & G. W. Ladd (Eds.), *Family-peer relationships: Modes of linkage.* Hillsdale, NJ: Erlbaum.

Elliot, A. J., & Devine, P. G. (1994). On the motivational nature of cognitive dissonance: Dissonance as psychological discomfort. *Journal of Personality and Social Psychology, 67,* 382–294.

Ellis, A. (1962). *Reason and emotion in psychotherapy.* Secaucus, NJ: Prentice-Hall.

Ellis, A. (1993). Fundamentals of rational-emotive therapy for the 1990s. In W. Dryden & L. K. Hill (Eds.), *Innovations in rational-emotive therapy.* Newbury Park, CA: Sage.

Ellis, H. C., & Hunt, R. R. (1993). *Fundamentals of cognitive psychology* (5th ed.). Madison, WA: Brown & Benchmark.

Ellis, W. D. (1938). *A source book of gestalt psychology.* London: Routledge & Kegan Paul.

Ellman, S. J., Spielman, A. J., Luck, D., Steiner, S. S., & Halperin, R. (1991). REM deprivation: A review. In S. J. Ellman & J. S. Antrobus (Eds.), *The mind in sleep* (2nd ed.). New York: Wiley.

Ellsworth, P. C. (1994). William James and emotion: Is a century of fame worth a century of misunderstanding? *Psychological Review, 101,* 222–229.

Elmes, D. G., Kantowitz, B. H., & Roediger, H. L., III. (1995). *Research methods in psychology* (5th ed.). St. Paul: West Publishing.

Engel, S. A., Rumelhart, D. E., Wandell, B. A., & Lee, A. T. (1994). MRI of human visual cortex. *Nature, 369,* 525.

Epel, E. S., McEwen, B. S., & Ickovics, J. R. (1998). Embodying psychological thriving: Physical thriving in response to stress. *Journal of Social Issues, 54,* 301–322.

Eppley, K., Abrams, A., & Shear, J. (1989). The differential effects of relaxation techniques on trait anxiety: A meta-analysis. *Journal of Clinical Psychology, 45,* 957–974.

Epstein, S. (1979). The stability of behavior: On predicting most of the people much of the time. *Journal of Personality and Social Psychology, 37,* 1097–1126.

Epstein, S. (1994). Trait theory as personality theory: Can the part be as great as the whole? *Psychological Inquiry, 5,* 120–122.

Erickson, M. A., & Kruschke, J. K. (1998). Rules and exemplars in category learning. *Journal of Experimental Psychology: General, 127,* 107–140.

Erickson, M. H. (1964). A hypnotic technique for resistant patients. *American Journal of Clinical Hypnosis, 7,* 8–32.

Ericsson, K. A., & Simon, H. A. (1993). *Verbal reports as data* (Rev. ed.). Cambridge, MA: MIT Press.

Erikson, E. (1963). *Childhood and society.* New York: Norton.

Erikson, E. (1968). *Identity: Youth and crisis.* New York: Norton.

Erikson, E. (1982). *The life cycle completed: Review.* New York: Norton.

Esser, J. K. (1998). Alive and well after 25 years: A review of groupthink research. *Organizational Behavior & Human Decision Processes, 73,* 116–141

Estes, W. K. (1992). Postscript on ability tests, testing, and public policy. *Psychological Science, 3,* 278.

Evans, E. F. (1982). Functions of the auditory system. In H. B. Barlow & J. D. Mollon (Eds.), *The senses.* Cambridge: Cambridge University Press.

Evans, G. W. (1997). Environmental stress and health. In A. Baum, T. Revenson, & J. E. Singer (Eds.), *Handbook of health psychology.* Hillsdale, NJ: Erlbaum.

Evans, G. W., Hygge, S., & Bullinger, M. (1995). Chronic noise and psychological stress. *Psychological Science, 6,* 333–338.

Eysenck, H. J. (1952). The effects of psychotherapy: An evaluation. *Journal of Consulting Psychology, 16,* 319–324.

Eysenck, H. J. (1970). *The structure of human personality* (3rd ed.). London: Methuen.

Eysenck, H. J. (1991). Dimensions of personality: 16, 5, or 3?ÑCriteria for a taxonomic paradigm. *Personality and Individual Differences, 12,* 773–790.

Eysenck, H. J., & Eysenck, S. B. G. (1975). *Manual of the Eysenck Personality Questionnaire.* San Diego: EdITS.

Eysenck, H. J., & Kamin, L. (1981). *The intelligence controversy: H. J. Eysenck vs. Leon Kamin.* New York: Wiley.

Fackelmann, K. A. (1993). Marijuana and the brain. *Science News, 143,* 88–94.

Fahy, T. A. (1988). The diagnosis of multiple personality: A critical review. *British Journal of Psychiatry, 153,* 597–606.

Fallon, A. E., & Rozin, P. (1985). Sex differences in perceptions of desirable body shape. *Journal of Abnormal Psychology, 94,* 102–105.

Fallon, A. E., Rozin, P., & Pliner, P. (1984). The child's conception of food: The development of food rejections with special reference to disgust and contamination sensitivity. *Child Development, 55,* 566–575.

Fantz, R. L. (1961, May). The origin of form perception. *Scientific American, 204,* 66–72.

Farah, M. J. (1988). Is visual imagery really visual? Overlooked evidence for neuropsychology. *Psychological Review, 95,* 307–317.

Farah, M. J. (1994). Specialization within visual object recognition: Clues from prosopagnosia and alexia. In M. J. Farah & G. Ratcliff (Eds.), *The neuropsychology of high-level vision.* Hillsdale, NJ: Erlbaum.

Faust, I. M. (1984). Role of the fat cell in energy balance physiology. In A. J. Stunkard & E. Stellar (Eds.), *Eating and its disorders.* New York: Raven.

Fava, M., & Rosenbaum, J. F. (1991). Suicide and fluoxetine: Is there a relationship? *Journal of Clinical Psychiatry, 52,* 108–111.

Fazio, R. H. (1986). How do attitudes guide behavior? In R. M. Sorrentino & E. T. Higgins (Eds.), *Handbook of motivation and cognition: Foundations of social behavior* (Vol. 1). New York: Guilford.

Fehr, B., & Russell, J. A. (1991). The concept of love: Viewed from a prototype perspective. *Journal of Personality and Social Psychology, 60,* 425–438.

Feingold, A. (1988). Matching for attractiveness in romantic partners and same-sex friends: A meta-analysis and theoretical critique. *Psychological Bulletin, 104,* 226–235.

Feingold, A. (1990). Gender differences in effects of physical attractiveness on romantic attraction: A comparison across five research paradigms. *Journal of Personality and Social Psychology, 59,* 981–993.

Feingold, A. (1992). Good-looking people are not what we think. *Psychological Bulletin, 111,* 304–341.

Feist, J. (1994). *Theories of personality* (3rd ed.). Fort Worth, TX: Harcourt Brace.

Feldman, M. D., & Christensen, J. F. (Eds.). (1997). *Behavioral medicine in primary care: A practical guide.* Stamford, CT: Appleton & Lange.

Ferguson, N. B. L., & Keesey, R. E. (1975). Effect of a quinine-adulterated diet upon body weight maintenance in male rats with ventromedial lesions. *Journal of Comparative and Physiological Psychology, 89,* 478–488.

Ferster, C. B., & Skinner, B. F. (1957). *Schedules of reinforcement.* New York: Appleton-Century-Crofts.

Festinger, L. (1957). *A theory of cognitive dissonance.* Stanford, CA: Stanford University Press.

Festinger, L., & Carlsmith, J. M. (1959). Cognitive consequences of forced compliance. *Journal of Abnormal and Social Psychology, 58,* 203–210.

Festinger, L., Riecken, H. W., & Schacter, S. (1956). *When prophecy fails.* Minneapolis: University of Minnesota Press.

Festinger, L., Schachter, S., & Black, K. (1950). *Social pressures in informal groups: A study of human factors in housing.* New York: Harper.

Fiedler, K. (1988). The dependence of the conjunction fallacy on subtle linguistic factors. *Psychological Research, 50,* 123–129.

Fischbach, G. D. (1992, September). Mind and brain. *Scientific American, 267,* 48–57.

Fishbain, D. A., & Goldberg, M. (1991). The misdiagnosis of conversion disorder in a psychiatric emergency service. *General Hospital Psychiatry, 13,* 177–181.

Fisher, C. B., & Younggren, J. N. (1997). The value and utility of the 1992 ethics code. *Professional Psychology—Research and Practice, 28,* 582–592.

Fiske, S. T. (1993). Social cognition and social perception. *Annual Review of Psychology, 44,* 155–194.

Fiss, H. (1991). Experimental strategies for the study of the function of dreaming. In S. J. Ellman & J. S. Antrobus (Eds.), *The mind in sleep* (2nd ed.). New York: Wiley.

Flavel, J. H. (1971). Stage-related properties of cognitive development. *Cognitive Psychology, 2,* 421–453.

Flavel, J. H., Miller, P. A., & Miller, S. A. (1993). *Cognitive development* (3rd ed.). Englewood Cliffs, NJ: Prentice-Hall.

Fleishman, E. A., & Parker, J. F., Jr. (1962). Factors in the retention and relearning of perceptual motor skill. *Journal of Experimental Psychology, 64,* 215–226.

Foa, E. B., & Riggs, D. S. (1995). Posttraumatic stress disorder following assault: Theoretical considerations and empirical findings. *Current Directions in Psychological Science, 4,* 61–65.

Fodor, J. A., & Pylyshyn, Z. W. (1981). How direct is visual perception? Some reflections on Gibson's "ecological approach." *Cognition, 9,* 139–196.

Foersterling, F., Buehner, M., & Gall, S. (1998). Attributions of depressed persons: How consistent are they with the covariation principle? *Journal of Personality & Social Psychology, 75,* 1047–1061.

Fong, G. T., Krantz, D. H., & Nisbett, R. E. (1986). The effects of statistical training on thinking about everyday problems. *Cognitive Psychology, 18,* 253–292.

Fong, G. T., & Nisbett, R. E. (1991). Immediate and delayed transfer of training effects in statistical reasoning. *Journal of Experimental Psychology: General, 120,* 34–45.

Forgas, J. P. (1998). On being happy and mistaken: Mood effects on the fundamental attribution error. *Journal of Personality & Social Psychology, 75,* 318–331.

Foulkes, D. (1985). *Dreaming: A cognitive-psychological analysis.* Hillsdale, NJ: Lawrence Erlbaum.

Frazer, J. G. (1890/1959). *The new golden bough: A study in magic and religion* (abridged ed., T. H. Gaster, Ed.). New York: Macmillan.

Fredericks, D. W., & Williams, L. W. (1998). New definition of mental retardation for the American Association of Mental Retardation. *Image-the Journal of Nursing Scholarship, 30,* 53–56.

Freedman, J. L. (1988). Television violence and aggression: What the evidence shows. In S. Oskamp (Ed.), *Television as a social issue* (Vol. 8). Beverly Hills, CA: Sage.

Freedman, J. L., & Fraser, S. C. (1966). Compliance without pressure: The foot-in-the-door technique. *Journal of Personality and Social Psychology, 4,* 195–202.

Freeman, H. L., & Stansfeld, S. A. (1998). Psychosocial effects of urban environments, noise, and crowding. In A. Lundberg (Ed), *The environment and mental health: A guide for clinicians.* Mahwah, NJ: Erlbaum.

Freud, S. (1900/1990). *The interpretation of dreams.* New York: Basic Books.

Freud, S. (1905/1962). *Three contributions to the theory of sexuality.* New York: Dutton.

Freud, S. (1910). The origin and development of psychoanalysis. *American Journal of Psychology, 21,* 181–218.

Freud, S. (1912/1964). The dynamics of transference. In J. Strachey (Trans. & Ed.), *The standard edition of the complete works of Sigmund Freud* (Vol. 12). London: Hogarth Press.

Freud, S. (1940). *An outline of psychoanalysis.* New York: Norton.

Freudenberger, H. J. (1974). Staff burnout. *Journal of Social Issues, 30,* 159–165.

Friedlander, L., Lumley, M. A., Farchione, T., & Doyal, G. (1997). Testing the alexithymia hypothesis: Physiological and subjective responses during relaxation and stress. *Journal of Nervous & Mental Disease, 185,* 233–239

Friedman, H. S., Hawley, P. H., & Tucker, J. S. (1994). Personality, health, and longevity. *Current Directions in Psychological Science, 3,* 37–41.

Friedman, M., & Rosenman, R. F. (1974). *Type A behavior and your heart.* New York: Knopf.

Friedrich-Cofer, L., & Huston, A. C. (1986). Television violence and aggression: The debate continues. *Psychological Bulletin, 100,* 364–371.

Frueh, B. C., de Arellano, M. A., & Turner, S. M. (1997). Systematic desensitization as an alternative exposure strategy for PTSD. *American Journal of Psychiatry, 154,* 287–288.

Fukuda, T., Kanada, K., & Saito, S. (1990). An ergonomic evaluation of lens accommodation related to visual circumstances. *Ergonomics, 33,* 811–831.

Fyer, A. J., Mannuzza, S., Gallops, M. S., Martin, L. Y., Aaronson, C., Gorman, J. M., Liebowitz, M. R., & Klein, D. F. (1990). Familial transmission of simple phobias and fears: A preliminary report. *Archives of General Psychiatry, 47,* 252–256.

Gabrieli, J.D.E. (1998). Cognitive neuroscience of human memory. *Annual Reviewer of Psychology, 49,* 87–115.

Gaetz, M., Weinberg, H., Rzempoluck, E., & Jantzen, K. J. (1998). Neural network classifications and correlational analysis of EEG and MEG activity accompanying spontaneous reversals of the Necker Cube. *Cognitive Brain Research, 6,* 335–346.

Gagnon, J., & Simon, W. (1973). *Sexual conduct: The social sources of human sexuality.* Chicago: Aldine.

Galef, B. G., Jr. (1985). Social learning in wild Norway rats. In T. D. Johnston & A. T. Pietrewicz (Eds.), *Issues in the ecological study of learning.* Hillsdale, NJ: Erlbaum.

Galton, F. (1869). *Hereditary genius: An inquiry into its laws and consequences.* New York: Appleton.

Galton, F. (1883). *Inquiries into human faculty and development.* London: Macmillan.

Gandelman, R. (1992). *Psychobiology of behavior development.* New York: Oxford University Press.

Gandevia, S. C., McCloskey, D. I., & Burke, D. (1992). Kinaestheticsignals and muscle contraction. *Trends in Neurosciences, 15,*62–65.

Gangestad, S. W., & Snyder, M. (1985). On the nature of self-monitoring: An examination of latent causal structure. In P. Shaver (Ed.), *Review of personality and social psychology* (Vol. 6). Beverly Hills, CA: Sage.

Garcia, J., & Koelling, R. A. (1966). Relation of cue to consequence in avoidance learning. *Psychonomic Science, 4,* 123–124.

Gardner, E. B., & Costanzo, R. H. (1981). Properties of kinesthetic neurons in somatosensory cortex of awake monkeys. *Brain Research, 214,* 301–319.

Gardner, E. L. (1997). Brain reward mechanisms. In J. H. Lowinson, P. Ruiz, R. B. Millman, & J. G. Langrod (Eds.), *Substance abuse: A comprehensive textbook.* Baltimore: Williams & Wilkins.

Gardner, H. (1983). *Frames of mind: The theory of multiple intelligences.* New York: Basic Books.

Gardner, H. (1993). *Multiple intelligences: The theory in practice.* New York: Basic Books.

Gardner, R. A., & Gardner, B. T. (1969). Teaching sign language to a chimpanzee. *Science, 165,* 664–672.

Gardner, R. A., Gardner, B. T., & Van Cantfort, T. E. (Eds.).(1989). *Teaching sign language to chimpanzees.* Albany, NY: SUNY Press.

Garland, A. F., & Zigler, E. (1993). Adolescent suicide prevention: Current research and social policy implications. *American Psychologist, 48,* 169–182.

Garrity, T. F., Stallones, L., Marx, M. B., & Johnson, T. P. (1989). Pet ownership and attachment as supportive factors in the health of the elderly. *Anthrozoos, 3,* 35–44.

Gazzaniga, M. (1967, August). The split brain in man. *Scientific American, 217,* 24–29.

Gazzaniga, M. S. (1970). *The bisected brain.* New York: Appleton-Century-Crofts.

Gazzaniga, M. S., Bogen, J. E., & Sperry, R. W. (1965). Observations on visual perception after disconnection of the cerebral hemispheres in man. *Brain, 88,* 221–236.

Gazzaniga, M. S., Eliassen, J. C., Nisenson, L., Wessinger, C. Mark, Fendrich, R., & Baynes, K. (1996). Collaboration between the hemispheres of a callosotomy patient: Emerging right hemisphere speech and the left hemisphere interpreter. *Brain, 119,* 1255–1263.

Gazzaniga, M. S., & LeDoux, J. E. (1978). *The integrated mind.* New York: Plenum.

Geiselman, R. E., Fisher, R. P., MacKinnon, D. P., & Holland, H. L. (1985). Eyewitness memory enhancement in the police interview: Cognitive retrieval mnemonics versus hypnosis. *Journal of Applied Psychology, 70,* 401–412.

Gelman, S. A., & Markman, E. M. (1986). Categories and induction in young children. *Cognition, 23,* 183–209.

Gerbner, G., & Gross, L. (1976). Living with television: The violence profile. *Journal of Communications, 26,* 172–199.

Gershon, E. S. (1990). Genetics. In F. K. Goodwin & K. R. Jamison (Eds.), *Manic-depressive illness.* New York: Oxford University Press.

Gershon, E. S., & Reider, R. O. (1992, April). Major disorders of mind and brain. *Scientific American, 267,* 126–133.

Gibbs, R. W., O'Brien, J. E., & Doolittle, S. (1995). Inferring meanings that are not intended: Speakers' intentions and irony comprehension. *Discourse Processes, 20,* 187–203.

Gibson, E. J., & Walk, R. D. (1960, April). The "visual cliff." *Scientific American, 202,* 64–71.

Gibson, J. J. (1966). *The senses considered as perceptual systems.* Boston: Houghton Mifflin.

Gibson, J. J. (1979). *The ecological approach to visual perception.* Boston: Houghton Mifflin.

Gick, M. L., & McGarry, S. J. (1992). Learning from mistakes: Inducing analogous solution failures to a source problem produces later successes in analogical transfer. *Journal of Experimental Psychology: Learning, Memory, & Cognition, 18,* 623–639.

Gigerenzer, G. (1996). On narrow norms and vague heuristics: A reply to Kahneman & Tversky. *Psychological Review, 103,* 592–596.

Gigerenzer, G. (1997). Ecological intelligence: An adaptation for frequencies. In D. Cummins & C. Allen (Eds.), *The evolution of mind.* New York: Oxford University Press.

Giguere, C., & Abel, S. M. (1993). Sound localization: Effects of reverberation time, speaker array, stimulus frequency, and stimulus rise/decay. *Journal of Acoustical Society of America, 94,* 769–776.

Gilbert, D. T. (1989). Thinking lightly about others: Automatic components of the social inference process. In J. S. Uleman & J. A. Bargh (Eds.), *Unintended thought.* New York: Guilford.

Gilligan, C. (1982). *In a different voice: Psychological theory and women's development.* Cambridge, MA: Harvard University Press.

Gillin, J. C. (1993). Clinical sleep-wake disorders in psychiatric practice: Dyssomnias. In D. L. Dunner (Ed.), *Current psychiatric therapy.* Philadelphia: Saunders.

Gladue, B. A. (1994). The biopsychology of sexual orientation. *Current Directions in Psychological Research, 3,* 150–154.

Glaser, B. G., & Strauss, A. L. (1968). *Time for dying.* Chicago: Aldine.

Glenberg, A. M., & Fernandez, A. (1989). Evidence for auditory temporal distinctiveness: Modality effects in order and frequency judgments. *Journal of Experimental Psychology: Learning, Memory, & Cognition, 14,* 728–737.

Goldberg, J., True, W. R., Eisen, S. A., & Henderson, W. G. (1990). A twin study of the effects of the Vietnam War on posttraumatic stress disorder. *Journal of the American Medical Association, 263,* 1227–1232.

Goldberg, L. R. (1993). The structure of phenotypic personality traits. *American Psychologist, 48,* 26–34.

Goldberger, L., & Breznitz, S. (Eds.). (1993). *Handbook of stress: Theoretical and clinical aspects.* New York: Free Press.

Goldstein, B. (1994). *Psychology.* Pacific Grove, CA: Brooks/Cole.

Goleman, D. (1995). *Emotional intelligence.* New York: Bantam.

Golub, S. (1992). *Periods: From menarche to menopause.* Newbury Park, CA: Sage.

Gonzalez-Quijano, M. I., Martin, M., Millan, S., & Lopez-Calderon, A. (1998). Lymphocyte response to mitogens: Influence of life events and personality. *Neuropsychobiology, 38,* 90–96.

Goodall, J. (1990). *Through a window: My thirty years with the chimpanzees of Gombe.* Boston: Houghton Mifflin.

Goodenough, D. R. (1991). Dream recall: History and current status of the field. In S. J. Ellman & J. S. Antrobus (Eds.), *The mind in sleep* (2nd ed.). New York: Wiley.

Goodwin, K. F., & Jamison, K. R. (1990). *Manic depressive illness.* New York: Oxford University Press.

Gopnick, A. (1982). Words and plans: Early language and the development of intelligent action. *Journal of Child Language, 9,* 303–318.

Gopnick, A. (1993). How we know our minds: The illusion of first-person knowledge in intentionality. *Behavioral and Brain Sciences, 16,* 1–14.

Gorwood, P., Bouvard, M., Mouren-Simeoni, M. C., Kipman, A., & Ades, J. Genetics and anorexia nervosa: A review of candidate genes. *Psychiatric Genetics, 8,* 1–12.

Gottesman, I. I. (1991). *Schizophrenia genesis: The origins of madness.* New York: Freeman.

Gould, M. S. (1990). Suicide clusters and media exposure. In S. J. Blumenthal & D. J. Kupfer (Eds.), *Suicide over the life cycle: Risk factors, assessments and treatment of suicidal patients.* Washington, D.C.: American Psychiatric Press.

Gould, R. L. (1978). *Transformations: Growth and change in adult life.* New York: Simon & Schuster.

Graber, J.A., Brooks-Gunn, J., & Warren, M.P. (1995). The antecedents of menarchael age: Heredity, family environment, and stressful life events. *Child Development, 66,* 346–359.

Graf, P., Mandler, G., & Haden, P. E. (1982). Simulating amnesic symptoms in normal subjects. *Science, 218,* 1243–1244.

Graf, P., & Schacter, D. L. (1985). Implicit and explicit memory for new associations in normal and amnesic subjects. *Journal of Experimental Psychology: Learning, Memory, & Cognition, 11,* 501–518.

Graffen, N. F., Ray, W. J., & Lundy, R. (1995). EEG concomitants of hypnosis and hypnotic susceptibility. *Journal of Abnormal Psychology, 104,* 123–131.

Graig, E. (1993). Stress as a consequence of the urban physical environment. In L. Goldberger & S. Breznitz (Eds.), *Handbook of stress: Theoretical and clinical aspects* (2nd ed.). New York: Free Press.

Granrud, C. E. (Ed.). (1993). *Visual perception and cognition in infancy.* Hillsdale, NJ: Erlbaum.

Granvold, D. K. (Ed.). (1994) *Cognitive and behavioral treatment: Methods and applications.* Pacific Grove, CA: Brooks/Cole.

Graziano, W. G., & Bryant, W. H. M. (1998). Self-monitoring and the self-attribution of positive emotions. *Journal of Personality & Social Psychology, 74,* 250–261.

Greenblatt, D. J., & Shader, R. I. (1978). Pharmacotherapy of anxiety with benzodiazepines and beta-adrenergic blockers. In M. Lipton, A. DiMascio, & F. Killiam (Eds.), *Psychopharmacology: A generation of progress.* New York: Raven.

Greene, R. L. (1992). *Human memory: Paradigms and paradoxes.* Hillsdale, NJ: Erlbaum.

Greenough, W. T., Black, J. E., & Wallace, C. S. (1987). Experience and brain development. *Child Development, 58,* 539–559.

Greenwald, A. G., & Banaji, M. R. (1995). Implicit social cognition: Attitides, self-esteem, and stereotypes. *Psychological Review, 102,* 4–27.

Greenwald, A. G., & Pratkanis, A. R. (1984). The self. In R. S. Wyer & T. K. Srull (Eds.), *Handbook of social cognition* (Vol. 3). Hillsdale, NJ: Erlbaum.

Greenwald, A. G., Schuh, E. S., & Klinger, M. R. (1995). Activation of marginally perceptible ("subliminal") stimuli: Dissociation of unconscious from conscious cognition. *Journal of Experimental Psychology: General, 124,* 22–42.

Greenwald, A. G., Spangenberg, E. R., Pratkanis, A. R., & Eskenazi, J. (1991). Double-blind tests of subliminal self-help audiotapes. *Psychological Science, 2,* 119–122.

Grencavage, L. M., & Norcross, J. C. (1990). Where are the common factors? *Professional Psychology: Research and Practice, 21,* 372–378.

Grice, H. P. (1975). Logic and conversation. In P. Cole & J. L. Morgan (Eds.), *Syntax and semantics: Vol. 3. Speech acts.* New York: Seminar Press.

Grill, H. J., & Kaplan, J. M. (1990). Caudal brainstem participates in the distributed neural control of feeding. In E. M. Stricker (Ed.), *Handbook of behavioral neurobiology* (Vol. 10). New York: Plenum.

Grochowitz, P. M., Schedlowski, M., Husband, A. J., King, M. G., Hibberd, A. D., & Bowen, K. M. (1991). Behavioral conditioning prolongs heart allograft survival in rats. *Brain, Behavior, and Immunity, 5,* 349–356.

Grossberg, S., & Rudd, M. E. (1992). Cortical dynamics of visual motion perception: Short-range and long-range apparent motion. *Psychological Review, 99,* 78–121.

Groves, P. M., & Thompson, R. F. (1970). Habituation: A dual-process theory. *Psychological Review, 77,* 419–450.

Gruneberg, M. M., Sykes, R. N., & Gillett, E. (1994). The facilitating effects of mnemonic strategies on two learning tasks in learning disabled adults. *Neuropsychological Rehabilitation, 4,* 241–254.

Gulick, W. L., Gescheider, G. A., & Frisina, R. D. (1989). *Hearing: Physiological acoustics, neural coding, and psychoacoustics.* New York: Oxford University Press.

Gunderson, J. G. (1992). Diagnostic controversies. In A. Tasman & M. B. Riba (Eds.), *Review of psychiatry* (Vol. 11). Washington, DC: American Psychiatric Press.

Gurman, E. B. (1994). Debriefing for all concerned: Ethical treatment of human subjects. *Psychological Science, 5,* 139.

Haan, N. (Ed.). (1977). *Coping and defending: Processes of self-environment organization.* New York: Academic Press.

Haan, N. (1993). The assessment of coping, defense, and stress. In L. Goldberger & S. Brezitz (Eds.), *Handbook of stress: Theoretical and clinical aspects* (2nd ed.). New York: Free Press.

Haerich, P. (1997). Long-term habituation and sensitization of the human acoustic startle response. *Journal of Psychophysiology, 11,* 103–114.

Hamer, D. H., Hu, S., Magnuson, V. L., Hu, N., & Pattatucci, A. M. L. (1993). A linkage between DNA markers on the X chromosome and male sexual orientation. *Science, 261,* 321–327.

Hansen, C. H. (1989). Priming sex-role stereotypic event schemas with rock music videos: Effects on impression favorability, trait inferences, and recall of a subsequent male-female interaction. *Basic and Applied Social Psychology, 10,* 371–391.

Hanson, V. L. (1990). Recall of order information by deaf signers: Phonetic coding in temporal order recall. *Memory & Cognition, 18,* 604–610.

Harlow, H. F., Harlow, M. K., & Meyer, D. R. (1971). From thought to therapy: Lessons from a primate laboratory. *American Scientist, 59,* 538–549.

Harlow, H. F., & Zimmerman, R. R. (1959). Affectional responses in the infant monkey. *Science, 130,* 421–432.

Harmon, T. M., Hynan, M. T., & Tyre, T. E. (1990). Improved obstetric outcomes using hypnotic analgesia and skill mastery combined with childbirth education. *Journal of Consulting and Clinical Psychology, 58,* 525–530.

Hartshorne, H., & May, A. (1928). *Studies in the nature of character: Vol. 1. Studies in deceit.* New York: Macmillan.

Harris, S. M., & Busby, D. M. (1998). Therapist physical attractiveness: An unexplored influence on client disclosure. *Journal of Marital & Family Therapy, 24,* 251–257.

Hart, P. (1998). Preventing groupthink revisited: Evaluating and reforming groups in government. *Organizational Behavior & Human Decision Processes, 73,* 306–326.

Hartup, W. W., & Stevens, N. (1997). Friendships and adaptation in the life course. *Psychological Bulletin, 121,* 355–370.

Harvey, S. (1987). Female sexual behavior: Fluctuations during the menstrual cycle. *Journal of Psychosomatic Research, 31,* 101–110.

Hasher, L., Stolzfus, E. R., Zacks, R. T., & Rypma, B. (1991). Age and inhibition. *Journal of Experimental Psychology: Learning, Memory, & Cognition, 17,* 163–169.

Hasher, L., & Zacks, R. R. (1979). Automatic and effortful processes in memory. *Journal of Experimental Psychology: General, 108,* 356–388.

Hasselmo, M. E., Rolls, E. T., & Baylis, G. C. (1989). The role of expression and identity in the face-selective responses of neurons in the temporal visual cortex of the monkey. *Behavioral Brain Research, 32,* 203–218.

Hasselmo, M.E., Wyble, B. P., & Wallenstein, G. V. (1996). Encoding and retrieval of episodic memories: Role of cholinergic and GABAergic modulation in the hippocampus. *Hippocampus, 6,* 693–708.

Hastie, R. (1991). A review from a high place: The field of judgment and decision making as revealed in its current textbooks. *Psychological Science, 2,* 135–138.

Hatfield, E. (1988). Passionate and companionate love. In R. J. Sternberg & M. L. Barnes (Eds.), *The psychology of love.* New Haven, CT: Yale University Press.

Hatfield, E., & Rapson, R. L. (1993). *Love, sex, and intimacy.* New York: HarperCollins.

Hauri, P. (1982). The sleep disorders. Kalamazoo, MI: Upjohn.

Hayes, C. (1952). *The ape in our house.* London: Gollacz.

Hayes, K. J., & Hayes, C. (1951). The intellectual development of a home-raised chimpanzee. *Proceedings of the American Philosophical Society, 95,* 105–109.

Hayes, S. C., & Heiby, E. (1996). Psychology's drug problem: Do we need a fix or should we just say no? *American Psychologist, 51,* 198–206.

Hearold, S. (1986). A synthesis of 1043 effects of television on social behavior. In G. Comstock (Ed.), *Public communication and behavior.* New York: Academic Press.

Hearst, E., & Franklin, S. R. (1977). Positive and negative relations between a signal and food: Approach-withdrawal behavior to the signal. *Journal of Experimental Psychology: Animal Behavior Processes, 3,* 37–52.

Hebb, D. O. (1949). The organization of behaviour. New York: Wiley-Interscience.

Hector, R. I. (1998). The use of clozapine in the treatment of aggressive schizophrenia. *Canadian Journal of Psychiatry, 43,* 466–472.

Heider, E. (1972). Universals of color naming and memory. *Journal of Experimental Psychology, 93,* 10–20.

Heider, F. (1944). Social perception and phenomenal causality. *Psychological Review, 51,* 358–374.

Heiman, G. A. (1995). *Research methods in psychology.* Boston: Houghton Mifflin.

Heimann, M. (1989). Neonatal imitation gaze aversion and mother-infant interaction. *Infant Behavior and Development, 12,* 495–505.

Hellige, J. B. (1990). Hemispheric asymmetry. *Annual Review of Psychology, 41,* 55–80.

Hellige, J. B. (1993). Unity of thought and action: Varieties of interaction between the left and right cerebral hemispheres. *Current Directions in Psychological Science, 2,* 21–25.

Helmes, E., & Reddon, J. R. (1993). A perspective on developments in assessing psychopathology: A critical review of the MMPI and MMPI-2. *Psychological Bulletin, 113,* 453–471.

Henderson-King, E. I., & Nisbett, R. E. (1996). Anti-black prejudice as a function of exposure to the negative behavior of a single Black person. *Journal of Personality and Social Psychology, 71,* 654–664.

Henley, N. M. (1989). Molehill or mountain? What we know and don't know about sex bias in language. In M. Crawford & M. Gentry (Eds.), *Gender and thought: Psychological perspectives.* New York: Springer-Verlag.

Herman, C. P., & Polivy, J. (1988). Studies of eating in normal dieters. In B. T. Walsh (Ed.), *Eating behavior in eating disorders.* Washington, DC: American Psychiatric Press.

Herrmann, D., Raybeck, D., & Gutman, D. (1993). *Improving student memory.* Seattle, WA: Hogrefe & Huber.

Herz, R. S., & Cahill, E. D. (1997). Differential use of sensory information in sexual behavior as a function of gender. *Human Nature, 8,* 1997, 275–286.

Hetherington, A. W., & Ranson, S. W. (1942). The relation of various hypothalamic lesions to adiposity in the rat. *Journal of Comparative Neurology, 76,* 475–499.

Higbee, K. L. (1988). *Your memory* (2nd ed.). Englewood Cliffs, NJ: Prentice-Hall.

Hilgard, E. R. (1965). *Hypnotic susceptibility.* New York: Harcourt, Brace, & World.

Hilgard, E. R. (1986). *Divided consciousness: Multiple controls in human thought and action* (Rev. ed.). New York: Wiley.

Hilgard, E. R. (1987). *Psychology in America: An historical survey.* New York: Harcourt Brace Jovanovich.

Hilgard, E. R. (1992). Dissociation and theories of hypnosis. In E. Fromm & M. Nash (Eds.), *Contemporary hypnosis research.* New York: Guilford.

Hill, J. O., & Peters, J. C. (1998). Environmental contributions to the obesity epidemic. *Science, 280,* 1371–1374.

Hilton, J. L., & von Hippel, W. (1996). Stereotypes. *Annual Review of Psychology, 47,* 237–271.

Hines, M. (1982). Prenatal gonadal hormones and sex differences in human behavior. *Psychological Bulletin, 92,* 56–80.

Hintzman, D. L. (1986). "Schema abstraction" in a multiple-trace memory model. *Psychological Review, 93,* 411–428.

Hirsh, I. J., & Watson, C. S. (1996). Auditory psychophysics and perception. *Annual Review of Psychology, 47,* 461–484.

Hitch, G. J., & Halliday, M. S. (1983). Working memory in children. *Philosophical Transactions of the Royal Society London B, 302,* 325–340.

Hobfoll, S. E., Shoham, S. B., & Ritter, C. (1991). Women's satisfaction with social support and their receipt of aid. *Journal of Personality and Social Psychology, 61,* 332–341.

Hobson, J. A. (1988). *The dreaming brain.* New York: Basic Books.

Hobson, J. A., & McCarley, R. W. (1977). The brain as a dream state generator: An activation-synthesis hypothesis of the dream process. *American Journal of Psychiatry, 134,* 1335–1348.

Hodges, J., & Tizard, B. (1989). IQ and behavioral adjustment of ex-institutional adolescents. *Journal of Child Psychology and Psychiatry, 30,* 53–75.

Hofferth, S. (1996). Child care in the United States today. *The Future of Children, 6,* 41–61.

Hoffman, M. L. (1986). Affect, cognition, motivation. In R. M. Sorrentino & E. T. Higgins (Eds.), *Handbook of motivation and cognition: Foundations of social behavior*. New York: Guilford.

Hoffmann, P. (1997). The endorphin hypothesis. In W. P. Morgan (Ed.), *Physical activity and mental health*. Washington, DC: Taylor & Francis.

Hofmann, S. G., Lehman, C. L., & Barlow, D. H. (1997). How specific are specific phobias? *Journal of Behavior Therapy & Experimental Psychiatry, 28*, 233–240.

Hofstadter, M.C., & Reznick, J.S. (1996). Response modality affects human infant delayed-response performance. *Child Development, 67*, 646–658.

Hogan, J. A. (1997). Energy models of motivation: A reconsideration. *Applied Animal Behaviour Science, 53*, 89–105.

Hohmann, G. W. (1966). Some effects of spinal cord lesions on experienced emotional feelings. *Psychophysiology, 3*, 143–156.

Holland, P. C. (1977). Conditioned stimulus as a determinant of the form of the Pavlovian conditioned response. *Journal of Experimental Psychology: Animal Behavior Processes, 3*, 77–104.

Holland, P. C., & Rescorla, R. A. (1975). The effects of two ways of devaluing the unconditioned stimulus after first- and second-order appetitive conditioning. *Journal of Experimental Psychology: Animal Behavior Processes, 1*, 355–363.

Holmes, D. S. (1976). Debriefing after psychological experiments: I. Effectiveness of postdeception dehoaxing. *American Psychologist, 31*, 858–867.

Holmes, D. S. (1987). The influence of meditation versus rest on physiological arousal: A second examination. In M. A. West (Ed.), *The psychology of meditation*. Oxford: Clarendon Press.

Holmes, T. H., & Rahe, R. H. (1967). The Social Readjustment Rating Scale. *Journal of Psychosomatic Research, 11*, 213–218.

Holt, E. B. (1931). *Animal drive and the learning process: An essay toward radical empiricism*. New York: Holt.

Homa, D. (1984). On the nature of categories. In G. H. Bower (Ed.), *The psychology of learning and motivation* (Vol. 18). Orlando, FL: Academic Press.

Honzik, M. P., Macfarlane, J. W., & Allen, L. (1948). The stability of mental test performance between two and eighteen years. *Journal of Experimental Education, 17*, 309–324.

Hooker, W. D., & Jones, R. T. (1987). Increased susceptibility to memory intrusions and the Stroop interference effect during acute marijuana intoxication. *Psychopharmacology, 91*, 20–24.

Hopkins, B. (1991). Facilitating early motor development: An intracultural study of West Indian mothers and their infants living in Britain. In J. K. Nugent, B. M. Lester, & T. B. Brazelton (Eds.), *The cultural context of infancy: Vol. 2. Multicultural and interdisciplinary approaches to parent-infant relations*. Norwood, NJ: Ablex.

Horgan, J. (1993, June). Eugenics revisited. *Scientific American, 268*, 123–131.

Horgan, J. (1994, July). Can science explain consciousness? *Scientific American, 271*, 88–94.

Horn, J. L. (1976). Human abilities: A review of research and theory in the early 1970s. *Annual Review of Psychology, 27*, 437–485.

Horn, J. L. (1982). The aging of human abilities. In J. Wolman (Ed.), *Handbook of developmental psychology*. Englewood Cliffs, NJ: Prentice-Hall.

Horn, J. L. (1985). Remodeling old models of intelligence. In B. B. Wolman (Ed.), *Handbook of intelligence*. New York: Wiley.

Horn, J. L., & Cattell, R. B. (1966). Refinement and test of the theory of fluid and crystallized ability intelligences. *Journal of Educational Psychology, 57*, 253–270.

Horn, J. L., & Noll, J. (1997). Human cognitive capabilities: Gf-Gc theory. In D. P. Flanagan & J. L. Genshaft (Eds.), *Contemporary intellectual assessment: Theories, tests, and issues*. New York: Guilford Press.

Horne, J. A. (1988). *Why we sleep: The functions of sleep in humans and other mammals*. Oxford: Oxford University Press.

Horne, J. A., & Minard, A. (1985). Sleep and sleepiness following a behaviourally "active" day. *Ergonomics, 28*, 567–575.

Horney, K. (1945). *Our inner conflicts: A constructive theory of neurosis*. New York: Norton.

Horney, K. (1967). *Feminine psychology*. New York: Norton.

Horvath, A. O., & Luborsky, L. (1993). The role of the therapeutic alliance in psychotherapy. *Journal of Consulting and Clinical Psychology, 61*, 561–573.

Horvath, P. (1988). Placebos and common factors in two decades of psychotherapy research. *Psychological Bulletin, 104*, 214–225.

Houle, M., McGrath, P. A., Moran, G., & Garrett, O. J. (1988). The efficacy of hypnosis- and relaxation-induced analgesia on two dimensions of pain for cold pressor and electrical tooth pulp stimulation. *Pain, 33*, 241–251.

Hser, Y., Anglin, M. D., & Powers, K. (1993). A 24–year follow-up of California narcotics addicts. *Archives of General Psychiatry, 50*, 577–584.

Hubbel, J. C. (1990, January). Animal rights war on medicine. *Reader's Digest*, 70–76.

Hubel, D. H., & Wiesel, T. N. (1962). Receptive fields, binocular interaction, and functional architecture in the cat's visual cortex. *Journal of Physiology, 160*, 106–154.

Hubel, D. H., & Wiesel, T. N. (1979, September). Brain mechanisms and vision. *Scientific American, 241*, 150–162.

Hull, C. L. (1943). *Principles of behavior*. New York: Appleton-Century.

Hull, J. G., & Bond, C. F., Jr. (1986). Social and behavioral consequences of alcohol consumption and expectancy: A meta-analysis. *Psychological Bulletin, 99*, 347–360.

Hunnicutt, C. P., & Newman, I. A. (1993). Adolescent dieting practices and nutrition knowledge. *Health Values, 17*, 35–40.

Hunt, E. (1985). The correlates of intelligence. In D. K. Detterman (Ed.), *Current topics in human intelligence* (Vol. 1). Norwood, NJ: Ablex.

Hunt, E., & Agnoli, F. (1991). The Whorfian hypothesis: A cognitive psychology perspective. *Psychological Review, 98*, 377–389.

Hunt, M. (1993). *The story of psychology*. New York: Anchor Books.

Hunt, R. R., & Einstein, G. O. (1981). Relational and item-specific information in memory. *Journal of Verbal Learning and Verbal Behavior, 20*, 497–514.

Hunt, R. R., & McDaniel, M. A. (1993). The enigma of organization and distinctiveness. *Journal of Memory and Language, 32*, 421–445.

Hurt, S. W., Reznikoff, M., & Clarkin, J. F. (1995). The Rorschach. In L. E. Beutler & M. R. Berren (Eds.), *Integrative assessment of adult personality*. New York: Guilford.

Hurvich, L. M., & Jameson, D. (1951). The binocular fusion of yellow in relation to color theories. *Science, 114*, 199–202.

Hyde, J. S., & Lin, M. C. (1988). Gender differences in verbal ability: A developmental meta-analysis. *Psychological Bulletin, 104*, 53–69.

Inoue-Nakamura, N., & Matsuzawa, T. (1997). Development of stone tool use by wild chimpanzees (Pan troglodytes). *Journal of Comparative Psychology, 111*, 159–713.

Ishai, A., & Sagi, D. (1997). Visual imagery: Effects of short- and long-term memory. *Journal of Cognitive Neuroscience, 9*, 734–742.

Izard, C. E. (1994). Innate and universal facial expressions: Evidence from developmental and cross-cultural research. *Psychological Bulletin, 115,* 288–299.

Jacobi, L., & Cash, T. F. (1994). In pursuit of the perfect appearance: Discrepancies among self-ideal percepts of multiple physical attributes. *Journal of Applied Social Psychology, 24,* 379–396.

Jacobson, E. (1938). *Progressive relaxation.* Chicago: University of Chicago Press.

Jacobson, J. L., & Jacobson, S. W. (1994). Prenatal alcohol exposure and neurobehavioral development: Where is the threshold? *Alcohol Health and Research World, 18,* 30–36.

Jacoby, L. L., & Witherspoon, D. (1982). Remembering without awareness. *Canadian Journal of Psychology, 36,* 300–324.

Jacoby, L. L., Woloshyn, V., & Kelley, C. M. (1989). Becoming famous without being recognized: Unconscious influences of memory produced by dividing attention. *Journal of Experimental Psychology: General, 118,* 115–125.

James, W. (1884). Some omissions of introspective psychology. *Mind, 9,* 1–26.

James, W. (1890). *The principles of psychology.* New York: Holt. (Reprinted Cambridge, MA: Harvard University Press, 1983).

James, W. (1894). The physical basis of emotion. *Psychological Review, 1,* 516–529.

Jamison, K. R. (1986). Suicide and bipolar disorders. *Annals of the New York Academy of Science, 487,* 301–315.

Jamison, K. R. (1989). Mood disorders and patterns of creativity in British writers and artists. *Psychiatry, 52,* 125–134.

Jamison, K. R., Gerner, R. H., Hammen, C., & Padesky, C. (1980). Clouds and silver linings: Positive experiences associated with primary affective disorders. *American Journal of Psychiatry, 137,* 198–202.

Janis, I. L. (1982). *Victims of groupthink* (2nd ed.). Boston: Houghton Mifflin.

Janis, I. L. (1989). *Crucial decisions: Leadership in policymaking and crisis management.* New York: Free Press.

Jarrad, L. E. (1993). On the role of the hippocampus in learning and memory in the rat. *Behavioral and Neural Biology, 60,* 9–26.

Jasper, J. H., & Tessier, J. (1969). Acetylcholine liberation from cerebral cortex during paradoxical (REM) sleep. *Science, 172,* 601–602.

Jausovec, N. (1997). Differences in EEG activity during the solution of closed and open problems. *Creativity Research Journal, 10,* 317–324.

Jaynes, J. (1976). *The origin of consciousness in the breakdown of the bicameral mind.* Boston: Houghton Mifflin.

Jenike, M. A. (1998). Neurosurgical treatment of obsessive-compulsive disorder. *British Journal of Psychiatry, 173,* 79–90.

Jenike, M. A., Baer, L., Ballantine, T., & Maetuga, R. L. (1991). Cingulotomy for refractory obsessive-compulsive disorder: A long-term follow-up of 33 cases. *Archives of General Psychiatry, 48,* 548–557.

Jenike, M. A., Baer, L., & Minichiello, W. E. (Eds.). (1986). *Obsessive-compulsive disorders: Theory and management.* Littleton, MA: PSG Publishing.

Jenkins, H. M., Barrera, F. J., Ireland, C., & Woodside, B. (1978). Signal-centered action patterns of dogs in appetitive classical conditioning. *Learning and Motivation, 9,* 272–296.

Jenkins, J. G., & Dallenbach, K. M. (1924). Obliviscence during sleep and waking. *American Journal of Psychology, 35,* 605–612.

Jenner, P. (1990). Parkinson's disease: Clues to the cause of cell death in the substantia nigra. *Seminars in the Neurosciences, 2,* 117–126.

Jennison, K. M. (1992). The impact of stressful life events and social support on drinking among older adults: A general population survey. *International Journal of Aging and Human Development, 35,* 99–123.

Jensen, A. R. (1992). Commentary: Vehicles of *g. Psychological Science, 3,* 275–278.

Jensen, A. R. (1993). Why is reaction time correlated with psychometric *g? Current Directions in Psychological Science, 2,* 53–56.

Jensen, A. R., & Weng, L. (1994). What is a good *g? Intelligence, 18,* 231–258.

Jensen, J. P., Bergin, A. E., & Greaves, D. W. (1990). The meaning of eclecticism: New survey and analysis of components. *Professional Psychology: Research and Practice, 21,* 124–130.

John, E. R., Prichep, L. S., Fridman, J., & Easton, P. (1988). Neurometrics: Computer-assisted differential diagnosis of brain dysfunction. *Science, 239,* 162–169.

Johnson, C. H., & Hastings, J. W. (1986). The elusive mechanism of the circadian clock. *American Scientist, 74,* 29–36.

Johnson, L. M., & Morris, E. K. (1987). Public information on research with nonhumans. *American Psychologist, 42,* 103–104.

Johnson, M. H., Dziurawiec, S., Ellis, H., & Morton, J. (1991). Newborns' preferential tracking of face-like stimuli and its subsequent decline. *Cognition, 40,* 1–19.

Johnson, R. C., McClearn, C. G., Yuen, S., Nagoshi, C. T., Ahern, F. M., & Cole, R. E. (1985). Galton's data a century later. *American Psychologist, 40,* 875–892.

Johnson, S. P. (1997). Young infants' perception of object unity: Implications for the development of attentional and cognitive skills. *Current Directions in Psychological Science, 6,* 5–11.

Jones, E. E. (1964). *Ingratiation.* New York: Appleton-Century-Crofts.

Jones, E. E. (1990). *Interpersonal perception.* New York: Freeman.

Jones, E. E., & Davis, K. E. (1965). A theory of correspondent inferences: From acts to dispositions. In L. Berkowitz (Ed.), *Advances in experimental social psychology* (Vol. 2). New York: Academic Press.

Jones, E. E., & Harris, V. A. (1967). The attribution of attitudes. *Journal of Experimental Social Psychology, 3,* 1–24.

Jones, E. R., & Childers, R. L. (1993). *Contemporary college physics* (2nd ed.). Reading, MA: Addison-Wesley.

Jones, G. V., & Martin, M. (1992). Misremembering a familiar object: Mnemonic illusions, not drawing bias. *Memory & Cognition, 20,* 211–213.

Jones, L. A. (1988). Motor illusions: What do they reveal about proprioception? *Psychological Bulletin, 103,* 72–86.

Jones, M. C. (1924). A laboratory study of fear: The case of Peter. *Pedagogical Seminary, 31,* 308–315.

Jones, R. T. (1971). Tetrahydrocannabinol and the marijuana-induced social "high" or the effects on the mind of marijuana. In A. J. Singer (Ed.), Marijuana: Chemistry, pharmacology, and patterns of social use. *Annals of the New York Academy of Sciences, 191,* 155–165.

Jou, J., Shanteau, J., & Harris, R. J. (1996). An information processing view of framing effects: The role of causal schemas in decision making. *Memory & Cognition, 24,* 1–15.

Joule, R. V. (1986). Twenty-five on: Yet another version of cognitive dissonance theory? *European Journal of Social Psychology, 16,* 65–78.

Jung, C. G. (1923). *Psychological types.* New York: Pantheon Books.

Justice, A. (1985). Review of the effects of stress on cancer in laboratory animals: Importance of time stress application and type of tumor. *Psychological Bulletin, 98,* 108–138.

Kagan, J. (1997). Temperament and the reactions to unfamiliarity. *Child Development, 68,* 139–143.

Kagan, J., & Snidman, N. (1991). Temperamental factors in human development. *American Psychologist, 46,* 856–862.

Kahn, R. S., Davidson, M., Knott, P., Stern, R. G., Apter, S., & Davis, K. L. (1993). Effect of neuroleptic medication on cerebrospinal fluid monoamine metabolite concentrations in schizophrenia: Serotonin-dopamine interactions as a target for treatment. *Archives of General Psychiatry, 50,* 599–605.

Kahneman, D. (1973). *Attention and effort.* Englewood Cliffs, NJ: Prentice-Hall.

Kahneman, D., Slovic, P., & Tversky, A. (Eds.). (1982). *Judgment under uncertainty: Heuristics and biases.* Cambridge: Cambridge University Press.

Kail, R. (1991). Developmental change in speed of processing during childhood and adolescence. *Psychological Bulletin, 109,* 490–501.

Kail, R., & Salthouse, T. A. (1994). Processing speed as a mental capacity. *Acta Psychologica, 86,* 199–225.

Kalat, J. W. (1992). *Biological psychology* (4th ed.). Belmont, CA: Wadsworth.

Kalat, J. W. (1996). *Introduction to psychology* (4th ed.). Pacific Grove, CA: Brooks/Cole.

Kaler, S. R., & Freeman, B. J. (1994). Analysis of environmental deprivation: Cognitive and social development in Romanian orphans. *Journal of Child Psychology and Psychiatry, 35,* 769–781.

Kales, A., & Kales, J. D. (1984). *Evaluation and treatment of insomnia.* New York: Oxford.

Kalichman, S. C., Belcher, L., Cherry, C., & Williams, E. A. (1997). Primary prevention of sexually transmitted HIV infections: Transferring behavioral research technology to community programs. *Journal of Primary Prevention, 18,* 149–172.

Kalick, S. M., Zebrowitz, L. A., Langlois, J. H., & Johnson, R. M. (1998). Does human facial attractiveness honestly advertise health? Longitudinal data on an evolutionary question. *Psychological Science, 9,* 8–13.

Kalter, N. (1998). Group interventions for children of divorce. In K. C. Stoiber & T. R. Kratochwill (Eds.), *Handbook of group intervention for children and families.* Boston, MA: Allyn & Bacon.

Kamen-Siegel, L., Rodin, J., Seligman, M. E. P., & Dwyer, J. (1991). Explanatory style and cell-mediated immunity in elderly men and women. *Health Psychology, 10,* 229–235.

Kamil, A. C., & Balda, R. P. (1990). Differential memory for different cache sites by Clark's nutcrackers (*Nucifraga columbiana*). *Journal of Experimental Psychology: Animal Behavior Processes, 16,* 162–168.

Kamin, L. J. (1968). "Attention-like" processes in classical conditioning. In M. R. Jones (Ed.), *Miami symposium on the prediction of behavior: Aversive stimulation.* Miami: University of Miami Press.

Kandel, E. R. (1991). Cellular mechanisms of learning and the biological basis of individuality. In E. R. Kandel, J. H. Schwartz, & T. M. Jessel (Eds.), *Principles of neural science* (3rd ed.). New York: Elsevier.

Kandel, E. R., & Schwartz, J. H. (1982). Molecular biology of learning: Modulation of transmitter release. *Science, 218,* 433–443.

Kane, J. M., & Marder, S. R. (1993). Psychopharmacologic treatment of schizophrenia. *Schizophrenia Bulletin, 19,* 287–302.

Kane, J. M., Woerner, M., Weinhold, P., Wegner, J., Kinon, B., & Bernstein, M. (1986). Incidence of tardive dyskinesia: Five-year data from a prospective study. *Psychopharmacology Bulletin, 20,* 387–389.

Kanner, A. D., Coyne, J. C., Schaefer, C., & Lazarus, R. S. (1981). Comparison of two modes of stress measurment: Daily hassles and uplifts versus major life events. *Journal of Behavioral Medicine, 4,* 1–39.

Kaplan, R. M. (1985). The controversy related to the use of psychological tests. In B. B. Wolman (Ed.), *Handbook of intelligence: Theories, measurements, and applications.* New York: Wiley.

Kapur, S., & Mann, J. J. (1993). Antidepressant action and the neurobiologic effects of ECT: Human studies. In C. E. Coffey (Ed.), *The clinical science of electroconvulsive therapy.* Washington, DC: American Psychiatric Press.

Karau, S. J., & Hart, J. W. (1998). Group cohesiveness and social loafing: Effects of a social interaction manipulation on individual motivation within groups. *Group Dynamics, 2,* 185–191.

Karau, S. J., & Williams, K. D. (1993). Social loafing: A meta-analytic review and theoretical integration. *Journal of Personality and Social Psychology, 65,* 681–706.

Karni, A., Tanne, D., Rubenstein, B. S., Askenasy, J., & Sagi, D. (1994). Dependence on REM sleep of overnight improvement of a perceptual skill. *Science, 265,* 679–682.

Kauer, J. S. (1987). Coding in the olfactory system. In T. E. Finger & W. L. Silver (Eds.), *Neurobiology of taste and smell.* New York: Wiley.

Kaufman, A. S., & Horn, J. L. (1996). Age changes on tests of fluid and crystallized ability for women and men on the Kaufman Adolescent and Adult Intelligence Test (KAIT) at ages 17–94 years. *Archives of Clinical Neuropsychology, 11,* 97–121.

Kausler, D. H. (1994). *Learning and memory in normal aging.* San Diego, CA: Academic Press.

Kaufman, M. H. (1997). The teratogenic effects of alcohol following exposure during pregnancy, and its influence on the chromosome constitution in the pre-ovulatory egg. *Alcohol & Alcoholism, 32,* 113–128.

Kazdin, A. E. (1982). The token economy: A decade later. *Journal of Applied Behavior Analysis, 15,* 431–445.

Keesey, R. E., & Powley, T. L. (1975). Hypothalamic regulation of body weight. *American Scientist, 63,* 558–565.

Keller, M. B., & Shapiro, R. W. (1982). Double depression: Superimposition of acute depressive episodes on chronic depressive disorders. *American Journal of Psychiatry, 139,* 438–442.

Kelley, H. H. (1967). Attribution theory in social interaction. In E. E. Jones, D. E. Kanouse, H. H. Kelley, R. E. Nisbett, S. Valins, & B. Weiner (Eds.), *Attribution: Perceiving the causes of behavior.* Morristown, NJ: General Learning Press.

Kelley, H. H. (1983). Love and commitment. In H. H. Kelley, E. Berscheid, A. Christensen, J. H. Harvey, T. L. Huston, G. Levinger, E. McClintock, L. A. Peplau, & D. R. Peterson (Eds.), *Close relationships.* New York: Freeman.

Keller, W. C., & Rueda, M. G. (1998). Mechanisms of action in dopaminergic agents in Parkinson's disease. *Neurology, 50,* 511–514.

Kelley, K. (1985). Sex, sex guilt, and authoritarianism: Differences in responses to explicit heterosexual and masturbatory slides. *Journal of Sex Research, 21,* 68–85.

Kellogg, W. N., & Kellogg, L. A. (1933). *The ape and the child.* New York: McGraw-Hill.

Kelly, D. D. (1991). Sleep and dreaming. In E. R. Kandel, J. H. Schwartz, & T. M. Jessell (Eds.), *Principles of neural science* (3rd ed.). New York: Elsevier.

Kemper, T. L. (1994). Neuroanatomical and neuropathological changes during aging and dementia. In M. L. Albert & J. E. Knoefel (Eds.), *Clinical neurology of aging* (2nd ed.). New York: Oxford University Press.

Kenrick, D. T., & Funder, D. C. (1988). Profiting from controversy: Lessons of the person-situation debate. *American Psychologist, 43*, 23–34.

Kenrick, D. T., Gutierres, S. E., & Goldberg, L. (1989). Influence of erotica on judgments of strangers and mates. *Journal of Experimental Social Psychology, 25*, 159–167.

Kenrick, D. T., McCreath, H. E., Govern, J., King, R., & Bordin, J. (1990). Person-environment intersections: Everyday settings and common trait dimensions. *Journal of Personality and Social Psychology, 58*, 685–698.

Keppel, G., & Underwood, B. J. (1962). Proactive inhibition in short-term retention of single items. *Journal of Verbal Learning and Verbal Behavior, 1*, 153–161.

Kerkhoff, G., Munssinger, U., & Meier, E. K. (1994). Neurovisual rehabilitation in cerebral blindness. *Archives of Neurology, 51*, 474–481.

Kessler, R. C., McGonagle, K. A., Shanyang, Z., Nelson, C. B., Hughes, M., Eshleman, S., Wittchen, H., & Kendler, K. S. (1994). Lifetime and 12–month prevalence of DSM-III-R psychiatric disorders in the United States. *Archives of General Psychiatry, 51*, 8–19.

Key, W. B. (1973). *Subliminal seduction.* Englewood Cliffs, NJ: Prentice-Hall.

Keysar, B., Barr, D. J., Balin, A., & Paekm T. S. (1998). Definite reference and mutual knowledge: Process models of common ground in comprehension. *Journal of Memory and Language, 39*, 1–20.

Kiecolt-Glaser, J. K., Garner, W., Speicher, C., Penn, G. M., Holliday, J., & Glaser, R. (1984). Psychosocial modifiers of immunocompetence in medical students. *Psychosomatic Medicine, 46*, 7–17.

Kiesler, C. A., & Sibulkin, A. E. (1987). *Mental hospitalization: Myths and facts about a national crisis.* Beverly Hills, CA: Sage.

Kihlstrom, J. (1985). Hypnosis. *Annual Review of Psychology, 36*, 385–418.

Kihlstrom, J., & Cantor, N. (1984). Mental representations of the self. In L. Berkowitz (Ed.), *Advances in experimental social psychology* (Vol. 17). New York: Academic Press.

Kihlstrom, J., & McConkey, K. M. (1990). William James and hypnosis: A centennial reflection. *Psychological Science, 1*, 174–178.

Kite, M. E. (1996). Age, gender, and occupational label. *Psychology of Women Quarterly, 20*, 361–374.

Kite, M. E., & Johnson, B. J. (1988). Attitudes toward older and younger adults: A meta-analysis. *Psychology and Aging, 3*, 233–244.

Kimble, G. A. (1993). A modest proposal for a minor revolution in the language of psychology. *Psychological Science, 4*, 253–255.

Kimelberg, H. K., & Norenberg, M. D. (1989, April). Astrocytes. *Scientific American, 260*, 66–76.

Kimura, D. (1992, September). Sex differences in the brain. *Scientific American, 267*, 118–125.

Kimura, D., & Hampson, E. (1994). Cognitive pattern in men and women is influenced by fluctuations in sex hormones. *Current Directions in Psychological Science, 3*, 57–61.

Kirchgessner, A. L., & Sclafani, A. (1988). PVN-hindbrain pathway involved in the hypothalamic hyperphagia-obesity syndrome. *Physiology and Behavior, 42*, 517–528.

Kirkcaldy, B. D., Cooper, C. L., & Furnham, A. F. (1999). The relationship between type A, internality-externality, emotional distress and perceived health. *Personality & Individual Differences, 26*, 223–235.

Klatzky, R. L. (1984). *Memory and awareness: An information-processing perspective.* New York: Freeman.

Klatzky, R. L., Lederman, S. J., & Metzger, V. A. (1985). Identifying objects by touch: An "expert system." *Perception & Psychophysics, 37*, 299–302.

Kline, P. (1991). *Intelligence: The psychometric view.* New York: Routledge, Chapman, & Hall.

Klinger, E. (1977). *Meaning and void: Inner experience and the incentive in people's lives.* Minneapolis: University of Minnesota Press.

Kluft, R. P. (1991). Multiple personality disorder. In A. Tasman & S. M. Goldfinger (Eds.), *Review of psychiatry* (Vol. 10). Washington, DC: American Psychiatric Press.

Kohlberg, L. (1963). The development of children's orientations toward a moral order: I. Sequence in the development of moral thought. *Vita Humana, 6*, 11–33.

Kohlberg, L. (1969). Stage and sequence: The cognitive-developmental approach to socialization. In D. A. Goslin (Ed.), *Handbook of socialization theory and research.* Chicago: Rand McNally.

Kohlberg, L. (1986). *The psychology of moral development.* New York: Harper & Row.

Kolb, B., & Whishaw, I. Q. (1990). *Fundamentals of human neuropsychology* (3rd ed.). New York: Freeman.

Konarski, E. A., Jr. (1985). The use of response deprivation to increase the academic performance of EMR students. *The Behavior Therapist, 8*, 61.

Kosky, R. J., Eshkevari, H. S., Goldney, R. D., & Hassan, R. (1998). *Suicide prevention: The global context.* New York: Plenum Press.

Kosslyn, S. M. (1983). *Ghosts in the mind's machine: Creating and using images in the brain.* New York: Horizon.

Kosslyn, S. M., Alpert, N. M., Thompson, W. L., & Maljkovic, V. (1993). Visual mental imagery activates topographically organized visual cortex: PET investigations. *Journal of Cognitive Neuroscience, 5*, 263–287.

Kosslyn, S. M., Ball, T. M., & Reiser, B. J. (1978). Visual images preserve metric spatial information: Evidence from studies of image scanning. *Journal of Experimental Psychology: Human Perception and Performance, 4*, 47–60.

Kosslyn, S. M., & Koenig, O. (1992). *Wet mind: The new cognitive neuroscience.* New York: Free Press.

Kraemer, P. J., & Golding, J. M. (1997). Adaptive forgetting in animals. *Psychonomic Bulletin & Review, 4*, 480–49.

Kramer, R. M. (1998). Revisiting the Bay of Pigs and Vietnam decisions 25 years later: How well has the groupthink hypothesis stood the test of time? *Organizational Behavior & Human Decision Processes, 73*, 236–271.

Kraepelin, E. (1921). *Manic-depressive insanity and paranoia.* London: Churchill Livingstone.

Kramer, A., & Buck, L. A. (1997). Encountering people labeled "schizophrenic." *Journal of Humanistic Psychology, 37*, 12–29.

Kramer, P. D. (1993). *Listening to Prozac.* New York: Viking.

Krantz, D. S., & Manuck, S. B. (1984). Acute psychophysiologic reactivity and risk of cardiovascular disease: A review and methodologic critique. *Psychological Bulletin, 96*, 435–464.

Kraus, S. J. (1995). Attitudes and the prediction of behavior. *Personality and Social Psychology Bulletin, 21*, 58–75.

Krause, N., & Liang, J. (1993). Stress, social support, and psychological distress among the Chinese elderly. *Journals of Gerontology, 48*, 282–291.

Krechevsky, M., & Seidel, S. (1998). Minds at work: Applying multiple intelligences in the classroom. In R. J. Sternberg & W. M. Williams, (Eds.), *Intelligence, instruction, and assessment: Theory into practice.* Mahwah, NJ: Lawrence Erlbaum Associates.

Krug, E. G., Kresnow, M., Peddicord, J., Dahlberg, L., Powell, K., Crosby, A., & Annest, J. (1998). Suicide after natural disasters. *New England Journal of Medicine, 338,* 373–378.

Krystal, A. D., & Coffey, C. E. (1997). Neuropsychiatric considerations in the use of electroconvulsive therapy. *Journal of Neuropsychiatry & Clinical Neurosciences, 9,* 283–292.

Kübler-Ross, E. (1969). *On death and dying.* New York: Macmillan.

Kübler-Ross, E. (1974). *Questions and answers on death and dying.* New York: Macmillan.

Kuhn, D. (1992). Cognitive development. In M. H. Bornstein & M. E. Lamb (Eds.), *Developmental psychology: An advanced textbook.* Hillsdale, NJ: Erlbaum.

Kuhn, W., Winkel, R., Woitalla, D., Meves, S., Przuntek, H., & Mueller, T. (1998). High prevalence of Parkinsonism after exposure to lead-sulfate batteries. *Neurology, 50,* 1885–1886.

Kutchinsky, B. (1992). The child sexual abuse panic. *Nordisk Sexoligi, 10,* 30–42.

Labouvie-Vief, G., Hakim-Larson, J., & Hobart, C. J. (1987). Age, ego level, and the life-span development of coping and defense processes. *Psychology and Aging, 2,* 286–293.

Labov, W. (1973). The boundaries of words and their meanings. In C. J. N. Bailey & R. W. Shiny (Eds.), *New ways of analyzing variation in English* (Vol. 1). Washington, DC: Georgetown University Press.

Lackner, J. R., & DiZio, P. (1991). Decreased susceptibility to motion sickness during exposure to visual inversion in microgravity. *Aviation, Space, and Environmental Medicine, 62,* 206–211.

Ladd, G. T. (1892). Contributions to the psychology of visual dreams. *Mind, 1,* 299–304.

Lafferty, P., Beutler, L. E., & Crago, M. (1991). Differences between more or less effective psychotherapists: A study of select therapist variables. *Journal of Consulting and Clinical Psychology, 57,* 76–80.

Lakoff, G. (1987). *Women, fire, and dangerous things: What categories reveal about the human mind.* Chicago: University of Chicago Press.

Lamb, M. E. (1998). Nonparental child care: Context, quality, correlates, and consequences. In I. E. Sigel & K. A. Renniger (Eds.), *Handbook of child psychology: Child psychology in practice* (4th ed.). New York: Wiley.

Lamb, M. E., Ketterlinus, R. D., & Fracasso, M. P. (1992). Parent-child relationships. In M. H. Bornstein & M. E. Lamb (Eds.), *Developmental psychology: An advanced textbook.* Hillsdale, NJ: Erlbaum.

Lamb, M. E., & Sternberg, K. L. (1990). Do we really know how day care affects children? *Journal of Applied Developmental Psychology, 11,* 351–379.

Lambert, M. J., & Bergin, A. E. (1994). The effectiveness of psychotherapy. In A. E. Bergin & S. L. Garfield (Eds.), *Handbook of psychotherapy and behavior change* (4th ed.). New York: Wiley.

Lamont, J. A. (1997). Sexuality. In D. E. Stewart & G. E. Robinson (Eds.), *A clinician's guide to menopause. Clinical practice.* Washington, DC: Health Press International.

Lancet, D., Gross-Isseroff, R., Margalit, T., & Seidemann, E. (1993). Olfaction: From signal transduction and termination to human genome mapping. *Chemical Senses, 18,* 217–225.

Landauer, T. K. (1962). Rate of implicit speech. *Perceptual and Motor Skills, 15,* 646.

Lane, R. D., Reiman, E. M., Ahern, G. L., & Schwartz, G. E. (1997). Neuroanatomical correlates of happiness, sadness, and disgust. *American Journal of Psychiatry, 154,* 926–933.

Lang, P. J. (1994). The varieties of emotional experience: A meditation on James-Lange theory. *Psychological Review, 101,* 211–221.

Langer, E. J. (1989). *Mindfulness.* Cambridge, MA: Addison-Wesley.

Langer, E. J., & Abelson, R. P. (1974). A patient by any other-name: Clinician group differences in labeling bias. *Journal of Consulting and Clinical Psychology, 42,* 4–9.

Langlois, J. H., & Roggman, L. A. (1990). Attractive faces are only average. *Psychological Science, 1,* 115–121.

Langlois, J. H., Roggman, L. A., Casey, R. J., Ritter, J. M., Rieser-Danner, L. A., & Jenkins, V. Y. (1987). Infant preferences for attractive faces: Rudiments of a stereotype? *Developmental Psychology, 23,* 363–369.

Langlois, J. H., Roggman, L. A., & Musselman, L. (1994). What is average and what is not average about attractive faces? *Psychological Science, 5,* 214–220.

Laprelle, J., Hoyle, R. H., Insko, C. A., & Bernthal, P. (1990). Interpersonal attraction and descriptions of the traits of others: Ideal similarity, self similarity, and liking. *Journal of Research in Personality, 24,* 216–240.

Larose, H., & Standing, L. (1998). Does the halo effect occur in the elderly? *Social Behavior & Personality, 26,* 147–150.

Latané, B. (1981). The psychology of social impact. *American Psychologist, 36,* 343–356.

Latané, B., & Nida, S. A. (1981). Ten years of research on group size and helping. *Psychological Bulletin, 89,* 308–324.

Latané, B., Williams, K., & Harkins, S. (1979). Many hands make light the work: The causes and consequences of social loafing. *Journal of Personality and Social Psychology, 37,* 822–832.

Laudenslager, M. L., Ryan, S. M., Drugen, R. L., Hyson, R. L., & Maier, S. F. (1983). Coping and immunosuppression: Inescapable but not escapable shock suppresses lymphocyte proliferation. *Science, 221,* 568–570.

Lawton, M. P., Kleban, M. H., & Rajagopal, D., & Dean, J. (1992). Dimensions of affective experience in three age groups. *Psychology and Aging, 7,* 171–184.

Lazarus, A. A., & Messer, S. B. (1991). Does chaos prevail? An exchange on technical eclecticism and assimilative integration. *Journal of Psychotherapy Integration, 1,* 143–158.

Lazarus, R. S. (1966). *Psychological stress and the coping process.* New York: McGraw-Hill.

Lazarus, R. S. (1991). *Emotion and adaptation.* New York: Oxford University Press.

Lazarus, R. S. (1993). Why we should think of stress as a subset of emotion. In L. Goldberger & S. Breznitz (Eds.), *Handbook of stress: Theoretical and clinical aspects* (2nd ed.). New York: Free Press.

Lazarus, R. S., & Folkman, S. (1984). *Stress, appraisal and coping.* New York: Springer.

Leach, M. M., & Harbin, J. J. (1997). Psychological ethics codes: A comparison of 24 countries. *International Journal of Psychology, 32,* 181–192.

Lebow, J. L., & Gurman, A. S. (1995). Research assessing couple and family therapy. *Annual Review of Psychology, 46,* 27–57.

Leclerc, G., Lefrancois, R., Dube, M., Hebert, R., & Gaulin, P. (1998). The self-actualization concept: A content validation. *Journal of Social Behavior & Personality, 11,* 69–84.

Lee, C. J., & Katz, A. N. (1998). The differential role of ridicule in sarcasm and irony. *Metaphor & Symbol, 13,* 1–15.

Lee, E. K. (1998). Periodic left temporal sharp waves during acute psychosis. *Journal of Epilepsy, 11,* 79–83.

Lee, P. (1997). Language in thinking and learning: Pedagogy and the new Whorfian framework. *Harvard Educational Review, 67,* 430–471.

Lefcourt, H. M. (1982). *Locus of control: Current trends in theory and research.* Waterloo, Ontario: University of Waterloo.

Legemaate, J. (1998). Legal protection in psychiatry: Balancing the rights and needs of patients and society. *European Psychiatry, 13,* 107s–112s.

Leibowitz, H. W. (1971). Sensory, learned, and cognitive mechanisms of size perception. *Annals of the New York Academy of Sciences, 188,* 47–62.

Leith, K. P., & Baumeister, R. F. (1996). Why do bad moods increase self-defeating behavior? Emotion, risk tasking, and self-regulation. *Journal of Personality & Social Psychology, 71,* 1250–1267.

Lenneberg, E. H. (1967). *Biological foundations of language.* New York: Wiley.

Leon, M. I., & Gallistel, C. R. (1998). Self-stimulating rats combine subjective reward magnitude and subjective reward rate multiplicatively. *Journal of Experimental Behavior: Animal Behavior Processes, 24,* 165–277.

Lepper, M. R., Greene, D., & Nisbett, R. E. (1973). Undermining children's intrinsic interest with external reward: A test of the "overjustification" hypothesis. *Journal of Personality and Social Psychology, 28,* 129–137.

Lerman, H. G. (1986). From Freud to feminist personality theory: Getting here from there. *Psychology of Women Quarterly, 10,* 1–18.

LeVay, S. (1991). A difference in hypothalamic structure between heterosexual and homosexual men. *Science, 253,* 1034–1037.

LeVay, S. (1996). *Queer science: The use and abuse of research into homosexuality.* Cambridge, MA: MIT Press.

Levenson, R. W. (1992). Autonomic nervous system differences among emotions. *Psychological Science, 3,* 23–27.

Levine, D. N., Warach, J., & Farah, M. J. (1985). Two visual systems in mental imagery: Dissociation of "what" and "where" in imagery disorders due to bilateral posterior cerebral lesions. *Neurology, 35,* 1010–1018.

Levine, G., & Parkinson, S. (1994). *Experimental methods in psychology.* Hillsdale, NJ: Erlbaum.

Levinson, D. J., Darow, C. N., Klein, E. B., Levinson, M. H., & McKee, B. (1978). *The seasons of a man's life.* New York: Knopf.

Lewis, M., & Brooks-Gunn, J. (1979). *Social cognition and the acquisition of self.* New York: Plenum.

Lewontin, R. (1976). Race and intelligence. In N. J. Block & G. Dworkin (Eds.), *The IQ controversy: Critical readings.* New York: Pantheon.

Li, X., Sano, H., & Merwin, J. C. (1996). Perception and reasoning abilities among American, Japanese, and Chinese adolescents. *Journal of Adolescent Research, 11,* 173–193.

Liberman, R. P., Kopelowicz, A., & Young, A. S. (1994). Biobehavioral treatment and rehabilitation of schizophrenia. *Behavior Therapy, 25,* 89–107.

Lickey, M. E., & Gordon, B. (1991). *Medicine and mental illness: The use of drugs in psychiatry.* New York: Freeman.

Liebert, R. M., & Liebert, L. L. (1995). *Science and behavior: An introduction to methods of psychological research* (4th ed.). Englewood Cliffs, NJ: Prentice-Hall.

Lilienfeld, S. O. (1994). Conceptual problems in the assessment of psychopathy. *Clinical Psychology Review, 14,* 17–38.

Linde, J. A., & Clark, L. A. (1998). Diagnostic assignment of criteria: Clinicians and DSM-IV. *Journal of Personality Disorders, 12,* 126–137.

Linde, L., & Bergstrom, M. (1992). The effect of one night without sleep on problem solving and immediate recall. *Psychological Research, 54,* 127–136.

Linden, W. (1990). *Autogenic training: A clinical guide.* New York: Guilford.

Lindsley, O. R., & Skinner, B. F. (1954). A method for the experimental analysis of psychotic patients. *American Psychologist, 9,* 419–420.

Lindvall, O., Rehncrona, S., Brundin, P., Gustavii, B., ∞stedt, B., Widner, H., Lindholm, T., Bjπrklund, A., Leenders, K. L., Rothwell, J. C., Frackowiak, R., Marsden, D., Johnels, B., Steg, G., Freedman, R., Hoffer, B. J., Seiger, A., Bygdeman, M., Strπmberg, I., & Olsen, L. (1989). Human fetal dopamine neurons grafted into the striatum in two patients with severe Parkinson's disease. *Archives of Neurology, 46,* 615–631.

Linton, M. (1975). Memory for real-world events. In D. A. Norman & D. E. Rumelhart (Eds.), *Explorations in cognition.* San Francisco: Freeman.

Linville, P. (1985). Self-complexity and affective extremity: Don't put all your eggs in one cognitive basket. *Social Cognition, 3,* 94–120.

Linville, P. (1987). Self-complexity as a cognitive buffer against stress-related illness and depression. *Journal of Personality and Social Psychology, 52,* 663–676.

Linville, P., & Carlston, D. E. (1994). Social cognition of the self. In P. G. Devine, D. L. Hamilton, & T. M. Ostrom (Eds.), *Socialcognition: Its impact on social psychology.* New York: Academic Press.

Lipsey, M. W., & Wilson, D. B. (1993). The efficacy of psychological, educational, and behavioral treatment: Confirmation from meta-analysis. *American Psychologist, 48,* 1181–1209.

Lisk, R. D. (1978). The regulation of sexual "heat." In J. B. Hutchinson (Ed.), *Biological determinants of sexual behaviour.* New York: Wiley.

Livingstone, M., & Hubel, D. H. (1988). Segregation of form, color, movement, and depth: Anatomy, physiology, and perception. *Science, 240,* 740–749.

Liu, Z. (1996). Viewpoint dependency in object representation and recognition. *Spatial Vision, 9,* 491–521.

Locke, J. L. (1994). Phases in the child's development of language. *American Scientist, 82,* 436–445.

Loftus, E. L. (1979). *Eyewitness testimony.* Cambridge, MA: Harvard University Press.

Loftus, E. L. (1991). *Witness for the defense.* New York: St. Martin's.

Loftus, E. L. (1993). The reality of repressed memories. *American Psychologist, 48,* 518–537.

Loftus, E. L., & Loftus, G. R. (1980). On the permanence of stored information in the brain. *American Psychologist, 35,* 409–420.

Loftus, E. L., & Palmer, J. C. (1974). Reconstruction of automobile destruction: An example of the interaction between language and memory. *Journal of Verbal Learning and Verbal Behavior, 13,* 585–589.

Loftus, E. L., Polonsky, S., & Fullilove, M. T. (1994). Memories of childhood sexual abuse. *Psychology of Women Quarterly, 18,* 67–84.

Logan, G. D. (1988). Toward an instance theory of automatization. *Psychological Review, 95,* 492–527.

Logan, G. D. (1991). Automaticity and memory. In W. E. Hockley & S. Lewandowsky (Eds.), *Relating theory and data: Essays on human memory in honor of Bennet B. Murdock.* Hillsdale, NJ: Erlbaum.

Lorenz, K. Z. (1958, December). The evolution of behavior. *Scientific American, 199,* 67–78.

Lovaas, O. I. (1987). Behavioral treatment and normal educational and intellectual functioning in young autistic children. *Journal of Consulting and Clinical Psychology, 55,* 3–9.

Lovaas, O. I., Koegel, R., Simmons, J. Q., & Long, J. S. (1973). Some generalization and follow-up measures on autistic children in behavior therapy. *Journal of Applied Behavior Analysis, 6*, 131–166.

Lovdal, L. T. (1989). Sex role messages in television commercials: An update. *Sex Roles, 21*, 715–724.

Lowe, J., & Carroll, D. (1985). The effects of spinal cord injury on the intensity of emotional experience. *British Journal of Clinical Psychology, 24*, 135–136.

Loewenstein, R. J. (1996). Dissociative amnesia and dissociative fugue. In L. K. Michelson, & W. J. Ray (Eds.), *Handbook of dissociation: Theoretical, empirical, and clinical perspectives*. New York: Plenum Press.

Luborsky, L., Barber, J. P., & Crits-Cristoph, P. (1990). Theory-based research for understanding the process of dynamic psychotherapy. *Journal of Consulting and Clinical Psychology, 58*, 281–287.

Lucy, J. A. (1997). Linguistic relativity. *Annual review of anthropology, 26*, 291–312.

Luria, A. R. (1968). *The mind of a mnemonist*. New York: Basic Books.

Lutz, C. (1982). The domain of emotion words in Ifaluk. *American Ethnologist, 9*, 113–128.

Lykken, D. T. (1998). *A tremor in the blood: Uses and abuses of the lie detector*. New York: Plenum Press.

Lyness, S. A. (1993). Predictors of differences between Type A and Type B individuals in heart rate and blood pressure reactivity. *Psychological Bulletin, 114*, 266–295.

Lynn, R. (1994). Some reinterpretations of the Minnesota transracial adoption study. *Intelligence, 19*, 21–27.

Lynn, S. J., Rhue, J. W., & Weekes, J. R. (1990). Hypnotic involuntariness: A social cognitive analysis. *Psychological Review, 97*, 169–184.

Mackay, D. G. (1983). Prescriptive grammar and the pronoun problem. In B. Thorne, C. Kramarae, & N. Henley (Eds.), *Language, gender, and society*. Rowley, MA: Newbury House.

MacKenzie, K. R. (1997). *Time-managed group psychotherapy: Effective clinical applications*. Washington, DC: American Psychiatric Press, Inc.

MacKinnon, D. W. (1962). The nature and nurture of creative talent. *American Psychologist, 17*, 484–495.

MacLean, C. R. K., Walton, K. G., Wenneberg, S. R., & Levitsky, D. K. (1997). Effects of the Transcendental Meditation program on adaptive mechanisms: Changes in hormone levels and responses to stress after 4 months of practice. *Psychoneuroendocrinology, 22*, 277–295.

Maier, N. R. F. (1931). Reasoning in humans II: The solution to a problem and its appearance in consciousness. *Journal of Comparative Psychology, 12*, 181–194.

Maier, N. R. F., & Burke, R. J. (1967). Response availability as a factor in the problem-solving performance of males and females. *Journal of Personality and Social Psychology, 5*, 304–310.

Maier, S. F., Watkins, L. R., & Fleshner, M. (1994). Psychoneuroimmunology: The interface between behavior, brain, and immunity. *American Psychologist, 49*, 1004–1017.

Maj, M. (1998). Critique of the DSM-IV operational diagnostic criteria for schizophrenia. *British Journal of Psychiatry, 172*, 458–460.

Malt, B. C., & Smith, E. E. (1984). Correlated properties in natural categories. *Journal of Verbal Learning and Verbal Behavior, 23*, 250–269.

Mandler, G., Nakamura, Y., & Van Zandt, B. J. S. (1987). Nonspecific effects of stimuli that cannot be recognized. *Journal of Experimental Psychology: Learning, Memory, & Cognition, 13*, 646–648.

Mandler, J. M. (1992). How to build a baby: II. Conceptual primitives. *Psychological Review, 99*, 587–604.

Mann, J. J. (1998). Neurobiological correlates of the antidepressant action of electroconvulsive therapy. *Journal of Ect, 14*, 172–180.

Mann, T. (1994). Informed consent for psychological research: Do subjects comprehend consent forms and understand their legal rights? *Psychological Science, 5*, 140–143.

Manson, S. M. (1995). Culture and major depression: Current challenges in the diagnosis of mood disorders. *Psychiatric Clinics of North America, 18*, 487–501.

Maratos, O. (1998). Neonatal, early and later imitation: Same order of phenomena? In F Simion, & G. Butterworth (Eds.). *The development of sensory, motor and cognitive capacities in early infancy: From perception to cognition*. Hove, England UK: Psychology Press/Erlbaum (UK) Taylor & Francis.

Marcia, J. E. (1966). Development and validation of ego identity status. *Journal of Personality and Social Psychology, 3*, 551–558.

Marcus, D. E., & Overton, W. F. (1978). The development of cognitive gender constancy and sex-role preferences. *Child Development, 49*, 434–444.

Markman, A. B. & Wisniewski, E. J. (1997). Similar and different: The differentiation of basic-level categories. *Journal of Experimental Psychology: Learning, Memory, & Cognition, 23*, 54–70.

Markus, H. (1977). Self-schemata and processing information about the self. *Journal of Personality and Social Psychology, 35*, 63–78.

Markus, H., & Kitayama, S. (1991). Culture and the self: Implications for cognition, emotion, and motivation. *Psychological Review, 98*, 224–253.

Markus, H., & Kitayama, S. (1994). A collective fear of the collective: Implications for selves and theories of selves. *Personality and Social Psychology Bulletin, 20*, 568–579.

Markus, H., & Nurius, P. (1986). Possible selves. *American Psychologist, 41*, 954–969.

Marlatt, G. A., & VandenBos, G. R. (Eds.). *Addictive behaviors: Readings on etiology, prevention, and treatment*. Washington, DC: American Psychological Association.

Marsh, R. L., Sebrechts, M. M., Hicks, J. L., & Landau, J. D. (1997). Processing strategies and secondary memory in very rapid forgetting. *Memory & Cognition, 25*, 173–181.

Marshall, G. D., & Zimbardo, P. G. (1979). Affective consequences of inadequately explained physiological arousal. *Journal of Personality and Social Psychology, 37*, 970–988.

Marshall, J. C., & Halligan, P. W. (1988). Blindsight and insight in visuo-spatial neglect. *Nature, 336*, 766–767.

Marson, L., & McKenna, K. E. (1994). Stimulation of the hypothalamus initiates the urethrogenital reflex in male rats. *Brain Research, 638*, 103–108.

Martin, K. M., & Aggleton, J. P. (1993). Contextual effects on the ability of divers to use decompression tables. *Applied Cognitive Psychology, 7*, 311–316.

Martin, P., & Bateson, P. (1993). *Measuring behavior: An introductory guide* (2nd ed.). Cambridge: Cambridge University Press.

Martin, R. J., White, B. D., & Hulsey, M. G. (1991). The regulation of body weight. *American Scientist, 79*, 528–541.

Marx, M. H., & Cronan-Hillix, W. A. (1987). *Systems and theories in psychology*. New York: McGraw-Hill.

Maser, J. D., Kaelber, C., & Weise, R. E. (1991). International use and attitudes toward DSM-III and DSM-III-R: Growing consensus in psychiatric classification. *Journal of Abnormal Psychology, 100*, 271–279.

Mash, D. C., Flynn, D. D., & Potter, L. T. (1985). Loss of M2 muscarine receptors in the cerebral cortex in Alzheimer's disease and experimental cholinergic denervation. *Science, 228,* 1115–1117.

Maslach, C. (1976). Burned out. *Human Behavior, 5,* 16–22.

Maslach, C. (1982). *Burnout—The cost of caring.* Englewood Cliffs, NJ: Prentice-Hall.

Maslach, C., & Jackson, S. E. (1981). The measurement of experienced burnout. *Journal of Occupational Behavior, 2,* 99–113.

Maslow, A. H. (1954). *Motivation and personality.* New York: Harper.

Mason, J. R., & Reidinger, R. F. (1982). Observational learning of aversions in red-winged blackbirds (*Agelaius phoeniceus*). *Auk, 99,* 548–554.

Mason, J. W. (1975). A historical view of the stress field. *Journal of Human Stress, 1,* 22–36.

Massaro, D. W., & Loftus, G. R. (1996). Sensory and perceptual storage: Data and theory. In E. L. Bjork & R. A. Bjork (Eds.), *Handbook of perception and cognition* (Vol. 10: Memory). New York: Academic Press.

Masson, J. (1984). *The assault on truth: Freud's suppression of the seduction theory.* New York: Farrar, Straus, & Giroux.

Masters, W. H., & Johnson, V. E. (1966). *Human sexual response.* Boston: Little, Brown.

Matano, R. A., Yalom, I. D., & Schwartz, Kim. (1997). Interactive group therapy for substance abusers. In J. L. Spira (Ed.), *Group therapy for medically ill patients.* New York: Guilford Press.

Matsumoto, D. (1987). The role of facial response in the experience of emotion: More methodological problems and a meta-analysis. *Journal of Personality and Social Psychology, 52,* 769–774.

Matsumoto, D. (1994). *People: Psychology from a cultural perspective.* Pacific Grove, CA: Brooks/Cole.

Mattay, V. S., Berman, K. F., Ostrem, J. L., Esposito, G., Van-Horn, J. D., Bigelow, L. B., & Weinberger, D. R. (1996). Dextroamphetamine enhances "neural network-specific" physiological signals: A positron-emission tomography rCBF study. *Journal of Neuroscience, 16,* 4816–4822.

Matthews, G. (1997). Intelligence, personality and information-processing: An adaptive perspective. In J. Kingma & W. Tomic, (Eds.), Advances in cognition and educational practice: Reflections on the concept of intelligence, Vol. 4. Greenwich, CT: Jai Press.

Matthews, K. A. (1992). Myths and realities of the menopause. *Psychosomatic Medicine, 54,* 1–9.

Matzel, L. D., Held, F. P., & Miller, R. R. (1988). Information and expression of simultaneous and backward associations: Implications for contiguity theory. *Learning and Motivation, 9,* 317–344.

Mauss, M. (1902/1972). *A general theory of magic* (R. Brain, Trans.). New York: Norton.

Mayer, D. J. (1953). Glucostatic mechanism of regulation of food intake. *New England Journal of Medicine, 249,* 13–16.

Mayer, J. D., & Salovey, P. (1997). What is emotional intelligence? In P. Salovey & D. Sluyter (Eds.), *Emotional development, emotional literacy, and emotional intelligence.* New York: Basic Books.

Mays, V. M., & Albee, G. W. (1992). Psychotherapy and ethnic minorities. In D. K. Freedheim (Ed.), *History of Psychotherapy: A century of change.* Washington, DC: American Psychological Association.

McAllister-Williams, R. H., Ferrier, I. N., & Young, A. (1998). Mood and neuropsychological function in depression: The role of corticosteriods and serotonin. *Psychological Medicine, 28,* 573–584.

McArthur, L. Z., & Berry, D. S. (1987). Cross-cultural agreement in perceptions of babyfaced adults. *Journal of Cross-Cultural Psychology, 18,* 165–192.

McCall, M. (1994). Decision theory and the sale of alcohol. *Journal of Applied Social Psychology, 24,* 1593–1611.

McCall, M. (1997). The effects of physical attractiveness on gaining access to alcohol: When social policy meets social decision making. *Addiction, 92,* 597–600.

McCall, R. B., & Carriger, M. S. (1993). A meta-analysis of infant habituation and recognition memory performance as predictors of later IQ. *Child Development, 64,* 57–79.

McCann, I. L., & Holmes, D. S. (1984). Influence of aerobic exercise on depression. *Journal of Personality and Social Psychology, 46,* 1142–1147.

McClelland, D. C. (1961). *The achieving society.* Princeton, NJ: Von Nostrand.

McClelland, D. C., Atkinson, J. W., Clark, R. A., & Lowell, E. W. (1953). *The achievement motive.* New York: Appleton-Century-Crofts.

McClelland, J. L., & Elman, J. L. (1986). The TRACE model of speech perception. *Cognitive Psychology, 18,* 1–86.

McCloskey, M., & Cohen, N. J. (1989). Catastrophic interference in connectionist networks: The sequential learning problem. In G. H. Bower (Ed.), *The psychology of learning and motivation.* New York: Academic Press.

McCrae, R. R., & Costa, P. T., Jr. (1985). Updating Norman's "adequate taxonomy": Intelligence and personality dimensions in natural language and in questionnaires. *Journal of Personality and Social Psychology, 49,* 710–721.

McCrae, R. R., & Costa, P. T., Jr. (1990). *Personality in adulthood.* New York: Guilford.

McCrae, R. R., & Costa, P. T., Jr. (1997). Personality trait structure as a human universal. *American Psychologist, 52,* 509–516.

McCrae, R. R., Costa, P. T., Jr., & Yik, M. S. M. (1996). Universal aspects of Chinese personality structure. In M. H. Bond (Ed.), *The handbook of Chinese psychology.* Hong Kong: Oxford University Press.

McDaniel, E., & Andersen, P. A. (1998). International patterns of interpersonal tactile communication: A field study. *Journal of Nonverbal Behavior, 22,* 59–75.

McDermott, K. B., & Roediger, H. L., III. (1994). Effects of imagery on perceptual implicit memory tests. *Journal of Experimental Psychology: Learning, Memory, & Cognition, 20,* 1379–1390.

McDermott, K. B., & Roediger, H. L., III (1998). Attempting to avoid illusory memories: Robust false recognition of associates persists under conditions of explicit warnings and immediate testing. *Journal of Memory and Language, 39,* 508–520.

McDonald, M. P., & Crawley, J.N. (1997). Galanin-acetylcholine interactions in rodent memory tasks and Alzheimer's disease. *Journal of Psychiatry and Neuroscience, 22,* 303–317.

McDougall, W. (1908). *An introduction to social psychology.* London: Methuen.

McFall, R. M. (1976). Behavioral training: A skill-acquisition approach to clinical problems. In J. T. Spence, R. C. Carson, & J. W. Thibaut (Eds.), *Behavioral approaches to therapy.* Morristown, NJ: General Learning Press.

McGhee, P. E., & Frueh, T. (1980). Television viewing and the learning of sex-role stereotypes. *Sex Roles, 6,* 179–188.

McGuire, P. K., Shah, G. M. S., & Murray, R. M. (1993). Increased blood flow in Broca's area during auditory hallucinations. *Lancet, 342,* 703–706.

McGuire, W. J. (1985). Attitudes and attitude change. In G. Lindzey & E. Aronson (Eds.), *Handbook of social psychology* (Vol. 2). New York: Random House.

McIntosh, D. N., Zajonc, R. B., Vig, P. S., & Emerick, S. W. (1997). Facial movement, breathing, temperature, and affect: Implications of the vascular theory of emotional efference. *Cognition & Emotion, 11,* 171–195.

McIntosh, A. R., Grady, C. L., Ungerleider, L. G., & Haxby, J. V. (1994). Network analysis of cortical visual pathways mapped with PET. *Journal of Neuroscience, 14,* 655–666.

McKenna, S. P., & Glendon, A. I. (1985). Occupational first aid training: Decay in cardiopulmonary resuscitation (CPR) skills. *Journal of Occupational Psychology, 58,* 109–117.

McKinlay, S. M., Brambilla, D. J., & Posner, J. G. (1992). The normal menopause transition. *Maturitas, 14,* 103–115.

McKnight, J. D., & Glass, D. C. Perceptions of control, burnout, and depressive symptomatology: A replication and extension. *Journal of Consulting & Clinical Psychology, 63,* 490–494

McLeod, J. D., Kessler, R. C., & Landis, K. R. (1992). Speed of recovery from major depressive episodes in a community sample of married men and women. *Journal of Abnormal Psychology, 101,* 277–286.

McNeil, B. J., Pauker, S. G., Cox, H. C., Jr., & Tversky, A. (1982). On the elicitation of preferences for alternative therapies. *New England Journal of Medicine, 306,* 1259–1262.

Medin, D. L. (1989). Concepts and conceptual structure. *American Psychologist, 44,* 1469–1481.

Medin, D. L., Goldstone, R. L., & Gentner, D. (1993). Respects for similarity. *Psychological Review, 100,* 254–278.

Medin, D. L., & Ross, B. H. (1992). *Cognitive psychology.* Fort Worth: Harcourt Brace Jovanovich.

Medin, D. L., & Shaffer, M. M. (1978). A context theory of classification learning. *Psychological Review, 85,* 207–238.

Mednick, S. A. (1962). The associative basis of the creative process. *Psychological Review, 69,* 220–232.

Meeus, W. H. J., & Raaijmakers, Q. A. W. (1987). Administrative obedience as a social phenomenon. In W. Doise & S. Moscovici (Eds.), *Current issues in European social psychology* (Vol. 2). Cambridge, England: Cambridge University Press.

Meisel, A., & Roth, L. H. (1983). Toward an informed discussion of informed consent: A review and critique of the empirical studies. *Arizona Law Review, 25,* 265–346.

Melamed, B. G., & Siegel, L. J. (1975). Reduction of anxiety in children facing hospitalization and surgery by use of filmed modeling. *Journal of Consulting and Clinical Psychology, 43,* 511–521.

Melzack, R. (1973). *The puzzle of pain.* New York: Basic Books.

Melzack, R., & Wall, P. D. (1965). Pain mechanisms: A new theory. *Science, 150,* 971–979.

Melzack, R., & Wall, P. D. (1982). *The challenge of pain.* Harmondsworth: Penguin.

Merikle, P. M. (1988). Subliminal auditory messages: An evaluation. *Psychology & Marketing, 5,* 355–372.

Merikle, P. M., & Skanes, H. E. (1992). Subliminal self-help audiotapes: A search for placebo effects. *Journal of Applied Psychology, 77,* 772–776.

Merton, R. (1948). The self-fulfilling prophecy. *Antioch Review, 8,* 193–210.

Mesulam, M. M. (1987). Neglect (selective inattention). In G. Adelman (Ed.), *Encyclopedia of neuroscience* (Vol. 2). Boston: Birkhauser.

Milgram, S. (1963). Behavioral study of obedience. *Journal of Abnormal and Social Psychology, 67,* 371–378.

Milgram, S. (1974). *Obedience to authority.* New York: Harper & Row.

Miller, D. B. (1977). Roles of naturalistic observation in comparative psychology. *American Psychologist, 32,* 211–219.

Miller, G. A. (1956). The magical number seven plus or minus two: Some limits on our capacity for processing information. *Psychological Review, 63,* 81–97.

Miller, G. A., Galanter, E., & Pribram, K. H. (1960). *Plans and the structure of behavior.* New York: Holt.

Miller, J. G. (1994). Cultural diversity in the morality of caring: Individually oriented versus duty-based interpersonal moral codes. *Cross-cultural Research: The Journal of Comparative Social Science, 28,* 3–39.

Miller, L. L., & Branconnier, R. J. (1983). Cannabis: Effects on memory and the cholinergic limbic system. *Psychological Bulletin, 93,* 441–456.

Miller, M. A., Rahe, R. H. (1997). Life changes scaling for the 1990s. *Journal of Psychosomatic Research, 43,* 279–292.

Miller, N. E. (1985). The value of behavioral research on animals. *American Psychologist, 40,* 423–440.

Miller, N. E. (1991). Commentary on Ulrich: Need to check truthfulness of statements by opponents of animal research. *Psychological Science, 2,* 422–424.

Miller, S. D. (1989). Optical differences in cases of multiple personality disorder. *Journal of Nervous and Mental Disease, 177,* 480–486.

Miller, T. W. (1993). The assessment of stressful life events. In L. Goldberger & S. Breznitz (Eds.), *Handbook of stress: Theoretical and clinical aspects* (2nd ed.). New York: Free Press.

Miller, W. R., Taylor, C. A., & West, J. C. (1980). Focused versus broad-spectrum behavior therapy for problem drinkers. *Journal of Consulting and Clinical Psychology, 48,* 590–601.

Millsaps, C. L., Azrin, R. L., & Mittenberg, W. (1994). Neuropsychological effects of chronic cannabis use on the memory and intelligence of adolescents. *Journal of Child and Adolescent Substance Abuse, 3,* 47–55.

Milner, A. D., & Rugg, M. D. (Eds.). (1992). *The neuropsychology of consciousness.* London: Academic Press.

Milner, B. (1966). Amnesia following operation on the temporal lobes. In C. W. M. Whitty & O. L. Zangwill (Eds.), *Amnesia.* London: Butterworths.

Mineka, S. (1987). A primate model of phobic fears. In H. Eysenck & I. Martin (Eds.), *Theoretical foundations of behavior therapy.* New York: Plenum.

Mirmiran, M., van Soneren, E. J. W., & Swaab, D. F. (1996). Is brain plasticity preserved during aging and in Alzheimer's disease? *Behavioral Brain Research, 78,* 43–48.

Mischel, W. (1968). *Personality and assessment.* New York: Wiley.

Mischel, W., & Peake, P. K. (1982). Beyond déja vu in the search for cross-situational consistency. *Psychological Review, 89,* 730–755.

Mischel, W., & Shoda, Y. (1995). A cognitive-affective system theory of personality: Reconceptualizing situations, dispositions, dynamics, and invariance in personality structure. *Psychological Review, 102,* 246–268.

Mischel, W., & Shoda, Y. (1998). Reconciling processing dynamics and personality dispositions. *Annual Review of Psychology, 49,* 229–258.

Moldin, S. Q., & Gottesman, I. I. (1997). Genes, experience, and chance in schizophrenia—Positioning for the 21st century. *Schizophrenia Bulletin, 23,* 547–561.

Moncrieff, J. (1997). Lithium: Evidence reconsidered. *British Journal of Psychiatry, 171,* 113–119.

Mook, D. G. (1995). *Motivation: The organization of action* (2nd ed.). New York: Norton.

Moray, N. (1959). Attention in dichotic listening: Affective cues and the influence of instructions. *Quarterly Journal of Experimental Psychology, 11,* 56–60.

Morelli, G. A., Rogoff, B., Oppenheim, D., & Goldsmith, D. (1992). Cultural variations in infants' sleeping arrangements: Questions of independence. *Developmental Psychology, 28,* 604–613.

Moret, V., Forster, A., Laverriere, M. C., & Lambert, H. (1991). Mechanism of analgesia induced by hypnosis and acupuncture: Is there a difference? *Pain, 45,* 135–140.

Moscovici, S., & Zavalloni, M. (1969). The group as a polarizer of attitudes. *Journal of Personality and Social Psychology, 12,* 125–135.

Moskowitz, H. (1985). Marihuana and driving. *Accident Analysis and Prevention, 17,* 323–345.

Mozel, M. M., Smith, B., Smith, P., Sullivan, R., & Swender, P. (1969). Nasal chemoreception in flavor identification. *Archives of Otolaryngology, 90,* 367–373.

Muchinsky, P. M. (1993). *Psychology applied to work.* Pacific Grove, CA: Brooks/Cole.

Mueller, C. M., & Dweck, C. S. (1998). Praise for intelligence can undermine children's motivation and performance. *Journal of Personality & Social Psychology, 75,* 33–52.

Mullen, M. (1994). Earliest recollection of childhood: A demographic analysis. *Cognition, 52,* 55–79.

Munakata, Y., McClelland, J.L., Johnson, M.H., & Siegler, R.S. (1997). Rethinking infant knowledge: Toward an adaptive process account of successes and failures in object permanence tasks. *Psychological Review, 104,* 686–713.

Murdock, B. B., Jr. (1960). The distinctiveness of stimuli. *Psychological Review, 67,* 16–31.

Murnen, S. K., & Stockton, M. (1997). Gender and self-reported sexual arousal in response to sexual stimuli: A meta-analytic review. *Sex Roles, 37,* 135–153

Murphy, G. L., & Lassaline, M. E. (1997). Hierarchical structure in concepts and the basic level of categorization. In K. Lamberts, D. R. Shanks, & David R. (Eds.), *Knowledge, concepts and categories: Studies in cognition.* Cambridge, MA: The MIT Press.

Murray, H. A. (1938). *Explorations in personality.* New York: Oxford University Press.

Muter, P. (1980). Very rapid forgetting. *Memory & Cognition, 8,* 174–179.

Myers, D. G. (1982). Polarizing effects of social interaction. In H. Brandstatter, J. H. Davis, & G. Stocker-Kreichgauer (Eds.), *Group decision making.* New York: Academic Press.

Myers, D. G., & Diener, E. (1995). Who is happy? *Psychological Science, 6,* 10–19.

Myers, D. G., & Ridl, J. (1979, August). Can we all be better than average? *Psychology Today,* pp. 89–98.

Myers, T. C., Wittrock, D. A., & Foreman, G. W. (1998) Appraisal of subjective stress in individuals with tension-type headache: The influence of baseline measures. *Journal of Behavioral Medicine. 21,* 469–484.

Nadon, R., Hoyt, I. P., Register, P. A., & Kihlstrom, J. F. (1991). Absorption and hypnotizability: Context effects reexamined. *Journal of Personality and Social Psychology, 60,* 144–153.

Nagar, D., & Panady, J. (1987). Affect and performance on cognitive tasks as a function of crowding and noise. *Journal of Applied Social Psychology, 17,* 147–157.

Nairne, J. S. (1990). A feature model of immediate memory. *Memory & Cognition, 18,* 251–269.

Nairne, J. S. (1996). Short-term/working memory. In E. L. Bjork & R. A. Bjork (Eds.), *Handbook of perception and cognition* (Vol.10: Memory). New York: Academic Press.

Nairne, J. S., & Rescorla, R. A. (1981). Second-order conditioning with diffuse auditory reinforcers in the pigeon. *Learning and Motivation, 12,* 65–91.

Naveh-Benjamin, M., & Ayres, T. J. (1986). Digit span, reading rate, and linguistic relativity. *Quarterly Journal of Experimental Psychology, 38A,* 739–751.

Neath, I. (1993). Distinctiveness and serial position effects in recognition. *Memory & Cognition, 21,* 689–698.

Neath, I. (1998). *Human memory: An introduction to research, data, and theory.* Pacific Grove, CA: Brooks/Cole.

Neisser, U. (1967). *Cognitive psychology.* New York: Appleton-Century-Crofts.

Neisser, U. (1978). Memory: What are the important questions? In M. M. Gruneberg, P. E. Morris, & R. N. Sykes (Eds.), *Practical aspects of memory.* London: Academic Press.

Neisser, U., & Harsch, N. (1992). Phantom flashbulbs: False recollections of hearing the news about Challenger. In E. Winograd & U. Neisser (Eds.), *Affect and accuracy in recall: Studies of "flashbulb memories."* Cambridge: Cambridge University Press.

Nelson, K. (1973). Structure and strategy in learning to talk. *Monographs of the Society for Research in Child Development, 38*(Serial No. 149).

Newcomb, A. F., & Bagwell, C. L. (1995). Children's friendship relations: A meta-analytic review. *Psychological Bulletin, 117,* 306–347.

Newell, A., & Simon, H. A. (1972). *Human problem solving.* Englewood Cliffs, NJ: Prentice-Hall.

Newsome, W. T., Shadlen, M. N., Zohary, E., Britten, K. H., & Movshon, J. A. (1995). Visual motion: Linking neuronal activity to psychophysical performance. In M. S. Gazzaniga (Ed.), *The cognitive neurosciences.* Cambridge, MA: MIT Press.

Nichols, D. S., & Greene, R. L. Dimensions of deception in personality assessment: The example of the MMPI-2. *Journal of Personality Assessment, 68,* 251–266.

Nickerson, R. S., & Adams, M. J. (1979). Long-term memory for a common object. *Cognitive Psychology, 11,* 287–307.

Nicolaus, L. K., & Nellis, D. W. (1987). The first evaluation of the use of conditioned taste aversion to control predation by mongooses upon eggs. *Applied Animal Behaviour Science, 17,* 329–346.

Nobel, K. D., Robinson, N. M., & Gunderson, S. A. (1993). All rivers lead to the sea: A follow-up study of gifted young adults. *Roeper Review, 15,* 124–130.

Norman, D. A. (1988). *The psychology of everyday things.* New York: Basic Books.

Nosofsky, R. M. (1986). Attention, similarity, and the identification-categorization relationship. *Journal of Experimental Psychology: General, 115,* 39–57.

Novick, L. R. (1988). Analogical transfer, problem similarity, and expertise. *Journal of Experimental Psychology: Learning, Memory, & Cognition, 14,* 510–520.

Nowakowski, R. S. (1987). Basic concepts of CNS development. *Child Development, 58,* 568–595.

Oakes, J. (1985). *Keeping track: How schools structure inequality.* New Haven, CT: Yale University Press.

Oakes, P. J., & Turner, J. C. (1990). Is limited information processing capacity the cause of social stereotyping? *European Review of Social Psychology, 1,* 112–135.

O'Donnell, P., & Grace, A. (1998). Dysfunctions in multiple interrelated systems as the neurobiological bases of schizophrenic symptom clusters. *Schizophrenia Bulletin, 24,* 267–283.

Offer, D., & Schonert-Reichl, K. A. (1992). Debunking the myths of adolescence. *Journal of the American Academy of Child and Adolescent Psychiatry, 31*, 1003–1013.

Ogden, J. A., & Corkin, S. (1991). Memories of HM. In W. C. Abraham, M. C. Corballis, & K. G. White (Eds.), *Memory mechanisms: A tribute to G. V. Goddard.* Hillsdale, NJ: Erlbaum.

Ogloff, J. R. P., Roberts, C. F., & Roesch, R. (1993). The insanity defense: Legal standards and clinical assessment. *Applied & Preventive Psychology, 2*, 163–178.

Okada, F., Okajima, K., & Tokumitsu, Y. (1998). Contradirect effects on neuronal activity in treating depression. *Human Psychopharmacology, 13*, 455–456.

Oldani, R. (1997). Causes of increases in acheivement motivation: Is the personality affected by prenatal environment? *Personality & Individual Differences, 22*, 403–410.

Olds, J. (1958). Satiation effects in self-stimulation of the brain. *Journal of Comparative and Physiological Psychology, 51*, 675–678.

Olson, J. M., & Zanna, M. P. (1993). Attitudes and attitude change. *Annual Review of Psychology, 44*, 117–154.

O'Mahony, M. (1978). Smell illusions and suggestion: Reports of smells contingent on tones played on television and radio. *Chemical Senses and Flavor, 3*, 183–187.

Orne, M. T. (1959). The nature of hypnosis: Artifact and essence. *Journal of Abnormal and Social Psychology, 58*, 277–299.

Orne, M. T. (1969). Demand characteristics and the concept of quasi-controls. In R. Rosenthal & R. L. Rosnow (Eds.), *Artifact in behavioral research.* New York: Academic Press.

Ortmann, A., & Hertwig, R. (1997). Is deception acceptable? *American Psychologist, 52*, 746–747.

Ortony, A., & Turner, T. J. (1990). What's basic about basic emotions? *Psychological Review, 97*, 315–331.

Oscar-Berman, M., Shagrin, B., Evert, D. L., & Epstein, C. (1997). Impairments of brain and behavior: The neurological effects of alcohol. *Alcohol Health & Reseach World, 21*, 65–75.

Otto, M. W., Demopulos, C. M., McLean, N. E., Pollack, M. H., & Fava, M. (1998). Additional findings on the association between anxiety sensitivity and hypochondriacal concerns: Examination of patients with major depression. *Journal of Anxiety Disorders, 12*, 225–232.

Pahl, J. J., Swayze, V. W., & Andreasen, N. C. (1990). Diagnostic advances in anatomical and functional brain imaging in schizophrenia. In A. Kales, C. N. Stefanis, & J. A. Talbott (Eds.), *Recent advances in schizophrenia.* New York: Springer-Verlag.

Paivio, A. (1971). *Imagery and verbal processes.* New York: Holt, Rinehart & Winston.

Palmore, E. B. (1990). *Ageism: Negative and positive.* New York: Springer.

Parkes, J. D., & Block, C. (1989). Genetic factors in sleep disorders. *Journal of Neurology, Neurosurgery, and Psychiatry, 52*, 101–108.

Parkin, A. J. (1993). *Memory: Phenomena, experiment, and theory.* Oxford, England: Blackwell.

Parmelee, A. H., & Sigman, M. D. (1983). Perinatal brain development and behavior. In M. M. Haith & J. J. Campos (Eds.), *Handbook of child psychology: Vol. 2. Infancy and developmental psychobiology.* New York: Wiley.

Parsons, J. E., Kaczala, C., & Meece, J. L. (1982). Socialization of achievement attitudes and beliefs: Classroom influences. *Child Development, 53*, 322–339.

Pasewark, R. A., & Seidenzahl, D. (1979). Opinions concerning the insanity plea and criminality among mental patients. *Bulletin of the American Academy of Psychiatry and Law, 7*, 199–202.

Pashler, H. (1992). Attentional limitations in doing two tasks at the same time. *Current Directions in Psychological Science, 1*, 44–48.

Pashler, H. (1998). *The psychology of attention.* Cambridge, MA: MIT Press.

Paul, G. L., & Lentz, R. J. (1977). *Psychosocial treatment of chronic mental patients: Milieu versus social learning programs.* Cambridge, MA: Harvard University Press.

Paulus, P. B. (1988). *Prison crowding: A psychological perspective.* New York: Springer.

Payne, J. W. (1994). Thinking aloud: Insights into information processing. *Psychological Science, 5*, 241–248.

Pedersen, D. M., & Wheeler, J. (1983). The MŸller-Lyer illusion among Navajos. *Journal of Social Psychology, 121*, 3–6.

Pedersen, J. B. (1998). Sexuality and aging. In I. H. Nordhus & G. R. VandenBos (Eds.), *Clinical geropsychology.* Washington, DC: American Psychological Association.

Penfield, W., & Perot, P. (1963). The brain's record of auditory and visual experience. *Brain, 86*, 595–696.

Pennebaker, J. W. (1990). *Opening up: The healing power of confiding in others.* New York: Morrow.

Pennebaker, J. W. (1997). Writing about emotional experiences as a therapeutic process. *Psychological Science, 8*, 162–166.

Penney, C. G. (1989). Modality effects and the structure of short-term verbal memory. *Memory & Cognition, 17*, 398–422.

Perls, F. S. (1969). *Gestalt therapy verbatim.* Moab, UT: Real People Press.

Perls, F. S., Hefferline, R. F., & Goodman, P. (1951). *Gestalt therapy.* New York: Julian.

Perner, J., Leekam, S., & Wimmer, H. (1987). Three-year-olds' difficulty understanding false belief: Cognitive limitation, lack of knowledge or pragmatic misunderstanding. *British Journal of Developmental Psychology, 5*, 125–137.

Perrett, D. I., & Mistlin, A. M. (1987). Visual neurones responsive to faces. *Trends in Neuroscience, 10*, 358–364.

Perry, W. (1970). *Forms of intellectual and ethical development in the college years.* New York: Holt, Rinehart & Winston.

Pert, C. B., & Snyder, S. H. (1973). The opiate receptor: Demonstration in nervous tissue. *Science, 179*, 1011–1014.

Peterson, A. C. (1988). Adolescent development. *Annual Review of Psychology, 39*, 583–607.

Peterson, C., & Seligman, M. E. P. (1987). Explanatory style and illness. *Journal of Personality, 55*, 237–265.

Peterson, C., Seligman, M. E. P., & Vaillant, G. E. (1988). Pessimistic explanatory style is a risk factor for physical illness: A thirty-five-year longitudinal study. *Journal of Personality and Social Psychology, 55*, 23–27.

Peterson, D. R. (1968). *The clinical study of social behavior.* New York: Appleton-Century-Crofts.

Peterson, L. R., & Peterson, M. J. (1959). Short-term retention of individual items. *Journal of Experimental Psychology, 58*, 193–198.

Petty, R. E., & Cacioppo, J. T. (1986). *Communication and persuasion: Central and peripheral routes to attitude change.* New York: Springer-Verlag.

Petty, R. E., & Wegener, D. T. (1997). Attitude change: Multiple roles for persuasion variables. In D. Gilbert, S. Fiske, & G. Lindzey (Eds.), *Handbook of social psychology* (4th ed.). New York: McGraw-Hill.

Petty, R. E., Wegener, D. T., & Fabrigar, L. R. (1997). Attitudes and attitude change. *Annual Review of Psychology, 48*, 609–647.

Pfaff, D. W., & Sakuma, Y. (1979). Deficit in the lordosis reflex of female rats caused by lesions in the ventromedial nucleus of the hypothalamus. *Journal of Physiology, 288*, 203–210.

Phelps, E. A., & Anderson, A. K. (1997). Emotional memory: What does the amygdala do? *Current Biology, 7*, 311–113.

Phillips, K., & Matheny, A. P., Jr. (1997). Evidence for genetic influence on both cross-situation and situation-specific components of behavior. *Journal of Personality and Social Psychology, 73*, 129–138.

Piaget, J. (1929). *The child's conception of the world.* New York: Harcourt Brace.

Piaget, J. (1952). *The origins of intelligence in children.* New York: International Universities Press.

Piaget, J. (1970). Piaget's theory. In P. H. Mussen (Ed.), *Carmichael's manual of child psychology* (Vol. 1). New York: Wiley.

Pickles, J. O. (1988). *An introduction to the physiology of hearing* (2nd ed.). London: Academic Press.

Pierce, T. W., Madden, D. J., Siegel, W. C., & Blumenthal, J. A. (1993). Effects of aerobic exercise on cognitive and psychosocial functioning in patients with mild hypertension. *Health Psychology, 12*, 286–291.

Pinel, J. P. J., & Treit, D. (1979). Conditioned defensive burying in rats: Availability of burying materials. *Animal Learning & Behavior, 7*, 392–396.

Pines, A. (1993). Burnout. In L. Goldberger & S. Breznitz (Eds.), *Handbook of stress: Theoretical and clinical aspects* (2nd ed.). New York: Free Press.

Pines, A., & Aronson, E. (1988). *Career burnout: Causes and cures* (2nd ed.). New York: Free Press.

Pinker, S. (1994). *The language instinct.* New York: HarperCollins.

Pinker, S. (1997). *How the mind works.* New York: Norton.

Piasecki, T. M., Fiore, M. C., & Baker, T. B. Profiles in discouragement: Two studies of variability in the time course of smoking withdrawal symptoms. *Journal of Abnormal Psychology, 107*, 238–251.

Pittenger, D. J. (1996). Reconsidering the overjustification effect: A guide to critical resources. *Teaching of Psychology, 23*, 234–236.

Plomin, R., Fulker, D. W., Corley, R., & DeFries, J. C. (1997). Nature, nurture, and cognitive development from 1 to 16 years: A parent-offspring adoption study. *Psychological Science, 8*, 442–447.

Plomin, R., Corley, R., Caspi, A., Fulker, D. W., & DeFries, J. (1998). Adoption results for self-reported personality: Evidence for nonadditive genetic effects? *Journal of Personality & Social Psychology, 75*, 211–218.

Plous, S. (1991). An attitude survey of animal rights activists. *Psychological Science, 2*, 194–196.

Porter, R. H., Makin, J. W., Davis, L. B., & Christensen, K. M. (1992). Breast-fed infants respond to olfactory clues from their own mother and unfamiliar lactating females. *Infant Behavior and Devlopment, 15*, 85–93.

Posner, M. I. (1993). Interaction of arousal and selection in the posterior attention network. In A. Baddeley & L. Weiskrantz (Eds.), *Attention: Selection, awareness, and control. A tribute to Donald Broadbent.* Oxford, England: Clarendon Press.

Posner, M. I., & Rothbart, M. K. (1992). Attentional mechanisms and conscious experience. In A. D. Milner & M. D. Rugg (Eds.), *The neuropsychology of consciousness.* London: Academic Press.

Postmes, T., & Spears, R. (1998). Deindividuation and antinormative behavior: A meta-analysis. *Psychological Bulletin, 123*, 238–259.

Potter, W. Z., & Manji, H. K. (1993). Are monamine metabolites in cerebral spinal fluid worth measuring? *Archives of General Psychiatry, 50*, 653–656.

Pratkanis, A. R., & Greenwald, A. G. (1989). A sociocognitive model of attitude structure and function. *Advances in Experimental Social Psychology, 22*, 245–285.

Pratt, G. J., Wood, D., & Alman, B. M. (1988). *A clinical hypnosis primer.* New York: Wiley.

Preilowski, B. (1975). Bilateral motor interaction: Perceptual-motor performance of partial and complete split-brain patients. In K. J. ZŸlch, O. Creutzfeldt, & G. C. Galbraith (Eds.), *Cerebral localization.* New York: Springer-Verlag.

Premack, D. (1962). Reversibility of the reinforcement relation. *Science, 136*, 255–257.

Premack, D. (1976). *Intelligence in ape and man.* Hillsdale, NJ: Erlbaum.

Proctor, F., Wagner, N., & Butler, J. (1974). The differentiation of male and female orgasm: An experimental study. In N. Wagner (Ed.), *Perspectives on human sexuality.* New York: Behavioral Publications.

Proctor, R. W., & Van Zandt, T. (1994). *Human factors in simple and complex designs.* Boston: Allyn & Bacon.

Provence, S. A., & Lipton, R. C. (1962). *Infants in institutions.* New York: International Universities Press.

Prud'homme, M. J. L., Cohen, D., & Kalaska, J. F. (1994). Tactile activity in primate somatosensory cortex during active arm movements: Cytoarchitectonic distribution. *Journal of Neurophysiology, 71*, 173–181.

Prudic, J., Sackeim, H. A., & Devanand, D. P. (1990). Medication resistance and clinical response to electroconvulsive therapy. *Psychiatry Research, 31*, 287–296.

Putnam, F. W., Guroff, J. J., Silberman, E. K., Barban, L., & Post, R. M. (1986). The clinical phenomenology of multiple personality disorder: Review of 100 recent cases. *Journal of Clinical Psychiatry, 47*, 285–293.

Quadagno, D. M. (1987). Pheromones and human sexuality. *Medical Aspects of Human Sexuality, 21*, 149–154.

Quirion, R. (1993). Cholinergic markers in Alzheimer's disease and the autoregulation of acetylcholine release. *Journal of Psychiatry and Neuroscience, 18*, 226–234.

Rachman, S. J. (1990). *Fear and courage.* New York: Freeman.

Ragland, D. R., & Brand, R. J. (1988). Type A behavior and mortality from coronary heart disease. *The New England Journal of Medicine, 318*, 65–69.

Raichle, M. E. (1994, April). Visualizing the mind. *Scientific American, 270*, 58–64.

Rakic, P. (1991). Plasticity of cortical development. In S. E. Brauth, W. S. Hall, & R. J. Dooling (Eds.), *Plasticity of development.* Cambridge, MA: Bradford/MIT Press.

Ralph, M. R., Foster, R. G., Davis, F. C., & Menaker, M. (1990). Transplanted suprachiasmatic nucleus determines circadian period. *Science, 247*, 975–978.

Ramachandran, V. S. (1992). Filling in gaps in perception: I. *Current Directions in Psychological Science, 1*, 199–205.

Ratcliff, R. (1990). Connectionist models of recognition memory: Constraints imposed by learning and forgetting functions. *Psychological Review, 97*, 285–308.

Ratnasuriya, R. H., Eisler, I., Szmuhter, G. I., & Russell, G. F. (1991). Anorexia nervosa: Outcome and prognostic factors after 20 years. *British Journal of Psychiatry, 158*, 495–502.

Raugh, M. R., & Atkinson, R. C. (1975). A mnemonic method for learning a second-language vocabulary. *Journal of Educational Psychology, 67*, 1–16.

Raven, J. C., Court, J. H., & Raven, J.(1985). *A manual for Raven's progressive matrices and vocabulary scales.* London: H. K. Lewis.

Rechtschaffen, A., & Bergmann, B. M. (1995). Sleep deprivation in the rat by the disk-over-water method. *Behavioural Brain Research, 69,* 55–63.

Ree, M. J., & Earles, J. A. (1992). Intelligence is the best predictor of job performance. *Current Directions in Psychological Science, 1,* 86–89.

Reed, T. E., & Jensen, A. R. (1992). Conduction velocity in a brain nerve pathway correlates with intelligence. *Intelligence, 16,* 259–272.

Reeve, J. (1992). *Understanding motivation and emotion.* Fort Worth, TX: Harcourt Brace Jovanovich.

Reisenzein, R. (1983). The Schachter theory of emotion: Two decades later. *Psychological Bulletin, 94,* 239–264.

Rescorla, R. A. (1968). Probability of shock in the presence and absence of CS in fear conditioning. *Journal of Comparative and Physiological Psychology, 66,* 1–5.

Rescorla, R. A. (1980). Simultaneous and successive associations in sensory preconditioning. *Journal of Experimental Psychology: Animal Behavior Processes, 6,* 207–216.

Rescorla, R. A. (1988). Pavlovian conditioning: It's not what you think it is. *American Psychologist, 43,* 151–160.

Rescorla, R. A. (1992). Hierarchical associative relations in Pavolvian conditioning and instrumental training. *Current Directions in Psychological Science, 1,* 66–70.

Resnick, S. M., Berenbaum, S. A., Gottesman, I. I., & Bouchard, T. J. (1986). Early hormonal influences on cognitive functioning in congenital adrenal hyperplasia. *Developmental Psychology, 22,* 191–198.

Revelle, W. (1995). Personality processes. *Annual Review of Psychology, 46,* 295–328.

Revusky, S. H., & Garcia, J. (1970). Learned associations over long delays. In G. H. Bower & J. T. Spence (Eds.), *The psychology of learning and motivation* (Vol. 4). New York: Academic Press.

Rhodes, G., & Tremewan, T. (1996). Averageness, exaggeration, and facial attractiveness. *Psychological Science, 7,* 105–110.

Ribaupierre, F. de. (1997). Acoustical information processing in the auditory thalamus and cerebral cortex. In G. Ehret & R. Romand (Eds.), *The central auditory system.* New York: Oxford University Press.

Richards, F. A., & Commons, M. L. (1990). Postformal cognitive-developmental theory and research: A review of its current status. In C. N. Alexander & E. J. Langer (Eds.), *Higher stages of human development: Perspectives on adult growth.* New York: Oxford University Press.

Richman, A. L., Miller, P. M., & LeVine, R. A. (1992). Cultural and educational variations in maternal responsiveness. *Developmental Psychology, 28,* 614–621.

Rickels, K., Schweizer, E., Case, W. G., & Greenblatt, D. J. (1990). Long-term therapeutic use of benzodiazepines. I. Effects of abrupt discontinuation. *Archives of General Psychiatry, 47,* 899–907.

Riegel, K. F. (1976). The dialectics of human development. *American Psychologist, 31,* 689–700.

Riggs, D. A., & Foa, E. B. (1993). Obsessive-compulsive disorder. In D. H. Barlow (Ed.), *Clinical handbook of psychological disorders* (2nd ed.). New York: Guilford.

Rijsdijk, F. V., Vernon, P. A., & Boomsma, D. I. (1998). The genetic basis of the relation between speed-of-information processing and IQ. *Behavioural Brain Research, 95,* 77–84.

Riley, E. P., Mattson, S. N., Sowell, E. R., Jernigon, T. L. (1995). Abnormalities of the corpus callosum in children prenatally exposed to alcohol. *Alcoholism: Clinical & Experimental Research, 19,* 1198–1202.

Rips, L. J. (1989). Similarity, typicality, and categorization. In S. Vosniadou & A. Ortony (Eds.), *Similarity and analogical reasoning.* Cambridge: Cambridge University Press.

Rivett, M. (1998). The family therapy journals in 1997: A thematic review. *Journal of Family Therapy, 20,* 423–430.

Robbins, T. W. (1997). Arousal systems and attentional processes. *Biological Psychology, 45,* 57–71.

Roberts, C. J., & Lowe, C. R. (1975). Where have all the conceptions gone? *Lancet, 1,* 498–499.

Robey, R. R., & Dalebout, S. D. (1998). A tutorial on conducting meta-analyses of clinical outcome research. *Journal of Speech Language & Hearing Research, 41,* 1227–1241.

Robinson, J. O., Rosen, M., Revill, S. I., David, H., & Rus, G. A. D. (1980). Self-administered intravenous and intramuscular pethidine. *Anaesthesia, 35,* 763–770.

Robinson, L. A., Berman, J. S., & Neimeyer, R. A. (1990). Psychotherapy for the treatment of depression: A comprehensive review of controlled outcome research. *Psychological Bulletin, 100,* 30–49.

Rodin, J. (1981). Current status of the internal-external hypothesis for obesity: What went wrong? *American Psychologist, 36,* 361–372.

Rodin, J., Schank, D., & Striegal-Moore, R. H. (1989). Psychological features of obesity. *Medical Clinics of North America, 73,* 47–66.

Roediger, H. L., III, & McDermott, K. B. (1993). Implicit memory in normal human subjects. In F. Boller & J. Grafman (Eds.), *Handbook of neuropsychology* (Vol. 8). Amsterdam: Elsevier.

Roediger, H. L., III, & McDermott, K. B. (1995). Creating false memories: Remembering words not presented in lists. *Journal of Experimental Psychology: Learning, Memory, & Cognition, 21,* 803–814.

Roediger, H. L., III, Weldon, M. S., Stadler, M. L., & Riegler, G. L. (1992). Direct comparison of two implicit memory tests: Word fragment and word stem completion. *Journal of Experimental Psychology: Learning, Memory, & Cognition, 18,* 1251–1269.

Roesler, A. & Witztum, E. (1998). Treatment of men with paraphilia with a long-acting analogue of gonadotropin-releasing hormone. *New England Journal of Medicine, 338,* 416–422.

Rogers, C. R. (1951). *Client-centered therapy.* Boston: Houghton Mifflin.

Rogers, C. R. (1961). *On becoming a person: A therapist's view of psychotherapy.* Boston: Houghton Mifflin.

Rogers, C. R. (1963). The actualizing tendency in relation to "motives" and to consciousness. In M. R. Jones (Ed.), *Nebraska symposium on motivation.* Lincoln: University of Nebraska.

Rogers, S. M., & Turner, C. F. (1991). Male-male sexual contact in the U.S.A.: Findings from five sample surveys, 1970–1990. *Journal of Sex Research, 28,* 491–519.

Roggman, L. A., Langlois, J. H., Hubbs-Tait, L., & Rieser-Danner, L. A. (1994). Infant day-care, attachment, and the "file drawer problem." *Child Development, 65,* 1429–1443.

Roitblat, H. L., & von Ferson, L. (1992). Comparitive cognition: Representations and processes in learning and memory. *Annual Review of Psychology, 43,* 671–710.

Rolls, E. T. (1995). Central taste anatomy and neurophysiology. In R. L. Doty (Ed.), *Handbook of olfaction and gustation.* New York: Dekker.

Rosch, E., & Mervis, C. B. (1975). Family resemblances: Studies in the internal structure of categories. *Cognitive Psychology, 7,* 573–605.

Rosch, E., Mervis, C. B., Gray, W. D., Johnson, D. M., & Bayes-Braem, P. (1976). Basic objects in natural categories. *Cognitive Psychology, 8,* 382–439.

Rosen, D. L., & Singh, S. (1992). An investigation of subliminal embed effect on multiple measures of advertising effectiveness. *Psychology & Marketing, 9,* 157–173.

Rosenbaum, M. E. (1986). The repulsion hypothesis: On the non-development of relationships. *Journal of Personality and Social Psychology, 51,* 1156–1166.

Rosenhan, D. L. (1973). On being sane in insane places. *Science, 179,* 250–258.

Rosenthal, R. (1966). *Experimenter effects in behavioral research.* New York: Appleton-Century-Crofts.

Rosenthal, R. (1994). Science and ethics in conducting, analyzing, and reporting psychological research. *Psychological Science, 5,* 127–134.

Rosenthal, R., & Jacobson, L. (1968). *Pygmalion in the classroom: Teachers' expectations and pupils' intellectual development.* New York: Holt, Rinehart & Winston.

Rosenthal R., & Rosnow, R. L. (Eds.). (1969). *Artifact in behavioral research.* New York: Academic Press.

Rosenthal, R., & Rosnow, R. L. (1975). *The volunteer subject.* New York: Wiley.

Rosenthal, R., & Rosnow, R. L. (1991). *Essentials of behavioral research: Methods and data analysis* (2nd ed.). New York: McGraw-Hill.

Rosenzweig, M. R. (1984). Experience, memory, and the brain. *American Psychologist, 39,* 365–376.

Rosenzweig, S. (1936). Some implicit common factors in diverse methods of psychotherapy. *American Journal of Orthopsychiatry, 6,* 422–425.

Rösler, F., Pechmann, T., Streb, J., Röder, B., & Hennighausen, E. (1998). Parsing of sentences in a language with varying word order: Word-by-word variations of processing demands are revealed by event-related potentials. *Journal of Memory and Language, 38,* 150–176.

Rosnow, R. L., & Rosenthal, R. (1996). *Beginning behavioral research: A conceptual primer* (2nd ed.). New York: Macmillan.

Ross, C. A., Miller, S. D., Reagor, P., Bjornson, L., Fraser, G. A., & Anderson, G. (1990). Structured interview data on 102 cases of multiple personality disorder from four centers. *American Journal of Psychiatry, 147,* 596–601.

Ross, L. (1977). The intuitive psychologist and his shortcomings: Distortions in the attribution process. In L. Berkowitz (Ed.), *Advances in experimental social psychology* (Vol. 10). New York: Academic Press.

Ross, L., & Nisbett, R. E. (1991). *The person and the situation: Perspectives of social psychology.* New York: McGraw-Hill.

Rothbart, M.K., & Ahadi, S.A. (1994). Temperament and the development of personality. *Journal of Abnormal Psychology, 103,* 55–66.

Rothlind, J., Posner, M. I., & Schaughency, E. (1991). Lateralized control of eye movements in attention deficit hyperactivity disorder. *Journal of Cognitive Neuroscience, 3,* 377–381.

Rotter, J. B. (1966). Generalized expectancies for internal versus external locus of control of reinforcement. *Psychological Monographs, 80*(Whole No. 609).

Rotter, J. B., Liverant, S., & Crowne, D. P. (1961). The growth and extinction of expectancies in change controlled and skilled tasks. *Journal of Psychology, 52,* 161–177.

Rouw, R., Kosslyn, S. M., & Hamel, R. (1997). Detecting high-level and low-level properties in visual images and visual percepts. *Cognition, 63,* 209–226.

Rovee-Collier, C. (1993). The capacity for long-term memory in infancy. *Current Directions in Psychological Science, 2,* 130–135.

Rozin, P. (1990). Development in the food domain. *Developmental Psychology, 26,* 555–562.

Rowan, J. (1998). Maslow amended. *Journal of Humanistic Psychology, 38,* 81–92.

Rowland, D. T. (1991). Family diversity and the life cycle. *Journal of Comparative Family Studies, 22,* 1–14.

Rozin, P., & Fallon, A. E. (1987). A perspective on disgust. *Psychological Review, 94,* 23–41.

Rozin, P., Hammer, L., Oster, H., Horowitz, T., & Marmara, V. (1986). The child's conception of food: Development of categories of accepted and rejected substances. *Journal of Nutrition Education, 18,* 75–81.

Rubinsky, H., Eckerman, D., Rubinsky, E., & Hoover, C. (1987). Early-phase physiological response patterns to psychosexual stimuli: Comparisons of male and female patterns. *Archives of Sexual Behavior, 16,* 45–55.

Ruble, D. N., Balaban, T., & Cooper, J. (1981). Gender constancy and the effects of sex-typed televised toy commercials. *Child Development, 52,* 667–673.

Rudman, L. A., & Borgida, E. (1995). The afterglow of construct accessibility: The behavioral consequences of priming men to view women as sexual objects. *Journal of Experimental Social Psychology, 31,* 493–517.

Rumbaugh, D. M. (Ed.). (1977). *Language learning by a chimpanzee: The Lana project.* New York: Academic Press.

Rumelhart, D. E., & McClelland, J. L. (Eds.). (1986). *Parallel distributed processing: Explorations in the microstructure of cognition* (Vol. 1). Cambridge, MA: MIT Press.

Rummel, A., & Feinberg, R. (1988). Cognitive evaluation theory: A meta-analytic review of the literature. *Social Behavior and Personality, 16,* 147–164.

Russek, M. (1971). Hepatic receptors and the neurophysiological mechanisms controlling feeding behavior. In S. Ehrenpreis (Ed.), *Neuroscience research.* New York: Academic Press.

Russell, J. A. (1994). Is there universal recognition of emotion from facial expression? A review of the cross-cultural studies. *Psychological Bulletin, 115,* 102–141.

Ryckman, R. M. (1993). *Theories of personality* (5th ed.). Pacific Grove, CA: Brooks/Cole.

Sagie, A., Elizur, D., & Yamauchi, H. (1996). The structure and strength of achievement motivation: A cross-cultural comparison. *Journal of Organizational Behavior, 17,* 431–444.

Saitoh, T., Kang, D., Mallory, M., DeTeresa, R., & Masliah, E. (1997). Glial cells in Alzheimer's disease. Preferential effect of APOE risk on scattered microglia. *Gerontology, 43,* 109–118.

Sakai, F., Stirling Meyer, J., Karacan, I., Yamaguchi, F., & Yamamoto, M. (1979). Narcolepsy: Regional cerebral blood flow during sleep and wakefulness. *Neurology, 29,* 61–67.

Salkovskis, P. M. (1985). Obsessional compulsive problems: A cognitive behavioral analysis. *Behaviour Research and Therapy, 23,* 571–577.

Salovey, P., & Mayer, J. D. (1990). Emotional intelligence. *Imagination, cognition, and personality, 9,* 185–211.

Salthouse, T. A. (1994). The nature of the influence of speed on adult age differences in cognition. *Developmental Psychology, 30,* 240–259.

Saltzstein, H. D. (Ed.) (1997). *Culture as a context for moral development: New perspectives on the particular and the universal.* San Francisco: Jossey-Bass, Inc.

Sameroff, A. J., Seifer, R., Baldwin, A., & Baldwin, C. (1993). Stability of intelligence from preschool to adolescence: The influence of social and family risk factors. *Child Development, 64,* 80–97.

Sanders, R. J. (1989). Sentence comprehension following agenesis of the corpus callosum. *Brain and Language, 37,* 59–72.

Sanderson, W. C., & Barlow, D. H. (1990). A description of patients diagnosed with a DSM-II-R anxiety disorder. *Journal of Nervous and Mental Disease, 178,* 588–591.

Sanson, A., & di-Muccio, C. (1993). The influence of aggressive and neutral cartoons and toys on the behaviour of preschool children. *Australian Psychologist, 28,* 93–99.

Sarason, I. G., Sarason, B. R., & Pierce, G. R. (1994). Social support: Global and relationship-based levels of analysis. *Journal of Social and Personal Relationships, 11,* 295–312.

Sarbin, T. R., & Coe, W. C. (1972). *Hypnosis: A social psychological analysis of influence communication.* New York: Holt, Rinehart & Winston.

Saron, C. D., & Davidson, R. J. (1989). Visual evoked potential measures of interhemispheric transfer times in humans. *Behavioral Neuroscience, 103,* 1115–1138.

Savage-Rumbaugh, S., McDonald, D., Sevcik, R., Hopkins, W., & Rupert, E. (1986). Spontaneous symbol acquisition and communicative use by pygmie chimpanzees. *Journal of Experimental Psychology: General, 115,* 211–235.

Savage-Rumbaugh, S., Murphy, J., Sevcik, R., Brakke, K., Williams, S., & Rumbaugh, D. M. (1993). Language comrephension in ape and child. *Monographs of the Society for Research in Child Development, 58* (3–4, Serial No. 233).

Saxe, L. (1994). Detection of deception: Polygraph and integrity tests. *Current Directions in Psychological Science, 3,* 69–72.

Scarborough, E., & Furumoto, L. (1987). *Untold lives: The first generation of American women psychologists.* New York: Columbia University Press.

Scarr, S. (1998). American child care today. *American Psychologist, 53,* 95–108.

Scarr, S., & Weinberg, R. A. (1976). IQ test performance of black children adopted by white familics. *American Psychologist, 31,* 726–739.

Schachter, S. (1971). *Emotion, obesity, and crime.* New York: Academic Press.

Schachter, S., & Gross, L. (1968). Manipulated time and eating behavior. *Journal of Personality and Social Psychology, 10,* 98–106.

Schachter, S., & Singer, J. E. (1962). Cognitive, social, and physiological determinants of emotional state. *Psychological Review, 69,* 379–399.

Schacter, D. L., Norman, K. A., & Koutstaal, W. (1998). The cognitive neuroscience of constructive memory. *Annual Review of Psychology, 49,* 289–318.

Schaie, K. W. (1983). The Seattle Longitudinal Study: A twenty-one-year exploration of psychometric intelligence in adulthood. In K. W. Schaie (Ed.), *Longitudinal studies of adult psychological development.* New York: Guilford.

Schaie, K. W. (1989). The hazards of cognitive aging. *Gerontologist, 29,* 484–493.

Schaie, K. W. (1993). The Seattle longitudinal studies of adult intelligence. *Current Directions in Psychological Science, 2,* 171–175.

Schaie, K. W. (1998). The Seattle Longitudinal Studies of adult intelligence. In M. P. Lawton, & T. A. Salthouse (Eds.), *Essential papers on the psychology of aging. Essential papers in psychoanalysis.* New York: New York University Press.

Schedlowski, M., Fluge, T., Richter, S., & Tewes, U. (1995). b-Endorphin, but not substance-P, is increased by acute stress in humans. *Psychoneuroendocrinology, 20,* 103–110.

Scheff, T. J. (1984). *Being mentally ill: A sociological theory.* New York: Aldine.

Scheich, H., & Zuschratter, W. (1995). Mapping of stimulus features and meaning in gerbil auditory cortex with 2–deoxyglucose and c-fos antibodies. *Behavioural Brain Research, 66,* 195–205.

Scheier, M. F., & Carver, C. S. (1993). On the power of positive thinking: The benefits of being optimistic. *Current Directions in Psychological Science, 2,* 26–30.

Scheier, M. F., Matthews, K. A., Owens, J. F., Magovern, G. J., Sr., Lefebvre, R. C., Abbott, R. A., & Carver, C. S. (1989). Dispositional optimism and recovery from coronary artery bypass surgery: The beneficial effects on physical and psychological well-being. *Journal of Personality and Social Psychology, 57,* 1024–1040.

Schelling, T. C. (1992). Addictive drugs: The cigarette experience. *Science, 255,* 430–433.

Schiller, P. H. (1996). On the specificity of neurons and visual areas. *Behavioural Brain Research, 76,* 21–35.

Schiller, P. H., Logothetis, N. K., & Charles, E. R. (1990). Functions of the colour-opponent and broad-channels of the visual system. *Nature, 343,* 68–70.

Schleifer, S. J., Keller, S. E., Meyerson, A. T., Raskin, M. J., Davis, K. L., & Stein, M. (1983). Suppression of lymphocyte stimulation following bereavement. *Journal of the American Medical Association, 250,* 374.

Schlenker, B. R., & Forsyth, D. R. (1977). On the ethics of psychological research. *Journal of Experimental Social Psychology, 13,* 369–396.

Schmahmann, J. D., & Sherman, J. C. (1998). The cerebellar cognitive affective syndrome. *Brain, 121,* 561–579.

Schmidt, F. L., & Hunter, J. E. (1993). Tacit knowledge, practical intelligence, general mental ability, and job knowledge. *Current Directions in Psychological Science, 2,* 8–9.

Schmidt, S. R. (1991). Can we have a distinctive theory of memory? *Memory & Cognition, 19,* 523–542.

Schmuckler, M. A. (1996). Development of visually-guided locomotion: Barrier crossing by toddlers. *Ecological Psychology, 8,* 209–236.

Schnapf, J. L., & Baylor, D. A. (1987, April). How photoreceptor cells respond to light. *Scientific American, 256,* 40–47.

Schneider, J. S., Sun, Z. Q., & Roeltgen, D. P. (1994). Effects of dopamine agonists on delayed response performance in chronic low-dose MPTP-treated monkeys. *Pharmacology, Biochemistry, and Behavior, 48,* 235–240.

Schneider, S. G., Taylor, S. E., Hammen, C., Kemeny, M. E., & Dudley, J. (1991). Factors influencing suicide intent in gay and bisexual suicide ideators: Differing models for men with and without human immunodeficiency virus. *Journal of Personality and Social Psychology, 61,* 776–788.

Schneiderman, N., Antoni, M. H., Ironson, G., Laperriere, A., & Fletcher, M. A. (1992). Applied psychological science and HIV-1 spectrum disease. *Applied and Preventive Psychology, 1,* 67–82.

Schreiber, F. (1973). *Sybil.* New York: Warner Books.

Schroeder, D. H., & Costa, P. T. (1984). Influence of life event stress on physical illnesss: Substantive effects or methodological flaws? *Journal of Personality and Social Psychology, 46,* 853–863.

Schwartz, B. (1990). The creation and destruction of value. *American Psychologist, 45,* 7–15.

Schwartz, C. E., Snidman, N., & Kagan, J. (1996). Early childhood temperament as a determinant of externalizing behavior in adolescence. *Development & Psychopathology, 8,* 527–537.

Schwartz, W. J. (1996). Internal timekeeping. *Science & Medicine, 3,* 44–53.

Schweickert, R., Guentert, L., & Hersberger, L. (1990). Phonological similarity, pronunciation rate, and memory span. *Psychological Science, 1,* 74–77.

Sclafani, A. (1994). Eating rates in normal and hypothalamic hyperphagic rats. *Physiology and Behavior, 55,* 489–494.

Scott, T. R., Plata-Salamn, C. R., & Smith-Swintosky, V. L. (1994). Gustatory neural coding in the monkey cortex: The quality of saltiness. *Journal of Neurophysiology, 71,* 1692–1701.

Sebrechts, M. M., Marsh, R. L., & Seamon, J. G. (1989). Secondary memory and very rapid forgetting. *Memory & Cognition, 17,* 693–700.

Sedikides, C., Campbell, W. K., Reeder, G. D., & Elliot, A. J. (1998). The self-serving bias in relational context. *Journal of Personality & Social Psychology, 74,* 378–386.

Seeman, P., Lee, T., Chau Wong, M., & Wong, K. (1976). Antipsychotic drug doses and neuroleptic/dopamine receptors. *Nature, 261,* 717–719.

Segall, M. H., Dasen, P. R., Berry, J. W., & Poortinga, Y. (1990). *Human behavior in global perspective.* New York: Pergamon.

Segerstrom, S. C., Taylor, S. E., Kemeny, M. E., & Fahey, J. L. (1998). Optimism is associated with mood, coping, and immune change in response to stress. *Journal of Personality & Social Psychology, 74,* 1646–1655.

Sekular, R., & Blake, R. (1990). *Perception* (2nd ed.). New York: McGraw-Hill.

Seligman, M. E. P. (1975). *Helplessness: On depression, development, and death.* San Francisco: Freeman.

Selkoe, D. J. (1992, September). Aging brain, aging mind. *Scientific American, 267,* 135–142.

Selye, H. (1936). A syndrome produced by diverse nocuous agents. *Nature, 138,* 32.

Selye, H. (1952). *The story of the adaptation syndrome.* Montreal: Acta.

Selye, H. (1974). *Stress without distress.* Philadelphia: Lippincott.

Sepple, C. P., & Read, N. W. (1989). Gastrointestinal correlates of the development of hunger in man. *Appetite, 13,* 183–191.

Shaffer, D. R. (1993). *Developmental psychology: Childhood and adolescence* (3rd ed.). Pacific Grove, CA: Brooks/Cole.

Shapiro, A. K. (1960). A contribution to a history of the placebo effect. *Behavioral Science, 5,* 109–135.

Shapley, R. (1990). Visual sensitivity and parallel retinocortical channels. *Annual Review of Psychology, 41,* 635–658.

Shapley, R., & Kaplan, E. (1989). Responses of magnocellular LGN neurons and M retinal ganglion cells to drifting heterochromatic gratings. *Investigative Ophthalmology and Visual Science, 30,* 323.

Sharma, K. N., Anand, B. K., Due, S., & Singh, B. (1961). Role of stomach in regulation of activities of hypothalamic feeding centers. *American Journal of Physiology, 201,* 593–598.

Shaywitz, S. E., Fletcher, J. M., & Shaywitz, B. A. (1994). Issues in the definition and classification of attention deficit disorder. *Topics in Language Disorders, 14,* 1–25.

Shepard, R. N. (1990). *Mind sights.* New York: W. H. Freeman.

Sheridan, C. L., & Radmacher, S. A. (1992). *Health psychology: Challenging the biomedical model.* New York: Wiley.

Shields, S. A. (1975). Functionalism, Darwinism, and the psychology of women: A study in social myth. *American Psychologist, 30,* 739–754.

Shiffrin, R. M., & Schneider, W. (1977). Controlled and automatic human information processing II: Perceptual learning, automatic attending, and a general theory. *Psychological Review, 84,* 127–190.

Shirley, M. M. (1933). *The first two years: A study of 25 babies. Vol. 1: Postural and locomotor development.* Minneapolis: University of Minnesota Press.

Shirley, S. G., & Persaud, K. C. (1990). The biochemistry of vertebrate olfaction and taste. *Seminars in the Neurosciences, 2,* 59–68.

Shweder, R. A., Mahapatra, M., & Miller, J. G. (1990). Culture and moral development. In J. W. Stigler, R. A. Shweder, & G. Herdt (Eds.), *Cultural psychology.* New York: Cambridge University Press.

Siegel, J. M. (1983). A behavioral approach to the analysis of reticular formation unit activity. In T. E. Robinson (Ed.), *Behavioral approaches to brain research.* New York: Oxford University Press.

Siegel, J. M. (1990). Stressful life events and use of physician services among the elderly: The moderating role of pet ownership. *Journal of Personality and Social Psychology, 58,* 1081–1086.

Siegel, S. (1983). Classical conditioning, drug tolerance, and drug dependence. In Y. Israel, F. B. Glaser, R. E. Popham, W. Schmidt, & R. G. Smart (Eds.), *Research advances in alcohol and drug problems* (Vol. 7). New York: Plenum.

Siegel, S. (1989). Pharmacological conditioning and drug effects. In A. J. Goudie & M. W. Emmett-Oglesby (Eds.), *Psychoactive drugs: Tolerance and sensitization.* Clifton, NJ: Humana Press.

Siegler, R. S. (1994). Cognitive variability: A key to understanding cognitive development. *Psychological Science, 3,* 1–5.

Siegler, R. S. (1996). *Children's thinking: Beyond the immaculate transition.* New York: Oxford University Press.

Sigelman, C. K., & Shaffer, D. R. (1995). *Life-span human development* (2nd ed.). Pacific Grove, CA: Brooks/Cole.

Sigmundson, H. K. (1994). Pharmacotherapy of schizophrenia: A review. *Canadian Journal of Psychiatry, 39,* 570–575.

Silver, E., Cirincione, C., & Steadman, H. J. (1994). Demythologizing inaccurate perceptions of the insanity defense. *Law and Human Behavior, 18,* 63–70.

Silverstein, B., Perdue, L., Peterson, B., & Kelly, E. (1986). The role of the mass media in promoting a thin standard of bodily attractiveness for women. *Sex Roles, 14,* 519–532.

Simon, H. A. (1969). *The sciences of the artificial.* Cambridge, MA: MIT Press.

Simon, H. A. (1992). What is an "explanation" of behavior? *Psychological Science, 3,* 150–161.

Sims, A. C. P., & Sims, D. (1998). The phenomenology of posttraumatic stress disorder: A symptomatic study of 70 victims of psychological trauma. *Psychopathology, 31,* 96–112.

Siqueland, E. R., & DeLucia, C. A. (1969). Visual reinforcement of nonnutritive sucking in human infants. *Science, 165,* 1144–1146.

Sivian, L. S., & White, S. D. (1933). On minimum audible sound fields. *Journal of Acoustical Society of America, 4,* 288–321.

Skinner, B. F. (1938). *The behavior of organisms: An experimental analysis.* New York: Appleton-Century.

Skinner, B. F. (1948). "Superstition" in the pigeon. *Journal of Experimental Psychology, 38,* 168–172.

Skinner, B. F. (1956). A case history in scientific method. *American Psychologist, 11,* 221–233.

Skinner, B. F. (1969). *Contingencies of reinforcement: A theoretical analysis.* New York: Appleton-Century-Crofts.

Slater, A., Von der Schulenburg, C., Brown, E., Badenoch, M., Butterworth, G., Parsons, S., & Samuels, C. (1998). Newborn infants prefer attractive faces. *Infant Behavior & Development, 21,* 345–354.

Slater, E., & Glithero, E. (1965). A follow-up of patients diagnosed as suffering from hysteria. *Journal of Psychosomatic Research, 9,* 9–13.

Sloane, R. B., Staples, F. R., Cristol, A. H., Yorkston, N. J., & Whipple, K. (1975). *Psychotherapy versus behavior therapy.* Cambridge, MA: Harvard University Press.

Slovic, P., Fischoff, B., & Lichtenstein, S. (1982). Facts versus fears: Understanding perceived risk. In D. Kahneman, P. Slovic, & A. Tversky (Eds.), *Judgment under uncertainty: Heuristics and biases.* Cambridge: Cambridge University Press.

Smiley, P. A., & Dweck, C. S. (1994). Individual differences in achievement goals among young children. *Child Development, 65,* 1723–1743.

Smith, E. E. (1989). Concepts and induction. In M. Posner (Ed.), *Foundations of cognitive science.* Cambridge, MA: MIT Press.

Smith, E. E., Patalano, A. L., & Jonides, J. (1998). Alternative strategies of categorization. *Cognition, 65,* 167–196.

Smith, E. R., & Mackie, D. M. (1995). *Social psychology.* New York: Worth.

Smith, E. R., Stewart, T. L., & Buttram, R. T. (1992). Inferring a trait from a behavior has long-term, highly-specific effects. *Journal of Personality and Social Psychology, 62,* 753–759.

Smith, E. R., & Zárate, M. A. (1992). Exemplar-based model of social judgment. *Psychological Review, 99,* 3–21.

Smith, F. J., & Campfield, L. A. (1993). Meal initiation occurs after experimental induction of transient declines in blood glucose. *American Journal of Physiology, 265,* R1423–R1429.

Smith, M. L., & Glass, G. V. (1977). Meta-analysis of psychotherapy outcome studies. *American Psychologist, 32,* 752–760.

Smith, M. L., Glass, G. V., & Miller, T. I. (1980). *The benefits of psychotherapy.* Baltimore, MD: Johns Hopkins University Press.

Snarey, J. R. (1995). In a communitarian voice: The sociological expansion of Kohlbergian theory, research, and practice. In W. M. Kurtines & J. L. Gewirtz (Eds.), *Moral development: An introduction.* Boston: Allyn & Bacon.

Snyder, C. R. (1989). Reality negotiation: From excuses to hope and beyond. Self-illusions: When are they adaptive? [Special issue] *Journal of Social and Clinical Psychology, 8,* 130–157.

Snyder, F. (1967). In quest of dreaming. In H. A. Witkin & H. B. Lewis (Eds.), *Experimental studies of dreaming.* New York: Random House.

Snyder, M. (1974). The self-monitoring of expressive behavior. *Journal of Personality and Social Psychology, 30,* 526–537.

Snyder, M. (1987). *Public appearances/Private realities: The psychology of self-monitoring.* New York: Freeman.

Snyder, M., Tanke, E. D., & Berscheid, E. (1977). Social perception and interpersonal behavior: On the self-fulfilling nature of social stereotypes. *Journal of Personality and Social Psychology, 35,* 656–666.

Snyder, S. H. (1976). The dopamine hypothesis of schizophrenia: Focus on the dopamine receptor. *American Journal of Psychiatry, 133,* 197–202.

Snyder, S. H., & D'Amato, R. J. (1986). MPTP: A neurotoxin relevant to the pathology of Parkinson's disease. *Neurology, 36,* 250–258.

Soudino, K. J., Plomin, R., & DeFries, J. C. (1996). Tester-rated temperament at 14, 20, and 24 months: Environmental change and genetic continuity. *British Journal of Developmental Psychology, 14,* 129–144.

Spanos, N. P. (1982). Hypnotic behavior: A cognitive, social psychological perspective. *Research Communications in Psychology, Psychiatry, and Behavior, 7,* 199–213.

Spanos, N. P. (1986). Hypnotic behavior: A social psychological interpretation of amnesia, analgesia, and "trance logic." *The Behavioral and Brain Sciences, 9,* 449–502.

Spanos, N. P. (1996). *Multiple identities and false memories: A sociocognitive perspective.* Washington, DC: American Psychological Association.

Spanos, N. P., Weeks, J. R., & Bertrand, L. D. (1985). Multiple personality: A social psychological perspective. *Journal of Abnormal Psychology, 92,* 362–376.

Sparks, D. L. (1988). Neural cartography: Sensory and motor maps in the mammalian superior colliculus. *Brain, Behavior, and Evolution, 31,* 49–56.

Spearman, C. (1904). "General intelligence," objectively determined and measured. *American Journal of Psychology, 15,* 201–293.

Spelke, E. S. (1991). Physical knowledge in infancy: Reflections on Piaget's theory. In S. Carey & R. Gelman (Eds.), *The epigenesis of mind: Essays on biology and cognition.* Hillsdale, NJ: Erlbaum.

Spelke, E. S., Breinlinger, K, Macomber, J., & Jacobson, K. (1992). Origins of knowledge. *Psychological Review, 99,* 605–632.

Spence, S., Shapiro, D., & Zaidel, E. (1996). The role of the right hemisphere in the physiological and cognitive components of emotional processing. *Psychophysiology, 33,* 112–122.

Sperling, G. (1960). The information available in brief visual presentations. *Psychological Monographs, 74*(Whole No. 48).

Speigel, D. (1995). Hypnosis and suggestion. In D. L. Schacter (Ed.), *Memory distortion.* Cambridge, MA: Harvard University Press.

Spiegel, D., Bloom, J. R., Kramer, H. C., & Gotheil, E. (1989). Effect of psychosocial treatment on survival of patients with metastatic breast cancer. *Lancet, 14,* 888–891.

Spiegler, M. D., & Guevremont, D. C. (1998). *Contemporary behavior therapy* (3rd ed.). Pacific Grove, CA, USA: Brooks/Cole Publishing Co.

Spitz, R. A. (1945). Hospitalism: An inquiry into the genesis of psychiatric conditions in early childhood. *Psychoanalytic Study of the Child, 1,* 53–74.

Spitzer, R. L. (1975). On pseudoscience in science, logic in remission, and psychiatric diagnosis: A critique of Rosenhan's "On being sane in insane places." *Journal of Abnormal Psychology, 84,* 442–452.

Spitzer, R. L., Gibbon, M., Skodol, A. E., Williams, J. B., & First, M. B. (Eds.). (1994). *DSM-IV Casebook.* Washington, DC: American Psychiatric Press.

Sponheim, S. R., Clementz, B. A., Iacono, W. G., & Beiser, M. (1994). Resting EEG in first episode and chronic schizophrenia. *Psychophysiology, 31,* 37–43.

Springer, S. P., & Deutsch, G. (1989). *Left brain, right brain.* (3rd ed.). New York: Freeman.

Squire, L. R. (1992). Memory and the hippocampus: A synthesis of findings with rats, monkeys, and humans. *Psychological Review, 99,* 195–231.

Squire, L. R., Ojemann, J. G., Miezin, F. M., Petersen, S. E., Videen, T. O., & Raichle, M. E. (1992). Activation of the hippocam-pus in normal humans: A functional anatomical study of memory. *Proceedings of the National Academy of Sciences, 89,* 1837–1841.

Staddon, J. E. R. (1998). The dynamics of memory in animal learning. In M. Sabourin (Ed.) et al. *Advances in psychological science, Vol. 2: Biological and cognitive aspects.* Hove, England: Psychology Press/Erlbaum.

Staddon, J. E. R., & Simmelhag, V. L. (1971). The "superstition" experiment: A reexamination of its implications for the principles of adaptive behavior. *Psychological Review, 78,* 3–43.

Steblay, N. M., & Bothwell, R. K. (1994). Evidence for hypnotically refreshed testimony: The view from the laboratory. *Law and Human Behavior, 18,* 635–651.

Steele, C. M., & Josephs, R. A. (1990). Alcohol myopia: Its prized and dangerous effects. *American Psychologist, 45,* 921–933.

Stein, M., & Miller, A. H. (1993). Stress, the immune system, and health and illness. In L. Goldberger & S. Breznitz (Eds.), *Handbook of stress: Theoretical and clinical aspects* (2nd ed.). New York: Free Press.

Stein, M., Ottenberg, P., & Roulet, N. (1958). A study of the development of olfactory preferences. *American Medical Association Archives of Neurology & Psychiatry, 80,* 264–266.

Stein, R. M., & Ellinwood, E. H. (1993). Stimulant use: Cocaine and amphetamine. In D. L. Dunner (Ed.), *Current psychiatric therapy.* Philadelphia: W. B. Saunders.

Steiner, J. E. (1977). Facial expressions of the neonate infant indicating the hedonics of food-related chemical stimuli. In J. M. Weiffenbach (Ed.), *Taste and development.* Bethesda, MD: Department of Health, Education, and Welfare.

Stern, R. S., & Cobb, J. P. (1978). Phenomenology of obsessive-compulsive neurosis. *British Journal of Psychiatry, 132,* 233–234.

Sternberg, R. J. (1977). *Intelligence, information processing, and analogical reasoning.* Hillsdale, NJ: Erlbaum.

Sternberg, R. J. (1985). *Beyond IQ: A triarchic theory of human intelligence.* New York: Cambridge University Press.

Sternberg, R. J. (1986). A triangular theory of love. *Psychological Review, 93,* 119–135.

Sternberg, R. J. (1988a). Triangulating love. In R. J. Sternberg & M. L. Barnes (Eds.), *The psychology of love.* New Haven, CT: Yale University Press.

Sternberg, R. J. (1988b). *The triarchic theory of mind: A new theory of human intelligence.* New York: Viking Press.

Sternberg, R. J. (1997). The concept of intelligence and its role in lifelong learning and success. *American Psychologist, 52,* 1030–1037.

Sternberg, R. J. Principles of teaching for successful intelligence. *Educational Psychologist, 33,* 65–72.

Sternberg, R. J., & Gardner, M. K. (1983). Unities in inductive reasoning. *Journal of Experimental Psychology: General, 112,* 80–116.

Sternberg, R. J., & Grajek, S. (1984). The nature of love. *Journal of Personality and Social Psychology, 47,* 312–329.

Sternberg, R. J., & Kaufman, J. C. (1998). Human abilities. *Annual Review of Psychology, 49,* 479–502.

Sternberg, R. J., Torff, B., Grigorenko, E. L. (1998). Teaching triarchically improves school achievement. *Journal of Educational Psychology, 90,* 374–384.

Sternberg, R. J., & Wagner, R. K. (1993). The g-ocentric view of intelligence and job performance is wrong. *Current Directions in Psychological Science, 2,* 1–5.

Stevens, S. S. (1939). Psychology and the science of science. *Psychological Bulletin, 36,* 221–263.

Stewart, D. D., & Stasser, G. (1995). Expert role assignment and information sampling during collective recall and decision making. *Journal of Personality & Social Psychology, 69,* 619–628.

Stewart, T. L., Doan, K. A., Gingrich, B. E., & Smith, E. R. (1998). The actor as context for social judgments: Effects of prior impressions and stereotypes. *Journal of Personality and Social Psychology, 75,* 1132–1154.

St. Jean, R., McInnis, K., Campbell-Mayne, L., & Swainson, P. (1994). Hypnotic underestimation of time: The busy beaver. *Journal of Abnormal Psychology, 103,* 565–569.

Stoyva, J. M., & Carlson, J. G. (1993). A coping/rest model of relaxation and stress management. In L. Goldberger & S. Breznitz (Eds.), *Handbook of stress: Theoretical and clincial aspects* (2nd ed.). New York: Free Press.

Strassman, R. J. (1992). Human hallucinogen interactions with drugs affecting serotonergic neurotransmission. *Neuropsychopharamacology, 7,* 241–243.

Streissguth, A. P., Randels, S. P., & Smith, D. F. (1991). A test-retest study of intelligence in patients with fetal alcohol syndrome: Implications for care. *Journal of the American Academy of Child and Adolescent, 30,* 584–587.

Stricker, L. J., Rock, D. A., & Burton, N. W. (1996). Using the SAT and high school record in academic guidance. *Educational and Psychological Measurement, 56,* 626–641.

Strombeck, R., & Levy, J. A. (1998). Educational strategies and interventions targeting adults age 50 and older for HIV/AIDS prevention. *Research on Aging, 20,* 912–936.

Sue, S., & Zane, N. (1987). The role of culture and cultural techniques in psychotherapy: A critique and reformulation. *American Psychologist, 42,* 37–45.

Sue, S., Zane, N., & Young, K. (1994). Research on psychotherapy with culturally diverse populations. In A. E. Bergin & S. L. Garfield (Eds.), *Handbook of psychotherapy and behavior change* (4th ed.). New York: Wiley.

Sullivan, P. F., Bulik, C. M., & Kendler, K. S. (1998). Genetic epidemiology of binging and vomiting. *British Journal of Psychiatry, 173,* 75–79.

Surra, C. A. (1998). Subjectivity and practicality in mating and parenting decisions. In A. Booth & A. C. Crouter (Eds.), *Men in families: When do they get involved? What difference does it make?* Mahway, NJ: Erlbaum.

Sussman, J. R., & Levitt, B. (1989). *Before you conceive: The complete pregnancy guide.* New York: Bantam Books.

Suzdak, P. D., Glowa, J. R., Crawley, J. N., Schwartz, R. D., Skolnick, P., & Paul, S. M. (1986). A selective imidazobenzodiazepine antagonist of ethanol in the rat. *Science, 234,* 1243–1247.

Swinson, R. P., Antony, M. M., Rachman, S., & Richter, M. A. (Eds.). (1998). *Obsessive-compulsive disorder: Theory, research, and treatment.* New York: The Guilford Press.

Szasz, T. (1961). *The myth of mental illness: Foundations of a theory of personal conduct.* New York: Hoeber-Harper.

Szasz, T. (1990). Law and psychiatry: The problems that will not go away. *The Journal of Mind and Behavior, 11,* 557–564.

Tanford, S., & Penrod, S. (1984). Social influence model: A formal integration of research on majority and minority influence processes. *Psychological Bulletin, 95,* 189–225.

Tanner, J. M. (1990). *Foetus into man: Physical growth from conception to maturity* (Rev. ed.). Cambridge, MA: Harvard University Press.

Tateyama, M., Asai, M., Hashimoto, M., Bartels, M., & Kasper, S. (1998). Transcultural study of schizophrenic delusions: Tokyo versus Vienna versus Tuebingen (Germany). *Psychopathology, 31,* 59–68.

Tavris, C. (1989). *Anger: The misunderstood emotion* (rev. ed.). New York, NY: Touchstone Books/Simon & Schuster, Inc.

Taylor, F. K. (1965). Cryptomnesia and plagiarism. *British Journal of Psychiatry, 111,* 1111–1118.

Taylor, F. W. (1911). *Principles of scientific management.* New York: Harper.

Taylor, H. (1997). The very different methods used to conduct telephone surveys of the public. *Journal of the Marketing Research Society, 39,* 421–432.

Taylor, S. E., Repetti, R., & Seeman, T. (1997). Health psychology: What is an unhealthy environment and how does it get under the skin? *Annual Review of Psychology, 48,* 411–447.

Teeter, J. H., & Brand, J. G. (1987). Peripheral mechanisms of gustation: Physiology and biochemistry. In T. E. Finger & W. L. Silver (Eds.), *Neurobiology of taste and smell.* New York: Wiley.

Tellegen, A., Lykken, D. T., Bouchard, T. J., Jr., Wilcox, K. J., Segal, N. L., & Rich, S. (1988). Personality similarity in twins reared apart and together. *Journal of Personality and Social Psychology, 54,* 1031–1039.

Templeton, J. J. (1998). Learning from others' mistakes: A paradox revisited. *Animal Behaviour, 55,* 79–85.

Tennes, K., & Kreye, M. (1985). Children's adrenocortical responses to classroom activities and tests in elementary school. *Psychosomatic Medicine, 47,* 451–460.

Terman, L. M. (1925). *Mental and physical traits of a thousand gifted children.* Stanford, CA: Stanford University Press.

Terman, L. M. (1954). The discovery and encouragement of exceptional talent. *American Psychologist, 9,* 221–238.

Terman, L. M., & Ogden, M. (1947). *Genetic studies of genius. Vol. 5. The gifted child grows up.* Stanford, CA: Stanford University Press.

Terrace, H. S. (1986). *Nim: A chimpanzee who learned sign language.* New York: Columbia University Press.

Tesser, A. (1993). The importance of heritability in psychological research: The case of attitudes. *Psychological Review, 100,* 129–142.

Thibos, L. N., Bradley, A., Still, D. L., & Zhang, X. (1990). Theory and measurement of ocular chromatic aberration. *Vision Research, 30,* 33–49.

Thigpen, C. H., & Cleckley, H. A. (1957). *Three faces of Eve.* New York: McGraw-Hill.

Thomas, A., & Chess, S. (1977). *Temperament and development.* New York: Bruner/Mazel.

Thompson, S. K. (1975). Gender labels and early sex-role development. *Child Development, 46,* 339–347.

Thomsen, P. H. (1994). Obsessive-compulsive disorder in children and adolescents: A review of the literature. *European Child and Adolescent Psychiatry, 3,* 138–158.

Thomsen, P. H. (1998). Obsessive-compulsive disorder in children and adolescents: Clinical guidlines. *European Child and Adolescent Psychiatry, 7,* 1–11.

Thoresen, C. E., & Powell, L. H. (1992). Type A behavior pattern: New perspectives on theory, assessment and intervention. *Journal of Consulting and Clinical Psychology, 60,* 595–604.

Thorndike, E. L. (1898). Animal intelligence: An experimental study of the associative processes in animals. *Psychological Review, Monograph Supplements, 2*(Serial No. 8).

Thorndike, E. L. (1911). *Animal intelligence: Experimental studies.* New York: Macmillan.

Thorndike, E. L. (1914). *The psychology of learning.* New York: Teacher's College.

Thurstone, L. L. (1938). *Primary mental abilities.* Chicago: University of Chicago Press.

Tienari, P. (1992). Implications of adoption studies on schizophrenia. *British Journal of Psychiatry, 161,* 52–58.

Tiffany, S. T. (1990). A cognitive model of drug urges and drug-use behavior: Role of automatic and nonautomatic processes. *Psychological Review, 97,* 147–168.

Timberlake, W. (1980). A molar equilibrium theory of learned performance. In G. H. Bower (Ed.), *The psychology of learning and motivation* (Vol. 14). New York: Academic Press.

Timberlake, W., & Silva, F. J. (1994). Observation of behavior, inference of function, and the study of learning. *Psychonomic Bulletin and Review, 1,* 73–88.

Tinbergen, N. (1951). *The study of instinct.* London: Oxford University Press.

Titchener, E. B. (1899). Structural and functional psychology. *Philosophical Review, 8,* 290–299.

Tolman, C. W. (1968). The role of the companion in social facilitation of animal behavior. In E. C. Simmel, R. A. Hoppe, & G. A. Milton (Eds.), *Social facilitation and imitative behavior.* Boston: Allyn & Bacon.

Tomaka, J., Blascovich, J., Kibler, J., & Ernst, J. M. (1997). Cognitive and physiological antecedents of threat and challenge appraisal. *Journal of Personality & Social Psychology, 73,* 63–72.

Tomkins, S. S. (1962). *Affect, imagery, and consciousness* (Vol. 1). New York: Springer.

Tomlinson-Keasey, C., & Little, T. D. (1990). Predicting educational attainment, occupational achievement, intellectual skill, and personal adjustment among gifted men and women. *Journal of Educational Psychology, 82,* 442–455.

Torrance, E. P. (1981). Empirical validation of criterion-referenced indicators of creative ability through a longitudinal study. *Creative Child and Adult Quarterly, 6,* 136–140.

Towler, G. (1986). From zero to one hundred: Coaction in a natural setting. *Perceptual and Motor Skills, 62,* 377–378.

Trafimow, D., Triandis, H. C., & Goto, S. G. (1991). Some tests of the distinction between the private self and the collective self. *Journal of Personality and Social Psychology, 60,* 649–655.

Treisman, A. (1960). Contextual cues in selective listening. *Quarterly Journal of Experimental Psychology, 12,* 242–248.

Triplett, N. (1898). The dynamogenic factors in pacemaking and competition. *American Journal of Psychology, 9,* 507–533.

Trope, Y., & Liberman, A. (1993). The use of trait conceptions to identify other people's behavior and to draw inferences about their personalities. *Personality and Social Psychology Bulletin, 19,* 553–562.

Trull, T. J., & McCrae, R. R. (1994). A five-factor perspective on personality disorder research. In P. T. Costa, Jr. & T. A. Widiger (Eds.), *Personality disorders and the five-factor model of personality.* Washington, DC: American Psychological Association.

Tseng, W., & McDermott, J. F. (1975). Psychotherapy:Historical roots, universal elements, and cultural variations. *American Journal of Psychiatry, 132,* 378–384.

Tuckman, B. W. (1998). Using tests as an incentive to motivate procrastinators to study. *Journal of Experimental Education, 66,* 141–147.

Tugrul, K. (1998). Newer antipsychotic agents: Impact on quality of life and alternative applications. *Journal of the American Psychiatric Nurses Association, 4,* S35–S41.

Tulving, E. (1983). *Elements of episodic memory.* Oxford, England: Oxford University Press.

Tulving, E., & Pearlstone, Z. (1966). Availability versus accessibility of information in memory for words. *Journal of Verbal Learning and Verbal Behavior, 5,* 381–391.

Tulving, E., & Thomson, D. M. (1973). Encoding specificity and retrieval processes in episodic memory. *Psychological Review, 80,* 352–373.

Turner, T. J., & Ortony, A. (1992). Basic emotions: Can conflicting criteria converge? *Psychological Review, 99,* 566–571.

Tversky, A., & Kahneman, D. (1973). On the psychology of prediction. *Psychological Review, 80,* 237–251.

Tversky, A., & Kahneman, D. (1974). Decision making under uncertainty: Heuristics and biases. *Science, 185,* 1124–1131.

Tversky, A., & Kahneman, D. (1983). Extensional versus intuitive reasoning: The conjunction fallacy in probability judgment. *Psychological Review, 90,* 293–315.

Tyler, J. M., & Tyler, C. L. (1997). Ethics in supervision: Managing supervisee rights and supervisor responsibilities. *Hatherleigh Guide to Ethics in Therapy, 10,* 75–95.

Ulrich, R. E. (1991). Commentary: Animal rights, animal wrongs and the question of balance. *Psychological Science, 2,* 197–201.

Usher, J. A., & Neisser, U. (1993). Childhood amnesia and the beginnings of memory for four early life events. *Journal of Experimental Psychology: General, 122,* 155–165.

Van Doornen, L. J., & Van Blokland, R. (1987). Serum-cholesterol: Sex-specific psychological correlates during rest and stress. *Journal of Psychosomatic Research, 31,* 239–249.

van Ijzendoorn, M. H., & Kroonenberg, P. M. (1988). Cross-cultural patterns of attachment: A meta-analysis of the strange situation. *Child Development, 59,* 147–156.

van Os, J., & Marcelis, M. (1998). The ecogenetics of schizophrenia: A review. *Schizophrenia Research, 32,* 127–135.

van Rijzingen, I. M. S., Gispen, W. H., & Spruijt, B. M. (1997). Postoperative environmental enrichment attenuates fimbria-fornix lesion-induced impairments in Morris maze performance. *Neurobiology of Learning and Memory, 67,* 21–28.

Ventura, J., Nuechterlein, K. H., Lukoff, D., & Hardesty, J. P. (1989). A prospective study of stressful life events and schizophrenia relapse. *Journal of Abnormal Behavior, 98,* 407–411.

Vernon, P. E. (1983). Speed of information processing and general intelligence. *Intelligence, 7,* 53–70.

Vernon, P. E., & Mori, M. (1992). Intelligence, reaction times, and peripheral nerve conduction velocity. *Intelligence, 16,* 273–288.

Verschueren, S., Cordo, P. J., & Swinnen, S. P. (1998). Representation of wrist joint kinematics by the ensemble of muscle spindles from synergistic muscles. *Journal of Neurophysiology, 79,* 2265–2276.

Victor, M. (1996). Conflicting communicative behavior in a split-brain patient: Support for dual consciousness. In S. Hameroff & A. W. Kaszniak (Eds.), *Toward a science of consciousness: The first Tucson discussions and debates.* Cambridge, MA: MIT Press.

Vitz, P. C. (1988). *Sigmund Freud's Christian unconscious.* New York: Guilford.

Vogel, G. W., Buffenstein, A., Minter, K., & Hennessey, A. (1990). Drug effects on REM sleep and on endogenous depression. *Neuroscience and Biobehavioral Reviews, 14,* 49–63.

Vokey, J. R., & Read, J. D. (1985). Subliminal messages: Between the media and the devil. *American Psychologist, 40,* 1231–1239.

von Frisch, K. (1967). *The dance language and orientation of bees.* Cambridge, MA: Belknap Press.

Vygotsky, L. S. (1978). *Mind in society: The development of higher psychological processes.* Cambridge MA: Harvard University Press.

Waddill, P. J., & McDaniel, M. A. (1998). Distinctiveness effects in free recall: Differential processing or privileged retrieval? *Memory & Cognition, 26,* 108–120.

Wagenaar, W. A. (1986). My memory: A study of autobiographical memory over six years. *Cognitive Psychology, 18,* 225–252.

Wagner, A. R. (1981). SOP: A model of automatic memory processing in animal behavior. In N. E. Spear & R. R. Miller (Eds.), *Information processing in animals: Memory mechanisms.* Hillsdale, NJ: Erlbaum.

Wagner, R. K. (1997). Intelligence, training, and employment. *American Psychologist, 52,* 1059–1069.

Wagner, R. K., & Sternberg, R. J. (1985). Practical intelligence in real-world pursuits: The role of tacit knowledge. *Journal of Personality and Social Psychology, 49,* 436–458.

Wahba, M. A., & Bridwell, L. G. (1976). Maslow reconsidered: A review of research on the need hierarchy theory. *Organizational Behavior and Human Performance, 15,* 212–240.

Waldman, I. D., Weinberg, R. A., & Scarr, S. (1994). Racial-group differences in IQ in the Minnesota Transracial Adoption Study: A reply to Levin and Lynn. *Intelligence, 19,* 29–44.

Walen, S. T., DiGuiseppe, R., & Dryden, W. (1992). *A practitioner's guide to rational-emotive therapy.* New York: Oxford University Press.

Walker, L. J. (1989). A longitudinal study of moral reasoning. *Child Development, 60,* 157–166.

Wallace, C. J. (1998). Social skills training in psychiatric rehabilitation: Recent findings. *International Review of Psychiatry, 10,* 9–10.

Wallhagen, M. I., Strawbridge, W., & Shema, S. (1997). *Perceived control: Mental health correlates in a population-based aging cohort.* Paper presented at the 50th Annual Scientific Meeting of the Gerontological Society of America.

Walters, J. M., & Gardner, H. (1986). The theory of multiple intelligences: Some issues and answers. In R. J. Sternberg & R. K. Wagner (Eds.), *Practical intelligence: Nature and origins of competence in the everyday world.* New York: Cambridge University Press.

Walton, G. E., & Bower, T. G. R. (1993). Newborns form "prototypes" in less than 1 minute. *Psychological Science, 4,* 203–205.

Wampold, B. E., Mondin, G. W., Moody, M., Stich, F., Benson, K., & Ahn, H. (1997). A meta-analysis of outcome studies comparing bona fide psychotherapies: Empiricially, "all must have prizes." *Psychological Bulletin, 122,* 203–215.

Washburn, M. F. (1908). *The animal mind.* New York: Macmillan.

Wasow, T. (1989). Grammatical theory. In M. I. Posner (Ed.), *Foundations of cognitive science.* Cambridge, MA: MIT Press.

Wasserman, E. A., & Miller, R. R. (1997). What's elementary about associative learning? *Annual Review of Psychology, 48,* 573–607.

Waters, E., Wippman, J., & Sroufe, L. A. (1979). Attachment, positive affect, and competence in the peer group: Two studies in construct validation. *Child Development, 50,* 821–829.

Watson, J. B. (1913). Psychology as a behaviorist views it. *Psychological Review, 20,* 158–177.

Watson, J. B. (1919*). Psychology from the standpoint of a behaviorist.* Philadelphia: Lippincott.

Watson, J. B., & Rayner, R. (1920). Conditioned emotional reactions. *Journal of Experimental Psychology, 3,* 1–14.

Webb, E. J., Campbell, D. T., Schwartz, R. D., Sechrist, L., & Grove, J. B. (1981). *Nonreactive research in the social sciences.* Boston: Houghton Mifflin.

Webb, W. B. (1981). The return of consciousness. *G. Stanley Hall Lecture Series, 1,* 129–152.

Webb, W. B. (1992). *Sleep: The gentle tyrant.* Bolton, MA: Anker Publishing.

Weber, R., & Crocker, J. (1993). Cognitive processes in the revision of stereotypic beliefs. *Journal of Personality and Social Psychology, 45,* 961–977.

Weinberg, R. A., Scarr, S., & Waldman, I. D. (1992). The Minnesota Transracial Adoption Study: A follow-up of IQ test performance at adolescence. *Intelligence, 16,* 117–135.

Weiner, R. D., & Coffey, C. E. (1988). Indications for use of electroconvulsive therapy. In A. J. Frances & R. E. Hales (Eds.), *Review of Psychiatry* (Vol. 7). Washington, DC: American Psychiatric Press.

Weingarten, H. P. (1983). Conditioned cues elicit feeding in sated rats: A role for learning in meal initiation. *Science, 220,* 431–433.

Weingarten, H. P., Chang, P. K., & McDonald, T. J. (1985). Comparison of the metabolic and behavioral disturbances following paraventricular and ventro-medial-hypothalamic lesions. *Brain Research Bulletin, 14,* 551–559.

Weinstein, L. N., Schwartz, D. G., & Arkin, A. M. (1991). Qualitative aspects of sleep mentation. In S. J. Ellman & J. S. Antrobus (Eds.), *The mind in sleep* (2nd ed.). New York: Wiley.

Weir, W. (1984, October). Another look at subliminal "facts." *Advertising Age,* 46.

Weisberg, H. F., Krosnick, J. A., & Bowen, B. D. (1989). *An introduction to survey research and data analysis* (2nd ed.). Glenview, IL: Scott, Foresman.

Weisberg, R. W. (1994). Genius and madness? A quasi-experimental test of the hypothesis that manic-depression increases creativity. *Psychological Science, 5,* 361–367.

Weiskrantz, L. (1992). Introduction: Dissociated issues. In A. D. Milner & M. D. Rugg (Eds.), *The neuropsychology of consciousness.* London: Academic Press.

Weiss, J. M. (1977). Psychological and behavioral influences on gastrointestinal lesions in animal models. In J. D. Maser & M. E. P. Seligman (Eds.), *Psychopathology: Experimental models.* San Francisco: Freeman.

Weiss, L., & Baum, A. (1987). Physiological aspects of environment-behavior relationships. In E. Zube & G. Morre (Eds.), *Advances in environmental psychology* (Vol. 1). New York: Plenum.

Weiten, W. (1995). *Psychology: Themes and variations* (3rd ed.). Pacific Grove, CA: Brooks/Cole.

Weldon, M. S., & Roediger, H. M., III. (1987). Altering retrieval demands reverses the picture superiority effect. *Memory & Cognition, 15,* 269–280.

Wellman, H. M., & Estes, D. (1986). Early understanding of mental entities: A reexamination of childhood realism. *Child Development, 57,* 910–923.

Wender, P. H., Kety, S. S., Rosenthal, D., Schlusinger, F., Ortmann, J., & Lunde, I. (1986). Psychiatric disorders in the biological and adoptive families of adopted individuals with affective disorders. *Archives of General Psychiatry, 43,* 923–929.

Wenner, A. (1998). Honey bee "dance language" controversy. In G. Greenberg & M. M. Haraway (Eds.), *Comparative psychology: A handbook.* New York: Garland.

Wernicke, C. (1874). *Der Aphasische Symptomenkomplex.* Breslau, Poland: Cohn & Weigert.

Wertheimer, M. (1987). *A brief history of psychology* (3rd ed.). New York: Holt, Rinehart & Winston.

Wertsch, J. V., & Tulviste, P. (1992). L. S. Vygotsky and contemporary developmental psychology. *Developmental Psychology, 28,* 548–557.

Wever, E. G. (1949). *Theory of hearing.* New York: Wiley.

Wheeler, L., & Kim, Y. (1997). What is beautiful is culturally good: The physical attractiveness stereotype has different content in collectivistic cultures. *Personality & Social Psychology Bulletin, 23,* 795–800.

Whitbourne, S. K. (1985). *The aging body.* New York: Springer.

Whitbourne, S. K., Zuschlag, M. K., Elliot, L. B., & Waterman, A. S. (1992). Psychosocial development in adulthood: A 22–year sequential study. *Journal of Personality and Social Psychology, 63,* 260–271.

White, L., Tursky, B., & Schwartz, G. E. (1985). *Placebo: Theory, research, and mechanisms.* New York: Guilford.

Whitely, B. E., Jr. (1990). The relationship of heterosexuals' attributions for the causes of homosexuality to attitudes toward lesbians and gay men. *Personality and Social Psychology Bulletin, 16,* 367–377.

Whorf, B. L. (1956). *Language, thought, and reality: Selected writings of Benjamin Lee Whorf.* New York: Wiley.

Widiger, T. A. (1998). Personality disorders. In D. F. Barone & M. Hersen (Eds.). *Advanced personality. The Plenum series in social/clinical psychology.* New York: Plenum Press.

Wigfield, A. (1994). Expectancy-value theory of achievement motivation: A developmental perspective. *Educational Psychology Review, 6,* 49–78.

Wiggins, J. S., & Pincus, A. L. (1992). Personality: Structure and assessment. *Annual Review of Psychology, 43,* 473–504.

Williams, D. A., Overmier, J. B., & LoLordo, V. M. (1992). A reevaluation of Rescorla's early dictums about Pavlovian conditioned inhibition. *Psychological Bulletin, 111,* 275–290.

Williams, L. M. (1992). Adult memories of childhood abuse: Preliminary findings from a longitudinal study. *The Advisor, 5,* 19–20.

Willingham, W. W., Lewis, C., Morgan, R., & Ramsit, L. (1990). *Predicting college grades: An analysis of institutional trends over two decades.* Princeton, NJ: Educational Testing Service.

Wilson, E. O. (1963, May). Pheromones. *Scientific American, 208,* 100–114.

Windgassen, K. (1992). Treatment with neuroleptics: The patient's perspective. *Acta Psychiatrica Scandinavica, 86,* 405–410.

Winett, R. A. (1995). A framework for health promotion and disease prevention programs. *American Psychologist, 50,* 341–350.

Winikoff, B. (1983). Nutritional patterns, social choices, and health. In D. Mechanic (Ed.), *Handbook of health, health care, and the health professions.* New York: Free Press.

Wise, R. A., & Bozarth, M. A. (1987). A psychomotor theory of addiction. *Psychological Review, 94,* 469–492.

Wise, R. A., & Rompre, P. P. (1989). Brain dopamine and reward. *Annual Review of Psychology, 40,* 191–225.

Wissler, C. (1901). The correlation of mental and physical tests. *Psychological Review, Monograph Supplement 3*(No. 6).

Witelson, S. F. (1992). Cognitive neuroanatomy: A new era. *Neurology, 42,* 709–713.

Wixted, J. T., & Ebbesen, E. B. (1991). On the form of forgetting. *Psychological Science, 2,* 409–415.

Wolff, N., Helminiak, T. W., & Tebes, J. K. (1997). Getting the cost right in cost-effectiveness analyses. *American Journal of Psychiatry, 154,* 736–743.

Wollberg, Z., & Newman, J. D. (1972). Auditory cortex of squirrel monkey: Response patterns of single cells to species-specific vocalizations. *Science, 175,* 212–214.

Wolpe, J. (1958). *Psychotherapy by reciprocal inhibition.* Stanford, CA: Stanford University Press.

Wolpe, J. (1975). Forward. In B. Sloane, F. Staples, A. Cristol, N. Yorkston, & K. Whipple (Eds.), *Psychotherapy versus behavior therapy.* Cambridge, MA: Harvard University Press.

Wolpe, J. (1982). *The practice of behavior therapy.* New York: Pergamon.

Wong, S. E., Martinez-Diaz, J. A., Massel, H. K., Edelstein, B. A., Wiegand, W., Bowen, L., & Liberman, R. P. (1993). Conversational skills training with schizophrenic inpatients: A study of generalization across settings and conversants. *Behavior Therapy, 24,* 285–304.

Woods, E. R., Lin, Y. G., Middleman, A., Beckford, P., Chase, L., & DuRant, R. (1997). The associations of suicide attempts in adolescents. *Pediatrics, 99,* 791–796.

Woods, S. C., Seeley, R. J., Porte, D., & Schwartz, M. W. (1998). Signals that regulate food intake and energy homeostasis. *Science, 280,* 1378–1383.

Woody, G. E., & Cacciola, J. (1997). Diagnosis and classification: DSM-IV and ICD-10. In J. H. Lowinson, P. Ruiz. R. B. Millman, & J. G. Langrod (Eds.), Substance abuse: A comprehensive textbook. Baltimore: Williams & Wilkins.

Worringham, C. J., & Messick, D. M. (1983). Social facilitation of running: An unobtrusive study. *Journal of Social Psychology, 121,* 23–29.

Wright, A. A. (1990). Memory processing by pigeons, monkeys, and people. In G. H. Bower (Ed.), *The psychology of learning and motivation* (Vol. 24). New York: Academic Press.

Wright, A. A., Santiago, H. C., Sands, S. F., Kendrick, D. F., & Cook, R. G. (1985). Memory processing of serial lists by pigeons, monkeys, and people. *Science, 229,* 287–289.

Wundt, W. (1896). *Outlines of psychology.* C. M. Judd (Trans.). New York: Stechart.

Wyer, R. S., Jr., & Srull, T. K. (1989). *Memory and cognition in its social context.* Hillsdale, NJ: Erlbaum.

Yalom, I. D. (1980). *Existential psychotherapy.* New York: Basic Books.

Yalom, I. D. (1995). *The theory and practice of group psychotherapy* (4th ed.). New York: Basic Books.

Yamamoto, T., Yuyama, N., & Kawamura, Y. (1981). Central processing of taste perception. In Y. Katsuki, R. Norgren, & M. Sato (Eds.), *Brain mechanisms of sensation.* New York: Wiley.

Yamaguchi, S., Tsuchiya, H., & Koboyashi, S. (1998). Visuospatial attention shift and motor responses in cerebellar disorders. *Journal of Cognitive Neuroscience, 10,* 95–107.

Yapko, M. D. (1994). Suggestibility and repressed memories of abuse: A survey of psychotherapists' beliefs. *American Journal of Clinical Hypnosis, 36,* 163–179.

Yates, F. A. (1966). *The art of memory.* Chicago: University of Chicago Press.

Yeomans, J. M., & Irwin, D. E. (1985). Stimulus duration and partial report performance. *Perception & Psychophysics, 37,* 163–169.

Yin, R.K. (1998). The abridged version of case study research: Design and method. In Leonard Bickman & Debra J. Rog (Eds.), *Handbook of applied social research methods.* Thousand Oaks, CA: Sage.

Young, J. E., Beck, A. T., & Weinberger, A. (1993). Depression. In D. H. Barlow (Ed.), *Clinical handbook of psychological disorders* (2nd ed.). New York: Guilford.

Zacks, R. T., & Hasher, L. (1994). Directed ignoring: Inhibitory regulation of working memory. In D. Dagenbach & T. H. Carr (Eds.), *Inhibitory processes in attention, memory, and language.* San Diego, CA: Academic Press.

Zahorik, D. M., Houpt, K. A., & Swartzman-Andert, J. (1990). Taste-aversion learning in three species of ruminants. *Applied Animal Behaviour Science, 26,* 27–39.

Zajonc, R. B. (1965). Social facilitation. *Science, 149,* 269–274.

Zajonc, R. B. (1968). Attitudinal effects of mere exposure. *Journal of Personality and Social Psychology, 9,* Monograph Supplement, No. 2, part 2.

Zajonc, R. B., Heingartner, A., & Herman, E. M. (1969). Social enhancement and impairment of performance in the cockroach. *Journal of Personality and Social Psychology, 13,* 83–92.

Zajonc, R. B., Murphy, S. T. & McIntosh, D. N. (1993). Brain temperature and subjective emotional experience. In M. Lewis & J. M. Haviland (Eds.), *Handbook of emotions.* New York, NY: Guilford Press.

Zametkin, A. J., Nordahl, T., Gross, M., King, A. C., Semple, W. E., Rumsey, J., Hamburger, S., & Cohen, R. M. (1990). Cerebral glucose metabolism in adults with hyperactivity of childhood onset. *New England Journal of Medicine, 323,* 1361–1366.

Zatorre, R. J., Evans, A. C., & Meyer, E. (1994). Neural mechanisms underlying melodic perception and memory for pitch. *Journal of Neuroscience, 14,* 1908–1919.

Zeki, S. (1992, September). The visual image in mind and brain. *Scientific American, 267,* 68–76.

Zelazo, P. R., Zelazo, N. A., & Kolb, S. (1972). "Walking" in the newborn. *Science, 176,* 314–315.

Zigler, E. F., & Stevenson, M. F. (1993). *Children in a changing world* (2nd ed.). Pacific Grove, CA: Brooks/Cole.

Zotterman, Y. (1959). Thermal sensations. In J. Fields, H. W. Magoun, & V. E. Hall (Eds.), *Handbook of physiology: Section I. Neurophysiology, 1,* 431–458. Washington, DC: Physiological Society.

Name Index

Subject Index

A

Abnormal behavior, 6, 545–551. *See also* Psychological disorders
  characteristics of, 546–549
  conceptualizing, 574–575
  criteria for, 548–549
  labeling of, 550–551
  medical model of, 549–550
Absolute threshold, 208, 209, 215
Abstract thought, beginnings of, 140
Accent, linguistic development of, 352
Accidental reinforcement, 288
Accommodation, 135, 173
Acetylcholine (ACh), 79, 238, 336
Achievement motivation, 426–427
Achievement tests, 41, 395
Acoustic errors, in short-term memory, 307–308
Acquisition
  in classical conditioning, 267–269, 275
  and shaping behavior, 287–288
Action, in learning, 278
Action factors, in psychotherapies, 608
Action potential, 75, 77–78, 83
Activation-synthesis hypothesis, 239–240, 254
Acute response phase, of immune response, 631
Adaptation. *See also* Sensory adaptation
  immune response and, 631
Adaptation level, judgments relative to, 450–451
Adaptive mind, 25–26
Adaptive perspective, 13
Adaptive problems, 5
  thinking about, 345
Adaptive tendencies, 12
Adaptive tools, 5
Addiction, to tobacco, 642–643
Adjustment, in decision making, 373–374
Adjustment problems, 9
Adler, Alfred, 478
Adolescence
  development during, 126–127, 164
  personal development during, 154–155
Adolescent suicide, 563
Adoption studies, 411–412
Adrenal glands, 106

Adulthood
  development during, 127–128
  personal development during, 154–156
Adults
  cognitive development of, 142–143
  development of, 164
Adventitious reinforcement, 288
Advertising, subliminal, 226
Aerobic exercise, 641–642, 647
Affective component, of attitude, 510
Afferent nerve pathways, 86
African Americans
  average IQ of, 410
  environmental influences on, 411–412
Age
  intelligence and old, 407–408
  of norm group in IQ tests, 399
Ageism, 159
Age regression, 249
Aggression
  punishment and, 291
  studies on, 58–59
Aging
  memory and, 133–135, 134
  physical, 127–128
  processes of, 159–160
  reaction time and, 128
Agonists, 80
Agoraphobia, 555
Agreeableness
  in personality disorders, 566
  as personality superfactor, 467, 468
AIDS (acquired immune deficiency syndrome), 644–645, 647
Akinetopsia, 180
Alarm reaction, in GAS, 620
Alcohol, effects of, 243–244
Algorithms, 366–367, 376
Allen, Karen, 638
Allport, Gordon, 469
Allport's trait theory, 469
Alpha waves, 233
Altruism, 517–519
Alzheimer's disease, 80, 128
  memory loss in, 336
Ambiguity, in personality tests, 471–472
American Psychological Association, 17, 63
  ethical guidelines of, 60, 61, 63

founding of, 15
American Sign Language, as learned by chimpanzees, 354
Ames Room, 192
Amnesia, 334–335, 339. *See also* Forgetting
  anterograde, 302, 334–335, 339
  childhood, 323
  dissociative, 558
  infantile, 323
Amphetamines, 244
Amplitude of sound, 195
Amygdala, 95
Anagrams, 366–367
Analogies, in problem solving, 369
Anal stage, 477
Analytic intelligence, 393, 394
Anchoring, 373–374
Andreasen, Nancy, 560
Androgens, 126
  sexual behavior and, 439–440
Angell, James Rowland, 15
Anger, 444, 450
  factors affecting, 423
  punishment and, 291
"Animal electricity," 82
Animal intelligence, 279–280
Animal Mind, The (Washburn), 17
Animal research, 67
  ethics in, 62–64
Animals
  learning in, 260
  sexuality in, 439
  shaping and training of, 289
Anorexia nervosa, 436, 456
Antagonists, 81
  of dopamine, 585–586
Anterograde amnesia, 302, 334–335, 339
"Anthropometric" laboratory, 386, 387
Antianxiety drugs, 587
Antidepressant drugs, 237, 586–587
Antipsychotic drugs, 585–586, 587
Antisocial personality disorder, 565
Anxiety, 80, 552
Anxiety disorders, 552–556, 575
Anxiety hierarchy, 601, 611
Appetitive stimulus, 281
Applied psychologists, 9, 28
Approximation technique, shaping behavior

731

surface and deep structure of, 350, 375–376
units of, 349
Latané, Bibb, 519
Latency period, 478
Latent content of dreams, 239, 474, 591
Lateral geniculate nucleus, 177
Lateral hypothalamus, 432
Law of effect, 278–280, 297
observational learning and, 293
Law of large numbers, 45
L-dopa, 80
Learned disorders, 572–573, 600
Learned helplessness, 571
Learning, 260–262. *See also* Classical conditioning; Instrumental conditioning
about consequences of behavior, 278–292, 295
about events, 263–265, 295, 296
biological constraints on, 288–289
inhibitory, 277
observational, 262, 292–294, 297
problems solved through, 262
REM sleep and, 238
through shaping, 288
Learning factors, in psychotherapies, 608
Legal insanity, 548
Lens, 173
LeVay, Simon, 443
Lie detectors, 449
Life events, stress and, 623–624, 628
Life problems, personality and, 490
Lifestyle, healthy, 641–645, 647
Light, 172, 214
Lightning calculation, 384, 391
Light spectrum, 172
Liking, determinants of, 531–533
Limbic system, 95
Linear perspective, 188
Linguistic intelligence, 392
Linguistic relativity hypothesis, 346
Linkword system, 317–318
Listening, dichotic, 223, 224
Lobes, brain, 95–96, 97–99
Lobotomy, prefrontal, 589
Loci, method of, 315–317, 338
Locus of control, 485–486
Logical-mathematical intelligence, 392
Logical thought, beginnings of, 139
Longitudinal design, 133
Longitudinal studies, of IQ scores, 407–408
Long-term habituation, 264–265, 296
Long-term memory, 303, 312–321, 337, 338
Looking and learning, in problem solving, 364, 369
Loudness, 214
Love, psychology of, 534–535
Loving, determinants of, 531–533
Lowball technique, 514–515
Lucas, Henry Lee, 465
Lying, detection of, 449

Lymphocytes, 630, 646
Lysergic acid diethylamide (LSD), 245

M
Madness, creativity and, 560
Magnetic resonance imaging (MRI), 91
Maier two-string problem, 364–365
Major depressive episode, 561
Male hormones, 106–107
"Male menopause," 127
Malleus, 196
Mania, 560, 562, 575
Manic state, 562
Manifest content of dreams, 239, 474
Mantras, 251, 255
Mapping, 22
Marijuana, 246, 247
Marriage/family problems, 9
Marriage partners, choosing, 531–533
Martin, Lillien, 17, 28
Maslow, Abraham, 19, 28, 480
humanistic approach of, 481–482
need hierarchy of, 429–430, 456, 481–482
Mate selection, 441–442, 456
Mathematics, gender differences in achievement in, 427
Mating rituals, 439
Maturation. *See also* Development
sexual, 126–127
McDougall, William, 424
M-channel, 177
Mean, 42
Meaning. *See also* Semantics
language structure and, 349
thinking about, 314
Means-ends analysis, 367
Median, 43
Medical care, aging and, 159
Medical model, of abnormal behavior, 549–550
Medical student syndrome, 556–557
Meditation, 222, 251–252, 251–252, 253, 255
Meditation training, 636
Medulla, 93
Membrane, cell, 77
Memories
accuracy of, 4, 325–327
repressed, 39–40
Memory, 302–337. *See also* Forgetting; Long-term memory; Short-term memory
aging and, 133–135, 134
auditory sensory, 306, 338
cueing and, 322–329, 337, 339
echoic, 306
episodic, 313, 338
eyewitness testimony and, 326–327
flashbulb, 316, 317
hippocampus and, 335–336
iconic, 304, 305–306
implicit and explicit, 327, 339

interference with, 331–332
long-term, 312–321, 337, 338
as primary mental ability, 388
procedural, 313, 338
reconstructive, 325–327, 339
repetition and, 320–321, 338
repression of, 333–334, 339
semantic, 313, 338
sensory, 304
short-term, 304–312, 336–337, 338
storage of, 335–336
studies of, 38
subliminal messages and, 226
updating, 329–336, 329–336, 337, 339
visualization and, 315–320, 338
visual sensory, 304–306, 338
working, 307
Memory capacity, short-term, 310–311
Memory enhancement, 249–250
Memory errors, 307–308
Memory illusions, 328–329. *See also* False memories
Memory principles, underwater experiment in, 58–59
Memory processes, 302–303
Memory schemas, 325–326, 327
Memory span, short-term, 310, 311, 338
Memory tests, implicit, 328
Men
casual sex and, 441
mate selection by, 441–442
sexual desire in, 440
suicide rate among, 563
Menarche, 126
Menopause, 127
sexual experience following, 440
Mental age, 398–400
Mental functioning, 222–229, 253
Mental images, 318–320. *See also* Imagery; Inner voice; Visual imagery
Mental processes, study of, 21
Mental retardation, 400
statistical deviance and, 546
Mental sets, 365
Mental speed, 389–390
Mental test performance, intelligence as measured by, 384, 387, 389, 391–393, 398–400, 401
Mescaline, 245
Meta-analysis, 606–607
Method of loci, 315–317, 338
Midbrain, 93–94, 96, 112
Middle age, personal development during, 155–156
Middle ear, 196
Milgram, Stanley, authority experiments by, 525–527
Mind, 7
as a *tabula rasa*, 10–11
computer model for, 21
Freud's theory of, 474
study of, 6–8, 28
Mind/body connection, 11–12

Credits

This page constitutes an extension of the copyright page. We have made every effort to trace the ownership of all copyrighted material and to secure permission from copyright holders. In the event of any question arising as to the use of any material, we will be pleased to make the necessary corrections in future printings. Thanks are due to the following authors, publishers, and agents for permission to use the material indicated.

CHAPTER 1
13: Figure 1.3 from *The Story of Psychology*, by R. C. Bolles, p. 277. Copyright ©1993 Brooks/Cole Publishing Co.

CHAPTER 3
104: Figure from *Introduction to Psychology*, Fourth Edition, by J. Kalat, p. 117, Brooks/Cole Publishing Company, 1996.

CHAPTER 4
123: Figure 4.3 adapted from *Life-Span Human Development*, by C. K. Sigelman and D. R. Shaffer, p. 92. Copyright ©1995 Brooks/Cole Publishing Co. **131:** Figure 4.8 graph adapted from *Cognition*, 40, by M. H. Johnson, S. Dziurawiec, H. Ellis, and J. Morton, "Newborns' Preferential Tracking of Face-Like Stimuli and Its Subsequent Decline," pp. 1–19, 1991, with kind permission of Elsevier Science–NL, Sara Burgerhartstraat 25, 1055 KV Amsterdam, The Netherlands.

CHAPTER 5
187: Figure 5.16 from "Higher-Level Vision," by I. Biederman. In D. H. Osherson, S. M. Kosslyn, & J. M. Hollerback (Eds.), *An Invitation to Cognitive Science: Visual Cognition and Action*, Vol. 2, p. 135. Copyright ©1990 MIT Press. Reprinted by permission. **193:** Figure 5.20 (b) from Mind Sights, by R. N. Shepard. Copyright ©1990 by Roger N. Shepard. Reprinted by permission of W. H. Freeman & Company.

CHAPTER 6
232: Figure 6.6 from *Current Concepts: The Sleep Disorders*, by P. Hauri, 1982, The Upjohn Company, Kalamazoo, Michigan. Reprinted by permission.

CHAPTER 7
261: Figure 7.1 graphs reprinted with permission from "Memory Processing of Serial Lists by Pigeons, Monkeys and People," by A. A. Wright, H. C. Santiago, S. F. Sands, D. F. Kendrick, and R. G. Cook, 1985, *Science*, 229, pp. 287–289. Copyright ©1985 American Association for the Advancement of Science.

CHAPTER 8
319: Figure 8.9 from "Long-Term Memory for a Common Object," by R. S. Nickerson and M. J. Adams, 1979, *Cognitive*

Psychology, 11, pp. 287–307. Used by permission of Academic Press and the author.

CHAPTER 9
358: Figure 9.5 from *Psychology*, by B. Goldstein, p. 324, Brooks/Cole Publishing Company, 1994.

CHAPTER 10
390: Figure 10.3 adapted from "Conduction Velocity in a Brain Nerve Pathway Correlates with Intelligence," by T. E. Reed and A. R. Jensen, 1992, *Intelligence*, 16, pp. 259–272. Copyright ©1992 Ablex Publishing Corp. Reprinted by permission. **403:** Figure 10.5 from *Psychology: Themes and Variations*, Third Edition, by W. Weiten, p. 343, Brooks/Cole Publishing Company, 1995. **402:** Excerpt from "The G-ocentric View of Intelligence and Job Performance Is Wrong," by R. J. Sternberg and R. K. Wagner, 1993, *Current Directions in Psychological Science*, 2, pp. 1–5. Copyright ©1993 Cambridge University Press. Reprinted by permission of Cambridge University Press.

CHAPTER 12
467: Figure 12.1 from "A 16PF Profile," by R. B. Cattell, 1973, *Psychology Today*, July 1973, pp. 40–46. Copyright ©1973 Sussex Publishers, Inc. Reprinted with permission from *Psychology Today Magazine*. **470:** Figure 12.4 adapted from *Psychology: Themes & Variations*, Third Edition, by W. Weiten, p. 509, Brooks/Cole Publishing Company, 1995. **492:** Figure 12.9 adapted from "Personality Similarity in Twins Reared Apart and Together," by A. Tellegen, D. T. Lykken, T. J. Bouchard, Jr., K. J. Wilcox, N. L. Segal, and S. Rich, 1988, *Journal of Personality and Social Psychology*, 54(6), 1031–1039. Copyright ©1988 by the American Psychological Association. Adapted by permission of the author.

CHAPTER 14
553: Figure 14.3 reprinted with permission from the *American Psychiatric Association Diagnostic and Statistical Manual of Mental Disorders*, Fourth Edition. Washington D.C., American Psychiatric Association, 1994.

CHAPTER 15
596: Figure 15.6 adapted from "Depression," by A. T. Beck and J. E. Young. In D. H. Barlow (Ed.), *Clinical Handbook of Psychological*

Disorders: A Step by Step Treatment Manual, pp. 667–668. Copyright ©1985 Guilford Press. Reprinted by permission.

CHAPTER 16

624: Table 16.1 reprinted by permission of the publisher from "The Social Readjustment Rating Scale," by T. H. Holmes and R. H. Rahe in *Journal of Psychosomatic Research*, 11, pp. 213–218. Copyright 1967 by Elsevier Science Inc. **640:** Figure 16.6 from Barlow, D. H., Rapee, R. M., *Daily Stress Record, Mastering Stress: A Lifestyle Approach*, 1991, p. 12. Reproduced with permission of American Health Publishing Company, Dallas, Texas. All rights reserved. For ordering information call 1-800-736-7323.

PHOTOS

CHAPTER 1

5: (top) John Livzey; (inset) Alfred Pasieka/SPL/Photo Researchers, Inc. **7:** (left) Richard Hutchings/Photo Researchers, Inc.; (right) Hank Morgan/PhotoResearchers, Inc. **12:** Corbis-Bettmann. **13:** Stephen Krasemann/Photo Researchers, Inc. **14:** copyright Charles Adams/*The New Yorker Magazine*. **15:** Corbis-Bettmann. **16:** (top) Corbis-Bettmann; (bottom) Archives of the History of American Psychology, University of Akron, OH. **17:** (top) Nina Leen/*Life Magazine;* (bottom) Courtesy of Wellesley College Archives/©Notman. **18:** (top) Archives of the History of American Psychology, University of Akron, OH; (bottom) Corbis-Bettmann. **20:** Corbis-Bettmann. **23:** (all) John Livzey. **25:** (left) Photodisc; (middle) Digital Stock; (right) Photodisc. **27:** (top) John Livzey; (inset) Alfred Pasieka/SPL/Photo Researchers, Inc.; (bottom) Photodisc. **28:** (top) Tom McCarthy/Rainbow; (bottom) Corbis-Bettmann.

CHAPTER 2

35: (left) NASA; (right) Photodisc. **37:** (top) Laura Dwight; (bottom) Dan McCoy Rainbow. **41:** Larua Dwight. **47:** (left) David Woo/Stock Boston; (right) Bob Daemmrich/Stock Boston. **48:** (left) A. Sieveking/Petit Format/Photo Researchers; (right) David M. Grossman. **50:** Bob Daemmrich/The Image Works. **56:** Tony Freeman/PhotoEdit. **61:** Brad Markel/Liaison International. **63:** (top left) Photodisc; (top right) Joel Gordon; (bottom left) Courtesy of the Foundation for Biomedical Research; (bottom right) Conklin/Monkmeyer Press. **65:** (top) Photodisc; (bottom) Joel Gordon. **66:** (top) Laura Dwight; (middle right) Laura Dwight; (bottom left) David Woo/Stock Boston; (bottom right) Tony Freeman/PhotoEdit. **67:** (top) Bob Daemmrich/The Image Works; (bottom left) Brad Markel/Liaison (bottom right) Photodisc.

CHAPTER 3

73: (top) Photodisc; (bottom) CNR/SPL/Photo Researchers, Inc. **80:** Corbis-Bettmann. **81:** (left) Photodisc; (right) Jack Fields/Photo Researchers, Inc.; (bottom) © Patrick Johns/Corbis-Bettmann. **88:** Dan McCoy/Rainbow. **90:** Richard Nowitz/Photo Researchers, Inc. **91:** (top) CEA/ORSAY/CNRI/Photo Researchers, Inc.; (bottom left) Courtesy of Siemens Medical Systems; (bottom right) Scott Camazine/Photo Researchers, Inc. **97:** Courtesy of Warren Museum, Harvard Medical School. **100:** John Livzey. **107:** (left) Peter Cade/Tony Stone Images; (right) Photodisc. **110:** Michael Newman/PhotoEdit. **111:** (top) Scott Camazine/Photo Researchers, Inc.; (bottom) Peter Cade/Tony Stone Images. **112:** CNR/SPL/Photo Researchers, Inc. **113:** Michael Newman/PhotoEdit.

CHAPTER 4

119: (top left) Gary Watson/SPL/Photo Researchers, Inc.; (middle) Laura Dwight; (top right) Smith/Monkmeyer Press. **120:** (left) Petit Format/Nestle/Photo Researchers, Inc.; (middle left) Petit Format/Nestle/Photo Researchers, Inc.; (middle right) James Stevenson/SPL/Photo Researchers, Inc.; (right) Petit Format/Nestle/Photo Researchers, Inc. **122:** (left) George Steinmetz; (right) Liaison Stock. **125:** (left) Victor Englebert/Photo Researchers, Inc.; (right) John Livzey. **126:** (top) Bob Daemmrich/The Image Works; (bottom) Bob Daemmrich/Stock Boston. **127:** Photodisc. **130:** Courtesy of Dr. Carolyn Rovee-Collier. **132:** (top) John Livzey; (bottom) Enrico Ferorelli. **135:** Bill Anderson/Monkmeyer Press. **136:** Bob Daemmrich/Stock Boston. **137:** (top left) Charles Gupton/Stock Boston; (middle right) Goodman/Monkmeyer Press; (bottom right) Goodman/Monkmeyer Press. **139:** David Young-Wolff/PhotoEdit. **141:** Corbis. **142:** Catherine Karnow/Woodfin Camp. 143: Kopstein/Monkmeyer Press. **146:** Laura Dwight. **147:** (top left) Martin Rogers/Stock Boston; (top right) Martin Rogers/Woodfin Camp; (bottom) Josef Polleross/The Image Works. **149:** Bob Daemmrich/Stock Boston. **151** (both) Liaison. **152:** (top left) Digital Stock; (top right) Michael Newman/PhotoEdit; (bottom) Corbis. **153:** Dan McCoy/Rainbow. **154:** UPI/Bettmann-Corbis. **155:** (top) Dana Schuerholz/Impact Visuals; (bottom) John Livzey. **156:** (left) Myrleen Cate/Tony Stone Images; (right) Photodisc. **157:** (left) Tom McCarthy/The Stock Market; (right) Suzanne Szasz/Photo Researchers, Inc. **158:** Bob Daemmrich/The Image Works. **160:** (top) Robert Brenner/PhotoEdit; (middle) James Schnepf/Gamma Liaison; (bottom) Bob Daemmrich/Stock Boston. **161:** (left) Joel Gordon; (right) Andy Levin. **162:** Gary Watson/SPL/Photo Researchers, Inc. **163:** (top) Digital Stock; (bottom) Smith/Monkmeyer Press. **164** (top) James Stevenson/SPL/Photo Researchers, Inc.; (bottom) David Young-Wolff/PhotoEdit. **165:** (left) Charles Gupton/Stock Boston; (right) Catherine Karnow/Woodfin Camp.

CHAPTER 5

175: (all) Enrico Ferorelli. **177:** Omikron/Photo Researchers, Inc. **180:** (top) D.F. Benson/Archives of Neurology/American Medical Association; (bottom) Courtesy of Dr. Patrick Dupont, Ph.D. **181:** Fritz Goro/Time/Warner, Inc. **186:** ©Bev Doolittle, "The Forest Has Eyes" - The Greenwich Workshop. **189:** (left) Denis Waugh/Tony Stone Images; (middle) Maggie Leonard/Rainbow; (right) John Elk III/Stock Boston. **192:** Richard Nowitz/Phototake, NYC. **195:** Enrico Ferorelli. **198:** Bob Daemmrich/Stock Boston. **199:** Tony Freeman/PhotoEdit. **201:** Photodisc. **202:** Peter Menzel/Stock Boston. **204:** Jerry Wachter/Photo Researchers, Inc. **206:** Rene Lynn/Photo Researchers, Inc. **207:** Omikron/Photo Researchers, Inc. **211:** (left) F. Pedrick/The Image Works; (right) M. Bernsau/The Image Works. **212:** (top) Omikron/Photo Researchers, Inc.; (bottom) Peter Menzel/Stock Boston. **213:** Omikron/Photo Researchers, Inc. **214:** (top) Enrico Ferorelli; (bottom) Jerry Wachter/Photo Researchers, Inc. **215:** Rene Lynn/Photo Researchers, Inc.

CHAPTER 6

220: Catherine Pouedras/SPL/Photo Researchers, Inc. **222:** (left) Coco McCoy/Rainbow; (middle left) Esbin-Anderson/The Image Works; (middle right) Hiller/Monkmeyer; (right) David Attie/Phototake, NYC. **224:** (top) Mark Richards/PhotoEdit; (bottom) David Young-Wolff/PhotoEdit. **225:** Jeff Dunn/Stock Boston. **228:** © Dan McCoy/Rainbow. **231:** (left) Wayne

Lankinen/DRK Photo; (right) Photodisc. **234:** David Grossman. **235:** Mike Mazzaschi/Stock Boston. **243:** (left) Hank Morgan/Rainbow; (right) M. Antman/The Image Works. **244:** Photodisc. **245:** Timothy Ross/The Image Works. **246:** A. Ramey/PhotoEdit. **248:** Jean-Loup Charmet/SPL/Photo Researchers, Inc. **249:** Bob Daemmrich/Stock Boston. **250:** Forsyth/Monkmeyer Press. **252:** Photodisc. **253:** (top left) Esbin-Anderson/ The Image Works; (middle) A. Ramey/PhotoEdit; (bottom) Forsyth/Monkmeyer Press. **254:** Mike Mazzaschi/Stock Boston. **255:** (top left) A. Ramey/PhotoEdit; (top right) Timothy Ross/The Image Works; (bottom) Bob Daemmrich/Stock Boston.

CHAPTER 7
262: (left) Chad Hutchings/Photo Researchers, Inc.; (middle) Stephen Krasemann/Photo Researchers, Inc.; (right) Anthony Wood/Stock Boston. **263:** Allan Roberts. **267:** Sovfoto. **271:** Simon Fraser/Royal Victoria Infirmary/Newcastle/Photo Researchers, Inc. **274:** Courtesy of Professor Benjamin Harris. **286:** Courtesy of Doctors Robert and Marian Breland Bailey. **288:** Stephen Green/Focus on Sports. **293:** Bob Daemmrich/Stock Boston. **294:** Richard Hutchings/Photo Researchers, Inc. **295:** (top) Anthony Wood/Stock Boston; (middle) Courtesy of Doctors Robert and Marian Breland Bailey; (bottom) Richard Hutchings/Photo Researchers, Inc. **297:** (top) Courtesy of Doctors Robert and Marian Breland Bailey; (bottom) Richard Hutchings/Photo Researchers, Inc.

CHAPTER 8
304: M. Douglas/The Image Works. **307:** Joel Gordon. **311:** (both) Leonard Lessin/Peter Arnold. **313:** Leanna Rathkelly/Tony Stone Images. **316:** J. Pat Carter/Gamma Liaison. **322:** Conklin/Monkmeyer. **324:** K. Harrison/The Image Works. **328:** Tony Freeman/PhotoEdit. **330:** Cobis-Bettmann. **332:** Bill Bachman/The Image Works. **335:** Mazziotta el al/SPL/PhotoResearchers, Inc. **337:** (top) Leanna Rathkelly/Tony Stone Images; (bottom) Mazziotta el al/SPL/PhotoResearchers, Inc. **338:** M. Douglas/The Image Works. **339** (top) Conklin/Monkmeyer Press; (bottom) John Lei/Stock Boston.

CHAPTER 9
345: (left) Charles Gupton/Stock Boston; (middle left) P. McCarten/PhotoEdit; (middle right) Robert Brenner/PhotoEdit; (right)Bryce Flynn/Stock Boston. **347:** (left) Martin Rogers/Stock Boston; (right) Ryan Beyer/Tony Stone Images. **348:** Scott Camazine/Photo Researchers, Inc. **352:** (left) Sheldon Secunda/Liaison; (right) Myrleen Ferguson/ PhotoEdit. **354:** (left) Susan Kuklin/Photo Researchers, Inc.; (right) Enrico Ferorelli. **356:** Jeff Greenberg/Rainbow. **357:** Alex Bartel/SPL/Photo Researchers, Inc. **359:** Dan McCoy/Rainbow. **361:** (left) Tim Davis/Photo Researchers, Inc. (middle) Tom & Pat Leeson/Photo Researchers, Inc. (right) Eric Neurath/Stock Boston. **362:** (left) Blair Seitz/Photo Researchers, Inc.; (right) Brady/Monkmeyer. **367:** Robert Brenner/PhotoEdit. **371:** Grantpix/Monkmeyer Press. **373:** Corbis-Bettmann. **375:** Martin Rogers/Stock Boston. **376:** (top) Scott Camazine/Photo Researchers, Inc.; (bottom) Enrico Ferorelli. **378:** Tom & Pat Leeson/Photo Researchers, Inc. **379:** Robert Brenner/PhotoEdit.

CHAPTER 10
384: (left) UPI/Corbis-Bettmann; (right) Tom Ulrich/Tony Stone Images. **386:** Craig Jones/Allsport. **387:** (both) Archives of the History of American Psychology. **392:** (left) A. Ramey/PhotoEdit; (right) Louise Gubb/The Imge Works. **396:** Bob

Daemmrich/Stock Boston. **398:** Archives of the History of American Psychology. **402:** Michael Rosenfeld/Tony Stone Images. **404:** Archives of the History of American Psychology. **406:** Laura Dwight/PhotoEdit. **408:** Morrison/Wulffraat/Retna. **411:** Lois Moulton/Tony Stone Images. **414:** Tom Ulrich/Tony Stone Images. **415:** Bob Daemrmich/Stock Boston. **416:** UPI/Corbis-Bettmann. **417:** (top) Bob Daemmrich/Stock Boston; (bottom) Michael Rosenfeld/Tony Stone Images.

CHAPTER 11
424: (left) Jean F. Stoick/Peter Arnold; (right) Capital Features/The Image Works. **426:** David Young-Wolff/PhotoEdit. **427:** (left) Charles Gupton/Stock Boston; (right) Bill Binzen/Rainbow. **428:** Jeff Greenberg/Rainbow. **432:** John Livzey. **433:** (top right) Richard Howard; (bottom left) Richard Pasley/Stock Boston; (bottom right) Xinhua/Gamma Liaison. **436:** (left) Alinari/Art Resource, NY; (middle) Dennis MacDonald/PhotoEdit; (right) Tony Freeman/PhotoEdit. **438:** Sid Bahrt/Photo Researchers, Inc. **445:** (top right) Bob Daemmrich/The Image Works; (top middle) Tom McCarthy/PhotoEdit; (bottom middle) R. Lord/The Image Works; (bottom right) Lawrence Migdale/Stock Boston. **446:** Myrleen Cate/PhotoEdit. **447:** John Livzey. **449:** Srulik Haramaty/Phototake, NYC. **451:** Reuters/Corbis-Bettmann. **456:** (top) David Young-Wolff/PhotoEdit; (bottom) Sid Bahrt/Photo Researchers, Inc. **457:** Tom McCarthy/PhotoEdit. **458:** Jean F. Stoick/Peter Arnold.

CHAPTER 12
465: (left) Bob Daemmrich/The Image Works; (right) Enrico Ferorelli. **469:** Betty Press/Woodfin Camp. **473:** Archiv/Photo Researchers, Inc. **476:** (left) David Young-Wolff/PhotoEdit; (right) David Waite/Gamma Liaison. **477:** © Erika Stone/Peter Arnold. **478:** Karsh/Woodfin Camp. **479:** Corbis-Bettmann. **481:** Bruce Ayres/Tony Stone Images. **483:** (all) Tony Freeman/PhotoEdit. **485:** David Ximeno Tejada/Tony Stone Images. **489:** Bob Daemmrich/The Image Works. **490:** Christopher Morrow/Stock Boston. **493:** Betty Press/Woodfin Camp. **495:** (top) Betty Press/Woodfin Camp; (middle right) Tony Freeman/PhotoEdit; (botto left) David Ximeno Tejada/Tony Stone Images.

CHAPTER 13
501: (left) Michael Newman/PhotoEdit; (middle) Corporal F. Stuart Westmorland/Photo Researchers, Inc. **503:** (left) Matthew McVay/Tony Stone Images; (middle) Matthew McVay/Tony Stone Images; (right) Palmer/Kane/Tony Stone Images. **508:** Courtesy of Columbia Tristar Television. **509:** Bill Gallery/Stock Boston. **512:** Spencer Grant/PhotoEdit. **517:** Bob Daemrmich/Stock Boston. **518:** Johnny Crawford/The Image Works. **520:** Topham/The Image Works. **521:** William Vandivert/Scientific American. **522:** Jack Kurtz/Impact Visuals. **523:** Dominique Buisson/Photo Researchers, Inc. **525:** Washington Post-Frank Johnston/Woodfin Camp. **526:** (all) Stanley Milgram, 1965 "Obedience"/Penn State University. **528:** John Lei/Stock Boston. **531:** Suzanne Murphy/Tony Stone Images. **533:** Stuart Cohen/Tony Stone Images. **536:** (top) Corporal F. Stuart Westmorland/Photo Researchers, Inc.; (bottom) Johnny Crawford/The Image Works. **537:** Stuart Cohen/Tony Stone Images. **538:** (top left) Matthey McVay/Tony Stone Images; (bottom right) Palmer/Kane/Tony Stone Images. **539:** (top left) Topham/The Image Works; (top right) Dominique Buisson/Photo Researchers, Inc.; (bottom) Joel Gordon.

CHAPTER 14
544: Ex-Rouchon/Photo Researchers, Inc. **546:** Gerd Ludwig/Woodfin Camp. **547:** (left) M. Schwarz/The Image Works; (right) Bob Strong/The Image Works. **548:** Reuters/Corbis-Bettmann. **551:** David Harry Stewart/Tony Stone Images. **555:** (left) Bill Luster/©Corbis-Bettmann; (middle) Bob Daemmrich/The Image Works; (right) Cathlyn Melloan/Tony Stone Images. **558:** Brad Wrisley/Gamma Liaison. **563:** Goldberg/Monkmeyer Press. **564:** Wellcome Department of Cognitive Neurology/SPL/Photo Researchers, Inc. **565:** Grunnitus/Monkmeyer Press. **568:** (top) Dr. R. Haier/Peter Arnold; (bottom) Paul S. Howell/Liaison. **572:** BUU/Gamma Liaison. **574:** Ex-Rouchon/Photo Researchers, Inc. **575:** (top) Cathlyn Melloan/Tony Stone Images; (bottom) Grunnitus/ Monkmeyer Press. **576:** (top) Gerd Ludwig/Woodfin Camp; (bottom) Wellcome Department of Cognitive Neurology/SPL/Photo Researchers, Inc. **577:** (top) Grunnitus/Monkmeyer Press; (bottom) Goldberg/Monkmeyer Press.

CHAPTER 15
583: (left) Hank Morgan/Photo Researchers, Inc.; (middle) Will & Deni McIntyre/Photo Researchers, Inc.; (right) Michael Newman/PhotoEdit. **584:** Corbis-Bettmann. **588:** Will & Deni McIntyre/Photo Researchers, Inc. **589:** UPI/Corbis-Bettmann. **591:** Corbis-Bettmann. **594:** Courtesy of The Institute for Rational-Emotive Therapy. **597:** Will & Deni McIntyre/Photo Researchers, Inc. **600:** Peter Southwick/Stock Boston. **601:** Archives of the History of American Psychology, University Akron, OH. **602:** Lester Sloan/Woodfin Camp. **609:** Michael Newman/PhotoEdit. **610:** Will & Deni McIntyre/Photo Researchers, Inc. **611:** (top) Peter Southwick/Stock Boston; (bottom) Michael Newman/PhotoEdit. **612:** Courtesy of The Institute for Rational-Emotive Therapy. **613:** Michael Newman/PhotoEdit.

CHAPTER 16
619: (left) Michael Newman/PhotoEdit; (right) Steven Peters/Tony Stone Images. **620:** S. Purdy Matthews/Tony Stone Images. **625:** Ed Prâitchard/Tony Stone Images. **627:** Collins/Monkmeyer Press. **630:** (top) J.Y. Rabeuf/The Image Works; (bottom) Joseph Sohm/Tony Stone Images. **633:** Kevin Moloney/Liaison. **635:** (top left) Carini/The Image Works; (bottom left) Jonathan Nourok/PhotoEdit; (bottom right) Tony Freeman/PhotoEdit. **638:** Seth Resnick/Liaison. **642:** Tom McCarthy/PhotoEdit. **643:** Peter Menzel/Stock Boston. **645:** David Young-Wolff/PhotoEdit. **646:** (top) S. Purdy Matthews/Tony Stone Images; (bottom) Collins/Monkmeyer Press. **647:** (top) Carini/The Image Works; (bottom) Seth Resnick/Liaison. **648:** Michael Newman/PhotoEdit. **649:** (left) Carini/The Image Works; (right) Kevin Moloney/Liaison

Your name: _____ Date: _____

May we quote you, either in promotion for *Psychology: The Adaptive Mind, 2/e*, or in future publishing ventures?

Yes: _____   No: _____

Sincerely yours,

James S. Nairne

TO THE OWNER OF THIS BOOK:

I hope that you have found *Psychology: The Adaptive Mind, 2/e* useful. So that this book can be improved in a future edition, would you take the time to complete this sheet and return it? Thank you.

School and address: _____

_____

Department: _____

Instructor's name: _____

1. What I like most about this book is: _____

_____

_____

2. What I like least about this book is: _____

_____

_____

3. My general reaction to this book is: _____

_____

_____

4. The name of the course in which I used this book is: _____

_____

5. Were all of the chapters of the book assigned for you to read? _____

   If not, which ones weren't? _____

6. In the space below, or on a separate sheet of paper, please write specific suggestions for improving this book and anything else you'd care to share about your experience in using this book.

_____

_____

_____

_____

_____

_____

_____